ETERNAL PEOPLE

*God in Relation to Israel:
Israel in the Tanakh and the New Testament*

WILLEM J. OUWENEEL

AN EVANGELICAL INTRODUCTION TO
REFORMATIONAL THEOLOGY
VOL IV/1A

PART IV: CONSUMMATION:
THE LIVED SHAPE OF THEOLOGY

AN EVANGELICAL INTRODUCTION TO REFORMATIONAL THEOLOGY

Part I: Scripture: The Revealed Source For Theology
   I/1 *The Eternal Word*: God Speaking To Us
   I/2 *The Eternal Torah*: Living Under God

Part II: God: The Personal Source Behind Theology
   II/1 *The Eternal God*: God Revealing Himself To Us
   II/2 *The Eternal Christ:* God With Us
   II/3 *The Eternal Spirit*: God Living In Us

Part III: Redemption: The Christ-Centered Heart of Theology
   III/1 *The Eternal Purpose*: Living In Christ
   III/2 *Eternal Righteousness*: Living Before God
   III/3 *Eternal Salvation*: Christ Dying For Us
   III/4 *Eternal Life*: Christ Living In Us

Part IV: Consummation: The Lived Shape of Theology
   IV/1a *The Eternal People*: God in Relation To Israel: Israel in the Tanakh and the New Testament
   IV/1b *The Eternal People*: God in Relation To Israel: Post-New Testament Israel
   IV/2 *The Eternal Covenant*: Living With God
   IV/3 *The Eternal Kingdom*: Living Under Christ

Part V: Method: The Comprehensive Foundation of Theology
   V/1 *Eternal Truth*: The Prolegomena of Theology

ETERNAL PEOPLE

*God in Relation to Israel:
Israel in the Tanakh and the New Testament*

WILLEM J. OUWENEEL

PAIDEIA
PRESS

PAIDEIA
PRESS

*The Eternal People: God in Relation to Israel
Israel in the Tanakh and the New Testament*

This English edition is a publication of Paideia Press (P.O. Box 1000, Jordan Station, Ontario, Canada L0R 1S0). Copyright © 2020 by Paideia Press. All rights reserved. Except for brief quotations in critical publications or reviews, no part of this book may be reproduced in any manner without prior written permission from Paideia Press at the address above.

Unless otherwise indicated, Scripture quotations are from the ESV® Bible (The Holy Bible, English Standard Version®). Copyright © 2001 by Crossway, a publishing ministry of Good News Publishers. Used by permission. All rights reserved.

Scripture quotations or references marked as NKJV are taken from the New King James Version®. Copyright © 1982 by Thomas Nelson, Inc. Used by permission. All rights reserved.

Scripture quotations or references marked as NIV are taken from the Holy Bible, New International Version®, NIV®. Copyright © 1973, 1978, 1984, 2011 by Biblica, Inc.™ Used by permission of Zondervan. All rights reserved worldwide. www.zondervan.com. The "NIV" and "New International Version" are trademarks registered in the United States Patent and Trademark Office by Biblica, Inc.™

Book Design by: Steven R. Martins

ISBN 978-0-88815-317-3

Printed in the United States of America

Who is like me?
Let him speak out!
Let him show me clearly what has been happening
*since I set up the **eternal people**;*
let him foretell future signs and events.

Isaiah 44:7 (CJB)

[N]either circumcision counts for anything,
nor uncircumcision,
but [whether one is] a new creation.
And as for all who walk by this rule,
peace and mercy be upon them,
and upon the Israel of God.

Galatians 6:15–16

*The battle that is fought today [ca. 1944/45] against the Jewish people shows through its frenzy that it goes not only, and not basically, against the present-day dissolved, unrecognizable people; it goes against the **eternal Israel**.*

Margarete Susman[1]

---

1. Susman (1996); originally written during and immediately after, and in response to, the Shoah; Margarete Susman was a German-Jewish poet and writer in Switzerland.

Table of Contents

Series Preface		i
Author's Preface		v
Abbreviations		xi
Chapter 1	The Calling of Israel	1
Chapter 2	The Destiny of Israel	49
Chapter 3	A Collision of Paradigms	99
Chapter 4	The Problem Politicized	145
Chapter 5	The Old and the New Covenants in the Tanakh	191
Chapter 6	The Physical and the Spiritual Israel	243
Chapter 7	The Old Testament Messianic Hope	289
Chapter 8	Jesus and the Jews	359
Chapter 9	Israel in Prophecy in the Tanakh	413
Chapter 10	Israel Is Not the Church	457
Chapter 11	The Ecclesia Is Not Israel	503
Chapter 12	The One People of God	547
Chapter 13	Israel in New Testament Prophecy: Gospels and Acts	591
Chapter 14	Israel in New Testament Prophecy: Paul and Revelation	629
Bibliography		673
Scripture Index		703
Subject Index		749

Table of Contents Expanded

Series Preface		i
Author's Preface		v
Abbreviations		xi
1	**The Calling of Israel**	**1**
1.1	Introduction	2
	1.1.1 The Eternal People	2
	1.1.2 The Name "Israel"	5
	1.1.3 The National Angels	7
1.2	Personal Development: Autobiographical Comments	11
	1.2.1 Early Experiences	11
	1.2.2 Visits to Israel	13
	1.2.3 A Multi-Faceted Front	15
1.3	The Navel of the Earth	18
	1.3.1 Jerusalem: Its Origins	18
	1.3.2 Jerusalem: Its Restoration	21
	1.3.3 Jerusalem or Rome?	23
1.4	The Starting Point: Calling	26
	1.4.1 The Calling of Abraham	26
	1.4.2 Israel in the Midst of the Nations	28
	1.4.3 "My Land"	30
1.5	Ally and Son	34
	1.5.1 The Two Abrahamic Covenants	34
	1.5.2 The Old and New Covenant	38
	1.5.3 Israel Son of God	41
1.6	Prophetic Promises	44
	1.6.1 Hermeneutical Keys	44
	1.6.2 More Examples	46

2	The Destiny of Israel		49
	2.1	Jacob and Esau	49
		2.1.1 The Face of *Elohim*	49
		2.1.2 Wrestling with the Angel	51
		2.1.3 Hosea 12	53
	2.2	The Crucial Blessing	55
		2.2.1 Blessing Jacob or Combating Him	55
		2.2.2 Jacob's Method of Fighting	58
		2.2.3 The Encounter with Esau	60
	2.3	The Restoration of Israel	64
		2.3.1 Twelve Components	64
		2.3.2 Two Kinds of Redemptive Prophecies	70
		2.3.3 Messiah the Center of Prophecy	73
		2.3.4 Connection Between the First and Second Exiles	75
	2.4	The "Times of the Gentiles"	81
		2.4.1 The Wild Waters	81
		2.4.2 Jonah As a Type van Israel	83
		2.4.3 Israel in the Dragon	86
	2.5	The Four World Empires	90
		2.5.1 Why Four?	90
		2.5.2 Zechariah, Daniel, and Revelation	92
		2.5.3 The Third and Fourth Empires	95
	2.6	Summary	97
3	A Collision of Paradigms		99
	3.1	Introduction	99
		3.1.1 Spiritualism or Literalism	99
		3.1.2 Replacement Theology	102
		3.1.3 What Is In a Name?	104
	3.2	Survey	106
		3.2.1 Five Replaced Components	106
		3.2.2 Three Considerations	109

		3.2.3	A Third Way	110
	3.3	Misunderstandings		112
		3.3.1	Two Paths of Salvation	112
		3.3.2	"Not Christocentric"	114
		3.3.3	More Misunderstandings by Paas	116
	3.4	Misconceptions by Robertson		118
		3.4.1	"Inconceivable"?	118
		3.4.2	Type and Fulfillment	119
		3.4.3	The New Creation	120
	3.5	Further Misconceptions		123
		3.5.1	Final Misunderstandings	123
		3.5.2	Misunderstandings: Epilogue	124
		3.5.3	Positive Israelology	126
	3.6	Recapitulation		129
		3.6.1	Philosophy of Science	129
		3.6.2	Seven Pillars	130
		3.6.3	Paradigm Shifts	134
	3.7	Various "-Isms"		136
		3.7.1	"Christian Zionism"	136
		3.7.2	"Israelism"	138
		3.7.3	A Right to the Land?	140
4	The Problem Politicized			145
	4.1	Politicizing the Problem		145
		4.1.1	The Constantinian Turn	145
		4.1.2	Two Consequences	148
		4.1.3	Two More Consequences	150
	4.2	Theological Developments		151
		4.2.1	The New Eschatology	151
		4.2.2	Paradigm Shift	154
		4.2.3	Augustine and the "De-Jewishified" Jew	156
	4.3	Protestant Eschatology		158
		4.3.1	Reformational Eschatology	158

		4.3.2	Power Thinking Versus Non-Violence	160
		4.3.3	Belgic Confession, Article 36	162
		4.3.4	Abraham Kuyper	164
	4.4	Mennonites: Evangelicals *Avant la Lettre*		166
		4.4.1	Anabaptists	166
		4.4.2	Mennonites and Jews	168
	4.5	Israel and the Netherlands		170
		4.5.1	The Second Reformation	170
		4.5.2	Réveil and Secession	173
		4.5.3	The Afrikaners	175
	4.6	Other Countries		176
		4.6.1	Europe and America	176
		4.6.2	Theology and Politics	178
		4.6.3	A Fitting Parable	180
	4.7	Recent Developments		183
		4.7.1	Recent Reformed Voices	183
		4.7.2	Classic and Moderate Dispensationalism	186
		4.7.3	Classic and Moderate Federalism	188
5	The Old and the New Covenants in the Tanakh			191
	5.1	Beginning with the New Testament		191
		5.1.1	The New Covenant Today	191
		5.1.2	The Place of the Nations	194
		5.1.3	The Covenant Partner	196
	5.2	Covenant and Israel		198
		5.2.1	The Same Israel As Before	198
		5.2.2	Biblical References	201
		5.2.3	Straddling the Fence	204
	5.3	The New Covenant		206
		5.3.1	When Effectuated?	206
		5.3.2	Seven Promises	207
		5.3.3	Minority and Majority	209

	5.4	Covenant and Church	210
		5.4.1 The Church of the Firstborn	210
		5.4.2 Differences	213
		5.4.3 The Messianic Torah	215
		5.4.4 Letter and Spirit	217
	5.5	The Significance of *Ha'Aretz*	219
		5.5.1 The Land: An Everlasting Inheritance	219
		5.5.2 God's Dwelling Place	222
		5.5.3 An Indissoluble Bond	225
	5.6	The Land of the Fathers	228
		5.6.1 The *T'shubah*	228
		5.6.2 A Second Dispersion?	230
		5.6.3 The Land During the Messianic Kingdom	231
	5.7	The Testimony of Other Prophets	234
		5.7.1 The Messiah: Branch, Powerful Ruler	234
		5.7.2 In Zion It Happens	237
		5.7.3 Where Does the Messiah Return?	239
6	The Physical and the Spiritual Israel		243
	6.1	Physical Israel	243
		6.1.1 Preterism	243
		6.1.2 More on Matthew 24	246
		6.1.3 Jesus' Return is Future	249
	6.2	Confirmation by the Apostle Paul	251
		6.2.1 The Place of Romans 9–11	251
		6.2.2 Isaiah's and Paul's Message	253
	6.3	No Church in the Tanakh	256
		6.3.1 The Meaning of *Ekklēsia*	256
		6.3.2 The Church is Post-Pentecost	258
	6.4	A "Spiritual Israel"? Four "Proofs" Refuted	261
		6.4.1 First "Proof"	261
		6.4.2 Second "Proof"	264
		6.4.3 Third "Proof"	265

	6.4.4	Fourth "Proof"	266
6.5	A "Spiritual Israel"? Four More "Proofs" Refuted		268
	6.5.1	Fifth "Proof"	268
	6.5.2	Sixth "Proof"	269
	6.5.3	Seventh "Proof"	271
	6.5.4	Eighth "Proof"	272
6.6	A "Spiritual Israel"? Four More "Proofs" Refuted		274
	6.6.1	Ninth "Proof"	274
	6.6.2	Tenth "Proof"	275
	6.6.3	Eleventh "Proof"	277
	6.6.4	Twelfth "Proof"	278
6.7	Summary		279
	6.7.1	Ethnic Israel Today	279
	6.7.2	Points of Attention	281
	6.7.3	No Two-Ways Doctrine	284
6.8	Two Types		286
	6.8.1	Jacob and His Two Wives	286
	6.8.2	The Loved and the Unloved Wife	287
7	The Old Testament Messianic Hope		289
	7.1	Messianic Hope in the Tanakh	289
	7.1.1	Many Messianic Prophecies	289
	7.1.2	The Tanakh and the New Testament	292
	7.1.3	The Gospels and Paul about the Tanakh	294
	7.2	Balance	295
	7.2.1	Interpretation and Application	295
	7.2.2	The *Entire* Torah Speaks of the Messiah	297
	7.2.3	Recognizable Messianic Predictions	299
	7.3	From Adam to Judah	300
	7.3.1	Adam	300
	7.3.2	Shem and Eber	302

	7.3.3	Abraham and Isaac	302
	7.3.4	Jacob	304
	7.3.5	Judah	306
7.4	The Shoot of Jesse	308
	7.4.1	Bethlehem	308
	7.4.2	Jesse	310
7.5	David	312
	7.5.1	"My Servant David"	312
	7.5.2	The Son of David	312
	7.5.3	David and Amos	314
7.6	Sons of David	315
	7.6.1	Ahaz	315
	7.6.2	Jechoniah	317
7.7	Son of God	318
	7.7.1	Psalm 2	318
	7.7.2	Isaiah 9:6-7	320
7.8	The Son of Man in Daniel 7	323
	7.8.1	*Ben-Adam*	323
	7.8.2	Daniel 7:13	324
	7.8.3	A Messianic Figure	325
7.9	The Son of Man in the Psalms	327
	7.9.1	Psalm 8 and Hebrews 2	327
	7.9.2	The Messianic Thrust	328
	7.9.3	Psalm 80	330
7.10	The Messianic Prophet	331
	7.10.1	The Prophet Announced by Moses	331
	7.10.2	More than Moses	332
7.11	The Messianic Priest	334
	7.11.1	Psalm 110:4	334
	7.11.2	Zechariah 6:12-13	336
7.12	The Messianic King	337
	7.12.1	Introduction	337
	7.12.2	Psalms	338

		7.12.3	Zechariah	341
	7.13		Other Messianic Psalms	342
		7.13.1	Psalm 16	342
		7.13.2	Psalm 22	344
		7.13.3	Psalm 40	345
		7.13.4	Psalm 69	346
		7.13.5	Psalm 110	347
		7.13.6	Psalm 118	348
	7.14		The Servant of the Lord	350
		7.14.1	The Four Poems	350
		7.14.2	Various Layers	352
		7.14.3	Servant-Messiah	354
	7.15		Two More Messianic Passages	356
		7.15.1	Daniel 9	356
		7.15.2	Hosea 11	358
8	Jesus and the Jews			359
	8.1		Jesus the Jew	359
		8.1.1	Judah and Joseph	359
		8.1.2	Jesus and the Pharisees	362
	8.2		Jesus and the Jews	364
		8.2.1	A Growing Chasm	364
		8.2.2	Four Similarities	366
		8.2.3	Three More Similarities	368
	8.3		Jesus, a Jewish Rabbi	370
		8.3.1	Jesus' Jewish Origin	370
		8.3.2	Jesus the Rabbi	372
	8.4		Jesus: A Different Person	374
		8.4.1	The New Moses	374
		8.4.2	Greater Than Moses	377
		8.4.3	Jesus the Son of Man	378
		8.4.4	Jesus the Son of David	379
		8.4.5	Jesus Claimed Divinity	380
	8.5		Jesus: A Different Ministry	382

	8.5.1	Jesus Claimed to Be the Only Way	382
	8.5.2	Jesus Claimed to Be the True Sin Offering	384
	8.5.3	Jesus "Insufficiently" Honored Israel's Election	387
	8.5.4	Jesus Also Welcomed Gentiles	389
8.6	Double Rejection		392
	8.6.1	The Leaders of Judaism Rejected Jesus	392
	8.6.2	The Breach	394
	8.6.3	Jesus Rejected the Leaders of Judaism	397
8.7	Two Transitional Parables		399
	8.7.1	The Wicked Tenants	399
	8.7.2	The Wedding Feast	402
8.8	Impediments From Christians for Jews		405
	8.8.1	Impediments 1–2	405
	8.8.2	Impediments 3–4	406
	8.8.3	Impediments 5–7	409
9 Israel in Prophecy in the Tanakh			413
9.1	Moses		414
	9.1.1	Deuteronomy 4:30	414
	9.1.2	Deuteronomy 32:35–43	415
9.2	Isaiah		417
	9.2.1	Isaiah 7:14	417
	9.2.2	Isaiah 9:6–7	418
	9.2.3	Isaiah 10–11	420
9.3	Vague or Detailed Interpretation		421
	9.3.1	The Neighboring Nations	421
	9.3.2	The Two and the Ten Tribes	423
9.4	More Isaiah Prophecies		425
	9.4.1	Isaiah 28:7–19	425
	9.4.2	Isaiah 52:13–53:12	426
9.5	Other Major Prophets		428

	9.5.1	Jeremiah	428
	9.5.2	Ezekiel 36	431
	9.5.3	Ezekiel 37:15–22	433
	9.5.4	Daniel	434
9.6		Some Minor Prophets	436
	9.6.1	Hosea	436
	9.6.2	Joel	437
	9.6.3	Micah	439
	9.6.4	Zechariah	440
9.7		Not Everything Literal	444
	9.7.1	Isaiah 11:6–8	444
	9.7.2	Isaiah 40:4	446
	9.7.3	Isaiah 55:12–13	447
9.8		Israel's Past and Future	448
	9.8.1	God's Faithfulness	448
	9.8.2	A Hermeneutical Key	451
	9.8.3	The First and the Second Exile	453
10	**Israel Is Not the Church**		**457**
10.1		Israel and the Ecclesia	457
	10.1.1	Three Models	457
	10.1.2	Similarities	460
	10.1.3	Differences	462
10.2		Israel Set Aside	465
	10.2.1	"Rejection"	465
	10.2.2	Always "God's People"?	467
	10.2.3	Election and Responsibility	469
10.3		Israel and the Ecclesia	471
	10.3.1	Which Bride?	471
	10.3.2	"The Others"	473
10.4		The Destruction of Jerusalem	476
	10.4.1	Predictions	476
	10.4.2	The Crimson Thread	478
	10.4.3	The Only Explanation	479

10.5	"Until"	481
	10.5.1 In the New Testament	481
	10.5.2 In the Tanakh: Isaiah	483
	10.5.3 In the Tanakh: Ezekiel	484
	10.5.4 In the Tanakh: Micah	485
10.6	The "Trees" of the End Time	486
	10.6.1 "The Fig Tree and All the Trees"	486
	10.6.2 The Neighbors	488
10.7	Two Other Visions	489
	10.7.1 The Valley of Dry Bones	489
	10.7.2 The Nation Scattered and Peeled	491
10.8	The Remnant of Israel	494
	10.8.1 Its Character	494
	10.8.2 Its Formation	496
10.9	"All Israel" or a "Remnant"?	498
	10.9.1 The Righteous and the Wicked	498
	10.9.2 "All Israel" Is the Repentant Remnant	499
	10.9.3 Final Redemption	500
11 The Ecclesia Is Not Israel		503
11.1	The Power of Tradition	503
	11.1.1 Introduction	503
	11.1.2 The Belgic Confession	505
	11.1.3 The Westminster Confession	507
11.2 The Heidelberg Catechism		508
	11.2.1 Quotations	508
	11.2.2 The Ecclesia and Eden	509
	11.2.3 A Paradigm Shift	511
11.3 The Ecclesia is Post-Pentecost		512
	11.3.1 No Unified Entity	512
	11.3.2 The Ecclesia: A Future Matter	513
	11.3.3 The Ecclesia: A Matter Formerly Hidden	514
	11.3.4 The Foundation of the Ecclesia	516

		11.3.5	The Position of John the Baptist	517
		11.3.6	The Significance of Jesus' Death	517
		11.3.7	The Significance of Jesus' Glorification	519
		11.3.8	The Ecclesia: Dwelling Place of the Holy Spirit	520
		11.3.9	The Ecclesia: A Spirit-Baptized Company	521
	11.4	Parallelisms Between Believers in the Tanakh and Believers in the New Testament		522
		11.4.1	Similarities	522
		11.4.2	Additional Similarities	526
		11.4.3	Metaphors	528
	11.5	Differences		530
		11.5.1	The Ecclesia As People of God	530
		11.5.2	The Ecclesia As the Family of God	531
		11.5.3	The Ecclesia As the Body of Christ	533
		11.5.4	The Ecclesia As Temple of the Holy Spirit	534
		11.5.5	Imitating the Tanakh	535
	11.6	A Trivial Difference?		537
		11.6.1	First Shepherds of Sheep, Then Fishers of People	537
		11.6.2	*Both* Shepherds of Sheep *and* Fishers of People	538
	11.7	New Approaches		540
		11.7.1	Two Peoples/One People	540
		11.7.2	Literal or Spiritual	542
		11.7.3	Ecclesia and Kingdom	544
12	The One People of God			547
	12.1	"All Israel"		547
		12.1.1	Jewish Privileges	547
		12.1.2	A Double Election	550
		12.1.3	Romans 11:26	552

12.2		Is the Olive Tree Israel?	554
	12.2.1	Features of the Tree	554
	12.2.2	Warning and Prophecy	556
12.3		The Covenant Tree	558
	12.3.1	God's Promises	558
	12.3.2	Kinds of "Children"	560
	12.3.3	Blessing and Grafting	561
12.4		God's People	563
	12.4.1	Two Peoples or One?	563
	12.4.2	Continuity and Discontinuity	565
	12.4.3	*'Am* and *Goy*, *Laos* and *Ethnos*	568
	12.4.4	Two Pairs: Two Rocks	569
	12.4.5	Two Dozens	570
12.5		People on a Pilgrimage	572
	12.5.1	A Double Exodus	572
	12.5.2	The Ecclesia On Its Way	573
12.6		Moses and Jesus	576
	12.6.1	Parallels	576
	12.6.2	Two Births	578
	12.6.3	Flavius Josephus	580
12.7		Lessons from the Torah	580
	12.7.1	Sinai and Zion	580
	12.7.2	Commemoration	584
	12.7.3	Forever Remembered	586
13 Israel in New Testament Prophecy: Gospels and Acts			591
13.1		"The Abomination" in Matthew 24	592
	13.1.1	Various Views	592
	13.1.2	Matthew 24 Versus Luke 21	593
13.2		Jesus' Reply	595
	13.2.1	The Great Tribulation	595
	13.2.2	Conclusion	597
13.3		Ways of Interpretation	600
	13.3.1	Four Options	600

	13.3.2	Approaches	601
	13.3.3	"The Abomination of Desolation"	603
13.4	Comparison with Luke 21		606
	13.4.1	Differences	606
	13.4.2	Harmony	608
13.5	Matthew 10:23		610
	13.5.1	A Difficult Verse?	610
	13.5.2	A Line to the Future	611
13.6	Other New Testament Passages		612
	13.6.1	Matthew 19:28 and Luke 22:29–30	612
	13.6.2	Acts 26:7 and James 1:1	613
	13.6.3	Conclusion	615
13.7	Acts 1:6–8		617
	13.7.1	A Question and an Answer	617
	13.7.2	Dreaming of an Earthly Kingdom	618
	13.7.3	Jesus' Additional Remark	620
13.8	Acts 3:19–26		621
	13.8.1	Israelocentric	621
	13.8.2	Messianic "Times"	622
	13.8.3	The Lame Shall Leap!	624
13.9	First Peter 2:9–12		625
	13.9.1	Jewish Addressees?	625
	13.9.2	Gentile-Like Jews	627
14	**Israel in New Testament Prophecy: Paul and Revelation**		**629**
14.1	Romans 11: Hardening Now, Salvation Later		629
	14.1.1	The Place of Romans 9–11	629
	14.1.2	Contrast: First Argument	632
	14.1.3	Contrast: Second Argument	633
14.2	Then Will Be the Restoration		635
	14.2.1	"Hardening"	635
	14.2.2	When and How?	637
	14.2.3	"Zion"	638

14.3		Romans 11 from Various Viewpoints	639
	14.3.1	The Supersessionist View	639
	14.3.2	Universalism	642
	14.3.3	Particularism	644
	14.3.4	Jesus' Testimony	645
14.4		Israel Elsewhere with Paul	648
	14.4.1	Second Corinthians 3:16	648
	14.4.2	Second Thessalonians 2:4	651
	14.4.3	The Two "Beasts"	653
14.5		Israel in Revelation 7–11	654
	14.5.1	Revelation 7:1–8	654
	14.5.2	Revelation 10:1–11:13	657
14.6		Revelation 12	660
	14.6.1	The Woman in Revelation 12	660
	14.6.2	Vicissitudes of the Woman	663
14.7		Israel in Revelation 13–16	665
	14.7.1	Revelation 13:14–18	665
	14.7.2	Revelation 14:1–5	666
	14.7.3	Revelation 16:13–16	668
14.8		The Two Jerusalems	669
	14.8.1	The Earthly Jerusalem	669
	14.8.2	The Heavenly Jerusalem	671
Bibliography			673
Scripture Index			703
Subject Index			749

Series Preface

BY MEANS OF THIS PREFACE, the editor and publisher of this series wish to help the reader both understand and process the content of these volumes.

The capacities and erudition of Dr. Willem Ouweneel need no demonstration or defense from us. His voluminous work and prodigious writing stand as a testimony to his love for the Lord Jesus Christ, God's Word, and God's people.

But these volumes present ideas that will surprise some, anger others, and possibly confuse still others. Both the editor and publisher disagree with some of Dr. Ouweneel's assertions and conclusions, but this is not the place for offering our counter-arguments. That requires an altogether different venue. Nevertheless, discerning readers will legitimately wonder why this editor and publisher invested effort and resources in putting these volumes into print.

At least three reasons justify that investment. Each of them is very sensitive.

The first reason is: *self-examination*. Some of our readers may conclude that, in presenting his exegetical, doctrinal, and historical case, Dr. Ouweneel is "coloring outside the lines" of what they have come to believe. He challenges deeply and firmly held convictions and beliefs, like those associated with Israel, with the law of God, with election and reprobation, with infant baptism, with covenant theology, and with justification. At each point, his challenges call us readers to self-examination, regarding our love for Scripture, for the God of Scripture, and for the Truth revealed and incarnated personally in Jesus Christ. One of Ouweneel's challenges is for us believers in Jesus Christ who are Reformed and Presbyterian church members to recognize that there are millions, even billions, of Jesus-believers who disagree with us *and are nevertheless genuine Christians*. And they ought to be acknowledged as such.

The second reason is: *repentance*. Coming, as they do, from one who lives and teaches outside the orbit of many of our readers, Dr. Ouweneel's observations about the state of our (numerous) churches and of our (interminable) doctrinal squabbles ought to embarrass us Reformed and Presbyterian church members. Our incessant polemicizing, our cantankerous stridency, and our offenses against the unity of Christ's church seriously compromise the gospel's witness to the watching world. Brothers and sisters, we must repent of these, for the sake of the gospel, for the sake of the church's witness, and for the sake of our children.

The third reason is: *ecumenicity*. This reason may indeed strike you as strange, but one of the salutary outcomes of reading Dr. Ouweneel's arguments can be this: *not* that you surrender your commitments and convictions that are being challenged, but instead that you come to *respect* and *love* those Jesus-believers who don't share them with you. These Christians are those whose spiritual pilgrimage and gospel-guided history have not brought them to the same place on the road, but who nonetheless are walking the same road as we.

You may well be asking: How, then, is this different from advocating doctrinal relativism? If these distinctive features of Reformed confession and theology are biblical, then why is Dr. Ouweneel being given a microphone for proclaiming his criticisms and rejections of these distinctive emphases of Reformed teaching? The short answer is this: So that from this brother in Christ, this close cousin in the faith, this fellow pilgrim-soldier, we may learn how to lock arms with other Jesus-believers as we face unbelief in our day, even if we can't hold hands. So that we may learn what it means to be Jesus-believers *first*, Reformed or Presbyterian confessors *second*, and only then, *thirdly, theological advocates*.

So we leave you with this challenge: Why do you believe what you believe? What is your biblical warrant? Dr. Ouweneel presents fairly the various positions prevalent within Christianity. The reader will learn why others believe what they believe, and why they don't emphasize certain teachings in the same way that we do.

These books, then, are *not* for the faint of faith. But they *are* for those wanting to grow up and mature into the unity of faith in our Lord Jesus Christ (John 17: 20–23; Eph. 4:13).

Nelson D. Kloosterman, editor
John Hultink, publisher

Author's Preface

IN THE NOVEL *Yesterday's Streets*, written by the Jewish German-American author Silvia Tennenbaum,[1] the Jewish businessman Eduard Wertheim declares that Jews are like anyone else, and if they were not, they should become so. Such was the viewpoint of this assimilated, wealthy Jew, who, during the first half of the twentieth century, had acquired a leading position in the German *bourgeoisie*. This lasted until 1933 when the Nazi era began and Wertheim was forced to flee. During this era, the world learned once again that the Jews are *not* like everyone else, and never will be. The early propagator of anti-Semitism, Haman, the *tzorēr hayyehudim* ("enemy of the Jews," Est. 3:10; 8:1; 9:10, 24), long ago told the Persian king: "There is a particular people scattered and dispersed among the peoples in all the provinces of your kingdom. Their laws are different from those of every other people; moreover, they don't observe the king's laws. It doesn't befit the king to tolerate them" (Est. 3:8).

For century after century, such intolerance has been encountered by the Jews among other nations: these people were a fly in the ointment, a thorn in their side, deserving to be ripped out, different from everyone else. The Gentiles could at least try as much as possible to ignore Israel — Jewish people isolated in their ghettos. Christians, too, have often responded this way throughout history. Christian theologians formulated their creeds, confessions, and catechisms, and penned their dogmatic handbooks without mentioning Israel or burying Israel in their footnotes. Ask yourself: Down through the centuries, which works of systematic theology have

---

1. Tennenbaum (1982).

included a chapter on the *locus* (topic) of Israelology,[2] the "doctrine of Israel"? Still today we encounter orthodox Christians who admit they are not particularly interested in Israel. This is like admitting that you are not very interested in your older brother. Wherever the Jews were not chased out, put to death, or forced to assimilate, many people have tried to ignore them.

Today, after and because of the Shoah (the Holocaust), ignoring Israel while formulating theological doctrine is no longer an option. Christian theologians must engage the numerous issues surrounding Israel, not just historical and political issues, but especially theological questions. The phenomenon of "Christian theology after Auschwitz" does exist, as one theologian has pointed out.[3] Whether the theology that I am seeking to formulate belongs to this phenomenon is another question altogether; but it is true that in their formulations, theologians will never again be able to ignore Israel.

In my opinion, rather than being an incidental discussion in systematic theology, Israelology is in fact one of its primary subjects. I hope to explicate and defend this claim in this book, which is intended to be an introduction to the *locus* of Israelology. This work presents a *theology* of Israel, rather than a history of Israel, or of Jewry and Judaism, or of the state of Israel, and so on, although all these matters will be touched upon. A theology of Israel is that part of systematic theology that analyzes the origin, place, significance, character, purpose, and future of Israel, as we find these matters expressed in both the Old Testament and the New Testament. Finally, this theology examines the significance of all these dimensions pertaining to Israel with a view to understanding the origin, place, significance, character, purpose, and future of Christianity.

This is not the first book that I have written about Israel. In addition to books specifically about Israel and Judaism,[4] I have penned other publications in which the Jewish people play an important

---

2. The term seems to have been coined by the Messianic Jew and theologian Arnold Fuchtenbaum (1994, title).
3. Jansen (1981, 1999).
4. Ouweneel (1982a; 1991; 1999; 2000a; 2001a; 2001b; 2002; 2014; 2019); see also Van de Kamp and Ouweneel (2013; written together with orthodox Rabbi Lody Van de Kamp).

role.⁵ However, until now far I have not provided a unified presentation of a developed Israelology; hence this work, which is a translation and elaboration of the first half of an earlier Dutch work.⁶ Various subjects that might have found a place in this volume have been discussed in some of my Dutch-language volumes.⁷

Why have I written so much about Israel? The fact that the great-grandmother of my mother's great-grandmother was a Lieberman was insufficient reason; I am as much of a *goy* as most of my readers. I was born in 1944, a year that has been called the most horrible year of all world history because it featured the nadir of the Shoah. But it was also a year of hope: I was born four days before Operation Overlord, the successful invasion of Nazi-occupied Western Europe by the Allied forces. My parents had married a year earlier. My mother's last employment involved caring for two children from a wealthy Jewish family. Their father had died in a concentration camp in early 1945; their mother had died while in hiding from the Nazis. The children had escaped; one became a well-known medical doctor in the United States.⁸ Throughout my life, Israel has always been a close companion. From the time I was around twenty years old, I have regularly visited the country of Israel. A good friend there is an orthodox rabbi, but I also know secular Jewish scholars there, as well as Messianic Jews and Evangelical Palestinians. If we were ever to be banned from the Netherlands, I hope my wife and I would be allowed to live in Jerusalem, despite our age.

The title of this book indicates that it is part of my "Eternal" series, whose volumes discuss a number of dogmatic subjects of eternal significance. (Please note, I do not claim that the books are of eternal significance, but their subjects are.) In a sense, the previous volumes are all related to this one: the "Eternal Word" is primarily the Tanakh,⁹ Israel's Holy Book, with its divinely inspired

---

5. Ouweneel (1998a; 2003a; 2010a; 2012a; 2012b).
6. Ouweneel (2019a).
7. Ouweneel (2010a; 2012a; 2014).
8. See his autobiography (Kan [2010]).
9. The term "Tanakh" refers to what Christians call the "Old Testament" (because of 2 Cor. 3:14); the Jewish word is an acronym: T = *Torah* (the five books of Moses), N = *Nebi'im* (the early and the later prophetic books: Joshua to Mala-

commentary: the New Testament, written by Jewish authors, as well.[10] The "Eternal Torah" is the Torah given first to Israel. The "Eternal God" is none other than the God of Israel. The "Eternal Christ [Anointed]" is primarily the Messiah (Anointed) of Israel. The "Eternal Purpose" refers primarily to the redemption of Israel.[11] The "Eternal Salvation" is based on the principle first revealed in the Tanakh (the Old Testament): "[W]ithout the shedding of blood there is no forgiveness of sins" (Heb. 9:22; cf. Lev. 17:11). The "Eternal Covenant" refers primarily to the covenants made with the patriarchs, and their offspring: the people of Israel.[12] And the "Eternal Kingdom" is the kingdom of the King set by God upon Zion, God's holy hill (Ps. 2:6).

Conversely, some people are "Judeophile" Christians, who seem to know about *nothing else* than Israel. This seems to me unhealthy as well. They ought not to forget that, for instance, sincere, Bible-believing Palestinian Christians—and these exist—are closer to them than any (not-yet-Jesus-confessing) Jew. What binds us together with Israel is the God of Israel, the Book of Israel, as well as the expectation of the coming Messiah. What binds us together with Jesus-believing Palestinians (as well as with Jesus-believing Jews and Jesus-believing people throughout the world) is the person of Jesus Christ, and our salvation in him.

Actually, I was challenged to write this book by a staunch supersessionist in the Netherlands, Dr. Steven Paas.[13] This may explain why my polemic against supersessionism occupies a larger place in this book than would perhaps have been the case in a more thetical treatment of the subject.

This is a two-volume project. The first volume focuses on the biblical Israel, the Israel we find throughout both the Tanakh and the New Testament. The second volume focuses on the Israel who lived in post-biblical times until today, and on its prophesied future.

---

chi), Kh = *Ketubim* or "writings" (from Psalms to Chronicles).

10. Perhaps with the exception of Luke, but he was presumably a Jewish proselyte before he met Jesus Christ.
11. Matt. 15:20; Luke 1:68–71; 2:25; Rom. 15:8.
12. Gen. 15 and 17; Exod. 19–24; Jer. 31:31–34; Heb. 8.
13. Cf. Paas (2012, 2014, 2015, 2018).

Author's Preface

Bible quotations in this book usually come from the English Standard Version. Unless otherwise noted, italics within Bible quotations have been added.

I warmly thank my editor, Dr. Nelson D. Kloosterman, and my publisher, John Hultink, for their constant support and encouragement.

Loerik (Houten, the Netherlands), Autumn 2020
Willem J. Ouweneel

From *Nabucco* (i.e., "Nebuchadnezzar," 1842), by Giuseppe Verdi. about the Israelites in exile (Italian text, Temistocle Solera, based on a French drama by Auguste Anicet-Bourgeois and Francis Cornu), the text of the famous "Chorus of the Hebrew Slaves":

Va, pensiero, sull'ali dorate;	Fix, my thoughts, on wings of gold;
va, ti posa sui clivi, sui colli,	Go settle upon the slopes and the hills,
ove olezzano tepide e molli	where, soft and mild, the sweet airs
l'aure dolci del suolo natal!	of my native land smell fragrant!
Del Giordano le rive saluta,	Greet the banks of the Jordan
di Sionne le torri atterrate.	And Zion's toppled towers.
O, mia patria sì bella e perduta!	Oh, my homeland, so lovely and so lost!
O, membranza, sì cara e fatal!	Oh, memory, so dear and so dead!
Arpa d'or dei fatidici vati,	Golden harp of the prophets of old,
perché muta dal salice pendi?	why do you now hang silent upon the willow?[1]
Le memorie nel petto raccendi,	Rekindle the memories in our hearts,
ci favella del tempo che fu!	And speak of times gone by!
O simile di Solima ai fati,	Mindful of the fate of [Jerusalem],[2]
traggi un suono di crudo lamento,	Let me cry out with sad lamentation,
o t'ispiri il Signore un concento	or else may the Lord strengthen me
che ne infonda al patire virtù!	to bear these sufferings![3]

---

1. Cf. Psalm 137:2.
2. Not "Solomon's temple," as several translations have it; the word "Solima" comes from *Hierosoluma*, a Gk. designation of Jerusalem.
3. "What to expect from *Nabucco*," study guide, Metropolitan Opera, September 2016, pages 25 and 33; available at https://en.wikipedia.org/wiki/Va,_pensiero.

Abbreviations

AMP	Amplified Bible
AMPC	Amplified Bible, Classic Edition
ASV	American Standard Version
BRG	BRG Bible
CEB	Common English Bible
CEV	Contemporary English Version
CJB	Complete Jewish Bible
DARBY	Darby Translation
DLNT	Disciples' Literal New Translation
DRA	Douay-Rheims 1899 American Edition
ERV	Easy-to-Read Version
ESV	English Standard Version
EXB	Expanded Bible
GNT	Good News Translation
GNV	1599 Geneva Bible
GW	God's Word Translation
HCSB	Holman Christian Standard Bible
ICB	International Children's Bible
ISV	International Standard Version
JUB	Jubilee Bible 2000
KJ21	21st Century King James Version
KJV	King James Version

LEB	Lexham English Bible
MEV	Modern English Version
MOUNCE	Mounce Reverse-Interlinear New Testament
MSG	The Message
NASB	New American Standard Bible
NIRV	New International Reader's Version
NMB	New Matthew Bible
NCV	New Century Version
NET	New English Translation
NIV	New International Version
NLV	New Life Version
NKJV	New King James Version
NOG	Names of God Bible
OJB	Orthodox Jewish Bible
PHILLIPS	J. B. Phillips
RSV	Revised Standard Version
TLB	Living Bible
TLV	Tree of Life Version
TPT	The Passion Translation
VOICE	The Voice
WE	Worldwide English (New Testament)
WEB	World English Bible
YLT	Young's Literal Translation

Other Sources

BT	Kelly, W., ed. 1856–1920. *Bible Treasury: A Monthly Review of Prophetic and Practical Subjects*. Available at https://bibletruthpublishers.com/bible-treasury/lpvl22465.

CD	Barth, K. 1956. *Church Dogmatics*. Translated by T. H. L. Parker et al. Vols. 1/1–4/4. Louisville, KY: Westminster John Knox.
COT	Commentaar op het Oude Testament
CNT	Commentaar op het Nieuwe Testament
CR	*Corpus Reformatorum*. 1st series and 2nd series. Vols. 1–87. Brunswick: Schwetschke, 1834–1900.
CW	Darby, J. N. n.d.-a *The Collected Writings of J. N. Darby*. Kingston-on-Thames: Stow Hill Bible and Tract Depot.
DJG	Green, J. B. and S. McKnight, eds. 1992. *Dictionary of Jesus and the Gospels*. Downers Grove, IL: InterVarsity Press.
EBC	The Expositor's Bible Commentary
EDR	Evangelische Dogmatische Reeks
EGT	Expositor's Greek Testament
EJ	Skolnik. F. 2007. *Encyclopedia Judaica*. 2nd ed. 14 vols. Farmington Hills, MI: Keter Publishing House Ltd.
KDC	Keil, C. F. and F. Delitzsch. 1976–1977. *Commentary on the Old Testament*. 10 vols. Grand Rapids, MI: Eerdmans.
KV	Korte Verklaring der Heilige Schrift
NICNT	New International Commentary on the New Testament
NICOT	New International Commentary on the Old Testament
NIGTC	New International Greek Testament Commentary
RC	Dennison, J. T., Jr., ed. 2008–2014. *Reformed Confessions of the 16th and 17th Centuries in English Translation*. 4 vols. Grand Rapids, MI: Reformation Heritage Books.
RD	Bavinck, H. 2002–2008. *Reformed Dogmatics*. Edited by J. Bolt. Translated by J. Vriend. 4

	vols. Grand Rapids, MI: Baker Academic.
SBB	Soncino Press Books of the Bible
ST	Chafer, L. S. 1983. *Systematic Theology*. 15th ed. 8 vols. Dallas, TX: Dallas Seminary Press.
SYN	Darby, J.N. n.d.-b. *Synopsis of the Books of the Bible*. 5 vols. London: G. Morrish.
TDNT	Kittel, G. et al., eds. 1964–1976. *Theological Dictionary of the New Testament*. Translated by G. W. Bromiley. 10 vols. Grand Rapids, MI: Eerdmans.
TNTC	Tyndale New Testament Commentaries

Chapter 1
The Calling of Israel

Im-eshkachekh[1] *Yerushalayim tishkakh y'mini.*
If I forget you, O Jerusalem,
>let my right hand forget its skill [or, wither away]!

>>Psalm 137:5
>>Quoted by J. A. Nederbragt[2]

Who will have pity on you, O Jerusalem,
>or who will grieve for you?
Who will turn aside
>to ask about your welfare?

>>Jeremiah 15:5

---

1. For our transliteration of biblical Heb. in this volume, the transliteration *kh* (Heb. *khet*) must be pronounced like the *ch* in Loch Ness, and the transliteration *ch* represents a sound between *h* and *kh*. The Heb. *aleph* is transliterated as [ʼ] and the Heb. *ayin* is transliterated as [ʻ]; within a transliterated word the diacritical [ʼ] can also represent a mute *e*, or it can divide two vowels that must be pronounced separately.
2. Nederbragt (1957, 5; also the title); Johan Alexander Nederbragt was the Dutch consul, from 1948 ambassador, to Israel (1946–1953).

THE ETERNAL PEOPLE: ISRAEL IN THE TANAKH AND THE NEW TESTAMENT

1.1 Introduction

1.1.1 The Eternal People

> Thus says *Adonai*,
> Isra'el's King and Redeemer,
> *Adonai-Tzva'ot* [i.e., Lord of hosts]:
> "I am the first, and I am the last;
> besides me there is no God.
> Who is like me? Let him speak out!
> Let him show me clearly what has been happening
> since I set up the *eternal people*;
> let him foretell future signs and events. . . ."

THIS IS WHAT WE READ in Isaiah 44:6–7 (CJB). The second to the last line contains the italicized phrase that renders the Hebrew *'am-olam*, usually translated as "the eternal people" (or, "an eternal people," LEB). Other translations have "ancient people" (ESV), "my people long ago" (NOG). Some expositors believe, however, that the context is pointing in another direction. They think these verses are referring to "the dead" (people who lived long ago, Ezek. 26:20), or to ancient ancestors before Noah's Flood (cf. Job 22:15),[3] or to Israel's patriarchs Abraham, Isaac, and Jacob.

Many other expositors see this "eternal people" as a reference to none other than Israel, a people that originated in distant antiquity, as Israel says through Jeremiah (31:3): "The Lord[4] appeared to me from ages past [others read: from afar], [saying], 'I have loved you with an everlasting love; therefore with lovingkindness I have drawn you [and] continued My faithfulness to you" (AMP). Israel is the "eternal people" because it originated long ago. Israel is the "eternal people" also because it is "everlasting": if the kingdom of

---

3. See http://biblehub.com/isaiah/44–7.htm.
4. The word Lord, printed in small capitals, which is always a rendering of the tetragrammaton (YHWH), appears in many English translations, following the rendering *Kurios* in the Septuagint (LXX, the ancient Gk. translation of the Tanakh by Jews) and *Dominus* in the Vulgate (the ancient Lat. translation of the Bible by Jerome). Where "Lord" appears in the New Testament I have taken the liberty of using small capitals where I believe the reference is to YHWH, especially in quotations from the Tanakh.

Israel ("the holy people of the Most High") is an "everlasting kingdom" (Dan. 7:27), then Israel itself is "everlasting."[5] They are an "eternal people," that is, a people from many ages past, and with many ages still future.

The indigenous peoples of North and South America and the Australian aboriginals presumably lived in their respective continents (long) before Israel lived in Canaan, that is, before the thirteenth or fifteenth century BC (the accepted date depends on the chronology used[6]). But how many nations (a) are far older than three thousand years, (b) formed a civilized and well-organized society so many centuries ago, and (c), still possess an identity as a distinct nation?[7]

Israel is in truth "the people of ages ago," and we may add, Israel is still "*God's* people of ages ago." The apostle[8] Paul called the faithful among them "the Israel of God" (Gal. 6:16).[9] To be sure, today the name *Lo-'Ammi* is *formally* written over the nation (Hos. 1:9), but this belongs to God's temporary providential ways with his people; *existentially*, Israel is and remains God's people, and one day this will become visible to all (1:12; 2:22). In the end times, it will be said, "The remnant of *my people* shall plunder them [i.e., the hostile neighbors], and the survivors of *my nation* shall possess them. This shall be their lot in return for their pride, because they taunted and boasted against the *people of the* LORD *of hosts*" (Zeph. 2:9–10).

These claims being asserted here might not (yet) be self-evident to some readers. Is *ethnic* Israel still formally "God's people"? Will they be so also in the end times? An affirmative answer to both of

---

5. We will see that the terms "everlasting" or "eternal" in such passages means "lasting forever as long as the present earth exists."

6. Many believe that the entrance into Canaan fits best historically and chronologically in the thirteenth century BC; those who take 1 Kings 6:1 literally (Solomon's temple-building [969 BC] began 480 years after the exodus from Egypt), believe it fits best in the fifteenth century BC; see Kitchen (2006).

7. Perhaps the Greeks? The Persians (Iranians)? The Kurds (who are largely the ancient Medes)?

8. An "apostle" (from Gk. *apostolos*) was an "emissary," Heb. *shaliach* (plur.: *sh'lichim*).

9. We will see later why those who think here of the church are mistaken (§6.2.2).

these questions comprises the thesis that I wish to defend in this two-volume work on Israelology. "[F]or the gifts and the calling of God are irrevocable"; he is not able and willing to come back on them (cf. Rom. 11:29), for this calling is based not only on God's promises, but also on his solemn *oaths*.[10] Thus, the reason that the nation of Israel still exists is because Israel still has a mighty God; he was explicitly and emphatically identified throughout Scripture as the "God of Israel," beginning in Exodus 5:1.[11]

Before leaving this introductory claim, I would issue my first challenge to supersessionists (Christians who believe that the church is the "spiritual Israel"): If indeed the Ecclesia[12] is now "(the spiritual) Israel," if there is no longer any room for ethnic Israel as such in the counsels and ways of God, why has God so obviously preserved ethnic Israel to this very day? Why have the Jews not been gradually swallowed up by the masses of the Gentile world, and lost their identity forever, as has happened to so many tribes and nations? I will have to direct many more questions to supersessionists throughout these two volumes, but this one is a good starter: *Why are the Jews still around?* Why has God allowed them to reestablish their own nation state? Let me reply immediately with an interrogatory assertion: Could it be because God is still the God of *ethnic* Israel?

Near the Qotel in Jerusalem, on a busy religious day, a Jew once asked me: "Are you Jewish?" My answer was: "No, but I love the God of Israel." His response: "He is the God of *all* people." My reply: "Yes, but he loves to call himself the God of Israel." His re-

---

10. Gen. 22:16; 24:7; 26:3; 50:24; Ps. 105:9; Isa. 62:8–9; Jer. 11:5; Micah 7:20; Heb. 6:13–14; actually, we should also mention here God's oaths concerning the unbelieving majority of Israel: Ps. 95:11; Amos 4:2; Heb. 3:11; 4:3 (cf. this "never" with the "never" in Isa. 62:8).

11. From Exod. 3:7 onward, God says many times in the Tanakh: "*my* people." Only when he is angry with Israel does he often say, "*your* people" (32:7), but even then, Moses keeps saying that they are "*your* people" (vv. 11–12).

12. I will often prefer this word "Ecclesia" to the word "church" because of all the misleading historical, denominational, and organizational connotations of the latter term, especially to Jewish ears. Since Acts 2, the *Ecclesia* is the body of Christ, the temple of the Holy Spirit, the totality of all Jesus-believers, irrespective of various ecclesiastical denominations and organizations (cf. Belgic Confession, Art. 27, first part).

sponse: a smile, after which he hastened on, for he was busy forming a *minyan*.[13] Indeed, God is called the "God of Israel" more than two hundred times in the Bible (including Matt. 15:1; Luke 1:68), in addition to those numerous times when God calls Israel "*my people*."

The story goes[14] that when the French king asked the French philosopher Voltaire for a proof of the supernatural, the latter simply replied: "The Jews, Sire, the Jews . . ." (Fr. *Les Juifs, Sire, les Juifs*). This is a profound truth, which apparently needed no further clarification. Follow intensely the history of the people of Israel, beginning with the liberation of Israel from Egyptian slavery until its liberation from the Nazi massacre, and it is difficult not to believe in the existence of God—as well as in the existence of the devil, for that matter. I once told a rabbi friend in Jerusalem that I believe anti-semitism is evidence for the existence of God. He understood my claim immediately.

1.1.2 The Name "Israel"

The meaning of the name "Israel" (Heb. *Yisra'ēl*) is less unambiguous than it may seem, whereas the name, as happens generally with Semitic names (think of Abraham [Gen. 17:5], Isaac [21:3–6], and Jacob [25:26]), should actually be a key to Israel's history. The Hebrew name consists of two parts: *yisra* and *ēl*. The latter means "Mighty One," and can be a synonym for *Elohim* ("God"). The word *yisra* comes from the Hebrew root *s-r-h*, which is related to *sar*, "prince, ruler," and thus means "to behave princely, rule, exert power," possibly "to fight." In Genesis 32:28, the meaning seems to be clear: henceforth, Jacob will be called "Israel," "*for you have striven [or, struggled, wrestled; Heb. sarita] with God and with men, and have prevailed*" (cf. v. 25, "a man wrestled [Heb. *wayyi'abēq*] with [Jacob]"; for the meaning of this phrase, see chapter 2 below). Hence, many expositors have explained the name "Israel" to mean "struggler with God" or "prince of God."

---

13. From the Heb. *minyan*, "number"; the term designates "the quorum of ten male adults, aged 13 years or over, necessary for public synagogue service and certain other religious ceremonies" (*EJ* 14:302, s.v. "Minyan").

14. I found the same story with regard to the French King Louis XIV and Blaise Pascal, and with regard to the Prussian King Frederic the Great and his pious physician; Larsson (1989, 36). Therefore, this might be only a fanciful legend.

The problem with such an interpretation is that ēl is not the subject of the phrase here, as for instance in the names Daniel ("God is my judge"), Raphael ("God heals"), or Samuel ("God hears"). If we understand the name in this sense, then the meaning is rather "God is prince/ruler" (perhaps in the sense of *my* prince/ruler), or "God rules/reigns," or possibly, "God battles (triumphs)."

Both meanings are appropriate designations to be written above the history of Israel. On the one hand, Israel is the "fighter[15] of God" or "prince of God." No matter how much Israel has been opposed, no matter how many mighty world empires have tried to exterminate Israel, from ancient Egypt until Nazi Germany and modern Muslim countries (Arabic, Turkish, Iranian), by God's grace and power Israel has repeatedly triumphed in these battles, to this day. If we start from the more primary meaning of the name "Israel," though, we must say that, throughout the centuries Israel definitely did not always behave in a princely way. Nevertheless, especially in "the Israel of God" — the faithful within the nation, the truly godly among Israel — the princely character emerged repeatedly. Israel is a prince, and in the future Messianic kingdom, it will function as a prince, a ruler: "Then the kingdom, the rulership and the greatness of the kingdoms under the whole heaven will be *given to the holy people of the Most High. Their kingdom is an everlasting kingdom, and all rulers will serve and obey them*" (Dan. 7:27 CJB). In line with the feminine character attributed to Israel in many metaphors used to describe her, we may also say that she will be the "queen" (Heb. *shēgal*) alongside the Messiah (Ps. 45:9).

On the other hand, "*God* is prince/ruler" ("*God* rules"). God is the *sar* ("prince, ruler") of Israel. This could be written above Israel's history, too: no matter what occurs, no matter what happens to Israel, and no matter what *will* happen to the nation, everything is under God's sway. The LORD is the almighty *sar* of Israel as well as of the entire world. Thus, God told his people while they were still in Babylon: "[R]emember the former things of old; for I am God, and there is no other; I am God, and there is none like me, declaring the end from the beginning and from ancient times things not yet done, saying, 'My counsel shall stand, and I will accomplish all my purpose'" (Isa. 46:9–10). Immediately after this, he revealed that he

---

15. Only in Gen. 32 would the rendering "fighter *with* God" be appropriate.

would use Cyrus the Persian to liberate Judah from Babylon, and to bring it back to its own country. Cyrus was God's "shepherd" (44:28), God's "anointed" (45:1), the "man of my counsel" (46:11), and as such he was a remarkable type (foreshadowing) of the Messiah. Just as God used Cyrus to restore Israel in *ha'Aretz* ("The Land," i.e., Israel), God will use the Messiah to restore Israel in *ha'Aretz*. God is the Ruler who, as the Supreme Lord of all kings, directs the hearts of all kings (and presidents, prime ministers, chancellors, or other leaders of nations) like "streams of water" (Prov. 21:1), so that they do—consciously or usually unconsciously, voluntarily or involuntarily—what is pleasing to him.

May I add here that, in contrast to the Hebrew name "Israel," the Greek word *ekklēsia* is rather prosaic. It means nothing but "(a group of people who are) called out," or, "called together," and thus "gathering," "assembly." The Ecclesia is a gathering of Jesus-believers, called out of every nation of the world (Jewish and Gentile) into one new company.

1.1.3   The National Angels

As we consider God's rule, we need to recall an extraordinary biblical state of affairs that I have discussed extensively elsewhere.[16] This discussion is worth repeating, because it helps us identify the most significant visible, and especially invisible, powers that guide and influence the history and spiritual status of Israel.

In Daniel 10, the prophet had an encounter with a celestial being telling him that he met with the "prince [Heb. *sar*] of the kingdom of Persia" (or "the prince of Persia," vv. 13, 20). He also spoke of the "prince [Heb. *sar*] of Greece" (v. 20), and in particular of the archangel Michael, called "your [i.e., Israel's] prince" (v. 21), "the great prince who has charge of your people" (12:1). From the context, it is evident that no earthly princes were intended here, but invisible powers in the spiritual world: angelic powers, who come to be understood as the guiding forces behind the various empires. Not the earthly rulers but these celestial beings are the actual powers behind the scenes, who govern and control the history of these respective empires and nations. Moreover, these celestial beings are—and this is very important—hostile toward the celestial messenger appear-

---

16. Ouweneel (2003a, §1.2.2 and chapter 2).

ing to Daniel, *and* toward Michael, the celestial "prince of Israel," and thus toward Israel itself. Here we find the most profound insight into the true nature of the four world empires (Dan. 2:7): they were governed by invisible angelic powers. These spiritual powers not only fight each other but they target especially Israel. In ordinary history, we might suppose that what occurred between Persia and Greece in the fourth century BC was merely a conflict. However, this was nothing but a chess match between two black kings. The real conflict in history is between *all* black kings, on the one hand, and the great White King along with his white pawns — his faithful ones — on the earth, on the other hand. The tiny people of Israel is the axis of world history, no matter how strange this may seem to the secular historian. This is because the God of Israel is the same as the "God of gods," the "King of kings," and the "Lord of lords."[17]

In Jewish tradition, the word *sar* is a well-known term for the angelic princes of the various nations. This word is used often to designate an earthly prince or ruler, but several times to designate celestial princes as well. In addition to Daniel 10:13, 20 and 12:1, consider Joshua 5:14, which tells us of the "commander [*sar*, captain, prince] of the army of the LORD." This is a celestial prince, who has been placed over an entire army of celestial beings. The battle of Israel against Canaan was not merely a conflict between two earthly nations, but it was fundamentally a spiritual battle between two invisible powers: the army (host) of Adonai and the evil spiritual army "behind" the Canaanite nations. The Bible has given us several glimpses of God's host in the higher world, especially when people belonging to God became involved in conflict situations.

One example involved Jacob:

> Early in the morning Laban arose and kissed his grandchildren and his daughters and blessed them. Then Laban departed and returned home. Jacob went on his way, and the angels of God met him. And when Jacob saw them he said, "This is God's camp!" So he called the name of that place Mahanayim [two camps[18]] (Gen. 31:55–32:2).

---

17. Deut. 10:17; Ps. 136:2; Dan. 2:47; 11:36; 1 Tim. 6:15; Rev. 19:16.
18. Rabbis Nachmanides and Jacob Sforno in Cohen (1983, ad loc.) argued that the two camps or armies were the celestial company of the angels and the earthly company of Jacob himself.

Another example involved the prophet Elisha:

When the servant of the man of God [i.e., Elisha] rose early in the morning and went out, behold, an army [from Syria] with horses and chariots was all around the city. And the servant said, "Alas, my master! What shall we do?" He [i.e., Elisha] said, "Do not be afraid, for those who are with us are more than those who are with them." Then Elisha prayed and said, "O Lord, please open his eyes that he may see." So the Lord opened the eyes of the young man, and he saw, and behold, the mountain was full of horses and chariots of fire all around Elisha (2 Kings 6:15-17; cf. also 7:6, "[T]he Lord had made the army of the Syrians to hear the sound of chariots and of horses; the sounded of a great army").

Each world power has its own *sar* (angelic prince), and when we consider the dragon in the book of Revelation (the "Devil and Satan," 12:9; 20:2), which is the angelic prince of the eschatological world power (cf. 12:3 with 13:1), then we see that this reality is no different today. In Daniel 11-12, Israel has a *sar*, too, but this seems to be an exception. To be sure, this *sar*, Michael, is the only one who in the Bible is called an "archangel" (i.e., chief angel, Jude 9; cf. 1 Thess. 4:16); he is truly great. Yet, the fact that Israel had an angelic prince at all — that is, an intermediary between itself and God — was because, since the fall of Jerusalem and the destruction of the temple (586 BC), Israel had temporarily become a *goy* ("nation") like all the others; through the prophet, God called Israel *Lo-'Ammi*, "Not-My-People" (Hos. 1:9; 2:22). But basically, God himself is the *sar* of Israel, something indicated in one possible interpretation of Israel's name (see §1.1.2 above).

According to what is likely the correct rendering, Deuteronomy 32:8-9 said: "When the Most High gave to the nations their inheritance, when he divided mankind, he fixed the borders [or, territories] of the peoples according to the number of the sons of God.[19] But the Lord's portion is his people, Jacob his allotted heritage." These verses are generally understood to mean that in antiquity

---

19. The reading "sons of God" is supported by various ancient translations (Symmachus, Vetus Latina, Syrohexaplaris), and today also by a reading found in a damaged Qumran manuscript (4 Q), where we read *benē ēl*. Thus, the text probably read originally "sons of God" (i.e., gods, angels) instead of *benē Yisra'ēl*, "sons of Israel" (see the apparatus of the *Biblia Hebraica Stuttgartensia*).

God divided the world into a number of nations, each with its own territory or inheritance, and that he assigned to each nation one of the angelic princes. He himself, however, received Israel as his inheritance (cf. Deut. 4:20). In other words, the LORD assigned the territories of the nations to the gods of the nations, and conversely, Deuteronomy 4:19 (the LORD has allotted the deified celestial bodies to the nations) and 29:26 (Israel served gods that the LORD "had not allotted to them") suggest that he assigned these gods (read: national angels, angelic princes) to these nations.

An inheritance (or "lot") refers to the possession allotted to a person when an entire estate is divided; each of the gods received its own nation, but the LORD received Israel. We find the same idea in Sirach 17:17, "He appointed an [angelic] ruler for every nation, but Israel is the Lord's own portion" (RSV). Consider Isaiah 26:13 as well: "O LORD our God, / other [angelic] lords[20] besides you have ruled over us, / but your name alone we bring to remembrance." It has been suggested that some of these angelic lords had specific names: Rahav (Rahab) seems to have been the name for the angelic prince of Egypt,[21] Sheshakh may have been the name of the angelic prince of Babylon (Jer. 25:26),[22] and perhaps Nahum 2:8 speaks of Huzzab (Hutzav), possibly the goddess of Nineveh (LEB: "Her [i.e., Nineveh's] goddess [Heb. *Hutzav*] is taken out and taken into exile").

In summary, each nation (every world power) has its own angelic prince in the spiritual world—princes who, as Daniel 10 shows, are persistently opposed to Israel because Israel is the people of the LORD. From the Exodus until this very day, there are virtually no exceptions to the rule that the world powers oppose Israel, with the exception of a few[23] Christian nations. This is only to say that the nations, usually including "Christian" nations, oppose the *God* of

---

20. Heb. *be'alunu* (from *ba'al*, "lord"); cf. 1 Cor. 8:5, "indeed there are many 'gods' and many 'lords' [Gk. *kurioi*]."

21. Isa. 51:9; Ps. 87:4; 89:11 (10); cf. Job 9:13; 26;12; Ezek. 29:3.

22. Or Sheshakh (*sh-sh-kh*) was a code name for Babylon (*b-b-l*), *b* being the second letter in the Hebrew alphabet, and *sh* the second to the last letter; *l* is the twelfth letter, and *k* is the twelfth letter from the end.

23. "A few": it seems that virtually all European countries have driven out the Jews at some time, except the Netherlands.

Israel. In times when Israel is *'Ammi* ("My People," Hos. 1–2), the LORD functions as Israel's *sar*. And even when Israel is externally *Lo-'Ammi*, in the background God still functions as its *sar*, who will prevent any world power from doing anything to Israel beyond his will. Those who fight against Israel are fighting against the *sar* of Israel, that is, against the God of gods, the King of kings, the Lord of lords. The conflict between Israel and these earthly powers is fundamentally this invisible battle in the "heavenly realm (places, spheres, regions)" (cf. Eph. 6:12). This essential point will play a significant role throughout our presentation of an Israelology. Those who touch Israel, touch the apple of God's eye,[24] that is, they touch him in one of his most sensitive parts.

1.2 Personal Development: Autobiographical Comments

1.2.1 Early Experiences

My spiritual awakening in the field of theology began during my eleventh year. In that year (1955), my maternal grandmother gave me a chart of biblical prophecy with an extensive description, with Israel forming the center of the chart. With that subject of prophecy—theologians would say, eschatology, the doctrine of what in Greek is called *ta eschata* ("the last things," the things of "the last days"[25])—my Bible study began, which over the years became the passion of my life in the scholarly domain, something that has continued uninterruptedly to this day. Throughout my adult life, I earned several doctorates: first, in the natural sciences (1970), later in philosophy (1986), while continually studying and preaching the Scriptures, and third, in systematic theology (1993).

I recall that during my high school period in Apeldoorn (the Netherlands), I took a German course, during which, because of the literature we were reading, the conversation turned one day to religious matters. I no longer recall the context, but at one point a classmate raised his hand and said, "There are even people who believe that Jesus will literally return on the Mount of Olives." I hardly heard the teacher's response because I was so impressed with the question. This was my first exposure to supersessionism,

---

24. Zech. 2:8; cf. Deut. 32:10; Ps. 17:8.
25. Acts 2:17; 2 Pet. 3:3; cf. Num. 24:14; Deut. 4:30; Isa. 2:2; 2 Tim. 3:1; Heb. 1:2; James 5:3; Heb. *acharit-hayamim* (so in the CJB).

the view that the church is the spiritual Israel. These Christians spiritualize all Old Testament prophecies, including references to "Israel," "Judah," as well as the "Mount of Olives." At that time in my life, I firmly believed that Jesus would come again on the Mount of Olives because of Zechariah 14:4-5 ("... On that day his feet shall stand on the Mount of Olives that lies before [i.e., to the east of] Jerusalem; and the Mount of Olives shall be split in two from east to west.... Then the LORD my God will come, and all the holy ones with him") and Acts 1:11 (after Jesus ascended from the Mount of Olives, two angels said, "This Jesus, who has been taken up from you into heaven, will come in the same way as you saw him go into heaven").

Six decades later, I still believe the very same thing. Not because I am stubborn, or literalistic, or biblicistic, but because my study of Scripture has led me to the conclusion that, everywhere in the Bible, terms like "Israel," "Judah," "Ephraim," and "Mount of Olives" must be taken literally. To be sure, the term "Jerusalem" is occasionally used in a spiritual sense, which is clear from the adjectives or appositions attached to it: "the Jerusalem [that is] above" (Gal. 4:26), "the heavenly Jerusalem" (Heb. 12:12), "the New Jerusalem" (Rev. 3:12; 21:2), "Jerusalem coming down out of heaven from God" (Rev. 21:10). But please note that these expressions detract nothing at all from the future reality of a *literal, earthly* Jerusalem, as I hope to show.

Moreover, I also wish to demonstrate that the term "Israel" must *always* be taken literally.[26] One of the greatest protagonists of the Calvinist Second Reformation in the Netherlands (seventeenth and eighteenth centuries), Wilhelmus à Brakel, wrote in his famous work, *The Christian's Reasonable Service*,[27] the following remarkable words: "In order to eliminate any secret doubts, one ought to know that throughout the entire New Testament the name Israel is never assigned to believers, that is, the church of the New Testament. Rather, it is always understood that this refers to the Jewish nation;

---

26. The only apparent exception is Rom. 9:6 (lit., "Not all who are from Israel are Israel"; CJB: "[N]ot everyone from Isra'el is truly part of Isra'el"), which simply means: "Not all those descended from Israel, beginning with the patriarchs, belong to the true Israel of God"; see extensively, §§6.2.2 and 6.5.2 below.

27. This title is an allusion to Rom. 12:1 (KJV).

that is, in distinction to and separation from all other nations."[28] In short: *in the New Testament the term "Israel"* ***always*** *refers to ethnic Israel*, or to the godly core of Israel (Gal. 6:16, "the Israel of God"). I will be furnishing ample proof for the claim that the term "Israel" *never* includes Gentile Jesus-believers.

1.2.2   Visits to Israel

Throughout my life, I have met many people from many different countries who proudly told me that they had been to Israel. Sometimes I have asked them: "To *which* Israel?" Their astonished look has led me to explain further: "Did you see—like so many others— only the Israel of the Old and New Testaments, the Israel of the Children's Bible and Sunday School? For instance, did you see only the places where Jesus once walked? Or did you see also the modern *state* of Israel? Did you attend synagogue services, and speak with orthodox[29] Jews, in order to understand their religion? Did you visit the graves of their great rabbis, and did you speak with the people there? Did you speak with secular Jews about their political convictions? Did you speak with Messianic Jews? Did you speak with Evangelical Palestinian Christians? *Which* Israel did you see?"

I fear that many viewed Israel only through the lens of their cameras, and at home they show their friends the pictures and videos associated with well-known Bible stories. In fact, they saw virtually *nothing*, because we can no longer identify with certainty the great majority of these "sacred" places. At any rate, these tourists scarcely saw modern Israel at all, except the people selling souvenirs and fruits, and the people serving in hotels and restaurants.

In 1982 I visited the state of Israel for the first time. Not as part of a travel group, but at the invitation of Palestinian Plymouth Brethren congregations in Galilee. On eleven consecutive evenings I delivered Bible lectures on a number of basic subjects; I usually preached in English, sometimes in French (depending on the translator), and was translated into Arabic by local brethren. In appreciation for my labors, two Palestinian Christians gave me a

---

28. Brakel (1995, 4:511).
29. Throughout this book, the phrase "orthodox Jews" refers to Jews with a rabbinic Talmudic orientation.

guided tour through the Holy Land.[30] Travelling with these two men afforded me a most remarkable way of seeing the land, viewing things through the eyes of two Palestinians, one of them being a Bible-believing Evangelical brother. We saw the well at Sychar (Shechem; John 4:5), the Samaritan sanctuary on Mount Gerizim, and in Hebron the tombs of the patriarchs in the cave of Machpelah. The highlight was Jerusalem, which we entered from the West Bank, from the north, at dusk. What a touching view! No hotel for us, but a guestroom in the home of an Arab Christian living within the ancient Turkish city walls, where my Evangelical Palestinian friend and I read together Psalm 122:

> I was glad when they said to me,
>   "Let us go to the house of the LORD!"
> Our feet have been standing
>   within your gates, O Jerusalem!
> Jerusalem — built as a city
>   that is bound firmly together, ...
> Pray for the peace of Jerusalem!
>   May they be secure who love you!
> Peace be within your walls
>   and security within your towers!"
> For my brothers and companions' sake
>   I will say, "Peace be within you!"
> For the sake of the house of the LORD our God,
>   I will seek your good.

Throughout my life, I have made nine visits to Israel. Twice I went with a few students of mine to participate, together with Israeli and German colleagues and students, in archeological excavations at Ramat Rachel (near Jerusalem). This is how I met secular Israeli scholars and became acquainted with a new side of modern

---

30. I use the phrase "Holy Land" when I wish to avoid the terms "Israel" and "Palestine." I am aware of the perfectly correct argument by Robertson (2000, 11) that, strictly speaking, the Land is holy only when, and insofar as, the *Shekhinah* dwells there. In the Bible, places as such are never holy (sacred); places are holy only if, when, and because God's glory sojourns there (see Exod. 3:5; cf. Deut. 33:16). However, I am also aware that Jerusalem is still called the "holy city" even though the *Shekhinah* no longer dwelt there, and at most only an afterglow of God's glory could be found (Matt. 4:5; 27:53; Rev. 11:2). Sometimes I will simply use the Heb. term *ha'Aretz* ("*The* Land").

Israel. I have led two tours that devoted special attention to the history of orthodox Judaism. This is how we became acquainted with *this* important dimension of Israel.

Israel, and in particular Jerusalem, continues to fascinate me like no other place on earth. And since I am not a supersessionist, I travel throughout that country with the thrilling thought: *this* is the place where "it" is going to happen! With this attitude, I survey the Mount of Olives (cf. Zech. 14:5), the Temple Square (cf. Ezek. 40–44), the Valley of Jehoshaphat (cf. Joel 3:2, 12), and in the northern region of the country, the Valley of Jezreel ("Armageddon," i.e., Mountain of Megiddo, Rev. 16:16). At the Dead Sea, I think of Ezekiel 47:8-10 ("wherever the river goes, every living creature that swarms will live, and there will be very many fish"). And most especially, in the little square in the Jewish quarter of old Jerusalem, near the reconstructed Hurva synagogue, I sit down on a bench to enjoy watching older people and playing children, all the while thinking of Zechariah 8:4-5:"Old men and old women shall again sit in the streets of Jerusalem, each with staff in hand because of great age. And the streets of the city shall be full of boys and girls playing in its streets."

In this way, I see the *past* everywhere around me, I see the *present* situation in Israel—and talk with as many Jews and Arabs as I can—and above all, look into the *future*.

> If I forget you, O Jerusalem,
>   let my right hand forget its skill!
> Let my tongue stick to the roof of my mouth,
>   if I do not remember you,
> if I do not set Jerusalem
>   above my highest joy! (Ps. 137:5-6).

1.2.3   A Multi-Faceted Front

No Christian dogmatics can present a discussion about "Israel as such" (Ger. *Israel an sich*). The Israelology that I am presenting is an explicitly Christian Israelology, or a New Testament-oriented Israelology. It is closely interwoven with many subjects within systematic theology, including ecclesiology (the doctrine of the Ecclesia, including the relationship between ethnic Israel and the Christian

Ecclesia),[31] eschatology (the doctrine of the last things, including the prophetically announced future of both Israel and the Ecclesia),[32] Christology (the doctrine of Christ, including the claim that Jesus is the Messiah of Israel),[33] election (in what sense Israel is a chosen nation, and how this relates to election in the Pauline sense [e.g., Eph. 1:3]),[34] foederology (the doctrine of the covenants, which are primarily covenants with Israel[35]) and basileology (the doctrine of the kingdom, which is primarily the Messianic kingdom of Israel),[36] and the Torah (the Sinaitic or Mosaic Torah in comparison with the Torah of Christ; Gal. 6:2).[37] Separate volumes in this dogmatic series have been devoted to these subjects.

This multi-faceted character of Israelogy makes the debate with supersessionism (erroneously called "replacement theology"[38]) rather difficult because the discussion must engage so many fronts simultaneously. My opposition to supersessionism engages it on the matter of the church (something the New Testament calls "the Ecclesia of God," the body of Christ and the temple of the Holy Spirit, which did not exist in the Old Testament), on the matter of the last things (amillennialism is unbiblical), on the matter of the covenants (all covenants are basically with Israel; covenantal universalism is mistaken), on the kingdom of God (the kingdom is not just spiritual, but it is also very physical), and on the Torah (the Mosaic Torah has been fulfilled but not abolished).

All these matters are interrelated. A debate on one of these subjects will usually find an opponent scurrying behind the other four (and more) subjects, imagining that their position on *that* matter is sufficiently persuasive. Try engaging on all these subjects simul-

---

31. Ouweneel (2010a; 2010b).
32. Ouweneel (2012a).
33. Ouweneel (2007b, especially chapter 5).
34. Ouweneel (2008b).
35. Even the Noahic Covenant is Shem-oriented, and thus Israel-oriented (Gen. 9–11).
36. Ouweneel (2011a).
37. Ouweneel (2020).
38. Supersessionism teaches that the church began with Adam and Eve; and thus, it cannot teach that Israel has been replaced by the church; see Paas (2014, 221; 2015, 174–78).

taneously! Moreover, this is decidedly not simply a matter of the straightforward interpretation of a number of Bible passages. Consider one of the most crucial passages, Romans 11:26, "all Israel will be saved"—a passage that has been heavily debated since the fourth century and will be debated until the moment it is fulfilled. You can be sure that both the supersessionist and the literalist *come to this text with an* a priori *conviction that determines how they read Romans 11:26*, since this text functions as the cornerstone of their paradigm. Supersessionist exegetes expend significant effort in discussing numerous exegetical details, yet the outcome of their argument can be known in advance: the term "Israel" refers not to ethnic Israel but to the church.[39] But I too work with an *a priori* conviction that I openly acknowledge: in Romans 11:26 the term "Israel" refers to ethnic Israel (recall Reformed theologian Brakel: in the New Testament "Israel" never refers to the church but always to ethnic Israel.)

To state the matter in terms of the philosophy of science: one's reading of such passages depends on one's functioning paradigm or the interpretive glasses one is wearing (see more extensively in §1.5 below). We are reminded here of Philip's question to the Ethiopian: "Do you *understand* what you are reading?" (Acts 8:30). Do you have the proper intellectual framework or paradigm for understanding a given passage? Recall what the Ethiopian was actually reading:

> Like a sheep he was led to the slaughter
> > and like a lamb before its shearer is silent,
> > so he opens not his mouth.
> In his humiliation justice was denied him.
> > Who can describe his generation?
> For his life is taken away from the earth
> (Acts 8:32–33, quoting Isa. 53:7-8).

To whom did the pronoun "he" refer? The answer depends on your glasses. Ask Philip, and he would answer: "Jesus" (Acts 8:35). Ask *early* orthodox rabbis, and they would reply: "The Messiah" (but not Jesus). Ask *later* orthodox rabbis (influenced by Christian interpretations), and they would answer: "Israel." Ask some modern Israelologists, and they would reply: "Jesus, but also Israel." *Four*

---

39. Robertson (2000); Maljaars (2015).

answers to the same question! *None* of them is a matter of "simply reading what the text says" (as many naïve Bible readers think), for Isaiah 53 did not tell us to whom the pronoun "he" referred. That is a matter of interpretation. And such interpretation is always embedded in some theological paradigm:[40] rabbinic Judaism, supersessionism, dispensationalism (classical or moderate), and the like.

The debate is complicated in advance by at least three realities:

(a) The multi-faceted character of Israelology; many subjects of systematic theology must be engaged simultaneously, whereas in reality we can deal with only one at a time.

(b) Multiple misunderstandings on the part of each side of the debate toward the other (see chapter 3 below).

(c) The paradigm/lens through which the debate is being viewed, about which the theologians involved often seem unaware (again, see chapter 3 below). A partial explanation of this unawareness is that theologians are among those scientists who seem least concerned about the philosophical foundation of their discipline, and who, as a consequence of the long-held suspicion of theologians toward philosophers, often seem *unwilling* to examine this foundation. No one should be considered an academic theologian who lacks proper training in the philosophy of science, especially regarding how scientific theories and paradigms are formed. No theology can be either scientific or scholarly that neglects the study of its own philosophical foundations.

1.3 The Navel of the Earth
1.3.1 Jerusalem: Its Origins

It sounds like a platitude to say that no city in the world is more fascinating than Jerusalem (Yerushalayim).[41] This city is more than forty centuries old, its origins lying in obscure antiquity. This city has known great wealth and the bitterest poverty, has been beaten and rose again to flourish, has been repeatedly trampled down and yet revived. In our own day this city stands again at the center of global interest, both because of the miracles that modern Israel has accomplished there, and because it is the most controversial political area in the world. This is the city where ancient civilizations

---

40. See extensively, Ouweneel (2013, chapters 6-14).
41. See Ouweneel (1977; 1999).

meet one another, where the great trade roads of antiquity intersect. This city lies at the "navel of the earth" (Ezek. 38:12 MSG, WYC; Heb. *tabbur ha'aretz*), "set in the center of the nations, with countries all around her" (Ezek. 5:5). This is spiritually true, because Deuteronomy 32:8 explains that all the nations of the world have been arranged, as it were, around Israel as their center; these territories are oriented toward God's land. It is also geographically true, since the Holy Land lies virtually at the point where the ancient continents of Asia, Africa, and Europe meet. It lies between Egypt to the southwest and Assyria to the northeast, to mention two of Israel's most significant neighbors.[42] Neither the advanced age nor the interesting geography of Jerusalem is what appeals to us most, nor its role in general world history or in modern political developments. What fascinates us most is the unique place that this wondrous city occupies in the plans and counsels of the Almighty, in the redemptive history of God with the world—not only in the past, but also in the end times. The stage where these divine counsels are being realized is the earth, viewed from the territory that, in God's mind, is the center of the earth. This is Canaan, known also as Palestine, known today as Israel. Consider the following series of what may be called seven concentric circles:

1. This world is *God's* world ("The earth is the LORD's and the fullness thereof, the world and those who dwell therein," Ps. 24:1).

2. Its center of this world is God's wonderful land ("the land[43] is mine," Lev. 25:23).

3. The magnificent center of this Holy Land is the "city of God."[44]

4. The magnificent center of this city is the temple, which is the "temple of the LORD."[45]

5. The glorious center of this temple is the Most Holy Place, the

---

42. Compare "the Kings of the South[west] and the North[east]" in Daniel 11.
43. It is important to know that the Heb. word for "land" here is the same Heb. word *eretz* translated as "earth" in Ps. 24:1.
44. Ps. 46:4; also see Ps. 48:1, 8; 87:3; 101:8; Isa. 60:14; cf. the New Jerusalem, called "the city of my God" (Rev. 3:12).
45. 1 Sam. 1:9; 2 Kings 24:13; Jer. 7:4; Ezek. 44:7.

Qodesh Qodeshim, "Holy of Holies" (AMP).[46]

6. The holiest of this Most Holy Place is the ark of the covenant.[47]

7. The holiest component of this ark is what has traditionally been called the "mercy-seat" (the "atonement lid," NET; Heb. *kapporet*), on which the *Shekhinah* rested between the golden cherubim.[48]

Noteworthy, as we will see, is that the Ecclesia of God (the body of Christ), has no such center. It is of a very different order. It is itself a (spiritual) city (Rev. 21:9–10) and a (spiritual) temple (1 Cor. 3:16; 2 Cor. 6:16; Eph. 2:20-22). And the *Shekhinah*, which rested on Christ—we will return to this—now rests in every place where believers are together in the name of Jesus (Matt. 18:20).[49] Christianity possesses no sacred places: no Rome, no Constantinople, no Wittenberg, no Geneva, no Westminster (or Canterbury), and so on. Christians and Messianic Jews have Jesus in common, and he is their all and everything. But Gentile Christians often have great trouble spiritually understanding those Messianic Jews who tell them that they look forward to the new temple of the Messianic kingdom. Yet, Gentile believers should understand *and* appreciate this. They face a choice: either they spiritualize all the Old Testament prophecies concerning the city and the temple of the Messianic kingdom—which is not Bible exposition but the refusal to exposit—or they take the Scriptures at face value—not only Ezekiel 40-44, but also passages such as the following (*all referring to the Messianic kingdom, as the context makes clear*):

(a) "And the foreigners who join themselves to the LORD to minister to him, to love the name of the LORD, and to be his servants, everyone who keeps the Sabbath and does not profane it, and holds fast to my covenant—these I will bring to my holy mountain, and make them joyful in my house of prayer; their burnt offerings and their sacrifices will be accepted on my altar; for my house shall be called a house of prayer for all peoples" (Isa. 56:6-7).

---

46. Exod. 26:33; during the Messianic kingdom: Ezek. 41:4; 42:13; 43:12; 44:13.
47. Cf. Exod. 26:33-34; 1 Kings 8:6; 2 Chron. 5:7; however, regarding the future, cf. Jer. 3:16.
48. Exod. 25:22; Num. 7:89; 1 Sam. 4:4; 2 Sam. 6:2; 2 Kings 19:15; 1 Chron. 13:6; Ps. 80:1; 99:1; Isa. 37:16.
49. Cf. Talmud: Aboth III.2 on Mal. 3:16 (see further in chapter 12 below).

(b) "Arise, shine [Jerusalem], for your light has come, and the glory of the Lord has risen upon you. . . . All the flocks of Kedar shall be gathered to you, the rams of Nebaioth shall minister to you; they shall come up with acceptance on my altar, and I beautify my beautiful house" (Isa. 60:1, 7).

(c) "It shall come to pass in the latter days that the mountain of the *house of the* Lord shall be established as the highest of the mountains, and it shall be lifted up above the hills; and peoples shall flow to it, and many nations shall come, and say: 'Come, let us go up to the mountain of the Lord, to the *house* of the God of Jacob, that he may teach[50] us his ways and that we may walk in his paths.' For out of Zion shall go forth *Torah* [or, teaching] and the word of the Lord from Jerusalem" (Micah 4:1-2).

(d) "Behold, the man whose name is the Branch: for he shall branch out from his place, and he shall build the temple *of the* Lord. It is he who shall build the temple *of the* Lord and shall bear royal honor, and shall sit and rule on his throne" (Zech. 6:12-13; this cannot refer to Zerubbabel, who never possessed a royal position).

(e) "[O]n that day [of Messianic rule], . . . the pots in the house *of the* Lord shall be [as holy] as the bowls before the altar. . . And there shall no longer a trader [or, Canaanite] in the house *of the* Lord of hosts on that day" (Zech. 14:20-21).

(f) "O Jerusalem, Jerusalem, ... See, your *house* is left to you desolate. For I tell you, you will not see me again, *until* you say, 'Blessed is he who comes in the name of the Lord'" (Matt. 23:37-39; cf. Ps. 118:26).

1.3.2 Jerusalem: Its Restoration

Some restoration prophecies concerning Israel in general, and Jerusalem in particular, were undoubtedly initially fulfilled after the Babylonian exile. When we read, "I am the Lord . . . who confirms the word of his servant and fulfills the counsel of his messengers, who says of Jerusalem, 'She shall be inhabited,' and of the cities of Judah, 'They shall be rebuilt, and I will *raise up* their ruins'" (Isa. 44:24-26), clearly the initial reference is to the restoration of the city linked with Judah's return from Babylon. This becomes still more

---

50. Heb. *w'yorēnu*, from the root *y-r-h*, from which also *Torah* was derived (see the next line).

clear from the following verses (v. 28; 45:1) that speak of Cyrus the Persian, who allowed Judah to return to their country and to rebuild city and temple. Yet, in these chapters[51] we find so many hints of the Messianic kingdom that we may claim to have here an initial confirmation of a general principle that will be confirmed many times: *ultimately, all writing prophets* (except the author of Jonah) *refer to the Messianic kingdom,* so that past restorations—like the one after the Babylonian exile—*are never the definitive fulfillments of their prophecies;* those prophecies possess a deeper dimension.

Here is an example from a later part of Isaiah:

> They [i.e., the Israelites] shall build up the ancient ruins; they shall raise up the former devastations; they shall repair the ruined cities, the devastations of many generations. Strangers shall stand and tend your flocks; foreigners shall be your plowmen and vinedressers; but you shall be called the priests of the Lord; they shall speak of you as the ministers of our God; you shall eat the wealth of the nations, and in their glory you shall boast. . . . Their offspring shall be known among the nations, and their descendants in the midst of the peoples; all who see them shall acknowledge them, that they are an offspring the Lord has blessed. . . . For as the earth brings forth its sprouts, and as a garden causes what is sown in it to sprout up, so the Lord God will cause righteousness and praise to sprout up before all the nations (61:4-11).

To conclude that all of this was fulfilled at the return of the exiles from Babylon constitutes a very superficial reading. *The prophet was speaking about Messianic times.*

Therefore, in view of this, let Israel, and Gentile believers with them, continue to pray for Jerusalem, "giving the Lord no rest":

> On your walls, O Jerusalem, I have set watchmen; all the day and all the night they shall never be silent. You who put the Lord in remembrance, take no rest, and give him no rest until he establishes Jerusalem and makes it a praise in the earth. The Lord has sworn by his right hand and by his mighty arm: "I will not again give your grain to be food for your enemies, and foreigners shall not drink your wine for which you have labored; but those who garner it shall eat it and praise the Lord, and those who gather it shall drink it in the courts of

---

51. See, e.g., Isa. 40:1–11; 41:17–20; 42:1–7; 43:16–21; 45:22–25.

my sanctuary" (Isa. 62:6-9).

This is the five-fold future restoration of Israel:

(a) the spiritual restoration of the faithful remnant of the people (e.g., Ezek. 36);

(b) the physical restoration of the land (e.g., Nahum 2:3);

(c) the restoration of the city (see the passages just quoted);

(d) the restoration of the throne of David (Isa. 16:5; Jer. 33:21; Luke 1:32); and

(e) the restoration of the temple, the altar, and the priestly ministry (Ezek. 40–45).

1.3.3 Jerusalem or Rome?

A city located at the "navel of the earth" (Ezek. 38:12 MSG, WYC), "set in the center of the nations, with countries all around her" (Ezek. 5:5), is indeed the center of the world. One might think that the earth's globe has no center, or that it should perhaps be located at one of the poles. Yet, the traditional representation of the countries of the world showed Israel as the center. In Numbers 2 we see how, during Israel's wilderness journey, the twelve tribes were arranged around the tabernacle. Similarly, the temple of Jerusalem formed the center of Israel, and therefore also of the entire world. This geographical center coincides with what might be called the spiritual center of the world: "As for me [says the LORD], I have set my King on Zion, my holy hill" (Ps. 2:6). "[M]any peoples shall come, and say: 'Come, let us go up to the mountain of the LORD, to the house of the God of Jacob, that he may teach us his ways and that we may walk in his paths.' For out of Zion shall go forth the law [*Torah*, teaching], and the word of the LORD from Jerusalem" (Isa. 2:3; Micah 4:2). "The sons of those who afflicted you shall come bending low to you, and all who despised you shall bow down at your feet; they shall call you the City of the LORD, the Zion of the Holy One of Israel" (Isa. 60:14).

The nearby great sea is called in the Bible the "hinder sea" (Zech. 14:8 KJV, Heb. *hayam ha'aharon*) because the Israelite facing the east (the sunrise)[52] has the sea behind them. In the medieval world, the

---

52. They are properly "oriented," since the Latin word *oriens* means the rising sun or the East; cf. Ps. 121:5–6: if you are "oriented," you need shade on your right side to protect from the midday sun.

sea was called the Mediterranean Sea, which literally means, the Sea in the Middle of the Earth (Lat. *in medio terrae*). Through this name, the location of the "middle" is moved westward, from the land of Israel to the vicinity of Rome, the capital of the Roman Empire in the West, from the eighth century BC to the fifth century AD. Supersessionism (Roman Catholic) would have us believe that the "middle" of the earth has been relocated from Jerusalem to Rome, along with a shift in allegiance from the Messiah to the Pope.

We do find in the Bible a remarkable hint of such a shift. In Daniel 4:10 we read about "a tree in the midst of the earth"; the (Latin) Vulgate reads here, *in medio terrae* (cf. Mediterranean). This tree represents the head of the Gentile world. In Daniel's day, this was King Nebuchadnezzar, but in the course of the history of the four world empires this was eventually the emperor of Rome. Please note that this was the pagan emperor, but since about AD 313 this was the (pseudo-)Christian (supersessionist) Emperor Constantine. The tree was so impressive that "it was visible to the end of the whole earth" (v. 11). In contrast to this, there was and is tiny Israel, and that other "tree": the cross of Calvary,[53] which Tertullian called "middle of the earth" (Lat. *medium terrae*).[54]

At the Synod of Mainz (AD 813), the "Roman" Emperor Charlemagne (Charles the Great, "founder of Europe") proclaimed the archangel Michael to be the patron saint of the "Roman" (Frankish Carolingian) Empire of those days.[55] We have seen that, in Daniel 12, Michael stood over against the four world empires, especially the Persian and the Greek empires. All those empires had their own angelic princes, as did Israel, which had Michael as its "prince" (see §1.1.3 above). The book of Revelation shows that the fourth (Roman) empire also had its angelic prince, who is none other than the "dragon" (see Rev. 12–13). Charlemagne was proud of his empire being the *"Christian"* successor to the ancient *pagan* Roman Empire. He sought to express this by adopting various Roman forms, techniques, and materials (bronze, marble), and applying them in so-called Carolingian architecture. The Pope had even given him

---

53. Acts 5:30; 10:39; 13:29; Gal. 3:13; 1 Pet. 2:24.
54. *Adversus Marcionem* I.198; Dante Alighieri used the expression in the same sense (*Inferno* XXXIV.13–14).
55. See Rosenberg (1956, 270–83).

the Latin title *Imperator Romanorum*, that is, "Emperor of the Romans." But what did Charlemagne do? His angelic prince was not the "dragon" — of course not, since this had been the angelic prince of the *pagan* Roman Empire — but none other than Michael, whom he had "adopted" from ancient Israel!

Charlemagne thought he could justify this on two grounds. First, the Christianization of the Roman Empire, which had occurred in fourth century, began with Emperor Constantine the Great; this required that the demonic prince be exchanged for a biblical one (see further in §4.1.2 below).

The second justification was found in supersessionist thinking, in which the Christianized Roman Empire had taken the place of the ancient kingdom of Israel. Thus, Charlemagne viewed himself not only as the successor of Augustus, Tiberius, and all the other great Roman emperors, but also explicitly as the successor of the Israelite kings David and Solomon. Therefore, in Charlemagne's thinking, Michael relocated, so to speak, from Jerusalem to the German city of Aachen, which had been developed from a Roman settlement and was at that time the center of the Frankish (Carolingian) empire. The extraordinary Dome there, where Charlemagne was later buried, was, as it were, the "temple" of that glorious empire. And thus, the same Michael was placed on the (Roman Catholic) Calendar of Saints. Israel's chief prince became a Christian saint![56] In a sense, you might say that September 29, Michael's day of commemoration, is one of the days for celebrating supersessionism. And yet, I would suggest that Michael, Israel's prince, feels more at home today in Jerusalem than in either Rome or Aachen.[57]

---

56. Some European cities have "St. Michael" as their patron saint, such as Zwolle (the Netherlands), Hamburg and Hildesheim (Germany); think also of Mont Saint Michel in France.

57. The *Jewish Encyclopedia* says of Charlemagne: ". . . He realized the advantages to be derived by the country from the business abilities of the Jews, and gave them complete freedom with regard to their commercial transactions. Some Jews seem to have occupied prominent places at his court. Thus, Charlemagne had for his physician one named Ferragut. A Hebrew named Isaac was a member of an embassy sent by Charlemagne to Harun al-Rashid, probably in the capacity of dragoman. . . . But if the Jews were free in their commercial dealings, their [rather bad] political status generally remained almost the same under Charlemagne as under his predecessors" (https://jewishencyclopedia.

1.4 Starting Point: Calling[58]
1.4.1 The Calling of Abraham

Israel's history will *end* in Jerusalem with a restored people, land, city, throne, and temple. But all of this history *began* with a solitary man from Ur, in the land of the Chaldees, a man who, after having left, was a man without a land and a city, to say nothing of a throne and a temple. This was Abram (Heb. *Avram*), since Genesis 17 called Abraham (Heb. *Av-Raham*). Abram means something like "The (divine) Father is exalted." The name "Abraham" is explained in Genesis 17:5, "No longer shall your name be called Abram, but your name shall be Abraham [father of a multitude], for I have made you the father of a multitude of nations." If I understand the names correctly, the former name refers to the God of this man, whereas the latter name refers to Abraham himself as the forefather of many nations (Heb. *av hamor goyyim*). These nations include the descendants of the twelve sons of Ishmael (Gen. 25:13–15), the six sons of Keturah (vv. 1–2), the five sons of Esau (Gen. 36), and the twelve sons of Jacob (Gen. 49). If we count them this way, the total number of 12 + 6 + 5 + 12 = 35 nations (families, tribes) who may call Abraham their father.

When, in the time of Noah, all humanity had descended into corruption and violence (Gen. 6:5, 11–12), God responded to this with the Flood. After the Flood, the heart of natural humanity turned out to be as evil as it had been before (Gen. 8:21). A new flood was not possible, as the rainbow in the clouds indicated (Gen. 9:13–16). Therefore, this time God followed a different course. As he had chosen Noah before the Flood in order to save him, after the Flood he again chose a man with whom he would continue his redemptive plans. He did not bring new judgment upon humanity but "allowed all the nations to walk in their own ways" (Acts 14:16). That is, he is not directly engaged with them, except in his universal providence. Instead, he chose one man, from whom he built his own nation.

From the new, post-Flood humanity, the path of election narrowed down first to Noah's son Shem (Gen. 9:26), then to his de-

---

com/articles/4250-charlemagne).
58. See extensively, Ouweneel (2011a; 2014, 33–47).

scendant Eber (Heb. *'ēber*) (Gen. 10:21, 24-25; 11:14-17),⁵⁹ and then to his descendant Terah, the father of Abram (Gen. 11:24-43). It was this Abram who was chosen by God as an only one from the entire humanity of the time. Centuries later, God told his people: "Look to Abraham your father and to Sarah who bore you; for he was but one when I called him, that I might bless him and multiply him" (Isa. 51:2). And through Joshua the LORD said, "Long ago, your fathers lived beyond the River [Euphrates], Terah, the father of Abraham and of Nahor; and they served other gods. Then I took your father Abraham from beyond the River [Euphrates]" (Josh. 24:2-3).

The "God of glory" (the glorious God of gods) appeared to Abram (Acts 7:2), and made this special seven-fold promise to him:

1. "I will make of you a great nation,
2. and I will bless you
3. and make your name great,
4. so that you will be a blessing.
5. I will bless those who bless you,
6. and him who dishonors you I will curse,
7. and in you all the families of the earth shall be blessed" (Gen. 12:2-3; cf. 28:14; Acts 3:25).

In summary:

(a) God does something *for* Abraham (1-3), making him numerous, blessed, and famous;

(b) God does something *through* Abraham (4 and 5), namely, supplying a blessing to millions of people;

(c) God does something *with* the people who come into contact with Abraham (6 and 7): they are either blessed or cursed (there is no third option). From now on, no human being can avoid Abraham and his progeny altogether: "in" him (through him, because of him) a person is blessed or is cursed, depending on what his attitude is toward Abraham and his (Jewish) progeny. God, who is

---

59. In the expression "Abram the Hebrew [Heb. *ha'ibri*]" (Gen. 14:13), the description "the Hebrew" is traditionally understood to refer to "the descendant of Eber (Heb. *'ēber*); others explain it as meaning "someone from the other side," viz., of the Euphrates (cf. Josh. 24:2) (from the root *'-b-r*, "to pass over/through").

also the God of all Gentile Jesus-believers, is first and foremost the God of Abraham, Isaac, and Jacob (Exod. 3:6, 15–16). You cannot be blessed by God if you do not "bless" the patriarchs and their descendants, that is, declare about them what is good (wholesome, beneficial, salutary).[60]

In anticipation of arguments coming later in this book, I would alert the reader to this: no Gentile (Christian, Muslim, or other theists) can belong to God without blessing the Jew. But this is something essentially different from claiming that Gentile Jesus-believers today must themselves become "Jews" (in some spiritualized sense), "in" or "through" whom humanity today is blessed. Jesus' statement remains true: "[S]alvation is from the Jews" (John 4:22), not from every individual Jew, but from Israel as a whole, due to the *God* of that nation and his promises to it. What other nation could Jesus have had in mind except the people of Israel? Please note, this is *ethnic* Israel, not some spiritual Israel or the Ecclesia. Gentile Jesus-believers *are* not Israel—as we will see through many proofs—but are saved *through* Israel. They *need* the Jews, which is something very different from *becoming* "Jews."

1.4.2 Israel in the Midst of the Nations

In God's words to Abraham, we find a clear distinction between the "nation" (Heb. *goy*) that would sprout from Abraham, viz., Israel, and the "nations" (Heb. *goyyim*, Gen. 18:18; 22:18; 26:4) that would be blessed "in" this man. These two, the nation and the nations, must never be confused. To that one nation, the land of Canaan was given, *forever*, without any restriction; as the LORD told Abraham, "Lift up your eyes and look from the place where you are, northward and southward and eastward and westward, for all the land that you see I will give to you and to your offspring *forever* [Heb. *'ad-'olam*]" (Gen. 13:14–15; cf. 15:18; 17:8). Later, God told Jacob, "Behold, I will make you fruitful and multiply you, and I will make of you a company of peoples and will give this land to your offspring after you for an *everlasting* possession" (Gen. 48:4).[61] Through the prophet, God told Israel in view of the Messianic kingdom: "Your

---

60. Cf. Gk. *eulogeō* and Lat. *benedicere*, i.e., "to bless," but literally: "to say what is good" (the Heb. root *b-r-kh* means "to praise, congratulate, wish someone well").

61. Cf. Exod. 32:13; Deut. 4:40; Josh. 14:9.

people shall all be righteous [Heb. *tzaddikim*]; they shall possess the land *forever*, the branch of my planting, the work of my hands, that I might be glorified [or, display my beauty]" (Isa. 60:21). And even more strongly: "I will let you dwell in this place, in the land I gave of old to your fathers *forever* [Heb. *l'min-'olam w''ad-'olam*, from erelong and forever]" (Jer. 7:7; cf. 25:5).

Only supersessionism is satisfied with translating the Hebrew word *eretz* in such passages as "earth"; the (supersessionist) KJV has "land" here, as well as in Isaiah 57:13 and 61:7. This matter is important, because some have asserted that the word "land" in Exod. 20:12 and Deuteronomy 5:16 has been changed in the citation of these verses in Ephesians 6:3 to the word "earth," which thereby does away with the entire land-promise.[62] The latter was a mistake, along with the conclusion people have drawn from the mistake. Both the Hebrew *eretz* and the Greek *gē* are ambiguous: both can mean both "earth" and "land." Several English translations and paraphrases (ESV, CJB, GNT) have retained the word "land" in Ephesians 6:3.

There can be no doubt that the "land" (Canaan) was given to Israel *forever*, that is, as long as the present earth remains. Due to their own sins, the people may have lost their land for a time, but this does not change God's promise. The land belongs to them, and will belong to them, as long as the present creation exists. What if Israel were to express the desire to return to *their own* land, reminding God of his many promises? What if God were to inform them that, from now on, they would have to understand that "the Promised Land" really means the entire earth? Intelligent as they are, they might answer, "Well, then, LORD, give us the *entire earth* for an inheritance; and if that is too much, we will be more than satisfied with that tiny piece of "earth" formerly known to us as the Promised Land.

No, God was sufficiently clear. Through Moses, he told his people that their future great spiritual restoration (we add: under the Messiah) would be linked to this:

> And the LORD your God will *bring you into the land that your fathers possessed*, that you may possess it. And he will make you more pros-

---

62. E.g., Paas (2014, 64).

perous and numerous than your fathers. And the Lord your God will circumcise your heart and the heart of your offspring, so that you will love the Lord your God with all your heart and with all your soul, that you may live. And the Lord your God will put all these curses on your foes and enemies who persecuted you. And you shall again obey the voice of the Lord and keep all his commandments that I command you today. The Lord your God will make you abundantly prosperous in all the work of your hand, in the fruit of your womb and in the fruit of your cattle and in the *fruit of your ground*. For the Lord will again take delight in prospering you, as he took delight in your fathers (Deut. 30:5–9).

Or consider this Messianic promise:

. . . the time is coming to gather all nations and tongues. And they shall come and shall see my glory, and I will set a sign among them. And from them I will send survivors to the nations, to Tarshish, Pul, and Lud, who draw the bow, to Tubal and Javan, to the coastlands far away, that have not heard my fame or seen my glory. And they shall declare my glory among the nations. And they shall bring all your brothers [Israel!] from all the nations as an offering to the Lord, on horses and in chariots and in litters and on mules and on dromedaries, *to my holy mountain Jerusalem*, . . . just as the Israelites bring their grain offering in a clean vessel to the house of the Lord. And some of them also I will take for priests and for Levites (Isa. 66:18–21).

Please notice the difference: what will happen is not that the nations *will become* "Jews" by believing in Jesus and will dwell in a spiritual "land," but rather that the nations *will bring together* the Jews from over all the earth to dwell in their own land, and specifically to his holy mountain, Jerusalem, that is, to the *city* of Jerusalem, and the holy *mountain* there, the Temple Mount.

1.4.3 "My Land"

In antiquity, Israel bordered mighty Egypt on one side, and bordered the Assyrian, Babylonian, and Persian empires on the other side. A person traveling overland from Europe or Asia to Africa, and *vice versa*, always had to pass through the land of Israel, between the Mediterranean Sea and the Arabian desert. In many cases, they would pass Jerusalem. From Ramat Rachel, near Jerusalem, I have often contemplated that ancient road, trying to imagine the thousands of merchants, soldiers, and other travelers who had passed here during thousands of years. No wonder that so many battles have been fought in this very land. This centralized location of the land Israel, both in the spiritual world and among the continents, has been indisputable to this very day.[63] The ultimate great battles of the future that we read about in the Bible—spiritualized by supersessionism—will all occur in this land, and nowhere else.

Consider this biblical testimony:

> I saw, coming out of the mouth of the dragon and out of the mouth of the beast and out of the mouth of the false prophet, three unclean spirits like frogs. For they are demonic spirits, performing signs, who go abroad to the kings of the whole world, to assemble them for battle on the great day of God the Almighty.... And they assembled them at the place that in Hebrew is called Armageddon [Mountain of Megiddo, overlooking the Valley of Jezreel]" (Rev. 16:13-16).

That this is definitely eschatological is clear from the sequel to these verses:

> I saw the beast and the kings of the earth with their armies gathered to make war against him who was sitting on the horse [i.e., Jesus, Rev. 19:11-16] and against his army. And the beast was captured, and with it the false prophet who in its presence had done the signs by which he deceived those who had received the mark of the beast and those who worshiped its image (Rev. 19:19-20).

(b) In a similar vein we read:

> [B]ehold, in those days and at that time, when I restore the fortunes of Judah and Jerusalem, I will gather all the nations and bring them down to the Valley of Jehoshaphat [= The LORD judges]. And I will enter into judgment with them there, on behalf of my people and my heritage Israel, because they have scattered them among the nations and have divided up my land (Joel 3:1-2).

Again, these words appear in a clearly eschatological context, namely, Joel 2:28-32 and 3:11-17.

(c) One more piece of evidence:

> Behold, I am against you, O Gog, chief prince of Meshech and Tubal.

---

63. See Ouweneel (2003a, especially chapters 2–4).

And I will turn you about and drive you forward, and bring you up from the uttermost parts of the north, and lead you against the mountains of Israel. Then I will strike your bow from your left hand, and will make your arrows drop out of your right hand. You shall fall on the mountains of Israel, you and all your hordes and the peoples who are with you. I will give you to birds of prey of every sort and to the beasts of the field to be devoured. You shall fall in the open field, for I have spoken (Ezek. 39:1–5).

Ezekiel 38–39 supplies us with all the fine details, and we can find the entire eschatological context in chapters 34–48.

"The land is mine," says the Lord (Lev. 25:23), and nowhere in Scripture has he indicated that one day this will no longer be the case or will be the case only in some spiritual way. On the contrary, the ongoing promise is this: *I will bring you back to the land that your fathers have possessed, and soon after this, the Messianic kingdom will begin.* Hands off my land! This is what Adonai told the foreign powers, but today he says this to advocates of supersessionism. On the one hand, he was angry with Israel because it had defiled *his* (God's!) land (Jer. 2:7; 16:18), and told them that he would remove them from this land that he had given them (2 Chron. 7:20). On the other hand, he was angry with the foreign powers that had laid their hands on *his* land, whether the Assyrians (Isa. 14:25; Joel 1:6; 3:2), or Edom with its allies (Ezek. 36:5). In the last days, he will allow Gog, that mysterious enemy,[64] to invade *his* (God's) land (Ezek. 38:16), but only in order that God will triumph over him, and will make himself known to Gog as the Holy One of Israel (Ezek. 39:7, 25).

Hands off God's land! This is true for Babylonians, Persians, Greeks, and Romans, but also for Mamluks, Turks, Britons, Arabs, and Iranians, and all those members of the United Nations who repeatedly vote against Israel. It is also true for "Christian" organizations worldwide that constantly criticize the state of Israel. And it is true for theologians who spiritualize the land, and thereby in the name of God rob Israel of its land. (If I promise you a million

---

64. And apparently yet well-known: "I spoke of you long ago through my servants the prophets of Isra'el. Back then, they prophesied for many years that I would have you invade them" (Ezek. 38:17 CJB); therefore, some have conjectured that he is the same as the Assyrians.

dollars, then tell you I meant this spiritually, am I not a robber?) Nowhere in Scripture do we read that, since Easter and Pentecost, the "land" must be viewed spiritually; this conclusion is an invention of supersessionism.

Abraham, Isaac, and Jacob dwelt in the Promised Land, but understood very well that the promise would be fulfilled only in their descendants, and that they themselves would never personally possess the land. Instead, they did two things:

(a) They firmly believed in the promise of the LORD to Abraham: "To your offspring I give *this land*, from the river of Egypt to the great river, the river Euphrates" (Gen. 15:18).[65] They rejoiced that their descendants would possess the Promised Land *forever*.

(b) For themselves, in view of the Messianic kingdom (when they would be risen saints in heaven!), they looked forward to "a heavenly country" (cf. Heb. 11:13–16). By what logic, then, do some conclude that this mention of "a heavenly country" means that the literal country must no longer count in God's plan?

Those who conclude that Gentile Jesus-believers must look forward to this Promised Land as "heaven" usually commit three errors. They believe that

(a) the Promised Land was always earthly, never heavenly;

(b) the Promised Land was intended only for the Jews, not for Gentiles; and

(c) the intermediate state (between death and resurrection) is not "heaven."[66]

Following the lead of the patriarchs, we maintain that *we*, Jewish and Gentile believers who pass away before the coming of Messiah, look forward to "a heavenly country" *at the resurrection*. This truth is just as valid as another truth: Jewish believers living on earth in those days will inherit the (very earthly) Promised Land.

Compare here this statement of the apostle Paul: "For the promise to Abraham and his offspring that he would be heir of the world did not come through the law [i.e, earning salvation by

---

65. Notice how often this promise was repeated: Gen. 12:7; 13:15; 17:8; 24:7; 26:3; 28:4, 13; 35:12; 48:4; Exod. 32:13; 33:1.

66. See Ouweneel (2020).

keeping the Torah] but through the righteousness of faith" (Rom. 4:13; cf. Gen. 15:6; Hab. 2:4). Does this mean that the Promised Land of the Tanakh has now become the entire world (Gk. *cosmos*)?[67] Not at all. Abraham in person will *not* belong to the chosen people who, during the Messianic kingdom, will dwell on the *earth* in their mortal bodies. He will belong to the *glorified* saints mentioned in the Tanakh as well as in the New Testament, who (from heaven) will share in the kingdom (cf. Matt. 8:11; Luke 13:28) and will reign with the Messiah over the *earth*. Paul told the Corinthians: "[D]o you not know that the saints will judge [or govern, rule] the world?" (1 Cor. 6:2). And in the book of Revelation, the twenty-four elders said about what God has done for believers: "[Y]ou have made them a kingdom and priests to our God, and they shall reign on [or, over] the earth" (5:10). Israel's risen and glorified saints will experience the Messianic kingdom from above, in heavenly glory, while Israel's surviving, earthly saints will experience this same kingdom from below, in their Promised Land — where else?

1.5 Ally and Son

1.5.1 The Two Abrahamic Covenants[68]

Abraham and his descendants were called to live in the world as witnesses of the true God, demonstrating the true service of God.[69] To this end, God made covenants, the first with Abram (Gen. 15, first Abrahamic Covenant), the second with Abraham (Gen. 17, second Abrahamic Covenant). These two covenants are one. Through them God offered a warrant both for the blessing that he would grant to Abr(ah)am's physical offspring and for the blessing that he would prepare for the Gentile world. The latter was also linked with Abraham because a "multitude" of nations was assigned to him.[70] According to Romans 4:11–13, this included a spiritual offspring, Gentiles who walked by the same faith as Abraham: he is "the father of all who believe without being circumcised, so that righteousness would be counted to them as well." Such Gentile be-

---

67. So Bailey (1994, 63); Robertson (2000, 26); cf. Chapman (1985, 227).
68. Regarding the covenants, see extensively, Ouweneel (2011a, chapters 1–4).
69. Isa. 43:9–12; 44:8; developed by Paul in Rom. 2:17–20.
70. Gen. 17:1–21; 28:3; 35:11; 48:4; Deut. 33:3 ("peoples" [Heb. ʿ*ammim*] = the tribes of Israel).

lievers are called "sons of Abraham" (Gal. 3:7); they are those who are blessed "in [with, through, and because of]" Abraham (Gen. 12:3).

In a sense, they are more Abraham's "children" than the *r'sha'im* ("wicked") in Israel were and are. As Jesus told the unbelieving and hostile leaders of Israel, "If you were Abraham's children, you would be doing the works Abraham did"; you would walk in his faith and devotion (John 8:39). Jesus did not deny that they were physical offspring of Abraham (v. 37), but being "children" is a spiritual designation that must be used with prudence. The repenting Jewish tax collector, Zakkai (Zacchaeus), was a "son of Abraham" (Luke 19:9), but not the impenitent Jews (cf. 18:9–14). The possessed woman who was set free from the devil was such a "daughter of Abraham" (Luke 13:16) — but not all Jewish women were.

No Jew is a true Jew only by being a physical descendant of Abraham. This is clear from the fact that all covenants are not one-sided, proceeding from God alone, but they are always two-sided, because the promises of God are accompanied by conditions that the partners must fulfill. The promises to Abraham are absolutely unconditional (cf. Rom. 11:29, God's calling is irrevocable) — yet, God addresses him as follows: "Walk before me, *and be blameless*" (Gen. 17:1). The blessings of the Abrahamic Covenant have experientially benefited only the remnant (Heb. *sha'ar*) of Israel, that is, those who walk in the footsteps of Abraham, "walking before God, blameless."

In a broader sense, the Abrahamic Covenant was the covenant with "the patriarchs" (Rom. 9:5): Abraham, Isaac, and Jacob.[71] It is also called an "everlasting covenant" (Heb. *b'rit 'olam*) because it will culminate in the "everlasting covenant" that for the faithful of Israel will be fulfilled in the Messianic kingdom.[72] It is not identical with subsequent covenants, especially the Sinaitic covenant, but it is the foundation and starting point for them. Therefore, when speaking of the Messianic kingdom and the restoration of Israel, the prophet declared: the LORD "will again have compassion on us;

---

71. Exod. 2:24; Lev. 26:42; 2 Kings 13:23; cf. the divine oath in Num. 32:11; Deut. 1:8; 6:10; 9:5; 29:13; 30:20; 34:4.

72. Gen. 17:7, 13, 19; 1 Chron. 16:17; Ps. 105:10; Isa. 61:8; Jer. 32:40; 50:5; Ezek. 16:60; 37:26; Heb. 13:20.

he will tread our iniquities underfoot. You will cast all our sins into the depths of the sea. You will show faithfulness to Jacob and steadfast love to Abraham, as you have sworn to our fathers from the days of old" (Micah 7:19-20). In other words, the promises to the patriarchs will benefit those, and only those, who have repented and have received the forgiveness of sins.

The sign of the covenant in Genesis 17 is circumcision, which was administered to all the males in Abraham's household; after Genesis 17, circumcision was administered to all the sons of the covenant partners, by which act these sons themselves also became covenant partners: "You shall be circumcised in the flesh of your foreskins, and it shall be a sign of the covenant between me and you. . . . Any uncircumcised male who is not circumcised in the flesh of his foreskin shall be cut off from his people; *he has broken my covenant*" (Gen. 17:11, 14). This is why Jesus' servant, Stephen, spoke in Acts 7:8 of the "covenant of [i.e., characterized by] the circumcision" (Gk. *diathēkē peritomēs*), which in Hebrew is called *b'rit milah*. But here again, this is spiritually true only for those covenant partners who also have a circumcised *heart*. Therefore, Moses said, "[C]ircumcise the foreskin of your heart" (Deut. 10:16), and about the great Messianic restoration of Israel he says, "And the LORD your God will circumcise your heart and the heart of your offspring, so that you will love the LORD your God with all your heart and with all your soul, that you may live" (Deut. 30:6). And Jeremiah declared, "Circumcise yourselves to the LORD; remove the foreskin of your hearts, O men of Judah and inhabitants of Jerusalem; lest my wrath go forth like fire, and burn with none to quench it, because of the evil of your deeds" (Jer. 4:4; cf. 9:25).

In perfect harmony with this, the apostle Paul stated, "[N]o one is a Jew who is merely one outwardly, nor is circumcision outward and physical. But a Jew is one inwardly, and circumcision is a matter of the heart, by the Spirit, not by the letter. His praise is not from man but from God" (Rom. 2:28-29). These are the true *physical* children of Abraham: those who, in addition to having been circumcised in the flesh, have a circumcised (i.e., repentant, forgiven, humble, God-devoted) heart, like Abraham had (viz., the Jewish *tzaddiqim*). Other believers are not physical children, but are definitely spiritual children of Abraham; that is, they have not been circumcised in the flesh (at least not for religious reasons), but they do possess a "circumcised" heart (viz., the Gentile *tzaddiqim*). What matters is the heart. From a very practical point of view, historically speaking, throughout the centuries Israel's identity was defined especially by Shabbat and circumcision, and in addition, by the food laws (Heb. *kashrut*) and the festivals (Heb. *Mo'adim*). Humanly speaking, as long as Israel practiced these two (or four) elements, to this very day Israel could not be assimilated into the masses of the Gentile world (as Haman, the supreme "enemy of the Jews," realized, Est. 3:8, 10).

It is therefore all the more remarkable that supersessionism has altered these very practices: Shabbat has been replaced with Sunday (discussed in the next volume), and circumcision has been replaced with infant baptism.[73] The replacement of those Jewish practices means that supersessionism really believes that Jews still keep Shabbat (on Saturdays) and still circumcise their little boys entirely in vain. In other words, supersessionism actually declares that the two main practices that have preserved Israel's identity to this day are now entirely obsolete. This teaching ignores three undeniable realities:

1. This saying of Jesus: "Do not think that I have come to abolish the Law (*Torah*) or the Prophets. I have come not to abolish them but to fulfill them" (Matt. 5:17). Indeed, we read that what will be celebrated in the Messianic kingdom will not be the Sunday but Shabbat.[74]

2. After they had come to faith in Jesus, the apostles went to the synagogue on Shabbat (Acts 13:14, 42, 44; 16:13; 17:2 ["as was his custom"]; 18:4), and Paul had no problem with circumcising Jews, even after they had come to faith in Jesus (Acts 16:3; cf. 21:21).

3. During the Messianic kingdom, what will be administered will not be infant baptism but that "everlasting" institution of God (Gen. 17:13): circumcision.[75]

Supersessionism spirtualizes all these Bible passages, so that these verses no longer mean what they seemed to mean, and

---

73. See Ouweneel (2011a, chapters 1–8).
74. Isa. 56:2, 4, 6; 66:23; Ezek. 44:24; 45:17; 46:1, 3–4, 12.
75. Implied in Isa. 52:1; Jer. 9:25–26; Ezek. 44:9.

what millions of Jews, as well as millions of Christians, have always thought they meant. Supersessionism rescue their theory by spiritualizing all those Bible passages that conflict with the theory, and applying them to the Ecclesia. But the Bible does not do this. Thankfully, the insight is gradually growing among Reformed Christians that Sunday did *not* replace Shabbat, and therefore is not the new Shabbat.[76] However, the idea that baptism did *not* replace circumcision—and that this is definitely not taught in Colossians 2:11-12—is an insight that will grow only very slowly.[77] Our Reformed brothers and sisters may well believe in the literal fulfillment of the prophecies concerning Israel, but if they continue to maintain that Shabbat has moved to Sunday and circumcision has been "replaced" by baptism, they remain committed in large part to "replacement theology" (see further in chapter 5).

1.5.2 The Old and New Covenant

Basically, only *two* covenants have been, or will be, made specifically with Israel, for the benefit of all humanity. These are the Old (Sinaitic, Mosaic) Covenant of Exodus 24 and the New Covenant of Jeremiah 31:31–34. Some speak of *three* covenants because of the covenant made with Israel in the fields of Moab just before Israel's entrance into the Promised Land (Deut. 29:1, 9, 12, 14). However, this was nothing more than the renewal of the Sinaitic Covenant; similar renewals are found under Joshua and Nehemiah, and the Kings David, Asa, Joash, Hezekiah, and Josiah.[78] Basically, there is just the Old and New Covenant.

The New Testament speaks explicitly or implicitly of a "first" and a "second covenant," the "good" and the "better covenant," the temporary and the "everlasting covenant," the "old" and the "new

---

76. This was the case with the Kuyperian supersessionist J. Douma (1996); for his version of supersessionism, see Douma (2008); cf. other Kuyperian supersessionists: Aalders (1949, n.d.); Boersma (1978); Van Delden (1985); Kamsteeg (n.d.); for Roman Catholic supersessionism, see Renckens (1962); Bartels et al. (1976).

77. But see the Reformed Rev. H. Biesma, http://www.kerkenisrael.nl/vrede-over-israel/voi42–4a.php; also see https://christenenvoorisrael.nl/2007/03/in-de-plaats-van-de-besnijdenis/.

78. Josh. 24:16–17, 21; Neh. 9:38; 1 Chron. 11:3; 2 Chron. 15:12–13; 23:3; 29:10–11; 2 Kings 23:3.

covenant," that is, the Sinaitic Covenant and the New Covenant of the Messianic day.[79] At the same time, the Old and New Covenant can easily be seen as basically one covenant. This is evident from the fact that the Old Covenant is also called an "everlasting covenant" (*b'rit 'olam*).[80] Therefore, we find that this one covenant is referred to in a twofold way: on the one hand, it is a covenant that has never been abolished (cf. Matt. 5:17), and on the other hand, in its original form, it is called "obsolete" because it must give way to what Jeremiah calls the "New Covenant": "In speaking of a new covenant, he makes the first one obsolete. And what is becoming obsolete [Gk. *palaioumenon*[81]] and growing old is ready to vanish away" (Heb. 8:13).[82] If the Old Covenant is everlasting, this must mean that the New Covenant is nothing else than a renewal (deepening and extension) of the Old Covenant.[83]

Renderings such as "everlasting" and "perpetual" are no weaker than "eternal" because they all express the same thought: as long as (ethnic) Israel exists, the covenant remains in force. We could also say, as long as the present *earth* exists, Israel will exist, and thus the covenant will exist as well. In Judges 2:1–2, the angel of the LORD said to Israel on behalf of the LORD himself, "I brought you up from Egypt and brought you into the land that I swore to give to your fathers. I said, 'I will never [*lo . . . l''olam*, not in eternity] break my covenant with you, and you [for your part] shall make no covenant with the inhabitants of this land; you shall break down their altars.'"

Here again are the two sides mentioned earlier: God's covenant with Israel will be forever—but in practice, it will be effectuated

---

79. Heb. 8:7, 13; 9:1, 15, 18; 7:22; 8:6; 13:20; 8:8, 13; 9:15; 12:24; cf. Luke 22:20; 2 Cor. 3:1.
80. Exod. 31:16; Lev. 24:8; 1 Chron. 16:17; Ps. 105:10; Isa. 24:5.
81. From the Gk. verb *palaioō*, which Louw and Nida explain (in §67.103) to mean "to cause to become old and obsolete, *and hence no longer valid*—'to make old to make out of date'" (italics added). This same supersessionist perspective governs the explanation of this word group in *TDNT* 5:717–720.
82. See Ouweneel (2020, chapter 4).
83. *Contra* Douma (2008, 123), who asserted that the Old Covenant was *replaced* by the New Covenant.

only with the faithful in Israel, the remnant (Heb. *sha'ar*) of Israel,[84] "the Israel of God." One side of the matter involves God's eternal and sovereign counsels, his irrevocable promises, his perpetual faithfulness. There *will* be a restored ethnic Israel in the Promised Land during the Messianic kingdom. The other side involves human responsibility. Those who have "broken the everlasting covenant" (Isa. 24:5) have forfeited the promises. How can something be "everlasting," and yet be "broken"? It will be everlasting for God's elect, but null and void for those who persist in their wickedness. The fact that the faithful will "enter" is just as certain as the fact that the wicked will not "enter."[85] As Romans 11:7 says, "What then? Israel failed to obtain what it was seeking. The elect [or, chosen] obtained it, but the rest were hardened." When it comes to God's ways with the earth, Israel is his "chosen people" (Deut. 7:6; 14:2). But when it comes to his eternal blessings, some among the "chosen" have been "chosen" for eternity, and others have not.

The fact that the Abrahamic Covenants, or the Old and New Covenant, are all called "eternal (everlasting)" does not mean that essentially only one divine covenant has been made with fallen humanity, namely, the one covenant that in Reformed theology is called "the covenant of grace." The covenants form a unity, but they are not identical. Nor should we speak one-sidedly here of a covenant of *grace*, since this covenant involves *both grace and works*, namely, the good works that are the fruit and proof of regeneration and faith. Only a theology that drives a wedge between divine sovereignty and human responsibility could construct the unfortunate distinction between a "covenant of works" and a "covenant of grace." *All* covenants, including those before the Fall and after the Exodus, are covenants of grace *and* works, unconditional as well as conditional, a subtle interplay between one hundred percent divine sovereignty (grace) and one hundred percent human responsibility (works). There is no grace apart from human responsibility to be fulfilled; but no human works exist apart from the divine grace through which alone they can be performed. *Each Israelite reaching the Messianic kingdom will be there wholly and entirely through God's*

---

84. Isa. 10:20–22; 11:11; 28:5; Jer. 31:6; Ezek. 6:8; Obad. 1:17; Micah 2:12; 5:6–7; Zeph. 2:7, 9; 3:13; Zech. 8:12; 9:7; Rom. 11:5.
85. Num. 14:22–23; Deut. 1:34; Ps. 95:11; Heb. 3:11, 18.

grace and mercy—and no Israelite will forever fall outside the divine blessings except due wholly and entirely to their own wickedness.[86] No Israelite who enters the Messianic kingdom will be able to glory in their own achievements; and no Israelite who is excluded from the kingdom will be able to blame God for that outcome.

1.5.3 Israel Son of God

Calvinism characteristically claims that the relationship between God and his people is always by definition "covenantal."[87] With respect to Gentile Jesus-believers this is certainly incorrect. Apart from the book of Hebrews (addressed to Jesus-believing *Jews*!), the New Testament rarely speaks of any covenant involving Gentile believers. The only two exceptions that I am aware of are these: "[T]his is my blood of the covenant, which is poured out for many [apparently including Gentiles[88]] for the forgiveness of sins" (Matt. 26:28; cf. Mark 14:24; Luke 22:20); and: God "has even made us competent to be workers serving a New Covenant, the essence of which is not a written text but the Spirit. For the written text brings death, but the Spirit gives life" (2 Cor. 3:6 CJB). That is, it is made effectual only through the power of the Holy Spirit.

In contrast to this, the New Testament often referred to a relationship that is much more intimate than a covenantal relationship: that between God the Father and his children.[89] One might mention the Bridegroom–bride relationship as well,[90] but it might be argued that this, too, is a relationship of a covenantal nature (Ezek. 16:8, 59–61; Mal. 2:14).

In Israel we find something similar. In a marvelous way, the apostle Paul summarized the seven characteristics of Israel—plus a special eighth one—of which the covenants are only one feature. They are as follows (Rom. 9:4–5; for more extensive discussion, see §12.1.1 below):

---

86. See extensively, Ouweneel (2008b; 2011a, chapters 2–4).
87. See, e.g., Jonker (1988, 82–83).
88. Cf. Matt. 20:28, "[T]he Son of Man did not come to be served, but to serve—and to give his life as a ransom for *many*."
89. E.g., Luke 20:36; John 1:12–13; Rom. 8:14–16, 19; 2 Cor. 6:18; Gal. 3:26; Eph. 5:1; Phil. 2:15; 1 John 3:1–2, 10; 5:2.
90. Matt. 9:15; 2 Cor. 11:2; Eph. 5:25–30; Rev. 21:2, 9–10; 22:17.

1. To them belong the adoption (being adopted as sons; see below),
2. the glory (the *Shekhinah*; this is the rabbinic expression for God's glorious presence in the midst of his people),
3. the covenants (all of them are Israel-oriented, including the Noahic covenant),
4. the giving of the *Torah* (an extremely important subject, which we will deal with extensively),
5. the worship (the ministry of priests offering sacrifices in the Temple),
6. the promises (directly to the patriarchs, and afterward to Israel through Moses and the later prophets; see §1.6);
7. the patriarchs (Abraham, Isaac, Jacob, and the latter's twelve sons, who are *Israel's* ancestors);
8. and from their race, according to the flesh [i.e., as far as his physical descent is concerned], came the Messiah.

At this point, we are considering only the first of these eight features: to Israel belongs "the sonship" or the "adoption as sons" (one word: Gk. *huiothesia*). Indeed, at the very beginning of Israel's national existence we hear these words from God's mouth: "Then you [i.e., Moses] shall say to Pharaoh, 'Thus says the LORD, Israel is my firstborn son'" (Exod. 4:22). The plural occurs as well: "You are the sons of the LORD your God" (Deut. 14:1). Looking back at the wilderness journey, the LORD said through Moses: ". . . the wilderness, where you have seen how the LORD your God carried you, as a man carries his son, all the way that you went until you came to this place" (1:31), and: ". . . as a man disciplines his son, the LORD your God disciplines you" (8:5). Centuries later he said through Hosea: "When Israel was a child, I loved him, and out of Egypt I called my son" (Hos. 11:1). The same book says about the future: "[T]he time will come when, instead of being told, 'You are not my people,' it will be said to them, 'You are the children [or, sons] of the living God'" (1:10 CJB).

If Israel is referred to as either God's "son," or his "sons," then it is fitting that God himself is called the "Father" of Israel, both in the sense of the One begetting and in the sense of the One caring for his people: "Is he not your father, who created you, who made you and established you?" (Deut. 32:6). "[Y]ou are our Father, though Abraham does not know us, and Israel does not acknowledge us; you, O Lord, are our Father, our Redeemer from of old is your name" (Isa. 63:16). "But now, O Lord, you are our Father; we are the clay, and you are our potter; we are all the work of your hand" (64:8). "Have we not all one Father? Has not one God created us?" (Mal. 2:10a). "As a father shows compassion to his children, so the Lord shows compassion to those who fear him" (Ps. 103:13).

In the Tanakh, such designations refer exclusively in an *external* way to Israel as the people of God; they tell us nothing about whether we are dealing with the *tzaddiqim* (the righteous, godly ones), or with the *r'sha'im* (the wicked ones) in Israel (cf., e.g., 1 Kings 8:32, "judge your servants, condemning the guilty by bringing his conduct on his own head, and vindicating the righteous by rewarding him according to his righteousness"). Every Jew is a "son" of the Lord because he or she belongs to the chosen people of God. But in the *limited* (spiritual, eternal) sense of the term, only these are "sons":

> I will sprinkle clean water on you, and you shall be clean from all your uncleannesses, and from all your idols I will cleanse you. And I will give you a new heart, and a new spirit I will put within you. And I will remove the heart of stone from your flesh and give you a heart of flesh. And I will put my Spirit within you, and cause you to walk in my statutes and be careful to obey my rules (Ezek. 36:25–27).

Notice that this is immediately linked with the Promised Land, as the adjacent verses show: "I will take you from the nations and gather you from all the countries and bring you into your own land. ... You shall dwell in the land that I gave to your fathers, and you shall be my people, and I will be your God" (vv. 24, 28). We find something similar in Isaiah 1:18–20,

> Come now, let us reason [or, dispute] together, says the Lord: though your sins are like scarlet, they shall be as white as snow; though they are red like crimson, they shall become like wool. If you are willing and obedient [the *tzaddiqim*], you shall eat the good of the land; but if you refuse and rebel [the *r'sha'im*], you shall be eaten by the sword; for the mouth of the Lord has spoken.

There is a natural Israel and a spiritual Israel. But notice this essential point: the expression "spiritual Israel" *is not an **extension** of the term "natural Israel,"* as the supersessionism claims, *but a restriction of that term*. The "spiritual Israel" is only a *part* of the "natural Israel," namely, the faithful part, the *tzaddiqim*, the "remnant" of Israel, "the Israel of God." Believing Gentiles are never called "Jews" or "Israel," as we will see more extensively. But at the same time, we remember that both the Jewish and the Gentile *tzaddiqim* are spiritual children of Abraham. This is far more important for a person's eternal blessing than being a natural descendant of Abraham. Spiritual children of Abraham—Jews or Gentiles—are those who walk in the confidence and devotion of Abraham, which constituted his response to God and his promises, and who walk in practical righteousness, as Abraham did. Notice the two most important verses in the Tanakh with regard to this confidence:

(a) Abraham "believed the LORD, and [the latter] counted it to him as righteousness" (Gen. 15:6), that is, God declared him to be a *tzaddiq*, not only because of his godly walk but because of his trust in God and his promises.

(b) "[T]he righteous shall live by his faith" (Hab. 2:4b); that is, the secret of their spiritual life is not only a righteous walk, important as this is, but their confidence, their trust in God, in all circumstances of life.

1.6   Prophetic Promises

1.6.1   Hermeneutical Keys[91]

Of course, the New Covenant is an everlasting covenant *par excellence*; all earlier forms of the covenant culminate in the New Covenant. Moreover, the passages below illustrate that this New Covenant is made only with ethnic Israel—i.e., with the faithful among Israel—*and is linked inextricably with the Promised Land*.

> Instead of your shame there shall be a double portion; instead of dishonor they shall rejoice in their lot; therefore *in their land* they shall possess a double portion; they shall have everlasting joy. For I the LORD love justice; I hate robbery and wrong; I will faithfully give them their recompense, and I will make an *everlasting covenant* with them. Their offspring shall be known among the nations, and their descen-

---

91. Hermeneutics is the science of exegesis, the study of the rules and starting points for the interpretation of texts.

dants in the midst of the peoples; all who see them shall acknowledge them, that they are an offspring the LORD has blessed (Isa. 61:7–9).[92]

Behold, I will gather them from all the countries to which I drove them in my anger and my wrath and in great indignation. I will *bring them back to this place* [i.e., the land of Israel], and I will make them dwell in safety. And they shall be my people, and I will be their God. I will give them one heart and one way, that they may fear me forever, for their own good and the good of their children after them. I will make with them an *everlasting covenant*, that I will not turn away from doing good to them. And I will put the fear of me in their hearts, that they may not turn from me. I will rejoice in doing them good, and I will plant them in this land in faithfulness, with all my heart and all my soul (Jer. 32:37–41).

Once again we observe that no unbiased reader can read in these passages anything other than that (a) Israel will be brought back to *the same land* from which they had been driven, and (b) this was not completely fulfilled after the Babylonian exile, but will be completely fulfilled when the "eternal covenant" is be fully realized, that is, under the Messiah. In the same context in the book of Jeremiah we read these verses: "[T]hey shall serve the LORD their God and David their king [i.e., the Messiah], whom I will raise up for them" (Jer. 30:9). "In those days and at that time I will cause a righteous Branch [i.e., the Messiah] to spring up for David, and he shall execute justice and righteousness in the land" (Jer. 33:15). Here we find two hermeneutical keys that will play an extremely important role in these two volumes on Israelology:

(a) The *promise* is this: You will return to the land where you yourselves, or your ancestors, have lived. This is not some kind of "spiritual land," like a "heavenly land." It is invalid to link these prophecies with the "heavenly country" of Hebrews 11:16, because the latter is a "land" where the Israelites or their fathers *have never lived before*. Moreover, you cannot say: "I promise A," only later to explain that you actually meant B. The promise: You shall return to *your own* country, can be explained in only one way, if Bible exegesis means anything. If Israel possessed a "double portion" in

---

92. Cf. Isa. 24:5; 55:3; 56:4; 59:21; see also 42:6 and 49:8 in connection with the Servant of the LORD.

the land (Isa. 61:7), then by necessity Israel formerly possessed a "single portion" in that same land.

(b) The ultimate fulfillment of the land promise is linked inextricably with the establishment of the Messianic kingdom. The Israelites will finally enjoy peace and justice in their own ancient land under the blessed rule of the Messiah *in that same land*. He will be seated in Zion, on the throne of his father David. No exegesis of the prophecies of the Tanakh can do justice to this if it is not placed in the context of the Messianic kingdom:

> For to us a child is born, to us a son is given; and the government shall be upon his shoulder, and his name shall be called Wonderful Counselor, Mighty God, Everlasting Father, Prince of Peace. Of the increase of his government and of peace there will be no end, on the throne of *David* and over *his* kingdom, to establish it and to uphold it with justice and with righteousness from this time forth and forevermore. The zeal of the LORD of hosts will do this (Isa. 9:6–7).

At this point, an essential question must be raised: With what validity does supersessionism claim that in terms of God's repeated promises to bring Israel back *to the same land where their fathers had lived*, this land will be replaced ultimately with a very different land, whether a "heavenly land" or the "new earth"? The only answer available to supersessionism is that these prophecies were completely fulfilled immediately after the Babylonian exile. But that generates a second essential question: How is it possible that these prophecies of return to the land are invariably linked with the *appearance of the Messiah* and culminate in the *Messianic kingdom of peace*, in the Promised Land and throughout the earth? In what follows, these questions will be asked repeatedly, because the *locus* of Israelology consists of the answers to these questions.

1.6.2 More Examples

"In those days and in that time, . . . the people of Israel [the ten tribes] and the people of Judah [the two tribes] shall come together, weeping as they come, and they shall seek the LORD their God. They shall ask the way to Zion, with faces turned toward it, saying, 'Come, let us join ourselves to the Lord in an *everlasting covenant* that will never be forgotten'" (Jer. 50:4–5). Not only the Judeans, as during the return from the Babylonian exile, but ultimately Israelites from all twelve tribes will return to Israel's own land. This land must be understood in the physical-concrete sense, as is evident from Ezekiel 48, where the land is apportioned to the twelve tribes according to a division very different from what they were familiar with. No expositor can do justice to the geographical details in this chapter by spiritualizing this land. Doing so will hollow out this chapter and dozens of prophetic chapters.

This new division of the land will be realized only in the Messianic kingdom, that is, by the Messiah himself, as we learn from the following passage:

> My servant David [i.e., the Messiah son of David] shall be king over them, and they shall all have one shepherd. They shall walk in my rules and be careful to obey my statutes. They shall *dwell in the land that I gave to my servant Jacob, where your fathers lived*. They and their children and their children's children shall dwell there *forever*, and David my servant shall be their prince *forever*. I will make a covenant of peace with them. It shall be an *everlasting covenant* with them. And I will set them in their land and multiply them, and will set my sanctuary in their midst *forevermore*. My dwelling place shall be with them, and I will be their God, and they shall be my people. Then the nations will know that I am the LORD who sanctifies Israel, when my sanctuary is in their midst *forevermore* (Ezek. 37:24–28).

Here again, several matters are being raised in an initial fashion that will be explained much more thoroughly later in these two volumes (see §5.6.3 below):

1. One day, the Messiah will rule in glory; and no matter how universal this rule may be, its center will be in the physical land of Israel.

2. Israel will dwell in its own land; this is explicitly the land where their "fathers" had lived. No other land, literal or spiritual, can be designated as the land where Israel had lived in earlier ages than *ha'Aretz* (Canaan, Palestine, Israel).

3. The Israelites will again have a sanctuary "forever" (i.e., as long as the present earth exists); in Ezekiel 40–44 and elsewhere this temple is described in detail.

4. Israel will be a blessing for all nations worldwide.

Please note that this is the very same situation that had been foretold to Abr(ah)am in the beginning:

1. The Messiah is *the* Seed of Abraham (see the remarkable argument of Paul in Gal. 3:15–18).

2. Abraham was to become a large nation.

3. This nation would dwell in the very land to which God had brought Abram in Genesis 12.

4. This nation would be a blessing for all the Gentile nations; Isaiah 60 is a beautiful description of the relationship between Israel and the Gentile nations during the Messianic kingdom.

Chapter 2
The Destiny of Israel

Two nations are in your womb,
>and two peoples from within you [or, from birth] shall be divided;

the one shall be stronger than the other,
>the older shall serve the younger.

Genesis 25:23

2.1   Jacob and Esau
2.1.1   The Face of *Elohim*

One important way to describe world history in a metahistorical manner is to say that basically it is governed by the battle between the Lamb and the dragon.[1] In the book of Revelation, the Lamb is the Messiah of Israel (cf. John 1:29; 1 Cor. 5:7; 1 Pet. 1:19), and the dragon (the Devil, Satan; 12:9; 20:2) is the angelic prince of the Roman Empire. Both terms appear in the Tanakh: in the early rabbinic interpretation of Isaiah 53, the Servant is the Messiah, and he is called the "Lamb led to the slaughter" (v. 7) — a picture of weakness and destruction, but also of atonement (cf. Exod. 2:1-13; 29:38-47). In the same book of Isaiah, the angelic prince of Babylon, the first of the four world empires, is called a "dragon" (Heb. *tannin*; 51:9 KJV;

---

1. See extensively, Ouweneel (2003a, §4.2 and Excursus 6); cf. De Graaff (1982).

cf. Jer. 51:34, 44; see below); he is the foreshadowing of the "dragon" who is the angelic prince of the last of the four world empires.

The fourth empire is the Roman Empire. This is the empire—together with its heir: Western (pseudo-)Christian nations—that in Jewish tradition is referred to as "Edom" (the nation descending from Jacob's brother Esau).[2] In other words, world history can be described as the conflict between Jacob/Israel—basically, the God and the Messiah of Israel—against Esau/Edom—basically, the diabolical angelic prince of Edom. Genesis 32 is the chapter where, according to an ancient rabbinic tradition, we meet with the angelic prince of Esau.

Imagine the situation. Esau and Jacob are twins born to Isaac and Rebekah. Before their birth, the two were struggling against each other (Gen. 25:22)—a bad sign. God told Rebekah (v. 23):

Two nations are in your womb,
> and two peoples from within you [or, from birth]
shall be divided;
the one shall be stronger than the other,
> the older shall serve the younger.

At birth, Esau appeared first, followed immediately by Jacob, whose hand grasped Esau's heel (Gen. 25:26). "Esau" means "hairy," and "Jacob" means "heel-holder," either in the negative sense of "cheater," "imposter"—at least this is the way Esau explained the name (Gen. 27:36)—or in the more neutral sense of "one who steps in the place of another."[3] Thus, on the one hand, holding Esau's heel at birth foreshadows Jacob's deceiving character. On the other hand, it also refers to Jacob's justified claims: the fact that he held Esau's heel implies that, according to divine right, he will take Esau's place. Ultimately this means that the Israelite empire of the Messiah will take the place of the Western (pseudo-Christian) world power.

We know the subsequent history of the brothers. As a conse-

---

2. E.g., Lev. Rabbah XIII; Abodah Zarah 10b.
3. Heb. 'aqēv, "heel"; 'aqav, "to take by the heel," and hence also "to cheat" (Jer. 9:4; cf. Hos. 12:4). Because 'aqēv in a derived sense also means "footsteps, footprints" (see Ps. 77:19; 89:51; Song 1:8), it is also conceivable that 'aqav means "tread in someone's footsteps," that is, "step in someone's place."

quence of his ignoble machinations, Jacob must flee from his brother's anger, and sojourn for twenty years outside the land that, through Isaac's blessing, had become his in the form of a promise. After this exile, foreshadowing all the later exiles of Israel, Jacob returned to Canaan at God's command, but in great fear of Esau: Would Esau go with him, or turn against him? Therefore, he tried to appease him through enormous gifts, especially after hearing that Esau was on his way to meet him with four hundred men.

When Jacob finally met Esau, he said to him (Gen. 33:10): ". . . I have seen your face, which is like seeing the face of God [Heb. *Elohim*], and you have accepted me." Usually, this statement is dismissed as flattery on Jacob's part, but in my view, these words have a much deeper sense. Jacob noticed here that he has seen the face of Esau, and that this was like seeing the face of *elohim*![4] What do these mysterious words mean? What similarity is intended here? And when did Jacob see the face of *elohim*? Who is this *elohim*? And what connection is there between the face of this *elohim* and the face of Esau? In my view, the most obvious answer—supplied by ancient rabbis—is this: this *elohim* was the angelic prince of Esau; his face corresponds with the face of Esau himself,[5] and Jacob had seen this face when he wrestled with *Esau's elohim* near the brook called Jabbok.

2.1.2 Wrestling with the Angel

We now arrive at that important event in Jacob's life, described in Genesis 32:24–31: Jacob wrestling with a "man." Many of the older expositors, both Christian and Jewish, understood this "man" who wrestled with Jacob to have been a good angel, an (or the) Angel of the LORD, or even the LORD himself. Some rabbis suggested that the angel was Michael,[6] or in general, an angel of God. However, on the whole, Jewish exegetes understood this angel to be the angelic prince of Esau, say, Edom, say, the Roman Empire and its (pseu-

---

4. Heb. *Elohim*, "God," but also "gods," or "a figure from the divine world" (angels; cf. Ps. 8:6 with Heb. 2:7), or "god-like being" (1 Sam. 28:13).
5. Cf. Acts 12:15 for the idea that a person's face is similar to that of his guardian angel.
6. See sources mentioned in Lueken (1898, 16); so also rabbi Chelbo in the Midrash: Gen. Rabbah 78, 1.

do-)Christian successors.[7] The great Jewish expositor Rashi (Rabbi Shlomo Yitzchaqi) wrote that, according to (Jewish) scholars, the "man" of verse 24 was the guardian angel of Esau.[8] According to one passage in Midrash Tanchuma,[9] this "man" was Samael, the angel of evil, but this Samael was none other than Satan,[10] that is, the angelic prince of Esau/Edom, that is, of the Roman Empire and of its (pseudo-)Christian successors.

The ancient rabbis understood that the angel whom Jacob met was not a good angel, evident from at least five facts:

1. It follows from Hosea 12:4–5, if this passage is correctly understood (see the next section): in the poetic parallelism of the text, Jacob's brother corresponds to the *elohim*.

2. This *elohim* comes to wrestle with Jacob not during the day but at night. It is a spirit of darkness. When the night has passed, the *elohim* asks Jacob to let him go *because* dawn has arrived (v. 26). If this had really been an angel of God, an angel of light, why would he come to Jacob in the dark, and apparently flee the daylight?

3. The easiest explanation of Genesis 33:10, then, is that Jacob appeals to Esau's clemency by reminding him of the fact that the previous night he had seen Esau's *elohim*, implying that he had prevailed over this guardian angel, *and* that the latter had blessed Jacob. If Esau's *elohim* had blessed Jacob, what else could Esau himself do? Remember that it is the duty of every human being to "bless" Abraham, Isaac, and Jacob in order to be blessed themselves (Gen. 12:3; 27:29).

4. If this had really been an angel of the LORD, how is it con-

---

7. Cohen (1983, ad loc.) implicitly gave both interpretations.

8. For Rashi's comments, see
https://www.chabad.org/library/bible_cdo/aid/8227/showrashi/true.

9. Midrash Tanchuma: a specific collection of Midrash; Midrash is a form of rabbinical Bible exegesis.

10. In the Tanakh, *Satan* was an "adversary" in God's celestial court (Job 1:6–13; 2:1–7; Zech. 3:1–2), who was not necessarily a negative figure, except in 1 Chron. 21:1 (where he incites David); in the New Testament, his evil character was far more explicit: he was *the* angelic prince, *the* "tempter" of God's people (Matt. 4:3; 1 Cor. 7:5; 1 Thess. 3:5), whose judgment was being announced (Rom. 16:20; Rev. 20); he was also called the "devil" (from Gk. *diabolos*, "slanderer").

ceivable that Jacob gained the victory (cf. v. 28, "you [Jacob] have prevailed"; see also Hos. 12:5)? Rather, the angel of the LORD would have gained the victory over Jacob. However, one essential point of the narrative is that not the *elohim* but Jacob prevailed, although at the precious cost of his disjointed hip (vv. 25, 31-32). Rabbi Shimeoni has pointed out that it is evident from the angel's words "Let me go" (lit., "Send me away"), that the sender is greater than the one sent, so that Jacob is greater than the angel.[11]

5. V. Hamilton, who was remarkably vague on the identity of the angel in Genesis 32, pointed to this remarkable parallelism: in verses 25-26, the angel "wrestles" (Heb. root *'-b-q*) with Jacob, and in Genesis 33:4 Esau "hugs" (Heb. *ch-b-q*) Jacob.[12] The angel embraces Jacob to fight with him, whereas Esau embraces Jacob to greet him. Together with this word play, we mention the names Jacob (Heb. *Ya'aqob*) and Jabbok (33:22, Heb. *yabboq*); the combination of the Hebrew letters *b-q* appears four times. Although Hamilton did not draw this conclusion, the connection seems to be an indication that the angel fighting with Jacob was Esau's guardian angel.

Returning to Genesis 33:10, we may conclude—as Jewish tradition does—that the angel was not only an evil one, but more specifically that it was the guardian angel of Esau. We may read the verse in such a way that Jacob was suggesting here a connection with the wrestling angel: he said as it were, that the face of the *elohim* with whom he had wrestled was the face of Esau himself. This can only be understood if the relationship between the angel and Esau was that of a guardian angel and the person guarded. This is precisely what the majority of the Jewish rabbis believed.[13] In Genesis 32, it is the battle between Israel and the angelic powers behind the "Edomite" (Roman) world.

2.1.3 Hosea 12

For an accurate exegesis of Genesis 31, it is helpful to consider Hosea 12:3-5 as well. This text says,

> In the womb he [Jacob] took his brother [Esau] by the heel,

---

11. Gen. Rabbah 78, 1; cf. Midrash Ps. 91, §6 (199b), 104, §3 (220b).
12. Hamilton (1995, 329).
13. E.g., Rashi; see Cohen (1983, 202); the Targum of Jeremiah says in Gen. 33:10: "I have seen your face as if I had seen the face of your angel."

> and in his manhood he [Jacob] strove with God [Heb. *Elohim*].
> He strove with the angel and prevailed;
>   he wept and sought his favor.
> He met him [ESV alternate reading] at Bethel,
>   and there he spoke with us—
> the LORD, the God of hosts,
>   the LORD is his memorial name.

First, we notice here the poetic parallelism in verse 3: in the womb he held Esau's heel, and in the strength of his manhood he fought with *elohim*. The parallelism clearly suggests a connection between Esau and *elohim*, so that we are strongly inclined to think of Esau's *elohim* again. Second, *elohim* corresponds with "angel" in the next line.

But then the crucial question arises: Who is the "he" of verse 4, second line: "he wept and sought his favor [Heb. root: *ch-n*, "grace"]"? In Genesis 32 we read that Jacob did beg the angel to bless him, but this is quite different from begging for grace. Such a supplication does not fit the one who overcame, but the one who *was* overcome. It is rather the angel—who has lost the struggle, who flees the dawn, and who finds himself in Jacob's headlock—who exclaims: "Let me go!" Therefore, along with Jewish sources,[14] I think it is the angel who weeps and begs for Jacob's favor: please, release me from this chokehold, and let me escape from the rising (and frightening) light!

This may become even clearer when we examine the rest of the passage. Hosea was seeing the situation from the angel's viewpoint, who was weeping and begging for grace, and then said (in my rendering): "At Bethel he [the angel] would meet him [Jacob]," that is, there they would appear together before the LORD: "There he [God] would speak with us [Jacob and the angel]," that is, there God would judge between me (the angel) and you (Jacob). The angel begs Jacob for grace, counts on appearing together with him before the LORD, and then states in an entreating way: "*There* God will judge between us." According to Rashi, this meant that God would reveal himself later, in Bethel (Gen. 35:10). There *he* will change your name and bless you. I too—i.e., the angel—will be there, and

---

14. E.g., Rashi, Abraham Ibn Ezra, David Kimchi, and the Talmud tract Chullin 92a (on Hos. 12:5).

will acknowledge your being entitled to the blessing. Thus, the angel's supplication is this: Please wait until *he* speaks with us, *then* I will bless you, that is, acknowledge your being entitled to the patriarchal blessing. But Jacob did not wish to wait that long, and forced the angel to acknowledge this right at Pniel; hence the emphasis on the word "there" in Genesis 32:30: the angel blessed him there, not only at Bethel.

As I see it, the angel's blessing upon Jacob has a double meaning: a general meaning, as in Genesis 12:3 — wishing Jacob well — and a specific meaning: accepting Jacob's acquired birthright and the blessing attached to it.

2.2 The Crucial Blessing
2.2.1 Blessing Jacob or Combating Him

Why did Esau's guardian angel come to wrestle with Jacob? The reason for this must be sought in the blessing that Isaac, after giving the great, actual patriarchal blessing to Jacob, had granted to Esau (Gen. 27:39-40):

> Behold, away from [or, Behold, of] the fatness of the earth shall your dwelling be,
> and away from [or, and of] the dew of heaven on high.
> By your sword you shall live,
> and you shall serve your brother;
> but when you grow restless [CJB: break loose]
> you shall break his yoke from your neck.

Isaac made clear that the blessing of the firstborn — which also involved the blessing of the coming Messiah and of the Messianic kingdom — rested with Jacob, and that if he rejected Jacob, Esau would forever remain deprived of that blessing. Therefore, only two ways were open to Esau. One way was to acknowledge Jacob's birthright, and thereby in and through him receive a share in the great blessing ("in you all the nations shall be blessed," Gen. 12:3). The other way was to keep contesting Jacob's birthright, and to try to annul the latter's priority: ". . . break his yoke from your neck." Here we find *one of the prominent basic features of all (Western) history*, especially when we consider that, in the rabbinic view, Esau/Edom represents the (pagan, later [pseudo-]Christian) Roman Empire.

Recall the crucial statement that God made and repeated to the patriarchs:

- (a) to Abraham: "[I]n *you* all the families [or, nations] of the earth shall be blessed" (Gen. 12:3; 18:8);

- (b) to Abraham again: "[I]n *your offspring* shall all the nations of the earth be blessed" (Gen. 22:18);

- (c) to Isaac: "[I]n *your offspring* all the nations of the earth shall be blessed" (Gen. 26:4);

- (d) to Jacob: "[I]n *you* and *your offspring* shall all the families of the earth be blessed" (Gen. 28:14).

This promise has a universal reach: regarding all the families and nations of the earth it is true that those who bless the patriarchs and Israel will themselves be blessed "in" (through, because of) them. To "bless" Israel is to proclaim what is good to and about Israel, to seek what is good for Israel, to strive for its well-being, and in this very way to share in Israel's blessing. This could and should have been the way of blessing for Esau. The same is true for Western culture as such; only these two options are available, which come to govern its history: either seek the blessing that is in and with Israel—that is, in and with the *God* of Israel—or reject Israel, which includes rejecting the *God* of Israel, and refuse Israel's priority, "shake his yoke off the neck," that is, persecute Israel, drive it out, exterminate it. Just as the destiny of the previous three world empires depended on their attitude toward the God of Israel, and toward Israel itself, the same destiny will befall the Roman Empire and its heir: the (pseudo-)Christian Western world. Therefore, the Shoah (Holocaust) is one of the forebodings of the decline of Western culture.[15] Salvation will be granted only to those who maintain a personal relationship with the God of Israel in and through the Messiah, and who give evidence of this by blessing (seeking the good for, supporting) Israel.[16]

---

15. This involves not just the decline of Nazi Germany and its allies, but also of all the Western countries—including North America—that to a great extent refused to receive the Jewish fugitives, and/or refused to bomb the railways to the concentration camps; for more extensive discussion of this matter, see the second volume.

16. This is primarily a spiritual matter; it does not necessarily mean approving

In Genesis 32, we see how Esau's angelic prince chose the second option and came to wrestle with Jacob. In the loneliness of the night, Jacob was attacked. But Jacob was strong, for an entire *army* of angels was given him to accompany and protect him (vv. 2–3). Esau's guardian angel saw that he would not succeed in throwing off Jacob's "yoke," nor in prevailing entirely over him. This is a general rule: Edom/Rome will never be able to entirely overcome Jacob/Israel because the LORD is on the latter's side. However, Edom/Rome is certainly able to hurt Israel severely, and has done so many times throughout world history. We see this here as well. Esau's angelic prince inflicted a serious injury on Jacob by striking his hip socket. This was not an arbitrary trauma. In the Bible, the hip, or the loins, are linked first of all with procreation: Jacob's sixty-six descendants "came out of his loins" (Gen. 46:26 KJV; Exod. 1:5; also Judg. 8:30 KJV). If Esau's guardian angel could not prevail over Jacob himself, he tried to hurt him in his offspring. This is exactly what has been happening to Israel for more than three thousand years now, from the time its newborn sons were thrown into the Nile River (Exod. 1) until the time his sons and daughters died in the gas chambers of Auschwitz or died in the wars that the state of Israel has had to fight with its neighbors.

Genesis 3:15 identified a broader principle behind this. God said to the serpent (i.e., the "dragon," the Devil and Satan; Rev. 12:9; 20:2):

> I will put enmity between you and the woman,
>   and between your offspring and her offspring;
> he shall bruise your head,
>   and you shall bruise his heel.

I understand this to be referring to two offsprings: that of the serpent and that of the woman. Physically, both will be born of Eve, but spiritually speaking, her wicked descendants are in fact "children of the devil" (see John 8:44; 1 John 3:10), of whom Cain was the very first. The other offspring, in accordance with Eve's character as the "mother of all *living*" (Gen. 3:20), are the children of God, the righteous, of whom Abel was the first. Throughout the ages, there would be enmity between the devil's offspring (the wicked) and

---

everything that the government of the *state* of Israel decides.

the woman's true offspring (the righteous). *Ultimately* the woman's offspring *par excellence*, the Messiah himself, will "bruise the head" of the dragon, and thus put an end to all the havoc and mischief he has caused. But *in the meantime*, before the serpent's end, the devil would time and again "bruise the heels" of the righteous. The first example of this was Abel, who was murdered by Cain (Gen. 4). Jesus spoke of "all the righteous bloodshed on earth, from the blood of righteous Abel" (Matt. 23:35; cf. Heb. 11:4). Abel was a type of Israel, whose "heel" was "bruised" a million times by the Cains of this world, not least by the (pseudo-)Christian world.

2.2.2 Jacob's Method of Fighting

How did Jacob conduct his battle against the angel? In Genesis 32:26 we get the impression that Jacob did not flee from the angel, but neither did he beat him up or destroy him. Jacob was not intending to exterminate Esau. He limited himself to placing his opponent in an iron grip, from which the latter could not free himself. As we saw, this evil angel fled from the daylight. Therefore, when dawn appeared, he called upon Jacob to let him go. He even cried, begging for Jacob's grace (see above). But Jacob did not release him; he told the angel: "I will not let you go unless you bless me" (v. 26).

To some expositors, this is one of the strongest indications that the angel is a representative of the LORD; whom else would Jacob ask for a blessing? But this argument forgets that Jacob did not need at all to ask *God* for a blessing because he *had* the great patriarchal blessing of God through Isaac (27:27-29). Moreover, we have considered the many passages in Genesis that speak of the *nations* blessing the patriarchs. Therefore, it is quite conceivable that Jacob was asking the angel for *this* blessing. It was Jacob's great desire that Esau—representative of so many families and nations—would "bless" *him*, not only by proclaiming good over Jacob, but by accepting with delight the blessing that *God* had in store for Jacob. Only when Esau "blesses" Jacob—by acknowledging the latter's birthright—could he himself be blessed. Jacob said to (the angelic prince of) Esau as it were: "If you bless me, you will be blessed yourself." This is exactly the way Rashi interpreted the passage: ". . . unless you bless me" means: ". . . unless you acknowledge my title to my father's blessings." Only *here* lies hidden all the blessing for Esau, and Edom, and the Western world.

Thus, until the dawn of the Messianic age, "Jacob" (Israel) still clasps the empire of the *goyyim*, especially "Edom," "Rome," the (pseudo-)Christian Western world. Israel does so because it *knows* that the blessing for the world will arrive only if and when the latter acknowledges Israel's birthright, and seeks its blessing there, namely, with the God and the Messiah of Israel. This is the blessing that Jacob forced from the angel: if the latter blessed him, Esau himself will be blessed. This is why Jacob did not let the angel go, not out of self-defense—for he only had to release him and the angel would have fled from the dawn—but out of love for Esau. This is no longer the deceitful Jacob, the heel-grabber and supplanter, but a princely man, thinking first not of his own victory but of the well-being of Esau. Therefore, the angel said (Gen. 32:28): "Your name shall no longer be called Jacob, but Israel,[17] for you have striven with [or, behaved princely toward] God [or "him"; Heb. *elohim*] and with men [see the "man" in v. 24], and have prevailed." According to Rashi, Esau's angelic prince said as it were that people would no longer find the name Jacob fitting for him as though he had attained the blessings by supplanting (root *'aqav* [cf. Gen. 27:36]) another, but the name Israel would befit him, since he had attained the blessings through superiority (root *sar*) over another, that is, through open battle and victory.

Jacob clung to the angel until the latter could do nothing else than bless him (Gen. 32:29). Jacob, who had been so much occupied with Esau's face (Gen. 32:20), says of this place (Gen. 32:30): "I have seen God [or "him"; Heb. *elohim*] face to face, and yet my life has been delivered." *This* was the outcome of the battle: Jacob did not lose his life, but on the contrary, he gained the victory, although at the cost of a serious injury, which to this day hurts him in his offspring, and threatens the fulfillment of God's promises. However, all this cannot cast doubt on the ultimate victory of Israel. When the sun of the Messianic kingdom rises (cf. Gen. 32:31 with Mal. 4:2),[18] Israel will be the victor, but this too will be true: Edom will be blessed insofar as it has blessed Israel. That is, Edom/Rome as a whole will, together with its angelic prince, necessarily face its final

---

17. Regarding the meaning of the name, see §1.1.2.
18. In Genesis, we twice find a setting sun (vv. 15:12, 17; 28:11), and twice a rising sun (19:23; 32:31), each time in a somewhat solemn context.

judgment, but there will be everlasting blessing for each "Edomite" who has "blessed" Israel, that is, has accepted the "salvation from the Jews" (John 4:22).

In his commentaries, the well-known church father Jerome mocked the Jewish expositors because they claimed that the Roman Empire would be destroyed, and that world dominion would then be given into the hands of the Jews.[19] This outcome was inconceivable to this supersessionist, who lived during the Christianization of the Roman Empire, in which Jesus Christ supposedly ruled the world through the Christian emperor. This was the fulfillment of the biblical prophecies! The Messianic kingdom had arrived! But Jerome was wrong. Daniel 7 teaches that the Roman Empire, (pseudo-)Christian or not, will cease to exist at the coming of the Son of Man, who will establish his own kingdom (vv. 13–14). And this kingdom will be a *Jewish* kingdom (v. 27 ESVUK): "And the kingdom and the dominion / and the greatness of the kingdoms under the whole heaven / shall be *given to the people of the saints of the Most High; / **their** kingdom shall be an everlasting kingdom, / and all dominions shall serve and obey **them**.*"

2.2.3 Jacob's Encounter with Esau

All of this had to receive a definitive shape in Jacob's encounter with Esau (Gen. 33). After the victory that Jacob had gained over Esau's guardian angel, Esau came with four hundred men to meet Jacob . Yet, he could do nothing else than reconcile himself with Jacob. For a moment, things still seemed about to go wrong when Esau refused the blessing that Jacob wished to grant him. This was risky, for it was vitally important that Esau accept this blessing. This was because apart from Jacob there could never be any blessing for him!

And then we hear those very significant words of Jacob. He did not say outright: "You *must* accept this, for I have prevailed over your *elohim*," but much more subtly (vv. 10–11): "No, please, if I have found favor [grace] in your sight, then accept my present from my hand. For I have seen your face, which is like seeing the face of *elohim*, and you have accepted me. Please accept my blessing [!] that is brought to you, because God has dealt graciously with me, and

---

19. Quoted by Kocken (1935, 7); see also Adamek (1938, 27–28).

because I have enough."

In two respects, this was the reverse of what we found in Genesis 32. First, earlier we found in Hosea 12 that it was the angel who begged for grace, but now, Jacob is the man who asks for Esau's grace. What humility on the part of Jacob, who had just prevailed over Esau's guardian angel!

Second, in Genesis 32 it was Jacob who begged to be blessed by the angel, but in Genesis 33 it was he who offered a blessing to Esau. Jacob said as it were: I have seen your *elohim*, I have wrestled with him, but then he did not say: I have prevailed over him, but: he has accepted me, that is, he was benevolent toward me, as was clear from the fact that he blessed me. Jacob was saying: Esau was now bound to that blessing. He—that is, his guardian angel—had blessed Jacob, and now Esau had to accept the blessing from Jacob: "I will bless those who bless you" (Gen. 12:3). At the present occasion, Esau was blessed by Jacob, that is, by the LORD, for the blessing that Jacob could grant him comes from the LORD himself, as Jacob explained. Just as Jacob had clung to the angel until the latter blessed *him*, so now he urged Esau fervently until Esau accepted the blessing from Jacob (v. 11b).

After this, the two men parted. Esau with his four hundred men and Jacob with his children and his flocks could not travel on together. They formed two totally different worlds. But they did not part forever. On the contrary, they only took different paths leading to the same goal. This is clear from Jacob's announcement that he, in his own time and in his own way, would come to Esau in Seir (the mountains of Edom) (v. 14). Some have viewed this as yet another subterfuge on Jacob's part; but why not accept that Jacob means this literally? The great Jewish expositor Rashi asked: "When will Jacob come in Seir?" He answered with a reference to Obadiah 21, "In the days of the Messiah, for it is said: 'And saviors shall go up to Mount Zion to rule Mount Esau.'" That is, in the Messianic kingdom the two will finally meet in peace.

What do all of these things teach us about the history of Western culture? The observation has already been registered that, in the rabbinic writings, the name Edom—the name for the people of Esau's descendants (Gen. 25:30; 36:1)—is a common designation for the Roman Empire, and after Rome's conversion, for Christianity.

This can be seen numerous times in the Targumim, the Midrashim, and the Talmud.[20] For the correctness of this identification, Jewish tradition finds important evidence in Numbers 24:17-19: one day, the star shall come out of Jacob, and a scepter shall rise out of Israel, which refers to the coming of the Messiah and to the arrival of God's kingdom:

> Edom shall be dispossessed;
>   Seir [the mountains of Edom] also, his [i.e., Israel's] enemies, shall be dispossessed.
> [But] Israel is doing valiantly.
> And one from Jacob [i.e., the Messiah] shall exercise dominion
>   and destroy the survivors of [the Edomite] cities!
> (Num. 24:18-19).

In the light of Daniel 2 and 7, we can understand how the dispersed Jews, when reading "Edom," thought of the fourth, Roman Empire, because this is the empire that, at the coming of the Messiah (the "one" of Num. 24:19), will be destroyed.[21] One could read Isaiah 34 and 63 as well, prophetic chapters about the defeat of "Edom," which seem to have a much wider scope than just that little neighbor of Israel.[22]

Viewed from a metahistorical standpoint, the history of Western culture exhibits as one of its chief traits the profound conflict between Jacob and Esau, that is, between, on the one hand, Israel and the God of Israel and, on the other hand, Satan, the "dragon," the angelic prince of Edom/Rome. The outcome of this conflict is a prophetic certainty: Western culture will be brought to an end by the coming of the Messiah of Israel and the establishment of the Messianic kingdom. However, before history will have advanced that far, this culture will repeatedly manifest the following main characteristics:

(a) Edom continually tries to shake off the yoke of Jacob. Western history is virtually one prolonged pogrom, with as its horrible nadir—so shortly before the end time—the Shoah (Holocaust). Es-

---

20. See Ouweneel (2003a, Excursus 7).
21. See extensively, ibid.
22. See Talmud: Makkoth 12a, where the "Edom" of Isa. 63 is identified as the Roman Empire.

au's guardian angel has struck Jacob's hip in a devastating manner: killed his children, tried to dash his hopes.

(b) Israel has never given up on Edom. It has never abandoned Western culture, on the contrary, Israel occupies crucial positions in that culture (see the second volume for many examples). "Jacob" clings to "Esau," and will not let him go until daybreak, no matter how badly he has been beaten by Esau. Israel clings to Edom, not to destroy it but in order that Edom will acknowledge Israel's birthright, and will convert to the God of Israel: "Salvation is from the Jews" (John 4:22).

(c) There is a discrepancy here, of course, because for Samael himself, the "dragon," the angelic prince of Rome, there is no hope, as the Bible makes clear: his end is in the lake of fire and sulfur (Rev. 20:10). For Western civilization as such there is no hope, either: the beast undergoes the same destiny as the dragon who seduced it. But the blessing that the angel gives to Jacob entails that, within Western culture, there will be the thousands who, in the last days, will acknowledge Israel as God's people, and will acknowledge God as the God of Israel. As Zechariah 8:23 says, "In those days ten men from the nations of every tongue shall take hold of the robe of a Jew, saying, 'Let us go with you, for we have heard that God is with you.'" There is a beautiful saying from Rabbi Resh Lakish suggesting that this will be 2,800 men per Jew, because all languages are represented—and Genesis 10 mentions seventy languages—and the robe of a Jew has four fringes[23]; so the formula is $10 \times 70 \times 4 = 2{,}800$.[24]

Let me conclude this discussion with the remarkable "oracle concerning Dumah" (i.e., Edom) in Isaiah 21:11–12:[25]

> One is calling to me from Seir,
> "Watchman, what time of the night [is it]?
> Watchman, what time of the night [is it]?"
> The watchman says:
> "Morning comes, and also the night.

---

23. This refers to the *tzitzit* or *tzitziyyot*, described in Num. 15:38–40; some presume that the sick woman of Matt. 9:20 touched these fringes on the garment of Jesus.
24. Talmud: Shabbath 32b.
25. Cf. Rashi and Talmud: Sanhedrin 94a.

> If you will inquire, inquire;
> come back again."

Many Christian expositors presumed that it was Edom asking the prophet how long its misery would last. But Rashi believed that it is *Israel* calling here from its exile in "Seir" (i.e., Edom, i.e., the Roman Empire): "Watchman [i.e., the prophet? perhaps God himself?], how long will Israel's exile in the Roman world last until the day of salvation finally arrives, that is, when the Messiah comes?" Rashi mentions several possible renderings of the divine answer (which is intentionally vague?) to this question:

(a) "Morning comes, but first the night will last a while longer," that is, it will last long before both the Babylonian and the "Edomite" exile will be over and the Messianic kingdom will arrive.

(b) "Morning [after the Babylonian exile] comes, but after this it will become night again" [viz., the second exile: the one in the "Edomite" world) (so Rabbi David Kimchi).

(c) "Morning comes for the righteous, but night for the wicked" (so Rashi and the Targum).

(d) Finally: "come back again" at a later time, *or*, "repent first" (so Rashi). There is no end to any exile without true repentance before God by the faithful remnant.

2.3 The Restoration of Israel

2.3.1 Twelve Components

The past and the future belong together; we can sufficiently understand the one only by comparing it with the other. So we cannot understand Israel's past correctly if we do not perceive in that past the continual anticipation of the Messianic kingdom in Jesus Christ; all Israel's history is to be understood from its Messianic future. Conversely, we cannot understand this future if we do not understand Israel in terms of its main characteristics as brought to us by Israel's past. There are twelve such characteristics.[26]

---

26. Cf. the eight "components" in Rom. 9:4–5, mentioned earlier (cf. the numbers inserted in the text): "They are Israelites, and to them belong the adoption [no. 3], the glory [no. 9], the covenants [implied in no. 2], the giving of the law [no. 4], the worship [nos. 8 and 10, and implied in nos. 6 and 7], and the

1. The *God* of Israel, the God who is the LORD of all the earth and of all people, but who delights to call himself the God of Israel (Exod. 5:1; 24:10; 32:27; 34:23).

2. The *patriarchs:* Abraham, Isaac, and Jacob, and the latter's twelve sons, the forefathers of the twelve tribes of Israel (Acts 7:8-9). In the Messianic kingdom, each of these twelve tribes will have its own territory (Ezek. 48).

3. The chosen *people*, who, since their stay at Mount Sinai, are God's covenant people; they are both "sons" of God (Deut. 14:1; Rom. 9:4) and "bride/wife" of God (Jer. 2:2; Ezek. 16:1-14; Hos. 2:14-23). During the Messianic kingdom, *this* elect nation will dwell in the Promised Land; nation and land belong together forever (see point [6] below).

4. Israel's *Torah*, the Sinaitic or Mosaic Law, is Israel's greatest treasure, and it will be thus also during the Messianic kingdom: "For out of Zion shall go forth the law [Heb. *torah*], and the word of the LORD from Jerusalem" (Isa. 2:3; Micah 4:2). It is said of the Messiah: ". . . the coastlands wait for his *Torah*" (Isa. 42:4), and the LORD promises: "Give attention to me, my people, and give ear to me, my nation; for *Torah* will go out from me, and I will set my justice for a light to the peoples" (Isa. 51:4). Notice especially this promise: "[T]his is the covenant that I will make with the house of Israel after those days, declares the LORD: I will put my *Torah* within them, and I will write it on their hearts. And I will be their God, and they shall be my people" (Jer. 31:32). Please note: just as Israel is the apple of God's eye (Deut. 32:10; Ps. 17:8; Zech. 2:8), the Torah is the apple of Israel's eye (Prov. 7:2, "[K]eep my commandments and live; keep my teaching [Heb. *torah*] as the apple of your eye"). God, Israel, and the Torah form a "threefold cord," which is "not quickly broken" (Eccl. 4:12).

5. Israel's chosen (Davidic) *king* will reign over them. David was the man after God's own heart (1 Sam. 13:14), and he is the one after whom even the Messiah will be named: "[M]y servant David shall be prince among them" (Ezek. 34:24). "My servant David shall be king over them, and they shall all have one shepherd. They shall walk in my rules and be careful to obey my statutes.

---

promises [implied in nos. 11 and 12]. To them belong the patriarchs [no. 2], and from their race, according to the flesh, is the Christ [no. 5]."

They shall dwell in the land that I gave to my servant Jacob, where your fathers lived. They and their children and their children's children shall dwell there forever, and David my servant shall be their prince forever" (Ezek. 37:24-25). "Afterward the children of Israel shall return and seek the LORD their God, and David their king, and they shall come in fear to the LORD and to his goodness in the latter days" (Hos. 3:5).

6. *Ha'Aretz*, Israel's "Holy Land," with its three names: Canaan, Israel, and Palestine; the "glorious [or, beautiful, pleasant] land," says Daniel 11:16, 41; "a pleasant land, a heritage most beautiful of all nations," says Jeremiah 3:19; "a land flowing with milk and honey, the most glorious of all lands," says Ezekiel 20:6, 15.

7. Israel's holy *city*, Jerusalem, "the city of the great King" (Ps. 48:1; Matt. 5:35); see the previous point. No believing Jew could ever be satisfied with any other city than this one, the only true city of God's promises. No "Jerusalem above" (cf. Gal. 4:26) has ever been promised to the Jew. For many centuries now, Israel has been en route, *not* first and foremost to the new heavens and the new earth that will arrive only *after* the present creation, *not* to the heavenly paradise (as the Jews say, *gan Eden*, the "garden of Eden"[27]) where the believing Jew supposedly goes when they die,[28] but to the city of which Israel speaks at least once a year, on Seder evening: *L'shana haba'a birushalayyim*, "Next year in Jerusalem." This is the Israelite's prayer:

> Send out your light and your truth;
>   let them lead me;
> let them bring me to *your holy hill* [i.e., Zion],
>   and to *your dwelling* [i.e., the temple on Zion]!
> Then I will go to the *altar of God*,
>   to God my exceeding joy,
> and I will praise you with the lyre,
>   O God, my God (Ps. 43:3-4).

8. Israel's holy *temple*: first the one built by Solomon, then the

---

27. See Ouweneel (2019b); this view of the "heavenly paradise" is *not* an originally Jewish idea; no doubt, Hellenism and Christian ideas about the hereafter have influenced this Jewish development.

28. This is a mistaken idea; see extensively, Ouweneel (2020).

one built by Zerubbabel—renewed and enlarged by Herod—and ultimately the temple built by the Messiah himself during his kingdom (Ezek. 40–44).

9. The *Shekhinah*, the glorious presence of God, which rested in and on the first temple (and departed from it just before its destruction; Ezek. 9–11)—it is not mentioned in connection with the second temple—and which will rest again in its visible form of appearance in and on the third temple: "As the glory of the Lord entered the temple by the gate facing east, the Spirit lifted me up and brought me into the inner court; and behold, the glory of the Lord filled the temple" (Ezek. 43:4–5).

10. Israel's *priesthood*: the priestly line runs from Levi through Aaron and his son Eleazar to the latter's descendant Zadok (2 Sam. 8:17), and from there to the distant descendants of Zadok in the Messianic kingdom: ". . . the priests . . . . These are the sons of Zadok, who alone among the sons of Levi may come near to the Lord to minister to him" (Ezek. 40:46; cf. 43:19; 44:15; 48:11).

11. Israel's *prophets* and the prophetic promises that they have proclaimed regarding Israel, and that, insofar as they are contained in the Tanakh, will *all* be fulfilled literally, and to the full, only in the Messianic kingdom.

12. Israel's Messianic *kingdom of peace and justice*, toward which its entire history is moving. It will be a spiritual-yet-earthly kingdom. Its peace will be spiritual peace ("Oh that you had paid attention to my commandments! Then your peace would have been like a river, and your righteousness like the waves of the sea," Isa. 48:18), but also peace between the nations ("[T]hey shall beat their swords into plowshares, and their spears into pruning hooks; nation shall not lift up sword against nation, neither shall they learn war anymore," Isa. 2:4).

Ultimately, these things involve not only Israel, but also God's plan and purpose for the entire world: the rule of the great King will be in the "city of the great King," but it will be over all the earth. "'As for me, I have set my King on Zion, my holy hill.' I will tell of the decree: The Lord said to me, 'You are my Son; today I have begotten you. Ask of me, and I will make the nations your heritage, and the ends of the earth your possession'" (Ps. 2:6–8). It will be "the time for restoring *all the things* about which God spoke by the mouth of his holy prophets long ago" (Acts 3:21). Only then will Jerusalem truly be the "City of Peace,"[29] when the "Prince of Peace" will be seated in its midst with justice and with righteousness (Isa. 9:6-7). But these blessings will involve the entire created world; the apostle Paul speaks of "the mystery of his will, according to his purpose, which he set forth in Christ as a plan for the fullness of time, to unite *all things* in him, *things in heaven and things on earth*" (Eph. 1:9-10). God's plan involves nothing less than this (cf. Isa. 2:1-4, which includes all the nations).

Biblical prophecy was never about Israel alone, but always about Israel in relation to the nations. Even the very first patriarchal promise referred to "all the families [or, nations] of the earth" (Gen. 12:3; 18:18; 22:18; 26:4). In a more negative sense, we see this at a moment in Israel's history when every hope for a better future for Israel seemed to be dashed. This was after the destruction of the city and the temple by King Nebuchadnezzar and the deportation of the people to Babylon. There were several metahistorical consequences:

1. The *Shekhinah*, the glorious presence of the LORD,[30] had left the temple shortly before its destruction (Ezek. 9-11). The glory of the LORD had withdrawn into heaven.

2. The designation "God of heaven" is connected—not exclusively but mainly—with this period (see especially in the books of Ezra, Nehemiah, and Daniel).

3. The spiritual world center has temporarily moved from Jerusalem to the world centers that are governed by the four successive world empires: the city of Babylon (in modern Iraq), "Susa the citadel" (in modern Iran), the various capitals of Alexander the Great (beginning with Macedonian Pella in modern Greece), and finally the city of Rome (in modern Italy).[31] Since then, other cities have claimed to be centers of world empires: Napoleonic Paris, Nazi Ber-

---

29. The name Jerusalem, Heb. *Yerushalayyim*, is related to Heb. *shalom*, "peace," and is usually explained as "City of Peace."

30. The Heb. Word *Shekhinah* is a rabbinic term that does not appear in the Bible, for which the latter uses the word *kabod*, "glory." *Shekhinah* comes from the root *sh-kh-n*, "to dwell"; cf. the related word *mishkan*, "dwelling," rendered in our translations as "tabernacle."

31. Two of the four cities are in Asia, two in Europe.

lin, Washington (the center of the greatest extant world power). But "the gifts and the calling of God are irrevocable" (Rom. 11:29). Ultimately, no city other than Jerusalem can be the center of the world.

Of course, the promises that God once made to the patriarchs cannot be severed from Israel's own responsibility (cf. §1.5.2). The promises are always *unconditional* in the sense that they depend on God's own sovereign counsel alone and will be fulfilled no matter the circumstances. However, these promises are also always *conditional*: they are fulfilled only for those who live righteous lives (the *tzaddiqim*). However, through repentance, conversion, and renewed devotion in the power of the Holy Spirit, *every* Israelite in principle can become a *tzaddiq*. We see this in the case of Abraham, the great example for every *tzaddiq*, despite his mistakes: "[W]alk before me, and be blameless" (Gen. 17:1). "I have chosen him, that he may command his children and his household after him to keep the way of the Lord by doing righteousness and justice, so that the Lord may bring to Abraham what he has promised him" (Gen. 18:19). "[I]n your offspring shall all the nations of the earth be blessed, *because you have obeyed my voice*" (Gen. 22:18). "Abraham obeyed my voice and kept my charge, my commandments, my statutes, and my laws" (Gen. 26:5).

Because of Israel's responsibility, part of Israel will ultimately fail to receive the promised blessings;[32] as the prophet declared: "In that day the *remnant* of Israel and the survivors of the house of Jacob will no more lean on him who struck them, but will lean on the Lord, the Holy One of Israel, in truth. A *remnant* will return, the remnant of Jacob, to the mighty God" (Isa. 10:20-21). "In the whole land, declares the Lord, two thirds shall be cut off and perish, and *one third* shall be left alive. And I will put this third into the fire, and refine them as one refines silver, and test them as gold is tested. They will call upon my name, and I will answer them. I will say, 'They are my people'; and they will say, 'The Lord is my God'" (Zech. 13:8-9). At the same time, however, God's promises are based upon his sovereign grace, *not* on pure human mer-

---

32. Regarding this complicated but very important relationship between God's sovereignty and human responsibility, see Ouweneel (2008b, especially chapter 10).

it.[33] And therefore, even in the greatest apostasy and the heaviest judgments, the unassailable promise of God remain, which are anchored in God himself (cf. Micah 7:18-20). In the end, the grace of God, centered in the Messiah, will turn everything for good in favor of the people of God (cf. Heb. 4:1, 9). Therefore, even in their predictions of judgment, the prophets always spoke of the ultimate blessing. This was true of Ezekiel and Jeremiah as well, who prophesied in the time of Jerusalem's destruction (586 BC).

In the darkest and saddest of all psalms, Psalm 88, there is no glimpse of hope, of a future restoration, of the ultimate Messianic blessing, nothing—*except* in the very first line: "O LORD, *God of my salvation* . . . ." This says it all. Whatever may follow—troubles, misery, death—the very first line points to the ultimate end of this all: "my salvation," declared Israel (with the words of the sons of Korah, who themselves had miraculously been saved; cf. Num. 16:32 and 26:11). In Hebrew this expression, "my salvation," is *y'shu'ati*, whose root reminds us immediately of the name *Yeshuah*, English "Jesus" (see §2.4.2).

2.3.2 Two Kinds of Redemptive Prophecies

Two kinds of prophecies that entail blessing must be distinguished, prophecies that were strongly connected in the words of the prophets under consideration. First, there was the promise of a restoration that would be fulfilled in the short term. Jeremiah mentioned the exact time; he received this message from the LORD:

> This whole land shall become a ruin and a waste, and these nations shall serve the king of Babylon *seventy years*. Then after *seventy years* are completed, I will punish the king of Babylon and that nation, the land of the Chaldeans, for their iniquity, declares the LORD, making the land an everlasting waste (Jer. 25:11-12).

"When seventy years are completed for Babylon, I will visit you, and I will fulfill to you my promise and *bring you back to this place*" (Jer. 29:10; cf. Dan. 9:2, where Daniel recalled this prophecy). For this return to Israel's own country, three motives were mentioned:

---

33. This notion of merit differs in degree but not in essence from the rabbinic notion of merit, and is similar to the New Testament's understanding of good works, which are the *fruit* of the circumcised human heart; cf. Talmud: Kiddushin 40a/b; Shabbath 127a/b.

1. After seventy years, the Holy Land would have received its "Sabbatical years": Nebuchadnezzar "took into exile in Babylon those who had escaped from the sword, and they became servants to him and to his sons until the establishment of the kingdom of Persia, to fulfill the word of the Lord by the mouth of Jeremiah, until the land had enjoyed its Sabbaths. All the days that it lay desolate it kept Sabbath, to fulfill seventy years" (2 Chron. 36:20-21). Every seventh year should have been a Sabbath, that is, a year of rest (Lev. 25:1-7). Because of Israel's unfaithfulness, the land was denied these years of rest. Therefore, it was entitled to 7 x 70 = 490 years, which was more or less from the beginning of the Davidic kingdom: the time from its beginning (ca. 1008 BC) until the consecration of the second temple (516 BC) was approximately 492 years. When we recall the beginning of the four hundred and ninety years (the conquest of Jebus by David, ca. 1000 BC; 2 Sam. 5:6-9), we will observe that the seed of Jerusalem's infidelity was sown at the very founding of the city.

2. After seventy years, the iniquity of the king of Babylon and his people would be complete, so to speak, and God would have to bring judgment upon them (Jer. 25:12).[34] Nebuchadnezzar was the Babylonian king to whom God had granted such a high position: "[B]ecause of the greatness that he [i.e., God] gave him, all peoples, nations, and languages trembled and feared before him. Whom he would, he killed, and whom he would, he kept alive; whom he would, he raised up, and whom he would, he humbled" (Dan. 5:19). To this king, God had granted the rule over all nations (the ones known in those days). Yet, he too had turned against the God of gods, and thus came under God's judgment. These people would be brought under servitude to the king of the Persians, who would become God's instrument for bringing the Jews back to their own land.[35] Babylon and the land of the Chaldees, however, would

---

34. The span of approximately seventy years can be seen to begin with the very first exiles being taken to Babylon (in 605 BC, when Nebuchadnezzar first besieged Jerusalem) and end with the beginning of the restoration of the temple (537 BC), which is sixty-eight years. Others have calculated this span to have extended from the destruction of the temple (586 BC) to the consecration of the new temple (516 BC), a period of seventy years.

35. 2 Chron. 36:22-23; Ezra 1:1-4; cf. Isa. 44:28; 45:1-8.

be devastated.[36]

3. However, the most important motive for the remnant of Israel to return to its own land was the unshakable faithfulness of God:

> I know the plans I have for you, declares the LORD, plans for welfare [or, peace] and not for evil, to give you a future and a hope. Then you will call upon me and come and pray to me, and I will hear you. You will seek me and find me, when you seek me with all your heart. I will be found by you, declares the LORD, and I will restore your fortunes and gather you from all the nations and all the places where I have driven you, declares the LORD, and I will *bring you back to the place from which I sent you into exile* (Jer. 29:11-14).

For these people, who had forfeited all their rights to blessing, God had "plans of peace." His grace effectuated their return. Please note: not a return to some kind of "spiritual country," but "to the place from which I sent you into exile." There can be no doubt as to what land was intended here.

This promise brings us to the second type of redemptive prophecies, namely, those prophecies that refer to events in a much more remote future; prophecies that have not yet been completely fulfilled today. To be sure, many of these prophecies have enjoyed a limited, partial fulfillment, but *no single* biblical prophecy viewed in its widest bearing and in its totality has been completely fulfilled. Such a complete fulfillment would be *impossible* because each prophetic book finds its complete fulfillment in the Messiah and in his Messianic kingdom. *No single* prophecy can be completely explained in isolation from that future; as the apostle Peter wrote: "[N]o prophecy of Scripture comes from someone's own interpretation" (2 Pet. 1:20). Each prophecy can be understood only if we see the Messiah as its center: "[A]ll the promises of God find their Yes in him. That is why it is through him that we utter our Amen to God for his glory" (2 Cor. 1:20). "[T]he testimony of Jesus is the spirit of prophecy" (Rev. 19:10), which either means the testimony *concerning* Jesus—he is the chief subject of prophecy—or the testimony that the Spirit of Christ himself gives through the prophets: concerning his sufferings as well as his glories (1 Pet. 1:11; cf. Luke

---

36. Cf. Isa. 13:17; 21:2; Jer. 25:14; 27:7; 51:11, 28; Dan. 5:30; 6:1; Zech. 6:8.

24:26).[37]

These two are key terms: suffering and glory.[38] They referred not only to Christ's first coming (including the sufferings that would befall the Messiah), but also to the subsequent glories; that is, the glory of his ascension (cf. Luke 24:26) and his enthronement in heaven as well as the glory of his return and his Messianic enthronement on earth, in Jerusalem. The prophets spoke of the "power and coming [read, the powerful coming] of our Lord Jesus Christ" (2 Pet. 1:16). Therefore, we can begin to understand the prophecies only when we continually view them against the background of God's great redemptive plan of uniting "all things in him [i.e., Christ], things in heaven and things on earth" (Eph. 1:10).

Thus, no single prophecy can be completely fulfilled today, as long as the Messiah has not yet been revealed in all his majesty, even though some prophecies in God's providential ways have already received a partial fulfillment. However, such an initial fulfillment, or preliminary fulfillment, occurs in God's providence, and such actions, which thus do not take place directly and visibly for all people, never form the actual subject of prophecy. In fact, prophecy is basically always about God's *direct* actions, whether in grace toward his people or in judgment upon the wicked (in Israel and elsewhere). If we keep such principles in clear view, then we will be holding an important hermeneutical key for understanding of the prophecies.

2.3.3 Messiah the Center of Prophecy

As we saw, during the time when Jerusalem was destroyed by the Babylonians redemptive prophecies were proclaimed that referred directly to the Messianic end times and the final Messianic blessings. We also saw that the Messiah occupies the central position in them. In the words of Jeremiah and Ezekiel, we often find him described in terms of a sharp contrast with the wicked Davidic kings, who were his ancestors, and who ruled over Judah in those days. In Jeremiah 23:5, he is the righteous and wise Branch of David, who protects and blesses the poor Jewish sheep who had been dispersed by their corrupt shepherds.

---

37. See Ouweneel (1990, ad loc.).
38. Rom. 8:17–18; Heb. 2:9–10; 1 Pet. 4:13; 5:1, 10.

In Ezekiel 17, we find an exceptionally beautiful prophecy about the Messiah. In this chapter, the royal house of David was being compared to a cedar, the uppermost of its young twigs (i.e., Jehoiachin) was carried by a great eagle (i.e., the king of Babylon) to a city of merchants (i.e., Babylon) (vv. 3-4). This eagle then took of the "seed" of the land (i.e., Zedekiah), who, through his care, grows to be a beautiful vine. By ingratitude and unfaithfulness, however, this vine twisted its roots toward another eagle (i.e., the Pharaoh of Egypt), and rebelled against Babylon, which had acted toward him in a benevolent way. Therefore, judgment comes upon it: the vine withers. But then God said,

> I myself will take a sprig from the lofty top of the cedar and will set it out. I will break off from the topmost of its young twigs a tender one, and I myself will plant it on a high and lofty mountain. On the mountain height of Israel will I plant it, that it may bear branches and produce fruit and become a noble cedar. And under it will dwell every kind of bird; in the shade of its branches birds of every sort will nest (Ezek. 17:22-23).

This was not Zerubbabel, who was indeed heir to the throne but never had any royal position in Judah. This "sprig" is none other than the Messiah, the last Branch from the house of David, and *he* will ultimately be the Davidic King as God always had him in mind, and about whom the prophets made their predictions.[39] Under the blessed rule of *this* King, there will be lasting peace and justice in the land of Israel. And please note: where will this King rule? From heaven? From the Christian Ecclesia? No, the text gives an unequivocal answer: *on the mountain height of Israel*.

In Ezekiel 21, too, we find an important reference to the Messiah, who formed a contrast to the last Davidic king of Judah: Zedekiah. This chapter describes God's judgment upon Jerusalem, and ends as follows:

> Because you have made your guilt to be remembered, in that your transgressions are uncovered, so that in all your deeds your sins appear—because you have come to remembrance, you shall be taken in hand. And you, O profane wicked one, prince of Israel [i.e., Zedeki-

---

39. Almost all Jewish and Christian expositors have understood the text in this way; so, e.g., the Targum and Rashi.

ah], whose day has come, the time of your final punishment, thus says the LORD God: "Remove the turban and take off the crown. Things shall not remain as they are. Exalt that which is low, and bring low that which is exalted. A ruin, ruin, ruin I will make it. This also shall not be, *until he comes, the one to whom judgment belongs* [or, *he whose right it is*], and I will give it to him" (Ezek. 21:24–27).

That is, Zedekiah is discarded, but after many vicissitudes, finally the Man will come to the throne "whose *right* it is" to sit on the throne of David on the basis, first, of his descent, secondly, of his redemptive work, and thirdly, of his personal qualities. The verse reminds us of Genesis 49:10, which we read along with the Septuagint, Syriac, and Targum as follows: "The scepter shall not depart from Judah, nor the ruler's staff from between his feet, *until he comes to whom it belongs*; and to him shall be the obedience of the peoples."

We will return to this point, but at this juncture we must beware of confusing the earthly throne of David with the celestial throne of God. To be sure, the throne of David was sometimes called the "throne of the LORD" (1 Chron. 29:23; cf. Jer. 3:17), but this was evidently an *earthly* throne because the Davidic kings were sitting upon it. Supersessionism is mistaken to think that this throne relocated to heaven. The angel Gabriel told Mary about her Son who was to be born: "He will be great and will be called the Son of the Most High. And the LORD God will give to him the throne of his father David, and he will reign over the house of Jacob forever, and of his kingdom there will be no end" (Luke 1:32–33). What evidence suggests that we must now view this throne as located in heaven? It was never there, and it never will be there. Jesus himself made this very clear in his letter to the church of Laodicea: "[a] The one who conquers, I will grant [future tense!] him to sit with me on *my throne* [i.e., the throne of David] [i.e., when I come again], [b] as I also conquered and sat down [past tense!] with my Father on *his throne* [i.e., since his ascension]" (Rev. 3:21).[40]

2.3.4 Connection Between the First and Second Exiles

So, then, in the midst of decline and judgment the LORD gives, these promises of ultimate blessing that still await their fulfillment. The

---

40. Heb. 8:1; 12:2; cf. Matt. 26:64; Eph. 1:20; Col. 3:1.

point deserving our careful attention is that these promises are often given in the context of promising Israel's return from Babylon, after the seventy years of the first exile, and this may be confusing to the reader. That is to say, when the text speaks of this return, it often mentions blessings that were not granted at all to Israel in those days, but that will be fulfilled in the future. *In concreto*, Israel will enjoy these blessings during the Messianic kingdom, such as:

(a) A King from the house of David, sitting again on the throne of David (e.g., Ps. 132:11);

(b) the reunion of Judah (the two tribes) and Israel (the ten tribes) (e.g., Ezek. 37:15–28);

(c) the utter and definitive fall of all Israel's enemies (e.g., Joel 3);

(d) the central position that Israel will occupy on earth, in the midst of all the nations worldwide (e.g., Isa. 61:9); and

(e) the peace, justice, and prosperity that will reign during the Messianic kingdom (e.g., Isa. 9:6–7).

From this, we see that in the prophecies the first return was very often identified with—or smoothly passes into—the end time return of Israel. One consequence of this is that the first exile of seventy years in Babylon is linked with the second exile, which began with the second destruction of Jerusalem in AD 70, and in a sense is still continuing, as long as foreign powers still occupy Jerusalem (think of the apostate Dome of the Rock and the Al-Aqsa Mosque on the sacred Temple Square). Jesus said, "Jerusalem will be trampled underfoot by the Gentiles, until the times of the Gentiles are fulfilled" (Luke 21:24). The "times of the Gentiles" are the times (a) in which there is no temple at Jerusalem, and (b) in which the foreign powers are still in charge. From the time of Jesus until now, these are, on the one hand, the Western Roman Empire and its (Western) successors, and, on the other hand, the Eastern Roman Empire and its (Eastern) successors: the Muslim world.[41]

---

41. In 1453, Constantinople (modern Istanbul), capital of the Eastern Roman Empire, was captured by the Turks, and since then has been Islamic. But Eastern Christianity continued not only in Greek Orthodoxy, and especially in Russian Orthodoxy. Thus, I see these as the four principal entities of the end time world: (a) the successors of the Western Roman Empire (especially Europe and its emigrants in North and South America, Australia, and New-Zealand), (b) the successors of the Eastern Roman Empire, namely, Eastern Orthodoxy and

To a great extent, Israel has returned to its land. Yet, the "times of the Gentiles" will continue in Jerusalem as long as Israel is (a) not independent of the Western powers (it cannot actually exist without the support of Europeans and especially Americans), and (b) not independent of the (Islamic) Eastern powers, which continue to exercise tremendous influence in the Promised Land. This is the same as saying that, despite the establishment of the state of Israel, the "times of the Gentiles" will continue until the coming of the Messiah. And this is the same as saying that the second exile will continue largely until this coming.

We find this, for instance, in the passage in Jeremiah 30-31, quoted above, where the return from the Babylonian exile is connected with the future Messianic blessings. We find the same in Hosea 3, where the people go into exile, and where the exile does not end before the coming of the future King "David" (the Messiah). In Deuteronomy 28, 30, and 32, the great prophetic chapters of Moses, we find the same principle: because of its infidelity and apostasy, Israel will fall. In Jeremiah's terms: "[M]any nations will pass by this city [i.e., Jerusalem], and every man will say to his neighbor, 'Why has the LORD dealt thus with this great city?'" (Jer. 22:8). This refers to both the first (586 BC) and the second sieges of Jerusalem (AD 70). After this, the various texts spoke of the first as well as of the second exiles, united into one, and the return to the land with the ultimate blessing and restoration. In Zechariah 2:7-8, for instance, we see how after the Babylonian captivity, God had mercy on the people of Israel again, and had them return to Zion from Babylon and all the nations. However, here too, the mentioned blessings will become a reality only in the future: "Sing and rejoice, O daughter of Zion, for behold, I come and I will dwell in your midst, declares the LORD. And many nations shall join themselves to the LORD in that day, and shall be my people. And I will dwell in your midst" (Zech. 2:10-11). This will become a reality only in the Messianic kingdom.

Please notice that here we find the key to understanding this connection between the first and the second exiles. It is this: during the period between the beginning of the first exile and the end of the second exile, *Israel is without the "glory"*; the *Shekhinah*, the glorious presence of the LORD, is not found in Israel. This is the case, first,

---

Islam, and (c) the great pagan powers in Asia (especially China and India).

because the *Shekhinah* never descended upon the temple of Zerubbabel—a point that has led to much debate among both Jewish and Christian expositors—and second, because for the greater part of this period (since AD 70) Israel had no temple at all.

The absence from Israel of the glory of God reminds us of what has been called the second of *all* five of Israel's exiles:

1. The first exile was the twenty years exile of Jacob—later called "Israel" (Gen. 35:10)—in Paddan-aram (see above), emblematic of all later Israelite exiles; the "vessel of God's promises" lived outside the Promised Land.

2. Next was the exile of Jacob's offspring in Egypt until the Exodus of the full-grown people of Israel (215 or 430 years, depending on the chosen reading of the text).

3. Then came the *Ichabod* period, when the ark of the covenant was in exile in the land of the Philistines. God's glory dwelt between the cherubim on the atonement lid on the ark, as we have seen. When the ark was captured by the Philistines—due to the folly of Israel's priests—the wife of the priest Phinehas gave birth to a boy whom she named *Ichabod* ("The glory is gone"), saying, "The glory has departed (or, gone into exile![42]) from Israel!" because the ark of God had been captured and because her father-in-law and her husband had died (1 Sam. 4:21–22). This was an ominous foreshadowing of the Babylonian exile and of the present exile (since AD 70), during which the *Shekhinah* again departed from Israel, until it returns to the land (Ezekiel 43).

4. The Babylonian exile, when not only the *Shekhinah* had left the temple, and thus the land, but Judah itself had been driven from the land.

5. The great exile from AD 70 until now: no *Shekhinah*, no temple, no city, no land; from this time, Israel has been wandering among the nations.

Formally, until the Messianic time Israel is still "Not-My-People" (Heb. *Lo-'Ammi*, Hos. 1:9). To a large extent, the people of Israel may be back in their own country today, but Hosea 3:4 is

---

42. Heb. *g-l-h*, cf. Isa. 5:13; Lam. 1:3; Ezek. 12:3–4; Amos 1:5; 5:5; 6:7; 7:11, 17; Micah 1:16; also cf. Hos. 10:5, ". . . the calf of Beth-aven [= Bethel]. / . . . [its glory] has departed [or, gone into exile] from them."

still true of them: "[T]he children of Israel shall dwell many days without king or prince, without sacrifice or pillar [memorial stone], without ephod or household gods [Heb. *teraphim*]." Today Israel has no king, but no foreign prince either. It has no sacrifices and priestly garments—for it has no temple—but it has no idolatry (sacred stones, household gods) either. In a certain sense, it exists in a spiritual no man's land, except for the vital things it has preserved throughout the centuries: the Sabbath, circumcision, *kashrut*, and *Mo'adim*, the *Torah* and its synagogues, and the *yeshivas*. And yet—Israel is profoundly incomplete without the temple and the restoration of the priestly sacrificial ministry. (As we will see, Jesus' own sacrifice did *not* abolish this sacrificial ministry at all; else why did the apostles participate in the temple sacrifices after Easter and Pentecost?)

All these designations coincide: *Lo-'Ammi*, the "times of the Gentiles," the absence of the *Shekhinah*, no matter the importance of the following matters: the state of Israel, and Israel's spiritual treasures: *Shabbat, B'rit milah, kashrut, Mo'adim, Torah*, not to mention the Talmud—Israel's cherished commentary on the Torah—and the prayers.

Neither the return of the remnant from Babylon, nor the return to *ha'Aretz* in the twentieth century, were a genuine restoration of the *nation*, because this restoration will include the restoration of the special connection between Israel and the God of Israel. Recall the small number of Judeans returning from Babylon; the great majority stayed behind in Babylon. Look at the numbers today: more than half of all the Jews worldwide (58%) live outside the Promised Land.[43] That is to say, there are more than twice as many Jews as there are Israelis. There are still more than twice as many Jews living in New York City (a recent estimate is 1,100,000) than there are Jews living in Jerusalem (546,100).[44] To be sure, the eschatological significance of the state of Israel is enormous. But its existence is still far from being the "restoration of Israel." The same was true regarding the return from Babylon. which involved the return of a relatively small group of Jews in order to establish a Jewish vassal

---

43. The percentage is even larger (64%) if we take into account "connected" Jewry, i.e., those who are partly Jewish.
44. See https://en.wikipedia.org/wiki/Jewish_population_by_country.

state, which after a relatively short period (about six centuries) was dissolved when the Jews went into exile again. *And during this entire period no Shekhinah descended to Israel.* This was a short period, for in biblical redemptive history we are told very little about this period,[45] while the four hundred years—the period between the Tanakh and the New Testament—remain entirely hidden in obscurity (except for some apocryphal books). One could put it this way: the "times of the Gentiles" are the times during which Israel had to live *without the Shekhinah*. This period is from 586 BC, or somewhat earlier (see Ezek. 9–11), until at least today, a period lasting nearly 2,800 years.[46]

What then was the purpose of the reestablishment of a Jewish society in *ha'Aretz* from 586 BC until AD 70, a society that after a relatively short period would again cease to exist? I can see only one main purpose, but this was a very important one. God brought a remnant back to the land in order to present to this relatively small company the Messiah—not in the royal dignity that he would possess in the future, but as the suffering Servant of the LORD (see especially Isa. 52–53; regarding this, see chapter 7 below). In rabbinic language: not yet as "Messiah son of David"—although Jesus *was* the Son of David (Matt. 1:1, 20)—but as "Messiah son of Joseph."[47] In the midst of this remnant of Israel, the Messiah was born in order to submit the people to the final and greatest test: their attitude toward the Anointed of the LORD. We know how the multitude of Jerusalem's inhabitants—except for a "remnant" within this "remnant"—rejected Jesus and became co-responsible for his execution.[48] After this, it took precisely one generation of forty years, from AD 30 to 70, before the people were driven out again, and Jerusalem with its beautiful—but empty—temple was destroyed again. All this occurred as the "times of the Gentiles," which had begun in 586

---

45. This is somewhat compensated for especially by the first book of the Maccabees.
46. An alternative view is given by the Talmud, Aboth III.2, which suggests that "[when] two sit together and there are words of Torah [spoken] between them, the *Shekhinah* abides among them," with reference to Mal. 3:16. Jesus may have been thinking of this when he spoke the words recorded in Matt. 18:20.
47. This, Jesus was too (Luke 3:24, 30; John 1:45; 6:42), although not in the traditional sense of referring to the *tribe* of Joseph.
48. See, e.g., John 19:12–16; Acts 2:23; 3:15; 5:30; 7:52.

BC, were continuing—Gentile times that are continuing still today, until the *Shekhinah* descends upon the new temple of the Messianic kingdom (Ezek. 43).

2.4 The "Times of the Gentiles"
2.4.1 The Wild Waters

Depending on whether we place the Exodus from Egypt in the thirteenth or the fifteenth century BC, the history of Israel as a nation encompasses between 3,250 and almost 3,500 years. During only three segments of this period was Israel as a nation both independent and united, having its own central government (omitting the period of the Judges).

1. The first period was the years of the kingship of David and Solomon, a period of exactly eighty years (1011–931 BC).[49] After this period, the nation divided into the northern kingdom (Israel) and the southern kingdom (Judah). It was no less than 821 years before another independent, unified Israel arose.

2. After the return from the Babylonian captivity, Judah developed a certain independence with the Hasmonean dynasty, descendants of the Maccabees, who had driven out the Syrians, and had purified the temple (164 BC; the feast of Chanukkah). This (more or less) independent "kingdom of Judea" lasted from about 110 to 63 BC, when the Romans conquered the land. This was a period of only 47 years, but if we begin to calculate from about 140 BC, when Judea became semi-autonomous, this is period of 77 years. If we reckon until the fall of the Hasmonean dynasty (37 BC)—to be replaced by the Herodian dynasty—this period expands to 103 years. The Hasmonean rulers were not Judeans, like David and Solomon, but Levites.

3. Only from 1948, no fewer than 2,010 years after the Roman conquest, we can speak again of a centrally ruled, relatively independent, unified Israel; in 2020, this state was seventy-two years old, which approaches the numbers mentioned under (1) and (2) above. In 1967 ancient Jerusalem was reconquered, and in 1980, Israel declared Jerusalem to be its (undivided) capital again. Thus, in 2020 a Jerusalem-centered Israel had existed for only fifty-three years. I trust that this state of Israel will be followed immediately

---

49. 2 Sam. 5:4; 1 Kings 2:11; 11:42; 1 Chron. 29:27; 2 Chron. 9:30.

by the Messianic kingdom, without a new (long) interval of time.

The "times of the Gentiles" began with the first fall of Jerusalem (586 BC), if we do not include the Hasmonean period. These were, and are, the times during which Israel was under the power of the heads of the four world empires—Babylonian to Roman—or during which Israel experienced the strong influence of the world powers. This is the case today. As we saw, these were, and are, also the times during which the *Shekhinah* did *not* dwell in a Jerusalem temple. The "times of the Gentiles" will continue in Israel as long as there are still pagan sanctuaries standing on the Temple Mount. These times will not end before the third temple is built, and the *Shekhinah* descends again (Ezek. 40-44). Prophecies about the return from the Babylonian exile smoothly transition into predictions about the return from the last great exile—an exile that has lasted so far no less than nineteen and a half centuries. Only then will Israel reach its destiny: the Messianic kingdom. The last Davidic king fell in 586 BC (2 Chron. 36:11-12); it will take more than 2,600 years before the new *and* last Davidic King will sit on the throne of David.

The Bible speaks optimistically about the "eternal people," in a land that was also created for "eternity," that is, as long as the present earth exists. People and land belong together; they were created for each other, and they are unbreakably linked together. Yet, the sad thing is that, for centuries the nation of Israel has rarely lived in its own land, having been submerged in the "sea" of the nations. As Isaiah says, "Ah, the thunder of many peoples; they thunder like the thundering of the sea! Ah, the roar of nations; they roar like the roaring of mighty waters" (Isa. 17:12). And the apostle John says, "The waters that you saw, . . . are peoples and multitudes and nations and languages" (Rev. 17:15). Israel went from the *land* into the *waters*. This future reminds us of the third day of creation: may *ha'Aretz* come into view again in the midst of the waters (cf. Gen. 1:9-10)!

On *Yom Kippur*, the Day of Atonement, the Jews still today read the history of Jonah, which is quite remarkable and fitting.[50] Jonah was a prophet (2 Kings 14:25), and his book is among the twelve Minor Prophets. One may wonder, though, what is so prophetic about this book. Jonah utters just one prophecy in this book, "Yet

---

50. See Ouweneel (2020, §5.4).

forty days, and Nineveh shall be overthrown!" (3:4) — and this one prophecy is not even fulfilled. Actually, there is a second prophecy in the book, and this one *was* fulfilled: "Pick me up and hurl me into the sea; then the sea will quiet down for you, for I know it is because of me that this great tempest has come upon you" (1:12). This prophecy did come true (v. 15), which is of great prophetic significance (as we shall see in the second volume). Thus, in my view the truly prophetic character of the book of Jonah can be grasped only if we see in it a type of both the Messiah and his people Israel, both in relation to the Gentile world.

Clearly, Jonah was a type of Christ, though a feeble one. Jesus himself draws the parallel between Jonah and his own person. In Matthew 12:40, he alluded to Jonah 2: "[J]ust as Jonah was three days and three nights in the belly of the great fish, so will the Son of Man be three days and three nights in the heart of the earth." Just as Jonah descended into the watery grave, Jesus sank into the depths of death. As he prophetically says in Psalm 69:1-2:[51] "Save me, O God! For the waters have come up to my neck. I sink in deep mire, where there is no foothold; I have come into deep waters, and the flood sweeps over me" (cf. Ps. 42:7). Here, Jonah is a type of Jesus in his sufferings and death. But in Luke 11:30, the comparison is more with Jonah 3: the preaching of the "resurrected" Jonah to Nineveh. Here we read: "[A]s Jonah became a sign to the people of Nineveh, so will the Son of Man be to this generation." Just as Jonah, so to speak, rose from death and addressed his preaching to the Ninevites, so too Jesus genuinely rose from death and, through his Holy Spirit, addressed his message of repentance to the Gentiles by means of the apostles. And just as the penitent Ninevites escaped God's judgment, the penitent Gentiles of our own day will be delivered from the "wrath to come" (1 Thess. 1:10).

2.4.2 Jonah As a Type of Israel

But there is more: Jonah was a type not only of Christ, but also of Israel.[52] For the first time in our discussion, we encounter an es-

---

51. Cf. Ps. 69:9 with John 2:17 and Rom. 15:3, and cf. v. 21 with Matt. 27:34, 48 in order to grasp the Messianic character of this Psalm.

52. From among Christian expositors, see the comments by Thomas K. Cheyne in the *Encyclopaedia Biblica*, edited by him and J. Sutherland Black (1903, 2:2565–66).

sential principle, which we will examine extensively: the Messiah is the true personification of Israel (see below). The Jews seem to be aware of this because, as we saw, they read this book annually in the synagogue on *Yom Kippur*. This practice highlights Jonah 2, where we read of Jonah's sojourn in the sea, which corresponds to Israel's history among the Gentiles. One hopes that they are also aware of the conclusion to be drawn from this correspondence: like Jonah, Israel too failed to be God's witness among the Gentiles. This had been Israel's calling: to be "a guide to the blind, a light to those who are in darkness, an instructor of the foolish, a teacher of children, having in the *Torah* the embodiment of knowledge and truth" (Rom. 2:19–20). Israel failed in this respect for the same reason Jonah did: their unwillingness to assume that God could possibly have any other plan with the Gentiles than to bring judgment upon them; they begrudged God's grace to the Gentiles (clear examples are Acts 13:45 and 17:5). This is why Israel was set aside for a time, swallowed up in the "sea" of the Gentiles. However, God preserved them there in a miraculous way until this very day, so that it did not lose its own identity, just as Jonah did not perish in the sea.

In the last days, the remnant of Israel—that is that portion that repents and confesses its sins—will be accepted again as God's people because of the atoning work of Christ. This is the very work to which *Yom Kippur* points in such a clear way: "[I]f the blood of goats and bulls, and the sprinkling of defiled persons with the ashes of a heifer, sanctify for the purification of the flesh, how much more will the blood of Christ, who through the eternal Spirit offered himself without blemish to God, purify our conscience from dead works to serve the living God" (Heb. 9:14). In the last days, Israel will be restored as God's witness to the world, just as Jonah received a new opportunity to fulfill his commission. The gospel of the coming Messianic kingdom will be preached especially by converted Jews, the "brothers" of the King (cf. Matt. 25:40 throughout the whole earth, so that a great multitude from the Gentiles will repent and believe, and will be saved from God's judgment.[53] Thus in the story of Jonah we receive a picture of the entire history

---

53. Regarding this, see Matt.10:16–23, especially v. 23; see also 24:14; 25:31–40; Rev. 7:9–19.

of Israel, including their restoration at the end. In accordance with God's commission, they will be a blessing for all the nations, just as Jonah, the restored preacher, was a blessing for the Ninevites.

To understand this better, let us pay special attention to Jonah's prayer, uttered when he had been swallowed by the sea and by the "great fish." It was, as it were, the prayer of the faithful of Israel throughout the centuries (2:2-9):

> I called out to the Lord, out of my distress,
>> and he answered me;
> out of the belly of *Sheol* [the grave, or the realm of death] I cried,
>> and you heard my voice.
> For you cast me into the deep,
>> into the heart of the seas,
>> and the flood surrounded me;
> all your waves and your billows
>> passed over me.
> Then I said, "I am driven away
>> from your sight;
> *yet I shall again look*
>> *upon your holy temple."* . . .
> I went down to the land
>> whose bars closed upon me forever;
> yet you brought up my life from the pit,
>> O Lord my God.
> When my life was fainting away,
>> I remembered the Lord,
> and my prayer came to you,
>> *into your holy temple.* . . .[54]
> But I *with the voice of thanksgiving*
>> *will sacrifice to you* [in your temple];
> what I have vowed I will pay.
>> Salvation belongs to the Lord!

---

54. Here the word "temple" seems to refer to the heavenly dwelling place of God (cf. 1 Kings 8:30–49), whereas the earlier mention of "temple" referred to the temple in Jerusalem.

This prayer is filled with quotations from the Psalms, psalms that are prophetically sung or prayed by the faithful remnant of Israel, the Israel of God. Jonah was employing the prophetic imperfect tense of Hebrew verbs; that is: in his mind he was viewing himself as already *beyond* his coming salvation. His deepest desire was not only to be set free from the water flood, but *to be allowed to minister to God again in the temple*, where he would offer with thankfulness his sacrifices of praise to God. This is all the more remarkable, if not all the more improbable, because Jonah prophesied among the ten tribes (2 Kings 14:25), who only with difficulty had access to the temple in Jerusalem (cf. 1 Kings 15:17). Jonah prayed, so to speak, an "impossible prayer" — like the "impossible prayer" that Israel has been praying for centuries: "Next year in Jerusalem," and as the Jews in Jerusalem have been praying: "Next year in the new temple."

How will Israel reach that goal? The answer is found in the last line of Jonah's prayer: "Salvation belongs to the LORD!" (Heb. *Y'shu'atah l'*YHWH). *In concreto*, salvation lies in him whose name is related to this word *y'shu'atah*: *Yeshuah*, in Greek *Iēsous*, in English "Jesus" (see §2.3.1 above). Jonah was quite aware of the powers that held him captive: the power of *Sheol* (v. 2), and the power of "the deep" (Heb. *t'hom*, v. 6; the deep water mass of Gen. 1:2; 7:11; Exod. 15:5). Jonah could make as many promises as he wanted, but these would not free him from these powers. He needed to realize that only the LORD could free him from these overwhelming forces of the deep and the dark. The moment Jonah no longer said "I will thus" and "I shall so," but "from *him* my salvation must come," the fish vomited him upon the dry land.[55] Once again, Israel finds "the land"! Via the route of humiliation, expecting everything from the LORD alone, Israel will reach its final destiny.

2.4.3 Israel in the Dragon

In Jeremiah 51 we find an important confirmation that we must view Jonah's history as a prophetic presentation of the history of Israel:[56]

> Nebuchadnezzar the king of Babylon has devoured me [i.e., Judah];

---

55. This is the same Heb. word *yabbashah* as in Gen. 1:9–10 (see previous section).
56. See more extensively, Ouweneel (2020, §3.3.3; 2003, 73n1).

he has crushed me; he has made me an empty vessel; he has swallowed me like a monster [Heb. *tannin*, dragon]; he has filled his stomach with my delicacies; he has rinsed me out. . . . I [i.e., the LORD] will punish Bel in Babylon, and take out of his mouth what he has swallowed. The nations shall no longer flow to him; the wall of Babylon has fallen (Jer. 51:34, 44).

Notice here the meaning of the term "dragon." Too easily we assume that Jonah 1–2 was telling us about an ordinary fish. But Jesus, too, spoke of a "sea monster" in connection with Jonah: "Jonah was three days and three nights in the belly of the sea monster" (Gk. *kētos*, Matt. 12:40 AMPC). Here we do not have the same Greek word *drakōn* ("dragon") that we find in Revelation 12:3–17 and elsewhere), but it is basically the same idea of a monster. Hebrew *tannin* and Greek *drakōn* are always references to Satan, or to one or some of his chief angelic companions: ". . . the great dragon, that ancient serpent, who is called the devil and Satan, the deceiver of the whole world" (Rev. 12:9; cf. 20:2).

Just as Jonah was travelling on the sea (a metaphor pointing to the wild masses of the nations) and ended up in the belly of the sea monster, so too Judah travelled the route of the Gentiles and ended up in the belly of the dragon, that is, Babylon. This referred either to the king of Babylon, Nebuchadnezzar, or the chief god of Babylon, Bel. Notice that in Jeremiah 51, the *king* swallowed Judah like a dragon, and the *god Bel* was forced to vomit Judah out again. Here, the king and his god were one, as is usually the case with the great powers. Just as God forced Babylon the dragon to spit out Judah, so too he forced the sea monster that had swallowed Jonah to spit him out. And just as Jonah was commanded to continue his commission, Judah was commanded to continue its calling to be a witness to the nations.[57] With respect to both Jonah and Judah, only the Messiah completely fulfilled this mission: "Christ became a servant to the circumcised [i.e., Israel] to show God's truthfulness, in order to confirm the promises given to the patriarchs, and in order that the Gentiles might glorify God for his mercy" (Rom. 15:8-9); "he came and preached peace to you who were far off [i.e., the Gentiles] and peace to those who were near [i.e., Israel]" (Eph. 2:17). However, in the last days, Israel will receive the opportunity

---

57. Cf. Jonah 3:1; Isa. 42:4–7; 49:3, 6; 52:10, 15; Rom. 2:19–20.

to walk in the footsteps of the Messiah.

In my view, it cannot be reasonably denied that Jonah was a type of the Messiah, nor can it be denied that he was a type of Israel. This points to a remarkable example of the profound inner connection between the Messiah and Israel, described as follows: the Messiah is the true personification of Israel. There are more examples of this, like this one in Psalm 80:

> You brought a vine out of Egypt;
> you drove out the nations and planted it. . . .
> Look down from heaven, and see;
> have regard for this vine,
> the stock that your right hand planted,
> and for the son whom you made strong for yourself.
> They have burned it with fire; they have cut it down;
> may they perish at the rebuke of your face!
> But let your hand be on the man of your right hand,
> the son of man whom you have made strong for yourself!
> (vv. 8, 14b–17).

These verses clearly refer to Israel, which God had brought out of Egypt and "planted" in the Promised Land. But the expressions in verse 17 are equally applicable to the Messiah: "the man of your right hand" (Heb. *ish y'minecha*, cf. Ps. 110:1) and "son of man" (Heb. *ben-adam*, Dan. 7:13; but also Ps. 8:4 in the light of Heb. 2:6). See also Hosea 11:1, "When Israel was a child, I loved him, and out of Egypt I called my son," which in Matthew 2:15 is applied to the child Jesus, called out of Egypt.

This profound connection between the Messiah and his people is crucial for penetrating more deeply into the prophecies in Isaiah 42–53 concerning the suffering servant of the LORD, and also into the book of Job.[58] The correct interpretation does not choose between the Messiah *or* Israel, but seeks the answer in the hidden connection between the two. This will culminate in the Messianic kingdom, where this connection will be made manifest.

Understanding the "dragon" as a reference to Satan himself or to his most powerful national angels is crucial for understanding Israel in relation to the "times of the Gentiles," i.e., the era of the four

---

58. Ouweneel (2000).

world empires (see the next section). In Isaiah 51:9, the national angel of Egypt was referred to as Rahab or the "sea monster" (Heb. *tannin*, "dragon"). In Jeremiah 51 we saw the "dragon" to be the angelic prince of the Babylonian empire, while in the book of Revelation the "dragon" is the angelic prince of the Roman Empire.[59] In connection with this dragon, we find two other figurative animals. One is the Lamb, the Messiah, who in Revelation is the great adversary of the dragon. The book of Revelation could be understood as describing the cosmic battle between the gigantic, all-powerful dragon and the tiny, humble Lamb, in which the Lamb emerges as the great Victor (Rev. 17:14). Another animal we encounter is the dove, which surprisingly was the meaning of Jonah's name. In Psalm 55, David expresses the feelings of the faithful remnant of Israel: "... Oh, that I had wings like a dove [Heb. *ka-jonah*]! / I would fly away and be at rest; / yes, I would wander far away; / I would lodge in the wilderness; / I would hurry to find a shelter / from the raging wind and tempest" (vv. 6–8). In Psalm 74, the situation is even more remarkable. First, Asaph says, "Yet God my King is from of old, / working salvation in the midst of the earth. / You divided the sea by your might; / you broke the heads of the sea monsters [Heb. *tanninim*, dragons] on the waters. / You crushed the heads of Leviathan; / you gave him as food for the creatures of the wilderness" (vv. 12–14). And then: "Remember this, O LORD, how the enemy scoffs, / and a foolish people reviles your name. / Do not deliver the soul of your turtledove [Heb. *tor*] to the wild beasts; / do not forget the life of your poor forever" (vv. 18–19).

In summary: the "times of the Gentiles" are

(a) the times of the *dragon*: Israel is swallowed by the wild "sea" of the Gentiles;

(b) the times of the *Lamb*: after AD 30 glorified at God's right hand, invisible to both Israel and the nations;

(c) the times of the *dove*, which must constantly try to escape from the clutches of the ferocious monsters; but at the same time, it is the name that the Bridegroom has for his beloved, to whom his heart goes out (Song 1:15; 2:14; 4:1; 5:2; 6:9).[60]

---

59. See much more extensively, Ouweneel (2003a).
60. See extensively, Ouweneel (1973).

2.5 The Four World Empires
2.5.1 Why Four?

The "times of the Gentiles," during which God has placed world dominion in the hands of the heads of the nations, will last from the destruction of Jerusalem by Nebuchadnezzar until the coming of the Son of Man on the clouds of heaven to establish the Messianic kingdom and to put an end to all world powers. These "times of the Gentiles" can be divided into four periods, according to the four world empires that arise successively during this period, namely, the Babylonian, the Medo-Persian, the Greco-Macedonian, and the Roman Empires (Dan. 2 and 7).[61] In the Bible, the number four is the number of the earth; think of the four winds (Zech. 6:5; Mark 13:27; Rev. 7:1) and the corresponding "ends of the earth." This number thus involves what in Greek is called the *oikoumenē*,[62] the inhabited world, which is fitting here when we consider that the world empires contained all nations lying within the prophetic field of vision. It was the world as far as the biblical prophets could see.

However, the number four points to another matter. It teaches us that world power has not remained in the hands of one nation, one dynasty; rather, in the course of the centuries it has passed from one nation or dynasty to another. The LORD placed world dominion in the hands of the head of the nation; as Daniel said to Nebuchadnezzar:

> You, O king, the king of kings, to whom the God of heaven has given the kingdom, the power, and the might, and the glory, and into whose hand he has given, wherever they dwell, the children of man, the beasts of the field, and the birds of the heavens, making you rule over them all—you are the head of gold (Dan. 2:37–38).

And to Belshazzar the prophet said,

> O king, the Most High God gave Nebuchadnezzar your father kingship and greatness and glory and majesty. And because of the greatness that he gave him, all peoples, nations, and languages trembled

---

61. The Assyrian empire is not part of this series, because it was terminated before the fall of Jerusalem.

62. This word sometimes designated the entire territory of the Roman Empire: Luke 2:1; 4:5 (here, the devil is the actual prince of this "inhabited world," as in Rev. 12:9 and 20:2 he is the dragon behind the [Roman] beast); Acts 17:6.

and feared before him. Whom he would, he killed, and whom he would, he kept alive; whom he would, he raised up, and whom he would, he humbled (Dan. 5:18–19).

However, three times world dominion was transferred to another nation. One after another of these mighty kings rendered himself unworthy of this power because they did not pay honor to him from whom they had received this power. As Daniel continued to Belshazzar:

> *But* when his heart was lifted up and his spirit was hardened so that he dealt proudly, he was brought down from his kingly throne, and his glory was taken from him. He was driven from among the children of mankind, and his mind was made like that of a beast, and his dwelling was with the wild donkeys. He was fed grass like an ox, and his body was wet with the dew of heaven, until he knew that the Most High God rules the kingdom of mankind and sets over it whom he will (Dan. 5:20–21).

The infidelity and disobedience that led to Israel's fall occurred also among the rulers of the empires, and their prospective judgment was just as certain as the final judgment upon the wicked in Israel. Therefore, in the closing scenes of the future, we see God's judgment executed upon both Israel and the last world empire, the Roman Empire with its historical successors. In the past, both Romans and Jews were guilty of the death of the Messiah. Only two options are available in the future. One is that the penitent among both the "Romans" (Western Christianity) and the Jews will find salvation in the same Messiah. The other option is that the wicked among both will follow their supreme head (see Rev. 13): the political "Anti-Messiah" (Antichrist) (the first beast) and the religious "Anti-Messiah" (the second beast, i.e., the false prophet).[63] Both will be destroyed together by Jesus Messiah at his coming:

> Then I saw heaven opened, and behold, a white horse! The one sitting on it is called Faithful and True, and in righteousness he judges and makes war. His eyes are like a flame of fire, and on his head are many diadems, and he has a name written that no one knows but himself. . . . From his mouth comes a sharp sword with which to strike down the nations, and he will rule them with a rod of iron [Ps. 2:9]. He

---

63. See extensively, Ouweneel (2012a, 233–35).

will tread the winepress of the fury of the wrath of God the Almighty. On his robe and on his thigh he has a name written, "King of kings and Lord of lords" . . . And I saw the beast and the kings of the earth with their armies gathered to make war against him who was sitting on the horse and against his army. And the beast was captured, and with it the false prophet who in its presence had done the signs by which he deceived those who had received the mark of the beast and those who worshiped its image. These two were thrown alive into the lake of fire that burns with sulfur (Rev. 19:11-12, 15-16, 19-20).

Thus, when the iniquity of both groups, the wicked of Israel and the wicked of the Western world empire, is complete, both will fall under the judgment of the Messiah. If, then, both Jews and Gentiles have failed in their commission, what will be God's response? He will choose a Man after his own heart (cf. 1 Sam. 13:14) and will bring forth from the house of David a Ruler, of whom it is said: "[T]he God of heaven will set up a kingdom that shall never be destroyed, nor shall the kingdom be left to another people. It shall break in pieces all these kingdoms and bring them to an end, and it shall stand forever" (Dan. 2:44). This Ruler "will be great and will be called the Son of the Most High. And the LORD God will give to him the throne of his father David, and he will reign over the house of Jacob forever, and of his kingdom there will be no end" (Luke 1:32). He will execute divine judgment upon the wicked in Israel and the wicked among the nations.

However, by the grace of God, a remnant" of Israel as well as a remnant from the nations will be brought to repentance and conversion by the Spirit of God:

> For thus says the One who is high and lifted up, who inhabits eternity, whose name is Holy: "I dwell in the high and holy place, and also with him who is of a contrite and lowly spirit, to revive the spirit of the lowly, and to revive the heart of the contrite. For I will not contend forever, nor will I always be angry" (Isa. 57:15-16).

They will embrace the Messiah as their Savior and King, and he will rule over them in the Messianic kingdom.

2.5.2 Zechariah, Daniel, and Revelation

The history of the world empires was foretold specifically by those prophets who started from the (temporary) setting aside of Israel,

The Destiny of Israel

and spoke of the intermediate times, the times when the nations have received the supreme power over the earth. These are the times of the four world empires, until the return of the Son of Man. These prophets are Daniel in the Tanakh and John in the book of Revelation, and partly also Zechariah (in the Tanakh). Thus, they must be sharply distinguished from those prophets who prophesied during the time when Israel was still more or less recognized by God, and his throne was still in Jerusalem (cf. 1 Chron. 29:23). At this time, the enemy of the people was especially Assyria, the rod of God's anger (Isa. 10:5), used by the LORD to punish the apostate nation — especially the ten tribes — for its idolatry. At the same time, however, judgment is pronounced upon Assyria itself, when it too rebels against the God of gods (see especially the prophecy of Nahum).

Daniel and John are in a very different position. They see the world dominion in the hands of the nations, namely, in the hands of the successive heads of the four world empires: Daniel during the first and second empire, John during the fourth empire. Of course, this creates a totally new relationship with Israel, which at this time is *Lo-'Ammi*, and stands under the dominion of the head of the nations. As a consequence, the prophecies of these two men are essentially different from those of the other writing prophets.[64]

In a brief but highly transparent way, we find the history of the four empires and of the subsequent kingdom of the Messiah explained in Zechariah 6:1-8, 13. They are presented here as four chariots.[65]

(a) The first chariot, with red horses, represented the Babylonian empire; red is suggestive of its violent shedding of blood.

(b) The second chariot, with black horses, represented the empire of the Medes and Persians; black suggests that it is an exceptionally dark period (think of Haman in the book of Esther). This chariot went to the north country, which means that the Medes and

---

64. Is this a reason why the rabbis never acknowledged the book of Daniel to be one of the prophetic books? Jesus, however, spoke explicitly of "Daniel the prophet" (Matt. 24:15).

65. So Rashi (cf. 1:18–21); see also Kelly (1970b, ad loc.); Gaebelein (2017, ad loc.); Denham Smith (n.d., ad loc.); in addition, very different explanations have been given of the four chariots and horses.

Persians conquered Chaldea and Babylonia under King Cyrus the Persian.

(c) The third chariot, with white horses, represented the Greco-Macedonian empire; it went after the previous chariot, which means that, under the guidance of Alexander the Great, it swallowed the entire Medo-Persian empire.

(d) The fourth chariot, with dappled horses—the Roman Empire—moved to the south country: Egypt. Indeed, the Romans went much further south than the other empires did. However, not only the South enticed them; no, they were the strong horses, with more power than any of the other empires had possessed (though these horses are less uniform: they are spotted; cf. Dan. 2:41). They "were impatient to go and patrol the earth," which they were allowed to do (v. 7).

This entire history is reviewed more extensively in the book of Daniel, viewed of course not merely from a historical point of view, but from the standpoint of God's thoughts concerning this world, and specifically concerning the role of Israel in the four empires. Thus, in Daniel 3 and 4, precisely the self-elevation and pride of the first and greatest imperial king were depicted quite extensively. He to whom God had given the greatest honor on earth (see above) used this honor to glorify himself. Fortunately, through God's judgment he came to his senses, and gave God the honor that belonged to him (4:34–37). However, the evil had crept in, and came to be manifested in his successors.

Apparently, his son (actually his grandson?) Belshazzar[66] totally despised the knowledge of the God of heaven, for he "praised the gods of gold and silver, bronze, iron, wood, and stone" (Dan. 5:4). Therefore, Daniel reminded him of the judgment that had come upon Nebuchadnezzar, and then told him:

> [Y]ou his son, Belshazzar, have not humbled your heart, though you knew all this, but you have lifted up yourself against the Lord of heaven. . . . And you have praised the gods of silver and gold, of bronze, iron, wood, and stone, which do not see or hear or know, but the God in whose hand is your breath, and whose are all your ways, you have

---

66. Secular history tells us that Belshazzar was a son of Nabonidus and possibly of a daughter of Nebuchadnezzar, but the latter point has been doubted.

not honored. . . . God has numbered the days of your kingdom and brought it to an end; . . . you have been weighed in the balances and found wanting; . . . your kingdom is divided and given to the Medes and Persians (Dan. 5:22–28).

That same night, King Belshazzar was killed because Babylon had been taken by surprise by the Persian King Cyrus (v. 30). This is what Zechariah 6:8 refers to, when the angel said, "Behold, those [i.e., the Medes and Persians] who go toward the north country [i.e., Babylonia] have set my Spirit at rest in the north country." They had executed God's wrath upon Babylon.

Thus, Cyrus was the rod God used to punish Belshazzar and to set God's Spirit at rest in Babylon. Cyrus (d. 530 BC) was the only Semite among the heads of the nations mentioned in the Bible. Therefore, humanly speaking it unsurprising that he was the very man who allowed the Jews to return to their own country and to rebuild the temple (2 Chron. 36:22–23; Ezra 1:1–4). The Bible speaks in a favorable way of this "shepherd" and "anointed" of the LORD, who in these qualities, and as head of the empire, can be viewed to some extent as a type of the Messiah (Isa. 44:28; 45:1; 46:10–11).

2.5.3 The Third and Fourth Empires

The conquest of the Medo-Persian empire by Alexander the Great (d. 323 BC) was described extensively by Daniel long before these events occurred.[67] In Daniel 8, we find the rise of the third empire in the visionary picture of the ram (the Persian empire) that is trampled down by the goat coming up from the West (Alexander the Great), while Daniel 11 told us more concretely about these matters:

> Behold, three more kings shall arise in Persia, and a fourth shall be far richer than all of them. And when he has become strong through his riches, he shall stir up all against the kingdom of Greece. Then a mighty king shall arise, who shall rule with great dominion and do as he wills. And as soon as he has arisen, his kingdom shall be broken and divided toward the four winds of heaven, . . . (Dan. 11:2–4).

This passage is self-explanatory and is completely confirmed by secular historiography. After Alexander's death, his empire was divided into four parts. The prophet then continued narrating the

---

67. This remark presupposes an early dating of the book of Daniel; cf. Ouweneel (2012c, §12.1.3 and references).

history of two of those parts the Syrian and the Egyptian parts. He did so because these countries were of special importance to Israel, which was situated exactly between the two. In verse 30, the fourth empire appeared for the first time: ". . . ships of Kittim [i.e., the Romans] shall come against him [i.e., the Syrian king]." Verse 35 brings us to the "time of the end," when the wicked ruler of Israel will meet his destiny.

A discussion of various details in this history would carry us too far afield.[68] For personal study, I recommend the general representations of the four empires together, namely, first the large image in Daniel 2, with its golden head (Babylonian), the silver arms and chest (Medo-Persian), the bronze middle and thighs (Greco-Macedonian), and the iron legs with the ten toes, partly of potter's clay, partly of iron (Roman). Further in Daniel 7, corresponding with the latter (but more in their true moral character, as God sees them), the four animals: the lion (cf. v. 4 with 2:37–38 and 4:16), the bear with its *two* sides (cf. v. 5 with 2:39: two arms, and 8:3–4, 20: two horns), the leopard with the *four* heads (cf. v. 6 with 2:39; 8:5, 21–22; 11:4: four horns), and finally the dreadful beast with the *ten* horns (cf. v. 7 with 2:40–41: ten toes). The latter empire is one of the great subjects of the book of Revelation, where we find in Revelation 13:1 ten horns and ten diadems, and in Revelation 17:3 and 10 ten horns, that is, ten kings or kingdoms.

In all these descriptions — and this is a very important hermeneutical principle — it is evident that the history of the four empires is not yet finished today. The reason is that *this history finishes only with the coming of the Messiah on the clouds of heaven,* when he will completely destroy this fourth empire (or its Western and Eastern successors) and will establish his Messianic kingdom. In Daniel 2:44 the God of heaven establishes this kingdom, in Daniel 7:13–14 the Son of Man does so (cf. Matt. 26:64), and in Zechariah 6:12–13 the Branch, the great Priest-King, does so.[69] In Revelation 17:14 he is the Lamb, and finally in Revelation 19:11–16 he is the One called "Faithful and True," "the Word of God," and the "King of kings

---

68. See much more extensively, Ouweneel (2012a, chapters 6–12).

69. I choose the reading of Zech. 6:13 indicated in the ESV footnote: "It is he [i.e., the Branch] who shall build the temple of the LORD and shall bear royal honor, and shall sit and rule on his throne. And he shall be a priest on his throne."

and Lord of lords."

2.6 Summary

These are the angelic princes at the head of Israel during the period when Israel is *Lo-'Ammi*:[70]

Exile	Angelic prince	Israel in/outside its land
First	*Egypt* ("Rahab"; cf. Isa. 30:7)	outside
Second	*Babylon* (Isa. 14:12-15; 51:9; cf. Jer. 51:34 and 44)	outside
	Persia (Dan. 10:13, 20)	outside > in
	Greece (Dan. 10:20)	in
Third	*Rome* (the "dragon" in Rev. 12-13; cf. 16:13; 20:2)	in > outside

Notes

1. Between the first and second exile, when Israel was *'Ammi* and dwelt in its own land, the LORD himself was its Prince (cf. Deut. 32:8-9).
2. During the second (and the third?) exile, Israel stands under the special protection of the archangel Michael (Dan. 10:21; 12:1; cf. Jude 9; Rev. 12:7).
3. Between the second and the third exiles, Israel, or a limited portion of it, is in *ha'Aretz*; yet, it is *Lo-'Ammi*, determined by the absence of the *Shekhinah*.
4. During the Messianic kingdom, when Israel will again be *'Ammi*, the LORD himself will be its Prince in the person of the Messiah (in addition to this, there will be a prince who apparently is the earthly representative of the Messiah: Ezek. 44:3; 45:7, 22; 46:16).
5. The periods in which Israel was *'Ammi* consistently coincide with the periods, from Exodus 40 to Ezekiel 9-11, that the *Shekhinah* was in its midst. (The only exception seems to be the time when the ark was captured by the Philistines [1 Sam. 4-6], and *Ichabod* ["gone is the glory," 4:21] had become true.)

---

70. Regarding these angelic princes, see much more extensively, Ouweneel (2003a).

A possible chronology

1. *First exile* (Israel in Egypt): somewhere between the nineteenth and the thirteenth centuries BC: a period of 215 or 430 years, depending on one's interpretation of Exod. 12:41 (Masoretic text or Septuagint) and Gal. 3:17 (following the Septuagint).
2. From the divine revelation at Mount Sinai to the first fall of Jerusalem: traditionally 1446 BC to 586 BC = 860 years (also based on the 480 years in 1 Kings 6:1, i.e., from 1446 to 966 BC).[71]
3. *Second exile* (Judah in Babylon): 586 to 516 BC = 70 years.[72]
4. From the restoration of the temple to the second fall of Jerusalem: 516 BC to AD 70 = 585 years.[73]
5. *Third exile* (Israel among the nations): 70 to 1948 (establishment of the state of Israel) or to 1967 (the reconquest of old Jerusalem) = 1878 or 1897 years (however, in fact the exile will continue until the arrival of the Messianic kingdom, as argued above).

---

71. See chapter 1 note 5.
72. Jer. 25:11–12; 29:10; Dan. 9:2; Zech. 1:12; 7:5.
73. Not 586 years, since there never was a year zero; from June in the year 1 BC to June in the year AD 1 is one year, not two years.

Chapter 3
A Collision of Paradigms

> "'I scattered you like the four winds of the sky . . .' [Zech. 2:6]. This is what [the Lord] meant: 'As the world cannot endure without winds, so too the world cannot exist without Israel.'"
>
> Talmud: Taanith 3b

3.1 Introduction
3.1.1 Spiritualism or Literalism

WORKS OF SYSTEMATIC THEOLOGY usually contain no separate *locus de Israel*,[1] a chapter on Israelology, unlike what one finds with a *locus de ecclesia* or an ecclesiology (chapter on the Ecclesia). So if we wish to deal with Israelology as an essential part of *Christian* theology, this *locus* must deal very concretely with Israel in relation to the totality of Christian theology. What was Israel's role in the Bible, not only in the Tanakh but also in the New Testament? What is the precise relationship between Israel as the people of God in the Tanakh, and the Ecclesia as the people of God in the New Testament? Are these two totally different "peoples of God," as classical dispensationalism[2] has always taught? Or are believers from the

---

1. The Latin Vulgate contains both the form *Israel* and the form *Israhel*.
2. The term "dispensation" is adopted from Eph. 1:10 (KJV), the "dispensation

Tanakh and those from the New Testament basically one people of God? Can the Ecclesia be identified as the true Israel, or the new Israel, or spiritual Israel? Or does (ethnic) Israel simply continue to be "Israel," until the end of history, remaining distinct from the Christian Ecclesia (even though the Ecclesia includes Jesus-believing Jews)? Is there still a special future for this ethnic Israel, or does its spiritual future coincide with that of the Christian Ecclesia?

Other related questions are these: What about the special promises that have been made to Israel, such as the return to the land where their fathers have lived, the appearance of the Messiah in the midst of Israel, and the establishment of the Messianic kingdom with the earthly Jerusalem as its center? Or is ethnic Israel, since its great majority has rejected its Messiah, no longer entitled to these promises? In other words, are these promises realized only for those from Israel who came and come to faith in Messiah Jesus, and have found their place within the body of Christ, the Ecclesia? Does this mean that these promises must be understood "spiritually": a spiritual people (the Ecclesia), a spiritual land (the "heavenly country"), a spiritual city (the New Jerusalem), and a spiritual temple (the Ecclesia)?

The opponents of the latter approach sometimes refer to this view as a form of spiritualism: it spiritualizes the prophecies in the Tanakh, or even spiritualizes them *away*.[3] Or must we understand these prophecies in a literal way, and thus as referring to the literal people of Israel, the literal land of Israel, the literal city of Jerusalem, and even a literal temple, which will be rebuilt during the Messianic kingdom? The opponents call *this* approach "literalism," which understands the prophecies in a way that, in their eyes, is highly exaggerated. Are these the only options: spiritualism or lit-

---

[Gk. *oikonomia*) of the fullness of times." Typical of classical dispensationalism is that the dispensation of the church is an intermezzo in God's dealings with Israel. This idea is just as unacceptable as saying that Israel is an intermezzo in God's dealings with the world; see Paas (2015, 28).

3. Miskotte (1964, 550–51): "The so-called spiritualizing of the Old Testament expectation of salvation has in every age been a great mistake of Christian apologetics, a mistake that has its roots in Hellenism, which has entirely unnecessarily increased the distance between synagogue and church, ..." In our day, De Jong (2011, 18) was among those who have defended this "spiritualizing" anew.

eralism? Or are other approaches possible?

Added to this is the problem of that section of systematic theology called *foederology*: the doctrine of the covenant (from Lat. *foedus*).[4] Who precisely is the partner in the covenant that God made with Abraham: only Israel (Abraham's physical offspring), or also the believing non-Jews (Abraham's spiritual offspring)? And if the latter, in what sense? Does the Sinaitic Covenant involve only Israel, or also believing non-Jews? Does the New Covenant, which is explicitly made with Israel and Judah (no Gentiles were mentioned), involve only the twelve tribes or also believing non-Jews? And if the latter, in what sense? What about the Law of Sinai, the Mosaic Torah, given to Israel? If it was not abolished by Jesus (Matt. 5:17), does it apply (a) only to ethnic Israel, or (b) also to Jesus-believing Jews, or (c) also to Jesus-believing non-Jews? What is the relationship between the Torah of Moses and the Torah of Christ (Gal. 6:2), what Jesus called his "commandments" (John 14:15, 21; 15:10), and what the apostle James called the "law of liberty" and the "royal law" (i.e., the law of the kingdom [of God]; 1:25; 2:8, 12)?

To this we may add the questions from the field of eschatology (the doctrine of the last things). Must we look forward to a Messianic kingdom on earth? (No, say the amillennialists, unless you simply mean the new heavens and the new earth.) And if so, will this kingdom arrive before (as post-millennialism affirms) or after the coming of the Messiah (as pre-millennialism affirms)?[5] These questions have everything to do with Israel: those who spiritualize the prophecies, and do not acknowledge a separate future for (a penitent) ethnic Israel in their own land, are committed particularly to amillennialism. And those who take the prophecies literally and acknowledge a separate future for ethnic Israel in their own land are committed particularly to pre-millennialism. Of course, this cannot be a coincidence. (Advocates of post-millennialism are divided over the matter, but they appear to constitute by far the smallest group.)

---

4. Such a combination of a Latin and a Greek word is infelicitous; though it is a neologism, the term "diathecology" would be better.

5. The terms "a-," "post-," and "pre-millennial" come from Lat. *mille*, "thousand" (see Rev. 20:1–6).

3.1.2 Replacement Theology

Christians who have reflected at all on these problems include many who are committed to amillennialism, and this usually also means that they are committed to *supersessionism* or *substitutionism*.[6] In English this is called "replacement theology," or "substitution theology": in the counsels and ways of God, the New Testament Ecclesia has replaced the ethnic Israel of the Tanakh. In the Anglo-Saxon world, especially O. Palmer Robertson and Stephen Sizer belong to this group.[7] In the German world, Joseph Ratzinger has defended his version of supersessionism.[8] In the Dutch world, some rather recent defenders of supersessionism have included J. Douma, H. de Jong, S. Paas, and A. Maljaars;[9] in addition to these we would mention B. Reitsma and H. Veldhuis.[10]

It is not difficult to understand why so many Christians remain committed to amillennialism: the official theology of the Roman Catholic Church and of the Eastern Orthodox churches is thoroughly supersessionist. The Reformers Martin Luther and John Calvin were as well, and in their wake followed the majority of traditional Protestants (with some interesting exceptions, as we will see). Anti-supersessionists are also found in the Reformed world,[11] but they

---

6. From Lat. *supersedere* and *substituere*, "to replace."
7. Robertson (2000); Sizer (2004, 2007).
8. Ratzinger (2018).
9. Douma (2008); De Jong (2011); Paas (2014; 2017); Maljaars (2015).
10. Reitsma (2006); Veldhuis (2012); a fascinating survey of the two positions was offered by Ten Berge (2011).
11. In addition to the Reformed W. ten Boom et al. (1933) and Johannes de Heer (1934, 1961, n.d.), we find sympathetic Reformed theologians like Berkhof (1973); Graafland (1978); Den Butter (1978); De Boer et al. (1983; 1987; 1988); Vreekamp (1988); Cohen Stuart (1989); Van der Spek-Begemann (1991); Paul et al. (1993); Glashouwer (1998, 2016); Janse (2000); Den Hertog (2003); Van der Graaf and Verboom (2004); Van Campen and Den Hertog (2005); Mulder and Noordegraaf (2007); Abma et al. (2011); articles in Plaisier and Spronk (2012); Hoek (2013); Paul (2013); Van der Kooi and Van den Brink (2017, 346–78); De Vries (2013); Westerman (2015). See also Drost (2007) on K. H. Miskotte, A. A. van Ruler, and H. Berkhof. Hyper-Calvinism has much affinity for the idea of a spiritual restoration of Israel in the end time, but little affinity for a literal land promise; cf. Boot (1995); Meeuwse et al. (2004); but see also Buijs (1974); Den Butter (1978); E. F. Vergunst in

inhabit mainly the Evangelical world.[12] Numerous theologians try carefully to navigate in between the two positions. One Reformed Old Testament scholar committed to supersessionism, T. C. Vriezen, wrote: "Over against Paul, there is no possibility to assert that the role of [ethnic] Israel as covenant people is over."[13] Pope John Paul II also argued that God has never renounced his covenant with Israel, emphatically meaning ethnic Israel. This thought also resounds in the newest Roman Catholic catechism, and in the apostolic exhortation *Evangelii Gaudium* by Pope Francis — which was later relativized by Benedict XVI, however: the Sinaitic covenant was replaced by the Christ covenant, the temple ministry by the Eucharist, the land promise by the "heavenly country"; the state of Israel has nothing to do with the biblical prophecies.[14]

Supersessionism asserts that in God's providential dealings with the earth, ethnic Israel as the people of God has been replaced by the New Testament Ecclesia; in other words, the Ecclesia is the "spiritual" (or "true") Israel. In this view, ethnic Israel as such no longer has a future; individual Israelites must come to faith in Jesus Christ and join the Christian Ecclesia, laying aside everything about them that is Jewish. In the Netherlands, this theology has been widely discredited in traditional Reformed circles, though many Reformed theologians still adhere to some milder form of

---

Boogaard et al. (1992, 60-66); R. Boogaard in Van Hell et al. (1992, chapter 4); Van Moolenbroek (2016).

12. In addition to my own work, see Bruijn (1960); Van der Meer (1974); Van Veelen (1983); Archbold (1993); Prince (1994); Pawson (1995); Te Dorsthorst (1996); Diprose (1997); Van Barneveld (1998; 2002; 2009; 2012; 2014); De Voogd van der Straaten (2007, chapter 19); Essid (2009); Van Dijk (2016); Michelson (n.d.). Messianic authors are on the same line as the Evangelicals, e.g., De Graaf-van Gelder (1969; n.d.); Christiaan Salomon Duijtsch (on him, see Haitsma [1991]); Lambert (1990); Juster (1995); Van der Rhee (1997); Stern (1997; 1999; 2009); Shulam (1998; 2010); Berkowitz (1999); various writers in Hoekendijk (2001); Heidler (2006).

13. Vriezen (1951, 246).

14. The Swiss Jesuit and Judaist Christian Rutishauser (https://www.nzz.ch/feuilleton/benedikt-xvi-ruft-den-juden-zu-an-christus-fuehrt-kein-weg-vorbei-ld.1401426) rightly asked: "Why does Benedict interpret the dispersion of the Jewish people theologically, but the Zionist return in terms of secular (profane) history?"

this theology.[15] Therefore, it is quite important to grasp the precise meaning of the term "replacement theology."

At the outset, some adherents of replacement theology will object to being identified by that phrase, and I understand why. They argue that, strictly speaking, the Ecclesia did not replace Israel, since the Israel of the Tanakh already was the Ecclesia, which in the New Testament is simply being expanded with millions of believing non-Jews. The (Gentile) Ecclesia and (the true) Israel constitute the one, true people of God, such that non-Jesus-believing Jews do not belong to this one people of God, and Jesus-believing non-Jews do. *Theologically* speaking, it is correct for those making this claim to reject the identifying phrase "replacement theology." But *phenomenologically* speaking, their rejection is mistaken. This is because in the supersessionist view, the (New Testament) Ecclesia, 99% of which are non-Jews, has *de facto* definitely replaced ethnic Israel, 98% of which are non-Jesus-believers. Thus, it is not mistaken to insist that on the basis of the supersessionist view, the predominantly non-Jewish Ecclesia has replaced ethnic Israel. This insistence is confirmed all the more strongly by the supersessionist conviction that God's promises have been transferred from ethnic Israel to the predominantly non-Jewish Ecclesia — the divine promises concerning the land, the earthly city of Jerusalem, the earthly temple, and the Davidic throne.

3.1.3 What Is In a Name?

The view that spiritualizes God's promises to Israel — especially the land promise — and transfers them from ethic Israel to the predominantly non-Jewish Ecclesia, is called *replacement theology* or *supersessionism*.[16] Some theologians reject this identification because they, like Augustine, believe in (the possibility of) a massive conversion to Jesus by many Jews in the end time. Consequently, they declare triumphantly: You see, we do *not* believe that ethnic Is-

---

15. See, e.g., the "Open Letter about Israel to Dutch Christians" (Dutch *Open brief over Israël aan Nederlandse christenen*), signed by seven theologians; see Paas (2014, 278–87); others holding this position include Matter (1953), Robertson (2000), Sizer (2004; 2007), Douma (2008), De Jong (2011), Maljaars (2015), Oostland and Siegers (2016). Still others wrestle with the subject, e.g., Van Bekkum and Mulder (2010).

16. *Contra* Douma (2008, 62–63).

rael has been set aside forever. However, this conviction about the conversion of many Jews has nothing to do with supersessionism. Even if *all* ethnic Jews were eventually to believe in Jesus (and thus join the Ecclesia), this conviction still rejects the literal land promise. Those who assert that the modern state of Israel has nothing to do with the biblical prophecies are supersessionists. The intense debates about Christianity between the orthodox and the liberal can be stopped quite simply by asking whether Jesus rose bodily from the dead. Similarly, the intense debates about supersessionism can be stopped quite simply by asking whether the literal land promise remains valid until the end time. Many Christians sincerely love Israel because of what it *was*; but ask them about the land promise, and they will show their true colors.

The claim that the (New Testament) Ecclesia is "(spiritual) Israel" is without foundation, as we will extensively show. This matter deserves heavy emphasis and scrutiny, because this (New Testament) Ecclesia scarcely resembles ancient Israel, which fits the paradigm of supersessionism exactly. This view has declared the Sinaitic Torah to have come to an end (despite Matt. 5:17, and with a mistaken appeal to Rom. 10:4); it continues to accept the Ten Commandments (though essentially changing the Fourth Commandment by moving the Sabbath to the Sunday), while insisting that the so-called "ceremonial" commandments must be spiritualized.[17] The Ecclesia seeks to be "Israel" but rejects everything that is thoroughly and basically Israelite: the Sabbath, circumcision, the *kashrut* (food laws), and the *Mo'adim* (festival times). It seeks to be Israel without resembling Israel. How can this be defended? If God has indeed abolished the ancient Sabbath, circumcision, the *kashrut* and the *Mo'adim*—which he has not—then why call this Ecclesia "Israel"? What is so "Israelite" about the Ecclesia, except that it serves the "God of Israel" and reads the "book of Israel"? This is like someone wanting to resemble David Ben Gurion, but who is totally bald, two foot taller, and has a narrow face.

Here we are facing vital questions, each of which requires dis-

---

17. The distinction between moral and ceremonial commandments is illogical and untenable; see Ouweneel (2020). For a discussion of the history and validity of this distinction in connection with the Belgic Confession, see Kloosterman (2011).

cussion. But at this juncture, the conclusion seems warranted that according to supersessionism, ethnic Israel, with its earthly king, earthly land, earthly temple, and earthly people—the people who are central in the Tanakh, as well as in the New Testament Gospels—has been replaced by the Ecclesia of the New Testament with its heavenly king, heavenly land, heavenly temple, and heavenly people, an Ecclesia that people nonetheless call "Israel." I too believe in this heavenly king, land, temple, and people—*but I also maintain the room that the Bible leaves for the earthly king, earthly land, earthly temple, and earthly people of future ethnic (converted) Israel.*

"Replacement theology," in the modern semi-technical sense of the term, involves not just the claim that the Ecclesia is Israel. It entails the theological view that the Ecclesia possesses the identity of Israel, such that this, according to God's will, excludes any other Israel-after-Israel, according to one author.[18] Consider this additional question: Does supersessionism realize how frustrating it must have been for the early Ecclesia, which had begun to believe that it was the true Israel, that the other Israel continued to exist, refusing to accept Jesus but maintaining that *they* were the true Israel? It was this frustration, and the accompanying desire to physically drive out ancient Israel, which forms the root of all (pseudo-)Christian anti-Semitism.

3.2 Survey

3.2.1 Five Replaced Components

These are the five replaced components in replacement theology:

1. The *circumcision* of Jewish boys mandated in the Tanakh has been replaced by *(infant) baptism.* Such a replacement is taught nowhere in the New Testament, not even in Colossians 2:11–12: "In him [i.e., Christ] also you were circumcised with a circumcision made without hands, by putting off the body of the flesh, by the circumcision of Christ, having been buried with him in baptism." This passage was not identifying any "replacement." On the contrary, this passage is not referring to physical circumcision, but rather to the spiritual circumcision of the heart[19]—viz., regeneration. This is

---

18. R. W. Jenson in Plaisier and Spronk (2012, 57).

19. Cf. Lev. 26:41; Deut. 10:12, 16; 30:6; Jer. 4:4; 9:26; Ezek. 44:7, 9; Acts 7:51; Rom. 2:29.

an inner purification, of which baptism is the external counterpart.

2. The Sabbath *Saturday* has been replaced by the *Sunday*; that is, the Sabbath is believed to have moved from the seventh to the first day of the week. This is not taught by the New Testament, either. On the one hand, the ordinary Sabbath was not abolished at all; the (Jewish) apostles simply continued observing the sacred days stipulated in the Tanakh, including the Sabbath.[20] On the other hand, the first day of the week was apparently viewed as a special day — it was the day of the resurrection of Jesus — but never as the new Sabbath. The Sunday is a festival day, but not an obligatory day of rest (despite what some Reformed and Presbyterian denominations teach). Applying the ancient Sabbath commandments to the Sunday belongs to supersessionism. We will return to this in volume 2.

3. The throne of *David* has been replaced by — or is identified with — the heavenly throne of God; that is, the throne of David has apparently been moved to heaven. Supersessionism understands that when Gabriel said that God would give Jesus the throne of his father David (Luke 1:32; cf. Isa. 9:7), he was referring to God's throne in heaven, where Christ is now seated at God's right hand. As we explained earlier, Jesus *now* sits in the throne of God the Father *in heaven,* as he will *soon* sit on the throne of his father David *on earth* (cf. Rev. 3:21; cf. §2.3.3 above).

4. The physical people of *Israel* has been replaced by the New Testament *Ecclesia*. Without any valid basis, the Ecclesia has annexed and spiritualized the promises that had been given exclusively to Israel, such as the land promise. It is very naïve to think that, when Hebrews 11 speaks of a "heavenly country," this is an encouragement to spiritualize Israel's land promise. Worse still, supersessionism has not only annexed (and spiritualized) Israel's promises, but it views the curses upon ethnic Israel as still valid. Throughout our study, we will learn that in the Tanakh Israel never was the Ecclesia (the church), and that in the New Testament the Ecclesia (the church) never was, and never will be, Israel in any sense of the term. Of all five replacements, this one is the most devastating and encompassing; when this one is shown to be erroneous, then the other four replacements are rendered dubious.

---

20. Acts 13:14, 27, 42, 44; 15:21; 16:13; 18:4; 20:16; 28:17; 1 Cor. 16:8.

5. The hope of the *earthly kingdom* — the Messianic kingdom after the second coming of the Son of Man — has been replaced by the hope of *heaven*: a "heavenly country," *not* in the sense of Hebrews 11 (which refers to the heavenly side of the Messianic kingdom), but in the sense of "going to heaven when you die." Perhaps this is one of the gravest errors of supersessionism.[21] Instead of looking forward to the Messianic kingdom, and eventually the new heaven and the new earth, for millions of Roman Catholics and traditional Protestants this has become their principal hope: when a believer dies, they go to "heaven," there to enjoy all their heart's desire. In fact, for most Jesus-believers, the return of Christ and the resurrection of the dead have become virtually superfluous, because already at death they supposedly receive heavenly bliss.[22] Scarcely any perspective remains that includes God's plans with this *earth*. It is forgotten that God is not concerned just with the salvation of individual souls but with his creation as a whole. The believer who passes away is "with Christ" (Phil. 1:23), but *at that point* they are waiting, along with Christ himself (Heb. 10:13), for the restoration of all things (Acts 3:21).

A striking instance of bundling together two supersessionist errors into one was this claim of about Jesus sitting on the throne of David (Luke 1:32): "That the Evangelist who recorded it held that it was fulfilled in the Kingdom of Heaven, the spiritual sovereignty of the Christ, is shown by the fact that he records it in the same Gospel as that which tells of the Crucifixion and Ascension."[23] This is a remarkable *non sequitur*. The two errors are these: first, the "kingdom of heaven" (which Luke actually does not mention at all — it is an expression found in Matthew alone) is taken to be the same as "heaven" instead of meaning a heavenly kingdom *on earth*.[24] Second, the "throne of David" is thought to be located in heaven instead of on earth.

---

21. See extensively, Ouweneel (2019b; 2020).

22. N. T. Wright, who himself is basically committed to supersessionism, has popped this balloon; see Wright (2008; 2016). Regarding this subject, see extensively, Ouweneel (2020).

23. https://www.biblehub.com/commentaries/luke/1-32.htm.

24. See again, Ouweneel (2020).

3.2.2 Three Considerations

Before we move on, consider the following matters.

(a) In the Tanakh, ethnic Israel was "the people of God," even though many Israelites never had any intimate faith-connection with the God of Israel. *Outwardly*, all Israelites belonged to "the people of God," but that included non-God-believing and Torah-unfaithful Israelites, on the one hand, and God-believing and Torah-faithful Israelites, on the other hand; in short, there were the *r'sha'im* (the "wicked") and the *tzaddiqim* (the "righteous"). The latter were not only ethnic, but also *spiritual* Israel, "the Israel of God" (Gal. 6:16).

(b) In the New Testament, the Ecclesia is "the people of God," even though many (not-really-Jesus-believing) "Christians" have no intimate faith-connection with Christ; *outwardly*, they are all "the people of God," but the Ecclesia includes non-Jesus-believing (non-Jesus-serving) as well as Jesus-believing (Jesus-serving) Christians (see the seven churches in Rev. 2–3).

(c) In addition to this, ever since Acts 2 ethnic Israel continues to exist — today with its own political nation state of Israel — and still claims to be "the people of God," whereas 98% of them reject Jesus as their Messiah. However, ethnic Israel today includes many sincerely Torah-faithful Israelites, who — as far as humans can assess — sometimes seem to be much closer to God than many (pseudo-)Christians.

All this does not make it easy to identify who are "the people of God" today: Jews and/or Christians. Consider this as one helpful descriptive definition: *The people of God today are all those who love the God of the Bible with all their heart and show this by walking in his commandments.*

- For the non-Jesus-believing Jews, the term "commandments" refers to the Mosaic Torah;
- For non-Jewish Christians, the term "commandments" refers to the Messianic Torah (the Torah of Christ, Gal. 6:2), which in its divine, eternal essence is identical with the Mosaic Torah;
- For "Messianic Jews,"[25] that is, the Jesus-believing Jews, the

---

25. Actually, this is a strange title, for *all* (orthodox) Jews confess the (coming)

term "commandments" refers to both the Mosaic Torah and the Messianic Torah.
- Notice that each of the first two groups still has their own blind spot:
- The blind spot of the great majority of the Jews pertains to Jesus; but when they turn to the LORD, the "veil" is taken away (2 Cor. 3:15–16).
- The blind spot of the great majority of Christians pertains to Israel; but one day, also the "veil" of the nations will be taken away (Isa. 25:7[26]).

3.2.3 A Third Way

At this juncture the reader may be prepared to learn about a third way between supersessionism, and (classical) dispensationalism. Here is the outline of that third way.

1. The Bible *never* identifies Israel in the Tanakh with the term *Ecclesia* in any sense that is comparable to the New Testament Ecclesia. Israel's "congregation [Gk. *ekklēsia*] in the wilderness" (Acts 7:38) was nothing but Israel's ordinary popular assembly (Heb. *'edah* or *qahal*), and has nothing to do with the New Testament bride or body of Christ or temple of the Holy Spirit. Why is supersessionism not consistent? If Acts 7:38 is cited to prove that Israel was the Old Testament ecclesia, why then are we not told that the assembly (the same Gk. word *ekklēsia*!) of Ephesus (Acts 19:32, 39–40) was its "church"? (It is remarkable that supersessionism often appeals to Acts 7:38, but never to 19:32, 39–40.)

2. The Bible nowhere states that the Ecclesia is the "spiritual Israel," or "the Israel of God" (certainly not in Gal. 6:16, which refers to the faithful within ethnic Israel), or is part of "Israel" in any sense, or has been "incorporated into Israel" (certainly not in Rom. 11:11–24, where the Israelites are not the "tree" but only the natural "branches"), or in any other way is allowed to bear the name "Israel."

3. Moreover, to "spiritualize" references in the prophecies of the Tanakh is a hermeneutical error of the first order. Contrary to what supersessionism often asserts, the writers of the New Testa-

---

Messiah, but not that *Jesus* is this Messiah.

26. The prophet does not specify, though, what exactly he means by this "veil."

ment *never* do this. The New Testament writers may make spiritual *applications* (e.g., the Ecclesia is a spiritual "city" or "temple"), but supersessionism constantly confuses this with the *exegesis* of the prophecies, as if, for instance, the coming of a "New Jerusalem" would automatically imply that there is no more place for *earthly* Jerusalem in the Messianic kingdom. It is just as illogical as asserting that, because some prophets saw the throne of God in *heaven*,[27] this implies that the throne of the Davidic king was no longer "throne of the LORD" (1 Chron. 29:23; cf. Jer. 3:17). Supersessionism argues that you cannot have both, i.e., a heavenly and an earthly throne, a heavenly and an earthly city, a heavenly and an earthly temple. My reply is: Of course you can—why not? Here is a clear example: the LORD is called the "LORD of hosts" (YHWH *Tz'baoth*), where "hosts" can mean (a) the people of Israel (Exod. 12:41), (b) the angels (1 Kings 22:19), and (c) the celestial bodies (Deut. 4:19).

4. In contrast to classical dispensationalists, however, who overemphasize the *differences* between the Israel of the Tanakh and the Ecclesia of the New Testament, I emphasize the deep *similarities* between the two, most especially with respect to the *tzaddiqim* in both groups) (see §10.1):

a. both groups are blessed "in" the patriarchs:
b. both groups live by God's Torah (either by the Mosaic Torah or by the Messianic Torah), yet completely by the grace of God and the power of his Spirit;
c. both groups are both sons of God and servants (slaves) of God;
d. both groups are a holy nation, a kingdom of priests, that is, a royal priesthood;
e. both groups were and are born of the same Holy Spirit;
f. both groups were (in anticipation) or are (in retrocipation) washed by the same blood of the Lamb;
g. both groups are justified by faith, but this must be a true faith, that is, a faith that results in acts pleasing to God.

---

27. Isa. 6:1; Ezek. 1:26; 10:1; Dan. 7:9; cf. Exod. 17:16.

3.3 Misunderstandings

3.3.1 Two Paths of Salvation?

Any fruitful debate about supersessionism must refuse to spread any misunderstandings about either position. People committed to supersessionism continue to spread misunderstandings about the literal land promise of those who defend the continuing special place and role of ethnic Israel. This involves no fewer than *twelve* such misunderstandings, each of which needs to be exposed and corrected.

First, supersessionism asserts that those who understand the prophecies about Israel's future literally — people whom Reformed theologian S. Paas calls "Israelists" — are defending two paths of salvation, as if one single Jew could ever be saved apart from Jesus Christ. They forget that these so-called "Israelists" also have John 14:6 and Acts 4:12 in their Bibles: "I [said Jesus] am the way, and the truth, and the life. No one comes to the Father except through me," and: "[T]here is salvation in no one else [other than Jesus], for there is no other name under heaven given among humans by which we must be saved." Therefore, the assertion of Reformed theologian J. Douma is totally unfounded, namely, that those who understand the prophecies about Israel's future literally believe "that there is both a Christian and a Jewish salvation."[28] No "Israelist" whom I know would ever claim such a thing.

The claim Douma has made results from logical fallacy: an argument draws conclusions from position A that are justified *only* on the basis of position B, not position A. Theologians and other scholars regularly commit this error because it requires hard work to "get into the skin" of one's opponent. One committed to position B views position A through B-lenses, and what they see resembles B more than A. And if one committed to position A is careless they will do the same: view B through A-lenses.

It is surprising that near the end of his book, Douma himself wrote about a "two-track policy with regard to the new Israel (the Ecclesia) and old Israel that is still hardened."[29] What is the basic difference between a two paths of salvation and a two-track policy?

---

28. Douma (2008, 88).
29. Ibid., 132.

A Collision of Paradigms

Classical dispensationalists see not two but seven different types of divine dealings in the seven dispensations that they distinguish (see the Scofield Reference Bible). But even the staunchest advocate of supersessionism must admit that God's dealings with Israel differ quite drastically from God's dealings with the New Testament Ecclesia. And yet, there is only *one path of salvation*: "The saying is trustworthy and deserving of full acceptance, that Christ Jesus came into the world to save sinners" (1 Tim. 1:15) — Jewish or Gentile.

> What then? Are we Jews any better off? No, not at all. For we have already charged that all, both Jews and Greeks [read, Gentiles], are under sin.... For there is no distinction: for all [Jews and Gentiles] have sinned and fall short of the glory of God, and are justified by his grace as a gift, through the redemption that is in Christ Jesus, whom God put forward as a propitiation by his blood, to be received by faith. This was to show God's righteousness, because in his divine forbearance he had passed over former sins. It was to show his righteousness at the present time, so that he might be just and the justifier of the one who has faith in Jesus (Rom. 3:9, 22–26).

During the time covered by the Tanakh, God "passed over" the sins of the penitent in anticipation of Christ's work of atonement; and in the "present time," he forgives the sins of the penitent by looking back at Christ's work of atonement.

An orthodox rabbi once asked me: "If I do not believe in Jesus, will I be lost forever?" My reply was: "The New Testament says that 'to those who by patience in well-doing seek for glory and honor and immortality, he [i.e., God] will give eternal life.... There will be ... glory and honor and peace for everyone who does good, the Jew first and also the Greek' [Rom. 2:7–10]. If you humbly and sincerely serve Adonai, these words will become true for you as well. But, as a Christian, I must add that, first, such salvation cannot be severed from Christ's atoning work — that is, you can be saved only through him — and second, that 'seeking for glory and honor' and 'doing good' is possible only through the power of the Holy Spirit."

We understood each other; and although this was our first encounter, at the end of our long conversation, we embraced each other.

3.3.2 "Not Christocentric"

Second, advocates of supersessionism suggest that *their* view of the prophecies about Israel's future is "Christocentric," while the views of others are not.[30] This accusation is both unwarranted and quite painful. One of these advocates asked, "Have the Scriptures been fulfilled in Christ *and* Israel, or have they been fulfilled in Christ *or* Israel? These two options exclude each other, therefore only one can be true."[31] This conclusion is not logical, since both options might be wrong—and in fact they are, because many prophecies have not been fulfilled yet. Worse still, the juxtaposition of the two options is simply absurd. Of course, the truth is that the Scripture have been, *and will be*, fulfilled "in Christ" (cf. 2 Cor. 1:20, all promises of God are yes and amen in Christ), namely, those concerning the Ecclesia, as well as those concerning Israel, as well as those concerning the world.

Interestingly, another advocate of supersessionism did *not* wish to assert "that every prophecy must be explained in a Christocentric way."[32] He did recognize that Jesus Christ is the key for understanding the entire Holy Scripture, but, according to him, this is true only "in the main things." But if this is the case, should not advocates of supersessionism figure out first whether they themselves are so "Christocentric" in their exposition of the Scriptures before accusing others of not being so?

Some critics have thought it is legitimate to ask whether dispensationalism reasons more from the viewpoint of the Abrahamic covenant than that of the cross. Is not its focus more upon the Jewish kingdom than upon the body of Christ? Does it not interpret the New Testament by means of Old Testament prophecies instead of interpreting these prophecies by means of the more complete revelation of the New Testament? And so on.[33]

This is one more series of entirely false contrasts. What Christian theologian can begin from the Abrahamic covenant and ne-

---

30. This is reflected in the titles of Paas's writings (2017; cf. 2014, 34), though he has rightly warned against making such a generalized accusation (2015, 29).
31. Paas (2017, 29).
32. Douma (2008, 96).
33. Bass (1960, 151); also see Sizer (2004, 257–61), who created similar false contrasts.

glect the cross of Christ? What believing theologian could deal with the Messianic kingdom without also pointing out the place that the body of Christ will have in this kingdom? And what theologian could interpret the prophecies of the Tanakh other than in the light of Israel's Messiah as he has been revealed in the New Testament? My own difficulty with classical dispensationalism is far more that it emphasizes the "heavenly" body of Christ to such an extent that it elevates it highly above the "earthly" people of God: Israel. This emphasis is—to quote two verses from the same chapter—more occupied with "every spiritual blessing in the heavenly places" (Eph. 1:3) than with the "fullness of time," in which "all things in heaven and on earth" will be united "in Christ" (v. 10), at which time both Israel and the Ecclesia will have their own places.

Third, one supersessionist has claimed that "the Old Testament prophecy at various points is obsolete. To be sure, much in the Old Testament is outdated. This is true not only for the law of Moses but also for the prophets."[34] Is this the general conviction within supersessionism that certain things in the Tanakh are "obsolete" and "outdated"? Nothing in the New Testament shows that *even a single "jot" or "tittle"* in the Mosaic Torah is obsolete (Matt. 5:18 [N] KJV). Acts 15 shows that this Torah is applicable only to Jews, not to Gentiles. But nothing in the Torah is "obsolete" or "outdated." One needs to read only Ezekiel 40–48 to see that it is basically the Mosaic Torah that will govern life in Israel during the Messianic kingdom. Recall as well what Isaiah said about the Messianic kingdom (Isa. 56:6–7).

Here we are touching on a principal difference between those whose who spiritualize the prophecies and those who understand them literally. The former—at least some of them—claim that certain things in the Tanakh are obsolete and outdated. In fact, classical dispensationalists implicitly claim the same, for in their view, certain things that were applicable in certain dispensations are not so in other dispensations. In contrast to these two views, I maintain that *basically* nothing in the Tanakh is obsolete or outdated. Of course, I do not mean this in any literalistic sense (we do not build arks, we do not have to leave our lands and families,), but certainly in the Christocentric sense, which includes the typological sense.

---

34. Douma (2008, 95).

(a) "Do not think that I have come to abolish the Law or the Prophets; I have not come to abolish them but to fulfill them" (Matt. 5:17). Has the basic difference between "abolishing" and "fulfilling" been truly honored by supersessionism?

(b) "[W]hatever was written in former days was written for our instruction, that through endurance and through the encouragement of the Scriptures we might have hope" (Rom. 15:3). In this instruction, nothing is obsolete or outdated.

(c) "[All] these things [that formerly happened to Israel] happened to them as an example, but they were written down for our instruction, on whom the end of the ages has come" (1 Cor. 10:11).

(d) "All Scripture is breathed out by God and profitable for teaching, for reproof, for correction, and for training in righteousness" (2 Tim. 3:16) — *all* Scriptures, without any exception.

3.3.3 More Misunderstandings by Paas

The fourth misunderstanding is somewhat less serious, but nevertheless disturbing. The Reformed Dutch theologian S. Paas has accused the "Israelists" (as he called them) of misunderstanding "the relationship between the Kingdom of God and Israel": "In principle, the Kingdom has already arrived, but at the same time it is not yet fully visible as it is ultimately intended. There is a tension between the *already* and the *not yet*."[35] I agree one hundred percent! Paas must deeply misunderstand his opponents if he thinks that they view the matter differently.[36] It seems that the opponents of supersessionism are seeing things more clearly than supersessionism does, because they distinguish clearly between the "present age"[37] and the "age to come," that is, the "age" of the Messianic kingdom[38] (see §3.4.3 on the difference between the "seventh" and the "eighth day").

Fifth, Paas's misunderstanding is related to that of B. Reitsma. In 2013, Reitsma gave a speech on the subject "Not Israel but God's kingdom is the climax."[39] If this title really covers the contents of

---

35. Paas (2014, 42).
36. See extensively, Ouweneel (2011a, chapters 9–14).
37. Mark 10:30; Gal. 1:4; 1 Tim. 6:17; Titus 2:12; Heb. 9:9.
38. Matt. 12:32; Luke 18:30; 20:35; Heb. 6:5.
39. Quoted in Paas (2014, 51n2).

that address, then we are being confronted with a false contrast! This is a striking example of comparing apples and oranges. Was this statement directed against those who understand the prophecies about future Israel literally? Of course, the climax (of redemptive history, I suppose) is the Messianic kingdom—and ultimately, the new heavens and the new earth—but the point is that Israel will play an essential role in this kingdom. These are simply false dilemmas: "It is not about the kingdom but about God," or "It is not about Israel but about Christ," or, "It is not about 'the land,' but about heaven." And so on.

Sixth, Paas suggested that what he calls "Israelism" implies a "turn back again to the weak and worthless elementary principles" mentioned in Galatians 4:9, and then went on to suggest "that this leads to a return to servitude, and in this way you become severed from Christ, and will fall away from grace."[40] This is quite a claim! If held consistently, one wonders whether "Israelists" can be saved. Indeed, at a conference, one well-known Reformed supersessionist in the Netherlands refused all cooperation, and even communication, with those who understand the prophecies about future Israel literally, and another one said in an e-mail to me that he doubted whether he could call me a brother. Apparently, only advocates of supersessionism can be saved!

The real issue is that Paas misunderstood not only so-called "Israelism," but also Galatians 4 and 5.[41] The Pauline letters teach an enormous difference between the *law* (the Mosaic Torah), from which Paul removes nothing at all,[42] and what we call *legalism*, the view that a person by their own strength, through works of the law, can obtain salvation. New Testament Greek had no word for "legalism," and therefore for both ideas Paul used the word *nomos*, which occasionally creates confusion and always requires careful exegesis.[43] Think of all the confusion surrounding Romans 10:4, "Christ is

---

40. Paas (2014, 48, 258; cf. 253: this is "a heterodox [euphemism for heretical] phenomenon."
41. See Ouweneel (1997).
42. See, e.g., Rom. 3:31; 8:4; 10:1–13; 13:8–10; Gal. 6:2; 1 Tim. 1:8–11; cf. Matt. 5:17.
43. Ouweneel (2020, 26–27, 88–89); this point has been stressed by Cranfield in his commentary on Romans (2004).

the end of the law for righteousness to everyone who believes"! According to Paul in the letter to the Galatians, Christians should not fall back into legalism—but this warning in no way diminishes the enduring role of the Torah, since the same Paul explains in chapter 6:2, "Bear one another's burdens, *and so fulfill the law of Christ.*"

Seventh, Paas asserted that "Israelists" would claim that the Reformers, who after all were supersessionists, would have excluded the Jews from conversion and salvation.[44] But who has ever claimed such a thing? I know no such "Israelists." Augustine left room for a massive conversion of Jews in the end time, and theologians of early Protestantism pointed to the possibility or probability of such a massive conversion. During the time of the Reformation, there were Jewish Christians in the Protestant churches. It is true, though, that we can blame the Reformers for uncritically following the Roman Catholic Church with respect to Israelology, leading them to leave no room for the literal land promise and the restoration of ethnic Israel in the Messianic kingdom. But this is quite a different matter.

3.4 Misconceptions by Robertson
3.4.1 "Inconceivable"?

Eighth, the Presbyterian American O. Palmer Robertson has argued that it is "inconceivable" that a possible temple, sacrifices, and priesthood during the Messianic kingdom could replace the high-priestly ministry of Jesus.[45] *Of course* this is inconceivable! How could Robertson believe or suggest that anyone who understands the prophecies about future Israel literally would hold such an "inconceivable" opinion? This is nothing but tilting at windmills.

Jesus is the Priest-King of the Messianic kingdom in the spirit and after the model of Melchizedek (Heb. 5-7). This must not be confused with the priesthood that will serve in the new temple, and that has an explicitly Levitical character (Ezek. 40-44). It is like the types: in addition to the *Judeans*, David, and Solomon—all of whom in a certain sense were also king-priests[46]—there were the *Levites*, Zadok and his sons, functioning as priests. Interestingly, a descendant of Zadok through his son Ahimaaz was Jehozadak,

---

44. Paas (2014, 96).

45. Robertson (2000, 81–83).

46. 2 Sam. 6:17; 24:25; 1 Kings 3:4; 8:63.

the last high priest before the Babylonian exile (1 Chron. 6:3–15), while his son Joshua, or Jeshua, was the first high priest after the exile (Zech. 3:1; Ezra 3:2, 8). This matter is important because, just as ultimately the great Son (distant Descendant) of David will be the Judean King, the "sons" (distant descendants) of Zadok will be priests during the Messianic kingdom.[47]

3.4.2 Type and Fulfillment

Ninth, O. Palmer Robertson committed another error that we encounter more often in supersessionism. This error can be described as the confusion between types and prophetic fulfillment.[48] Typology and prophecy are completely different. Colossians 2:16–17 must serve here as an argument: "Therefore let no one pass judgment on you in questions of food and drink, or with regard to a festival or a new moon or a Sabbath. These are a *shadow* of the things to come, but the substance belongs to Christ."

Notice what is said here: the "shadows" in the Tanakh give way to the New Testament reality in Christ; this is true of typology, but not of prophecy. The confusion consists of the assumption that when the shadow has been fulfilled, the reality that cast the shadow disappears and no longer plays a role. So if the Sabbath is fulfilled in Christ, then the Sabbath is no longer needed. Supersessionism seeks to be wiser than the apostles, who observed the Sabbath and the other holy days as they had done earlier, *despite their fulfillment in Christ*.[49]

The *types* vary from Moses to the bronze serpent, from Aaron to the ark of the covenant. All of them found their realization in Christ, the true Moses (e.g., Heb. 3:1–6), the true bronze serpent (John 3:14–15), the true Aaron (e.g., Heb. 5:1–10), the true ark, on which rested the glory of God (Heb. 9:1–5). However, it is illegitimate to conclude from this that *therefore* the Holy Land, or the city of Jerusalem, or the temple of Jerusalem, have been replaced by some new, spiritual reality. These *are* types or shadows: the Holy Land may be taken as a type of the "heavenly places" (Eph. 1:3),

---

47. See Ezek. 40:46; 43:19; 44:15; 48:11.
48. Robertson (2000, 5–7, 13–17); actually, his entire book is based on this mistake.
49. Acts 3:1; 13:14, 27, 42, 44; 15:21; 16:13; 17:2; 18:4; 20:16.

the city and the temple of Jerusalem may be viewed as types of the New Testament Ecclesia. But this does not mean that these types are identical with *prophecies*, which may now be viewed as fulfilled in Christ and his Ecclesia.

This matter is exceedingly important. The Holy Land may be a *type* of the "heavenly place," but this has nothing to do with the *prophecies* concerning the Holy Land in view of end times Israel. The city and the temple of Jerusalem may be viewed as *types* of the New Testament Ecclesia, but this has nothing to do with the *prophecies* concerning the city and the temple in view of end times Israel. This important point must be registered now, though later we will deal much more extensively with the New Testament significance of land, city, and temple, as well as with the prophetic significance of the literal land, city, and temple.

3.4.3 The New Creation

Tenth, maintaining the literal land promise does not mean that those who take the prophecies about future Israel literally fail to understand that, *ultimately*, God's plans involve the entire cosmos.[50] The Lamb of God takes away the sin of the *world* (John 1:29), God has loved the *world* (John 3:16), and "in Christ God was reconciling the *world* to himself" (2 Cor. 5:19), to mention just a few examples. And this is not just a New Testament insight. The prophecies in the Tanakh make abundantly clear that God's plans do not involve only Israel, but all the nations of the world. Immediately following the sacrifice of his son—a type of the sacrifice of God's Son (Heb. 11:17-19)—God announced to Abraham: "[I]n your offspring [i.e., the Messiah] shall all the nations of the earth be blessed" (Gen. 22:18). Through David he said to the Messiah: "Ask of me, and I will make the nations your heritage, and the ends of the earth your possession" (Ps. 2:8). And Isaiah told us many times about the blessings that will extend to all the nations during the Messianic kingdom (see, e.g., Isa. 60–66). Though Israel was the chosen people, *from the beginning* God had the entire cosmos in view.

One of the great problems in supersessionism is that it usually acknowledges the new heavens and the new earth, but not the future Messianic kingdom. We could also express it this way (follow-

---

50. Cf. Robertson (2000, 9–10).

ing an old interpretation of Genesis 1 by both some rabbis and some church fathers): supersessionism does not distinguish between the "seventh day" (the Messianic kingdom) and the "eighth day" of world history (the new heavens and the new earth). The "seventh day" is the last day of the "week," a Sabbath in which the entire week finds its consummation. Thus, Psalm 92, which is "A Song for the Sabbath," is a hymn about the Messianic kingdom (consider its place in the entire series of Psalms 90–100, which is filled with attention to the coming of the Lord and his reign over the world). But an "eighth day," which is the first day of a new week, is a new beginning.

During the "seventh day" of the Messianic kingdom, the literal Zion—often a poetic designation for the entire city of Jerusalem and the salvation linked with it—will be the center of the world; to that place the nations will flow (Isa. 2:1-4). But during the "eighth day," there will be no mention of Zion nor of distinct nations (Rev. 21:1-8). By not distinguishing these things, some interpreters mistakenly view the Jerusalem of the Messianic kingdom (including the temple of Ezekiel) as having been fulfilled in the New Jerusalem, which will not contain any temple at all, since God himself will be its temple (Rev. 21:22).[51] Using my terminology, this interpretation confuses the (literal) temple of the "seventh day" with the (figurative) temple of the "eighth day."

It might be theoretically possible to imagine forms of millennialism that are linked with supersessionism. Practically, however, supersessionism seems most easily defended when linked with a strict amillennialism. This makes any debate of supersessionism between amillennialists and pre-millennialists impossible, because the outcome is certain *a priori*. Amillennialists and pre-millennialists do not see the same thing because they are looking through different glasses. The same is true about debates regarding the "thousand years" of Revelation 20:1-6 between supersessionists and those who take the prophecies about future Israel literally. Again, this debate occurs between people wearing differing presuppositional glasses. Those who take the prophecies about future Israel literally identify the "thousand years" with the Messianic kingdom, whereas supersessionism argues away the "thousand years"

---

51. Ibid., 25n23; also cf. G. K. Beale in Paas (2017, chapter 3).

because *a priori* it has no room for a Messianic kingdom between Jesus' second coming and the arrival of the new heaven and earth. In other words, the conclusions of supersessionism are not based upon strict and accurate exegesis of the text itself, but upon eschatological models that *precede* exegesis.

A striking example of this was Abraham Kuyper's enormous eschatological work, "On the Consummation [of all things]" (Dutch *Van de voleinding*).[52] In contrast with other supersessionists and amillennialists, Kuyper honestly admitted that it is exegetically impossible to place the "thousand years" of Revelation 20 *before* the second coming of Christ, described in Revelation 19. What a wonderful insight! All supersessionists and amillennialists could learn from this. But . . . Kuyper himself was a supersessionist and amillennialist. So what does he do? He indeed places the "thousand years" *after* the second coming of Christ, and then . . . virtually reduces the thousand years to zero. This illustrates what happens when exegesis is governed by dogmatics: the prejudices of one's dogmatic system determine how a certain text must be read. The entire discussion about the "thousand years" is dominated by paradigms. This renders useless any quarrel about the exegesis of Revelation 20; far better—but also infinitely more complicated—to debate the underlying paradigm commitments.

Let me extend the typology of the days of creation a bit further. Robertson also confused—in my terminology—the "seventh day" with the "sixth day," that is, the present age (see above), the time between the Day of Pentecost (Acts 2) and the second coming of Christ.[53] In other words, the form of the kingdom of God in the present era differs considerably from its form during the "age to come," that is, the era of the Messianic kingdom. Here are several differences.

- The present age is characterized by a hidden Christ (Col. 3:3, "your life is hidden with Christ in God"), the "age to come" by a manifest Christ (Rev. 1:7, "he is coming with the clouds, and every eye will see him").
- In the present age, Israel is still formally *Lo-'Ammi*—although

---

52. Kuyper (1931).
53. Robertson (2000, chapter 5).

God is providentially working in and with Israel — but in the "age to come" Israel will be accepted and renewed as the manifest people of God (*'Ammi*).

- Today, the emphasis is on the work God is doing among the Gentiles, gathering the Ecclesia, which is the body of Christ. Soon, when the Ecclesia will be in a glorified state in heaven, the emphasis will again be on restored Israel and on the nations that will flow to Zion.
- Today is still the age of misery, conflict, and persecution; soon it will be the age of peace and justice.

3.5 Further Misconceptions

3.5.1 Final Misunderstandings

Eleventh, one author suggested that the literal-Israel view has gnostic traits.[54] This is an effective, though deceptive, technique: attribute one "-ism" to another "-ism" that your readers know is a villainous heresy, so you need not supply any further refutation of that one "-ism." This author's argumentation, however, failed to identify and explain the allegedly gnostic features of our view of Israel. The allegation was little more than a cheap insinuation. The same technique often happens when people label their opponent "Arminian." At that point, every Calvinist is supposed to sense intuitively that interacting any further with this opponent's views is pointless.

Twelfth, another mistake made by an advocate of supersessionism involves confusing *a literal view* with *literalism*.[55] According to him, a person who interprets Zechariah 14 literally — that is, believes that Jesus will return on the Mount of Olives, and that the prophecy involves a literal Jerusalem and Israel — is obliged to interpret every detail literally, to the point of the absurd. But *nobody* treats literary texts this way; nor would any supersessionist do this. Later, in chapter 9, I will mention a number of metaphors in prophecies, metaphors that I do not interpret literally. However, because an *exaggerated* literalistic exegesis is invalid does not require us to dismiss *all* literal exegesis.

---

54. R. Potgieter, in Paas (2017, chapter 9).
55. In Paas (2017, 295–96). Cf. Sizer (2004, 108): "ultra-literal"; Paas (2014, 24): "literality delusion."

A few examples will show the absurdity of this.⁵⁶ Do those who accept the historicity of Genesis 3 believe that the serpent, after having been cursed, henceforth eats literal dust (Gen. 3:14; cf. Isa. 65:25)? Or, when Genesis 3:21 says that God made garment of animals' skins and covered Adam and Eve with them, does this mean God is a tanner or a dressmaker?⁵⁷ Do those who interpret the plagues of Egypt literally really believe that the water in Egypt changed into literal blood: a biological liquid tissue full of red and white blood cells and platelets (Exod. 7:17–21)? Who believes that, during Jesus' sufferings on the cross, the sun "ceased shining" (which is the correct rendering of Luke 23:45, Gk. *tou hēliou eklipontes*)? Who believes that the land of Malta approached the ship of Paul (as we read literally in Acts 27:27!),⁵⁸ instead of the reverse? Nobody. But who would be so foolish as to use these examples to claim that Genesis 1–3, Exodus 7, Luke 23 or Acts 27 *therefore* cannot be true historical descriptions of concrete events?

3.5.2 Misunderstandings: Epilogue

Many more misunderstandings within supersessionism could be identified, errors that constantly trouble the discussion with those who take the Israel prophecies about future Israel literally. By way of supplying a kind of bonus, let me mention a thirteenth mistake: supersessionist critics claiming that a "pseudo-theology" places the Old Covenant above the New Covenant [?], thereby reducing the Ecclesia to the status of a concubine [?] in order to make Israel the Bride of Christ.⁵⁹ *Every* phrase in this claim is not only mistaken, but absurd. Who could be so foolish to place the Old Covenant above the New Covenant, when the New Covenant is the crown and fulfillment of the Old Covenant? Moreover, if one wishes to apply the bride metaphor consistently, the Ecclesia is the bride or wife of Jesus as the glorified Lord at God's right hand, whereas Israel is the bride and wife of Jesus as the Messiah of Israel. The church father Ambrose saw Jacob with his two wives, Leah and Rachel, as a type

---

56. Cf. Ouweneel (2012c, §11.1.1).
57. This example is from Calvin, *Comm. Genesis* ad loc.
58. The latter two examples make the point so clearly that no English translation seems prepared to render them literally, not even the KJV.
59. Bilezikian in Sizer (2007, first of the unnumbered pages).

of Christ with his two wives.⁶⁰ His mistake involved confusing the types: Ambrose thought that Leah represented Israel, who had to yield to Rachel, the Ecclesia. I am convinced that the reverse is true: Jacob served in order to obtain Rachel, but received Leah instead, though in the end he also received Rachel. Jesus served in order to obtain Israel, but received the Ecclesia instead, though in the end he will also receive Israel (see further in §6.7.3 below).⁶¹

Enough with misunderstandings! Let the explanations of twelve misunderstandings that we have supplied be sufficient to provide an impression of the thinking of some influential advocates of supersessionism.

Misconceptions like those I have described show that one has not thoroughly grasped or understood the opponent's view. Or one is simply looking through the lens of their own paradigm and ending up misrepresenting crucial points or accusing their opponent of something the opponent has never said, intended, believed, or taught. This resembles the regrettable way Roman Catholics and Protestants fought each other in the sixteenth century; consider, for example, the decrees of the Council of Trent, as well as Protestant distortions of Roman Catholic thinking. Careful scrutiny of this polemical history will help identify misunderstandings on both sides. But here is the issue: Did, and do, opponents really *listen* to each other? Or do they merely shoot at the other side from the safety of their own bulwarks, without ever hitting the other party? Are they merely trying to convince their own people, who in fact *are* already convinced?

It is hard to blame the opponents, really, since such tilting at windmills happens all the time, on both sides of the debate. But I fervently hope that similar things will not be said about my treatment of supersessionism. For one of the main objections in many debates is that the one party has inadequately grasped the views of the other party, and therefore renders those views incorrectly or one-sidedly. Usually this is not a matter of unwillingness or bad intentions; it is a matter of *intellectual incapacity* due to the tremendous force of one's own paradigm. It seems that this phenomenon is more psychological than theological, the more so when people's

---

60. Ambrose, *De Iacob et vita beata* 2.5.25, in Schenkle (1897).
61. See Jukes (1976) under "Jacob," including the reference to Ambrose.

denominational choices and academic positions are at stake. In this way, A reviews the work of B, and concludes by saying, "B has not convinced me." *Of course not*; when each party is imprisoned in its own paradigm, denomination, and academy, this is bound to be the outcome. The cost of changing one's mind can be far too high. It is as though A is locked (partly voluntarily) in their own prison, and says, "B has not shown me a way out." B's reply could be, "But do you really *want* to get out?"[62] And vice versa.

Another point to consider is that advocates of supersessionism might maintain that they are not convinced by my refutation of their alleged misunderstandings. They might claim that I am in fact defending a two-ways-of-salvation heresy, or that I am in fact denying Christ his central position in the way I interpret the prophecies. I do not agree with this, but of course, my opponents are allowed to believe these things. Conversely, advocates of supersessionism may continue to deny adamantly that they adhere to replacement theology, but nonetheless I maintain that they actually do. (By replacement theology I mean the view that the New Testament Ecclesia has replaced ethnic Israel as God's covenant people, so that ethnic Israel *as such* no longer has a redemptive-historical future in its own land.) Those who deny the literal land promise for Israel are supersessionists. From the fourth century, the roots of anti-Semitism have been embedded in this theology. As we continue to develop our Israelology in these volumes, we labor in the hope that progress in this discussion can and will be made, for the well-being of everyone involved.

3.5.3 Positive Israelology

These two volumes on Israelology are presented not as an *antithetical* work designed merely to oppose supersessionism. Its adherents are still many, and their influence is widespread; therefore, I cannot avoid referring to them often. But these two volumes are designed first and foremost as a *thetical* work, a positive exposition of a theology of Israel arising from my encounter with Scripture.

The debate is complicated by the perspectives of millennialists and amillennialists, covenant universalists and covenant particu-

---

62. Regarding these crucial issues, belonging to the philosophical questions fundamental to theology, see Ouweneel (2013).

larists (see §3.6.2), to mention just a few contrasts. However, the core question is actually quite simple: Must we interpret the biblical prophecies about future Israel, especially the land promise, literally—involving ethnic Israel in the Holy Land—or must we interpret them figuratively, spiritualizing them, applying them to the New Testament Ecclesia?[63] Of course, some advocates of supersessionism claim that they *do* interpret them literally, since today, "Israel" is the Ecclesia! For that reason, we must constantly explain what we mean by the word "literal": with the word "Israel," I am referring to the physical descendants of the sons of Jacob, called the twelve patriarchs, and I am referring to the land that today lies between Dan and Beersheba, between the Hermon and the Negev. I am referring to the Jerusalem that is today the capital of the state of Israel, and I am referring to the Mount of Olives and Mount Zion[64] in the immediate environs of this city.

Literal or spiritual? Millions of Christians reply, The prophecies must be interpreted literally: "the land" is Palestine. Millions of other Christians reply, The prophecies must be interpreted spiritually: "the land" is either the "heavenly places" of Ephesians, or "heaven" as the place where believers go when they die,[65] or the new heaven and earth. The former group believes that the present state of Israel has *everything* to do with the biblical prophecies; the latter group believes that the present state of Israel has *nothing* to do with the biblical prophecies.[66] An intermediate position is scarcely

---

63. E.g., Van de Beek (2002, 362): "Also for the land it is true that the wall between Israel and the nations has been broken down. This means that there can no longer be such thing as a specific land for Israel." (In his view, for Israel today "the land" is what it has always been for the priestly tribe of Levi: the LORD was their portion [heritage]; Num. 18:20–23.) But this claim is a *non sequitur*: Van de Beek alludes to Eph. 2:14–15, to which we shall return extensively.

64. Old Zion is *not* what is called "Zion" today, the mountain at the southwest corner of the old city (think of the "Zion Gate"), but the mountain on which was situated the "city of David" (east of the old city; 2 Sam. 5:7; 1 Kings 8:1), and the adjacent Temple Mount, God's dwelling place (Ps. 20:2; 74:2; 76:2). In the Psalms and the prophetic books, "Zion" is often simply a poetic name for Jerusalem, without referring to any single mountain. The meaning of the name "Zion" (Heb. *Tziyyon*) is very uncertain.

65. Regarding this mistaken idea, cf. the discussion in Ouweneel (2020).

66. As one member of the latter group put it: the founding of the state of Israel in 1948 has just as little to do with biblical prophecies as the founding of the

conceivable. Yet, a third group does exist, which includes millions of Christians. These Christians are simply uninterested in these matters since they do not affect their personal lives. They rarely meet Jews and are uninterested in a country thousands of miles away. They may be very much interested in preaching the gospel: "If you wish to be saved, you must believe in Jesus." But it appears to be irrelevant for themselves and for their gospel preaching that this Jesus was a Jew, and that he was and is the Messiah *of Israel*. These people will likely not read this book. But if some of them do, I hope that they will see that these matters are far more relevant to them than they might have thought. Perhaps this point will find shared agreement among both advocates of supersessionism and advocates of literal interpretations of prophecies about future Israel. Christianity involves infinitely more than individual salvation and personal happiness.

An additional point to keep in mind is that this debate does not involve only traditional Protestants (especially Reformed) and Evangelicals. The cleft between advocates of supersessionism and advocates of the literal interpretation of prophecies about future Israel exists in both groups. Reformed theologian Steven Paas mentioned many Reformed examples of both views. Rather soon after the Reformation, during the Dutch Second Reformation (seventeenth and eighteenth centuries), this cleft was manifested very deeply within the Reformed community, especially in the Netherlands (see the next chapter).[67] With regard to the Evangelicals, adherents of both views are found among them, both among the Evangelicals belonging to the traditional Protestant churches and among the free church Evangelicals.

Unfortunately, many Christians are simply uninterested in this discussion. They might enjoy visiting the land of Israel ("because Jesus walked there"), but they are not very interested in (1) the prophetic and historical backgrounds of modern Israel, (2) the state of Israel as such, (3) historic and modern Judaism, and (4) the future of Israel. This is like going to visit the United States of America only to learn about and enjoy the native Americans. To be sure, they are a vital part of the story,

United States in 1776.

67. See Van Campen (2007).

but the United States involves infinitely more than that.

3.6 Recapitulation

3.6.1 Philosophy of Science

It is important to realize that because supersessionism is an encompassing paradigm, it can be combated effectively only by attacking it on all fronts simultaneously. Confronting it only on this or that point will simply enable advocates of supersessionism to hide behind other components of the paradigm (the so-called waterbed effect). Perhaps such an advocate might even admit that the counter-arguments are rather strong and may have exposed a weakness in the paradigm. Despite this exposure, however, such an advocate is certain that their paradigm will survive unscathed.[68]

This phenomenon is familiar in the philosophy of science. An isolated hypothesis might perhaps be attacked effectively, but not a complete paradigm (framework of thought), which encompasses many different parts of a particular science, including a number of underlying hermeneutical principles. As I indicated in chapter 1, Israelology is closely related to the subjects of ecclesiology and eschatology, but also to Messianology, the doctrine of election, the doctrine of the covenant, and the doctrine of the kingdom, as well as the doctrine of the Torah (whether the Mosaic Torah or the Messianic Torah, the Torah of Christ). The goal of these two volumes is to gather together all of the Bible's teaching about Israel into a single coherent, consistent, and encompassing totality.

Consider this advice: "We must not let Paul say *what* we would wish to hear or how we should wish to hear it, we must not *enforce* an answer to our questions: and: the answer that we give must *materially* not contradict what Paul said if it must remain an answer by Paul."[69] This advice is fundamentally incorrect, because this advice assumes *a priori* that what Paul meant is objectively certain, and then exhorts us not to force Paul to say something else. However, in many cases, *it is not at all certain* a priori *what Paul meant*. What

---

68. By way of comparison, the same phenomenon occurs in the debate about evolution: biologists hide behind geologists, paleontologists, morphologists, embryologists, and so on, and these do the very same: hide behind the others; see Ouweneel (2018).

69. From W. G. Kümmel, cited in Maljaars (2015, 9).

Paul meant can be determined only by means of thorough exegesis; this is the result, not the precondition, of careful exegesis.[70] And those who, *on the basis of their paradigm*, believe that Paul meant "A," should not blame those who, *on the basis of another paradigm*, believe that Paul meats "B." The difference is not between what Paul ("objectively") did not or did not mean, but what people *think*, on the basis their paradigm, that Paul meant. One's chosen paradigm determines the route (and conclusions) of one's exegesis. This truth certainly pertains to advocates of supersessionism, but just as certainly also to me and to other theologians who interpret the biblical prophecies about future Israel literally.

3.6.2 Seven Pillars

Supersessionism is constructed on at least seven pillars. My thesis claims that each of these pillars is in the process of collapsing, but each weakened pillar is still being supported by the other six.

1. *Spiritualism* ("spiritualizing theology"): prophecies that require a literal interpretation according to respectable grammatical-historical exegesis are interpreted figuratively. These prophecies are no longer applied to ethnic Israel but to "spiritual Israel," the New Testament Ecclesia. These prophecies involve the biblical people, the land, the city, the temple, the altar, the throne of David, and so on.

My comment: Over against this view, I endorse what advocates of supersessionism erroneously call "literalism": the literal—but not literalistic!—interpretation of the biblical prophecies, taking into account common metaphors and other stylistic figures, according to ordinary principles of grammatical-historical exegesis. For instance, a promise like "I will bring you back to the land where your fathers lived" means "I will bring you (Israelites) back to the land (Israel) where your (Israelite) fathers lived."

2. The doctrine of the *kingdom of God*: this kingdom is viewed in an exclusively spiritual sense, with erroneous appeals to John 3:5 ("unless one is born of water and the Spirit, he cannot enter the kingdom of God") and John 18:36 ("My kingdom is not of this

---

70. A concomitant problem is that this exegesis contains its own biases. Many have pointed out that we are dealing here with a "hermeneutical circle," from which no investigator can escape; see Ouweneel (2013, §6.6.2).

world"), Romans 14:17 ("the kingdom of God is not a matter of eating and drinking but of righteousness and peace and joy in the Holy Spirit"), and similar passages. Especially the expression "kingdom of heaven" (which was Matthew's designation for what the other evangelists called the "kingdom of God") is entirely misunderstood by those who interpret it to refer to heaven as such.[71]

My comment: In "my" Israelology, I understand the kingdom of God to be primarily spiritual, too—but this by no means excludes the physical aspects of the kingdom: in the Messianic kingdom, *here on earth*, there will be literal, earthly nations and literal, earthly territories, as well as a literal temple and a literal throne. The spiritual and the physical are not mutually exclusive alternatives: every human being is both spiritual and physical. The "kingdom of heaven" is definitely a heavenly kingdom *on earth*, as a careful study of Matthew clearly shows (cf. Dan. 4:26, "Heaven rules"—in earthly kingdoms).

3. The typically Reformed covenant universalism, which comes to light in speaking of "the" covenant (of grace), as if, for instance, the covenant of Abraham and the New Covenant are more or less identical, or constitute forms of one and the same covenant of grace.[72] This is a theological construct, which does not function properly in practice.

My comment: Over against this, I endorse what I call a form of covenant particularism: there is not *only one* covenant (of grace), but there are *at least seven* covenants (of grace): (1) the Noahic Covenant (Gen. 8–9), (2) the Abrahamic Covenant (Gen. 15 and 17), (3) the Sinaitic Covenant (Exod. 19–24), (4) the Levitical Covenant (Mal. 2:4–5, 8), (5) the Deuteronomic Covenant (Deut. 29:1–14), (6) the Davidic Covenant (2 Sam. 23:5), and (7) the New Covenant.[73] Interestingly, all these covenants continue to have significance even,

---

71. Regarding this and similar errors, see extensively, Ouweneel (2020).
72. The extent to which covenant theology permeates the present discussions about Israel is seen, for instance, in Sizer (2004, 261–64), who places a "covenant alternative" over against what he calls "Christian Zionism."
73. Some investigators identify still more covenants: in addition to those mentioned, they identify a covenant with Adam (Hos. 6:7), one with the celestial bodies (Jer. 33:25), and one with Levi (Mal. 2:4–5, 8; cf. Num. 25:11–13); see Ouweneel (2011a, §1.3).

or especially, in the Messianic kingdom.[74]

4. Emphasis on the strong continuity between the Tanakh and the New Testament, which comes to expression in speaking of the one people of God, for which the terms "church" and "spiritual Israel" function as equivalent identifiers.

My comment: Of course, I accept this continuity to some extent (cf. chapters 5, 7, and 8), but I also emphasize the discontinuity, arising with the first coming of the Messiah as well as Israel's rejection of the Messiah (see chapter 8). Moreover, I claim that I have a more sharply defined view of the *continuity* of Tanakh and New Testament, because within my formulation of a biblical Israelology the term "Israel" possesses identical meanings in both the Tanakh and the New Testament.

5. In line with the preceding point, some believe that "the church" constitutes a community existing from Adam. The argument is simple: the church is the community of believers in the biblical sense, and there were such believers in the book of Genesis, beginning in chapter 3. All believers of every age belong to this one church.

My comment: Over against this, I strongly emphasize the differences between Israel and the Ecclesia (or "church"), that is to say, the New Testament Ecclesia — and I know of no other Ecclesia. It is the body of the glorified Man Jesus Christ, seated at the right hand of God (Eph. 1:22-23). The Ecclesia is "a holy congregation and gathering of true *Christian* believers" (cf. the Belgic Confession, Art. 27), not of pre-Christian believers, although these too have their important place in God's counsels and ways. This Ecclesia has existed since the Day of Pentecost (Acts 2, the outpouring of the Holy Spirit), not since the time of Adam, because this Ecclesia is called the temple of the Holy Spirit (1 Cor. 3:16; Eph. 2:20-22). However, over against classical dispensationalists, I also strongly emphasize the *similarities* between believers in the Tanakh and believers in the New Testament, because these similarities are equally undeniable (see §10.1 below).

6. In Christ, the Mosaic Torah has come to an end (Rom. 10:4). In him, it has not only been fulfilled but also abolished, for many,

---

74. This matter is not further elaborated in this volume; see Ouweneel (2011a, chapters 1–4).

with the exception of the Ten Commandments. Orthodox Jews as well as Messianic Jews are utterly mistaken in trying to observe commandments that God has declared to be no longer valid.

My comment: Over against this, I claim that the Mosaic Torah has not been abolished at all. It is explicitly and emphatically an "everlasting law," which for Israel, whether "Messianic" or not, is still fully in place, now and one day in the Messianic kingdom (see Ezek. 40-45). There is no intrinsic reason to formally or morally exempt the Ten Commandments from this.[75] The godly Israelite acknowledged the everlasting validity of the Torah, for the inspired Psalm 119 says, "I will keep your law continually, *forever and ever*" (v. 44). "I incline my heart to perform your statutes *forever, to the end*" (v. 112); "every one of your righteous rules *endures forever*" (v. 160). God's Torah is eternal, just as he who *is* in his person the "eternal Torah" is eternal.[76] After Easter and Pentecost, Jesus-believing Jews (think of Peter, John, and Paul) continued to participate in the sacrificial ministry in the temple.[77] To claim that this was a "weakness" is to beg the question (Lat. *petitio principii*); such an assertion is designed only to save one's theory. Instead, these sacrifices were a consequence of the apostolic conviction that the sacrificial ministry had not been abolished at all. Just as the sacrifices stipulated in the Tanakh looked *forward* to the sacrifice of Christ,[78] the sacrifices after Calvary look *back* to the sacrifice of Christ, whether or not those who offer them are aware of this.

7. The biblical notion of the Messianic kingdom is best represented by amillennialism, that is, by rejecting the notion of a future kingdom of peace lasting a thousand years, or possibly the

---

75. See extensively, Ouweneel (2020), where I explain that nine of the Ten Commandments (with the exception of the Sabbath commandment) are contained in a much richer form in the Torah of Christ, and as such are binding upon all Jesus-believers.

76. Cf. Jer. 31:33 and 2 Cor. 3:3, where "Torah" and "Christ" are comparable: Christ is written on "fleshly tablets" of the heart, just as the Mosaic Torah had been written on "tablets of stone."

77. See Acts 3:1 (the evening offering in the temple); 21:26 (Paul sacrificing in the temple); 24:17 (Paul explaining that he came to Jerusalem to bring sacrifices); and 28:17 (Paul explaining to Jewish leaders that he had never departed from the "customs of our fathers").

78. See Heb. 7:27; 8:3–4; 9:7–26; 10:1–14; cf. also 1 Cor. 5:7; 1 Pet. 1:19.

idea that, already today, we are living some form of such a thousand-years kingdom (in which the "thousand years" of Rev. 20:1-6 must be taken figuratively, of course).

My comment: Over against this, I believe that a biblical Israelology has the greatest affinity to pre-millennialism. This view respects the order presented in Revelation 19-21: first, the return of Christ (Rev. 19), then, his thousand-years reign (Rev. 20), and then, the new heavens and earth (Rev. 21).

3.6.3 Paradigm Shifts

Every theologian with some self-awareness knows how difficult it is to alter one's paradigm, or to undergo what is termed a "paradigm shift."[79] The stages of this challenge can be explained this way.

(a) Opponents misunderstand each other because they do not take into account the other's *entire* paradigm (although having an overview of an entire paradigm is almost superhuman).

(b) Counter-arguments avail nothing, but to see why they are impotent, one needs to encounter other components of the other's paradigm. The difficulty involves trying to explode the entire fortress-paradigm at once, when in reality, it can be dismantled only one stone at a time. And the inhabitants of the fortress-paradigm always have a corner to which they retreat and feel safe.

(c) Both sides adduce Bible passages familiar to each side but which function very differently in each paradigm. Bible passages must be *interpreted*, and this always occurs within a paradigmatic context.[80] Once again we encounter the famous "hermeneutical circle": one's exegesis influences one's presuppositions, but presuppositions influence exegesis.

Very few theologians have a *complete* overview of, and insight

---

79. The phrase comes from Thomas Kuhn (1996), one of the most influential philosophers of science in the twentieth century. Remarkable examples of paradigm shifts in theology include that of Karen Armstrong (1993), who moved from a strict Catholic paradigm to a liberal syncretistic paradigm, and that of Eta Linnemann (1990), who shifted from a liberal (Bultmannian) paradigm to an orthodox Evangelical paradigm.

80. This matter is discussed extensively in my work on the philosophy of theology (Ouweneel [2013, chapters 6-14]).

into, their opponent's paradigm, and yet disagree with it.[81] Therefore, the debate often resembles "beating the air" (cf. 1 Cor. 9:26): do opponents *listen* to each other? Moreover, confessional and denominational factors also play an enormous role. What must a theologian say if the Forms of Unity teach that the Ecclesia existed from Adam, that (infant) baptism is the replacement of circumcision, and that the Sunday is the Ecclesia's "Sabbath"? The debate seems futile from the outset.

The structure of such a collision interests me deeply, from the viewpoints both of theology and of the philosophy of science, as well as of psychology. *The great majority of those who advocate supersessionism were socialized in supersessionism from their early youth,* but they fight for their view as though it were the most obvious standpoint in the world. Let us also consider what is at stake, also for those who take the Israel prophecies literally. A paradigm shift of this magnitude is almost as drastic as a conversion: *every* chapter of one's systematic theology will look differently! In some cases, rather than engage in fervent but futile debates, the convert could do better by looking for a different church denomination.

It seems to be an ironclad rule that someone who openly defends a certain view can rarely be won over to the alternative paradigm. Their authority and reputation are at stake. Therefore, I have not written this presentation of Israelology to convince opposing colleagues,[82] at least in this subject (on the great Nicene aspects of Christianity we fortunately agree!). Such debates must instead be targeted toward only one group: those (mostly younger) Christians who are not (yet) *bound* in any paradigmatic, confessional, denominational, or professional respect, so that from a psychological point of view, they are still open to considering various lines of thinking and to an honest examination of available options. One consolation is this: in our postmodern times, this group is much larger than it has ever been.

---

81. In my judgment, J. Douma (2008) is one of the few advocates of supersessionism who has thoroughly examined the viewpoints of his opponents.

82. See Robertson (2000); De Jong (2002; 2011; 2012); Douma (2008); Maljaars (1976; 2015); Fijnvandraat et al. (1979); Paas (2012; 2014); and Sizer (2004; 2007).

3.7 Various "-Isms"
3.7.1 "Christian Zionism"

In a confrontation between two paradigms, each party inevitably develops certain designations for the other party, which could be experienced as somewhat demeaning. Thus, advocates of supersessionism dislike being called "replacement theologians," and certainly reject the label "anti-Semites" (which is understandable). However, I know of no better terms than supersessionism and replacement theology because these terms simply describe the conviction held by these advocates that the picture in the Tanakh—ethnic Israel in a literal land with a literal temple—has been "replaced" or "superseded by" by the New Testament picture of a "spiritual Israel" in a spiritual land and with a spiritual temple. Therefore, it is difficult to understand the inaccuracy or inappropriateness of designations like supersessionism and replacement theology, as well as a designation like spiritualism. Moreover, not designations but contents are at issue.

Conversely, some designations of the other side of this debate are not always experienced as pleasant or appropriate, either. One such phrase is "Christian Zionism."[83] I avoid it because I do not self-identify as a (Christian or non-Christian) "Zionist."[84] Zionism is the nationalist movement of the Jewish people—and their friends—that advocates the re-establishment of and support for a Jewish state in Palestine. I do support such a state—as do many advocates of supersessionism!—because we are very happy for the Jewish people that, after centuries of oppression and after the horrible Shoah, they now have their own land and state, and can live in relative safety. Moreover—and with this, advocates of supersessionism do *not* agree—I definitely see in this phenomenon as part of the fulfillment of biblical prophecies. But the reason the term "Zionism" is problematic is that this refers to a secular movement, very different from what I, along with many Jews, see as the ultimate goal of the state of Israel: *conversion*

---

83. The phrase "Christian Zionism" seems to have been used first by Theodor Herzl, in reference to Henri Dunant, the Swiss philanthropist and founder of the Red Cross; see Sizer (2004, 19).

84. For a Jewish analysis of "Christian Zionism," see rabbi Dan Cohn-Sherbock (2006); for a Christian analysis, see Sizer (2004).

to the God of Israel and to the book of Israel.

Such a conversion—and here, many Jews do *not* agree with me—cannot happen apart from the person and work of Jesus Christ, and from the power of the Holy Spirit. God's mighty hand brought the people of Israel to the land of Israel, and that same mighty hand will guide many Jews to the conversion, especially when Yeshuah haMashiach appears. As the apostle John exclaims: "Look! He is coming with the clouds [Dan. 7:13]! Every eye will see him, including those who pierced him [Zech. 12:10; John 19:37]; and all the tribes of the Land[85] will mourn him" (Rev. 1:7 CJB). The establishment of the state of Israel in 1948 was not the ultimate fulfillment of any biblical prophecy as such; but it was most definitely a precursor to that final fulfillment. That fulfillment will involve this: "[A] partial hardening has come upon Israel, until the fullness of the Gentiles has come in. And in this way all Israel will be saved, as it is written, 'The Deliverer will come from Zion, he will banish ungodliness from Jacob' [Isa. 27:9; 59:20]; 'and this will be my covenant with them when I take away their sins' [Jer. 31:31-34]" (Rom. 11:25-27).

Today in the land of Israel we are seeing the preparatory work, *under God's guidance*, for the ultimate fulfillment of God's prophecies in the Messianic kingdom. This is exactly what I find in Ezekiel 37:1-14 (the vision of the valley of dry bones), where we clearly see a restoration in two stages:[86]

(a) a *national* restoration, represented by the bones that are joined together to become corpses (vv. 4-8)—a tremendous miracle, but obviously inadequate as the ultimate goal;

(b) a *spiritual* restoration, represented by the corpses coming alive (vv. 9-14); to be sure, this spiritual element was present within Israel from the very beginning, and it is increasing; but it is not yet the massive revival that God seems to have in mind. The increase involves a truly godly Jewry, devoted to God and to the Torah, as well as (especially since about 1980) the formation of "Messianic" (Jesus-believing Jewish) congregations.

---

85. Advocates of supersessionism read the word "earth" here.
86. See, e.g., Grant (1931); Gaebelein (1972); Walvoord (1991).

3.7.2 "Israelism"

Another designation for what I consider to be a biblical Israelology comes from S. Paas: "Israelism," and one who advocates this view is an "Israelist." If these designations intend to identify someone who loves Israel and loves God's promises to Israel, then they are unproblematic, despite personal discomfort with any "-ism". But Paas said this about Israelism: "The driving force of Israelism is not a heavenly but an earthly Zion."[87] If this is correct, then I am not an Israelist, and I know no such (Christian) Israelists. These designations involve a basic misunderstanding about the Israelology being presented here. Advocates of supersessionism seem to think that we must choose between believing in a spiritual future for (earthly) Jerusalem (and Zion, and the temple,), or believing in the "New Jerusalem" (and a spiritual, or heavenly Zion).

These advocates seem somehow unable to accommodate a theology that accepts *both* the earthly Zion and the heavenly Zion. They forget that Hebrews 12 is found also in the Bibles of "the Israelists":

> [Y]ou have come to Mount *Zion* and to the city of the living God, the heavenly *Jerusalem*, and to innumerable *angels* in festal gathering, and to the assembly of the *firstborn* who are enrolled in heaven, and to *God*, the judge of all, and to the spirits of the *righteous* made perfect, and to *Jesus*, the mediator of a new covenant, and to the sprinkled *blood* that speaks a better word than the blood of Abel (vv. 22–24).[88]

Here, "Zion" is a figurative designation for the entire system of mercy and atonement that has been introduced by Jesus Christ, by his person and his work, over against any form of legalism that aims to please God by good works, performed in one's own strength.

The apostle Paul deals with the same subject in Galatians 4:21–31, where he presents us with the following seven contrasts, all expressing more or less the same matter:[89]

1. The *Old* Covenant versus the *New* Covenant.
2. Hagar versus Sarah.
3. Hagar's son Ishmael versus Sarah's son Isaac.

---

87. Paas (2014, 19).

88. For a detailed exegesis, see Ouweneel (1982b, ad loc.).

89. For a detailed exegesis, see Ouweneel (1997, ad loc.).

4. Mount Sinai versus Mount Zion.
5. The *earthly* Jerusalem versus the *heavenly* Jerusalem.
6. The children of the *slave* (bondwoman) versus the children of the *free* woman.
7. Slavery versus freedom.

Biblical Israelology *acknowledges* the heavenly Zion, but refuses to choose between the earthly Zion and the heavenly Zion. It firmly maintains the presentations in Galatians 4 and Hebrews 12, *but it also maintains the promises of God for ethnic Israel*. There is no hermeneutical principle or rule that compels us to choose one or the other. We Gentile Jesus-believers have no part in the earthly Jerusalem; we do have a part in the heavenly Jerusalem. But this does not allow us to purloin God's promises concerning the earthly Jerusalem from our Jewish friends, and to spiritualize them for ourselves.

Other false dilemmas will go undiscussed here, like the choice that a person interested in prophecy is either a spiritualist or a literalist. One can interpret biblical prophecies literally — leaving room for metaphors and the like — without being a litera*list*. But at the same time one can also interpret these prophecies spiritually, in the sense that they are never *only* about the land, or the city, or the temple. No fulfillment of these prophecies can occur without the spiritual side: humbling oneself before the LORD, repenting, living (again) according to the commandments of God (see the following section).

The decisive hermeneutical issue is this: the New Testament speaks of Zion, Jerusalem, the "heavenly country," and the Ecclesia being a spiritual temple, and so on, but it *never* suggests that *therefore* the literal land, the literal city, the literal Mount Zion, the literal Israel, and the literal Judah have ceased to exist. This latter conclusion is something that advocates of supersessionism read into the New Testament because their paradigm demands it.[90] The New Testament does occasionally make *applications* of land, city, and temple, but it never identifies this to be the *meaning* or the *exe-*

---

90. During the public defense of his doctoral dissertation, Reformed theologian H. R. van de Kamp (1990) said that he had sought to read the book of Revelation in an "unbiased" way (which is fundamentally impossible). And what was the result? He discovered that in Revelation, "Israel" is the church!

gesis of these terms in the sense that there is no longer any room in the ways of God for the literal land, city, and temple. The New Testament Ecclesia may be a spiritual temple and a spiritual city, on its way to the "heavenly country," but it is a hermeneutical mistake of the first order to suggest that *therefore* God's promises regarding literal Israel, the literal land, the literal city of Jerusalem, and the literal temple have become obsolete.

In the coming chapters, all these things will be explained in detail. And we will see that all the mentioned biases—exegetical, dogmatic, paradigmatic, confessional, denominational, professional, and psychological—play an essential role in this.

3.7.3 A Right to the Land?

For a non-specialist in the field of international law, this is a complicated section: are the people of Israel legally entitled to *ha'Aretz*, or to part of it? In some respects, the answer is "Yes," and in some respects the answer is "Not yet." First, with regard to the "Yes":

1. There is no historical doubt that *this* is the land that the Israelites had inhabited for at least thirteen, and perhaps fifteen, centuries,[91] when such an entity as a "Palestinian nation" did not exist.

2. There is no theological doubt that *this* is the land that God will give back to the Israelites ("the land that your father possessed," Deut. 30:5[92]), not only the territory of the modern state of Israel, but also what today is called the West Bank, historical Judea and Samaria.

3. Even more broadly than this: "To your offspring I give this land, from the river of Egypt[93] to the great river, the river Euphrates" (Gen. 15:18). A pre-fulfillment of this occurred in the time of Solomon: "Solomon ruled over all the kingdoms from the Euphrates to the land of the Philistines and to the border of Egypt" (1 Kings 4:21).

4. Something many Christians—and many Muslims!—do not seem to know is that the Quran also clearly says that the Holy Land was given to Israel, and not to Arabs: "O my people, enter the Holy

---

91. This depends on the date of the Exodus: fifteenth or thirteenth century BC.
92. Cf. Jer. 7:7; 25:5; 35:15; Ezek. 20:42; 36:28; 37:25.
93. Opinions differ about whether the Nile is meant here, or the more proximate Wadi El-Arish.

Land which God has assigned for you, and do not turn back, lest you return as losers" (Surah 5:21). "We [i.e., Allah] said to the Children of Israel, 'Inhabit the land, and when the promise of the Hereafter [or rather, the ultimate promise] arrives, We will bring you all together'" (17:104).[94] The Quran never assigned this land to any Arabs, but only to Israel.

But there is also the aspect of the "not yet." Both Jews and Christians must ask themselves why God drove the Jews out of their land nineteen and a half centuries ago. Let me explain with two analogies.

This expulsion was like a father sending his child out of the room because the child misbehaved. Sometime later, the child re-enters the room, and says, "As a child I am entitled to be in this room." How will the father respond? He will say, "You are allowed to enter if you first offer your apologies for what you did a while ago." The child definitely has a right to be in the room, just as Israel definitely has a right to the land. But when the child has been sent out, the child must first humble themselves and repent. This is what many Jews did when they returned to the Holy Land—but many have not, yet.

Here is a more biblical analogy: Israel's expulsion from the land was like a husband who sends his wife out of the house because of here adulterous behavior; indeed, Israel was compared several times with a repeatedly unfaithful wife.[95] The husband tells her that he does not divorce her forever, but if she wishes to come back, she must show that she repents of her sins, that she has quit her adulterous life, and that she seeks to be faithful to her husband again. Imagine that this woman returned to the house one day, and said, "Here is where I have always lived, and I have a right to live here again." Imagine that her husband is so gracious that he lets her in, and watches her unobtrusively to see whether her attitude has changed, and whether she engages in relations with other men again. What is the situation in Israel today? Some have not humbled themselves at all; there is no repentance, and no confidence in God. But they do talk about "rights" ("this is our land, where are ancestors have lived for so many centuries"), without much reflec-

---

94. https://www.clearquran.com.
95. Isa. 50 and 54; Ezek. 16 and 23; Hos. 2 and 3.

tion on the past.

However, others have humbled themselves before the Lord, and have entrusted themselves to his mercy. Listen to their prayers on Tish'ah b'Av, the Ninth of the month Av, when the faithful in Israel commemorate five main calamities that devastated Israel in the past, especially the two destructions of Jerusalem, and at least seven more recent tragedies. One of the main prayers consists of the entire book of Lamentations read in the synagogues, while in many Sephardic congregations, the book of Job is also read. The Jews who genuinely identify with Lamentations are those who say in their hearts: "Jerusalem sinned grievously; therefore she became filthy; all who honored her despise her, for they have seen her nakedness; she herself groans and turns her face away" (1:8). "Why should a living man complain, a man, about the punishment of his sins?" (3:39). "This was for the sins of her prophets and the iniquities of her priests, who shed in the midst of her the blood of the righteous" (4:13).[96] And although Job was not guilty of the gross evils that his friends had accused him of, he does say in the end: "I despise myself, and repent in dust and ashes" (42:6).

Here is the answer: those who have returned not only to the land, but also to the Lord, are those who are entitled to be there:

> [W]hen all these things come upon you, the blessing and the curse, which I [i.e., Moses] have set before you, and you call them to mind among all the nations where the Lord your God has driven you, and *return* to the Lord your God, you and your children, and obey his voice in all that I command you today, with all your heart and with all your soul, then the Lord your God will *restore your fortunes* and have mercy on you, and he will gather you again from all the peoples where the Lord your God has scattered you. . . . And the Lord your God will bring you into the land that your fathers possessed, that you may possess it. And he will make you more prosperous and numerous than your fathers. And the Lord your God will circumcise your heart and the heart of your offspring, so that you will love the Lord your God with all your heart and with all your soul, that you may live (Deut. 30:1–6).

---

96. Cf. Talmud: Shabbat 119b, where many sins are enumerated for which Jerusalem was destroyed.

There is a word in this text, the Hebrew root *sh-v(u)-b*, which occurs with two meanings: a spiritual "return" to the LORD (vv. 2 and 10, repent, convert to him), and a physical "return" to the land (v. 3a, *w'shab et-shebutcha*, "turn your captivity" or "restore your fortunes"; cf. v. 5, "bring you into the land").[97] These two meanings are closely attached: *there can be no "return" to the Promised Land without a true "return" to the LORD*.

This penitent humility characterized the attitude of Daniel. He found in the book of Jeremiah (25:11–12; 29:10) that Judah's captivity would last seventy years (Dan. 9:2). Daniel realized that these seventy years had almost ended. But he did not turn to the LORD to remind him of his promise and to claim Judah's "rights." Instead, although personally innocent, he humbled himself before God, thus representing the repenting remnant of Israel: "[W]e have sinned and done wrong and acted wickedly and rebelled, turning aside from your commandments and rules" (Dan. 9:5; repeated in vv. 8, 11 and 15). Today this attitude is shared by many Jews in the Holy Land: no "claiming" of anything without true penitent humility before the LORD. "Claiming" (banging one's fists on the table) makes a person big; penitent humility makes them small: "I dwell in the high and holy place, and also with him who is of a contrite and lowly spirit, to revive the spirit of the lowly, and to revive the heart of the contrite" (Isa. 57:15).

Too many Zionists were interested only in returning to the land, and not in returning to the LORD. But many have truly returned to the LORD as well. A rough indication of this might be that more than half of all Israelis observe Tish'ah b'Av to some extent, and about half of *these* observe it as a day of fasting. Another rough indication of this penitent humility is the observance of *Yom Kippur*, which is observed as a day of fasting by almost three-fourths of the Jewish people in Israel. Of course, outward observance does not tell us much about the inward attitude; yet these numbers are encouraging. During the *Yamim Nora'im* ("Days of Awe"), the ten days preceding *Yom Kippur*, the godly Jew meditates about who and what they are before God, in order that all their iniquities may be taken away on *Yom Kippur* (Lev. 16:16, 21, 30, 34). The greatest

---

97. This Heb. root appears also in vv. 3b, 8, and 9, where it is often rendered as "again"; e.g., v. 3b, lit. "turn and gather" is "gather again."

"Yom Kippur" will be the day when the Messiah appears: the seventy "weeks" (490 years) that remain until that day will end this way: "Seventy weeks are decreed about your people and your holy city, to finish the transgression, to put an end to sin, and to atone for iniquity, to bring in everlasting righteousness" (Dan. 9:24). Elaboration of this point will have to wait for a later chapter.

Chapter 4
The Problem Politicized

It has been taught, Rabbi Nehemiah said: "In the generation of Messiah's coming impudence will increase, [mutual] esteem be perverted, the vine yield its fruit, yet shall wine be dear, and the Kingdom will be converted to heresy[1] [i.e., Christianity, Heb. minuth] with none to rebuke them." This supports Rabbi Isaac, who said: "The son of David will not come until the whole world is converted to the belief of the heretics [i.e., Christians]."

Talmud: Sanhedrin 97a

4.1 Politicizing the Problem
4.1.1 The Constantinian Turn

OF ALL THE SUBJECTS treated in systematic theology, ecclesiology (the doctrine concerning the Ecclesia) and eschatology (the doctrine concerning the last things) have been politicized the most. This is because these subjects—especially the church as an immanent phe-

---

1. Cf. the comment in the Soncino edition of the Talmud: "By 'the Kingdom' is meant the Roman Empire, and the statement is a remarkable forecast by R. Nehemia (150 c.e.) of the conversion of Rome to Christianity under Constantine the Great in 313; v. however, Herford [2003], *Christianity in the Talmud*, 207ff." My question: how can this be said to have happened "in the generation of Messiah's coming"?

nomenon—are closely related to general world history. The same is even more clearly the case with Israelology (the doctrine concerning Israel), because Israel was and is an ethnic entity that lives constantly in relation with other ethnic entities (nations, empires). It is impossible to speak of Israel's present and future except on the basis of a certain general view of world history and the modern world situation. This influences one's ecclesiology: notice the different ways we speak about (1) the church in the Middle Ages, when the Roman Catholic Church was virtually the only representation of the body of Christ (in the East along with the Eastern Orthodox Churches); or (2) in the post-Reformation Protestant countries, where the Lutheran church or the Calvinist church was occasionally the only (permitted) church; or (3) in the nineteenth century, when free churches began to flourish.

Similarly, eschatology has changed in tandem with Israelology throughout the centuries. The Christian view of Israel was very different (a) in the early centuries (as we discover from the writings of the church fathers), (b) after the Constantinian shift (when the Roman Empire became a "Christian" empire), (c) after the Reformation, and (d) after the resurgence of the literal-Israel view. This dependence on historical situations clearly illustrates that eschatology and Israeology—as all the other sciences—can be practiced only within a chosen paradigm. And such paradigms change over time for a number of reasons, with political and historical circumstances being not unimportant ones. Perhaps the most striking and tumultuous paradigm shift occurred in the fourth century of our era.[2] In the year 312, the Roman Emperor Constantine the Great was "converted" to Christianity (our quote marks indicate our uncertainty about the spiritual quality and content of this event), and in 313 he issued the Edict of Milan (formulated along with his co-emperor Licinius), in which complete freedom of religion was announced for the entire Empire. This was important especially for Christians, who had been so bitterly oppressed and persecuted throughout the first three centuries of the Christian era. Sixty-seven years later, in 380, Emperor Theodosius I, along with his co-emperors Gratian and Valentinian II, declared Nicene (anti-Arian, Catholic) Christi-

---

2. See extensively, Ouweneel (2003a, chapter 4; 2014, chapter 11); also see Froom (1950, ad loc.).

anity to be implicitly the state religion of the Roman Empire. In this way, a remarkable development was completed. As we have seen, the Babylonian, the Medo-Persian, the Greco-Macedonian, and (so far) the Roman Empire had all been pagan empires, in which the gods of the consecutive nations always stood in opposition to the God of Israel. But now, 1,132 years since the founding of the city of Rome in 753 BC, the Roman Empire had explicitly become a *Christian* empire.[3] Or it had become at least a pseudo-Christian empire: thousands of people were baptized, seemingly without much inner conviction. They seem to have done so mainly in order to obtain the best jobs and political positions in this reconstituted Empire.

Without entering too much into the political and historical circumstances, let us instead focus on the consequences of this Constantinian shift for eschatology and Israelology. We will see that the church fathers living before this shift, insofar as they expressed themselves on the matter, were oriented to a pre-millennial view. That is to say, as far as I can tell, they believed basically what millions believe still today: they anticipated a Messianic kingdom to be erected at the second coming of Christ, in which they saw a place for a converted Israel. Alas, the idea of a "Christian" Roman Empire caused the decline of the former view concerning the second coming of Christ and the establishment of the Messianic kingdom. Why continue anticipating such a kingdom if this very kingdom of Christ was realized *here and now*, not only spiritually, but also politically and historically? Initially, Christians had eagerly expected the second coming of Christ, who would establish his kingdom in power and majesty in this world. *Now* the idea predominated that Christ rules already now, namely, by means of the two heads or leaders of the Christian world: the political head, the emperor, and later the pope as the spiritual head of this Christian commonwealth. In the early centuries, the emphasis lay still on the emperor, who acted as the actual head of the church and as the chairman of its gatherings. Christ rules in heaven, and the emperor is his visible representative on earth. The Ecclesia maintained its faith in the sec-

---

3. From the founding of the city of Rome in 753 BC to the formal Christianization of the Empire in AD 380 (the pagan stage) was 1,132 years; from this Christianization until the Reformation in 1517 (the Roman Catholic stage) was 1,137 years—nearly as long. The time from the Reformation until today is almost half this length.

ond coming of Christ, but this would take place "only" at the end of world history, and this is by definition always "far away." This is the practical view of millions of orthodox Roman Catholics and traditional Protestants until today.

A church that is taking the lead in the politics and the wars of this world, and that recognizes the emperor as its actual head—not because he is a Christian[4] but because he is the emperor—such a church will naturally develop totally new understandings of prophecy. Formerly, the *pagan* Roman Empire had been viewed as the great adversary of the church—and thus also of the God of Israel—and therefore also as *the* instrument of the "dragon."[5] Since the Constantinian shift, the character of the empire had turned one hundred and eighty degrees: it had now become the ally of the church, and thus an instrument of God in the development of a new, "Christian" empire, or even: *the* Messianic kingdom. But what did this *really* mean for the Ecclesia—and for (its view of) Israel?

4.1.2 Two Consequences

The question must be asked whether the new situation in the Empire meant that Christians were *still* under the sway of the "dragon," who had merely changed his face: from a "roaring lion" (1 Pet. 1:8) he had changed into an "angel of light" (2 Cor. 11:14). Compare the history of Samson: the "angel of light," Delilah (Judg. 16:4–21), was in fact far more dangerous than the lion that Samson encountered at the beginning of his story (Judg. 13:5–6). He was able to withstand the "roaring lion," but, unfortunately, not the "angel of light." The very same thing happened to Christianity from the fourth century onward.

In this and the next section, consider the following four aspects of the Constantinian shift, each of which is more dragon-like than Christ-like.[6]

1. *Caesaropapism*: the church was made subservient to the state,

---

4. After his "conversion," Constantine continued living basically as a pagan idolator; he formally joined the Christian church on his deathbed by being baptized.
5. The book of Revelation was written mainly to encourage Christians who were living in the Roman Empire, that is, under the rule of the "dragon."
6. Cf. Ouweneel (2003a; chapter 5; 2014, chapter 11).

and church leaders were made subservient to the emperor (later, to other heads of state), entirely without regard for the personal faith of this emperor or these heads of state. A symptom of this was that Emperor Constantine the Great possessed the highest authority during the—formally ecclesiastical—Council of Nicaea (325), whereas it is very doubtful whether at that time he was a genuine Christian.[7] Orthodox Protestants believe the content of the Nicene Creed because they believe it corresponds with the Bible; but Roman Catholics and Eastern Orthodox basically believe it because it is invested with the authority of the Council—which was essentially the authority of an emperor who was at that time still pagan.

2. For my purpose here, we must notice especially the rise of *Jewish persecution*; it is a most remarkable thing that *the end of the pagan persecution of the Christians coincided with the beginning of "Christian" persecution of the Jews* because the latter did not wish to accommodate to the now all powerful Roman Catholic Church. Two years after religious freedom for Christians was announced, in 315, the first decree was levelled against the Jews; in that decree, they were forbidden, under the threat of being burned, to attack converted Jews, or to convert non-Jews (who now virtually had become "Christians") to Judaism. In this decree, the Jews were called a "pernicious" (Lat. *feralem*) and "nefarious sect" (Lat. *nefariam sectam*)! Many decrees followed: Jews were not allowed to have Christian slaves (though Christians were allowed to have Jewish slaves), Christians were not allowed to convert to Judaism, and Jewish religious gatherings were curtailed. This was not the Spirit of Christ— it was the spirit of the dragon.

Whereas before the Great Shift, the Christian feast of Easter coincided with Pesach, the Council of Nicaea chose a new date, so that the two usually no longer coincided. Metahistorically this was an incredibly important event in God's history with this world: *now Jews and Christians were going to part ways for many centuries*. In a sense, their two paths intersected again in the twentieth century,

---

7. This caesaropapism still exists in the Church of England, whose head is the British monarch. To some extent, it also existed in the Netherlands of the seventeenth century, where it was the States-General (the Parliament) under whose auspices the Synod of Dordt (1618–19) met, and who also ordered the preparation of the Statenvertaling (States [!] Translation) of the Bible (completed in 1637) (see §4.4.1).

after the Shoah. The motivation of the fathers in Nicaea was this:

> It would be unworthy if, in this sacred feast, we would follow the custom of the Jews, who have tarnished their hands with the most heinous crime [read, the death of Jesus], and have remained spiritually blind. Henceforth, we do not wish to have anything in common anymore with the hostile people of the Jews, for our Savior has pointed a different way for us.

There was, however, a positive feature to various conciliar decrees: in 330 and 331, the officials in the synagogues were exempted by decree from obligations to the state.

4.1.3 Two More Consequences

3. The beginning of Jewish persecution coincided with the beginning of *anti-millennialism*. Notice the difference: most church fathers of the second and third centuries looked forward to the second coming of Christ and to the Messianic kingdom that he would establish on earth; these expectations corresponded entirely with the predictions of the Jewish prophets. But in the fourth century, this changed drastically. The existence of a "Christian" Roman Empire had effectively led to the demise of this expectation of a future Messianic kingdom; Christians now believed that the Messianic kingdom had been realized *here and now* in this "Christian" empire.

This was yet another point at which the ways of Jews and Christians parted: for the Jews, the Messianic kingdom was and remained a future matter, but for the majority of Christians, this Messianic kingdom had been realized within the "Christian" Roman Empire — the very same empire that at the same time had begun to persecute the Jews. *From now on, anti-millennialism and anti-Semitism would form a strong bond,* that would last until the Shoah; humanly speaking, the Holocaust was possible only because the majority in the Lutheran church had embraced Luther's supersessionism (see the next point) and, to some extent, even his anti-Semitism (see the second volume). This does not mean that every advocate of anti-millennialism or supersessionism in our time is an anti-Semite — of course not — but the historical link cannot be denied.

4. Indeed, anti-millennialism is almost always closely linked with *supersessionism* (substitutionism, replacement theology); both views insist that ethnic Israel as such no longer plays a role in God's

redemptive-historical dealings with the world. The (New Testament) Ecclesia has *actually* replaced ethnic Israel spoken about in the Tanakh. Imagine: there *are* no longer any blessings for ethnic Israel. All the blessings promised in the Tanakh have been spiritualized, and annexed by the Christian Ecclesia, though it was happy to leave all the predicted curses to Israel. For Roman Catholics this meant that Rome had actually replaced Jerusalem, the Roman emperor had replaced the Davidic king, the emperor's throne was the ancient "throne of David," and the central church of Rome, the old, and later the new, Saint Peter's Basilica, *de facto* fulfilled the role of the ancient temple in Jerusalem. In §1.3.3 above, we saw that this led the "Christian" "Roman" Emperor Charlemagne to adopt the angelic prince of Israel: archangel Michael.

Protestants subsequently spiritualized many of these views: they no longer claimed any sacred cities, a Davidic throne, a central church, and least of all a special angelic prince. Yet, with the emphasis of supersessionist Protestants on the spirituality of city, temple, and throne, they adhered to the same line of thinking: these matters no longer belong to ethnic Israel, but to those who claim to be the "spiritual Israel," having stripped these realities of everything Jewish. This is a historical and theological riddle: spiritually, supersessionism claims as *many features and realities* of being "Israel" as possible; practically, it demonstrates as *few features* of being "Israel" as possible.

4.2 Theological Developments
4.2.1 The New Eschatology

The earlier church fathers saw in the image of Nebuchadnezzar in Daniel 2 the four pagan empires, the last of which was the Roman Empire. However, after the early decades of the fourth empire, no pagan world empire existed any longer; it had been succeeded by a "Christian" empire. In Daniel 2, the last pagan empire, the Roman one, is succeeded by the kingdom of Christ. Thus, what was more obvious than to suppose that the "Christian" empire established during the fourth century was the promised Messianic kingdom, which destroyed all the previous pagan empires? The territory of the "Christianized" Roman Empire was also the territory in which the kingdom of Christ would emerge, and the establishment of the earthly Ecclesia through human hands would be the means through which the kingdom of Christ would be realized, and entity in which the biblical prophecies would be fulfilled.

What a poor reasoning this was, for two reasons.

1. *Theological.* Daniel 2 can be understood only as the parallel of Daniel 7, where the same four empires are described, along with the way these four empires will be destroyed. The comparison shows that the "stone" of Daniel 2:34-35 (and 45) — the stone that "struck the image on its feet of iron and clay, and broke them in pieces" and "became a great mountain and filled the whole earth" — corresponds with Daniel 7:13-14:

> [B]ehold, with the clouds of heaven there came one like a son of man. . . . And to him was given dominion and glory and a kingdom, that all peoples, nations, and languages should serve him; his dominion is an everlasting dominion, which shall not pass away, and his kingdom one that shall not be destroyed.

This cannot possibly be the "Christian kingdom" that began in the fourth century, because all Christians[8] agree that the coming of the "Son of Man" on the clouds of heaven is still future. In other words, this parallelism clearly shows that the fifth empire in Daniel 2 is not at all the "Christian kingdom" that began in the fourth century, but the kingdom of the Son of Man, which will begin only after his second coming.

2. *Historical.* In the fourth century, there was no question of a "Christian" kingdom that henceforth subdued all the pagan powers. On the contrary, the exact opposite occurred: the realm of the "dragon" was not placed under Christ, but the "Christian" kingdom was held in the claws of the "dragon." In other words, the church did not Christianize the empire, but the — still very pagan — empire secularized and paganized the church. I am not speaking of the — no doubt thousands of — faithful Christians who sincerely followed and served Christ. I am speaking of the *system* of the (caesaropapist) "church," which found security in the arms of the pagan gods. *One of the obvious consequences of this was the beginning of the persecution and oppression of the Jews.* If the Lamb were the head of this kingdom, such a development would have been unthinkable;

---

8. Except the preterists, of course, who believe that the second coming of Christ occurred in AD 70 (see §6.1.1 below).

rather, the "dragon" was its true head, who was all too eager to "swallow" the Jews again.

Who were the "gods" of this "Christian" empire? Let me mention only the most important one: the Council of Ephesus (431) declared the Virgin Mary to be the "Mother of God." The populace of Ephesus was enthusiastic about this because early Christianity had taken from them Artemis, the Mother Goddess, and now they received the "Mother of God." For most people, there would have been little difference between "Mother Goddess" (the divine Mother of the gods) and "Mother of God." This pagan Mary was gradually given many attributes and titles adopted from paganism. One of her main Latin titles is *Regina Coeli*, "queen of heaven," a title originally borne by the Semitic chief goddess, in Assyrian called Ishtar and in Phoenician Astarte.[9] In Mesopotamia, she was known as *sharrat shamē*, "queen of heaven." In Jeremiah 7:18 and 44:17–19, 25, we read how the people of Jerusalem made cakes for her, bearing her image and burning incense for this "queen of heaven."[10]

It is of interest to point out that certain Christian nations and countries acknowledge a certain saint as their patron. A well-known example is St. George, the patron saint of England. In the same way, cities too can have a patron saint; thus, St. Dionys(i)us (*Saint Denys*) is the patron saint of Paris (and France), St. Joseph is the patron saint of Berlin, and St. Nicholas is the patron saint of Amsterdam. This idea of a patron saint or guardian saint is the continuation of the pagan notion of *genius*, a "divine" power taking under its protection against specific powers a certain nation, country, or city. The existence of such patron saints shows that many of the saints of the Roman Catholic Church, the Eastern Orthodox Church, along with some who appear on the religious calendars of Anglicans and Lutherans, go back to ancient pagan idols. Of course, this does not deny that saints like George or Nicholas, for example, may have existed, and even been very godly people, who were later canonized. The calendar of saints contains many names of historical persons. But that does not at all contradict the reality

---

9. Heb. *Ashtarot* (Judg. 2:13; 10:6; 1 Sam. 7:3–4; 12:10; 31:10) or *Ashtoret* (1 Kings 11:5,33; 2 Kings 23:13); the form *Astarte* is the Greek transcription of the name; see extensively, Ouweneel (1998a).

10. See further Ouweneel (1998a).

that the notion of guardian saints arose from the pagan (and Christianized) notion of "divine" *genii* (guardian angels). These few examples could be multiplied greatly.[11]

4.2.2 Paradigm Shift

After the Great Shift, theology was both supersessionist and anti-millennialist. These insights did not arise from renewed Bible study but merely from the changed political circumstances in the Roman Empire. Some of the new theological insights were quite disgusting. In his eulogy on Constantine, the Christian historian Eusebius compared him several times with Moses.[12] Indeed, a new, Mosaic theocracy had arisen, aping that of ancient Israel, which had become obsolete.[13] For the first time, genuine "churches" arose, magnificent buildings, which to some extent were imitations of Israel's tabernacle and temple, with an outer court for the non-consecrated, the actual temple for the laymen, and the screened-off sanctuary with the altar, accessible only to the priests. No one wondered how Jews within the empire might feel about these things. They were outcasts, whose opinions did not count.

Before the Great Shift, Eusebius taught that Isaiah 35 and Psalm 46 referred to the future Messianic kingdom; after the shift he applied these chapters to the new church buildings of his time, such as the church in Tyre, which he referred to as a "new and much better Jerusalem."[14] He also asserted that the magnificent church that Constantine wished to build in old Jerusalem—the Church of the Holy Sepulchre—might be the fulfillment of the prophecy concerning the New Jerusalem (Rev. 21). He explained the dragon's being cast out of heaven (Rev. 12) as Constantine's victory over the pagan Roman Empire. When Constantine had his sons and a nephew share in his imperial rule, Eusebius saw in this the fulfillment

---

11. See extensively, Ouweneel (1998a; 2003a).
12. *Vita Constantini*, chapters 12, 20, 38–39; see https://www.documentacatholicaomnia.eu/03d/0265-0339,_Eusebius_Caesariensis,_Vita_Constantini_%5bSchaff%5d,_EN.pdf).
13. For clarifying descriptions of the views of various church fathers, see Froom (1950).
14. In addition to his *Vita Constantini* (see note 12 above), see especially his *Historia Ecclesiastica* ("Church History") and his *Laudes Constantini* ("Praises of Constantine").

of Daniel 7:17, ". . . the saints of the Most High shall receive the kingdom."

The roots of supersessionism and anti-millennialism grew in the period of history fed by these attitudes. That Protestants subsequently developed a softened, more spiritualized version of these views does not affect this claim at all. The great paradigm shift in ecclesiology, eschatology, and Israelology was clearly illustrated in the new thinking of Eusebius, as well as in that of various other teachers of the Ecclesia, and was soon to be summarized by the greatest of them, Augustine.

Try to imagine the import of the Great Shift. For three centuries — the first centuries of church history — great figures in the church, like Justin Martyr, Irenaeus, Tertullian, Hippolytus, and Lactantius, unanimously believed in a thousand-year[15] kingdom after the second coming of Christ. No wonder.

1. This had been the conviction of the prophets in the Tanakh: first the coming of the Messiah in glory and power, then the establishment of his kingdom (first, Dan. 7:13, then v. 14; first, Zech. 14:5, then v. 9; first, Isa. 30:4-5, then 32:1).

2. This is also the message of the New Testament: first the second coming (Rev. 19), then the thousand-year kingdom (Rev. 20), then the new heaven and earth (Rev. 21).

Tanakh, New Testament, and the early teachers of the Ecclesia were all of one mind. However, after the Great Shift, the situation drastically changed. Eusebius, Ambrose, Prudentius, and Jerome (the great composer of the Vulgate, the authoritative Latin Bible translation), rejected millennialism out of hand. In addition, we must mention the Donatist[16] Tichonius, who is rather unknown, but who was the main source of Augustine's views. Tichonius replaced the idea of a *future* thousand-year kingdom with the idea of a *present* thousand-year kingdom (beginning with the resurrection of Christ), while the second coming of Christ was pushed to the end

---

15. It does not matter whether the "thousand years" were understood literally or figuratively; at a minimum they referred to a well-defined period between the second coming of Christ and the arrival of the new heavens and the new earth.

16. Donatism was a strictly orthodox, reformation-minded movement within fourth-century Christianity, whose member had left the Roman Catholic Church.

of world history.

Imagine what this meant. Supposedly, not only Christian pre-millennialists but also Jewish teachers were and are utterly mistaken. Both the Bible-believing Christian as well as the Tanakh-believing Jew have written in their heart: "Perhaps today!" *Today* might be the day that the Messiah appears on the clouds of heaven, so that *today* the Messianic kingdom could begin. No, says the post-millennialist, you are both wrong: the thousand-year reign is indeed future, but these thousand years will occur *before* the appearance of the Messiah, and therefore the Messiah cannot come today. But no, says the amillennialist, you are *all three* wrong: the thousand-year kingdom already exists now—tell this to the thousands of Christians and Jews who are still being persecuted for their faith!—and the second coming will occur on the last day of world history.

4.2.3 Augustine and the "De-Jewishified" Jew

Augustine was the most important church father who expanded the new view of the Messianic kingdom within a century after the Great Shift. According to him, (a) the Messianic rule was not to be postponed to the future—it operated already *now*. To be sure, the kingdom is manifested wherever people are devoted to Christ, submit to his commandments, and follow him. But who can fail to see the enormous difference between this rule and the time when the Messiah will have appeared in glory and majesty, and will subject all nations to his powerful authority? Today, the kingdom is still "hidden" because the King is still "hidden" (Col. 3:3)—on that day, all eyes will see him (Rev. 1:7), and all knees will bow down before him (Phil. 2:9–11).

(b) Augustine taught that the Messianic kingdom receives its form within the Roman Empire under the guidance of the emperor, namely, through the church under the guidance of the bishop of Rome. It is quite amazing that both Martin Luther (a former Augustinian monk) and John Calvin were pupils of Augustine—and absorbed these ideas rather uncritically. In many respects the Reformation was definitely a return, a going back to the Word—but this return did not occur in the fields of eschatology and Israelology.

(c) Revelation 20:1–6 was understood as entirely fulfilled: Satan is "bound" (although this "bound" Satan still goes around freely as the roaring lion [1 Pet. 5:8], apparently bound with a very long chain!), and the "first resurrection" was spiritualized and applied to regeneration—as if the notion of resurrection mentioned in these few verses (Rev. 20:4–6) actually involves two completely different realities: a spiritual resurrection and a physical resurrection. The interpretation of the remaining details of these verses is pious fantasy: the "pit" in which Satan is bound is the totality of yet unconverted nations; the thrones in verse 4 are the present ecclesiastical seats. The "camp of the saints" in verse 9 is the worldwide (universal, catholic) church. *Any future for the Jews involved both being converted to this (largely pagan) church and completely abandoning everything Jewish.* This latter feature was perhaps the bitterest pill to swallow: Jews who wished to be saved had to abandon every trace of their Jewishness, in order to enter the "spiritual Israel."[17] They had to move from Jerusalem to Rome (and later, to the centers of Protestantism). The Roman Catholic Church was the stone in Daniel 2, which destroyed the image and grew to be the new (Christianized) world power.

Supposedly, this church is the New Jerusalem of Revelation 21. There is room in this church for everyone who believes, on the condition that people abandon their former religion. Converts from paganism must forsake their idols, and converts from Judaism must forsake the religion given to them not by false gods but *by the God of the Bible.* Unlike the first century, the process of conversion involves not converts from paganism being welcomed into the company of Jewish believers, but (forced) converts from Judaism laying aside their Jewishness in order to be received into a company of converted pagans that has appropriated for itself the name "Israel." *Precisely this is one of the reasons Jews have so much difficulty accepting Jesus:* they are under the impression that doing so requires them to join the church-with-99%-former-pagans (the "new Israel"), and to cease 100% being Jews. This impression is a persistent Jewish error, but one that is due entirely to what (pseudo-)Christians have been teaching for centuries.

---

17. During the Middle Ages, the Spanish Inquisition carefully scrutinized Jewish Christian converts, and if, for instance, they refused to make a fire on the Sabbath (cf. Exod. 35:3), the Inquisitors had them burned at the stake.

This tragic misunderstanding will infect the hearts of most Jews until the appearance of the Messiah, I am afraid. It is the fault of anti-Jewish, anti-millennialist supersessionism. Of course, many advocates of supersessionism hate anti-Semitism. They may be very kind to Jews. During World War II, some of them helped Jews in Nazi-occupied Europe. But at the end of the day, this is their message to the Jews: if you wish to be saved, *you must stop being Jewish* and join the Christian church. No longer are the nations of the earth blessed "in" (through, because of) the offspring of the patriarchs, but the reverse is the case: Jews can be blessed only "in" (through, because of) the Gentile church. To be sure, salvation is primarily "from Christ." But this salvation no longer comes "from the Jews" to the Gentiles (John 4:22), but from the Gentiles to the Jews (if the latter are prepared to take off the robe of their Jewishness and put on the Gentile garment). This is one of the saddest fruits of supersessionism: it does not kill the Jew, but it destroys the Jewishness of the Jew.

4.3 Protestant Eschatology

4.3.1 Reformational Eschatology

History has shown the dramatic consequences of supersessionism. One century later, around 500, Rome's bishop had become the sole ruler within the Roman Catholic Church;[18] the see of the emperor, namely, Rome, also became the see of the prince of the church, namely, the bishop of Rome, called the pope (from Lat. *papa*, father). On the theological level, supersessionism and anti-millennialism in particular caused the catholic (universal, worldwide) church to become the *Roman* Catholic Church.[19] Remarkably, large segments of early Protestantism did not perceive this. On the contrary, although they saw the consequences, they clung tenaciously to supersessionism and anti-millennialism. Apparently, the tremendous metahistorical significance of these "-isms" completely escaped the notice of the Reformers and their successors. Or perhaps we should say that the Reformers were confronted with so many changes and challenges simultaneously that they were unequipped to submit

---

18. See more extensively, Ouweneel (2003a, §6.4).

19. This name actually contains a contradiction: a church cannot simultaneously be Roman (i.e., limited) and catholic (universal).

Augustine's eschatology and Israelology to sharp scrutiny. "I have not found your works complete in the sight of my God," said the Lord (Rev. 3:2); on the point of eschatology and Israelology, several centuries would pass before the Ecclesia could arrive at better insights.

Because Luther and Calvin continued Roman supersessionism and anti-millennialism, they failed miserably with regard to the Jewish people. Initially, Luther sharply opposed the persecution of the Jews, especially because he was convinced that he could win them in relation to his new approach to Scripture. Although Jews did express their gratitude for his courageous support, they remained loyal to the faith of their fathers. How different this would, or could, have been had Luther (a) rejected supersessionism and anti-millennialism, (b) made clear to the Jews that a great prophetic future was awaiting them (and joined with them in this matter), and (c) also made clear to them that, in order to be saved, they did not have to join the church of the Reformation, but could establish their own Messianic (Jesus-believing) congregations.

Alas, these insights developed only later. To be sure, the second of these insights began to penetrate the world of the Dutch Second Reformation before the end of the sixteenth century (see below), but the third insight began to emerge near the end of the nineteenth century. The first of these insights is now beginning to attract more and more believers in the Reformational world, but a majority of them still remain unpersuaded.

Martin Luther was so disappointed about the negative response of the Jewish world that he changed from a warm defender into a bitter adversary. Unfortunately, in this respect Luther aligned entirely with the Counter-Reformation. Many believe that his horrible writings against the Jews (1543) were his worst mistake and severely damaged his reputation. The Reformation involved a re-formation of church structures, and the Second Reformation involved a restoration of true personal spiritual life. Ecclesiology and soteriology were rehabilitated, so to speak. But the time was not yet ripe for a thorough revision of eschatology and Israelology.

Even in cases where these insights emerged, no one had the courage to completely abandon supersessionism and anti-millennialism. This shows the enormous power of an erroneous paradigm.

The insights emerged fully for the first time at the beginning of the nineteenth century. But, despite how harsh the observation may sound, perhaps nothing has shone greater light on eschatology and Israelology than the Shoah. God used this heinous calamity to open the eyes of more Christians than ever before. Sadly, those who still advocate supersessionism and anti-millennialism *after* the Shoah (and *after* the establishment of the state of Israel) are afflicted with severe blindness. As Blaise Pascal once said, There is light enough for those who *wish* to see.

4.3.2 Power Thinking Versus Non-Violence

Because the Reformed leaders advocated supersessionism, thinking in terms of power was not foreign to them. What the pope had been before, this was what the Reformed city magistrates became at the Reformation: representatives of God's dominion on earth, exercising this divine power with all their strength. Of course, they appealed to Romans 13:1-7, where the authorities are God's servant commanded to suppress evil. Paul was referring to pagan powers, but now these "Christian" powers began using this passage to destroy their theological adversaries. As if this could ever have been Paul's intention! When he spoke of heresies, it was the Ecclesia that had to deal with them through admonition, and eventually excommunication. But all of this was strictly non-violent.

In a sense, the Roman Catholic Church never used violence against heretics. The Spanish Inquisition was a church organization, but the (alleged) heretics they found were handed over to the Spanish government, who executed them. The church could always wash its hands and claim innocence (cf. Matt. 27:24). Nothing changed after the Reformation. The church itself never executed heretics. But it ensured that the city magistrates were as thoroughly Protestant as they themselves—and it was the Protestant city magistrates who executed the heretics.

We need only recall Calvin's regrettable cooperation with the execution of the "heretic" Michael Servetus in Geneva (1553). Or recall the Calvinist reign of terror in the Flemish city of Ghent (1577-1584), implemented by the Calvinist city magistrate but instigated by none other than the well-known city preacher Petrus

Datheen.[20] Or recall the purely political coup d'état by prince Maurice of Orange (son of William the Silent) in 1618, supported by the Contra-Remonstrant pastors, which was one of the factors that led to the regrettable execution of the innocent (but Remonstrant, i.e., Arminian) Grand Pensionary (a kind of prime minister) Johan van Oldenbarnevelt (1619).

This entire Reformed show of force, which in fact came to an end only with the revision of the Constitution in the Netherlands in 1848 — two to three centuries later! — meant that, for centuries, only Reformed men were allowed to serve in political office, since they alone viewed themselves as the representatives of the true divine government on earth. In and through them, the Messianic kingdom was realized in the Netherlands, they believed. On average, Protestant rulers were certainly less violent toward their adversaries than Catholic rulers had been. But the principle remained the same: (alleged) heretics must be opposed with every possible means, including violence. Please note that, *this line of thinking would have been impossible apart from supersessionism, anti-millennialism,* and the like. "The Messianic kingdom is *now*, and *we* are the ones called by God to enforce and maintain it."

One could provide Lutheran and Anabaptist examples of the same error. Think of the heinous Anabaptist rule in the German city of Münster (1534-1536), under the guidance of John of Leyden, who turned the city into a millenarian Anabaptist theocracy, proclaiming himself to be the King of New Jerusalem. Or think of the absurd rule of government, established at the Peace of Augsburg (1555): *cuius regio, eius religio,* according to which the religion of the German regions was determined by the (Roman Catholic or Lutheran) religion of the ruler (to the exclusion of Calvinism, Zwinglianism, and Anabaptism). All these extravagances were inconceivable apart from supersessionism and anti-millennialism. God's millennial kingdom is *now*, and *we* are the rulers, whether Roman Catholics, Calvinists, Lutherans, Zwinglians, or Anabaptists. These groups were very different, and they often violently attacked each

---

20. Different from the very tolerant William of Orange, founder of the Netherlands, Datheen believed that the authorities were called to support the Reformed religion, and ought not tolerate any other religion. Datheen introduced and defended the Heidelberg Catechism in the Netherlands.

other, but they shared one important loyalty: supersessionism and anti-millennialism.

Indeed, history shows that theological views can result in the enormous political consequences of religious arrogance, power abuse, and violence. Jews have always been the first witnesses of such arrogance and violence in every century of church history.

4.3.3 Belgic Confession, Article 36

Clear evidence of the underlying erroneous paradigm is found in the (unaltered, original) Article 36 of the Belgic Confession, which is crucial to this discussion. It declares that the government is mandated to "protect the sacred ministry, and thus may remove and prevent all idolatry and false worship, that the kingdom of the antichrist may be thus destroyed and the kingdom of Christ promoted."[21] This claim is a pure example of supersessionism: the church must promote the Messianic kingdom, if necessary, with power and violence against the non-Reformed (Catholic, Lutheran,) adversaries.

The Reformed Church in America (RCA) has officially commented on Article 36 as follows: "The Reformed Church in America retains the original full text [of the Belgic Confession], choosing to recognize that the confession was written within a historical context which may not accurately describe the situation that pertains today."[22] But this evasive and inaccurate statement does not at all touch the core of the matter. The point is not that the historical circumstances are different today, *but that the underlying theology was and is wrong*. If the RCA were right, then if the circumstances in the USA were to resemble those in the Netherlands of the sixteenth and seventeenth centuries, the church would have to begin "destroying all idolatry and false worship of the Antichrist" all over again. The RCA *could not* do this because the American Constitution (fortunately) renders it impossible. However, far more importantly, the RCA *should not wish* to do so, because such an approach embodies a mistaken ideology.

Moreover, we must remember what the phrases "all idolatry and false worship" and "kingdom of antichrist" meant when

---

21. Dennison (*RC*, 2:447).

22. https://www.crcna.org/welcome/beliefs/confessions/belgic-confession.

the Belgic Confession was written (1561): they referred to Roman Catholicism. Is this what some Reformed advocates of supersessionism believe? That if the historical context were favorable, they would be obligated to destroy Roman Catholicism wherever possible? If not, why do they no longer think so? Why do Reformed advocates of supersessionism think differently about these things today? What has changed? Only the cultural climate? The only reason *ought* to be that such advocates are prepared to review their *theology* today. The Christianized Roman Empire fought paganism, and the early Reformed magistrates fought Roman Catholicism (and other alleged heresies). But the underlying ideology was the same: the Messianic kingdom exists *today*, and the power of Christ that characterizes this kingdom has been given to the earthly rulers, from emperors to city magistrates. They must use this power—if necessary, with violence—to destroy their adversaries. Even the Belgic Confession originally said so.

In reality, the power of the Antichrist will be broken only at the second coming of Christ, and not before (see, e.g., 2 Thess. 2:3–10; Rev. 19:19–20).[23] The kingdom of the Antichrist will have to yield to the kingdom of the Messiah, and this will occur only when the Son of Man comes on the clouds of heaven. However, if you believe that the Messianic kingdom exists *now*, then it stands to reason that you would consider yourself an instrument in God's hand to destroy the kingdom of the Antichrist as much as possible already now, which kingdom has historically referred to Judaism, then Roman Catholicism, and subsequently rival forms of Protestantism. The kingdom of God must become manifest more and more openly and clearly, not only by the preaching of the Word of God but also through active suppression of every false (in the Belgic Confession: all non-Reformed) religion. State and church must work together in this suppression: the church by exposing the evil, the state by punishing this evil.

So then, the emperor (the state) and the pope (the church) must together fight the enemies of God—with swords and with words—only this time in a Reformed manner, viz., as Reformed magistrates and Reformed church leaders. In practice, the magistrates in the Netherlands rarely used violence, and did not formally forbid

---

23. For the name "Antichrist," see 1 John 2:18, 22; 4:3; 2 John 1:7.

all non-Reformed religions. What they did, though, was tell the non-Reformed believers to meet only in buildings that were not outwardly recognizable as church buildings. This situation lasted until the French occupation, beginning in 1795. In the Netherlands, many such "clandestine churches" (Dutch *schuilkerken*) existed — Roman Catholic, Lutheran, Mennonite, Remonstrant (Arminian) — many of which are still being used as church buildings. To this may be added the synagogues, for naturally the Jews were just as dangerous as the Catholics and the Remonstrants, if not more so.

4.3.4 Abraham Kuyper

Although Abraham Kuyper was a staunch ally of supersessionism and anti-millennialism, he did reject the mistaken implications of the original Article 36 of the Belgic Confession. In the Reformed Churches in the Netherlands, which under his guidance broke away from the Dutch Reformed Church in 1886, Article 36 was formally revised, and accepted only in the abridged form; no longer did it speak of "destroying all idolatry and false worship." The political party that Kuyper founded, the Anti-Revolutionary Party (a name inspired by Guillaume Groen van Prinsterer[24]), chose a radically different political philosophy, rooted in Kuyper's doctrine of sphere sovereignty: the state is sovereign only within its own sphere; that is, its task is limited to the maintenance of public justice. The state is not entitled to interfere with the internal life and functioning of other spheres, such as the church (denominations and local churches), marriage, the family, the school, the business company, the party, and so on. In this respect, Kuyper made tremendous progress; his notion of sphere sovereignty inspired Herman Dooyeweerd to develop his theory of the modal aspects.[25] However, one thing that Kuyper never did, as far as I am aware, is this: *he never questioned the underlying supersessionist theology of Article 36*. Kuyper did well, but he was not consistent. His view entailed tremendous progress: during his time of leadership as prime minister of the Netherlands (1901–1905), the States-General could not possibly have convened a National Synod, as had happened

---

24. Here the prefix "Anti" does not mean "contra" but "instead of": instead of revolution, the gospel. (N.B. "Groen" is not a first name, but the first part of the family name.)

25. See Ouweneel (2014).

in 1618–19 (the Synod of Dordt).²⁶ Such interference by the state in church matters had become unthinkable in Kuyper's day (and today even more so, though no longer on theological but on secular grounds). However, Kuyper did maintain the underlying theology and ideology of supersessionism from which the Belgic Confession in 1561 and the States-General in 1618 had adopted the idea of a government fighting for Christian truth.

Interestingly, in the Netherlands today there is a hyper-Calvinist political party, the SGP (*Staatkundig Gereformeerde Partij*, "Political Reformed Party"), which in fact is the oldest existing political party in the country. In the first sentence of its party platform it says that it strives for "a government that is entirely based upon the ordering of God as revealed in Holy Scripture." "*Therefore*," the party "stands for the maintenance of the unabridged Article 36 of the Belgic Confession" (italics added). This is a stunning *non sequitur*. The leaders of the SGP have often been asked whether, if they were to gain the majority in the Dutch Parliament, they would outlaw the Roman Catholic Church, and perhaps also the Evangelical free churches. Their answers have usually been evasive (which perhaps explains why the SGP's constituency has always been minuscule).

In 2015, a Reformed lawyer in the Netherlands (Cor Verkade) wrote that the theocratic ideas of the SGP should never have been included in its party platform because these ideas were rooted in the objectionable replacement theology.²⁷ He argued that the founders of the SGP believed that the Bible calls for the (true) Christians to establish a divinely ordered national state in the sense of the Messianic kingdom (Dutch *heilstaat*), whereas such a commandment was given to Israel alone.²⁸ Exactly! How appropriate! But what if you think you *are* (spiritual) Israel? Verkade is a Reformed thinker who explicitly exposed the underlying supersessionism of both the Belgic Confession and this hyper-Calvinist political party. We will see in a moment (§4.5 below) how various forms of the "Netherlands = Israel" delusion function in this type of thinking.

---

26. See note 7 above.
27. https://www.rd.nl/opinie/theocratie-is-restant-vervangingstheologie-1.445753.
28. https://www.trouw.nl/home/sgp-ers-vragen-zich-af-willen-we-nog-wel-een-christelijke-heilstaat~a845c098/.

4.4 Mennonites: Evangelicals *Avant la Lettre*
4.4.1 Anabaptists

The era of the Reformation, like others, showed us that eschatology cannot be severed from the political *powers*. The prevailing powers — the winners of history — leave behind the authoritative writings. Thus, how we think about Montanism (second/third century) has been determined by the *ruling* church of that time because they alone have left behind explanatory writings. The same is true for Donatism, a movement of the fourth and fifth centuries, which was partly influenced by Montanism. Independent sources might have shed quite a different light on these movements, perhaps allowing us to view them as early harbingers of the Reformation.

The same type of *power thinking* also plays a role in our judgment of the Anabaptist movement. I am not referring here to the vicious eschatology of the extreme Anabaptists, who, under the guidance of John of Leyden and others, created havoc in the German city of Münster (§4.3.2). No, I am referring to the moderate Mennonites, the totally non-violent followers of the Frisian preacher Menno Simons, who through their diligence and simple lifestyle made an enormous contribution to the Dutch economy, and elsewhere. From the seventeenth to the nineteenth centuries, the Reformed *powers* suppressed the Mennonites (as they did with the Roman Catholics and the Remonstrants [Arminians]), initially with fire and sword.

A striking example is the following. In 1523 the Swiss Reformer Ulrich Zwingli advocated believers' baptism, on simple biblical grounds ("Whoever believes and is baptized will be saved," Mark 16:16). However, for political reasons the city council of the Swiss city of Zürich did not wish to renounce infant baptism because it was crucially important for registration with the civil authorities.[29] This led Zwingli to change his position so radically that he soon became a fierce opponent of the Anabaptists.[30] His main argument against the Anabaptist view seems not to have been theological at all, but rather political, supported with a (mistaken) appeal to the Bible: those who rebelled against infant baptism were rebelling against the legal authorities (Rom. 13:2–5). In other words, the *gov-*

---

29. The same was true in the Netherlands until 1811.
30. See, e.g., Strübind (2003).

ernment of city, province, or state decided what people must believe. In 1526, with Zwingli's full support, the city council legislated the death penalty for the Anabaptists, and in 1527, Felix Mantz was the first Anabaptist who was executed by drowning in the Lake of Zürich—a punishment specifically designed for people who had immersed others in baptism in that same Lake.

Thus, the three great Reformers always chose the side of the Protestant authorities. Zwingli did this in Zürich, Calvin did it in Geneva, and Luther did it when he chose the side of the powers against the poor peasants with their justified demands for justice (the German Peasants' War, 1524–1526). The Dutch Calvinists did it, for instance, when they allowed the Dutch civil authorities to convene the Synod of Dordt, and order the production of the States Translation of the Bible (see §4.3.2). Of course, no violence was involved—although the Remonstrants were illegally and forcibly expelled from the Synod—but it was all the very same principle: the state was ruling the church. Today, this is most clearly seen in the Church of England, whose head is the British monarch, whether or not he or she is a believer. New bishops are first chosen by the king, then the prime minister (who may be an atheist) "advises" the monarch, who then formally "nominates" the prime minister's choice. Thereafter, the diocese's College of Canons meets to "elect" the new bishop. The odor of caesaropapism (see §4.1.2) fills the air.

In opposition to all this power politics of the three best known Reformers stood the Mennonites, followers of that other Reformer, Menno Simons, who definitely deserves a place alongside the others. The Mennonites oppose(d) all violence, all use of weapons, all power thinking, all formation of Protestant national churches and state churches, all ties between governments and churches, and so on. Menno Simons sharply condemned John of Leyden, and wrote emphatically that the enemies of God, including the false religions, would be condemned—not by Protestant magistrates today but— only at the second coming of Christ.[31] Simons looked forward to the second coming because at that time the earthly manifestation of the kingdom of God would be announced: "[I]f someone declares himself king in the kingdom and dominion of Christ, as John of Leyden did in Münster, together with Adonijah he will not remain unpun-

---

31. Wenger (1956, 47).

ished, for the true Solomon, Christ Jesus himself, must possess the kingdom, and sit eternally on the throne of David [1 Kings 2]."[32]

In contrast with Luther and Calvin, the Mennonite leaders lived in the strong expectation of the Lord's imminent return. In the meantime, they lived non-violently, happily prepared to undergo the martyr's death, if necessary. Just as the Reformers were closely allied with the Augustine of the post-Constantinian shift, the Mennonites were instead allied with the Christians of the pre-Constantinian shift, those of the first centuries of the Christian era: believers *now* suffering with Christ, who will *soon* be sharing in the kingdom at his coming.[33] Thus, there were clear pre-millennialist tendencies within the non-violent, peaceful segment of the Mennonites, though it seems that they became more outspoken for the first time in the nineteenth century.[34]

4.4.2 Mennonites and Jews

All this does not mean that Mennonite relationships with the Jews were of one kind.[35] Some early Anabaptists converted to Judaism, while others formed a kind of Amish-Jewish cult, which still exists in a few places in the United States and in Australia. Some American families seem to maintain a kind of Jewish-Mennonite interfaith lifestyle in their homes.

The so-called "Amish," the strictest of all Mennonites, have a natural affection for orthodox Jews; their lifestyle and that of certain (ultra-)orthodox Jewish groups exhibit various similarities when it comes to (modest, old-fashioned) dress, culture (isolation, strict family life), and language (Pennsylvania Dutch [*deutsch* = German] and Yiddish are both basically Germanic dialects, both maintained even in non-German-speaking environments like Russia and North America). At the same time, Mennonites also believe that the Jews in general are guilty of the death of Jesus, and some of them believe that WASPs (White Anglo-Saxon Protestants) are the true descendants of the twelve tribes of Israel.[36]

---

32. Ibid., 199; see also P. Patterson in Bingham and Kreider (2016, 337–54).
33. Cf. Rom. 8:17; 2 Tim. 2:12; 1 Pet. 4:12–13; Rev. 20:4–6.
34. Regarding Mennonite dogmatics, see Wenger (1952) and Lehman (1971).
35. https://en.wikipedia.org/wiki/Anabaptist–Jewish_relations.
36. Cf. the so-called British-Israel Church of God; see http://www.british-israel.ca/

Quite remarkably, in 2011 some Amish and other Mennonites travelled to Israel to confess the sins of Anabaptist anti-Semitism and indifference to Jewish suffering, especially during the Shoah. They declared themselves to be "Christian Zionists." In a letter, they wrote: "On this day, we, representing Anabaptist people, humble ourselves and seek your forgiveness for our collective sin of pride and selfishness by ignoring the plight of the Jewish people and the nation of Israel."[37] Other Mennonites have done the opposite, and have sided with Palestinian Christians against the Israelis.

In the twentieth century, the Dutch Anabaptists became more and more liberal, and as a consequence also largely lost their eschatological interests. Nevertheless, orthodox European Mennonites can be viewed as the forerunners of the Evangelical movement arising in the nineteenth century. In this movement, supersessionism, amillennialism, and covenantal universalism were radically rejected, along with all violent power thinking—and usually also infant baptism. The first Baptist churches in the Netherlands (1845) emerged from the English Baptist movement, which in 1609 had originated through contacts with Dutch Anabaptists. The first member of the Plymouth Brethren in the Netherlands, from 1851, was the former Anabaptist G. Willink. Especially the Plymouth Brethren, first and foremost J. N. Darby, opposed all kinds of political power thinking, and have revitalized (pre-)millennialism and therefore also the attitude of early Evangelicals toward the Jews. Interestingly, Darby and several other early Plymouth Brethren were "household baptists" (nearly paedo-baptists), not credo-baptists.

The Catholic-Apostolic movement, too, which originated in England more or less at the same time as the Plymouth Brethren, was thoroughly pre-millennialist, and opposed to all political power thinking. If J. N. Darby was the most original and influential thinker among (early) Plymouth Brethren, E. Irving played this role among the Catholic-Apostolic congregations. In the Netherlands, members of the patrician family of Van Oordt played a role among both Catholic-Apostolic and Plymouth Brethren. The important Dutch organization "Christians for Israel" (Dutch *Christenen voor*

BETATEST/about.html.
37. http://www.mennoworld.org/archived/2011/1/3/anabaptists-visit-israel-seek-reconciliation-among/?page=1.

Israël), established in 1980, was and is led to this day by members of the Van Oordt family.

4.5 Israel and the Netherlands

4.5.1 The Second Reformation

Reformed supersessionism and amillennialism, linked with speculations concerning something called "spiritual Israel," have generated very strange parallelisms drawn since the sixteenth century between Israel and various Western Christian countries.

Let us look first at the assumed parallelisms between Israel and the Netherlands. One Dutch author put it this way: "The house of slavery in Egypt and the Spanish tyranny, the Pharaoh and [the Spanish king] Philip II, Moses and Willem of Orange, Israel and the Netherlands. . . . How many times have comparisons been made between these situations, persons, and countries since the origin of the Netherlands as an independent state?"[38]

The national anthem of the Netherlands—the oldest extant national anthem in the world—is about William of Orange,[39] *pater patriae* ("Father of the Fatherland"), founder of the independent Netherlands, and is accordingly entitled the *Wilhelmus*.[40] It has no fewer than fifteen stanzas.[41] In the eighth stanza, the (unknown) poet suggests a parallel between King David and Willem of Orange, and between Israel and the Netherlands:[42]

> O David, thou soughtest shelter
> From King Saul's tyranny.
> Even so I [William] fled this welter
> And many a lord with me.
> But God the LORD did save me
> From exile and its hell

---

38. Golverdingen (1971, 121).
39. Nicknamed William the Silent, not to be confused with men of the same name, such as the later William of Orange who became king William III of England in 1689.
40. "Wilhelmus" is the Latinized form of the name Willem (Wilhelm, William).
41. For a poetic translation, see https://en.wikipedia.org/wiki/Wilhelmus.
42. The Dutch reads: "Als David moeste vluchten voor Saul den tyran: soo heb ick moeten suchten met menich edelman: maer Godt heeft hem verheven, verlost uit alder noot, een coninckrijk ghegheven in Israel seer groot."

And, in His mercy, gave him
A realm [lit., kingdom] in Israel.

I also think here of a poem of one of the greatest Dutch poets, Joost van den Vondel: *Verghelijckinge van de verlossinge der kinderen Israels met de vrijwordinge der vereenichde Nederlandtsche Provincien* ("Comparison between the Redemption of the Children of Israel and the Liberation of the United Dutch Provinces"). And a well-known pastor from the Second Reformation, Herman Witsius, in his *Twist des Heeren met zynen wyngaert* ("The LORD's Quarrel with his Vineyard," an allusion to Isa. 5), extensively elaborated this comparison, and even spoke of the *Neerlandts Israël* ("Dutch Israel").[43] The Dutch historian Gerrit Groenhuis wrote:

> We find the comparisons between the Netherlands and Israel mostly in the writings of the orthodox Reformed pastors: in the work of figures such as the Teellincks [especially Willem, d. 1629], [Godefridus] Udemans [d. 1649], [Daniel] Souterius [d. 1634], and later in the seventeenth century [Jodocus] Van Lodensteyn [d. 1677], [Abraham] Van de Velde [d. 1677] and [Herman] Witsius.... It is here that it can be established that the parallelisms between the Netherlands and Israel are more than fashion or parlance. Especially among the representatives of the Second Reformation, it turns out that the frequent references to Israel belong to the core of the radical Reformed conviction.[44]

In short: *we Dutch are the true Israel in God's eyes* — at least according to some Dutch.

In his historical work, *De wonderen des Allerhoogsten* ("The Miracles of the Most High," 1668), Dutch theologian Abraham van de Velde (just mentioned) formulated a complete identification of Israel and the Netherlands: "... for YHWH has redeemed Jacob, and has glorified himself in Israel [cf. Isa. 44:23], and has made known this miracles to the [Dutch] Provinces." Some sympathizers who lived abroad also called the Netherlands the "New Jerusalem"; Van de Velde himself spoke of "Israel, our Fatherland." It has been observed that this kind of thinking was inconceivable apart from Reformed covenantal theology, including the notion of something

---

43. For these and many other examples, see Groenhuis (1977, 77–87).
44. Ibid., 81.

called "spiritual Israel" (supersessionism)[45] — and this seems to me perfectly correct.[46]

The Dutch theologian M. van Campen has written extensively about the "Dutch Israel" (or "our Reformed Judah") in his dissertation, *Gans Israël* ("All Israel").[47] Some of the best-known theologians who strongly advocated this idea were the Voetians[48] Abraham Hellenbroek (*Bybelsche Keurstoffen*), Herman Witsius (already mentioned), and Theodorus van der Groe (especially in his *Biddags-predikatiën*), and the Cocceian Joachim Mobachius (*De Basuine aan den Mond*). They loved to speak of *Neêrlands Israël* ("Dutch Israel: Jacob, Jerusalem, Zion"), and called the God of Israel *Nederlands God* ("the Netherlands' God"). In this way, they were not only describing the (supposed) special blessings and privileges given to the Netherlands, but they were also warning about the responsibilities that such advantages entailed, and which the Dutch were supposed to live out.

Especially two points amaze us in such an identification of Israel and the Netherlands. First, why this special focus on the Netherlands? Why not include *every* Christian country? Was this pure nationalism (and thus a work of the flesh)? Why would not England, for example, equally deserve such an identification? The answer would probably have been that England had not enjoyed such a wondrous liberation from "Egypt" (read, Spain). Actually, we will see that Christians in other Christian countries claimed similar identifications with Israel.

Second, how did these Reformed authors feel about the ethnic (non-Jesus-believing) Jews living among them? These, of course, could not be considered to be part of this blessed and privileged country of the Netherlands, but these Jews did claim to be the one and only Israel (together with Jews living all over the world). How very irritating! Such a self-identification by the Reformed with "Is-

---

45. Ibid., 85–86.

46. See also Kuiper (2009), though, who showed that various Calvinist theologians rejected this identification of Israel and the Netherlands.

47. Van Campen (2007, 223–25, 248–50, 272, 529–32, 571); see also Huisman (1983); Op 't Hof (1984); Bisschop (1993); Van Eijnatten (1993).

48. Voetians were followers of theological leader Gisbertus Voetius; Cocceians were followers of theological leader Johannes Cocceius.

rael" can hardly be separated from bad feelings toward the Jews living among them. Here were two groups each claiming to be the true and only Israel.

4.5.2 Réveil and Secession

The Israel-Holland identification was still very much alive during the Réveil, a European revival movement during the early half of the nineteenth century. The leaders of the early Réveil like the poets Willem Bilderdijk and Isaac da Costa[49] — himself of Portuguese-Jewish descent! — viewed the Netherlands as a "second Israel," and stated that there "exists a special relationship between our fatherland and God," "a most special Providence of God regarding the Netherlands."[50] Historian and politician Guillaume Groen van Prinsterer expressed himself more carefully, when he wrote: "In how far can the Netherlands be called *a second Israel*? Not by *identification* but by *comparison*. The blessings of the gospel have been granted to the Netherlands not *exclusively*, but certainly *par excellence*."[51] In Groen's view, a middle position is expressed in the 1573 statement of prince William of Orange, that "we have made such a firm covenant with the supreme Potentate of Potentates that we are entirely assured that we, and all those who fully confide in this, will ultimately be set free by his magnificent and powerful hand, despite all his and our enemies; . . . ."[52]

The Reformed historian G. J. Schutte spoke, rather negatively, of

> the wet-blankets from the evening ferry of ultra-orthodoxy. People like the pastor of Ulrum, Hendrik de Cock, who wished to reinstate the doctrine of the Synod of Dordt 1618–1619, including the theocratic dominance of the public church in the ancient Republic [of the Seven United Provinces of the Netherlands]. Or his colleague from Benthui-

---

49. So, e.g., in his poem *Geestelijke wapenkreet* ("Spiritual Battle Cry"): "O Netherlands, one day you will become again the Israel of the West! God will gird your Church with light, your Kings with David's honor!"
50. Quoted in Smitskamp (1947, 18).
51. Groen van Prinsterer (1928, §105; also see §107).
52. Quoted in ibid., §165 (cf. §195); the quotation comes from a letter addressed at the city magistrate of the city of Alkmaar when it was being besieged by the Spaniards.

zen, the very bizarre pastor L. G. C. Ledeboer, who wept and lamented over the breach of Zion [Lam. 2:13], the broken covenant between God and the Netherlands, the lost Dutch Israel.[53]

These were all children of the great Secession (Dutch *Afscheiding*) of 1834, when many Reformed people left the national church because the latter had become like unfaithful and apostate Israel.

In the twentieth century, a pastor sympathizing with Ledeboer, G. H. Kersten, took the statement of William the Silent as the unassailable evidence that the Dutch people are "a covenant nation of the living God."[54] He repeatedly drew attention in his sermons to the striking similarities between Israel and the Netherlands, and between Moses and William of Orange.[55] According to Kersten, God had made a covenant with the Netherlands, and had thereby given this nation a special place among the nations, just as Israel once occupied such a position. Of course, he and others realized that the Netherlands as a whole had not remained very faithful to God and his Word; but they were confident that the orthodox Reformed were the faithful remnant of "Israel" in the midst of an apostate nation.

Abraham Kuyper, though he was a thoroughly Reformed advocate of supersessionism, understood very well that such nationalist ideas were completely mistaken. This is evident especially in his theory of sphere sovereignty, mentioned above, in which church and state were sharply distinguished.[56] Kuyper identified any talk of a *vaderlandse kerk* ("church of the fatherland," "national church") as a "tearing up" of the body of Christ (actually, this description as such is just as objectionable![57]), and he identified the idea of a *volkskerk* (national church, "church of the nation," in which church and nation are virtually identical) as "Jewish" in the sense that Israel as a nation and Israel as a religious community coincided, but today

---

53. Schutte (1992, 691 and references).
54. Kersten (1918, 12).
55. See references in Golverdingen (1971, 122–23).
56. See extensively, Ouweneel (2017, §6.5).
57. A church in the sense of a denomination or a local church can be torn apart according to its external form, but the true body of Christ, the Ecclesia, can never be torn apart.

a nation and a church can never coincide.[58] It is obvious why today most Reformed Christians in the Netherlands feel unsympathetic to ideas like those of the men of the Réveil and of Kersten. All of this leaves us with three options: "Israel" is the church, or "Israel" is the Netherlands, or . . . "Israel" is (ethnic) Israel, as it always was.

4.5.3 The Afrikaners

The Afrikaner nation—the Boers of South Africa—are a mixture consisting of approximately one-half Dutch, one-quarter Germans, and one-quarter French (originally Huguenots). Especially the Dutch and the French had deeply religious, Calvinist roots, to which the German immigrants quickly adapted. The Afrikaners had two types of enemies: the British at the Cape of Good Hope (who in 1804 had conquered the Dutch at the Cape), and the Bantu nations to the east and northeast of South Africa. In 1836, many Afrikaners began the Great Trek, away from the hostile and repressive British at the Cape, moving northeast to the regions later called the Orange Free State and Transvaal.

Especially during, and as a consequence of, this Great Trek, the Afrikaners, well-versed in the Bible as they were, had a strong sense of being a new Israel. They viewed themselves as having been sent to southern Africa to be a people of God over against the pagan (Bantu) nations in the area.[59] The Great Trek was seen as a parallel to Israel's wilderness journey, away from Egypt, the house of slavery, and on their way to the Promised Land, which was at the time still unknown to them. The most severe crisis of the Great Trek was the Battle of Blood River (1838), where fewer than five hundred *Voortrekkers* ("Pioneers") fought against an estimated 10,000 to 15,000 Zulus, led by King Dingane. The Boers' great victory—after their loud cries to the LORD, their psalm singing, and their famous vow to him—was evidence that God was on their side against the pagans, and that they were entitled to possess the Promised Land that they had reached. The Tugela River was their Jordan through which they reached this land that God had given to them. As God's covenant people, they not only felt superior to the pagans around them, but also, like Israel, felt obliged to maintain their position of

---

58. Kuyper (1905, 41–42); cf. Noordmans (1978, 380–81).

59. An important presentation of this idea was given by Willemse (1911).

separation, isolation, and purity (a view that was to become one of the roots of the later apartheid system).

Here again, we may presume that Afrikaner history would have been quite different if the Calvinist Afrikaners—especially the limited group of seceded Calvinists nicknamed the "Doppers"—had not adhered to supersessionism. This was the view that inculcated within them the sense of being a kind of Israel with a strong calling and a divinely chosen destiny, and thus a great sense of superiority.

4.6 Other Countries

4.6.1 Europe and America

Other Protestant nations construed and maintained similar views regarding their own countries.[60] Thus, the Prussian historian Heinrich Leo stated that in a special way God had been with the Brandenburg dynasty; in this respect it is interesting to note that, at the beginning of the seventeenth century, the Electors[61] of Brandenburg switched from the Lutheranism to Calvinism.

The English dictator, Oliver Cromwell, just like the English poet John Milton, was convinced that England was a chosen nation, a designation that actually referred to its faithful remnant: the (Reformed) Puritans. Because of Cromwell's supersessionism, it was self-evident that (Calvinist) England, like Judah and the house of David, was called to rule with and for God. England was the new Israel, and Cromwell himself the new Moses, views that clearly resounded in his most important speeches to the English Parliament, and in many of his letters.[62] Even today, the British-Israel Church of God proclaims, among other things: "We believe in the Throne of David as established within the British Commonwealth of Nations."[63] Their goal is to "preach and teach the truth about the true identity of the Anglo-Saxon-Celtic peoples, that we are God's covenant people." Every year, in the Royal Albert Hall in London, at the Last Night of the Proms, a poem by William Blake is sung, entitled "Jerusalem," put to music by Hubert Parry (1916). In this poem,

---

60. Smitskamp (1940, 151; 1947, 18); cf. Golverdingen (1971, 142).
61. An Elector was a German ruler who belonged to the limited company of rulers who elected the German emperor.
62. Hill (1990); Hale (1996).
63. See note 35 above.

both the holy Lamb of God and the New Jerusalem are situated in England: "I will not cease from mental fight, or shall my sword sleep in my hand: till we have built Jerusalem in England's green and pleasant land." This sentiment is far worse than ordinary replacement theology: this time, the spiritual Israel is not the church but the England itself.

As far as France is concerned, the anti-Enlightenment thinker, Count Joseph de Maistre, considered France to be the chosen nation with a special religious calling. Interestingly, this time the inspiration to this type of thinking came not from Reformed thinkers but from Roman Catholics. This is not really amazing: when it comes to supersessionism, the two have much in common.

And then, of course, the United States has been viewed as God's chosen country *par excellence*, a notion going back to the early (still Reformed) Puritans. Entirely in line with supersessionism, they freely applied the Bible's Israel passages to the USA. In 1900, the American senator Alfred J. Beveridge (Methodist, but sympathizing with the Puritans) said in a speech occasioned by the annexation of the "barbarian" Philippines:

> [O]f all our race [i.e., humanity] He [i.e., God] has marked the American people as His chosen nation to finally lead in the regeneration of the world. This is the divine mission of America, and it holds for us all the profit, all the glory, all the happiness possible to man. We are trustees of the world's progress, guardians of its righteous peace. The judgment of the Master is upon us: "Ye have been faithful over a few things; I will make you ruler over many things" [Matt. 25:21, 23].[64]

This kind of Americanism views the center of the world as no longer Jerusalem, not even Rome, but Washington DC, and Americans being the "new Romans," as Gerhard Mehrtens aptly described it.[65] Just as Charlemagne viewed his empire, which was (Frankish-) Roman, at the same time as a new Israel (§1.3.), Americans can be, at the same time, both the "new Romans" and a new Israel, destined to rule the world.

The view of the Second Reformation regarding the Netherlands, or that of the Puritans regarding England or the United States, as

---

64. www.mtholyoke.edu/acad/intrel/ajb72.htm.

65. Mehrtens (1987).

the "covenant people of Israel" was a typical product of an astonishing religious nationalism. In the case of the Dutch Guillaume Groen van Prinsterer and the American Alfred Beveridge, this view was possibly strengthened by Romanticism with its typical *Volksidee* ("idea of the nation"). At the basis of this delusion lay an overripe Calvinist covenant theology combined with the supersessionist delusion about the "spiritual Israel." It is extreme federalism, supersessionism, and of course also amillennialism, all in one. Taken together this constitutes a striking example of the extreme ideas resulting from mistaken starting points.

4.6.2 Theology and Politics

The remainder of this work will focus on the theological argumentation. But I ask the reader not to ignore for one moment the political and historical dimensions of all the issues that involve Israel. Advocates of supersessionism may write thick volumes full of theological arguments, and I respect this. But the roots of their paradigm lie not as much in theology as in politics, and this has been the case from the fourth to the twentieth centuries. It was supersessionist Roman Catholics who, during the Middle Ages, violently persecuted the pre-millennialist Waldenses, Cathars, Albigenses, Taborites, and Bohemian Brethren. It was supersessionist Protestants who violently persecuted the Anabaptists, and in England other deviant movements. Dutch supersessionists defended, until the nineteenth century (until the new Constitution of 1848), the right (or duty) of the state to meddle in religious matters, and to suppress heretical (read: non-Reformed) views. Without supersessionism and amillennialism, such a view would be unthinkable. The (Christian) rulers allegedly represent the King of kings in the present Messianic kingdom, even in violently suppressing everything that opposes Christ (read: opposes prevailing opinions).

How many violent pre-millennialists were prepared to persecute, or even execute, fellow Christians for their views? Of course, I am not claiming that modern supersessionists still advocate violence. They, too, have developed over time. But again, let them consider where the roots of this religious violence among Christians must be found: in ancient and medieval supersessionism. The moment a person begins to believe that people live already today in the Messianic kingdom, and that the (New Testament) Ecclesia is spiritual Israel, and that *Christ reigns today through ecclesiastical and political authorities,* then a Protestant government will arrogate to itself the supposedly God-given right and duty to restrain and punish all those who act in alleged opposition to Christ. Whether the leader is the pope, or a Protestant ruler, or a Reformed city magistrate before 1848 (in the Netherlands), such a leader views himself as the deputy (substitute, representative) of Christ on earth, whose authority must be established everywhere, with or without violence.

The Latin term for such a deputy or representative is *vicarius Christi*, literally: "vicar [deputy, substitute, representative] of Christ." This remarkable term has been applied in the past to the (Christian) emperor, to bishops, and to popes, and may be compared with the title "Supreme Governor of the Church of England," who is the English (later British) monarch. In a sense, in line with supersessionism, the title could be applied also to Protestant rulers, presidents, (prime) ministers, and even city magistrates. If Christ is the ruling King of kings, then every king or other type of ruler is his representative on earth. Therefore, we must recall the original version of Article 36 of the Belgic Confession is so important: "[The government's] office is not only to have regard unto and watch for the welfare of the civil state, but also that they protect the sacred ministry, and thus may remove and prevent all idolatry and false worship, that the kingdom of the antichrist may be thus destroyed and *the kingdom of Christ promoted.*"[66] Traditional (not necessarily modern!) supersessionism insisted that the kingdom of Jesus Christ be promoted in two ways: *positively* by preaching the gospel and founding churches, *negatively* by violently suppressing all that opposed Christ (read: the ruling opinion). But this is precisely what is attributed and assigned to the Messiah in Psalm 101, presupposing a *direct* Messianic rule over the "land" (earth), as foreshadowed by King David. We read on the one hand (v. 6): "I will look with favor on the faithful in the land, that they may dwell with me; he who walks in the way that is blameless shall minister to me." And on the other hand (vv. 7–8): "No one who practices deceit shall dwell in my house; no one who utters lies shall continue before my eyes. Morning by morning I will destroy all the wicked in the land, cut-

---

66. Dennison (*RC* 2:447–48).

ting off all the evildoers from the city of the LORD."

4.6.3 A Fitting Parable

Quite fitting in this context is, I think, the parable of the two slaves in Matthew 24:

> Who then is the faithful and wise servant, whom his master has set over his household, to give them their food at the proper time? Blessed is that servant whom his master will find so doing when he comes. Truly, I say to you, he will set him over all his possessions. But if that wicked servant says to himself, "My master is delayed," and begins to beat his fellow servants and eats and drinks with drunkards, the master of that servant will come on a day when he does not expect him and at an hour he does not know and will cut him in pieces and put him with the hypocrites. In that place there will be weeping and gnashing of teeth (vv. 45–51).

If we translate this text accurately, as do the ESV and others, we see that this is actually not at all a parable about *two* servants but rather about one and the same servant. This is because verse 48 says, "But if *that* wicked servant says . . . ," that is (as I read it): the faithful and wise servant of verse 45 has become a "wicked" servant in verse 48. With others,[67] I interpret this as representing two stages of church history. During the first stage, the Ecclesia is still living in the ardent expectation of the imminent return of Christ and his kingdom. However, this changed in the fourth century, first politically, later also theologically. The Messianic kingdom is no longer something to be looking forward to, because it is now viewed as something that *has already arrived*. The second coming of Christ has been identified with the end of world history, which by definition is far away. When Christ returns, history will cease, and the eternal state will begin. For the first time in church history, the expectation of Christ's second coming has died a sweet death — except for a handful of faithful ones who keep looking forward to that return. The servant, who in the meantime has become a "wicked" servant, says, "My master is delayed" (GNT: "will not come back for a long time"). In other words, "We have got the place to ourselves." This thought has been dominant now for over 1,700 years, that as long as Jesus stays away, the Christian authorities — Roman Catho-

---

67. See, e.g., Kelly (1896, ad loc.); Gaebelein (1910, ad loc.).

lic, Eastern Orthodox, or Protestant—run the place, bossing others around as if the world is theirs. At least, this view was dominant until the nineteenth century, when the Christian hope was finally revived.

The consequences of this view are certainly not only theological in nature: *the wicked servant begins to beat his fellow servants.* The leaders of the newly arisen "Christian" empire, and later of the "Christian" countries, initially Roman Catholics, subsequently Protestants, find their warrant in supersessionism because of the slogan: "Christ is reigning already now, namely, through us." And thus, the leaders begin to "beat"—often beat to death—all those who do not agree with their views: Donatists, Waldenses, Cathars, Albigenses, Taborites, Bohemian Brethren, Hussites, and later Protestants. However, the latter group, the Protestants, when they achieved power, exhibited the same supersessionist drive, and the Reformed were the fiercest of all: they began to suppress the Roman Catholics, the Anabaptists, the Remonstrants (Arminians), and even the Lutherans. Certainly during the earliest period, violence was sometimes definitely involved in this suppression.

However, even in the nineteenth century, those who took part in the Secession (see above) were persecuted by the "Reformed" King William I; their church gatherings were disrupted, their leaders were imprisoned. During those difficult decades, many of these Seceders emigrated to North America, where they eventually formed the Christian Reformed Church. Some of them were led by one of the foremen of the Secession, pastor H. P. Scholte, who went with his people to Pella, Iowa. Interestingly, Scholte was a pre-millennialist. In 1842, while still in the Netherlands, he had translated and published a book with lectures by J. N. Darby, given in French at Geneva, about the subject: *The Hope of the Church of Christ.* Darby was a pre-millennialist and one of the founders of the Plymouth Brethren. After Scholte's death, his second wife and two of his sons joined the Plymouth Brethren. The tables had turned: the violent oppression by so many supersessionist and anti-millennialist authorities was transformed into the peaceful and submissive attitude of the pre-millennialists.

Let us return to the parable of Matthew 24. The Master of the wicked slave ultimately returns on a day when the latter does not expect him, and at an hour when he is unaware of the possibility. No wonder: the servant expects his Master at the very end of world history, on the "last day."[68] He is not only badly surprised, but also severely judged. During the period preceding the coming of the Master, something happened that was not explained in this parable, but in the next one: the parable of the ten virgins (Matt. 25:1–13). There too, we find the same situation: the "bridegroom was delayed" (v. 5); he came "after a long time" (cf. v. 19, belonging to a third parable: that of the talents). All ten girls fell asleep. It is only "at midnight" that a cry is heard: "Here is the bridegroom! Come out to meet him" (v. 6).

I believe this is what happened during the first decades of the nineteenth century, an event of which Darby was only a part, and of which the Dutch Réveil, with W. Bilderdijk and I. da Costa (see above), was another part. This period of several decades was not just a matter of intense Bible study and new theological insights. Something happened, a call was heard, thousands of Christians awoke, precisely as we just read in Matthew 25: "'Here is the bridegroom! Come out to meet him.' Then *all those virgins rose and trimmed their lamps*" (vv. 6–7).[69] This new movement of pre-millennialism, involving the rediscovery of all the prophecies concerning Israel, was the tremendous countermovement against the supersessionism, anti-millennialism, and covenant universalism of so many centuries.

Here is one example: Dutch Bible teacher, H. C. Voorhoeve, wrote a book in 1866, called *De toekomst onzes Heeren Jezus Christus* ("The Future of Our Lord Jesus Christ").[70] In this book, he carefully examined the biblical prophecies, and accurately predicted the return of the Jews to the Promised Land, the establishment of their own state, the conversion of part of the Jews in the land, and many other aspects. Consider this: he wrote this book long before the Turks would be driven out of the Holy Land (which happened in 1917)! And remember that this state of Israel was established in

---

68. John 6:39–40, 44, 54; 11:24; 12:48.

69. When we notice that not only the wise awoke, but also the foolish girls, we think here especially of the Jehovah's Witnesses and the Mormons, prophetically active in that same century.

70. Voorhoeve (repr. 1922).

1948. But Voorhoeve described it all as if he had been present at the events himself—*all on the basis of what he found in the biblical prophecies*. He committed only one significant mistake: he thought that all these events would take place after the rapture of the Ecclesia, and this has turned out to be wrong. For the rest, he was perfectly right (see further in §4.7.2).

4.7 Recent Developments

4.7.1 Recent Reformed Voices

The reader may be wondering why, in addition to the thetical parts in this book, I am opposing especially the supersessionism of (in alphabetical order) J. Douma, A. Maljaars, S. Paas, O. P. Robertson, and S. Sizer. To be sure, their publications are relatively recent, and deserve a refutation because many Christians seem to agree with them. Yet, could it be the case that these five and several others are really involved in a rearguard action? You see, precisely in the Reformed world various newer, positive developments are happening. In chapter 3 above (note 11), I mentioned a large number of relatively recent Reformed publications in which—in a reluctant or a very outspoken way—other non- or no-longer-supersessionist sounds may be heard.

Here are a few interesting examples. Here and there, I will be referring to the Annotations to the States Translation of 1637, because these comments continue to be authoritative for many Reformed Bible readers. However, it is worthwhile to place these Annotations alongside several volumes of the Dutch series *Commentaar op het Nieuwe Testament, Derde Serie* ("Commentary on the New Testament, Third Series"), written by various Reformed authors in the Netherlands under the chief editorship of Jacob van Bruggen, who belongs to the Reformed Churches Liberated (in North America called Canadian Reformed and American Reformed Churches). I am referring particularly to Van Bruggen's commentaries on Romans[71] and Galatians,[72] in which traditional Reformed views are criticized in a refreshingly new way, for instance, with regard to Romans 9-11, and the place of Israel in the counsels and ways of God.

---

71. Van Bruggen (2013a); see also his colleague, H. Jager (1978, 234–37).
72. Van Bruggen (2013b).

On the other end of the spectrum are the congregations in North-America called the Netherlands Reformed Congregations. At the conclusion of the General Synod of 2007 in the Netherlands, the chairman of the Synod said that in the Netherlands Reformed Congregations, the time of the replacement theology was over. This was quite remarkable because, until that moment, in these Congregations Kuyperian supersessionism dominated the view of God's plan with Israel. One consequence was that people no longer believed that "Israel" in Romans 9-11 was "the church." They now believed that special promises remain and continue for the Jewish nation as "the beloved for the sake of their forefathers" (Rom. 11:28), both with regard to their conversion to God and the land promise, although on this last point the opinions are still not univocal. A process of examining and searching continues among these believers. But one thing is sure: their love for, and the prayers for, God's ancient covenant people have greatly multiplied among these congregations. This is not to say that all supersessionism has disappeared, but the changes are evident and widespread in this Reformed denomination.

Another example is the conference that was held in 2018 at the Theological University of Kampen (NL) on the subject of Israel. The conference had been organized by the research group *Biblical Exegesis and Systematic Theology (BEST)* of the (Reformed) Theological Universities of Apeldoorn and Kampen, and the Groningen university chair of the *Gereformeerde Bond* ("Reformed Alliance") within the Protestant Church in the Netherlands. Here, various participants from theological educational institutions, and from Reformed and other denominations, clearly stated that a revised theological view of Israel was strongly needed. Surprising criticism of traditional Reformed views was expressed, which is very encouraging and promising.

Among especially the Old Testament professors and Reformed professors of systematic theology, I mention in particular H. Berkhof,[73] and in recent times, M. J. Paul,[74] and the collaborative work of C. Van der Kooi and G. van den Brink.[75] Their publications offer in-

---

73. Berkhof (1986).

74. Paul (2013); M. J. Paul in Van Campen and Vergunst (2015).

75. Van der Kooi and Van den Brink (2017).

sights regarding Israel about which an Evangelical theologian can only rejoice.

Within Roman Catholicism, for instance, Hans Küng was an unsurprisingly ardent advocate of supersessionism. And yet, Küng displayed surprisingly nuanced insights regarding Israel.[76] The same was true earlier with Lutheran theologian J. Moltmann.[77]

Consider this quotation from H. Berkhof:

> The church keeps believing *for* Israel (that the people and its messiah will find each other), and therefore also *in* Israel (that within the way of this people the signs of God's covenant will always and afresh be and become visible). In the era of salvation we live in now, it retains, as the special address of the faithfulness and the promises of God, its own form as a separate people with a separate land and a separate way of judgment and grace, and thus with separate promises for the future (Romans 9:1-5; 11:28f.). This separateness can become a temptation to Israel to a proud isolationism, and an offense to the church because it shows her the limits of her universality. But for both it is a reminder that the present era of salvation is only provisional, which makes us look forward to a future when we will recognize each other and come together on the basis of the messiah Jesus, of which future the Christians out of Israel are through the ages the sign and guarantee (Romans 11:1f.).[78]

From Van der Kooi and Van den Brink, systematic theologians in the Protestant Church in the Netherlands (the former from a Kuyperian Reformed background, the latter from a Dutch Reformed background), we read these sentiments: it is

> Thus, it is plausible to see the return of the people of Israel to their land in 1948 as a hopeful sign of God's abiding faithfulness to his covenant. On the other hand, this promise may never be used in a political sense. It is unclear how God will fulfill his promises eschatologically,[79] but it is impossible to bring this fulfillment closer by human means, as some Orthodox Jews are well aware (note Gen 27 for the misery this effort will cause). . . . With respect to the land and the Palestinian conflict,

---

76. Küng (1992).
77. Moltmann (1996).
78. Berkhof (1986, 267).
79. This is a bit too modest, given that the prophets speak endlessly about it.

this perspective means that, for the sake of justice and compassion, which both Torah and gospel demand, solutions and compromises must be sought on the basis of current international law.[80]

This subject will be discussed more extensively in the second volume, where the present situation of Israel will be considered.

4.7.2 Classic and Moderate Dispensationalism

These recent Reformed developments exhibit something that seemed unthinkable when paradigms stood in rigid opposition to each other, but which began to emerge almost thirty years ago.[81] At that time, the church was confronted with classic *dispensationalism*, the theory of successive dispensations, distinct epochs in God's redemptive history in the world. It appears that today this form is defended by few academic theologians; instead, among them we encounter much more moderate and nuanced forms of dispensationalism. For example, in classic dispensationalism, the dispensations were so sharply separated that God could not possibly continue his dealings with Israel as long as the Ecclesia was still on earth. I think this consideration was the main basis for the doctrine of the secret rapture *before* the Great Tribulation. This rapture is described in 1 Thessalonians 4:17 (AMP), "Then we who are alive and remain [on the earth] will *simultaneously* be caught up (raptured) together with them [the resurrected ones] in the clouds to meet the Lord in the air, and so we will always be with the Lord!" All orthodox Christians believe in this rapture at the return of Christ, but not necessarily in this kind of rapture a number of years *before* Jesus' return. Nor is this what the text says.[82] The doctrine of pre-tribulationism (the doctrine that the Ecclesia will be brought from earth to heaven before the Great Tribulation) was thought to be necessary in order not to intermingle the distinct dispensations.

Recall the dispensationalist H. C. Voorhoeve (§4.6.3), who accu-

---

80. Van der Kooi and Van den Brink (2017, 377).

81. Ouweneel (1991).

82. *The* preeminent passage adduced as evidence for this is Rev. 3:10, "Because you have kept my word about patient endurance, I will keep you from the hour of trial that is coming on the whole world, to try those who dwell on the earth." The expression "keep you *from*" is understood to mean: make sure that you will be caught up from the earth before this "hour of trial" (i.e., the Great Tribulation) begins.

rately described in 1866 the future return of Israel to the Promised Land, and the establishment of their own state in that land. But as a pre-tribulationist, Voorhoeve was convinced that the restoration of Israel could occur only after the rapture of the Ecclesia.[83] In some dispensationalist presentations, the period involving the rapture of the Ecclesia itself constitutes a dispensation, although this period is supposed to last no longer than approximately seven years. These seven years are the last of the seventy "weeks" (periods of seven years) described by Daniel (9:24–27). The last half of this "week" is described in the book of Revelation as consisting of forty-two months (11:2; 13:5), or 1,260 days (11:3; 12:6; cf. the 1,290 days in Dan. 12:11), or "a time [read: a year], and times [read: two years] and half a time" (Rev. 12:14; cf. Dan. 7:25; 12:7).

Today, this type of dispensationalism is rarely defended by academic theologians. The demarcations between the dispensations have become far more flexible. We see this at the beginning of the New Testament dispensation, where until AD 70 or shortly thereafter, a Jesus-believing Jewish community existed as a distinct movement *within Judaism*, a movement with its own synagogues that also participated in the sacrificial ministry of the temple.[84] As a virtual parallel to this, we have experienced since the mid-twentieth century not only the resurgence of the state of Israel, but also the rise of a global Jesus-believing Jewish community, including in the land of Israel. This movement wishes to identify itself first and foremost as a distinct community *within* Judaism, and not as a denomination within Christianity.

From the pre-tribulationist standpoint, this Jesus-believing Jewish community occupies a rather ambiguous situation: this community is without doubt a part of the body of Christ. Does this mean that, therefore, these believers would be caught up in heaven at the rapture, and does this mean that, during the Great Tribulation, a new Jewish remnant would have to arise? Or, in the words of leading Messianic Jew David Stern,[85] must these Jesus-believing Jews

---

83. See also the prophetic chart by H. A. Ironside: https://www.jesusissavior.com/BTP/Dr_Harry_Ironside/ revelation_chart.htm, and a similar chart by A. E. Booth (1999).
84. See especially Acts 3:1; 21:18–26; 24:17; cf. 28:17.
85. Stern (1999, 804).

choose between being raptured along with (the rest of) the Christian Ecclesia before the Great Tribulation, *or*, in solidarity with (the rest of) Israel, passing through the Great Tribulation? This is a fair question, though not a valid theological argument. Yet, in the entire discussion between pre-, mid-, and post-tribulationists,[86] this subject ought not to be overlooked. The historical facts have not refuted the biblical data as such—of course they haven't—but have definitely cast doubt on the dispensationalist-pre-tribulationist interpretation of them.

4.7.3 Classic and Moderate Federalism

Classic federalism, or classic covenant theology, basically acknowledges no other covenants than the covenant of works and the covenant of grace, and does not divide human history into a series of dispensations. The last thirty years has seen the rise and growth of a much more moderate federal theology. For instance, some Reformed theologians are led by their careful exegesis of Scripture to question the notion of a covenant of works, including the idea that the Sinaitic Covenant would be a kind of covenant of works.[87] These reconsiderations have significant consequences for Israelology, especially with regard to Israel as continuing to live under the Sinaitic Covenant. How could God, certainly after the Fall, have given to his own people a covenant in which their salvation would depend on their good works and on their own strength? How could any Israelite have been saved under this Covenant? How does this view of the Sinaitic Covenant fit with God's words after this Covenant had been broken by Israel: "The LORD, the LORD, a God merciful and gracious, slow to anger, and abounding in steadfast love and faithfulness, . . ." (Exod. 34:6). Did not and does not all salvation, also under this Covenant, ultimately depend on the mercy and grace of God?

Advocates of classic federalism might be quite astonished by the following remark made by orthodox Jew Pinchas Lapide, who was a professor of New Testament.[88] He argued that the rabbis never viewed the Mosaic Torah as a way to salvation. On the contrary,

---

86. See Ouweneel (2012a, chapter 10).

87. See Ouweneel (2011a, chapter 4).

88. Quoted in Wilson (1989, 21).

Lapide claimed that the Jews view salvation as God's exclusive prerogative, and that the Jews therefore advocated pure grace. He claimed that all the masters of the Talmud taught that salvation can be attained only by means of God's gracious love.

Judaism as a religion of pure grace! It sounds quite Reformational. The reader who may find this perplexing and confusing will find the solution in a careful study of biblical Israelology. This study should include meditation on this phrase that appears seven times in the Tanakh (six times after Exod. 34:6): "[Y]ou, O LORD, are a God merciful and gracious, slow to anger and abounding in steadfast love and faithfulness."[89] And if I limit myself to the terms "gracious" and "merciful," I think of this wonderful passage: "[I]f you [during your captivity] return [Heb. root: *shub*] to the LORD, your brothers and your children will find compassion with their captors and return [Heb. root: *shub*] to this land. For the LORD your God is gracious and merciful and will not turn away his face from you, if you return to him" (2 Chron. 30:9). This shows us at least these two things: (1) there is no true and lasting return to the land without a true and lasting return to the LORD, and (2) both of these returns are inconceivable apart from the mercy and grace of God.

Newer developments within covenant theology are correlative to a newer perspective regarding Israel and Judaism. Classic dispensationalism largely has developed much more nuanced expressions, and classic federalism underwent a similar development, so that the two positions can come together much more easily. In the summary by Reformed theologians Van der Kooi and Van den Brink: "Since the 1970s a new consensus has developed that supersessionism has no biblical basis but has its roots primarily in the ancient estrangement between church and synagogue. *Israel as a concrete nation retains an enduring theological significance.*" (italics added).[90]

---

89. Ps. 86:15; cf. 103:8; 145:8; Neh. 9:17; Joel 2:13; Jonah 4:2.
90. Van der Kooi and Van den Brink (2017, 347).

Chapter 5
The Old and New Covenants in the Tanakh

Rabbi Eleazar of Modin said: "One who profanes things sacred, and one who slights the festivals, and one who causes his fellow-man's face to blanch[1] in public, and one who nullifies the covenant of our father Abraham – peace be upon him – and he who exhibits impudence towards the Torah, even though he has to his credit [knowledge of the] Torah and good deeds, he has not a share in the life of the world to come."

Talmud: Aboth 11

By taking upon himself the Yoke of the Law, Israel has been self-doomed to a life of trial.

Morris Joseph[2]

5.1 Beginning with the New Testament

5.1.1 The New Covenant Today

ACCORDING TO Jeremiah 31 and Hebrews 8, the New Covenant was formally established with the twelve tribes of Israel:

---

1. I.e., puts him to shame.
2. Joseph (2005, 154).

"Behold, the days are coming," declares the LORD, "when I will make a new covenant with the house of Israel and the house of Judah, not like the covenant that I made with their fathers on the day when I took them by the hand to bring them out of the land of Egypt, my covenant that they broke, though I was their husband," declares the LORD (Jer. 31:31–32; cf. Heb. 8:8–9).

Verse 32 makes clear that the house of Israel (the ten tribes) and the house of Judah (the two tribes)[3] in verse 31 are literal references, and do not refer to some "spiritual Israel"; these are the descendants of the people with whom God made a covenant after the exodus from Egypt.

Please note here that the letter to the Hebrews is not addressed to "the Ecclesia" (99% of which consists of Gentiles) but *to Jesus-believing Jews* – literally "Hebrew people." Many of the things dealt with in Hebrews can be properly understood only from this viewpoint. There are many aspects that can definitely be *applied* to Gentile Jesus-believers, such as atonement through the blood of Christ, but the actual scope and purpose of the letter must always be kept in view.

We will later see how important it is that the New Covenant was established explicitly with the twelve tribes of Israel. Nowhere in either the Tanakh or the New Testament do the identities of "Israel" and "Judah" include a large number of people from outside the nation,[4] nor do they refer to a company called "the Ecclesia," 99% of which consists of non-Jews. (New Testament passages that have been taken by advocates of supersessionism to mean otherwise are discussed in the next chapter.)

Ample evidence for this claim will be supplied in this and the next chapters. But at this point, notice that in Jeremiah 31 the Gentiles are not *partners in* but only *witnesses to* this renewed covenant that God is making with the ten tribes and the two tribes: "Hear the word of the LORD, O nations, and declare it in the coastlands far away; say, 'He who scattered Israel will gather him, and will keep

---

3. Evidence that these are indeed the ten and the two tribes is found in, e.g., 2 Sam. 2:10; 1 Kings 12:21; Jer. 3:18; 5:11; 11:10, 17; 12:14; 13:11.

4. An exception, of course, are Jewish proselytes: non-Jews fully joining Judaism through circumcision (if male) and *mikveh* (proselyte baptism), and submission to the entire Mosaic Torah.

him as a shepherd keeps his flock'" (v. 10). This difference is clearly evident in Jeremiah 33:7–9 as well:

> I [says the LORD] will restore the fortunes of Judah and the fortunes of Israel, and rebuild them as they were at first. I will cleanse them from all the guilt of their sin against me, and I will forgive all the guilt of their sin and rebellion against me. And it [i.e., Jerusalem] shall be to me a name of joy, a praise and a glory before all the nations of the earth who shall hear of all the good that I do for them [i.e., the twelve tribes]. They shall fear and tremble because of all the good and all the prosperity I provide for it.

Two more passages may help us see the difference between Israel and the nations:

> . . . I will faithfully give them [i.e., Israel] their recompense, / and *I will make an everlasting covenant with them.* / Their offspring shall be known among the nations, / and their descendants in the midst of the peoples; / all who see them shall acknowledge them, / that they are an offspring the LORD has blessed (Isa. 61:8–9).

> *I will make a covenant of peace with them* [i.e., Israel]. It shall be an *everlasting covenant* with them. And I will set them [in their land] and multiply them, and will set my sanctuary in their midst forevermore. My dwelling place shall be with them, and I will be their God, and they shall be my people. Then the nations will know that I am the LORD who sanctifies Israel, when my sanctuary is in their midst forevermore (Ezek. 37:26–28).

Supersessionists clearly distinguish the Ecclesia (also called the "spiritual Israel") from the *unbelieving*, and often *hostile* Gentile world. But in the two passages just quoted, the Gentile nations are not unbelieving and hostile at all: they "acknowledge" that Israel is "an offspring the LORD has blessed," and they "know" that God is "the LORD who sanctifies Israel." How must we understand this today? Where are the Gentiles who are *not* part of the Ecclesia, and yet acknowledge the God of this Ecclesia? And what is this "sanctuary" that the Gentiles see standing in the midst of this Ecclesia? Supersessionists cannot explain the details of such prophecies. But those who take these prophecies at face value understand them much more straightforwardly: the passages refer to the twelve tribes of Israel that are richly blessed *in their own land* during the Messianic kingdom, with the rebuilt sanctuary in their midst (cf. Ezek. 40–45). This Israel remains clearly distinct from the nations that do serve the God of Israel and are allowed into this kingdom (cf. Matt. 25:31–46), but never become part of Israel as such. Neither are they included in Israel as proselytes, nor are they seen as part of the so-called "spiritual Israel."

5.1.2 The Place of the Nations

Only a few times are the nations identified explicitly as beneficiaries of the New Covenant, and these appear only in Isaiah. God says to the Servant of the LORD: "I am the LORD; I have called you in righteousness; / I will take you by the hand and keep you; / I will give you as a covenant for the people, a light for the nations" (42:6). Here, it is not literally said that the New Covenant, which is "for the people," is also a blessing for the Gentile nations, but the poetic parallelism does suggest such a blessing. The emphasis is on the Servant *himself* being a "covenant" for the people: in him are found all the blessings of the covenant.

More concrete is Isaiah 56:6–7:

> ... [T]he foreigners who join themselves to the LORD, / to minister to him, to love the name of the LORD, and to be his servants, / everyone who keeps the Sabbath and does not profane it, / and holds fast my covenant—these I will bring to my holy mountain, / and make them joyful in my house of prayer; / their burnt offerings and their sacrifices / will be accepted on my altar; / for my house shall be called a house of prayer / for all peoples.

Here is an interesting exegetical nut for supersessionists to crack: who are these "foreigners," *who are never said to become part of Israel*, but who come under the blessings of the New Covenant?

Only in the New Testament do the nations become much more prominent. Consider Jesus' reference to the "many" at the institution of the Lord's Supper recorded in Matthew 26:28, "... my blood of the covenant, which is poured out for many for the forgiveness of sins" (cf. Mark 14:24). Here, the covenant includes many more than simply the disciples,[5] and more than just Israel: these are the

---

5. The "disciples" of Rabbi Jesus (Yeshuah) (Mark 9:5; 10:51; 11:21; 14:45) are what the Jews would call his *talmidim*.

"many" who "will come from east and west and recline at table with Abraham, Isaac, and Jacob in the kingdom of heaven [i.e., the heavenly kingdom on earth]" (Matt. 8:11; cf. Luke 13:28; see also Matt. 20:28, "[T]he Son of Man came not to be served but to serve, and to give his life as a ransom for many"). Another reference to the many Gentiles that will be added to Jesus' followers is found in John 10:16, "I have other [viz., Gentile sheep] sheep that are not of this fold [viz., Israel]. I must bring them also, and they will listen to my voice. So there will be one flock, one shepherd." But notice the difference: the words of Matthew 8:11 will be fulfilled in the "age to come" (see next section); in the present, Jesus-believing Jews and Jesus-believing non-Jews have been joined into "one flock," one Ecclesia, one body of Christ (see extensively, Eph. 2 and 3, discussed below in chapters 11 and 12). No amalgamation will exist in the future Messianic kingdom: believing Israel and the believing Gentiles will remain distinct.

Consider as well 1 Corinthians 11:25 ("This cup is the new covenant in my blood"), where the (largely) non-Jewish Corinthian Christians are described as fellow partakers in the blessings of the New Covenant. The same is taught in 2 Corinthians 3:2–3 (cf. the parallelism between v. 3 and Jer. 31:33) and verse 6 ("ministers of a new covenant"). The same description is given of the (largely) non-Jewish Galatian Christians, who are called "sons of Abraham" (Gal. 3:7) and "children of promise" (4:28) according to the model of Isaac. This is the great *similarity* between the "present age"[6] and the "age to come,"[7] that is, the "age" of the Messianic kingdom. In both "ages" (redemptive-historical epochs), believing non-Jews are brought into the New Covenant. It is like the Abrahamic Covenant, which was established with Abraham and his offspring, but "in" whom also the nations were to be blessed. Similarly, the New Covenant was established with the twelve tribes of Israel, but "in" and "through" them also believing Gentiles are blessed.

In addition to this similarity between the present age and the age to come, there is this enormous *difference*: only in the present age are Jesus-believing Jews and Jesus-believing non-Jews merged

---

6. Gal. 1:4; 1 Tim. 6:17; Titus 2:12; cf. "this age," Matt. 12:3; 13:40; Luke 16:8; 20:34; 1 Cor. 1:20; 3:18; 2 Cor. 4:4; Eph. 1:21.
7. Matt. 12:32; Mark 10:30; Luke 18:30; Eph. 1:21; Heb. 6:5.

into the one body of Christ. The present age features this unity of Jesus-believing Jews and Gentiles; in the age to come, the Ecclesia will be in heaven, whereas on the earth, there will be a distinct believing Israel and distinct believing Gentiles. Instead of there being one single church that exists from Adam until the end of history, God's dealings with the world throughout consecutive redemptive-historical epochs involve various and differing believing groups.

The main point here is that *enjoying the blessings of a covenant is very different from being a partner to this covenant*. Here is a simple analogy: when two world powers adopt a peace treaty, the entire world benefits from it, because the possibility of war has been drastically reduced. But this does not mean that those nations who benefit are also *partners* to that treaty.

5.1.3 The Covenant Partner

In the debate with covenant theologians and supersessionists (the two groups often coincide), the crucial question is this: Who is God's actual covenant partner in the New Covenant? This is crucial, first, because these advocates acknowledge the existence of only one covenant people: the church since Adam (or since Abraham), that is (since the exodus from Egypt) the people of Israel, or more specifically, the reborn among them (the "true" or "spiritual Israel"). When Jeremiah 31 and Hebrews 8 tell us that this New Covenant is being established with "Israel," this is understood to refer to the church as identical with this "spiritual Israel."

Second, advocates of supersessionism believe that this New Covenant has been actualized or realized in the present era, whereas, according to Jeremiah 31 and other passages in the Tanakh, viewed in the light of the New Testament, the implementation of this covenant will occur at the second coming of Christ, namely, at the beginning of the Messianic kingdom (Heb. *'olam habba*, the "age [or world] to come"). This is not to deny, however, that the New Covenant has great spiritual significance already today. To be sure, it has not yet been formally effectuated or activated. But as we have seen, believers belonging to the (New Testament) body of Christ, Jews and non-Jews, have, so to speak, already been brought into the New Covenant. This is something like a marriage, which in Malachi 2 is also called a covenant: the marriage itself may not yet have been formally activated or effectuated, but already the couple-to-be-wed grants an abundance of gifts to all the wedding guests.

New Testament Jesus-believers have been brought under the Mediator of the New Covenant, who is their life, and whose blood, on which the New Covenant is founded, has cleansed them: "Therefore he is the mediator of a new covenant, so that those who are called may receive the promised eternal inheritance, since a death has occurred that redeems them from the transgressions committed under the first covenant" (Heb. 9:15; cf. 8:6); "... Jesus, the mediator of a new covenant, and to the sprinkled blood that speaks a better word than the blood of Abel" (12:24). "This cup that is poured out for you is the new covenant in my blood" (Luke 22:20; cf. 1 Cor. 11:25). However, in all of this, God's *actual covenant partner, the Israel that will be spiritually and geographically restored*, is not yet in the picture, except for the few Jesus-believing Jews who by faith have become members of the body of Christ. This the core of the matter: the New Covenant will be effectuated when the present era of the Ecclesia has come to a close, and at that time the converted and restored Israel will be the earthly center of the Messianic kingdom. The elaboration of these important biblical data will fill the following chapters in this book.

In the meantime, we might say that the realization of the blessings of the New Covenant already in the present age is, so to speak, God's program for God's kingdom. In the main passages concerning the New Covenant, Jeremiah 30–31 and Ezekiel 37, the Messiah occupies the central position: the Israelites "shall serve the LORD their God and David their king, whom I will raise up for them" (Jer. 30:9).

> "Their prince [i.e., the Messiah] shall be one of themselves [i.e., Israel]; their ruler shall come out from their midst; I will make him draw near, and he shall approach me, for who would dare of himself to approach me [without having been invited]?" declares the LORD. "And you shall be my people, and I will be your God" (vv. 21–22).

> My servant David shall be king over them, and they shall all have one shepherd. They shall walk in my rules and be careful to obey my statutes. *They shall dwell in the land that I gave to my servant Jacob, where your fathers lived.* They and their children and their children's children shall

dwell there *forever*, and David my servant shall be their prince *forever*. I will make a *covenant of peace* with them. It shall be an *everlasting covenant* with them. And I will set them [in their land] and multiply them, and will set my sanctuary in their midst forevermore (Ezek. 37:24-26).

When the King himself institutes what is called the Lord's Supper for his subjects—his followers, subjects, disciples (Heb. *talmidim*)—he does so in a clearly eschatological context by referring both to the kingdom of God and to the New Covenant, with an explicit reference to the future, to the Messianic kingdom: "I tell you that from now on I will not drink of the fruit of the vine until the kingdom of God comes.... This cup that is poured out for you is the new covenant in my blood" (Luke 22:18, 20). This is the context in which Jesus-believers—Jesus' *talmidim*—celebrate the Lord's Supper. They not only look back to the cross by eating and drinking "in remembrance of him," but they also look forward to the appearance of the King in glory because Jesus' followers know that, as often as they eat the bread and drink the cup, they "proclaim the Lord's death *until he comes*" (1 Cor. 11:26), that is, until the time when the kingdom of God and the New Covenant will have become full reality.[8]

5.2 Covenant and Israel

5.2.1 The Same Israel As Before

In Hebrews 8:8 we read, "For he [i.e., the LORD] finds fault with them [i.e., Israel] when he says: 'Behold, the days are coming,' declares the LORD, 'when I will establish a new covenant with the house of Israel and with the house of Judah.'" The opening words of this verse remarkably suggest that establishing the New Covenant entailed a kind of reprimand of Israel.[9] If the Israelites had fulfilled their responsibilities under the Old Covenant—which they could not have done in their own strength—then a New Covenant would not have been necessary. The Old Covenant failed, not because of its nature—how could this be, since God himself had given it—but because of the sinfulness and sins of Israel; as Psalm 119:126 says, "It is time for the LORD to act, for *your law has been broken.*" And the prophet says, "... [T]hey have transgressed the laws, /

---

8. See Ouweneel (2010b, chapters 8–9).
9. See Ouweneel (1982, 1:109–110).

violated the statutes, / *broken the everlasting covenant*" (Isa. 24:5). "They have turned back to the iniquities of their forefathers, who refused to hear my words. They have gone after other gods to serve them. The house of Israel and the house of Judah have broken my covenant that I made with their fathers" (Jer. 11:10). "Behold, the days are coming, . . . when I will make a new covenant with the house of Israel and the house of Judah, not like the covenant that I made with their fathers on the day when I took them by the hand to bring them out of the land of Egypt, *my covenant that they broke*" (31:31-32). Therefore, humanly speaking, God *had to* make a New Covenant with them, if he still wished to bless them. And this is indeed what God wishes to do.

Notice the phrase, "they have . . . broken the everlasting covenant." How can something that is everlasting be broken and thereby ruined? The Old Covenant is everlasting in the sense that the New Covenant is nothing other than *a renewal of* the Old Covenant. In other words, in the form of the New Covenant the Old Covenant will last forever. But this renewal is indeed necessary *for the very reason that it has been broken*. It must be restored on a new footing: one where the emphasis no longer lies on the (failed) responsibility of the people but on the infinite, sovereign grace and mercy of God.

In summary, then, the idea of the Ecclesia as the "spiritual Israel" is truly despicable.[10] It is not true that, because the Old Covenant with Israel had failed, God now established a brand new covenant with a group, 99% of which consists of Jesus-believing Gentiles. Do not argue that this *is* the new Israel. It is not. The Bible nowhere suggests that it is, as we will see further in chapter 6. Such a mistaken claim is like promising to A that you wish to make a new beginning with the same A — but then it turns out that you actually mean B. Ethnic Israel still exists; to *them* the Lord promises to *restore* the covenant. The Ecclesia is not the group that has failed under the Old Covenant and thus must be restored. Israel failed, and must be restored, and will be restored.

Nowhere in the Bible did God make a covenant with the Ecclesia *as such*. That New Testament believers benefit from the *blessings* of the New Covenant, that they have been placed under the cover of the New Covenant, is a different matter altogether. This differ-

---

10. See also Ouweneel (2010a, chapter 3).

ence consists especially in this: what is *proper* to the Ecclesia, as the body of the glorified Christ and as the temple of the Holy Spirit, cannot be assigned to this New Covenant, but far surpasses it. The New Covenant is made not with the "church of the Gentiles," nor with some "spiritual Israel," but with the *same twelve tribes of Israel to whom the Old Covenant had been given, which they had broken.* (Actually, of course, it is made only with the faithful among them, the *tzaddiqim,* the repentant and believing remnant, "the Israel of God," as has always been the case).

Notice the quotation at the head of this chapter: "By taking upon himself the Yoke of the Law, Israel has been self-doomed to a life of trial." Three times the Israelites said to the LORD, "All that the LORD has spoken we will do" (Exod. 19:8; 24:3, 7). This was taking the yoke of the Torah upon themselves. That yoke was not simply placed on them, but they *accepted* it through their threefold vow. This vow laid a tremendous responsibility upon the people. Someone who, on their own, without any urging or forcing, makes such a promise, and does so three times, must stand for what they declare. King Solomon said,

> Be not rash with your mouth, nor let your heart be hasty to utter a word before God, for God is in heaven and you are on earth. Therefore let your words be few. . . . When you vow a vow to God, do not delay paying it, for he has no pleasure in fools. Pay what you vow. It is better that you should not vow than that you should vow and not pay (Eccl. 5:2–5).

Israel has indeed vowed, but did not live up to its vow. It utterly failed, already before Moses had descended from Mount Sinai. They said, "*All* that the LORD has spoken we will do"; in reality, the majority of them did *nothing* of what the LORD had told them.

However, to this very same nation God gives a second chance — to A, not to B that claims to be A, or that supposedly replaced A. *The Ecclesia is not Israel!* God's promises to Israel are for Israel. More concretely: the prophets tell us that the *same* Israel that failed will be restored by the mercy of God. Except for sharing the universal basis of atonement laid down by Christ, these concrete plans that God still has for Israel have basically nothing to do with the concrete plans that God has for the Ecclesia.

If the Old Covenant with Israel has failed, God makes a New Covenant with that same Israel, specifically the ten and the two tribes of Israel (Jer. 31:31; Heb. 8:8). In practice this means that it is actually made with those who repent and believe, and return to the LORD. The context of Jeremiah 31 makes this perfectly clear. Jeremiah 30 and 31 speak of the return of Israel, after having been punished and sent into exile. The return to the LORD and the return to the land coincide: Israel returns *to its own country*, to the land where their fathers had lived, a land from which they had been driven by God. You cannot turn this into a spiritual nation and a spiritual land. Of course, there is a primary reference here to the return from the Babylonian captivity, but it is evident that the prophecy has a much wider scope by culminating in the Messianic kingdom. This is the order: Israel in its own land fails – Israel is driven out of its own land into exile – Israel repents – God in his mercy brings it back to the same land where it had lived before – it is in this land that it will be blessed under the rule of the Messiah. Into this sequence and portrait you simply cannot force-fit the alien components of Ecclesia and heaven!

5.2.2 Biblical References

To underscore what I just argued, let me adduce some relevant Bible passages, including those that mention, or imply, the New Covenant.

1. Its effectuation will occur in the "latter days" (Jer. 23:20; 30:24; Heb. *b'acharith-hayyamim*, "in the last [or, end] of the days" [cf. CJB]). In connection with Israel, this expression *always* refers to the Messianic kingdom and to certain preceding or accompanying events.[11] This claim contradicts, for instance, the argument that "with the coming of Christ in the flesh, his sufferings and death, culminating in his resurrection, the 'latter days' have begun."[12] But Hosea 3:5,

---

11. Gen. 49:1 (showing that Jacob's blessings had eschatological significance); Num. 24:14; Deut. 4:30; Isa. 2:2; Jer. 48:47; 49:39; Ezek. 38:16; Dan. 2:28; 10:14; Hos. 3:5; Micah 4:1; cf. the "last days" (Gk. *eschatai hēmerai*) in Acts 2:17; 2 Tim. 3:1; James 5:3; 2 Pet. 3:3. The only exception is Heb. 1:1 ("in these last days he has spoken to us by his Son"), where the end times are viewed as having already begun (cf. 1 Cor. 10:11; 1 John 2:18).

12. Maljaars (2015, 29–30); cf. the "consummation of the age(s)," which in Heb. 9:26 refers to the first coming of Christ, but in Matt. 13:40, 49 and 24:4 to

for example, was certainly not fulfilled in the time of the Gospels and the book of Acts: "Afterward the children of Israel shall return and seek the LORD their God, and David their king, and they shall come in fear to the LORD and to his goodness *in the latter days*." Nor was Micah 4:1 fulfilled in those days: "It shall come to pass *in the latter days* that the mountain of the house of the LORD shall be established as the highest of the mountains, and it shall be lifted up above the hills; and peoples shall flow to it."

2. Israel will be restored to its own land, not to some "heavenly country," but to the land where its fathers had lived in previous centuries.[13] In the prophecies about their return this always refers explicitly to the literal, physical land of Israel, not some new "land," physical or spiritual. Through this link with the past ("you will again live in the *same* land"), there can be no doubt about what land is intended. Those who believe that all these prophecies, including the Messianic promises, were fulfilled when Judah returned from the Babylonian captivity, must consider this *post-exilic* verse, Zechariah 10:9, which in a literal translation says, "I will sow them among the people: and they shall remember me in far countries; and they shall live with their children, and turn again" (KJV; cf. ASV, BRG, CJB). Here God seems to announce a *new captivity* that will occur after the return from Babylon (which we know to have begun in AD 70), this time in "far countries," and a new return from there, with this Messianic promise: ". . . The pride of Assyria shall be laid low, and the scepter of Egypt shall depart. I will make them strong in the LORD, and they shall walk in his name" (Zech. 10:11–12; see further in §5.6.2).

3. This ultimate restoration of Israel is preceded by the Great Tribulation: ". . . a time of distress for Jacob; yet he shall be saved out of it" (Jer. 30:7); "there shall be a time of trouble, such as never has been since there was a nation till that time. But at that time your people shall be delivered, everyone whose name shall be found written in the book" (Dan. 12:1). "For then there will be great tribulation, such as has not been from the beginning of the world until now, no, and never will be. And if those days had not been cut short, no human being would be saved. But for the sake of the elect

---

the latter days and the second coming of Christ.

13. Jer. 30:3; 31:23; 32:37, 41; 33:11, 15; 50:4–5; cf. Isa. 61:7; Ezek. 37:25–26.

those days will be cut short" (Matt. 24:21-22; cf. Rev. 3:10).

4. The unbelieving, wicked portion of the nation will be judged, that is, they will not be allowed to enter the Messianic kingdom: "I am with you to save you . . . ; I will make a full end of all the nations among whom I scattered you, but of you I will not make a full end. I will discipline you in just measure, and I will by no means leave you unpunished" (Jer. 30:11). "But everyone shall die for his own iniquity [cf. Ezek. 18:20]. Each man who eats sour grapes, his teeth shall be set on edge" (Jer. 31:30).

> In the whole land, . . . two thirds shall be cut off and perish, and one third shall be left alive. And I will put this third into the fire, and refine them as one refines silver, and test them as gold is tested. They will call upon my name, and I will answer them. I will say, "They are my people"; and they will say, "The LORD is my God" (Zech. 13:8-9).

5. All nations, especially those that have assailed Israel, will be judged and be subjected to the Messiah (Jer. 30:6-8, 11, and many more passages).

6. The one who triumphs over them will indeed be the Messiah, the Son of David, who will be the cause, the center, and the ultimate goal of the spiritual and physical restoration of Israel.[14]

7. Other than at the return from the Babylonian captivity, the future restoration of Israel will involve not only the two but also the ten tribes.[15]

8. This return is not (only) from Babylon (modern Iraq) but *from all nations worldwide*.[16] This has begun to become a reality only since the end of the nineteenth century, or even later: Jews returning to the land of Israel from all the continents of the world.

9. Justice, joy, and peace will rule in Israel without being disturbed ever again (which definitely was not the case after the return from Babylon—on the contrary).[17]

10. All the things just mentioned will constitute the fulfillment

---

14. Isa. 9:7; 16:5; Jer. 23:5; 30:9, 21; 33:15, 17, 22; cf. Ezek. 34:23-24; 37:24-25; Hos. 3:4-5; Amos 9:11; Luke 1:32, 69.
15. Isa. 11:12-14; Jer. 3:18; 31:27, 31; 33:4, 14; Ezek. 37:15-28; Zech. 8:13.
16. Isa. 5:26; 43:6; 66:20; Jer. 29:14; 43:5; 46:28.
17. Isa. 9:6-7; 32:14-18; 60:17-22; Jer. 30:18-20; 31:4-7, 12-14, 24-25, 38-40.

and realization of the New Covenant.[18] This is in line with the letter to the Hebrews (see especially chapters 8–9 of that epistle), which never speaks of "heaven" as the place where deceased believers supposedly go, but several times of the coming Messianic kingdom: the "world to come" (2:5), the "Sabbath rest" (4:9), the "age to come" (6:5), the "good things to come" (10:1), the "future[19] blessings" (11:20), the "kingdom that cannot be shaken" (12:18), the "city that is to come" (13:14; comparable to the "heavenly country" in Heb. 11:16, which apparently refers to the heavenly side of the Messianic kingdom).

From a hermeneutical viewpoint, these ten points are crucially important. No one should imagine have been freed from supersessionism without believing in the literal land promise. But some remaining advocates of supersessionism, though they believe in a literal national restoration of ethnic Israel in its own land and city, still maintain the idea of the Ecclesia as the "spiritual Israel," for which idea they spiritualize the same prophecies they have accepted for the literal restoration of ethnic Israel (spiritualism). It is difficult to find people who once advocated supersessionism but later abandoned the view *completely*; in most cases some old leaven remains. People must be consistent and choose: either the "spiritual" interpretation is the correct exegesis—I am not talking of spiritual "applications"—but that leaves no room for a literal national restoration of Israel in its own land. Or the prophecies are understood straightforwardly, so that "Israel" means ethnic Israel and "Jerusalem" means the physical Jerusalem. You cannot have both.

5.2.3 Straddling the Fence

When people began to identify the Ecclesia as the "spiritual Israel," they unsurprisingly began to dismiss the literal national restoration of ethnic Israel. This correlation can also be reversed: when Christians in the early centuries of church history dismissed ethnic Israel because "Israel rejected the Messiah!," they began to apply to themselves the promises given to Israel, thinking: "*We* are Israel, for *we* accepted Israel's Messiah." The true "Israel," then, was identified

---

18. Isa. 42:6; 54:10; 55:3; 59:21; 61:8; Jer. 31:31–33; 32:40; 50:5; Ezek. 16:60–62; 34:25; 37:26.

19. The word "future" renders the Gk. participle *mellōn*, "to come," found in Heb. 2:5; 6:5; 10:1; 13:14.

with those who accept the Messiah of Israel. But you cannot hold both positions; you cannot hold out a place for ethnic Israel in the plans of God, while at the same time describing the Ecclesia as the true "spiritual Israel." Too many Christians today want to have it both ways. But you will have to choose.

(a) Either the New Covenant *has been made* with the Ecclesia as the "spiritual Israel" (which may include *individual* Jews who come to faith in Jesus and join the Gentile church) — but in this case we must forget about any literal national restoration of ethnic Israel. Or the New Covenant *will be made* with ethnic Israel (or the faithful remnant of it), but then the Ecclesia as such cannot be smuggled in as one of the covenant partners.[20]

(b) Either the Saturday is the Sabbath also under the New Covenant — as indeed it will be honored as such during the Messianic kingdom[21] — or the Sunday has become the Sabbath under this Covenant. There is an essential correlation between viewing the Ecclesia as the "new Israel" that has come in the place of (ancient) Israel and viewing the Sunday as the "new Sabbath" that has come in the place of the Saturday Sabbath.

(c) I must add here the matter of baptism. My point is not so much whether infant baptism is more or less biblical than believers' baptism (I accept the valid discussions on this matter). Rather, my point is the way infant baptism is explained and defended, especially in Reformed theology, namely, as having replaced the circumcision of the Tanakh. Either circumcision will be the entrance portal for renewed Israel also under the New Covenant (cf. Isa. 52:1; Ezek. 44:7, 9), or circumcision has been replaced by infant baptism. Here again, there is an essential correlation between viewing the Ecclesia as the "new Israel" that has come in the place of (ancient) Israel and viewing infant baptism as the new introductory rite that has come in the place of circumcision.[22] I refer here again to Colossians 2:11-12, "In him [i.e., Christ] also you were circumcised with a circumcision made without hands, by putting off the body

---

20. It is a most embarrassing solution to assume that the New Testament is speaking of *two* "New Covenants," as Chafer (*ST* 4:325) thought; cf. Ryrie (1953, 105-25).
21. Isa. 56:2-6; 66:23, Ezek. 44:24; 45:17; 46:1, 3-4, 12.
22. See extensively, Ouweneel (2011a, chapters 1-8).

of the flesh, by the circumcision of Christ, having been buried with him in baptism." Understanding this passage as the advocates of supersessionism do enables one to conclude that (infant) baptism is the God-ordained substitute for circumcision.[23] In reality, the apostle was not *referring* to physical circumcision, but rather to the spiritual circumcision of the heart (regeneration), of which baptism is the outward sign.[24] One could find an argument in this passage for believers' baptism: baptism is only for those who have undergone the spiritual circumcision of the heart. But the apostle was not pointing to any "replacement" here: baptism did not replace circumcision, but baptism and circumcision are two *different* sides of the *same* matter: baptism is the external side (a visible sign), and regeneration is the internal reality (a matter of the heart).

5.3 The New Covenant

5.3.1 When Effectuated?

When will the New Covenant be effectuated? The letter to the Hebrews makes clear that, although this covenant will be formally effectuated by the Messiah only at the beginning of the Messianic kingdom, the foundation for this covenant was laid at the moment when the Messiah shed his blood on Golgotha, and offered himself as the true atoning sacrifice:

> [W]hen Christ appeared as a high priest of the good things that have come, then . . . he entered once for all into the holy places, not by means of the blood of goats and calves but by means of his own blood, thus securing an eternal redemption. For if the blood of goats and bulls, and the sprinkling of defiled persons with the ashes of a heifer, sanctify for the purification of the flesh, how much more will the blood of Christ, who through the eternal Spirit offered himself without blemish to God, purify our conscience from dead works to serve the living God. Therefore he is the mediator of a new covenant, so that those who are called may receive the promised eternal inheritance, since a death has occurred that redeems them from the transgressions committed under the first covenant (Heb. 9:11–15).

Thus, all the blessings that will be granted on that day to the restored nation of Israel, at the beginning of the Messianic king-

---

23. See, e.g., Van Leeuwen (1953, 38–39).
24. Ouweneel (2011a, §6.2).

dom (cf. Dan. 9:24; Zech. 13:1), can be granted *already today* to the believers from Israel who in the present era have joined the body of Christ, whose members are being gathered from both Israel and the Gentiles. Yes, *all* the members of Christ's Ecclesia, yes, *all* believers of all time, also those who lived before Israel, as well as those who will be born during the Messianic kingdom,[25] can stand before God on no other foundation than on the "blood of the New Covenant,"[26] the blood of Christ. *But this does not mean that they are all New Covenant partners*. The Ecclesia shares in the blessings of a covenant that is made with *Israel*. This does not make *them* "Israel" too. The Ecclesia and Israel are peoples of God with a different origin, a different character, and a different destiny.

According to F. W. Grant, how can the New Covenant be applied to non-Jewish believers? From the totality of biblical data the answer must be that this covenant is indeed *not made with them*, but all of its blessings can certainly *be administered to them*.[27] J. D. Pentecost emphasized the other side of the matter: that the blood of the New Covenant is applicable also to non-Jewish believers does not deny that this covenant is made with Israel, and not with the Ecclesia; and its applicability to the Ecclesia does not at all change God's essential promises made to Israel in this covenant.[28] Indeed, the blood of the covenant is being applied already now, but the actual effectuation and fulfillment of the covenant is yet unfulfilled; these await the reappearance of the Messiah himself.

5.3.2 Seven Promises

Because of the blood of the covenant, God — reverently speaking — can do nothing other than bless those who are covered by this blood. Therefore, the announcement of the New Covenant contains no demand from God, but only promises of divine action, expressed by seven verbs with future tenses (Jer. 31:31-34; Heb. 8:8-12):

> [1] *I will make* a new covenant with the house of Israel and the house of Judah, ...

---

25. Cf. Ps. 22:30–31; 78:4; Isa. 65:19–23.
26 Cf. Luke 22:20; 1 Cor. 11:25; Heb. 9:20; 10:29; 12:24; 13:20.
27. Grant (1902, 48).
28. Pentecost (1964, 124–25).

[2] For this is the covenant that *I will make* with the house of Israel after those days, . . . : [3] *I will put* my law within them, and [4] *I will write* it on their hearts. [5] And *I will be* their God, and they shall be my people.

[6] For *I will forgive* their iniquity, and [7] *I will remember* their sin no more."

The "laws" (Heb. *torot*) involved are not placed as a heavy yoke on the shoulders of weak people (cf. Acts 15:10). Rather, they are written in their hearts,[29] in order to be observed *from within* by the power of the Holy Spirit; as the apostle Paul puts it:

God has done what the law, weakened by the [human] flesh, could not do. By sending his own Son in the likeness of sinful flesh and for sin, he condemned sin in the flesh [through Jesus' death on the cross], in order that the righteous requirement of the law might be fulfilled *in us* [not "by" us], who walk not according to the flesh but according to the Spirit (Rom. 8:3–4).

This is the Spirit's activity within believers (cf. the great eschatological significance of Ezek. 36:26–27).

Three times, the Israelites vowed, with a complete lack of self-knowledge, at Mount Sinai that they would fulfill all that God's commandments would command them (Exod. 19:8; 24:3, 7). They vowed this either out of fear or with the best of intentions—or both—but without realizing that they would be able to do so only in God's strength, and thus only in humility and self-surrender to him. The LORD "said nothing" to their vow, and thus their vow "stood" (cf. the cases in Num. 30:4, 7, 14); it could not be annulled, so Israel had to bear its full consequence. In a sense one might say that, humanly speaking, God was obligated, but also that it was an act of God's *love*, to place the Torah on the people's shoulders in order to prove to them that they would be unable, by their own strength, to fulfill the least of all God's commandments (cf. James 2:10, "[W]hoever keeps the whole law but fails in one point has become guilty of all of it"). The people were not only sinful, but they were unaware of being so (cf. Rom. 3:20; 7:7). The Israelites were still minors, and thus under guardianship (cf. Gal. 4:1–7). In addition to other purposes, the Torah was lovingly given to Israel

---

29. Jer. 31:33; cf. Ps. 37:31; 40:8; Isa. 51:7; 2 Cor. 3:3.

in order to show them their incapacity to do God's will, and to lead them to humble themselves and confess not only their sins, but also their powerlessness to do good.

5.3.3 Minority and Majority

Hebrews 8:9 beautifully emphasizes this childhood through the expression "I took them by the hand," as a parent does with a child, sometimes even carrying the child: "The LORD your God who goes before you will himself fight for you, just as he did for you in Egypt before your eyes, and in the wilderness, where you have seen how the LORD your God carried you, *as a man carries his son*, all the way that you went until you came to this place" (Deut. 1:30–31). "Know then in your heart that, as a man disciplines his son, the LORD your God disciplines you" (Deut. 8:5). By contrast, believers under the New Covenant have reached the age of majority, they have come of age, and have become mature children of God who have learned to know both God and themselves (cf. Heb. 8:11b), because the Spirit of God's Son has been poured out into their hearts, through whom they say, "Abba! Father!" They are not only *children* of God *begotten* by the Spirit (John 3:5), but *sons* of God *led* by the Spirit (Rom. 8:14).[30] Notice the difference.

When the Israelites made their threefold vow to the LORD at Sinai, they were speaking like little children; they knew not what they were saying (cf. the childish talk of the disciple Peter, Luke 9:33). God did not reproach them at the time; he knew what was in his people's hearts. He began the long, long journey with them, from Mount Sinai in the wilderness to Mount Zion in the Messianic kingdom. This was a long journey of maturing, of deepened understanding of themselves, of God, of the significance of his Torah, and of the importance of the Messianic redemption. They needed deliverance not only from their *outward* enemies, but also from their greatest enemy, the one within them: "Then you will remember your evil ways, and your deeds that were not good, and you will loathe yourselves for your iniquities and your abominations" (Ezek. 36:31).

This was written not in view of the wilderness journey — during the childhood period — but in view of the end times: the times of

---

30. See Ouweneel (2009b, 112–16).

maturing. True wisdom is for the mature (1 Cor. 2:6; cf. Col. 1:28; Heb. 5:14). Maturing was the heart of Israel's redemptive history— from the Exodus to the Messianic kingdom—just as it is for the Ecclesia: Jesus Christ

> gave the apostles, the prophets, the evangelists, the shepherds and teachers,
>
> to equip the saints for the work of ministry, for building up the body of Christ,
>
> until we all attain to the unity of the faith and of the knowledge of the Son of God,
>
> to *mature manhood*, to the measure of the stature of the fullness of Christ,
>
> so that we may no longer be children (Eph. 4:11–14).

In the "latter days," the times of Israel's dispersion and distress (Jer. 30:7) will be over, and the days of the Messianic kingdom will begin. They will be the "days of the Son of Man," as Jesus calls them himself (Luke 17:22, 26). Then, and no earlier, the New Covenant with Israel will be "cut,"[31] or "completed" (Heb. 8:8 LEB[32]). This New Covenant, which will be formally effectuated with Israel *at that time*, is being administered to Jesus-believers *already now* (2 Cor. 3:3, 6), so that the blessings of this covenant anticipate its effectuation.

5.4 Covenant and Ecclesia

5.4.1 The Ecclesia of the Firstborn

The Bible does not speak of a covenant made in the literal sense with the Ecclesia as such. That Gentile Jesus-believers were formerly "foreign to the commonwealth of Israel and strangers to the covenants of promise" (Eph. 2:12) does not mean that now they *do* belong to the "commonwealth of Israel" and have become partners in the New Covenant. In coming chapters, this claim will be dis-

---

31. So literally in Heb., *k-r-t b'rit*, possibly alluding to the sacrificial animals that are "cut" to formally establish the covenant (cf. Gen. 15:10).
32. Gk. *sunteleso*, from *telos*, "end, goal," i.e., a completing covenant will be made, perfecting the beneficiaries of it (Delitzsch, 1857, ad loc.); cf. Dan. 9:24, "... to finish the transgression, to put an end to sin, and to atone for iniquity, to bring in everlasting righteousness."

cussed extensively because of its importance in the present debate.

Our conclusion must be that the New Covenant is not at all *the* specific description of the Christian position, as federalists claim.[33] The specific relationship of non-Jewish Jesus-believers is *not* primarily covenantal but rather characterized by two other relationships, neither of which is covenantal:

1. The Father-child relationship. Israel was God's "son" (Exod. 4:22; Hos. 11:1), but this does not mean either that sonship is inherent to all biblical covenants—it is not—or, conversely, that any father-son relationship is covenantal in nature. Fathers do not make covenants with their sons, and if they did, it would not be in their capacity as fathers and sons. To me, the fact that God is my Father—because I have been born of him (John 1:12–13)—is infinitely more precious to me than that he would be my Covenant God. In a King-vassal covenant, the King promises his goodness and protection to his vassals, as God does in the biblical covenants. But the Father is not good and protective to me because he has promised such, but simply because he is *my Father*; these benefits proceed not from what he said but from his very *nature*.

2. Two other New Testament relationships exist that are not covenantal at all: being members of the body of Christ and being living stones in the temple of the Holy Spirit.[34] Not only has Christ died for believers (this involves his work), but believers have been united with the glorified Man in heaven (this involves his person). This unity is due to our new nature and our new life—*Christ* being our life (Col. 3:4)—not to some covenant. To use a platitude: my eyes and ears, my hands and feet, are not part of me because of some covenant but because I was born with them; they are *part* of me. And so, through new birth and faith in Christ, we have become his eyes and ears, his hands and feet; we have become *part* of him (Rom. 12:3–8; 1 Cor. 12:4–31).

Yet, the New Covenant is definitely precious to the Jesus-believer—Jewish or Gentile—because the blood of this Covenant is the foundation on which they are standing, together with *all* believers of *all* redemptive-historical epochs, from Adam and Eve to the end

---

33. Regarding this, see Ouweneel (1982, 1:108–09; 2010a, §4.5).

34. I do not mention the Bridegroom-bride relationship because it might be argued that marriage is a form of covenant (cf. Mal. 2:14).

of the Messianic kingdom, in all eternity. According to its moral, spiritual nature it is neither typically Jewish nor typically Christian. The blood of Christ is only the *foundation*, for the relationship first between God and Israel, and then also for that between God and the Ecclesia. It is the divine foundation for the individual as well, since the forgiveness of sins and the writing of the Messianic *torot* in the hearts of believers are primarily individual matters.

In the letter to the Hebrews, blessings are discussed that far surpass what was explicitly promised in the New Covenant as such. An important example is the entrance of believers into the sanctuary as priestly sons (though the term "priest" is never explicitly applied to believers in Heb.): ". . . those who draw near to God through him" (7:25); "we have confidence to enter the holy places by the blood of Jesus, by the new and living way that he opened for us through the curtain, that is, through his flesh" (10:19–20). All Jesus-believers are priests.[35] But under the New Covenant, this blessing is *not* promised to every individual covenant partner; in the Messianic kingdom, too, this principle of entering into the sanctuary will be reserved for the priestly family of Zadok (Ezek. 44:15–31; cf. Jer. 33:17–18, "David shall never lack a man to sit on the throne of the house of Israel, and the Levitical priests shall never lack a man in my presence to offer burnt offerings, to burn grain offerings, and to make sacrifices forever"). But in the Ecclesia — consisting of Jesus-believing Jews along with Jesus-believing Gentiles of the present era — *every* member belongs to the priestly family, that is, to the "house" (i.e., family) of the "great priest": "Christ [our 'high priest,' v. 1] . . . we are his house, if indeed we hold fast our confidence and our boasting in our hope" (Heb. 3:6); "we have a great priest over the house of God" (10:21).

This priestly character of the *entire* Ecclesia — in contrast to Israel, where only one family was and will be priestly — is exceedingly important. The Ecclesia is called "the assembly of the firstborn who are enrolled in heaven" (12:23); this seems to be a clear reference to the firstborn of Israel,[36] who were later replaced by the tribe of the Levites:

---

35. In addition to the passages in Hebrews, see 1 Pet. 2:5, 9; Rev. 1:6; 5:10; 20:6.
36. Cf. Exod. 24:5, where it refers to the "young men" of Israel who offered the sacrifices; later, this was done by the Aaronic family alone.

Behold, I have taken the Levites from among the people of Israel instead of every firstborn who opens the womb among the people of Israel. The Levites shall be mine, for all the firstborn are mine. On the day that I struck down all the firstborn in the land of Egypt, I consecrated for my own all the firstborn in Israel, both of man and of beast. They shall be mine: I am the LORD (Num. 3:12–13).

In other words, the Ecclesia of the firstborn is the Levitical Ecclesia, the Ecclesia of those—the Levitical priests in particular—who are privileged to draw near to the LORD in his sanctuary.

5.4.2 Differences

This was the first difference: during the Messianic kingdom, the actual covenant partners, the twelve tribes of Israel, will observe the difference between those who are allowed to draw near to the LORD in his sanctuary, and those who are not. Therefore we cannot interpret Ezekiel 44:15–31 "spiritually," as if this is passage is being fulfilled today in the Ecclesia. It is not. *All* Ecclesia members are priests, but during the Messianic kingdom Israel will still have its distinct priestly (Aaronic) family. This example shows that supersessionist spiritualizing is invalid; it yields a number of insoluble contradictions.

The second difference is that during the Messianic kingdom Israel will have an earthly sanctuary,[37] whereas the Ecclesia has a heavenly sanctuary, already today. Israel's sanctuary will not only be earthly, but will be found in the "land of Israel," and nowhere else (Ezek. 40:2; 45:1, 4, 7–8, 16, 22). Consider especially Ezekiel 48:29, "This is the land that you shall allot as an inheritance among the tribes of Israel, and these are their portions"—twelve portions, for each tribe one portion. What remains of this when this chapter, too, is entirely spiritualized? Nothing. As clearly as there is the earthly Promised Land, there is the heavenly Promised Land, so to speak. As clearly as there is the earthly sanctuary, there is the heavenly sanctuary: "[W]e have such a high priest, one who is seated at the right hand of the throne of the Majesty in heaven, a minister in the *holy places,* in the *true tent that the* LORD *set up,* not man" (Heb. 8:1–2).

[W]hen Christ appeared as a high priest of the good things that have

---

37. Isa. 56:5–7; 60:7; 66:20; Ezek. 40–44; Zech. 6:12–15; 14:20–21.

come, then through the greater and more perfect tent (not made with hands, that is, not of this creation) he entered once for all into the *holy places*, not by means of the blood of goats and calves but by means of his own blood, thus securing an eternal redemption (9:11-12).

"Christ has entered, not into *holy places* made with hands, which are copies of the true things, but into *heaven itself*, now to appear in the presence of God on our behalf" (vv. 24; see above, Heb. 10:19-21).

The members of God's Ecclesia have the privilege of entering the heavenly "holy places" as a family of worshipers because Christ—typologically speaking—has sprinkled the "blood of the New Covenant" before and upon the "ark of the covenant" (cf. Lev. 16:14-15). But this concerns an "ark of the covenant" *in heaven*: "God's temple in heaven was opened, and the ark of his covenant was seen within his temple" (Rev. 11:19). Both this heavenly ark and this entering the heavenly sanctuary, potentially by *all* Jesus-believers, and the fellowship with divine persons in the heavenly sanctuary, far surpass all the specific blessings of the New Covenant.

Let us explain a bit more specifically the spiritual aspects of the New Covenant (in addition to the physical aspects: the Promised Land, the holy city, the throne of David, the temple of God). This is described precisely in Jeremiah 31:31-34.

(a) A work accomplished *for* the beneficiaries, namely the forgiveness of their sins: "I will forgive their iniquity, and I will remember their sin no more." This corresponds with what in 2 Corinthians 3:9 is called the *ministry of righteousness*, and which is further explained in chapter 5:21: "For our sake he [i.e., God] made him [i.e., Jesus on the cross] to be sin who knew no sin [i.e., Jesus was sinless], so that in him we might become the righteousness of God."

(b) A work accomplished *in* the beneficiaries, namely, "I will put my law within them and I will write it on their hearts," with all the blessings that result from this: ". . . And I will be their God, and they shall be my people. And no longer shall each one teach his neighbor and each his brother, saying, 'Know the LORD,' for they shall all know me, from the least of them to the greatest." This corresponds with what in 2 Corinthians 3:8 is called the *ministry of the Spirit*. This is because in verse 3 it is the Holy Spirit who writes the *torot* on the fleshly tables of the hearts of believers. These *torot* are summarized here in one word: Christ: "[Y]ou are a letter from [or, concerning] Christ delivered by us, written not with ink but with the Spirit of the living God, not on tablets of stone [as the Ten Commandments had been] but on tablets of human hearts."

Under the Old Covenant, the Law had been imposed upon Israel as a strict "yoke ... that neither our fathers nor we have been able to bear," that is, we have been unable to completely fulfill the Law (Acts 15:10). On the one hand, remember Israel's vow: "All that the LORD has spoken we will do" (Exod. 19:8; 24:3, 7). On the other hand, remember James 2:10, "[W]hoever keeps the whole law but fails in one point has become guilty of all of it." As Paul said, "the wages of sin is death" (Rom. 6:23); strictly according to the stipulations, death had to be the portion of every Israelite. The LORD said, "You shall therefore keep my statutes and my rules; if a person does them, he shall live by them."[38] In this case, the reverse is also valid: a person who does *not* keep "my statutes and my rules" shall *die* by them. As Paul said, "[W]e know that whatever the law [i.e., the Mosaic Torah] says it speaks to those who are under the law, so that every mouth may be stopped, and the whole world [not only the Gentiles who were not under the Torah, but also the Jews who were under it] may be held accountable to God" (Rom. 3:19).

5.4.3 The Messianic Torah

The Old Covenant guaranteed life to those who kept the covenant, but death to those who broke it. Therefore, this covenant was called a *ministry of death* (2 Cor. 3:7). This death was not a consequence of the nature of the Old Covenant as such; how could it be, given that God himself had established it? No, death was a consequence of the sinful nature of the people. As King Solomon said, "[T]here is no one who does not sin."[39] Therefore, a covenant can be *good*, and yet inevitably bring death upon *evil* people. Moreover, within the stipulations of the Old Covenant, there was no promise of the Holy Spirit who would work *for* them, let alone work *in* them. In their threefold vow at Sinai, the Israelites implied that they would be able to fulfill God's commandments in their own strength.

And yet, there were so many true believers under the Old Cov-

---

38. Lev. 18:5; Ezek. 20:11; Luke 10:28; Gal. 3:12.
39. 1 Kings 8:46; cf. Job 14:1–4; 15:14–15; 25:4–6; Ps. 51:5; Rom. 3:19–20, 23.

enant! Moses, Joshua, many judges, the prophets, some kings, and some ordinary people, were splendid examples of this. And such *tzaddiqim* existed in the time of Jesus as well; it is said of the parents of John the Baptist (in more Hebrew language: Yochanan the Immerser, CJB): "[T]hey were both righteous before God, walking blamelessly in all the commandments and statutes of the LORD." How could this be? Were Zechariah and Elizabeth not included under Solomon's word: "[T]here is no one who does not sin"? They were. They were *tzaddiqim* because of two things that far surpassed the boundaries of the Old Covenant as such, but were nevertheless granted to all those who humbly acknowledged their own sinfulness and entrusted themselves to God's mercy. In the Tanakh, these two things are described nowhere better than in a prophecy that actually refers to the beginning of the Messianic kingdom (Ezek. 36:25-27):

(1) "I will sprinkle clean water on you [i.e., the repentant ones among Israel], and you shall be clean from all your uncleannesses, and from all your idols I will cleanse you. And I will give you a new heart, and a new spirit I will put within you. And I will remove the heart of stone from your flesh and give you a heart of flesh" (cf. 11:19; Jer. 32:39). This is the work of *regeneration* or *rebirth (new birth)*; as Jesus said, "Truly, truly, I say to you, unless one is born of water and the Spirit, he cannot enter the kingdom of God" (John 3:5).

(2) "And I will put my Spirit within you, and cause you to walk in my statutes and be careful to obey my rules." What we found under (1) is the work of the Spirit *upon* us: regenerating us. But here, under (2), the Holy Spirit comes to dwell personally *within* the believer, and it is through his power that the believer can now fulfill God's commandments. As Paul says, the "righteous requirement of the law" is "fulfilled in us, who walk not according to the flesh but according to the Spirit" (Rom. 8:4).

These things far surpass the stipulations of the Old Covenant and belong to the sphere of the New Covenant.[40] The beneficiaries of the New Covenant *as such* have been inwardly cleansed and atoned, and have received a "new heart and a new spirit" (Ezek. 18:31; 36:26). They possess no higher desire than to fulfill the Mes-

---

40. Cf. Ouweneel (2009b, 92–95).

sianic Torah, *and* through the Holy Spirit they are basically able to do so. As an example, here are seven of the typically Messianic commandments:[41]

1. "You shall love and serve only the one God, the Father, and the one Lord, Jesus Messiah, and do his will" (the elaboration of the first and second of the Ten Commandments; cf., e.g., 1 Cor. 8:2-6).

2. "You shall love and serve God so much that you only use his name to confess him, pray to him, praise him, worship him" (the elaboration of the third of the Ten Commandments; cf., e.g., 1 John 4:20-21).

3. "You shall love your parents at all costs — although you shall always love God more — and take care of them even in your own most difficult circumstances" (the elaboration of the fifth of the Ten Commandments; cf., e.g., Eph. 6:1-3).

4. "You shall love your brother so much that you are prepared to lay down your life for him" (the elaboration of the sixth of the Ten Commandments; cf., e.g., 1 John 3:16).

5. "You shall love your wife so much that you are prepared to lay down your life for her" (the elaboration of the seventh [and tenth] of the Ten Commandments; cf., e.g., Eph. 5:25-26).

6. "You shall love your brother so much that you are prepared to share everything you have with him" (the elaboration of the eighth [and tenth] of the Ten Commandments; cf., e.g., Eph. 4:28).

7. "You shall love your fellow Christian so much that you are prepared to serve him with the truth, in a truthful way" (the elaboration of the ninth of the Ten Commandments; cf., e.g., Eph. 4:25).

The beneficiaries of the New Covenant no longer bear the Torah as a yoke, but cherish it in their hearts (actually, this occurred already under the Old Covenant: Prov. 3:3; 7:13). For them, the Torah is "not burdensome" (1 John 5:3; this occurred under the Old Covenant: Deut. 30:11). It is written in their heart and in their mind, just as it was for the Messiah (Ps. 40:8), and just as it has been for the *tzaddiqim*, those Israelites who were truly "born again" (cf. Ps. 119:11, 34, 36, 112, 129).

5.4.4 Letter and Spirit

Jesus is not only the example for believers, but he is also the con-

---

41. See extensively, Ouweneel (2020).

tent of the Messianic Torah.⁴² According to 2 Corinthians 3:3 and 6, the Holy Spirit, through the apostles administers to the hearts of believers no one less than Christ in his own person. Here Paul was making a remarkable distinction between the Old and the New Covenants. Under the Old Covenant, the Mosaic Torah was written on tablets of stone. But under the New Covenant, the Messianic Torah—*that is Christ himself*—is written on tablets that are the hearts of believers. Look at the seven commandments just mentioned, which *all* say: "You shall love." Jesus is not only the example of such loving, but he *is* that love. When Paul wrote, "Love is patient and kind; love does not envy or boast; it is not arrogant or rude. It does not insist on its own way; it is not irritable or resentful; it does not rejoice at wrongdoing, but rejoices with the truth. Love bears all things, believes all things, hopes all things, endures all things" (1 Cor. 13:4-7), he could just as well have written: "*Jesus* is patient and kind; *Jesus* does not envy or boast; he is not arrogant or rude. He does not insist on his own way; he is not irritable or resentful; he does not rejoice at wrongdoing, but rejoices with the truth. *Jesus* bears all things, believes all things, hopes all things, endures all things."

The New Covenant that is administered to the Ecclesia is not "of the letter, but of the Spirit" (2 Cor. 3:6). The word "letter" (Gk. *gramma*) here refers back to the word "written" (Gk. *engegrammenē*) in verse 3.⁴³ This law is not what was literally engraved upon tablets of stone, but what the Holy Spirit figuratively writes in the hearts. On the hearts of restored Israel, the Torah of the Messianic kingdom will be written, which is essentially identical to the Mosaic Torah.⁴⁴ On the hearts of the Jesus-believers, the Messianic Torah (the "law of Christ," 1 Cor. 9:21; Gal. 6:2) will be written, whose spirit is Christ in person. One day, restored Israel will cherish the Torah in its inward parts, know it in a spiritual way, as Jesus had expounded it in the Sermon of the Mount (Matt. 5-7), and as Jesus' apostles had explained it in their letters. In those days, Israel will not be able to know and love the Torah apart from knowing and loving

---

42. Ouweneel (2020, 207–13, 359–68).
43. Cf. Barnett (1997, 176–77); *contra* Bernard (1979, 54), who thought the "letter" referred to the law itself, not to the writing of the law.
44. See Ouweneel (2020, 277–92, 337–44).

the Messiah. And conversely, the Jesus who cherishes his Ecclesia in his heart will be the One who is the Lord, the Spirit of the Tanakh, a Lord whom no one can know and love apart from knowing and loving his Torah, the commandments of Jesus: "If you love me, you will keep my commandments.... Whoever has my commandments and keeps them, he it is who loves me. And he who loves me will be loved by my Father, and I will love him and manifest myself to him" (John 14:15, 21). "If you keep my commandments, you will abide in my love, just as I have kept my Father's commandments and abide in his love" (15:10).

> [B]y this we know that we have come to know him, if we keep his commandments. Whoever says 'I know him' but does not keep his commandments is a liar, and the truth is not in him, but whoever keeps his word, in him truly the love of God is perfected. By this we may know that we are in him: whoever says he abides in him ought to walk in the same way in which he walked (1 John 2:3–4; cf. 3:22, 24; 5:2–3).

The Torah will be put into the *minds* of believers (Heb. 8:10), so that they comprehend, grasp, and understand it, and it is put into their *hearts*, their deepest inner self, the spiritual center of all their thinking, willing, and feeling, of all their considerations, decisions, emotions, and affections.[45] Thus, they love God, but also the Messiah, with all their heart and with all their soul and with all their strength and with all their mind (cf. Luke 10:27), that is, with all the facets of their renewed humanity. Thus, from the heart the relationship with God is restored in the power of the Holy Spirit: he will be their God, and they will be his people—and expression that frequently occurs in the prophecies,[46] and is also quoted several times in the New Testament.[47]

5.5 The Significance of *Ha'Aretz*

5.5.1 The Land: An Everlasting Inheritance

The Old as well as the New Covenants involve not only the people of Israel and its spiritual blessings; they also involve the indissol-

---

45. Cf. Ouweneel (2008a, 117–21).
46. E.g., Exod. 29:45; Lev. 26:12; Jer. 24:7; 30:22; 31:1; 32:38; Ezek. 11:20; 14:11; 37:27; Zech. 8:8).
47. 2 Cor. 6:16; Heb. 8:10; Rev. 21:7.

uble bond between Israel and the land. Regarding the patriarchs God said, "I established my covenant with them *to give them the land of Canaan*, the land in which they lived as sojourners" (Exod. 6:4). When Israel would be in exile (because of their sins), the LORD would say, "I will remember my covenant with Jacob, and I will remember my covenant with Isaac and my covenant with Abraham, and *I will remember the land*" (Lev. 26:42). Joshua warned: "[I]f you transgress the covenant of the LORD your God, which he commanded you, and go and serve other gods and bow down to them, then the anger of the LORD will be kindled against you, and you shall perish quickly from off the *good land* that he has given to you" (Josh. 23:16). God made with Abraham "the covenant *to give to his offspring the land* of the Canaanite, the Hittite, the Amorite, the Perizzite, the Jebusite, and the Girgashite. And you [, LORD,] have kept your promise, for you are righteous" (Neh. 9:8).

In §5.4.3 above, you will read an extensive citation of Ezekiel 36:25–27 about the renewal of the people's hearts, and the indwelling of God's Holy Spirit as conditions for entering the Messianic kingdom. However, we should not overlook the preceding verse 24: "I will take you from the nations and gather you from all the countries and bring you into your own land." Israel's return to their own land is inseparable from Israel's return to the LORD, and their return to the LORD is inseparable from their return to their own land.

Non-Jewish believers can scarcely imagine what *ha'Aretz* means to the Jews. The Dutch and the English may love their respective countries, and Americans and Canadians may do the same. But this cannot be compared with the *religious* significance of the land of Israel to the people of Israel. In their romantic, poetic descriptions, the Dutch, the Afrikaners, the British, or the Americans may speak of their country as "holy," and even refer to it as the "Promised Land" (see §§4.5 and 4.6). But this is not the same. Israel is the Holy Land, and Jerusalem is the holy city, not for romantic or poetic reasons, but *because the Shekhinah dwelt there*. Israel is the Promised Land because the LORD explicitly promised it to the patriarchs and through the prophets. For Christians, according to true Christian criteria no land can be called "holy" (although the British-Israel people may call England "holy"), and no city that could be called "holy" (although Roman Catholics may call Rome "holy," just as the Roman Empire was called the *Holy* Roman Empire from the thirteenth century until 1806).

In the book of Revelation, the New Jerusalem is called the "holy city" (21:2, 10; 22:19), but so too is the old Jerusalem: "Rise and measure the temple of God and the altar and those who worship there, but do not measure the court outside the temple; leave that out, for it is given over to the nations, and they will trample the holy city for forty-two months" (11:1-2). Even after the *Shekhinah* had left the temple and the city (Ezek. 9–11) — and as of today, has never returned — the afterglow of that presence remained in and over it, so that in subsequent history Jerusalem was still called the "holy city."[48] And what will it be like when the city is one day again called "holy" when the Messianic kingdom has arrived:

> Awake, awake,
> > put on your strength, O Zion;
> put on your beautiful garments,
> > O *Jerusalem, the holy city*;
> for there shall no more come into you
> > the uncircumcised and the unclean.
> Shake yourself from the dust and arise;
> > be seated, O Jerusalem;
> loose the bonds from your neck,
> > O captive daughter of Zion (Isa. 52:1-2).

Even before the *Shekhinah* descended on the temple of Solomon, the Promised Land was holy for the simple reason that it was *God's* land (and also because the *Shekhinah* had rested on the ark from the time recorded in Exod. 40, until Solomon's time). Of course, the whole earth is the LORD's (Ps. 24:1), but there is one country that he specifically calls *his* country. Recall our discussion in §1.1.3 above, regarding the "national angels"; all the countries of the world had been placed under such angels except Israel: the LORD had taken it for himself. Because the land is God's personal possession, he told Israel, ". . . the land belongs to me—you are only foreigners and temporary residents with me" (Lev. 25:23). To the two and a half

---

48. Neh. 11:1, 18; Matt. 4:5; Dan. 9:24; Matt. 4:5; 27:53.

Israelite tribes that chose to live beyond the Jordan, Joshua says, "[I]f the land of your possession is unclean, pass over into *the LORD's land where the LORD's tabernacle stands*, and take for yourselves a possession among us" (Josh. 22:19). In other words, your land, there beyond Jordan, is not truly "God's land"; you'd better come over to us.

The prophet predicted:

[T]he LORD will have compassion on Jacob and will again choose Israel, and will set them *in their own land*, and sojourners will join them and will attach themselves to the house of Jacob. And the peoples will take them and bring them *to their place*, and the house of Israel will possess them in the LORD's *land* as male and female servants. They will take captive those who were their captors, and rule over those who oppressed them (Isa. 14:1–2).

On the one hand, ha'Aretz belongs to Israel alone, throughout the ages—despites their exiles from the land—and to no other nation. On the other hand, ha'Aretz belongs to the LORD alone; the Israelites are only sojourners with him, and they dwell in the land only when, and insofar as, the LORD allows them.

5.5.2 God's Dwelling Place

The land is holy because it is the LORD's land; but more than that: it is holy because the holy city is there, or more specifically, Mount Zion (cf. Ps. 78:54); ". . . the LORD will inherit Judah as his portion in the holy land, and will again choose Jerusalem" (Zech. 2:12). The land is holy because of the holy city, and the city is holy because of its holy temple,[49] standing on God's holy mountain.[50] In all these cases, the word "holy" has basically the same meaning: a place is "holy" if and when the glorious presence of the holy God is there. This is where we find the *Shekhinah* (although this rabbinic term, derived from the Heb. verb *sh-kh-n*, "to dwell," is never used in the Tanakh[51]).

---

49. Ps. 5:7; 11:4; 79:1; 138:2; Jonah 2:4, 7; Micah 1:2; Hab. 2:20.
50. Ps. 48:1; 87:1; 99:9; Isa. 11:9; 27:13; 56:7; 57:13; 65:11, 25; 66:20; Jer. 31:23; Ezek. 20:40; Dan. 11:45; Joel 2:1; 3:17; Obad. 1:16; Zech. 3:11; 8:3. In 2 Pet. 1:18 the expression is used for the Mount of Transfiguration, which was holy because the transfigured Jesus was there.
51. But see a passage like this: "The glory of the LORD dwelt [Heb. *wayyishkan*

1. God "dwelt" in the burning bush near Mount Horeb or Sinai (Deut. 33:16 KJV), where he said to Moses, "Do not come near; take your sandals off your feet, for the place on which you are standing is holy ground" (Exod. 3:5) ("dwelt" is here from the Heb. root *sh-kh-n*, the same root as in *Shekhinah* as well as in *mishkan*, the Heb. term for "tabernacle").

2. God "dwelt" in the midst of Israel (Exod. 29:45–46), especially in the *mishkan* ("tabernacle," lit. "dwelling"; 25:8), specifically between the cherubim on the atonement lid on the ark of the covenant (although the Heb. verb used here is not *sh-kh-n* but *y-sh-b*, "to sit, to be enthroned").[52] In this mobile dwelling, God moved with the people through the wilderness, from Mount Sinai to the Promised Land. Here, the tabernacle ended up in Gibeon,[53] whereas the ark moved from Gibeah (Judg. 20:27), Shiloh (1 Sam. 4:3–4), Kiriath-Jearim (1 Sam. 6:21; 7:1–2), the house of Obed-Edom (2 Sam. 6:10–11), to the tent that David pitched for it (1 Chron. 15:1).

3. Finally, the ark was transferred to the temple of Solomon, and placed in the Most Holy place, just as it had been in the Most Holy place of the tabernacle (1 Kings 8). This temple remained the dwelling place of the LORD, who was enthroned on the ark, until the *Shekhinah* departed from the temple shortly before its destruction by the Babylonians (Ezek. 9–11).

4. The *Shekhinah* will return to the new temple in the Messianic kingdom:

> [B]ehold, the glory of the God of Israel was coming from the east. And the sound of his coming was like the sound of many waters, and the earth shone with his glory. . . . And I fell on my face. As the glory of the LORD entered the temple by the gate facing east, the Spirit lifted me up and brought me into the inner court; and behold, the glory of the LORD filled the temple (Ezek. 43:2–5).

Another way to describe the glory of the LORD dwelling in Jeru-

---

(from *sh-kh-n*) *k'bod JHWH*] on Mount Sinai" (Exod. 24:16); see also Ps. 26:8, "I love the habitation of your house and the place where your glory dwells [Heb. *um'qom mishkan* (from *sh-kh-n*) *k'bodĕka*)]."

52. 1 Sam. 4:4; 2 Sam. 6:2; 2 Kings 19:15; 1 Chron. 13:6; Ps. 80:1; 99:1; Isa. 37:16.

53. 1 Kings 3:4; 1 Chron. 16:39; 21:29; 2 Chron. 1:3, 13.

salem is the reference to his *name* as expressing his being, his glory: "Since the day that I brought my people Israel out of Egypt, I chose no city out of all the tribes of Israel in which to build a house, that my name [my glory] might be there" (1 Kings 8:16; cf. 11:36; 2 Kings 23:27). This was the place that God had already designated through Moses: when you will arrive in the Promised Land,

> you shall seek the place that the LORD your God will choose out of all your tribes to put his name and make his habitation there. There you shall go, and there you shall bring your burnt offerings and your sacrifices, your tithes and the contribution that you present, your vow offerings, your freewill offerings, and the firstborn of your herd and of your flock (Deut. 12:5–6).[54]

The ark is the heart of the Most Holy place, the Most Holy place is the heart of the temple, the temple is heart of Jerusalem, Jerusalem is the heart of the land, and the land is the heart of the world. After Israel had left Egypt, and was en route to the Promised Land, *this* is the part of the land on which they were focused:[55]

> You have led in your steadfast love
> > the people whom you have redeemed;
> you have guided [prophetic future tense] them by your strength
> > to your *holy abode*. . . .
> You will bring them in and plant them
> > on your own mountain,
> the place, O LORD, which you have made for *your abode*,
> > the *sanctuary*, O LORD, which your hands have established
> (Exod. 15:13, 17).

The Hebrew of the phrase "your holy abode" (v. 13) is *n'wē qodshēka*, the "habitation of your holiness"; the Hebrew of the words "your abode" (v. 17) is *shibt'ka*, from the root *y-sh-b*, mentioned above. The LORD had told his people that after their arrival in the land, they would have to "*seek* the place that the LORD your God will choose out of all your tribes to put his name and make his habitation [Heb. *shikhno*, from *shēkhēn*, from *sh-kh-n*] there" (Deut. 12:5).

---

54. Cf. Deut. 12:11, 21; 14:23–24; 16:2, 6, 11; 26:2; also see Ezra 6:12; Neh. 1:9; Jer. 7:12.

55. No doubt under the guidance of the Holy Spirit; the people's sinful flesh took over again soon thereafter (Exod. 15:24).

It is surprising that, immediately after having left Egypt, they were filled with the expectation of this sanctuary. Thus, all the more remarkably, after the entrance into Canaan, the Israelites seemed to have forgotten all about seeking the place where God would put his glory and make his dwelling place. It took centuries before Israel, or the faithful ones among them, had "found" this place. Notice the conspicuous mentioning of David's "finding" in Psalm 132:4-5, "I will not give sleep to my eyes or slumber to my eyelids, until I find a place for the LORD, a dwelling place for the Mighty One of Jacob."

5.5.3 An Indissoluble Bond

From the time of the patriarchs, an indissoluble bond existed between their offspring, the people of Israel, and the Promised Land, *ha'Aretz*, the land that is called the "land of Israel" (repeatedly from 1 Sam. 13:19 to Matt. 2:21). Abram is led from Ur of the Chaldeans to *this* land (Gen. 12:1), and immediately upon his arrival, God promises to give this land to Abram's offspring (v. 7), and to do so "forever" (Heb. *l'olam*), which in the Tanakh always means as long as the present earth exists, that is, at least including the Messianic kingdom: "Lift up your eyes and look from the place where you are, northward and southward and eastward and westward, for all the land that you see I will give to you and to your offspring *forever*" (Gen. 13:14-15).[56] There have been times when, because of its sins, Israel was driven out of the land, but it always returned to *this* land. Under neither the Old nor the New Covenants could the *people* of Israel possibly have been permanently severed from the *land* of Israel; in God's promises, they are linked indissolubly.

The view of some Christians that we must understand this land "spiritually" has no validity.

(a) There is not the slightest basis for this view in the New Testament, as we will see more extensively; the fact that the patriarchs—who knew that they themselves would never possess the Promised Land in person—looked forward to a "heavenly country" (Heb. 11:16) provides not the slightest basis for spiritualizing the earthly land.

---

56. Cf. Jer. 7:7; 25:5, Hebr. *l'min-'olam w'ad-'olam*, literally: "from of old [i.e., from the time of the patriarchs] and forever," i.e., until the end of this earth; cf. Douma (2008, 55–56).

(b) Spiritualizing the land is illogical. God told his people that he would bring them back to the same land where their fathers had once lived; but the spiritualizers turn it into a totally *different* land, some kind of "spiritual" land.

(c) That the Jews who came to faith in Jesus as their Messiah and Savior adopted this idea—often under pressure, however—makes the matter even worse. They allowed the land promise to be stolen from them by supersessionist denominations (Roman Catholic, Eastern Orthodox, traditional Protestant) through joining them. Fortunately, this is changing. I know a Jewish Christian who was once Reformed, and therefore an ardent supersessionist. However, he gradually became aware of his Jewish roots, left his supersessionist Reformed church, joined a Messianic Jewish community, and now lives in Israel together with so many other Messianic Jews (i.e., Jesus-believing Jews). In these "latter days"—and as a divine sign *of* these "latter days"—there are hundreds of thousands of Jews worldwide who believe in Yeshuah as their Messiah, Savior, and Lord, *and* observe the Mosaic Torah, cling to the literal land promise and the "world to come," the Messianic kingdom, the center of which will be Jerusalem.[57] And today, millions of non-Jewish Jesus-believers support their viewpoint. I have no doubt that this has been, and still is, a work of God's Spirit. This renewed view of the kingdom of God is part of the "gospel of the kingdom," which is being "proclaimed throughout the whole world as a testimony to all nations, and then the end will come" (Matt. 24:14), that is, the end of the present age (v. 3).

(d) Believing in the literal land promise is not optional, given that a divine *commandment* obligates Israel, if this is practically possible, to live in the country of Israel, and nowhere else. This commandment has never been annulled: "You shall dwell in the land that I gave to your fathers, and you shall be my people, and I will be your God" (Ezek. 36:28). The tense that is used here—"You shall"—has both an indicative and an imperative meaning, *just as in the Ten Commandments!* The Hebrew Bible ends with these poignant words, spoken by the Persian King Cyrus: "The LORD, the God of heaven, has given me all the kingdoms of the earth, and he has charged me to build him a house at Jerusalem, which is in Judah.

---

57. See extensively, Ouweneel (2020, §4.3 and chapter 8).

Whoever is among you of all his people, may the LORD his God be with him. *Let him go up*" (2 Chron. 36:23). The latter four words are one Hebrew word: *w'ya'al*, from the Hebrew root *y-'-l*, "to go up." The Tanakh — which ends with Second Chronicles — thus ends with a divine command, given through his "shepherd" and "anointed" Cyrus (Isa. 44:28; 45:1): "Go up!" This Hebrew root underlies the modern word *Aliyah*, which literally means "going up," and is used as a synonym for the emigration of Jews to the land of Israel. We tell the Jews, "Go up" to *ha'Aretz*, for as Jews that is your home. When a believing Jew in New York, or Minsk, or Buenos Aires, has finished reading the Tanakh, these words may still reverberate in their ears and heart: "Go up!"

For me, it is difficult to understand that so many Jews venerated Rabbi Menachem Mendel Schneerson (1902–1994) as Messiah, since throughout his life the man rarely left New York, nor did he even visit the Promised Land. He must have known perfectly well that Israel and the land belong together. The Covenant and the land belong together. The promises and the land belong together. The Messiah and the land belong together. There are no Messianic figures outside the land. The Messiah will sit on the throne of David, a throne that will be located not in New York but in Jerusalem:

> [T]he government shall be upon his shoulder, and his name shall be called Wonderful Counselor, Mighty God, Everlasting Father, Prince of Peace. Of the increase of his government and of peace there will be no end, on the throne of David and over his kingdom, to establish it and to uphold it with justice and with righteousness from this time forth and forevermore (Isa. 9:6–7).

One day, when the Messianic kingdom has arrived, the LORD will ensure that the last Jews are brought from the four corners of the earth to the Promised Land:

> [T]hey shall bring all your brothers from all the nations as an offering to the LORD, on horses and in chariots and in litters and on mules and on dromedaries, to my holy mountain Jerusalem . . ., just as the Israelites bring their grain offering in a clean vessel to the house of the LORD (Isa. 66:20).

It requires an enormous imagination to spiritualize *that*!

5.6 The Land of the Fathers
5.6.1 The *T'shubah*

In order to underscore the everlasting validity of the *aliyah* command (see previous section), we need only one thing: Bible passages that tell us in the same breath

(a) that Israel returns to its land,

(b) during the time that we call the "end time" or the "latter days,"

(c) that this is explicitly the *very same* land as the one their fathers lived in, and

(d) that this return is linked with the establishment of the Messianic kingdom of peace and justice on earth, during which the Messiah will reign from Jerusalem, sitting on the ancient throne of David.

It is not difficult to find such passages. Deuteronomy 30:1–10 provides the important link between (a) and (c), namely, in what Jewish tradition calls the *t'shubah* (usually pronounced as *t'shuvah*). This word comes from the Hebrew root *sh-v(u)-b* (or *shub*) and means both physical return (here, to the Promised Land) and conversion (penitent return to the LORD). We have seen earlier that in the Bible these two matters are closely connected, and we will see this again. I put in italics all the seven derivations of this Hebrew root occurring in this passage (NKJV):

> [1] Now it shall come to pass, when all these things come upon you, the blessing and the curse which I have set before you, and you call [them] to mind among all the nations where the LORD your God drives you, and you *return* [Heb. *v'shabta*] to the LORD your God and obey His voice, according to all that I command you today, you and your children, with all your heart and with all your soul, [2, 3] that the LORD your God *will bring you back from captivity* [*v'shab* ... *et-sh'butkha*[58]], and have compassion on you, [4] and gather you *again* [*v'shab*] from all the nations where the LORD your God has scattered you.... Then the LORD your God will bring you to the land which your fathers possessed, and you shall possess it.... [5] And you will *again* [*tashub*, or, you will

---

58. The Heb. for "bring back from captivity" (v. 3) is *shub et-shebutcha*, literally, "turn your captivity" (if *sh'but* comes from *shub*), "bring you back, restore you," or "turn your fortunes."

return and] obey the voice of the LORD and do all His commandments which I command you today. . . . [6] For the LORD will *again* [*yashub*] rejoice over you for good as He rejoiced over your fathers, if you obey the voice of the LORD your God, to keep His commandments and His statutes which are written in this Book of the Law, [and] [7] if you turn [*tashub*] to the LORD your God with all your heart and with all your soul.

In summary: (a) Israel returns to the LORD, (b) Israel returns to the Promised Land, and (c) the LORD returns to his people with blessing. Here we clearly see what "the land" means in this context:

(a) The Israelites will *return* to this land, the land where they had lived before—not some other land, or some figurative "land."

(b) Moreover, the fact that God refers to the same land is expressed in verse 5: "Then the LORD your God will bring you to *the land which your fathers possessed*, and you shall possess it." Some "spiritual" land (heaven?) is not a land where the fathers had lived before. Moses was speaking of the land of Abraham, Isaac, and Jacob. This clearly and emphatically excludes any spiritualizing of "the land."

(c) In a literal, physical land the people will "abound in all the work of your hand, in the fruit of your body, in the increase of your livestock, and in the produce of your land for good" (v. 9). Will children be born to believers in heaven or on the new earth? Will cows and goats, wheat and barley, exist in heaven or on the new earth?

Now supersessionists will hasten to tell us that Moses' prophecy was entirely fulfilled at the return of Judah from the Babylonian captivity. But, first, God was speaking here about the entire nation, that is, the *twelve* tribes, not just the two tribes.

Second, he was speaking here about a nation brought back "from all the nations where the LORD your God has scattered you" (v. 3), a situation that obtained only after the people had been dispersed again, this time among *all* the nations of the earth.

Third, at the return from the Babylonian captivity, there was no question of God putting "all these curses on your enemies and on those who hate you, who persecuted you." This is fulfilled only through the Messiah, at the beginning of his kingdom. The time of God's ultimate restoration of Israel will coincide with the time of

God's ultimate judgment upon all the wicked among the nations.

Fourth, at and after the return from the Babylonian captivity, no peace and justice obtained in Israel, nor among all the nations, as will be the case during the Messianic kingdom. In other words, none of these things will be fulfilled before the appearance of the Messiah on the clouds of heaven.

5.6.2 A Second Dispersion?

Zechariah 10:9-10, written *after* the return from the Babylonian captivity, is quite remarkable. It literally says (NKJV),

> I will sow[59] them [i.e., Israel] among the peoples, and they shall remember Me in far countries; They shall live, together with their children, and they shall return. I will also bring them back from the land of Egypt, and gather them from Assyria. I will bring them into the land of Gilead and Lebanon, until no [more room] is found for them, ..."

Here, biblical prophecy speaks *again* of a dispersion among the nations, which, unfortunately, began again in AD 70. And *again*, the LORD promised that ultimately he will allow his people to return, this time not only from Babylon but also from Egypt and Assyria, even from *all the nations among which God had dispersed them.*[60] It is possible to view this as a limiting phrase: to those (few) countries among which God had dispersed them, but elsewhere this is not possible: "I will take you from the nations and gather you from all the countries and bring you into your own land" (Ezek. 36:24). The fulfillment of this statement began for the first time in the nineteenth century, and is being fulfilled to this very day.

In Zechariah 13:7 we find something similar. Here, God said about the Messiah: "Awake, O sword, against my shepherd, against the man who stands next to me. . . . Strike the shepherd, and the sheep will be scattered" (cf. the quotation of this in Matt. 26:31). Again, the post-exilic prophet was speaking of a *future* scattering (dispersion) of Israel, specifically of the sheep of the good Shepherd (cf. John 10:1-18). About this, Joseph Ratzinger asserted, "Zechariah, in a mysterious vision, had spoken of a Messiah who suffers

---

59. It seems that the prophet means "sow *again*" (as the LORD had done at the Babylonian exile); expositors pay scant attention to this point.

60. Isa. 66:20; Jer. 16:15; 23:3, 8; 29:14; 32:37; 43:5.

death, after which Israel is once again dispersed.[61]

However, today the dispersed Jews are returning home! This must be a difficult point for supersessionists. Israel was driven out of its own land and dispersed among the nations; on the supersessionist standpoint, it would have been ten times more likely that the dispersed Israel—no longer God's people—had totally become completely engulfed by the nations, and had completely lost its identity. But no, they are returning as this is being written, and the time is coming when *all* Israelites will return from all the countries of the world to the land where their fathers had once lived. This is perfectly clear language. A person is temporarily banned from his house, but one day he has the opportunity to return to the house where he had lived earlier. But what can supersessionists make of this? If the Ecclesia is "spiritual Israel," there *is* no return to the land where either Israel or the early Christians had lived. Supersessionists can only reply that the Ecclesia consists of believers from all countries and nations, en route to their *heavenly* homeland *where they have never been before*. But this is not valid Bible exposition.

5.6.3   The Land During the Messianic Kingdom

The return of Israel from *all* lands and nations can be described in even more powerful terms: God "will raise a signal for the nations and will assemble the banished of Israel, and gather the dispersed of Judah *from the four corners of the earth*" (Isa. 11:12). This return will be infinitely greater than a return from Babylon, or even from the entire Middle East. This involves the return of all the twelve tribes (cf. v. 13) that have been dispersed all over the earth and will be brought back from the four corners of the earth, from South America to East Asia, from Greenland to New Zealand. I have seen their synagogues, or their ruins, in the forests of South America and in the cities of China. Their emptiness is quite touching, especially since that emptiness is due either to the Shoah or to the Aliyah: the Jews involved have been murdered (which is horrible)—or have returned to their land (which is fantastic, because that is where they belong).

My supersessionist friends may well be affected by the former, the Shoah, and this is good. However, they seem not to be as affect-

---

61. Ratzinger (2011, 150).

ed by the latter, the Aliyah, and that is a pity. They mourn the Jews who died in the gas chambers; they seem to shed no tears of joy for the Jews already now sitting under their vines and their fig trees, even though the Messianic kingdom has not even begun.

I myself have visited concentration camps such as Buchenwald (Germany) and Auschwitz-Birkenau (Poland), and I have wept there. But I have also wept in the Promised Land, seeing how they have built up a land again "flowing with milk and honey," a land that had been neglected for centuries by Bedouins and Turks. I weep, not only out of happiness for the Jews who are back in their own land, where they can enjoy a certain amount of peace and safety, but especially because I dream of the Messianic times that soon will arrive *in this very country*. Let us look a little more closely at Isaiah 11:1–10, which deal with

(a) the birth and work of the Messiah (vv. 1–5; cf. Acts 13:22–23);

(b) the paradisal[62] circumstances for the earth that will arrive with him (vv. 7–8);

(c) "the earth shall be full of the knowledge of the LORD as the waters cover the sea [bottom]. In that day the root[63] of Jesse [i.e., his descendant, the Messiah], who shall stand as a signal for the peoples—of him shall the nations inquire, and his resting place shall be glorious" (vv. 9–10; cf. Rom. 15:12).

Here we need to elaborate several conclusions drawn earlier from Ezekiel 37:24–28 (see §1.6.2 above).

(a) The Messiah is described in Ezekiel 37 as "my servant David" and the "one shepherd." There can be only one throne from where a Scion of David can execute his earthly dominion: the "throne of David."[64] Compare Ezekiel 34:23–24, where the LORD says, "I will set up over them one shepherd, my servant David, and he shall feed them: he shall feed them and be their shepherd. And I, the LORD, will be their God, and my servant David shall be prince among them." "For thus says the LORD: 'David shall never lack a

---

62. See extensively, Ouweneel (2019b).

63. The word for "root" (Heb. *shoresh*) here refers to something shooting *out* of a root: "shoot, scion," or simply "son" or "descendant"; cf. Isa. 11:1b, "branch" (Heb. *netzer*) from Jesse's "root" (Heb. *shoresh*); cf. the quotations in Rom. 15:12; Rev. 1:16; 5:5.

64. Luke 1:32; cf. 1 Kings 2:12; Ps. 132:11–12; Isa. 9:6–7; 16:5; Jer. 33:17.

man to sit on the throne of the house of Israel'" (Jer. 33:17).

(b) Israel will dwell again in its own land; this is explicitly the land where their fathers had lived. What Jew, then or now, Jesus-believing or not, could ever seriously believe that this was referring to a figurative Israel and a figurative land, where no Jew has ever dwelt before? The text speaks of the land where Israel's ancestors had lived, with their children and their cattle (Deut. 30:9). Even the thoroughly secularized Zionist Jew Theodor Herzl, who had considered every possible homeland for Israel (in Russia, in South America), finally could not avoid the fact that only one land is eligible as the homeland for the Jews, and this was and is ancient *Eretz Yisra'el*.[65]

(c) This involves an "everlasting" kingdom; this implies that, as soon as the Messianic kingdom has begun, Jerusalem can never be destroyed again,[66] and Israel can never be dispersed again. It will last as long as the present earth will last, that is, during the entire Messianic kingdom. (This well be the case afterward as well, but expositors differ on the question whether Israel will still be a distinct entity after the Messianic kingdom, on the new earth.)

(d) "My dwelling place shall be with them," the LORD said (Ezek. 37:27). Notice the difference with the supersessionist understanding of this statement. If the Ecclesia is the "spiritual Israel," it is not only "Israel," but also the "(spiritual) city" and the "(spiritual) temple." The New Testament clearly speaks of the Ecclesia in such terms—but it is a serious mistake to interpret such descriptions as the fulfillment of these prophecies in the Tanakh. The Ecclesia *is* a (figurative) "temple," but Israel will *not* be some kind of "temple." It will have a temple in its midst, but this holy place will be carefully separated from the common people, no matter how sacred this renewed Israel may be. The new temple area will have "a wall around it, 500 cubits long and 500 cubits broad, to make a separa-

---

65. See his writings: Herzl (1905).
66. Just *before* the beginning of the Messianic kingdom, Jerusalem may still go through hard times: "I will gather all the nations against Jerusalem to battle, and the city shall be taken and the houses plundered and the women raped. Half of the city shall go out into exile, but the rest of the people shall not be cut off from the city. Then the LORD will go out and fight against those nations as when he fights on a day of battle" (Zech. 14:2–3).

tion between the holy and the common" (Ezek. 42:20). How can supersessionists spiritualize this?

(e) "Then the nations will know that I am the LORD who sanctifies Israel, when my sanctuary is in their midst forevermore" (Ezek. 37:28). Israel with its blessed circumstances will be a mighty testimony to the majesty and glory of God and to his saving grace. The emphasis here is on the new temple. What will astonish the nations worldwide after the return of the Messiah more than seeing this glorious new temple on the ancient Temple Mount? Who truly *believes* in the reappearance of God's temple at all? If today an earthquake (or a bomb) would destroy the Dome of the Rock and/or the El Aqsa Mosque, I fear that even the Western "Christian" countries would offer millions of dollars to the pitiful Muslims to have these buildings restored.

5.7 The Testimony of Other Prophets
5.7.1 The Messiah: Branch, Powerful Ruler

As we have seen, the throne of David is sometimes called the "throne of the LORD" (see 1 Chron. 29:23, where Solomon takes his place on this throne), but the reverse never occurs: God's throne *in heaven* is never called "throne of David." Consider again Revelation 3:21, where Christ described himself as sitting *now* in the throne of the Father (in heaven), and as sitting *later* on his *own* throne, where he will sit here on earth, in Jerusalem.

Jeremiah 3 also referred to the "throne of the LORD": during the Messianic age,

> Jerusalem shall be called the throne of the LORD, and all nations shall gather to it, to the presence of the LORD in Jerusalem, and they shall no more stubbornly follow their own evil heart. In those days the house of Judah shall join the house of Israel, and together they shall come from the land of the north to the land that I gave your fathers for a heritage (vv. 17–18).

How could anyone seriously believe that all this was fulfilled at the return of Judah from the Babylonian captivity? First, there was no reunion of the two tribes and the twelve tribes. Second, the nations worldwide did not flock to Jerusalem, in order to serve the LORD, the God of Israel. Third, a new temple was built but the *Shekhinah* did not descend to it; there was no question at all of a (renewed) "presence of the LORD in Jerusalem."

What a wonderful description of the Messianic kingdom this is! The name of the LORD will dwell again in Jerusalem, as a testimony for all the Gentile nations. They will all come to Jerusalem, where the new temple will stand, and where not only Israel but all the nations will serve the LORD.[67] Compare this again with the supersessionist interpretation, in which the Ecclesia, the temple, and the nations serving God *all completely coincide*. They are all one and the same thing. But in the literal interpretation, these realities are sharply distinguished: Israel is distinguished from its temple, Israel is distinguished from "all the nations," and "all the nations" are distinguished from the temple. Israel serves in God's temple, and the nations serve in God's temple, but distinct from Israel. None of these elements survive in the supersessionist interpretation, since it does not do justice to such prophetic passages, but must limit itself to vague, generalized statements.

Supersessionist commentaries on the prophetic books in the Tanakh often display the following. On the one hand, the actual exegesis can be rather precise, *as if* the text must be taken literally. But then, at the end of a prophetic chapter, lo and behold, we learn how the fulfillment of this chapter is to be found in the Ecclesia. The expositor offers an explanation of this in only a few lines, without entering into the details.[68]

God said to Jeremiah:

> ... Then I will gather the remnant of my flock out of all the countries where I have driven them, and I will bring them back to their fold, and they shall be fruitful and multiply.... Behold, the days are coming, ... when I will raise up for David a righteous Branch, and he shall reign as king and deal wisely, and shall execute justice and righteousness in the land. In his days Judah will be saved, and Israel will dwell securely. And this is the name by which he will be called: "The LORD is our righteousness." Therefore, behold, the days are coming, ... when they shall no longer say, "As the LORD lives who brought up the people of Israel out of the land of Egypt," but "As the LORD lives who brought

---

67. Cf. Isa. 2:3; Ezek. 40-44; Micah 4:2; Zech. 6:12–13; 8:22–23; 14:8-11, 16-21.
68. The Dutch Bible commentary series *Korte Verklaring* (featuring numerous volumes! [Eng. edition, "Bible Student's Commentary"]) is a remarkable example of this (see the Bibliography).

up and led the offspring of the house of Israel out of the north country and out of all the countries where he had driven them.' Then they shall dwell in their own land (23:3–8).

This passage was describing the ultimate return of all twelve tribes to the Promised Land, where the true David (the Branch, the Messiah) will be King over them, and not only over them but over all the earth. Israel will be safe, and the earth will be full of God's righteousness.

> Behold, I will restore the fortunes of the tents of Jacob and have compassion on his dwellings; the city [i.e., Jerusalem] shall be rebuilt on its mound, and the palace shall stand where it used to be. Out of them shall come songs of thanksgiving, and the voices of those who celebrate. I will multiply them, and they shall not be few.... Their prince [i.e., the Messiah] shall be one of themselves [i.e., of Israel]; their ruler shall come out from their midst; I will make him draw near, and he shall approach me.... And you shall be my people, and I will be your God (Jer. 30:18–22).

Here we read about (a) the return of Israel to its own, ancient land, (b) the restoration of Jerusalem, (c) the worship of the LORD by Israel, (d) the Messiah (Prince, Ruler) stands in their midst as their King.

We read repeatedly that these are the stages of Israel's restoration: (1) return to the land, (2) reunion of the two tribes with the ten tribes, (3) restoration of the temple, (4) return of the Messiah, (5) submission to the Messiah. As we read elsewhere:

> [T]he children of Israel shall dwell many days without king or prince, without sacrifice or pillar, without ephod or household gods. Afterward the children of Israel shall return and seek the LORD their God, and David their king [i.e., the Messiah], and they shall come in fear to the LORD and to his goodness in the latter days (Hos. 3:4–5).

Notice here the connection between Davidic royalty and Aaronic priesthood. The two belong together forever, and find their ultimate fulfillment in the Messiah, the great King-Priest (Zech.

6:13).⁶⁹ King Melchizedek was his great prototype.⁷⁰ As we read in Jeremiah 33:17–18, "David shall never lack a man to sit on the throne of the house of Israel, and the Levitical priests shall never lack a man in my presence to offer burnt offerings, to burn grain offerings, and to make sacrifices forever."

5.7.2   In Zion It Happens

"[B]ehold, in those days and at that time, when I restore the fortunes [Heb. *shub et-sh'but*] of Judah and Jerusalem, I will gather all the nations and bring them down to the Valley of Jehoshaphat. And I will enter into judgment with them there, on behalf of my people and my heritage Israel, because they have scattered them among the nations and have divided up my land, ..." Put in the sickle, for the harvest is ripe. Go in, tread, for the winepress is full. The vats overflow, for their evil is great. Multitudes, multitudes, in the valley of decision! For the day of the LORD is near in the valley of decision. . . . The LORD roars from Zion, and utters his voice from Jerusalem, and the heavens and the earth quake. But the LORD is a refuge to his people, a stronghold to the people of Israel. "So you shall know that I am the LORD your God, who dwells in Zion, my holy mountain." And Jerusalem shall be holy, and strangers shall never again pass through it. And in that day the mountains shall drip sweet wine, and the hills shall flow with milk, and all the streambeds of Judah shall flow with water; and a fountain shall come forth from the house of the LORD and water the Valley of Shittim (Joel 3:1–2, 13–18).

Here again, we find the familiar pattern: (a) Israel's return to its own land, (b) judgment upon the nations, (c) the LORD's personal intervention (implying the appearance of the Messiah), (d) God dwelling again on his "holy mountain" (implying the new temple, the "house of the LORD"), (e) everlasting blessing for land and people. Imagine the embarrassment of the supersessionists: Zion, God's holy mountain, the temple, the city of Jerusalem, Judah, Israel — these various names and realities are insignificant for exegesis, since in their view these all refer to and are fulfilled in the Ecclesia.

Our conclusion must be that the prophecies mentioned here

---

69. The text is ambiguous: either King and Priest are one person here (KJV), or the two are distinct (ESV).
70. Gen. 14:18–20; Ps. 110:1–7; Heb. 7:1–2; see Ouweneel (2014, 47–49).

cannot possibly refer (only) to Judah's return from Babylon because in each these prophecies, *all* the people of Israel return, they experience the appearance and intervention of the Messiah, Israel is spiritually restored, it serves the Lord in his temple, and through it all the nations of the earth are blessed. There can be no doubt that the Messiah will appear—not as a baby in Bethlehem but as the Son of Man on the clouds of heaven—in the land of Israel, where he will find a returned Israel, with a restored societal life, and with rebuilt cities and villages.

I just alluded to a key passage in the Tanakh:

> I saw in the night visions, and behold, with the clouds of heaven there came one like a son of man, and he came to the Ancient of Days and was presented before him. And to him was given dominion and glory and a kingdom, that all peoples, nations, and languages should serve him; his dominion is an everlasting dominion, which shall not pass away, and his kingdom one that shall not be destroyed (Dan. 7:13-14).

Jesus used the designation "Son of Man" many times, and unmistakably applied it to himself, especially when he referred to his sufferings, death, and resurrection.[71] In several cases, the Israelite context is very clear:

> So when you see the abomination of desolation spoken of by the prophet Daniel, standing in the holy place . . ., then let those who are in Judea flee to the mountains. . . . Pray that your flight may not be in winter or on a Sabbath. For then there will be great tribulation, such as has not been from the beginning of the world until now, no, and never will be. . . . [A]s the lightning comes from the east and shines as far as the west, so will be the coming of the Son of Man. . . . Then will appear in heaven the sign of the Son of Man, and then all the tribes of the earth will mourn, and they will see the Son of Man coming on the clouds of heaven with power and great glory (Matt. 24:15-16, 20-22, 27, 30)[72]

This takes us back to Daniel 7, where we hear not only about the Son of Man and his everlasting kingdom, but also about who will be the people first and foremost involved in this kingdom. These

---

71. E.g., Matt. 8:20; 12:40; 17:9, 12, 22; 20:18, 28; also in the other Gospels.

72. Matt. 24:15-21, 27, 30; cf. 13:41; 16:27-28, referring to his transfiguration on the mountain, 17:1-8; 19:28; 25:31; 26:64.

are the saints who have suffered so badly under the four world empires (from the Babylonian to the Roman one): the faithful among the Israelites, the *tzaddiqim* ("righteous"), the *chasidim* ("godly").[73] Of *them* the text tells us this: "[T]he holy ones of the Most High will receive the kingdom and possess the kingdom forever, yes, forever and ever" (Dan. 7:18 CJB); "the Ancient of Days came, judgment was given in favor of the holy ones of the Most High, and the time came for the holy ones to take over the kingdom" (v. 22 CJB). "And the kingdom, the rulership and the greatness of the kingdoms under the whole heaven will be given to the holy people of the Most High. Their kingdom is an everlasting kingdom, and all rulers will serve and obey them" (v. 27 CJB). In other words, the coming of the Son of Man was closely linked here with the people of Israel, which together with him receives world dominion. That is, world dominion *on earth*, to be clearly distinguished from the dominion that the *heavenly* saints will share with Christ.[74]

5.7.3 Where Does the Messiah Return?

Acts 1 tells us about the ascension of the risen Jesus from the Mount of Olives. Immediately after this event, two angels appear, who tell the *talmidim* (disciples) of Rabbi Jesus: "Men of Galilee, why do you stand looking into heaven? This Jesus, who was taken up from you into heaven, will come in the same way as you saw him go into heaven" (Acts 1:11). These words refer not only to the *way* Jesus ascended and will descend again, namely, with clouds, but also to the *place* where he will descend, namely, the Mount of Olives.

This thought seems to be clearly corroborated by Zechariah 14. In this chapter, Israel was viewed as living in its land and its city, though threatened again by its enemies. After this we read:

Then the LORD will go out and fight against those nations as when he fights on a day of battle. On that day his feet shall stand on the Mount of Olives that lies before Jerusalem on the east, ... Then the LORD my God will come, and all the holy ones[75] with him. .

---

73. I am not using these terms with the limited senses they often have in Judaism.
74. 1 Cor. 6:2; 2 Tim. 2:12; Rev. 5:10; 20:4, 6; 22:5.
75. The "holy ones" in Dan. 7 (see above) are holy ones *on earth*, the "holy ones" in Zech. 14 are descending *from heaven*; they may refer to angels (Matt. 16:27; 25:31) or to glorified saints (Col. 3:4; 1 Thess. 3:13; Rev. 17:14; 19:14).

. . And the LORD will be king over all the earth. On that day the LORD will be one and his name one. The whole land shall be turned into a plain from Geba to Rimmon south of Jerusalem. But Jerusalem shall remain aloft on its site from the Gate of Benjamin to the place of the former gate, to the Corner Gate, and from the Tower of Hananel to the king's winepresses. And it shall be inhabited, for there shall never again be a decree of utter destruction. Jerusalem shall dwell in security (vv. 3–11).

This passage dealt with the appearance of the LORD, who intervenes in order to save his people, and especially his city, and to this end he personally descends on the Mount of Olives. He really and concretely stands with his feet on this Mount. He not only redeems Israel, but also immediately establishes his kingdom of peace and justice. The rest of the chapter dealt with this kingdom, in which the nations of the world will go up to Jerusalem to serve the LORD there, and to celebrate *Sukkot* (the Feast of Booths) (vv. 16–19). This also presupposed the rebuilding of the temple, evident from verses 20–21 about the "house of the LORD." Therefore, there can be no doubt that the appearance of the Messiah is included in this descent of the LORD.

In the New Testament this matter is clear: in Isaiah 6:1–5, the prophet recorded a glimpse of the glory of the LORD, who spoke to him, and John 12:41 tells us that this was none other than the glory of the pre-incarnate Christ that Isaiah beheld. Hebrews 1:10–12 applies to Jesus the words of Psalm 102:24–27; in the words of Hebrews: "You, Lord [the LORD of Ps. 102], laid the foundation of the earth in the beginning, and the heavens are the work of your hands; they will perish, but you remain; they will all wear out like a garment, like a robe you will roll them up, like a garment they will be changed. But you are the same, and your years will have no end."[76] He is God and Man in one person, the One who will descend to the Mount of Olives in order to definitively save Israel and to establish the Messianic kingdom. This is what the angels tell Jesus' disciples: this Jesus who ascended from this place to heaven, he is the One who will descend again from heaven upon the Mount of Olives.

More passages in the Tanakh tell us that the establishment of the Messianic kingdom begins with the appearance of the LORD in

---

76. See further Ouweneel (2007b, §8.1.1).

Jerusalem (and we add: in the person of the returning Christ). A beautiful example is this:

> As a lion or a young lion growls over his prey, and when a band of shepherds is called out against him he is not terrified by their shouting or daunted at their noise, so the LORD of hosts will come down to fight on Mount Zion and on its hill. Like birds hovering, so the LORD of hosts will protect Jerusalem; he will protect and deliver it; he will spare and rescue it (Isa. 31:4–5).

A few verses later, we read:

> Behold, a king will reign in righteousness, and princes will rule in justice. Each will be like a hiding place from the wind, a shelter from the storm, like streams of water in a dry place, like the shade of a great rock in a weary land. Then the eyes of those who see will not be closed, and the ears of those who hear will give attention. The heart of the hasty will understand and know, and the tongue of the stammerers will hasten to speak distinctly (Isa. 32:1–4).

The Messianic kingdom follows here upon the LORD's descent to "Zion" — not necessarily one particular mountain, but a general poetic reference to Jerusalem and the mountains beneath and around it.

Chapter 6
The Physical and the Spiritual Israel

> [T]o this day the same veil remains over them [i.e., the Jews] when they read the Old Covenant; it has not been unveiled, because only by the Messiah is the veil taken away. Yes, till today, whenever Moshe is read, a veil lies over their heart. "But," says the Torah, "whenever someone turns to **Adonai**, the veil is taken away." [Exod. 34:34] Now, "Adonai" in this text means the Spirit. And where the Spirit of Adonai is, there is freedom. So all of us, with faces unveiled, see as in a mirror the glory of the Lord; and we are being changed into his very image, from one degree of glory to the next, by Adonai the Spirit.
>
> 2 Corinthians 3:14–18 (CJB)

6.1 Physical Israel
6.1.1 Preterism

AS WE NOW CONTINUE with our subject, we will first explain another erroneous teaching, in addition to supersessionism, namely, preterism. Supersessionism has been around for many centuries, but preterism is relatively new. Preterism asserts that all prophecies about Israel, including those about the return of the Messiah, were fulfilled in and around AD 70; this is called "full preterism." There is also a milder form, called "partial preterism." Some claim that the most important, relatively recent defender of such a "partial preterism" was D. Chilton.[1] He did leave room for a second coming of Christ at the end of time, but understood Matthew 24 as having been entirely fulfilled in AD 70, including the references to the "coming" of the Son of Man.

Full preterism is closely related to supersessionism; in fact, the former is a fruit of the latter. We could call it a form of consistent supersessionism; in other words, if you are a supersessionist, and you wish to be consistent, then I cannot see how you would not eventually be convinced of full preterism. That is, if you believe that Matthew 24 described the time around the fall of Jerusalem in AD 70, then you must also believe that Jesus came back in those days, because verses 29–30 said,

> *Immediately* after the tribulation of those days [i.e., ostensibly around AD 70] the sun will be darkened, and the moon will not give its light, and the stars will fall from heaven, and the powers of the heavens will be shaken. Then will appear in heaven the sign of the Son of Man, and then all the tribes of the earth will mourn, and they will see the Son of Man coming on the clouds of heaven with power and great glory.

Of course, not many supersessionists would like to be *that* consistent; most of them do believe in a future second coming of Christ.

The most important arguments adduced for preterism are passages that supposedly suggest that Jesus will return within one generation. For instance: "Truly, I say to you, there are some standing here who will not taste death until they see the Son of Man coming in his kingdom" (Matt. 16:28). This is understood to mean that, when Jesus returns, some of them standing there would still be alive. Preterists forget that Jesus himself spoke a different language in the three parables of Matthew 24–25. The wicked servant says, "My master is *delayed*" (24:48), which no Christian would have said if the Lord had come back within that generation's lifetime. The second parable says, "Then the kingdom of heaven will be like ten virgins who took their lamps and went to meet the bridegroom. . .

---

1. See, e.g., Chilton (1987; 2007).

. As the bridegroom was *delayed*, they all became drowsy and slept. But *at midnight* there was a cry, 'Here is the bridegroom! Come out to meet him'" (25:1-6). That is, Jesus would stay away so unexpectedly long as a bridegroom who, instead of arriving in daytime, arrives at midnight.

The third parable, that of the talents, says, "*[A]fter a long time* the master of those servants came and settled accounts with them" (v. 19). This language is clear enough, too: Jesus would stay away "a long time," which by now has been almost two thousand years. This is not in conflict with Revelation 22, where Jesus says three times, "Behold, I am coming soon" (vv. 7, 12, 20), given the fact that, for God, "a thousand years . . . are but as yesterday when it is past" (Ps. 90:4; cf. 2 Pet. 3:8).

As far as Matthew 16:28 is concerned, clearly Jesus was referring to the event that would follow immediately after his words: his transfiguration on the mount, where Moses and Elijah appeared to him, and together with him, to the three disciples. The former two represented the heavenly saints during the Messianic kingdom, the latter three the earthly saints during that same kingdom, and Jesus stood in their midst in all the glory and majesty with which he will be invested during the Messianic kingdom. The fact that this scene indeed prefigured the "age to come" and the "world to God" (Heb. 2:5; 6:5) was confirmed by the apostle Peter, who emphasized the eschatological dimension of the transfiguration on the mount:

> [W]e [i.e., Jesus' disciples] did not follow cleverly devised myths when we made known to you the power and *coming of our Lord Jesus Christ*, but we were eyewitnesses of his majesty. For when he received honor and glory from God the Father, and the voice was borne to him by the Majestic Glory, "This is my beloved Son, with whom I am well pleased," we ourselves heard this very voice borne from heaven, for we were with him on the holy mountain. And we have the prophetic word more fully confirmed, to which you will do well to pay attention as to a lamp shining in a dark place, until the day dawns and the morning star rises in your hearts (2 Pet. 1:16-19).

Another passage that preterists love to quote is Matthew 24:34, "Truly, I say to you, this generation will not pass away until all these things take place." Here again, preterists suggest that, according to Jesus himself, he would come again within one generation (about forty years). However, at least three alternative explanations of this verse are plausible:

(a) "This generation" referred to the people living when these signs and events will begin (so the AMP; cf. EXB): the "generation" of the "latter days."

(b) The CJB renders: "I tell you that this people will certainly not pass away before all these things happen." David Stern suggests that Jesus "is guaranteeing [here] that the Jews will persist as a people until the second coming,"[2] with reference to Jeremiah 31:35–37, where the LORD guaranteed that, as long as the fixed order of the celestial bodies is not be disturbed, so long will the "offspring of Israel" last before him.

(c) Others have suggested that the Greek word *genea* ("generation") must be explained from Matthew 17:17, where Jesus said to his own disciples: "O faithless and twisted generation, how long am I to be with you? How long am I to bear with you?" Here the sense seems to be not so much people living during the same period, but a group of people — a "race" — of a certain (im)moral character: an "evil and adulterous generation" (12:39, 45; 16:4). The sense in Matthew 24:34 could thus be: this kind of (evil) people will be around all the time, until the arrival of the Messianic kingdom; you will never be able to get rid of them. As Jesus explained in the parable of the weeds: "Let both [i.e., wheat and weed] grow together until the harvest, and at harvest time I will tell the reapers, 'Gather the weeds first and bind them in bundles to be burned, but gather the wheat into my barn'" (Matt. 13:30).

6.1.2 More on Matthew 24

It may be clear that, in this context, Matthew 24 is the most important Bible passage about which many battles have raged for centuries (see more extensively, §13.1). To begin with, let us look at verse 14: "[T]his gospel of the kingdom will be proclaimed throughout the whole world as a testimony to all nations, and then the end will come." First, this gospel is not exactly the same as the gospel of God's grace for poor sinners, which has been preached for many centuries. It is rather the "gospel of the kingdom," and I venture to

---

2. Stern (1999, 75).

The Physical and the Spiritual Israel

say that this has received the full attention of theologians only since the nineteenth century, and especially since the twentieth century. The gospel of grace says more or less this: "You are a sinner, but if you believe in Jesus, you may know that he bore your sins on the cross, so that you will be saved." The gospel of the kingdom says more or less this: "You are part of the evil kingdom of Satan,[3] and you will perish with him, unless you accept Jesus as your Lord and King, so that you will not perish with Satan's kingdom, but will enter into, and prevail with, Messiah's kingdom."

Second, around AD 70 gospel had reached neither the entire Middle East nor the "whole world." Only since the twentieth century has the preaching of the gospel to all the nations of the world begun to be fulfilled to some extent. Conclusion: it is difficult to imagine how the announcement of Jesus, and thus also his further exposition, could ever have been fulfilled before the twentieth century. Conversely, this means that, today more than ever before, we have every reason to anticipate the imminent reappearance of Jesus the Messiah.

Another point that may strike us in Matthew 24 is "the abomination of desolation" mentioned in verse 15. This expression was obviously derived from the book of Daniel, which spoke of an "abomination that makes desolate (or, brings desolation)" (11:31; 12:11; cf. 9:27). A study of Daniel shows that this referred to an idolatrous image like the one that the Syrian King Antiochus IV Epiphanes had placed in the temple at Jerusalem in 167 BC. In AD 70, such an "abomination"—an idolatrous image in some form—*did not at all exist in the temple*. Preterists quote various pagan and Christian writers from that time who described miraculous natural phenomena occurring around AD 70. But nothing of these things even vaguely resembled the second coming of Christ as it is described in the New Testament: on the clouds of heaven, visible for all people (cf. Rev. 1:7). *There was no abomination in the temple, and there was no visible Messianic appearance from heaven.*

Look also at verse 24, "[F]alse christs [or, messiah's] and false prophets will arise and perform great signs and wonders, so as to

---

3. Cf. Matt. 12:26–28, "if Satan casts out Satan, he is divided against himself. How then will his kingdom stand? . . . But if it is by the Spirit of God that I cast out demons, then the kingdom of God has come upon you."

lead astray, if possible, even the elect." We may quietly say that such a crowd of false messiahs and false prophets did not exist in Israel around AD 70. These things lead me to a conclusion that will be corroborated by our further studies of this chapter, and that is of great significance: *verses 15–31 do not refer at all to the time around AD 70* but rather to the "latter days," when Israel will be back in its land, as has indeed been the case, physically and partially spiritually, since the establishment of the state of Israel in 1948.[4] For us who are not preterists, this conclusion is confirmed by a point of enormous significance: *this time of the restored Israel in its own land will end with the coming of the Son of Man, that is, the Messiah* (notice the "immediately" in v. 29). The expression "Son of Man" appears seven times in this End Time Sermon of Jesus:

(1) ". . . as the lightning comes from the east and shines as far as the west, so will be the coming of the *Son of Man*" (24:27).

(2, 3) "Immediately after the tribulation of those days the sun will be darkened, and the moon will not give its light, and the stars will fall from heaven, and the powers of the heavens will be shaken. Then will appear in heaven the sign of the *Son of Man*, and then all the tribes of the earth [better: of the land] will mourn, and they will see the *Son of Man* coming on the clouds of heaven with power and great glory. And he will send out his angels with a loud trumpet call, and they will gather his elect from the four winds, from one end of heaven to the other" (vv. 30–31).

(4, 5) "[A]s were the days of Noah, so will be the coming of the *Son of Man*. For as in those days before the flood they were eating and drinking, marrying and giving in marriage, until the day when Noah entered the ark, and they were unaware until the flood came and swept them all away, so will be the coming of the *Son of Man*" (vv. 37–39).

(6) "Therefore you also must be ready, for the *Son of Man* is coming at an hour you do not expect" (v. 44).

(7) "When the *Son of Man* comes in his glory, and all the angels with him, then he will sit on his glorious throne" (25:31).

---

4. Notice the difference with Luke 21, which does refer to the events of AD 70, and where there are the (long) "times of the Gentiles" (v. 24) between these events and the second coming of Christ.

6.1.3 Jesus' Return is Future

Should preterists not gain some wisdom from the reality that, in the first centuries of church history, no Christian writer, such as church historian Eusebius and so many others, ever came to the discovery that Jesus had already returned in AD 70? How can it be explained that all the ancient church creeds, such as the Apostles' Creed, the Nicene Creed, and the Athanasian Creed ("He will come again with glory to judge the living and the dead") — all composed long *after* AD 70 — speak of a *future* return of Christ? In other words, the writers of these Creeds were convinced that the following verses were all to be fulfilled in the future: Christ "is the one appointed by God to be judge of the living and the dead" (Acts 10:42). "[T]o this end Christ died and lived again, that he might be Lord both of the dead and of the living" (Rom. 14:9). "I charge you in the presence of God and of Christ Jesus, who is to judge the living and the dead, and by his appearing and his kingdom . . ." (2 Tim. 4:1). The wicked "will give account to him who is ready to judge the living and the dead" (1 Pet. 4:5).

The Bible connects the second coming of Christ with an entire series of events, *none of which occurred around* AD 70. Let me give some examples.

(a) Jesus will come on the clouds of heaven, and "every eye will see him, even those who pierced him" (Rev. 1:7; cf. Matt. 24:30). This did not happen in those days.

(b) The wicked enemies of Christ will be judged, and the devil will be shut up for a time, so that he can no longer deceive the people (Rev. 17:14; 19:11–20:3). This did not happen in those days; the devil still moves around freely (1 Pet. 5:8).

(c) When Christ comes in all his glory, he will sit down on his "glorious throne," and all the nations will be gathered before him in order to be judged by him (Matt. 25:31-46). This did not happen in AD 70.

(d) The angel Gabriel promised to Mary that God would give to Jesus the throne of his father David (Luke 1:32); this is the throne of David's kingship over Israel (2 Sam. 3:10; 1 Kings 2:12). This throne is still in Jerusalem (Ps. 133:3-5) — perhaps not literally, but at any rate there is where it should stand; it never stood anywhere else. As we have seen, it is definitely not the throne of God in heaven. When

Jesus comes again, he will sit on *this* throne, and forever there will be peace and justice on earth (Isa. 9:6-7). *None of these things were fulfilled in or around AD 70*—unless all these Bible passages are "spiritualized away" (see below). (And if you do such a thing, you can make the Bible say whatever you like.)

Jesus will return on the Mount of Olives (Acts 1:11); in his person, God himself will place his feet on the Mount of Olives (Zech. 14:4). There, his glorious kingdom over Israel, but also over all the nations, will begin; all these nations will go up to physical Jerusalem in physical Israel (vv. 9-19). There, on Mount Zion, they will learn the Torah—which therefore cannot have been annulled—and they shall beat their swords into plowshares, and enjoy peace (Micah 4:1-4; Isa. 2:1-4). Moreover, at Jesus' second coming all deceased believers will rise bodily from the dead in order to be brought into the Father's house,[5] and to reign with Christ (Rev. 20:4, 6). Again, *none of these things were fulfilled in or around AD 70*; no dead believers rose from the dead (unless preterists adhere to the ancient heresy of only some "spiritual" resurrection; cf. 2 Tim. 2:18), and least of all have they been brought into the Father's house.

Preterism is a sad appendage of supersessionism. According to this doctrine, the present events in and around the state of Israel ostensibly have nothing to do with biblical prophecies. Supersessionists tell us that these must all be understood spiritually; preterists tell us that they were all fulfilled around AD 70. The only exception, according to partial preterists, is the second coming of Christ, which must still occur, but in a setting that has nothing to do with the Israelite setting of Matthew 24. And here we have the key to refute this entire doctrine: in Matthew 24, the appearance of the Son of Man on the clouds of heaven *has everything to do with ethnic Israel living in its own country (again)*. Just before the (re-)appearance of the Messiah, in the physical city of Jerusalem, there will be a physical "holy place," where a physical "abomination of desolation" will dwell, which will be destroyed by the Messiah himself.

The preterists are right on one point, namely, in claiming that the second coming of Christ will occur while (ethnic) Israel is in its own land. Traditional supersessionists are also right on one point, namely, in believing that the second coming of Christ is an event

---

5. John 14:1-3; 1 Cor. 15:50-57; 1 Thess. 4:13-17; Phil. 3:20-21.

that still lies in the future. What if these advocates would sit down together and develop a new insight combining the best of these two worlds? The second coming still lies in the future, and *when* it occurs, *Israel will be living in its own country (again)*. We will deal with this subject more extensively in chapter 13.

6.2 Confirmation by the Apostle Paul
6.2.1 The Place of Romans 9–11

I have decided that the best approach is to deal with my subject in bits and pieces. The disadvantage of this approach is that, time and again, I need to deal with a theme only briefly, while a more extensive treatment will have to wait until a later point, or even more than one later point, in these volumes. From a didactic point of view, though, this seems to me the safest route to follow, so that readers—especially those coming from a supersessionist background—will gradually be made familiar with the numerous aspects of our subject.

For instance, at a later point we must consider more extensively how dangerous and misleading it is to spiritualize, in many Bible passages, designations like "Zion," "Jerusalem," "Judah," and "Israel," and to identify these as the Ecclesia. In the Dutch States Translation, this mistake appears constantly in the headings and the Annotations associated with the prophetic books. In this way, all consolation for Zion as it existed in the days of the prophets, and will exist in the latter times, is effectively removed.[6]

The apostle Paul, I suppose, would have had little sympathy for this, if I read his letter to the Romans correctly. I cannot image that any sensible expositor could ever have doubted that in Romans 9–11 the apostle was speaking about ethnic Israel, his "brothers," his "kinsmen according to the flesh . . . Israelites" (9:3-4). We need only follow the argument of Paul in Romans. He first demonstrates that all people have sinned, both Jews and Gentiles (2:9; 3:9), and that God offers salvation to both groups because both equally need

---

6. During a sermon that for me was incomprehensible—I was perhaps ten years old—I read those headings in the Bible that I had borrowed for that church service. I read about "the church such" and the "church so," and I read those chapters to find mention of the "church," but without success. What I did find was Zion, Jerusalem, Judah, Israel, and so on. I could not understand this—and now, two-thirds of a century later, I still do not understand it.

it (1:16); in these elementary respects there is *no* difference between Jews and Gentiles (10:12). In the course of Romans 1–8 not one advantage is identified that the Jew has over the Gentile. You might think that possessing the Torah is such an advantage, but if a Jew is a sinful person, who disobeys the Torah, then possessing the Torah is rather a disadvantage than an advantage because they are judged according to that very same Torah (3:12–29).

After chapters 1–8, Paul dealt with the question raised already in 3:1, "Then what advantage has the Jew?" What difference does it make to be a Jew? What might be the unique calling and destiny of Israel in the further plans of God? This is worked out in Romans 9–11. It is one of those subjects that we can deal with extensively only later in these volumes, especially when we examine the significance of the olive tree in Romans 11 (see §§12.1 and 14.1). At this point, we limit ourselves to the apostle's conclusion: "[I]n this way all Israel will be saved, as it is written, 'The Deliverer will come from Zion, he will banish ungodliness from Jacob'; 'and this will be my covenant with them when I take away their sins'" (11:26–27). Here the point to consider is not that some supersessionists (like John Calvin[7]) were able to discover in these verses a "spiritual Israel," that is, the Ecclesia. This simply exhibits the blinding power of mistaken paradigms. For three entire chapters Paul had been speaking unmistakably about ethnic Israel—but then, suddenly, in chapter 11:26, he must have been referring to the Ecclesia? This has nothing to do with serious exegesis. The only reason for this conclusion is the supersessionist bias, which governs exegesis. *Where dogmatics dominates exegesis, the result is always bad theology.*

Apart from this point, it is fascinating and significant to notice how Paul quoted the Tanakh here (vv. 26–27). Presumably, various passages were present in his mind at the same time, but this is the most important one to which he alludes:

> "And a Redeemer will come to Zion, / to those in Jacob who turn from transgression," / declares the LORD. / "And as for me, this is my covenant with them," says the LORD: "My Spirit that is upon you, and my words that I have put in your mouth, shall not depart out of your mouth, or out of the mouth of your offspring, or out of the mouth of

---

7. Calvin (n.d., ad loc.); see also Paas (2014, 53–55), and especially Maljaars (2015).

your children's offspring," says the LORD, "from this time forth and forevermore" (Isa. 59:20-21).

This is the enormous significance of these verses: in Romans 9-11 Paul was speaking unequivocally about ethnic Israel, as we will see, and underscored this with a quotation from the Tanakh that, according to him, *was dealing with ethnic Israel*. Paul did not spiritualize such statements of Isaiah, but understood them literally.

6.2.2 Isaiah's and Paul's Message

What Yesha'yahu (the prophet Isaiah) and Rabbi Sha'ul (the apostle Paul) wished to teach us is this: one day, "all Israel" will return (convert) to the God of Israel. The expression turns out to mean in practice: the humbled and repenting *part* of Israel, that is, those who indeed confess their sins before God (cf. 57:14-21; 59:9-13). See earlier in 10:21-22, "A remnant will return [Heb. *sh'ar yashub*[8]], the remnant of Jacob, to the mighty God. For though your people Israel be as the sand of the sea, only a remnant of them will return." For this remnant idea, see also 17:4-6:

> [I]n that day the glory of Jacob will be brought low, and the fat of his flesh will grow lean. And it shall be as when the reaper gathers standing grain and his arm harvests the ears, and as when one gleans the ears of grain in the Valley of Rephaim. Gleanings will be left in it, as when an olive tree is beaten—two or three berries in the top of the highest bough, four or five on the branches of a fruit tree.

How can the "remnant" of Israel ultimately be called "all Israel"? The answer is that the Israel that will be allowed into the Messianic kingdom consists entirely of *tzaddiqim*: "In the LORD all the offspring of Israel shall be justified [of, shall be(come) righteous; Heb. *yitzd'qu*, root *tz-d-q*] and shall glory" (Isa. 45:25). "Your people shall all be righteous [*tzaddiqim*, root *tz-d-q*]; they shall possess the land forever, the branch of my planting, the work of my hands, that I might be glorified" (60:21). We have not the slightest reason or right to *extend* the term "all Israel" to non-Jewish Jesus-believers, but must do the very opposite: we must *limit* the term to the "true" Israel, "the Israel of God," that is, the faithful, the humble, the pen-

---

8. Interestingly, one of Isaiah's sons had this name: "Then *Adonai* said to Yesha'yahu, 'Go out now to meet Achaz, you and your son Sh'ar Yashuv'" (Isa. 7:3 CJB).

itent. This is an important principle, which we will encounter several times, at quite different places: the phrase "spiritual Israel" is quite acceptable as long as it is not *extended* (to non-Israel) but *limited* (to the true core of Israel). This, and none other, is the "all Israel" that will be saved, and will be allowed into the Messianic kingdom. *More* than these will be allowed into the kingdom (e.g., Matt. 25:31-34), but these are Gentile *tzaddiqim*; they are never called "Israel."

Compare here Paul's famous saying, whose literal form is this: "For not all those who are of [or, from, Gk. *ex*] Israel are Israel" (Rom. 9:6). This can be—and has been—read in two different ways: the *extensive* way, which, according to the context, is the wrong way, and the *restrictive* way, which is the correct way: (a) In the former case—the *extensive*, that is, the *wrong* way[9]—the text is read as follows: not all those who eventually are "(spiritual) Israel" were originally born of ethnic Israel (or, of the patriarchs). In the entire context, there is not the slightest reason to read the text in such an extending way; on the contrary, it goes against the entire spirit of the passage, and such a reading is rooted in nothing but supersessionist bias.

(b) In the latter case—the *restrictive*, that is the *correct* way—the text is read as follows: not all those who were born of ethnic Israel's root (or, of the patriarchs) eventually belonged to Israel, the blessed people of God (and this explains why, today as well, not all Israelites belong to the true Israel of God) (see further in §6.5.2). For instance, Ishmael was a son of Abraham, yet fell outside the sphere of blessing. Esau was a grandson of Abraham, and even a twin brother of Jacob, yet he did not receive the great patriarchal blessing, either. Paul's argument was this: not every Abrahamite "automatically" receives the covenant blessing, *not*: there are more "Israelites" than the physical descendants of the patriarchs. Supersessionists read the text in a way that is the very opposite of what the context permits.

The future conversion of Israel is clearly localized in time: it will occur when the Deliverer (read, the Messiah) comes "to Zion" (Paul wrote, "from [or, out of] Zion," but for our argument this makes no difference; perhaps Paul had Ps. 14:7; 50:2; 53:7 in mind).

---

9. Rom. 9:6 plays an important role in the way Maljaars (2015, e.g., 69–71) spiritualizes Rom. 11:26; see Maljaars (1976).

Thus, the great restoration is linked with "Zion," which is the poetic designation of the physical Jerusalem during the Messianic kingdom. With this restored Israel the New Covenant is made, as Jeremiah 31:31–34 makes clear: with the ten and the two tribes of Israel. The fact that Gentile Jesus-believers profit from this New Covenant does not make them "Israel."

Sometimes, however, the apostle Paul seemed to spiritualize certain prophecies, for instance, by applying Hosea 1:10 and 2:22 to believers from the Gentile world:

> ... us whom he has called, not from the Jews only but also from the Gentiles? As indeed he says in Hosea, "Those who were not my people I will call 'my people,' and her who was not beloved I will call 'beloved.'" "And in the very place where it was said to them, 'You are not my people,' there they will be called 'sons of the living God'" (Rom. 9:24–26).

However, we will see that this is rather an example of a midrashic application, not of real exegesis, as everyone must be able to see, whether supersessionist or not. Hosea said: Israel was first *Lo-'Ammi* ("Not-My-People"), but one day will be accepted and will become *'Ammi* ("My-People") again. Paul said, Look, it is similar with the Gentile nations: first they were not God's people, but when they come to faith in Christ, they begin to belong to God's people.

Paul could never have intended this as grammatical-historical exegesis! If he had, he would simply have blundered: in Hosea *Lo-'Ammi* was not the Gentile world at all, but God's own people of Israel, set aside for a time. Of course, Paul was fully aware of this. Everyone can see that he gives a midrashic (that is, homiletic, typological) application. He sees a similarity between Israel who had been set aside and the Gentiles—both becoming "people of God" by faith—without ignoring the essential differences. It is a hermeneutical error (a) to read Paul as if he is giving here grammatical-historical exegesis, and (b) to deduce from this how we should read Hosea 1–2.[10]

---

10. We find a similar midrashic application in 2 Cor. 6:16b ("I will make my dwelling among them and walk among them, and I will be their God, and they shall be my people"), which goes back to Lev. 26:12 (cf. Ezek. 37:27): what one day will happen with (the remnant of) ethnic Israel (grammatical-histori-

6.3 No Ecclesia in the Tanakh
6.3.1 The Meaning of *Ekklēsia*

As we have seen, supersessionism (or substitutionism) is often called "replacement theology." This doctrine says that, in God's governmental ways with the earth, the ethnic Israel of the Tanakh continues as the people of God in the (New Testament, post-Pentecost) Ecclesia, and that this Ecclesia is the spiritual Israel. Supersessionism claims that ethnic Israel as such has no spiritual future, with one exception: the *individual* Jew can come to faith in Jesus, then join a Christian denomination, abandoning all those Jewish elements they had possessed throughout their life: no more circumcision (except in the spiritual sense), no more Sabbath on Saturday, no more *kashrut* ("food laws"), no more Jewish festivals, no more submission to any specific element in the Mosaic Torah. This is one of the strangest aspects of supersessionism, if not an outright paradox: *you can become a member of spiritual Israel only by laying aside everything that is Israelite*. The stress on being the spiritual Israel is correlative to the denial and abandonment of all those Jewish elements. Therefore, so-called "Messianic Jews" are looked at with suspicion and rejection, on the one hand by orthodox Jews, on the other hand by Roman Catholic and Protestant supersessionists.

Actually, I know of no theologian who will openly admit to being a replacement theologian (or a supersessionist, or a substitutionist). These are dirty words. Similarly, no Jew or Christian will ever say that he or she is "legalistic," or that he or she has no sense of humor. Yet, "we," the others, firmly believe that some people *are* inclined to "legalism" (finding rules more important than people, or inclined to imposing [often self-made] rules on people), and many people have only a limited sense of humor. Similarly, many theologians are replacement theologians, whether or not they appreciate this label. I venture to say that, if you reject the literal land promise, you adhere to some form of replacement theology. If you claim that circumcision has been replaced by infant baptism, you adhere to some form of replacement theology. If you say that the biblical Sabbath is to be observed on Sunday and no longer on Saturday, you adhere to some form of replacement theology.

I even venture to say that, if you wish to be a *consistent* Roman

---

cal exegesis) resembles what is happening today with the Gentile world.

Catholic, or Lutheran, or Reformed believer, you must adhere to replacement theology. On the one hand, you cannot say, for instance, that today the Ecclesia is God's covenant people, and at the same time reject replacement theology. But on the other hand, if you deny that the Ecclesia is God's covenant people, then how can you call yourself Reformed?

The Greek word *ekklēsia* is the usual New Testament word for "church," or "assembly," or "congregation," in their ecclesiastical meanings. This term *ekklēsia* and its Hebrew equivalents (*'edah* or *qahal*) were never used in the Tanakh to refer to anything that even vaguely resembles what in the New Testament is called "church." The latter is the body of the glorified Christ in heaven (Eph. 1:20-23)—but in the Tanakh there was not yet any glorified *Man* at the right hand of God in heaven. The Ecclesia is the house or the temple of God the Holy Spirit (1 Cor. 3:16; 2 Cor. 6:16; Eph. 2:20-22)—but in the Tanakh, the Holy Spirit had not yet been poured out as happened in Acts 2: before the Day of Pentecost, the Holy Spirit *worked* on earth, since Genesis 1:2, but never *dwelt* on earth, as he now dwells in the Ecclesia. In the Tanakh, Israel was the bride or wife of God (e.g., Ezek. 16; Hos. 2)—but there could be no question of a community being the bride or wife of the glorified *Lamb* in heaven (cf. Rev. 19:7; 21:9).

The Tanakh spoke of the people's "congregation" in Egypt or in the wilderness (see from Exod. 12:3, 6, 19, 47 and later), and for this, used words like *'edah* or *qahal*, in the Septuagint rendered as *ekklēsia* (see Acts 7:38, "This [Moses] is the one who was in the assembly in the wilderness with the angel who spoke to him on Mount Sinai"). But to say that "therefore" the New Testament *ekklēsia* is the same as this *ekklēsia* in the Tanakh is just as invalid as saying that the *ekklēsia* of Christ is the same as the *ekklēsia* ("city assembly") of Ephesus (Acts 19:32, 39-40).

Apart from these considerations, in what possible sense could one speak of any kind of "church" in the Tanakh? The Belgic Confession says in Article 27:

> We believe and profess one catholic or universal Church, which is a holy congregation of true Christian believers, all expecting their salvation in Jesus Christ, being washed by His blood, sanctified, and sealed by the Holy Spirit.

This church has been from the beginning of the world, and will be to the end thereof; . . . .[11]

I perceive a strange inconsistency in this Article. The first part of it is an excellent description of the *New Testament* Ecclesia: not one ethnic nation, but a worldwide Ecclesia; not simply God-believers but Christ-believers (*christgelovigen*, as the original Dutch text said), "all expecting their salvation in Jesus Christ, being washed by His blood" (believers in the Tanakh looked forward to the Messiah, but they could not know very much about him; and did they await the salvation *from their sins* from him?). And last but not least: being "sanctified and sealed by the Holy Spirit" is a typically New Testament phenomenon,[12] a post-Pentecost matter, which in this way could never have been said of believers in the Tanakh. And then, after this fully *New Testament* description of the Ecclesia, the Confession—unexpectedly and without warrant—adds that *this* Ecclesia "has been from the beginning of the world, and will be to the end thereof." But (a) there was no Ecclesia before the Fall, and (b) before Acts 2, there was no Ecclesia of Jesus-believers who were washed by his blood and sealed with the Holy Spirit.

6.3.2 The Ecclesia is Post-Pentecost

How could we ever say that ethnic Israel was the Ecclesia in the Tanakh? There are no Bible passages suggesting such a thing, but there is a lot of negative evidence for it. First, Israel always consisted of both a faithful part, which loved God and served him by keeping his Torah (the *tzaddiqim*), and a large unfaithful part of non-believers and pseudo-believers. Could we then say, perhaps, that "the Israel of God" (the faithful *sha'ar* or "remnant") was "the Ecclesia of God" in the Tanakh? No, we could not, because if we did so, we would bypass all the believers in the Tanakh who did *not* belong to Israel.

(a) *Pre-Israel times:* especially Adam and Eve, Abel, Enoch, Lamech and his son Noah (Gen. 5), and the three patriarchs—you could not possibly say that Abraham was an Israelite—nor Jacob's son Joseph, and a contemporary of Abraham such as King Melchizedek (Gen. 14:18–20). Interestingly, some rabbis even spoke

---

11. Dennison (*RC* 2:440).
12. Rom. 15:16; 1 Cor. 6:11; 2 Cor. 1:21–22; Eph. 1:13; 4:30.

of *seven* non-Jewish *prophets* of God, namely, Balaam and his father Beor (Num. 22:5), Job, Eliphaz the Temanite, Bildad the Shuhite, Zophar the Naamathite (Job 2:11), and Elihu the son of Barachel (32:2).[13]

(b) *During the time of Israel:* Moses' father-in-law Jethro (Exod. 18:1–12), Rahab in Jericho (Josh. 2), Ruth the Moabitess (Ruth 1–4), Naaman the Syrian (2 Kings 5), Ebed-melech the Ethiopian (Jer. 38:7–12), and perhaps Hiram the king of Tyre (1 Kings 5:7), the widow in Zarephath (1 Kings 17), and the Shunammite (2 Kings 4). There were more than two dozen non-Israelite believers in the Tanakh, but of course there must have been many more.

The simple core of the matter is that in the Tanakh we do indeed encounter the chosen people of Israel, but *not* a clearly identifiable community of born again, God fearing *tzaddiqim*, stemming from before Israel, from Israel itself, and from outside Israel. At best, there were—what Jesus called—the "scattered children of God" (John 11:52 CJB).[14] This seems to refer not so much to the Jews in the Diaspora, but rather to Jewish as well as non-Jewish believers in and outside the land of Israel. The fact that Gentiles are included here is clear from the context: the reference is not to "the nation only," that is, Israel, but especially to the Gentile children of God. As Jesus had said one chapter earlier: "I have other sheep [i.e., Gentiles] that are not of this fold [i.e., Israel]. I must bring them also, and they will listen to my voice. So there will be one flock, one shepherd" (12:16).[15] It was only Jesus, and no one earlier, who created one single "flock" consisting of *both* the true sheep from the fold of Israel *and* the true sheep from outside Israel.

Before this, from the beginning of humanity, there had been only "scattered children of God" who had never formed a *unity* that could be called "Ecclesia." In the Ecclesia, the totality is always more than the mere sum of the parts; one cannot simply add all those "scattered children of God" mentioned in the Tanakh, and then claim that this sum is the Ecclesia in the Tanakh.

This is the reason why Jesus spoke of the Ecclesia in the future

---

13. Talmud: Baba Bathra 15b.
14. See extensively, Ouweneel (2010a, §2.2.2).
15. Ibid., §2.2.1.

tense: "I tell you, you are Peter [i.e., "rock"], and on this rock [Gk. *petra*, i.e., on "rocks" such as Peter] I *will* build my Ecclesia, and the gates of Hades [i.e., the realm of death, Heb. *sh'ol*] shall not prevail against it" (Matt. 16:18).[16] In other words, *before Matthew 16, or Acts 2, no Ecclesia of God existed in any biblical sense*.[17]

The Ecclesia is not simply the sum of all the *tzaddiqim* of all time. We will never understand the Ecclesia if we do not discern the *collective* aspects of the Ecclesia. It is the aggregate of all those who, as one single "body," have been unified to their glorified "head" in heaven (see especially Eph. and Col.). It is the aggregate of all those who, as "living stones," "are being built up as a spiritual house, to be a holy priesthood, to offer spiritual sacrifices acceptable to God through Jesus Christ" (1 Pet. 2:5). This is the "house" of which the apostle Paul said, "Do you not know that you are God's temple and that God's Spirit dwells in you?" (1 Cor. 3:16). And: the Ecclesia is being "built together for a dwelling place of God in the Spirit" (Eph. 2:22).

This dwelling of the Spirit is a key element. To be sure, the Holy Spirit worked on the earth throughout the times of the Tanakh. But he was never said to have *dwelt* on earth; there was only a *promise* in this respect.[18] Since the Fall, the Spirit was like the "dove"[19] that "found no place to set her foot" (Gen. 8:9) in this wicked world. The first time the Spirit found such a place was when Jesus appeared on earth and was baptized by John the Baptist: when Jesus "had been baptized and was praying, the heavens were opened, and the Holy Spirit descended on him in bodily form, like a dove; and a voice came from heaven, 'You are my beloved Son; with you I am well pleased'" (Luke 3:21–22). However, even then, there was not yet a *unified company* in which the Holy Spirit could dwell. Therefore, it was said about Jesus' day: ". . . the Spirit was not yet present, because Jesus had not yet been glorified" (John 7:39 MOUNCE). In other words, first, Jesus had to be glorified—which happened at his as-

---

16. Ibid., §2.1.2–2.1.3.

17. It might seem that in Matt. 18:17 "the church" was viewed as something already existing at that point; but one need only ask where this community had existed at that time.

18. Isa. 44:3; Ezek. 36:27; 37:14; 39:29; Joel 2:28–29.

19. Cf. the "hovering" of God's *ruach* over the waters in Gen. 1:2.

cension into heaven (Acts 1) — and only then could the Holy Spirit come to dwell on earth (Acts 2).

Therefore, the ignorant disciples in Ephesus could say, "[W]e did not so much as hear whether the Holy Spirit was [given]" (Acts 19:2 ASV; or, "whether the Holy Spirit had [come]").[20] Only at the moment the Holy Spirit was poured out could the Ecclesia be formed: "For in one Spirit we were all baptized into one body — Jews or Greeks, slaves or free — and all were made to drink of one Spirit" (1 Cor. 12:13).[21] In my view, this means that it was through the Holy Spirit that the "scattered children of God" were forged together into one body ("Spirit baptism").

6.4 A "Spiritual Israel"? Four "Proofs" Refuted

6.4.1 First "Proof"

We have now finally come to the point where we must evaluate the claim that the Ecclesia is the "spiritual Israel." It is my thesis that the Bible nowhere teaches this or anything that remotely resembles it. Yet, supersessionists come up with a number of biblical "proofs," which, however, are not at all valid but are nevertheless badly needed in support of the position. The claim that the Ecclesia is the spiritual Israel is one of the main pillars of supersessionism. But I hope to show that it is a pillar resting on sand. As with the house in Matthew 7:27, the rain falls, and the floods come, and the winds blow and beat against that pillar, and it falls, and great is its fall.

I will briefly deal with no fewer than twelve biblical passages, and seek to convince the reader that, if these are read properly — that is, according to correct standards of grammatical-historical exegesis — supersessionism lacks any basis. The passages are dealt with in a more or less arbitrary order.[22]

---

20. Most translations wrongly render: "whether there is any Holy Spirit" (as if disciples of John the Baptist could possibly be that ignorant about the Holy Spirit).

21. This most likely referred not to water baptism, but to Spirit baptism (cf. Matt. 3:11; John 1:33; Acts 1:5; 11:16): as the human body is immersed in water, so the human Spirit is "immersed" in the Holy Spirit.

22. See extensively, Ouweneel (2010a, chapter 3, especially for references to other publications).

The first passage that is adduced is Ephesians 2:11-13:

> Therefore remember that at one time you Gentiles in the flesh, called "the uncircumcision" by what is called "the circumcision," which is made in the flesh by hands — remember that you were at that time separated from Christ, alienated from [or, foreign to] the commonwealth of Israel and strangers to the covenants of promise, having no hope and without God in the world. But now in Christ Jesus you who once were far off have been brought near by the blood of Christ.

The supersessionist argument is this: formerly, the Gentiles were "foreigners to the commonwealth of Israel," *but now* apparently this is no longer the case. *Now* Gentile believers are *part* of the commonwealth of Israel.[23] In short, now they *do* belong to Israel, not in the ethnic sense but in the spiritual sense. The Ecclesia is the "commonwealth of Israel" in the present redemptive-historical epoch.

But this is a logical error. The text does not say that Gentile believers are now part of the commonwealth of Israel, and according to the context this could not have been Paul's intention. Paul was *never* interested, as we will see, in suggesting that Gentile believers have now become a part of "Israel," or have become "Israel," or anything like that. Paul's point is rather that Jesus-believing Jews *from* Israel and Jesus-believing non-Jews *from* the Gentile world now constitute *something entirely new*, namely, the Ecclesia of God, the body of Christ, the temple of the Holy Spirit. Paul's argument is *not*: formerly non-A, but now A, but rather: formerly, to be sure, non-A, but now something that is very different from and much more beautiful than A. It is like a daddy in Orlando telling his kids, "You were never a Chicagoan; that's true. But you have something that is much better than being a Chicagoan for we have Disney World and SeaWorld!" Here is a paraphrase of Ephesians 2:11-13: it is true, Gentile brothers and sisters, that you never had any part in the commonwealth of Israel; but don't worry, now you have received something much better than becoming a Jewish proselyte: you have become members of the body of Christ, and stones in the temple of the Lord, the dwelling place of the Holy Spirit!

In Ephesians 3:3-6 Paul speaks of "the mystery" that

---

23. Cf., e.g., Douma (2008, 63–64).

was made known to me by revelation, as I have written briefly. When you read this, you can perceive my insight into the mystery of Christ, which was not made known to the sons of men in other generations as it has now been revealed to his holy apostles and prophets by the Spirit. This mystery is that the Gentiles are fellow heirs, members of the same body, and partakers of the promise in Christ Jesus through the gospel.

Notice especially the expression "the mystery of Christ, which was not made known to the sons of men in other generations as it has now been revealed to his holy apostles and prophets." In an earlier publication,[24] A. Maljaars and I quarreled about the meaning of this sentence. In Maljaars's view, the sentence means: the mystery was not made known *to the extent that* it has been revealed now. In other words, the "mystery" is not really new; part of it was made known already in the time of the Tanakh, though not in the fullness in which it has been revealed now. My reply was—and after more than forty years I still believe the same—first, that the point of a "mystery" (i.e., a hidden thing) is that there was a time that it was not yet known at all; this was the time before the secret was unveiled. Second, I quoted a few parallel passages: verse 3 ("the mystery was made known to me by revelation," that is, before this, hitherto it was *un*known); and especially Colossians 1:26 ("the mystery hidden for ages and generations but now revealed to his saints") and Romans 16:25 ("the revelation of the mystery that was kept secret for long ages").

Third, the mystery was *not* known "to *some* extent" already in the Tanakh. Where then in the Tanakh is any corner of the veil lifted as to the contents of what Paul calls the "mystery"? Where in the Tanakh is there a hint of a future company, which would be the "body" of Christ—the glorified Man at God's right hand—the "temple" of the Holy Spirit (descended on earth and dwelling in the Ecclesia), and the "bride" or "wife" of the Lamb? A company in which Jews remain Jews, and Gentiles remain Gentiles (just as "in Christ" "there is no male and female" [Gal. 3:28], whereas also in the Ecclesia men remain men, and women remain women) but on equal footing, as members of the one body of Christ, as stones in the one temple of God? The future creation of such a company was a

---

24. Fijnvandraat et al. (1979).

perfect "mystery" (entirely hidden) in the Tanakh.[25]

6.4.2 Second "Proof"

I would like to ask this interesting question of supersessionists: If the Ecclesia is the real Israel in the present time, is it possible or allowed to still use that same name for ethnic Israel? I would think that, from the supersessionist standpoint, this is hardly warranted: there can be only one real Israel. Yet, the apostle Paul, who *never* uses the designation "Israel" for the Ecclesia—as this chapter is intended to demonstrate—*several* times used the designation "Israel" for contemporaneous ethnic Israel, including, or especially referring to, non-believing Jews. Of the latter he wrote: "They are Israelites" (Rom. 9:4). He said "that Israel who pursued a law that would lead to righteousness did not succeed in reaching that law" (i.e., they tried to make themselves righteous before God by keeping the Torah, but did not succeed; 9:31; cf. 11:7, 11, 25). Or he said, "Consider the people of Israel: are not those who eat the sacrifices participants in the altar?" (1 Cor. 10:18).

After having come to faith in Christ, the apostle Paul still could say: "I am a Jew," or, "I myself am an Israelite,"[26] which definitely did not mean "I am a member of the spiritual Israel, that is, the Ecclesia." And indirectly, the apostle Peter did the same: "You yourselves know how unlawful it is for a Jew to associate with or to visit anyone of another nation" (Acts 10:28; see also Gal. 2:14–15). In the Ecclesia of God, Jews are still Jews, and Australians are still Australians—and Jewish Australians are still Jewish Australians—but they have been made one in Christ. And if the Jesus-believing Jews are still Jews, then certainly the non-believing Jews are as well.

Perhaps the clearest example is 1 Corinthians 10:32, where Paul says, "Give no offense to Jews or to Greeks [i.e., Gentiles] or to the church of God." Paul clearly distinguishes between the three communities and calls them by their old names: the Jews are still Jews, and they are not to be confused with the "church of God." If this is so, how then could the Ecclesia in Paul's mind be the new "Israel," and how could Jesus-believers be the new "Jews" (in any sense)? In the book of Acts, we find the same thing: nowhere is the impression

---

25. Eph. 1:9; 3:1–12; 5:32; Col. 1:26–27; 2:2; 4:3.
26. Acts 21:39; 22:3; Rom. 11:1; 2 Cor. 11:22; Phil. 3:5.

given that the Ecclesia is now actually the (new or true) "Israel"; on the contrary throughout the book, "Israel" (or "the Jews") and the Ecclesia (or the Christians) remain clearly distinct. First, non-Jesus-believing Jews are viewed as erring, but they are definitely not viewed as no-longer-Jews. Second, Jesus-believing Jews are nowhere viewed as being more "Jewish" than the other Jews (nor as being less "Jewish"). Third, Jesus-believing Gentiles are viewed as being on the right track, but they are never viewed as Jews-in-a-certain-sense, or as more "Jewish" (in some spiritual sense) than ordinary Jews. Israel is and remains Israel, and the Ecclesia is the Ecclesia.

In a certain sense, one could say that a Jesus-believing Gentile is more a child of Abraham than a non-Jesus-believing Jew because spiritual descent is more significant than physical descent (cf. John 8:39 and Rom. 4:11–12) — but "Jews" and "children of Abraham" are never synonymous notions (see below).

6.4.3 Third "Proof"

We come now to another remarkable example of a logical error. This involves Paul's statement in Romans 2:28–29:[27] "[N]o one is a Jew who is merely one outwardly, nor is circumcision outward and physical. But a Jew is one inwardly, and circumcision is a matter of the heart, by the Spirit, not by the letter. His praise is not from man but from God."

Numerous supersessionists conclude from this that every person who has a "circumcised heart" is a "Jew" (whether in an ethnic sense or a spiritual sense).[28] But first, this is a logical error that claims A = B, and C = B, therefore A = C. Or more concretely: a sheep is a mammal, a cow is a mammal, so a cow is a sheep. A true Jew has a circumcised heart, a believing Gentile has a circumcised heart, so a believing Gentile is a true Jew.

Second, the entire idea itself would not fit the context of Romans 2:28–29. Paul was referring here to the difference between a true Jew and a false Jew; Gentiles are entirely outside his range of argument. The false Jew is a Jew in the sense that though one is

---

27. E.g., Robertson (2000, 38–39); Paas (2014, 283); Maljaars (2015, 41, 79, 148).
28. Of the commentators, see, e.g., Moo (1996, 175).

physically circumcised, one is not spiritually circumcised, that is, circumcised in their heart.[29] The true Jew is a Jew not only outwardly—physical circumcision—but also inwardly: the circumcision of the heart and, we may add, of the lips (cf. Exod. 6:12, 30). There was no reference in these verses to Gentiles, and therefore, we cannot draw any conclusion about Gentiles.[30]

Decades ago, I debated a rabbi at the Western Wall in Jerusalem. The subject of circumcision was raised, and I told him that I believed I was circumcised in my heart. He straightened his back, and proudly replied: "*I have circumcised lips, a circumcised heart, and a circumcised member!*" I could not compete with him there.

6.4.4 Fourth "Proof"

There is another, even more famous supersessionist "proof"—one of the "standard proofs," we might say—that supposedly demonstrates that the Ecclesia is "spiritual Israel." This is Galatians 6:16, "[N]either circumcision counts for anything, nor uncircumcision, but a new creation. And as for all who walk by this rule, peace and mercy be upon them, and upon the Israel of God." Supersessionists believe that this verse shows that the Ecclesia of God—the assembly of Jewish and non-Jewish Jesus-believers—is this "Israel of God," but the text no basis for this claim. Roman Catholic theologian Hans Küng said that the Ecclesia is the "new people of God," and adds: "Only at one point in the New Testament is the name Israel applied to the new people of God, and that only polemically and in parentheses: this must be the meaning of the phrase 'the Israel of God' (Gal 6:16)."[31]

In reality, every reader can see that Paul distinguishes *two* groups: "all who walk by this rule" *and* "the Israel of God." The first group consists of the Jesus-believing non-Jews in Galatia, who do not have to submit to the Mosaic Torah, but exclusively to the "rule" that belongs to the "new creation" (v. 15), which is the Law of Christ (v. 2). The second group, "the Israel of God," either con-

---

29. Cf. Deut. 10:16; 30:6; Jer. 4:4; 9:25–26; cf. Lev. 26:41; Ezek. 44:7–9; Acts 7:51.
30. So correctly (Reformed!) Ridderbos (1959, 69); Juster (1995, 104–05); Stern (1999, 336–40, 571–76); cf. Ouweneel (2020, 477).
31. Küng (1967, 115).

sists of those in Israel who, when they learned about the Messiah, received him in faith—that is, the Jesus-believing Jews—or the expression anticipates the "all Israel" that ultimately is saved (Rom. 11:26). We might read Paul's statement as follows: in the end, it is not physical circumcision that counts (cf. 3:28, what matters is "neither Jew nor Greek, there is neither slave nor free, there is no male and female, for you are all one in Christ Jesus"), but whether one, by faith, belongs to the "new creation" (cf. 2 Cor. 5:17), and thus lives by the "rule" of this new creation." May peace and mercy be upon them. But also—Paul added, almost as an afterthought—on "the Israel of God," that is, on those who *did* receive physical circumcision, but, just like us, are under the rules of the "new creation."[32]

Interestingly, the (supersessionist) Annotations to the Dutch States Translation provided this comment on the expression "upon the Israel of God": "That is, upon all true believers, who are true Israelites, and so acknowledged by God, which he adds to distinguish from the Israelites after the flesh; see Rom. 2:28–29 and Rom. 9:6, and so on."[33] This is a correct interpretation, apart from the question whether these commentators also viewed the Gentile believers as "sincere Israelites."

Many translators suffer to a certain extent from the bias of supersessionism. So how do they render this verse? The AMP says, ". . . upon the [true] Israel of God (Jewish believers)." The EXB says (cf. ICB), ". . . . and to all of God's people [the Israel of God; either: (1) Jewish Christians or (2) the Ecclesia as the 'new Israel']."

Apparently, some translators, like some expositors, interpreted the "and" here as an epexegetical *kai*, that is, a so-called explanatory "and." In this case, the reading would be something like this: "all who walk by this rule, peace and mercy be upon them, *namely*, upon the Israel of God." This is apparently the way the NIV and the RSV wish to read the text.[34] However, this is what we call begging the question: must this rendering prove one's preconceived idea

---

32. See Ouweneel (1991, 34, 50; 1997, 400–02; 2001a, 257 note 1).
33. Haak (1918, ad loc.).
34. See also J. B. Lightfoot, M. Zerwick, W. Gutbrod; cf. Robertson (2000, 41–43); Paas (2014, 56), and Maljaars (2015, 144–47); see references in Fung (1988, 310n61).

(the Ecclesia = Israel), and at the same time, must this preconceived idea support the rendering? This does not sound very convincing (or very scholarly).

Moreover, from a linguistic point of view, it is not very obvious to assume an exegetical *kai* here; on the contrary, the Greek *autous* ("them") and *Israel* are too far apart to require such an exegetical *kai*. In addition, the preposition *epi* ("upon") is repeated here before "the Israel of God." In other words, an epexegetical *kai* is, according to Greek grammar, simply highly unlikely here. Actually, the *kai* is exactly what one could expect here: don't despise uncircumcised believers, as if they would be second-class. What counts is being a born-again Jesus-believer—and that is also the only thing that counts for those who *have* been circumcised: also for them, the thing that really matters is to be born-again Jesus-believers. Peace and mercy be on *both* groups, which have now been united in Christ: "[I]n Christ Jesus you are all sons of God, through faith. For as many of you as were baptized into Christ have put on Christ. There is neither Jew nor Greek, there is neither slave nor free, there is no male and female, for you are all one in Christ Jesus" (Gal. 3:26–28).

6.5 A "Spiritual Israel"? Four More "Proofs" Refuted
6.5.1 Fifth "Proof"

The apostle Paul speaks about "Israel according to the flesh" (1 Cor. 10:18 LEB). Astonishingly, this has been taken as evidence that there should also be an "Israel according to the Spirit." Again we ask: By what logic? Does the expression "forefather according to the flesh' (Rom. 4:1) necessarily imply "forefathers according to the Spirit"? Does the expression "masters according to the flesh" (Eph. 6:5; Col. 3:22) necessarily imply "masters according to the Spirit"?

If the first error is logical, the second one is linguistic. We must remember here that the word "flesh" (Gk. *sarx*) has two quite different meanings in the New Testament. It can refer to the "flesh" as the carrier of the sinful nature, and in this case, there can be a clear distinction with the Spirit; for instance: "For those who live according to the flesh set their minds on the things of the flesh, but those who live according to the Spirit set their minds on the things of the Spirit. For to set the mind on the flesh is death, but to set the

The Physical and the Spiritual Israel

mind on the Spirit is life and peace" (Rom. 8:5–6). And: "[W]alk by the Spirit, and you will not gratify the desires of the flesh. For the desires of the flesh are against the Spirit, and the desires of the Spirit are against the flesh, for these are opposed to each other, to keep you from doing the things you want to do. But if you are led by the Spirit, you are not under the law" (Gal. 5:16–18). The assumption of some "Israel according to the Spirit" in contrast with "Israel according to the flesh" proceeds from this meaning of "flesh," namely, sinful flesh.

However, in 1 Corinthians 10:18 ("Israel according to the flesh") the "flesh" has a neutral meaning, as in the expression "Christ according to the flesh" (2 Cor. 5:16), which simply means "Christ as a tangible Man on earth." Similarly, "Israel according to the flesh" is physical Israel, a tangible ethnic community here on earth, without any necessary implication of sinfulness. Just as "Christ according to the flesh" does not demand a contrast with some "Christ according to the Spirit," the expression "Israel according to the flesh" does not necessarily imply an "Israel according to the Spirit."

Yet, in itself I do not object to a contrast with "Israel according to the Spirit," but only if this is taken in the following sense: such an "Israel according to the Spirit" could be taken to mean "the Israel of God," as in Galatians 6:16, the faithful core of Israel. In neither case is there any hint in the text of the Ecclesia, or of non-Jewish Jesus-believers. In Romans 9:3, Paul speaks of his "kinsmen according to the flesh," that is, his — mostly non-Jesus-believing — physical relatives: the Jews. The Jesus-believers could be called his "kinsmen according to the Spirit," whether they were Jews or Gentiles. But this does not render the latter group "Jewish." Let me say this once more:

* Gentile Jesus-believers have *not* become citizens of Israel,* nor have Jewish Jesus-believers become Gentiles (by becoming members of the predominantly Gentile church), but

* *both* Gentile and Jewish Jesus-believers have become "fellow citizens of the household of God" (Eph. 2:19), which is *never* called "Israel."

6.5.2 Sixth "Proof"

Back in §6.2.2, the famous but difficult verse, Romans 9:6, came up for discussion, which literally says: "For not all those who are of [or, from, Gk. *ex*] Israel are Israel." After briefly repeating what we wrote earlier, we will enter a little further into the difficulties of the text.

Some supersessionists read this verse in the *extending* way, which I think is mistaken.[35] That is to say, in their view, the text means that not all those who eventually are "(spiritual) Israel" were originally born of ethnic Israel (or, of the patriarchs). However, the context provides no reason for understanding the text in such an extending way. Instead of reading the sentence in the *extending* way, the context makes clear that it must rather be read in a *limiting* way: not all those who were born of ethnic Israel (or, of the patriarchs) eventually belonged to Israel, the blessed people of God. This understanding of the verse, first, fits better with the Greek original, and second, fits better within the entire context. For Paul is doing a lot of limiting here:

(a) You may be a son of Abraham, and yet fall outside God's covenant blessing (as in the case of Ishmael and his descendants).

(b) You may be a son of Isaac, and yet fall outside God's covenant blessing (as in the case of Esau and his descendants).

(c) You may be a descendant of the twelve patriarchs, and yet fall outside God's covenant blessing — not only because you are not elect (God's sovereign choice) but because you are wicked (human responsibility).

In short, what Paul wished to demonstrate here is that not all descendants of the patriarchs are automatically saved. Everyone could see the truth of this, for many Jews were wicked in their personal behavior and/or in their attitude toward Jesus. Paul's readers may have been amazed that only a limited number of Jews had believed in their Messiah. Paul answered: It was always like this — only part (a "remnant," v. 27) will be saved. This is the logical way of reading the text. But supersessionists turn the meaning around. Paul said that not every Abrahamite shares in the ultimate blessings. The supersessionists read: all those who share in the ultimate blessings become (spiritual) Abrahamites, or "Israel."

---

35. E.g., Fung (1988, 311 note 67).

6.5.3 Seventh "Proof"

The apostle Paulus wrote, "[L]ook out for those who mutilate the flesh [ancient term: concision; KJV]. For we are the circumcision, who worship by the Spirit of God and glory in Christ Jesus and put no confidence in the flesh" (Phil. 3:2–3). In the KJV, "concision" and "circumcision" form a wordplay, which goes back to a wordplay in the Greek: *katatomē* and *peritomē*, respectively.[36]

A. Maljaars wrote: "Another word for *Israel* is also the term *circumcision*, ... which he [i.e., Paul] even ventures at one occasion ... to emphatically designate the church (Phil. 3:3)."[37] The expression "the circumcision" can mean various things; for instance, sometimes it simply refers to the totality of the circumcised, that is, the Jews (cf. literally "the circumcision" in the KJV, more freely "the circumcised" in the ESV[38]). However, in Philippians 3:3, Paul wrote, "*[W]e are the circumcision*," which apparently refers to all Jesus-believers, Jews and Gentiles; he was thus referring here to the spiritually circumcised (see note 28). It is important to distinguish them: there are physically circumcised who are not spiritually circumcised, and the reverse; there are those who are both, and those who are neither of the two. Those who have been spiritually circumcised—whether they have been physically circumcised or not—in the present time constitute the Ecclesia of God.

Paul was opposing in this passage against those we call "Judaizers": those who teach that believers of non-Jewish descent cannot be saved unless they—if they are males—get circumcised. As Acts 15:1 reported: "[S]ome men came down from Judea and were teaching the brothers, 'Unless you are circumcised according to the custom of Moses, you cannot be saved.'" In Galatians 5:2, Paul tells us the reverse: "I, Paul, say to you that if you accept circumcision, Christ will be of no advantage to you." Men who give in to the Judaizers and became circumcised, were mockingly—or angrily—called by Paul the "concised" (men mutilated in the flesh). From a purely physical point of view, concision and circumcision are exactly the same. From a spiritual point of view, they are each other's

---

36. In many languages, translators have tried to maintain the wordplay: German: *Zerschneidung* and *Beschneidung*; Dutch: *versnijdenis* and *besnijdenis*.

37. Maljaars (2015, 148).

38. Rom. 3:30; Gal. 2:9, 12; Col. 4:11; Titus 1:10.

opposites. Concision was applied to on *non-Jewish* believers who have been deluded that circumcision is essential for someone's eternal salvation. Paul's conclusion was that only those are saved whose *hearts* have been circumcised, whether they are physically circumcised Jews, or physically uncircumcised Gentiles. Compare this warning word by Paul: "Was anyone at the time of his call uncircumcised? Let him not seek circumcision. For neither circumcision counts for anything nor uncircumcision, but keeping the commandments of God" (1 Cor. 7:18b, 19).

Maljaars and other supersessionists have concluded that the "spiritual circumcision" of Gentiles believers entails that they, too, have now become "Israel." However, the New Testament contains no indication that having become "spiritually circumcised" is the same as having become "Israel." "Spiritual circumcision" is a much wider concept than being Jewish. *All* believers of all time, wherever they lived, were "spiritually circumcised" — but the friends of Job were not Israelites, and Naaman and Ebed-melech, though "spiritually circumcised" (a description supersessionists would accept, I suppose) never became Israelites. Today it is no different: not every physically circumcised man is a Jew, and even less so is every "spiritually circumcised" person a "Jew." Still less do these things mean that the prophecies in the Tanakh concerning Israel have been transferred to the (New Testament) Ecclesia. Those who believe otherwise are committing the logical fallacy of *non sequitur*.

6.5.4 Eighth "Proof"

Another argument that has been drawn from 1 Peter 2:9-10:

> [Y]ou are a chosen race, a royal priesthood, a holy nation, a people for his own possession, that you may proclaim the excellencies of him who called you out of darkness into his marvelous light. Once you were not a people, but now you are God's people; once you had not received mercy, but now you have received mercy.

The apostle Peter alluded here to things that are said in the Tanakh about Israel (Exod. 19:6; Hos. 1:10; 2:22), and were applied here to the Ecclesia. The last allusion by Peter, to the book of Hosea, is also found with the apostle Paul, who applied the text even more explicitly to non-Jews:

... us whom he has called, not from the Jews only but also from the Gentiles? As indeed he says in Hosea, "Those who were not my people I will call 'my people,' and her who was not beloved I will call 'beloved.'" "And in the very place where it was said to them, 'You are not my people,' there they will be called 'sons of the living God.'"

Those who read Hosea's statement within its context will find that Hosea was speaking about ethnic Israel, which, because of its sins, had been temporarily called Not-My-People (*Lo-'Ammi*). For a time, God had oppressed his people, but through Hosea he promised that one day he was going to restore it. Israel went through these three stages: *'Ammi – Lo-'Ammi – 'Ammi*. This clearly shows that Peter and Paul were merely making an *allusion* because the Gentiles had never been *'Ammi* before. Such allusions are made several times in the New Testament. For instance, everyone can see the difference between Jeremiah 31:15 ("A voice is heard in Ramah, lamentation and bitter weeping. Rachel is weeping for her children; she refuses to be comforted for her children, because they are no more") and the way Matthew used this verse in Matthew 2:18. However, the *principle* behind the original passage and the quotation is the same: mourning about dead children. Another example: to show that the Gentiles, too, have now heard the gospel, Paul quoted Psalm 19:4; in his words: "Their voice has gone out to all the earth, and their words to the ends of the world." Again, one can easily see that this is not exegesis, for the psalm was speaking about celestial bodies. The *principle* behind the original passage and the quotation is the same: God causes a "voice" to go out through all the earth.

These examples may help us understand what method Peter and Paul were using. The *principle* behind the promised restoration was this: those who, formerly, were not God's people are now God's people. This principle can be applied very well to believers from the Gentile nations. Indeed, they were not *'Ammi – Lo-'Ammi – 'Ammi*, but they were definitely *Lo-'Ammi – 'Ammi*.

Now, whatever we may think of the way Peter and Paul handled the Tanakh, at least they did not assert that, because Israel will be *'Ammi* again, and because the Gentile believers have become *'Ammi*, too, therefore Gentiles have become Israel. Peter and Paul said no such thing at all; but the supersessionists say this. They commit this type of logical error: believing Israel is *'Ammi* (A = C), and believing Gentiles are *'Ammi* (B = C), so therefore A = B (believing Gentiles are believing Israel). Both (restored) Israel and the Ecclesia are people of God, just as the Germans and the French are people of Europe, without making them identical.

6.6 A "Spiritual Israel"? Four More "Proofs" Refuted
6.6.1 Ninth "Proof"

The apostle Paul wrote: "[W]hatever was written in former days [i.e., in the Tanakh] was written for our instruction, that through endurance and through the encouragement of the Scriptures we might have hope" (Rom. 15:4), and: "Now these things took place as examples [Gk. *typoi*] for us, that we might not desire evil as they did.... [T]hese things happened to them [i.e., Israel] as an example [Gk. *typikōs*, "type-wise"], but they were written down for our instruction, on whom the end of the ages has come" (1 Cor. 10:6, 11). In other words, the entire Tanakh was written for us, or in view of us, Jesus-believers of the New Testament. This can be understood in at least two senses. First, there is general moral admonition in all the books of the Tanakh that can be easily be applied to the (both Jewish and Gentile) believers of the New Testament Ecclesia.

In addition to this exhortative aspect, there is the typological aspect, hinted at with the Greek words *typoi* and *typikōs*.[39] And as we saw earlier, typology and fulfillment must never be confused. Israel's exodus from Egypt, Israel's passage through the Red Sea, and Israel's wilderness journey are "types" (models, foreshadowings; CJB: "prefigurative historical events") of the exodus of Jesus-believers from the slavery of sin and death, their having been baptized into Christ, and their journey through the wilderness of the evil world until the Messianic kingdom. In exactly the same sense, the restoration of Israel is a type of the many aspects that concern the Ecclesia, as we have been considering many times: the land, the people, the city, the temple, the altar—they all have a spiritual meaning as reflected in the (New Testament) Ecclesia. But this is something essentially different from *fulfillment*. There is obviously a typological connection. But this does not change the fact that Israel's deliverance from Egypt and its journey to the Promised Land

---

39. Two standard works: Habershon (1974); Jukes (1976).

also have a redemptive-historical meaning of their own, entirely apart from any typological application to the Ecclesia. Similarly, the prophecies concerning the restoration of Israel, its land, its people, its city, its temple, its altar, have a redemptive-historical meaning of their own, entirely apart from any typological connection with the Ecclesia.

The very fact that, as Paul said, event A is a *typos* of event B shows that A and B are not identical. If we can say that, to some extent, Israel in the Tanakh was a type of the New Testament Ecclesia, this is proof in itself that Israel and the Ecclesia are two different things. The Ecclesia can learn much from Israel—but this does not *constitute* the Ecclesia to be Israel; on the contrary, it underscores the distinction between the two. If supersessionists wish to use the passages mentioned as argument for their central thesis, the result turns out to be the opposite of their claim: Israel and the Ecclesia are in fact two (very) different entities.

6.6.2 Tenth "Proof"

An important weapon in the arsenal of supersessionism is Paul's parable of the olive tree in Romans 11:16–24: "[I]f the root is holy, so are the branches. But if some of the branches were broken off, and you, although a wild olive shoot, were grafted in among the others and now share in the nourishing root of the olive tree, do not be arrogant toward the branches," and so on. Several commentators and expositors have claimed that the "olive tree" is Israel. An interesting example is the Dutch Reformed rhymed version of Psalm 87 (from 1773). This version says something that the psalm itself does not say, namely, that believers have been *bij Israel ingelijfd*, that is, "engrafted into Israel." The expression is so precious to supersessionists that the new rhymed version of 1968 has carefully retained it. Even the rhymed version of the Reformed Liberated Churches contains it! (However, the newer rhymed version of 2020, and the ancient ones by Reformed pastors Petrus Datheen and Jacob Revius, do not.)

Ask a Reformed Christian in the Netherlands why they believe that every believer belongs to (the new, spiritual) "Israel," and this rhymed version of the Psalms might easily be their first piece of "evidence." Psalm 87 is not directly related to Romans 11, but the various rhymed versions have certainly helped to imagine "Israel" in the olive tree. Being engrafted into the olive tree is an image similar to being incorporated into Israel. If this were correct, this would be strong evidence for supersessionism.

However, it is not correct. The tree is *not* a representation of Israel; it is explicitly the *natural branches* of the tree that represent Israel (vv. 17–21), not the tree as such. Branches belong to the tree, but they are not the tree. So what is the tree? Verse 16b helps us to understand this: "[I]f the root is holy, so are the branches." This holy "root" can be nothing else than God's promises to the patriarchs, in which people of "all [believing Jewish and non-Jewish] families" and "all [believing] nations"[40] have received a share. In this, the fact comes to light that also non-Jewish Jesus-believers are called "sons/children of Abraham";[41] see especially Romans 4, where Abraham is called "the father of all who believe without being circumcised, so that righteousness would be counted to them as well, and to make him the father of the circumcised who are not merely circumcised but who also walk in the footsteps of the faith that our father Abraham had before he was circumcised" (vv. 11–12).

Gentile Jesus-believers are (spiritual) "sons/children of Abraham"—but they are never called "Israel," and they are never viewed as engrafted or incorporated into "Israel" (in any sense of the term), as supersessionists keep telling us. The only thing we are allowed to conclude is that, in addition to having physical descendants, Abraham also has spiritual descendants. We will deal with this important subject more extensively in chapter 12.

As to Psalm 87, the Annotations to the Dutch States Translation tell us that "Zion" is the church, being "born" occurs through the preaching of the holy gospel, and the term "register" in verse 6 means: "namely, those who will join the Christian church." This is not interpretation, but pure imagination. Psalm 87, as so many psalms, is a glorious description of the Messianic kingdom, when Zion will be the center of the world, the capital of the kingdom of

---

40. Cf. Gen. 12:3; 18:18; 22:18; 26:4; 28:14.
41. Gal. 3:7; cf. vv. 9 and 14; also see John 8:39–40, where only true believers are viewed as "children of Abraham," whether or not they have descended from him.

God,[42] just as we find it elsewhere:

> It shall come to pass in the latter days that the mountain of the house of the Lord shall be established as the highest of the mountains, and shall be lifted up above the hills; and all the nations shall flow to it, and many peoples shall come, and say: "Come, let us go up to the mountain of the Lord, to the house of the God of Jacob, that he may teach us his ways and that we may walk in his paths." For out of Zion shall go forth the law, and the word of the Lord from Jerusalem. He shall judge between the nations, and shall decide disputes for many peoples; and they shall beat their swords into plowshares, and their spears into pruning hooks; nation shall not lift up sword against nation, neither shall they learn war anymore (Isa. 2:2–4).[43]

6.6.3 Eleventh "Proof"

Supersessionist A. Maljaars has mentioned several other passages from the letters of Paul that are supposed to show that Paul applied certain synonyms for "Israel" "without hesitation to the church of Christ."[44] In reality, none of his quotations indicates that Paul viewed the Ecclesia as "Israel." Sometimes, these passages were rather far removed from such a thought. For instance, Maljaars mentions Galatians 4:26, where Paul says, "[T]he Jerusalem above is free, and she is our mother." Maljaars is here mistaken in not one but two respects: neither Israel nor the Ecclesia was being referred to here.

First, the "Jerusalem above" is not a synonym for Israel; rather it is the opposite because Paul placed it over against the "present Jerusalem," the capital of physical Israel (v. 25). Second, there is not a reference to the Ecclesia here either. Paul placed the Judaizing order—not present in the Tanakh!—of legalism and slavery over against the divine (New Testament) order of grace and liberty (see earlier in §3.7.2). Again, there is here no hint that the Ecclesia is "(spiritual) Israel." The New Testament contains three figurative "Jerusalems":

(a) The "Jerusalem above" in Galatians 4 is a figurative term for the order of grace and liberty that has been introduced by God in

---

42. Cohen (1985, 283–84).
43. Cf. Micah 4:1–3; Isa. 56:6–7; Jer. 3:17; Zech. 2:10–11.
44. Maljaars (2015, 147–48).

the person of, and through the work of, Jesus Christ.

(b) The "heavenly Jerusalem" of Hebrews 12:22 can, in my view—given the total perspective of the letter to the Hebrews (described in preceding chapters)—be best defined as the "city that is to come" (13:14), that is, the heavenly capital of the "world" and "age to come" (2:5; 6:5), the Messianic kingdom (12:28), the counterpart of the earthly Jerusalem, the two going to be functioning at the same time.

(c) The "new Jerusalem" is the Ecclesia, the bride of the Lamb: "Then came one of the seven angels . . . saying, 'Come, I will show you the Bride, the wife of the Lamb.' And he carried me away in the Spirit to a great, high mountain, and showed me the holy city Jerusalem coming down out of heaven from God" (Rev. 21:9-10); this is the celestial city called the "new Jerusalem" in verse 2 and earlier in 3:12.

Even if the "new Jerusalem" is the Ecclesia, or if the "Jerusalem above" or the "heavenly Jerusalem" were the Ecclesia, this does not mean that the old Jerusalem has been done away with, nor that the Ecclesia is "(spiritual) Israel," nor that all the promises in the Tanakh concerning Israel have been transferred to the (New Testament) Ecclesia. Supersessionism teaches this—the Bible does not.

6.6.4 Twelfth "Proof"

The same considerations apply to Galatians 3:7 and 29: "Know then that it is those of faith who are the sons of Abraham. . . . [I]f you are Christ's, then you are Abraham's offspring, heirs according to promise." Such passages demonstrate that there are surely numerous *similarities* between (post-Abrahamic) believers in the Tanakh and New Testament believers. These similarities have often been neglected in classical dispensationalism in order to focus on the *differences* between Israel and the Ecclesia. But such neglect is careless exegesis.

Fear of supersessionism should not impede us from underscoring and dealing honestly with the similarities between Israel and the Ecclesia. Both are "children of Abraham" (see §6.6.1), both are called "people of God," both live by the Torah, whether the Mosaic Torah or the Messianic Torah (which differ only gradually). But *this does not mean they are the same.*

Galatians 3 does not demonstrate that the Ecclesia is "(spiritual) Israel," and it certainly does not prove that all prophecies in the Tanakh about Israel have been transferred to the (New Testament) Ecclesia, or that the physical offspring of Abraham as such—that is, ethnic Israel—is no longer important. Some children of Abraham are Israelite; this does not mean that all other children of Abraham are Israelite, too. Some mammals are sheep; this does not mean that all other mammals are sheep, too.

6.7 Summary

6.7.1 Ethnic Israel Today

In summary, we may conclude that the New Testament nowhere says or suggests that (a) non-Jewish Jesus-believers in some way or another have become "Jews," or that the Ecclesia in some way or another is "(spiritual) Israel"; (b) even less does the New Testament suggest that this "spiritual Israel" could claim to have taken over all the prophecies in the Tanakh about ethnic Israel; (c) even less does the New Testament give us any hint that these prophecies in the Tanakh must be robbed of their—obviously intended—literal meaning, and must be spiritualized in order to become applicable to the (New Testament) Ecclesia.

I continue to find it incredible that Christians could have ever believed such a thing. *There is no biblical basis for supersessionism.* As we have seen, the only basis for supersessionism has been a historical one—above all The Great Shift in the fourth century—coupled with a resistance to ethnic Israel that bordered, and borders, on anti-Semitism. One must be all the more astonished about the fact that Christianity—Roman Catholicism, Eastern Orthodoxy, traditional Protestantism—has adhered to this doctrine for so many centuries: "*We* are (spiritual) Israel." Two points that help us to understand this phenomenon are these:

(a) The enormous lack of real interest in eschatological matters, and especially in the related questions of Israelology.

(b) The enormous power of tradition, both among Roman Catholics and among traditional Protestants: many think it is inconceivable that so many generations of theologians, including Augustine, Thomas Aquinas, Luther and Calvin, could have been mistaken as to these matters.

We must add here an important point. Supersessionists assert that the Ecclesia is "spiritual Israel," or something similar, such as "Christians are the true Jews." However, such statements are not sufficient to distinguish between the various kinds of supersessionists. If we wish to use the term "supersessionism" in a meaningful, unambiguous way, it is essential to establish what is the supersessionist's *attitude toward present-day ethnic Israel.*

(a) The weak (less harmful) variety of this theology takes the land and temple promise in the Tanakh literally, and teaches that God still has special promises for *ethnic* Israel as such. Nevertheless, here we are dealing with a variety of supersessionism, because it teaches that the Israel that returns to God somewhere in the future will be received in and absorbed by the Christian Ecclesia. *Extra Ecclesiam nulla salus* ("outside the Ecclesia there is no salvation");[45] in this view, this is also true for Israel. Behind this is the ancient view of the existence of a "church since Adam": believing Israelites under the Old Covenant were part of the "church," and it will be no different under the New Covenant. This variety of supersessionism has grown in popularity among those Christians who, since 1948, have been impressed by the establishment of the state of Israel. They have begun to see a connection with the promises in the Tanakh, but at the same time, they — consciously or unconsciously — wish to retain as much of the traditional view as possible.

(b) The harmful and objectionable variety of supersessionism is the one that spiritualizes the land and temple promise in the Tanakh, and sees them as fulfilled in the Ecclesia. In this view, there are no longer any special promises for ethnic Israel, although it reckons with the possibility that, in the end times, a massive part of ethnic Israel will be saved (as Augustine already taught) — but this group of converts to Jesus will simply become a part of the Ecclesia (see the previous variety). The "church" is the encompassing term for all regenerated of all time, from Adam till the end of history, and in fact this term is a synonym for "Israel," that is, for all believers of all time since the Sinaitic Covenant. The similarity with the previous variety is this belief in a "church throughout all time"; the difference is the attitude toward the land promise. In fact, this variety is

---

45. The expression has been encountered first with Cyprian of Carthage (third century).

more consistent than the previous one: you cannot have the traditional view, and at the same time believe in the literal land promise. This is why the subject is so complicated: so many theological issues are at stake simultaneously.

(c) The most harmful and most objectionable variety of supersessionism is the one that adheres not only to the same things that the previous variety believes, but it also believes that the vicissitudes of ethnic Israel during the preceding nearly two thousand years must be viewed in terms of divine punishment because the Jews have rejected their Messiah, and have made themselves co-responsible for his death. It is this inherent anti-Semitism that makes supersessionism (in its most consistent and radical form) so obnoxious. It is especially this third variety that has led so often to those heinous atrocities as forced assimilation, expulsion, and even robbery, rape, and murder.

6.7.2 Points of Attention

Let me finally mention three points that, in my view, are of essential significance in our studies concerning the physical and the spiritual Israel.

(a) Sometimes, the term "replacement theology" has been given a meaning that is far too broad, so that it lost its distinctive meaning. When, one day, the Messiah will appear on the clouds of heaven, many Jews will recognize in him Jesus of Nazareth: they will "look on him whom they have pierced."[46] Yes, at that time many Jews will believe in Jesus, their Messiah, Savior and Lord. So, in the end Christians will have it their way after all: ultimately, many Jews do become Christians. Judaism is "replaced" by Christianity, the Torah is "replaced" by the New Testament, Israel must give way to the Ecclesia.

This argument is based on several misunderstandings. Judaism will never be "replaced" by Christianity, as if one religion would be replaced by another one. Jews will ultimately find their promises, and in fact their entire existential identity, fulfilled in Jesus Christ, who was and is the Messiah of Israel before he was and is anything else. Jews do not become Christians, such as becoming Roman Catholic, or Anglican, or Evangelical. Rather, they will fi-

---

46. Zech. 12:10; John 19:37; Rev. 1:7; cf. Ps. 22:16; Isa. 53:5.

nally find their fulfillment *as Jews*. They will never be more Jewish than when they find their Jewish Messiah, who is also their Redeemer. Second, the Torah will never be "replaced" by the New Testament; Jews who find Jesus also find in the New Testament the most perfect interpretation of the Tanakh. Third, Israel will never give way to the Ecclesia; rather, they will be each other's complement. During the Messianic kingdom, the Ecclesia will be glorified in heaven, and converted Israel will be blessed on earth in peace and righteousness.

If supersessionism entails the view that many Jews in the end will believe in Jesus, then I am a supersessionist, too. But this kind of argument leads us nowhere. The difference between supersessionists and non-supersessionists is not *Jesus*, but *the Ecclesia*. Those who claim that all Jesus-believing Jews, *including those in the Messianic kingdom*, ultimately become part of the Ecclesia (which traditionally also implied abandoning everything that is typically Jewish) are supersessionists, no matter what variety they espouse. I have no difficulty with the idea that ultimately, in eternity, there will be only "one people of God," the gathering of all those, from all time, washed in the same blood of Christ. But don't call this "the Ecclesia"! Such a people of God will constitute a much wider notion than the New Testament Ecclesia, which is the body of the glorified Christ, the temple of the Holy Spirit, the bride of the Lamb.

(b) The (erroneous) view that Gentiles who have converted to Christ have been engrafted or incorporated into Israel, might lead to the idea that the two groups — Jesus-believing Jews and Jesus-believing Gentiles — must now resemble each other as much as possible. This mistaken idea may arise in two contrary, but equally objectionable ways. The one is the traditional way: Jews must become Gentiles by *abandoning* everything that is typically Jewish: circumcision, Sabbath, food laws, festivals.[47] The other way, equally objectionable, is that Gentiles must become Jews by *adopting* everything that is typically Jewish: Sabbath, food laws, festivals, and sometimes even circumcision of male believers. The effect is the

---

47. Under the Spanish Inquisition, if a marrano (a Spanish Jew who by force had become a [pseudo-]Christian) refused to make fire on the Sabbath—and thus proved to be still a Jew (Exod. 35:3)— this refusal could warrant the death penalty.

same: Jewish and Gentile believers become as similar as possible.

In recent times, the latter error has become stronger by the decade: in certain circles, non-Jewish Christian men are pushed to have themselves and their little boys circumcised, and to place themselves under the Jewish food laws, the Sabbath, and the Jewish festivals. It is undeniable that the Mosaic Torah was never abolished (see, e.g., Matt. 5:17); from this fact, these Gentile Christians conclude that therefore they must keep it. Or some of them argue that Christians must obey the "commandments of Jesus,"[48] and that these are obviously equal to the Mosaic commandments. They forget that not only was the Mosaic Torah never abolished, but neither was it imposed upon Gentile Jesus-believers. On the contrary, the apostles in Acts 15 explicitly prohibited this.

Of course, Gentile Christians who become circumcised know about Acts 15; but they have found various ways to escape its force. One way to do this is misquote James: "Therefore my judgment is that we should not trouble those of the Gentiles who turn to God. . . . For from ancient generations Moses has had in every city those who proclaim him, for he is read every Sabbath in the synagogues" (Acts 15:19–21). This is explained as follows: Do not trouble those newly converted Gentiles *right now*; but let them keep going to the synagogues, as good Jewish proselytes, and there they will hear the Mosaic Torah, and gradually begin to understand what God asks of them as well.[49] Of course, this argument strongly conflicts with Galatians 2, 5, and 6, where the apostle Paul earnestly warned Gentile Christians against becoming circumcised.[50] Or consider this plain statement by Paul: "Was anyone at the time of his call uncircumcised? Let him not seek circumcision" (1 Cor. 7:18b).

The view of these Christian Gentile circumcisers seems to be the very opposite of that of the supersessionists, who wished, and wish, to free Jesus-believing Jews from everything Jewish. However, the two views do share one important element: they fail to grasp the difference between Israel and the Ecclesia. It is just as

---

48. John 14:15, 21; 15:10–17; 1 John 2:3–4; 3:22–24; 5:2–3; 2 John 1:6; cf. Gal. 6:2; 2 Pet. 3:2.

49. Cf. the various ways Stern (1999, 279) reads Acts 15:21, including the way just mentioned.

50. Regarding this subject, see extensively, Ouweneel (1997).

bad to force Jesus-believing Jews to live as Gentiles—as Roman Catholics, Eastern Orthodox, and traditional Protestants, including some Evangelicals, have been doing for centuries—as it is to force Jesus-believing Gentiles to live as Jews.

6.7.3 No Two-Ways Doctrine

(c) The view presented here is *not* a two-ways doctrine, as has been asserted.[51] A genuine two-ways doctrine teaches that Christians reach salvation through Christ, but Jews—or other people—can reach this same salvation through another route. In such a case, there would be two different entrances into the kingdom of God: one through Christ, and one through some other way (usually some variety of the many ways—Jewish or Gentile—of "leading a decent life"). Generally speaking, among those who take the prophecies about Israel literally, I am aware of no one who teaches such a two-ways doctrine. To be sure, throughout the history of the last two thousand years, God has been going different ways with Israel and with the Ecclesia, and this will continue until the coming of the Messiah and the establishment of his kingdom. See what I wrote in §2.2.3 about the different ways of "Jacob" (Israel) and "Esau" (Edom, Christianity): the two cannot move forward together. They form two totally different worlds. But they do not part forever; remember that Jacob said that in his own time and in his own way, he would come to Esau in Seir (the mountains of Edom) (Exod. 33:14). Rashi asks: "When will Jacob come in Seir?" He answers with a reference to Obadiah 1:21, "In the days of the Messiah, for it is said: 'And saviors shall go up to Mount Zion to rule Mount Esau.'"[52] That is, in the Messianic kingdom the two will finally meet in peace.

In New Testament terms: in the end, godly Jews and godly Christians will find each other in the one Messiah, in the one salvation based upon his blood, and in the one kingdom of God (*not* in the one "Ecclesia"). God-serving Jews and God-serving Christians basically live by the *same* Messianic hope (I say this despite the many different details in their expectations): the appearance of the Messiah, the establishment of his kingdom, where he will sit on the throne of David, when peace and justice will fill Israel, and even

---

51. Cf. Paas (2014, 21).
52. Cohen (1983, 203).

the entire world. In this way, the two will find each other in the Messiah. But Jews will never become church members, and (Gentile) church people will never become Jews. As I said, I reckon with the possibility that ultimately, in the new heaven and on the new earth, there will be one people of God. But as I see it, this people will not be called "the Ecclesia" (as if Jews after all have become church members), and it will not be called "Israel" either (as if Gentiles have become Jews after all). Revelation 21:3 (NIV) states, "And I heard a loud voice from the throne saying, 'Look! God's dwelling place is now among the *people*, and he will dwell with them. They will be *his people*, and God himself will be with them and be their God."

The common expectation of the godly Jew and the godly Gentile is beautifully expressed in Article 1 of the Church Order of the Protestant Church in the Netherlands (the PKN; formerly the Dutch Reformed Church):[53] "According to its confession, the Protestant Church in the Netherlands is a form of the one holy, apostolic and catholic (or worldwide) Christian church, which, *sharing in the expectation granted to Israel*, reaches out for the coming of the Kingdom of God" (italics added).[54] Notice especially this comment that came from theologians in the PKN:

> The church does not take the place of Israel but sees itself as a community that is privileged to share in the expectation that was given to Israel. . . . Likewise, the church of today cannot, despite its perspective on Jesus of Nazareth differing from that of Judaism, regard Israel as a something of the past that is no longer relevant. Both Israel and the church cherish the expectation of a future in which God is recognized as the God of all nations and of the entire earth, as their universal perspective. Israel lived with this perspective before the church came into being.[55]

Here, the Ecclesia is being discussed in terms of its strictly New Testament sense, and this is — rightly — the ongoing approach of

---

53. This statement was adopted despite the objections of a group of liberal theologians within the PKN, especially those who strongly sympathize with "the Palestinians."

54. https://www.protestantsekerk.nl/actief-in-de-kerk/kerkorde/kerkorde-en-ordinanties.

55. Van der Kooi and Van den Brink (2017, 342–43).

the authors from whom I borrowed the quotation just given.[56] Israel was there long before the (New Testament) Ecclesia came about. The authors, both systematic theologians belonging to the PKN, do not speak of a kind of "church since Adam," which in the Old Testament was "Israel," and in the New Testament is supposedly some "(spiritual) Israel." They rightly abandon this idea. There *is* no "church since Adam." There is Israel from Exodus 19 to the eternal state, and there is the Christian Ecclesia from Acts 2 to the eternal state. And one day the two will meet: when "Jacob" meets "Esau" in Seir, that is, in the Messianic kingdom. But Jacob will never become Esau, or vice versa.

6.8 Two Types

6.8.1 Jacob and His Two Wives

In §3.5.2 I already briefly mentioned the two wives of the patriarch Jacob: Leah and Rachel.[57] Thus, God, or the Messiah, in typological language also has two "wives": Israel and the Ecclesia. Those who can appreciate typology will grasp this. The church father Ambrose saw in Jacob with his two wives, Leah and Rachel, a type of Christ with his two wives: Israel and the Ecclesia. But who of the two is Leah, and who is Rachel? Of course, the supersessionists, including Ambrose,[58] said, and say, that Leah represented Israel, who had to give way to Rachel, the Ecclesia. Leah is the despised one, the Ecclesia is the beloved one—so, naturally, Leah represents Israel, and Rachel represents the Ecclesia. Leah had to give way to Rachel, Leah's eldest son, Reuben, had to give way to Rachel's eldest son, Joseph.

But I am convinced that the truth is the reverse. Jacob worked for Rachel, but after seven years of labor, he got Leah instead. However, in the end he *also got* Rachel. It is the very same with the Messiah: Jesus came with the express purpose of ministering to Israel (cf. Matt. 15:24; Rom. 15:8), but—so to speak—he got the Ecclesia instead. However, in the end, during the Messianic kingdom, he

---

56. See especially Van der Kooi and Van den Brink (2017, chapter 14).

57. A little detail: Jacob had two "wives" and "two female servants" (who also bore him sons) (Gen. 32:22), not four "wives." This is different with Hagar, who is explicitly said to have become Abraham's "wife" (Gen. 16:3).

58. See chapter 3, note 60, above.

will get Israel as well. And then he will have both! During the Messianic kingdom, the Ecclesia will be his heavenly wife, and Israel on earth will be his earthly bride.[59] One thing is certain: the two women never become one wife: Leah never becomes Rachel, and Rachel never becomes Leah; that is, Israel never becomes the Ecclesia, and the Ecclesia never becomes Israel. In other words, in whatever way Leah and Rachel are explained, they never offer us any support for supersessionism: Leah is not a "spiritual Rachel," and Rachel is not a "spiritual Leah." (I say this realizing, of course, that no biblical truth can be proven through types alone.)

6.8.2 The Loved and the Unloved Wife

The Tanakh spoke of yet another type of a man with two wives, which we may consider here. It offered a counterpart to the previous type:

> If a man has two wives, the one loved and the other unloved,[60] and both the loved and the unloved have borne him children, and if the firstborn son belongs to the unloved, then on the day when he assigns his possessions as an inheritance to his sons, he may not treat the son of the loved as the firstborn in preference to the son of the unloved, who is the firstborn, but he shall acknowledge the firstborn, the son of the unloved, by giving him a double portion of all that he has, for he is the firstfruits of his strength. The right of the firstborn is his (Deut. 21:15–17).

In the former type, Rachel (Israel) is the beloved, and Leah (the Ecclesia) is the less loved wife of God. The son of Rachel (Israel), Joseph, not Reuben, receives the right of the firstborn (1 Chron. 5:1–2), and thus is the type of the Messiah.[61] However, in the latter type mentioned it is precisely the son of the less loved wife who receives the right of the firstborn. This sheds light on another aspect of the matter: if Israel has become *Lo-'Ammi*, and has been moved aside, it seems that the Ecclesia has now become the beloved wife of God, or of the Messiah, and Israel has become the less loved, or even "hated" one (as the text literally says). However, when the Messiah

---

59. Regarding this difference, see extensively, Ouweneel (2012a).
60. Lit., "hated," here in the sense of "loved less than the other."
61. Apart from this, Judah, Leah's son, too, is a type of the Messiah; cf. Gen. 49:8–10.

appears, all Gentiles, including Gentile Christians, will be reminded of the fact that the Messiah is a son of *Israel*, not of the Ecclesia. A *Jew* will rule the world—a son of the despised and hated wife, for centuries mocked, beaten, driven out. *Her* son was born not in Rome but in Bethlehem. And one day, he will come forth, not out of the cathedrals, but out of the ghettos.

Chapter 7
The Old Testament Messianic Hope[1]

Our Rabbis taught, The Holy One, blessed be He, will say to the Messiah, the Son of David (May he reveal himself speedily in our days!), "Ask of me anything, and I will give it to thee", as it is said, I will tell of the decree etc. this day have I begotten thee, ask of me and I will give the nations for thy inheritance [Ps. 2:7–8]. But when he will see that the Messiah the son of Joseph is slain, he will say to Him, "Lord of the Universe, I ask of Thee only the gift of life". "As to life", He would answer him, "Your father David has already prophesied this concerning you", as it is said, He asked life of thee, thou gavest it him [even length of days for ever and ever] [Ps. 21:5].

Talmud: Sukkah 52a

7.1 Messianic Hope in the Tanakh
7.1.1 Many Messianic Prophecies

I ONCE HEARD AN orthodox rabbi say that Jesus did not fulfill *any* Messianic prophecy. He needed to believe this, for else he would

---
1. See extensively, Ouweneel (2007b), chapter 4.

have had to acknowledge that Jesus is the Messiah.[2] This is because these prophecies were given for this very purpose: in order that Jews would recognize their Messiah the moment he appeared. The apostle Matthew wrote the first New Testament book to show how and why the "gospel of the kingdom"[3] had shifted from Israel to the world at large. To this end, he first demonstrates that Israel had rejected its Messiah despite the fact that Jesus had fulfilled many prophecies in the Tanakh. For instance, look at the following expressions regarding Jesus:

(a) "took place/this was to fulfill": 1:22; 2:15; 8:17; 12:17; 13:35; 21:4; "written/spoken by the prophet": 2:5; 3:3; 24:15;

(b) "then was fulfilled": Matt. 2:17; 4:14; 27:9;

(c) "might be fulfilled": 2:23; 4:14; 26:56;

(d) "is fulfilled": 13:14–15.

(e) "Well did Isaiah prophesy": 15:7;

(f) "how ... be fulfilled": 26:54.

In addition, there are passages in which prophecies are unmistakably implied, such as 26:64.

In fact, the entire New Testament is full of the painful message that the entire Tanakh is saturated with Jesus, but that the people of the Tanakh did not discern this. This resembles the star that appeared to the wise men from the East but failed to interest the rabbis; that is, they knew the prophecies, but apparently were not interested in their fulfillment (Matt. 2). It is as Jesus said to one of the leading rabbis of his days, Nicodemus: without having been born of "water" (God's Word[4]) and Spirit you will be unable to "see" the kingdom of God, and unable to enter it (John 3:3, 5). Jesus also referred to Isaiah 6:9, "This is why I speak to them [i.e., Israel] in parables [i.e., in a hidden form], because seeing they do not see, and hearing they do not hear, nor do they understand. Indeed, in their case the prophecy of Isaiah is fulfilled that says: 'You will indeed

---

2. Heb. *mashiach*, "anointed," from *m-sh-ch*, "to anoint"; cf. Gk. *christos*, from *chriō*, "to anoint"; see extensively, Schirrmacher (2001); Raymond (2003).
   In New Testament references to the Tanakh, sometimes I take the liberty of rendering "Messiah" instead of "Christ."

3. Cf. Matt. 4:23; 9:35; 24:14; cf. 4:17; Mark 1:15; Luke 4:43; 16:16; Acts 8:12.

4. Cf. John 15:3; Eph. 5:26; Titus 3:5.

hear but never understand, and you will indeed see but never perceive'" (Matt. 13:13-14).

On another occasion, a rabbi told me that the term *mashiach* ("anointed") does not appear in the Tanakh with its Messianic meaning ("Messiah"). This is indeed remarkable: the word *mashiach* occurs many times in the Tanakh with the meaning of "anointed," whether a king or a priest, but rarely in the truly Messianic sense. Yet, there is one clear example: Daniel 9:24-27.[5] When the rabbi read the passage, he exclaimed: "That is something else!" But I challenged him to tell me *who* could possibly be this *Mashiach* ("anointed one") of whom the text was speaking:

> [D]iscern that seven weeks [of years] will elapse between the issuing of the decree to restore and rebuild Yerushalayim until an anointed prince comes. It [i.e., Jerusalem] will remain built for sixty-two weeks [of years], with open spaces and moats; but these will be troubled times. Then, after the sixty-two weeks [i.e., a total of 69 "weeks," i.e., 483 years], *Mashiach* will be cut off and have nothing" (vv. 25-26 CJB).

Who was this *Mashiach* who, 483 years after the Persian order to rebuild Jerusalem, was "cut off" in this city?

I told him about the Jewish tradition that, in the year 6 of our era, the orthodox Jews tore their robes on the Temple Square because the Romans had taken away from them the last piece of their sovereignty, the *ius gladii* (the "right of the sword," i.e., the right to carry out the death penalty). They cried: "Woe unto us, for the scepter has been taken away from Judah, but Shiloh has not come!" (cf. Gen. 49:10 NKJV).[6] They did not know that, at that very moment, Jesus was living in Nazareth, perhaps ten or twelve years old. In other words, both Daniel 9 and the event of AD 6 could have been sufficient to demonstrate that a Jewish personality living in the first decades of the first century must have been the Messiah of Israel. How many alternatives for Jesus within Israel could present-day Jewish scholars identify during that same period?

In reality, Jesus has fulfilled *numerous* prophecies of the Tanakh. Some investigators claim that Jesus has fulfilled more than three hundred prophecies. In many cases this is quite obvious; many of

---

5. See extensively, §7.15.1 and Ouweneel (2012a, §6.5).
6. Montefiore (1927, 283-300).

them are quoted in the New Testament and linked to Jesus. (For my top-thirty see this footnote.[7]) Some of them refer to Jesus' birth, others to his earthly ministry, others to his death, his resurrection, and his glorification.

7.1.2 The Tanakh and the New Testament

The Tanakh is saturated with the expectation of the Messiah, that is, the anointed king from the tribe of Judah, and as became clear over time, from the house of David. The Messiah is the eschatological king who will receive world dominion, and who will establish peace and righteousness, not only for Israel but for the entire world. If we pass over for a moment Genesis 3:15 (see §7.3.1), and a number of Messianic foreshadowings in Genesis, we find his first announcement in the blessing of Jacob: "The scepter shall not depart from Judah, nor the ruler's staff from between his feet, until Shiloh comes, and to him [shall be] the obedience of the peoples" (Gen. 49:10 NASB; see §7.3.5).

In the first century of our era, the Messianic expectation among the Jews was universal.[8] Even a Samaritan outcast could say, "I know that the Messiah is coming . . . . When he comes, he will tell us all things" (John 4:25). The Jewish fisherman Andrew told his brother Simon, "We have found the Messiah," apparently in the sense of the One we were looking for (John 1:42). Interestingly, in these two passages we find the Greek word *Messias*, related to the Hebrew term *Mashiach*; usually, the New Testament uses *Christos* ("anointed") as a rendering of *Mashiach*.

According to Christians, the appearance of Jesus in this world was the (partial) fulfillment of this Messianic hope of the Tanakh, and according to most Jews, it was not. This does not change the existence of this Messianic hope as such, and it deserves our full attention. This matter involves the relationship between the Tana-

---

7. Gen. 3:15; 49:10; Num. 24:17; Deut. 18:15–16; 2 Sam. 7:12–16; Ps. 8:4–6; 16:1–11; 22:1–22; 40:6–8; 45:1–18; 69:4, 21; 110:1–7; 118:22–26; Isa. 7:14; 9:6–7; 11:1–10; 42:1–7; 49:1–7; 50:4–11; 52:13–53:12; 61:1; Jer. 23:5; 33:15; Ezek. 34:23–24; 37:24; Dan. 7:13–14; 9:26; Micah 5:2; Zech. 9:9; 11:12–13.

8. Regarding the Messianic hope (including that of the pagan nations), from the second century BC until the second century after the beginning of our era, see Oegema (1991).

kh and the New Testament. The twentieth century saw significant debate on this matter. Not a few theologians underestimated the significance of the Tanakh in comparison with the New Testament, or at least they devalued the Messiological exegesis of the Tanakh.[9] For instance, W. E. Vischer strongly defended this exegesis,[10] whereas E. Hirsch viewed the Tanakh only as the proclamation of a legalistic religion, which supposedly had been annulled by Jesus.[11]

In addition, some seek to do justice to the Tanakh by interpreting it alone, apart from any light or influence from the New Testament. For example, the New Testament appeals extensively to the Tanakh to make clear that Jesus is the fulfillment of the Messianic predictions. But this does not mean that in all these quotations the actual grammatical-historical exegesis of these passages in the Tanakh was being presupposed. In some cases we are dealing with Messianic applications of statements in the Tanakh that refer to the Davidic king in general (see, e.g., Ps. 2:7 and 2 Sam. 7:14 in Heb. 1:5). In other cases, the relationship is even weaker; these involve midrashic (i.e., typological) applications of the Tanakh that could never have derived from ordinary grammatical-historical exegesis (see, e.g., Hos. 11:1 in Matt. 2:15, and Jer. 31:15 in Matt. 2:18).[12]

However, it is equally true that exegesis must never consciously exclude the New Testament's testimony. For instance, it cannot be insignificant to expositors that a Jewish man, Peter, provided in Acts 2:25–31 a Messianic interpretation of Psalm 16:8–11. Another Jewish man, unknown to us, did the same in Hebrews 2:6–9 with respect to Psalm 2:5–7,[13] a third Jewish man, the apostle John, gave in John 12:41 a Christological interpretation of Isaiah 6, and a fourth Jewish man in Acts 8:32–35, the evangelist Philip, interpreted

---

9. See Berkouwer (1954, chapter 7).

10. Vischer (1949).

11. Hirsch (1936); I have tried to refute this error in Ouweneel (2020).

12. The rabbis speak here of a *pesher* interpretation, in which the expositor taps into a "deeper" layer of the text than the one to which ordinary (grammatical-historical) exegesis refers (*pesher* overlaps here with midrash).

13. He does so by adopting the Septuagint reading of Ps. 8:5: *elohim* = "angels," and does the same in Heb. 10:5 with Ps. 40:6, in the phrase *ears you have dug for me* the Septuagint takes "ears" as a *pars pro toto* by rendering: "a body have you prepared for me."

Isaiah 53 Christologically.

7.1.3 The Gospels and Paul about the Tanakh

The enormous emphasis of especially the Gospels regarding the overall Messianic significance of the Tanakh is unmistakable.[14] Jesus himself said, "the Scriptures [i.e., the Tanakh] . . . bear witness about me" (John 5:39), and, "Moses . . . wrote of me" (v. 45). Philip said, "We have found him of whom Moses in the Law and also the prophets wrote, Jesus of Nazareth, the son of Joseph" (John 1:45). And to the Emmaus disciples Jesus said,

> "O foolish ones, and slow of heart to believe all that the prophets have spoken! Was it not necessary that the Messiah should suffer these things and [thus] enter into his glory?" And beginning with Moses and all the Prophets, he interpreted to them in all the Scriptures the things concerning himself (Luke 24:25-27).

And a little later:

> "These are my words that I spoke to you while I was still with you, that everything written about me in the Law of Moses and the Prophets and the Psalms[15] must be fulfilled." Then he opened their minds to understand the Scriptures, and said to them, "Thus it is written, that the Messiah should suffer and on the third day rise from the dead, and that repentance for the forgiveness of sins should be proclaimed in his name to all nations, beginning from Jerusalem" (vv. 44-47).

Thus, the apostle Peter wrote that the "Spirit of the Messiah" within the prophets of the Tanakh "predicted the sufferings of Christ and the subsequent glories" (1 Pet. 1:11).

The apostle Paul, too, made a direct connection between the predictions in the Tanakh and the life and sufferings of Jesus: ". . . the utterances of the prophets, which are read every Sabbath, [his enemies] fulfilled them by condemning him. . . . And when they had carried out all that was written of him, they took him down from the tree [i.e., the cross] and laid him in a tomb" (Acts 13:27, 29). Thus, Paul could testify that, in all his ministry, he had been

---

14. See "Old Testament in the Gospels," by C. A. Evans (*DJG* 579–90).

15. This formulation agrees with the Jewish threefold arrangement of the Tanakh: T-N-Kh = *Torah*, *Nebi'im* (= prophets) and *K'tubim* (= [other] writings, of which the Psalms are the first and largest book).

"saying nothing but what the prophets and Moses said would come to pass: that the Messiah must suffer and that, by being the first to rise from the dead, he would proclaim light both to our people and to the Gentiles" (Acts 26:22-23). And when the Ethiopian eunuch asked whether the prophet in Isaiah 53 was speaking about himself or someone else, "Philip opened his mouth, and beginning with this Scripture he told him the good news about Jesus" (Acts 8:34-35).

Nowhere does the New Testament speak critically of the Tanakh; on the contrary: "Scripture [i.e., the Tanakh] cannot be broken" (John 10:35). Nowhere do we find any suggestion of some breach between the New Testament and the Tanakh.[16] With regard to the Tanakh, the New Testament has at least a threefold function: it is the fulfillment, *and* the continuation, *and* the interpretation of the Tanakh. Berkouwer said of this "Christian" (read: Messianic) character of the Tanakh:

> When the church or theology spoke of promise and fulfillment it was this undeniable interconnection they were referring to; one can also say: they were referring to the Christian character of the Old Testament. One can boil down the church's credo regarding the Scriptures into the statement that it is no anachronism to say that the Old Testament is Christian.[17]

In other words, the Christological (or Messiological) interpretation is not being read into the Tanakh; rather, the Tanakh is explicitly Messianic, concerning both the person and the redemptive work of the Messiah.

7.2 Balance
7.2.1 Interpretation and Application

It is important to maintain a balanced approach here.[18] On the one hand, the *entire* Tanakh is fundamentally Messianic, from the

---

16. Some have suggested such a breach in the six "antitheses" of Matt. 5:21–22, 27–28, 31–32, 33–34, 38–39, and 43–44 ("You have heard . . . but I say to you"); however, Jesus *never* turned against the Torah as such but only against certain rabbinic (mis)interpretations of it; see Vermes (1993, 37); Ouweneel (2020, 261–62).
17. Berkouwer (1954, 117).
18. Cf. Heyns (1988, 232).

promise in Genesis 3:15 (the woman's scion will bruise the head of the serpent, i.e., the devil and Satan; cf. Rev. 12:9; 20:2) to the rise of the "sun of righteousness" in Malachi 4:2, no doubt a reference to the Messiah.[19] The scope of the Tanakh is thoroughly Messiological. I maintain this over against some Christian historical-critical exegesis, which has rejected the Messianic interpretation of, for instance, Genesis 3:15, Psalm 22, and the songs of the Servant of the LORD in Isaiah 42–53,[20] and has entirely psychologized away the Messianic hope as such.[21]

On the other hand, the legitimacy of grammatical-historical exegesis must never be despised. It takes priority over typological (or allegorical,[22] or midrashic) interpretation of any passage in the Tanakh. In rabbinic terms, the *peshat* (grammatical-historical exegesis) always comes before, and must not be contradicted by, *remez* (allegorical exegesis), *derash* (midrashic exegesis), and *sod* (mystical-esoteric exegesis).[23] In a somewhat simplified formulation, we would insist that *interpretation* must always be distinguished from, and always precede, *application*. There is no doubt that the New Testament's use of the Tanakh often has more to do with application (Spirit-inspired application!) than with strict interpretation.

In such an approach, it is quite easy to lose the balance, such that one theologian places more emphasis on a strictly grammatical-historical exegesis (a typically Western imbalance), and another theologian more on a typological, allegorical, or midrashic approach (more in line with certain rabbinic schools). Personally, I am most averse to any approach that detracts from the thoroughly Messianic character of the Tanakh (when that is properly understood). This includes any approach that affects the way the New Testament deals with the Tanakh. To summarize: grammatical-historical exegesis must always precede any form of typological exegesis, without detracting anything from the legitimacy of typological exegesis, as the New Testament itself extensively demonstrates. However, this exegesis must never go beyond the New Testament

---

19. Cf. Matt. 17:2; Acts 26:13; Rev. 1:16; also see 2 Sam. 23:3–4.
20. See, e.g., Von Rad (1935).
21. Regarding this, see Berkouwer (1954, 142–52).
22. Regarding the difference between typology and allegory, see §7.6.1 below.
23. Regarding typology in the Psalms, see Thompson (1996, 51–59).

midrashic exegesis of the Tanakh, and never be carried out at the expense of the *sensus literalis*, that is, of the grammatical-historical exegesis of the Tanakh.

In brief, the balance must be maintained between grammatical-historical exegesis and midrashic or typological exegesis. Only in this way can we do justice to the Messiological scope of the Tanakh, as I hope to show. On the one hand, many passages in the Tanakh that, according to the New Testament midrashic exegesis, are Messiological are not so according to their *sensus literalis*, and this must be fully maintained. On the other hand, we do well to heed Berkouwer's wise caution: "No one may say that a given part of the Old Testament is without bearing on Jesus Christ, even though certain parts do not belong to what are generally called Messianic prophecies."[24]

7.2.2 The *Entire* Torah Speaks of the Messiah

The decisive point is not *how many* prophecies of the Tanakh Jesus has fulfilled, but rather that the *entire* Tanakh is Messianic. In stronger terms, *everything* in the Tanakh involves the Messiah: the patriarchs in Genesis, the priests, and the sacrifices in Exodus to Deuteronomy,[25] the judges in the book of Judges, the kings in 1 Samuel to 2 Chronicles, and the Psalms. Even the wisdom in Proverbs is, in person, none other than the Messiah (Prov. 8; cf. 1 Cor. 1:24; Col. 2:3),[26] and in my view, he is also the "man" in Ecclesiastes 7:28 ("One man among a thousand I found, but a woman among all these I have not found") and 9:15 ("there was found in [the city] a poor, wise man, and he by his wisdom delivered the city. Yet no one remembered that poor man"). He is identified typologically not only with Melchizedek, Isaac, Joseph, Moses, and David, but also with Joshua in the book of Joshua, with Boaz in the book of Ruth, with Elijah/Elisha in the book of Kings, with Mordecai in the book of Esther,[27] with Job in the book of Job,[28] with the bridegroom

---

24. Berkouwer (1954, 128).
25. Ouweneel (n.d.-a).
26. Ouweneel (1998a, 50–51).
27. Ouweneel (n.d.-b).
28. Ouweneel (2000).

in the Song of Solomon,[29] with Jonah in the book of Jonah (cf. Matt. 12:40),[30] and so on.

With regard to Jesus' statement concerning all that was written *about* him in the Law of Moses (Luke 24:44), Klaas Schilder rightly argued that it was no use "nosing around" in the Mosaic literature to try to "dig up" some "nugget" that might "lend" itself to a Messianic interpretation.[31] On the contrary, Christ is the all-pervading subject of the *entire* Torah (Pentateuch), as well as of the rest of the Tanakh. Schilder explained this in his unique way:

> Thus, [in Luke 24:27, 44; John 5:39] Christ . . . will *not* have been thinking especially of some detail A, or type B, or event C, or text D, or priestly garment E, or tabernacle piece F, or festival day G, or festival menu H, *but* rather of the *foundational lines*: Moses was a *mediator*; what is mediatorship? Moses wished to *die* for others, but he was not allowed or able to do this [Exod. 32:32-33]; what is mediatorship-without-exhaustive-sacrifice? Moses gave laws, laws, laws, but how can he [in Deut. 30:11-14] . . . posit as the ultimate commandment-with-a-threat: Now don't produce your ultimate forced effort, but acknowledge that the bread-from-heaven has been setting on your table for a long time already as cut bread, within your reach, yes, in your mouth, yes, already in your heart (cf. Rom. 10:6-8)? And then: Moses wrote the history of the *toledoth*,[32] of the decisive births and turns in history. All these *toledoth* are *my toledoth*, Christ wishes to say. And Moses wrote about Melchizedek [cf. Heb. 7:1-10], and about Isaac, in whom the promised seed [i.e., Christ; Gal. 3:16] would be called, would be begotten. I am *the* Begotten One! It is about *me* that Moses wrote, also in those historical portions.[33]

The *entire* Tanakh, not just certain Messianic prophecies, spoke of the Messiah—notice that Schilder cannot avoid foregrounding some elements from the Torah that illustrated most clearly this Messiological character. This same reality will guide us in the re-

---

29. Ouweneel (1973).
30. Ouweneel (1989).
31. Schilder (1949, 309).
32. *Toledoth* = births, origins, history (Gen. 2:4; 6:9; 10:1; 11:10, 27; 25:12, 19; 36:1, 9).
33. Schilder (1949, 310–11).

mainder of this chapter.

7.2.3 Recognizable Messianic Predictions

We do well here to distinguish between Messianic prophecies that are recognizable as such only in the light of the New Testament, and those that seem to have been explicitly intended as such by the writers of the Tanakh, and hence were acknowledged as such by the rabbis. A Jewish counting discerned seventy-five Messianic prophecies in the Torah, 243 in the prophetic books, and 138 in the writings.[34] We therefore also listen to orthodox Jewish testimony, even though this has certainly suffered from constantly opposing the Christological interpretations in the New Testament with regard to the Tanakh.

There is an evident tension here: Jews blame Christians for reading their "Jesus faith" into the Tanakh, while Christians, together with the apostle Paul, speak of a "veil" (2 Cor. 3:14) through which Jews are kept from reading the Tanakh as they should.[35] But here, too, there is a difference. On the one hand, for instance the orthodox Jewish theologian Hans-Joachim Schoeps turned sharply against the Christological interpretation of the Tanakh.[36] On the other hand, the equally orthodox Jewish theologian Pinchas Lapide assumed a much milder attitude: for him, it was a not an implausible possibility that the Messiah expected according to the Tanakh would turn out to be Jesus of Nazareth; he said that Christians and Jews expect one and the same consummation as fulfillment of the promises.[37]

An obvious example of recognizable Messianic prophecies are many psalms. Some of these (Ps. 2, 45, 72, 132) have been accepted by the rabbis as Messianic, at least indirectly or secondarily. But other psalms were not accepted by them as such; *Jesus-followers* recognize them as Messianic only because the New Testament treats them as such; take, for instance, Psalm 8 (see Heb. 2:5–9), 16 (see Acts 2:31; 13:35), 22 (see Matt. 27:39, 43, 46; John 19:24; Heb. 2:12), 40 (see Heb. 10:5–10), 69 (see John 2:17; Rom. 15:3), and 102 (see Heb.

---

34. So Edelkoort (1941, 507).
35. Berkouwer (1954, 142).
36. Schoeps (1932, 25).
37. In Rahner and Lapide (1987, 66–67).

1:10–12). Please note that for Jesus-followers the New Testament is the divinely inspired key to the Tanakh, which cannot be surpassed by any rabbinic comments. For instance, where early Jewish expositors had no difficulty recognizing the Messiah in Isaiah 53, later rabbis rejected this interpretation because it came too close to the New Testament interpretation of it[38] (see further in §7.14 below).

There is an obvious tension here. I once suggested to an orthodox rabbi that the difference is this: Jews read the Tanakh through the glasses of the Talmud, and Christians read it through the glasses of the New Testament. He agreed.

We may add here, though, that both sides today receive unexpected assistance. The Jews receive assistance from liberal Christian theologians who reject many Christological interpretations of passages in the Tanakh. The Soncino Books of the Bible series contains many rather triumphant references to such liberal—I venture to say, unbelieving—expositors, who inadvertently come to the aid of Jewish scholars by denying the application of many passages to Jesus. But conversely, there are also orthodox Jewish theologians who have come much closer to the Christian approach. I once asked an orthodox rabbi: Some Jewish authors have argued that, according to orthodox Jews, Jesus could not have been the Messiah—but when, one day, the Messiah will appear, they would not be amazed if he would turn out to have the traits of Jesus of Nazareth. What do you think of that? He fully agreed without any hesitation, in front of an auditorium filled with listeners!

Without any hesitation we declare that (conservative, non-supersessionist) Christians and (orthodox) Jews are looking forward to that one great and glorious event: the appearance of the Messiah of Israel on the clouds of heaven (Dan. 7:13), who will sit on the throne of David to rule over Israel (Isa. 9:7), and from there over all the earth (Ps. 72:8; Isa. 49:6).

7.3 From Adam to Judah

7.3.1 Adam

The New Testament opens with calling Jesus, in retrospect, "son of David, son of Abraham" (Matt. 1:1), and ultimately "son of Adam" (Luke 3:23–38). The messages concerning the Davidic descent of the

---

38. Cf. Matt. 8:17; Luke 22:37; Acts 8:32–33; 1 Pet. 2:22, 24.

Messiah (according to his human nature) are gradually narrowing down throughout the Tanakh. They begin with Adam.

In Genesis 3:15, we find a promise that has been referred to as the Proto-Evangelium: "I will put enmity between you [i.e., the serpent] and the woman, and between your offspring and her offspring; he [i.e., the woman's offspring] shall bruise your head, and you shall bruise his heel." Conservative Christian expositors invariably find here a Messianic prophesy: the Anointed One of God is the woman's offspring, and thus also Adam's offspring (Luke 3:23–38), and the serpent is Satan (cf. Rev. 12:9; 20:2, "that ancient serpent, who is called the devil and Satan, the deceiver of the whole world"). No doubt the references in the book of Revelation have strongly supported this exegesis.

Jewish expositors have never discerned a Messianic prophecy here. Nor do modernist Christian expositors see any Messianic prediction here (on this point, these two groups are allies); liberals believe that traditionally far too much has been read into the text. This complaint is not entirely without basis: American scholars Francis A. Schaeffer and Josh McDowell thought they had found a reference to Jesus' virgin birth in the text.[39]

In the primary sense (*peshat*, see §7.2.1), the text was obviously referring to two actual progenies: real snakes and real people (cf. Isa. 65:25). In the secondary sense (*remez* or *derash*), the text was referring to two families: that of Satan (in addition to Rev., see John 8:44, "You are of your father the devil") and that of the (reborn) woman, that is, the family of death and the family of life, respectively (cf. Gen. 3:20, "Eve" = life). Cain and Abel constituted the first fulfillment of Genesis 3:15 because they were the first representatives of these two spiritual families, respectively. Cain, as an instrument of Satan, was the first to "bruise the heel" of the woman's offspring, the family of life. That is, he inflicted upon it a crippling but not ultimately destructive blow. This describes the entire course of history, from the murder of Abel[40] to the murder of Jesus.[41] Conversely, one day Satan's "head" will be "bruised," and this will entail his ultimate destruction. Even Messiah's followers

---

39. McDowell (1972, 116); Schaeffer (1982, 73–74).
40. Cf. Matt. 23:35; Luke 11:51; Heb. 12:24.
41. Cf. Acts 2:23; 3:15; 5:30; 7:52; 13:28.

will be involved in this—"The God of peace will soon crush Satan under your feet" (Rom. 16:20)—but the ultimate conqueror of Satan will be the Messiah.[42]

The prediction of Genesis 3:15 could be called an indirect Messianic prophecy: the time when the Messiah was "pierced" (Zech. 12:10)—"they have pierced my hands and feet" (Ps. 22:16); "he was pierced for our transgressions; he was crushed for our iniquities" (Isa. 53:5)—was the same as the time when, figuratively speaking, Messiah's "heel" was "bruised." But it turned out to be also the time when he "bruised" the serpent's "head."

7.3.2 Shem and Eber

In Genesis, the Messianic line runs from Adam through Seth, Enosh (Gen. 4:25-26), Noah (6-9), Shem, Eber (10:21), Terah, and the patriarchs (11:27). All of these were representatives of the woman's offspring not only in the physical but also in the spiritual sense.

The insider knows how, in light of the historical continuation throughout the Tanakh, in Noah's predictions concerning his sons the line of Shem will become the Messianic line, or at least the line of the divine blessing: "May God enlarge Japheth, and let him dwell in the tents of Shem" (Gen. 9:27). That is, for Japheth the divine blessing can be realized only in and through the "tents of Shem." In subsequent parts of the Tanakh, it becomes evident that the divine blessing, which also extends to the Japhethites, is realized through Shem's descendant, the Messiah. But the attentive reader of the Torah knows this in principle already in Genesis 9:27.

In Genesis 10:21, the line is narrowed still further: Shem in particular was the ancestor of Eber, and this Eber was, according to Genesis 11:10-27, the forefather of Abr(ah)am, who was nicknamed "the Hebrew" (Heb. *'ibri*, Gen. 14:13). This expression can mean two things: either descendant of Eber (Heb. *'eber*, "Eberite"), or the one who has crossed the Euphrates (from *'br*, "to cross, to pass") (cf. Josh. 24:2).

7.3.3 Abraham and Isaac

The LORD said about Abraham under oath: "In your seed all the nations of the earth shall be blessed" (Gen. 22:18 NKJV). In Gala-

---

42. Heb. 2:14; 1 John 3:8; cf. Rev. 17:14; 20:1, 10.

tians 3:16, the apostle Paul, in a midrashic way of arguing, draws from this the conclusion that the text was speaking ultimately of *the* seed of Abraham, that is, the Messiah. This argument of Paul is not "just" a "Jewish method of Scripture exegesis" and the "Jewish redemptive pattern of his days," but a responsible exposition of Genesis 22:18.[43] Abraham's seed, his offspring, is the people of Israel. But, as we will observe repeatedly, the Messiah is the true, personified Israel; in his person, the true Israel of God is consolidated, as it were. Therefore, *the* seed of Abraham is ultimately the Messiah.

Interestingly, Paul suggested that, if the Galatian believers had listened carefully to the Torah (see Gal. 4:21), they could have deduced what Paul deduced here from Genesis. That is, as far as we can assess, Paul did not follow some existing Jewish interpretation, nor did he himself invent some explanation; he was convinced that his exegesis followed from the text itself.[44] In the same self-evident way he draws far-reaching conclusions from the story of Sarah and Hagar (in Gal. 4:21–31), and from the stories of Israel's travels through the wilderness (in 1 Cor. 10:1–12).

The seed of Abraham involves three things. First, it referred to the people of Israel because it is Abraham's "seed" that will inherit the promised land.[45] Second, it referred to the Messiah, who is the true Israel (see later in this chapter). And third—we should not forget this—it is Abraham's physical son Isaac. After Abraham, the first new stage in the Messianic line was Isaac: "In Isaac your seed shall be called" (Gen. 21:12 NKJV), and to Isaac it was said, "[I]n your seed all the nations shall be blessed" (26:4 NKJV).

Isaac was not only the Messiah's forefather but also a model, a *type*. Abraham had many sons (cf. Gen. 25:2), yet in a certain sense he had only *one* son: the one whom he so dearly loved (22:2). Similarly, Isaac had millions of descendants, yet in a certain sense he had only *one* descendant: the one beloved son, the Messiah. If the Messiah is both "son of Abraham," which son Isaac physically was, and "son of David" (Matt. 1:1), we may think here of Solomon as well. Just like Abraham, David had many sons, yet there was only one son who was particularly loved by the LORD. The LORD gave

---

43. *Contra* Loonstra (1994, 50–51).
44. See more extensively, Ouweneel (1997, 203–206, 287–89).
45. Cf. Gen. 17:9; 21:12; 26:3, 24; 28:4, 13.

him the name Jedidiah, which means "beloved of the LORD" (2 Sam. 12:24–25). Isaac, the son of his father's love, and Solomon, the son of God's love, remind us of the great son of both Isaac and Solomon: the One who is called "the son of his [i.e., the Father's] love" (Col. 1:13 ASV). The same Gospel that tells us that Jesus was the (beloved) son of Abraham and the (beloved) son of David, also tells us that three times God called him *his* beloved (Matt. 3:17; 12:18; 17:5).

The writer of the letter to the Hebrews (Jesus-believing Jews), who was so strong in his midrashic approach to the Tanakh, implicitly presents Isaac as a *type* of the Messiah:

> By faith Abraham, when he was tested, offered up Isaac, and he who had received the promises was in the act of offering up his only son, of whom it was said, "Through Isaac shall your offspring be named" [Gen. 21:12]. He considered that God was able even to raise him from the dead, from which, figuratively speaking, he did receive him back (Heb. 11:17–19).

The son of his father's love had to be sacrificed, and in a figurative way, the son did indeed pass through death and was given back to his father through resurrection.

7.3.4 Jacob

The name "Israel" was first given to a person, who is usually called Jacob, but sometimes is called by his name Israel.[46] Thus, the primary person who could be called the Israel—so literally that he was the first to carry the name "Israel"—was Jacob. In this sense, Jacob, too, prefigured (foreshadowed, constituted a *type* of) the Messiah, despite the vicissitudes of his life due mainly to his own mistakes. In Isaiah, the servant of the LORD is primarily "Israel, my servant, Jacob."[47] But sometimes this s/Servant is distinguished from Israel: "And now the LORD says, he who formed me from the womb to be his servant, to bring Jacob back to him; and that Israel might be gathered to him. . . . 'It is too light a thing that you should be my servant to raise up the tribes of Jacob and to bring back the preserved of Israel'" (49:5-6). The *servant* is Jacob/Israel—the *Servant* is the true (self of) Jacob/Israel, who brings the latter back to the

---

46. Gen. 32:28; 35:10, 21–22; 37:3, 13; 42:5; 43:6, 8, 11; 45:21, 28; 46:1–2, 5, 8, 29–30; 47:27, 29, 31.

47. Isa. 41:8; 44:1, 21; 45:4; 49:3.

Lord (see §7.14). Jacob is a type of the Messiah—and at the same time, he is the one who will be brought back by the Messiah.

Of the two sons of Isaac, Jacob became the bearer of the Messianic promise. As the apostle Paul wrote,

> [W]hen Rebekah had conceived children by one man, our forefather Isaac, though they were not yet born and had done nothing either good or bad—in order that God's purpose of election might continue, not because of works but because of him who calls—she was told, "The older will serve the younger" [Gen. 25:23]. As it is written, "Jacob I loved, but Esau I hated" [Mal. 1:2]. (Rom. 9:10–13).

God told Jacob: "[I]n you and in your seed [Israel *and* the true Israel: the Messiah] all the families of the earth shall be blessed" (Gen. 28:14 NKJV).

The remarkable prophecy by the false prophet Balaam (from whom we, interestingly, hear only God-inspired prophecies) related to this:

> [A] star shall come out of Jacob, and a scepter shall rise out of Israel; it shall crush the forehead of Moab and break down all the sons of Sheth. Edom shall be dispossessed; Seir also, his enemies, shall be dispossessed. Israel is doing valiantly. And one from Jacob shall exercise dominion and destroy the survivors of cities! (Num. 24:17–19).

This "star" turned out to be a ruler,[48] also because of the parallel with "scepter." This ruler will triumph over all neighboring peoples around Israel, including Balaam's own sponsor: Moab.

One might argue that these words were fulfilled in David's victories over Moab and Edom (2 Sam. 8:2, 13–14; 1 Kings 11:15–16), but this was at best only a preliminary fulfillment because both Moab and Edom later regained their power. Therefore, the prophecy will be definitively fulfilled in the Messiah only.[49] The Targums of Onkelos and of Jonathan understood the text to be Messianic. Also great Jewish expositors—Rashbam (Rabbi Shemuel ben Meir, grandson of Rashi) and Nachmanides—thought of the Messiah in Numbers 24.[50] It is all the more remarkable that someone like Mar-

---

48. Cf. Isa. 14:12; Ezek. 32:7; Rev. 22:16; also see 2 Sam. 23:3 (KJV).
49. Allen (1990, 909–911); Ashley (1993, 502–503, and references).
50. Cohen (1983, 926); also see jerTaanith 68.4; Debarim Rabba chapter 1;

tin Luther refused to understand the passage as Messianic because he deemed Balaam to be unworthy prophet for such a lofty subject.[51] Church fathers like Justin Martyr and Athanasius had no difficulty with the Messianic interpretation, nor did many expositors who followed Luther.

7.3.5 Judah

The Messianic line narrowed again. First of all, notice that Jacob's prophecies concerning his twelve sons referred explicitly to the "last days," or the "end of days" (Gen. 49:1) — Hebrew *acharith-hayyamim*. In connection with the *b'ney Yisra'el* ("sons of Israel"), this expression *always* referred to the Messianic kingdom and to certain preceding or accompanying events (see §5.2.2 above). That is, Jacob's prophecies had an emphatic eschatological significance, describing both the Israel after the flesh and the Israel of God to be restored in the end times under the blessed rule of the Messiah.

Among the twelve sons of Jacob, Joseph is the clearest *type* of the Messiah in his person (Gen. 49:22-26, ". . . him who was set apart from his brothers," v. 26; see §8.1.1) and in his life (from glory to humiliation — sold by his own brothers — and then back to even higher glory). It is remarkable that, after Reuben's fall, the right of the firstborn was given not to Judah, but to Joseph (1 Chron. 5:1; see again §8.1.1). Joseph became what is said of Jesus as well: ". . . the firstborn among many brothers" (Rom. 8:29).

Yet, interestingly, Judah was the bearer of the Messianic promise: "[I]t is evident that our Lord was descended from Judah."[52] Of great significance is Jacob's prophecy concerning his son Judah, and thus concerning the tribe of Judah:

> The scepter shall not depart from Judah,
> > nor the ruler's staff from between his feet,
> until tribute [or, Shiloh] comes to him;
> > and to him shall be the obedience of the peoples (Gen. 49:10).

The first difficulty is the Hebrew word *shiloh*. Is it a name (as so many traditional translators render it), or an ordinary word that

---

Pesiqta Sotarta 58.1; Qumran scrolls: 1QM:VII.
51. Mentioned in Bornkamm (1969, 240n72).
52. 1 Chron. 2–4; Heb. 7:14; cf. Matt. 1:3; Rev. 5:5.

must be translated? Some render as follows: "he whose right it is to come" (CSB), or "he whose right it is comes" (HCSB), or "he to whom it belongs shall come" (NIV). Others, "until tribute comes to him" (ESV). If Shiloh is a location (see, e.g., 1 Sam. 1:3, 9, 24), it is possible to render as "until he comes to Shiloh" (EXB alternate). All these possible renderings have been defended by expositors.[53] The usual rendering is problematic, first, because a feminine subject ("Shiloh") is connected here with a masculine verbal form ("comes"), and second, because in the Tanakh, Shiloh is exclusively the name of a location, not in Judah but in Ephraim. Nonetheless, many Jewish and Christian expositors have understood the name Shiloh here as referring to the Messiah. Some have suggested that is has the same root as *shalom*, "peace," so that the meaning could be something like *sar-shalom*, "prince of peace," a title found in Isaiah 9:6.

The rendering in the Septuagint is clearly Messianic: ". . . until the things come that are kept in store for him." One could think here of (his title to) the Davidic scepter and the "ruler's staff," these two expressions being more or less synonymous. It is significant that the Dead Sea scrolls also view the passage as Messianic by speaking explicitly of "the Messiah of righteousness, the branch of David."[54] Those from the tribe of Judah who would wield the scepter would do so in expectation of him to whom kingship would truly belong.[55] And this would not only be a royal rule over the *tribes* of Israel, but over the *nations* of the world.[56] No Davidic king ever possessed *this* kingship, though Solomon approached it most closely (1 Kings 4:21, 24; cf. the heading of Ps. 72).

Genesis 49 does not seem to leave open the possibility that there would ever be a time when this (royal) scepter would no longer be available to Judah; the royal tribe would keep it until he would come "whose right it is," or "to whom it belongs." We think here of another Messianic reference: "A ruin, ruin, ruin I will make it [i.e., Judah/Jerusalem]. This also shall not be, until *he comes, the one to whom judgment belongs* [lit., *whose right* (Heb. *mishpat*) *it is*], and I

---

53. See the extensive discussions of Sailhamer (1990, 279–80) and Hamilton (1995, 659–62, including the references).
54. 4QPBless, quoted in Hamilton (1995, 660).
55. Sailhamer (1990, 276).
56. Cf. Ps. 2:8; 72:8–11; Isa. 49:5–6; Dan. 7:13–14; Rev. 5:5, 9.

will give it to him" (Ezek. 21:27; in some Bibles v. 32).[57]

Even after the fall of the Davidic royal house, Israel retained a certain measure of independence under the Persians (cf. Ezra 1:5, 8), later under the Greeks, and still later under the Romans. Therefore, we can understand what happened when the Romans, in the year 6 of our era, took from Judea its last piece of sovereignty, namely, the *ius gladii*, the "right of the sword" (the right to execute the death penalty; cf. John 18:31). We read that pious Jews sprinkled ashes on their heads, covered themselves with sackcloth, and shouted: "Woe over us, for the scepter has departed from Judah, and the Messiah has not come!"[58] They did not know about a certain boy, perhaps ten or twelve years old, who was living at that very moment in the inconspicuous town of Nazareth. Of this boy, the angel Gabriel had said, "[T]he LORD God will give to him the throne of his father David" (Luke 1:32). That same year 6, or shortly after, was the time that this same boy, at Pesach, sat in the temple in the midst of the rabbis, and told his astonished parents that he had to be busy with his Father's business (Luke 2:49 NKJV). The *ius gladii* had been taken away, but Shiloh's work only just begun.

7.4 The Shoot of Jesse

7.4.1 Bethlehem

Jesse, or Isai, the father of David (Ruth 4:17), is called a few times Jesse the Bethlehemite (1 Sam. 16:1, 18; 17:58), and once "an Ephrathite of Bethlehem in Judah, named Jesse" (17:12). At a much later time, when it was generally known that the Messiah would come from the house of David, Micah explicitly referred to "Bethlehem Ephrathah" (Bethlehem of the Ephrathites, to distinguish it from other Bethlehems), the dwelling place of Jesse, the "city of David," and thus the city of the Messiah:[59]

> [Y]ou, O Bethlehem Ephrathah, who are too little to be among the clans of Judah, from you shall come forth for me one who is to be ruler in Israel, whose coming forth is from of old, from ancient days. Therefore he shall give them up until the time when she who is in labor has

---

57. Fisch (1978, 141).
58. Jerusalem Talmud: Sanhedrin 24.
59. Bethlehem must share the title "city of David" (Luke 2:4, 11) with Jerusalem (2 Sam. 5:7, 9; 6:10, 12, 16).

given birth; then the rest of his brothers shall return to the people of Israel (Micah 5:2-3; some Bibles: 5:1-2).[60]

Interestingly, the Jewish scholars in Herod's day did not hesitate for a moment to interpret this passage as Messianic (Matt. 2:4-6; cf. John 7:42). We may assume that this was common at that time. However, in the days of the early Ecclesia, some Jewish expositors, as a reaction to the Christian interpretation of the passage, tried to empty it of its Messianic meaning, for instance by applying it to Zerubbabel.[61]

Since 2 Samuel 7:12-16 (cf. Heb. 1:5), every Israelite could already presume that the Messiah would be born of the house of David, and, we may add, from the royal line. Apart from David himself, the Davidic kings would generally have been born in Jerusalem. It is all the more remarkable that, according to the prophet Micah, the Messiah would be born not in Jerusalem but in the same city as David had been. In spite of its low reputation, Bethlehem Ephrathah was chosen as the birthplace, not only of David but also of his greatest Son, *the* ruler of Israel. The parallel goes even further: both are shepherds,[62] and both have been chosen by God "for himself" (cf. the remarkable "for me" in Micah 5:2 and in 1 Sam. 16:1; cf. 13:14 and Acts 13:22).

The city is the "woman" who will give birth to the Messiah; at least, this is a possible explanation of verse 3 because the "she" in this verse must be a figure mentioned a little earlier in the text.[63] Many others, however, think of Israel as a whole, one argument being that the "daughter of troops" in Micah 5:1 (some Bibles: 4:14) might be Israel as well; but this might also be "Zion" (Jerusalem; cf. v. 13). Indeed, Rashi (acronym of Rabbi Shlomo Yitzchaqi) and Malbim (acronym of Meir Leibush ben Yechiel Michel) find here a reference to "Zion" (cf. Isa. 66:8).[64] The underlying question is

---

60. See more extensively on this passage, Ouweneel in Knevel and Paul (1995, 168–83).
61. Keil (KDC 10:480–81).
62. 1 Sam. 16:11; Micah 5:4; cf. vv. 5–6, 8; Ezek. 34:23; 37:24.
63. McComiskey (1985, 428); the suggestion by Allen (1976, 345) that the "she" must be linked with Isaiah 7:14 is far-fetched and unnecessary.
64. Goldman in Cohen (1980, 175).

whether verse 3 does indeed speak of Messiah's birth, or rather of Zion "giving birth" in the end time (cf. 4:9-10), during which the believing remnant of Israel is born (cf. Isa. 49:21; 54:1; 66:8).

Especially for supersessionists, I may add that the fulfillment of the prophecy refers to the end time, when "the rest of his brothers shall return to the people of Israel," and the Messiah will shepherd his people (v. 4), and will have triumphed over all his enemies (vv. 5-9). As literally as "Bethlehem" means Bethlehem in verse 2, just as surely does the phrase "our land" in verses 5-6 mean the land of Israel, "Assyria" in verses 5-6 means Assyria,[65] and the "remnant of Jacob" in verses 7-8 means the remnant of Jacob.

About the remarkable words at the end of verse 2: "whose coming forth is from of old, from ancient days" (cf. NKJV: "Whose goings forth [are] from of old, from everlasting"; DRA: "his going forth is from the beginning, from the days of eternity") I have written elsewhere.[66] They suggest that the origin of the Messiah lay not just in his birth in Bethlehem, but in past eternity. This corresponds with what the New Testament tells us about him who is from "before the foundation of the world" (John 17:24; cf. 1:1-14; 8:58).

Finally, notice the remarkable fact that the wise men mentioned in Matthew 2 immediately went to Bethlehem to find the newborn King there, but that none of the rabbis went with them to investigate whether a son might have been born in Bethlehem who might become the "King of the Jews." In other words, the rabbis knew the evidence, but it is questionable whether they *wanted* to check this evidence. As the French philosopher Blaise Pascal wrote: "There is light enough for those who want to see."[67]

7.4.2 Jesse

In Romans 15:12, Paul quoted Isaiah 11:10, where the Messiah is called the "root of Jesse." The full verses 1 and 10 say this: "There shall come forth a shoot from the stump of Jesse, and a branch from his roots shall bear fruit. . . . In that day the root of Jesse, who shall stand as a signal for the peoples—of him shall the nations inquire, and his resting place shall be glorious."

---

65. See Ouweneel (2012a, §12.4.1).

66. Ouweneel (2007b, §7.2.1).

67. Pensées 430.

The Old Testament Messianic Hope

The army of Assyria resembling a forest (10:33-34) will be reduced to stumps, whereas from the "stump of Jesse" a shoot, a branch will come forth. It said Jesse, not David. In opposition to the pride of Assyria, the emphasis lay not on some royal figure but on a plain Judean farmer: Jesse—although the point of the passage of course was to refer to David and his offspring (cf. 9:6-7; 16:5).[68]

The remarkable traditional rendering "root [Heb. *choter*] of Jesse" is basically mistaken. If A is the root of B, then B comes forth from A; but what the text said is that A (the shoot) comes forth from B (Jesse). We have the same problem in Revelation 5:5 and 22:16: the Messiah is not the "root" (Gk. *rhiza*) of David (as though David sprouted from *him*) but the "shoot" (descendant) of David.

Jewish tradition does not doubt that Isaiah 11 refers to the Messiah, an interpretation acknowledged, for instance, by the Targum, the Talmud, and Rashi.[69] Above the interpretation of Isaiah 11, Rabbi Israel W. Slotki placed the words *The Messianic Age*.[70] The New Testament alludes to the passage several times.[71]

By the time the Messiah would be born, the house of David would have become a "stump" (cf. 6:13; 53:2); it still existed but for six centuries it had not produced a king. Indeed, it was like this at the beginning of our present era. Just as in Genesis 49, the prophecy extends to all nations: "In that day the shoot of Jesse . . . — of him shall the nations inquire." In Isaiah, the expression "in that day" consistently referred to the Messianic time: *then* the Messiah "shall stand as a signal" (or, banner, ensign), which will exert attractive power on all the nations.[72]

In the imagery of Isaiah, the Messiah is a "shoot," a "branch" (cf. 4:2; 6:13), a metaphor that we will meet again later.

---

68. Grogan (1986, 87); Oswalt (1986, 278–79).
69. Sanhedrin 93b.
70. Slotki (1983, 56).
71. Matt. 2:23; Acts 13:22–23; Rom. 15:12; Eph. 1:17; Rev. 5:5; 19:11, 15, 21; 22:16; also see Isa. 11:4c ("with the breath of his lips he shall kill the wicked"), which we find back in 2 Thess. 2:8.
72. Cf. Isa. 2:1–4; 49:6; 60:1–3; also see John 12:32.

7.5 David

7.5.1 "My Servant David"

In some passages in the Tanakh about David, such as Psalm 2, the interpretive question is whether they were speaking about David himself or about the great son of David, the Messiah,[73] or about both (see §7.7.1). Of course, there is a profound coherence between these two interpretations because, in the Tanakh, David is one of the great types (prefigures, foreshadows) of the Messiah. This extends to the point that the Messiah is sometimes called "David" himself. At least, there can be no doubt who was meant in Hosea 3:4–5: "[T]he children of Israel shall dwell many days without king or prince, without sacrifice or pillar, without ephod or household gods. Afterward the children of Israel shall return and seek the LORD their God, and David their king, and they shall come in fear to the LORD and to his goodness in the latter days." These last words, "in the latter days," are characteristic for (the beginning of) the Messianic age.[74] Indeed, the Targum identifies "David their king" here as the Messiah. "Seeking" the Messiah can hardly refer to the first coming of the Messiah in the person of Jesus Christ; it will be fulfilled only in the Messianic kingdom.[75]

The same name, "David," is found in Ezekiel: "I will set up over them one shepherd, my servant David, and he shall feed them: he shall feed them and be their shepherd. And I, the LORD, will be their God, and my servant David shall be prince among them" (34:23–24). "My servant David shall be king over them, and they shall all have one shepherd. They shall walk in my rules and be careful to obey my statutes. They shall dwell in the land that I gave to my servant Jacob, where your fathers lived. They and their children and their children's children shall dwell there forever, and David my servant shall be their prince forever" (37:24–25). There can be no reasonable doubt that here "David" is a name for the Messiah.[76]

7.5.2 The Son of David

Other passages spoke about the seed (descendant) or son of Da-

---

73. See "Son of David," by D. R. Bauer (*DJG* 766–69).
74. Lehrman in Cohen (1980, 13).
75. Isa. 12:1–6; 66:23; Jer. 33:11; Ezek. 20:40; see Wood (1985, 183).
76. Mulder in Knevel and Paul (1995, 127–29, 136–38).

vid, where the reference was to the Messiah. We find the latter in the background of the prophecy of Nathan, given to David (2 Sam. 7:12-16). Hebrews 1:5 applies 2 Samuel 7:14 to the Messiah. One rabbi wrote on this passage that the promise given in it concerning an everlasting kingship of the house of David strongly influenced the development of Messianic hope in Israel.[77] And one Protestant commentator wrote: "Even though this prophecy, viewed by itself, is originally not a Messianic promise, the Messianic expectation did sprout from it under certain conditions."[78]

Indeed, these verses contain a Messianic perspective, one that unfolds throughout the subsequent divine revelation. Therefore, it is certainly going too far to say that, in 2 Samuel 7, David was "allowed to hear that the Messiah would come forth from his family."[79] Yet, the *root* of the Messianic hope in Israel can certainly be sought here (cf. Ps. 89:19-29).[80] For the first time in history, it is implicitly suggested that the great Messianic king would sprout from the house of David, and nowhere else.

There has been some debate about whether David's "seed" and "son" in verse 12 referred to Solomon alone, or to each Davidic king.[81] In both cases, the warning was understandable, though not applicable to the Messiah: "When he commits iniquity, I will discipline him with the rod of men, with the stripes of the sons of men" (v. 14). However, verse 16, with its promise of a continual Davidic house and kingship and a throne that is fixed forever, does find its ultimate fulfillment in the Messiah. If the passage was referring primarily to Solomon, the literal son of David, he was a type (prefigure, foreshadow) of the Messiah (cf. Matt. 12:42). As we heard the angel Gabriel say to the Virgin Mary about the boy she would bear, "[T]he Lord God will give to him the throne of his father Da-

---

77. Goldmann (1983, 229).
78. Van der Woude (1973, 5–6).
79. Edelkoort (1941, 162).
80. Brown (1994, 130, 156–60) saw a second phase in the Messianic hope in, e.g., Isa. 7:14; 9:6–7; 11:1–5; Micah 5:2; Jer. 23:5; 30:9; Ezek. 17:23; 34:23–24; 37:24–25, and a third, post-exilic phase in, e.g., Zech. 9:9–10, the Psalms of Solomon, the Dead Sea scrolls, and 1 Enoch.
81. In addition to Goslinga (1962, 139–40), see Peels in Knevel and Paul (1995, 45).

vid" (Luke 1:32).

7.5.3 David and Amos

David himself had some awareness of the coming Messiah, as can be seen in Psalm 110:1 ("The LORD says to *my Lord*: 'Sit at my right hand, until I make your enemies your footstool'") (see the interpretation given by Jesus in Matthew 22:42–45; see further discussion in §7.12.2). In 2 Samuel 23:3–5, God was speaking either in general terms about how a good ruler should behave (so, many translations), or in more specific terms about the coming Messiah:

> The Rock of Israel said to me: "One shall come who rules righteously, who rules in the fear of God. He shall be as the light of the morning; a cloudless sunrise when the tender grass springs forth upon the earth; as sunshine after rain." And it is my family He has chosen! Yes, God has made an everlasting covenant with me; his agreement is eternal, final, sealed (TLB).

In my view, it is clearly unproblematic to claim that the Messiah was being referred to with the words "he dawns on them like the morning light, like the sun shining forth on a cloudless morning" (v. 4 ESV), at least in the ultimate sense of these words. They remind us of Malachi 4:2, where many expositors see in the expression "the sun of righteousness" a reference to the Messiah.

In Amos 9:11–12 we read: "'In that day I will raise up the booth of David that is fallen and repair its breaches, and raise up its ruins and rebuild it as in the days of old, that they may possess the remnant of Edom and all the nations who are called by my name,' declares the LORD who does this." In Acts 15:16–17, these words were quoted by Jesus' brother James (cf. Gal. 1:19). He gave the quotation mainly in the Septuagint version, with the implication that, in the end time, David's "booth" or "tent" would be restored in the great son of David, and that this would have tremendous consequences for Israel and all the earth. It is sufficient to note here that the perspective in Amos 9:11–15 is clearly Messianic,[82] and that this is also the way James understood it in Acts 15.[83]

---

82. So also Lehrman in Cohen (1980, 123).

83. The strange differences between the Masoretic text and the Septuagint, and between the Septuagint and Acts 15, need not occupy us here; see, e.g., Bruce (1988, 293–94); and Mudde in Knevel and Paul (1995, 157–66).

The notion of a "booth" or "tent" may suggest that, at the time of fulfillment, David's house or dynasty will have shrunk to nothingness. Yet, in Isaiah 16:5 we find this term "tent," too, without any notion of little esteem: ". . . a throne will be established in steadfast love, and on it will sit in faithfulness in the tent of David one who judges and seeks justice and is swift to do righteousness."

7.6 Sons of David

7.6.1 Ahaz

In Isaiah 7, the Messianic line is narrowed to King Ahaz: from him the Messiah would come forth. This is not so astonishing: apart from Joahaz and Zedekiah, *all* Davidic kings were forefathers of the Messiah (Matt. 1:6–11). In this respect, it is remarkable that the prophet Isaiah in 7:13 did not give the promise to King Ahaz, but more generally to the "house of David," as if the wicked Ahaz had personally forfeited all promises.

Most conspicuous is verse 14, "Behold, the virgin shall conceive and bear a son, and shall call his name Immanuel." Not only conspicuous, but confusing; it is said that there are at least eight different interpretations of the verse.[84] Discussing all eight opinions would lead us too far afield. I believe that Matthew 1:18–23, where the verse is applied to Jesus, offers not only a "figurative" or "associative" exegesis but a genuine grammatical-historical exegesis. My two core arguments are these:

(a) The text may certainly refer to a "virgin" (see below). (b) Whether Isaiah 7:14 speaks directly about the Messiah or about a son who would be born in the near future but would be a type (prefigure) of the Messiah, at any rate this Messianic dimension is present *in the text itself,* and was not read into the text by Matthew.

As to point (a): indeed, the Hebrew text does not use the common Hebrew word for "virgin," *b'tulah,* but the word *almah,* which means "girl" or "young woman." However, in the seven places where *almah* (singular) occurs in the Tanakh, it always refers to a girl who is unmarried and chaste. Thus, Genesis 24 calls Rebekah both a *b'tulah* (v. 16) and an *almah* (v. 43). Although *almah* is linked less directly than *b'tulah* with virginity, in common Hebrew par-

---

84. In Knevel and Paul (1995, 78–85); see also Berkouwer (1965, 113–17); Grogan (986, 62–66); Oswalt (1986, 206–13).

lance it certainly did refer to an unmarried, chaste young woman, that is, a "virgin."[85] Therefore, it is perfectly understandable that the Septuagint rendered *almah* in Isaiah 7:14 with a word that unambiguously means "virgin," namely, *parthenos*. From the Septuagint, *parthenos* was adopted in Matthew 1:23. Luther was said to have promised a hundred guilders to anyone who could prove to him that *almah* could refer to a married woman.

If the text had a primary fulfillment in a child that would be born soon, then the young woman intended—whether she was a princess at Ahaz' court,[86] or the future wife of Isaiah (Isa. 8:3)—was still a virgin at the moment of the prophecy. If the text had no initial fulfillment but was fulfilled directly in the Messiah (see further point [b]), the text indicates that, during her pregnancy, the *almah* would still be a virgin.

As to point (b): whether the text has one or two fulfillments—opinions may differ on this point without any problem—at any rate the text itself contains a depth-dimension that surpasses a short-term fulfillment. First, the "sign" in 7:11-14 is a *miraculous* sign, which goes far beyond the mere fact that a young married woman would get pregnant and give birth to a child. Second, the sign is not given directly to Ahaz, but to the "house of David" (v. 13), which seems to favor the notion of a long-term fulfillment. And particularly third, Immanuel is not just any child: all the land of Israel is *his* land (8:8). Of what prince could such a thing be said (except of Hezekiah, but his birth was very ordinary; moreover, he probably had already been born at the time of Isaiah 7). The land belongs to the LORD (Lev. 25:23; Hos. 9:3); indeed, "Immanu-El" is "God with us." This is indeed the setting of these chapters: not some "spiritual" land, but the ancient physical land of Israel—the land of God, the land of the Messiah, the land of Immanuel.

Especially on behalf of supersessionists, we must consider here that these passages belong to one lengthy prophecy stretching from Isaiah 7:1 to 9:7. This means that 7:14 and 8:8 find their climax in 9:6-7: the Child born, the given Son given, is the Messiah from the house of David, who one day will rule in justice and righteousness, on the throne of David (§7.7.2). Even if Isaiah 7:14 had a contempo-

---

85. Bloesch (1997, 94).
86. Loonstra (1994, 49).

raneous fulfillment, Matthew quoted the verse correctly by viewing it as being basically and ultimately fulfilled in the Messiah. The same is true for the Messianic prophecy of Isaiah 16:4-5, which tied in directly with 9:6-7:[87] "When the oppressor is no more, and destruction has ceased, and he who tramples underfoot has vanished from the land, then a throne will be established in steadfast love, and on it will sit in faithfulness in the tent of David one who judges and seeks justice and is swift to do righteousness."

7.6.2 Jechoniah

The prophecies in Jeremiah concerning the "Branch" (23:5; 33:15; Heb. *tz'mach*) were given after a remarkable divine statement concerning Jechoniah, or, as he is called elsewhere, Jehoiachin (e.g., 2 Kings 24:6) or Coniah (e.g., Jer. 22:24). The statement is this: "Write this man down as childless, a man who shall not succeed in his days, for none of his offspring shall succeed in sitting on the throne of David and ruling again in Judah." This verse is remarkable because Jechoniah as well as his son Shealtiel and the latter's son Zerubbabel appear in Matthew 1:12 in the legitimate pedigree of Jesus (legitimate because it is the genealogy of Joseph, legitimate father of Jesus and heir to the throne of David). In the genealogy of Luke 3:23-38, Zerubbabel and Shealtiel occur as well, but not Jechoniah; in verse 27 Shealtiel is called a son of Neri. Perhaps we should take Jeremiah 22:30 to means literally that Jechoniah himself had no sons but that Shealtiel was appointed as his legitimate heir.[88] Other ingenious solutions have been proposed, such as levirate marriages. The solutions are made difficult by the great diversity of the manuscript varieties in the genealogies in the Tanakh, both in the Masoretic text and in the Septuagint.

If indeed Jechoniah himself had seven biological sons, including Shealtiel (1 Chron. 3:17-18), Jeremiah 22:30 might only be telling us that none of the seven direct sons of Jechoniah would occupy the Davidic throne.[89] It is all the more remarkable that, a few verses later, the Messiah from the house of David was announced: "Be-

---

87. Oswalt (1986, 343).
88. See Godet (1879, ad loc.); Plummer (1922, ad loc.). In Talmud tract Sanhedrin 37b, it is supposed that Jechoniah received forgiveness (cf. 2 Kings 25:27-30), and therefore yet received his son Shealtiel.
89. So Irenaeus, *Adversus Haereses* 3.21.9.

hold, the days are coming, ... when I will raise up for David a righteous Branch, and he shall reign as king and deal wisely, and shall execute justice and righteousness in the land. In his days Judah will be saved, and Israel will dwell securely. And this is the name by which he will be called: 'The LORD is our righteousness'" (Jer. 23:5-6; cf. 33:14-16). The name of the Messiah, "The LORD our righteousness" (YHWH *Tzidkēnu*), is an obvious allusion to the name of the last pre-exilic Davidic king, Zedekiah (Heb. *Tzidqiyyahu*, "The LORD, my righteousness"), who could be called a kind of anti-messiah (cf. the concept of the *antichristos*, "anti-messiah," or "antichrist," in 1 John 2:18, 22; 4:2; 2 John 1:7).

The notion of the "Branch" reminds us of Isaiah 11:1, although the Hebrew term there is different (§7.4.2). After the exile, we find it again in Zechariah: "[B]ehold, I will bring my servant the Branch [Heb. *tz'mach*] . . . and I will remove the iniquity of this land in a single day. In that day, . . . every one of you will invite his neighbor to come under his vine and under his fig tree" (Zech. 3:8-10; cf. 1 Kings 2:25; Micah 4:4). "Behold, the man whose name is the Branch: for he shall branch out from his place, and he shall build the temple of the LORD . . . and shall bear royal honor, and shall sit and rule on his throne. And there [or, he] shall be a priest on his throne, and the counsel of peace shall be between them both" (Zech. 6:12-13). The Branch metaphor does not mean here that the Messiah—for he is the one being referred to, as the Targum of Jonathan tells us already—is a Branch from the tree of David, but he "branches out from his place," possibly a reference to his humble and unclear origin.

Just as in Jeremiah 23 and 33, the eschatological terminology used can refer only to the Messianic kingdom; the temple here cannot be anything other than the temple described in Ezekiel 40-44 (cf. Isa. 2:2-4; Hagg. 2:7-10). The priesthood of the Branch in Zechariah 6 will be discussed in §7.11.2 below.

7.7   Son of God
7.7.1   Psalm 2

As we now speak of the Messiah as "Son of God," we are reviewing the clues in the Tanakh itself, without discussing at this point the

New Testament view of the "Son of God" (see chapter 8).⁹⁰ First and foremost, Israel among the nations was referred to as God's "firstborn son" (Exod. 4:22–23; cf. Hos. 11:1, "out of Egypt I called my son"; cf. the plural "sons" in Deut. 14:1). Next, the Davidic king in particular was described as God's "son" (2 Sam. 7:14; Ps. 2:7; 89:26–27): "Israel's privileged status as God's firstborn is personified in the king; he embodies the dignity of Israel in person."⁹¹ This is expressed in the formulation that the Messiah is the true Israel.

In various passages in the New Testament, the Tanakh was quoted to fortify the notion of Jesus' divine sonship. In Acts 13:33, the apostle Paul applied Psalm 2:7 ("You are my Son; today I have begotten you") to Jesus, and the same occurred in Hebrews 5:5. In Hebrews 1:5, the passages of Psalm 2:7 and 2 Samuel 7:14 ("I will be to him a father, and he shall be to me a son") were applied to him. Remarkably enough, one highly relevant passage was nowhere quoted: "For to us a child is born, to us a son is given" (Isa. 9:6; see next section).

With regard to Psalm 2, in Acts 4:25-26 (quoting Ps. 2:1-2) and in Revelation 2:27 and 19:14 (quoting Ps. 2:9), a Messianic interpretation of Psalm 2 is implied. It is also assumed that God's words to the Messiah—"You are my beloved Son" (Mark 1:11; Luke 3:22)—are an allusion to Psalm 2:7. However, this does not mean that the psalm was primarily a Messianic psalm.⁹² Many expositors, such as John Calvin, have thought first of an ordinary Davidic king, who did prefigure *the* great son of David.⁹³ Yet, we can also understand those who identify the psalm as prophetic and Messianic.⁹⁴ This is because the full reality of the psalm clearly reaches way beyond every Davidic king, including Solomon, especially because of the mentioned world rule of the anointed king (vv. 8-9; cf. Rev. 19:19-21; 20:7-9).

Jewish expositors have wrestled with the same problem: Is the psalm primarily or secondarily Messianic? Rashi wrote: "Our Rab-

---

90. Cf. Wentsel (1981, 278–86).
91. Ratzinger (2007, 336).
92. Cf. Van Estrik in Knevel and Paul (1995, 53, 55–56).
93. Ridderbos (1955, 19); VanGemeren (1991, 65).
94. Delitzsch (KDC 5:89–91).

bis expound [the psalm] as relating to king Messiah; but according to its plain meaning it is proper to interpret it in connection with David, in the light op the statement: *And when the Philistines heard that David was anointed king over Israel, all the Philistines went up to seek David* (2 Sam. v. 17)."[95] Not a son of David, but David himself would thus be the "begotten" (i.e., set, installed; v. 6) son of verse 7. However, in the Dead Sea scrolls Psalm 2 seems to be viewed as primarily Messianic.[96]

If in Psalm 2:7 the "you are my son" is thought to refer to David, in 2 Samuel 7:14 and Psalm 89:26 a similar expression is applied to Solomon, the son of David—but in their ultimate significance, these passages are Messianic as well. In its primary meaning, this sonship does not necessarily tell us anything about the king's descent. Even less must we think here of a deification of the Davidic king, similar to the practice of certain heathen nations with their own kings. The only point is an adoption in the sense of an official relationship between God and his anointed one, namely, on the day of the latter's enthronement. No doubt the expression also involves favor and familiarity, but as such it does not necessarily point to an ontic relationship between God and his anointed one.[97] Only in its Messianic *application* can it refer to the divine birth of the Messianic (cf. Isa. 9:6; Micah 5:2 and Luke 1:35). However, even in Acts 13:32–33, the verb "begotten," quoted from Psalm 2:7, does not signify a "begetting" in the womb but an installing in the Messianic office, either in connection with Christ's resurrection from the dead (cf. Rom. 1:4), or not.[98] Therefore, some translations render verse 33 as follows: "Today I have begotten (or fathered) you" (NKJV), but others: "Today I have become your father" (NIV).

7.7.2   Isaiah 9:6–7

Of quite a different nature is Isaiah 9:6–7:

---

95. Quoted in Cohen (1985, 3).

96. Quotations in Longenecker (1981, 426), which also refer to 2 Sam. 7:14; here again some have primarily thought of a Messianic meaning, e.g., Schneider (1953, ad loc.).

97. Thus also Goslinga (1962, 143–44) on 2 Sam. 7:14.

98. This is related to how one interprets the verb "to beget" in v. 33 *and* v. 34; cf. Knowling (1979, 295–96); Longenecker (1981, 428); Bruce (1988, 259–60).

> For to us a child is born, to us a son is given; and the government shall be upon his shoulder, and his name shall be called Wonderful Counselor, Mighty God, Everlasting Father,[99] Prince of Peace. Of the increase of his government and of peace there will be no end, on the throne of David and over his kingdom, to establish it and to uphold it with justice and with righteousness from this time forth and forevermore. The zeal of the LORD of hosts will do this.

The first point of interest is that this passage is even more explicitly Messianic than, for instance, Isaiah 7:14 or Psalm 2:7, yet is never quoted in the New Testament (although Isa. 9:2 is quoted in Matt. 4:15-16). Another, almost as clearly Messianic, passage is Psalm 72, which is not quoted in the New Testament, either.

The second point of interest is that Isaiah emphasized the *childhood* of the redeemer, just as he did in 7:14 in comparison with 8:1-4 and 18. The Talmud and medieval Jewish expositors tried to combat the Christological exegesis of the passage by asserting that the text was referring only to the birth of crown prince Hezekiah. However, this does not agree with the chronology of Hezekiah's life. Others argue that the four verbs of verse 6 must refer to the same moment in time, and this moment must be either before Hezekiah's birth, or after his enthronement.[100] Neither view can be historically correct: the prophecy of Isaiah 7:1-9:7 dates from the time of the Syro-Ephraimite war (734-732 BC); at that time, Hezekiah had already been born (c. 741 BC), but he was not yet co-regent (c. 729 BC), and not yet king (c. 716 BC).

Moreover, the text evidently implies that this is not an ordinary man; among his names are "Mighty God" (Heb. *El Gibbor*) and "Everlasting Father" (Heb. *Abi-'Ad*), and he receives an eternal rule.[101] Therefore, the Targum says emphatically that this refers to the "anointed one, in whose days there will be peace for us." However, this does not necessarily mean that the Targum was thinking here of *the* Messiah in the eschatological sense. Rabbi Samson H. Levey assumed that the word "Messiah" (anointed one) in the Tar-

---

99. It is remarkable that the given "son" is described, among other things, as "Everlasting Father," i.e., someone who, as the God-king, is the father of his people.
100. Alexander (1980, 203); others have thought of different crown princes; see Buitink-Heijblom in Knevel and Paul (1995, 88–90).
101. Oswalt (1986, 245).

gum referred only to Hezekiah.[102] It is interesting to note here that, according to one rabbinic tradition, God originally wished to make Hezekiah the Messiah, but he changed his mind after Hezekiah had failed to sing a hymn to him after his miraculous healing.[103] (We ourselves would rather point to a more serious failure of Hezekiah: see Isa. 39.) The greatest "Messianic" kings in the Tanakh are no doubt David, Solomon, Hezekiah, and Josiah—but they all failed miserably, each in his own way. There is only One who will never fail, and he is the One to whom these persons point.

Rabbi Slotki hid behind "modern non-Jewish exegetes" (read: liberal Christian theologians) who thought of a "contemporary person," namely, Hezekiah, and quoted rabbi Isaac Abarbanel, who put the names in a separate sentence: "Wonderful in counsel is God the Mighty, the Everlasting Father, the Ruler of Peace."[104] Here, not only is the link with the context severed, but this view also ignores that, according to verse 7, the born child himself is the Peace-Bringer.[105] However, this cannot refer to Hezekiah because he himself waged war, and was attacked by others.

In the parallel phrases "to us a child is born" and "to us a son is given," the former refers to the human origin of the Messiah; he is the child that was born of the virgin (Isa. 7:14). In the light of the New Testament, the latter phrase, concerning the *given* Son, seems to point to his divine nature, like the names mentioned ("Mighty God, Everlasting Father").[106] I will return to these names later; here I will consider only the name "Son." Some have claimed that the two names "Child" and "Son" refer to the humanity and deity of the Savior,[107] but, of course, this is not exegesis but an interpretation in retrospect, inspired by the New Testament. The "given Son," who is a divine Son, explains for us the identity of the Father of the Son born of the virgin (Isa. 7:14). According to his divine nature, he

---

102. Quoted by Buitink-Heijblom in Knevel and Paul (1995, 88).

103. Sanhedrin 94a.

104. Slotki (1983, 44.

105. Rashi and Kimchi solve this by translating: "And the Wonderful One, the Counselor, the Mighty God, the Everlasting Father calls his [= Hezekiah's] name Prince of Peace."

106. See extensively, Davis (2004).

107. Bultema (1981, 123).

is the Son of the Father; according to his human nature, he is the child of the virgin.

7.8 The Son of Man in Daniel 7

7.8.1 *Ben-Adam*

As we saw earlier, Jesus referred to himself many times as the "Son of Man," thirty times in the Gospel of Matthew alone. In the New Testament Gospels, no person except Jesus himself ever uses this title for Jesus, and outside the Gospels three others did so: Stephen (Acts 7:56), the writer of Hebrews 2:6, and the apostle John (Rev. 1:13 and 14:14).[108]

The remarkable fact that Jesus so often called himself the Son of Man can be understood only from the Tanakh (as can most other key notions in the New Testament). The Hebrew expression *ben-adam*, literally "son of a (or, the) man (human)," primarily means simply "member of the human race," "human being."[109] Because the Hebrew word *adam* does not have a plural form, the notion of "humans" is often rendered as *b'nē-(ha)adam*, "humans, people" (lit., "sons of a/the human," members of the human race).

The singular *ben-adam* with the simple meaning of "human being" occurs more than ninety times in Ezekiel, where the LORD addressed the prophet in this way (2:1, 3, 6, 8). The phrase is here "a depicting of weakness and mortality, powerlessness and dependence, humility and submission."[110] At the same time, the association of *ben-adam* ("Son of Man") with the Messiah is so strong that one commentator saw in this title in Ezekiel a foreshadow of the Messiah.[111] Not only kings and priests, but also prophets can be types of the Messiah (cf. Isaiah in Isa. 8:18 and Heb. 2:13b).

For the sake of completeness, we find the expression "son of

---

108. This fact that, apart from Jesus, hardly anyone uses this title for Jesus has led to ardent debates; see Ratzinger (2007, 321–35).
109. See the extensive study by Michel (1992); cf. Wentsel (1981, 270–78); Sevenster (1986, 1749–52); see "Son of Man," by I. H. Marshall (*DJG* 775–81).
110. Noordtzij (1932, 1:56); cf. Alexander (1986, 761); cf. Job 25:6; Isa. 51:12, and especially in contrast with God's greatness: Num. 23:19; Job 35:7–8; Ps. 146:3.
111. Grant and Bloore (1931, 24).

man" (*ben-adam*) in Psalm 8:4, but we encounter it also in Psalm 80:17, "[L]et your hand be on the man of your right hand, the son of man whom you have made strong for yourself!" The Targum renders verse 15 as follows: "... King Messiah whom you made strong for yourself," and various rabbis have expressed their agreement with this. However, others were of the opinion that the designation here refers to Israel.[112] The two interpretations are not that different if we remember again that the Messiah is the true Israel.

7.8.2   Daniel 7:13

Sometimes, "son of man" is in Hebrew *ben-enosh* ("son of a mortal"), as in Psalm 144:3. The Aramaic text of Daniel 7:13 used the expression *bar-enash*, "son of (mortal) man." In Daniel 2:38 and 5:21, the Aramaic *b'nē-anasha* means "children of man" (humans, people). Within the context of Daniel 7, as in other places, the primary meaning of *ben-enosh* is no more than "human being"; the term does not yet have here the specific meaning that it acquired later. In Daniel 7:13, there is someone "*like* a son of man" appearing—actually simply someone who looked like a human being (cf. Ezek. 1:26, "a likeness with a human appearance"; Rev. 1:13 GNT: "like a human being").[113] There are at least two major differences with what we find earlier in Daniel 7: the four "beasts."

(a) The "beasts" *come up* out of the "sea" (Dan. 7:2), presumably a picture of the restless nations (cf. Isa. 17:12; Rev. 17:15), whereas the Son of Man *comes down* from heaven. The "beasts" are products of human history, the Son of Man is a divine intervention from above.

(b) The "beasts" are *like* a lion, a bear, a leopard, respectively (Dan. 7:4-6)—the fourth "beast" was "different" (vv. 7, 23-24)—whereas the person coming down is "*like* a son of man" ("like a human being," GNT); he is not a beast but a human, someone of the species of *Homo sapiens*.

Indeed, we sense immediately that this is not just an ordinary man; and this is our experience wherever this title is used in the Bi-

---

112. See https://biblehub.com/commentaries/psalms/80-17.htm for the various interpretations; so too Cohen (1985, 266).

113. *Contra* Van Genderen and Velema (2008, 442–43), who understood the title "Son of Man" in Dan. 7:13 as a title of highness.

ble. "In the Son of Man, man is revealed as he truly ought to be."[114] In Daniel 7, he is the Human of humans, just like the fourth "beast" is a kind of "Beast of the beasts" ("terrifying and dreadful and exceedingly strong. It had great iron teeth; it devoured and broke in pieces and stamped what was left with its feet. It was different from all the beasts that were before it," v. 7).

The *bar-enash*, this Man *par excellence*, comes with the clouds of heaven, and receives from God (the "Ancient of days," v. 9) "dominion and glory and a kingdom, that all peoples, nations, and languages should serve him; his dominion is an everlasting dominion, which shall not pass away, and his kingdom one that shall not be destroyed" (v. 14). Again, there is a contrast with the fourth "beast," which strives for world dominion: "[I]t shall devour the whole earth, and trample it down, and break it to pieces" (v. 23). The beast's kingdom comes to an end, the Son of Man's kingdom is everlasting. The beast's kingdom is destructive, the Son of Man's kingdom brings peace and justice.

7.8.3 A Messianic Figure

It is no wonder that, from ancient times, Jewish expositors have understood Daniel 7:13–14 to be referring to the Messiah, even though on modern Jewish exegete wishes to think here, in the light of verse 27, of the reborn nation of Israel.[115] (We presume that he did not wish to come near the current Christological interpretation of the text.) The rabbis did feel a tension, though, with Zechariah 9:9: will the Messiah come on the clouds of heaven, or mounted on a donkey? In the Talmud, one of them says, "If they [i.e., Israel] are meritorious, [he will come] with the clouds of heaven; if not, lowly and riding upon an ass."[116] This is not the place to enter into the difficulties of such a view; but we observe that *both* prophecies are unconditional, and *both* must have their fulfillment—only (as the New Testament shows) at different times.

What comes to expression more clearly in the Septuagint than in the Targum and in the Greek translation by Theodotion is that

---

114. Ratzinger (2007, 325); cf. 334–35: such a human we should become too (1 Cor. 15:48–49; Eph. 4:24; Col. 3:9–11).
115. Slotki (1985, 60, 63).
116. Sanhedrin 98a.

the "Son of Man" receives nothing less than God's own authority as judge. It has been suggested that the idea of a pre-existent Messiah is already implied here.[117] This is supported by the interesting fact that, in verse 13, the Septuagint renders Hebrew *im* ("with") as Greek *epi* ("upon"), whereas appearing *on* clouds normally is said of God alone (cf. Ps. 68:33–34; 97:2; 104:3; Lam. 3:44; and especially Isa. 19:1).

In Jewish apocalyptic writings, the "Son of Man" grew into an important Messianic figure.[118] In the parables of 1 Enoch, he is the object of the hope of a pious community. He is the chosen One, the righteous One, the representative of God's righteousness and wisdom, One who had existed before the foundation of the world, One who enters into the Messianic conflict with the spiritual powers, and comes out of this as the Overcomer (1 Enoch 46:3; 48:2; 62:7). The Enoch passages are clearly related to Daniel 7, but also to the psalms and the prophets, especially Isaiah. We must be careful with 1 Enoch, though, because it is possible that there are Christian influences in the writing (it originated between 40 and 70 of our era, the parables possibly even later).[119] We can conclude, however, that 1 Enoch understood the Son of Man in Daniel 7 to be a Messianic *figure*, without the expression "Son of Man" having become already a Messianic *title*.

In 2 Esdras (= 4 Ezra) 13, the expression "Son of Man" also referred to a Messianic figure, though One who is quite different from 1 Enoch. Especially the fantastic imagery is remarkable here. At any rate, the apocalyptic literature is important in the transition to the New Testament period, in which the title "Son of Man" plays a great role within the Jewish community. Here, Jesus applies this title unhesitatingly to himself, with all Messianic connotations involved in this.

One Jewish commentator seemed to clearly identify the Son of Man in Daniel 7:13 with the Davidic Messiah; there are more such

---

117. Hengel (1995, 183–84 and references); regarding Jewish ideas concerning a pre-existent Messiah, see e.g., http://jewishencyclopedia.com/articles/12339-preexistence.

118. Michel (1992, 614–17); Zwiep (2003, 17–31); Knight (2004, 117–20).

119. Brown (1994, 93).

suggestions in rabbinic tradition, as well as in the Talmud.[120]

7.9 The Son of Man in the Psalms

7.9.1 Psalm 8 and Hebrews 2

In Hebrews 2:6–8, the writer quoted Psalm 8:4–6 and applied it to Jesus. The text of the psalm said,

> [W]hat is man [Heb. *enosh*] that you are mindful of him, and the son of man [*ben-adam*] that you care for him? Yet you have made him a little lower than the heavenly beings [or gods, or God, Heb. *elohim*] and crowned him with glory and honor. You have given him dominion over the works of your hands; you have put all things under his feet.

It is quite remarkable to see how the writer of Hebrews applied this, because the latter is an excellent example of passage in the Tanakh where the grammatical-historical exegesis, whether by Jews or by Christians, would hardly arrive at a Messianic interpretation.[121] At any rate, as far as I know, Jewish exegesis has never presumed a Messianic depth dimension in this psalm. On the contrary, the primary meaning of the psalm is evident: God has established humanity as lord over the earth, and endowed humanity with powers that make them only little less than God himself (or, than the heavenly beings).[122]

All the more striking, then, that the writer of Hebrews 2 discerned a Messianic impulse in the psalm. The "Son of Man" is now the One "who for a little while was made lower than the angels, namely Jesus, crowned with glory and honor because of the suffering of death, so that by the grace of God he might taste death for everyone" (v.9). It is quite possible that the writer was well aware of the primary—if one wishes, literal-historical—meaning of Psalm 8, but in addition to this knew of the eschatological depth dimension in the psalm.

Interestingly, the idea of a Messianic significance of the psalm is not an idea exclusive to the writer of Hebrews. If Jesus, in Matthew 21:16, quotes the saying from Psalm 8:2—"Out of the mouth

---

120. Hagigah 14a; Sanhedrin 38b (see Strack 1:238; 4:871, 1104–1105); see Hengel (1995, 194–95).
121. See more extensively Ouweneel (1982b, 1:32–37).
122. See Cohen (1985, 18–19).

of infants and nursing babies you have prepared praise" — is this based only on an acoustic association? Or was he not actually saying that he was claiming for himself the honor that is brought to God because he, Jesus, is the Messianic God-Man? At a minimum, he assigned to the psalm a Messianic tendency. The apostle Paul did the same by quoting twice the words of verse 6b ("you have put all things under his feet"), both times applying them to the Messiah (1 Cor. 15:27; Eph. 1:22). Thus, we are not dealing with view peculiar to the writer of Hebrews, for Jesus and especially Paul testified indirectly to the Messianic thrust of Psalm 8.

7.9.2 The Messianic Thrust

What arguments could we adduce for claiming that this Messianic significance must be embedded in the psalm itself, and was not read into it later in order to salvage certain quotations in the New Testament? First, we notice the idealizing way in which the psalm spoke about "man" (the human race). How can Psalm 8 offer us such an optimistic picture of man as ruler over the creation? Did David not know about the Fall and its consequences? Compare this with Psalm 144:3–4: "O LORD, what is man [Heb. *adam*] that you regard him, or the son of man [Heb. *ben-enosh*] that you think of him? Man is like a breath; his days are like a passing shadow." Is not the picture of Psalm 144 far more realistic? Here, David wondered how God could care for such tiny and unworthy things as humans.

However, in Psalm 8:4–6, David asked almost the same question, but now considering the *greatness* of humanity; only the Hebrew terms *enosh* and *adam* are reversed. Ps144 represents the overall teaching of the Tanakh: what is tiny humanity that God should be at all interested in it? In my view, Psalm 8 is the striking *exception*: what is man that God has elevated him to such a height that man is allowed to rule over all God's works, yes, all created things have been put under his feet? It may be true that the psalm was primarily describing the greatness of the *first* Adam, though with a remarkable optimism and idealism that totally overlooked the human Fall (Gen. 3). However, secondarily, the psalm spoke of the *last* Adam (cf. 1 Cor. 15:45). It did so in a language that, to make the parallelism between the first and the last Adam quite clear, obviously drew on Genesis 1. On the one hand, Psalm 8 celebrated what the first Adam had possessed but forfeited through the Fall, and on the other hand, it anticipated what the last Adam will possess during the Messianic kingdom (cf., e.g., Isa. 11:1-10; 65:21-25).

The moment we open ourselves to this understanding of Psalm 8, we can begin to understand how Psalm 8:5 was understood in Hebrews 2: "[Y]ou have made him a little lower than the *elohim*, and crowned him with glory and honor." Let us first remember that it was not the letter to the Hebrews but the Septuagint that first entertained the idea of translating the Hebrew word *elohim* as "angels." Why the Septuagint did this seems to be obvious: the thought that humanity would be just a little lower than the LORD seemed almost blasphemous. Others have preferred the rendering "gods,"[123] but this change is as big as that between the Hebrew and the Septuagint since the "gods" in the Bible are created angelic powers (cf. Col. 1:16).[124] At any rate, the translation "angels" or "gods" (ESV: "heavenly beings") is not only acceptable but also preferable to the rendering "God."

Notice that the verb "crowned" is the Greek word *estephanōsas*, which is related to *stephanos*; this is not a royal crown—a "diadem" as in Revelation 12:3; 13:1; 19:12—but a wreath of leaves like the one given to a victor.[125] In Genesis 1 and 2, Adam was not such a victor; in Hebrews 2, *Jesus* is the Victor, who had passed through death and resurrection before the wreath of victory was figuratively placed on his head.

The "Son of Man" has been "made a little lower than the heavenly beings." What a wonderful example of a "twofold level" these words constitute! From the standpoint of the first Adam they refer to his *greatness*: in the creation order he is only a little lower than the "gods" (angelic powers). But from the standpoint of the last Adam they refer to his *humiliation* in his incarnation, and in his sufferings and death, he was placed even below the angels.

In summary, I agree here with the conclusion that the psalm is not Messianic in the narrower sense of the term, yet is applicable in a Messianic way in the sense that Jesus is perfect Man, and has realized God's expectation of humanity in perfect obedience and

---

123. Ridderbos (1955, 74–75).
124. See Ouweneel (2003a, especially chapter 2); soon to appear in English.
125. Cf. 1 Cor. 9:25; 2 Tim. 4:8; James 1:12; 1 Pet. 5:4; Rev. 2:10; 4:4, 10.

holiness.¹²⁶ At the same time, I wish to emphasize that the psalm goes further than this: it refers to the Messiah not only in the moral sense but especially in the eschatological sense, that is, as the ultimate human ruler of the world (the Messianic kingdom).

7.9.3   Psalm 80

There is one more passage that demands our attention when it comes to the expression "son of man." This is Psalm 80:17, "[L]et your hand be on the man of your right hand [Heb. *ish y'minekha*], the son of man (Heb. *ben-adam*) whom you have made strong for yourself," especially together with verse 15: ". . . the stock that your right hand planted, and for the son [Heb. *ben*; others: branch] whom you made strong for yourself." In the light of the preceding verse, verse 15 was clearly referring to Israel, which came under judgment because of its infidelity. Over against this, the faithful ones now place their hope on the son of David, referred to as "the man of your right hand" (cf. Ps. 110:1) and the "Son of Man," who ultimately is *the* son of David, the Messiah.¹²⁷ Both the Targum and many older Christian expositors have understood this to be referring to the Messiah.

One commentator could not accept such a transition from the collective referent (in v. 15) to an individual referent (in v.17).¹²⁸ However, on the basis of many passages in the Tanakh — discussed in depth in this chapter — we find that the collective referent (Israel) and the individual referent (the Messiah) often merge because, as we have seen and will see, the Messiah is the true (i.e., faithful) Israel.¹²⁹

Charles Spurgeon wrote about Psalm 18:17:

> There is no doubt here an outlook to the Messiah, for whom believing Jews had learned to look as the Saviour in time of trouble. . . . It is by the man Christ Jesus that fallen Israel is yet to rise, and indeed through him, who deigns to call himself the Son of Man, the world

---

126. VanGemeren (2008, 110).
127. See ibid., 527–28 and the references there.
128. Ridderbos (1958, 315).
129. Ouweneel (2000, chapter 2).

is to be delivered from the dominion of Satan and the curse of sin.[130]

And Joseph Ratzinger wrote: "Psalm 80:17 closely associates 'Son of Man' with the vine [v. 14]. Conversely: Although the Son has now himself become the vine, this is precisely his method for remaining one with his own, with all the scattered children of God whom he has come to gather (cf. Jn 11:52)."[131] The vine taken out of Egypt (Ps. 80:8, 14) corresponds with the son called out of Egypt (Hos. 11:1). Both find their primary meaning in Israel, but their secondary meaning lies in the Messiah, the Vine and Son *par excellence* (cf. Matt. 2:15; John 15:1).

One last remark: the Hebrew expression *ish y'minekha* in Psalm 80:17 resembles the Hebrew expression *ish y'mini* in Esther 2:5, said of Mordecai. The Hebrew expression *ish y'mini* literally means "man of (my) right hand," but all agree that here it must mean "Benjaminite," descendant of Benjamin (Ben-Yamin), a name meaning "son of the right hand" (cf. Gen. 35:18). Actually, both Benjamin and Mordecai are Messianic types in their own right. The Messiah is truly the Man of God's right hand (Ps. 110:1).

7.10 The Messianic Prophet
7.10.1 The Prophet Announced by Moses

It is an ancient custom in theology, especially since Calvin and in the Reformed tradition, to distinguish in the ministry of the Messiah his threefold office (Lat. *munus triplex*). These three offices have in common that all of them are based on *anointing*: the office of *prophet* (cf. 1 Kings 19:16; Isa. 61:1–3; see the parallelism in Ps. 105:15), the office of *priest* (cf. Exod. 29:7; 30:30; Lev. 8:12; Num. 3:3), and the office of *king* (cf. 1 Sam. 16:13; 2 Sam. 2:4; 5:3).

The first and most important reference to the Messiah as prophet is found in the following words of Moses:

> The LORD your God will raise up for you a prophet like me from among you, from your brothers – it is to him you shall listen – just as you desired of the LORD your God at Horeb on the day of the assembly, when you said, "Let me not hear again the voice of the LORD my God or see this great fire any more, lest I die" 'They are right in what they have

---

130. Spurgeon (2004, 2:184–85); also cf. Alexander Pirie, quoted by him (197–98).
131. Ratzinger (2007, 260).

spoken. I will raise up for them a prophet like you from among their brothers. And I will put my words in his mouth, and he shall speak to them all that I command him" (Deut. 18:15-18).

From the New Testament it is clear that the Jews in Jesus' days understood this passage eschatologically.[132] They expected a special prophet, shown by their question to John the Baptist: "Are you the Prophet?" (John 1:21, 25); at the same time, this passage shows that, to these people, it was not self-evident that the Messiah and the Prophet would be identical because they distinguished between the two: "They asked him, 'Then why are you baptizing, if you are neither the Christ [= Messiah], nor Elijah, nor the Prophet?'" (v. 25). When Philip told Nathanael, "We have found him of whom Moses in the Law and also the prophets wrote, Jesus of Nazareth, the son of Joseph" (v. 45), it was likely that he was thinking of Deuteronomy 18 (cf. John 5:46). In John 6:14, some Jewish people were saying about Jesus, "This is indeed the Prophet who is to come into the world!" In Acts 3:22-23, the apostle Peter applied our text to Jesus, and not to the prophets in general, in contrast to many expositors of Deuteronomy 18 and Acts 3.[133]

These examples do not necessarily imply that Deuteronomy 18:15-18 is basically Messianic.[134] Moses was primarily announcing a successor (Joshua? Samuel? see 1 Sam. 3:20; Acts 13:20), and after him an entire series of prophets, who usually did not prophesy simultaneously, but one after the other. The singular prophet is no problem here; in Deuteronomy 17:14-20, Moses also spoke of "the king" (singular), whereas there have been many kings in Israel. However, in addition to this primary meaning there clearly has been some expectation of one very special prophet, as is clear from the Gospels. Thus, Rabbi Levi ben Gershom (or Gersonides) in his *Sefer Milhamot Adonai* ("Book of the Wars of the LORD," finished 1329) expressed the belief that Moses' words referred to the Messiah.

7.10.2 More than Moses

Perhaps the expectation of the Prophet was inspired more by Deu-

---

132. Cf. also 1QS IX,9–10; 4QTest. and see Hengel (1995, 39).

133. Cohen (1983, 1085); Edelkoort (1941, 76–78).

134. Craigie (1976, 262); Paul in Knevel and Paul (1995, 33–36).

teronomy 34:10–12 than by 18:15–18. There we read:

> [T]here has not arisen a prophet since in Israel like Moses, whom the LORD knew face to face, none like him for all the signs and the wonders that the LORD sent him to do in the land of Egypt, to Pharaoh and to all his servants and to all his land, and for all the mighty power and all the great deeds of terror that Moses did in the sight of all Israel.

As decline in Israel increased, the longing for a "second Moses" deepened. The faithful wanted a prophet of his stature (cf. Num. 12:6–8), who would perform equally great or even greater miracles over against the people's enemies and would accomplish definitive redemption.[135]

What Israel needed most is a prophet like Moses, "whom the LORD knew face to face." As the LORD himself said, "With him I speak mouth to mouth, clearly, and not in riddles, and he beholds the form of the LORD" (Num. 12:8). This is the Prophet with a capital P:

> He shows us the face of God, and in so doing he shows us the path that we have to take.... [T]he characteristic of this "prophet" will be that he converses with God face-to-face, as a friend does with a friend [Exod. 33:11]. His distinguishing note will be his immediate relation with God, which enables him to communicate God's will and word firsthand and unadulterated. And that is the saving intervention which Israel—indeed, the whole of humanity—is waiting for.[136]

Recall that Moses was allowed to see only God's "back" (Exod. 33:20–23); therefore, the expectation of the "new Moses" (*novus Moses*; cf. Heb. 3:1–6) included that to him would be granted what had not been granted to the first Moses:

> ... a real, immediate vision of the face of God, and thus the ability to speak entirely from seeing, not just from looking at God's back.... [Jesus] lives before the face of God, not just as a friend, but as a Son; he lives in the most intimate unity with the Father.... Jesus' teaching ... originates from immediate contact with the Father, from the "face-to-face" dialogue—from the vision of the one who rests close to the

---

135. Craigie (1976, 406–407).
136. Ratzinger (2007, 4–5; see 1–8).

Father's heart [John 1:18].[137]

From John 1:25 and 7:40–41 ("When they heard these words, some of the people said, 'This really is the Prophet.' Others said, 'This is the Messiah'") it is clear that in New Testament times a distinction was made between the Prophet and the Messiah; the former was possibly viewed as the forerunner of the latter, such as John the Baptist indeed has been.

Isaiah 61:1–3 is not necessarily primarily Messianic, either:

> The Spirit of the Lord God is upon me, because the Lord has anointed me to bring good news to the poor; he has sent me to bind up the brokenhearted, to proclaim liberty to the captives, and the opening of the prison to those who are bound; to proclaim the year of the Lord's favor, ...

The speaker here was first of all the prophetic writer, who secondarily, in his very quality as prophet, may be understood as a type of the Messiah. In the synagogue of Nazareth, Jesus applied the prophecy to himself (Luke 4:17–21), which again is an example of a *pesher* interpretation.[138] The latter is highly important, but does not prove that the prophecy as such is primarily Messianic; it can be taken to refer to the prophets in general.[139] It is equally clear, though, that only in the Messiah does the prophecy finds its ultimate, highest, and most complete fulfillment.[140] And it is equally important that this very prophecy makes the notion of the Messiah accessible to believers from among the Gentiles: the Man with the anointing oil will bring the happy message of healing, redemption, and deliverance.[141]

7.11 The Messianic Priest

7.11.1 Psalm 110:4

We read in Psalm 110:4, "The Lord has sworn and will not change his mind, 'You are a priest forever after the order of Melchizedek.'" These words are quoted several times in Hebrews (5:6, 10; 6:20; 7:11,

---

137. Ibid., 5–7.
138. See note 12 above.
139. Calvin (*Comm. Isaiah* ad loc.).
140. Young (1972, 458–59).
141. Cf. Grün (2002, 134–36).

17).[142] This could be one of the passages in the Tanakh of which the Jews were thinking when they said, "We have heard from the Law [Torah, here in the sense of Tanakh] that the Messiah remains forever" (John 12:34). Other possible passages in the Tanakh are Isaiah 9:7, Daniel 7:14, and Micah 5:2 (see also Luke 1:32-33).

Rabbi Abraham Cohen distanced himself not only from the Christological exegesis of Psalm 110,[143] but also from the view that the protagonist was Simon the Maccabee, who combined the monarchy with the office of high priest.[144] Cohen referred to Rashi, who thought of Abraham (Gen. 14), and to Ibn Ezra, Bible scholar Alexander F. Kirkpatrick, and chief rabbi Hermann Adler, who, like Cohen, thought of David (see also §7.12.2). David was priest, not in the Levitical sense, but "after the order" (i.e., the ideal model, example) of Mechizedek, who was both king and priest (Gen. 14:18). Others drew a connection between king David and the Zadokian priesthood.[145]

Thinking of David here is highly suggestive because to some extent all *three* offices mentioned were combined in him.

(a) Especially in 2 Samuel 23:1-7 (apart from many prophetic psalms) he is clearly a *prophet*: "The oracle of David, the son of Jesse, the oracle of the man who was raised on high, the anointed of the God of Jacob, the sweet psalmist of Israel: 'The Spirit of the LORD speaks by me; his word is on my tongue,' . . . ."

(b) In passages like 2 Samuel 6:13-18 and 1 Chronicles 21:28, David acted like a *priest*: he offered sacrifices, was clothed like a priest (2 Sam. 6:14), and pronounced a priestly blessing upon the people (v. 18). (David's son, Solomon, offered sacrifices as well, and blessed the people [1 Kings 8:14, 55, 62-64], while the Levitical high priest stood under his authority [2:27, 35].)

(c) And of course, David was a *king*, as we will consider below.

As we saw elsewhere, Psalm 110 is not primarily Messianic but generally applicable in this case to the Davidic kings.[146] But here

---

142. See more extensively Ouweneel (1982, 1: 68, 84–85, 91–94).
143. See Berkouwer (1952, 145) on the (non-)Messianic character of Ps. 110.
144. Cohen (1985, 371).
145. Rowley (1950).
146. Cf. Paul (1987); VanGemeren (1991, 696–700); Hengel (1995, chapter 3).

again, we must say that the psalm is understood in its full depth only when its Messianic thrust is recognized, as we learn from the New Testament. Interestingly, Jesus himself pointed to the remarkable fact that in verse 1 David addressed the protagonist as "my Lord" (Matt. 22:43–45 par.). How can David speak of either himself or of one of his own descendants as "my Lord," unless this very special "son of David" is the Messiah himself?

7.11.2 Zechariah 6:12–13

Zechariah 6:12–13, too, suggests a remarkable connection between kingship and priesthood:

> Behold, the man whose name is the Branch: for he shall branch out from his place, and he shall build the temple of the Lord. It is he who shall build the temple of the Lord and shall bear royal honor, and shall sit and rule on his throne. And there [or, he] shall be a priest on his throne, and the counsel of peace shall be between them both.

Notice here the two different renderings in verse 13, which can both be defended: either "[in addition to the king] there shall be a priest on his throne," or "he [i.e., the king] shall [also] be a priest on his throne."

The Dead Sea scrolls referred to two Messianic figures: a high priest of the house of Phinehas (cf. Num. 25:10–13; hence the "sons of Zadok" in Ezek. 40:46; 43:19; 44:15; 48:11) and a king from the house of David. Rabbi Eli Cashdan also wished to read the text in this way, and assumed as self-evident that the Branch was Zerubbabel (though with Messianic overtones; Zech. 4:6–10), and that the intended priest was Joshua (3:1–9; 6:11).[147]

The difficulties with this interpretation are, first, that in chapter Zechariah 3:8 the Branch is presented as future, whereas Zerubbabel was already present, and second, that the latter has never received any royal dignity and never occupied a royal throne. What is even more remarkable is that in 6:11 not Zerubbabel but Joshua received a crown, although he himself never received the office of king-priest.[148] This argument supports translating verse 13 not as

---

147. In Cohen (1980, 293); Edelkoort (1941 and 1945) connected this with various speculations about whether Haggai and Zechariah might have erroneously understood the Messiah to have been linked to Zerubbabel.

148. The suggestion by Edelkoort (1945, 81; cf. 83) and others that in v. 11 we

"there will be a priest," but as "he will be priest."[149] Thus, the ending of verse 13, "the counsel of peace shall be between them both," means nothing other than that, within the Messiah, there will be perfect harmony within himself between the two offices of king and priest. Zerubbabel and Joshua,[150] the two "messiahs" ("anointed ones," 4:14), together constitute a type prefiguring the one Messiah, the one crowned King-Priest on the throne.[151]

Joseph Ratzinger pointed to another, deeper clue about Jesus' priesthood.[152] The high priest Aaron, who in addition to Melchizedek was the great prototype of all biblical priesthood, was called in Psalm 106:16 "the holy one of the LORD." Something similar was also written on his turban, on a golden plate: "Holy to the LORD," that is, "Consecrated to the LORD" (Exod. 28:36; 39:30). In Hebrew, the word for "consecrating" to the priesthood comes from the same root *qdsh*, "to hallow, sanctify" (28:3, 41; 29:1, 21, 33, 44; Lev. 8:12, 30). Given these facts, it is remarkable that the apostle Peter said of Jesus: "[W]e have believed, and have come to know, that you are the Holy One of God" (John 6:69; cf. Mark 1:24; Luke 4:34). He said this immediately after Jesus' exposition that he would give his "flesh" for the life of the world (v. 51), which is a priestly (sacrificial) act (cf. Heb. 2:17, Jesus was "a merciful and faithful high priest in the service of God, to make propitiation for the sins of the people").

7.12 The Messiah King
7.12.1 Introduction
As we saw, the title "Messiah," the Anointed One, is related to all three Messianic offices: prophet, priest, and king. Nevertheless, the title was linked especially with Messiah's kingship; especially in the Psalms, the "anointed one" is usually the king (2:2; 18:50; 89:51; 132:10, 17), often with obvious Messianic traits. However, in some cases, all the people of Israel may have been intended, viewed as an "anointed" people. Notice especially the poetic parallelism in

---

must read "Zerubbabel" does not find any support in the manuscripts.
149. Ridderbos (1932, 105); Baldwin (1972, 137); Barker (1985, 640).
150. In Ezra and Nehemia the latter is called "Jeshua," in the Septuagint rendered as *Iēsous*, "Jesus" (cf. Heb. 4:8 *Iēsous* = Joshua).
151. Unger (1962, 609–10); Barker (1985, 638–41).
152. Ratzinger (2007, 302).

Psalm 28:8-9: "The LORD is the strength of his people; / he is the saving refuge of his anointed. / Oh, save your people and bless your heritage! / Be their shepherd and carry them forever" (cf. also 20:6; 84:9; 89:38). This may be another example of the way the Messiah and God's people "coincide," or the way the Messiah is the true personification of the entire nation of Israel.

In the New Testament, the phrase "the Christ" (Gk. *ho christos*, "the anointed one") was originally simply the Greek rendering of "the Messiah"; but gradually this title developed into a name, often without the article. In the combination "Jesus Christ," "Christ" is hardly recognizable as a title. Especially where "Christ" occurs as a subject, without the article and without the addition "Jesus" (Rom. 5:6, 8; 6:4, 9), it has become a full name. As Joseph Ratzinger expressed it, the term "Christ" ". . . began as an interpretation [and] ended up as a name, and therein lies a deeper message: He is completely one with his office; his task and his person are totally inseparable from each other. It was thus right for his task to become a part of his name."[153] This name always reminds us of the link with Israel: he is the Messiah of *Israel*. "Christ [Messiah!] became a servant to the circumcised [i.e., Israel] to show God's truthfulness, in order to confirm the promises given to the patriarchs" (Rom. 15:8) — promises that are irrevocable (cf. 11:29).

7.12.2 Psalms

The Son of Man is the King of the world, yet always first and foremost specifically the anointed King of Israel. The title "Messiah," that is, the Anointed One, could be linked with all three offices of Jesus, for it was kings, priests, as well as (sometimes) prophets who were anointed in the Tanakh.[154] Nonetheless, the title is mainly linked with his kingship; especially in the Psalms, the "anointed one" is usually the king,[155] often with clearly Messianic features. In the New Testament, "Christ" is hardly still recognizable as a title. Especially where "Christ" occurs as a subject, without the article and without the addition "Jesus" (Rom. 5:6, 8; 6:4, 9), it has become a complete name. As Joseph Ratzinger expressed it: "What began

---

153. Ibid., 368.
154. 1 Kings 19:16; Isa. 61:1; cf. the parallelism in Ps. 105:15.
155. Ps. 2:2; 18:50; 20:6; 28:8; 45:7; 84:9; 89:38, 51; 132:10, 17.

as an interpretation [Christ] ended up as a name, and therein lies a deeper message: He is completely one with his office; his task and his person are totally inseparable from each other. It was thus right for his task to become a part of his name.[156]

We have already considered many examples of the Messianic royal office, such as Genesis 49:10 and Daniel 7:13–14, and passages that link the Messiah with (the house of) David. In this section, some other royal psalms will be discussed.

Psalm 72 offers the ideal picture of the Davidic king, with a strong emphasis on righteousness and peace, as is common in Messianic prophecies.[157] Rabbinic tradition, too, discerns in the psalm a Messianic thrust; see Targum and Talmud.[158] Rashi interpreted the psalm as David's prayer for his son Solomon; compare the first Hebrew words: *lish'lomoh*, which can mean "*of* Solomon" (ESV, NIV) but also "*for* Solomon" (NKJV). Connected with this is the question what translational form is chosen: declaration ("He *will* judge Your people with righteousness, and Your poor with justice," v.2 NKJV), or subjunctive wish ("May he judge your people with righteousness, and your poor with justice," ESV). Obviously, the declaration one better suits the Messianic thrust.

We must now look at Psalm 110:1. No verse in the Tanakh is alluded to more often in the New Testament: "The LORD says to my Lord: 'Sit at my right hand, until I make your enemies your footstool.'"[159] No wonder: no passage in the Tanakh seems to speak more clearly than this one about the ascension and heavenly glorification of the Messiah (cf. Acts 2:34–35). Jesus did *not* link the sitting at God's right hand with, for instance, the temple on earth, where the ark of the covenant had been located earlier, which sometimes was also called the throne of God.[160] Rather, he linked it with heaven by adding immediately that he would come down from there on the clouds of heaven (Matt. 26:64 par.). All the relevant New Tes-

---

156. Ratzinger (2007, 319).
157. VanGemeren (1991, 469).
158. Cohen (1985, 227).
159. See Matt. 22:44; Mark 12:36; Luke 20:42; Acts 2:34; 1 Cor. 15:25; Heb. 1:13; 10:12–13.
160. 1 Sam. 4:4; 2 Sam. 6:2; 2 Kings 19:15; 1 Chron. 13:6; Ps. 80:1; 99:1; Isa. 37:16.

tament passages that speak of the Messiah's sitting at God's right hand *in heaven*[161] go back to Psalm 110:1.

Yet, as we saw, this psalm does not necessarily have a primary Messianic meaning. For instance, Psalm 110:1 can be linked with 1 Chronicles 29:23, where Solomon is sitting on the "throne of the LORD" (cf. 28:5, "the throne of the kingdom of the LORD over Israel"). Psalm 110:1 did not explain where the protagonist sits down at God's right hand, and a simple earthly referent is most natural. Verse 1b finds a direct application to David in 1 Kings 5:3, where Solomon says, "You know that David my father could not build a house for the name of the LORD his God because of the warfare with which his enemies surrounded him, *until the LORD put them under the soles of his feet.*" Secondarily, however, it cannot be denied that the psalm finds its highest and most complete fulfillment in the Messianic King-Priest, just as do Psalms 2, 45, 72, and 132.

Of special interest with regard to Messiah's kingship is Isaiah 32:1–2 (GNT), "Behold, a King shall reign in justice, and the princes shall rule in judgment. And [that] man shall be as an hiding place from the wind, and as a refuge for the tempest, ..." Some medieval rabbis thought here of King Hezekiah, but Isaac Abarbanel[162] identified rabbis who referred the passage to the Messiah.[163] The prophecy stands in a long line of Messianic prophecies that refer to the Messianic kingdom.[164] According to Rabbi David Kimchi, the "princes" in verse 1b are the judges and other officials of the king. Verse 3 tells us that the so-called seeing ones will really see, the so-called hearing ones will really hear (one could also translate: those who are *able* to see and hear will indeed do so). Verse 4 tell us that the "rash" ones will receive understanding, and that the stammerers will speak plainly. The fool (i.e., the former apostate, or the oppressor) will become wise (vv. 5a, 6), and the scoundrel (i.e., the former extortionist) will become generous (vv. 5b, 7–8). One only has to wonder how all these things could be viewed as having been fulfilled during the reign of King Hezekiah!

---

161. E.g., Acts 7:55–56; Rom. 8:34; Eph. 1:20; Col. 3:1; Heb. 1:3; 1 Pet. 3:22.
162. Regarding him, see Ouweneel (2014, 377–78).
163. Slotki (1983, i.l.).
164. Isa. 9:6–7; 11:1–10; 24:23–27:13; 28:5–6; 29:5–8, 17–24; 30:18–26.

7.12.3 Zechariah

The final part of Zechariah contains some remarkable Messianic references, of which we will consider the two most obvious passages.[165] The first says,

> Rejoice greatly, O daughter of Zion! Shout aloud, O daughter of Jerusalem! Behold, your king is coming to you; righteous and having salvation is he, humble and mounted on a donkey, on a colt, the foal of a donkey. I will cut off the chariot from Ephraim and the war horse from Jerusalem; and the battle bow shall be cut off, and he shall speak peace to the nations; his rule shall be from sea to sea, and from the River to the ends of the earth (9:9–10).

Rabbi Abraham Ibn Ezra saw here a reference to Judas the Maccabee, others to Nehemiah, but Rashi believed that the passage "can only refer to King Messiah of whom it is said, 'And his dominion shall be from sea to sea,' [Ps. 72:8] since we do not find any ruler with such wide dominion during the days of the Second Temple."[166] Rabbi Cashdan recognized in verse 10a the "first effect of the Messianic age: the destruction of all implements of war."[167]

Matthew 21:4–5 and John 12:14–15 connect this passage to Jesus, specifically to his entry into Jerusalem, riding on a young donkey. Three things are said of him: (a) he is "righteous," (b) he is "saved" or "salvation bringing" (Heb. *nosha'*).[168] (NRSV: "victorious"), and (b) he is "humble." Here is an incidental comment for supersessionists: of course, Jesus' entry into Jerusalem could only be a preliminary fulfillment; ultimately, the passage refers to the Messianic kingdom of peace (v. 10). In those days we expect an entry that will be more in line with Psalm 24:7, "Lift up your heads, O gates [of Jerusalem]! / And be lifted up, O ancient doors, / that the King of glory may come in." *No written biblical*[169] *prophecy – viewed in its context – has*

---

165. See P. Siebesma in Knevel and Paul (1995, 184–99).
166. Quoted in Cohen (1980, 305).
167. Ibid., 306.
168. Cf. Septuagint: *sōzōn*, Vulgate: *salvator*; Hebr. *nosha'*, from *y-sh-'*, "to save" (from which also the name *Yēshuah*, "Jesus," is derived).
169. "Written biblical" must be distinguished from "oral biblical," such as the prophecies of Elijah (1 Kings 17:1) and Agabus (Acts 11:28), which are never eschatological in nature.

been completely fulfilled so far; they find their main and definitive fulfillment in the Messianic kingdom.

Zechariah 12:10 is the second important Messianic passage: "I will pour on the house of David and on the inhabitants of Jerusalem the Spirit of grace and supplication; then they will look on Me whom they pierced. Yes, they will mourn for Him as one mourns for [his] only [son], and grieve for Him as one grieves for a firstborn" (NKJV). The middle part is quite remarkable; one could even read here: ". . . they will look on *me* because they pierced him." Many Jewish expositors believe that "they" are the nations, and that "him" refers to Israel. But Rashi refers the passage to the so-called "Messiah son of Joseph," who is supposed to die in battle.[170] Again, Cashdan unfortunately hides behind liberal Christian expositors, who avoid finding any Christological meaning in the text but think of some unknown martyr.[171]

The apostle John said of Jesus on the cross: "And again another Scripture says, 'They will look on him whom they have pierced'" (John 19:37). Elsewhere John said, "Behold, he is coming with the clouds, and every eye will see him, even those who pierced him, and all tribes of the earth will wail on account of him" (Rev. 1:7). Evidently, the piercing was in the past; but of course, the full significance of Zechariah's prophecy lies in the end times: the mourning will be at the return of the Messiah, followed by the Messianic kingdom as described in the remainder of the book of Zechariah.

7.13 Other Messianic Psalms

7.13.1 Psalm 16

Psalm 16 is one of the many Psalms whose parts are related to the Messiah in the New Testament. The apostle Peter in Acts 2:24–32, and the apostle Paul in 13:35–37, adduced Psalm 16:10 as evidence for the resurrection of the Messiah. The verse says, "For you will not abandon my soul to Sheol, or let your holy one see corruption [or, see the pit]." To us, this may seem a rather weak piece of evidence; but Peter in Acts 2 gives a real *pesher* interpretation. At first sight, the text simply seems to say that David was confident that

---

170. In reference to Sukkah 52a, Kimchi, and Ibn Ezra; cf. De Wilde (1929, 247 and further).

171. In Cohen (1980, 321–22).

God would *keep* him from death, and not that God would *raise* him from death. However, the verse also allows for a different interpretation. The expression "you will not abandon my soul to Sheol" can mean: You will make sure that I will never get there; but it can also mean: After I have arrived in Sheol, you will not abandon me to it (or, leave me there), that is, you will raise me from death. The second line is perhaps even clearer: "you will not . . . let your holy one see corruption." This can mean: You will make sure that I do not die (and thereby "see corruption"), but also: You will make sure that, when I am in Sheol, I will not see corruption.

The Septuagint seems to go more into the direction of this second interpretation than the Masoretic text does: "You will not abandon my soul to [in the sense of: leave my soul in] the Sheol." This means: my soul will have to spend some (short) time in Sheol, but not forever. We must consider here that the Septuagint, as a Jewish translation, reflects to some extent the Jewish *understanding* of the text, and such a few centuries before the birth of Christ. It is also virtually the text of the Septuagint that is quoted by Peter and Paul.

Thus, this psalm has a deeper significance that Peter and Paul had in view.[172] Their argument is: nobody can claim that *David* was rescued from the tomb, and therefore the text must prophetically refer to another person. This was someone who was prefigured by David but was himself greater than David: the Son of David, the Messiah. As far as we can still assess, the apostles were following the current Jewish exegesis, that is, an older exegesis, which could not yet be (anti-)Christologically biased.

Rabbinic tradition sees in this verse a reference to the immortality of the righteous.[173] The text is also used in the liturgy with this meaning. Some rabbis saw here a hint of the Messiah. That is to say, there is a midrash of the Psalms in which a line in Psalm 16:9 is as follows: "[M]y glory[174] rejoices in the Lord, the Messiah, who will come forth from me [i.e., David]." This midrash was written at a much later time than the book of Acts; this means that after the arrival of Christianity some rabbis associated Psalm 16 with the Messiah.

---

172. Cf. Ridderbos (1955, 131–32); VanGemeren (1991, 159).

173. Cohen (1985, 39).

174. Heb. *k'bodi*, i.e. here, "my heart"; cf. Ps. 30:13; 57:9.

There is yet another interesting connection between the apostolic and the rabbinic interpretations. According to tradition, it was Rabbi Hillel (who lived just before Jesus) who put together some rules for the midrash. The second of these rules was that of "word analogy" (Heb. *g'zērah shawah*). This means that, if in two Bible passages the same key terms occur, the interpretation of the one passage is also true for the other one. The apostle Peter apparently followed this rule. He first quoted Psalm 16:8–11, and then Psalm 110:1. In both psalms, we find the expression "at my right hand," so that these two passages can be linked together. This implies that, if Psalm 110 is Messianic, Psalm 16 is too. The apostle Paul used a similar argument in Acts 13. He first quoted Isaiah 55:3, and then Psalm 16:10. In both passages, we find the Hebrew term *chesed* (Gk. *hosios*) (rendered as "mercies" and "merciful/godly/faithful," respectively). Because this term is shared by the two passages, a connection can be made between them, so that both can be applied to the resurrection of Christ.

7.13.2 Psalm 22

As for Psalm 22, Rabbi Abraham Cohen, who wished to give an *orthodox* interpretation, hid behind *liberal* Christian expositors in order to avoid the Christological application of the psalm.[175] He preferred the interpretation according to which an unknown protagonist expresses his feelings here as a member of the suffering nation of Israel (cf. Rabbi David Kimchi, who thought in particular of the time of Esther).

At the present time, we no longer have any difficulty admitting that this psalm is not primarily Messianic;[176] thus, John Calvin suggested that the psalm presents David as suffering under Saul (although there are many objections against this interpretation[177]). Only secondarily, in his descriptions, David was speaking about himself, so that the psalm received a Messianic significance.[178] Hence the many Messianic allusions to this psalm in the New Testament, not only to verse 2 ("My God, my God, why have you for-

---

175. Cohen (1985, 61); cf. Mudde in Knevel and Paul (1995, 60–61).
176. *Contra* many church fathers; see Mudde in ibid., 59–60, 67–68.
177. Ridderbos (1955, 185–86).
178. Ibid., 182–86; VanGemeren (1991, 199).

saken me?" Matt. 27:46; Mark 15:34), but also to other verses, such as verses 8–9 (see Matt. 27:39, 43); verse 14 (see 1 Pet. 5:8); the end of verse 17 (see John 19:18; 20:25, 27); verse 19 (see John 19:24); verse 23 (see John 20:17; Heb. 2:12); verse 25 (Heb. 5:7), and verse 28 (Rev. 15:4).

At the deepest level, we may wonder whether any godly man or woman was forsaken by God. The idea conflicts with other statements in the Psalms, such as 9:10 ("you, O LORD, have not forsaken those who seek you"), 37:25 ("I have not seen the righteous forsaken"), and 94:14 ("the LORD will not forsake his people"). David may have *felt* forsaken in Psalm 22:2, but only Jesus was *really, truly* forsaken on the cross, when the "chastisement" of God was upon him because of the sins of his people (Isa. 53:4–5).

7.13.3 Psalm 40

Psalm 40 seems suited to the time of David's flight from King Saul. Here again, this psalm is at most indirectly Messianic. (One may wonder here how many *direct* Messianic psalms there are at all – possibly none.) Rabbi Abraham Cohen does not mention any possible Messianic overtones, while others are remarkably brief on this point.[179]

Nevertheless, in Hebrews 10:5-7, the writer quoted Psalm 40:6–8 and applied it in a Messianic way: "In sacrifice and offering you have not delighted, but you have given me an open ear. Burnt offering and sin offering you have not required. Then I said, 'Behold, I have come; in the scroll of the book it is written of me: I delight to do your will, O my God; your law is within my heart.'" This quotation cannot be dismissed as a loose interpretation of Psalm 40, which for the further understanding of the psalm supposedly is not relevant.[180]

First of all, there is the remarkable way in which the Septuagint renders the words "you have given me an open ear" (better: "ears you have dug for me," ESV note), namely, "a body you have prepared for me." Whereas the Hebrew text speaks only of the preparation of the ears (which, of course, presupposes an entire body), the Septuagint takes the liberty of extending this phrase to the en-

---

179. Noordtzij (1934, 129); Ridderbos (1955, 354); VanGemeren (1991, 321).
180. See more extensively Ouweneel (1982, 2:28–31).

tire body. These words receive their proper sense only in the incarnation of the Logos because the text presupposes a "me" who had existed before his human body was prepared.

Second, the quotation of Psalm 40:6–8 in Hebrews 10 is one of the clearest proofs in the Tanakh that animal sacrifices as such could not supply any real satisfaction to God in view of sin, and that a Redeemer was needed who could and would present himself as the true sacrifice:

> For if the blood of goats and bulls, and the sprinkling of defiled persons with the ashes of a heifer, sanctify for the purification of the flesh, how much more will the blood of the Messiah, who through the eternal Spirit offered himself without blemish to God, purify our conscience from dead works to serve the living God (Heb. 9:13–14; cf. 10:4, 11).

Third, there is the line "in the scroll of the book it is written of me," which I prefer to relate to the book of God's eternal counsel,[181] as in 1 Peter 1:19–20, which spoke of the "lamb without blemish or spot . . . foreknown before the foundation of the world." The letter to the Hebrews based so many important conclusions on Psalm 40:6–8 that, if we accept the unity of the Bible, its use could not possibly have been a random allusion. Therefore, I appreciate commentaries that, in addition to providing the primary interpretation, endeavor to follow these Messianic lines in the remainder of the psalm.[182]

7.13.4 Psalm 45

Originally, this psalm was a matrimonial psalm for some (or, any) Davidic king; but the Targum referred to it as a Messianic psalm. Ultimately, the "king" of verses 1, 5, 11, 14–15 cannot be anyone other than the Messiah. Only he is truly "the most handsome of the sons of men," and it is only upon his lips that true grace is poured out (v. 2; cf. Luke 4:22). If verse 2 refers to Messiah's first coming, verses 3–5 refer to his second coming, with the emphasis on the military judgments that he will bring on his enemies (to be distinguished from his tribunal judgments).

---

181. See ibid., 30.

182. See, e.g., Grant (1897, 165–69); Gaebelein (1965, 175–81); Spurgeon (2004, 1:548–67).

Most remarkable — and for Jewish expositors most difficult — is the way the Messiah is addressed: "Your throne, *O God*, is forever and ever. The scepter of your kingdom is a scepter of uprightness; you have loved righteousness and hated wickedness. Therefore *God, your God*,[183] has anointed you with the oil of gladness beyond your companions" (vv. 6-7). In Hebrews 1:8, we hear God speaking to the Messiah; so it is God who addresses the Messiah as "God," and in one breath speaks of Messiah's God. Only in the light of the full New Testament revelation can this state of affairs be properly grasped: the Messiah is God and Man in one person. He is "God manifest in the flesh" (1 Tim. 3:16), *and* he is a godly Man who places his confidence in his God (cf. Ps. 16:1 and Heb. 2:13a). I say "grasped," for here we encounter the mystery of Messiah's personality, which surpasses all human understanding.

The anointing of which verse 7 speaks is not the one that makes Messiah to be *Messiah* (the Anointed One), but refers to the "gladness" of his wedding with his bride, the faithful remnant of Israel. Or perhaps we should say that the bride is Jerusalem (cf. Song 6:4; Jer. 2:2; cf. also Rev. 21:2), whilst the "virgin companions" of verse 14 may refer to the other cities of Israel. Compare this beautiful verse (Song 3:11):

> Go out, O daughters of Zion,
>   and look upon King Solomon,
> with the crown with which his mother crowned him
>   on the day of his wedding,
>   on the day of the gladness of his heart.

7.13.5 Psalm 69

Psalm 69 describes an episode from the life of the persecuted David, but the New Testament quotations reveal a Messianic thrust: verse 4b is quoted in John 15:25; verse 9a in John 2:17; verse 9b in Romans 15:3; verses 22-23 in Romans 11:9-10; verse 25 in Acts 1:20. And last but not least, John 19:28 ("I thirst") alludes to Psalm 69:21. In this way, Psalm 69 receives Messianic traits, which sheds an interesting light on lines such as verse 4 (end, ASV): "That which I took not away I have to restore." This sounds like a reference to

---

183. The Dutch States Translation reads, "Therefore, *O God, your God,* has anointed you . . . ."

the doctrine of sacrificial substitution (the innocent one paying for the trespasser).

However, clearly large sections of the psalm do not refer to the Messiah at all but rather to believing Israel, such as verse 5 ("the wrongs I have done"; cf. v.19). Thus, in Psalm 69 we primarily see the suffering David, and subsequently the suffering (but not innocent) faithful in Israel, with whom the Spirit of Christ apparently identifies himself.

Something similar—a reference to Israel, especially the righteous among them, which then in the New Testament is applied to the Messiah[184]—is seen at various places in the Psalms. Let me mention only Psalm 34:20 (cf. Exod. 12:46; Num. 9:12), applied to Jesus in John 19:36. For Psalm 22:1, see Matthew 27:46 and Mark 15:34. For Psalm 41:9 see John 13:18. For Psalm 109:25 see Matthew 27:39 and Mark 15:29. Sometimes the subject is specifically David (see, e.g., Ps. 89:27 in Rev. 1:5). Remember, the Messiah is the true Israel.

7.13.6 Psalm 110

David was clearly aware of the coming Messiah; one of his beautiful statements was this:

> The Spirit of the LORD speaks by me; his word is on my tongue. The God of Israel has spoken; the Rock of Israel has said to me: "When one [or, The One who] rules justly over men, ruling in the fear of God, he dawns on them like the morning light, like the sun shining forth on a cloudless morning, like rain that makes grass to sprout from the earth" (2 Sam. 23:2-4).

We may wonder, though, how many psalms that we now call Messianic reveal David's awareness that they extended far beyond his own person (although this is not decisive; cf. 1 Pet. 1:10-12). Think, for instance, of Psalm 22 (v. 1, "My God, my God, why have you forsaken me?" cf. Matt. 27:46) and 40 (v. 7, "Behold, I have come; in the scroll of the book it is written of me"; cf. Heb. 10:7-9). I think especially of Psalm 110:1. There is no verse in the Tanakh to which the New Testament alludes more often than this one: "The LORD says to my Lord: 'Sit at my right hand, until I make your en-

---

184. The reverse occurs as well: the clearly Messianic prophecy in Isaiah 50:8–9 is generalized in Romans 8:33–34, and then referred to all believers.

emies your footstool'" (v. 1).[185] This is no wonder: as we have seen, no passage in the Tanakh testifies more clearly about the ascension and glorification of Christ than this one.

Jesus used this verse to challenge the Pharisees: if the Messiah is a "son" (descendant) of David, how can David call his own scion "Lord," thus placing the latter above himself? Jesus could have asked this question only if the Pharisees, too, had been convinced that the text was a Messianic prophecy. Who would the Messiah truly be if he is called "Lord" by his forefather David? Since the Pharisees knew that Jesus presented himself as the Messiah, they sensed the tremendous appeal embedded in the question: If David calls his own scion "Lord," why do you not have more respect for him?

There is even more here. Jesus did not link this sitting at God's right hand with the temple in Jerusalem, where the ark of the covenant was housed, which was also called the throne of God.[186] The common rabbinic interpretation is that the Messiah was placing himself alongside the ark in the sanctuary.[187] All the more shocking for the Jewish Council, then, that Jesus claimed that he would place himself *in heaven* at God's right hand, for it was *from there* that he would come down on the clouds of heaven (Matt. 26:64-68). Indeed, all New Testament passages that speak of Jesus' sitting at God's right hand link this with heaven[188] — and in fact all these passages go back to Psalm 110:1. Jesus' claim about himself to the Jewish Council was tremendous: not only would he rise from the dead, as he had announced several times, but he would ascend to heaven, and there he would take his place "at the right hand of the Majesty on high" (Heb. 1:3).

For the Jew (and Gentile) who wishes to believe it: in the last moments of his earthly life, the martyr Stephen saw Jesus standing at the right hand of God *in heaven* (Acts 7:55-56) — standing, as if he were ready to return immediately if the Jews at that moment

---

185. See Matt. 22:44; Mark 12:36; Luke 20:42; Acts 2:34–35; 1 Cor. 15:25; Heb. 1:13; 10:12–13.

186. Cf. 1 Sam. 4:4; 2 Sam. 6:2; 2 Kings 19:15; 1 Chron. 13:6; Ps. 80:1; 99:1; Isa. 37:16.

187. Cohen (1985, 371).

188. Rom. 8:34; Eph. 1:20; Col. 3:1; Heb. 1:3; 1 Pet. 3:22.

would have believed in him after all (cf. Peter's appeal in 3:19-21). However, instead of ceasing their stoning and bowing down before the glorified Lord, the furious crown murdered this special witness of Jesus.

7.13.7 Psalm 118

As for Psalm 118, it is remarkable that, in New Testament times, Israel's spiritual leaders still clearly understood and accepted the Messianic significance of this psalm. Here again, the New Testament supplied a *pesher* interpretation of the text. Verses 22-23 say, "The stone that the builders rejected has become the cornerstone. This is the LORD's doing; it is marvelous in our eyes" (for this passage, see Matthew 21:42 par.; Acts 4:11; 1 Peter 2:7).

Verses 25-26 say, "Save us, we pray, O LORD! O LORD, we pray, give us success! Blessed is he who comes in the name of the LORD! We bless you from the house of the LORD" (for this passage, see Matthew 21:9 par.; 23:39 par.). Here, the phrase "save us please" is Hebrew *hoshi'ah na*, from which the word "Hosanna" (Luther Bible: "Hosianna") was derived (Matt. 21:9, 15 par.).

Unfortunately, the Messianic significance of the psalm disappear from later Jewish tradition due to a negative reaction to Christianity. This occurred in many other cases where the rabbis became aware of the Christological use that theologians made of certain passages from the Tanakh. For instance, Rabbi Abraham Cohen applied verse 22 to Israel,[189] as in so many cases where the text speaks of the suffering *tzaddiq* (see further in §7.14).

7.14 The Servant of the LORD

7.14.1 The Four Poems

In the prophetic books, Isaiah in his person was occasionally a type of the Messiah (see 8:17 in Heb. 2:13; cf. 61:1-2 in Luke 4:18-19), or Eliakim was such (see Isa. 22:20-22 in Rev. 3:7), as well as the prophet Zechariah.[190] But the most remarkable Messianic figure in the prophetic books was no doubt the suffering servant of the LORD, described in four distinct poems in the second part of the book of Isaiah, namely, in 42:1-7; 49:1-7 (or -9a), 50:4-11, and

---

189. Cohen (1985, 392).

190. See Zech. 11:4-7 in Luke 15:1-7; John 10:11, 14; Zech. 11:9-14 in Matt. 27:9-10; cf. Zech. 13:7 in Matt. 26:31.

52:13—53:12.[191] The interpretation of these four "servant songs" has a complicated history. The traditional Jewish interpretation sees in the servant of the LORD either the suffering people of Israel, or the prophet himself, or another biblical figure such as Moses, Uzziah, Hezekiah, Josiah, Zerubbabel, Jehoiachin, Cyrus, Jeremiah, or Ezekiel, or reads some verses to have referred to the people, and other verses to a certain person. However, there were definitely also Jewish traditions and expositors who saw references to the Messiah in certain passages on the servant of the LORD.[192] Thus, the Targum of Jonathan reads in Isaiah 52:13a "my servant the Messiah" (even though it applied the next verses to Israel). Rabbis Ibn Ezra, Rashi, Abarbanel, and others, who themselves had abandoned the Messianic interpretation, recognized that this interpretation is the oldest Jewish interpretation.[193] Detailed evidence appeared in the ancient Jewish writings that, according to the early Jewish view, Isaiah 53 referred to the Messiah.[194] Some interpreters believed that the later Jews had abandoned their earlier interpretation due to their polemic resistance to the Christians.[195] Both the Midrash Tanchuma and Yalkut Shimeoni, as well as more recent rabbis, understood Isaiah 53 to be referring to the Messiah. The *Zohar*, the famous medieval kabbalistic work of Moses de León,[196] linked the Messiah explicitly with Isaiah 53. A prayer by early Rabbi Eleazar HaQalir is read in the synagogues on Yom Kippur, in which Isaiah 53 is unambiguously related to the sufferings of the Messiah.[197]

With the rise of Christianity, the Messianic interpretation of Isaiah 53 was relegated more and more to the background in Judaism. However, the Jewish men (including the proselyte Luke) who wrote the New Testament had been raised in Judaism and prom-

---

191. See more extensively, Ouweneel (2000, chapter 2, for many more references); see Ouweneel in Knevel and Paul (1995, 94–112); also see "Servant of Yahweh," by R. T. France (*DJG* 744–47).
192. So Ridderbos (1934, 33); Oswalt (1998, 110).
193. Alexander (1980, 129, 285, and references).
194. Hengstenberg (1956, 292–94).
195. Gesenius (2012, 1:l).
196. Regarding him, see Ouweneel (2014, 371–73).
197. Santala (1997, 300, 303–04, 307–08, 310–11); also see Wolff (1984) on the interpretation of Isa. 53 in Second Temple Judaism.

inently related Isaiah 53 to the Messiah. John the Baptist seemed to be alluding to Isaiah 53:4 and 7 in John 1:29 ("Behold, the lamb of God"). In teaching the Ethiopian eunuch, the evangelist Philip immediately applied Isaiah 53 to the Messiah (Acts 8:30–35). In Matthew 20:28 par. ("give his life as a ransom for many"), Jesus himself seemed to be alluding to Isaiah 53:10 ("his death was a sacrifice to bring forgiveness," GNT). In Luke 22:37, Jesus referred to Isaiah 53:12 ("was numbered with the transgressors"), and in Luke 18:31 and 24:16 — entering into glory through sufferings — probably to Isaiah 53 in general.[198] The apostolic writers followed the same interpretation. Thus, the message of Isaiah 52–53 was interpreted in John 12:38 and in Romans 10:16 and 15:21 as the message concerning the Messiah. And some verses in Isaiah 53 were directly related to him: verse 4 in Matthew 8:17; verses 5 and 9 in 1 Peter 2:22–25, verses 7–8 in Acts 8:32–33, and verse 12 in Luke 22:37.[199]

In general, Jews see Israel in Isaiah 53, and Christians see Jesus. However, the reverse occurs as well. On the one hand, we saw that the earlier rabbis definitely saw the Messiah in Isaiah 53. On the other hand, especially in recent times there have been Christian expositors who saw in the prophecies concerning the servant of the LORD primarily, or exclusively, Israel. They are prepared to admit that Isaiah can be *applied* to Jesus, since this was done in the New Testament. Yet they are of the opinion that the primary referent of the prophecy concerns Israel. Several authors have properly summarized the multi-faceted and complicated problem of these prophecies.[200]

7.14.2 Various Layers

It is unsurprising that the interpretation of the prophecies concerning the suffering servant of God appears to be so complicated. In

---

198. Also cf. Matt. 8:16–17; 12:15–21; Mark 9:12b; 14:24; John 12:37–38.

199. Also cf. Rom. 4:25; 1 Cor. 15:3; 2 Cor. 5:21; Heb. 9:28; 1 Peter 1:11, 19; 3:18; 1 John 2:1–2; 3:5. See extensively, Wolff (1984, 71–143) on references to Isa. 53 in early Christian literature. See also the quotation of 42:1–4 in Matt. 12:18–21, and of 49:6 in Luke 2:32; Acts 13:47; 26:23. The only passage where Isa. 53 was not applied to Jesus is Acts 13:47; here, Paul and Barnabas apply the notion of the servant to themselves.

200. Ridderbos (1934, 33–36); Rowley (1952, 49–53, 61–88); North (1956, 192–219); Wolff (1984).

studying Isaiah 40–53 we soon find that the expressions "my servant," and "his servant," and "servant of the LORD," sometimes refer to Israel, and to Israel alone.[201] And if one believes that Isaiah was referring in certain passages to the Messiah, such that the prophet seems to have been speaking of *two* servants, one can still be confused by the striking similarities between the servant Israel and the servant Messiah within the four songs.

However, in addition to the similarities there are also significant differences between the two. In 42:19-22 Israel is the blind and imprisoned servant, whereas just before, in verses 6-7, the servant is the very one who opens the eyes of the blind and brings out the prisoners from the dungeon (cf. 49:8-9; 61:1-2). Similarly, in 44:21-22 God blots out the sins of unfaithful servant (Israel), but in 53:5-12 it is the very servant who blots out the sins of Israel[202] through his atoning sufferings.

This is the general line: in the passages mentioned, Israel, God's servant, was comforted and was promised redemption (from Babylon); but the true servant, the Messiah, the true "Israel" (49:3), is the One *through whom* the redemption will be brought about. Generally speaking, it is evident to which of the two servants Isaiah is referring; at various places, the two are contrasted with each other. Thus, the servant was given as a covenant for the people of Israel (42:6; 49:8); he was called to bring back Israel to God (49:5-6; cf. 42:3); he was the One despised by Israel (49:7; cf. 50:6; 53:2-4); he had a message for Israel (50:10); he was stricken for the transgression of "my people," says the LORD (53:8). In all these cases, the servant was sharply distinguished from the people of Israel.

However, what was distinguished here must not be disconnected. Especially in the first two songs, it cannot be excluded that the prophet was (also) thinking of Israel, or at least of the faithful remnant of Israel. We need only think of Isaiah 49:3, where the prophet explicitly uses the name "Israel" for the servant of the LORD. In

---

201. Isa. 41:8–9; 43:10; 44:1–2, 21, 26; 45:4; 48:20; cf. also the plural "servants" in 54:17.

202. *Not* the nations, as some expositors have it, because God speaks of "*my* people" (53:8); it is not Israel vicariously suffering for the nations—a thought unknown in the Tanakh—but the Messiah vicariously suffering for God's people.

summary, the following "layers" have been distinguished in the prophecies concerning the servant of the LORD:

(1) Apart from the four songs mentioned, the servant was always the people of Israel.

(2) In the earlier of the four songs, it is possible that (also) Israel, or the remnant of Israel—the true Israel—was still in the prophet's mind: the true people of God. However, the very first prophecy (42:1-7) had a very personal character (see especially vv. 2-4), and here the servant was being contrasted with the entire nation, including the faithful remnant.

(3) Especially in the later songs, the prophet had one individual in mind, one who was rejected by the people, and atoningly suffered for them. According to many (older) Jewish sources as well as the New Testament, this person is the Messiah.

7.14.3 Servant-Messiah

Isaiah 52:13 links immediately with verses 11-12, where the remnant of Israel was described as leaving Babylon at the end of the exile (cf. 48:20) and returning to Zion. Additionally, Isaiah 52-53 clearly has a depth dimension, for the ultimate fulfillment is seen in the kingdom of the Messiah (cf. 52:7-10, 15; 53:12). However, this Messianic kingdom cannot be established without having blotted out the many sins of the people, which had led to the exile. The people must also recognize that their sins cannot be taken away by anyone but the Messiah, the One whom they themselves, remarkably enough, had rejected. This insight is expressed in the fourth servant song. It is the LORD, the same One who in 52:12 brings his people back to the promised land, who in verse 13 draws their attention to the Messiah.

Indeed, the Messiah is the One who, although he was rejected by Israel, was nonetheless *God's* servant (cf. 42:1; 49:3). As such, he was sharply contrasted with Israel itself, the unfaithful servant of the LORD. In Isaiah 41:8-9; 43:10; 44:1-2; 45:4; 48:20, Israel, God's servant, was comforted, and its deliverance was prophesied. However, this redemption was not possible without a sin offering for all the sins committed. Therefore, Isaiah 52:13-53:12 is needed to show *how* and *through whom* the redemption is at all possible: the Messiah is both God's sin offering for the people, and the Redeemer, the One who delivers from Babylon and from all the other powers that have oppressed Israel, *and* the One who redeems Israel from itself, from its sins and trespasses. The Messiah is the divine *basis* for God's forgiveness and redemption, as well as the *instrument* through whom the deliverance is brought about.

In Isaiah 53 the servant of the LORD must primarily be one single person, that is, this person is first and foremost the Messiah; secondarily we see contained in him the true Israel. Apparently, the servant is a man; the literal translation of verse 3 is: "He was despised and ceasing [or, taking an end] [among the] *men* [Heb. *ishim*], a *man* [*ish*] of sorrows." Subsequently, this man is literally killed. Verse 5 says that he was "pierced," and verse 10, that it was God's will to "crush" him. Verse 7 compares him with a "lamb led to the slaughter"; verse 8 calls him "cut off out of the land of the living." Verse 9 even puts it in still stronger terms: "[T]hey made his grave with the wicked and with a rich man in his death." In verse 10 he dies the death of a guilt offering, and verse 12 says: "[H]e poured out his soul to death."

By way of conclusion, we may say that the four prophecies concerning the servant of the LORD, especially the last one, give us a clear picture of the Messiah, the One who is described in the New Testament as the Redeemer who, on the cross of Golgotha, bore the sins and sicknesses of his people, as well as of all those who would believe in him. At the same time, the many passages mentioned in which the servant of the LORD is clearly Israel indicate that, in the description of God's servant, the true Israel was being referred to as well. Both the Messiah and (the true) Israel are "chosen," "called from the womb," "upheld," led by God's "Spirit," are in the "shadow of his hand," and he "glorifies himself" in them.[203]

Viewed in this way, there is only one servant in Isaiah: the Messiah who is the true Israel, or rather the true personification of the remnant of Israel, faithful Israel. However, at the same time there is a profound internal tension involving, on the one hand, the servant is the One who takes away the sins of the people (53:8–12), and on the other hand, the servant is the one whose sins are taken away (44:21–22). Throughout the centuries, the servant (Israel) has

---

203. One the one hand, see Isa. 41:8–10; 43:10; 44:1–3, 23; 45:4; 46:3; 51:16, on the other hand, see 42:1 and 49:1–5.

been the "scapegoat" (cf. Lev. 16:10, 20–22) of all nations. And at the same time, the servant (Messiah) has been the "scapegoat" for the faithful from all nations as well as from Israel itself. Thus, in the widest sense, the "we" in 53:1–6 basically includes every faithful person in every age, of multiple nations. The true faithful one is he/she who finds his/her eternal salvation in Israel's Messiah, *and* grieves over what has been inflicted upon Israel throughout the ages. Salvation is from the Messiah, but this is the same as saying that salvation is from the Jews (John 4:22). The Messiah cannot be separated from Israel, and *vice versa*. Israel is God's firstborn son (Exod. 4:22), and the Messiah is God's firstborn Son (Rom. 8:29; Col. 1:15; Heb. 1:6), and yet, God can have only one firstborn son. When thinking of the *true* Israel, that is, the chosen and regenerate Israel, "the Israel of God," it is no exaggeration to say: Israel is Jesus, and Jesus is Israel.

7.15 Two More Messianic Passages
7.15.1 Daniel 9

It is highly interesting that, in the entire Tanakh, only one passage features the word *mashiach* with a meaning that could be truly Messianic, and this is Daniel 9:24–27:

> Seventy weeks [lit., sevens] are decreed about your people and your holy city, to finish the transgression, to put an end to sin, and to atone for iniquity, to bring in everlasting righteousness, to seal both vision and prophet, and to anoint a most holy place. Know therefore and understand that from the going out of the word to restore and build Jerusalem to the coming of Messiah, the prince, there shall be seven weeks and sixty-two weeks: it shall be built again with squares and moat, but in a troubled time. And after the sixty-two weeks, the Messiah shall be cut off and shall have nothing. And the people of the prince who is to come shall destroy the city and the sanctuary. Its end shall come with a flood, and to the end there shall be war. Desolations are decreed. And he shall make a strong covenant with many for one week, and for half of the week he shall put an end to sacrifice and offering. And on the wing of abominations shall come one who makes desolate, until the decreed end is poured out on the desolator (ESV, with a few adaptations from the NKJV).

The Hebrew text is very complicated, and at various points alternative translations are conceivable; this is not the place to enter into all the details.[204] I agree with commentaries that interpret the text in a Messianic sense, and need not repeat their arguments.[205] In brief: I understand the "weeks" (literally "sevens") to be sevens of years. They must be counted from the moment that the order was given to rebuild the city; in 457 BC, Ezra received from the Persian king Artaxerxes I Longimanus the order to rebuild the temple (Ezra 7:12–26), and Ezra rightly concluded that this also implied the restoration of the walls (9:9); no safe restoration of the temple was possible without the restoration of the city as such. From this royal command, it was seven "sevens" (forty-nine years) for the restoration of city and temple. This meant seven plus sixty-two "sevens," that is, 483 years, until the Messiah. Verse 24 makes clear that the seventy "sevens" terminate when Israel's unrighteousness is be atoned for; this will be fully realized at the beginning of the Messianic kingdom. On the basis of both internal and external exegetical arguments, I believe, with many other expositors, that there is a large gap between the sixty-ninth and the seventieth "seven."[206] If we begin in the year 457 BC, then the sixty-nine "sevens" (483 years) bring us just about to the beginning of Jesus' ministry in Israel (AD 27).

The text says that, after the sixty-nine "sevens" the Messiah is "cut off." This is followed by the mysterious Hebrew words *l'ēn lo*, which is literally: "and not for (or, to, against) him." These words have been interpreted in various ways: (a) "he shall have nothing" (i.e., he dies poor and destitute), (b) "it will not be for himself" (i.e., he dies for others), (c) "there is nothing against him" (i.e., he dies innocently), (d) "there is no one for him" (i.e., no one defends him or helps him). Each of these interpretations is applicable to Jesus. Interpretations (b) and (c) present him as the innocent substitute. This suggests a connection with verse 24, which becomes apparent

---

204. Regarding this, see Ouweneel (1999, §1.7; 2012a, §6.5).

205. See, e.g., Anderson (1990, ad loc.); Kelly (1952, ad loc.); Gaebelein (1911, ad loc.); Lang (1942, ad loc.); Hoehner (1977, 117); McDowell (1979, 15–22); Maier (1982, ad loc.); Archer (1982, 289–92); Fijnvandraat (1990, ad loc.).

206. Internal: v. 26 mentions events that apparently occur after the sixty-ninth but before the seventieth "seven"; external: v. 26 has been entirely fulfilled, but v. 27 not at all.

only in the light of the New Testament: the One who atones for the unrighteousness is the One who dies innocently for others.

7.15.2 Hosea 11

Last of all, we consider Hosea 11:1, "When Israel was a child, I loved him, and out of Egypt I called my son." This verse must be mentioned because in Matthew 2:15 it is applied to the Messiah. The theological basis that Matthew had for this application lay in the profound unity between Israel and its Messiah. We have seen several times that the Messiah is the true Israel. This implies that, in his life, the entire history of Israel repeats itself in a nutshell, in such a way that he, in contrast with Israel, magnificently remains upright. Thus, Jesus calls himself the true vine (John 15:1), and there can hardly be any doubt that he was contrasting himself to Israel, which is often compared to a vine.[207] Whereas, in all these passages, Israel was pictured as an unfaithful and guilty, "false vine," not producing true fruit, Jesus presents himself as the "true vine."

Since Israel was viewed in Psalm 80 as a "vine" "dug up [or, uprooted] from Egypt" (v. 8 HCSB), and was also called "son" (v. 15), there seems to be a parallel here with Hosea 11:1. We have seen (§7.9.3) that the text in Psalm 80:15 and 17 seems to move smoothly from Israel to the Messiah. Verse 15 might still refer to Israel—Israel is the firstborn "son" of God (Exod. 4:22)—but although verse 17 unmistakably speaks of the same figure as verse 15, this figure assumes in verse 17 unmistakably Messianic features. In the light of the New Testament, terms such as "man of your right hand" and "son of man" receive their full significance in the Messiah. If this line of thought is correct, it is not only the New Testament but the Tanakh writer himself who merges the figures of Israel and the Messiah.

---

207. Ps. 80:8–15; Isa. 5:1–7; Jer. 2:21; Ezek. 15; 19:10; Hos. 10:1.

Chapter 8
Jesus and the Jews

*In two things chiefly does the fundamental difference appear between Christianity and all other religious systems, notably Rabbinism. . . . Subjectively, they concern **sin** and the **sinner**; or, to put it objectively, the forgiveness of sin and the welcome to the sinner. But Rabbinism, . . . can only generally point to God for the forgiveness of sin. What here is merely an abstraction, has become a concrete reality in Christ. He speaks forgiveness on earth, because He is its embodiment.*

Alfred Edersheim (1883)[1]

King Jannai[2] said to his wife, "Fear not the Pharisees and the non-Pharisees but the hypocrites who ape the Pharisees; because their deeds are the deeds of Zimri [Num. 25:14] but they expect a reward like Phinehas [Num. 14:11–13]."

Talmud: Sotah 22b

8.1 Jesus the Jew
8.1.1 Judah and Joseph

THROUGHOUT THIS BOOK, I refer to the Messiah several times as the

---

1. Edersheim (1971, 1:507); Alfred Edersheim was a European Christian Jew and Bible scholar.
2. I.e., the Hasmonaean Alexander Jannaeus, d. 76 BC.

true Israel. To put it another way: the Messiah *is* Israel personified. No Jew should forget this: their true identity lies in the Messiah. No supersessionist should forget this: the "Israel of God" is not the Ecclesia but the Messiah, and it includes the ethnic character of this Israel. No Jew or Gentile is anything apart from *Israel's* Messiah: "salvation is from the Jews" (John 4:22). As someone has put it: "There is no contrast between Israel and the Messiah. They are one and the same. They cannot be played off one against the other."[3] Therefore, many statements in the Tanakh can be linked both with the Messiah and with Israel. The most remarkable example of this are the four prophecies about the suffering Servant of the LORD in the book of Isaiah (see §7.14).

Indeed, no one can really understand Israel — its origin, its character, its position, its history, its future — without knowing the essentials of Israel's Messiah and Messianic hope: the expectation of the anointed[4] King from the house of David, who will establish peace and justice in Israel and throughout the entire world. If we leave David out of consideration for a moment, this expectation existed already in Genesis 49. This chapter has an emphatically prophetic character, for Jacob tells his sons: "Gather yourselves together, that I may tell you what shall happen to you in days to come. Assemble and listen, O sons of Jacob, listen to Israel your father" (Gen. 49:1b, 2). "Days to come"[5] (Heb. *b'acharit hayyamim*) is more accurately "the latter days" (ASV), "the last days" (KJV), or "the end of days" (DARBY). It is not simply "the future"; the last days are explicitly the *days of the Messiah*, or, as Jesus called them, the "days of the Son of Man" (Luke 17:22, 26).

The Messianic character clearly comes to light in this chapter in not one but two sons of Jacob: in Judah, the fourth son of Leah (he received a birthright beyond them because the first three sons had failed, vv. 3-7), and in Joseph, the first son of Rachel, who received

---

3. Van de Beek (2002, 109).

4. Remember: "Messiah" comes from Heb. *mashiach*, "anointed," from *m-sh-ch*, "to anoint"; cf. Gk. *christos*, from *chriō*, "to anoint"; see extensively, Schirrmacher (2001); Raymond (2003).

5. Why this weak rendering? Is it the fear of reading too much prophecy into this chapter? Cf. Num. 24:14; Isa. 2:2; Ezek. 38:16; Dan. 2:28; 10:14; Hos. 3:5; Micah 4:1.

the birthright. Consider 1 Chronicles 5:1-2,

> The sons of Reuben the firstborn of Israel (for he was the firstborn, but because he defiled his father's couch, his birthright was given to the sons of Joseph the son of Israel, so that he could not be enrolled as the oldest son; though Judah became strong among his brothers and a chief came from him, yet the birthright belonged to Joseph).

Judah was the physical ancestor of David, and through him of the Messiah. But Joseph was, so the speak, the spiritual ancestor of the Messiah because not Judah but Joseph was Jacob's "firstborn."

Of Judah, Jacob had said: "The scepter shall not depart from Judah, nor the ruler's staff from between his feet, until tribute comes to him [or, until Shiloh comes; see §7.3.5]; and to him shall be the obedience of the peoples." In this prophecy, as well as in 2 Samuel 7:12-16 (God's prophecy to David and his house), lay the root of Israel's Messianic hope. But let us not overlook Joseph, who, to be sure, was not the physical ancestor of the Messiah, but was certainly one of the most important and magnificent *types* (prefigures, foreshadows) of him. Joseph's description is the most extensive in Genesis 49:

> Joseph is a fruitful bough, / a fruitful bough by a spring; / his branches run over the wall. / The archers bitterly attacked him, / shot at him, and harassed him severely, / yet his bow remained unmoved; / his arms were made agile by the hands of the Mighty One of Jacob / (from there is the Shepherd, the Stone of Israel), / by the God of your father who will help you, / by the Almighty who will bless you / with blessings of heaven above, / blessings of the deep that crouches beneath, / blessings of the breasts and of the womb. / The blessings of your father / are mighty beyond the blessings of my parents, / up to the bounties of the everlasting hills. / May they be on the head of Joseph, / and on the brow of him who was set apart from his brothers (vv. 22-26).

Notice the following seven points:[6]

1. Literally, Joseph was a "fruitful son"; Rashi: a "lovely son"; Rashbam: a "fruitful vine"; Jacob Sforno: a tree that offers protection (to Jacob and his sons; Gen. 45-50).

---

6. For rabbinic references, see Cohen (1983, ad loc.).

2. Nachmanides: the "branches" are Joseph's sons: Ephraim and Manasseh. Or, Joseph's fruitfulness reaches over the wall, indicating that Messiah's blessings reach out, not only to Israel but, to the nations.[7]

3. Jacob Sforno suggests that the hateful "archers" are Joseph's brothers (Gen. 37), Potiphar and his wife (Gen. 39), and the cupbearer (Gen. 40).

4. A complicated phrase: is God the Shepherd (cf. Gen. 48:15), who strengthened Joseph (and thus the Messiah)? Rashi and others believe that Joseph himself is here the shepherd, the rock of Israel; and as such, he is an excellent type of the Messiah.[8]

5. God has blessed Joseph, and thus *will* bless the Messiah, with rain and sunshine, with water from the earth, and with fruitfulness of humans and cattle.

6. Jacob's blessing for Joseph was greater than that of Abraham and Isaac; I take this to mean that, in the glorified Messiah, the blessing for Israel will be greater than the blessing for the patriarchs.

7. "Set apart" is Hebrew *nazir*; Joseph is the "consecrated one" among his brothers (cf. Deut. 33:16). Spiritually speaking, he was the true Nazirite of Numbers 6, as also the Messiah would be: the One set apart to the LORD.

8.1.2 Jesus and the Pharisees

The last point in the previous section—the Messiah as the One "set apart"—takes us to the confrontation between Jesus and the Pharisees. The latter was a Jewish religious party, whose name came from Hebrew *parush*, plural *p'rushim*, from the root *p-r-sh*, "to set apart." Jesus was not literally a *nazir* because he drank wine (Matt. 11:19; cf. Num. 6:3).[9] But he was a spiritual *nazir*, because he was

---

7. Others translate: "Joseph is a wild donkey, a wild donkey beside a spring, his wild colts beside the wall" (ESV note).
8. Cf. Isa. 40:11; Ezek. 34:23; 37:24; John 10:11; Heb. 13:20; 1 Pet. 5:4.
9. By contrast, his forerunner, John the Baptist, *was* a literal *nazir*, at least when it came to wine drinking (Luke 1:15; cf. the Rechabites in Jer. 35).

totally consecrated to God, as he himself said, "My food is to do the will of him who sent me and to accomplish his work" (John 4:34). "I always do the things that are pleasing to him" (John 8:29). Opposing him was a party of religious people calling themselves the ones "set apart for," or "separated (consecrated) to," the Lord. The confrontations between Jesus and the Pharisees were the saddest and most solemn ever to occur in redemptive history.

Christians believe that Jesus is the Messiah of Israel, but most Jews do not believe so. On no point do Jews and Christians part ways so painfully as they do with respect to Jesus. At the same time, Jesus resembled no party in Israel more closely than these very Pharisees. It was no coincidence that a leading Pharisee, Nicodemus visited Jesus at night and became his disciple (John 3:1-21; 7:50-51; 19:38-39). In the book of Acts we do not explicitly find that Sadducees became followers of Jesus,[10] but we do read that many Pharisees did (Acts 15:5). The Sadducees accepted only the Torah as Holy Scripture, but Jesus and the Pharisees accepted the entire Tanakh as Scripture. No wonder that Jesus' most influential representative and preacher was Rabbi Sha'ul, the later apostle Paul, a converted Pharisee. In his conflict with the Jewish Council, the Pharisees chose Paul's side against the Sadducees (Acts 23:6-10). When the Jesus-believing Paul looked back on his past, he did not say, "I *was*," but "I *am* a Pharisee" (Acts 23:6; cf. 26:5; Phil. 3:6). Jesus-believing Pharisee Saul/Paul (Sha'ul/Paulos) implicitly assumed an unbroken continuum between the beliefs of the Pharisees and the Christian faith.[11] Of course, a wide chasm existed between those Pharisees who kept following the old line and those Pharisees who became followers of Jesus.[12]

No wonder that some authors have claimed that Jesus *was* a Pharisee[13] — a sincere one,[14] like Nicodemus, Saul of Tarsus (the later apostle Paul), and Rabbi Gamaliel (Acts 5:34; 22:3), better known

---

10. Many priests did become followers, though (Acts 6:7), and we know that many priests were Sadducees.
11. Dunn (2006, 326).
12. A. Noordegraaf in Mulder and Noordegraaf (2007, 208).
13. See, e.g., Maccoby (1986).
14. The rabbis were aware of the fact that many Pharisees had not been sincere; cf. the famous seven types of Pharisees in the Talmud: Sotah 22b.

among the Jews as Gamliel I (d. AD 58), a grandson of the famous Rabbi Hillel, and a member of the school of Hillel.[15] Not only was Jesus sincere, but he opposed the many additions to the Torah (see his Sermon on the Mount, Matt. 5-7) — something to which the Pharisees were inclined, and which eventually received shape in the Talmud. Jesus warned that such additions could obscure and vitiate the true meaning of the Tanakh. (The same happens today with so many "Christian" sects and cults that wrap the Bible in their own interpretations and additions.)

Indeed, Jesus was far more critical of rabbinic tradition than the Pharisees were, but at least he shared with them a deep respect for the Tanakh, and like them, he held to "the hope and the resurrection of the dead" (cf. Acts 23:6, and v. 8, "the Sadducees say that there is no resurrection, nor angel, nor spirit, but the Pharisees acknowledge them all"). Especially in their Messianic hope, the two — Jesus and the Pharisees — were very close.

(a) The Pharisees believed in the resurrection of the dead, as Jesus did: he predicted his own resurrection (Matt. 16:21; 17:23) as well as the resurrection of the dead in general (22:23-32; John 5:28-29; in 11:24-25 he declared himself to be the Resurrection).

(b) The Pharisees believed in the coming of the Son of Man on the clouds of heaven, as did Jesus, who identified himself as this "Son of Man" (Matt. 24:30; 26:64).

(c) The Pharisees believed that the Messiah would be the Son of David, and one day would sit on the throne of David. Jesus believed the same — as did the crowd, at least when he entered Jerusalem riding on a donkey, for they shouted: "Hosanna to the Son of David! Blessed is he who comes in the name of the LORD! Hosanna in the highest!" (Matt. 21:9), and: "'Blessed is the King who comes in the name of the LORD! Peace in heaven and glory in the highest!" Actually, some of the *Pharisees* in the crowd said to him, "'Teacher, rebuke your disciples.' He answered, 'I tell you, if these were silent, the very stones would cry out'" (Luke 19:38-40).

8.2 Jesus and the Jews
8.2.1 A Growing Chasm

The eschatology of Jesus and the Pharisees was identical; the great

---

15. Regarding him, see Ouweneel (2014, 111–16).

difference between them was this: the latter were not prepared to apply the Messianic features in the Tanakh to Jesus. Today the situation is different: orthodox Jews, that is, Jews thinking along rabbinic-Talmudic lines, the spiritual descendants of the Pharisees, still deny that Jesus *was* the Messiah, but some of them cautiously suggest that, when the Messiah does appear, he may turn out to be Jesus. This is new; it is a joyful sign of the last days. Jews and (non-supersessionist) Christians both believe in the Messiah, who will appear in Jerusalem, and there will sit on the throne of David. But most orthodox Jews cannot believe that the Jesus of the Gospels was the Messiah. We will need to consider why they cannot believe this—and try to understand their reasons.

This confrontation has been a sad phenomenon. For many centuries, Jesus (and his followers) and the Pharisees (and their successors, rabbinic-Talmudic Jews) have parted ways. After the fall of Jerusalem (AD 70), the further development of rabbinic Judaism was partly determined by their opposition to early Christianity.[16] No wonder that *their* picture of "the Jew," as well as *their* picture of "the Messiah," had less and less room for Jesus, precisely because these pictures were construed—largely inadvertently, we may assume—in such a way that they implicitly *opposed* Jesus. The more Jesus could be branded as un-Jewish, and the more the picture of the Messiah deviated from that of Jesus, the easier it was to assert that Jesus could not possibly have been the Messiah. Add to this that Jews were increasingly under the (erroneous) impression that Jews who believed that Jesus was the Messiah would stop being Jews, and would have betrayed their heritage by joining a Christian denomination. It was largely the fault of supersessionism that Jews began to believe this. It was and is one of the saddest falsehoods peddled to the Jews by supersessionism. In the time of the book of Acts, it was not easy for a Jew to become a Jesus-believer. Today, it is hundred times more difficult, first, because of so many theological falsehoods, and second, because of seventeen centuries of supersessionist oppression of Jews.

In a certain sense, one could speak of a hate-love relationship

---

16. Actually, this was less the case in Babylon (where the Babylonian Talmud would be composed) because the number of Christians there was very limited, and thus, Jewish knowledge of Christianity was very limited.

between, on the one hand, the Pharisees and later rabbinic Judaism and, on the other hand, Jesus and his (Jewish and Gentile) followers. Jesus heavily criticized the *hypocritical* Pharisees,[17] but so did later rabbis (see note 14 above). Every honest Jew or Christian, or any human being, should abhor hypocrisy. Yet, at the same time, Jesus said of the scribes (Torah experts) and the Pharisees: "The scribes and the Pharisees sit on Moses' seat, so *do and observe whatever they tell you*" (Matt. 23:2–3). The apostle Paul, too, said to the leaders of Judaism in Rome: "I had done nothing against our people or *the customs of our fathers,*"[18] and such customs point much more to the Pharisees than to the Sadducees or other religious parties. Therefore, in a sense there is also a different hate-love relationship between, *on the one hand, the Pharisees, later rabbinic Jews,* **and Jesus** *and, on the other hand, supersessionist Christianity.*

8.2.2 Four Similarities

Until today, a deep connection has existed between (non-supersessionist) Christians and orthodox Jews—if only both parties were prepared to admit it. And given the misery of church history with all its persecution of the Jews, this is not easy. I see *seven* vital similarities between (non-Jesus-believing) Jews and Christians.

1. Both (godly) Jews and (godly) Christians love the God of Israel, that is, the God of the Bible.
    * There is this great difference, though: Christians believe that this God has revealed himself not only through the prophets in the *Tanakh*, but especially in the person of his Son, Jesus Christ.
2. Both (godly) Jews and (godly) Christians believe in the *Tanakh* (the Old Testament), that is, in what, for Jesus and the apostles, was "Scripture" or "the Scriptures," as they put it many times.
    * The difference is that Christians read the Tanakh from a New Testament perspective, and Jews read it from a Talmudic—or more broadly, rabbinic—perspective, the latter being a perspective that became more and more anti-Jesus.

---

17. Cf. Matt. 6:2, 5, 16; 7:5; 15:7; 22:18; 23:13, 15, 23, 25, 27–29.
18. Acts 28:17; cf. 24:12–13; 25:8; Gal. 1:14.

3. Both (godly) Jews and (godly) Christians believe in the *coming Messiah*, the Son of Man, who will descend on the "clouds of heaven" (Dan. 7:13) and will be seated on the throne of his forefather, King David (Isa. 9:7), in the Messianic age, during the Messianic kingdom.
   * The difference is that, according to Christians, this Messiah has sojourned in this world, namely, in the person of Jesus Christ. But some orthodox Jews who deny that Jesus was the Messiah do reckon with the possibility that the coming Messiah will have the face of Jesus.
4. Both (godly) Jews and (godly) Christians believe that there can be no true reconciliation with God without a *penitent* heart and without a *sin offering* prescribed by God: "[T]he life of the flesh is in the blood, and I have given it for you on the altar to make atonement for your souls, for it is the blood that makes atonement by the life" (Lev. 17:11; cf. Heb. 9:22, "[U]nder the law almost everything is purified with blood, and without the shedding of blood there is no forgiveness of sins").
   * The difference is that, according to Christians, Jesus Christ has personally become the true and only sin offering: "[W]hen Christ had offered for all time a single sacrifice for sins, he sat down at the right hand of God, waiting from that time until his enemies should be made a footstool for his feet. For by a single offering he has perfected for all time those who are being sanctified" (Heb. 10:12–14).

We must add here that orthodox Jews, because of the no-longer-functioning temple, are inclined to make the facile claim that prayers and alms and the like can replace such sacrifices. The danger is here that the solemnity of the "dwelling many days without sacrifice" (Hos. 3:4) is weakened.[19]

---

19. Here is an example from Aboth de-Rabbi Nathan, quoted in Armstrong (1993, 72): when Rabbi Joshua complains that, since the temple has been destroyed, no penitence for sins can be rendered, Rabbi Jochanan ben Zakkai answers that there is another penitence that is just as good. This is loving-kindness; for it is said, "[W]hat I desire is mercy, not sacrifices" (Hos. 6:6 CJB; cf. Matt. 9:13; 12:7). But was it Hosea's intention to set aside the entire sacrificial ministry, as if the Torah no longer mattered? Or was he referring to the attitude of the

8.2.3 Three More Similarities

5. Both (godly) Jews and (godly) Christians believe that, when the Messiah appears, they will be obligated to *follow* and *obey* him: "I will set up over them one shepherd, my servant David [i.e., the Messiah], and he shall feed them: he shall feed them and be their shepherd. And I, the LORD, will be their God, and my servant David shall be prince among them" (Ezek. 34:23-24). "My servant David shall be king over them, and they shall all have one shepherd. They shall walk in my rules and be careful to obey my statutes" (37:24).

   * The difference is that, according to Christians, Jesus is this Messiah, and his followers are obligated now to obey his "Torah": "Bear one another's burdens, and so fulfill the Torah of Christ" (Gal. 6:2; cf. 1 Cor. 9:21, I am "outside the Torah of God but under the Torah of Christ"). Jesus himself said, "If you love me, you will keep my commandments. . . . Whoever has my commandments and keeps them, he it is who loves me. And he who loves me will be loved by my Father, and I will love him and manifest myself to him. . . . If anyone loves me, he will keep my word, and my Father will love him, and we will come to him and make our home with him" (John 14:15, 21, 23). "As the Father has loved me, so have I loved you. Abide in my love. If you keep my commandments, you will abide in my love, just as I have kept my Father's commandments and abide in his love" (John 15:9-10). Keeping the Torah of the Messiah means becoming like the Master himself (cf. Matt. 10:25). Moses was not a perfect example, but Jesus was (cf. Phil. 2:5-6).

6. Both (godly) Jews and (godly) Christians believe that it is essential—and God's will *par* excellence for humans—that a person becomes a *tzaddiq*, a "righteous" person, for instance in the sense of Luke 1:6, ". . . righteous before God, walking blamelessly in all the commandments and statutes of the LORD." In the Tanakh, this means of course keeping the Torah of Moses. But it also involves this rule: ". . . the righteous shall live by his faith [i.e., confidence in God]" (Hab.

---

heart on the part of the offerer?

2:4). This point was picked up by Jesus' apostles; Paul made this statement the core of his letters to the Romans (1:17) and to the Galatians (3:11; cf. Heb. 10:38). Someone who keeps God's commandments but does not live by trusting confidence in God is not a true *tzaddiq*. Actually, someone who lives by faith but does not keep God's commandments is not a true *tzaddiq*, either. Hebrews 11 is a chapter full of examples of *tzaddiqim*, "righteous ones," in the Tanakh who both kept God's commandments and lived by their faith (confidence) in him.

* The difference is that, according to Christians, faith in God is related not only to a person's earthly circumstances, but especially to their eternal destiny. And what is more: faith has a concrete object. It is faith in *Jesus*, who died for the sins of all those who believe in him *and* who will lead his people safely to the Messianic kingdom. At present, faith, and righteousness are "the righteousness of God through faith in *Jesus Christ* for all who believe" (Rom. 3:22). God is righteous *and* he is the One who makes righteous (or, justifies) who have faith in Jesus (v. 26; cf. Gal. 2:16).

7. Both (godly) Jews and (godly) Christians live out of the promises of God. *The* great example of a man who was declared to be righteous because of his faith (confidence) in God was the patriarch Abraham: "[H]e believed the LORD, and he [i.e., the LORD] counted it to him as righteousness" (Gen. 15:6), declaring him to be righteous because of this faith, namely, his faith in the promises of God, including the promise of a son for very old Abraham. This point is so important that the apostles quote or allude to this verse several times.[20]

    * The difference is this: Abraham believed that God would make his promises come true in the "son of promise," Isaac. Christians believe that God will make his promises come true in *the* "Son of promise," Jesus Christ:

For all the promises of God find their Yes in him. That is why it is through him that we utter our Amen to God for his glory. And it is God who establishes us with you in Christ, and has anointed us,

---

20. Rom. 4:3, 9, 18, 22; Gal. 3:6; James 2:23.

and who has also put his seal on us and given us his Spirit in our hearts as a guarantee (2 Cor. 1:20-22).

8.3 Jesus, a Jewish Rabbi

8.3.1 Jesus' Jewish Origin

Jesus was a Jew, born of a Jewish mother, Mary (Heb.: Miriam, named after the sister of Moses),[21] "born under the Torah" (Gal. 4:4), that is, born as a member of the nation to which God had entrusted the Torah (cf. Rom. 3:2, "the Jews were entrusted with the oracles [or, messages, very words] of God"). If, as one tradition suggests, Luke 3:23-38 provides us with the ancestry of Mary, then Jesus was a descendent of David also through his maternal line.[22] At any rate, Jesus' legal father was a descendant of David (Matt. 1:20), through the royal line (vv. 1-17).[23] Because Jesus was born of the legal marriage of Joseph and Mary, he shared in all the rights of this royal line. Moreover, this was apparently rather widely known because it was quite common that people addressed him not only as "Son of Joseph" (John 1:45), but also as "Son of David."[24]

At his birth, Jesus received the Hebrew name *Yeshuah*, that is, "The LORD saves," both from his father (Matt. 1:21) and from his mother (Luke 1:31). The name resembles that of Joshua (Heb. *Y'shuah*). In the Greek of the New Testament, both names are rendered as *Iēsous*,[25] which through the Latin *Iesus* became "Jesus" (Jésus, Jesús, Gesù, Jezus, Isus,) in our modern languages. Entirely according to the Torah, Jesus was circumcised on the eighth day.[26] On the fortieth day, the child was presented in the temple, which was linked with a special sacrificial ritual, prescribed in the Torah, because he was a firstborn son.[27]

---

21. Mary was a very common name; four other women in the New Testament were named Mary: Luke 8:2; 10:39; Acts 12:12; Rom. 16:6.
22. It remains difficult to understand how Mary could be related to—the undoubtedly Levitical—Elizabeth (Luke 1:36).
23. The last Davidic king from whom Jesus legally descended was Jechoniah (Matt. 1:11–12); also called Jehoiachin (2 Kings 24:8–17).
24. Matt. 9:27; 12:23; 15:22; 20:30–31.; 21:9, 15
25. By way of exception, in Heb. 4:8 *Iēsous* means Joshua, not Jesus.
26. Luke 1:21; cf. Gen. 17:12; Lev. 12:3; as a sign of Jewishness, see Phil. 3:3.
27. Luke 1:22–24; cf. Exod. 13:12–15; Lev. 12:1–8.

A rabbi once told me that Christians cannot have it both ways: Jesus was either the son of Joseph, but then he was not the Son of God; or he was the Son of God, but then he was not the son of Joseph. It is not easy to explain to an orthodox rabbi the New Testament teaching about Jesus being both truly God and truly Man. According to his divine nature, Jesus was the Son of God; according to his human nature, Jesus was the son of Joseph and Mary (cf. Luke 1:32–35). Or take a few illustrations found in the Tanakh: Jesus was the *child* that was born, and the *Son* who was given (Isa. 9:6). On the one hand, he was the human Baby born of a woman in Bethlehem, while on the other hand, he was the One "whose coming forth is from of old, from ancient days [or even, from eternity, from everlasting; NASB, KJV]," referring to his divine origin (Micah 5:2).

When Jesus was twelve years old, he accompanied his parents for the first time to the temple in Jerusalem in order to celebrate Pesach (Passover) (Luke 2:41–52). This age suggests that a ritual was performed in Jesus' day that in later times developed into the Bar Mitzvah, "son of the commandment," the ritual through which the Jewish boy at age thirteen becomes religiously mature.[28] It was quite remarkable that on this occasion, Jesus found the temple to be his natural environment: he sat among the Torah-experts, listened to them, and asked them questions (Luke 2:46): "And all who heard him were amazed at his understanding and his answers" (Luke 2:47).

What is almost more impressive was Jesus' reply to the reproachful questions of his parents: "Son, why have you treated us so? Behold, your father and I have been searching for you in great distress." Young Jesus said to them, "Why were you looking for me? Did you not know that I must be in my Father's house [or about my Father's business; Gk. *en tois tou patros mou*]?" (Luke 2:49). His parents did not understand this, and none of the teachers could have understood it: a Jewish boy speaking about God as his personal Father! Moreover, this event indicates that at an early age Jesus was aware of his unique origin, as expressed by the apostle Paul: "[W]hen the fullness of time had come, God sent forth his Son, born of woman, born under the Torah" (Gal. 4:4).

---

28. In more liberal Jewish circles, the *Bat Mitzvah* ("daughter of the covenant") was later developed for girls.

8.3.2 Jesus the Rabbi

When Jesus was about thirty years old, he began his preaching ministry (Luke 3:23). Today, we realize better than ever how closely this preaching of Jesus resembled the teaching of the rabbis of his time. For the first time, in recent decades more light has been shed on this matter, especially—interestingly enough—through publications of orthodox Jews like David Flusser and Pinchas Lapide.[29] For example, we have learned that elements of what is called the Lord's Prayer ("Our Father in heaven . . . ," Matt. 6:9-13) in several respects resemble elements in certain Jewish prayers, such as Shemoneh Esrei, Qedushah, and the New Year's Prayer. In fact, the sevenfold Lord's Prayer *basically contains nothing that an orthodox Jew could not pray*:

Our Father in heaven,

(1) hallowed be your name.

(2) Your kingdom come,

(3) your will be done, on earth as it is in heaven.

(4) Give us this day our daily bread,

(5) and forgive us our debts, as we also have forgiven our debtors.

(6) And lead us not into temptation,

(7) but deliver us from evil.

Therefore, it is rather strange that Christians began viewing the Lord's prayer as *the* Christian prayer *par excellence*, since it is basically a Jewish prayer At the same time, it is a blessing that this prayer connects Christians with religious Jews.[30]

---

29. See, e.g., Flusser (1981; 2001); Lapide (1983; 1984; 2004; 2011); Rahner and Lapide (1987).

30. Conversely, the Creed of Maimonides—see Ouweneel (2014, 342–46)—contains virtually nothing that Christians could not confess as well; in a very brief summary: (1) God has created and governs all things, (2) he is one [which does *not* contradict the Trinity doctrine, if correctly understood; see §8.8.3], (3) he has no body or form, (4) he is eternal, (5) he is the only One to be worshiped, (6) all the words of the prophets are true, (7) the prophecy of Moses is true, he being the father of all prophets [including Christ and the apostles, we may add!], (8) the entire Torah was given to Moses, (9) this Torah is immutable and irrevocable, (10) God knows, and sees through, all human actions, (11)

In view of these newer developments, people sometimes speak about "bringing Jesus (back) home" (Ger. *Heimholung Jesu*), referring to returning Jesus to his Jewish context, so to speak, for only in this way we can truly begin to understand him. Jesus is allowed to be a Jew again, by both Jews and Christians. In stronger terms: as long as we do not see him primarily as a Jew, we will be unable to view his entire mission in its proper perspective.

No wonder people sometimes called Jesus "Rabbi" or "Rabboni," especially in John's Gospel.[31] They meant this in the sense of "my (revered) Teacher" or "Master." Jesus warned his disciples: "[Y]ou are not to be called rabbi, for you have one teacher, and you are all brothers" (Matt. 23:8). This seems to mean at least two things: first, if Jesus was their Rabbi, they should never claim this title for themselves; and second, his followers should not resemble the Jewish rabbis of that time. He himself allowed people to call *him* "Rabbi," but clearly distinguished himself from other rabbis: "[H]e was teaching them [i.e., the people] as one who had authority, and not as their scribes" (Matt. 7:29). That is, he stood head and shoulders above the Torah-experts of his day. This was so both because he was God's Son, and because he, as a human being, had been anointed with the Holy Spirit at his baptism by John the Baptist (Luke 3:22; Acts 10:38).

To see the latter in its proper perspective, we must consider the fact that, according to a Talmudic statement, the Holy Spirit had departed from Israel at the death of Israel's last prophet: Malachi.[32] Thus, none of Jesus' contemporaries would ever have claimed to speak directly through the Holy Spirit. But Jesus did speak and act through the Holy Spirit (Luke 4:1, 14; 10:21), as he himself also testified (Matt. 12:28; John 3:34). The only new prophet who was still to be expected was the Messiah himself (Deut. 18:15-18; cf. Acts 3:22-23; 7:37). But Jesus said of John the Baptist that he was "more than a prophet" (Matt. 11:9; cf. 14:5; 21:26); and he referred to him-

---

the Creator rewards or punishes people according to whether they obey his commandments [the latter being possible only through the Holy Spirit], (12) the Messiah will come, and (13) there will be a resurrection of the dead.

31. Matt. 26:25, 49; Mark 9:5; 10:51; 11:21; John 1:39, 50; 3:2, 26; 4:31; 6:25; 9:2; 11:8; 20:16.
32. Talmud: Sotah 48b.

self as a prophet, directly or indirectly (Matt. 13:57; Luke 13:33). The people often agreed with this.³³

One day while visiting Jerusalem, I overheard a Jewish guide, standing near the pool of Siloam, telling an orthodox Jewish family about the "rabbi from Galilee" who at that place had healed a blind man (John 9). The remarkable thing was that he did not mention the name "Jesus," but he did call him "rabbi." Not every Jewish teacher agrees with this, of course. A rabbi once told me that Jesus could not be called a "rabbi" because he had not received a *s'michah*, that is, a consecration through the laying on of hands. My counter-question was this: What authority could or should or would have given Jesus this *s'michah*, or whose *talmid* (disciple, pupil) would he have been? It is like asking whether Moses could be called a "rabbi" because no one had given *him* the *s'michah*. Jesus says through the prophet: "The LORD God has given me the tongue of those who are taught, that I may know how to sustain with a word him who is weary. Morning by morning he awakens; he awakens my ear to hear as those who are taught" (Isa. 50:4), and: "I have more understanding than all my teachers, for your testimonies are my meditation. I understand more than the aged, for I keep your precepts" (Ps. 119:99–100).

In recent decades, more light has been shed on the similarities between the Sermon on the Mount (Matt. 5–7) and the rabbinic teaching of Jesus' time and shortly before (especially the time of the great Rabbis Hillel and Shammai). This has made Jesus more Jewish than he had been for centuries. And of course, in doing so one can also exaggerate Jesus' Jewishness, especially in the modern rabbinic sense: Jesus was no more than one of the many contemporary rabbis in Israel. Formerly, Jesus had been viewed as very un-Jewish, whereas today he can often be portrayed as too Jewish. In this way, the tremendous *differences* between him and other rabbis are completely overlooked. Therefore, the time has come for us to examine these differences.

8.4 Jesus: A Different Person
8.4.1 The New Moses
Jesus' preaching and that of contemporaneous rabbis shared at least

---

33. Matt. 16:14; 21:11; Luke 7:16; John 4:19; 6:14; 7:40; 9:17.

seven significant differences, which made Jesus absolutely unique within Judaism.[34]

1.[35] Jesus not only interpreted Moses but presented himself implicitly as what the church fathers called a *novus Moses*, a "new Moses" (unheard of!).[36] The New Testament mentions the following similarities:

* Moses lifted up the snake in the desert; similarly the Son of Man was lifted up (John 3:14).
* Moses gave the bread from heaven; the Father gave his own Son as the bread from heaven (6:32).
* Moses was a prophet; Jesus was also a prophet.
* Moses was (at times) rejected by his people (cf. Acts 7:23–29); Jesus was too.
* Each of them could be described as "mighty in his words and deeds" (Acts 7:22; see vv. 20–28, 51–52).
* Israel was "baptized" into Moses (1 Cor. 10:2; cf. Isa. 63:11); Jesus-believers are baptized into the Messiah (Rom. 6:3).
* The Egyptian magicians, Jannes and Jambres,[37] opposed Moses (2 Tim. 3:8); the heretics of today oppose (the doctrine concerning) the Messiah (2 John 1:9).
* The song of Moses is parallel to the song of the Lamb (Rev. 15:3).
* Moses was accompanied by twelve princes of Israel's tribes and seventy(-two) elders (Num. 1:44; 11:16, 24–25; Exod. 24:1, 9); Jesus was accompanied by, and sent out, twelve apostles corresponding to the Israel's tribes as well as seventy(-two) messengers (Matt. 19:28; Luke 22:30; 10:1).[38]

---

34. Ouweneel (2020, 368–76; 2003a, 345–47).
35. Points 2., 3., and following, are considered in §8.4.3 and following.
36. See Davies (1969, 10–16); for a Jewish view, see Schoeps (1949, 87–116).
37. Mentioned in the Targum Jonathan 7:11–8:19.
38. Cf. Pseudo-Clement, *Recognitiones* I.40–41, on this parallel. Rabbinic tradition, referred to by Schoeps (1949, 96), tells us that Moses originally had seventy-two elders (including Eldad and Medad); similarly, some manuscripts in Luke 10:1, 17 have seventy, but others have seventy-two messengers, six for each tribe.

- Some rabbis believed that the *Shekhinah* rested on Moses;[39] similarly, it is implicitly stated that the *Shekhinah* rested on Jesus.[40]
- Interestingly, the Targum (Aramaic paraphrase) of the Psalms applies Psalm 68:18 ("You ascended on high, leading a host of captives in your train and receiving gifts among men") to Moses ("You, prophet Moses, ascended to the sky, you took captives captive, you taught the words of the Torah, and gave them as gifts to the children of men"), whereas Ephesians 4:8 applies the verse to Jesus ("When he ascended on high he led a host of captives, and he gave gifts to men").

There are also *a fortiori* arguments:

- "Moses permitted ... I tell you [however]" (Matt. 19:8–9).
- Those who do not listen to Moses will listen even less to one rising from the dead (especially Jesus himself) (Luke 16:31).
- "The Torah was given through Moses; grace and truth came through Jesus Messiah" (John 1:17).
- Those who do not listen to the writings of Moses, will listen even less to the words of Jesus (John 5:45–47).

Scripture also mentions contrasts:

- Moses was the mediator of the Old Covenant, and Jesus of the New Covenant.[41]
- Moses brought the "ministry of death," whereas Jesus brought the "ministry of the Spirit" (2 Cor. 3:7–8).
- Moses was a servant in God's house, but Jesus is Son over God's house (Heb. 3:1–6).
- The covenant of Moses was consecrated with the blood of animals, that of Jesus with his own blood (Heb. 9:18–23).
- Moses was connected with Mount Sinai, the mountain of judgment, but Jesus with Mount Zion, the mountain of grace (Heb. 12:18–22).

---

39. Talmud: Sanhedrin 11a.
40. Cf. Matt. 18:20; Luke 9:34–35 (see also 1:35, "overshadow," and cf. Exod. 40:34 LXX); John 2:19–21.
41. Deut. 5:5; Gal. 3:19; 1 Tim. 2:5; Heb. 8:6; 9:15; 12:24.

* In Moses' case, Sinai was the mountain of the Torah-giving, but Jesus gave his Torah at another mountain (Matt. 5–7).

8.4.2 Greater Than Moses

When Peter on the Mount of Transfiguration seemed to place Jesus, Moses, and Elijah on one level—which, viewed superficially, could have been understood as a compliment: was Jesus equal to Moses and Elijah, these giants of the Tanakh!?—heaven protested immediately: "*This* is my *Son*, my Chosen One; listen to *him*!" (Luke 9:35), and no longer only to Moses or Elijah; or perhaps more strongly: Jesus' words have the priority over those of Moses and Elijah.

Imagine the response of the Jews toward someone claiming to be greater than Moses! When the Messiah appears, and he is much greater than the people had expected, two reactions are possible: either exaltation because of this superior greatness . . . or indignant rejection: who does he think he is!? Even if he were the Messiah, he cannot be greater than Moses, or he cannot be the Son of God, he cannot be the true sin offering, and so on. Conqueror of the Romans, King on David's throne—this fit the expectations. Being greater than Moses, being God incarnate, being the true sin offering—these characterizations go much too far. Jesus must have been an imposter, or a dreamer. Yet, he healed the sick, he raised the dead, he multiplied bread, he walked on water. The question of Pilate becomes relevant: "Then what shall I do with Jesus who is called Messiah . . . ?" (Matt. 27:22).

Jesus rarely causes pure indifference (except among those who hardly know him): he causes either exhilaration or irritation; it is virtually impossible to remain neutral toward his person and teaching. Since Jesus, there have been dozens of false messiahs among the Jews, but as far as I know, *none* of them ever claimed to be greater than Moses, to be God incarnate, and to be the true sin offering for the sins of the people. Whether Jesus is the true Messiah or a false messiah, he is completely unique, in both positive *and* negative senses.

Imagine that the Father told Jesus' followers that they had to listen not only to Moses, through whom God gave his Torah to his people, and not only to Elijah, who restored the people to the obedience of the Torah, but *above all* to Jesus. This divine word was a direct allusion to Deuteronomy 18:15, "The LORD your God will raise up for you a prophet like me from among you, from your brothers—*it is to him you shall listen*." The words "like me" underscore the similarity between Moses and Christ (cf. Acts 3:22; 7:37). Philip told Nathanael, "We have found him of whom Moses in the Law and also the prophets wrote" (John 1:45), and Jesus himself said, "Moses . . . wrote of me" (John 5:46). The people exclaimed: "This is indeed the Prophet who is to come into the world!" (John 6:14; cf. 7:40). After his resurrection Jesus told some disciples:

> "O foolish ones, and slow of heart to believe all that the prophets have spoken! Was it not necessary that the Christ should suffer these things and [thus] enter into his glory?" And beginning with Moses and all the Prophets, he interpreted to them in all the Scriptures the things concerning himself (Luke 24:25–27).

Just as Moses had received the Torah on Mount Sinai, so too Jesus proclaimed *his* commandments from a mountain, which in the Christian tradition was going to be called the Mount of Beatitudes, near the Sea of Galilee. What rabbi would have dared to say, "You have heard that it was said to those of old, 'You shall not . . . .' But *I* say to you . . . ."?[42] Some have mistakenly concluded from these statements that Jesus was contradicting Moses! *But this was never the case.* Jesus did not come with an alternative Torah, an improved version of the Mosaic Torah. Rather, he revealed the true meaning and depth of the Torah in a way no rabbi had ever done or *could* have done. What I am calling in this study the Torah of the Messiah (cf. Gal. 6:2), or the Messianic Torah, does nothing else than make explicit the spiritual meaning and depth of the Mosaic Torah: "[H]e was teaching them [i.e., the people] as one who had authority, and not as their scribes" (7:29; see §8.3.2). His teaching was not only better than these, but it was essentially *different* from these because his authority came from above.

8.4.3 Jesus the Son of Man

2. Jesus presented himself under several titles that no ordinary rabbi, or any other person in Israel, would have dared to claim for himself. First, Jesus presented himself as the Son of Man, and thus as the fulfillment of Daniel 7:13 (NKJV), ". . . behold, [One] like the

---

42. Matt. 5:21–22, 27–28, 31–32, 33–34, 38–39, 43–44.

Son of Man, coming with the clouds of heaven!" (see more extensively §7.8). Here we find the Aramaic *bar enash* (literally "son of a mortal"), whereas we find the Hebrew *ben-adam* in Psalm 8:4, in Hebrews 2:6 applied to the Messiah, and in Psalm 80:17 (applied by some to the Messiah, by others to Israel; §7.8.1).

Some have asserted that in using this expression, Jesus meant some other person; but in many passages[43] it is undeniable that Jesus was referring to himself. This means that, when he spoke of the Son of Man coming on the clouds of heaven, we must assume that he was speaking of himself as well, in reference to the future.[44] We see this especially when we compare Luke 12:8 (". . . everyone who acknowledges me before men, the Son of Man also will acknowledge before the angels of God") with the parallel text Matthew 10:32, where we find "I" instead of "Son of Man." In other words, although modernists have often denied it, there can be no doubt that Jesus was presenting himself in this and other ways as the Son of Man of Daniel 7, that is, as the Messiah. When the high priest asked him, "Are you the Christ [= Messiah], the Son of the Blessed?" Jesus answered straightforwardly, "I am," and immediately added: ". . . and you will see the Son of Man seated at the right hand of Power, and coming with the clouds of heaven" (Mark 14:61-62).[45]

8.4.4 Jesus the Son of David

Second, Jesus accepted the title "Son of David" (§7.5.2), with which people often addressed him. By doing this, Jesus implicitly acknowledged his title to the throne of David, exactly as the angel had promised (Luke 1:32, "the Lord God will give to him [i.e., Jesus] the throne of his father David"). This corresponded with what Isaiah had announced (Isa. 9:6-7; 16:4-5). It was also in agreement with the miracles that Jesus performed and that could be expected from the Messiah (e.g., Isa. 29:18; 32:1-4; 35:5-6; 42:7). In the Gospel of Mark, these miracles involved especially the expulsion of demons—beginning in Mark 1:21-28—with this important comment

---

43. Such as Matt. 8:20; 11:19; 12:40; 17:9; 26:2, 24, 64.
44. E.g., Matt. 10:23; 13:41; 16:27-28; 24:27, 30, 37, 39, 44.
45. The words in the parallel passages, "You have said so" (Matt. 26:64), and "You say that I am" (Luke 22:70), have exactly the same meaning with the same connotations.

in Matthew 12:28: "[I]f it is by the Spirit of God that I cast out demons, then the kingdom of God has come upon you."

The kingdom of God is never anything other than the Davidic kingdom, the kingdom of the great Son of David. And when Jesus says elsewhere, "[T]he kingdom of God is in the midst of you" (Luke 17:21), this cannot mean anything else than that, according to Jesus, in *his* person the kingdom of God had arrived and was being realized. He presented himself as the King, and to all Jews this necessarily implied that he was the great Son of David.

It is highly interesting that Pontius Pilate ordered this title to be written above Jesus' cross (John 19:19):

> Greek: *Iēsous ho Nazōraios ho basileus tōn Ioudaiōn*
> Latin: *Iesus Nazarenus Rex Iudaeorum*
> Hebrew: *Yēshuah haNotzri Melekh hayy'hudim*

In English these mean *Jesus the Nazarene* (or, *of Nazareth*), *the King of the Jews*. Especially the Greek version, including the article, makes clear that Jesus is not just *one among many* Davidic kings, but he is *the* Davidic king, *the* Anointed One, the Messiah. Pilate did not necessarily believe this himself; but apparently he had the inner urge — no doubt generated by God himself — to make this announcement to the cultural world (Greek), the political world (Latin), and the religious world (Hebrew). It does not matter whether he did so mockingly or cynically; he *said* it: this is *the* King of Israel.

8.4.5 Jesus Claimed Divinity[46]

3. Throughout the centuries, orthodox Jews either have shrugged their shoulders about Jesus' Messianic claims, in the light of the dozens of other figures who throughout history have pretended to be the Messiah. Or they did what the high priest did, tearing their robes — literally or figuratively — over such wicked blasphemy. I assume that Caiaphas did so not primarily because Jesus claimed to be the Messiah, but especially because of

(a) Jesus' claim to be the "Son of the Blessed" (Mark 14:51), as well as

(b) Jesus' claim that he would sit down at the right hand of

---

46. See extensively, Ouweneel (2007b, chapters 7–8).

God—not in the temple but—*in heaven* (cf. Ps. 110:1; see §7.12.2), as well as

(c) Jesus' claim that from there he would one day descend on the clouds of heaven (Dan. 7:13; Matt. 26:64).

As C. S. Lewis stated the matter, such claims were rooted either in Jesus' (pious or proud) imagination (he believed in his own stories), or in conscious deceit, or they were simply true.[47] There is no fourth possibility: Jesus was a dreamer, or an imposter, or a truth-teller.

Especially in John's Gospel, Jesus' claims are characterized as blasphemy "because . . . he was even calling God his own Father, making himself equal with God" (John 5:18; cf. 10:33, ". . . you, being a man, make yourself God"). For Judaism, such a claim was totally unacceptable. This is somewhat strange because of claims made in the Tanakh itself, if not about Messiah's deity, then at least about his divinity: "You are my Son" (Ps. 2:7). "Your throne, O God, is forever and ever" (45:6; addressed to the Messiah!); "Mighty God, Everlasting Father" (Isa. 9:6, said of the Messiah); ". . . whose goings forth have been from of old, from everlasting" (Micah 5:2, about the Messiah). For the apostles—Jesus' messengers to the world—this divinity of Jesus was of primary significance. Notice, for instance, the progress in the argumentation of Hebrews 1:[48]

(a) *Verse 5:* Jesus is Son of God on the basis of Psalm 2:7 and 2 Samuel 7:14; this is still hardly shocking because it need mean nothing more than that God adopted each royal son of David as his own son, as was expressed at each new coronation of a Davidic scion.

(b) *Verse 6:* "Let all God's angels worship him" (Ps. 97:7); this goes a step further, although both the Hebrew and the Greek term for "worship" need mean nothing more than "to bow down" or "to pay homage." This does make the honored person very special, possibly divine, but not necessarily so.

(c) *Verse 8:* "Your throne, o God . . ." (Ps. 45:6); here, the Messiah is addressed as "God," which for Jewish expositors is

---

47. See Lewis (1952, 40–41).
48. See the explanation in Ouweneel (1982b, ad loc.).

embarrassing.[49] Yet, one might still evade the conclusion of divinity, for instance by appealing to Jesus' own words in John 10:33-36, where he himself seems to relativize the designation "g/God" on the basis of Psalm 82:6.

(d) *Verses 10-12*: this quotation from Psalm 102:25-27 is referred here to Christ, *but in Psalm 102 it refers to the* LORD. To the writer of Hebrews these were apparently the same. Indeed, this is either the most glorious truth — the LORD (YHWH) is Father, Son and Holy Spirit — or it is the most wicked blasphemy, which in orthodox Jewish ears indeed it is. Compare John 12:41, where the apostle John said that, when Isaiah saw the glory of the LORD, he saw the glory of *Christ*, and spoke of *him*.[50]

8.5 Jesus: A Different Ministry

8.5.1 Jesus Claimed to Be the Only Way

4. Jesus stated that people can come to God only through him. No rabbi would have ventured to make such a claim. The Torah is the billboard pointing to God, and rabbis are at best just interpreters of the Torah. Although some rabbis have become very famous, the person of the rabbi is not what matters. Rather it is the Torah interpreted by him that matters, or more correctly: the God to whom the Torah refers. Rabbis of different schools may sometimes behave as rivals, such as Shammai and Hillel, or the Baal Shem Tov and the Vilna Gaon, but in the end they remain colleagues: guides to the same God through the same Torah, even if they differ in its interpretation.

Jesus was very different. He stated openly, "I am the way, and the truth, and the life. No one comes to the Father *except through me*" (John 14:6). This was unheard of. The apostle Peter later confirmed this by arguing that "there is salvation in no one else, for there is no other name under heaven given among men by which we must be saved" (Acts 4:12). Jesus' followers proclaimed not only Jesus' teaching — like ordinary disciples of a regular rabbi would do with regard to their master, since it is not his person who matters, but his

---

49. See Cohen (1985, ad loc.).

50. To complete the picture: Paul stated that the person speaking in Isa. 6 was the Holy Spirit (Acts 28:25–26).

interpretation of the Torah. However, Jesus' followers proclaimed in particular Jesus' *person*. Peter said, "[H]e is lord [Gk. *Kyrios*] of all" (Acts 10:36); this is, he is not only a great Teacher—he is that too—but he is the *Kyrios* of the world.

This is remarkable for two reasons. First, *Kyrios* was the title of the Roman emperor.[51] But Jesus was the *basileus heteros*, the "different King" of the Roman "world" (Acts 17:6-7). The word in Acts 17:6 is Greek *oikoumenē*, the "inhabited [world]," which seems to refer here especially to the Roman Empire (cf. Luke 2:1, where the emperor Augustus wished to have registered "all the *oikoumenē*," that is, that part of the inhabited world over which he was emperor). In other words, the apostles presented the risen and glorified Jesus as the alternative Ruler of the Roman Empire. What Jews would ever had presented their rabbi as the rival king of the world?

Second, the title *Kyrios* referred to God himself. In the book of Acts, it referred either to God or to Jesus. In New Testament quotations from the Tanakh, the divine name, YHWH, was consistently rendered as *Kyrios*.[52] Now, the peculiar thing is that some of these quotations referred to Jesus himself, so that he was being identified with the *Kyrios* in the Tanakh. The most remarkable example is Hebrews 1:10-12 (see previous section).

In order to understand how the crucified Jesus could be the *Kyrios* of the world, it was important that the apostles proclaimed his resurrection from the dead.[53] They preached not only a doctrine, not only a person, but an event, a historical fact. They proclaimed that Jesus was raised from death because God's salvation is founded upon the death *and* resurrection of Jesus. A beautiful example, among many others, is Romans 4: God "raised from the dead Jesus our Lord, who was delivered up for our trespasses and raised for our justification" (vv. 24-25).

Such preaching was totally new and strange: salvation is not attained by accepting a certain doctrine, or by following a certain way of life, or by performing certain (sacrificial or other) rituals, or by doing certain good works—although all these things are defi-

---

51. See Jesus as *Kyrios* also in Acts 2:36; 11:20; Rom. 10:12; 14:9.
52. See Matt. 3:3; 4:7, 10; 5:33; Acts 2:21, 25, 34; 3:22.
53. Acts 2:24, 32; 3:15; 4:10; 5:30; 10:40; 13:30, 34, 37; 17:31.

nitely involved—but by believing in the once-dead-and-now-risen Jesus Christ. The rabbis said, Observe the Torah, and you will reach God. Jesus says, You *cannot* observe the Torah by your own strength, but I have died to atone for your trespasses to make you a new person and to give you the power to serve God.

Jesus was sometimes called Rabbi or Rabboni, but at the same time it became more and more evident that he was and is much more than that. As far as I know, no Jew has ever appealed to people to "believe in" Rabbi Aqiva or in Rabbi Maimonides. Modern orthodox Jews would probably need to ponder whether one can say that you must "believe in the Messiah" when he appears. If you must believe, then believe in *God*, as we find it since Genesis 15:6 ("[Abraham] believed the LORD"). If there was a question of believing in an ordinary man, that occurred in direct connection with believing in God: "Israel saw the great power that the LORD used against the Egyptians, so the people feared the LORD, and they believed in the LORD and in his servant Moses" (Exod. 14:31). Moses and the Messiah—according to the common Jewish presentation—are in the end nothing but mediators between God and his people, or a billboard pointing to God. This is true for Jesus, too (1 Tim. 2:5; Heb. 9:15; 12:24).

And yet, Jesus is more. He told his followers: "Believe in God [or, You believe in God]; believe also in me" (John 14:1). Again, such a thing was unheard of. Therefore, the responses to him were and are so radical and so contrary: either you reject his pretenses with indignation—and are prepared to support his execution—or you surrender to him and worship him. Jesus was the "stumbling stone," in whom one could believe or over whom one could stumble.[54] For the godly, orthodox Jew, a middle position is virtually inconceivable, it seems. But in the last hundred years, we have seen initial hints of a middle position. Some rabbis have argued that Jesus could not possibly have been the Messiah—but when the Messiah appears, they reckon with the possibility that he might have the features of Jesus.

8.5.2 Jesus Claimed to Be the True Sin Offering

5. Jesus not only announced his own death—other people have

---

54. Rom. 9:32–33; see Isa. 8:14; 28:16; 1 Pet. 2:6–8.

done the same — but he added two elements that no prophet or rabbi has ever claimed or would venture to claim. First, he announced that he would have to "go to Jerusalem and suffer many things from the elders and chief priests and scribes, and be killed, and *on the third day be raised*" (Matt. 6:21; cf. 17:22-23; 20:18-19). And that is what happened, as the apostles and hundreds of other people (1 Cor. 15:6) have testified. The apostle Peter spoke of "us who had been chosen by God as witnesses, who ate and drank with him after he rose from the dead" (Acts 10:41).[55]

Second, more remarkably, Jesus announced that he would not just die, but that he would die *vicariously* for all those who would believe in him. Of course, Israel was familiar with the thought that an innocent sacrificial animal took the place of the sinner to die in their stead. But it was *not* familiar with a *Man* who said such a thing of himself. They had never been struck by the remarkable contrast in Psalm 40:6-7 (cf. Heb. 10:5-7):

In sacrifice and offering you have not delighted,
> but ears you have dug for me [Septuagint: a body have you prepared for me].

Burnt offering and sin offering
> you have not required [or, in them you have taken no pleasure].

Then *I* said, "Behold, *I* have come;
> in the scroll of the book it is written of me."

When we read Psalm 40 in the light of Hebrews 10, the contrast becomes evident: the animal sacrifices make place for — are replaced by — a *man*, who in his own person becomes the true

(a) "sacrifice" (Heb. *zebach*, here: *zebach sh'lamim*, "peace offering"; Lev. 3 and 7);

(b) "offering" (Heb. *mincha*, here: "grain offering"; Lev. 2);

(c) "burnt offering" (Heb. *'olah*; Lev. 1); and

(d) "sin offering" (Heb. *chata'ah*; Lev. 4-5).[56]

---

55. See Matt. 28; Mark 16; Luke 24; John 20–21; 1 Cor. 15:4–8; orthodox Jewish scholar Pinchas Lapide (1983) was of the opinion that Jesus really rose from death.

56. These are four of the five offerings of Lev. 1–7, the fifth being the "guilt offering" (Heb. *asam*).

Jesus himself clearly referred to this, for instance, by stating that "the Son of Man came not to be served but to serve, and to give his life as a ransom for many" (Matt. 20:28; cf. 1 Tim. 2:5), that is, to pay the ransom in order to release them from the power of sin, death, and the devil. At the institution of the Lord's Supper, Jesus announced that his blood would be "poured out for many for the forgiveness of sins" (26:28). Here "for" (Gk. *peri*) means "for the sake of," or "instead of"; it is a preposition characteristic of sacrificial terminology. See for instance Romans 8:3, *peri hamartias*, "for sin" ("By sending his own Son in the likeness of sinful flesh and for sin [or, and as a sin offering], he condemned sin in the flesh"; cf. Heb. 10:6, 18, 26; 13:11); the Septuagint uses this expression to refer to the sin offering.

In fact, through such statements, Jesus presented himself as the true atonement offering. In this way, he fulfilled the prophecy concerning the Servant of the LORD in Isaiah 53:5-6 and 10:

> But he was pierced for our transgressions;
>> he was crushed for our iniquities;
> upon him was the chastisement that brought us peace,
>> and with his wounds we are healed. . . .
> . . . [T]he LORD has laid on him
>> the iniquity of us all. . . .
> [W]hen his soul makes [or, when you make his soul] an offering for guilt,
>> he shall see his offspring; he shall prolong his days; . . . .

Jesus is not only the true high priest, he is also the sin offering that the high priest brings in order to reconcile the people with God: ". . . a merciful and faithful high priest in the service of God, to make propitiation for the sins of the people" (Heb. 2:17).

> [I]f the blood of goats and bulls, and the sprinkling of defiled persons with the ashes of a heifer, sanctify for the purification of the flesh, how much more will the blood of Christ, who through the eternal Spirit offered himself without blemish to God, purify our conscience from dead works to serve the living God (Heb. 9:13-14).

Christ "has appeared once for all at the end of the ages to put away sin by the sacrifice of himself" (Heb. 9:26; cf. 10:5-10).

The matter is very important in the dialogue between Jews and Christians. Since AD 70, Israel has had no temple and no sacrificial ministry: "[T]he children of Israel shall dwell many days without king or prince, without sacrifice. . ." (Hos. 3:4). How then can there be atonement for their sins?[57] The statement of Hebrews 9:22, "without the shedding of blood there is no forgiveness of sins," is fully rooted in the Tanakh: "[T]he life of the flesh is in the blood, and I have given it for you on the altar to make atonement for your souls, for it is the blood that makes atonement by the life" (Lev. 17:11). When one day, Israel will be restored, where will it find the blood that will make atonement for them (cf. Dan. 9:24, ". . . to finish the transgression, to put an end to sin, and to atone for iniquity, to bring in everlasting righteousness")? The answer was supplied by Psalm 40: no animal sacrifices will suffice, but the One who took their place: the One of whom is written in the scroll of the book, the true David—not only King and Priest, but also sin offering.[58]

8.5.3 Jesus "Insufficiently" Honored Israel's Election

6. One of the difficult, and for many Jews unpalatable, realities about Jesus was that he did not seem to respect the exceptional position of the chosen people of Israel in the counsel and the ways of God. Thus, he demanded, as John the Baptist had done before him, that Jews should repent of their sins and convert to God. Actually, this was not very new, for the prophets in the Tanakh had called upon Israel many times to repent and return to the LORD. But John, along with Jesus' disciples (John 3:22–23), administered water baptism to Jews, a rite that until then had been reserved for Gentiles who wished to join Judaism; this was the so-called proselyte baptism. Now the Jews were being told that they, too, had to undergo the same "baptism of repentance for the forgiveness of sins" (Mark 1:4) in order to receive a share in the kingdom of God. Many

---

57. Sacrifices can never be replaced by prayers (see note 19); passages in the Tanakh that seem to speak negatively about sacrifices (e.g., Isa. 1:11, 13; Hos. 6:6; 8:13; 9:4; Amos 5:22; Micah 6:6–8) do so not because God considers them to be superfluous or replaceable—*he instituted these sacrifices himself*—but because they were not being offered with the right attitude of heart.

58. This question cannot be answered by referring to future sacrifices mentioned in Ezek. 40–46; these future sacrifices will refer back to the one and only sacrifice of Jesus Christ on the cross.

viewed this demand as humiliating and hurtful. Nevertheless, the biblical truth is that no one, Jew or Gentile, Pharisee or criminal, can find peace with God without repentance and conversion.

The parable of the Pharisee and the tax collector makes this clear in the most painful way (Luke 18:9-14). How on earth was it possible that the godly Pharisee was rejected, and that the tax collector — that corrupt extortionist, who was cozy with the Roman occupier — received the grace of God? There can be only one answer: the Pharisee came pleading his own "righteousness," and did not humble himself before God about his sins. The latter attitude was the very attitude of the tax collector. Pharisees were and are not rejected because they are Pharisees, nor are they privileged because they are Pharisees. Conversely, tax collectors are not accepted, or rejected, simply because they are tax collectors. For the Pharisee and the tax collector, there is one and the same rule: "The sacrifices of God are a broken spirit; a broken and contrite heart, O God, you will not despise" (Ps. 51:17). "I dwell in the high and holy place, and also with him who is of a contrite and lowly spirit" (Isa. 57:15). For everyone, entering the kingdom of God occurs along the pathway of self-humbling, repentance, and conversion.

Jesus had told Nicodemus, who was "*the* teacher of Israel" (John 3:10), one of the spiritual leaders of the nation: "You [plural] must be born again" (v. 7), that is, no one can enter the kingdom of God without having been "born" of water and Spirit (v. 5). Without this "new birth," people will not be able to "see" it, that is, to spiritually discern it (v. 3). The godliest and most learned Jew could not enter the kingdom of God except through repentance, conversion, and regeneration. Jesus reproached Nicodemus for not understanding "new birth," which he could and should have known about through Ezekiel 36:22-32. In this prophecy, "water" — which I take to mean the "water" of God's Word (John 15:3; Eph. 5:26) — and "Spirit" are mentioned as the means by which God will introduce penitent Israelites into the Messianic kingdom.

John 8 is a clear example of how the Jewish leaders felt hurt with regard to these things. At Jesus' accusing words they responded in protest: "We are offspring of Abraham and have never been enslaved to anyone. How is it that you say, 'You will become free'?" (v. 33) But Jesus replied that they were indeed (physical) descendants but not genuine children of Abraham (v. 39); rather, they were children of the devil (v. 44).[59] He argued that they were "slaves of sin," who had to be set free by the Son of God (vv. 34–36). Genuine children of Abraham are those who also walk in the faith of Abraham (Rom. 4:11-12).[60]

8.5.4 Jesus Also Welcomed Gentiles

7. The consequence of the previous point was something that, for many Jews, was perhaps more objectionable: if a Jew could enter the kingdom of God only through repentance and faith — that is, *not* merely on the basis of descent and privileged position — then there was no longer any reason why a Gentile could not enter the kingdom of God on the very same conditions.

Jesus was stepping on the toes of many of his very orthodox listeners when he told the cities of Galilea:

> Woe to you, Chorazin! Woe to you, Bethsaida! For if the mighty works done in you had been done in Tyre and Sidon, they would have repented long ago in sackcloth and ashes. But I tell you, it will be more bearable on the day of judgment for Tyre and Sidon than for you. And you, Capernaum, will you be exalted to heaven? You will be brought down to Hades. For if the mighty works done in you had been done in Sodom, it would have remained until this day. But I tell you that it will be more tolerable on the day of judgment for the land of Sodom than for you (Matt. 11:21-24).

Jesus did not say that the Gentile cities Tyre, Sidon, and Sodom *had* repented. They had not. Rather he said that, if they had experienced the same marvelous testimony of God's divine power that the Galilean cities Chorazin, Bethsaida, and Capernaum had experienced, they would have repented much more easily and quickly than the latter had done. Tyre, Sidon, and Sodom were wicked, but Chorazin, Bethsaida, and Capernaum were even more corrupt, or at least less inclined to repentance.

Jesus also announced that he had found a greater faith here

---

59. Cf. Rev. 2:9 and 3:9; Jews persecuting Christians are not real Jews but belong to Satan.

60. Cf. the Corinthians (1 Cor. 4:14), the Thessalonians (1 Thess. 2:7, 11), Timothy (1 Tim. 1:2, 18; 2 Tim. 1:2; 2:1), and Titus (1:4), who were spiritual children of the apostle Paul.

and there among Gentiles than he had ever encountered in Israel. About a Roman centurion he said: "Truly, I tell you, with no one in Israel have I found such faith [i.e., confidence in God and in me]" (Matt. 8:10; cf. 15:28), about a Canaanite woman: "[G]reat is your faith!"), and added: "I tell you, many will come from east and west and recline at table with Abraham, Isaac, and Jacob in the kingdom of heaven, while the sons of the kingdom [i.e., the Israelites] will be thrown into the outer darkness. In that place there will be weeping and gnashing of teeth" (Matt. 8:11-12). Those for whom the kingdom had originally been intended, must give way to people for whom it had originally *not* been intended. The kingdom is for the penitent, for believers, for the godly, for the *tzaddiqim*, whether Jewish or Gentile. The *tzaddiqim* live by God's commandments, whether it is the Mosaic Torah, or, in the case of the Gentiles, the "requirements of the law written on their hearts" (Rom. 2:12-16 NKJV).

Can we imagine how painful it was for the spiritual leaders to hear Jesus telling them: "Truly, I say to you, the [Jewish] tax collectors and the [Jewish] prostitutes go into the kingdom of God before you" (Matt. 21:31)? Yet, it was even more painful for them to hear that *Gentiles* would go before them into the kingdom of God:

> In that place [i.e., hell] there will be weeping and gnashing of teeth, when you [i.e., Jews] see Abraham and Isaac and Jacob and all the prophets in the kingdom of God but you yourselves cast out. And people will come from east and west, and from north and south, and recline at table in the kingdom of God. And behold, some are last [i.e., Gentiles] who will be first, and some are first [i.e., Jews] who will be last (Luke 13:28-30).

The latter are rejected, not because they are Jews—of course not—but because they do not come to Jesus on the humble path of repentance and faith. The doors of the kingdom are still wide open for every Jew to find their Messiah—but throughout the last nineteen centuries the large majority of those who have come to the Messiah has been converted Gentiles. The gate to the kingdom of God is "narrow" (Matt. 7:13-14); one must become very "small," and lay down all of one's pride and self-conceit in order to be able to enter through it. "Strive to enter through the narrow door. For many, I tell you, will seek to enter and will not be able" (Luke 13:24).

The apostle Paul is a striking example of how converted Jews viewed their descent and former privileges:

> If anyone else thinks he has reason for confidence in the flesh, I have more: circumcised on the eighth day, of the people of Israel, of the tribe of Benjamin, a Hebrew of Hebrews; as to the law, a Pharisee; as to zeal, a persecutor of the Ecclesia; as to righteousness under the law, blameless. But *whatever gain I had, I counted as loss for the sake of Christ.* Indeed, I count everything as loss because of the surpassing worth of knowing Christ Jesus my Lord. For his sake I have suffered the loss of all things and count them as rubbish, in order that I may gain Christ (Phil. 3:4–8).

In other words, Paul's natural privileges could not begin to measure up to what he had received in Christ; for him, these natural privileges had become impediments to this blessing. No Jew is saved because of descent and natural privileges; they are saved in the same way *any* human being is saved: the way of repentance, conversion, and faith.

It is told that for a time, F. Rosenzweig—co-translator of the Tanakh together with Martin Buber—considered becoming a Christian. But then he was reminded of John 14:6 ("No one comes to the Father except through me"), and said to himself: "This is not true for me, for we Jews *are* already with the Father."[61] Apparently, he did not realize that the apostle Peter had said to *Jews*, "[T]here is salvation in no one else [but Jesus], for there is no other name under heaven given among men by which we must be saved" (Acts 4:12). When it is a matter of coming to the Father, there is no difference between Jew and Gentile because they *both* need salvation from their sins:

> What then? Are we Jews any better off? No, not at all. For we have already charged that all, both Jews and Greeks, are under sin.... For there is no distinction: for all have sinned and fall short of the glory of God, and are justified by his grace as a gift, through the redemption that is in Christ Jesus, whom God put forward as a propitiation by his blood, to be received by faith (Rom. 3:9, 22–25).

---

61. See Rosenzweig on Christianity in Rosenstock-Huessy (2011).

8.6 Double Rejection

8.6.1 The Leaders of Judaism Rejected Jesus

In light of the previous points, it is no wonder that, according to the rabbis, Jesus cannot be the Messiah, because he did not, for example, establish the Messianic kingdom of peace and justice. However, some of these rabbis presumed that Jesus nevertheless might have had a special mission for, and among, the Gentiles.[62] They were prepared to acknowledge that this was a *God-given* mission in order to make known to the Gentile world the God of Israel. But what they did not want to acknowledge—and what many Christians seem to forget as well—is that Jesus was *not* sent by God especially for the Gentiles; he was sent by God first and foremost *to* and *for Israel*.

When an angel came to tell Joseph about the child with whom Mary was pregnant, he said, "[Y]ou shall call his name Jesus, for he will save *his people* from their sins" (Matt. 1:21). He did not speak of the Gentile world at all, but of "his people," that is, Israel. The angel Gabriel, when announcing Jesus' conception (Luke 1:32-33), did not refer to the Gentile world, either: "He will be great and will be called the Son of the Most High. And the LORD God will give to him the throne of his father David, and he will reign over the *house of Jacob* forever, and of his kingdom there will be no end" (cf. the prophecy by Zechariah in 1:67-79). And to the shepherds, after Jesus' birth, the angel said, "Fear not, for behold, I bring you good news of great joy that will be for *all the people* [of Israel]. For unto *you* [plural, i.e., Israel] is born this day in the city of David a Savior, who is Christ [i.e., the long-expected Messiah] the Lord [Heb. *Mashiach Adonai*]" (2:10-11).

The apostle Paul put it this way: "I tell you that Christ became a *servant to the circumcised* [i.e., Israel] to show God's truthfulness, in order to confirm the promises given to the patriarchs, and"—then, secondarily, he adds—"in order that the Gentiles might glorify God for his mercy" (Rom. 15:8-9). In this order: Jesus came first for Israel, and only after this do the Gentile nations come in view.

---

62. This was the view of Jewish scholars like Jehuda Halevi, Moses Maimonides, Jakob Emden, and Samson Raphael Hirsch; see also http://cjcuc.com/site/2015/12/03/orthodox-rabbinic-statement-on-christianity/. Regarding this view, see Ouweneel (2014, 119–20).

Even the (Gentile!) wise men from the East ask: "Where is he who has been born king *of the Jews*?" (Matt. 2:2). That is, this birth was certainly also for them—why else would the star have been shown to them?—but it was primarily for the Jews. Thus the constant pattern of Paul's ministry was: ". . . to the Jew first and also the Greek" (Rom 1:16).[63]

The apostle John told us: "He came to his own [note the ESV: to his own things, i.e., to his own domain], and his own people did not receive him" (John 1:11). Jesus did *not* come to Israel in order to found a new religion. This is a very serious, even absurd error, encountered among both Jews and Christians (to say nothing about millions of "outsiders"). Jesus did not found Christianity! Jesus came to bring *Judaism to its fulness*! For when the Messiah appears, Israel will finally reach its destiny; only in this way, and not before. However, the mass of Israel refused to accept him, for each of the seven reasons that I mentioned in the previous sections. In addition, through both his miracles and his personal claims, Jesus threatened the position of the political and religious authorities. *Jesus did not fit into the human-made system of the leaders*. We might express this as follows (with some reservations): Jesus came to *Israel*, was accepted by a great number of Jews,[64] but was rejected by *the leaders of Judaism*.

The apostle Paul put it this way:

> What shall we say, then? That Gentiles who did not pursue righteousness have attained it, that is, a righteousness that is by faith; but that [the leaders of] Israel who pursued a Torah that would lead to righteousness [i.e., keeping the Torah in one's own strength] did not succeed in reaching that Torah. Why? Because they did not pursue it by faith, but as if it were based on works [i.e., on one's own achievements]. They have stumbled over the stumbling stone, as it is written, "Behold, I am laying in Zion a stone of stumbling, and a rock of offense; and whoever believes in him will not be put to shame" [Isa. 8:14; 28:16]. Brothers, my heart's desire and prayer to God for them is that they may be saved. For I bear them witness that they have a zeal for God, but not according to knowledge [or, proper understanding].

---

63. Cf. Acts 13:5, 14; 14:1; 17:1–3, 10; 18:4; 19:8; Rom. 2:9–10.

64. Acts 21:20 does not speak of "many thousands of Jews," as many translations have it, but of "many *tens of* thousands of Jews" (CJB, CEV, ISV, TPT).

For, being ignorant of the righteousness of God, and seeking to establish their own, they did not submit to God's righteousness. For Christ is the end of the Torah [i.e., the end of the order in which people "seek their own righteousness" by trying to keep the Torah; i.e., "the end of legalism"] for righteousness to everyone who believes (Rom. 9:30–10:4).

Some leaders of Judaism in Jesus' day *elevated* the Jew as if they, in their own strength, would be able to enter the kingdom of God, as persons privileged above all Gentiles. Over against this, Jesus proclaimed nothing new, but rather these basic principles taught in the Tanakh: each human, Jewish or Gentile, can be saved only (a) through repenting of sins committed, (b) through acknowledging one's own incapacity to inherit the kingdom of God, and (c) through believing surrender, as Abraham had done: "[H]e believed the LORD, and he [i.e., the LORD] counted it to him as righteousness," that is, declared him to be a *tzaddiq* (a righteous one), not (just) on the basis of any achievements on Abraham's behalf, but (primarily) on the basis of his trusting confidence in God.[65] The secret is not *pretense* (of one's self-righteousness) but *confidence* (in the God who forgives a person's trespasses, and empowers them to serve God).

8.6.2 The Breach

The breach between Jesus and — not so much the nation of Israel as such but rather — the leaders of Judaism is made visible in a remarkable way in the story of the man born blind (John 9). After he had been healed by Jesus, the man came into conflict with the Jewish leaders because the healing had occurred on a Sabbath. The enormous, even eschatological significance of the miracle (see, e.g., Isa. 32:1–3) escaped the leaders; they clung to a single detail, which was all the more strange because the Torah does not at all forbid healing on a Sabbath. Jesus rightly said of them: "Woe to you, scribes and Pharisees, hypocrites! For you tithe mint and dill and cumin, and have neglected the weightier matters of the law: justice and mercy and faithfulness" (Matt. 23:23). They were so meticulous that they strained out the smallest gnats from their wine cups but if — so to speak — a camel were swimming around in it, they would swallow

---

65. Gen. 15:6; cf. Rom. 4:3, 9, 18, 22; Gal. 3:6; James 2:23.

it.⁶⁶ This is typical of many sects and cults (Jewish, Christian, or otherwise): they strongly emphasize many legalistic details, but overlook the real essence of things.

When the healed man challenged the leaders, "they reviled him, saying, 'You are his disciple, but we are disciples of Moses. We know that God has spoken to Moses, but as for this man, we do not know where he comes from'" (John 9:28–29). According to them Jesus could not be a disciple of Moses, even though they could never catch him transgressing the Mosaic Torah. The reality was that he simply did not fit into the religious system that they had constructed around Moses. To some extent they were honest about it: ". . . we do not know where he comes from." That is, they could not situate him precisely. Jesus did not fit into their system, their order of thinking; but unfortunately, they did not give him the opportunity to break through their frame of thinking, and thus *lead them back to this very Moses*, that is, to the true core of the Mosaic Torah (see above: "justice and mercy and faithfulness"; in Luke 11:42, "justice and the love of God").⁶⁷

About such people Jesus said, "No one who drinks old wine wants new wine. They say, 'The old wine is just fine'" (Luke 5:39 ERV). The traditionalist always clings to the old, even if they could get something better. John Gill gave an interesting example, referring to Rabbi Jose bar Juda, who said, "He that learns of young men, to what is he like? To him that eats unripe grapes, and drinks wine out of the fat; but he that learns of old men, to what is he like? To him that eats ripe grapes, and drinks 'old wine.'"⁶⁸ Every traditionalist is convinced that truly new insights are inconceivable. Many Christians like to quote Deuteronomy 19:14, "You shall not move your neighbor's landmark, which the men of old have set, in the inheritance that you will hold in the land that the LORD your God is giving you to possess." Don't move the landmarks that "the men

---

66. Jewish scholar Immanuel Velikovsky somewhere illustrated the same point by telling the story of a biologist's helpers who brokenheartedly told him that a crocodile had just swallowed his bride. The biologist's sober answer was: "That's not possible, there are no crocodiles here; it must have been a caiman."
67. These are the four Hebrew ethical core concepts: respectively, *mishpat* ("justice"), *chesed* ("mercy"), *emet* ("faithfulness"), and *ahabah* ("love").
68. Pirke Abot 4.20 (https://biblehub.com/commentaries/luke/5-39.htm).

of old have set"! One wonders how both traditionalist Jews and traditionalist Christians will ever be able to recognize and accept their Messiah when he appears on the clouds of heaven, because he might not fit into their preconceived frames of thinking, or into the dozens of *different* Jewish, and hundreds of *different* Christian, frames of thinking. When the Son of Man appears, we fear that at least *some* Jews and *some* Christians will definitely reject him because he will not fit their expectations.

In John 9, the leaders of Judaism knew only one response to the healing of the man born blind: they "cast him out" (v. 34; cf. v. 22, "the Jews had already agreed that if anyone should confess Jesus to be Christ [i.e., Messiah], he was to be put out of the synagogue"; see also 12:42; 16:2). The leaders said, as it were: Within our order of things there is no place for people like this Man. In a sense, they were perfectly correct, of course. In the same way they would cast out Jesus himself. Strictly speaking Jesus was not rejected by the people of Israel but by the leaders of Judaism, represented by the majority of the Jewish spiritual leaders. The *true* Israel was represented by people who were "righteous before God, walking blamelessly in all the commandments and statutes of the LORD" (Luke 1:6), of whom it could be said, ". . . a good and righteous man" (Luke 23:50), and "Behold, an Israelite indeed, in whom there is no deceit!" (John 1:47). We know of no New Testament Jewish person of whom such a testimony was given, who nevertheless rejected Jesus.[69]

In Matthew's Gospel, the breach was described in a different way. Here, the nadir was reached in Matthew 12:24, where the Pharisees accused Jesus of casting out demons with the help of "Beelzebul,[70] the prince of demons" (read: Satan). Jesus answered this wicked accusation in five ways.

1. Jesus demonstrated how illogical and foolish this accusation is: how could Satan cast out his own servants, the demons (v. 26, "if Satan casts out Satan, he is divided against himself")?

---

69. A possible exception might seem to be the "rich young man" of Mark 10:12–22: Jesus loved him (apparently for his sincerity), yet the man turned away. He did not *reject* Jesus, but thought the cost of following him was too high.

70. Heb. *Ba'al-Zebul*, "lord of the house"; KJV and others read Beelzebub (*Ba'al-Zebub*, "lord of the flies"), a mocking Jewish distortion of the name Beelzebul.

2. Jesus argued that he cast out the demons by the Spirit of God, and that this is evidence that the kingdom of God was busy breaking through in Israel (v. 28).
3. Jesus made implicitly clear that these Pharisees were blaspheming the Holy Spirit, namely, by identifying this Spirit with Beelzebul, and that there would be no forgiveness for this sin (vv. 31-32, 36-37).
4. Jesus announced his sufferings, death, and resurrection, which would be the consequence of his rejection by the majority of the people (v. 40).
5. Jesus announced that many Gentiles would listen to God better than many Jews:

> The men of Nineveh will rise up at the judgment with this generation and condemn it, for they repented at the preaching of Jonah [see Jonah 3], and behold, something greater than Jonah is here. The queen of the South [i.e., of Sheba; 1 Kings 10] will rise up at the judgment with this generation and condemn it, for she came from the ends of the earth to hear the wisdom of Solomon, and behold, something greater than Solomon is here (Matt. 12:41-42).

In other words, Gentiles bowed before Jonah and Solomon, but the leaders of Judaism refused to bow before the One who was so much greater than Jonah or Solomon.

8.6.3 Jesus Rejected the Leaders of Judaism

In the previous section, I quoted both John 9 and Matthew 12 as two examples of the tragic turning point in the relationship between Jesus and Judaism. It is very important to consider with accuracy precisely how Jesus responded to this. In John 10—the immediate sequel of the story of John 9—he did so by presenting himself as the good Shepherd, who does at least three important things:

1. He gives his life for his sheep (i.e., all the true believers, Jewish or Gentile), as Jesus emphasized three times (vv. 11, 15, 17); giving his life into death implies life for his sheep: "I came that they may have life and have it abundantly" (v. 10); "I give them eternal life, and they will never perish, and no one will snatch them out of my hand" (v. 28).

2. He leads his Jewish sheep out of the sheepfold of—not Israel but—Judaism. After the violent "out" (Gk. *exō*) of John 9:34 follows the gentle "leads them out" (*exagei*) of 10:3. Judaism *casts* Jesus' followers out, Jesus *leads* them out.

3. Afterward, he unites these Jewish sheep with the sheep from the Gentile world: "I have other sheep that are not of this fold. I must bring them also, and they will listen to my voice. So there will be one flock, one shepherd" (v. 16). This is the same as what John 11:52 tells us about gathering "into one the children of God who are scattered abroad," and what Jesus himself described as "my Ecclesia" (Matt. 16:16).

In Matthew 13, Jesus made clear in the parables of the sower and of the weeds what will happen next after the majority of Israel rejected him. The key statement is this: "The field is the world" (v. 38).[71] From now on, the seed of the gospel of the kingdom is sown among all nations, not only among the Jews (although among them, too). Jesus describes what will be the further vicissitudes of this kingdom, but at this moment this is not our subject.[72] The point is this: first, the leaders of Judaism reject Jesus (John 9; Matthew 12). Second, Jesus led his own disciples "out"—thus rejecting the leaders of Judaism—and announced that, from now on, the gospel of the kingdom would go to all the nations. At a later point, he said: "[T]his gospel of the kingdom will be proclaimed *throughout the whole world* as a testimony to *all nations*" (Matt. 24:14), and: "Go therefore and make disciples of *all nations*" (28:19).

Now, we realize that it was God's intention all along that the salvation that Jesus brought would come to the Gentile world as well. For if Israel had accepted its Messiah, the Messianic kingdom would have arrived, and the Messianic blessings would have come to the Gentile world after all. However, because Jesus was rejected by the leaders of Judaism, this involvement of the Gentiles *now* occurred in a painfully different way: now it was not Israel *plus* the Gentile world, but the Gentile world *instead of* the majority of the Jewish people. The apostle Paul put it this way:

---

71. Richard Trench (2018, ad loc.) astonishingly called this one of the most cumbersome texts in the entire New Testament.
72. See extensively, Ouweneel (2011a, chapter 10).

> It was necessary that the word of God be spoken first to you [i.e., the Jews]. Since you thrust it aside and judge yourselves unworthy of eternal life, behold, we are turning to the Gentiles. For so the LORD has commanded us, saying, "I have made you a light for the Gentiles, that you may bring salvation to the ends of the earth [Isa. 49:6]" (Acts 13:46–47).

The latter quotation deserves to be written in full. God was speaking to his s/Servant, who is primarily Israel (Isa. 49:3) but later is the One who is Israel, the Messiah. He told him: "It is too light a thing that you should be my servant to raise up the tribes of Jacob and to bring back the preserved of Israel; I will make you as a light for the nations, that my salvation may reach to the end of the earth" (v. 6).

This transition from Israel to the Gentile world is no small thing, announced by Jesus in passing. For him, in his person, it was linked with the greatest suffering. When he approached Jerusalem for the last time during his earthly life, "he *wept* over it, saying, 'Would that you, even you, had known on this day the things that make for peace! But now they are hidden from your eyes'" (Luke 19:41–42). He wept especially because he foresaw the imminent destruction of the city by the Romans after exactly forty years (AD 70) (vv. 43–44). During that same time, Jesus also said,

> O Jerusalem, Jerusalem, the city that kills the prophets and stones those who are sent to it! How often would I have gathered your children together as a hen gathers her brood under her wings, and you were not willing! See, your house [i.e., the temple] is left to you desolate. For I tell you, you will not see me again, until you say, "Blessed is he who comes in the name of the LORD [Ps. 118:26]" (Matt. 23:37–39).

Here again, the sadness of Jesus was evident in the reproach that the city refused to listen, the announcement of its destruction, as well as the great "until": the implicit announcement of the great restoration of Israel.

8.7 Two Transitional Parables

8.7.1 The Wicked Tenants

The transition from Judaism to Christianity just described was sharply illustrated by Jesus in several kingdom parables.[73] First, in

---
73. See more extensively, Ouweneel (2011a, §10.3).

the parable of the tenants (Matt. 21:33–41), God entrusted his "vineyard" (Israel, see Isa. 5:1–7) to the spiritual leaders of the people, but they did not produce the required and expected fruits. God sent his servants, the prophets, to them, but they killed these. Finally, he sent his beloved Son, but when the spiritual leaders of Israel saw him, they said, "This is the heir. Come, let us kill him and have his inheritance" (v. 38). This statement implied that according to Jesus, Israel's leaders, who had just asked, "By what authority are you doing these things, and who gave you this authority?" (v. 23), knew very well the answer to this question. They *knew* who Jesus was—"This is the heir" (cf. Heb. 1:2)—and in spite of this, or rather for this very reason, they killed him. He stood in their way and opposed their religious system; if they eliminated him, they would be free to do as they liked.[74]

By the "tenants" Jesus understood the spiritual leaders of Israel. The "vineyard" of Israel, and thus the kingdom of God, was taken away from them, and "given to a people producing its fruits" (v. 43). Please notice the following difference. Some parables (the weeds, the net, the two servants, the ten virgins, the talents; see Matt. 13 and 24–25) put the greatest emphasis on what will happen "at the end of the age," that is, shortly before and at the time of Messiah's second coming. But the parables of the tenants and the wedding feast put the emphasis on what occurred right after Jesus' first coming: *the kingdom formally passed from Israel to the new — Jewish and Gentile — people of God* (the "people" of v. 43). This new people of God consisted of (a) faithful, penitent Israelites, who acknowledged their Messiah and learned to follow him, and (b) all those from the nations who would accept the Messiah of Israel as their personal Savior and Lord and would learn to follow him. The Ecclesia is not "Israel" in some spiritual sense, but a different people, the "other tenants" (Matt. 21:41), the "others" (Gk. *allois*) in the parallel account in Luke 20:16, distinct from the leaders of Judaism.

In the debate with supersessionists, this is an interesting point. The latter might argue: You see, the Israel of the Tanakh *is replaced* by the New Testament Ecclesia; so there you have it: a kind of re-

---

74. It is striking that the grand inquisitor in Dostoevsky's *The Brothers Karamazov* followed a similar reasoning, saying to Jesus: Stay out of the way, then we will have the (Christian) world all for ourselves; see extensively, Ouweneel (2003b).

placement theology after all. In a sense, this is true of course. But this is not the issue. The issue is that this Ecclesia is not at all a kind of "spiritual Israel," that is, the same old Israel but now, ostensibly, enlarged with millions of Gentile believers. No, the Ecclesia is *another* people, a people *other than* Israel. In Matthew 16:18 (cf. 18:17), Jesus referred to this new community as *his* Ecclesia, which he was going to build (future!). I mention this debate to show how both sides can claim the term "replacement," and to what terminological confusion this may lead. Therefore, the real issue at stake is not some form of "replacement," or the similarities and differences between Israel and the Ecclesia. Rather, it is this question: Is there, after this exchange of people, still a literal land promise left to ethnic Israel?

The most dramatic expression in our parable is the phrase "taken away": "Therefore I tell you, the kingdom of God will be *taken away* [Gk. *arthēsetai*] from you" (Matt. 21:43). This means *in concreto*: no longer is there any possibility left that a person could enter the kingdom of God merely and purely because he had been born a Jew, or because he was keeping the Torah, or even because he had become a Jewish proselyte. Neither descent, nor circumcision, nor keeping the Torah gives a Jew entrance into the kingdom of God. Already Ezekiel 11:19 and 36:26 had made this very clear:[75] Israel will be able to enter the kingdom of God in no other way than with a new heart and a new spirit. This is what the New Testament calls new birth or regeneration.[76] This never occurs on the basis of a person's own achievements, but only by the grace of God, through the work of the Holy Spirit. It was like this in Genesis 3, and it will be like this until the end of the present world.

The kingdom is "given to a people producing its fruits" (Matt. 21:43), that is, who bear the fruits in which God can rejoice. This is what the grapes entail: they are an image of joy (cf. Judg. 9:13; Ps. 104:15; see also Isa. 5:2c, 4c). For Israel, this implied the fruit of gratitude, praise, worship, servitude, surrender, and consecration. But if this is the criterion for true and wholesome fruit, there is, in God's thought, no reason why salvation could or should be limited to Is-

---

75. Cf. also Deut. 30:2, 10; Ps. 32:1–5; 51:10, 14, 17; 130:1–4; and Isa. 57:14–21.

76. John 3:3–7; Titus 3:5; 1 Pet. 1:3, 23; Ouweneel (2009b, 71–98).

rael. The "other" people (Matt. 21:41, 43) consist of all those, Jewish as well as Gentile, who will bear fruit for God, and thus show themselves to be true disciples and good servants of the kingdom of God through their surrender, consecration, and obedience to the King.

8.7.2 The Wedding Feast

Immediately after the parable of the tenants we read the parable of the royal wedding feast (Matt. 22:1-14), which in certain important respects corresponds with the previous parable. The vineyard has been replaced by a wedding feast, and the tenants of the vineyard correspond with the people invited to the feast. The latter are the first to qualify for attending the wedding feast. Here again we have a picture of Israel, the ones who were originally the "sons of the kingdom" (8:12).[77] First the Jew, then the Greek (Rom. 1:16; 2:9-10). These invitees behave in a way similar to that of the tenants in the previous parable: they do not satisfy the desires of the master. The tenants refuse to pay the fruits of the vineyard, and the invitees refuse to accept the invitation. The tenants killed the servants of the master, and some invitees did the same. In this way, both groups show their disinterest in and contempt for the master. Thus, in the interpretation of the parables, Jesus argued that tenants and invitees may be interested in religiosity and (outward) piety, but they are not interested in God.

Of course, this characterization is limited to Jews; in the "last days," there are also (pseudo)Christians who are "lovers of pleasure rather than lovers of God, having the appearance of godliness, but denying its power" (2 Tim. 3:4-5). It is a widespread phenomenon: people who are (outwardly) religious but are not really interested in God; they are basically interested only in themselves.

Matthew 22:5 identifies two responses: indifference and violence. The former respondents are neutral — if that were possible — the latter are overt opponents. As to this second group: both the tenants and second group of the invitees used violence against all the servants of God who threatened their religious system and their interests. Such violence went further than just contempt and indif-

---

77. The expression "royal children, or sons" is a common rabbinic expression for Israel; see Talmud: Shabbat 66b, 67a, 111a, 128a. It is remarkable that in Matthew 13:38 the expression refers to the true subjects of the kingdom of God (Jewish or Gentile).

ference; it involved outright hatred. Jesus says, "If the world hates you, know that it has *hated* me before it hated you.... If I had not done among them the works that no one else did, they would not be guilty of sin, but now they have seen and *hated* both me and my Father" (John 15:18, 24; see also 7:7; cf. Luke 19:14, "his citizens *hated* him," and Stephen in Acts 7:51–53).

Those in the parable who in the end responded to the invitation were the have-nots. Those who already "have" something, or believe they do, did not come; only those who did not "have" anything. If the original invitees had taken part in the wedding feast, they would have done so on the basis of their status, that is, of being entitled to attend. Those who, in the end, do indeed take part, do so on the basis of the king's pure grace and benevolence. Compare the laborers in the vineyard, where the workers of the eleventh hour also depended on the master's grace and benevolence (Matt. 20:1–16).

In the parable of the wedding feast we find the remarkable indirect prophecy, lacking in the parable of the tenants: "The king was angry, and he sent his troops and destroyed those murderers and burned their city" (Matt. 22:7). Compare the parable of the ten minas, where we find a similar statement: "But as for these enemies of mine, who did not want me to reign over them, bring them here and slaughter them before me" (Luke 19:27). These implicit prophecies concerning the fall of Jerusalem, forty years later, are directly ascribed here to God's personal intervention; the Roman armies are even called here *his* armies. Compare Isaiah 10:5 and Habakkuk 1:6, where the armies of the Assyrians and the Babylonians, respectively, were *God's* armies against Israel as well. In our parable, God sent "his" army *against* Jerusalem, explicitly because the city was the killer of God's servants: "O Jerusalem, Jerusalem, the city that kills the prophets and stones those who are sent to it!" (Matt. 23:37).

Jesus explained that this was the reason the kingdom of God was taken away from (the unbelieving majority of) Israel and given to a new (Jewish-Gentile) people of God. *The former were not worthy of it:*

> "The wedding feast is ready, but those invited were not worthy. Go therefore to the main roads and invite to the wedding feast as many as you find." And those servants went out into the roads and gath-

ered all whom they found, both bad [viz., those who refused the wedding garment] and good.⁷⁸ So the wedding hall was filled with guests (Matt. 22:8–10).

Notice the term "worthy": only those are "worthy" of the kingdom who confess their personal utter *unworthiness* and entrust themselves to the grace and mercy of God.

This parable contained a double judgment. The first judgment was pronounced upon the invitees, that is, the natural, religious, but essentially God-less part of Israel. After this, the "sinners" may come in, both from Israel and from the nations. However, those among them who thought they can attend without a garment that is fitting for the king—that is, they came with garments of their own "righteous deeds" (cf. Isa. 64:6) — fell basically under the same divine judgment as the religious, but God-less part of Israel. In Jesus' day, Israel was a mixture of *tzaddiqim* ("righteous ones," who were allowed to enter God's kingdom) and *r'sha'im* (the "wicked," God-less ones, no matter how religious they were). In its present form, the kingdom of God, consisting of Jews and Gentiles, is also a mixture of *tzaddiqim* (who at the appearance of Christ will be allowed to enter the Messianic kingdom) and *r'sha'im*. The judgment is exactly the same: the righteous enter the kingdom of God (in its present or in its future form, respectively), and the wicked come under God's judgment.

In my view, the final conclusion of verse 14 — "For many are called, but few are chosen" — is true in both cases: the called or invited ones are many, whether this involves the Israelites in Jesus' day, or the (mostly Gentile) children of the kingdom in the present time. This indicates the breadth of God's gospel: the entire world. But the *truthful* ones among them, the faithful, the righteous, the genuine disciples of the King, the good servants, are far fewer in number. The many "called" ones who indeed come to join God's people consist, both formerly and now—and even afterward in the Messianic kingdom—of good ones (the "chosen" of v. 14) and evil ones. In the end, the only point that matters is not whether one is a

---

78. For this important phrase, see Ouweneel (2011a, chapter 10): it is not the distinction between those who are *innately* good or bad, but between those who humbly accept the king's conditions for entering, and those who think they can enter on their own conditions.

Jew or a Greek, Catholic or Protestant, churchgoer or not, of high or low descent, a spiritual leader or an outcast, but whether one is a true righteous one (that is, one who lives by God's grace and according to his commandments), or a God-less one.

8.8 Impediments from Christians for Jews
8.8.1 Impediments 1–2

Earlier I mentioned seven reasons why it was and is difficult for Jews to accept Jesus as their Messiah. Humanly speaking, I understand this attitude. Yet, Christians—including me—believe that these seven reasons are not valid; otherwise, how could they themselves have come to faith in Jesus as the Messiah of Israel? However, what is far worse is that, throughout the centuries, Christians have presented arguments to Israel to solidify the Jewish rejection of Jesus. If, today, a Jew refuses to accept Jesus as Messiah, this is not only because of the seven reasons mentioned earlier, but especially because of these *new* seven reasons, invented by Christians (or so-called Christians). If, today, Jews refuse to accept Jesus as the Messiah, Christianity is just as responsible for this refusal as the Jews themselves are. The Jews in Jesus' day who refused were more culpable than the Jews in our day who refuse, and that is the fault of Christians.

Let us have a brief look at these seven impediments that Christians place in the path of Jews.

1. Christians have divested Jesus of (many of) his Jewish characteristics. Many Caucasians have come to depict Christ as an Aryan with blond hair and blue eyes, an honorary member (or even pope, patriarch, archbishop, pastor) of a typically Western church, with Western features, such as a Western way of thinking. Due to the strong Hellenist-Roman influence that the church underwent from the beginning, theology, too, since Origen, became a strongly Hellenist-Roman matter, with its rationalism and scientism, both of which are foreign to orthodox Judaism.[79] Thus, the Jesus who is usually presented to the Jew today is especially the Jesus of the Western church and Western theology. He resembles far more the

---

79. Rabbinic Judaism also clearly exhibits Hellenist influences (especially in the more intellectual school of Maimonides). To give one example: there are thousands of Greek loanwords in the Talmud—and along with these words often come their meanings as well; see Krauss (2009).

Hellenist teacher (who he never was) than the Jewish rabbi (who he was). *This* Jesus is strongly alienated from traditional Judaism; who can blame the Jews for not finding *this* Jesus appealing? Only in recent decades has interest in the *Jewish* Jesus been renewed.

2. During the twentieth century, the accusation could be heard that "the Jews" had killed Jesus, and that, since the crucifixion, all Jews of all time and places are co-responsible for this act. Not only this—many Christians took upon themselves, "in the name of God," the role of executioner to punish the Jews for this murder. We can scarcely imagine the enormous damage done by robbing and killing Jews, raping their wives and daughters, setting their synagogues and Talmudim on fire, at many places and throughout many centuries, all *in the name of Jesus*.

A simple biblical answer to this is that the apostles never accused *all* Jews indiscriminately of murdering Jesus. They accused only the shouting mob in Jerusalem (see the emphatic "they" in Acts 13:27–29, where Paul blames the Jews in Jerusalem at the time of Jesus, not the Pisidian Jews he was addressing at that moment). Moreover, it is a biblical principle that you can blame people only for their own sins, not for the sins of their forefathers (Ezek. 18:20). People may make themselves one with the sins of their ancestors (cf. the "*we* have sinned" in Dan. 9:5, 8, 11, 15), and they may have to bear the *consequences* of the sins of their forebears (Exod. 20:5), but in the end they are judged only for their *own* sins.

The consequence of the enormous guilt of "Christians" toward Jews is that Jesus-believers cannot evangelize Jews in the same way they evangelize other people in the world, as if nothing has happened. It is naïve to think that you can persuade Jews to follow a Jesus who, for centuries, brought them only misery. Yes, there is indeed room to bear witness to Jews, but only with the greatest modesty, with a profound awareness of the results of so many centuries of "Christian" anti-Semitism. As a German Jewess once told me: "In the name of Jesus my entire family has been killed; but in the name of *Yeshuah* I have found eternal salvation."

8.8.2 Impediments 3–4

3. For Christians who advocate supersessionism it had become a source of great irritation that a small ethnic group continues to

maintain that *they* are the "true" Israel. But conversely, for the Jews it has become a source of irritation that an ever larger and stronger church arose that claimed that *they* were the only people of God, claiming for itself the name of the "true Israel," or the "spiritual Israel," or the "Israel of God." In other words, in order to find salvation in Jesus, a Jew was forced to believe that they were not really a Jew but could become one by joining a community consisting almost exclusively of Gentiles. In order to become a "true Jew," they had to eliminate all their typically Jewish characteristics (with a false appeal to, e.g., Rom. 2:28-29 or Gal. 6:16). From a Jewish viewpoint, it is difficult to imagine anything more irritating than this. A Jew can become a true Jew only by henceforth relinquishing all their Jewishness? What a foolish idea!

As time passed, the question was no longer whether Jesus was the Messiah of Israel. It was the *church* that mattered: *Extra Ecclesiam nulla salus*, "Outside the *church* there is no salvation," referring, moreover, to the organizational, denominational church. For the Jew, this implied an irritating paradox: You, a Jew, can become a true Jew only by joining the church of the Gentiles. To this end, you must surrender your Sabbath, your Jewish festivals, and your food laws. You must learn to observe Sunday, to eat pork, and forego circumcising your little boys. No wonder that few Jews were willing to voluntarily accept this insane paradox: to become a Jew you must lay down your Jewish identity and accept a Gentile one. Moreover, in the medieval Roman Catholic Church, the Inquisition, *under penalty of death*, carefully watched whether the Jews who had become "Christians" had really surrendered everything that was typically Jewish. Quite a few "converted" (baptized) Jews met the end of their life at the stake.

4. The Jewish people always kept alive their desire to return one day to *ha'Aretz*, the land where their forefathers had lived. At every Seder meal they sighed, "Next year in Jerusalem." But now Christians tell them that they were thoroughly wrong. To their utter embarrassment, the Jews had to discover that "Christians" had stolen the age-old land promise, and had given to it their own, spiritualized interpretation. In other words, if a Jew were to consider becoming a Christian, they were given to understand that they would have to surrender one of their greatest and deepest desires:

the land.⁸⁰ With an appeal to the "heavenly country" (Heb. 11:14-16), or perhaps the "New Jerusalem" (Rev. 3:12; 21:2, 9), or perhaps the spiritual "Zion,"⁸¹ such a convert did receive an ethereal "land" instead, but this was not at all what they had been hoping for.⁸²

If throughout history, "Christians" were interested in the Holy Land at all, that interest came to expression in the crusades. On the way to the Holy Land, during the first crusade (1095–1099), they killed as many Jews in the Rhineland as they could, and once they arrived in Jerusalem, they murdered both Jews and Muslims. The link between Christians and *ha'Aretz* evokes only negative feelings among Jews.

In a highly touching way, Israel brings the age-old hope of the promised land to expression—against all "Christian" suppression—in a song of Naftali Herz Imber, called *HaTikvah* ("The Hope"), the first version of which dates from 1877, and which has since then become the national anthem of the state of Israel:

> As long as in the heart, within,
>
> the soul of a Jew still yearns,
>
> and onward, towards the ends of the east,
>
> an eye still gazes toward Zion,
>
> our hope is not yet lost,
>
> the two-thousand-year-old hope,
>
> to be a free nation in our land,
>
> the land of Zion and Jerusalem.

Supersessionism has never been able to quench this hope, although it has tried everything possible. And what no supersessionist would ever have expected or thought possible—and what all Christians faithful to the prophecies knew would happen one day—occurred in the twentieth century: the state of Israel was born.

---

80. Cf. Paul (2013, 45).

81. Rom. 9:33; 11:26; Heb. 12:22; 1 Pet. 2:6; Rev. 14:1.

82. The pious Jew received this "heavenly country" anyway: already during the intertestamentary period, the thought was developed that at their death the *tzaddiqim* go to the heavenly paradise (Heb. *Gan Eden*, "Garden of Eden"); see, e.g., http://jewishencyclopedia.com/articles/11900-paradise.

8.8.3 Impediments 5–7

5. The words of the Messiah in Psalm 40:8b, "[Y]our Torah is within my heart [lit., my bowels]," characterize each godly Jew, as do these words: ". . . your Torah is my delight. . . . Oh how I love your Torah! It is my meditation all the day."[83] Moreover, the Jew knows from the Tanakh that this Torah is not of a transient nature: "I will keep your law continually, forever and ever. . . . Your commandment . . . is ever with me. . . . I incline my heart to perform your statutes forever, to the end. . . . Your testimonies are righteous forever; . . . every one of your righteous rules endures forever (Ps. 119:44, 98, 112, 144, 160).

Israel is the apple of *God's* eye (Deut. 32:10; Zech. 2:8), and the Torah is the apple of *Israel's* eye (cf. the metaphor in Prov. 7:2). The Sinaitic Torah is Israel's greatest treasure, certainly as long as Israel is not living in the Promised Land (for Zion and the temple belong to its greatest treasures as well). And now, here comes the "Christian" and tells the Jew that this Torah has found its *end* in Christ (despite Matt. 5:17 and a wrong understanding of Rom. 10:4). In other words, Jews are deluded by "Christians" who tell them that, in order to find eternal salvation, they must surrender their greatest treasure. This is said despite this explicit statement by the apostle Paul: "Do we then overthrow the Torah by this faith? By no means! On the contrary, *we uphold the Torah*" (Rom. 3:31). We cannot say that the Mosaic Torah has been annulled (more on this elsewhere in this volume). Here the point is that, in our dialogue with Jews, the worst conceivable starting point is to assure them that the Torah has been abolished. This is like telling a couple that has fallen in love that matrimonial relationships have been abolished.

6. Our next point is difficult for supersessionists to digest. *Must the Jew become a Christian in order to be saved?* My reply is "no," if becoming a Christian required Jews to set aside their Jewishness and join a Christian denomination. But those same Jews cannot reproach Christians for insisting that *outside Christ, there is no salvation* (think of John 14:6 and Acts 4:12). However, these two sentences are not claiming the same thing, as many have erroneously thought. If the Jew serves the God of Israel with all their heart, I hope that

---

83. Ps. 119:77b, 97, 174; cf. 70, 92, 112, 163, 165; also see 1:2; 19:7–8.

when the Messiah appears, they should recognize him to be Jesus, and find that all their hope and blessing lie in him. But this does not imply or require that they must cease being a Jew, or must change from one religion to another. Converting to Jesus (Yeshuah) does not mean converting to a different religion than the one a Jew has received. On the contrary, it means finding the highest fulfillment of their Jewishness and of that religion. By becoming a Christian, the Jew does *not* lay down their Jewishness to become something different—in some ways even contrary to what they were—*but they will become a Jew in a sense more profound than ever before.*

Eternal salvation, atonement, forgiveness of sins, and reconciliation with God, do not lie in the church—no matter what meaning one gives that term—but in Christ, that is, the Messiah of Israel, and in him alone. However, it will be extremely hard for the Jew to grasp this, after "Christians" have told them for centuries: If you wish to be saved, turn your back on your Jewishness, and join our church!

7. Finally, Christians have made it harder for Jews to accept Jesus as their Messiah by giving a very distorted presentation of the Trinity. They have often given the impression that Christians do serve the God of Israel—the God of the Tanakh—but have, like polytheists, added two other "gods" to the God of Israel: Jesus and the Holy Spirit. Jews often respond to this with indignation. As a rabbi once told me, You, Christians, would never be able to recite the *Shema*—"the LORD is one" (Deut. 6:4)—for you people do not have one God, but three gods. His claim was completely mistaken, but I could hardly blame him for making it; it has been *our* "Christian" fault that Jews have received this impression. It is an egregiously error to suggest that the God of the Tanakh suddenly in the New Testament turns out to have a Son, who himself is God, too. (So, now you have two.) Rather, orthodox Christians believe that the *one* God of the Tanakh, called YHWH—with the emphasis on *one*—in the New Testament reveals himself to be who he always was: Father, Son, and Holy Spirit, still remaining *one* God.

Of course, this is a very deep and complicated subject, one that we cannot elaborate here.[84] At this point it is sufficient to observe

---

84. See extensively, Ouweneel (2007b, especially chapters 2 and 8).

that, if Christians had given a clearer presentation of the Trinity,[85] they might have frightened away fewer Jews. I can wholeheartedly confess together with Jews — and have done so many times — the *Shema, Yisra'ēl, Adonai Elohēnu Adonai echad* ("Hear, O Israel: The LORD our God, the LORD is one; or, The LORD our God is one LORD; or, The LORD is our God, the LORD is one; or, The LORD is our God, the LORD alone"). I confess to being a strict monotheist, whether or not Jews believe me.

---

85. Even the word Trinity, derived from Tri-unity, is somewhat unfortunate because it emphasizes the *tri-* more than the *unity*.

Chapter 9
Israel in Prophecy
in the Tanakh

In the whole of the Hexateuch[1] there is probably no idea more important than that expressed in terms of the land promised and later granted by Yahweh.

Gerhard von Rad[2]

[O]f all the promises made to the patriarchs it was that of the land that was most prominent and decisive.

William D. Davies[3]

*[T]he land is the central, if not **the central theme** of biblical faith. . . . [I]t will no longer do to talk about Yahweh and his people but we must speak about Yahweh and his people **and his land**.*

Walter Brueggeman[4]

So far as the Arabs are [concerned]. . . , I hope that . . . they will not grudge that small notch . . . in what are now

---

1. That is, the five books of Moses plus the book of Joshua.
2. Von Rad (1966, 79).
3. Davies (1974, 24; cf. also 1991).
4. Brueggeman (1977, 3, 126).

> *Arab territories being given to the people who for all these hundreds of years have been separated from it.*
> Arthur J. Balfour (July 12, 1920)[5]

9.1 Moses
9.1.1 Deuteronomy 4:30

IF AN EXEGETICAL APPROACH is correct, it is like a door-fitting key that fits exactly the texts involved; if it is wrong, it will not be able to open the doors, or will do so only by force. In my view, supersessionism is such a key, which manages to open a few doors, and triumphantly announces this to the world—but do not look at the force needed to pull it off. It does not take long to discover that people are using the wrong key for the door.

To this end, let us consider some prophecies as examples. In particular, I will deal with Messianic prophecies because expositors at least agree that the prophecies referring to the birth and the earthly life of the Messiah must be taken literally. Supersessionists, however, view the eschatological context in which these prophecies are framed to be figurative. They switch facilely from the literal to the figurative interpretation, and vice versa, all according to their paradigmatic biases. They have no fixed interpretative key for making such switches; it is purely arbitrary. Let me give some striking examples, first from the book of Deuteronomy.

In Deuteronomy 4:30 we read, "When you are in tribulation, and all these things come upon you in the latter days, you will return to the LORD your God and obey his voice." Some translations have something like "In time to come," but the Hebrew text is quite specific: *b'acharit hayyamim*, that is, "in the end (last; lit., most behind) of the days." It is not something vague—somewhere in the future—but it is unmistakably an eschatological statement: in the Tanakh this expression *always* refers (basically) to the Messianic age, or the time that immediately precedes it, the so-called "end time."[6] The expression corresponds with what the New Testament calls in Greek *ep' eschatou tōn hēmerōn [toutōn]*, "in the last of the/

---

5. http://cojs.org/july-12th-1920-sir-arthur-balfour/.
6. Gen. 49:1; Num. 24:14; Deut. 31:29; Isa. 2:2; Jer. 23:20; 30:24; 48:47; 49:39; Ezek. 38:16; Dan. 10:14; Hos. 3:5; Micah 4:1.

these days" (Heb. 1:2; 2 Pet. 3:3), or *en [tais] eschatais hēmerais*, "in [the] last days (Acts 2:17; 2 Tim. 3:1).[7] These passages refer to the "end time," that is, a time that, for the authors too, still lay in the future.

The interesting exception is Hebrews 1:1-2, ". . . in these last days [God] has spoken to us by his Son." Here, the Messianic age was viewed as beginning already with the first coming of the Messiah (cf. 1 John 2:18, "Children, it *is* the last hour," and 1 Cor. 10:11, "the end of the ages" (have come on us) (Gk. *ta telē tōn aiōnōn*). At the same time, the author of Hebrews knew very well that "the world to come" (Heb. 2:5, the world of the Messianic kingdom of peace), "the age to come" Heb. 6:5, the age of the Messianic kingdom) and "the city that is to come" (Heb. 13:14, the heavenly capital of the Messianic kingdom) were still realities belonging to the (distant) future (cf. also Heb. 11:20 KJV, "things to come," and 12:28, the [future] "kingdom that cannot be shaken").

9.1.2   Deuteronomy 32:35-43

In §5.6.1 attention was given to the important prophecy of Deuteronomy 30:1-10, the direct sequel of chapter 29, in which the blessing and the curse had been declared to Israel. Recall the fascinating double meaning of Hebrew verb *shub*, "to return" (to the promised land of the fathers) as well as "to convert," that is, "to return" to the LORD (vv. 2-3, 10). What we found in this passage was a remarkable eschatological description of the ultimate redemption of Israel.[8]

Deuteronomy 32 may count as a prophecy as well, namely, one by Moses the prophet (cf. 18:15, 18; 34:10). We read in verses 35-43:

> "Vengeance is mine, and recompense, for the time when their foot [i.e., the wicked's foot] shall slip; for the day of their calamity is at hand, and their doom comes swiftly." For the LORD will vindicate his people and have compassion on his servants, when he sees that their power is gone and there is none remaining, bond or free. Then he will say, . . . "I kill and I make alive; I wound and I heal; and there

---

7. Cf. Gk. *en husterois kairois*, "in latter times" (1 Tim. 4:1), *eschatē hōra*, "last hour" (1 John 2:18), and *ep' eschatou [tou] chronou*, "in the end of time" (Jude 18).

8. See further Ps. 14:7; 53:6; Jer. 31:23; 33:7, 11, 26; Hos. 6:11; Joel 3:1; Amos 9:14; Zeph. 3:20; other nations: Jer. 48:47; 49:6; Ezek. 29:14.

is none that can deliver out of my hand... I will take vengeance on my adversaries and will repay those who hate me. I will make my arrows drunk with blood, and my sword shall devour flesh — with the blood of the slain and the captives, from the long-haired heads of the enemy." Rejoice with him, O heavens bow down to him, all gods, for he avenges the blood of his children and takes vengeance on his adversaries. He repays those who hate him and cleanses *his people's land*.

This last verse (v. 43) says in Hebrew, "... atones for his land, his people" (perhaps, "for the land *of* his people," as the Septuagint and the Vulgate render the text). Various theologians of the Dutch Second Reformation (in the seventeenth and eighteenth centuries) have paid much attention to Deuteronomy 32, people like Johannes Cocceius, Henricus Groenewegen, and David Flud van Giffen.[9] For Cocceius, verse 43 was teaching atonement for Israel as a nation, as well as for the promised land, to which Israel would no doubt return, and where it would restore the city of Jerusalem. To this end, Cocceius referred to Luke 21:24 ("Jerusalem will be trampled underfoot by the Gentiles, *until* the times of the Gentiles are fulfilled") and Romans 11:25-27 ("... all Israel will be saved, 'The Deliverer will come from Zion...'").

Groenewegen saw in Deuteronomy 32:42 God's judgment of the wicked, especially — according to him — of popery, which he thought the book of Revelation was referring to as the false prophet, and in verse 42 as "the hairy head of the enemy." After having mentioned this future judgment, Moses described the blessed condition of the Ecclesia on earth, including the restoration of Israel in its own country. God was going to make the promised land the "garden-planting of his church," whatever he meant by this. Like other sympathetic theologians of his day, Groenewegen was an adherent of post-millennialism, which implied a future blossoming of the church on earth. But for now, the important point in his view was that he and other Reformed theologians believed in a national restoration of ethnic Israel in its own land, the ancient land of Israel. They believed that the text was perfectly clear: God would make atonement not only for his people, but also for the land where, according to God's promises, these people belong. This tied in with what Moses had said before:

---

9. Van Campen (2007, 300, 409–11, 429).

If your outcasts are in the uttermost parts of heaven, from there the LORD your God will gather you, and from there he will take you. And the LORD your God will bring you into the land that your fathers possessed, that you may possess it. And he will make you more prosperous and numerous than your fathers (Deut. 30:4-5).

9.2 Isaiah

9.2.1 Isaiah 7:14

In Isaiah 7 we find the well-known prophecy of verse 14, mentioned earlier: "Behold, the virgin shall conceive and bear a son, and shall call his name Immanuel."[10] It is important to note that this prophecy appeared in the context of the battle against, and the decline of, Assyria. Orthodox exegetes who interpret verse 14 literally should do the same with this eschatological battle against Assyria (cf. 10:12; 14:25; but see also 19:23-25). In the prophecies about Assyria's defeat, there were references to the *preliminary* blow that was administered to Assyria at the time of King Sennacherib (37:36), but at other places Assyria's decline was clearly linked with the coming of the Messiah and the establishment of his kingdom (see especially Isa. 28-32).

Now look at this passage about Immanuel—a passage understood literally by orthodox Jews and many Christians, but figuratively by supersessionists:

> [T]herefore, behold, the LORD is bringing up against them [i.e., Israel] the waters of the River [i.e., the Euphrates], mighty and many, the king of Assyria and all his glory. And it will rise over all its channels and go over all its banks, and it will sweep on into Judah, it will overflow and pass on, reaching even to the neck, and its outspread wings will fill the breadth of your land, O Immanuel [Heb. *'Immanu El*]. Be broken [or, evil], you peoples, and be shattered [or, dismayed]; give ear, all you far countries; strap on your armor and be shattered; strap on your armor and be shattered. Take counsel together, but it will come to nothing; speak a word, but it will not stand, for God is with us [Heb. *ki 'immanu El*] (Isa. 8:7-10).

Look at what happens here. At the time of Sennacherib, Immanuel had not yet been born; many centuries would pass before

---

10. Ouweneel (2007b, 168–71).

his birth. Nevertheless, the fall of Assyria was connected with his person. In the book of Isaiah, "Assyria," regardless of its name in the end time—geographically, it corresponds with modern Iraq, along with Syria—was the *same* power that, in the end time, will turn against Israel and Jerusalem, and will then be defeated *under the guidance of Immanuel*. After this, the Messiah will establish his kingdom in *that same* Israel and Jerusalem, not in some spiritual Israel or Jerusalem (Isa. 30-32). God will be with his people—this is what the name "Immanuel" expresses—in the person of him who is called Immanuel. The final victory over Israel's enemies will occur in and through the Messiah.

We are dealing here with an important underlying hermeneutical principle concerning the biblical prophecies: if a power that existed in the past (Assyria, the Roman Empire) appears in unmistakably eschatological prophecies—that is, prophecies culminating in the Messianic kingdom—and if this power is destroyed at—or just before—the appearance of the Messiah, then, in the end time, this power must exist again on earth, even if, in the meantime, this power may have temporarily disappeared. Therefore, I believe that in the end time, a power will exist that the prophets refer to as Assyria, one that will also have a certain historical and geographical link with ancient Assyria. This power threatened Jerusalem not only in the days of King Hezekiah and the later Davidic kings, but will do so again in the end time, and will be destroyed by the Messiah himself.

9.2.2 Isaiah 9:6-7

In Isaiah 9:6-7 one of the key questions is what we must understand by the "throne of David." No wonder that one supersessionist commentator understood it to be the heavenly throne of God:[11] Christ, "who already now is seated in the throne of glory in order to carry out the Father's pleasure, and one day will cause the kingdom of peace to arrive," by which he understood the new heavens and the new earth. Another commentator spoke explicitly of "figurative language in verse 7."[12] We could have some sympathy for this view since the throne of King Solomon in 1 Chronicles 29:23 is called the

---

11. Ridderbos (1985, 104).

12. Alexander (1953, 1:205).

"throne of the LORD." One might assume that, if the throne of David is sometimes called "throne of the LORD," then the throne of the LORD in heaven may be called the "throne of David."

However, the latter claim is logically invalid. If Saul was called king, it does not mean that any king may be called Saul. Both the throne of David in Jerusalem and the throne of God in heaven may be called "thrones of the LORD," but they definitely are not the same. Nowhere was the heavenly throne called the "throne of David," or something similar. In Revelation 3:21, Jesus himself clearly distinguished between the two thrones: "The one who conquers, I *will* grant him to sit with me on *my* throne, as I also conquered and *sat* down with my Father on *his* throne." There is the throne of Jesus' Father, on which he has *already* been sitting since his ascension to and glorification in heaven.[13] *And* there is Jesus' *own* throne, on which he *will* sit in the future. The latter apparently is the "throne of David,"[14] exactly as the angel Gabriel had foretold: "He [i.e., Jesus] will be great and will be called the Son of the Most High. And the LORD God will give to him the throne of his father David, and he will reign over the house of Jacob forever, and of his kingdom there will be no end" (Luke 1:32-33).

How could Mary, or any godly Jew in those days, have understood these words other than in relation to the throne of David *in Jerusalem* (cf. Jer. 13:13; 17:25) and the literal "house of Jacob" (Israel)? This was the very essence of Gabriel's message: for centuries, the house of David had possessed no heir who had occupied David's throne. This was now going to change, since Mary was going to give birth to a Son of David who *was* going to occupy the throne. Mary could never have grasped the incongruous idea that this throne of David had moved to heaven, and would from then on coincide with the throne of God—nor the idea that the "house of Jacob" would consist virtually exclusively of Gentiles. This cannot be called serious exegesis; I am most sympathetic to the confusion Mary or any godly Jew would have experienced.

At the same time, it is fascinating to see how Jewish expositors have wrestled with the same passage, Isaiah 9:6-7, and have arrived at the opposite solution: the verses are not Messianic at all but

---

13. See, e.g., Acts 2:33–34; Eph. 1:20; Heb. 1:3; 8:1; 10:12; 12:2; 1 Pet. 3:22.
14. Ps. 132:11; Isa. 9:7; Jer. 13:13; 17:25; 22:2, 4, 30; 29:16; 33:17; 36:30.

refer to King Ahaz.[15] How about that? How could anyone fail to see the Messianic bearing at least of verse 7? And if one sees this, how could one fail to interpret verse 6 along similar lines? Sometimes, orthodox Jews and supersessionists seem to be playing on the same team, by arguing away a Bible passage if it cannot be handled according to the principles of their paradigm.

9.2.3 Isaiah 10–11

Isaiah 7:14 is followed by verses 17–18, 20; 8:4, 7; 10:5, in which Assyria was identified as *the* adversary of Judah in Isaiah's days. However, Assyria is such an adversary in the end time too, since this power is definitively defeated only when "the LORD has finished all his work on Mount Zion and on Jerusalem" (10:12). After the attack by eschatological Assyria, the Messianic kingdom will appear immediately:

> Behold, the LORD God of hosts will lop the boughs [i.e., Assyria] with terrifying power. . . . He will cut down the thickets of the forest with an axe, and Lebanon will fall by the Majestic One. There shall come forth a shoot [i.e., the Messiah] from the stump of Jesse, and a branch from his roots shall bear fruit. And the Spirit of the LORD shall rest upon him. . . . He shall not judge by what his eyes see, or decide disputes by what his ears hear, but with righteousness he shall judge the poor, and decide with equity for the meek of the earth; and he shall strike the earth with the rod of his mouth, and with the breath of his lips he shall kill the wicked (Isa. 10:33–11:4).

In this instance the (non-inspired) division of Bible books into chapters regrettably obscures the coherence between the last verses of Isaiah 10 and the first verse of Isaiah 11. We must read it as one passage, however. This is a text that does speak in metaphorical (botanical) language (boughs, thickets, shoot, stump, branch, roots), but whose content must be taken literally, which applied not only to the origin of the Messiah from the dynasty of Jesse (the father of David), but just as much to the fall of Assyria. The text forms the introduction to a description of the Messianic kingdom, which is entirely localized in Israel: "None will harm or destroy another on *My entire holy mountain*, for *the land* will be as full of the knowledge of the LORD as the sea is filled with water" (Isa. 11:9 HCSB). The

---

15. Slotki (1983, 44).

Hebrew *eretz* can certainly mean "earth," and this would certainly fit into the verse (see most translations). But in my view, what was intended here is (primarily) the "land" (cf. CSB, CEV, GNT, WYC), namely, the land to which the dispersed of Israel are carried back:

> In that day the LORD will extend his hand yet a second time to recover the remnant that remains of his people, from Assyria, from Egypt, from Pathros, from Cush, from Elam, from Shinar, from Hamath, and from the coastlands of the sea. He will raise a signal for the nations and will assemble the banished of Israel, and gather the dispersed of Judah from the four corners of the earth. . . . [T]hey shall swoop down on the shoulder of the Philistines [i.e., Palestine] in the west, and together they shall plunder the people of the east. They shall put out their hand against Edom and Moab, and the Ammonites shall obey them. . . . And there will be a highway from Assyria for the remnant that remains of his people, as there was for Israel when they came up from the land of Egypt (Isa. 11:11–16).

9.3 Vague or Detailed Interpretation
9.3.1 The Neighboring Nations

The entire description given in the previous section is one that, today, is beginning to be literally fulfilled, constituting the prelude to the Messianic kingdom. Now let us note how this passage was distorted by one supersessionist commentator. He claimed that this passage was dealing with "the salvation the church of God[!] received in principle at Christ's first coming and will receive in perfection at His second coming. Especially pronounced are the experience of God's grace and the communion of saints, of which life in Canaan is the symbol. . . ."[16]

Perhaps a few questions can clarify matters here. First, who are all those nations from which Israel is gathered again (please note, many *more* nations than were involved in the return from the Babylonian exile)? Second, who constitutes this "remnant[17] that remains of his people," the "banished of Israel," and the "dispersed of Judah"? Third, from a supersessionist viewpoint, who are here the Philistines, the Edomites and the Moabites that are being attacked by God's people? Fourth, who are Judah and Ephraim? How can

---
16. Ridderbos (1985, 132).
17. Heb. *sha'ar*, from the root *sh-'-r*, "to remain, to be left over."

the distinction between the two be accounted for within supersessionism? Fifth, what is that "highway from Assyria"? As we have seen, supersessionism can offer us only vagueness, whereas a literal interpretation takes all the details seriously, so that they all neatly fall into place.

(a) The words "Philistines" and "Palestine" are etymologically identical. It was the ancient Romans who named the land of Israel after Israel's archenemies: Palestine (land of the Philistines). Formerly, the land of the Philistines/Palestine contained five cities: Gaza, Gath, Ekron, Ashdod, and Ashkelon (Josh. 13:3). Today, the latter four are situated within the state of Israel. Gaza and the region around it constitute what today is called the Gaza Strip — the hotbed of Palestinian (or, "Philistine") resistance against Israel.

(b) Today *Moab* is the middle part of the country of Jordan, and *Ammon* is the northern part of it. The capital of Jordan, Amman, stills sounds like the ancient Ammon (cf. Gen. 19:34-38, about the two sons of Lot).

(c) Ancient *Edom* is distributed across what is today the state of Israel, in the Negev desert, and the southern part of Jordan; the famous ancient city of Petra is part of it.

(d) As we have seen, the ancient *Assyrian* empire is distributed today across two countries in the Middle East: Iraq and Syria. The name "Syria" was clearly derived from "Assyria," but its ancient center lay more in what today is Iraq, not far from modern Bagdad.

(e) *Elam*, which is sometimes mentioned in the prophetic books of the Tanakh, belongs to modern Iran (ancient name: Persia). Media and Elam (Isa. 21:2; Jer. 25:25) are the ancient Medes and Persians (Est. 1:19; Dan. 5:28; 6:8, 12, 15). Descendants of the Medes are the Kurds, who nowadays can be found in northern Iraq (Southern Kurdistan), northwestern Iran (Eastern Kurdistan), southeastern Turkey (Northern Kurdistan), and northern Syria (Western Kurdistan). In view of the end time, the Persians are mentioned in Ezekiel 38:4-5,

> ... I will turn you [i.e., Gog] about and put hooks into your jaws, and I will bring you out, and all your army, horses and horsemen, all of them clothed in full armor, a great host, all of them with buckler and shield, wielding swords. Persia, Cush, and Put are with them, all of

them with shield and helmet; . . . .

9.3.2 The Two and the Ten Tribes

Isaiah 11 and many other passages make the historical distinction between the ten tribes (the northern kingdom) and the two tribes of Israel (the southern kingdom). It is an exegetical *tour de force* to view the ten tribes ("Ephraim") as the nations of the worlds and to ascribe this view to the apostle Paul because of a certain *application* he made.[18]

When the prophets in the Tanakh spoke of Ephraim and Judah, they pointed out that formerly the two belonged together, that due to their own sins they grew apart, and that each went into exile separately (Assyrian and Babylonian, respectively). But they also prophesied that one day, Ephraim as well as Judah would be brought back to the land of their fathers, and that the two would be rejoined. This would occur through the Messiah, at the beginning of his kingdom; see, for instance, Isaiah 11:12–13, where the two *together* turn against the neighboring nations.[19] How could anyone view *these* ten tribes as the nations of the world, or the church from the Gentiles, or something similar? These two, Jesus-believing Jews and Jesus-believing Gentiles, *never* belonged together before, *never* grew apart due to their sins, *never* went into exile separately. Here, Bible passages are being stretched on a Procrustean bed in order to make them fit one's own dogmatic biases.

It is remarkable to see how the supersessionist J. Ridderbos argued here.[20] First, he took the millennialist interpretation off the table by arguing that, if this approach were correct, the temple of Jerusalem would also have to be rebuilt, which from his perspective was unthinkable. Second, Ridderbos argued that millennialism would render the prophecy contradictory, for in Isaiah 11:4–5 it speaks of peace, and in verse 14–15 of battle. Ridderbos forgot that supersessionists are faced with precisely the same exegetical problem: How can the text speak of peace in verses 4–5, and of battle in verses 14–15? But this is precisely the essence of the matter: supersessionists do not have to bother about such details. According to

---

18. Maljaars (2015, 66–120).
19. Cf. Jer. 3:18; 30:3; 31:33; Ezek. 37:15-28.
20. Ridderbos (1985, 124–26).

Ridderbos, "The New Testament shows that the promises given to Israel pass over to the church of the new era . . . ; this is the true Israel, ..." Of course, the New Testament does nothing of the kind. But notice the actual point Ridderbos was making: once you believe that "Israel" in Isaiah 11 is "the church," you are liberated from the duty of interpreting all the details of the text. You need not bother about all those neighboring nations, you need not bother about the ten and the two tribes. It is more than enough that you understand that "Israel" is here "the church."

How could Ridderbos arrive at such an interpretation of the text? He worked within a tradition from which he could not separate himself. The Dutch States Translation wrote above Isaiah 11: "Prophecy that Christ would be . . . setting up a Kingdom by the preaching of his Word 4. And that the members of his church should live together in peace and unity, 6. And should at length get the victory over their spiritual enemies, they being brought to the knowledge of the Gospel, 11, 12, etc."[21]

Further comments are unnecessary.

What a blessing that, today, millions of Christians have come to see that, in Isaiah 11:9-16, God's holy mountain means God's holy mountain, Assyria means Assyria, Egypt means Egypt, Ephraim means Ephraim, Judah means Judah, and that Philistines, Edom, and Moab mean Philistines, Edom and Moab. There is always room for alternative interpretations, for instance, as to whether certain elements are literal or figurative. Are the wolf and the lamb, the cow and the bear in verses 6-7 to be taken literally or figuratively? Is "swooping down on someone's shoulder" in verse 14, and "waving the hand" over the Euphrates in verse 15, and the "highway" from Assyria to be taken literally or figuratively? Such questions leave the essence of the chapter unaffected. They are of a totally different order than a view that discovers "the church" in these verses and turns "defeated" Gentiles into "converted" Gentiles. The former questions have to do with common grammatical-historical *exegesis*; the latter betrays little more than pious *fantasy*.

---

21. Haak (1918, ad loc.).

9.4 More Isaiah Prophecies
9.4.1 Isaiah 28:7-19

The verses 7-19 in Isaiah 28 appear in a clearly Messianic context, given verse 16:

> Behold, I am the one who has laid as a foundation in Zion,
>   a stone, a tested stone,
> a precious cornerstone, of a sure foundation:
>   "Whoever believes will not be in haste [LXX: be put to shame]."

In the New Testament, this verse is quoted several times[22] and applied to Christ. Israel's adversary is the "overwhelming whip" (vv. 15, 18; cf. v. 2, "a storm of mighty, overflowing waters"). This is Assyria as we have already seen from Isaiah 8:7-8,

> [B]ehold, the LORD is bringing up against them the waters of the River [Euphrates], mighty and many, the king of Assyria and all his glory. And it will rise over all its channels and go over all its banks, and it will sweep on into Judah, it will overflow and pass on, reaching even to the neck, and its outspread wings will fill the breadth of your land, O Immanuel.

In Isaiah 28, we find four different parties: (a) the enemy threatening from outside, which is Assyria; (b) the unbelieving multitude of Israel; (c) the ally trusted (in vain) by Israel in order to protect it from Assyria; and (d) the believing remnant of Israel. It will be similar in the end time: there is the threatening enemy from outside, the unbelieving multitude and the believing remnant of Israel, and the false ally, which in the end time seems to be the restored Roman Empire, the "beast" of Revelation 13 and 17.

Although Assyria is the enemy in Isaiah 28—an enemy one might suppose belonged entirely to the past—this part of the book (chapters 28-29) culminates in prophecies about the Messianic kingdom:

> Is it not yet a very little while / until Lebanon shall be turned into a fruitful field, / and the fruitful field shall be regarded as a forest? / In that day the deaf shall hear the words of a book [or, the Book], / and out of their gloom and darkness the eyes of the blind shall see [cf.

---

22. Rom. 9:33; 10:11; Eph. 2:20; 1 Pet. 2:6-8; cf. Ps. 118:22; Matt. 21:42; Acts 4:11.

32:1-3]. ... / Jacob shall no more be ashamed, / no more shall his face grow pale. / For when he sees his children, / the work of my hands, in his midst, / they will sanctify my name; / they will sanctify the Holy One of Jacob / and will stand in awe of the God of Israel. / And those who go astray in spirit will come to understanding, / and those who murmur will accept instruction (Isa. 29:17-18, 22-24).

9.4.2 Isaiah 52:13-53:12

The fourth prophecy concerning the Servant of the LORD (see §7.14) is found in Isaiah 52:13-53:12. Orthodox Christian expositors agree that this Servant is the Messiah, and also that many details in this passage must be taken literally: his sufferings, his being pierced, his vicariously bearing the punishment, his grave "with a rich man," his expiating his people's sins, and so on.[23] Why, then, do supersessionists not take the rest of the passage literally as well, where we hear of the restoration and the re-acceptance of Israel that had previously been "cast off" (Isa. 54)? Why do they suddenly wish to abandon the literal interpretation, and refer these things — casting off and restoring — to the church?

The Annotations to the Dutch States Translation commented on Isaiah 54:1, "Here the Prophet speaketh to the Church of believing Jews, that should live at the time when the Gospel should begin to be preached, as may be gathered from *Gal. chap. 4, verse 27*, where these words are quoted, ..."[24] However, Galatians 4 does not at all refer to the first-century "congregation of believing Jews." The apostle Paul was juxtaposing two orders of things: the order of Judaistic legalism (Hagar, Sinai) and the order of sovereign grace (Sarah, Zion). Each (religious) person belongs to either of the two orders, whether he or she is a Jew or a Gentile. This has nothing to do with either the first-century "congregation of the believing Jews," or with Israel in the end time, for that matter. Paul was simply freely applying the fundamental principle of Isaiah 54:1.

No, the authors of the Annotations, or other supersessionists, cannot afford to continue lounging in exegetical vagueness and fuzziness; we need accurate exegesis here. If they are on the right

---

23. Cf. extensively, Ouweneel (2000, chapter 2).
24. Haak (1918, ad loc.); cf. also the exegetical attempts of some ancient authors at http://bible.cc/isaiah/54-6.htm.

track, let them explain to us how they wish to view Israel's restoration here as entirely fulfilled in the return from the Babylonian exile, whereas the text was clearly referring to the work of Christ on the cross, as well as to the Messanic kingdom (53:12; 54:10-14). The text unambiguously refers to the restoration of the Israel that was once cast off, within the framework of the establishment of the Messianic kingdom. Applying these things to the Ecclesia—in whatever ingenious way—has been inspired only by the supersessionist bias.

Or take this example from the book of Zechariah: "I will strengthen the house of Judah, and I will save the house of Joseph. I will bring them back because I have compassion on them, and *they shall be as though I had not rejected them,* for I am the LORD their God and I will answer them" (Zech. 10:6). I ask supersessionists to explain the following points: (a) the distinction between Judah (the two tribes) and Joseph (the ten tribes), (b) the "bringing back" (from where to where?), (c) the "rejection" as well as the re-acceptance of the people. In reference to Israel, this is all crystal clear; in reference to the Ecclesia, this is all murky and cloudy—unless the "rejected" people is ethnic Israel and the re-accepted people is the New Testament Ecclesia, which are two totally *different* peoples. What is lacking is common grammatical-historical interpretation, and what we are given is biased imagination.

Supersessionist Bible expositors do not know what to do with such passages as the ones mentioned. They limit themselves to some vague, general references to the Ecclesia of Christ without taking the trouble of indicating how, then, all the rich details of the texts have been fulfilled in the Ecclesia. If we believe in the inspiration of the Scriptures, must we not assume that all those details have their divinely given sense and meaning? Supersessionist exegesis neglects the details. What are the "pinnacles," the "gates" and the "wall" in Isaiah 54:12? To what city was the text referring? What would the first readers have understood by the text?

It goes on like this almost infinitely: what mountains and hills and what marvelous trees are meant in Isaiah 55:12-13? What is God's "house" and "walls," the "holy mountain," the "house of prayer," the burnt offerings and sacrifices and "my altar" (56:5-7)? It is all spiritualized, and thus effectively argued away. Supersessionists do not listen to Jesus, who knew perfectly well what the text was talking about: *he explicitly applied it to the literal temple in Jerusalem* (Matt. 21:13), and this should be an example to all expositors. We do not have the right to understand the text differently than Jesus did. He did not make some kind of midrashic application, but he simply took the passages at face value, as every contemporary Jew would have done: God's "house" is the literal temple, God's "altar" is the literal altar, God's "mountain" was the Temple Mount, north of the City of David. The offerings and sacrifices were literal animal offerings on altar of burnt offering in the temple.

Now the fascinating thing about Isaiah 54 and subsequent chapters is that these features were linked with the end time and with the Messianic kingdom. Does this necessarily change their meanings? Of course not. On the contrary, the prophecies in the Tanakh are full of indications that there will still be a literal temple on a literal mountain, with a literal altar and with literal offerings (Ezek. 40–45 and many other places). The fact that, in the New Testament, there are also references to a spiritual (figurative, symbolic) temple and a spiritual altar, a spiritual mountain and spiritual offerings, does not affect this at all. Only the supersessionist bias asserts that these spiritual things have replaced the literal things, or that texts about the literal things must now be interpreted in the light of these spiritual things. Hermeneutically, there is not the slightest basis for such an approach. We understand Isaiah 54–56 as Jesus apparently understood these prophecies, as Jesus' contemporaries apparently understood them, and as the first Jesus-believers apparently understood them. They would all have been filled with astonishment, or worse, indignation, if they could have seen and heard what supersessionists make of them. Hermeneutically speaking, it is a mortal sin if dogmatics dominates exegesis instead of the other way around. The question *What does the Bible say?* should never surrender to the question *What does our theology say that the Bible is supposed to say?*

9.5   Other Major Prophets
9.5.1   Jeremiah

For the covenant theology of Reformed supersessionists, Jeremiah 31:31–34, dealing with the New Covenant, is of the utmost importance. Rightly so. As we have seen several times, the passage clearly appears in a Messianic context (see 30:9 on "David their king"; see also 33:14-22). However, it also appears in the midst of the great "return prophecies": Israel as well as Judah will return to the promised land and will rebuild the land and the city (30:3, 18; 31:8, 19; 32:37).

This leads us immediately to the central question: Is it possible or conceivable that the establishment of the New Covenant is eschatological, whereas in the return prophecies the fulfillment would be suddenly restricted to the return from the Babylonian exile? However, in Jeremiah 32:37-40, the people of Israel who are gathered from all the lands to which they had been dispersed are the *same* people as the ones with whom God makes his "eternal covenant"! So what is it? The return prophecies refer to the return from the Babylonian captivity, and thus must be interpreted *literally*, whereas the establishment of the New Covenant refers to the Ecclesia, so that now the ten tribes and the two tribes must suddenly be understood *figuratively*? However, in the text these matters cannot be separated at all: God made his covenant with the returning *twelve* tribes, and did so nowhere else than in the promised land, and did so under nothing but the blessed rule of the Messiah in his kingdom. The text is that simple and straightforward. Supersessionists force a separation upon the text that—I repeat—has been inspired by their biases but not at all by the text itself.[25]

Believers from the Gentile world, too, come under the blessings of the New Covenant, as we have seen in chapter 5.[26] But this is not the subject here. The text was speaking of the New Covenant that would be made with no one other than the house of Israel (the ten tribes) and the house of Judah (the two tribes), which have returned from the lands to which they had been dispersed. They are restored to the land of promise and enter the Messianic kingdom of peace and justice. This can be understood only if it is not restricted to the restoration after the Babylonian exile, but includes especially the eschatological restoration of Israel, which is explicitly linked with the establishment of the Messianic kingdom: "[T]hey shall serve the LORD their God and David their king, whom I will raise up for them" (Jer. 30:9). See especially the conclusion of this part of Jere-

---

25. So, e.g., Aalders (1925, 77-94).
26. See extensively, Ouweneel (2011a, chapters 1-4).

miah (33:14–16):

> Behold, the days are coming, ... when I will fulfill the promise I made to the house of Israel and the house of Judah. In those days and at that time I will cause a righteous Branch to spring up for David, and he shall execute justice and righteousness in the land. In those days Judah will be saved, and Jerusalem will dwell securely. And this is the name by which it will be called: "The LORD is our righteousness."[27]

Some may spiritualize these things to refer to the Ecclesia, to being redeemed from the power of sin and death and devil, and to being placed under the blessed rule of Christ in heaven. However, this is the central hermeneutical question: *How do these expositors know that this is the right approach?* On the basis of the text as such? No—they know this exclusively because of the supersessionist bias. *But what does the text say?* The Jews are dispersed among the nations. But one day, God will bring them back to the land from which their fathers had been driven away, and then he will place them under the blessed rule of the Messiah, in their *own* land, in their *own* city, in their *own* temple, and then the earth will be full of righteousness and justice.

This is what the text says. And why is the text not allowed to simply say what it says? The Ecclesia *is* not Israel; it is something very different. Something very beautiful, but different. And when God is nearly finished with it ("when the fullness of the Gentiles has come in," Rom. 11:25), he will pick up the thread with his ancient people of Israel (presuming he had let go of this thread in the first place). Today, Israel is returning to its own land, according to God's own promises—to the land where their forefathers had lived for so many (thirteen or fifteen) centuries. (Israelites have been living in the land of Israel virtually uninterruptedly for the last 3250 or 3550 years.) And then the Messiah will come (for the second time, this time not on a donkey, but on the clouds of heaven), and will establish among them, as God had promised many times, his kingdom of peace and justice, a kingdom extending over all the earth. This is the plain story that these prophetic texts are telling us. No supersessionist theories will be able to eliminate the plain meaning of these texts.

---

27. Cf. Jer. 23:5–6; Zech. 3:8–10; 6:12–13; see Ouweneel (2007b, 170–71).

9.5.2 Ezekiel 36

In Ezekiel 34-37, we find clear references to the coming Messianic kingdom, in which the Messiah, referred to as "David," will rule (34:23-24; 37:24-25). Here the Messiah is King over Israel. This is enormously significant, for it places these chapters in an unmistakably eschatological context. *Everything* that was being described in these chapters stands in this framework of the restoration of Israel and the introduction of the Messianic kingdom.

First, God will judge all the nations that throughout history have treated Israel badly (Ezek. 36:3-7). These are literal nations just as Israel is a literal nation; it is the end of serious exegesis when some apply this to the "spiritual powers" that throughout the centuries have threatened God's Ecclesia. The angelic princes behind these nations are "spiritual powers,"[28] but never the nations as such. Countries such as Egypt and Babylon may serve a typological function in the Bible, but this never means that they no longer have a literal role in the subsequent history of Israel.

Second, God will bring the people of Israel back to the promised land, where it will flourish again and will dwell in safety (Ezek. 36:8-15). It is exegetically untenable to apply this to the Ecclesia because it is impossible to explain this promised "land" as a land *where the Ecclesia had formerly dwelt*. The escape routes taken by supersessionists are either "heaven" — usually mistakenly understood as the end station where believers go when they die[29] — or the new heavens and the new earth. However, either in "heaven" (the hereafter) or on the new earth, will all the different trees that have been promised for the Messianic kingdom continue to grow?[30] Or are these spiritual trees? And will babies continue to be born in heaven or on the new earth?[31] Or are these spiritual babies? But in particular: the Ecclesia has never before lived in "heaven" (the hereafter) or on the new earth, therefore these can never be places to which the Ecclesia is *brought back*. People A (Israel) returns to place B (Israel); this is "fulfilled" in people C (the Ecclesia) going

---

28. See extensively, Ouweneel (2003a).
29. See extensively, Ouweneel (2020).
30. See, e.g., Isa. 41:19; 55:13; 60:13; Ezek. 34:27; Micah 4:4.
31. See, e.g., Ps. 22:31; 78:6; Isa. 65:20, 25.

(not returning!) to place D (heaven or the new earth)!?

Third, there is here also a judgment coming upon Israel because this nation has shed innocent blood in its land, has served the idols there—the gods of the neighboring nations—and has desecrated God's name among the Gentiles. God will manifest himself as the Holy One to his own people. Applying this in detail to the Ecclesia requires an overactive exegetical imagination.

Fourth, God will richly bless Israel spiritually, but also materially (Ezek. 36:29-39). This spiritual aspect might be easily applied to the Ecclesia, but with the material aspect this is far more difficult:

> I will summon the grain and make it abundant and lay no famine upon you. I will make the fruit of the tree and the increase of the field abundant, that you may never again suffer the disgrace of famine among the nations. Then you will remember your evil ways, and your deeds that were not good, and you will loathe yourselves for your iniquities and your abominations. . . . On the day that I cleanse you from all your iniquities, I will cause the cities to be inhabited, and the waste places shall be rebuilt. And the land that was desolate shall be tilled, instead of being the desolation that it was in the sight of all who passed by. And they will say, "This land that was desolate has become like the garden of Eden, and the waste and desolate and ruined cities are now fortified and inhabited." Then the nations that are left all around you shall know that I am the LORD; I have rebuilt the ruined places and replanted that which was desolate. I am the LORD; I have spoken, and I will do it (Ezek. 36:29-36).

Not a single concrete application to the Ecclesia is possible here; again, supersessionist exegesis must degenerate into a number of fuzzy spiritualizations. This is always the approach: the literal character of the restoration prophecies are referred to—and limited to—Judah's return from the Babylonian captivity,[32] and the Messianic prophecies—which are inextricably interwoven in these texts—are kidnapped from them and applied to the Ecclesia.[33] This exegetical

---

32. Noordtzij (1932, 2:112): "Thus, justice is done to these verses in chapter 37 only if in them Israel's imminent future is disclosed, and to the doubting nation is given the assurance of the return [from Babylon], soon to be expected, to the land of the fathers."

33. Cf. the comments above Ezek. 36 in the Dutch States Translation: "By the speech directed to the mountains of Israel, God foretelleth that he will in great

approach of ripping from the text certain verses that appear within in a *coherent totality*, in order to interpret them in a way very different from that of surrounding verses, is a mortal sin. No science of literature could ever allow this approach to ancient texts. Again, dogmatics is dominating exegesis here. This is bad it itself, but it is even worse when the superimposed dogmatics is mistaken.

9.5.3   Ezekiel 37:15-22

Quite remarkable is also the supersessionist exegesis of Ezekiel 37:15-22, which deals with the reunion of the two tribes (Judah) and the ten tribes (Israel). This exegesis raises certain questions: Was the intention of the text that this reunion will occur at the beginning of the Messianic kingdom? If yes, where do these ten tribes come from? Or is the reunion something that occurs gradually throughout Israel's history? In addition to Judah and Benjamin (cf. Phil. 3:5), there were Levites (Luke 10:32; John 1:19; Acts 4:36) and Asherites (Luke 2:36) (and Ephraimites? John 11:54) in New Testament Jewry. Quite a few modern Israelis claim their descent from the ten tribes.

Far more complicated is the supersessionist interpretation. The Dutch States Translation writes above Ezekiel 37: "... He prophesieth also under the token of joining two sticks together in one hand, that he will gather his catholic Church of Jews and Gentiles, and unite them under one King and Shepherd, the Messiah Jesus Christ, ..."[34] Compare this with what the prophet is telling us. The ten *Israelite* and the two *Israelite* tribes—no Gentiles—will all be gathered from the Gentile nations among which they had been dispersed (as a punishment!), and will be brought back to *their own land*, the ancient land of Israel, and joined together on the *mountains of Israel* (vv. 21-22). I fail to see how the text can be twisted to say that the ten tribes are now Gentiles, the two tribes, are Jews, and how "the land" can be the Ecclesia. Among what countries has the Ecclesia been dispersed by way of punishment? To what land—where it had formerly dwelt!—has the Ecclesia been brought *back*? What objective reader could ever characterize this as valid exegesis? It is in-

---

zeal execute vengeance upon the enemies of his Church, that had derided, oppressed, and made havoc of her, ... and that he will most gloriously restore, multiply, and bless her, ..."

34. Haak (1918, ad loc.).

valid *eisegesis*, reading into the text whatever one wishes, inspired by the theological biases of supersessionism.

Here indeed, there is a veil over people's faces (cf. 2 Cor. 3:13-15); the similarity to non-Jesus-believing Jews is striking: the majority of Israel does not do justice to the Messiah prophecies, and the majority of Christianity does not do justice to the Israel prophecies. One day, believing Israel will acknowledge its Messiah, and one day, believing supersessionists will acknowledge Israel. In both cases, the veil will be removed (cf. 2 Cor. 3:16). Both events will occur in the kingdom of Jesus Christ, whose center will be the throne of David in Jerusalem. Many orthodox Jews do not believe in such a Christ-centered kingdom—but one day, some of them will. Many orthodox Christians do not believe in such an earthly kingdom, either—but one day, some of them will.

The LORD "will swallow up on this mountain the covering that is cast over all peoples, the veil that is spread over all nations" (Isa. 25:7). The blind spot of (the majority of) Israel is Jesus; the blind spot of (the majority) of Christianity is Israel. One day, from both groups many will be healed if they convert to the Messiah of Israel. For the Jews, the emphasis will lie on "Messiah": Jesus is their Messiah. For the Christians, the emphasis will lie on "Messiah *of Israel*": Jesus is first and foremost the Messiah of Israel, the people restored to their land who will become the center of the earth.

9.5.4 Daniel

We turn now to consider a few passages in Daniel that shed light on the future of the people of Israel, which has suffered so much under the four world empires (from the Babylonian to the Roman one). The time will come when their sufferings will be over; that is, when the Messiah will appear, and will establish his kingdom:

(a) After the description of the descent of the Son of Man to whom all power and dominion are given (Dan. 7:13-14), we read that he will share this dominion with the "people of the saints of the Most High," which, in the context of this book, cannot be anything other than the people of Israel (cf. vv. 15, 22, 25):

> And the kingdom and the dominion
> > and the greatness of the kingdoms under the whole heaven

shall be given to the *people of the saints of the Most High*;
their kingdom shall be an everlasting kingdom,
   and all dominions shall serve and obey them (Dan. 7:27 ESV note).

In the English rendering, the words "their" and "them" must be used because "people" in English is a plural term; the Hebrew text uses the singular because "people" (Heb. *'am*) is singular. One might properly render: ". . . the holy nation of the Most High; its kingdom shall be an everlasting kingdom, and all dominions shall serve and obey it." Just as long ago, Joseph's brothers bowed down before him (Gen. 44:14; cf. 37:7-8), so one day the nations of the world will bow down before Israel.[35]

(b) In §7.1.1, we briefly considered Daniel 9:24-27, the prophecy of the seventy weeks, that is, weeks of seven years each. The center of the prophecy is the Messiah, who is cut off after sixty-nine weeks (483 years) have passed. His being cut off (his death) is essential for making the fulfillment of verse 24 possible: "Seventy weeks are decreed about your people and your holy city, to finish the transgression, to put an end to sin, and to atone for iniquity, to bring in everlasting righteousness, to seal both vision and prophet, and to anoint a most holy place."

There can be no doubt about what people the angel Gabriel meant when he spoke to Daniel about "your people and your holy city." It was *their* purification, justification, and restoration that was in view, in order to fulfill all the prophecies, including the anointing of "the Most Holy": the sanctuary in the restored temple, the "holy of holies."

(c) In Daniel 12:1-3 we read:

At that time [i.e., the time of the end, 11:35, 40[36]] shall arise Michael, the great prince who has charge of your people [i.e., Israel]. And there shall be a time of trouble, such as never has been since there was a nation till that time. But at that time your people shall be delivered, everyone whose name shall be found written in the book [i.e., the book of life, or the book of God's counsels]. And many of those [among your people] who sleep in the dust of the earth shall awake, some to

---

35. Cf. Gen. 27:29; Isa. 45:14; 49:23; 60:14.

36. I am omitting here an analysis of the complicated passage in Daniel 11:36–45, which would require us to consider too many exegetical details.

everlasting life, and some to shame and everlasting contempt. And those who are wise shall shine like the brightness of the sky above; and those who turn many to righteousness, like the stars forever and ever.

The Hebrew word for "the wise," mentioned in verse 3, but also in 11:33, 35 and 12:10, is *maskilim*,[37] "those who have spiritual insight and understanding." In chapter 11, these overlap with the wise men in the days of the Maccabees; but in the end time in Israel (Dan. 12), these are the "teachers" who will instruct the people insofar as the latter are open to divine instruction and understanding (see further in §10.7.2).

9.6 Some Minor Prophets

9.6.1 Hosea

The prophet Hosea proclaimed:

> [T]he children of Israel shall dwell many days without king or prince, without sacrifice or pillar, without ephod or household gods. Afterward the children of Israel shall return and seek the LORD their God, and David their king, and they shall come in fear to the LORD and to his goodness in the latter days (Hos. 3:4–5).

Nobody doubts that the expression "David their king" referred here to the Messiah, and that verse 4 refers to the destiny of Israel, which is the consequence of its sins. They will be without the means of atonement, and even without their idols. Why, then, would anyone doubt what is said here about the restoration of Israel "in the latter days"? Earlier we considered the eschatological significance of this technical expression. The *same* Israel that, through its own apostasy, has been forced to endure such a long physical and spiritual exile, will ultimately meet its "David" (the Messiah) and enjoy God's salvation in the Messianic kingdom.

Interestingly, this was one of the Bible passages that, for instance, during the Dutch Second Reformation, led Johannes Cocceius and Wilhelmus à Brakel to the conviction of Israel's future

---

37. From Heb. *haskalah*, "enlightenment, understanding"; cf. also the Heb. term *Maskil* above thirteen Psalms (32–42), possibly meaning something like "skillful" or "instructive [poem]."

spiritual as well as national restoration.[38] In my opinion they were absolutely correct.

9.6.2 Joel

Joel 2 is known to virtually all Christians because the apostle Peter quoted it on the Day of Pentecost (Acts 2). Let me quote it in Peter's version (Acts 2:17-21; see Joel 2:28-32a):

> And in the last days it shall be . . .
> that I will pour out my Spirit on all flesh,
> and your sons and your daughters shall prophesy,
> > and your young men shall see visions,
> > and your old men shall dream dreams;
> even on my male servants and female servants
> > in those days I will pour out my Spirit, and they shall prophesy.
> And I will show wonders in the heavens above
> > and signs on the earth below,
> > blood, and fire, and vapor of smoke;
> the sun shall be turned to darkness
> > and the moon to blood,
> > before the day of the LORD comes, the great and magnificent day
> And it shall come to pass that everyone who calls
> > upon the name of the LORD shall be saved.

Because Peter quoted these words in connection with the outpouring of the Holt Spirit, people might easily think that what happened on that day reported in Acts 2 was the *entire* fulfillment of Joel 2:28-32a. Yet, Peter does not use the word "fulfill"; he uses the less specific and more careful expression: "This is what was uttered through the prophet Joel" (v. 16). No wonder: there is at best resemblance, or preliminary fulfillment, but certainly not *complete* fulfillment. In Acts 2, there were definitely *no* "wonders in the heavens above and signs on the earth below, blood, and fire, and vapor of smoke," and the sun was *not* "turned to darkness and the moon to blood." If it had been otherwise, the Bible would have certainly told us. At the *complete* fulfillment, these miraculous signs in the sky *will* indeed happen (cf. Matt. 24:29; Rev. 6:12; 8:12); this complete fulfillment will occur at the beginning of the Messianic kingdom, when there will be another outpouring of the Holy Spirit, announced by

---
38. Van Campen (2007, 196, 297); cf. Brakel (1949); Graafland (1978).

the prophets.[39]

If we make this important distinction between a preliminary and a complete fulfillment, we will better understand the sequel as we find it in Joel 3:

> For behold, in those days and at that time, when I restore the fortunes of Judah and Jerusalem, I will gather all the nations and bring them down to the Valley of Jehoshaphat. And I will enter into judgment with them there, on behalf of my people and my heritage Israel, because they have scattered them among the nations and have divided up my land, and have cast lots for my people, and have traded a boy for a prostitute, and have sold a girl for wine and have drunk it (vv. 1–3).

In the light of Acts 2, the outpouring of the Spirit as described in Joel 2:28 is understood literally. But what about these words in Joel 3? Must we now suddenly begin to spiritualize: Judah and Jerusalem are the Ecclesia? The Valley of Jehoshaphat—a particular valley near Jerusalem—must be taken figuratively? And tell us, what does it mean that "the nations" have *scattered* God's Ecclesia among "the nations," nations that have "divided up" God's land? *What* land? Again, supersessionists must resort here to vagueness and imagination, whereas a literal understanding renders the main line of the passage immediately clear. At the time of Israel's restoration, God will gather the nations near Jerusalem, and judge them there for all the evil things they have done to Israel, such as scattering it among the nations, and dividing up the land of Israel for themselves.

God said to the nations: "I will sell your sons and your daughters into the hand of the people of Judah, and they will sell them to the Sabeans, to a nation far away" (Joel 3:8). Try to spiritualize this! And then there is this triumphant final word:

> The LORD roars from Zion, / and utters his voice from Jerusalem, / and the heavens and the earth quake. / But the LORD is a refuge to his people, / a stronghold to the people of Israel. / "So you shall know that I am the LORD your God, / who dwells in Zion, my holy mountain. / And Jerusalem shall be holy, / and strangers shall never again pass through it." . . . / "Egypt shall become a desolation / and Edom a desolate wilderness, / for the violence done to the people of

---

39. Isa. 32:15; 44:3; Ezek. 36:27; 37:14; Zech. 12:10.

Judah, / because they have shed innocent blood in their land. / But Judah shall be inhabited forever, / and Jerusalem to all generations. / I will avenge their blood, / blood I have not avenged, / for the LORD dwells in Zion" (Joel 3:16-21).

This is one of those many biblical-prophetic descriptions—brief though it is—of the blessings of the Messianic kingdom: Judah will dwell in its own land again, Jerusalem will be in peace, and even the LORD himself will dwell in Zion, in the midst of his people.

9.6.3 Micah

The prophet Micah told us:

> [Y]ou, O Bethlehem Ephrathah,
>   who are too little to be among the clans of Judah,
> from you shall come forth for me
>   one who is to be ruler in Israel,
> whose coming forth is from of old,
>   from ancient days (Micah 5:2).

The verse belongs to the well-known Messianic texts that are often quoted during Christmas, but usually out of context (just as happens with Isaiah 9:6). Each Christian sees this text literally fulfilled in Matthew 2:1-12 and Luke 2:1-7, where Jesus' birth in Bethlehem is described. Is it not obvious then that we should take the sequel just as literally?

> Therefore he [i.e., God] shall give them [i.e., Israel] up until the time when she who is in labor has given birth [i.e., presumably; the time of Israel's labor pains,[40] i.e., the Great Tribulation[41]]; then the rest of his brothers [i.e., the Jewish brothers of the Messiah] shall return to [or, with (the rest of)] the people of Israel [i.e., Israel will be one again, both nationally and spiritually]. And he [i.e., the Messiah] shall stand and shepherd his flock in the strength of the LORD, in the majesty of the name of the LORD his God. And they shall dwell secure, for now he shall be great to the ends of the earth. And he shall be their peace. When the Assyrian comes into our land and treads in our palaces, then we will raise against him seven shepherds and eight princes of

---

40. Cf. McComiskey (1985, 428); e.g., Allen (1976, 345), however, thinks of Mary, the mother of the promised Messiah.
41. Cf. Jer. 30:7; Dan. 12:1; Matt. 24:21; Rev. 7:14.

men; they shall shepherd the land of Assyria with the sword, and the land of Nimrod at its entrances; and he shall deliver us from the Assyrian when he comes into our land and treads within our border. Then the remnant of Jacob shall be in the midst of many peoples like dew from the LORD, like showers on the grass, which delay not for a man nor wait for the children of man (Micah 5:3-7).

Apart from a few difficult matters of exegesis, we find here basically the same pattern as in so many other prophecies:[42] the literal Messiah, literally born in Bethlehem, will be the ruler of a literal Israel, which will literally return to the other literal Israelites who had remained behind in the literal land. Then, the literal Assyria will be defeated, and be driven out of the literal land of Israel, after which the literal Israel will enjoy the blessed dominion of the literal Messiah. It is hard to read the text in a different way when we abandon theological biases, like those we find in what the Dutch States Translation wrote above Micah 5: "A Prophecy . . . of his [i.e., Christ's] royal feeding and governing of his, and of the power and means of his Church against her enemies . . . of the wonderful growth, terribleness, victoriousness, safety and holiness of the Church, and God's vengeance against the disobedient."[43] This is also the spirit in which J. Ridderbos wrote: "As to the *fulfillment* [of vv. 2-6], at the last day [!] the world power that is hostile to God and his people is fully put down. But a preliminary fulfillment is given every time he uses the power granted to him (Matt. 28:18) to curb the powers threatening his church."[44]

9.6.4 Zechariah

(a) The prophet Zechariah made this appeal in 9:9:

> Rejoice greatly, O daughter of Zion!
> Shout aloud, O daughter of Jerusalem!
> Behold, your king is coming to you;
> righteous and having salvation is he,
> humble and mounted on a donkey,
> on a colt, the foal of a donkey.

---

42. I am ignoring the speculative hypothesis that in Micah very different parties were speaking alternately.
43. Haak (1918, ad loc.).
44. Ridderbos (1930, 98).

Everyone understands this prophecy in a literal sense, also because of its quotation in Matthew 21:5 and John 12:15 (Jesus' entry into Jerusalem on a donkey). Why do so many Christians not do the same with the following verse

> I will cut off the chariot from Ephraim
>   and the war horse from Jerusalem;
> and the battle bow shall be cut off,
>   and he shall speak peace to the nations;
> his rule shall be from sea to sea,
>   and from the River [Euphrates] to the ends of the earth
> (Zech. 9:10).

This described the restoration of Israel to its own land, the definitive abolition of war, and the introduction of the Messianic kingdom of peace and justice. But no, J. Ridderbos again smoothly moves from the literal to the figurative interpretation: "Through these two names [i.e., Jerusalem and Ephraim], the prophet wishes to describe the future people of God [read, the Ecclesia] in its fullness" (cf. the superscription of Ezek. 37 in the States Translation, quoted above).[45]

About the following verses (Zech. 9:11–10:3a), Ridderbos wrote,

> [T]he essential fulfillment is brought about here too by Christ's twofold coming, and lies, on the one hand, in the gathering of the elect from all nations, today [gathered] to the spiritual Zion, the Ecclesia of God, and one day to the heavenly Jerusalem; on the other hand, in the protection that Christ grants his Ecclesia today, and in the final victory over all the power of the enemy that he will grant her one day.[46]

How does this exegesis do justice to the text? It does not, but it is *imposed* upon the text because of the dogmatic (supersessionist) bias.

(b) The middle part of Zechariah 12:10 (KJV), "[T]hey shall look upon me whom they have pierced," is understood literally by each Christian, especially because of the quotation in John 19:35–37, "[O]ne of the soldiers pierced his side with a spear, and at once there came out blood and water. . . . For these things took place that the

---

45. Ridderbos (1952,129).
46. Ibid., 136.

Scripture might be fulfilled: 'Not one of his bones will be broken' [Exod. 12:46; Num. 9:12]. And again another Scripture says, 'They will look on him whom they have pierced.'" However, if we understand this literally, why do we not interpret the context literally?

> And I will pour out on the house of David and the inhabitants of Jerusalem a spirit [or, the Spirit] of grace and pleas for mercy, so that, when they look on me, on him whom they have pierced, they shall mourn for him, as one mourns for an only child, and weep bitterly over him, as one weeps over a firstborn. On that day the mourning in Jerusalem will be as great as the mourning for Hadad-rimmon in the plain of Megiddo.[47] The land shall mourn, each family by itself: the family of the house of David by itself, and their wives by themselves; the family of the house of Nathan by itself, and their wives by themselves; the family of the house of Levi by itself, and their wives by themselves; the family of the Shimeites by itself, and their wives by themselves; and all the families that are left, each by itself, and their wives by themselves (Zech. 12:10-14).

When we view the broader context, the entire passage culminates in the Messianic kingdom (Zech. 13-14). We hear about the outpouring of the Holy Spirit upon Israel at the beginning of Messiah's kingdom of peace (12:10;[48] cf. note 37), when the veil is removed from Israel (2 Cor. 3:16) and it recognizes its Messiah, and wails over him. This was what Joseph's brothers did when the royal brother, whom they had thought dead, manifested himself to them (Gen. 45). We are dealing here with literal Israel, literal Jerusalem, and the literal houses of David, Nathan, and Shimei (Zech. 12:12-14).[49]

What did J. Ridderbos make of this? This prophecy referred first to the outpouring of the Spirit on the Day of Pentecost. The fact

---

47. This presumably referred to the mourning for the fallen King Josiah (2 Kings 23:29; 2 Chron. 35:22), who, as a godly Davidic king, was a type of the Messiah.

48. Here I am following the translations and commentaries that have "Spirit," not "spirit."

49. Nathan is here the son of David (2 Sam. 5:14), and Shimei the grandson of Levi (Num. 3:1–2, 21); they stand here prototypically for the entire house of David and that of Levi, respectively, that is, for the royal and religious leaders of Israel.

that the Spirit who was then poured out is the Spirit of grace and of pleas for mercy, who inclines the hearts to the Pierced One, has become manifest first in those who, on the Day of Pentecost, were "cut to the heart" by Peter's preaching [Acts 2:37], ...[50]

Ridderbos went on to assert that from this it is "evident that the prophecy is not a literal copy of the fulfillment." But this interpretation does not do justice to the prophecy. Without any proof, Ridderbos stated in this context that "the prediction that *all* the people take part in the mourning is not fulfilled in the Israel according to the flesh, but only in the new Israel, gathered from Jews and Gentiles." Clearly this exegesis was being governed by replacement theology: the ethnic Israel has been replaced by the "new Israel."

Contrary to this, I believe that the *same* Israel "according to the flesh" that had once "pierced" the Messiah,[51] in the end repents of, and confesses, its sin, and thus is restored to its own land under the blessed rule of the Messiah (Zech. 14). The quotation from Ridderbos just given exposed one the most awkward aspects of supersessionism, namely its view that even though Israel according to the flesh that had committed the sin — and had to undergo the punishment for it — it is "Israel according to the Spirit" that supposedly undergoes the restoration and receives the Messianic blessings. For ethnic Israel there are, and remain, all the curses, for the "spiritual Israel" there are all the blessings. We are dealing here with two "Israels" that scarcely overlap: the one (98% non-Jesus-believing) has committed the sin and bears the curse for it; the other "Israel" (99% non-Jews) receives the forgiveness for this same sin, as well as the concomitant blessings. The reality, however, is that the latter "Israel" is no "Israel" at all, in any sense of the term.

I find in the Tanakh and in the New Testament only one Israel, as well as only one "Israel of God," that is, the penitent, believing, faithful, godly remnant of ethnic Israel. When Jesus returns, ethnic Israel will dwell in the land of Israel, as it does today. When the Messiah appears, many of them will repent and accept their Messiah in faith, mourning over what Israel had done to him. These Jews

---

50. Ridderbos (1952, 172).

51. One might argue that it was literally the Romans who crucified Jesus, but many Jews had made themselves co-responsible for this (Acts 2:23, 36; 4:10, three times "*you* crucified").

will not be *personally* responsible for the piercing of Jesus, but they will make themselves one with their ancestors, as Daniel had done in Daniel 9 ("*we* have sinned," vv. 5, 8, 11, 15). *This* is the "new Israel": the remnant of penitent, believing, faithful, godly Jews, who will be admitted to the Messianic kingdom and there enjoy God's blessings. All the time, it is and has been *one and the same Israel*: the ethnic Israel that failed, the ethnic Israel that repents, the ethnic Israel that is restored—thus constituting the "Israel of God"—and the ethnic Israel that enters the Messianic kingdom. The Ecclesia, the body of Christ, (even though containing a small number of believing Jews as well) is a very different phenomenon.

9.7 Not Everything Literal
9.7.1 Isaiah 11:6–8

To our arguments given so far, we must add that, of course, the word "literal" should not be understood too literally, in order to avoid the snare of literalism (exaggerated literality). Understanding prophecies literally does not require us to ignore the many metaphors and other stylistic figures that prophetic texts contain.[52] However, doing justice to metaphors and stylistic figures is something essentially different from spiritualizing terms like "Israel," "Judah," "Jerusalem," and "Zion" in order to apply these to the Ecclesia. Some examples from Isaiah may help to clarify the underlying hermeneutical principle.

> The wolf shall dwell with the lamb, / and the leopard shall lie down with the young goat, / and the calf and the lion and the fattened calf together; / and a little child shall lead them. / The cow and the bear shall graze [together]; / their young shall lie down together; and the lion shall eat straw like the ox. / The nursing child shall play over the hole of the cobra, / and the weaned child shall put his hand on the adder's den [without being hurt] (Isa. 11:6–8).

From the context it is evident, as is generally acknowledged, that the text was referring to the Messianic kingdom. Later, I will try to show that this is not the present form of the kingdom of God—everybody agrees on this point—but neither is it a description of the eternal state (the new heavens and the new earth), and

---

52. This may help Paas (2014, 24–27) to see that at least *my* "literality delusion" is not so bad after all.

certainly not of "heaven."⁵³ This is so because the text assumed that there are "the poor" who will be judged in righteousness (v. 4), and nations that will come to Israel to meet the Messiah there (vv. 9–10).

The subject of Isaiah 11 is the Messianic kingdom of peace, during which Israel will dwell again in its own land, and the Son of David will reign on the throne of David (cf. 9:7). However, this requires us to understand every detail in the text literally. For instance, one might debate whether the contrasts within the animal kingdom will be literally removed, as the text suggests (see also Isa. 65:25, "The wolf and the lamb shall graze together; the lion shall eat straw like the ox"). The exegesis of this passage also depends on the interpretation of Genesis 1:30, "[T]o every beast of the earth and to every bird of the heavens and to everything that creeps on the earth, everything that has the breath of life, I have given every green plant for food." Does this mean that before the Fall lions ate only vegetative food? In that case, they were no lions, for a lion has been designed, from head to tail, for hunting prey animals, and its intestinal tract cannot digest vegetative food.⁵⁴ Or does the text mean that, ultimately, all food of humans and animals goes back to vegetative food (e.g., lions eat herbivores)?⁵⁵

We need spend no more time on this matter. It is sufficient to state that a literal view of a Messianic kingdom after the second coming of Christ, with Israel as its center, does not necessarily demand a literal interpretation of all the details. In the case discussed here, we might be dealing with metaphors that represent the peace and righteousness of the Messianic kingdom. As far as wolf and sheep are concerned, one could think, for instance, of the same metaphors as in John 10:12 ("He who is a hired hand and not a shepherd, who does not own the sheep, sees the wolf coming and leaves the sheep and flees, and the wolf snatches them and scatters them"). As John Oswalt put it, "The most helpless and innocent will be at ease with those who were formerly the most rapacious

---

53. See extensively, Ouweneel (2020).

54. If we must assume that the change came through the Fall, we cannot say that God changed lions, for how must these have lived before the Fall? As non-predators? Rather, we would have to assume that God created the carnivores for the first time after the Fall—an idea that directly conflicts with Gen. 2:1.

55. Cf. Gispen (1974, 82).

and violent."[56] The Annotations to the Dutch States Translation might be right this time when commenting on Isaiah 11:8 (if we simply replace the word "church" by "Israel"): "... the meanest in the Church of God shall be in no fear or danger, that the great and mighty ones should any way hurt of mischieve them, forasmuch as they shall be converted unto Christ, as well as the meanest, as appeareth further, verse 9."[57]

9.7.2 Isaiah 40:4

In Isaiah 40:4: we read: "Every valley shall be lifted up, and every mountain and hill be made low; the uneven ground shall become level, and the rough places a plain"; compare 49:11, "I will make all my mountains a road, and my highways shall be raised up." Here, with even greater certainty, we can claim that the literal interpretation is not obvious. This is because, also during the Messianic kingdom, there will be mountains and hills: "It shall come to pass in the latter days that the mountain of the house of the LORD shall be established as the highest of the mountains, and shall be lifted up above the hills; and all the nations shall flow to it" (Isa. 2:2; also 55:12, "the mountains and the hills before you shall break forth into singing").

> But you, O mountains of Israel, shall shoot forth your branches [again] and yield your fruit to my people Israel, for they will soon come home. For behold, I am for you, and I will turn to you, and you shall be tilled and sown. And I will multiply people on you, the whole house of Israel, all of it. The cities shall be inhabited and the waste places rebuilt. And I will multiply on you man and beast, and they shall multiply and be fruitful. And I will cause you to be inhabited as in your former times, and will do more good to you than ever before. Then you will know that I am the LORD. I will let people walk on you, even my people Israel. And they shall possess you, and you shall be their inheritance, and you shall no longer bereave them of children" (Ezek. 36:8–12; cf. 37:22; Joel 3:18).

For a figurative interpretation, we may think, for instance, of the words spoken by Hannah, the mother of Samuel: "The LORD makes poor and makes rich; he brings low and he exalts. He raises up the

---

56. Oswalt (1986, 283).
57. Haak (1918, ad loc.).

poor from the dust; he lifts the needy from the ash heap to make them sit with princes and inherit a seat of honor" (1 Sam. 2:7–8; cf. Ps. 113:7–8), and the parallel words by Mary, the mother of Jesus: "He has shown strength with his arm; he has scattered the proud in the thoughts of their hearts; he has brought down the mighty from their thrones and exalted those of humble estate" (Luke 1:51–52).

9.7.3 Isaiah 55:12-13

We read in Isaiah 55:12–13:

> [Y]ou shall go out in joy and be led forth in peace; the mountains and the hills before you shall break forth into singing, and all the trees of the field shall clap their hands. Instead of the thorn shall come up the cypress; instead of the brier shall come up the myrtle; and it shall make a name for the LORD, an everlasting sign that shall not be cut off.

Here, the metaphorical meaning is even clearer than in the previous examples, certainly in verse 12, which speaks of singing mountains and clapping trees.[58]

Actually, it is possible that more was involved here. Elsewhere, I have argued that perhaps we must think here of elemental spirits, that is, spiritual powers that are associated with material elements: mountains, hills, trees, rivers, celestial bodies.[59] In Psalm 89:12, mention of praising mountains follows mention of Rahab, the prince of the chaos powers, especially Egypt;[60] thus, the notion of angelic powers is not far away. In Psalm 96:11–12, mention of the exulting field and the singing trees follows mention that the LORD is "to be feared above all gods" (v. 4), that is, angelic powers;[61] here again, the notion of angelic powers lies in the context.

That the heavens and the earth are exulting might be taken to mean that the inhabitants of heaven and earth are exulting.[62] However, in the case of the sea, the field, and the trees it is very well

---

58. Cf. 1 Chron. 16:33; Ps. 89:12; 96:11–12; 98:7–8; Isa. 35:1–2; 44:23; 49:13; 55:12.
59. See Ouweneel (2003a, 33–36, 319–20).
60. Ibid., 51–52, 93, 316–17.
61. Ibid., chapter 2; cf. Ps. 95:3–5, where the "gods" appear to be connected with earth and mountains, the sea and dry land; so too Ps. 97:9 and cf. vv. 2–5.
62. Cf. Job 15:15; Ps. 89:6; 96:1–3, 9–10; 97:1; 98:3–4; 99:1; 100:1.

possible to think of angels, the "gods" of the sea, the field, and the forest. Rivers "clapping their hands" (Ps. 98:8) is considered to be an even stronger anthropomorphism than "singing" or "exulting." This provides an even stronger indication that we must think here of the elemental spirits of rivers and mountains. Rivers and mountains do not have hands, but angels do.[63]

In Isaiah 44:23, especially the call to the "depths of the earth" is interesting because these remind us of Ephesians 4:9. This latter passage refers to the dark powers of the netherworld (*Sheol* or *Hades*, the realm of death). One day, these powers had to give back Christ from death, and in these passages in the Tanakh they are forced to exult over the redemption of Israel. This reminds us of Philippians 2:10, where Christ is brought homage by those who are in heaven and on earth, as well as those who are "underground" (Gk. *katachthonioi*): the powers of death and darkness. However, if these "depths of the earth" are linked with angelic powers, then it seems legitimate to assume this link also for the mountains and the trees in the passages quoted, as well as in Isaiah 49:13; 55:12.

9.8   Israel's Past and Future[64]
9.8.1   God's Faithfulness

The point has been made, and will continue to be made: the Ecclesia is not some "spiritual Israel"; it is a separate "project" of God, with very different characteristics. Therefore, the Ecclesia cannot adopt the promises and blessings of Israel. No doubt it *shares* certain blessings with Israel, but this is a very different matter. If A and B share certain features—like churches and synagogues sharing certain features—this does not mean they are identical; on the contrary, the fact of the sharing underscores their being distinct.

As we have seen, viewing the Ecclesia as the new "Israel" is a disastrous doctrine, basically tending to anti-Semitism,[65] that leaves the divine curses (Lev. 26; Deut. 28–29) to ethnic Israel, and transfers the divine blessings from ethnic Israel to some spiritual Israel,

---

63. Num. 22:23, 31; Judg. 6:21; 2 Sam. 24:16–17 par.; Rev. 8:4; 10:8, 10; 20:1.
64. Part of the following sections is an elaboration and extension of material from Ouweneel (1999, chapters 2–11).
65. I mean here genuine anti-Semitism, not only anti-Judaism; cf. Van Delden (1985, 63–64).

the Ecclesia. Of course, supersessionists argue repeatedly that this is not at all a different community but basically the same community that has existed from the beginning, though it has been expanded with millions of non-Jewish believers. But this is exactly *quod est demonstrandum*: the point that must be demonstrated. I have adduced many arguments for the following four considerations.

1. The Ecclesia of Jesus Christ did *not* begin with Adam and Eve, but began on the Day of Pentecost (recorded in Acts 2); that is, the Ecclesia is nowhere described as the collective term for all the regenerate of all time; this notion is nothing but a human invention.

2. There are not only phenomenological, but essential-theological differences between Israel and the Ecclesia, as we will see, so that it is impossible to believe that the two are basically the same.

3. The (believing) Israel of the Tanakh is never called "Ecclesia"; Acts 7:38 refers to the (not at all spiritual) assembly of natural ethnic Israel, and Acts 19:32 and 39–40 refer to the civic assembly or *ecclesia* of Ephesus.

4. In the New Testament, the Ecclesia—that is mainly, Gentile Jesus-believers—is never called "Israel," or is identified as belonging to Israel (in chapter 12, we will see more extensively that the olive tree of Romans 11 is *not* "Israel"); on the contrary, it is clearly distinguished from Israel (1 Cor. 10:32).

The only spiritual Israel that exists is the "Israel of God" mentioned in Galatians 6:16, that is, the Jesus-believing part of Israel, or more broadly, the godly part of Israel that has existed since Israel's beginning until today. These are Israelites who love the LORD and love his Torah, the *tzaddiqim*, the righteous and faithful ones. To *this* nation, the only true Israel known in the Bible, belong the promises and blessings of Israel; *this* is the "all Israel" that ultimately will be saved (Rom. 11:26; see further in chapter 12).

Romans 11:29 says that "the gifts and the calling of God are irrevocable." The Greek word for "gifts" is *charismata*, from *charis*, "grace"; these are gifts produced by God's mercy. The "calling" refers to Israel's calling by God. The term "irrevocable" (Gk. *ametamelēta*) means that God never regrets them, repents of them, never takes them back, or grants them to a different community, the Ecclesia. In principle, the unconditional promises once made to the patriarchs—promises concerning a concrete-physical land and a concrete-physical nation—are totally non-dependent on the responsibility of Israel as a whole. This is because they are not rooted in anything that human beings do or achieve, but entirely in the sovereign grace of God. To this must be added that the concrete, practical *application* of this grace can never be severed from human responsibility,[66] that is, they are granted to a faithful remnant, which has humbled itself, has repented, has been reborn through the Holy Spirit, and confides in God and his Torah.

Therefore, even in the greatest apostasy and the heaviest judgments, an unshakable promise remains, rooted in God's own being (Micah 7:18-20):

> Who is a God like you, pardoning iniquity
>   and passing over transgression
>   for the remnant of his inheritance?
> He does not retain his anger forever,
>   because he delights in steadfast love.
> He will again have compassion on us;
>   he will tread our iniquities underfoot.
> You will cast all our sins
>   into the depths of the sea.
> You will show faithfulness to Jacob
>   and steadfast love to Abraham,
> as you have sworn to our fathers
>   from the days of old.

Ultimately, the grace of God, centered in the person of Christ, will turn all things for the good of God's people: "Therefore, while the promise of entering his rest [i.e., the rest of the Messianic kingdom] still stands, let us fear lest any of you [i.e., Jewish Jesus-confessors!] should seem to have failed to reach it. . . . So then, there remains a Sabbath rest for the people of God [i.e., the Israel of God]" (Heb. 4:1, 9).[67] The Greek word for "Sabbath rest" is *sabbatismos*, derived from Hebrew *shabbat*. Thus, even in the context of announcing the most severe judgment, the prophets spoke of Israel's ultimate restoration as well, and of its future blessings under the

---

66. Regarding this vast subject, see Ouweneel (2008b).

67. It is strange that Stern (1999, 673) reads in this an admonition to keep the Shabbat, a matter that lies entirely outside the scope of Heb. 4.

glorious rule of the Messiah. This was done by Ezekiel and Jeremiah, despite the fact that they were prophesying during the time of the (first) fall of Jerusalem.

In this respect, we must clearly distinguish between the partial, short-term fulfillment of the restoration promises—in particular the return from Babylon after the seventy years of captivity[68]—and the eschatological, complete, and definitive fulfillment of the restoration promises, connected with the coming of the Messiah and the establishment of his kingdom in power and glory. The prophets speak not only of the first coming of the Messiah and the sufferings that would come upon him, but also of the "subsequent glories" (1 Pet. 1:11).

9.8.2 A Hermeneutical Key

What we have just now considered constitutes an essential hermeneutical key to understanding the biblical prophecies. It is this: *no single biblical prophecy has yet been completely fulfilled*. I am speaking here of written prophecies, not oral prophecies, spoken by certain prophets and recorded by certain authors. That is, I am not referring to a prophecy such as this one by the man of God from Judah, who spoke against King Jeroboam's altar: "O altar, altar, thus says the LORD: 'Behold, a son shall be born to the house of David, Josiah by name, and he shall sacrifice on you the priests of the high places who make offerings on you, and human bones shall be burned on you.'" (1 Kings 13:2). Or take this example of Elijah, who spoke to King Ahab: "As the LORD, the God of Israel, lives, before whom I stand, there shall be neither dew nor rain these years, except by my word" (17:1). These were not *written* prophecies; they were *oral* prophecies, recorded afterward in written form. There are many of them; but they are not my subject right now.

What I mean is this: even written prophecies that clearly refer to the first coming of the Messiah—his birth, his preaching, his sufferings, his death, and resurrection—have *never* been fulfilled in all their details. They *always* refer also to the coming of the Messianic kingdom, when the hostile nations will be judged, Israel will be the center of the world, the Messiah will sit on the throne of David, and peace and justice will fill the earth. These descriptions of the Mes-

---

68. Jer. 25:11–12; 29:10–14; cf. 2 Chron. 36:21; Dan. 9:2.

sianic kingdom, no matter how dismissive supersessionists may be regarding their literal meaning, are always formulated in the most "earthly" terms. This is because Christ will be the *literal* king of a *literal* ethnic nation, Israel, and beyond this, of the entire world, seated upon the *literal* throne of David. Therefore, in Jeremiah and Ezekiel, he is explicitly contrasted with the wicked kings from the house of David, his ancestors, who at the time ruled over Judah.

Consider Jeremiah 23:1–8, at the center which we read about the Branch sprouting from the Davidic tree, that is, the Messiah: "Behold, the days are coming, . . . when I will raise up for David a righteous Branch, and he shall reign as king and deal wisely, and shall execute justice and righteousness in the land" (v. 5), that is, in the *same* land over which, and on the *same* throne on which, the false kings were reigning, *not* some "spiritual" land or some "heavenly" throne. If we claim the latter, we ruin the entire thrust of the prophecy. The prophet was arguing that, one day, a *good* (righteous) King would rule over that same land, sitting on the same throne. He would have made a fool of himself had he intended to say that one day, the bad Davidic kings would be replaced by a good King, the Messiah, though in a different land, and sitting on a different throne in a context that has nothing to do with ethnic Israel. This interpretation eviscerates the power of the prophecy.

The same pertains to Ezekiel 17, which speaks of the unfaithfulness and apostasy of King Zedekiah; it is contrasted as follows:

> I myself will take a sprig from the lofty top of the cedar [i.e., the house of David] and will set it out [in the soil]. I will break off from the topmost of its young twigs a tender one, and I myself will plant it on a high and lofty mountain. On the mountain height of Israel will I plant it, that it may bear branches and produce fruit and become a noble cedar. And under it will dwell every kind of bird; in the shade of its branches birds of every sort will nest. And all the trees of the field shall know that I am the Lord; I bring low the high tree, and make high the low tree, dry up the green tree, and make the dry tree flourish. I am the Lord; I have spoken, and I will do it (Ezek. 17:22–24).

The language of the entire chapter is metaphorical (the cedar, the twig, the eagles), but the meaning is literal: instead of the false Judean kings, especially the last one, Zedekiah, one day a one of their distant descendants, the Messiah, would reign, over that same land, over that same people, and on that same throne, the ancient throne of David (see further in Jer. 30–33).

Very sharp is the contrast in Ezekiel 21:25–27:

> And you, O profane wicked one, prince of Israel [i.e., Zedekiah], whose day has come, the time of your final punishment, thus says the LORD God: "Remove the turban and take off the crown. Things shall not remain as they are. Exalt that which is low, and bring low that which is exalted. A ruin, ruin, ruin I will make it. This also shall not be, until he comes, the one to whom judgment belongs [or, the one who is entitled to it], and I will give it to him [i.e., the Messiah]" (see further in Ezek. 33–39).

9.8.3 The First and the Second Exile

The final promises for Israel are often strongly linked to the first return to the land of Israel after the seventy years of exile in Babylon. When the prophecy spoke of this return, blessings were often mentioned that the people in those days did not receive; rather, they would receive them in the future. Such blessings include a king from the house of David, seated on the throne of David in Jerusalem, the reunion of the two and the ten tribes, the judgment over all the enemies of the people, the central place that they would occupy in the earth, the peace and justice, the prosperity and rest in the Messianic kingdom. In other words, in the prophecies (sixth century BC), the first return (from Babylon) merged as it were with the return in the end time, a return from *all* the countries of the world.

A consequence of this is that the first exile, that is, the seventy years in Babylon, merged with the second exile,[69] which began with the second destruction of Jerusalem in AD 70, and to some extent will be going one until the (re-)appearance of the Messiah (only then, the last Jews will return to the land). We find this, for instance, in Jeremiah 30–31, where the return from the Babylonian exile was linked to the future blessings of the Messianic kingdom. We find

---

69. Sometimes called the third exile, so that the one in Egypt was the first, and the one in Babylon the second (cf. §2.3.4); for the parallels between the Egyptian and the Babylonian exiles, cf. e.g., Isa. 43:14–21; 51:9–11. The Egyptian exile was not literally punishment, although certainly the consequence of a sin: selling Joseph to Ishmaelites and eventually into slavery in Egypt (Gen. 37).

the same in Hosea 3, where the people went into exile, and where the exile ended with the future King "David." In Deuteronomy 28–32, too, the great prophecy of Moses, we find the same principle: because of Israel's unfaithfulness and apostasy, the great city would fall. This referred both to the first (586 BC) and to the second (AD 70) conquests of Jerusalem. After this, we hear of the first as well as the second exiles, united into one, and the eschatological return with the ultimate blessing and restoration.

In Zechariah 2:7–12, too, we see how, after the Babylonian exile, God shows mercy to his people again, and how the people return from Babylon to Zion. But here again, the blessing mentioned will become reality only in the future. This is because we read: "'[B]ehold, I come and I will dwell in your midst,' declares the LORD. And many nations shall join themselves to the LORD in that day, and shall be my people. 'And I will dwell in your midst'" (vv. 10–11). Nowhere in Ezra and Nehemiah do we read that the *Shekhinah* (the glorious presence of the LORD) descended upon the new temple that was built by the Davidic royal son Zerubbabel and the high priest Jeshua (or Joshua). This is quite remarkable![70] The *Shekhinah*, which left the former temple at the time of King Zedekiah (Ezek. 9–10), would return to the temple at the beginning of the Messianic kingdom (Ezek. 43). This is the same as saying that the LORD would come again to dwell in the midst of Israel.

This point is very important for the correct translation of Ezra 1:3 and similar passages. The Hebrew says, . . . *et-bêth* YHWH *Elohē Yisraēl hu ha'Elohim asher birushalayyim*, literally: ". . . the house of the LORD, the God of Israel—he is God—which/who is in Jerusalem." There are two options: it is either "the God of Israel who is [dwells] in Jerusalem," or "the house of the LORD, the God of Israel, which is in Jerusalem." Some translations have "who," others have "which." On the basis of verses 4 and 5, it seems clear that the second translation is the correct one because in these verses the middle words are lacking, so that we read: ". . . the house of God (or, the LORD) that is in Jerusalem." We cannot say that, during the Second Temple period, God "dwelt" in Jerusalem, because the *Shekhinah*

---

70. Presumably, this lack formed the background for Haggai 2:4 (the glory of the new temple was so much less than that of the former one).

Israel in Prophecy in the Tanakh

had not descended.[71] The *house* of God was in Jerusalem, but not the *God* of that house. Rabbinic tradition, too, has acknowledged this problem, and has searched for the significance of this remarkable fact.[72]

Here we have the key for understanding the link between the first and the second exiles. In the period comprising these exiles, the people were without the *Shekhinah*, without God's presence in their midst. Formally, it is not even God's people anymore: *Lo-'Ammi* ("Not-My-People") is written over Israel (Hos. 1:9). Nor was this the time of (i.e., characterized by) *the* nation, but the "times of the nations" (Luke 21:24 DRA), a period that will end only with the end of the second exile. Thus, the return of the remnant from Babylon was not a restoration of the special connection between Israel and its God. How small was that handful of people that returned from Babylon (in Ezra 2:64 only 42,360)! This was a fraction of all Jewry, whereas by far the great majority of them remained in the (former) Babylonian empire. This return was not the restoration of the entire nation, but the return of only a small group of Jews in order to found a Jewish state, which after a "short while" (about six hundred years) would be dispersed again. Also spiritually, this was a "short while" indeed, for in the redemptive history in the Bible very little was told us about this period, and the four hundred years between the Tanakh and the New Testament remain largely obscure (apart from Daniel's predictions about the period until the Syrian King — "king of the North" — Antiochus IV Epiphanes; Dan. 7-11).

What then was the intention of this re-establishment of a Jewish state, which was dependent on the world powers, which lacked the *Shekhinah*, and which would cease to exist after a few centuries? From a redemptive-historical point of view, especially *this* seemed to be the main intention: God brought a remnant back to the land in order to present to this small remnant the Messiah — not in the

---

71. Therefore, Jesus, standing next to the temple of Herod, could say that his body was the true temple (John 2:19), for the *Shekhinah* dwelt in him, not in the temple.

72. According to Rabbi Samuel ben Inia (Talmud: Yoma 21b), five things were lacking in the new temple as compared with the previous one: the ark (cf. Jer. 3:16), the holy fire (cf. 2 Chron. 7:1), the *Shekhinah*, the Holy Spirit (but see Hagg. 2:6), and the Urim and Thummim (but Ezra 2:63 and Neh. 7:65 do refer to them).

royal dignity that he will publicly possess in the future, but as the suffering Servant of the LORD (see the four prophecies on him in Isa. 42–53). This was in order to submit part of the nation to God's last and also greatest test: their attitude toward the Anointed of the LORD. We know how, in this greatest trial, the people of Jerusalem failed most miserably by rejecting their Messiah and killing him. As one of the earliest martyrs, Stephen, put it:

> You stiff-necked people, uncircumcised in heart and ears, you always resist the Holy Spirit. As your fathers did, so do you. Which of the prophets did your fathers not persecute? And they killed those who announced beforehand the coming of the Righteous One, whom you have now betrayed and murdered, you who received the Torah as delivered by angels and did not keep it (Acts 7:51–53).

After this, the Jewish nation, to the extent that it lived in Jerusalem and Judea, was driven away again under God's providence, and Jerusalem with its temple was destroyed again. And all of this under the ongoing dominion of the world powers, that is, the "times of the nations."

Chapter 10
Israel is Not the Ecclesia

[B]rothers, I want you to understand this truth which God formerly concealed but has now revealed, so that you won't imagine you know more than you actually do. It is that stoniness, to a degree, has come upon Isra'el, until the Gentile world enters in its fullness; and that it is in this way that all Isra'el will be saved. As the Tanakh says, "**Out of Tziyon will come the Redeemer; he will turn away ungodliness from Ya'akov and this will be my covenant with them**, . . . **when I take away their sins**."

Romans 11:25–27 (CJB)

Give no offense to [these three very different groups:]
   Jews or to
   Greeks [i.e., Gentiles] *or to*
   the church of God.

1 Corinthians 10:32

10.1 Israel and the Ecclesia
10.1.1 Three Models

IF WE WISH TO SEE the place Israel occupied in the biblical prophecies, we must choose from among three available models:[1]

(1) *Supersessionism (replacement theology)*: the Ecclesia (the church of the New Testament)[2] is the "spiritual Israel," that is, the redemptive-historical continuation of ethnic Israel featured in the Tanakh. It is basically the same Israel as in the Tanakh, although, on the one hand, it is limited to the Jesus-believing part of Israel and, on the other hand, it has been expanded with millions of Gentile Jesus-believers. The latter are now "spiritual Jews." The prophecies in the Tanakh concerning Israel are being fulfilled in the Ecclesia. In these prophecies, there is no room for a national and spiritual future of ethnic Israel as such. Thus, the land promise is no longer literally applicable; it must be understood according to its spiritual sense.

There *is* room, though, for the conversion of each individual Jew, even for many Jews. This conversion entails that such Jews come to faith in Jesus Christ as their Messiah and Redeemer. In this way, they become members of the Ecclesia, the body of Christ, and are supposed to join one of the many Christian denominations, setting aside everything that is specifically Jewish.

(2) *Dispensationalism*: this is the doctrine of dispensations, that is, successive, and very distinct, epochs in redemptive history. The Ecclesia is a divine project, fundamentally distinct from Israel. The Israel prophecies in the Tanakh are understood literally; in the end time, they are fulfilled in ethnic Israel, in the literal land of Israel. The Ecclesia and Israel are, redemptive-historically, two distinct "peoples of God," each with its own character, its own calling, and its own destiny. They *are* linked, though, because both are founded upon the one atoning work of Christ; this means that dispensationalism does not teach two paths of salvation;[3] there is only one path for receiving eternal salvation, and this is through (faith in) Christ and his redemptive work.

This model, though, does not exclude the possibility that, after redemptive history has ended, in the eternal state, that is, in the

---

1. Cf. Ouweneel (2010a, chapter 3).

2. I am avoiding the term "church" because of its organizational and denominational connotations, certainly to Jewish ears. I will use the New Testament term Ecclesia, which is the (basically invisible) body of Christ, consisting of all true Jesus-believers, Jewish and Gentile.

3. The term comes from Rosenzweig (1996); cf. Hoek (2004, 82–84).

new heavens and on the new earth, there is ultimately *one* "people of God." Thus, there are several varieties of thought within dispensationalism:[4]

- Classical dispensationalism (J. N. Darby, C. I. Scofield, L. S. Chafer).
- Revised dispensationalism (Charles C. Ryrie, John F. Walvoord).
- Apocalyptic dispensationalism (Hal Lindsey, Tim LaHaye).
- Messianic dispensationalism (Moishe Rosen, Arnold Fruchtenbaum).
- Progressive dispensationalism (Craig A. Blaising, Darrell L. Bock).

The subtle distinctions between these varieties need not occupy us now.

(3) *Intermediate model*: there is only one "people of God," in the Tanakh and the New Testament, and in the end time, there is a people that might be called both "Israel" (in the broad spiritual sense of the term) and the Ecclesia. That is, the Ecclesia is "Israel" in the spiritual sense (which does not mean that ethnic Israel has been done away with), and the true Israel in the Tanakh was the Ecclesia. In the end time, the Israel prophecies are literally fulfilled in ethnic Israel. That is, there is a national as well as a spiritual restoration of ethnic Israel, in the literal land of Israel, such that the Jesus-believing Jews find their place within the Ecclesia.

The correspondence between model (1) and model (3) is that, in both cases, the Ecclesia has existed since Adam and Eve, an Ecclesia that, since the Exodus, may be called the "spiritual Israel," or the "Israel of God."

The similarity between model (2) and model (3) is that, in both cases, the Israel prophecies in the Tanakh are understood literally: in the end time, there is a national and spiritual of ethnic Israel in its own land.

J. B. Payne was a Christian thinker who chose model (3), and explicitly criticized both model (1) and model (2).[5] He maintained

---

4. Cf. Sizer (2004, 119).
5. Payne (1980, 107).

both the reality of the coming kingdom of Israel on earth, and, at the same time, the confidence that Israel's saved citizens will belong to the New Testament Ecclesia. The supersessionists reject the first half of this statement, and the dispensationalists reject the second half. Payne criticized both parties for thereby rejecting the truth. It seems that in the Netherlands and elsewhere, a growing number of Reformed theologians are adopting a similar position.[6]

10.1.2 Similarities

In fact, my choice among these three models was made already in my ecclesiology.[7] I have extensively defended the following claims:[8]

(a) The Ecclesia in the true New Testament sense is the body of the glorified Man, Jesus Christ, at the right hand of God (see more extensively the next chapter); as such, it cannot date from the time of Adam and Eve. The Ecclesia began on the Day of Pentecost (Acts 2).

(b) In the Tanakh, the Ecclesia was a "mystery," a concealed matter, which was revealed only by the apostles, in particular the apostle Paul.[9] If the Ecclesia existed already in the time of the Tanakh, how could she have been a hidden thing in those days?

(c) Jesus explicitly presented the Ecclesia as a thing that, at the moment he spoke of it, was still a matter of the future: "... on this rock *I will build my church* [Ecclesia], and the gates of Hades shall not prevail against it" (Matt. 16:18).

(d) The Ecclesia's existence as the body of Christ and temple of the Holy Spirit presupposes the glorification of Christ and the outpouring of the Holy Spirit; see John 7:39 ("as yet the Spirit had not been given, because Jesus was not yet glorified") and Ephesians 1:22–23 (God "put all things under his [i.e., Christ's] feet and gave him as head over all things to the church, which is his body, the fullness of him who fills all in all").

(e) The Ecclesia is "built on the foundation of the apostles and prophets, Christ Jesus himself being the cornerstone" (Eph. 2:20). In this order, "apostles and prophets," it is always the New Testa-

---

6. For a survey see Hoek (2004, 43–89).
7. Ouweneel (2010a; 2010b).
8. Cf. Ouweneel (2010a, §§2.4 and 3.1).
9. Eph. 1:9–11; 3:3–4, 9; Col. 1:24–27; cf. Rom. 16:25; 1 Cor. 2:7.

ment prophets who are meant. See Ephesians 3:5 (the mystery of the Ecclesia "has *now* been revealed to his holy apostles and prophets by the Spirit") and 4:11 (Christ gave to his church "apostles and prophets"; cf. 1 Cor. 12:28; Rev. 18:20). In Luke 11:49-51 and in 2 Peter 3:2, the order is reversed; here, clearly the prophets of the Tanakh are meant.

Actually, I would describe my own view as a (very) *moderate* form of dispensationalism. Thus, I do acknowledge, much more clearly than classical dispensationalism did and does, the undeniable fact that there are many *similarities* between believers in the Tanakh and believers of the Ecclesia.[10] I count at least seven similarities, which I briefly mention here (for a further elaboration of these points, see §11.4.1):

(1) Both groups of believers are — as far as it concerns post-Abrahamic believers — "sons," "seed," or "children" of Abraham, some of them only in the spiritual sense, others in both the physical and the spiritual senses.[11]

(2) Both groups love the Torah and live by it. This is the Torah of Moses or the Torah of Christ, respectively, which are nothing other than varieties of the one Eternal Torah.[12] At the same time, both groups live by the sovereign grace and mercy of God.[13]

(3) The members of both groups are described both as servants (slaves) of God and as sons of God, without these two terms being mutually contradictory.[14]

(4) Both groups are a holy nation, people of God, both royal and priestly in character (a kingdom of priests, a royal priesthood; Exod. 19:5-6; 1 Pet. 2:9).

(5) Both groups have been born again by the same Holy Spirit.[15]

(6) Both groups have been washed — either looking ahead or looking back in history — by the same blood of Jesus Christ (Heb. 9-10).

---

10. Ouweneel (2010a, §3.2.1).
11. Matt. 3:9; John 8:39; Rom. 4:11–12; Gal. 3:7, 29.
12. See extensively, Ouweneel (2020).
13. Exod. 34:6; Ps. 103:8; Eph. 2:5, 8; Gal. 6:2.
14. Lev. 25:55; Deut. 14:1; Rom. 6:18–22; 8:14–16; 2 Cor. 6:4, 18.
15. Ezek. 11:19; 36:25–27; John 1:12–13; 3:3–5; Titus 3:5.

(7) Both groups are justified (i.e., declared to be righteous) on the basis not of works, but of faith, though this is a faith "working through love" (Gal. 5:6), that is, a faith *confirmed by* and *demonstrated in* appropriate deeds; and this commandment of love is the Torah of Christ.[16]

10.1.3 Differences

The similarities mentioned in the previous section are not evidence that Israel and the Ecclesia are one and the same thing. Israel and the Ecclesia, despite their similarities, are clearly two different divine projects. This becomes clear when we consider not only their similarities, but also their basic *differences*.[17] Again, I will mention seven such differences (see much more extensively, §11.4.2).

(1) Israel is a natural people, of which one becomes a member through physical birth; even if we consider only the "Israel of God," what binds these members together is primarily their physical relationship. The Ecclesia, however, is a purely spiritual people, of which one becomes a member through rebirth (regeneration; John 3:3–5) and the sealing with the Holy Spirit (Eph. 1:13).

We must relativize this difference a little, though, by pointing out, on the one hand, that in the Tanakh sometimes the term "Israel" referred to the true (spiritual, regenerate) "Israel," which is the faithful remnant of ethnic Israel (cf. Isa. 45:25; 60:21): the "Israel of God." On the other hand, "the church," considered outwardly and according to its responsibility, can also include nominal Christians, that is, unbelievers.[18] What remains, however, is the strictly ethnic character of Israel, the physical descendants of the twelve patriarchs. Such an ethnic character is entirely foreign to the Ecclesia, which is a multitude "from every nation, from all tribes and peoples and languages" (Rev. 7:9).

(2) For Israel, the highest blessing will lie in the Messianic kingdom; for the Ecclesia, the highest blessing will lie in the Father's house.[19]

Here again, some relativizing is needed. Ultimately, the high-

---

16. Gal. 6:2; cf. John 13:34; 1 Cor. 9:21; James 2:8-12.
17. Ouweneel (2010a, §3.2.2).
18. Rev. 2 and 3; cf. 2 Tim. 3:4–5; 4:3–4; 1 Pet. 4:17.
19. Regarding this, see Ouweneel (2012a, §13.2.2).

est blessing for both groups lies in the person of *Christ*; and since the "Father's house" is also compared to the temple (John 2:16), we may wonder whether the Father's house is not the heavenly place of worship during the Messianic kingdom. In this case, for *both* groups the Messianic kingdom is the important prospect, and afterward the eternal state (the new heaven and the new earth). In a certain sense, the Father's house may be viewed as what is going to be the heavenly counterpart of the earthly temple of Ezekiel 40-44.

(3) Israel as such was never associated with a glorified Man in heaven, at God's right hand. God dwelt (in the tabernacle, later in Solomon' temple) *in the midst of* the Israelites. The Tanakh never spoke of an individual dwelling of the Holy Spirit within a believer.[20] Insofar as the Tanakh spoke of the Holy Spirit working in and through the faithful of Israel, it was always referring to judges and prophets and to the divine power they needed for their ministry.[21] It was never a matter of the *person* of the Holy Spirit permanently dwelling *within* individual believers. Therefore, David could pray, "[T]ake not your Holy Spirit from me" (Ps. 51:11), whereas New Testament believers have heard Jesus saying: "I will ask the Father, and he will give you another Helper *to be with you forever*, even the Spirit of truth, whom the world cannot receive, because it neither sees him nor knows him. You know him, for he dwells with you and *will be in you*" (John 14:16-17).

The Ecclesia is the body of its glorified head in heaven, Jesus Christ, seated since his ascension at the right hand of God.[22] Moreover, the Ecclesia is the temple of God on earth, in which the Holy Spirit dwells permanently, while individual believers have been baptized in, and sealed and anointed with the Holy Spirit, both individually and collectively.[23] This makes the Ecclesia an absolutely special and unique phenomenon in all of redemptive history.

(4) We have seen that in the New Testament the Ecclesia was never described as some "spiritual Israel," nor as the "new Israel,"

---

20. Isa. 32:15; 44:3; Ezek. 36:27; Zech. 12:10 is eschatological.
21. E.g., Num. 11:25; Judg. 3:10; 6:34; 11:29; 13:25; 14:6, 19; 15:14; many times in Ezek.
22. Eph. 1:22-23; 4:15-16; 5:23; Col. 1:18; 2:19.
23. 1 Cor. 3:16; 6:19; 12:13; 2 Cor. 1:21-22; 6:16; Eph. 1:13; 2:20-22; 4:30; 1 John 2:20, 27.

nor as a part of Israel (in any sense of the term), nor have Jesus-believers been "grafted" into Israel (see §6.6.2 and below), or "incorporated" into Israel.[24] On the contrary, from Ephesians 2:11-22 and 3:3-11 it is evident that believers *from* the Gentiles as well as believers *from* Israel together form an entirely new project of God: the body of Christ (cf. also the "one flock" in John 10:16). In the New Testament, Israel and the Ecclesia always remain distinct entities. Consider, for instance, 1 Corinthians 10:32, where "the Jews" (Israel) and the "Ecclesia of God" stood distinctly alongside each other. Or consider Revelation 7, where the 144,000 from Israel (vv. 1-8) were clearly distinguished from the "great multitude that no one could number, from every nation, from all tribes and peoples and languages" (v. 9).

(5) In Galatians 6:16, the "Israel of God" cannot be the Ecclesia because the latter is clearly distinguished from it: what counts is whether one is "a new creation. And as for all who walk by this rule, peace and mercy be upon them, ***and*** upon the Israel of God." Although the expression "Israel of God" occurs only here, it refers to what—both in the Tanakh and in the New Testament—was described as the remnant of Israel, the humble, repentant, faithful, believing part of Israel, the *tzaddiqim*. One may differ about whether today this "Israel of God" is entirely part of the Ecclesia, or whether there are also *tzaddiqim* in Israel who are indeed humble, repentant, faithful, believing, though still blind to their Messiah, those whose eyes will be opened only at his second coming. Nobody can answer this question, I suppose; only God knows the answer.

Other passages[25] do not alter this total picture that the Ecclesia is *not* some "spiritual Israel" (see extensively, chapter 6). In Romans 11, the olive tree is *not* an image of Israel, into which believers from the Gentiles would have been grafted. This can be easily demonstrated: in Paul's description, Israel is not represented y the tree but only by the natural branches *of* this tree. These branches can be removed—and they *have* been partially cut off—while the tree remains the same. The best interpretation that is that the tree represents the Abrahamic blessings and promises—fulfilled in the person and work of Jesus Christ—a share in which Gentile believ-

---

24. Ouweneel (2010a, §3.3).
25. E.g., Acts 1:6; Rom. 2:28–29; 9:25–26; Heb. 8:8–12; 1 Pet. 2:10.

ers, too, have received according to God's promise (see previous section).[26]

(6) None of the undeniable parallelisms between Israel and the Ecclesia imply that the two would be identical. On the contrary, terms like "parallelisms," "similarities," and "correspondences" already indicate that we are speaking of two different matters, each of which retains its own character and position.[27] On the contrary, precisely because Israel and the Ecclesia are very different, the latter can never impede the blessings of ethnic Israel or take them over from Israel.

(7) The Ecclesia is a spiritual people (Acts 15:14; Titus 2:14), a spiritual temple (1 Cor. 3:16; Eph. 2:20-22), and looks forward to a "spiritual country" (cf. Heb. 11:16). It is a fundamental hermeneutical error to assume that, *therefore*, the physical Israel, the literal temple and city, and the literal land of promise have been done away with. The fact that the Ecclesia is a spiritual temple and city, is entirely distinct from the fact that, for ethnic Israel, there is the unshakable promise that, during the Messianic kingdom of peace and justice, literal Israel will dwell again in the literal land of promise, and in the literal city of promise, and will have a literal temple of promise with a literal altar of promise on the literal Mount Zion of promise. God will fulfill his promises to Israel, no matter how Gentile believers may have tried to poach them for themselves.

10.2 Israel Set Aside

10.2.1 "Rejection"

We must now discuss further the importance of Israel being set aside during the last nineteen-and-a-half centuries in connection with God's redemptive-historical dealings with the world. That Israel has been "rejected" for a time was the consequence of its rejection of its Messiah. This event—this "double rejection"—can best be summarized in these words by the apostles Paul and Barnabas, spoken to the Jews in Pisidian Antioch: "It was necessary that the word of God be spoken first to you. Since you thrust it aside and judge yourselves unworthy of eternal life, behold, we are turning to the Gentiles" (Acts 13:46) (see §§8.6 and 8.7). Indeed, Israel has

---

26. Ouweneel (2010a, §3.4).
27. Ouweneel (2010a, §3.5).

become *Lo-'Ammi*, as has become visible in the new exile that began in AD 70. At the same time, God began a great work among the Gentiles.

However, the book of Hosea (1:8–11: 2:1, 23), where we find the expression *Lo-'Ammi*, also makes clear that this condition will be only temporary: Hosea's wife "conceived and bore a son":

> And the LORD said, "Call his name Not My People [Heb. *Lo-'Ammi*],
>> for you [i.e., Israel] are not my people [Heb. *lo-'ammi*], and I am not your God."
> Yet [one day] the number of the children of Israel shall be like the sand of the sea,
>> which cannot be measured or numbered.
> And in the place where it was said to them, "You are Not My People [Heb. *Lo-'Ammi*],"
>> it shall be said to them, "Children of the living God" (Hos. 1:9–10).
>
> ... [A]nd I will say to Not My People [Heb. *Lo-'Ammi*], "You are my people [Heb. *'Ammi*]";
>> and he [i.e., Hosea's son, representing Israel] shall say, "You are my God" (Hos. 2:23).

We must not be afraid to use the term "rejection" here. When R. Pfisterer spoke of the "myth of the rejection" (of Israel),[28] he was discussing the idea of a *definitive* rejection. However, in the present context, election and reprobation do not stand in opposition to each other as they do in the Reformed doctrine of predestination.[29] H. Kraemer, was perfectly correct with regard to ethnic Israel: "Once chosen, always chosen."[30] However, please note that this is a *national* election essentially different from *eternal individual* election, in view of *eternal* salvation, which belongs to all true believers (e.g., Eph. 1:3–4). With regard to Israel, we are dealing with its *temporary* election as a chosen people *on earth*, irrespective of whether individual Israelites are saved for eternity. For this important distinction, see Romans 11:7, "Israel failed to obtain what it was seeking. The elect obtained it, but the rest were hardened." Here the *elect*

---

28. Pfisterer (1959, 274); see the interesting discussion of G. C. Berkouwer (1972, 326–34).
29. See Ouweneel (2008b, chapter 12).
30. Kraemer (1941, 27).

are those who were chosen for *eternal* salvation. But these *and* the "rest of Israel" that was "hardened" *all belong to Israel, the chosen people of God*. This one "chosen" people contains both eternally elect and eternally reprobate Israelites, depending on the presence or absence of *their* repentance and faith. The chosen *people* includes chosen *individuals* and non-chosen *individuals*!

Within the framework of Israel's *temporary* election as a chosen people *on earth* — temporary because it lasts only as long as the present earth will last — being temporarily set aside (until the second coming of the Messiah) need not be a contradiction at all. Romans 11:15 speaks explicitly of Israel's "rejection" (Gk. *apobolē*, from *apoballō*, "to cast away," "to reject"),[31] and says at the same time: "God has *not* rejected [Gk. *apotheomai*] his people" (v. 2), and this is because "the gifts and the calling of God are irrevocable" (v. 29). God has (temporarily) "rejected" his people in order to "accept" them again after this time (v. 15). What is "accepted" here is not the Ecclesia, but ethnic Israel, to the extent that it repents and returns to the LORD.

10.2.2 Always "God's People"?

Israel must never cling to its election as if being temporarily set aside were impossible. Consider Jeremiah's preaching in the temple (Jer. 7:1–15), where Israel responded to his appeal with indignation, as if being set aside were inconceivable: "This is the temple of the LORD, the temple of the LORD, the temple of the LORD" (v. 4); in other words: How could it be conceivable that God would have *his own* temple destroyed? And yet it happened. God is not bound to the temple; he can temporarily set it aside, just as he can temporarily set aside the entire city, or set aside the entire nation. But in every case the emphasis lies on the word "temporarily." On the one hand, being rejected is a terrible thing — let us not soften this by stressing the word "temporary." On the other hand, let us speak freely of Israel's having been set aside for a while — but with the emphasis on "for a while."

Being *Lo-'Ammi* is a full and gruesome truth. But the certainty that those who are *Lo-'Ammi* will become *'Ammi* again is a full and

---

31. Assuming that the text is speaking of God's rejection of Israel, and not Israel's rejection of the Messiah; see the discussion of this problem by Moo (1996, 693).

glorious truth. Let us not soften the truth of the *Lo-'Ammi*—but let us never speak of *Lo-'Ammi* without stressing the future *'Ammi* in response to supersessionists. Being *Lo-'Ammi* is a disciplinary measure in the sense that the *'Ammi* can never be undone. In my view, if someone were to ask whether Israel today is *'Ammi* or *Lo-'Ammi*, the answer ought to be: Israel is *always* God's people—but sometimes, in God's providential and redemptive-historical ways, the status of *Lo-'Ammi* must be applied to Israel. And be sure that this is not just a formality! The son always remains son, even when, as a temporary disciplinary measure, he must sit in his room during family meals.

The chance of being set aside is all the greater *because* Israel is God's chosen people—just as a good police officer is tougher on his own son than on the other boys in the gang. Notice the force of Amos 3:2,

> You only have I known
>   of all the families of the earth;
> *therefore* I will punish you
>   for all your iniquities.

Indeed, Israel can even be reduced in status to an ordinary nation: "Are you not like the Cushites to me, O people of Israel? . . . Did I not bring up Israel from the land of Egypt, and the Philistines from Caphtor and the Syrians from Kir?" (Amos 9:7). The LORD explicitly said: "I will remove Judah also out of my sight, as I have removed Israel, and I will cast off this city that I have chosen, Jerusalem, and the house of which I said, 'My name shall be there'" (2 Kings 23:27).

The rejection of Israel is a fact. So too is its future re-acceptance. And this works two ways. On the one hand, "Israel fans"—Steven Paas calls them "Israelists"[32]—exclaiming today that Israel is "God's people," should at least try to tell us *when* and *how* Israel, as *Lo-'Ammi*, has become *'Ammi* again. On the other hand, Paas and other supersessionists should answer the same question: When did *Lo-'Ammi*—which is one and the same people as *'Ammi*—become *'Ammi* again? I am afraid that, in their eyes, ethnic Israel is still, and

---

32. Basically, *all* Christians should be "Israelists" in the sense that all those who love the God of Israel and the Messiah of Israel should love the people of Israel, too, and rejoice in its glorious restoration.

will always remain, *Lo-'Ammi*, whereas the Ecclesia is now *'Ammi*. According to Hosea, the real answer to both the "Israelists" and the supersessionists must be this: Israel will become *'Ammi* again when it humbles itself and repents, returns to the LORD, and accepts its Messiah. Today, this is happening with a relatively small number of Jews; at the return of the Messiah, it will happen with a large multitude of them. This will be the —ethnic *and* believing—Israel that will enter the Messianic kingdom: "In the LORD all the offspring of Israel shall be justified [or, declared righteous] and shall glory" (Isa. 45:25). Or even more explicitly (because Israel's salvation is linked here to the Promised Land):

> Your people shall all be righteous;
> > they shall possess the land forever,
> the branch of my planting, the work of my hands,
> > that I might be glorified (Isa. 60:21).

10.2.3 Election and Responsibility

Israel's divine election definitely correlates with human responsibility, as is true for *all* divine election. Abraham was the first example of this. God said of him, "I have *chosen* him, that he may command his children and his household after him to keep the way of the LORD by doing righteousness and justice, so that the LORD may bring to Abraham what he has promised him" (Gen. 18:19). Notice both sides: on the one hand, sovereign election, on the other hand, the fulfillment of what God promised depends on a righteous life of Abraham and his offspring; as God had said earlier, "I am God Almighty; *walk before me, and be blameless*, that I may make my covenant between me and you, and may multiply you greatly" (Gen. 17:1-2). And later God said, "Abraham obeyed my voice and kept my charge, my commandments, my statutes, and my laws" (26:5).

The same applies to Israel as a whole. On the one hand, Israel's election is *unconditional*, depending on God's sovereign grace alone:

> The LORD your God has chosen you to be a people for his treasured possession, out of all the peoples who are on the face of the earth. It was not because you were more in number than any other people that the LORD set his love on you and chose you, for you were the fewest of all peoples, but it is because the LORD loves you and is keeping the oath that he swore to your fathers (Deut. 7:6-8).

And especially this passage showed us God's love for Israel, which is the guarantee for its future restoration (Jer. 31:2-6):

> The people who survived the sword [of Pharaoh]
>   found grace in the wilderness;
> when Israel sought for rest,
> the LORD appeared to him from far away.
> I have loved you with an everlasting love;
> therefore I have continued my faithfulness to you.
> Again I will build you, and you shall be built,
> O virgin[33] Israel!
> Again you shall adorn yourself with tambourines
> and shall go forth in the dance of the merrymakers.
> Again you shall plant vineyards
> on the mountains of Samaria;
> the planters shall plant
> and shall enjoy the fruit.
> For there shall be a day when watchmen will call
> in the hill country of Ephraim:
> "Arise, and let us go up to Zion,
> to the LORD our God."

This is the one side: God's electing love will guarantee the fulfillment of his promises to Israel: they will be "rebuilt" in their own land. That this goes much further than Judah's return to the Promised Land after the Babylonian captivity is shown especially by verse 6: the watchmen of Ephraim will encourage the ten tribes to go up to Mount Zion again, to serve the LORD there, thereby implying the reunion of the ten and the two tribes.

The other side is this: God makes the fulfillment of his promises dependent on Israel's faithfulness: "*[I]f* you will indeed obey my voice and keep my covenant, you shall be my treasured possession among all peoples, for all the earth is mine" (Exod. 19:5). "Pay attention to what I say. *Then* I will be your God, and you will be my people. In everything, live according to the way that I order you, *so that* things will go well for you" (Jer. 7:23 CJB). In God's *counsel*, it is certain that Israel is God's people, and will remain God's people as long as the present earth exists. But in God's *ways*, it is entirely

---

33. A remarkable designation, referring to the chaste character of the true "Israel of God" (cf. 2 Cor. 11:2).

conceivable that Israel is set aside for a time, and indeed has been, and that a substantial part of the people is lost forever.[34] In other words, Israel's ultimate restoration is certain because it is based upon God's irrevocable counsel. But as far as human responsibility is concerned, no restoration is conceivable without repentance and conversion, as will occur with the remnant of the people.

This seems to be a fixed order of things, confirmed in many respects, also with respect to God's church: (a) decline, (b) apostasy, (c) judgment upon the multitude of the company, (d) salvation for a humbled and penitent remnant.

10.3 Israel and the Ecclesia

10.3.1 Which Bride?

For centuries, then, Israel has been the rejected one, *and* at the same time it was, and always remained, the chosen one. In God's providential ways, it was Not-My-People (Heb. *Lo-'Ammi*) *and* at the same time, according to God's irrevocable counsel, it was, and always remained, My-People (Heb. *'Ammi*). In God's providential ways with Israel, the latter is the "disowned wife," the "wife cast off" (cf. Isa. 50:1, "for your transgressions your mother was sent away"; 54:6, ". . . a wife deserted and grieved in spirit, a wife of youth when she is cast off"). And at the same time, she is, and remains, God's married "wife." The imagery is sensitive: "'For I hate divorce!' says the LORD, the God of Israel. 'To divorce your wife is to overwhelm her with cruelty,' says the LORD of Heaven's Armies" (Mal. 2:16 NLT[35]). If God hates divorcing one's wife, then this must certainly be true for himself with regard to his own "wife," Israel. He may "disown" her for a while, but he can never "divorce" her forever (see the well-known "bridal" chapters: Isa. 54; Ezek. 16; Hos. 2).

In Romans 11:28 we find this very important and enlightening statement: "As regards the gospel, they [i.e., Israel] are enemies for your sake. But as regards election, they are beloved for the sake of

---

34. Regarding this very important subject of God's "counsel" and God's "ways," see Ouweneel (2008b, chapter 4).

35. To be sure, other renderings have been given as well, e.g., ESV: "For the man who does not love his wife but divorces her, says the LORD, the God of Israel, covers his garment with violence, says the LORD of hosts."

their forefathers." Israel is both of these things: enemies, because of their hostile response to Christ and the gospel, and beloved, because of God's irrevocable promises. Notice again that this is *one and the same* Israel. It is utterly mistaken to suggest that ethnic Israel are the enemies, and the Ecclesia ("spiritual Israel") are the beloved. Israel is Israel, and the Ecclesia are the "others" (Luke 20:16). No doubt, they are God's people in the present time, but *without* having adopted the promises and blessings that belong to the remnant of ethnic Israel alone.

What supersessionists suggest is this: God has "divorced" ethnic Israel, and instead, he (or, Christ) has "married" the Ecclesia. *But this is not graciously re-accepting the former wife*. This is rather as we read in Jacob's story: "Behold, it was Leah!" (Gen. 29:25). Can we not see the basic difference between, on the one hand, taking your former wife back—despite her former adultery—if she repents, and on the other hand, abandoning the former wife and marrying another woman? I repeat, the Ecclesia is not "Israel" in any sense; she is the "other one." (Actually, the parallelism with Jacob's story goes even deeper: God *has* associated himself with the Ecclesia, but in the end Jacob also gets his "Rachel," the woman who preceded Leah in Jacob's love! See §6.8.1.)

Hosea's story is the most beautiful—and touching—illustration of this. God tells the prophet: "Go, take to yourself a wife of whoredom and have children of whoredom, for the land commits great whoredom by forsaking the LORD" (1:2). God asks Hosea to marry a woman who God predicts will be unfaithful to Hosea, and will fall into adultery. Hosea does so; he marries Gomer. In verse 3 we read that Gomer "bore *him* a son," but with the next children (vv. 6 and 8) this "him" was conspicuously lacking; these must have been children born of "whoredom." In Hosea 2, this story is applied to God and Israel, but the restoration of the "marriage" was also foretold:

> I will remove the names of the Baals from her mouth, and they shall be remembered by name no more. . . . And I will betroth you to me forever. I will betroth you to me in righteousness and in justice, in steadfast love and in mercy. I will betroth you to me in faithfulness. And you shall know the LORD (vv. 17–20).

Hosea himself had to enact this by taking back unfaithful Gomer; at least this is the way I (and many others) read Hosea 3:1 (CJB): "*Adonai* said to me, 'Go once more, and show love to [this] wife [of yours] who has been loved by her boyfriend, to this adulteress—just as *Adonai* loves the people of Isra'el, even though they turn to other gods and love the raisin cakes [offered to them]." This cannot possibly refer to the Ecclesia. The *very same people* that had fallen into adultery—by serving the idols—was accepted by God again, as was explained in the remainder of Hosea 3: "For the children of Israel shall dwell many days without king or prince, without sacrifice or pillar, without ephod or household gods. Afterward the children of Israel shall return and seek the LORD their God, and David their king, and they shall come in fear to the LORD and to his goodness in the latter days" (vv. 4-5). How could anyone possibly understand this to be referring to church history?

10.3.2 "The Others"

In Luke 20:16, Israel is Israel, and the Ecclesia are "the others":[36] the owner of the vineyard "will come and destroy those tenants and give the vineyard to *others*" (Luke 20:16; cf. Matt. 21:43, "[T]he kingdom of God will be taken away from you and given to a people producing its fruits"). Israel is one "people," and the Ecclesia is the "other people."

Earlier we considered the parables of the wicked tenants and of the guests of the wedding feast; both parables illustrated the way Israel has been set aside (for a time). We now consider the parable of the excuses (Luke 14:15-24); here, the invitees did not wish to come, either, after which those are invited who are in the "streets and lanes of the city" (these were, I suppose, the remnant of Israel) and those on the "highways" and in the "hedges" (I take these to be believers from among the Gentiles). Each of these parables taught about the setting aside of unwilling Israel, and the message of salvation subsequently addressed to the *Gentiles* (the "others"). This truth was very extensively expounded for us in Romans 9-11 (see chapter 14 below).

In this way, salvation comes to the Gentiles, and thus the Eccle-

---

36. Gk. *alloi*, not *heteroi*; this means that here the emphasis is not that the Ecclesia *differs* from Israel—although it does—but that, after Israel's failure, she is God's alternative.

sia is formed. This is not some "spiritual Israel" — the Ecclesia are "the others," different from the set-aside-Israel. The Ecclesia is not some "spiritual Israel" to which millions of "spiritual Jews" from the Gentiles have been added. No, the Ecclesia is the company in which there is "neither Jew nor Greek" (Gal. 3:28; Col. 3:11); that is, converted Gentiles have not become some sort of "spiritual Jews," nor have converted Jews become some sort of "spiritual Gentiles" (although the official church has often forced them to behave like Gentiles). It is an altogether different company, neither Jewish nor Gentile. It is a special, and even unique, divine project.

Practically speaking, it is no wonder that all Jewish characteristics *did* disappear after a while in a church that has come eventually to consist of more than ninety-nine percent believers of Gentile descent. The Ecclesia began on the Day of Pentecost in Jerusalem (Acts 2), and for a time it was still completely Jewish. Notice the words of the brothers in Jerusalem to the apostle Paul: "You see, brother, how many tens of thousands of believers there are among the Judeans, and they are all zealots for the Torah" (Acts 21:20 CJB). Therefore, it was no doubt a work of God that already in Acts 8:1 and 4, after Stephen had been stoned to death, "there arose on that day a great persecution against the church in Jerusalem, and they [i.e., the believers in and around Jerusalem] were all scattered throughout the regions of Judea and Samaria." Thus, the gospel was spread throughout the entire land through the powerful testimony of Jesus-believing Jews.

Next, notice the transition to the Gentiles:

> Now those who were scattered because of the persecution that arose over Stephen traveled as far as Phoenicia and Cyprus and Antioch, speaking the word to no one except Jews. But there were some of them, men of Cyprus and Cyrene, who on coming to Antioch spoke to the Hellenists [i.e., Greek-speaking Gentiles] also, preaching the Lord Jesus (Acts 11:19–20).

A solemn moment! The gospel of Jesus Christ reached the Gentiles: Greek-speaking Jews testified to Greek-speaking Gentiles. The first local church in the Gentile world arose in Antioch, a Greek-speaking city in Syria, and today in Turkey.

Interestingly (and perhaps surprisingly), the apostles remained strongly tied to Jerusalem (cf. Acts 8:1). They were the only ones who stayed behind in the city, although it was to them that Jesus had given the command to go out over all the earth to preach to gospel to all the nations:

> Thus it is written, that the Christ should suffer and on the third day rise from the dead, and that repentance for the forgiveness of sins should be proclaimed in his name to all nations, beginning from Jerusalem. You are witnesses of these things. And behold, I am sending the promise of my Father upon you [i.e., the promise of the Holy Spirit]. But stay in the city until you are clothed with power [of the Spirit] from on high.[37]

The point is that the apostles did the last thing mentioned — stay in the city — but for a while failed to do the first thing mentioned — preach the gospel in the name of Jesus *to all nations*.

Although the apostle Peter was sent to guide the Roman centurion Cornelis and his people into the Ecclesia (Acts 10), Peter's ministry generally remained limited to Israel. Afterward, they even made a deal with the apostle Paul:

> [W]hen they [i.e., the believers in Jerusalem] saw that I had been entrusted with the gospel to the uncircumcised [i.e., the Gentiles], just as Peter had been entrusted with the gospel to the circumcised [i.e., the Jews] (for he who worked through Peter for his apostolic ministry to the circumcised worked also through me for mine to the Gentiles), and when James and Cephas [i.e., Peter] and John, who seemed to be pillars, perceived the grace that was given to me, they gave the right hand of fellowship to Barnabas and me, that we should go to the Gentiles and they to the circumcised (Gal. 2:7-9).[38]

In a sense, one could say that this Jesus-believing ministry among the Jews was spiritually ended at the destruction of Jerusalem (AD 70), when there was hardly a Jewish "church" remaining in the city (most Jewish Jesus-believers had fled to Pella in the region of Decapolis across the Jordan River). At this moment the typically

---

37. Luke 24:46-49; cf. Matt. 24:14; 28:19; Mark 16:15; Acts 1:8.
38. I believe that there are still good arguments for assuming that 1 and 2 Pet. were addressed mainly to Jewish Jesus-believers; cf., e.g., Grant (1902, 142–43); Tenney (1961, 347); if this is incorrect (as many expositors believe), then the arrangement of Gal. 2:7–9 was of short duration.

Jewish ministry of Peter and his colleagues made room for the ministry of Paul, to whom the true character of the Ecclesia had been revealed, as he explained it mainly in his letters to the Ephesians and the Colossians: the Ecclesia is the body of Christ, the house of God, the temple as the dwelling place of the Holy Spirit, the bride or wife of the glorified Man in heaven. None of these apostles—least of all Paul—proclaimed that this Ecclesia was the continuation of ancient Israel or *was* "(spiritual) Israel."

10.4 The Destruction of Jerusalem

10.4.1 Predictions

If we may believe certain theologians,[39] *all* the books of the New Testament were written before the fall of Jerusalem (AD 70). Many others have argued that at least Matthew, Mark, and Luke were written before this event. If this is correct, it is all the more remarkable that we find in the New Testament such specific prophecies about the destruction of Jerusalem by the Roman commander Titus.

The most direct prophecies were spoken by Jesus himself, about forty years before their fulfillment.[40] Without assigning these forty years more meaning than is warranted, I would note that in the Bible this was the biblical number of responsibility, of training (preparation), but also of warning. Think of Moses' forty years in the wilderness (Acts 7:30), his three times forty days on Mount Sinai, Israel's forty years in the wilderness (7:42; 13:18), Jesus' forty days in the wilderness, the forty days he spent with his disciples after his resurrection (1:3), and the like.

In the parable of the wedding feast, we heard about a city whose king sent an invitation to certain honored people for the wedding of his son (Matt. 22:1–14). But the citizens of this city rejected the invitation and killed the messengers of the king. What should the king do with such a city? "The king was angry, and he sent his troops and destroyed those murderers and burned their city" (v. 7). This was the judgment that would fall upon Jerusalem: it would fall to the flames because it had rejected the message of salvation.

The parable of the ten minas contains a similar announcement:

---

39. See, e.g., Robinson (2000).

40. I have argued elsewhere (Ouweneel, 2007b, §11.3.1) that I believe the year of Jesus' death and resurrection to have been AD 30 (not AD 33).

"... But his citizens hated him [i.e., the future king] and sent a delegation after him, saying, 'We do not want this man to reign over us'. . . . [The king:] 'But as for these enemies of mine, who did not want me to reign over them, bring them here and slaughter them before me'" (Luke 19:14, 27; cf. John 19:15, "Pilate said to them, 'Shall I crucify your King?' The chief priests answered, 'We have no king but Caesar'").

Jesus spoke directly about this judgment to (the inhabitants of) Jerusalem:

> [W]hen he drew near and saw the city, he wept over it, saying, "Would that you, even you, had known on this day the things that make for peace! But now they are hidden from your eyes. For the days will come upon you, when your enemies will set up a barricade around you and surround you and hem you in on every side and tear you down to the ground, you and your children within you. And they will not leave one stone upon another in you, because you did not know the time of your visitation [i.e., the time that God in his grace and mercy visited you]" (Luke 19:41–44).

These people did not understand what they were despising, and in their sinfulness they rejected salvation in Christ. They were blind to what could have saved them. Therefore, they would have to bear the consequences.[41] As Jesus said a bit later:

> [W]hen you see Jerusalem surrounded by armies, then know that its desolation has come near. Then let those who are in Judea flee to the mountains, and let those who are inside the city depart, and let not those who are out in the country enter it, for these are days of vengeance, to fulfill all that is written. Alas for women who are pregnant and for those who are nursing infants in those days! For there will be great distress upon the earth and wrath against this people. They will fall by the edge of the sword and be led captive among all nations, and Jerusalem will be trampled underfoot by the Gentiles, until the times of the Gentiles are fulfilled (Luke 21:20–24).

---

41. In Gal. 6:7, this principle is described as follows: "[W]hatever one sows, that will he also reap." Cf. Job 4:8, "[T]hose who plow iniquity and sow trouble reap the same"; and Prov. 22:8, "Whoever sows injustice will reap calamity, and the rod of his fury will fail."

10.4.2 The Crimson Thread

Jesus Christ died, rose again, and ascended to heaven in AD 30. This was forty years before the fall and destruction of Jerusalem. We find a highly remarkable passage in the (Babylonian) Talmud:

> Our Rabbis taught: "During the last forty years before the destruction of the Temple [i.e., since AD 30!] the lot ["For the LORD"] did not come up in the right hand [of the high priest, on *Yom Kippur*, half a year after Jesus' Pesach sacrifice]; nor did the crimson-colored strap [of the scape goat] become white; nor did the western-most light [in the sanctuary] shine; and the doors of the *Hekal* [Temple] would [each time] open by themselves."[42]

The Jerusalem Talmud says, "Forty years before the destruction of the Temple the western light went out, the crimson thread remained crimson, and the lot for the LORD always came up in the left hand. They would close the gates of the Temple by night and get up in the morning and find them wide open."[43]

Here, four spectacular miracles are mentioned, all of which occurred between AD 30 and 70:

(1) Before 30, on *Yom Kippur* (the Day of Atonement), when the lots were cast (see Lev. 16:8), the lot called "For the LORD" often — in fifty percent of the cases or more frequently? — appeared in the right hand of the high priest (cf. Prov. 16:33, "the decision [of the lot] is from the LORD"), and the other lot, the one "For Azazel" (concerning the scape goat) in the left hand. However, between AD 30 and 70, each year this occurred invariably the other way around. According to statistics, the lot for the LORD should appear in about fifty percent of the cases in the high priest's right hand; the chance that this is zero percent is 1 in 5,500,000,000!

(2) When the scapegoat was sent into the wilderness, a crimson thread was attached to its horns. In due course, this thread always turned white. The Jews took this as a sign that God had accepted the sin offering, and that the sins of the people had been erased. However, every year between AD 30 and 70 this thread remained crimson. Of course, one could presume that the thread after some time would have been bleached by the sun. But why did this not

---

42. Talmud: Yoma 39b.
43. Neusner (2008, 156–57).

occur during these forty years?

(3) On the west side, the "eternal light" (the Menorah, the seven-branched candlestick) shone in the temple as a reference to God's permanent presence there. Of course, this light was never to be extinguished (cf. Lev. 24:2–4). However, between AD 30 and 70 this light went out every night. Of course, such a thing can happen accidentally. But not every night for forty years, more than 146,000 nights.

(4) In the evening, the doors of the sanctuary were closed by the priests, and in the morning, the priests opened the doors again. However, everybody was frightened to see that, between AD 30 and 40, the doors opened every night by themselves.

On the basis of these utterly remarkable facts, Rabbi Jochanan ben Zakkai (founder of rabbinic-Talmudic Judaism) prophesied that, apparently, the temple had been done away with, and was going to be burned by fire.[44] He referred to Zechariah 11:1, "Open your doors, O Lebanon, that the fire may devour your cedars!" where for the name Lebanon he substituted the temple, because the latter had been built with cedar wood from Lebanon (cf. 1 Kings 7:2).

10.4.3 The Only Explanation

One might reject all these stories as Jewish legends, which one should not take historically seriously. This would certainly be true if these involved Christian legends, for Christians would have deep interest in seeing AD 30 as a very special year. However, it was rabbis who indirectly indicated that in the year 30 an utterly remarkable change took place. This change apparently suggested that, between AD 30 and 70, God no longer accepted the sin offering of *Yom Kippur*! Christians know immediately why this was the case: in AD 30, on the cross Christ had brought the true sin offering, which took away once and for all the sins of God's people.[45] Were the rabbis unaware that the Christians would draw such a conclusion immediately? It is all the more remarkable that, in the Talmud, they referred to this enormous change in AD 30.

Orthodox rabbi Tovia Singer was quite aware of this Christian

---

44. See note 43.
45. Heb.2:17; 9:11–15, 25–28; 10:1–14; also cf. Matt. 26:28; Rom. 8:3; 2 Cor. 5:21.

conclusion. He was rather angry about it (Christians misusing the Talmud to prove that Jesus is the Messiah!), and suggested that "the reason this miracle [i.e., the crimson thread turning white] ended 40 years before the destruction of the Second Temple was due to the deplorable lack of social justice and brotherly kindness among the Jewish people."[46] Farfetched, and not very convincing. Why then precisely in AD 30? Moreover, the same Talmud tract asks this question: "[W]hy was the second Sanctuary destroyed, seeing that in its time they were occupying themselves with Torah, [observance of] precepts, and the practice of charity?"[47] And moreover, if Singer were right, was atonement of the people not all the more necessary?

No, from AD 30, the one and only blood, the only blood that can take away sins, stands before God in the heavenly sanctuary:

> [W]hen Christ appeared as a high priest of the good things that have come, then through the greater and more perfect tent (not made with hands, that is, not of this creation) he entered once for all into the holy places, not by means of the blood of goats and calves but by means of his own blood, thus securing an eternal redemption (Heb. 9:11-12).

Every Day of Atonement before AD 30 wonderfully prefigured the sin offering that Christ would bring. However, after AD 30 God gave a wonderful testimony that *Yom Kippur had been fulfilled*. And as far as the "eternal light" in the temple was concerned, Jesus himself was the "light of the world."[48] Since this light of the world had been extinguished, the light of the temple was extinguished as well, no matter how often the lamp was lit again.

Over against Tovia Singer, we maintain that Christians do not need the Talmud to prove that Jesus is the Messiah, nor do we use it for that purpose. Rather, Christians are astonished about this unexpected, Jewish fourfold testimony concerning this wondrous year of AD 30. Singer dealt only with the crimson thread, not with the three other miracles. And neither he nor other rabbis (as far as I am aware) have come up with a satisfactory explanation concerning these four miracles. Is it strange, then, that Christians suggest there

---

46. https://outreachjudaism.org/yomkippur/.
47. Talmud: Yoma 9b.
48. John 1:4-9; 3:19-21; 8:12; 9:5; 12:35-36, 46.

might be a relationship with the Easter events on Golgotha in April of AD 30? In other words, if orthodox Jews do not have a reasonable explanation of the four miracles, we might modestly suggest the explanation supplied by the New Testament.

10.5 "Until"

10.5.1 In the New Testament

The destruction of Jerusalem had become inevitable; Jesus himself had predicted it as a certain fact. But at the same time, we must remember that this announcement of judgment can never undo the promises that God had once made to the patriarchs. These promises were unconditional and had been given by God to his chosen ones; the promises are the unshakable foundation of the future blessing of Israel (cf. Micah 7:18–20). God's providential judgments upon Israel are never definitive. Thus, if judgment was pronounced upon Israel, we must distinguish between two *types* of judgment:

(a) *Definitive* judgment upon the dead and raised wicked ones, both from Israel and the Gentiles, before the great white throne of God and the Lamb: ". . . if anyone's name was not found written in the book of life, he was thrown into the lake of fire" (Rev. 20:15).

(b) *Temporary* judgment upon the people of Israel in the providential ways of God with them—such as destruction of city and land, and subsequent exile—which has this twofold outcome:

* definitive judgment upon the impenitent and stiff-necked multitude of the people; in the end, if they do not repent, then through death and resurrection they fall under the judgment mentioned under (a).

* deliverance and salvation for the humble, penitent, faithful, righteous remnant of Israel, from which God time and again builds a new ethnic Israel; specifically, the "Israel of God." This remnant is destined ultimately for the Messianic kingdom, and ultimately for the new heavens and the new earth.

This faithful remnant does not have a privileged position in Israel since, historically speaking, it has always had to suffer together with the unfaithful multitude of the nation. Moses, Joshua, and Caleb had to travel through the wilderness for forty years, together with the entire nation, although they personally had not deserved this ordeal. Daniel and Ezekiel were carried away into captivity in

Babylon together with the rest of Judah, although they personally had no part in the apostasy and idolatry of the people that had led to the exile. These five men belonged to the *tzaddiqim*, the righteous who lived by their faith (Hab. 2:4b). This is the confidence that the *tzaddiqim* have: one day God will put an end to their misery and will lead them back to their land, where they will enjoy God's blessings.

This sure and certain end of the misery is expressed in the joyful word "until." When Jesus speaks of the coming destruction of Jerusalem, he uses this word in order to refer to the end of the period of Israel's having been put aside. Thus, we read in Matthew 23:37–39 (cf. also Luke 13:34–35):

> "O Jerusalem, Jerusalem, the city
>   that kills the prophets and stones those who are sent to it!
> How often would I have gathered your children together
>   as a hen gathers her brood under her wings,
>   and you were not willing!
> See, your house is left to you desolate.
>   For I tell you, you will not see me again, ***until*** [Gk. *heōs an*] you say,
>   'Blessed is he who comes in the name of the LORD.'"

This important prophecy consists of three parts. First, the people would be set aside. Second, their "house" would be destroyed; this was the temple of the Jews, which was no longer the house of Jesus' Father (cf. John 2:16).[49] For a long time, this house would remain desolate, and they would no longer see the Lord. But then, third, one day the people would shout the words that were shouted on the occasion of Jesus' entry into Jerusalem (Matt. 21:9), namely, when the Messiah returned and once again entered the city in triumph (Ps. 24 and 118).[50] Only on the occasion of *this* entry would peace be announced to the nations, and the Messiah would rule to the ends of the earth (Zech. 9:9–10).

---

49. Thus, Israel's feasts are "*my* appointed feasts," God said (Lev. 23:2; Ezek. 44:24), but in John's Gospel they are consistently called the "feasts of the Jews" (5:1; 6:4; 7:2).

50. I draw your attention here to the important prophetic meaning of the Psalms: Jesus "is revealed as the true subject of the Psalms, the 'David' from whom they come and through whom they acquire meaning," according to Ratzinger (2011, 67).

The apostle Paul uses the word "until" in a similar exuberant sense. The people of Israel could not possibly be set aside by God forever; for, "[a]s regards the gospel, they are enemies for your sake. But as regards election, they are beloved for the sake of their forefathers. For the gifts and the calling of God are irrevocable" (Rom. 11:28-29). Therefore, although the people had failed, and salvation had now come to the Gentiles, there remained a promise of blessing for Israel:

> Lest you be wise in your own sight,
> I do not want you to be unaware of this mystery, brothers:
> a partial hardening has come upon Israel,
> ***until*** [Gk. *achris hou*] the fullness of the Gentiles has come in.
> And in this way all Israel will be saved, as it is written,
> "The Deliverer will come from Zion,
> he will banish ungodliness from Jacob";
> "and this will be my covenant with them
> when I take away their sins" (Rom. 11:24-27).

For the most part, Israel is now being "hardened," but it will not stay like this. When the full number from the Gentiles has received its share in the "tree of promise,"[51] the moment will have arrived when the true (remnant of) Israel will be saved. Thus, there remains an "until," and this important word is the key to the future blessing of Israel.[52]

10.5.2 In the Tanakh: Isaiah

This hopeful "until" that indicates the end of Jerusalem's destruction and of Israel's rejection is expressed in exactly the same way in the Tanakh. Let me mention a few prophecies that refer to the destruction of Jerusalem and link it with the ultimate restoration in the end time. Notice what this means in the supersessionist perspective: Jerusalem will remain destroyed until . . . a totally different Jerusalem—the "New Jerusalem," the "heavenly Jerusalem"—arises at a totally different place. If cities were personified, this is like the English city of York being destroyed, and people trying to comfort her by saying that it will be "rebuilt" as New York, a totally different city on a totally different continent. York might reply that

---

51. Cf. Ouweneel (2010a, 105–107).
52. Regarding these "untils," see Glashouwer (2007, chapters 5–7).

this is no comfort to her at all; it wishes to be rebuilt *herself*. And this is exactly the same thing that Jerusalem would tell the supersessionists: You may well have your "New Jerusalem" (Rev. 3:12; 21:2, 9), or your "heavenly Jerusalem" (Heb. 12:22), or your "Jerusalem that is above" (Gal. 4:26) — but that is no comfort to me. God has promised that *I* will be rebuilt! If Jerusalem would speak this way, it would be perfectly correct.

My first example is Isaiah 32:9-15, where we find a touching announcement of the coming judgment over Jerusalem. This prophecy ends in verses 14-15 as follows:

[T]he palace is forsaken,
>   the populous city deserted;
> the hill and the watchtower
>   will become dens forever,
>   a joy of wild donkeys,
>   a pasture of flocks;
> *until* the Spirit is poured upon us from on high,
>   and the wilderness becomes a fruitful field,
>   and the fruitful field is deemed a forest.

The solitude of the city will come to an end when the Holy Spirit is poured out on the people of Israel and Jerusalem.[53] The once deserted city will be rebuilt and repopulated; try to apply this to some "spiritual Jerusalem"!

The outpouring mentioned here is not the outpouring of the Spirit that occurred on the Day of Pentecost. On that occasion, only a pre-fulfillment took place for a very small part of Israel (see §9.6.2). In the prophecies mentioned, however, we are dealing with the entire restored people of Israel. *Then*, the glorious time of blessing will begin, during which peace and justice will dwell on earth, and God's people will enjoy undisturbed rest.

10.5.3 In the Tanakh: Ezekiel

We see the same in Ezekiel 21:18-27, in which the destructions of Jerusalem by Nebuchadnezzar and by Titus are identified, as it were. Terrible would be the judgment of God over the city, only a ruin of which would remain. However, then we read (vv. 26-27): "Exalt that which is low, and bring low that which is exalted. A ruin, ruin,

---

53. Cf. Isa. 44:3; Ezek. 36:27; 37:14; 39:29; Joel 2:28-32; Zech. 12:10.

ruin I will make it. This also shall not be, *until* he [i.e., the Messiah] comes, the one to whom judgment belongs, and I will give it to him." The curse resting on the ruined city will be removed only when the Messiah comes, who will rule over the restored city. This does not refer to his first coming because the city was destroyed again later. The text refers to Messiah's second coming, which will usher in the definitive restoration of the people, the land, the city, and the temple.

10.5.4 In the Tanakh: Micah

We find a similar line of thinking in Micah 3:9–4:5, even though the word "until" is missing here; but it is implicitly there. In this passage again, important principles are subsequently developed.[54] First, the awful condition of the people's leaders, who built Zion with blood and Jerusalem with injustice; corruption and hypocrisy dominated the city. Second, what did God's reply to such evil have to be? Read the last verse of Micah 3 and the first verse of the following chapter (CJB):

> Therefore, because of you,
> Tziyon will be plowed under like a field,
> Yerushalayim will become heaps of ruins,
> and the mountain of the house like a forested height.
> ***But*** in the *acharit-hayamim* [i.e, in the last days] it will come about
> that the mountain of ADONAI's house
> will be established as the most important mountain.
> It will be regarded more highly than the other hills,
> and peoples will stream there.

Third, the "But" in Micah 4:1 is equivalent to the "until" in other passages.[55] Chapter 3:9 depicts the fall and destruction of Jeru-

---

54. Astonishing is the statement by Hendriksen (1959, 27), who said that Micah 4:1–4 has nothing to do with some millennial kingdom, which according to many will be established by Christ at his return. How did Hendriksen know that? Because, according to his paradigm, there will not be any millennial kingdom.
55. The "But" is here the simple Hebrew prefix *v-*, which in some translations is not rendered at all (ESV), or rendered as "And" or "Now." However, in the light of 3:9 the "But" seems to me highly preferable. Not seeing this connection is the consequence of the unfortunate division of the chapters, I suppose.

salem and the temple. The *"But"* in chapter 4:1 makes clear that it will not remain this way. In other words, Jerusalem and the temple will remain destroyed *until* the last days, that is, the end time, just before or at the coming of the Messiah. Then both will be rebuilt through the hand of the Messiah himself

What do supersessionists make of the "mountain of the LORD's house," which "will be established as the most important mountain"? Nothing at all. The text itself is clear enough: for a long time, the temple mount will be a ruin, but "in the last days" — an expression invariably referring to the Messianic age — a new temple will appear on that same mountain. This is followed by a description of the Messianic kingdom (almost verbally corresponding with Isa. 2:1-4), when the LORD/Messiah will execute his government and his jurisdiction from Mount Zion, ruling over — and between — many nations. In those days, war will have disappeared, and God's people will walk in the name of the LORD, their God, forever and ever.

Today, we live in the time after the destruction of Jerusalem, the time during which the Ecclesia is being gathered. This is what we find hidden in the words of Isaiah 8:14-18. Here again, we first find the judgment upon de inhabitants of Jerusalem (Isa. 8:14-15), and then — under the image of the prophet himself — the Man Christ, as the rejected One waiting upon the LORD, together with the children whom the LORD has given him, who would be signs and portents in Israel. This is the era of the Ecclesia (see the clear hint in Heb. 2:11-13), in which only a remnant of Israel is saved (Rom. 11:5, 7). If we relate this to the passage in Hebrews 2, we find here again the notion of the hopeful "until." This is because in verses 5-9 it is explained that the Lord, who is now seen in the midst of the Ecclesia, is not yet seen as the One to whom all things have been submitted. But one day, he, the rejected Son of Man of Psalm 8, who "for a little while was made lower than the angels" (Heb. 2:9), will rule over the "world to come" (v. 5), and be set over all the works of God's hands.

10.6 The "Trees" of the End Time
10.6.1 "The Fig Tree and All the Trees"
During the events in the end time, of which the prophecies spoke,

we find the people of Israel back in their own land, the land of irrevocable promise, as a restored Jewish nation. The "until" prophecies in the Tanakh and in the New Testament, too, presuppose that, after the great exile after AD 70, the Jewish people will be back in their country.

An example of this is Daniel 9, where we read in verse 26: "[T]he people of the prince who is to come shall destroy the city and the sanctuary. Its end shall come with a flood, and to the end there shall be war. Desolations are decreed." The "people" referred to here are the Romans, their "prince" can be none other than the Roman "beast" described in Revelation 13-19. The destruction of the city and the "sanctuary" (temple) refers to the event of AD 70. This will be after the end of the sixty-nine "weeks" (of years, that is, 483 years). But then, in verse 27, we find ourselves in the end time,[56] that is, the period just before the things already described in verse 24: "Seventy weeks are decreed about your people and your holy city, to finish the transgression, to put an end to sin, and to atone for iniquity, to bring in everlasting righteousness, to seal both vision and prophet, and to anoint a most holy place." This is obviously the announcement of the beginning of the Messianic kingdom.[57]

In verse 27, after the long interlude between the sixty-ninth and the seventieth "week," we suddenly find the people of Israel back in their country. They are described as "the many" (not "many"; EHV), that is, the unbelieving majority of the Jewish people. The fact that they are unbelieving—have little confidence in God—is evident from the fact that they make a covenant with those same Romans, that is, modern allied Western powers, who constitute the literal and spiritual descendants of the Roman Empire in Western and Middle Europe, and around the Mediterranean.[58] Apparently, they engage in the sacrificial ministry, although the Messianic tem-

---

56. Between the sixty-nine "weeks" and the seventieth "week" there seems to be a gap, because v. 26 describes events that take place *after* the sixty-ninth but *before* the seventieth "week."

57. See Ouweneel (2012a, §6.5) regarding the seventy "weeks" (of years) in Dan. 9:24–27.

58. Cf. the parallel with Isa. 28, where the unbelieving majority of Israel makes a covenant with Egypt in order to protect itself against the Assyrians, whereas the faithful trust in their God.

ple has not yet been built. Thus, what we find is, on the one hand, the prophetic announcement of the destruction of Jerusalem and the dispersion of Israel among the nations, but on the other hand, in the end time, a restored people in a restored city, *before* the coming of the Messiah and his kingdom. And not only this: *Israel's neighboring nations as well as "Assyria" as well as the "Roman Empire" appear again as well*, regardless of their precise names in the end time (see next section).

When will the re-establishment of the Jewish state occur? About this Jesus said, "Look at the fig tree, and all the trees. As soon as they come out in leaf, you see for yourselves and know that the summer is already near. So also, when you see these things taking place, you know that the kingdom of God is near" (Luke 21:29–31).

10.6.2 The Neighbors

The fig tree's "coming out in leaf," that is, the restoration of Israel,[59] is linked to "*all* the trees" "coming out in leaf." That is, reviving the dormant stump of Israel is accompanied with a universal agitation among the nations. This has been occurring especially after the First World War, with the fall of the Ottoman empire. This led to the rise of a number of independent states in the Middle East, each of which will play the role allotted to them in the prophecies:[60]

- Egypt: an independent state since 1922;
- Philistia (the Palestinians): since 1988 an independent state *de jure*, recognized as such by a number of other states;
- Ammon and Moab, that is, Jordan, an independent state since 1922;
- Edom, which is part of modern Saudi Arabia, an independent unified state since 1932;
- Iraq, part of ancient Assyria, an independent state since 1932;
- Syria, part of ancient Assyria, an independent state since 1936;
- Iran (Elam/Persia), reasonably independent in the last centuries until today;

---

59. See, e.g., Kelly (1896, ad loc.); Grant (1897, ad loc.); Gaebelein (1910, ad loc.).
60. Cf. Ps. 83:5–8; Isa. 11:11–16; 19:23–25; Jer. 12:14–15; Dan. 11:41–43; see §9.3.1.

- The "Roman Empire": the European Union (founded in 1955), either viewed as such, or in association with the United States and Canada (think of NATO, founded in 1947–1949).

The latter tree is of special interest because the Roman Empire has been revived in these latter days, though in another, more federal form, as was predicted by Daniel 2 (ten "toes") and 7 (ten "horns") and by the apostle John in Revelation 13 and 17 (ten "horns," that is, ten "kings" or "kingdoms"). It is the final form of the ancient "tree" that we find in Daniel 4, in the person of King Nebuchadnezzar. Assyria (Iraq/Syria?), too, the great eschatological power from the North (cf. "Gog" in Ezek. 38–39[61]), is presented as a tree (Ezek. 31:3). The tremendous development of all these "trees," which usher in the end time, is the infallible sign for the "fig tree coming out in leaf": the restoration of the Jewish state.

We do well to remember that anti-supersessionism was revived in the Dutch Second Reformation (seventeenth/eighteenth centuries), and came to full bloom in the nineteenth century, *when none of these "trees" had begun its new life ("coming out in leaf")*. The expositors involved, from the Reformed theologians in the seventeenth to the Evangelical theologians in the nineteenth centuries, simply believed the Scriptures, and thus announced the re-appearance of all these trees. What a lesson for all those who, *after* the re-appearance of these trees, still cling to supersessionism.

10.7 Two Other Visions

10.7.1 The Valley of Dry Bones

How will this restoration occur? There will be a return of the people and a restoration of the nation in *Ha'Aretz*, but at first largely — not entirely — in unbelief. This is represented in the well-known vision of Ezekiel 37 concerning the valley of the dry bones, an image of the restoration of Israel in the end time (for the interpretation, see vv. 11–14):

> Son of man, these bones are the whole house of Israel. Behold, they say, "Our bones are dried up, and our hope is lost; we are indeed cut off." Therefore prophesy, and say to them, "Thus says the Lord God:

---

61. "Gog" dwells in the "uttermost parts of the north" (Ezek. 38:6, 15; 39:2), which points to a power further north than Syria/Iraq (Russia?); some (NKJV) translate in 38:2–3; 39:1 "prince of Rosh," which some suppose to be Russia.

'Behold, I will open your graves and raise you from your graves, O my people. And I will bring you into the land of Israel. And you shall know that I am the LORD, when I open your graves, and raise you from your graves, O my people. And I will put my Spirit within you, and you shall live, and I will place you in your own land. Then you shall know that I am the LORD; I have spoken, and I will do it,' declares the LORD."

In the vision, we see that Israel's restoration consists of two stages. When the prophet began to prophesy, the first stage began: the dry bones joined together, sinews and flesh were beginning to cover the bones, and a skin covered them: "And I looked, and behold, there were sinews on them, and flesh had come upon them, and skin had covered them. *But there was no breath in them*" (v. 8). The bones had become corpses, and this was a great miracle. At the same time, it was an incomplete miracle: of what use are dead corpses? The explanation of this is given in verses 21–22:

> Behold, I will take the people of Israel from the nations among which they have gone, and will gather them from all around, and bring them to their own land. And I will make them one nation in the land, on the mountains of Israel. And one king shall be king over them all, and they shall be no longer two nations, and no longer divided into two kingdoms.

The initial fulfillment of this prophecy occurred at the return from the Babylonian captivity, but given the sequel, this exile merges with the subsequent exile, and brings us to the end time. We find here a joining of the bones, without, however, "spirit" in them. That is, the great majority of the Israelis has not yet been touched by the Spirit of God (cf. v. 14).

Therefore, the prophet must prophecy another time, after which the second stage of the restoration begins: the spirit (human life) entered the corpses, so that they were revived: "'Come from the four winds, O breath, and breathe on these slain, that they may live.' So I prophesied as he commanded me, and the breath came into them, and they lived and stood on their feet, an exceedingly great army" (vv. 9–10).[62] Here, the principle of 1 Corinthians 15:46

---

62. Please note that the Hebrew word for "wind," "breath," "spirit," and "Spirit" in Ezek. 37 is always the same word: *ruach*. In this way, the inner coherence of the

is shown: the natural is first, then the spiritual. The natural restoration of (the state of) Israel began, so to speak, with Theodor Herzl, and was fulfilled in the establishment of the state of Israel (1948). In the spiritual restoration of the people within the state of Israel, I distinguish three aspects:

(1) In 1948, there were some Hebrew Christians in Israel (converted Jews, who had joined certain Christian denominations and had largely laid down their Jewish features), but since around 1980 we see the rise of "Messianic" (i.e., Jesus-believing) Jewry, which is roughly estimated to contain some ten thousand Jews in Israel, and some hundreds of thousands worldwide. Insofar as these Jews are really reborn, the Spirit of God dwells in them.

(2) However, I also mention the growth of orthodox Jewry in Israel, among whom are no doubt many who sincerely love the God of Israel, and the Torah of this God. I am convinced that many of them are spiritually prepared for the encounter with their Messiah, when the "scales" will fall from their eyes (cf. Acts 9:18 concerning that remarkable Jew: Rabbi Shaul ben Y'mini, better known as the apostle Paul, the Benjaminite).

(3) The events described under (1) and (2) are occurring today, before our very eyes; event (3) is future: when the Messiah (re-)appears, many Jews will recognize and acknowledge him—prepared for this by the Holy Spirit—and then, as those penitent and reborn, they will be filled with this same Spirit.

10.7.2 The Nation Scattered and Peeled

There is another Bible passage showing that Israel's national restoration in unbelief precedes its spiritual restoration, namely, Isaiah 18, but I do admit that there two very different interpretations of this chapter. In the KJV, verse 2 speaks of

> ... a nation scattered and peeled,
> ... a people terrible [or, feared] from their beginning hitherto;
> A nation meted out [by God's judgments] and trodden down,
> Whose land the rivers [of invading armies] have spoiled [cf. 8:7]!

Here, it is not difficult to understand this to be referring to Is-

---

vision and its interpretation becomes much clearer.

rael, as Matthew Henry did.⁶³ However, most modern translations give us a different rendering,⁶⁴ in which the words quoted refer to Cush (probably Nubia, or countries further away, or also countries around the Euphrates); consider the rendering of the NIV:

> Go, swift messengers,
>> to a people tall and smooth-skinned,
>> to a people feared far and wide,
> an aggressive nation of strange speech,
>> whose land is divided by rivers.

Only if we follow the former interpretation⁶⁵ can we discern here the people of Israel, dispersed among the nations, bereft of its land and possessions, a fearful and wondrous people, more miraculous than any other people in world history. In this interpretation—which, we must admit, is doubted by many—this passage foretells that Israel, waiting for centuries for its restoration, one day will "lift up an ensign on the mountains [of Israel], will blow the trumpet" (Isa. 28:3). And all the "inhabitants of the world, and dwellers on the earth" will see the ensign, and hear the trumpet, and will be astonished. Israel will take possession of the land again, helped in this by a "land shadowing with wings, which is beyond the rivers of Cush" (the Nile and the Euphrates), that is a remote land, outside Israel's field of vision.⁶⁶

However, how will this national restoration take place? The banner is lifted up on the mountains, but it does not say that God does this. The people do this in their own strength, and what must God say of this? He tells the prophet: "I will take my rest, and I will consider in my dwelling place like a clear heat upon herbs, and like a cloud of dew in the heat of harvest" (Isa. 18:4). This is taken to mean that God is indeed behind the events, but invisibly in the

---

63. https://biblehub.com/commentaries/isaiah/18-2.htm.
64. Cf. Grogan (1986, 122–23); Oswalt (1986, 359–60).
65. See Bultema (1981, 189–93), with reference to the rabbis; see Slotki (1983, 85); see the commentaries of J. Calvin, S. Horsley, W. A. Kay, W. Kelly, I. da Costa, A. C. Gaebelein, and others; see also the Annotations to the Dutch States Translation.
66. Some have thought of Great Britain because of the latter's important role in the Middle East in the first half of the twentieth century, including the establishment of the state of Israel.

background, letting the people have their way.[67] He does not interfere, but at the same time *he* is the One who opens the way for his people, and makes possible its political independence. This is, as I would put it, because in these returned Jewish people, he already discerns the remnant that will be formed, and that will be "like heat shimmering in the sun, like a cloud of dew in the heat of harvest" (v. 4 CJB). And to be sure, no matter how secular the entire establishment of the state of Israel has been, the faithful *tzaddiqim* were there right from the beginning. The state of Israel was, humanly speaking, mainly the achievement of very secular Jews (especially socialists and communists). But spiritually speaking, it was a gift of God in answer to the prayers of the *tzaddiqim* who were there as well.

However, notice verse 5: "For afore the harvest, when the bud is perfect, / and the sour grape is ripening in the flower, / he shall both cut off the sprigs with pruning hooks, / and take away and cut down the branches." In the interpretation that we are following this means that, during the "harvest," the good wheat will be gathered, but the wicked ones will be cut off and be destroyed: "They shall be left together unto the fowls of the mountains, and to the beasts of the earth: and the fowls shall summer upon them, and all the beasts of the earth shall winter upon them" (v. 6; cf. Rev. 14:18–20; 19:15, 17–18). This is what the state of Israel has been from the beginning: a miracle of God as well as a place where the *tzaddiqim* are intermingled with the *r'sha'im*, the wicked. The former—the remnant, the "Israel of God"—are spiritually prepared for the Messianic kingdom; the latter are being prepared for judgment. As the prophet Zechariah (13:8–9) put it:

> "In the whole land," declares the LORD,
>   "two thirds shall be cut off and perish,
>   and one third shall be left alive.
> And I will put this third into the fire,
>   and refine them as one refines silver,
>   and test them as gold is tested.

---

67. It is striking that in the "Declaration of the Establishment of the State of Israel," the name of God is not mentioned; it only contains a reference to the "Rock of Israel" (2 Sam. 23:3); see https://mfa.gov.il/mfa/foreignpolicy/peace/guide/pages/declaration%20of%20establishment%20of%20state%20of%20israel.aspx.

> They will call upon my name,
>> and I will answer them.
> I will say, 'They are my people';
>> and they will say, 'The LORD is my God.'"

10.8 The Remnant of Israel

10.8.1 Its Character

After discussing these more politically oriented events, we turn now to a very important subject, namely, the formation of a believing, faithful remnant in the midst of the wicked majority of the people of Israel. In addition to all the prophetic events that will occur, the prophecies paid special attention to the weak and — already today — oppressed group of Jews who, in the midst of all the spiritual decline, repent and convert to the God of Israel and his Messiah. These faithful ones will receive the mercy of God in the midst of all the oppression and distress.[68]

Let us now consider how this remnant will be formed, and what will happen to them initially. As an example of this, we take the story in 2 Kings 18–19, describing the battle of the kingdom of Judah against the invading king of Assyria. This event has been viewed by various expositors as a type of the future battle of Judah against the "Assyria" of the end time. Actually, this must be the reason why we find the same story in Isaiah 36–39 as well, chapters that form a part of the totality of Isaiah's prophetic messages; in other words, they themselves are understood to have a prophetic character.[69]

In this story, we find by way of typological expression that in the end time there will be a remnant, especially in Jerusalem, which will come to great glory after the Assyrian power has been defeated (2 Kings 19:31; cf. Isa. 37:22): "[O]ut of Jerusalem shall go a *remnant*, and out of Mount Zion a band of survivors. The zeal of the LORD will do this."

In Isaiah 10 as well, the formation of this remnant was linked to the fall of the Assyrian and with Zion. Isaiah 10:5 explained that the

---

68. We remember here that, in the end time, there such faithful ones will be among the orthodox Jews as well, who are prepared by the Holy Spirit to meet and recognize and acknowledge their Messiah when he comes (again).
69. See, e.g., Vine (1971, ad loc.).

Assyrian, who was the "rod of God's anger" to chastise the people, turned against the LORD, and therefore would perish itself: "When the LORD has finished all his work on Mount Zion and on Jerusalem, he will punish the speech of the arrogant heart of the king of Assyria and the boastful look in his eyes" (Isa. 10:12). A bit later, the remnant was introduced (Isa. 10:20–25):

> In that day the *remnant* of Israel and the survivors of the house of Jacob will no more lean on him who struck them, but will lean on the LORD, the Holy One of Israel, in truth. A *remnant* will return,[70] the *remnant* of Jacob, to the mighty God. For though your people Israel be as the sand of the sea, only a *remnant* of them will return.[71] Destruction is decreed, overflowing with righteousness. For the LORD God of hosts will make a full end, as decreed, in the midst of all the earth [or rather, all the land]. Therefore thus says the LORD God of hosts: "O my people, who dwell in Zion, be not afraid of the Assyrians when they strike with the rod and lift up their staff against you as the Egyptians did. For in a very little while my fury will come to an end, and my anger will be directed to their destruction" (italics added).

We see here how a remnant is formed, again viewed here in connection with Zion. This remnant learns to confide in the LORD in the midst of all the oppression by its enemies, the neighboring nations as well as the wicked in Israel itself, in the final stage before the Messianic kingdom. The text spoke of "destruction" (Heb. *kilyon* or *kalah*) and of "what has been decreed" by God (Heb. *charutz* or *necheratzah*, both from the root *ch-r-tz*), a formula also used in Daniel 9:27 (Heb. *kalah v'necheratsah*, lit. "destruction and [divine] decree [or, determination]"). Divinely decreed destruction will be poured out upon the wicked of Israel and the Assyrians. However, the remnant of Israel will be saved when the "appointed time" of God's indignation will come to an end (cf. Dan. 8:19; 11:36). It is from this remnant that the new Israel—"all Israel" in Romans 11:26—will be formed, the Israel that will be privileged to enter the Messianic kingdom.

---

70. Heb. *Sh'ar yashub*, which always implies both "return to the land" and "return to the LORD." Notice that this was also the name of one of Isaiah's sons (Isa. 7:3, "Shear-jashub, your son").

71. One could also translate: ". . . yet, [fortunately] there will still be a *remnant* that . . . ."

10.8.2 Its Formation

How will this remnant be formed? In the book of Daniel, we find that its formation will begin with a group of special men of God, in Hebrew called *maskilim* (see earlier in §9.5.4), the "wise," the men with spiritual understanding of the counsels and the ways of God with regard to his people and to the entire world (cf. Daniel himself, 1:4, 17; 5:11–12, 14), in order to instruct others in these things ("teachers"): "... the wise among the people shall make many [people] [spiritually] understand" (11:33); "none of the wicked shall understand, but those who are wise shall understand" (12:10), that is, they understand what God is doing, and what he will do to his people in the latter days.

Especially in times of severe backsliding, God will look for such men and women: "The LORD looks down from heaven on the children of man, to see if there are any who understand [or, act wisely, Heb. *hayēsh maskil*]" (Ps. 14:2; cf. 53:2). "Understand, O dullest of the people! Fools, when will you be wise [Heb. *taskilu*]?" (Ps. 94:8). God will say to his people: "[L]et him who boasts boast in this, that he understands [Heb. *haskēl*] and knows me, that I am the LORD who practices steadfast love, justice, and righteousness in the earth. For in these things I delight." Jesus himself was characterized by this "understanding," both in his ministry on earth ("Behold, my servant shall act wisely [Heb. *yiskil*]," Isa. 52:13) and in the future in the Messianic kingdom (11:2). Similarly, there will be people in Israel of whom others will say, "The fear of the LORD is the beginning of wisdom; all those who practice it have a good understanding [Heb. *sekhel*[72]]" (Ps. 111:10; cf. Prov. 1:1–7).

These *maskilim* ("wise" men) will not attempt first to improve the wicked condition of the people, for "he who is prudent [Heb. *hamaskil*] will keep silent in such a time, for it is an evil time" (Amos 5:13). Rather, they will be witnesses of God to the people, and in this way "turn many to righteousness [Heb. *matzdiqē*, from the root *tz-d-q*]" (Dan. 12:3); that is, through their ministry, God will turn these Jews into *tzaddiqim*. Or, as Daniel 11:32–33 puts it: "... the people who know their God shall stand firm and take action. And the wise [Heb. *maskilim*] among the people shall make many under-

---

72. All the Hebrew words mentioned between [ ] come from the root *s-kh-l*.

stand,"[73] namely, the deeper sense of the Torah. In the midst of the wicked people, the LORD will notice these faithful ones:

> Then those who feared the LORD spoke with one another. The LORD paid attention and heard them, and a book of remembrance was written before him of those who feared the Lord and esteemed his name. "They shall be mine," says the LORD of hosts, "in the day when I make up my treasured possession, and I will spare them as a man spares his son who serves him" (Mal. 3:16–17).

Before the final trials come upon Israel, God will take measures beforehand to protect his remnant against the approaching judgments. This we find in Revelation 7:1–8. God sends an angel who has the seal of the living God. Before the judgments break out, the servants of God are sealed on their foreheads (cf. Ezek. 9:4, "Pass through the city, through Jerusalem, and put a mark on the foreheads of the men who sigh and groan over all the abominations that are committed in it"). With this seal, God makes these Israelites his inalienable property—his precious treasure. From each tribe, twelve thousand persons are chosen, not only from the two tribes.[74] These chosen and sealed ones are God's servants, his faithful ones, the righteous remnant. The sealing implies that until the second coming of Christ, they will remain living on earth, although many others of the remnant will be killed as martyrs for the Master. It is not very important whether we interpret the numbers 12,000 and 144,000 as literal or figurative numbers.[75] In any case, for God it will be a fullness of chosen ones, whom he will save from each tribe of Israel. (On the supersessionist standpoint, we are of course curious to know for what part of the Ecclesia each "tribe" stands.)

---

73. This refers primarily to the time of the Maccabees, but it is also a foreshadowing of the end time (Heb. *et qēts*, vv. 35, 40; 8:17; 12:4, 9; cf. Heb. *moʿēd qēts* in Dan. 8:19).

74. In the enumeration of the twelve tribes, Manasseh and Joseph are mentioned together, although Manasseh actually belongs to Joseph. Apparently, "Joseph" stands here for Ephraim, and presumably the name "Ephraim" is not mentioned here because of the heinous sins of the northern kingdom (see especially Hos.). The tribe of Dan is not mentioned, either.

75. As to the literal number, two passages are suggestive: "one third" of Israel in Zech. 13:8, and even much less in Isa. 17:6, "Gleanings will be left in it, as when an olive tree is beaten—two or three berries in the top of the highest bough, four or five on the branches of a fruit tree."

At the beginning of the Messianic kingdom, these chosen ones will be found not only within the state of Israel; many of them will still be living in the Diaspora. These Jews will be brought to Zion as a gift made by the nations:

> ". . . I will send survivors to the nations, to Tarshish, Pul, and Lud, who draw the bow, to Tubal and Javan, to the coastlands far away, that have not heard my fame or seen my glory. And they shall declare my glory among the nations. And they [i.e., these nations] shall bring all your brothers from all the nations as an offering to the LORD, on horses and in chariots and in litters and on mules and on dromedaries, to my holy mountain Jerusalem," says the LORD, "just as the Israelites bring their grain offering in a clean vessel to the house of the LORD. And some of them also I will take for priests and for Levites," says the LORD (Isa. 66:19-21).

10.9 "All Israel" or a "Remnant"?
10.9.1 The Righteous and the Wicked

No doubt, there is a certain tension between the statement, "a remnant will return (to the LORD)" (Isa. 10:21), and the statement, "all Israel will be saved" (Rom. 11:26). Some Bible teachers have claimed that, according to Romans 11:26, *all* Jews worldwide will be saved at the moment when the Redeemer appears. Even the greatest Jewish criminal would be saved! Some go as far as saying that, according to this verse, all Jews of all time will be saved, teaching a kind of universalism, especially for Israel. But this is not the way it works, of course. No human being, Jew or Gentile, has ever been saved or will ever be saved without repenting from his or her sins and turning to God, and no doubt many Jews, just like many Gentiles, have died as atheists, or at least as people like the (Jewish!) judge who said, "I neither fear God, nor respect man" (Luke 18:4). There is no redemption without repentance and faith.

Another biblical fact is that, in the end time, those who repent will be saved ("in Christ," as we know from the New Testament), but *the wicked will be judged*, including those in Israel. Never has a conversion of an entire nation occurred in which every individual member of that nation was saved, nor will this occur in the end time; see Zechariah 13:8-9, quoted in §10.6.3.

One of the passages in the Tanakh underlying Romans 11:26-27 is Isaiah 59:20, "And a Redeemer will come to Zion, / to those in Jacob who turn from transgression, ..." That is, the Redeemer will come, not for *all* Jews but for the *penitent* Jews! Immediately before this, we therefore read of the wicked (including those of Israel; cf. vv. 1-8!):

> According to their deeds, so will he repay,
>> wrath to his adversaries, repayment to his enemies;
> to the coastlands he will render repayment.
> So they shall fear the name of the LORD from the west,
>> and his glory from the rising of the sun;
> for he will come like a rushing stream,
>> which the wind [or, Spirit] of the LORD drives. (Isa 59:18-19).

If we consider these verses carefully, we clearly see the eschatological context: the prophet was speaking about the appearance of the LORD in the person of the Messiah (Isa. 60:1-2):

> Arise, shine, for your light has come,
>> and the glory of the LORD has risen upon you.
> For behold, darkness shall cover the earth,
>> and thick darkness the peoples;
> but the LORD will arise upon you,
>> and his glory will be seen upon you."

10.9.2 "All Israel" Is the Repentant Remnant

When this happens, the wicked will be judged, but the penitent will be saved; *from that time the "all Israel" of Romans 11:26 will be formed.*[76] Compare, for instance, Isaiah 57:13, "When you cry out, let your collection of idols deliver you! / The wind will carry them all off, / a breath will take them away. / But he who takes refuge in me shall possess the land / and shall inherit my holy mountain." A bit later we find this magnificent description of this salvation of "all Israel" — but with an ominous ending! God says (vv. 17-21),

> "Because of the iniquity of his[77] unjust gain I was angry,

---

76. Cf. the Pentateuch and Joshua: the "all Israel" that ultimately reached the Promised Land, was only the remnant of "all Israel" that had left Egypt (cf. Num. 14:21-24).

77. The "his" refers to wicked Israel; but the "him" in vv. 18-19 is the same Israel, now viewed, however, as the object of God's saving mercy.

> I struck him; I hid my face and was angry,
>> but he went on backsliding in the way of his own heart.
> I have seen his ways, but I will heal him;
>> I will lead him and restore comfort to him and [or, namely] *his mourners*,
> creating the fruit of the lips.
> Peace, peace, to the far and to the near," says the LORD,
>> "and I will heal him.
> *But* the wicked are like the tossing sea;
>> for it cannot be quiet,
>> and its waters toss up mire and dirt.
> There is no peace," says my God, "for the wicked."

The message is clear: *the people* are ultimately saved, but then specifically the "mourners," or "those who are sad" (about their own sins and about the vicissitudes of suffering Israel). Not the wicked. The wicked descendants of the patriarchs do not belong to the "Israel of God," and never did. We must always add, though, that when the most wicked person repents and returns to the God of Israel and his Torah, they will be saved. There is room for godly Davidic kings such as Solomon, Hezekiah, and Josiah (although they all had their failures, from which they had to repent) but also for the once wicked king Manasseh. First, we read of him: "Manasseh led Judah and the inhabitants of Jerusalem astray, to do more evil than the nations whom the LORD destroyed before the people of Israel" (2 Chron. 33:9), But second, we read of him: "[W]hen he was in distress, he entreated the favor of the LORD his God and humbled himself greatly before the God of his fathers. He prayed to him, and God was moved by his entreaty and heard his plea and brought him again to Jerusalem into his kingdom. Then Manasseh knew that the LORD was God" (vv. 12-13).[78]

John 3–4 shows the double principle: *John 3:* even a great teacher of Israel (see v. 10) can enter the kingdom of God only through rebirth, which implies repentance and faith. *John 4:* even a sinful woman—a non-Jew!—can be saved through repentance and faith.

10.9.3 Final Redemption

In Isaiah 63:7–64:12 we find a long prayer of the "mourners" (the

---

78. See the apocryphal Prayer of Manasseh, e.g., in the CEB.

humble, the penitent, the lamenting)[79] among Israel to the God of Israel, the core of which is this: Please accept us again! The faithful beg for a personal "descent" of God (64:1): "Oh that you would rend the heavens and come down, / that the mountains might quake at your presence— . . . !" This prayer is ultimately answered in the appearance of the God-Man on the clouds of heaven. In Isaiah 65, the prayer is followed by the LORD's long reply: he will set the faithful free and admit them to the blessings of the Messianic kingdom (vv. 17-25). But the wicked of Israel will receive no share in this. God addresses them directly, and compares them with his "servants" (the faithful among the people) (Isa. 65:13-14):

> . . . Behold, my servants shall eat,
> > but you shall be hungry;
> behold, my servants shall drink,
> > but you shall be thirsty;
> behold, my servants shall rejoice,
> > but you shall be put to shame.
> behold, my servants shall sing for gladness of heart,
> > but you shall cry out for pain of heart
> > and shall wail for breaking of spirit.

In short, "all Israel" will be saved in the sense that only those are saved to whom truly belongs the name of "Israel," that is, the "Israel of God" (Gal. 6:16) (see more extensively in chapter 12). These are the *tzaddiqim*, the "righteous ones," or the *chasidim*,[80] the "godly, faithful" ones (the penitent, God's servants). This is what the LORD says about the Messianic age that will come (Isa. 60:18-22):

> Violence shall no more be heard in your land,
> > devastation or destruction within your borders;
> you shall call your walls Salvation,
> > and your gates Praise.
> The sun shall be no more
> > your light by day,
> nor for brightness shall the moon

---

79. Cf. Jesus' word: "Blessed are those who mourn, for they shall be comforted" (Matt. 5:4); "theirs is the kingdom of heaven" (cf. vv. 3, 10).

80. In the broad sense; not (exclusively) referring to the movement known as the Hasidim.

give you light;
but the L ORD will be your everlasting light,
and your God will be your glory.
Your sun shall no more go down,
nor your moon withdraw itself;
for the L ORD will be your everlasting light,
and your days of mourning shall be ended.
Your people shall all be righteous;
they shall possess the land forever,
the branch of my planting, the work of my hands,
that I might be glorified.
The least one shall become a clan,
and the smallest one a mighty nation;
I am the L ORD;
in its time I will hasten it.

Chapter 11
The Ecclesia Is Not Israel

> In order to take all secret doubts away, people must know that throughout the entire New Testament the word Israel is never called the believing Church of the New Testament, but rather that by it always the Jewish nation is understood in contrast with, and in distinction from, all other nations.
>
> Wilhelmus à Brakel[1]

11.1 The Power of Tradition
11.1.1 Introduction

WE TURN NOW TO examine a matter that belongs to the core of our evaluation of supersessionism: how the New Testament connects the Ecclesia to the people of Israel in the Tanakh.[2] In earlier chapters I have claimed that the Ecclesia, in the sense the New Testament understands the term, did not yet exist in the Tanakh. I have argued that this could not have been otherwise, because the existence of the Ecclesia presupposes the glorified Man at the right hand of God, who is the head of his body, the Ecclesia: God raised Christ

---

1. Quoted in Van Campen (2007, 196); Wilhelmus à Brakel was a leading figure in the Dutch (Calvinist) so-called "Second Reformation" (Dutch: *Nadere Reformatie*).
2. See extensively, Ouweneel (2010a; 2010b).

> ... from the dead and seated him at his right hand in the heavenly places, far above all rule and authority and power and dominion, and above every name that is named, not only in this age but also in the one to come. And he put all things under his feet and gave him as head over all things to the Ecclesia, which is his body, the fullness of him who fills all in all (Eph. 1:20–23).

Moreover, if the Ecclesia is essentially identical with the Israel of the Tanakh—or if one so wishes, the *true* Israel of the Tanakh—why is the Ecclesia never called "Israel," and Israel is never called "Ecclesia"? Acts 7:38 simply speaks of the people's gathering in the wilderness. If *this* is supposed to be evidence that Israel deserves the name "Ecclesia," then one has to be consistent, and call the people's gathering in Ephesus (Acts 19:32, 39–40) also "church." *Israel was never the body of the glorified Christ in heaven*, and the Ecclesia was never an ethnic people.

That the Ecclesia did not yet exist in the Tanakh does not mean, of course, that during that period there were no reborn people, no believers, no *tzaddiqim*. It only means that these people did not belong to the Ecclesia in the strictly New Testament sense of the term. We therefore must begin by doing something that seems almost inconceivable for supersessionists: we must surrender the idea that the Ecclesia consists of all regenerate people of all time, from the Garden of Eden until the last day. The Bible reader unprepared to do this will find the idea that the Ecclesia—in its true, New Testament sense—exists only from the Day of Pentecost (Acts 2) to be incomprehensible and absurd.

Herman Bavinck described the view of Roman Catholics and of traditional Protestants this way:

> In its broadest sense [the church] embraces all who have been saved by faith in Christ or will be saved thus. . . . Belonging to it, accordingly, are all the believers who lived on earth from the time of the paradisal promise to this very moment and were taken up . . . into heaven ([Heb.] 12:23). Belonging to it are all the believers who still live on earth now. And belonging to it, in a sense, are also those who will later, even to the end of the ages.[3]

Very simply, the Ecclesia contains all believers of all time. All

---

3. Bavinck (*RD* 4:300–301).

regenerate people of all time together constitute the Ecclesia. Thus, it is inconceivable that there could be regenerate people who do not belong to the Ecclesia.

This is what I call the power of tradition. If everybody says that the Ecclesia contains all believers of all time, then it must be true. Yet, this thesis must be demonstrated from the Bible. But this thesis is entirely mistaken, and in contrast to the defense of this thesis by supersessionism, I endeavor to demonstrate that the Ecclesia is entirely a New Testament matter.

11.1.2 The Belgic Confession

Bavinck's explanation supplied above is entirely in line with the Reformational confessions and catechisms. In Article 27 of the Belgic Confession we read:

> We believe and profess one catholic or universal Church [Ecclesia], which is a holy congregation of true Christian believers, all expecting their salvation in Jesus Christ, being washed by His blood, sanctified and sealed by the Holy Spirit.
>
> This church [Ecclesia] has been from the beginning of the world, and will be to the end thereof; which is evident from this that Christ is an eternal King, which without subjects He cannot be.[4]

Here it is stated that the Ecclesia has existed since the beginning of history: it is "the church of all ages."[5] The justification for this claim given by author Guido de Brès is rather puzzling: Christ is an eternal King, who therefore must always have subjects. Our questions multiply here.

(a) Can we say that Christ has been King from eternity? In the Tanakh, the (triune) *God* is King from eternity to eternity[6] — but that is not the same. The eternal Son became Man, being sent into this world, in order to *become* a King *as Man*. Within time, he was *set* or *anointed*[7] as King over Zion (Ps. 2:6), namely, through his being

---

4. Dennison (*RC* 2:440).
5. Berkouwer (1976, 165); in his entire chapter 7, he proceeds from the unfounded assumption that the Ecclesia has existed in all ages, that is, since Adam and Eve.
6. Exod. 15:18; Ps. 10:16; 29:10; 146:10; Jer. 10:10; 1 Tim. 1:17.
7. Heb. *nasakti*, "set": LXX, Vulgate, and many modern translations; "anointed":

anointed with the Holy Spirit (Acts 10:38); this can refer only to his baptism in the river Jordan (Luke 3:21–22).[8]

(b) If God is King from eternity, then he certainly had *no* subjects until the creation of angels and humans.

(c) Is the kingdom of God the same as the Ecclesia? In other words, does the fact that God had subjects also in the period of the Tanakh have anything to do with the Ecclesia as we know it from the New Testament? Moreover, are not *all* human beings God's subjects, and not only believers? So what is the force of the argument used in the Belgic Confession?

(d) Why did the Confession not try to adduce positive arguments for the thesis that the Ecclesia has existed since Adam and Eve? Was this because the Belgic Confession would have great trouble finding such arguments? The only supposed evidence for an Ecclesia since Eden is the biased assumption that all believers of all time necessarily constitute one community, and this community is necessarily identical with what the New Testament calls the Ecclesia—but these are precisely the points that must first be proven if we wish to avoid committing a logical fallacy.

(e) Of particular importance is whether the first part of the quotation contradicts the second part. In other words: Can believers in the period of the Tanakh be identified as "true Christian believers, all expecting their salvation in Jesus Christ, being washed by His blood, sanctified and sealed by the Holy Spirit"? Of course not. I do believe that, by way of anticipation, all believers in the period of the Tanakh were washed by the blood of Christ, but I also believe that at most only a very few of them "awaited their entire [eternal!] salvation" in the coming Messiah, insofar as they had any notion. And the assertion that they were sealed with the Holy Spirit is even less defensible. The Holy Spirit rested upon only a few of believers in the Tanakh, namely, especially judges and prophets, and this was never called a "sealing" with the Spirit.[9] This sealing became

---

several other translations.

8. To be sure, the wise from the Orient ask where the *king of the Jews* was born (Matt. 2:2), but that is no different than saying that the Dutch *King* Willem-Alexander was born in 1967, although he has truly been king only since 2013.

9. Cf. 2 Cor. 1:22; Eph. 4:30; see also Rev. 7:1–2.

possible only through the outpouring of the Holy Spirit on the Day of Pentecost, according to Jesus' promise: ". . . the Father . . . will give you another Helper, to be with you forever, even the Spirit of truth" (John 14:16-17).

It is interesting to see that this description in this Article the Belgic Confession appears initially to be thinking exclusively of the New Testament Ecclesia, and then, as a kind of afterthought, includes the believers in the period of the Tanakh as well. The Article is excellent without the last sentence.

11.1.3 The Westminster Confession

By way of comparison, consider the Westminster Confession chapter 25.1, which declares: "The catholic or universal Church, which is invisible, consists of the whole number of the elect, that have been, are, or shall be gathered into one, under Christ the Head thereof; and is the spouse, the body, the fulness of Him that filleth all in all (Eph. 1:10, 22-23; 5:23, 27, 32; Col. 1:18)."[10] As in the Belgic Confession, here a typically and exclusively New Testament characteristic—Christ the head and bridegroom of his Ecclesia—is applied to the presumed "Ecclesia since Adam." But how can we possibly overlook the fact that, during the period of the Tanakh, (a) the Logos had not yet become flesh, (b) a glorified *Man* was not yet in heaven, seated at the right hand of God, and (c) therefore Christ was not yet the bridegroom of his Ecclesia?

Basically, we are dealing here not primarily with an ecclesiological or Israelological, but with a Christological problem. It is this: Can we simply and straightforwardly transfer features that specifically characterize the—humbled and then glorified—*Man* Christus Jesus to the pre-incarnate Logos? Is this not a serious confusion of the divine and the human natures of Christ, that is, a confusion of the eternal *Son*, from eternity in the bosom of the *Father* (John 1:18), and the *Man* Christ Jesus, since his ascension the glorified *Man* at the right hand of *God*? To suggest that this all refers to one and the same reality betrays very little understanding of both the Trinity and the two natures of Christ, and this touches upon the deepest mysteries of Christianity. The divine nature that the Son has possessed from eternity is essentially different, though inseparable,

---

10. Dennison (*RC* 4:264).

from the human nature that he has possessed only from his incarnation, a human nature that is essential to understand his character as the glorified Man at God's right hand.[11]

In other words, what sense does it make to assert that in the Tanakh the pre-incarnate Logos was head of his body? About whom, and about what, are we talking then? Is not supersessionism on this point in danger of drowning in the deep waters of Christology and Trinitarianism? Failure to properly distinguish between the divine and the human natures of Christ is far more serious than failure to properly distinguish between Israel and the Ecclesia! *Of course* the Ecclesia is associated with God the *Son*; but we cannot properly say that she has been made *one* with God the Son because this would suggest that ordinary humans have become divine. The Ecclesia, as a company of Spirit-given human beings, can be made one (be united) with the Son *only after he had become Man*; it is with the glorified *Man* that she has been united—and of this glorified Man we can speak only since his ascension and glorification, and since the outpouring of the Holy Spirit (cf. John 7:39, ". . . as yet the Spirit had not been given, because Jesus was not yet glorified").

11.2   The Heidelberg Catechism

11.2.1   Quotations

The Heidelberg Catechism, too, seems at first to refer unequivocally to the New Testament Ecclesia (Q/A 50): "*50. Why is it added: "And sitteth at the right hand of God"?* Because Christ ascended into heaven for this end, that He might there appear as the Head of His Church (Eph. 1:20–23; Col. 1:18), by whom the Father governs all things (John 5:22)."[12] This is perfectly correct: Christ, as the glorified Lord, is the head of his body; how, then, could the Ecclesia have existed before the glorification of Christ (which occurred after his ascension)?

However, later (Q/A 54) we read:

> *54. What do you believe concerning the "Holy Catholic Church"?*

That out of the whole human race (Gen. 26:4), from the beginning

---

11. See extensively, Ouweneel (2007b).
12. Dennison (*RC* 2:780).

to the end of the world (John 10:10), the Son of God (Eph. 1:10–13), by His Spirit and Word (Rom. 1:16; Isa. 59:21; Rom. 10:14–17; Eph. 5:26), gathers, defends, and preserves for Himself unto everlasting life a chosen communion (Rom. 8:29–30; Matt. 16:18; Eph. 4:3–6) in the unity of the true faith (Acts 2:46; Ps. 71:18; 1 Cor. 11:26; John 10:28–30; 1 Cor. 1:8–9); and that I am and forever shall remain a living member of this communion (1 John 3:21; 1 John 2:19).[13]

With the words "from the beginning of the world to its end," the Catechism, or its editors, refer to three Bible passages: Psalm 71:17–18; Isaiah 59:21, and 1 Corinthians 11:26. The first passage dealt with youth and old age, the second one spoke of the covenant, and the third passage referred to celebrating the Lord's Supper. It is beyond difficult to understand how the Heidelberg theologians thought that these verses prove that the Ecclesia exists from Adam to the last day.[14]

This would be less difficult to understood had these theologians referred to Acts 7:38, where the word *ecclesia* refers to people's gathering of Israel in the wilderness (although one would need only to consult Acts 19:32 and 39–40, where the word refers to the people's gathering in Ephesus, to see how inappropriate even this reference would have been). This would also have been less difficult to understand had these theologians referred to Romans 4:11 and 16, or to Galatians 3:7–9, 14, and 29, and 4:28, where we read that New Testament believers are blessed with Abraham, and are his spiritual descendants ("sons/children"). This shows that believers in the time of both the Tanakh and the New Testament came and come under the blessed promised made to Abraham. This does not at all prove that believers in the period of the Tanakh also belong to the Ecclesia, or that the Ecclesia would belong to Israel. But at least one could understand the relevance of such references better than the relevance of the passages that *were* mentioned, but which appear to be totally irrelevant.

11.2.2 The Ecclesia and Eden

Following in the line of the church father Augustine, the idea that the Ecclesia has existed since the Garden of Eden continues to be

---

13. Ibid., 2:781; cf. the consent of Moerkerken (2004, 297).
14. See Ouweneel (2016, ad loc.).

propounded by both Roman Catholics and traditional Protestants. Thus, S. Paas called it the "classic Christian doctrine."[15] Such designations are often successful discussion stoppers for the uninformed, because only spiritual agitators dare to deviate from the "classic" line. Yet, throughout the centuries, many theologians have dared to break with all sorts of "classic" positions, Martin Luther being one of the best known. Theology has often been advanced by those who ventured to leave the beaten track. Later generations must evaluate such derring-do: the daredevils are either condemned (rightly or falsely), or others pick up the new trail that they have pioneered, and totally new developments occur.

To which category did Dietrich Bonhoeffer belong, at least when it comes to the Ecclesia? In 1932–1933, in his courses on Genesis 1–3 he taught that chapter 2:23 ("This at last is bone of my bones and flesh of my flesh") revealed the Ecclesia in its original form.[16] The Bible reader familiar with typology might think that Bonhoeffer was speaking here of Eve as a type of the Ecclesia.[17] But no: what Bonhoeffer wished to say was that humanity is now, for the first time, more than one person, that this is the simplest form of community, and that the Ecclesia supposedly arose in this way. One cannot be a community; you need at least two or three (Matt. 18:20).

In his view, the Ecclesia did not exist only since the Fall; it is not only a community of redeemed people. Rather, Bonhoeffer argued that it existed before the Fall, as soon as human fellowship came into existence, which in turn was grounded in God himself. All God-given community of humans is "church"! This is perhaps the broadest definition of "Ecclesia" that I have encountered, and the reader will understand that it holds little appeal for me.

More specifically—as far as Israel is concerned—L. Berkhof expressed the matter as follows: "The New Testament Church is essentially one with the Church of the old Dispensation."[18] And J. I. Packer argued that the Ecclesia is *not* simply a New Testament

---

15. Paas (2014, 21).
16. Bonhoeffer (1997, 99).
17. Origen viewed Eve, Sarah, Tamar, Rahab, the woman of Prov. 31, the Virgin Mary, and Mary Magdalene as types of the Ecclesia; see Dulles (1987, 19); cf. Congar (1970, 44); Denham Smith (n.d.).
18. Berkhof (1981, 632).

phenomenon; rather it is the historical continuation of Israel in the Tanakh.[19] Biblical proof is not given; why would you need to demonstrate what "everybody" already believes?

Yet, it seems that today Reformed people are dealing with the notion of the "one Church since Adam" in a more nuanced way. A. Noordegraaf made a clear distinction between the people of Israel and the (New Testament) Ecclesia of Christ.[20] He spoke of the "church of all time," but on the same page of his publication he spoke of the "new [!] people of God from Jews, but especially from Gentiles."[21] Elsewhere he said "that in the Ecclesia the Messianic congregation of the end time has become manifest, rooted in Israel"[22] — a description with which I could live, at least with respect to the immanent-historical (not the eternal-transcendent) aspect of the Ecclesia.[23]

11.2.3 A Paradigm Shift

B. Wentsel claimed that "the church consists of the people of God from all times and dispensations,"[24] or somewhat more precisely:

> The Church goes back to, and is rooted in, the covenant of God with *Abraham*, our representative, in whom the entire ecumenism is contained [Gen. 12:17; Rom. 4:16-17]. . . . If we continue the line even further back, it turns out that the Church goes back to *Adam*, image of God, steward of the creation, representative of all humanity, with whom God twice made a covenant (Gen. 2:15-17).[25]

And a little earlier he had written: "This Pentecost event in Jerusalem [Acts 2] was not the birthday of the Church, because after

---

19. J. I. Packer in Henry (1962, 242).
20. A. Noordegraaf in Van 't Spijker et al. (1999, 19–62).
21. Ibid., 29.
22. Ibid., 47.
23. E.g., W. Balke makes a different sound: "In the one church of Christ, church and Israel belong together" (ibid., 264); logically this is a strange statement: how can the church be a part of itself?
24. Wentsel (1995, 368).
25. Wentsel (1998a, 26–27). The concluding statement refers to God's covenant-making both before and after the Fall; is this alluding to the Reformed theory of the covenant of works and the covenant of grace?

all the latter had been called into existence much earlier."[26] Notice this expression "because after all" (Dutch: *immers*), which accepts as self-evident the very point that must be demonstrated.[27]

This kind of "self-evidentness" is one of the most dangerous things in any form of science and scholarship. It means that within a community that adheres to a particular paradigm, nobody takes the trouble to supply us with evidence for a certain postulate, because all the people within that community have already accepted that postulate as *self*-evident or necessarily true. What is required is a paradigm shift. What is required is an Antoine Lavoisier (chemistry), a Georg Cantor (mathematics), or an Albert Einstein (physics) to burst the bubble, that is, *to call into question what is "self-evident."* Where is the Roman Catholic, or Lutheran, or Calvinist, or other theologian who will supply us with *independent* biblical evidence that what the New Testament calls the Ecclesia has existed since Adam? When will theologians stop assuming as self-evident what is not at all self-evident?

Yet, we are making progress, though not as quickly as happened with Lavoisier, Cantor, and Einstein; progress is more step by step. Consider this point for instance: B. Wentsel refused to call the Ecclesia "spiritual Israel": "[T]he name Israel cannot be transferred to the Church just like that; Israel keeps its name, and also its own identity."[28] This is remarkable and gratifying. Had Wentsel consistently developed this, however, he would have seen that if the Ecclesia is not Israel, can we not safely conclude that Israel (or the remnant of Israel) is not the Ecclesia? Can we not assuredly conclude that the two are very different divine projects? If Wentsel wishes to find one single caption for the two together, he might consider not using the term "Ecclesia," but the (one) "people of God." Thereby the cleft would have been bridged, and the dispute would have disappeared!

11.3 The Ecclesia is Post-Pentecost
11.3.1 No Unified Entity

Let me explain why the Ecclesia, in the sense in which the New Tes-

---

26. Ibid., 25.
27. However, see also the sequel of Wentsel's quotation below in our §11.7.1.
28. Ibid., 223.

tament wrote about it, necessarily exists only from the Day of Pentecost. Several of these nine arguments that I am going to mention in this and the next eight sections have been briefly touched upon already, but must be explained in a bit more detail.[29]

First, there was no unified entity consisting of all the regenerate before the Day of Pentecost. In the Tanakh, the "people of God," ethnic Israel, consisted of regenerate and non-regenerate people, while there were also regenerate people outside Israel.[30] In other words, there *was* not yet such a thing as "a holy congregation of true Christian believers" (Belgic Confession, Art. 27), in which all true "children of God [Jewish and Gentile] who are scattered abroad" were "gathered into one" (John 11:52). It is absurd to suggest that there existed such a thing as the Ecclesia in the sense of the totality and unity of all the regenerate worldwide. *The whole is more than the sum of the parts.* That is, mentally we may add together all the regenerate in the period of the Tanakh, but the sum does not necessarily imply a whole. A totality that was more than such a simple addition of individuals *did not exist*, something that could be called "Ecclesia," or even the *one* "people of God." If we could speak of an "Israel of God" in the Tanakh—and we can—then non-regenerate Israelites were not part of it—*but regenerate Gentiles were not part of it either!*

The Ecclesia is a unique entity, with very specific characteristics, to be mentioned below. And if we say that *Israel* of the Tanakh was the Ecclesia during that period of the Tanakh, two questions must be answered. First, what about all the regenerate outside Israel? And second, what about all the non-regenerate within Israel?

11.3.2 The Ecclesia: A Future Matter

Second, as we have seen, Jesus speaks of "his Ecclesia" in the future sense: "On this rock I *will* build my church" (Matt. 16:18);[31] the Jews have their *ekklēsia* (Acts 7:38), and each Gentile city has its *ekklē-*

---

29. Cf. Chafer (*ST* 4:45–46); Demarest (1997, 338–39).

30. Adam and Eve, Abel, Enoch, Lamech and his son Noah, Abraham, Isaac, Jacob, and at least his son Joseph, Melchizedek, Job, Eliphaz (?), Bildad (?), Zophar (?), Elihu, Jethro, Rahab, Ruth, Naaman, Ebed-melech, Hiram (?), the widow of Zarephath (1 Kings 17), the Shunammite (see §6.3.2).

31. F. Hahn in Kertelge (1977, 552) rejects attempts to view this future form as a voluntative "I will" in the sense of "I wish," "I want."

sia (Acts 19:32, 39, 41), but Jesus is going to have *his own* Ecclesia, which he will build on the rock (which is either [people such as] Peter, or Jesus himself as Peter had confessed him). This Ecclesia is the "one flock" with the "one shepherd," which, according to Jesus' statement in John 10:16, was still future. And the unified entity that would be created out of the "scattered children of God" was, according to Jesus' statement in John 11:52, still future as well.

This is why until the Day of Pentecost (Acts 2) the New Testament *never* spoke of the Ecclesia as a present reality. The word was not even mentioned, except in Matthew 16:18 and 18:17, where it referred to a future reality. However, after the Day of Pentecost, beginning with Acts 5:11 ("the whole church" of Jerusalem), the word appeared more than twenty times. Luke used this word in Acts, the book he wrote, but never in his Gospel. Apparently, according to him there *was* no Ecclesia before Acts 2.

As Millard J. Erickson put it: "It would seem that he [i.e., Luke] did not regard the church as present until the period covered in Acts. (While Acts 7:38 uses the Gk. term *ekklēsia* in reference to the people of Israel in the wilderness, it is likely that the term is here being used in a non-technical sense.) We conclude that the church originated at Pentecost."[32] Thus, the fact that the Septuagint rendered the Hebrew word *qahal* used in the Tanakh as *ekklēsia* does not prove that this is the same as the Ecclesia in the New Testament.[33] Using the same word is not necessarily proof that the same matter is meant, just as Naamah the daughter of Lamech is not the same as Naamah, the mother of Rehoboam (Gen. 4:19-22; 1 Kings 14:21).

11.3.3 The Ecclesia: A Matter Formerly Hidden

Third, during the centuries that comprise the Tanakh, the Ecclesia had existed in the heart and mind of God, so to speak, but for human beings it had been a "mystery," which is not something "mysterious," but simply a secret, hidden matter (Eph. 3:4-6):

---

32. Erickson (1998, 1058). Actually, he did believe that the believers in the Tanakh were included in the Ecclesia (1058–59), so that we may wonder what difference it makes for his view whether the Ecclesia began with Adam and Eve, or on the Day of Pentecost.

33. *Contra* Ridderbos (1975, 328).

> ... the mystery of Christ, which was not made known to the sons of men in other generations as it has now been revealed to his holy apostles and prophets by the Spirit. This mystery is that the Gentiles are fellow heirs [together with the Jewish believers], members of the same body [as the Jewish believers], and partakers of the promise in Christ Jesus through the gospel.

And as the apostle Paul said elsewhere, Christ's

> body, that is, the church, of which I became a minister according to the stewardship from God that was given to me for you, to make the word of God fully known, the mystery hidden for ages and generations but now revealed to his saints. To them God chose to make known how great among the Gentiles are the riches of the glory of this mystery, which is Christ in you [Gentile believers, as one with the Jewish believers], the hope of glory (Col. 1:24–27).[34]

The "mystery" (secret matter) did not mean that the Ecclesia existed in the Tanakh but was not recognized as such in those days. Of course, it did not yet exist: there was no company in which Jewish and Gentile Jesus-believers were members on equal footing of the one and the same body of Christ, that is, a body in which Christ was personally present, in both Jewish and Gentile believers. That Gentile believers could be joined to *Israel* as proselytes, and thus became full-fletched Jews, was no mystery at all.[35] The significance of the Ecclesia is not that Gentile believers are added to "Israel,"[36] but that Jesus-believers *from* Israel and Jesus-believers *from* the Gentiles have been joined together into something entirely new, into an entity about which formerly nobody could have had the faintest idea.

Please note that the Ecclesia

(a) was totally hidden to *all* people before Jesus came,

(b) was hidden to the disciples, even after the Day of Pentecost, until it was fully revealed to the apostles by the Holy Spirit, in particular through the apostle Paul (especially in Eph. and Col.), and

(c) is still hidden to those who, even today, do not understand the true character of the Ecclesia, despite its having been revealed

---

34. Cf. also Rom. 16:25; 1 Cor. 2:7 KJV.
35. See Ouweneel (2010a, §2.4.1).
36. Ibid., §3.4.

in Holy Scripture, and is being explained to us by the Holy Spirit (according to 1 Cor. 2:6-7 the wisdom concerning the "mystery" is revealed only to the "mature").

11.3.4 The Foundation of the Ecclesia

Fourth, in the previous section, we saw that the "mystery" of the Ecclesia, that is, its being a hidden matter in former centuries, entails the fact that the body of Christ has been unified with its glorified head in heaven. In the Gospels as well, this was still a hidden thing, because there *was* as yet no glorified Man in heaven. In the early chapters of Acts, this was still a hidden thing, because there *was* now indeed a glorified Man in heaven but no one had yet explained to Jesus-believers what this meant. But since Ephesians and Colossians, it is no longer a hidden matter: "the mystery hidden for ages and generations but now revealed to his saints" (Col. 1:26); ". . . the mystery of Christ, which was not made known to the sons of men in other generations as it has now been revealed to his holy apostles and prophets by the Spirit" (Eph. 3:4-5).

We read in Ephesians 2:19-21:

> So then you [i.e., Gentile believers] are no longer strangers and aliens [or, sojourners], but you are fellow citizens with the [Jewish] saints and [together with them you are] members of the household of God, built on the foundation of the *apostles and prophets*, Christ Jesus himself being the cornerstone, in whom the whole structure, being joined together, grows into a holy temple in the Lord.

As I have argued in §10.1.2, these "apostles and prophets" are definitely "apostles and *New Testament* prophets," as in 3:5 and 4:11 (Christ gave to his church "apostles and prophets"). This implies that the Ecclesia could not have existed before these New Testament apostles and prophets had appeared, because these were the men who laid the foundation of the Ecclesia. It is impossible that a building exists before its foundation has been laid.[37]

One cannot escape this argument by asserting that the term "Ecclesia" always refers to "the Ecclesia according to the specific character it has developed since the Day of Pentecost." First, the Bible never says such a thing; this idea is a human invention. The New Testament always speaks of "*the* Ecclesia," and what it means

---
37. Ibid., §2.1.3.

by that is *the* Ecclesia. Second, this assertion is neither useful nor profitable because the Ecclesia did not exist before the Day of Pentecost. *The* Ecclesia has existed only since the apostles and prophets, by the Holy Spirit, laid its foundation through their preaching and their inspired writings. And they could do this only after, and because, Jesus Christ became the glorified Man at God's right hand.

11.3.5 The Position of John the Baptist

Fifth, it is implicitly evident from two New Testament passages that Jesus' forerunner, John the Baptist, did *not* belong to the new dispensation of the Ecclesia. At one point Jesus said, "Truly, I say to you, among those born of women there has arisen no one greater than John the Baptist. Yet the one who is least in the kingdom of heaven is greater than he" (Matt. 11:11). This cannot be understood as a moral observation—as though every member of the kingdom of God would be morally superior to John the Baptist—but it is a redemptive-historical observation: John did not yet have any share in the kingdom of God because the kingdom arrived only in the person of Jesus (cf. Luke 17:21), and more specifically with his resurrection and glorification (cf. Matt. 28:18, "Jesus came and said to them, 'All authority in heaven and on earth has been given to me'").

John the Baptist himself said, "The one who has the bride is the bridegroom. The friend of the bridegroom, who stands and hears him, rejoices greatly at the bridegroom's voice" (John 3:29). John knew that he did not belong to the (bridal) Ecclesia; just like all the other great figures from the Tanakh he belonged "only" to the "friends" of the bridegroom (the groomsmen, so to speak). Revelation 19:7–9 tied in with this in the sense that, here, a distinction was made between the wife of the Lamb and those who have been invited to the wedding feast. A bride is not invited to her own wedding. On the one hand, there is the "bride" or "wife," which is the Ecclesia (cf. 21:9–10), and on the other hand, there are the "friends," all believers who lived before the death and resurrection of Christ who have not belonged to the (bridal) Ecclesia.

11.3.6 The Significance of Jesus' Death

Sixth, God's Ecclesia could originate only after Jesus accomplished the following in his self-surrender unto death:

> For he [i.e., Christ] himself is our *shalom* — he has made us [i.e., Jewish and Gentile believers] both one and has broken down the *m'chitzah* [i.e., partition wall[38]] which divided us by destroying in his own body the enmity occasioned by the *Torah*,[39] with its commands set forth in the form of ordinances. He did this in order to create in union with himself from the two groups a single new humanity and thus make *shalom*, and in order to reconcile to God both in a single body by being executed on a stake as a criminal and thus in himself killing that enmity (Eph. 2:14–16 CJB).

Through his death, Jesus broke down the dividing wall between Jews and Gentiles, occasioned by the Torah in the sense that Israel proudly boasted in the Torah, to the irritation and enmity of the Gentiles. Thus, the Torah made a division between the two, not because something was wrong with the Torah as such but because of the sinful nature of both Jews and Gentiles. Through his death, Jesus bridged the divide between the two groups. Thus, the way was opened to reconciling these two parties, (believing) Jews and (believing) Gentiles, to each other in one "body," the Ecclesia, the body of the glorified Christ. The "mystery" (secret) concerning the Ecclesia entails that Jewish and Gentile believers enter and live in this Ecclesia on equal footing (Eph. 2:11–22; 3:1–12), none of the members being more indispensable than the others (cf. 1 Cor. 12:14–31). The unique Pauline term "body," which does not appear in the Tanakh with regard to the Ecclesia, brings to light the Ecclesia's unique, specific character in the clearest way.[40]

It is important to understand this correctly. Believers in the Tanakh enjoyed many blessings in anticipation of and founded upon Jesus' death. Each of these believers possessed forgiveness of sins on the basis of the blood of Christ (cf. Rom. 3:23–26), although this was to be shed much later, and explained much later.

---

38. In Judaism, a *m'chitzah* is a partition (fence or wall), in particular the one between men and women in a synagogue, but also, for instance, at the Western Wall in Jerusalem.

39. The text does *not* say that Jesus abolished the Torah, as several translations suggest — a statement that would contradict many other New Testament statements (e.g., Matt. 5:17; Rom. 3:31; 8:4; 13:8–10; Gal. 6:2); see Ouweneel (2020).

40. Cf. Ridderbos (1975, 327–28, and chapter 9).

However, what did not yet exist in the Tanakh was the abolition of the enmity between Israel and the Gentiles, that is, removing the partition wall.

11.3.7 The Significance of Jesus' Glorification

Seventh, during the last night of his human life on earth, the Son asked the Father: "I glorified you on earth, having accomplished the work that you gave me to do. And now, Father, glorify me in your own presence with the glory that I had with you before the world existed" (John 17:4–5). This glorification occurred when Jesus entered heaven after his ascension and sat down at God's right hand.[41] The apostle Paul prays that believers may know

> what is the immeasurable greatness of his power toward us who believe, according to the working of his great might that he worked in Christ when he raised him from the dead and seated him at his right hand in the heavenly places, far above all rule and authority and power and dominion, and above every name that is named, not only in this age but also in the one to come. And he put all things under his feet and gave him as head over all things to the church, which is his body, the fullness of him who fills all in all (Eph. 1:19–23; cf. 4:15; 5:23).

Paul said that Christ was given as head to the Ecclesia at his glorification in heaven—*not before*. So, Christ was not the head of the Ecclesia in the Tanakh? The simple answer is: No, first because the Ecclesia did *not yet* exist, and second, the glorified Man had *not yet* ascended to heaven. Jesus *became* the Glorified Man on Ascension Day, and his Ecclesia originated ten days later, on the Day of Pentecost. During the time of the Tanakh, the *Triune* God was the head of humanity, and the *God* of all believers; it is a serious matter for Christians to be ignorant about the essential difference between, on the one hand, this situation during the time of the Tanakh and, on the other hand, the glorified *Man* in heaven, the head of the Ecclesia in the present time.

As the "firstborn from the dead"—the first of all those who gloriously rise from death: first in time and first in ranking—he is "the head of the body, the Ecclesia" (Col. 1:18; cf. 2:19). The Ecclesia is

---

41. At this moment, Jesus' *risen* body also became his *glorious* body (Phil. 3:21)—a glory that overwhelmed Saul near Damascus (Acts 22:11), and John on Patmos (Rev. 1:16–17).

inconceivable apart from the Lord Jesus Christ's resurrection from the dead and glorification in heaven. This is not just a matter of timing; in order to understand what the Ecclesia is, we must see that, "in Christ Jesus," she is "seated with him in the heavenly places" (Eph. 2:6). In the Tanakh there could not be a people of God in Christ seated in the heavenly places as long as Christ himself, as the Man who had died, was raised, and was glorified, had not been seated there. Ultimately this means that the Ecclesia could not exist as long as the Son of God had not yet become Man. This is precisely what the Greek phrase *kainos anthrōpos* ("new man," "new self," "new humanity," "new person"; Eph. 4:22-24; Col. 3:9-11) means: participation in the glorified humanity of Christ himself.

Of course, this important matter can be understood only if the deity and humanity of Christ are properly distinguished;[42] those who do not see any essential difference between the pre-incarnate Christ in heaven and the glorified Christ in heaven will never grasp it. The pre-incarnate Christ was God but not Man, the glorified Christ is both God and Man, and such forever. The pre-incarnate Christ did not have a body, the glorified Christ has a body (cf. Col. 2:8, "in him the whole fullness of deity dwells [present tense!] *bodily*"). The consequence is this: believers could not be united to the pre-incarnate Christ, but they can be united to the glorified *Man* Christ, as his body (collectively), and they can share in his "new humanity" (individually).

11.3.8 The Ecclesia: Dwelling Place of the Holy Spirit

Eighth, the Ecclesia is the temple of the Holy Spirit on earth,[43] and she can be this only after the outpouring of the Holy Spirit in Acts 2. *There was no temple of the Spirit before this day.* Earlier we saw that the Holy Spirit *worked* on earth during the period of the Tanakh, since Genesis 1:2; later, especially through judges and prophets. But it is never said that the Holy Spirit *dwelt* on earth during that period. He rested on God's servants, but in cases of backsliding he could also leave them (cf. Ps. 51:11). From Acts 2 onward, the situation is very different: the Holy Spirit *dwells* in individual believers, and in the Ecclesia as a whole. And this "dwelling" means that he can, and

---

42. See extensively, Ouweneel (2007b, chapters 8–9).
43. 1 Cor. 3:16; Eph. 2:20–22; cf. 1 Cor. 6:19; 2 Cor. 6:16.

will, never leave her; the Ecclesia is the Holy Spirit's permanent, everlasting dwelling place, as Jesus said, "I will ask the Father, and he will give you another Helper, *to be with you forever*, even the Spirit of truth" (John 14:16).

Jews commonly say that God dwells in heaven, and humans dwell on earth (cf. Ps. 115:3, 16). But Christians can truly declare and celebrate these two highly remarkable characteristics of Christianity, which seem to be the very opposite: first, since Jesus' ascension there is a glorified *Man* in heaven at God's right hand,[44] and since the Day of Pentecost, *God* the Holy Spirit dwells on earth (viz., in the Ecclesia).[45] Thus, someone has described the essence of the Ecclesia as "a community created by the Spirit,"[46] and observed that the Ecclesia is God's personal presence in the world by means of the Spirit.[47] This is another of the many essential differences between Israel and the Ecclesia: in Israel, the Spirit *rested on some*, but never permanently; in the Ecclesia, the Spirit *dwells in all*, and does so forever. Believers may not always be *filled* with the Spirit—otherwise, the admonition of Ephesians 5:18 would be superfluous—but he always *dwells* in them. (The dwelling has to do more with the Spirit as a divine person, whereas the filling has to do with the Spirit as a divine power.)

11.3.9 The Ecclesia: A Spirit-Baptized Company

Ninth, one way to describe the "body of Christ" is to say that it is the totality of all those who have been "baptized" in the Holy Spirit. I am referring here to 1 Corinthians 12:13, which I would render more or less as follows (ASV): "For in one Spirit were we all baptized into one body, whether Jews or Greeks, whether bond or free; and were all made to drink of one Spirit."[48] Was the apostle Paul speaking here of water baptism ("in [the power of] the one Spirit") or of Spirit baptism, that is, the believer's human spirit being figuratively immersed in the Holy Spirit,[49] just as the body is literally immersed

---

44. See Ouweneel (2007b, 431–33).
45. See Ouweneel (2007a, chapter 7).
46. Van Gelder (2000, title, 24–25, 112–13).
47. Ibid., 25.
48. Cf. Ouweneel (2007a, §7.1).
49. Cf. Matt. 3:11; Mark 1:8; Luke 3:16; John 1:33; Acts 1:5; 11:16; in all these

in water? I believe it is the latter. The effect of this Spirit baptism is, as Paul indicates, that all New Testament believers who have been baptized in the one Spirit have now become part of the one body of Christ. "Baptism" is: the person's spirit goes into the Spirit; "making to drink" is the opposite: the Spirit goes into the person.

This description of the Ecclesia as the totality of all people baptized in the Spirit is another of those essential differences with Israel in the Tanakh. This Spirit baptism occurred no earlier than in Acts 2. Even in Acts 1, the Spirit baptism was something future, although at that moment it was very imminent; as Jesus said (Acts 2:5), "John baptized with water [Gk. *hydaiti*, without a preposition], but you will be baptized in [Gk. *en*] the Holy Spirit not many days from now." On the Day of Pentecost, the one hundred twenty followers of Jesus Christ were baptized (spiritually immersed) in the Holy Spirit, and as a consequence, at that very moment the Ecclesia of Christ originated, as we now know in retrospect. From the beginning of its existence, the Ecclesia was the temple in which the Holy Spirit dwelt and will dwell forever. It was also the body of Christ, formed together by the one Spirit-baptism, united to its glorified head in heaven, and in him seated in the heavenly places (Eph. 2:6).

11.4 Parallelisms Between Believers in the Tanakh and Believers in the New Testament

11.4.1 Similarities

The classic dispensationalist Lewis Sperry Chafer mentioned a number of contrasts between Israel and the Ecclesia that, in my view (as a very moderate dispensationalist), are partial similarities instead. This may seem to play into the hands of the supersessionists, but this should not frighten us away. Why should we not acknowledge that believers in the Tanakh and believers in the New Testament have many things in common? However, such commonalities do not prove that the two are identical. On the contrary: if there are commonalities between A and B, this suggests instead that the two are *not* identical. I think of the following points (see earlier, much more briefly, §10.1.2).[50]

(1) *Seed of Abraham*. The apostle Paul said that Abraham is "the

---

cases, read "baptize in," not "with" ("immersing with" is linguistic nonsense).
50. Chafer (*ST* 4:47–53).

father of all who believe without being circumcised [i.e., Gentile Jesus-believers], so that righteousness would be counted to them [i.e., they would be declared righteous (= justified)] as well, and to make him the father of the circumcised [i.e., Jewish Jesus-believers] who are not merely circumcised but who also walk in the footsteps of the faith that our father Abraham had before he was circumcised."[51] The former group consists of spiritual children of Abraham (cf. Gal. 3:7, 29). The latter group consists of both physical and spiritual children of Abraham; this is the "Israel of God" (Gal. 6:16).[52]

The latter, the Jewish *tzaddiqim*, must be distinguished from those who are physical but not spiritual children of Abraham. Jesus acknowledged that the religious but non-believing leaders of Israel were "offspring" of Abraham, but he refused to give them the title "children" of Abraham:

> They answered him, "Abraham is our father." Jesus said to them, "If you were Abraham's children, you would be doing the works Abraham did, but now you seek to kill me, a man who has told you the truth that I heard from God. This is not what Abraham did. You are doing the works your father did. . . . You are of your father, the devil" (John 8:37-41, 44).

In other words, the believing Gentile is more "child" of Abraham than the unbelieving Jew because walking in the same faith as Abraham is more important than physical descent. "Sons of Abraham" coincides with "sons of God," as Paul made clear (Gal. 3:7, 26).

(2) *Mission.* Both Israel and the Ecclesia share the mission to make known to the nations the one true God, the God of Israel. Unfortunately, the similarity goes further than this: both have miserably failed in this task. The apostle Paul says to the Jews:

> [I]f you are sure that you yourself are a guide to the blind, a light to those who are in darkness, an instructor of the foolish, a teacher of children, having in the Torah the embodiment of knowledge and

---

51. Rom. 4:11, 16; cf. Gal. 3:7-9, 14, 29; 4:28; cf. Matt. 3:9 par.; Luke 13:16; 19:9.
52. Wentsel (1995, 367 [cf. 1998a, 81-83]): "Abraham, the representative of all believers, remains for Israel and the church the historical common primordial father, and the promise-bearer who links the two together."

truth—you then who teach others, do you not teach yourself? While you preach against stealing, do you steal? . . . You who boast in the Torah dishonor God by breaking the Torah. For, as it is written, "The name of God is blasphemed among the Gentiles because of you" [Isa. 52:5; Ezek. 36:23] (Rom. 2:19-24).

Concerning the Ecclesia's mission, Paul spoke of "the revelation of the mystery that was kept secret for long ages but has now been disclosed and through the prophetic writings [i.e., of the New Testament] has been made known to all nations, according to the command of the eternal God, to bring about the obedience of faith" (Rom. 16:25-26).

But after almost two thousand years, Paul no doubt would have said that Christians have equally dishonored God by not living up to the message they preach. They were supposed to preach the "gospel of the *kingdom*" (Matt. 24:14)—but how many of the 2.3 billion "Christians" in the modern world have really submitted to the King, and live according to his commandments? And speaking of "the revelation of the mystery," how many of them have really understood—with their hearts and their minds—the "mystery" of the Ecclesia?

(3) *Law and grace.* It has been often claimed that the governing principle in Israel had been the *law*, and that of the Ecclesia has been *grace*, but this is not a genuine contrast at all. On the one hand, the "Israel of God" has *always* lived by the grace and mercy of God. The people failed already at Mount Sinai, but on that same mountain God proclaimed: "The LORD, the LORD, a God merciful and gracious, slow to anger, and abounding in steadfast love and faithfulness, keeping steadfast love for thousands, forgiving iniquity and transgression and sin" (Exod. 34:5-6).

And recall the words of David:

The LORD is merciful and gracious,
    slow to anger and abounding in steadfast love.
He will not always chide,
    nor will he keep his anger forever.
He does not deal with us according to our sins,
    nor repay us according to our iniquities (Ps. 103:8-10).

Thus, the Ecclesia lives by grace, but the "Israel of God" does as well. Conversely, Israel is under the Torah, but the Ecclesia is as well, namely, the "Torah of Christ."[53] Jesus-believers are justified (declared righteous) by their faith in Jesus, but genuine faith is "faith working through love," that is, faith functioning according to the commandment of love.[54]

(4) *Position*. The position of Israel is that of servants, and the position of the Ecclesia is that of sons, but this is not a real contrast, either. On the one hand, of Israel — or at least of the "Israel of God" — it was said, "You are the sons of the LORD, your God" (Deut. 14:1), or, in the singular: "Israel is my firstborn son" (Exod. 4:22; cf. Hos. 11:1). On the other hand, Paul said of Jesus-believing Gentiles: "[N]ow that you have been set free from sin and have become slaves [or, servants] of God, the fruit you get leads to sanctification and its end, eternal life" (Rom. 6:22).

(5) *Priesthood*. Chafer claimed that Israel *had* a priesthood, whereas the Ecclesia *is* a priesthood. But again, this is inaccurate. God called Israel a "kingdom of priests" (Exod. 19:6; DRA: "a priestly kingdom"), and he said of restored Israel: "[Y]ou shall be called the priests of the LORD" (Isa. 61:6). Similarly, the Ecclesia was called a "holy priesthood" and a "royal priesthood (1 Pet. 2:5, 9). The apostle John wrote that Christ "made us a kingdom, priests to his God and Father" (Rev. 1:6; cf. 5:10; 20:6).

(6) *Future judgment*. According to Chafer, Israel would be on the way to God's future judgment, whereas the Ecclesia would not. Again, this is astonishingly inaccurate. The true "Israel of God" is *not* on the way to God's judgment[55] but to glory. But if we look at both Israel and the church from the viewpoint of human responsibility, then many "Christians" will fall under God's judgment along with many ungodly Jews: "[I]t is time for judgment to begin at the household of God [i.e, the church]; and if it begins with us, what will be the outcome for those who do not obey the gospel of

---

53. 1 Cor. 9:21; Gal. 6:2; cf. John 14:15, 21, 23; 15:10; Rom. 8:4; 13:8–10; James 1:25; 2:8, 12.
54. Cf. John 13:34–35; 14:15, 21; 15:10, 12, 17; 1 John 3:23; 4:21; 5:2–3; 2 John 1:5–6.
55. Except in the general sense of the judgment seat of Christ, where *all* believers' lives will be judged in view of the reward that will be given (Rom. 14:10; 2 Cor. 5:10).

God?" (1 Pet. 4:17). Compare the judgments pronounced on most of the seven churches in Revelation 2–3, and on the "great prostitute" in chapter 17, which I believe is the false church.

11.4.2 Additional Similarities

Thus, there are more similarities between Israel and the Ecclesia than classic dispensationalists seem prepared to acknowledge. Let me elaborate this point a little further by adding the following similarities between believers in the Tanakh and believers in the New Testament.[56]

(7) *Rebirth.* Both groups are born again by the same Holy Spirit (Ezek. 36:25–26; John 3:3–5), that is, they have the same life from God, have a new nature that is not able to sin; what still sins in them is the old nature, the "flesh" (Rom. 7–8). As far as believers in the Tanakh are concerned, we have possible proof of this in 1 Peter 4:6 (NIV): "For this is the reason the gospel was preached even to those who are now dead, so that they might be judged according to human standards in regard to the body, but *live according to God* in regard to the spirit."

Both groups can be called *chasidim*, that is, "godly ones," faithful and devoted to God and his commandments, which for us today is the Torah of Christ (see [3] above).

(8) *Cleansing.* Both groups were, and are, cleansed by the same blood of Christ: "[I]f the blood of goats and bulls, and the sprinkling of defiled persons with the ashes of a heifer, sanctify for the purification of the flesh, how much more will the blood of Christ, who through the eternal Spirit offered himself without blemish to God, purify our conscience from dead works to serve the living God" (Heb. 9:13–14).

By way of anticipation, believers in the Tanakh must have been purified by the same blood of Christ because there is no other blood by which people can be cleansed. I think that the apostle Paul expressed this by making the following distinction between the Tanakh era and the New Testament era; he spoke of

> ... the redemption that is in Christ Jesus, whom God put forward as a propitiation by his blood, to be received by faith. This was to show God's righteousness, because in his divine forbearance he had passed

---

56. See Ouweneel (2009b, §3.5,8.1–8.2), and Clowney (1995, chapters 2–3).

over *former* sins [i.e., sins during the Tanakh era]. It was to show his righteousness at the *present* time [i.e., the New Testament era], so that he might be just and the justifier of the one who has faith in Jesus (Rom. 3:24–26).

That is, God could "forbear" the sins committed by believers in the Tanakh because he looked forward to the work of atonement that Jesus would accomplish.

(9) *Justification.* Both groups have been justified, that is, have been declared righteous, have become—or were acknowledged as—*tzaddiqim*, righteous ones, first and foremost because of their devotion to, and confidence in, God. The great example of this was Abraham: "[H]e believed the Lord, and he [i.e., God] counted it to him as righteousness" (Gen. 15:6). That is, because of his faith (confidence) in God and his promises, God declared him to be a righteous man. His position before God, like the position of believers in the Tanakh and believers in the New Testament, was not based upon certain achievements of believers, but upon God himself and his justifying grace. Faith is not merely the acceptance of certain doctrines but submission to, and confidence in, *God himself*: "[T]he righteous shall live by his faith."[57]

To be sure, such faith cannot be separated from righteous *deeds*, but these works that are the *fruit* of salvation, not the condition for it. A beautiful example of pre-Pentecost believers were Zechariah and Elizabeth (Luke 1:6): "[T]hey were both righteous before God, walking blamelessly in all the commandments and statutes of the Lord." Such a description, if properly understood, is essentially true for all those serving God, both in the Tanakh and in the New Testament.

(10) *The New Covenant.* The previous points also imply that the blessings of the New Covenant, in which all previous covenants culminate, are granted not only to the "Israel of God," but also to all Gentile Jesus-believers.[58] That is, the covenant is formally made only with the twelve tribes of Israel, but it benefits all believers from every nation.

---

57. Hab. 2:4, quoted in Rom. 1:17; Gal. 3:11; Heb. 10:38.
58. Luke 22:20; 1 Cor. 11:25; 2 Cor. 3:6; Gal. 3:15–18; 4:21–31; Heb. 7:22; 8:6; 9:15; 12:24; 13:20.

11.4.3 Metaphors

The Bible often uses the same metaphors for Israel as for the Ecclesia; here are seven of them.[59]

(1) Israel is the "people of God" (Exod. 5:1), and the Ecclesia is also this (Acts 15:14; Titus 2:14; 1 Pet. 2:9–10). The difference is that in Israel's case, strictly speaking this is not a metaphor: Israel *is*, in the literal sense of the word a "people" (or "nation"), that is, a community of humans linked by ethnicity, language, history, culture, and territory. The Ecclesia is a people only in the figurative sense: she is a people made up of humans "from every nation, from all tribes and peoples and languages" (Rev. 7:9).

(2) The Israelites are "sons" or "children" of God (Deut. 14:1; Hos. 1:10), and so are the members of Christ's body (Rom. 8:14–16). The difference is that the Israelites are this in a formal sense, without this necessarily implying regeneration. In the Ecclesia, regeneration (rebirth) is a prerequisite of sonship/childhood: "[T]o all who did receive him, who believed in his name, he gave the right to become children of God, who were born, not of blood nor of the will of the flesh nor of the will of man, but of God" (John 1:12-13).

(3) Israel is the "bride" or "wife" of God, or of the Messiah,[60] the Ecclesia is the "bride" or "wife" of Christ: ". . . I betrothed you to one husband, to present you as a pure virgin to Christ" (2 Cor. 11:2)[61]

(4) Israel is compared to a "vine,"[62] and Christ and his followers are too: "I am the true vine, and my Father is the vinedresser. Every branch in me that does not bear fruit he takes away, and every branch that does bear fruit he prunes, that it may bear more fruit" (John 15:1-2).

---

59. Some have been mentioned by Clowney (1995, 29–30).
60. Isa. 49:18; 61:10; 62:5; Hos. 2:18–20; but see also the image of the wife cast off and received again: Isa. 50:1; 54:6–8; Jer. 2; Ezek. 16.
61. Cf. Eph. 5:25–32; Rev. 21:2, 9. Regarding the subject of these two "brides" or "wives," see §6.8 above.
62. Ps. 80:8; Ezek. 15; Hos. 10:1; sometimes also with a vineyard, e.g., Isa. 5:1–7.

(5) Israel is the "flock" of God,[63] and so is the Ecclesia:[64] "I have other sheep that are not of this fold. I must bring them also, and they will listen to my voice. So there will be one flock, one shepherd" (John 10:16).

(6) Israel is the "field" of God (see, e.g., Ezek. 36:9), and the Ecclesia is too: "He who plants and he who waters are one, and each will receive his wages according to his labor. For we are God's fellow workers. You are God's field" (1 Cor. 3:8–9).

(7) Israel was destined to be a "light" for the world,[65] as was the Ecclesia[66] (and, as I said before, both failed in this respect): "You are the light of the world. A city set on a hill cannot be hidden . . . let your light shine before others, so that they may see your good works and give glory to your Father who is in heaven" (Matt. 5:14–16).

Believers in the Tanakh and believers in the New Testament have much more in common than classic dispensationalists often think. They share the same regeneration, the same propitiation, the same salvation, the same spiritual father Abraham, the same Messiah, the same sacrifice, the same covenant, the same future (ultimately the new heavens and the new earth). Some statements referring to physical Israel are freely applied to the Ecclesia.[67]

These connections and similarities are so important that, in *this* sense, we might ultimately speak of one "people of God." However, one should not call this one people either "Israel" or the "Ecclesia (church)," just as, after the reunion of Judah and Ephraim (Ezek. 37:16, 19), the sum must not be called either Judah *or* Ephraim. Those who speak this way distinguish the similarities while failing to honor the differences between believers in the Tanakh and

---

63. Num. 27:17; Ps. 80:1; Isa. 40:11; 63:11 etc. It is striking that the patriarchs and the greatest leaders of ancient Israel were shepherds at one time: Abraham, Isaac, Jacob, Moses, David; see §11.6.
64. Acts 20:28–29; 1 Pet. 5:2–3; Heb. 13:20; also cf. Matt. 18:10–14.
65. Isa. 49:6 (cf. v. 3!); Rom. 2:19; the Jews called some of their greatest rabbis "lamp of light," or "lamp of Israel"; see, e.g., Talmud: Berakoth 28b; Kethuboth 17a.
66. Cf. John 8:12; 9:5; Phil. 2:15; Rev. 1:13; Rev. 2:1, 5.
67. Exod. 19:5 in 1 Pet. 2:9; Hos. 1:10 and 2:23 in Rom. 9:24–25; 1 Pet. 2:10; and Joel 2:28–32 in Acts 2:17–21.

believers in the New Testament. It is a mistake, but not a heresy, when people teach that the Ecclesia began with Adam, or with Abraham, for that matter. But those who do so truly lose sight of the enormous differences between believers in the Tanakh and believers in the New Testament.

11.5 Differences

11.5.1 The Ecclesia As People of God

In §10.1.3 we discussed seven differences between believers in the Tanakh and believers in the New Testament. Now let's consider these differences from the viewpoint of four great characteristics of the Ecclesia: people of God, family of God, body of Christ, and temple of the Holy Spirit.

First, the Ecclesia as the people of God. Although the true Israel (the "Israel of God" in Gal. 6:16) is certainly a spiritual people, Israel as such is primarily a natural, ethnic, national people. This is the same as saying that a person becomes a member of this nation through physical birth, just as a person becomes a Canadian by being born of Canadian parents. With the Ecclesia, this is very different: a person becomes a member of it not through physical birth but only through spiritual birth.[68] The children of believing parents who themselves do not yet believe are certainly part of the Christian community in the wider sense, for Paul tells us that they are "holy" (i.e. here, set apart) through their believing parents (1 Cor. 7:14). However, in the stricter sense, the church is "a holy congregation of true Christian believers" (Belgic Confession, Art. 27), not of the "children of Christian believers." This point plays a role in the various Christian views on baptism:[69] the Ecclesia consists of believers, which does not include their not-yet-believing children.[70]

With Israel it is different. Spiritually speaking, it has indeed

---

68. Pannenberg (1998, 98): "Unlike the people of Israel, the church is not a hereditary fellowship consisting of one generation of members after another. It is by nature a fellowship of individuals who are regenerated by faith and baptism."

69. See extensively, Ouweneel (2011a, chapters 5–8; 2016 on Lord's Days 26 and 27).

70. Therefore, Reformed Baptists (C. H. Spurgeon, J. C. Philpot, and many others), as well as most Evangelicals, baptize(d) their children only when these children (had) come to personal faith.

been called *out* of the nations,⁷¹ but this does not change the fact that, ethnically speaking, it is a nation among the nations, a natural, ethnic people like all other nations. Actually, this is emphasized especially when Israel goes astray, because this makes Israel equivalent to the other nations (and sometimes this is exactly what Israel wanted; see, e.g., 1 Sam. 8:5, 20). Or the prophet does this, for instance, in Amos 1-2, where the judgments on Judah and Israel are treated like those on the (other) nations (see also Amos 9:7, "Are you not like the Cushites to me, O people of Israel? . . . Did I not bring up Israel from the land of Egypt, and the Philistines from Caphtor and the Syrians from Kir?").

However, the point here is that Israel today is a nation in the ethnic sense,⁷² whereas the Ecclesia emphatically is not. The latter consists of believers who have been taken from all nations: "God first visited the Gentiles, to take *from* them a people for his name" (Acts 15:14). These "people" never become a natural, ethnic people among the peoples, a nation like all the other nations. Israel is international because there are Jews of almost every nationality on earth; but the Ecclesia is international because its members have been *born* of almost every nation on earth. This difference between Israel and the Ecclesia is obscured by objectionable notions like "national church" (Dutch *volkskerk*, or Ger. *Volkskirche*), a church that in principle includes an entire ethnic nation. Even worse is the notion of a "baptized nation," as advocated especially by P. J. Hoedemaker.⁷³

11.5.2 The Ecclesia As the Family of God

By the phrase "family of God" we understand the company of which God is the Father, and the members are his children. Of Israel it is said, "You are the sons of the LORD, your God" (see §11.4.1), and God is called their Father because he is the Creator and Sustainer of his people.⁷⁴ Formally this is true of every Israelite, due

---

71. Exod. 19:5; 33:16; Lev. 20:24; Deut. 7:6; 10:15; 2 Sam. 7:23; 1 Kings 8:53.
72. It has sometimes been argued that throughout the centuries, Israel largely lost its ethnic character—there are Caucasian Jews, African Jews, East Asian Jews, and the like—yet, every real Jew still boasts of their physical descent from Abraham, despite all ethnic mixtures.
73. See, e.g., Hoedemaker (1897).
74. Ps. 103:13; Isa. 63:16; 64:8; Mal. 2:10.

purely to his or her physical descent. But in the Ecclesia, the family of God is a spiritual matter: the members are children of God through rebirth, as we learn from John 1:12-13. In the Ecclesia, the *spiritual* children of God among Israel and the spiritual children of God from the Gentiles have been gathered into one people, according to the prophecy of John 11:52. And God is their Father, not in the general sense of Creator and Sustainer, but because they have received the Son as their life, the eternal Father of the eternal Son is now *their* Father.[75] About this the apostle Paul wrote:

> [Y]ou did not receive the spirit of slavery to fall back into fear, but you have received the Spirit of adoption as sons, by whom we cry, "Abba! Father!" The Spirit himself bears witness with our spirit that we are children of God, and if children, then heirs—heirs of God and fellow heirs with Christ, provided we suffer with him in order that we may also be glorified with him (Rom. 8:15-17).[76]

The family of God is the company of all those who have received life from God, life in the sense of the new creation, including eternal life. For believers in the Tanakh, eternal life involved the blessings of the Messianic kingdom;[77] for New Testament believers, eternal life involves the blessings of the heavenly house of the Father (John 14:1-3), including the person of Christ himself (John 17:3; 1 John 5:20). As we have learned (§10.1.3), this does not necessarily imply a great difference: since the "Father's house" is also compared to the temple (John 2:16), the Father's house might be the heavenly place of worship during the Messianic kingdom. Perhaps the Father's house can be viewed as what is going to be the heavenly counterpart of the earthly temple of Ezekiel 40-44.

The family of God is the company of those who have fellowship with the Father and the Son in the power of the Holy Spirit (cf. 2 Cor. 13:14). It is not just the life of rebirth, but "life abundantly" (John 10:10), divine life in its richest form, because believers have received Jesus Christ himself as their life (Col. 3:4; 1 John 5:11-12, 20).[78] Thus, the title "brother" or "sister" is not just a designation of

---

75. John 16:27; 20:17; 1 John 3:1; 5:12, 20.
76. See also Rom. 9:8; Eph. 5:1; Phil. 2:15; 1 John 3:1, 10; 5:2.
77. Ps. 133:3; Dan. 12:1–2; cf. Matt. 19:16; 25:34, 46; Luke 10:25.
78. See extensively, Ouweneel (2009b, §4.1–4.2).

attachment and affection, or of a physical relationship: because believers were born of God, and have the life of God in common, they are far more family than in any formal or physical sense.

11.5.3 The Ecclesia As the Body of Christ

As we have seen, the New Testament believers are the body of Christ, unified with their glorified head in heaven; they are as united as any head and body can be. Husband and wife may be separated for a while, but head and body can never be separated. Believers know him in this respect at least in the following seven qualities:

(1) Jesus is their *advocate* [Gk. *paraklētos*], their *helper*, their *intercessor*, their *defender* with the Father: "Christ Jesus is the one who died—more than that, who was raised—who is at the right hand of God, who indeed is interceding for us"; "we have an advocate with the Father, Jesus Christ the righteous."[79]

(2) Jesus is the *head* of the body (Eph. 1:19-23), the One coordinating all the members (4:15-16; Col. 2:19); the One granting the gifts to the body:

> ... it says, "When he ascended on high he led a host of captives, and he gave gifts to men." In saying, "He ascended," what does it mean but that he had also descended into the lower regions, the earth? He who descended is the one who also ascended far above all the heavens, that he might fill all things. And he gave the apostles, the prophets, the evangelists, the shepherds and teachers (Eph. 4:8–11).

(3) Jesus is the *victor* over the spiritual powers: "He disarmed the [demonic] rulers and authorities and put them to open shame, by triumphing over them in him [or, in it, i.e., the cross]."[80] This is of great practical importance for their own spiritual battle (Eph. 6:12-18).

(4) Jesus is the *center, goal, and content* of the hidden Christian life with God: "If then you have been raised with Christ, seek the things that are above, where Christ is, seated at the right hand of God. Set your minds on things that are above, not on things that are on earth. For you have died, and your life is hidden with Christ in

---

79. Rom. 8:34 and 1 John 2:1; cf. Luke 22:31–32; Heb. 4:16; 7:25.
80. Col. 2:15 ("God" [acting in Christ] is the subject here); Eph. 1:19–21; Heb. 1:3, 13; 10:12–13; 1 Pet. 3:21–22.

God" (Col. 3:1–3).

(5) Jesus is the heavenly *worship leader* of believers:[81] "We have such a High Priest, who is seated at the right hand of the throne of the Majesty in the heavens, a Minister [Gk. *leitourgos*, "liturgist"] of the sanctuary and of the true tabernacle which the LORD erected, and not man."

(6) Jesus is the *example* and the final *goal* of the Christian "race": "[O]ne thing I do: forgetting what lies behind and straining forward to what lies ahead, I press on toward the goal for the prize of the upward call of God in Christ Jesus" (Phil 3:13–14). "[L]et us lay aside every weight, and sin which clings so closely, and let us run with endurance the race that is set before us, looking to Jesus, the founder and perfecter of our faith" (Heb. 12:1–2).[82]

(7) Jesus is *looking forward* to his final triumph: Christ "sat down at the right hand of God, waiting from that time [together with his people] until his enemies should be made a footstool for his feet" (Heb. 10:12–13).

11.5.4 The Ecclesia As Temple of the Holy Spirit

Collectively, the Ecclesia is the house or the temple of God as the dwelling place of the Holy Spirit (1 Cor. 3:16; Eph. 2:20–22). The Ecclesia is a body, a bride or wife, a flock, a field, and last but not least, a house or temple. It is a figurative house whose figurative stones are believers: "As you come to him [i.e., Christ], a living stone rejected by men but in the sight of God chosen and precious, you yourselves like living stones are being built up as a spiritual house, to be a holy priesthood, to offer spiritual sacrifices acceptable to God through Jesus Christ" (1 Pet. 2:4–5).

Or — in a different use of the imagery — the Ecclesia is a house in which believers dwell (Eph. 2:19). It is a figurative temple in which God dwells as he did in the physical temple in Jerusalem. It is also a figurative temple as a place of worship in the power of the Spirit.

Individually, believers have been baptized in (Acts 1:5; 11:16–17), sealed, and anointed with,[83] and — in their optimum spiritual state — even filled with, the Holy Spirit (Eph. 5:18). During pre-Pen-

---

81. Heb. 8:1–2 (NKJV); cf. 2:11–12; 7:25; 10:19–22; 13:15.
82. Cf. 1 Cor. 9:24, 26; Gal. 2:2; 5:7; Phil. 2:16; 2 Tim. 4:7.
83. 2 Cor. 1:21–22; Eph. 1:13; 4:30; cf. Acts 10:38; 1 John 2:20, 27.

tecost times, an anointing with the Spirit (Isa. 61:1; cf. 1 Sam. 16:13) and being filled with the Spirit[84] did occur occasionally, but only in individual cases. A *people* was never collectively anointed with the Spirit. Nor was there ever a baptism in the Holy Spirit, for this event was announced as a future event,[85] and occurred on and after the Day of Pentecost.[86]

In the period of the Tanakh, the gift of the Spirit was limited to a few, with a view to a single task and for a limited period. And the act of anointing with oil—a picture of the anointing with the Spirit—was limited to kings, priests, and prophets. However, according to the promises in the Tanakh,[87] the anointing with the Spirit would be granted to *all* believers—as happened on the Day of Pentecost—and this would last forever (Acts 2:16-21; John 14:16-17). In other words, since Acts 2 *all* believers are anointed kings, priests, and prophets.[88] Due to the gift (Gk. *dōrea*)—the being given—of the Spirit, New Testament believer possesses the gifts (Gk. *charismata*) of the Spirit: gifts granted by the grace (Gk. *charis*) of God through the Holy Spirit to all believers who are open to receive them.

11.5.5 Imitating the Tanakh

Obscuring the differences between believers in the Tanakh and in the New Testament leads to regrettable consequences. Many New Testament believers are too little aware of their New Testament privileges and blessings, and therefore begin to identify themselves too easily in terms of the lifestyle and experiences of believers in the Tanakh. Remaining on the level of the Tanakh, so to speak, is a form of spiritual childhood (cf. 1 Cor. 2:6; 1 Pet. 2:1-5).

Here are some examples.

(a) The church building is viewed as a temple in the sense of the Tanakh, especially by Roman Catholics. The Greek Orthodox have a sanctuary in their churches that is accessible only to their priests, as was the case with the temple in the period of the Tanakh.

(b) The Sabbath is thought to have moved to the Sunday, and

---

84. E.g., Num. 11:24-29; 1 Sam. 10:10; 19:20, 23; Luke 1:15, 41, 67.
85. Matt. 3:11; Mark 1:8; Luke 3:16; John 1:33; Acts 1:5; 11:16.
86. Acts 1:5; 11:16; cf. 1 Cor. 12:13; Ouweneel (2007a, 170-87).
87. Isa. 32:15; 44:3; Ezek. 36:27; Joel 2:28-31; Zech. 12:10 ("Spirit," not "spirit").
88. 1 Cor. 14:24; 1 Pet. 2:9; Rev. 1:6; 5:10; 20:6.

is celebrated by hyper-Calvinists according to the rules of Sabbath that were prescribed in the Tanakh. But according to Acts 15, Gentile Jesus-believers are not under the Mosaic Torah at all (cf. Col. 2:16).

(c) Reformed Christians view Jewish circumcision, the sign of the Abrahamic Covenant, as having been replaced by infant baptism, the sign of the New Covenant. But circumcision never involved or pictured being incorporated into the death of Christ (Rom. 6:3-4; Col. 2:11-12).

(d) Many Christians love to sing—or limit themselves to singing—the Psalms of the Tanakh instead of singing rhymed portions of the New Testament.[89] Apparently, it does not matter to them that the Psalms do not speak of the most essential Christian blessings: resting in the finished work of Christ, union with the glorified Lord in heaven, eternal life in the Johannine sense, the sonship of all believers, the gifts and operations of the Holy Spirit, and so on. Such Christians hardly seem to notice the absence of these blessings in the Psalms, perhaps because these blessings may be absent from their own experience. Interestingly, the apostle Paul encourages us to sing not only psalms but also "hymns and spiritual songs" (Eph. 5:19; Col. 3:16).[90]

Here we see how failing to distinguish the nature and being of the Ecclesia, especially under the influence of supersessionism, can have the greatest practical consequences. The more people identify themselves in terms of the psalms in the Tanakh, the more easily they believe that "the church has existed since Adam." Personally, I enjoy singing the psalms of the Tanakh, rhymed or not, in various versions, since I also recognize the Christian blessings I enjoy in Christ. However, those unfamiliar with enjoying these Christian blessings will not be overcome that unfamiliarity by singing psalms only.

---

89. Phil. 2:6–11 is considered by many to be an example of an early Christian hymn.

90. It is debatable whether Paul was writing here about the psalms in the Tanakh: "There were *Christian* psalms—psalms which the Holy Spirit moved the primitive Christians to utter when they came together in worship (1 Cor. xiv, 15, 26), as He moved them to speak with tongues," according to Salmond (1979, 363); cf. Peake (1979, 541).

11.6 A Trivial Difference?

11.6.1 First Shepherds of Sheep, Then Fishers of People

It is remarkable that the patriarchs, as well as the greatest leaders of Israel in the Tanakh, began their careers as shepherds: Abraham, Isaac, and Jacob, together with his sons, were independent shepherd princes, Moses shepherded the flock of his father-in-law for forty years, and David, as a young man, shepherded his father's flock (not to mention Abel, the first martyr in the Tanakh). This apparent divine preference for shepherds cannot be coincidental. Jesus exhibited a similar preference by calling himself the good Shepherd.[91] Moreover, he appointed the apostle Peter as a spiritual shepherd ("Feed my lambs.... Tend my sheep.... Feed my sheep," John 21:15–17), and the apostles speak of the Ecclesia as a flock, and of its pastors (literally, "shepherds") caring for believers.[92]

And yet, Jesus did not choose a single (literal) shepherd as disciple or apostle, despite an apparently adequate number of shepherds in Israel in those days (cf. Luke 2:8–20). On the contrary, more than half of the twelve disciples were anglers! We know this to be true of Peter, the brothers John and James, Thomas, Nathanael (i.e., Bartholomew), and of two unnamed disciples (presumably Philip and Peter's brother, Andrew; John 21:2; cf. 1:40–45). This cannot have been coincidental, either.

Perhaps we may say that no animal was more characteristic for Israel than the lamb (or, the young ram) (see Gen. 22:7–8). At the very first Israelite festival, Pesach—the only festival instituted in Egypt before the exodus (Exod. 12)—the lamb was the focus and center. The daily morning and evening burnt offerings at the tabernacle, and later at the temple, involved lambs (Exod. 29:38–46). Even the Messiah was compared to a lamb:

> He was oppressed, and he was afflicted,
>   yet he opened not his mouth;
> like a lamb that is led to the slaughter,
>   and like a sheep that before its shearers is silent,
>   so he opened not his mouth (Isa. 53:7).

---

91. John 10:11, 14; cf. Matt. 2:6; 25:32; 26:31; Luke 15:1–7; Heb. 13:20; 1 Pet. 2:25; 5:4; Rev. 7:17.

92. Acts 2:28–29; Eph. 4:11; 1 Pet. 5:1–4.

However, from the earliest time the characteristic animal of Christianity has been the fish; we find it depicted already in the catacombs of Rome, where the early Christians met in secret. The Greek word for "fish" is *ichthus*, whose five letters (*i-ch-th-u-s*) have been explained as an acronym for *Iēsous CHristos THeou hUios Sōter*, "Jesus Christ, Son of God, Savior." Moreover, the fish has been associated with the baptism in water, and with the two miracles of the catch of fish (Luke 5:1-7; John 21:1-6; we do not hear of miracles of Jesus involving sheep).

We ignore here the New Age explanation, which equates the era of Israel in the Tanakh with the astrological age of the Ram, and the Christian era with the astrological age of the Fishes (and the post-Christian era with the astrological age of Aquarius for that matter, whatever this is supposed to mean).[93] But if we do not seek our solution in this direction, what else could be the explanation?

11.6.2 *Both* Shepherds of Sheep *and* Fishers of People

Israel as a people arose in a natural way, through natural birth from the sons of Jacob, during their captivity in Egypt (Exod. 1:1-7). It subsequently needed a shepherd, who would lead them out of Egypt: Moses, who kept them, fed them, tended them, as a good shepherd does with the flock. Moses had been practicing for this task during the forty years when he was a literal shepherd (Exod. 3:1; cf. Acts 7:30). In Numbers 27:17, he describes Israel, "the congregation of the LORD," as "sheep" with a "shepherd," namely, his successor, who was to be Joshua. Indeed, if the Ecclesia were simply the continuation of Israel from the Tanakh, it would have simply needed more shepherds to tend them.

However, with the Ecclesia things are different: *the Ecclesia was not the continuation of anything, but was constructed out of nothing*. Jesus made an altogether new beginning by telling his disciples: "Follow me, and I will turn you into *fishers of people*" (Matt. 4:19 NET). Here, the opening sentence of Matthew 13 is significant: "That same day Jesus went out of the house and sat beside the sea." In Matthew 12, the nadir had been reached in the rejection of Jesus by the leaders of Israel; in chapter 13, from now on the gospel of the kingdom of heaven would go to all the nations (v. 38, "The field

---

93. Regarding this, see Ankerberg and Weldon (2011).

is the world"). Thus, the seventh parable in Matthew 13 tells us: "Again, the kingdom of heaven is like a net that was thrown into the sea and gathered fish of every kind. When it was full, men drew it ashore and sat down and sorted the good into containers but threw away the bad" (Matt. 13:47–48). Jesus has left the "house" of Israel, and now turns to the turbulent "sea" of the nations (cf. Isa. 17:12; Rev. 17:15). His apostles are the "fishers of people," who "catch" the new people of God from all the nations of the world and gather them together in vessels.

Israel had its shepherds (cf. 2 Sam. 5:2; 7:7), and the Ecclesia has them, too (see above). However, Israel never had "fishers of people," no real "evangelists."[94] The shepherds of Israel kept the flock together, and the rabbis today do the same. However, in addition to shepherds of sheep, the Ecclesia also has fishers of people, through whose labor the Ecclesia is constantly extended worldwide. A person was and is an Israelite through birth, but a person becomes a member of the Ecclesia through personal conversion and rebirth, regardless of whether one's parents were Christians. The shepherds in the Ecclesia keep the flock together as well, but the fishers of people see to it that many tens of thousands of new "fishes" are added daily to the Ecclesia. As a result of this, today there are about hundred and fifty times as many Christians than Jews in the world. *Jewish leaders are shepherds of sheep, whereas Christian leaders are shepherds of sheep as well as fishers of people.*

Some view Jesus appointing "fishers of people" as a fulfillment of Jeremiah 16:16: "Behold, I am sending for many fishers, . . . and they shall catch them. And afterward I will send for many hunters, and they shall hunt them from every mountain and every hill, and out of the clefts of the rocks." This verse is then applied to the return from the exile, such that (especially Christian) "fishers of people" have helped the Jews living in the various countries to which they had been dispersed to return to the Promised Land, especially in the twentieth century. However, the majority of expositors agree that the "fishers of people," just like the "hunters" in this verse, are not friends but enemies of Israel, who catch and hunt them with the exile as the consequence. In my view they have nothing to do with

---

94. Cf. Acts 21:8; Eph. 4:11; 2 Tim. 4:5; see also the many references to "preaching the gospel (Gk. *evangelion*)."

Jesus' fishers of people.

11.7 New Approaches

11.7.1 Two Peoples/One People

In opposition to supersessionism, the proper understanding of the essential differences between Israel and the Ecclesia is being received by more and more Christians. Charles Ryrie insisted that the Ecclesia is different from Israel, that she began on the Day of Pentecost, and therefore did not exist in the period of the Tanakh.[95] David L. Smith insisted that no arguments can be adduced for the existence of the Ecclesia in the Tanakh, neither linguistically nor theologically. Israel is called "people of God," and so the Ecclesia too. Both are part of the kingdom of God. But this does not mean they are one and the same. The church has replaced Israel as God's chosen one until his plans for the nations (the Gentiles) have been fulfilled. At that time, Israel will again take its place as God's people, according to Smith.[96]

Notice here how carefully we must handle the phrase "replacement theology." Superficially speaking, one might think that Smith is a supersessionist, but in fact he is the very opposite of what we understand by supersessionism. What is decisive is not the (confusing) term "replacement" but whether a certain theology has room for a future restoration of Israel as an ethnic, though believing, people of God in its own land and its own city.

G. E. Ladd also argued that in both the Tanakh and the New Testament there is only one people of God, but this does not mean that believers in the Tanakh belonged to the Ecclesia, nor should we see an Ecclesia in the Tanakh. On the contrary, the Ecclesia was born on the Day of Pentecost, for the Ecclesia consists of all those who in the Spirit have been baptized into one body (1 Cor. 12:13), and this baptismal work began on the Day of Pentecost.[97]

All these authors are trying to find a suitable middle way between the ancient supersessionist idea of an "Ecclesia since Adam" and the sharp dispensationalist separation between Israel and the Ecclesia. Smith and Ladd both said that the two are different, that

---

95. Ryrie (1986, 399).
96. Smith (1996, 314).
97. Ladd (1959, 117).

the Ecclesia began in Acts 2, *and* that basically all believers of all time form one people of God. Thus, we can agree with Edmund P. Clowney that Pentecost did not create the people of God but renewed it[98] — as long as we do not substitute "Ecclesia" here for "people of God." Indeed, we discern such a people of God especially since the covenants that God made with Abraham, and later with Moses.[99] The apostle Paul clearly described a connection with Abraham (Rom. 4; Gal. 3). This is all well and good, as long as we do not assert that New Testament believers have been incorporated into Israel, or call Israel in the Tanakh the "Ecclesia" of those days. Marriage may fuse husband and wife together, but the husband never *becomes* the wife, and vice versa.

In seeking an acceptable middle position, D. Watson called Israel the "shadow" of the church.[100] R. Bijlsma called the Christian church the complementing and completing counterpart of Israel as a people of faith, reflecting and needing each other.[101] J. A. Heyns spoke of the embryonic origins of the church in her prehistory in the Tanakh.[102] B. Wentsel believed that the church dates from long before the Day of Pentecost, but added that the outpouring of the Holy Spirit on this Day had fundamental and redemptive-historical significance for the origin of the World Church, consisting of Jewish and Gentile believers.[103]

This struggle for the most accurate description of the relationship between Israel and the Ecclesia may continue forever, but it does not answer the decisive question: Is there still a future for ethnic Israel as God's people *in its own land*, the land of their fathers? If the answer is affirmative, it is unimportant whether an author views the Ecclesia as having begun with Adam, or with Abraham, or with Moses, or with Jesus, or in Acts 2. To a certain extent, this is a semantic question. What really matters is the interpretation of the prophecies about Israel: literal or spiritual?

---

98. Clowney (1995, 53).
99. Cf. Minear (1960, 70–71).
100. Watson (1978, 66).
101. Bijlsma (1981, 47).
102. Heyns (1988, 355).
103. Wentsel (1998a, 25).

11.7.2 Literal or Spiritual

As we have seen, supersessionism was formulated by Augustine, but traces of it can be found in the so-called Letter of Barnabas (second century) and with the church father John Chrysostom in his anti-Semitic *Adversus Judaeos* ("Against the Jews").[104] This doctrine has dominated Roman Catholic thinking ever since; it has been fed by anti-Semitism, and it has been feeding anti-Semitism throughout Christian history.[105] It is inconceivable that a leading Roman Catholic theologian, propounding the ecclesiology of his church, would at the same time interpret the prophecies about Israel literally. Spiritualizing interpretation pervades the view of Israel in that denomination.

With Protestantism, things are different. To be sure, the earliest Protestant theologians—Lutheran, Reformed, Anglican—were all supersessionists. One might admit that during the sixteenth century, too many other crucial subjects demanded attention, especially in the fields of soteriology (the doctrine of salvation) and ecclesiology (the doctrine of the church), together with the doctrine of the sacraments. We still see the detrimental effects of supersessionism in the Annotations to the Dutch States Translation and its captions. But we have also seen that during the Dutch Second Reformation, things began to change.[106] Fine examples included Theodorus van der Groe and Wilhelmus à Brakel, who did take the prophecies about Israel literally, and believed in the future restoration of Israel *in its own land*.

The point is, whereas Roman Catholic theology cannot conceivably understand the prophecies about Israel literally, not so with Protestant theology. It took a while before Protestant theologians began to discover this and set out to free themselves from this portion of Roman Catholic leaven, as they had done with so many other portions. Today, Reformed theologians in increasingly number are abandoning the spiritualized interpretation of the prophe-

---

104. See Wentsel (1995, 365).

105. It has been argued that German Nazism was inconceivable without Lutheran anti-Semitism, and that this anti-Semitism was inconceivable without supersessionism—which does not mean that every supersessionist is an anti-Semite, of course!

106. See the groundbreaking work by Van Campen (2007).

cies about Israel and understanding them literally. Recently some Dutch theologians wrote: "It directly goes against the biblical testimony to wish to tear Jews apart from their ancient inheritance, and to graft them into a Gentile-Christian church, which as the new and spiritual Israel supposedly has taken its place."[107] One theologian has written that replacement theology "is a theory and a lifestyle that totally conflicts with the Bible, and especially with what Paul writes in Romans 9–11.... The scarlet thread running through Romans 9–11 is that God's promises are indeed destined for the entire Gentile world, but that his promises for the people of Israel have not expired or have not been withdrawn."[108] Another wrote: "In my view, replacement theology is present where all openness for God's eschatological redemptive dealing with Israel *as a nation* is absent," which he sharply condemned.[109] This view is shared today by a number of others.[110] J. van Genderen wrote that "those who confess Jesus as the Messiah are the new Israel,"[111] but he also wrote: "One cannot possibly deduce from the New Testament, including the image of the olive tree in Romans 11, that those who believe must be incorporated into Israel in order to be the people of God."[112]

Thankfully, there is another side to the views in the Roman Catholic Church. The Second Vatican Council carefully avoided identifying the people of God directly with the Roman Catholic Church and claiming that the church has replaced Israel as people of God. The Council described the church as the "new people of God" continuous with Israel. It did not suggest that the election of the church as the people of God entailed the rejection of Israel, but instead viewed it as an extension of God's kingdom.[113] If this is a correct rendering of Vatican II, it is certainly an improvement. But the decisive question remains: Are theologians, from any background, prepared to accept the literal fulfillment of the prophecies

---

107. Den Boer et al. (1983, 40).
108. Verkuyl (1992, 369).
109. Hoek (2013, 24).
110. Paul (2013); Glashouwer (2007); Den Hertog (2003); also Van Campen & Den Hertog (2005).
111. Van Genderen and Velema (2008, 681).
112. Ibid., 633.
113. McGrath (2007, 407–408).

about Israel in the end time?

11.7.3 Ecclesia and Kingdom

Imagine two very different situations, the present one and the future one, that is, during the future Messianic kingdom.

In the *present* situation, a believing remnant, the "Israel of God," is taken *out* of the nation of Israel, the latter being either secularized (agnostic) or Judaist. At the same time, Gentiles come to faith in Jesus, and are taken *out* of the Gentile world, the latter being either secularized or (pseudo-)religious. The two groups, Jesus-believing Jews and Jesus-believing Gentiles, are joined into the one Ecclesia, the one body of Christ, the one temple of the Holy Spirit, the one bride of the Lamb. In doing so, Jesus-believing Jews do not become Gentiles, and Jesus-believing Gentiles do not become Jews. On the contrary, together they have become something entirely new: the Ecclesia. Of her, Paul said, "[A]s many of you as were baptized into Christ have put on Christ. There is neither Jew nor Greek, there is neither slave nor free, there is no male and female, for you are all one in Christ Jesus" (Gal. 3:27–28).

It is evident that, in practical life, the differences between slaves and free people, and between males and females still play a role; for instance, there are Christian employers and employees, and there are also Christian husbands and wives. The same is true of Jews and Gentiles. The Gentile believer is under the Torah of Christ, and the Jewish believer is under both the Torah of Moses and the Torah of Christ. But when it comes to their spiritual position in Christ, the differences are gone forever.

In the *future* situation, that is, during the Messianic kingdom, things are quite different. (Remember, during this kingdom, the Ecclesia will be with Christ in glory, with glorified bodies, reigning with him from heaven.) Here, the distinction between Jews and Gentiles is fully maintained. The Jews who will believe in Jesus when he returns, and who will enter the Messianic kingdom, will be in the physical, literal Promised Land, of which physical, literal Zion will be the center—as it will be the center of the world—and the Gentiles will come to worship there: "All the nations you have made shall come / and worship before you, O Lord, / and shall glorify your name" (Ps. 86:9).

Isaiah spoke of "the foreigners who join themselves to the LORD, / to minister to him, to love the name of the LORD, / and to be his servants, / everyone who keeps the Sabbath and does not profane it, / and holds fast my covenant" (Isa. 56:6). And Jeremiah said that, if Israel would return to the LORD, "then nations shall bless themselves in him, / and in him shall they glory" (Jer. 4:1-2). In such passages, it is never said that these converted Gentiles become Jews, nor is it said that Jews become Gentiles. Jews will remain Jews, and Gentiles will remain Gentiles, *without believers from these two groups being joined together into something entirely new: the Ecclesia.*

In summary: the Ecclesia is something of the *present* era (although, of course, it will exist in the next era as well, but then glorified in heaven). The Messianic kingdom is something of the *"age to come"* (although the kingdom of God exists already today, though only in hidden form[114]). The life of both the Ecclesia and of Jesus-believers dwelling on earth in the coming age arises from the person and the atoning work of Christ—but these groups are not the same. However, neither in the present era nor in the future era do Jews ever become Gentiles, nor do Gentiles ever become Jews.

---

114. See extensively, Ouweneel (2011a, chapters 9–14).

Chapter 12
The One People of God

[When there are] ten sitting together and occupying themselves with Torah, the Shekhinah abides among them . . . and whence [do we infer that the same applies] even [when there are only] two? [From] that which is said: "Then they that fear the LORD spoke one with another,[1] and the LORD hearkened, and heard, ..."

Talmud: Aboth III

[Jesus said,] "[W]herever two or three are assembled in my name, I[2] am there with them."

Matthew 18:20

12.1 "All Israel"[3]
12.1.1 Jewish Privileges

TO THIS POINT, Romans 9–11 has been mentioned several times. Now we must enter somewhat more deeply into this passage. Their proper understanding is vital for grasping the difference between Israel and the Ecclesia, as expositors have realized throughout the centuries. In Romans 1–8, the apostle Paul emphasized that, when

---

1. Mal. 3:16, lit. "a man with his neighbor," that is, just two persons.
2. I.e., "I" as the One on whom rests the *Shekhinah* (Luke 1:35; 9:34; John 2:19).
3. See Ouweneel (1991, 58–60; 2001a, 251–54).

it comes to human misery and the way of salvation, there is no difference between Jew and Gentile:

> What then? Are we [Jews] any better off [than the Gentiles]? No, not at all. For we have already charged that all, *both Jews and Greeks* [i.e., Gentiles], are under sin, as it is written: "None [neither Jew, nor Gentile] is righteous, no, not one; / no one understands; / no one seeks for God. / All have turned aside; together they have become worthless; / no one does good, not even one" [Ps. 14:3; 53:3]. . . . Now we know that whatever the Torah [here: the entire Tanakh] says it speaks to those who are under the Torah [i.e., to the Jews], so that every mouth [Gentile *and* Jewish] may be stopped, and the whole world [Gentiles *and* Jews] may be held accountable to God. . . . For there is no distinction: for all [Gentiles *and* Jews] have sinned and fall short of the glory of God, and are justified by his grace as a gift, through the redemption that is in Christ Jesus" (Rom. 3:9-12, 19, 22-24).

Later, in Romans 9-11, we read:

> [T]he Scripture says, "Everyone who believes in him will not be put to shame" [Isa. 28:16 Sept.]. For *there is no distinction between Jew and Greek* [i.e., Gentile]; for the same LORD is LORD of all, bestowing his riches on all who call on him. For "everyone who calls on the name of the LORD will be saved" [Joel 2:32]" (Rom. 10:11-13).

However, if there is no *distinction between Jew and Gentile* when it comes to sinfulness and salvation, what remains of the particular calling, position, and destiny of Israel as compared with the Gentile nations? As Paul had asked in Romans 3:1-2: "Then what advantage has the Jew? Or what is the value of circumcision? Much in every way. To begin with, the Jews were entrusted with the oracles of God." And this is just one of the many privileges of Israel, privileges that Paul identified in Romans 9:4-5 (see §1.5.3 above).

(1) To Israel belongs the *adoption* (the being adopted as sons; see Exod. 4:22; Deut. 14:1; Hos. 1:10 ["sons"]; 11:1); that is, among all the nations, only the Israelites were called the "son," or "sons," of God. No converted Gentiles were ever described this way before Israel was called as God's "son(s)."[4]

---

4. An exception seems to be Adam (Luke 3:38), but he was "son" of God purely in a creational way.

(2) To Israel belongs the *glory*, that is, the *Shekhinah*, God's glorious presence in their midst. Among no other people in all of world history has the glory of God dwelt visibly, first on Mount Sinai, then on and in the tabernacle of Moses, then on and in the temple of Solomon.

(3) To Israel belong the *covenants*; that is, all the covenants of the Bible are Israel-oriented, including the Noahic covenant, as we saw; and the New Covenant (Jer. 31:31–34), too, is explicitly made with the ten tribes and the two tribes of Israel. It is only secondarily that Gentiles, too, are graciously allowed to benefit from this covenant's blessings.

(4) To Israel belongs the giving of the *Torah*: to no other people has God ever given the Torah (in the broad sense, the Tanakh),[5] or, as Romans 3:2 said, the "oracles[6] of God." No Gentile should ever forget that the Bible they hold in their hands came from the Jews.

(5) To Israel belongs the *worship*,[7] that is, the ministry of priests offering sacrifices in the temple, the only building in world history where God gloriously dwelt *and* was worshiped the way he himself had prescribed (Exod. – Lev.) (apart from human weakness in the realization of it).

(6) To Israel belong the *promises*, namely, those given directly to the patriarchs (beginning with the seven promises of Gen. 12:2[8]), and later to Israel through Moses and the later prophets of Israel.[9]

---

5. In the still wider sense, including the New Testament, written by seven Jews (Matthew, Mark, John, Paul, James, Peter, and Jude) and one Jewish proselyte (Luke). Cf. Israel's Declaration of Independence, which says that Israel "gave to the world the eternal Book of Books" (https://www.mfa.gov.il/mfa/foreign-policy/peace/ guide/pages/declaration%20of%20establishment%20of%20 state%20of%20israel.aspx).

6. Gk. *logia*, "statements, messages," more broadly: "revelations, teachings"; *oracle* comes from Lat. *oraculum*, "divine message," derived from *orare*, 'to speak."

7. Gk. *latreia*, a word we today know mainly in negative expressions: "idolatry," "Mariolatry," "bibliolatry," "iconolatry," "papolatry," "necrolatry," "angelolatry," "astrolatry."

8. Or some might argue, the promise contained in Noah's prophecy: Gen. 9:26–27, God will be the God of Shem, the ancestor of Israel.

9. In our Bibles, the last promises are those of Mal. 4; in the Hebrew Bible, the last promise is the one implicitly contained in 2 Chron. 36:23, the promise of the new temple and Judah's return to the Holy Land.

These promises are much older than any promises given to Gentiles.

(7) To Israel belong the *patriarchs* (Abraham, Isaac, Jacob, and his twelve sons); they "belong" to Israel in the sense that they are their physical ancestors, which no Gentile can say (although Abraham is the spiritual father also of Gentile Jesus-believers, Rom. 4:11-12).

(8) ". . . and from Israel's race, according to the flesh [i.e., as far as his physical descent is concerned], came the Messiah." No Gentile, whether believing or not, should ever forget that the primary and most influential figure of world history, Jesus Christ, was not only a Jew but the Messiah (Anointed King) of Israel before he was anything to the Gentiles.[10]

12.1.2 A Double Election

The point of Romans 9-11 is to make clear the enduring value of Israel's enormous privileges. In order to understand these Pauline passages, it is essential to understand that the apostle was constantly maintaining the distinction between Israel and the Ecclesia.[11] We should have no doubt at all that in these chapters "Israel" always and exclusively means "Israel," Paul's "kinsmen according to the flesh."[12] Only Romans 9:6b might raise some doubt; we have discussed this verse extensively (§6.5.2), and suggested that it means that all those who have the same physical roots as Israel, namely, the patriarchs, are not themselves always "Israel": Ishmael and Esau were descendants of Abraham, yet did not share in the promises made to Abraham and his physical offspring. So even in Romans 9:6, "Israel" means Israel.

"Israel" *always* means "Israel" in Romans 9-11. It violates all decent rules of exegesis to suddenly insert "the church" into Romans 11:26 ("all Israel will be saved"). The enormous power of a mistaken paradigm explains why great theologians, with good intentions, could ever do such a thing: replace "Israel" with "the church" in three chapters that speak exclusively of Israel in the ethnic sense. We can only be thankful that, since the seventeenth cen-

---

10. Cf. Matt. 2:2; 10:6; 15:24; 22:11, 37; John 4:22; 10:2-4, 16; Rom. 15:8.
11. Though this latter term does not appear in Rom. 9-11, it does appear five times in chapter 16.
12. Rom. 9:3; 11:14; see further especially 9:4, 31; 10:19, 21; 11:1-2, 7, 11, 25.

tury (see the quotation from Wilhelmus à Brakel above in chapter 11!), traditional Protestant theologians have come increasingly to see and acknowledge this.

To be more precise, the apostle Paul distinguished in Israel between the unbelieving, "hardened" (stubborn) part of Israel (Rom. 11:7, 25) and the "remnant chosen by grace" (v. 5). With respect to Israel, election (chosenness) has two very different meanings:

(a) All Israel has been chosen for a particular place and calling here *on earth*, since Exodus 19:5, ". . . you shall be my treasured possession among all peoples": "[Y]ou are a people holy to the LORD your God. The LORD your God has chosen you to be a people for his treasured possession, out of all the peoples who are on the face of the earth" (Deut. 7:6; 14:2).

(b) However, only a part of this chosen nation will receive *eternal salvation*; "the rest were hardened" (Rom. 11:7).

> [T]he God and Father of our Lord Jesus Christ . . . has blessed us[13] in Christ with every spiritual blessing in the heavenly places, even as he *chose* us in him before the foundation of the world, that we should be holy and blameless before him. In love he *predestined* [i.e., from eternity ordained] us for adoption to himself as sons through Jesus Christ, according to the purpose of his will (Eph. 1:3-5).

The implication is that there are two kinds of "Israel," *not* an ethnic-Jewish Israel and a Gentile Israel, *nor* an Israel of the Tanakh and a New Testament spiritual Israel, but:

(a) a Jesus-believing part of ethnic Israel, including a crypto-Jesus-believing part: the godly Jews whose eyes will be opened when the Messiah re-appears, and

(b) a non-Jesus-believing part, which will stubbornly reject him when he re-appears.

Not for a second does the apostle Paul give the impression in these chapters that the term "Israel" can and does refer also to the Ecclesia. On the one hand, he calls the unbelieving part of Israel still "Israel" or "Jews" (e.g., 1 Cor. 10:32), while on the other hand, he never calls believing Gentiles "Israel" or "Jews."

As to the double election, notice that, on the one hand, Israel's

---

13. I.e., both Jewish and Gentile Jesus-believers.

election as a "chosen people" is limited (to one ethnic nation) and temporary (lasting until the end of the present earth). On the other hand, the election of Jesus-believers, Jewish and Gentile, is *from* all eternity (as we just read in Ephesians 1:3-5) and *for* all eternity. The term "predestined" means "destined" "before the foundation of the world" (cf. Rom. 8:29-30; Eph. 1:11). In this sense, we could even say that the Ecclesia is "older" than Israel, for Israel and the Messianic kingdom belong to the things that are "*since* the foundation of the world" (Matt. 13:35; 25:34), but the roots of the Ecclesia go back "*before* the foundation of the world."[14] The former is from the beginning to the end of this world; the latter is from eternity and to eternity.

12.1.3 Romans 11:26

Therefore, it is exegetically untenable, and completely arbitrary when John Calvin, and several theologians after him[15] wish to insert the church into Romans 11:26. When Paul wrote, "In this way all Israel will be saved," the term "Israel" must now refer to the church, consisting of believing Jews and believing Gentiles. Calvin observed:

> Many understand this of the Jewish people, as though Paul had said, that religion would again be restored among them as before: but I extend the word Israel to all the people of God, according to this meaning, – "When the Gentiles shall come in, the Jews also shall return from their defection to the obedience of faith; and thus shall be completed the salvation of the whole Israel of God, which must be gathered from both; and yet in such a way that the Jews shall obtain the first place, being as it were the first-born in God's family.[16]

However, every objective reader can see that the text itself presents not the slightest reason for this extension of the meaning. We must conclude that Calvin's insertion is inspired by his Augustinian bias, that is, by his dogmatic paradigm, which was governing his exegesis. Paul said that one day, "Israel" — that is, the "Israel of God" — will finally receive the fulfillment of God's promises and be

---

14. Eph. 1:4; Rev. 13:8; cf. the Son of God: John 17:24; the Lamb: 1 Pet. 1:20.
15. In our modern day, e.g., Robertson (2000, chapter 6); Douma (2008); Paas (2014); Maljaars (2015, 35–41).
16. https://biblehub.com/commentaries/calvin/romans/11.htm.

saved. In saying this, he was not making any statement about the eternal destiny of Gentiles, whether believing or unbelieving. This was simply not his subject at this point.

After Calvin, many theologians have struggled to distance themselves from his mistaken example. For instance, J. D. G. Dunn acknowledged that "all Israel" in Romans 11:26 can refer only to historic, ethnic Israel; yet, he still wished to see in some way or another Gentile believers included in this "all Israel."[17] J. S. Vos was much more consistent when he wrote: "'All Israel' means here the sum of the already believing and the yet hardened Israel,"[18] and "Not only the totality of the argumentation from [Rom.] 11:11 but also Paul's use of the notion of 'Israel' in Romans 9-11 forbids to view the 'all Israel' of 11:26 as the people of God from Jews and Gentiles."[19]

We find convincing what V. Gäckle wrote:

> This view [i.e., that "Israel" in v. 26 is the church], adhered to by Augustine, Theodoret, Luther and others, fails because of the language used. For, apart from Romans 9:6,[20] "Israel" in Romans 9-11 always means the ancient covenant people of Israel. . . . The fact that exclusively the Jews are meant here is evident also from the two juxtapositions of the "fullness of the Gentiles" and "all Israel," and also of "Israel partially" and "all Israel" in verses 25 and 26.[21]

This is the third time we encounter a logical error in the thinking of supersessionism, namely, an *extension* of the meaning of the text in cases where a *restriction* is intended.

(a) Romans 2:28-29: not every Jew is a true Jew; only those are such who have been circumcised not only in their flesh but also in their heart. That is, the number of true Jews is smaller than that of physical Jews. The verse says nothing about Gentiles with circumcised hearts.

Supersessionists understand this to be saying that the number

---

17. Dunn (1998, 526–29).
18. In Baarda et al. (1984, 137).
19. Ibid., 143.
20. But even here, "Israel" basically means "Israel"; see §§6.5.2 and 12.1.2.
21. Gäckle (2009, 32).

of true Jews is *larger* than that of physical Jews, for, when a Gentile has been spiritually circumcised, he is a true "Jew."

(b) Romans 9:6: "Not all are Israel who are from Israel," that is, even though you may descend from Israel's physical ancestors, you are not necessarily a Jew. That is, the number of true Jews is smaller than that of physical descendants of Israel's forefathers.

Supersessionists understand this to be saying that the number of true Jews is *larger* than that of physical Jews, for, if you belong to the spiritual offspring of the patriarchs, you are a true "Jew."

(c) Romans 11:26: "thus all Israel will be saved," that is, in the end, the *remnant* of Israel will be saved, and from this, God builds the new ethnic Israel, the "Israel of God" that will enter the Messianic kingdom.

Supersessionists understand this to be saying that Jesus-believing Gentiles are saved as well, and thus they belong to this "all Israel."

None of these passages was saying anything about Gentiles, and therefore we are not allowed to draw any conclusion concerning the latter. In all these three cases, the following error is made: A = B, C = B, therefore A = C.

(a) The true Jew is spiritually circumcised; the Jesus-believing Gentile is spiritually circumcised; therefore this Gentile is a true Jew. (As if there could not be spiritually circumcised non-Jews.)

(b) The Jesus-believing Jew is a spiritual descendant of the patriarchs; the Jesus-believing Gentile is a spiritual descendant of the patriarchs; therefore this Gentile is a Jew. (As if there could not be spiritual descendants of the patriarchs who are not Jews.)

(c) The Jesus-believing Israel is saved; the Jesus-believing Gentiles are saved; therefore the latter are now "Israel" too. (As if there could not be persons who are saved who are not "Israel.")

These three logical errors are due to the enormous sway of the supersessionist paradigm.

12.2 Is the Olive Tree Israel?
12.2.1 Features of the Tree

In line with the arguments presented above, we now come to the parable of the olive tree in Romans 11:16–24. What exactly does the tree represent? Supersessionists usually claim that the tree is an image of Israel,[22] so that the believing Gentiles who are grafted in the tree thus become part of "(spiritual) Israel." Interestingly, avowed supersessionist Steven Paas rejects the view that the olive tree represents Israel.[23] He believes that the tree represents Christ, which does not seem to me very accurate. How can we say that unbelievers in Israel had a share in Christ? Can we say that the natural branches that have been broken off *had been* "in Christ" before, and then had been cut off from him? If so, in what sense had they been "in Christ"? And if this really involved a vital connection, would not Paul have taught here an apostasy of the saints?

However, the fact that Paas clearly sees that it is only the "natural branches" (vv. 21, 24; cf. vv. 16-19) that represent Israel is great progress, and should be noticed by the other supersessionists. If Paas is right on this point—and I am convinced he is—then it is no longer possible to assert that Jesus-believing Gentiles (branches from a "wild" olive tree) are "grafted" or "incorporated" into Israel and thus themselves become Israelite.

C. van der Kooi and G. van den Brink have argued that Israel is the "trunk" of the olive tree, whereas in Romans 11 it is of course the "natural branches" that are Israel. Yet, the authors had just written that "Christians from the gentiles *have been incorporated in the already existing covenant* with Israel," which is a more felicitous formulation.[24]

So what, then, does the tree represent? Let us first look at the various components of the apostle Paul's imagery. We must distinguish between:

(a) the "nourishing root"[25] of the olive tree (vv. 16-17);
(b) the "cultivated olive tree"[26] as such (v. 24),

---

22. E.g., Berkouwer (1963, 123,129); Heyns (1988, 358); Wentsel (1995, 369); Moo (1996, 702); Douma (2008, 63); see Fruchtenbaum (1994, 94–97, 198–201, 290–95) for an extensive discussion of this erroneous view.
23. Paas (2014, 28).
24. Van der Kooi and Van den Brink (2017, 359; italics original).
25. Gk. *tēs rizēs tēs piotētos*, literally, "of the root [and] fatness," or "of the root of fatness," in which "fatness" has the sense of "rich nourishment."
26. Gk. *kallielaios*, the (cultivated) garden olive tree as opposed to the *agrielaios*,

(c) the "natural branches" of this olive tree (vv. 21, 24), which are obviously Israel;

(d) the "wild olive tree" (vv. 17, 24), which obviously represents the Gentile world; and

(e) the "branches" of the latter tree, which represent the Gentiles.

Moreover, we must distinguish here between four events:

(a) certain "natural branches" are broken off; these are the Jews who refused to accept their Messiah;

(b) certain "wild branches" are grafted in because these Gentiles did believe in the Jewish Messiah;

(c) certain broken off "natural branches" may later be grafted in again if these Jews, at a later stage, do accept their Messiah in faith; and

(d) certain grafted in "wild branches" may later be broken off again if these Gentiles (nominal Christians) fall into backsliding and apostasy, thus drifting away from the Jesus they had accepted at first.

So what does the "cultivated olive tree" with its "nourishing root" represent? It cannot represent Christ as such. Nor can it represent Israel, for only the "natural branches" represent Israel. These branches may be broken off, whereas the tree still remains the tree. This is similar to what we read about the vine in John 15:1–8: believers are the branches of the vine, but they are not the vine as such. (The comparison extends no further: the vine is Jesus, but the olive tree is not Jesus.)

12.2.2 Warning and Prophecy

In order to find an answer, let us look somewhat more closely at the Pauline text.

> But if some of the branches were broken off, and you, although a wild olive shoot, were grafted in among the others and now share in the nourishing root of the olive tree, do not be arrogant toward the branches.... [Y]ou will say, "Branches were broken off so that I might be grafted in." That is true. They were broken off because of their

---

the uncultivated (wild) olive tree in the fields.

unbelief, but you stand fast through faith. So do not become proud, but fear. For if God did not spare the natural branches, neither will he spare you.... And even they, if they do not continue in their unbelief, will be grafted in, for God has the power to graft them in again. For if you were cut from what is by nature a wild olive tree, and grafted, contrary to nature, into a cultivated olive tree, how much more will these, the natural branches, be grafted back into their own olive tree (Rom. 11:17-24).

Paul's argument appears to be: the olive tree is a "noble" (cultivated) olive tree, with natural branches, that is, branches proper to the tree; these apparently represent Israel. The Jews who have refused to accept Jesus are the natural branches that have been broken off the tree. The natural branches that remain on the tree are the Jesus-believing Jews. Other branches, which have been taken from a "wild olive tree"—that is, Gentile Jesus-believers—have been cut off that wild tree and grafted into the cultivated tree. In this way, they have filled the places of the branches that had been broken off.

According to Paul's presentation in verses 22-23, it is possible that, in the future, these "wild" branches, which were grafted into the cultivated tree, are broken off again because of apostasy,[27] and it is equally possible that the natural branches, when they come to faith in Jesus—especially in the future, when Jesus returns—are grafted again into their own tree. Paul made this point as a warning: do not boast against the natural branches that were broken off, because, if you Gentile do not stay in the faith, the very same thing will happen to you. This warning remains valid throughout all of church history.

What was depicted in verses 22-23 as a possibility becomes a *prophetic reality* in verses 22-27. In other words, what begins as a warning ("If you ..., then A will happen"), ends with a prediction ("A *will* indeed happen"). Thus, the text depicted the present situation: natural branches have been broken off, wild branches have been grafted in. But then the text went on to depict the future situation as well: some of the wild branches *will be* broken off again— which entails God's judgment on nominal Christianity—and some

---

27. For the possibility of such apostasy of (pseudo-)Christians, see, e.g., Paul's "provided that" or "if indeed" ("if at least") (Gk. *eiper* or *ei ge* or *ean[per]*) (Rom. 8:17; 2 Cor. 5:3; Col. 1:23; cf. Heb. 3:6, 14).

natural branches *will be* grafted in again: this is the restoration of Israel insofar as it accepts its Messiah, and returns to the "tree" under Messiah's blessed rule.

More exegesis of these verses will follow below in chapter 14, especially regarding the future restoration of Israel. Here my point is that the olive tree and the natural branches cannot be identical: the branches *are* not the tree, they are *of* (and *on*) the tree. Unbelieving Jews are broken off the tree, while Jews who, at a later stage come to faith in their Messiah, are grafted into the tree again.

12.3 The Covenant Tree
12.3.1 God's Promises

So, what *is* the olive tree? We are not left with many choices. I would put it this way: if, as supersessionism claims, the Bible knows only one people of God, to which both natural and wild branches now belong, where did this one people begin? In other words, where or what is the "root" of the tree (Rom. 11:17-18)? In the first eleven chapters of Genesis, there is not really a "people" of God; it is mainly a matter of individual believers, like Adam, Enoch, Noah, and Shem. But then notice the seven promises of Genesis 12:2-3 that Gods gives to Abram (NKJV):[28]

(1) "I will make you a great nation;
(2) I will bless you
(3) and (I will) make your name great;
(4) and you shall be a blessing.
(5) I will bless those who bless you,
(6) and I will curse him who curses you;
(7) and in you all the families of the earth shall be blessed."

Here, the "great nation" is undoubtedly Israel. But notice Genesis 17:4-5:

> Behold, my covenant is with you, and you shall be the father of a multitude of nations [Heb. *ab hamon goyyim*]. No longer shall your name be called Abram [i.e., exalted father], but your name shall be Abraham

---

28. In some renderings, such as the ESV, the sevenfold blessing is less clear because certain phrases are rendered as subclauses, alongside main clauses; notice that the "you" here is always singular, and thus refers to Abram in person.

[i.e., father of many (nations)], for I have made you the father of a multitude of nations [Heb. *ab hamon goyyim*].

This is what the true and complete people of God is: not just the faithful of Israel, but also the faithful from many different nations; in short: all those who have been circumcised in their hearts, and thus are spiritual descendants of Abraham, whether or not they are physical descendants of Abraham (Rom. 4:11–12). Thus, the root is Abraham, or rather, God's promises to Abraham, or God's covenant that he made with Abraham (Gen. 15 and 17). It is the "line of promise on earth," as William Kelly put it.[29] And in the words of Jesus-believing Jew Arnold Fruchtenbaum: the olive tree is the place of blessing rooted in the Abrahamic Covenant rather than Israel as such,[30] and it is the place of blessing as comprised in the "Jewish" (more accurately: the Abrahamic) Covenant.[31] J. Verkuyl called the olive tree "the people of God" in the broadest sense.[32]

In verse 16, Paul's starting point was this: "If the dough offered as firstfruits is holy, so is the whole lump, and if the root is holy, so are the branches." Here Paul switched from one type of imagery to another, as he often did. The former image has been adopted from the Sinaitic laws concerning the grain offerings (Num. 15:17–21, "Some of the first of your dough you shall give to the LORD"). The latter image formed the introduction to the entire parable of the cultivated olive tree. It is no wonder that expositors have seen Abraham, or possibly the patriarchs, in the "root."[33] This is because Paul said that the patriarchs belong to Israel (Rom. 9:5), and that with regard to election, the Israelites are beloved for the sake of their forefathers (11:28), that is, Abraham, Isaac, and Jacob. All covenant promises and blessings began with the patriarchs; and these are promises and blessings not just for their physical (Jewish) descendants, but just as much for their spiritual (believing Gentile) descendants.

---

29. W. Kelly (*BT* 9, 24).
30. Fruchtenbaum (1994, 97).
31. Ibid., 175 (cf. 744).
32. Verkuyl (1992, 370).
33. E.g., Grant (1901, 270); Murray (1968, 2:85); Moo (1996, 699); Smith (1996, 205).

Indeed, right from the beginning God told the patriarchs these three things, amounting to a single mighty promise:

(a) "[I]n you [i.e., Abraham] shall all the *families* of the earth be blessed" (Gen. 12:3; cf. 18:18; Gal. 3:8).

(b) "[I]n your offspring shall all the *nations* of the earth be blessed" (22:18; 26:4; cf. Acts 3:25).

(c) In combination: "[I]n you [i.e. here, Jacob] *and* in your offspring shall all the families (or, nations) of the earth be blessed" (28:14).

The phrase "in you" is not "by you" (CJB), or "with you," but rather "through you," or "because of you"; that is, from now on, no person on earth can receive true spiritual blessing apart from you (any of the patriarchs), or from your offspring (Israel), that is, apart from my promises to you and your offspring; as Jesus said: "[S]alvation is from the Jews" (John 4:22).

12.3.2 Kinds of "Children"

All branches of the "tree of promise," the natural branches that were allowed to stay on the tree (the "Israel of God") and the Gentile branches grafted into it from elsewhere, are "children" of Abraham; Jewish and Gentile "children," respectively; but the most important thing is that both are *"children"*: children/sons of Abraham and children/sons of God (cf. Gal. 3:7, 26, 29). The branches that had been broken off are physical "offspring" of Abraham, but not "children" in the true, spiritual sense of the world. Just like Gentiles who refuse to accept Jesus, they are "children of the devil." This sounds very harsh, but we have a threefold testimony for this truth:

(1) John the Baptist did not use the word "devil," but "vipers," which amounted to the same thing;[34] he refused the title "children" to those who rejected his preaching: "You brood of vipers! Who warned you to flee from the wrath to come? Bear fruit in keeping with repentance. And do not presume to say to yourselves, 'We have Abraham as our father,' for I tell you, God is able from these stones to raise up children for Abraham" (Matt. 3:7-9).

(2) Jesus told the Jewish leaders, who had consciously rejected him:

---

34. Cf. Matt. 23:33; Luke 10:19; 2 Cor. 11:3; Rev. 12:9; 20:2.

You are of your father the devil, and your will is to do your father's desires. He was a murderer from the beginning, and does not stand in the truth, because there is no truth in him. When he lies, he speaks out of his own character, for he is a liar and the father of lies. But because I tell the truth, you do not believe me (John 8:44-45; cf. the contrast in vv. 33, 37 and 39-44).

(3) The apostle John said more in general terms:

Whoever makes a practice of sinning is of the devil, for the devil has been sinning from the beginning. . . . By this it is evident who are the children of God, and who are the children of the devil: whoever does not practice righteousness is not of God, nor is the one who does not love his brother (1 John 3:8-10).

All the "children of God" have a place in the cultivated olive tree — irrespective of their original tree — and all the "children of the devil" do not have a place in this tree, again, irrespective of their original tree. All the branches of the tree, natural and engrafted, are "supported" by the "root" (v. 18), that is, they are spiritual sons and heirs of Abraham, "children of promise."[35] Basically, the designations "sons/children of God" and "sons/children of Abraham" coincide, as we just saw (Gal. 3:7, 26, 29), not because Abraham is God, but because no Jew or Gentile can become a son of God apart from Abraham and the promises made to him. It is *from* God, and *through* (his promises to) Abraham, that these "sons/children" receive justification and divine life (Gal. 3:6, 11-12, 21, 24). Being grafted into the olive tree by faith is identical to becoming a child/son/offspring of Abraham, that is, receiving a share in the Abrahamic blessings. Romans 11 never says that Gentile Jesus-believers are incorporated into *Israel*, but I suppose we *can* say they are incorporated into *the people of God* in the broadest sense: all the "children of Abraham," no matter whether they are of Jewish or of Gentile origin.

12.3.3 Blessing and Grafting

Interestingly, the Hebrew "root" *b-r-kh* means both "to bless" and "to graft."[36] Therefore, one might translate Genesis 12:3b as follows:

---

35. Rom. 4:11, 16; 9:8; Gal. 3:7, 29; 4:28.
36. Shulam (1998, 363, 370, 387); the meaning "to graft" does not appear in the Tanakh.

"[I]nto you [Abraham], all the [believing] families of the earth shall be grafted." We have a remarkable example of this in the Talmud: "Rabbi Eleazar further stated: 'What is meant by the text, *And in thee shall the families of the earth be blessed* [b-r-kh, Gen. 12:3]? The Holy One, blessed be He, said to Abraham, 'I have two goodly shoots to engraft [b-r-kh] on you: Ruth the Moabitess [Ruth 4] and Naamah the Ammonitess [1 Kings 14:31].'"[37] Moab and Ammon were related to Israel (Gen. 19:37-38), yet they were idolatrous Gentile nations, hostile to Israel. But God opened the way for some of them to join the people of God (in spite of Deut. 23:3): Ruth became the wife of Boaz, and thus even the foremother of the entire David dynasty (Ruth 4:13-22). Naamah became one of the wives of King Solomon, and thus became the mother of King Rehoboam, and through him the foremother of such noble kings as Asa, Jehoshaphat, Hezekiah, and Josiah. Ruth and Naamah became valuable shoots grafted into God's people,[38] or more specifically, into Abraham.

Gentile Jesus-believers are not incorporated into Israel. In other words, Christians are not Jewish proselytes. If it were otherwise, and if we consider the fact that the circumcision of the flesh, the Sabbath (on the seventh day of the week), and the Festivals, as well as the food laws, have never been abolished for Israel, *Gentile Jesus-believers would have to observe all the commandments involved in these things*. In fact, this is precisely what some of them try to do. This error is as grave as that of the supersessionists, who claim that Gentile Jesus-believers indeed belong to "Israel," but at the same time assert that the circumcision of the flesh, the Sabbath (on the seventh day of the week), and the Festivals, as well as the food laws, have been abolished.

The two groups make the opposite mistake, but both mistakes are rooted in the same fundamental error, namely, believing that *Gentile Jesus-believers have been incorporated into Israel*. Both groups proudly tell us that they have become "Jews." For the former group this means "living as Jews," which is a fundamental mistake. For

---

37. Talmud: Yebamoth 63a.
38. *Not* "'grafted' upon the stock of Israel," as the comments in the Soncino edition of the Talmud say. Both Gen. 12:3 and Rabbi Eleazar say "in/on you," i.e., Abraham. Here, the commentators make the same mistake as the supersessionists, though for different reasons.

the latter group this means joining a supposed "Israel" that has been unrecognizably mutilated ("de-Israelized"), which is equally wrong. I do not know which error is worse.

It is one of those points where orthodox Jews exhibit more spiritual insight than the two groups just mentioned. I do not know what they (rightly!) detest more: Gentile Jesus-believers "living as Jews" without having become regular Jewish proselytes, or Gentile Jesus-believers claiming that *they* are the true Israel—but then an Israel without the circumcision of the flesh, the Sabbath (on the seventh day of the week), the Festivals, and the food laws. Orthodox Jews may discover here that I reject these two groups just as strongly as they do! On the one hand: *Gentile Jesus-believers have not been incorporated into Israel*. On the other hand, the circumcision of the flesh, the Sabbath (on the seventh day of the week), the Festivals, and the food laws *have not been abrogated*. Israel, even today, stands under the Mosaic Torah, as they have these last thirty-three or thirty-five centuries, that is, since their stay at Mount Sinai. Christian wish "blind" Jews would listen to *them*—but sometimes "blind" Christians could learn a lot from (orthodox) Jews. Unfortunately, usually both groups stop their ears from listening to each other (cf. Zech. 7:11; Acts 7:57).

12.4 God's People

12.4.1 Two Peoples or One?

Against the supersessionists, I have argued extensively that the Ecclesia is not "Israel," neither some "new Israel," nor some "spiritual Israel." Gentile Jesus-believers have *not* become "Jews," they have *not* been incorporated into or "grafted into" Israel. The Ecclesia, which is the body of the glorified Man Christ at God's right hand, constitutes a fully distinct "project" of God. As such, it differs essentially from that other "project" of God, the ethnic people of Israel, an earthly nation with an earthly calling and destiny.

However, against the classic dispensationalists, I emphasize the immanent-historical links and similarities between these two "projects." In the broadest sense of the word, all those who know, sincerely love and serve the God of Adam, Noah, Abraham, and Israel, and look forward to—or have placed their confidence in—the Messiah of Israel, are one people of God.

This is not entirely self-evident. Israel is explicitly called "the people of God," or, "my [i.e., God's] people."[39] But of the Ecclesia, the apostle James said, "God first visited the Gentiles, to take from them a people for his name" (Acts 15:14). Strictly speaking, this is not even "the" Ecclesia, but only the Gentile part of it. In other words, James used the word "people" here in a rather non-specific sense. Conversely, the apostle Peter wrote (presumably [mainly] to the Jewish Jesus-believers): "[Y]ou are a chosen race, a royal priesthood, a holy nation, a people for his own possession, that you may proclaim the excellencies of him who called you out of darkness into his marvelous light. Once you were not a people, but now you are God's people" (1 Pet. 2:9-10).

And the apostle Paul said in a general way: ". . . our great God and Savior Jesus Christ, who gave himself for us to redeem us from all lawlessness and to purify for himself a people for his own possession who are zealous for good works" (Titus 2:13-14).

Thus, in one sense there are two "peoples of God": Israel is called such, and the Ecclesia is as well, and these two are not the same. At the same time, there is *one* "people of God" in the sense of the *one* family of Abraham: the totality of all the spiritual descendants of Abraham, that is, all those throughout history about whom the following can be said, as it was said of Abraham (cf. Rom. 4:11-12):[40]

(a) They have placed their confidence in God with respect to all the things that he has promised to his people (cf. Gen. 15:6).

(b) They command their children and their households after them to keep the way of the Lord by doing righteousness and justice (cf. Gen. 18:19).

(c) They obey God's voice and keep his charge, his commandments, his statutes, and his laws (cf. Gen. 26:5).

We can look at this family from the transcendent-eternal and from the immanent-historical viewpoint.

(a) *Transcendent-eternal:* all those who, from eternity, have been

---

39. Exod. 3:7, 10; 5:1; Judg. 20:2; 2 Sam. 14:13.
40. Cf. here David's beautiful prayer: "O Lord, the God of Abraham, Isaac, and Israel, our fathers, keep forever such purposes and thoughts in the hearts of your people, and direct their hearts toward you" (1 Chron. 29:18).

chosen by God to become members of this family, from Abraham himself to the Jewish and Gentile believers living during the Messianic kingdom.

(b) *Immanent-historical:* in the present time, this family of Abraham is the totality of all Jesus-believing Jews and Gentiles, to the exclusion of all non-Jesus-believing Jews and Gentiles (among whom are still many Jews and Gentiles who will one day come to faith as well).

So, one or two peoples of God? In one sense: two peoples, which differ very much from each other. In another sense: one people, in the broad sense of the Abrahamic family, including the pre-Abrahamic saints. I discern seven subgroups of this family:

(1) Pre- Abrahamic believers, such as Adam, Abel, Enoch, and Noah.
(2) *Jews:* godly, righteous Jews in the Tanakh (the *tzaddiqim*);
(3) *Gentiles*: Gentiles in the Tanakh who loved and served Israel's God;
(4) *Jews:* the Jewish part of the Ecclesia;
(5) *Gentiles*: the Gentile part of the Ecclesia;
(6) *Jews:* Jews who will come to faith in the Messiah at his (re-) appearance; and
(7) *Gentiles*: godly Gentiles during the Messianic kingdom.

Notice that the groups (2), (4), and (6) constitute the "Israel of God" in the broadest sense.

12.4.2 Continuity and Discontinuity

Although we have repeatedly stressed the similarities between Israel and the Ecclesia, we must never lose sight of the differences. The term "similarities" itself indicates that we are referring to two things that are not identical. In and with the Ecclesia, God made an entirely new beginning in redemptive history. If the Ecclesia were the "spiritual Israel," or the spiritual continuation of the Israel of the Tanakh, we would have to place full emphasis on the *continuity* between Tanakh and New Testament. But now that we are going to underscore the remarkable parallelisms between the beginning of Israel and the beginning of the Ecclesia, this indirectly emphasizes the *discontinuity*. God begins something entirely new in redemptive history: not a new phase in the history of Israel, but a new people of God. However, notice these two features:

(a) This new people of God does not annul that other people of God, ancient Israel, which retains its ancient promises and blessings.

(b) This new people is not something *radically* new; it exhibits remarkable parallelisms with the earlier people of God.

We must keep the balance here: the differences demonstrate that the Ecclesia is something *different* than Israel; here we find discontinuity. But the similarities point to the continuity between the Tanakh and the New Testament.

Almost from the beginning of Israel's existence as a nation, God called it "my people": "I have surely seen the affliction of *my people* who are in Egypt and have heard their cry because of their taskmasters" (Exod. 3:7). "Thus says the LORD, the *God of Israel*, 'Let *my people* go,

that they may hold a feast to me in the wilderness'" (5:1; cf. 6:7; 7:16). In Exodus 19:5–6, the LORD says to Israel through Moses: "[I]f you will indeed obey my voice and keep my covenant, you shall be *my treasured possession* among all peoples, for all the earth is mine; and you shall be to me a kingdom of priests and a holy nation.'"

We find these words again in the New Testament, almost literally, but now applied to the Ecclesia (1 Pet. 2:9; cf. vv. 5 and 10; Titus 2:13–14). Committed supersessionists have interpreted these passages to mean that the Ecclesia is "(spiritual) Israel." Other supersessionists, though, have expressed themselves more carefully. Thus, L. Berkhof wrote: "The New Testament Church is essentially one with the Church of the old dispensation. As far as their essential nature is concerned, they both consist of true believers, and of true believers only. And in their external organization both represent a mixture of good and evil."[41] Of course, I cannot accept the second word "Church" in the first sentence. But if Berkhof had written: "The New Testament believers are essentially one with the believers of the old dispensation," I would have raised no objection. This is, in fact, what Berkhof expresses in the second sentence: the true Israel, the "Israel of God," consists of true *tzaddiqim*, and the true

---

41. Berkhof (1981, 632).

Ecclesia consists of true *tzaddiqim* as well, specifically: those justified by faith in the person and the work of Jesus Christ. In a third sentence, Berkhof touches upon the outward appearance of both Israel and the church: the two companies consist of true believers, but also including indifferent members, including people who in fact are outright enemies of the God of the Bible (cf. five of the seven churches in Rev. 2–3).

Another example was H. Ridderbos, who wrote: "... the church is *the continuation and fulfillment of the historical people of God* that in Abraham God chose for himself from all peoples [of the earth] and to which he bound himself by making the covenant and promises."[42] With such a sentence we need to have little difficulty, except for one thing: it stresses the unity of the Abrahamic family, but does not exhibit any awareness of the different, unique character of the Ecclesia in comparison with the situation of the Tanakh. I suggest we read: the church is the continuation and fulfillment of the historical Abrahamic family, and at the same time constitutes a different, unique part of this family. Where classical dispensationalists overemphasize the differences between believers in the Tanakh and New Testament believers, we stress the unity of the one Abrahamic family. And whereas supersessionists overemphasize the unity and identity of believers in the Tanakh and New Testament believers, we stress the unique character of the Ecclesia in comparison with Israel.

Even when it comes to the term "people," the uniqueness of the Ecclesia is evident. The words of the apostle James, "God first visited the Gentiles, to take from them a people for his name" (Acts 15:14), underscores the fact that God has begun a totally new work; we could never say that in the time of the Tanakh, God was "taking from the Gentiles a people for his name." And in Titus 2:13–14, we underscore the word "own": Christ "gave himself for us ... to purify *for himself* a people *for his own possession*." This is a people that had never existed before in this form, in the sense of Matthew 16:18: Jews and Gentiles may have *their* "ecclesias" (Acts 7:38; 19:32, 39–40), but Jesus announces that he is going to build *his own* Ecclesia (future tense!).

---

42. Ridderbos (1975, 327).

12.4.3 *'Am* and *Goy, Laos* and *Ethnos*

It is worthwhile to look a little more closely at the statement by James in Acts 15:14, about God "taking from the Gentiles [Gk. *ethnē*, plural of *ethnos*] a people [Gk. *laos*] for his name." Compare this with the words of the apostle Peter in Acts 15:7-9,

> Brothers, you know that in the early days God made a choice among you, that by my mouth the Gentiles [*ethnē*] should hear the word of the gospel and believe. And God, who knows the heart, bore witness to them, by giving them the Holy Spirit just as he did to us, and he made no distinction between us and them, having cleansed their hearts by faith.

James spoke (in v. 14) not of Israel but of an entirely *new* "people," which was being gathered from all nations, Jewish and here especially Gentile.[43] There is not a single suggestion here that this "people" or "nation" would be identical with Israel, or could be called "Israel," or would be the continuation of former Israel. On the contrary, *Israel (Jesus-believing or not) simply continues observing the Sinaitic Torah*, as James argues (v. 21), whereas this Torah is not imposed upon the Jesus-believing Gentiles. Supersessionists believe that the Mosaic Torah has been abolished, but James reassured Jesus-believing Jews by stating that "Moses" (i.e., the Mosaic Torah) would keep being read in all the synagogues, as had been the case for centuries, and has remained the case in the many centuries thereafter.[44]

Some expositors make a subtle distinction between Greek *ethnos* and *laos*,[45] a similar distinction as the one made between Hebrew *goy* and *'am*. James, presumably speaking Hebrew or Aramaic, said something like this: God was "taking from the Gentiles [Heb. *goyyim*] a people [Heb. *'am*] for his name." Such a distinction must be made in John 11:50 as well, where the high priest Caiaphas says, "[You do not] understand that it is better for you that one man

---

43. Bruce (1988, 293).

44. These same supersessionists must shake their heads about the fact that the Jesus-believing Jews in Acts 21:20 continued to be "zealous for the Torah." However, Luke and Paul apparently found this entirely normal (see Paul in vv. 21–26).

45. Cf. the English terms "ethnic" (from *ethnos*), and "laity" and "laical" (from *laos*).

The One People of God

should die for the people [Gk. *laos*], not that the whole nation [Gk. *ethnos*] should perish." The distinction must not be exaggerated, because several exceptions may be mentioned. Yet, it seems that *'am* and *laos* usually refer to God's chosen people, whereas *goyyim* and *ethnē* are a more general reference to the nations of the world (of whom Israel is but one).[46] In Acts 15:14, the "people" taken from the Gentiles are another such "chosen people," though distinguished from Israel. In the Tanakh, Israel is sometimes referred to as a *goy*, which does not necessarily have negative connotations. But when God speaks of Israel as "his people," it is *'am* (see especially Hos. 1–2). In Acts 11:50, Jesus is the Man who died for *God's people* (*'am, laos*) in order that Israel would not perish like any other nation (*goy, ethnos*).

The fact that God *had* "his own people ['*am, laos*]," but since Acts 2 *is gathering* a *laos* (*'am*) from the Gentiles, is remarkable because this time the *laos* is not Israel, but a "people" consisting of believing Gentiles. J. A. Bengel spoke here of an "eminent paradox" (Lat. *egregium paradoxon*).[47] We seem to be forced to say that God chose *twice* from the Gentile world a people for himself:

(a) First, he chose a purely *ethnic* people, Israel, a single *goy* from the many *goyyim*, which by God's grace became his own people (*'am, laos*).

(b) Second, he chose a purely spiritual people, the individual members being taken from *all* the *goyyim* (*ethnē*): the Ecclesia.

In both cases, one could say that we are dealing with a nation chosen from the nations, but of course, the difference is obvious: Israel was a single, well defined *goy*, one of the many *goyyim*, taken out of their midst. But the Ecclesia is not a *goy* (*ethnos*), like the Dutch or the Americans form a *goy* (*ethnos*); it is a *laos* (Titus 2:14; 1 Pet. 2:9), a gathering of individuals taken *out of all* the *goyyim* (*ethnē*) of this world.

12.4.4 Two Pairs: Two Rocks

The immanent-historical development of both Israel and the Eccle-

---

46. See Trench (1953, 367–68).
47. Bengel (1862, 449).

sia begins with a *rock*.⁴⁸ In Isaiah 51:1-2 the LORD said:

> Listen to me, you who pursue righteousness,
>   you who seek the LORD:
> look to the rock from which you were hewn,
>   and to the quarry from which you were dug.
> Look to Abraham your father
>   and to Sarah who bore you;
> for he was but one [or, alone] when I called him,
>   that I might bless him and multiply him.

Here, Abraham is the rock from which Israel was hewn, as Jewish tradition has loved to emphasize, too: "The ancestors of the nation are compared to a quarry and its members to the stones hewn therefrom."⁴⁹

In contrast to this the disciple (later apostle) Peter is the rock on which Christ would build his Ecclesia (not in the Roman Catholic sense of Peter being the first pope, but of Peter being the prototype of all true Jesus-worshipers): "I tell you, you are Peter [Gk. *petros*], and on this rock [Gk. *petra*] I will build my Ecclesia, and the gates of Hades shall not prevail against it" (Matt. 16:18).⁵⁰

The parallelism can hardly be coincidental. To be sure, this metaphor was not used in identical ways in the two cases: a rock *from* which stones are hewn is not the same as a rock *upon* which stones are built. Yet, it is remarkable that both "peoples of God" (or both forms of the one "people of God") began with a "rock" on which the further development of the peoples depended. In this, we do not forget, of course, that God himself is the actual Rock on which the two people have been and are being built.⁵¹

12.4.2 Two Dozens

It has often been noticed that the history of Israel begins with twelve men, namely, the patriarchs (the sons of Jacob), and that the history of the Ecclesia also begins with twelve men: the apostles.⁵² Actually,

---

48. Pop (1999, 402).
49. Slotki (1983, 250).
50. See Ouweneel (2010a, §2.1).
51. Cf. Deut. 32:4, 15, 18, 30–31; Ps. 89:26; Isa. 17:10; 30:29.
52. Wentsel (1998a, 475–76). Bilezikian (2001, 85) says that the twelve disciples

in both cases the numbers are a bit uncertain: the descendants of Joseph's sons, Ephraim and Manasseh, were counted as full-fledged tribes in Israel, so that the number was actually thirteen! At various places, the tribes of Israel are enumerated in such a way that the total is always twelve, so that one of the tribes must be omitted.[53]

There is a similar obscurity in the names of the apostles. In total, we find fifteen names, but it is generally accepted that Bartholomew and Nathanael are one and the same person, as well as Thaddeus, Lebbaeus, and Judas son of James; this brings the number to twelve. At any rate, the Bible clearly says there are *twelve* sons of Jacob (Gen. 35:22), hence twelve tribes (49:28); and there are *twelve* apostles (Matt. 10:2).

Interestingly, some of the names in the two groups are similar: we find the name of father *Ya'aqov* (in English Bibles "Jacob") identical to two apostles called *Iakōbos* (in English Bibles "James"): the son of Zebedee and the son of Alphaeus. We meet the name of the patriarch *Shim'on* ("Simeon") in the name of two apostles called *Simōn*: Simon Peter and Simon the Zealot. The name of the patriarch *Yehudah* ("Judah") is similar to that of the disciples *Ioudas* ("Judas"): Judas the son of James and Judas Iscarioth.[54] This is no fewer than half of the twelve disciples. (The patriarchs can also be divided in two groups of six: there were six sons of Leah and six sons of the other three women; Simeon and Judah both belonged to the sons of Leah.)

The close connection between the twelve tribes of Israel and the twelve apostles is remarkably underscored by Matthew 19:28 (NKJV): "Assuredly I say to you, that in the regeneration, when the

---

had taken the places of the twelve patriarchs, as judges over the people (Matt. 19:18).

53. See, e.g., Rev. 7:5-8 (Dan omitted); in many cases, Levi is identified separately, so that again twelve tribes remain (e.g., Num. 2; Ezek. 48).

54. The small differences in the names, e.g., Judah/Judas, are caused by the different origins: Hebrew and Greek, respectively. A third "Judas" in the New Testament, the "brother of James," is traditionally written as "Jude" (see Jude 1). Of course, Judas Iscarioth was a disciple, but not an apostle; Matthias became the new twelfth apostle (Acts 1:21–26). As to the confusion of twelve and thirteen, it has sometimes been argued that the apostle Paul, the "thirteenth apostle," was actually the "twelfth," since the choice of Matthias was viewed as precipitous.

Son of Man sits on the throne of His glory, you who have followed Me [i.e., the apostles] will also sit on twelve thrones, judging the twelve tribes of Israel." Of the New Jerusalem we are told (Rev. 21:12–14): "It had a great, high wall, with twelve gates, ... and on the gates the names of the twelve tribes of the *sons* of Israel were inscribed.... And the wall of the city had twelve foundations, and on them were the twelve names of the twelve *apostles* of the Lamb."

At the same time, this parallelism excellently underscores our claim that Israel, identified as the "twelve tribes of the sons of Israel," cannot be identical with the Ecclesia, identified as the "twelve apostles of the Lamb." If two objects can resemble each other only because they are not identical. Jesus-believing Gentiles are not identified with the twelve patriarchs; the Ecclesia has her own dozen men.

12.5   People of a Pilgrimage
12.5.1   A Double Exodus

Both the history of Israel and that of the Ecclesia begins with an *exodus*. N. T. Wright wrote that the story of Israel is the story of going out and returning home, of slavery and subsequent exodus, of exile and subsequent restoration. It is also the story that Jesus told in his words and deeds, and in particular through his death and resurrection.[55] In other words, Jesus' own story is one of going out and coming back, of entering captivity and coming out again.

We know of Israel's exodus through the book of Exodus, in Hebrew called *Sh'mot*, "Names," because of Exodus 1:1, which in the Septuagint received the name *Ex(h)odos*, from Greek *ex* ("out of") and *hodos*, "way," or "way out." The word occurs several times in the Septuagint as a designation for Israel's "going out" of Egypt.[56] It refers to Israel's deliverance from the captivity and slavery that it had endured in that land: "I am the LORD your God, who brought you out of the land of Egypt, out of the house of slavery" (Exod. 20:2; Deut. 5:6).

With regard to Jesus, the word occurs in the Greek text of Luke 9:29–31 (the story of the transfiguration on the mountain): "And as he [i.e., Jesus] was praying, the appearance of his face was al-

---

55. Wright (2007, 74–75).
56. Exod. 19:1; Num. 33:38; Ps. 114:1 (LXX: 113:1).

tered, and his clothing became dazzling white. And behold, two men were talking with him, Moses and Elijah, who appeared in glory and spoke of his departure [Gk. *exodos*] which he was about to accomplish at Jerusalem."[57] Here, the meaning of the word *exodos* is "to depart" (in the euphemistic sense), that is, "to die" (see the same word in 2 Pet. 1:15, "after my departure . . . ," i.e., my death). Just as Israel's exodus formed the foundation for its existence as a nation, Jesus' "exodus" out of this life formed the foundation on which he built his Ecclesia: "Christ loved the church and gave himself up for her" (Eph. 5:25; cf. Titus 2:13–14, ". . . Jesus Christ, who gave himself for us . . . to purify for himself a people for his own possession").

God's dealings with the Ecclesia are "exodus actions: as a pilgrimaging people they constantly must depart from sin on their way to the promised fatherland."[58] Several times we hear: "'Therefore *go out from their midst*, and be separate from them,' says the LORD, 'and touch no unclean thing; then I will welcome you, and I will be a father to you, and you shall be sons and daughters to me,' says the LORD Almighty" (2 Cor. 6:17–18). "*Come out of her* [i.e., the Great Babylon], my people,   lest you take part in her sins, lest you share in her plagues; for her sins are heaped high as heaven, and God has remembered her iniquities (Rev. 18:4–5)"[59] Very concretely, the apostle Paul suggested a typological link between Israel's exodus and the "exodus" of the Ecclesia: "[O]ur fathers [i.e., Israel] were all under the [pillar of] cloud, and all passed through the sea [i.e., Red Sea], and all were baptized into Moses in the cloud and in the sea. . . . Now these things took place as examples for us" (1 Cor. 10:1–6).

12.5.2 The Ecclesia On Its Way

N. T. Wright observed that when the apostle Paul spoke of the Spirit as the "down payment of our inheritance" (Eph. 1:13–14), he was

---

57. Cf. Heitink (2007, 26): "In his [i.e., Jesus'] life, the new exodus from the bonds of sin and death is realized."

58. Heyns (1988, 360); cf. Küng (1967, xi, 33, 95, 122–23, 131–32, 289, 329, 341, 344, 489); Bijlsma (1981, 39); Verkuyl (1992, 378); Rahner (1966 title: 'The Pilgrimaging Church," although the notion of the "pilgrimage" is hardly dealt with in this book); cf. Phil. 3:20; Heb. 11:13–16; 13:14; 1 Pet. 2:11–12.

59. Cf. Isa. 48:20; 52:11; Jer. 51:6, 45.

evoking, just as Jesus had done, the entire Exodus tradition, the story that began with Pesach and ended in the Promised Land. Paul said, in fact, that Christians are now the people of the true exodus, people on their way to their inheritance. But, argued Wright, this "inheritance" is not some bodyless heaven,[60] nor is it simply a small country among others (read: the land of Israel). The entire world is now God's Holy Land. In our pilgrimage from Pesach to the Promised Land, the Spirit plays the same role as he played in the ancient story with the pillar of cloud and fire.[61]

Wright is a supersessionist, as we may notice in this passage; yet, it is definitely true that the Ecclesia is an "exodus people," too, just like Israel in the Tanakh, a people on its way to the Promised Land, not to the "hereafter" but to the kingdom of God. Just as Israel was "on its way" from Egypt, or Babylon, back home, the Ecclesia is the "Exodus Church,"[62] "God people are on pilgrimage, on the way,"[63] from the land of captivity and slavery to the land of freedom and peace, the Messianic kingdom. As the Messiah himself said (Isa. 61:1; cf. Luke 4:18):

> The Spirit of the LORD God is upon me,
>   because the LORD has anointed me
> to bring good news to the poor;
>   he has sent me to bind up the brokenhearted,
> to proclaim *liberty to the captives,*
>   and the opening of the prison to those who are bound; . . . .

This "Exodus Church" is *called* "the Way" (Gk. *hodos*, as in *ex(h) odos*): ". . . any belonging to the Way . . ."[64] Just as the Israelites were "strangers and sojourners," so too are New Testament believers.[65] The English term "parish" comes from Greek *paroikia*, "sojourning" (1 Pet. 1:17 KJV, "the time of your sojourning"). This word is related to *paroikos*, "sojourner." Thus, the word "parish" expresses (without people usually realizing it) that the local church is a company of

---

60. Cf. extensively Ouweneel (2021).
61. Wright (2007, 114–15)
62. Cf. Moltmann (1977, 76–85).
63. Heitink (2007, 26).
64. Acts 9:2; cf. 19:9, 23; 22:4; 24:14, 22.
65. Lev. 25:23; 1 Chron. 29:15; Heb. 11:13; 1 Pet. 2:11.

"strangers and sojourners," "in a social structure that had not been invented *by* them."[66] It was invented *for* them in the sense that God makes of every Jesus-believer a person who is no longer "at home," but "on their way" to the kingdom of God. For both Israel and the Ecclesia, Abraham is the pilgrim par excellence, as the LORD told him: "Go from your land and your kindred and your father's house to the land that I will show you" (Gen. 12:1; cf. Acts 7:3; Heb. 11:8). The New Delhi Report on Witness spoke of the "pilgrim church," which, like Abraham, boldly moves into the unknown future, unafraid to leave behind the securities of its conventional structure, glad to dwell in the tent of continual adaptation, looking forward to the city whose designer and builder is God (Heb. 11:10).[67]

As part of the medieval pilgrim's blessing for those who are on their way to Santiago de Compostela in Spain (the alleged burial site of the apostle James son of Zebedee), this statement is made: "Oh God, you who took up your servant Abraham from the city of Ur of the Chaldeans, watching over him in all his wanderings, you who were the guide of the Hebrew people in the desert, we ask that you deign to take care of these your servants who, for love of your name, make a pilgrimage to Compostela, ..."[68]

In a different context, one sociologist has argued that if the market, which artificially generates desires and temporarily satisfies them, becomes *the* model for life, we are no longer pilgrims but tourists.[69] This is an enormous danger for Christians in a capitalist society. It reminds us of the two and a half tribes, who desired to stay on the eastern side of the river Jordan because they found a good life there; they had no longing to move into the Promised Land in order to dwell *there* (Num. 32). It is no wonder that these tribes were the first to be conquered by foreign powers (2 Kings 10:33) and carried away in exile (1 Chron. 5:26). Those who have no desire for "the land" are the first to be removed from it.

---

66. R. H. Reeling Brouwer in Jonkers and Bruinsma-de Beer (2000, 55).

67. Quoted in Visser 't Hoofd (1962, 90).

68. See, e.g., http://www.206tours.com/info/elcamino/prayers.htm; I myself made this walking trip in 2005, and on the way heard this blessing.

69. Bauman (1998, 77–102).

12.6 Moses and Jesus
12.6.1 Parallels

The history of Israel begins with the birth of Moses, their first leader and the greatest Israelite prophet who ever lived (Deut. 34:10) until Jesus, who built further on the foundation laid by Moses. The history of the Ecclesia begins with the birth of Jesus Christ, the Messiah of Israel, King of kings and Lord of lords (Rev. 19:16). The Bible understandably sees various parallelisms between these two giants, Moses and Jesus. This is important for our study because Jesus Christ appears after the eight world empires (from Egypt to Rome; cf. Rev. 17:10–11), whereas Moses as a miraculous deliverer stands at the very beginning of the history of the world empires. The God-sent opponent of the "first king," Pharaoh, is thus a type of the last, the Ninth King, who is the opponent of all his eight diabolical predecessors.[70]

The New Testament mentions, for instance, the following similarities and contrasts (three times seven).[71]

(1) Moses gave Israel the bread from heaven (Exod. 16:4; cf. Ps. 78:25; 132:15); the Father gave his people his Son as the bread from heaven (John 6:32; cf. Matt. 14:15–21).

(2) Moses gave access to physical water (Exod. 17:6); Jesus gave access to spiritual water (John 7:37–39).

(3) Moses and his family rode on a donkey (Exod. 4:20); Jesus rode on a donkey (Zech. 9:9; Matt. 21:2–7).

(4) Moses was a prophet, the greatest of all in the Tanakh (Deut. 34:10); Jesus is one too, the greatest of all (Deut. 18:15–18; Acts 3:22; cf. Matt. 17:5).

(5) Moses was accompanied by twelve princes from the tribes of Israel, and by seventy(-two)[72] elders from the people (Exod. 24:1, 9; Num. 1:44; 11:16, 24–25); Jesus was accompanied by twelve apostles, and sent them out, just as he sent out seventy(-two)[73] elders

---

70. See extensively, Ouweneel (2003a).

71. See Ouweneel (2020, 220–26, 368–76; see also 2003a, 345–47).

72. Rabbinic tradition says that Moses originally had seventy-two elders, including Eldad and Medad; so Schoeps (1949, 96).

73. Some manuscripts read in Luke 10:1 and 17 seventy, others seventy-two, that is, six for every tribe of Israel.

(Luke 10:1, 17).[74]

(6) The Torah was given through Moses (Israel was founded on the Mosaic Torah); grace and truth came through Jesus Christ (John 1:17) (the Ecclesia is founded on the Torah of Christ, 1 Cor. 9:21; Gal. 6:2).

(7) Moses was the great lawgiver of Israel; Jesus is the "new Moses" (Lat. *novus Moses*), the great lawgiver of the Ecclesia.[75]

(8) Moses was connected with Mount Sinai (the mountain of judgment), Jesus with Mount Zion (the mountain of grace) (Heb. 12:18-22).

(9) Those who do not listen to the written words of Moses, will listen even less to the spoken words of Jesus (John 5:45-47), and even less to someone rising from the dead, Jesus himself in particular (Luke 16:31).

(10) Moses lifted up the serpent in the wilderness; thus also the Son of Man was lifted up (John 3:14).

(11) Moses brought the Old Covenant (which, because of sin, was in effect a ministry of death); Jesus brought the New Covenant (which is the ministry of the Spirit in glory) (2 Cor. 3:7-8).

(12) Moses was a servant in the house of God; Jesus is Son over God's house (Heb. 3:1-6).

(13) Moses was rejected by his own people; Jesus was too (Acts 7:20-28, 51-52).

(14) The covenant of Moses was consecrated with the blood of animals, that of Jesus with his own blood (Heb. 9:18-23).

(15) Israel was baptized into Moses; New Testament believers are baptized into Christ (1 Cor. 10:2).

(16) The Egyptian sorcerers, Jannes and Jambres, opposed Moses; the heretics of today oppose (the truth of) Christ (2 Tim. 3:8).

(17) The song of Moses is parallel to the song of the Lamb (Rev. 15:3).

(18) The Targum (the Aramaic paraphrase of the Tanakh) applied Psalm 68:18 to Moses, whereas Ephesians 4:8 applied the verse to Jesus.

---

74. Cf. Pseudo-Clement, *Recognitiones* I.40–41 regarding this parallel.
75. See Davies (1969, 10–16); for a Jewish view, see Schoeps (1949, 87–116).

(19) The rabbis said that the *Shekhinah* rested on Moses;[76] similarly the *Shekhinah* rested on Jesus (Luke 1:35; 9:34; John 2:19).[77]

(20) Under Moses ten miracles happened, namely, the ten plagues of Egypt (called "signs" in Exod. 7:3; 8:23; 10:1-2); the rabbis expected the same from the Messiah.[78] Indeed, after having described Jesus as the second Moses teaching on the new "Sinai" (the mountain of the Sermon on the Mount, Matt. 5-7), Matthew mentions exactly ten miracles performed by Jesus (Matt. 8:1-9:34).

(21) An ancient Jewish tradition says that the light of the Messiah's face would shine more brightly than that of Moses' face (Exod. 34:29-30, 35).[79] Indeed, on three occasions the face of Jesus shone as brightly as the sun, or even more brightly (Matt. 17:2; Acts 26:13; Rev. 1:16).

12.6.2 Two Births

If we now consider specifically the birth of Moses and that of Jesus, we again discover several parallelisms.

(1) The book of Exodus begins with a *genealogy* before the circumstances of Israel and the birth of Moses are described (Exod. 1:1-5). Amram was a grandson of Levi, and a great grandson of Jacob (Exod. 6:15-19).

The Gospel of Matthew also begins with a *genealogy* before the birth of Jesus is described (Matt. 1:1-17). We even encounter the same names: Joseph was a son of Jacob (Matt. 1:16), and a great grandson of Levi (Luke 3:24).

(2) In the days of Moses, Israel suffered under *foreign oppressors*; it was a nation of slaves under the power of Egypt, with Pharaoh at its head, who promulgated despotic decrees: heavy forced labor (Exod. 1:11, 14; 5:6-9).

At the time of Jesus, Israel was again suffering under *foreign dominion*; it was a nation of slaves (cf. Ezra 9:8-9; Neh. 9:36-37) under the power of the Romans, with the emperor at their head (emphasized by Luke) as well as the Edomite king, Herod

---

76. Talmud: Sanhedrin 11a.
77. Ouweneel (2020, §6.2.1).
78. Mishnah: Aboth V.5.
79. Midrash Psalms 21, 179.

(emphasized by Matthew). Israel was subjugated to the despotic decrees of Augustus: the registration involved a census and an assessment in view of heavy taxes (Luke 2:1).

(3) Against the background of Moses' birth, we hear of a terrible *massacre* of little boys (Exod. 1:16,22): Pharaoh had all the newborn boys thrown into the Nile. Moses, however, was kept hidden by his parents (Heb. 11:23).

Against the background of Jesus' birth we also hear of a terrible *massacre* of little boys (Matt. 2:16): king Herod had all the boys up to two years old slaughtered at Bethlehem. The child Jesus, however, was taken by his parents and escaped.

(4) Jochebed saw that her child was "beautiful" (Exod. 2:2; Heb. 11:23), that is, "beautiful in God's sight" (Acts 7:20), and hid him for *three months*.

During her pregnancy Mary spent *three months* in quietness with Elizabeth (Luke 1:56); after the birth, others honored her child, and she herself "treasured up all these things, pondering them in her heart" (Luke 2:19, 51).

(5) Jochebed put her child into an exceptional "cradle," a basket of bulrushes, because there was no room for the boy in society; a young woman stayed near the basket: Miriam (Gk. *Mariam*) (Exod. 2:3–4).

Mary (Gk. *Maria[m]*), too, put her child into an exceptional "cradle": a manger, that is, a food-trough for animals, because there was no room for the boy in the inn; the young Mary (Gk. *Mariam*) sat at the manger (Luke 2:7, 16).

(6) Strangers came to see the child of Jochebed in his strange cradle: the daughter of Pharaoh with her servants discovered little Moses (Exod. 2:5).

Strangers came to see the child of Mary in his strange cradle: the shepherds came to the child, with the manger functioning as one of the signs of recognition (Luke 2:12, 16); later, wise men from the East came as well (Matt. 2:1–12).

(7) Moses spent the first years of his life in Egypt.

Jesus, too, spent the first years of his life in Egypt (Matt. 2:13–15).

12.6.3 Flavius Josephus

The Jewish historian Josephus supplied us with several other details about the birth of Moses, which are not mentioned in the Tanakh. If we assume that Josephus did not invent these details, he must have obtained them from oral Jewish tradition. We may assume that Matthew and his Jewish readers were familiar with these details.[80]

(a) An Egyptian astrologer predicted the birth of a Hebrew boy who would defeat Egypt and deliver Israel. Because of this, Pharaoh decreed that all Hebrew boys were to be killed.

"Wise men" (Gk. *magoi*, that is, astrologers) from the East predicted the birth of a Jewish boy, who would be king over Israel (which also implied that he would deliver his people from the Romans). Because of this, Herod decreed the massacre of the innocent little boys in Bethlehem (Matt. 2:1-18).

(b) Moses' father, Amram, was a distinguished man among his people.

Joseph was a distinguished man, being a descendant of David (Matt. 1:20; Luke 2:4). (The difference: Amram was from the tribe of Levi, Joseph from the tribe of Judah.)

(c) God appeared to Amram in a dream to enlighten him about the significance of the child that his wife was expecting, including the words, "He will deliver his people from slavery."

An angel of the LORD appeared to Joseph in a dream to enlighten him about the significance of the child that his wife was expecting (Matt. 1:20-23), including the words, "He will save his people from their sins" (v. 21).

(d) Josephus called Moses the greatest person who has ever lived among the Hebrews.

Jesus is the greatest person in the New Testament, even in the entire Bible, all literature, all humanity.

12.7 Lessons from the Torah

12.7.1 Sinai and Zion

Of course, there lies a deeper meaning in the fact that the outpouring of the Holy Spirit in Acts 2 occurred during the Jewish Feast of

---

80. Jewish Antiquities II.5.

Weeks (*Shavu'ot*, Jewish Pentecost).[81] Originally, this was a harvest feast (Lev. 23:15-21; Deut. 16:9-11), but after the destruction of Jerusalem and the temple, and the dispersion of Israel, this harvest aspect receded into the background. At least since the second century of our era, but probably already centuries before this, this feast had become what is called in Hebrew *z'man mattan toratēnu*, the "time of the giving of our Torah," the feast of the Torah-giving on Mount Sinai. According to the rabbis, *Shavu'ot* is celebrated on the same day as the day on which the Torah was given, the sixth day of the third month of the religious year,.[82]

The Torah-giving on Mount Sinai was also the moment when the covenant between God and his people was made. Therefore, *Shavu'ot* was also a covenant feast; the people

> were gathered at Jerusalem in the third month of the fifteenth year of the reign of Asa. They sacrificed to the LORD on that day from the spoil that they had brought 700 oxen and 7,000 sheep. And they entered into a covenant to seek the LORD, the God of their fathers, with all their heart and with all their soul (2 Chron. 15:10-12).

The Jewish book of Jubilees (second century BC) linked the Feast of Weeks explicitly with the covenants, in particular the Noahic Covenant.[83] The Essene sect of Qumran (first century of our era) spoke about a feast of the New Covenant, which very probably refers to the Feast of Weeks.[84]

Originally, *Shavu'ot* was the Feast of the Old Covenant, while the Day of Pentecost of Acts 2, the Feast of the New Covenant, is linked with another mountain, Zion.[85] Concerning this link the prophet was said: the LORD says, "In those days and in that time, . . . the people of Israel and the people of Judah shall come together, weeping as they come, and they shall seek the LORD their God. They shall ask the way to Zion, with faces turned toward it, saying, 'Come, let us join ourselves to the LORD in an everlasting covenant

---

81. See more extensively, Ouweneel (2020, 259–69).
82. Cf. Talmud: Shabbath 88a.
83. Jub. VI.15–22; XLIV.1–5.
84. E.g., 4QDa [4Q266] 11, 17; 1QS II.19–26; V.20–24; VI.
85. Actually, not apart from *Sukkoth*, the Feast of Booths, which is *the* eschatological feast of the Messianic kingdom; cf. Zech. 14:16–19.

that will never be forgotten'" (Jer. 50:4–5). Whereas Israel remembers at *Shavu'ot* the Torah-giving on Mount Sinai (Exod. 20), the Ecclesia remembers at Pentecost the outpouring of the Holy Spirit on Zion. These might seem to be very different things, but the parallelism goes much deeper than might appear at first sight.

(a) During the *first* Day of Pentecost in history, Israel was born on Mount Sinai as the covenant people of God: the people of the Old Covenant. During the *first* Day of Pentecost after Messiah's death and resurrection, the Ecclesia was born on Mount Zion as the covenant people of God: the people of the New Covenant.

(b) On both occasions, on Mount Sinai in Exodus 19–20 and on Mount Zion in Acts 2, people heard voices[86] and saw fire (or tongues like fire) (Exod. 19:16, 19; Acts 2:3). The Torah/Logos is compared to fire (Jer. 23:29), and also to water (Eph. 5:26), just as the Spirit is compared to fire and water.[87]

(c) On both mountains, God gave a precious gift to his newborn people: on Mount Sinai, it was the Torah, on Mount Zion it was the Holy Spirit. It is noteworthy that, in Hebrew, both *torah* (lit., "instruction") and *ruach* ("breath, Spirit") are feminine words. Some rabbis have described the Torah as the "daughter of God," initially lying in the bosom of God, then given in marriage to Israel.[88] And concerning God's *ruach*, Genesis 1:2 describes her as a Lady, hovering over the world, watching over it as a good Mother. The Christian notion of Sophia ("Wisdom") exhibits links with both the Torah (Heb. *Chokhmah*, "Wisdom," of Prov. 8) and the Spirit, as in the painting of Michelangelo (Sistine Chapel, the Vatican), where God creates Adam with the help of his "daughter," Sophia, that is, through the power of the Holy Spirit.[89]

(d) The links between the Torah and the Holy Spirit are numerous.[90] Giving the Torah was like giving the Spirit, just as breaking the Torah is like grieving the Spirit (Isa. 63:20–21; Eph. 4:30). Under

---

86. Exod. 19:16, "thunders," Heb. *qolot*, lit. "voices"; Acts 2:4, Gk. *glōssais*, "tongues."
87. See Ouweneel (2007a, 206–207).
88. See, e.g., Exod. Rabbah 33 (94a).
89. See more extensively Ouweneel (1998a, §2.3.3).
90. Ouweneel (2020, 259–61).

the New Covenant, the Spirit of the living God is writing "Christ" in the hearts of believers, which is the same as saying that the Torah is being written in their hearts (2 Cor. 3:3; Heb. 8:10). Living by the Spirit is the same as living under the Torah of Christ (Gal. 5:13–6:2; 2 Cor. 3:6). Where the Spirit is, there is liberty (2 Cor. 3:17), therefore the Torah of Christ is the "law of liberty" (James 1:25; 2:12). Just as the Torah (i.e., literally "teaching"!) led and taught God's people, the Spirit leads and teaches God's people (John 14:26; 16:13; Rom. 8:14). Just as the Torah makes alive and enlightens the eyes (Ps. 119:93; 19:8), the Spirit makes alive and enlightens the eyes (2 Cor. 3:6; Eph. 1:17–18). The Torah had been written "by the finger of God" (Exod. 31:18; Deut. 9:10 CJB), while Jesus acted "by the finger of God," that is, by the Spirit of God (Luke 11:20; compare Matt. 12:28, finger = Spirit). True sons of God are those who keep the Torah (Deut. 8:5–6), that is, they are those who are led by the Spirit (Rom. 8:14). Both the Torah and the Spirit convict people concerning sin, righteousness and judgment (compare Rom. 3:20; 5:20; 7:7–11; Gal. 3:19 with John 16:8). Rejecting the Torah amounts to resisting the Holy Spirit (Acts 7:38–51). By the power of the Holy Spirit, the righteous requirement of the Torah is fulfilled in believers (Rom. 8:4).

We learn about the contrast between Sinai and Zion also from Galatians 4:24–27 and Hebrews 12:18–24.[91] In the former passage, we find in juxtaposition: (a) Sinai and Zion (see in v. 27 the quotation from Isa. 54:1 and cf. 49:14), (b) Hagar and Sarah, (c) Ishmael and Isaac, (d) the "present" Jerusalem (the Judaistic order of things) and the "Jerusalem above" (the New Testament order of things). These two orders of things are being contrasted here, the old order and the new one, such that the new one replaces the old one. The old one characterizes Judaism, whereas the new one characterizes the Ecclesia.

Again, this speaking of Zion in a spiritual sense does not at all mean that the literal Zion has been done away with in God's plans with Israel and the world. Read again Isaiah 2:2–3, and ask how one can do justice to the details in these verses if Zion is spiritualized here:

---

91. Ouweneel (1982b, 2:83–90; 1997, 292–98); cf. Pop (1999, 335).

It shall come to pass in the latter days
>that the mountain [i.e., Zion] of the house of the LORD
shall be established as the highest of the mountains,
>and shall be lifted up above the hills;
and all the nations shall flow to it,
>and many peoples shall come, and say:
"Come, let us go up to the mountain of the LORD,
>to the house [i.e., temple] of the God of Jacob,
that he may teach us his ways
>and that we may walk in his paths."
For out of Zion shall go forth the Torah,
>and the word of the LORD from Jerusalem.

On the supersessionist standpoint, in these verses, what is this mountain? What is the house of the LORD? What is Zion? Of what Torah was the text speaking? What time was this, when many peoples would go to Zion, and (see v. 4) the wicked would be judged, the swords would be beaten into plowshares, and there would be peace and justice between the nations? If we do not have any sensible answers to such questions, our exegesis is apparently on the wrong track.

12.7.2 Commemoration

To "commemorate" means to remember a thing or event in a solemn way. It means "celebrating" that thing or event, and we usually do this on fixed "memorial days" in the year. In the Bible, this notion of commemoration is very important. When Jesus instituted the Lord's Supper, "he took bread, and when he had given thanks, he broke it and gave it to them, saying, 'This is my body, which is given for you. Do this [i.e., eating] in *remembrance* of me'" (Luke 22:19; cf. 1 Cor. 11:24–25). This means: "commemorate me (in my sufferings and death)"; as Paul said, "For as often as you eat this bread and drink the cup, you proclaim the Lord's death until he comes" (1 Cor. 11:26).

God is set on helping us never to forget certain things; they must always remain in our conscious memory, whether for positive or for negative reasons. The Hebrew verb for "remember" or "commemorate" is *z-kh-r*, a root that we encounter, for instance, in the name Zechariah. In the Bible, this name was borne by at least four persons.[92] The name means, "The LORD commemorates" or "remembers." This can be a comfort to the bearer of the name ("the LORD thinks of me, he does not forget me"), but in case he is a prophet, the message of that name for the majority of listeners was: Remember, the LORD does not forget a single sin (negative), or (to the remnant), Be comforted, the LORD does not forget any of his promises (positive).

Many Jewish festivals are actually memorial days or times: *Pesach* (Passover) remembers the exodus from Egypt, *Shavu'ot* (Pentecost) remembers the Torah-giving on Mount Sinai, *Sukkot* (the Feast of Booths) remembers the wilderness journey, *Hanukkah* recalls the re-dedication of the Second Temple (after its desecration by King Antiochus IV), and *Purim* commemorates the deliverance under Queen Esther. It is no different with the Christian holidays: Christmas commemorates the birth of Jesus, Good Friday remembers his death on the cross, Easter celebrates his resurrection, Ascension Day recalls his ascension to heaven, and Pentecost commemorates the outpouring of the Holy Spirit.

Of four Jewish festival days it is said in particular that they are days of commemoration, of remembrance:

(a) "This day [i.e., *Pesach*] shall be for you a memorial day [one Heb. word: *zikkaron*, from *zkhr*], and you shall keep it as a feast to the LORD" (Exod. 12:14).

(b) Of *Matzot* (the Feast of the Unleavened Loaves) it is said: "You shall eat no leavened bread with it. Seven days you shall eat it with unleavened bread, the bread of affliction—for you came out of the land of Egypt in haste—that all the days of your life you may remember [Heb. *zkhr*] the day when you came out of the land of Egypt" (Deut. 16:3).

(c) *Shavu'ot* (Pentecost): "You shall remember [Heb. *z-kh-r*] that you were a slave in Egypt; and you shall be careful to observe these statutes" (Deut. 16:12).

(d) *Rosh haShanah* (New Year):[93] "In the seventh month, on the first day of the month, you shall observe a day of solemn rest, a me-

---

92. 2 Kings 15:8-11; 2 Chron. 24:20; Zech. 1:7; Luke 1:5.

93. On the religious calendar as described in Lev. 23, this is actually the first day not of the first month, but of the seventh month.

morial [Heb. *zikron*, from *z-kh-r*] proclaimed with blast of trumpets [i.e., the *shofar*], a holy convocation" (Lev. 23:24). The rabbis view this as a day of "reminding" God of his promises and covenants.[94]

Commemoration is made easier when there are concrete, tangible memorial signs, such as monuments. The latter word comes from Latin *monere*, "to warn, to advise." When it is rendered this way, negative events in particular are remembered, which people hope will never be repeated: never again slavery in Egypt, never again a wilderness journey, never again an Antiochus, never again a Haman (or, as a small German sign in Auschwitz says: *Nie wieder*, "Never again"). But of course, all these negative memories are also linked with joyful celebrations: deliverance, Torah-giving, arrival in the Promised Land, re-dedication.

The Ecclesia knows such a monument, too: every time she celebrates the Lord's Supper, she constructs a concrete, tangible monument, so to speak. Israel was also familiar with a literal memorial or monument. After the passage through the Jordan, Joshua ordered to make a heap of twelve stones taken from the river, in order to commemorate this joyful event, saying: "[T]hese stones shall be to the people of Israel a memorial [Heb. *zikkaron*] forever" (Josh. 4:7). Every time the Israelites saw this heap of stones, they would remember their triumphant entry into the Holy Land.[95] One of the most beautiful things is what will *not* be remembered in eternity; as the LORD said at the announcement of the New Covenant: "I will forgive their iniquity, and I will remember their sin no more" (Jer. 31:34).[96]

12.7.3 Forever Remembered

Three things are mentioned in the Psalms that *will* be remembered forever, both in the sense of "not forgotten" and of "commemorated":

(1) The name of the Messiah: "I will cause your name to be re-

---

94. Rashi: the sounding of the ram's [!] horn is a memorial to God on Israel's behalf of the "binding" of Isaac, instead of whom a ram was offered (Gen. 22); see Cohen (1983, 753).
95. Haughty people like Saul (1 Sam. 15:12) and Absalom (2 Sam. 18:18) made such monuments for themselves!
96. Cf. Heb. 8:12; see also Isa. 64:9.

membered in all generations; therefore nations will praise you forever and ever" (45:18).

(2) The covenant with his people: "He remembers his covenant forever, the word that he commanded, for a thousand generations" (105:8; cf. 111:5).

(3) The *tzaddiq*: "[T]he righteous will never be moved; he will be remembered forever" (112:6).

Notice the importance of these three: the Messiah, God's covenant, the righteous. This reminds us of the tremendous eschatological significance of the seven Jewish festivals.

(1) *Pesach* (Passover) looks forward to the Messianic kingdom, in which the Passover Lamb[97] will forever take his central position. Moreover, Israel reads the Song of Solomon during the feast, reminding the people of Israel's early bridal days (Jer. 2:2), and its wonderful future as the bride and wife of the Messiah.[98]

(2) *Shavu'oth* (Pentecost) looks forward to the Messianic kingdom, when the Torah will be proclaimed to, and will be loved and observed by, all the nations.[99] Moreover, Israel reads the book of Ruth during the feast, reminding the people of the roots of their great King David.[100]

(3) *Rosh haShanah* (New Year): if Rashi was right (see note 94), on this day God is "reminded" of Isaac's burnt offering (Gen. 22), as Messiah's burnt offering will be the foundation for all Messianic blessings, ". . . to finish the transgression, to put an end to sin, and to atone for iniquity, to bring in everlasting righteousness" (Dan. 9:24).

(4) *Yom Kippur* (Day of Atonement) looks forward to the time when the great King-Priest will return from the heavenly sanctuary, to bring to Israel the great message of the atonement that he has accomplished.[101] On that day, the book of Jonah is read, in which Jonah is a type of Israel, preserved throughout all its misery,

---

97. Cf. 1 Cor. 5:7, and also Gen. 22:7–8; Exod. 29:38–46; Isa. 53:7; John 1:29 (cf. 19:36 with Exod. 12:46); 1 Pet. 1:18–19; Rev. 5–21.
98. Ps. 45; Isa. 54:6–8; 61:10; 62:5; Ezek. 16:8, 60; Hos. 2:18–19.
99. Isa. 2:3; 51:4, 7; Jer. 31:33; Ezek. 44:24; Micah 4:2; Mal. 4:4.
100. Ruth 4:18–22; Ezek. 34:23–24; 37:24–25; Hos. 3:5.
101. Lev. 16:18; cf. Dan. 9:24; Rev. 11:19; 14:17; 15:5–8.

set free from the mouth of the "dragon,"[102] and again restored as a witness to the nations.

(5) *Sukkoth* (Feast of Booths): not only Israel but all the world will be filled with joy during the Messianic kingdom; see Zechariah 14:16-19 for the significance of this feast: the Messianic kingdom will be the great harvest feast, in which the redemptive history of God's people will come to a close. During the feast, the book of Ecclesiastes is read, in which joy plays a great role (3:12, 22; 5:19; 8:15; 11:8-9), just as the period of *Sukkoth* is closed with *Simchat Torah*, "Joy of the Law."

(6) *Hannukkah* (Dedication) looks forward to the time of the new temple, to be built by the Messiah, where the *Shekhinah* will descend again (Ezek. 43) (an event that did *not* occur in the Second Temple, neither before nor after its desecration and rededication).

(7) *Purim* ("Lots") looks forward to the time when Israel will have been ultimately delivered from all the "Hamans" of history, and of the end time world, as s explained in the book of Esther (which is read during the feast), and the true Mordecai will appear, of whom we read: "[H]e was great among the Jews and popular with the multitude of his brothers, for he sought the welfare of his people and spoke peace to all his people" (Est. 10:3).

Let me add a few words more on joy as described in the book of Ecclesiastes (see above under *Sukkoth*). The Torah — whether we think of the Mosaic Torah or the Messianic Torah — tells God's people what they must do. Ecclesiastes tells them about themselves, about the many questions they may have as people thrown into a world that in many respects is absurd, and about their stubbornness in following the path of practical wisdom: doing good, avoiding evil. The Torah is the objective, Ecclesiastes the subjective, aspect of *Sukkoth* preaching. Both sources bring joy; as to the Torah:

> Your testimonies are my heritage forever,
>   for they are the joy of my heart.
> I incline my heart to perform your statutes
>   forever, to the end. (Ps. 119:111-112).[103]

---

102. Matt. 12:40 (CJB); cf. Isa. 51:9; Jer. 51:34, 44, where Babylon is the sea monster.

103. Cf. vv. 14, 16, 24, 35, 47, 70, 77, 92, 143, 162, and especially 174: "[Y]our

And the book of Ecclesiastes says, "I perceived that there is nothing better for them [i.e., the humans] than to be joyful and to do good as long as they live; also that everyone should eat and drink and take pleasure in all his toil—this is God's gift to man [i.e., humanity]" (Eccl. 3:12-13). "Rejoice, O young man, in your youth, and let your heart cheer you in the days of your youth. Walk in the ways of your heart and the sight of your eyes. But know that for all these things God will bring you into judgment" (Eccl. 11:9)—that is, there is no true joy than the one that moves within the boundaries of God's Torah. True joy is for those who can truly say, "Oh how I love your Torah!" (Ps. 119:97)—because they love God. And Jesus said,

> As the Father has loved me, so have I loved you.
> > Abide in my love.
>
> If you keep my commandments,
> > you will abide in my love,
> > just as I have kept my Father's commandments and abide in his love.
>
> These things I have spoken to you,
> > that *my joy* may be in you,
> > and that *your joy* may be full (John 15:9-11).

Torah is my delight."

Chapter 13
Israel in New Testament Prophecy: Gospels and Acts

So when you see the abomination that causes devastation spoken about through the prophet Dani'el standing in the Holy Place . . . , that will be the time for those in Y'hudah to escape to the hills. . : Pray that you will not have to escape in winter or on Shabbat. For there will be trouble then worse than there has ever been from the beginning of the world until now, and there will be nothing like it again! . . .

At that time, if someone says to you, "Look! Here's the Messiah!" or, "There he is!" don't believe him. For there will appear false Messiahs and false prophets performing great miracles — amazing things! — so as to fool even the chosen, if possible. . . . For when the Son of Man does come, it will be like lightning that flashes out of the east and fills the sky to the western horizon.

Matthew 24:15–27 (CJB)

13.1 "The abomination" in Matthew 24
13.1.1 Various Views

SUPERSESSIONISTS HAVE CLAIMED that the New Testament does not support a literal interpretation of the prophecies in the Tanakh about Israel, in particular a literal land promise.[1] In this and the next chapter, we will investigate to what extent this is correct, beginning with the End Times Sermon given by Jesus. We find a report of this sermon in the synoptic Gospels: in Matthew 24-25 (in the narrower sense: 24:1-44), Mark 13, and Luke 21:5-36. In all three versions, two predicted events play an essential role: the destruction of the temple in Jerusalem in AD 70 as well as the coming of the Son of Man on the clouds of heaven. These two events are the elliptical focal points of Jesus' exposé. Jesus links these two events very closely. In general, this leads to three type of interpretations[2] (for a more nuanced distinction, see §13.3.1).

(a) *Both* events occurred in AD 70; this is the viewpoint of full preterism (§3.6.1). The strength of this view is that it keeps both events together. Its weakness is that the claim is completely unacceptable that Jesus returned in AD 70 "on the clouds of heaven," seen by all (Rev. 1:7), so that no subsequent coming of Jesus is to be expected (unless one would have to assume not only a second but also a third coming?). Moreover, when and how will the resurrection of the dead take place? Will there be a Messianic kingdom? Clearly, full preterism is little more than a form of supersessionism, with no room for a literal fulfillment of the prophecies of the Tanakh. Thus, it weaves together two significant errors.

(b) *Both* events will be fulfilled in the end times; this is the futuristic viewpoint of dispensationalism. Again, the strength of this view is that it keeps both events together. Its weakness is that it seems obvious to many that in his Sermon Jesus was referring to the Jewish War of AD 66-70, and to nothing else. However, there is a variant of this standpoint that I find the most satisfactory inter-

---

1. See, e.g., De Jong (2011, 26): "When, namely, all these prophetic promises concerning the restoration of the land must be taken literally, it is difficult to understand that the New Testament hardly pays any attention to this. It is only a few times that the land is brought up, and then only in a spiritualizing sense." See also Haacker (1997, 210); Maljaars (2015, chapter 2).

2. Hays et al. (2007, 318–20).

pretation, especially of Matthew 24, as I will explain further below.

(c) The fall of Jerusalem occurred in AD 70, whereas the second coming of Christ will occur at the end of time; this is the viewpoint of many traditional expositors, including supersessionists. It is an "already–not yet" view (partly fulfilled, partly not). The strength of this view is that it avoids the weaknesses of the two previous views. Its weakness, however, is that the two events mentioned are separated; at present, nineteen-and-a-half centuries lie between them. What remains here of the "*Immediately* after the tribulation of those days . . ." (Matt. 24:29), which suggests *no* (long) interval lies between the two events? Moreover, in AD 70 there *was* no "abomination of desolation" (i.e., an idol that brings destruction) in the Jerusalem temple (cf. Matt. 24:15). These objections are so serious as to render this entire view just as unacceptable as (a). My conclusion, therefore, is that only an improved variant of (b) is acceptable.[3]

13.1.2 Matthew 24 Versus Luke 21

To understand the view I am defending, it is essential to note the differences between Matthew 24 and Mark 13 on the one hand, and Luke 21 on the other. The Holy Spirit has inspired the Gospel writers to present us with two versions of Jesus' End Times Sermon, as we find this several times in the Gospels. Mark 13 contains no new eschatological viewpoints with respect to Matthew 24, so that I will limit myself to the vital eschatological differences between Matthew 24 and Luke 21. The matter is complicated because I defend the view that Luke 21 was largely fulfilled in AD 70, though the second coming of Jesus, of course, is future. Between these two events lies a period that is described as the "times of the Gentiles" (v. 24). Matthew 24, however, is largely future; here again, the important interval was identified in verse 14: "[T]his gospel of the kingdom will be proclaimed throughout the whole world as a testimony to all nations, and *then the end will come.*" In other words, *verses 15 and following described the end times.*

Indeed, if the Holy Spirit gave us two, or perhaps three, versions of the End Times Sermon, why could he not have given us each of these versions with a different accent? Think of that other sermon of Jesus, the Sermon on the Mount (Matt. 5–7), which clear-

---

3. Cf. Kelly (1896); Grant (1897); Gaebelein (1910); Walvoord (1974).

ly differs from its parallel in Luke 6. Or think of the parable of the talents (Matt. 25) and that of the minas (Luke 19), which seem to have arisen on the same occasion but yet differ in important respects.

To understand the differences between Matthew 24 and Luke 21, we must begin with the starting points of each version. When the disciples drew Jesus' attention to the magnificent temple buildings, he said, "You see all these, do you not? Truly, I say to you, there will not be left here one stone upon another that will not be thrown down" (Matt. 24:1–2). Thus, Jesus' starting point for his entire End Times Sermon is his announcement of the destruction of the temple. Now notice the subsequent questions of the disciples: "Tell us, [a] when will these things be, and [b] what will be the sign of your coming and [c] of the end of the age?" (Matt. 24:3). The disciples were asking about three specific matters.

This is very different in Luke 21, where the disciples ask only this: "Teacher, when will these things be, and what will be the sign when these things are about to take place?" (v. 7). Of the three questions reported in Matthew 24, only one remains here: "[W]hen will these things be," namely, the destruction of the temple that had just been announced by Jesus? The second question in Luke 21 refers to this same event, whereas in Matthew 24 the disciples ask explicitly about Jesus' second coming, although Jesus himself had made no reference to his coming. The third question in Matthew 24 is entirely absent in Luke 21. concerning the "end of the [present] age." Implicitly, this is also a question about the beginning of the "age to come," that is, the age of the Messianic kingdom (cf. Matt. 13:39–40, 49; 28:20).

We may put it this way: in Luke 21, the disciples' interest was focused on the announced destruction of the temple; their questions made no mention of the eschatological dimension. However, in Matthew 24 that eschatological dimension is precisely what comes to the fore: the disciples wished to know more about the end of the present age, about the second coming of Jesus, and thus also about the beginning of the new age, the age of the Messianic kingdom. In short: in Luke, the disciples wished to know about the *imminent* future; in Matthew, the disciples wished to know about the *distant* future. In each Gospel report, Jesus gave them the answers they were seeking: in Luke, he emphasized the destruction of Jerusalem as it would occur in AD 70; in Matthew, he emphasized the end of the present age and his second coming.

13.2 Jesus' Reply
13.2.1 The Great Tribulation

Some have argued that the first question of the disciples (Matt. 24:3) was answered Matthew 24:4-35; that is, "these things" were entirely fulfilled in AD 70, even if they constituted a foreshadowing of (the events around) Jesus' second coming. We will have to consider whether this is an acceptable approach. J. Gibbs believed that the second and third questions ("what will be the sign of your coming and of the end of the age?") were answered in Matthew 24:36-25:46.[4] This illustrates the central problem for interpreting Matthew 24-25: in these chapters, what referred to the imminent future (AD 66-70), and what referred to the distant future (the second coming and the events connected with it)? Specifically, were verses 15-28 (viewed from Jesus' time) describing the *imminent* future or the *distant* future?

In the first part of his reply, Jesus spoke very generally of what has often been called the "signs of the times":[5] false christs (messiahs), wars and rumors of wars, famines and earthquakes (Matt. 24:4-7). However, these are only forebodings of the end time; they are just the "beginning of the birth pains" (v. 8). These events are followed by tribulations and martyrdoms, stumbling, mutual betrayal, false prophets, deceptions, increasing lawlessness, and decreasing love (Matt. 24:9-12; cf. 2 Tim. 3:1-5). By this time, the pressure has become so great that the faithful are called upon to endure (v. 13). In the meantime, according to Matthew 24:14, the "gospel of the kingdom" is proclaimed "as a testimony to all nations," and this will go on until the "end" (Gk. *telos*). The latter is a key term, coinciding with the other word for "end" (Gk. *synteleia*) — the "end of the age" in verse 3.

The latter is quite important because it means that *verses 15 and*

---

4. See extensively, Gibbs (2001).
5. See Ouweneel (2012a, §4.1.3); the expression "sign of the times" is adopted from Matt. 16:3, where it actually has a quite different meaning, connected with the earthly ministry of Jesus.

following were describing the "end time," as may become clearer from our discussion of the following verses.⁶ We will first deal with verses 15–20, but first underscore the eschatological significance of these verses by pointing out what immediately followed them. Verse 21 refers to the "great tribulation, such as has not been from the beginning of the world until now, no, and never will be." The Greek expression, *thlipsis megalē*, also appears in Revelation 2:22 (regarding unbelievers in Thyatira) and in Revelation 7:14 (the 144,000 coming from the "great tribulation"), in both instances with the same strictly eschatological meaning. Also given the strongly Jewish character of Matthew 24:15–20, this event seems to be identical to the one in, for instance, Jeremiah 30:7,

> Alas! That day is so great
>   there is none like it;
> it is a time of distress [Heb. *'ēt tzarah*] for Jacob;
>   yet he shall be saved out of it.

Equally clear is Daniel 12:1 (notice the linguistic resemblance to Matt. 24:21),

> At that time shall arise Michael, the great prince who has charge of your people. And there shall be a time of trouble [Heb. *'ēt tzarah*],⁷ such as never has been since there was a nation till that time. But at that time your people shall be delivered, everyone whose name shall be found written in the book.

Many other passages in the Tanakh seem to point—directly or typologically—to the same eschatological event of tribulation and distress that will come upon God's people.⁸

To properly understand Matthew 24, it is important to see that this "great tribulation" will *immediately* precede the Messianic kingdom.⁹ We see this in Matthew 24:27–30:

---

6. Maljaars (2015, 23) and others have completely overlooked this possibility.

7. LXX: *hēmera thlipseōs*, "day of tribulation."

8. Ps. 20:1 ("day of trouble"); 37:39 "time of trouble"); 50:15 ("day of trouble"); Isa. 33:2 ("time of trouble"); 37:3 ("day of distress"); Jer. 15:11 ("time of distress"); 16:19 ("day of trouble"); Obadiah 1:12 ("day of his misfortune"), 14 ("day of distress"); Nahum 1:7 ("day of trouble"); Hab. 3:16 ("day of trouble"); Zeph. 1:15 ("day of distress").

9. *Contra*, e.g., Kimball (1984); Chilton (1987), Bray (1996), and Gibbs (2001),

Israel in New Testament Prophecy: Gospels & Acts

> For as the lightning comes from the east and shines as far as the west, so will be the coming of the Son of Man. . . . *Immediately* after the tribulation of those days the sun will be darkened. . . . Then will appear in heaven the sign of the Son of Man, and then all the tribes of the earth[10] will mourn, and they will see the Son of Man coming on the clouds of heaven with power and great glory.

The same sequence appeared in Jeremiah 30:7, where the "time of distress" was followed by the restoration of Israel and the coming of the Messianic kingdom in Jeremiah 30–33. Likewise in Daniel 12:1, where the same "time of distress" was followed by the consummation of God's ways with Israel and the world. In Revelation 7:14 the "great tribulation" is followed by the blessings of the Messianic kingdom.

Here we face a crucial question regarding the interpretation of the entire End Time Sermon. If Matthew 24:21–30 was speaking of the "end of the age," to what time were verses 15–20 referring? After Jesus' remark in verse 2, one might think that the passage was referring to the Jewish War of AD 66–70, and indeed, this is what expositors usually assume. However, this interpretation faces two insurmountable difficulties.

(1) The reference to "the abomination of desolation" in verse 15 becomes problematic, because, as we will see, such an abominable idol did *not* exist in the temple in the years 66–70;

(2) The eschatological context of verses 14–30 becomes problematic: notice "the end" in verse 14, notice the "For" in verse 21: the things described in verses 15–20 are described as "great tribulation," apparently immediately followed by the coming of the Son of Man.

13.2.2 Conclusion

Given the entire context of Matthew 24:15–20, I interpret these verses as referring to the end time:

> So when you see the abomination of desolation spoken of by the

---

who believed that the "great tribulation" is not future, but occurred in AD 66–70.

10. Better: "the land"; the passage is about Israel! We cannot legitimately interpret this as suddenly referring to all the nations of the earth (*contra* Maljaars [2015, 134]).

prophet Daniel, standing in the holy place (let the reader understand), then let those who are in Judea flee to the mountains. Let the one who is on the housetop not go down to take what is in his house, and let the one who is in the field not turn back to take his cloak. And alas for women who are pregnant and for those who are nursing infants in those days! Pray that your flight may not be in winter or on a Sabbath.

Of course, one might understand this to refer to an initial partial fulfillment in AD 70, and to a definitive complete fulfillment in the end time, as F. W. Grosheide proposed: "Therefore, verse 15 must first of all refer to the destruction of the temple, but ultimately— and this is the chief point, to which Daniel referred as well—to the appearance of the antichrist."[11] To be sure, Grosheide spiritualized this ultimate fulfillment, but in itself it was a good thing that he viewed this ultimate fulfillment as the main fulfillment. H. Ridderbos gave a similar interpretation; he thought of "the destruction of Jerusalem and the concomitant great tribulation" (AD 70), but at the same time saw this event "as the great omen of the Lord's coming and the paragon of the tribulation of the last days."[12] Even though these expositors were supersessionists, they were aware of the necessary *eschatological* significance of verses 15–20.

We might go one step further. Matthew 24:15-20 might remind us of AD 70 in some vague sense, but not in the concrete sense, simply because at that time there was no "abomination of desolation" in the temple of Herod. The Annotations to the Dutch States Translation circumvent this problem by explaining it as "the abominable destroying army of the Romans" because of Luke 21:20 ("But when you see Jerusalem surrounded by armies, then know that its desolation has come near").[13] This view goes entirely against the spirit of Daniel, because the latter uses the term to refer to the abominable idol that the Syrian King Antiochus IV had placed in the Second Temple.

Joseph Ratzinger did not even give any explanation when he asserted that "[i]t cannot be determined which event or reality it was that the Christians identified as the sign of the 'abomination

---

11. Grosheide (1954, 363); Hill (1972, i.l.).
12. Ridderbos (1987, 443).
13. Haak (1918, ad loc.); so also Matthew Henry, John Wesley (bible.cc/matthew/24-15.htm), and Anthony Hoekema (1979, 156).

that makes desolate', precipitating their departure, but there was no shortage of possible candidates—incidents in the course of the Jewish War that could be interpreted as this sign foretold by Jesus."[14]

Interestingly, Herman Ridderbos acknowledged that such interpretations were not legitimate:

> Some commentators have tried to determine more precisely what this desecration was; their suggestions include the erecting of an idol in the temple and the atrocities of the Zealots before the fall of Jerusalem. The former suggest is mere conjecture, however, and the Zealots' murders in the temple are too limited in scope for Jesus' intent.[15]

Thus, he proposed his own solution: "The 'abomination that causes desolation' should probably be understood more generally as the profanation of the temple that took place before and during Jerusalem's capture."[16]

However, this interpretation is hardly acceptable. Jesus spoke explicitly of "the abomination of desolation spoken of by the prophet Daniel, standing in the holy place [i.e., the temple]," and not of something that was only vaguely "abominable." The book of Daniel referred to it three times:

(1) In 9:27, we read about an event from the last half "week," that is, shortly before the "end of the age."[17]

(2) In 11:31, the prophet referred to the time of Antiochus IV Epiphanes (cf. 8:13), whereas Jesus was referring to a future event, just like Daniel 9:27.

(3) In 12:11, Daniel referred to the end time again, as he had in

---

14. Ratzinger (2011, 28–29). He also claimed (35–36) that, from the beginning, Christians had not taken part in the temple ministry (because for them the temple had been done away with; cf. 209, 230). However, this assertion conflicts with Acts 2:46; 3:1; 21:26; cf. 28:17.
15. Ridderbos (1987, 443).
16. Ibid.
17. Regarding the seventy "weeks (of years)" in Dan. 9:24–27, see extensively, Ouweneel (2012a, §6.5.3). The last half "week" involves the period of three-and-a-half years before the second coming of Christ, i.e., forty-two months (Rev. 11:2; 13:5), or 1,260 days (Rev. 11:3; 12:6; cf. Dan. 12:11–12), or "a time [year], and times [two years], and half a time" (Rev. 12:14; Dan. 7:25; 12:7).

9:27; also notice the 1,290 days, which clearly referred to (a small extension of) the last half "week."

It is essential that we understand two things. First, we must grasp the eschatological significance of Daniel 9:27 and 12:11, especially in connection with the expression "the time of the end" in 8:17 (Heb. *'et qētz*) and 19 (Heb. *mo'ēd qētz*), in 11:35 (Heb. *'ēt qētz . . . lammo'ēd*) and 40; 12:4, 9 (Heb. *'ēt qētz*). Second, we must understand *that Jesus was referring to the very same end time* (see the word "end" in Matt. 24:3, 6, 13–14). This is shown also by his description of this period as "great tribulation," immediately followed by his second coming.

13.3 Ways of Interpretation

13.3.1 Four Options

We are now focusing on Matthew 24:15–20, for which there appear to be only six interpretative options (possibly with several variations), two of which cannot be taken seriously.

(1) Jesus simply erred with respect to the future; this approach does not fit my view of Jesus, nor into my view of the inspired Scriptures.

(2) In verses 27–30, Jesus did not speak of his second coming at all (see §13.3.2, R.T. France); this interpretation cannot be taken seriously, because of Jesus' obvious allusion to Daniel 7:13, which spoke of the Son of Man coming on the clouds of heaven.[18]

(3) Jesus was speaking of the events of AD 70 (as the parallel with Luke 21 suggests, too), but then in eschatological terms, which possibly receive a very generally formulated ultimate fulfillment in the end time (so, e.g., Grosheide, mentioned above). Objection: no "abomination of desolation" occurred in AD 70.

(4) Jesus was blending the period around AD 70 and the end time as if they were one event, thus bypassing the centuries between these two events. Objection: notice again the important word "immediately" in verse 29.

(5) Jesus meant that the Son of Man *might* come again during or immediately after the destruction of city and temple, provided that Israel would repent, and that Christians would have carried

---

18. See also Matt. 26:64 and cf. 10:23; 16:27–28; 24:37, 39, 44; 25:31.

out the Great Mission of verse 14.[19] Objection: this interpretation conflicts with the assurance with which Jesus spoke no fewer than four times about his second coming, in verses 30, 37, 39, and 44.

(6) Jesus was referring to the city of Jerusalem, the temple, and the people of Israel in the end time, beyond the destruction of AD 70. Only in this way can we understand how Jesus could speak of "the abomination of desolation" in the temple in the sense that Daniel had meant it, namely, in the last half "week" of Daniel 9:27 and 12:11.

Apart from some details of exegesis, this latter is held by many expositors and seems preferable.[20] The most important reason for rejecting this interpretation would be the supersessionist bias against a future literal fulfilment of the land promise in the New Testament, whether in Matthew 24 or elsewhere. But this is exactly the issue: Matthew 24 did speak of the "time of the end," of the "great tribulation," "immediately" followed by the second coming of Christ. Without the supersessionist bias, this would be perfectly obvious for any objective reader of Matthew 24. And notice what this implies: *in the end time, Jesus views Israel as dwelling in its own land*, meaning that before this time, Israel must have returned to its land from all the countries to which it had been dispersed.

Notice here the circular argument, pointed out, for instance, in note 1. Because of the supersessionist bias, people do not see any reference here to a literal land promise in the New Testament. And this is then used as an argument *for* supersessionism! But without this bias, interpreters would see the literal land promise in Matthew 24, in Romans 11, and in Revelation 7 and 11, and several other places. If your bias prevents you from seeing something, you cannot use your not seeing that something as an argument to defend your bias.

13.3.2 Approaches

The prophecies about Israel in the Tanakh tell us that in the time of the end, there will again be a people of Israel, returned from

---

19. So Ford (1979, 76).
20. Kelly (1896); Grant (1897, ad loc.); Zahn (1903, ad loc.); Gaebelein (1910, ad loc.); Schuyler English (1935, ad loc.); Lagrange (1948, ad loc.); Schniewind (1956, ad loc.); Schlatter (1963, ad loc.); Walvoord (1974, ad loc.).

all countries in the world to its own land according to God's unbreakable promises. There they will have a "holy place," where the "Roman" (Western) "prince" of Daniel 9:27—that is, the Roman "beast" of Revelation 13:14–15—will erect "the abomination of desolation," midway through the last of the seventy "weeks" (periods of seven years) of Daniel.[21] Supersessionists do not accept the literal interpretation of the prophecies about Israel. However, what I just described is exactly the picture painted by Jesus in Matthew 24:15–20: when that idolatrous image stands in the "holy place"—an image that was *not* there in AD 70—the Judeans must flee to the surrounding mountains in order to find refuge there, as long as the "beast's" raging lasts.

The differences with AD 70 are not just that in those days there was no abominable idol in the temple, but also that after the destruction of city and temple, the Jews were dispersed for many centuries throughout many countries. However, at the time of the end there *will* be ""the abomination of desolation," and the tribulation will last only three-and-a-half years (half a "week"). After this relatively short period, the Son of Man will return on the clouds of heaven and establish his Messianic kingdom in the midst of the Jews.

Remarkably, D. A. Carson used precisely the opposite argument. He believed that Matthew 24:15–20 cannot refer to the time of the Antichrist because "the details in vv. 16–21 are too limited geographically and culturally to justify that view."[22] In other words, the "Antichrist" (read: the Roman "beast") has worldwide significance, whereas Matthew 24:15–20 deal with Jerusalem and Judah only. However, this is the core of the matter. Indeed, the "beast" will have universal significance, but this did not prevent Jesus from limiting himself in his sermon to the events in Jerusalem and Judah. This is because he was speaking here to his followers in Israel, and beyond them to their spiritual descendants in end-time Jerusalem and Judah. He as pointing forward to the time just before his second coming, when again there would be a people of Israel—observing the Sabbath (v. 20)—in the Holy Land, and when there would even

---

21. Dan. 9:27; 12:11; Rev. 13:14–15; 14:9–11; 15:2; 16:2; 19:20; 20:4; cf. 2 Thess. 2:4.

22. Carson (1984, 499).

be a "holy place" in Jerusalem, where the "beast" would place "the abomination of desolation."

Equally remarkable was the approach of R. T. France. Since Matthew 24:15–20 must refer to the destruction of city and temple in AD 70, and since no gap appeared in Matthew 24 between this destruction and the "coming of the Son of Man," verses 27 and 30–31 could not refer literally to the second coming.[23] The difference between this interpretation and that of full preterism has become very small. Personally, we prefer the interpretation that these verses definitely were referring to the second coming, as is the case elsewhere in Matthew.[24] The consequence of this is that verses 15–20 must have described primarily the time of the end, too, which end found a very preliminary fulfillment in AD 66–70.

13.3.3 "The Abomination of Desolation"

Regarding the suggestions that have sought to localize "the abomination of desolation" in the Jewish War (AD 66–70), let me mention three explanations that appear quite inadequate.[25]

(1) In AD 40, Emperor Gaius gave order to erect an image of himself in the temple of Jerusalem. This was thirty years before AD 70—far too long ago. Moreover, he was murdered a year after he had given this order, so it was never implemented. Thus, this event not only never occurred, but was also too early.

(2) Probably during the winter of AD 67/68, the Zealots—a Jewish guerrilla movement directed against the Roman occupying army—took the temple and made it their headquarters. They allegedly mocked the temple rituals, which seems to conflict with their "zeal" (as indicated by their name) for the holiness of God. They are said to have polluted the temple with blood because of the fights that broke out there.[26] However, such events had nothing to do with the kind of *pagan* pollution that Daniel and Jesus had in mind, namely, the erection of an idolatrous image.

(3) To be sure, when the Roman soldiers ultimately entered the temple, they did place their (idolatrous) banners in the holy courts,

---

23. France (2007, 890–94).
24. Matt. 10:23; 16:27–28; 24:37, 39, 44; 25:31; 26:64; cf. 13:41–42; 19:28.
25. France (2007, 913).
26. Flavius Josephus (*Jewish War* IV.150–57, 196–207).

and brought sacrifices to them.[27] However, when this occurred, the destiny of temple, city, and people had already been decided upon. That is, at that moment there was no longer time for the Jews to flee, whereas Jesus said that the idolatrous image itself would be the sign calling for their flight. In light of Daniel, we must assume that placing this idolatrous image would occur a half "week" (three-and-a-half years) before the appearance of the Son of Man.

Rather than adopt these solutions, it would be far better simply to acknowledge that in AD 70 there *was* in the temple no "abomination of desolation" in the spirit of that to which Daniel was referring. We are left then with only two solutions regarding Matthew 24:15: either Jesus was mistaken, or he was referring not to AD 70 but to an event that would occur three-and-a-half years before the return of the Messiah.

Please notice the consequence of the latter solution. If it is correct, then Matthew 24 makes clear that, near the time of Christ's return, there will be indeed a people of Israel dwelling in the Holy Land. This may seem strange: how could Jesus move in his teaching from his own time to the time of the end, and entirely bypass the dispersion of Israel among all the nations of the world? Strange or not—he did the same earlier (cf. Matthew 10; see §13.5.1). He sent out his disciples to preach the gospel of the kingdom, and then said: "When they persecute you in one town, flee to the next, for truly, I say to you, you will not have gone through all the towns of Israel before the Son of Man comes" (Matt. 10:23). Many expositors have racked their brains over this remarkable statement: Jesus' disciples would not be finished with their preaching before the second coming of Jesus? In my view, the simplest explanation is that Jesus, here again, moved in his teaching from his own time to the time of the end, *when disciples of Jesus would again preach the gospel of the kingdom to the towns in the land of Israel*—which very thing is happening today in Israel.

In summary, Matthew 24:15-20 tells us the following:

(a) A moment will arrive when, at a "holy place" in Jerusalem (three-and-a-half years before the second coming of Christ?), an idolatrous image will be erected. Expositors have thought here of

---

27. Ibid., 616.

the image mentioned in Revelation 13:13–15:[28] the second beast (later in Rev. called the "false prophet," 16:13; 19:20; 20:10)

> performs great signs, even making fire come down from heaven to earth in front of people, and by the signs that it is allowed to work in the presence of the [first, Roman] beast it deceives those who dwell on earth, telling them to make an image for the beast that was wounded by the sword and yet lived. And it was allowed to give breath to the image of the beast, so that the image of the beast might even speak and might cause those who would not worship the image of the beast to be slain.

(b) The placing of this image in the "holy place" will be the sign for the "Israel of God" to escape from this idolatry by fleeing to the mountains as soon as they can (Matt. 24:15–20).

(c) The last three-and-a-half years will be a "great tribulation" for Israel, descending especially upon the wicked in Israel, but the faithful will have to suffer under it as well. They are the "elect" in verse 22 (see also v. 31) for whose sake the time of this tribulation will be cut short.

(d) This time of idolatry and apostasy will be worsened by many false messiahs and false prophets, who will try to mislead even the *tzaddiqim* (vv. 23–26).

(e) At the end of this period, Jesus will come again:

> For as the lightning comes from the east and shines as far as the west, so will be the coming of the Son of Man. . . . Immediately after the tribulation of those days the sun will be darkened, and the moon will not give its light, and the stars will fall from heaven, and the powers of the heavens will be shaken. Then will appear in heaven the sign of the Son of Man, and then all the tribes of the earth [read: land] will mourn, and they will see the Son of Man coming on the clouds of heaven with power and great glory" (Matt. 24:27–30).

---

28. Cf. Rev. 11:1, "Rise and measure the temple of God [at Jerusalem] and the altar and those who worship there, but do not measure the court outside the temple; leave that out, for it is given over to the nations, and they will trample the holy city [i.e., Jerusalem] for forty-two months [i.e., three-and-a-half years]."

13.4 Comparison with Luke 21

13.4.1 Differences

The differences between Matthew 24 and Luke 21 are considerable. As clearly as Matthew 24 referred to the Jerusalem of the end time, so clearly did Luke 21 refer to the destruction of Jerusalem in AD 70. This does not necessarily mean that Jesus gave *two* End Time Sermons, just as he did not necessarily give two Sermons on the Mount, despite the great differences between the two versions in Matthew 5–7 and Luke 6:20-49. This kind of differences in the description of identical events constitutes a general synoptic phenomenon; one could almost say that, if it were otherwise, we could just as well have received one instead of three such Gospels.[29] The synoptic Gospels differ in the choice and the arrangement of events, and in the way each event is described. They are not historiographic or journalist reports; rather than offering photographic reproductions, they offer portraits of Jesus, his person and his work, which tell us much about Jesus, but also much about the purpose of the Holy Spirit in each Gospel.

Therefore, the great differences between Matthew 24 and Luke 21 should not be a concern to us. Matthew 24 presented us with the following order of things:

(a) *Verses 4–14:* a long period of "birth pains" and distress, lasting until the time of "the end." This period encompasses the last nineteen centuries.

(b) *Verses 15–28:* the period of the "great tribulation": the pressure that Jerusalem and Judah must endure in the "time of the end."

(c) *Verses 29–31:* immediately after the previous period, the coming of the Son of Man on the clouds of heaven will occur.

Luke 21 presented us with the following order of things:

(a) *Verses 8–19:* a relatively short period of "birth pains" and distress, lasting until the Jewish War of AD 66–70.

(b) *Verses 20–23:* the Jewish War of AD 66–70, the destruction of Jerusalem and the temple by the Romans.

(c) *Verse 24:* the "times of the Gentiles,"[30] that is, the long peri-

---

29. See extensively, Ouweneel (2012c, §13.5).

30. The mention of this period, lasting as long as world power remains in the hands of the Gentiles, seems to have been overlooked by Paas (2014, 212), for

od between AD 70 and the "time of the end."

(d) *Verse 25–28:* the end of the "time of the end," marked by the coming of the Son of Man on the clouds of heaven.

Notice that both in Matthew 24 and in Luke 21, there was a long period lasting until the "time of the end" (necessarily so, because AD 70 is nineteen-and-a-half centuries behind us, but the second coming of Christ has not yet occurred). In Matthew, this is the period between Jesus' days and the "end time," while in Luke this is the period between the destruction of Jerusalem (AD 70) and the "end time." That is, in Matthew 24 the second coming of Christ follows *immediately* upon the "great tribulation" (v. 29), whereas in Luke 21 there are the "times of the Gentiles" in between the fall of Jerusalem and the "end time." It is only when these "times of the Gentiles" have been fulfilled that the second coming of Christ will occur (v. 27).

Of great importance for the interpretation of Matthew 24 and Luke 21 is that Matthew spoke of "the abomination of desolation," and Luke did not. Whereas we had to conclude that Mathew's description of Jerusalem's distress could not have referred to the events of AD 66–70, there is nothing to prevent us from indeed applying Luke 21:20–24 to these very events:

> [W]hen you see Jerusalem surrounded by armies, then know that its desolation has come near. Then let those who are in Judea flee to the mountains, and let those who are inside the city depart, and let not those who are out in the country enter it, for these are days of vengeance, to fulfill all that is written.[31] Alas for women who are pregnant and for those who are nursing infants in those days! For there will be great distress upon the earth and wrath against this people. They will fall by the edge of the sword and be led captive among all nations, and Jerusalem will be trampled underfoot by the Gentiles, until the times of the Gentiles are fulfilled.

As we have seen, the transition to the "time of the end" was

---

he asserts that Luke 21:24 points to the *end* of earthly Jerusalem.

31. The clearest direct reference to the destruction that occurred in AD 70 is Dan. 9:26 (NKJV), "And after the sixty-two weeks Messiah shall be cut off, but not for Himself; And the people of the [Roman] prince who is to come shall destroy the city and the sanctuary."

referred to as the "times of the Gentiles" that must be "fulfilled," that is, brought to an end. In Daniel 7 the coming of the Son of Man on the clouds of heaven would occur at the end of the time of the four great world empires. Therefore, the "times of the Gentiles" are apparently identical to the times of the four world empires. In other words, the second coming of Christ marks the end of the fourth world empire. It is the same picture as in the book of Revelation: the power of the Roman "beast" comes to an end only at the time of Jesus' return (Rev. 19:11-21). Elsewhere, I have argued that the Roman Empire has continued to exist—though often in a rather hidden way—until our own time.[32]

Thus, we may assume that, in Luke 21:25-27, we find a description of the "time of the end":

> And there will be signs in sun and moon and stars, and on the earth distress of nations in perplexity because of the roaring of the sea and the waves, people fainting with fear and with foreboding of what is coming on the world. For the powers of the heavens will be shaken. And then they will see the Son of Man coming in a cloud with power and great glory.

13.4.2 Harmony

In summary, if we were to harmonize or blend the events mentioned in Matthew 24 and Luke 16, the following chronological picture emerges.

(1) The period between the End Time Sermon and the Jewish War (AD 30-66).

(2) The *Jewish War* (AD 66-70) (Luke): Jerusalem will be surrounded by Roman armies; this will lead to the destruction of the city and the temple, and the death of hundreds of Jews. The (Messiah-believing) remnant in Judea and Jerusalem will flee to the mountains. These will be the "days of vengeance, to fulfill all that is written" (v. 22). "And I will scatter you among the nations, and I will unsheathe the sword after you, and your land shall be a desolation, and your cities shall be a waste. . . . And you shall perish among the nations, and the land of your enemies shall eat you up" (Lev. 26:33, 38).

---

32. See Ouweneel (2003a, chapter 9; 2012a, §6.1.1).

(3) The *"times of the nations"* (AD 70–present) (Luke): at present, we live during the time when Jerusalem is "trampled underfoot" by the nations (21:24); after many centuries, since 1967 this has finally ended in the literal sense. As long as the continuation of the state of Israel still depends on the world powers, though, and as long as there are still two false "sanctuaries" in the temple square, we may say that paganism is still triumphing in Jerusalem.[33]

(4) However, there is an "until," as we discovered earlier (see §10.5). God's judgment over Jerusalem will end when the "times of the Gentile" have been "fulfilled." This means, among other things, that the "fulness of the Gentiles" will have "come in" (Rom. 11:25). It also means that God will "restore the fortunes of Judah and Jerusalem," namely, by gathering "all the nations" and bringing "them down to the Valley of Jehoshaphat. And I will enter into judgment with them there, on behalf of my people and my heritage Israel, because they have scattered them among the nations and have divided up my land, and have cast lots for my people" (Joel 3:1–3).

As we have seen, the "times of the Gentiles" referred to the era of the dominion of the nations, in particular of four world empires (Dan. 7).[34] In the time of the end, a Western power will appear that will be the spiritual heir of the ancient Roman Empire.

(5) The *end time "birth pains"* (Matthew/Luke): the end of the present era will be characterized by horrible signs, which Matthew 24:8 describes as "birth pains" (through them, the new era, the age of the Messiah, will be "born"), and Luke 21:25-26 says, "[T]here will be signs in sun and moon and stars, and on the earth distress of nations in perplexity because of the roaring of the sea and the waves, people fainting with fear and with foreboding of what is coming on the world. For the powers of the heavens will be shaken."

(6) The *"great tribulation"* (Matthew): in the time of the end, there will again be (as in 167–164 BC) an "abomination of desolation" (an abominable idol that will bring devastation) in the then existing "holy place" in Jerusalem. The faithful remnant in Israel

---

33. On a positive note, we may also say that these are the "times" during which the gospel goes out to all nations (Matt. 24:14; Mark 13:10); see Ratzinger (2011, 41–45).
34. Ouweneel (2012a, chapters 5 and 6).

will again flee to the mountains (history repeats itself). This period was described as the "great tribulation" (or, the "time of distress," the "time of trouble").

(7) The *descending of the Son of Man*, that is, the second coming of Christ (Matthew/Luke), which will occur "with power and great glory." Not some largely invisible event, as the full preterists maintain, but "every eye will see him" (Rev. 1:7). The returned Messiah will destroy the world powers, will deliver his faithful, will restore his city and his temple, and will establish his kingdom of peace and justice.

13.5 Matthew 10:23

13.5.1 A Difficult Verse?

In Matthew 10, Jesus commissioned his disciples to go throughout all Israel in order to heal the sick and to cast out demons (v. 8), using the opportunity to warn them against the coming persecutions that the followers of Jesus would have to endure. In this context, he makes this remarkable statement: "When they persecute you in one town, flee to the next, for truly, I say to you, you will not have gone through all the towns of Israel before the Son of Man comes" (v. 23; see earlier in §13.3.3).

There can be no doubt that Jesus was referring here to his second coming, his descent as the Son of Man on the clouds of heaven (Dan. 7:13), as mentioned so often in Matthew.[35] Jesus saw the preaching by his followers being continued until the time of the end of the present era. Of course, some have suggested that this means that Jesus erroneously expected his second coming to be very soon. On the contrary, elsewhere in Matthew, Jesus indicates that this period would last a long time; the parables of chapter 13 strongly suggest this (see Matt. 24:48; 25:5, 19).

As we found in Matthew 24, Jesus seemed to bypass the entire intermediate period between his ascension and the time of the end, and to see a direct continuity between the activities of his disciples in the time of his own end and those of his disciples in the end time. Notice that this is explicitly an activity within the land of Israel. Jesus' words presuppose an Israel that, also in the end time,

---

35. Matt. 16:27–28; 24:27, 30, 37, 39, 44; 25:31; 26:64; compare parallel passages in the other Gospels.

will dwell in the Promised Land, and a believing part in Israel—the faithful remnant—that will proclaim the gospel of the kingdom, that is, of the King himself, among the cities and villages of Israel. They will be busy carrying out this ministry until the moment that the Son of Man returns.

Herman Ridderbos spoke here of "the tendency of prophecy to condense":

> In prophecy it often happens that different great events lying in the future are seen and described by the prophet on a single plane, even though they will prove to be separated by centuries. In Old Testament prophecy, for example, the final judgment of the world is regarded as the immediate background to or even as coincident with the judgment of Edom and Assyria.[36]

There is some truth in this statement, as long as we do not suggest that, in biblical prophecy, earlier and later prophetic events are mixed together. Rather, I believe that, also in the time of the end, there will again an "Edom" and an "Assyria," and also an Israel in the Promised Land. Instead of this, in his exegesis Ridderbos made a supersessionist move away from pointing to the tribulation of Israel to concluding that "no matter how violent the opposition to Christ's church may become before He appears in glory, a place will always remain for it."[37]

13.5.2 A Line to the Future

On the one hand, Jesus clearly indicated that his coming might take much more time than his disciples thought, but on the other hand, in Matthew he did draw a direct line from his own time to the end time. Thus, he said: "For the Son of Man is going to come with his angels in the glory of his Father, and then he will repay each person according to what he has done. Truly, I say to you, there are some standing here who will not taste death until they see the Son of Man coming in his kingdom" (Matt. 16:27-28). These words were fulfilled primarily in Jesus' transfiguration on the mountain (Matt. 17:1-8),[38] but they continue in force until the time of the end.

---

36. Ridderbos (1987, 204; cf. 53).
37. Ibid., 204.
38. Cf. Ouweneel (2007b, 461; 2011a, §9.5.1).

It is the same with Matthew 24:34, "Truly, I say to you, this generation [Gk. *genea*] will not pass away until all these things take place." In this statement, *genea* was not referring only to "generation" (people belonging to the same period of about thirty or forty years) but also to "this kind of people"; for this meaning compare the similar word *genos* in Mark 9:29, where it means "this kind of demons." If the expositors prefer the meaning "generation" (as indeed most translations do), we may have here another example of Jesus bypassing many centuries in order to blend his own generation with that of the end time.

D. A. Carson may have been exaggerating when he called Matthew 10:23 perhaps the most difficult verse in the New Testament, and mentioned no fewer than seven interpretations of the verse.[39] Some expositors made the matter unnecessarily complicated by suggesting other meanings of the expression "coming" (of the Son of Man) than the obvious meaning: the second coming of Christ.[40] The early church wrestled with the verse, as can be concluded from the fact that some ancient manuscripts (Codex Vaticanus, Codex Bezae) omit the words "of Israel." Perhaps the copyists could not imagine any disciples of Jesus still preaching in the end time among the cities and villages of Israel. If this interpretation of the manuscript omission is correct, we must conclude that supersessionism has affected even the copying of Bible manuscripts.

Some interpreters wished to understand "Israel" here to refer to the world, or to the church, which in Matthew is simply inconceivable. Matthew was very well aware of the difference between Israel and the Ecclesia (see 16:18; 18:17). All exegetical problems disappear the moment the reader is prepared to accept that, in the end time, there will again be an Israel in the Promised Land, and followers of Jesus who there proclaim his gospel of the coming kingdom (which then will be nearer than ever before).

13.6 Other New Testament Passages
13.6.1 Matthew 19:28 and Luke 22:29–30

Jesus spoke the following words to his disciples (on the same occasion, or on different occasions): "Truly, I say to you, in the new

---

39. Carson (2010, ad loc.).
40. E.g., France (2007, 395–98).

world,[41] when the Son of Man will sit on his glorious throne, you who have followed me will also sit on twelve thrones, judging the twelve tribes of Israel" (Matt. 19:28). And these words: "I assign to you, as my Father assigned to me, a kingdom, that you may eat and drink at my table in my kingdom and sit on thrones judging the twelve tribes of Israel." (Luke 22:29-30).

In the light of my previous considerations, it will not be surprising that here again, I prefer the literal interpretation: there is a divine future for the twelve tribes of ethnic Israel in the coming Messianic kingdom of Jesus Christ. Herman Ridderbos chose the supersessionist interpretation by spiritualizing these twelve tribes of Israel, identifying them as "the people of God of the great future, which, to be sure, for the greatest part will not be gathered from Israel, cf. 8:11-12, but which yet finds its type and principle in Israel. In this context, the twelve thrones and twelve tribes must not be taken literally either." But how could Ridderbos be so sure of this? And what did he presume would the disciples and the first readers of Matthew have taken these words to mean? How could they have possibly understood Matthew to mean here other than what he himself, as well as the entire New Testament, meant everywhere else, namely, that "(the twelve tribes of) Israel" means (the twelve tribes of) Israel, just as "thrones" are always thrones?

13.6.2 Acts 26:7 and James 1:1

If I say that I understand "the tribes of Israel" everywhere as a literal reference, I consider Acts 26:6-7 as a good example; here we read that the apostle Paul said to King Agrippa (who was partly Jewish): "I stand here on trial because of my hope in the promise made by God to our fathers, to which our twelve tribes hope to attain, as they earnestly worship night and day. And for this hope I am accused by Jews, O king!"

To what "twelve tribes" would he have referred before his judges? How could they have possibly thought of the Ecclesia? Moreover, is it not fascinating that Paul said here that "our twelve tribes" hope to attain to the "hope in the promise made by God to our fathers'? How could we read this passage to mean anything

---

41. Gk. *en tēi palingenesiai*, lit., "in the regeneration" (of the world); the same word as in Titus 3:5, where it refers to individual regeneration (rebirth).

else than that Paul was speaking about God's promises to the patriarchs concerning the literal people of Israel in the literal land of Israel? Either Paul was mistaken here, or he was misleading his judges on purpose—or the supersessionists are mistaken. In the New Testament the apostle Paul was the great specialist with regard to the divine project of the Ecclesia. And *he* never called the Ecclesia "Israel." And *he* was the one who spoke to his judges about the promise that God made regarding *Israel*, a promise whose fulfillment the *twelve tribes of Israel* hoped to enjoy. Did Paul say things just to please his judges? Or must we assume instead that Paul was not a supersessionist? The answer is clear: Paul really believed in God's promises regarding the twelve "tribes" — "tribes" in the only meaning in which both Paul and his judges understood the term.

Supersessionist A. Maljaars concluded with a certain aplomb (the italics are his): "*From these Bible passages* [Acts 23:6; 28:20] *it is evident that the hope for Israel lies exclusively in the resurrection of Jesus Christ.*"[42] Of course. Where else? By putting the words in italics, Maljaars seemed to suggest that others, such as those who take the land promise literally, think otherwise, which of course is not the case at all. In short, such a sentence in italics is just a smokescreen hiding the real problem at issue. The real question is whether there is still any future for ethnic Israel, and whether we must take the land promise literally. If we do so, then, indeed, the basis lies "exclusively in the resurrection of Jesus Christ." But that is not the point right now: the point is whether we interpret God's promises literally. It is mistaken to suggest that those who do so could believe that the restoration of ethnic Israel could have any basis other than the death and resurrection of Christ.

Maljaars indeed seemed to think so, as is evident from the "Open Letter" of 2012, written by supersessionists and also signed by him.[43] This Letter wrongly and misleadingly suggested that those who interpret God's Word literally effectively deny the central significance of Jesus' resurrection, or believe in a way of salvation for Israel that would be separate from Jesus' work of redemption. It is one of the most cruel accusations launched by supersessionists. It suggests that those who do not accept their view cannot be true

---

42. Maljaars (2015, 34).
43. See Paas (2014, 278–87).

Christians—and this is exactly what Maljaars wrote about them. You are either a supersessionist, or you are a non-Christian heretic.

In the meantime, we keep taking God's Word literally, just as the apostle James did at the beginning of his letter: "James, a servant of God and of the Lord Jesus Christ,

to the twelve tribes in the Dispersion: greetings" (James 1:1).

Here again, the reference is not to "spiritual Israel," but rather to the literal twelve tribes of Israel.[44] His entire letter suggests that he was addressing Jesus-believing Jews in the land of Israel, which he apparently viewed as representative for the entire nation: the "twelve tribes" in the Diaspora. The term "Dispersion" indeed referred, in the wider sense, to the dispersed Israelites among the nations of the world (cf. 1 Pet. 1:1, "elect exiles of the Dispersion"), or perhaps, in the narrower sense, to the dispersion of Jesus-believing Jews within the boundaries of the Holy Land (cf. Acts 8:1 DRA, "they were all dispersed through the countries of Judea, and Samaria").

In James' letter, too, his references to Israel stood in the broader context of the time of the end and the second coming of Christ: "Be patient, therefore, brothers, until the coming of the Lord. See how the farmer waits for the precious fruit of the earth, being patient about it, until it receives the early and the late rains. You also, be patient. Establish your hearts, for the coming of the Lord is at hand" (James 5:7-8). Compare also his reference to the Messianic kingdom: "Listen, my beloved brothers, has not God chosen those who are poor in the world to be rich in faith and heirs of the kingdom, which he has promised to those who love him?" (James 2:5). In addition, because of this Jewish context, we can understand James's great interest in the Torah, which he described as the "Torah of liberty" (1:25; 2:12) and the "royal Torah" (2:8), or, rendered somewhat more freely: the "Torah of the kingdom of God."

13.6.3 Conclusion

If, then, the phrase "the twelve tribes" must be interpreted literally in Acts 26 and James 1, why not in Matthew 19 and Luke 22?

Or consider these words from the apostle John about the New Jerusalem: "It had a great, high wall, with twelve gates, and at the gates twelve angels, and on the gates the names of the twelve tribes

---

44. See Ouweneel (1981, ad loc.).

of the sons of Israel were inscribed . . " (Rev. 21:12). Was John referring here to the literal tribes or to some figurative tribes of Israel? How could he have expected his readers to understand that he had meant the latter? And what, then, do these names of the twelve tribes stand for? Can supersessionists tell us what part of the Ecclesia is represented by each of these twelve names? Why could we not simply accept that John was thinking of the literal tribes of Israel? And if Paul did so in Acts 26, and James in James 1, why could Jesus not have been thinking of the literal tribes of Israel in Matthew 19 and Luke 22? What substantial objection exists to the interpretation that one day the twelve literal apostles of Christ, sitting on twelve literal thrones (cf. Rev. 20:4), will be judging the twelve tribes of Israel? In my view, "judging" here means not only the separation of the faithful from the wicked in Israel, but also reigning over the "Israel of God" during the Messianic kingdom that will be established here on earth after Jesus' second coming.

Let me add here one of the supersessionist arguments concerning these matters. S. Greijdanus understood Luke 22:29-30 to be presenting imagery: "In earthly forms, heavenly life is now presented with its beauty and glory."[45] *Heavenly life?*[46] The passage was not speaking of heaven at all, but of the Messianic kingdom *on earth*. Moreover, how must we understand the twelve apostles "judging" (pronouncing verdicts over) people who are already "in heaven"?[47] Greijdanus, too, understood the term "Israel" to refer to "the Lord's church, the Israel of God."

We may be thankful that many other expositors of Matthew 19 and Luke 22 did understand the term "Israel" literally,[48] entirely in line with the fact that in the Gospels the term "Israel" *always* referred to ethnic Israel. Thus, Jesus' prediction unambiguously indicates that the Messianic kingdom will involve the twelve literal

---

45. Greijdanus (1955, 226).

46. Cf. my view of this "heavenly life" in Ouweneel (2021).

47. Notice that passages speaking of the "judgment seat of God/Christ" (Rom. 14:10; 2 Cor. 5:10), or the "great white throne" (Rev. 20:11–15), or the "glorious throne" of Christ judging (Matt. 25:31–46), never localize this seat or throne "in heaven."

48. See the following commentaries ad loc.: Kelly (1896); Grant (1897); Gaebelein (1910); Walvoord (1974); Carson (2010); Liefeld (2009).

tribes of literal Israel, in accord with what many other prophecies tell us about this.

13.7 Acts 1:6-8
13.7.1 A Question and an Answer

After his resurrection, Jesus had daily conversations with his disciples about this single subject (others are not mentioned): the kingdom of God (Acts 1:1-3). I suppose that Jesus spoke of the kingdom both in the form it has in the present era, and in the form it would have in the age to come: the Messianic kingdom of peace and justice. We should not be disappointed that so little of this teaching was preserved in Acts 1, because everything we need to know about the kingdom of God right now can be found in the rest of the Tanakh and the New Testament.

From these forty days of conversation at least one question of the disciples, along with Jesus' answer, have been preserved for us. In view of our studies, this question and its answer are very significant (vv. 6-8):[49]

> So when they [i.e., the disciples] had come together, they asked him [i.e., Jesus], "Lord, will you at this time restore the kingdom to Israel?" He said to them, "It is not for you to know times or seasons that the Father has fixed by his own authority. But you will receive power when the Holy Spirit has come upon you, and you will be my witnesses in Jerusalem and in all Judea and Samaria, and to the end of the earth" (Acts 1:6-8).

It is astonishing how many expositors have assumed without any basis that this was a very wrong-headed, outdated, mistaken question.[50] John Calvin asserted that the question contained "as many errors as words."[51] In the Greek text, the disciples' question contains eleven words; it would be interesting to learn how Calvin could find in this question no fewer than eleven errors. In my view, the question contains no errors at all.

G. H. Kersten commented on this question: "Even the disciples

---

49. See Ouweneel (2011a, §§11.1.2 and 11.4.2).
50. Fortunately, a supersessionist like Robertson (2000, 131–37) left some room for a different approach.
51. Calvin (n.d., ad loc.); see also J. van Meggelen in Paas (2017, 175).

were not yet cleansed from that Jewish leaven. That is why they asked ... whether the Lord would 'at this time' restore again the Kingdom to Israel, ... Time and again the Lord Jesus rebuked them for doing so, ..."[52] This is astonishing: is belief in the kingdom as belonging to Israel "Jewish leaven"? And when did Jesus "rebuke" his disciples for this type of question? No one reading Acts 1 will be able to discover any tinge of rebuke in Jesus' reply. He does not say that their question was mistaken; on the contrary, *he indirectly confirms that the Father was going to restore the kingdom to Israel* — the only point was that the disciples were not allowed to know *when* this was going to happen.

Notice the difference between not identifying *when* something is going to happen, and declaring that this something is not going to happen. Too many interpreters join Kersten in wondering: How could the disciples ask such a foolish and uninformed question? But Jesus said: That is a very *good* question because one day I *will* restore the kingdom of Israel — but when this will occur is known to the Father alone.

Many interpreters mistakenly agree with this sentiment: "No doubt the thoughts of the disciples still moved within the narrow circle of Jewish national hopes" — even though Knowling acknowledged that "with these thoughts of the redemption of Israel there mingled higher thoughts of the need of repentance and righteousness for the Messianic kingdom."[53] Many of them refer positively to the hymns of Zechariah (Luke 1:67-79) and Simeon (Luke 2:28-32). Did not Zechariah speak through the Holy Spirit about the redemption of *Israel*, according to the promises made to the patriarchs? And did not Simeon not speak about *both* a light for revelation to the *Gentiles* and glory to *God's people of Israel*? Apparently, these hymns did not "still move within the narrow circle of Jewish national hopes," especially because Zechariah was "filled with the Spirit" when he uttered his hymn. And were Zechariah and Simeon guilty of not yet having "been purified from that Jewish leaven"?

13.7.2 Dreaming of an Earthly Kingdom

The reader must be crystal clear about the issue at hand. Consider

---

52. Kersten (1980, 2:544–45).

53. Knowling (1979, 56).

this comment made by a preacher in his sermon on this passage:

> When the Lord Jesus is leaving the earth, the disciples cannot resist asking once more, "Lord, will you at this time restore the kingdom to Israel?" The Lord Jesus had continually pointed out to his disciples that his Kingdom was there. Where? This Kingdom is where there is a people in the world that bows down before God in the dust.[54]

Notice again the preacher's implicit rebuke of the disciples (who "cannot resist") and the irrelevant observation that has nothing to do with either the disciples' question or the Lord's answer. Is the Lord going to restore one day the kingdom to Israel, yes or no? And where are all those many passages in which Jesus explained that the kingdom is there where "a people" "bows down before God in the dust" (aside from, perhaps, a misunderstood Luke 17:21)? This is nothing short of pious fantasy. There are passages, however, unmentioned by Jesus, where we read that Israel's *enemies* will have to bow down before Israel's king.[55]

The disciples were indeed convinced that one day the Davidic kingdom would be restored to Israel, and that a Son of David would again sit on the throne of David in a free and glorious kingdom: the kingdom of the Messiah, in which Zion will be the center of the world. And *it was perfectly correct that they expected this*, for this was exactly what God had promised through his *Spirit-inspired* prophets. After the four *Gentile* world empires, run by Satanic powers, the *Jewish* empire will arise, run by the Son of Man from heaven. Daniel 7:14 tells us that to the Son of Man "was given dominion and glory and a kingdom, that all peoples, nations, and languages should serve him; his dominion is an everlasting dominion, which shall not pass away, and his kingdom one that shall not be destroyed." But verse 27 supplies us with this essential addition:

> And the kingdom and the dominion
> > and the greatness of the kingdoms under the whole heaven
> > shall be given to the *people* [i.e., Israel] *of the saints of the Most High*;
> > *their* kingdom shall be an everlasting kingdom,
> > and all dominions shall serve and obey *them*.

---

54. Moerkerken (2004, 665).
55. Gen. 27:29; Ps. 72:9; 78:27; Isa. 25:12; 49:23.

The preacher cited earlier continued by saying that "in our day people will probably no longer be thinking of an earthly kingdom of the Messiah, of which the disciples were dreaming." On the contrary, millions of Christians worldwide are still dreaming of this earthly Messianic kingdom, which actually will also be a heavenly-spiritual kingdom. What people ignore is that not only the disciples, but Israel's ancient seers dreamed of it, inspired by the Holy Spirit. Again, please notice that in Acts 1:6-8, we do not read that Jesus *in any way whatsoever* corrected the disciples in this respect. On the contrary, he declared implicitly that *they were correct* to expect such a kingdom—the only thing disallowed was knowing *when* this kingdom would be established. The time when this would happen had been fixed by the Father "by his own authority."

13.7.3 Jesus' Additional Remark

In Jesus' conversation with his disciples about the restoration of the Davidic kingdom, we notice these words added by Jesus: "But you will receive power when the Holy Spirit has come upon you, and you will be my witnesses in Jerusalem and in all Judea and Samaria, and to the end of the earth."

It is as if Jesus were saying, "It will still take a while before the kingdom will be restored to Israel, and you will need all the patience and endurance you can procure. However, in the meantime, you will receive something that is marvelous, too: you will receive the Holy Spirit (as we read about in Acts 2) and through this, you will receive the power needed to spread the gospel of my kingdom to the ends of the earth." Two promised gifts, two unspeakable blessings. Which, then, is better: the restoration of the Davidic kingdom, or the gift of the Holy Spirit? They are incomparable—both are magnificent!

When the Messianic kingdom will be restored to Israel, it will be a blessing to all the Gentiles who will receive a share in it; but first, the nations will be spiritually prepared for this by the proclamation of the kingdom to them in the power of the Holy Spirit. And this has been going on by now for more than nineteen hundred years, and what a wondrous fruit the Spirit has produced!

The rest of Acts 1 described an important preparatory act: if the *twelve* apostles are going to be sent out into the world, the betrayer,

Judas, must first be replaced, so that their number will be complete again (Acts 1:14–26).[56] For the history of the Ecclesia, the full number of twelve seems to be less important, especially because soon afterward Saul of Tarsus was called, who became the apostle Paul (the thirteenth apostle, as some have called him[57]). However, for Israel the number twelve *is* prophetically important; as we have seen, the number twelve reminds us of the twelve tribes of Israel, and refer to the twelve thrones on which the twelve apostles will sit in order to reign over the twelve tribes; and it also refers to the twelve gates and foundations of the New Jerusalem.[58] The twelve apostles are as essential for the Ecclesia as the twelve patriarchs are for Israel (see further in §12.4.2).

13.8 Acts 3:19–26
13.8.1 Israelocentric

Shortly after the Day of Pentecost, and immediately after the healing of the lame man near the Beautiful Gate of the temple, the apostle Peter spoke these words to the gathered Israelites:

> Repent therefore, and turn back, that your sins may be blotted out, that times of refreshing may come from the presence of the Lord, and that he may send the Christ [i.e., Messiah] appointed for you, Jesus, whom heaven must receive until the time for restoring all the things about which God spoke by the mouth of his holy prophets long ago. . . . And all the prophets who have spoken, from Samuel and those who came after him, also proclaimed these days. You are the sons of the prophets and of the covenant that God made with your fathers, saying to Abraham, "And in your offspring shall all the families of the earth be blessed." God, having raised up his servant [i.e., Jesus], sent him to you first, to bless you by turning every one of you from your wickedness (Acts 3:19–26).

This passage is quite remarkable for several reasons.

First, notice the strongly Israelocentric character of salvation: Jesus is the Messiah destined for Israel, that is, their Anointed King; compare Psalm 2:2, 6 (AMP):

---

56. See the explicit mention of the *eleven* remaining disciples in Matt. 28:16; Mark 16:14; Luke 24:9, 33; Acts 1:26.
57. Altaf (2013, title).
58. Matt. 19:28; Luke 22:30; Rev. 21:12–14.

The kings of the earth take their stand;
And the rulers take counsel together
Against the Lord and His Anointed (the Davidic King, the Messiah, the Christ)...
Yet as for Me, I have anointed *and* firmly installed My King
Upon Zion, My holy mountain.

Moreover, notice that Peter called the Israelites the "sons of the prophets" who "proclaimed these days," namely, the days of the Messiah and his salvation, as well as "sons" of the covenant that God had made with the patriarchs of Israel. And also after his resurrection — or does "raised up" refer to Jesus' being begotten by God?[59] — Jesus, through his servants, went to Israel first, in order that it would come to repentance and faith and would receive a share in the divine blessing, beginning with the forgiveness of their sins.

13.8.2 Messianic "Times"

Second, Peter announced that if Israel would indeed repent, "times" would arrive that he described as "times of refreshing" (Gk. *kairoi anapsyxeōs*) and the "time for restoring all the things" (Gk. *chronōn apokatastaseōs pantōn*).[60]

(a) These "times" are familiar to the people because the prophets had written about them. Thus, Peter was explicitly referring to the Messianic kingdom, about which virtually *all* the writing prophets in the Tanakh had written.[61]

(b) These "times" will begin with the (second) coming of the Messiah (at his ascension, God took him up into heaven, but at the right time, God will send him again into the world).

(c) These "times" are intended for "all the families of the earth," as God had promised to Abraham, Isaac, and Jacob (Gen. 12:3; 18:18; 22:18; 26:4; 28:14).

---

59. See the discussion in Longenecker (1981, 300); Bruce (1988, 88).

60. The Gk. word *kairos* is means "time" in a qualitative sense, whereas the Gk. word *chronos* means "time" more in a quantitative sense; see Ouweneel (2011a, §4.2.2).

61. Remarkably, *none* of the great non-writing prophets (Elijah, Elisha) spoke of the Messianic kingdom, whereas *all* of the writing prophets (except Jonah) did (including Obadiah 21).

(d) These families, however, will receive the Messianic blessing only "in" (through, because of) Abraham's offspring: Israel (and, we may add, in him who is the true Israel: the Messiah; Gal. 3:16).

We conclude that Peter is referring unambiguously to the Messianic kingdom, in which Israel will receive the central position, while all nations will be blessed in and through Israel; this kingdom will arrive when Israel repents. Humanly speaking, if Israel had accepted Peter's word at this point in history, and had repented, Jesus would have returned immediately, and the Messianic kingdom would have arrived then. Compare the preaching of Stephen, who at the end of his sermon said, "Behold, I see the heavens opened, and the Son of Man *standing* at the right hand of God" (Acts 7:56) — "standing" as if (as some have presumed) Jesus was ready to descend if Israel had only repented at that moment.

Israel as a nation did *not* repent in response to Peter's preaching (as recorded in Acts 3), but the principle remains the same: the times of the Messianic kingdom arrive when Israel repents and converts, and when the Messiah comes back from heaven. This kingdom will involve "refreshment" and "restoration of all things," first for Israel itself, and then "in" Israel for the other nations insofar as these Israelites and Gentiles repent and convert to God and his Messiah.

The healing of the paralyzed man — on which occasion Peter gave this speech — reminds us of another lame man who had been miraculously healed: the man at the Pool of Bethesda (John 5:1–18). John tells us that this man "had been an invalid for thirty-eight years" (v. 5) — a remarkable number, because it corresponds with the time that the people of Israel spent in the wilderness, from the time they left Mount Sinai until they arrived in the "field of Moab" (cf. Num. 10:11; 21:20 ASV). No wonder that some[62] have seen in this lame man an image of "lame" natural Israel, which — not after thirty-eight years but after more than thirty centuries — obtains its final healing through its Messiah. That is, the healing will be only for those who indeed *wish* to be healed (cf. John 5:6). The ultimate

---

62. The Pulpit Commentary (https://biblehub.com/commentaries/john/5-5.htm) refers to Hengstenberg, Wordsworth, and Westcott (in part). But the Expositor's Greek Testament (same website) says: "To find in the man's thirty-eight years' imbecility a symbol of Israel's thirty-eight years in the wilderness is itself an imbecility." This latter statement is merely scolding, not arguing.

healing of Israel will occur on the great "Sabbath" (vv. 9–16), the seventh "day" of world history, that is, the time of the Messianic kingdom.

13.8.3 The Lame Shall Leap!

The healing of the two paralyzed men (see previous section) was a foreshadowing of this great eschatological restoration of Israel (Isa 35:4–6):

> Say to those who have an anxious heart,
>   "Be strong; fear not!
> Behold, your God
> will come with vengeance,
> with the recompense of God.
>   He will come and save you."
> Then the eyes of the blind shall be opened,
>   and the ears of the deaf unstopped;
> then shall *the lame man* leap like a deer,
>   and the tongue of the mute sing for joy (Isa. 35:4–6).

The "lame" — physically lame or spiritually "lame" — will be healed in the Messianic age:

> In that day, declares the LORD,
>   I will assemble *the lame*
> and gather those who have been driven away
>   and those whom I have afflicted;
> and *the lame* I will make the remnant,
>   and those who were cast off, a strong nation;
> and the LORD will reign over them in Mount Zion
>   from this time forth and forevermore (Micah 4:6–7).

And here is another great promise for the "lame" :

> But I will leave in your midst
>   a people humble and lowly.
> They shall seek refuge in the name of the LORD,
>   those who are left in Israel; . . .
> For they shall graze and lie down,
>   and none shall make them afraid. . . .
> The King of Israel, the LORD, is in your midst;
>   you shall never again fear evil.

On that day it shall be said to Jerusalem:
> "Fear not, O Zion;
> let not your hands grow weak.
>
> The LORD your God is in your midst,
> a mighty one who will save;
>
> he will rejoice over you with gladness;
> he will quiet you by his love;
> he will exult over you with loud singing." . . .
>
> Behold, at that time I will deal
> with all your oppressors.
>
> And I will *save the lame*
> and gather the outcast,
>
> and I will change their shame into praise
> and renown in all the earth. . . .
>
> . . . for I will make you renowned and praised
> among all the peoples of the earth,
>
> when I restore your fortunes
> before your eyes," says the LORD (Zeph. 3:12–20).

For non-supersessionists, these prophetic passages speak clearly about Israel's place in the coming Messianic Kingdom.

13.9 First Peter 2:9–12

13.9.1 Jewish Addressees?

Next, let us consider these remarkable words of the apostle Peter:

> [Y]ou are a chosen race, a royal priesthood, a holy nation, a people for his own possession, that you may proclaim the excellencies of him who called you out of darkness into his marvelous light. Once you were not a people, but now you are God's people; once you had not received mercy, but now you have received mercy. Beloved, I urge you as sojourners and exiles to abstain from the passions of the flesh, which wage war against your soul. Keep your conduct among the Gentiles honorable, so that when they speak against you as evildoers, they may see your good deeds and glorify God on the day of visitation (1 Pet. 2:9–12).

One's theological prejudices will determine whether one supposes that Peter's letter was addressed to believers (mainly) from the Gentiles *or* (mainly) from Israel.[63] Supersessionists will take the typically Jewish characteristics of the letter as evidence for the idea that Peter viewed the Ecclesia as a kind of "spiritual Israel." However, from an Israelocentric standpoint, these features can also be viewed as evidence that Peter's readers were in particular Jesus-believing Jews, as in the letter to the Hebrews. The choice begins already in 1:1, because the letter was said to be addressed "to the elect who are sojourners of the Dispersion [Gk. *diaspora*] in Pontus, Galatia, Cappadocia, Asia, and Bithynia" (ASV). As in James 1:1 ("To the twelve tribes in the Dispersion"), this seems to point to believers from Israel. Recall the Jews' question recorded in John 7:35, "Does he [Jesus] intend to go to the Dispersion [i.e., the dispersed Jews] among the Greeks?" Moreover, from an earlier time, an explicit agreement had been made that the apostle Paul would go (mainly) to the Gentiles, and the apostle Peter (mainly) to the Jews.

Also 1 Peter 1:8 seems to presuppose a typically Jewish problem: "Though you have not seen him, you love him. Though you do not now see him, you believe in him and rejoice with joy that is inexpressible and filled with glory." The typically Jewish problem is how a Jew could have faith in a Messiah who, first, has died, and, second, is invisible. The same problem emerges in 1 Peter 1:10–12:

> Concerning this salvation, the prophets [in the Tanakh] who prophesied about the grace that was to be *yours* [!] searched and inquired carefully, inquiring what person or time the Spirit of Christ in them was indicating when he predicted the sufferings of Christ and the subsequent glories. It was revealed to them that they were serving not themselves but *you* [!], in the things that have now been announced to *you* [!] through those who preached the good news to you by the Holy Spirit sent from heaven, things into which angels long to look.

Who are the "you" and "yours" in this passage? In other words, to whom and about whom had the prophets spoken? Not the Gentiles, but Israel! The same is true for the "you" in 1 Peter 2:6–7 (see Isa. 28:16). And when Peter spoke of strangers and sojourners (1 Pet. 1:1, 17; 2:11), he used a typically Israelite expression.[64] Peter's

---

63. For a discussion of this choice, see Guthrie (1990, 792–95).
64. Lev. 25:23, 35, 47; 1 Chron. 29:15; Heb. 11:13 (to be sure, there were also Gentile "strangers and sojourners" *among* Israel; Num. 9:14; 15:15; 35:15).

feminine readers are "daughters of Sarah" (1 Pet. 3:6). These are not definitive proofs that Peter's readers were (mainly) of Jewish descent, but they are certainly important hints of that, unless we are led by supersessionist biases.

13.9.2 Gentile-Like Jews

Some have adduced 1 Peter 4:1-3 as a counter-argument against the idea that Peter's readers were (mainly) of Jewish descent.[65]

> Since therefore Christ suffered in the flesh, arm yourselves with the same way of thinking, for whoever has suffered in the flesh has ceased from sin, so as to live for the rest of the time in the flesh no longer for human passions but for the will of God. For the time that is past suffices for doing what the Gentiles want to do, living in sensuality, passions, drunkenness, orgies, drinking parties, and lawless idolatry.

To some, this seems to point to former pagans rather than to Jews (cf. Rom. 1:22-32). Yet, consider that (a) some of the Jews had lived as degenerate Gentiles, and (b) the expression "what the Gentiles want to do" (literally: "the will of the Gentiles") might be interpreted to suggest that Peter was speaking here of Jews who formerly had done what the Gentiles wanted to do, that is, had lived like these Gentiles. This may be understood to mean that they themselves had not been Gentiles.

Over against the disobedient "builders" — the *Jewish* leaders — who had rejected the "cornerstone" (i.e., the Messiah; Matt. 21:42-43 par.), stands the believing remnant of Israel. It seems to me that Peter is especially addressing, not the people in its totality but these faithful ones, the true Israel, the "Israel of God" (Gal. 6:16), from which the "all Israel" of Romans 11:26 will one day be built. In my view, it is to them in particular that he applies the designations of Exodus 19:5-6: "my treasured possession . . . a kingdom of priests and a holy nation." In the words of Peter:

> "[Y]ou are a chosen race, a royal priesthood, a holy nation, a people for his own possession, that you may proclaim the excellencies of him who called you out of darkness into his marvelous light. Once you were not a people [Heb. *Lo-'Ammi*, "Not-My-People"], but now you are God's people [Heb. *'Ammi*, "My-People"]; once you had not re-

---

65. E.g., Tenney (1961, 347).

ceived mercy [Heb. *Lo-Ruchamah*, "No Mercy"], but now you have received mercy [Heb. *Ruchamah*, "Mercy"] (1 Pet. 2:9–10).

The latter designations refer back to Hosea 1:6–11 (cf. Hos. 2:23), a quotation supporting the Jewish character of Peter's words. This does not mean that these expressions could not be *applied* to Gentile believers (cf. Rom. 9:25–26), but then they constitute an application, not an interpretation. One day, all Israel will again be *'Ammi*, "My People"; but in the present time, this designation can be applied to the remnant of Israel, the "Israel of God," that in Jesus Christ has found its Messiah.

Chapter 14
Israel in New Testament Prophecy: Paul and Revelation

> ... And when the exiles are assembled, judgment will be visited on the wicked. ... And when judgment is visited on the wicked, transgressors cease. ... And when the transgressors have disappeared, the horn of the righteous is exalted. ... And where is the horn of the righteous exalted? In Jerusalem. ... And when Jerusalem is built, David will come [Hos. 3:5]. ... And when David comes, prayer will come. ... And when prayer has come, the Temple service will come. ... And when the service comes, thanksgiving will come.
>
> Talmud: Megillah 17b–18a

14.1 Romans 11: Hardening Now, Salvation Later
14.1.1 The Place of Romans 9–11

EARLIER, IN CHAPTER 12, we investigated several aspects of Romans 9–11, especially the meaning of the olive tree in Romans 11; we also made several comments about Romans 11:26. Now we need to investigate Romans 9–11 as a whole. These chapters are of crucial importance for understanding the present and future position of Israel. The prophecies in the Tanakh must certainly be interpreted on their own terms, which means that the end time prophecies concerning Israel must be taken just as literally as the prophecies concerning the first coming of the Messiah. However, it is very important to investigate whether this approach is corroborated by the New Testament. This certainly occurs in Matthew 24 and Revelation 7, but particularly in Romans 9-11. For my exegesis, I have profited from many authors,[1] without identifying their contributions at every point in what follows. I will not provide a detailed, verse-by-verse exegesis; I must limit myself to the eschatological main lines, which are relevant for an evaluation of the prophecies about Israel.

In Romans 1-8 the apostle Paul was making clear that all people, Jews and Gentiles, by nature are equally sinful, that they all need divine redemption, and that God causes his saving grace in Christ to be proclaimed indiscriminately to all people, both to Jews and to Gentiles. In Romans 9-11 we read Paul's discussion of what, then, remains of the unique position of Israel in the counsels and the ways of God. His discussion proceeded as follows:

(a) *Romans 9:1-29* deals with God's sovereignty and electing grace toward Israel in comparison to the Gentile nations. Israel *is* special (see §1.5.3 above regarding verses 1-5), and its unique position will never be altered or removed. This is shown in the Tanakh, but the same Tanakh also predicts that God's salvation will also affect believing Gentiles.

(b) *Romans 9:30-10:21* deals with Israel's failure, especially with regard to confiding in their own (supposed) righteousness, rooted in works of the Torah. In opposition to this, Paul explains the gospel of the Messiah: trust not yourself and your merits, but only God and only Jesus, his person and his redemptive work.

(c) *Romans 11* deals with Israel's future: in spite of its failures, God will not forget his promises: when the Messiah appears, "all Israel" will be saved. The starting point of chapter 11 is this: "I ask, then, has God rejected his people? By no means!"

The apostle Paul demonstrates this basically in three ways.

(1) Even in the *past*, God never definitively rejected his people

---

1. Kelly (*BT* 8 and 9); Brockhaus (n.d.); Grant (1901); Roozemeijer (1911); Coates (n.d.); Van Leeuwen and Jacobs (1952); Ridderbos (1959); Gaebelein (1970); Denney (1979); Medema (1985); Moo (1996); Shulam (1998); Stern (1999); Darby (*SYN*; *CW* 26).

(vv. 2–24). In the dark days of the prophet Elijah, God considered the "seven thousand in Israel, all the knees that have not bowed to Baal, and every mouth that has not kissed him" (1 Kings 19:18). Even during the darkest periods in the history of Israel, there remained a "remnant" of faithful ones, who formed a sharp contrast to the wicked majority of the people. Even in the most wicked conditions in Israel, there remained God's promise that a remnant will "return" (repent and convert) to the God of Israel.[2] Israel's condition was never hopeless, because God always procures for himself this "remnant," from which he will build the "all Israel" of verse 26.

(2) In the *present*, too, God has not rejected his people; the full-blooded Israelite Saul/Paul was a striking example of this (v. 1), and together with him "at the present time there is a remnant, chosen by grace.[3] But if it is by grace, it is no longer on the basis of works; otherwise grace would no longer be grace" (v. 5–6). This means that any remnant is Israel never owes its existence to the people's righteousness, that is, to their own merits, but always (objectively) to God's electing grace, and (subjectively) to faith toward God and toward Jesus, his person and his work. In the present era, this remnant has found a place in the Ecclesia of God, the body of Christ.

(3) Similarly, in the *future*, God will not reject his people; however, at that point it will no longer be a small remnant. On the contrary, "all Israel" will be saved (v. 26). More precisely: at that time again a remnant will return to the LORD, and from this, God will build the new Israel, which will consist entirely of *tzaddiqim*, "righteous ones" (Isa. 45:25; 60:21).

As in all previous centuries, there exists today a twofold Israel. As far as its place in God's redemptive history is concerned, Israel is and will remain—as long as the present earth exists—the "chosen people of God." However, considered from a spiritual, eternal viewpoint, this chosen nation consists of two groups: the elect and the hardened: "What then? Israel failed to obtain what it was seeking. The elect obtained it, but the rest were hardened."[4] The *elect* part of the *chosen* people has received God's blessing but the rest of

---

2. Cf. Isa. 10:21–22; 11:11, 16; 28:5; 37:31–32; 46:3.
3. Literally, "remnant according to election of grace."
4. Rom. 11:7, with reference to Isa. 29:10, 6:9, and Ps. 69:23, respectively.

the *chosen* people became hardened. However, this hardening that has come over the majority of the Jewish people is not definitive; the ultimate goal of God in his ways with Israel is not their fall, but their restoration (v. 11).

Please note that the group of *hardened Jews* and the group of *non-Jesus-believing Jews* are not necessarily identical. This is because every not-yet-Jesus-believing Jew can become a Jesus-believing Jew. This likely happens almost every day. And it will certainly happen on a much larger scale when the Son of Man (re-)appears.

14.1.2 Contrast: First Argument

In a remarkable way, the apostle Paul contrasts the Israelites of the present era (*now*) with those of the future era (*soon*).[5] Prepare to consider the following claim: just as there are literal Jewish converts in the present era, so too there will be literal Jewish converts in the following era.

Here is Paul's first argument: "[I]f their trespass [*now*] means riches for the world, and if their failure [*now*] means riches for the Gentiles, how much more will their fullness mean [*soon*]!" Israel's failure means riches for the Gentiles because—humanly speaking—Israel's having been set aside temporarily is the reason that the gospel of Christ could now go out to all the Gentiles.[6] How much more will their "fulness" (consummation, full restoration as a nation) *soon* be a blessing for all the world. Of course, I know that the "now" and the "soon" are not in the text; I have added them to bring out what I think is the sense of Paul's argument (cf. v. 15). To this end, three additional comments are warranted.

(a) Paul endeavored to make his fellow Jews "jealous" in the *now* (the present era) (vv. 11–14), so that they would begin to grasp what blessings the acceptance of the gospel might contain for them as well. By accepting it, they would belong to the "remnant according to election of grace" (v. 5). This concerns only "some of them" (v. 14); that is, Paul's ministry did not lead to the restoration of *all* Israel (v. 26), for this would occur only at the second coming of Christ.

---

5. I believe that if Maljaars (2015, especially 60–71) would have honored this contrast, his argument would have been different (cf. his chapter 8).
6. Cf. Matt. 13:38; 21:41; 24:14; 28:18–19.

(b) The road to Israel's ultimate salvation runs, remarkably enough, through the mission among the Gentiles: before the "fullness" of Israel (v. 12) arrives, the "fullness" of the nations must first come in (v. 25). It is only via the detour of Gentile "fullness" that Israel will ultimately and finally arrive at *its* "fullness."

(c) The notion of Israel's "fullness" coming *soon* stands over against the notion of a "remnant" existing *now*: at present it is only a minority, soon it will be a majority of Messiah-believing Israelites (v. 26).

14.1.3 Contrast: Second Argument

Now notice Paul's second argument: "For if their rejection [*now*] means the reconciliation of the world, what will their acceptance [*soon*] mean but life from the dead?" (Rom. 11:15).

Literally speaking, the acceptance of Israel will involve a remnant as well, but this remnant will be the repentant and converted majority of Israel, from which God will build the new "all Israel" (v. 26). Today, Israel as a nation has been set aside by God; the nation is *Lo-'Ammi*, except for a "remnant, chosen by grace" (v. 5). This temporary rejection has paved the way for the mission among the Gentiles, from which a great harvest has been gathered ("the reconciliation of the world"). This itself is spectacular enough. How magnificent, then, will it be when "*all Israel*" will be accepted again by God. It will be like a resurrection from the dead.[7]

When people make the supersessionist exegetical move in Romans 11 from literal Jews *now* to spiritual "Jews" coming *soon*, they are neglecting the logic of verses 12 and 15. The apostle Paul was claiming that *now* a remnant of Jews and a multitude from the Gentiles would exist, but *soon* also a multitude from the Jews. Supersessionists assert: That multitude from the Gentiles consist of "spiritual Jews," and is thus identical with that multitude from the Jews. Such reasoning violates Paul's entire argument. Paul was arguing: *Now* a remnant of Israel, *soon* all Israel. He was speaking twice of *the same Israel*.

In fact, Romans 11:12 and 15 have the character of prophetic

---

7. Consider Isa. 26:19; Ezek. 37:1–14; Dan. 12:1–2; Hos. 6:1–3, which contain both literal and figurative references to resurrection.

words. Verse 12: one day, the "fullness"[8] of Israel will arrive: "Now, if their leaving triggered this worldwide coming of non-Jewish outsiders to God's kingdom, just imagine the effect of their coming back! What a homecoming!" (MSG). Verse 15 (MSG): "If their falling out initiated this worldwide coming together, their recovery is going to set off something even better: mass homecoming! If the first thing the Jews did, even though it was wrong for them, turned out for your good, just think what's going to happen when they get it right!"

Thirdly, after the *warning* of verses 21-22, we find a *prophecy* in the parable of the olive tree (v. 23-24; cf. §12.2.2). This follows a common procedure used by the prophets: initially prophecies are conditional: "if you do not repent . . . then," and subsequently become unconditional: "such and such is surely going to happen to you because you are so wicked." We read:

> And even they [i.e., Jews], if they do not continue in their unbelief, will be grafted in, for God has the power to graft them in again. For if you [i.e., Gentile believers] were cut from what is by nature a wild olive tree, and grafted, contrary to nature, into a cultivated olive tree, how much more will these, the natural branches, be grafted back into their own olive tree.

This is no longer the description of a *possible* scenario in the end time but an outright *prediction*: the natural branches *will* be grafted back into their own olive tree. That is, they *will* come to faith in their Messiah, and be accepted again by the God of Israel. Those who do not "continue" in the kindness of God will be cut off (v. 22); but those who do not "continue" in their unbelief—that is, come to faith—will be grafted back into God's people.

In arboriculture, such grafting in of branches that had been broken off is highly unusual. What Paul was saying is that the restoration of Israel will indeed be a magnificent miracle of God. The adding of believing Gentiles is an "ordinary" miracle, so to speak— every conversion is a miracle—one that we may see happen around us every day. But the restoration of Israel—which is a very different thing—will be a miracle whose magnificence far surpass this. It is

---

8. AMPC: "their full reinstatement," CEV: "full return," ESV: "full inclusion," HCSB: "full number."

Israel that one day will confess:

> This is the Lord's doing;
> > it is *marvelous* in our eyes.
>
> This is the day that the Lord has made;
> > let us rejoice and be glad in it.
>
> Save us, we pray,[9] O Lord!
> > O Lord, we pray, give us success!
>
> Blessed is he who comes in the name of the Lord![10]
> > We bless you from the house of the Lord.
>
> The Lord is God,
> > and he has made his light to shine upon us (Ps. 118:23–27).

14.2 Then Will Be the Restoration
14.2.1 "Hardening"

In Romans 11:25, the apostle Paul used even stronger language; what in verses 21–22 was still just a possibility is in verse 23 a certainty. It is remarkable that Paul spoke here of a "mystery" (Gk. *mystērion*)—not something "mysterious," but something "hidden" (concealed, unknown). This does not mean that the coming ultimate restoration of Israel was unknown in the Tanakh—on the contrary. However, only in the New Testament did the scope, fullness, and clarity of this restoration become visible. This is because people could hardly have grasped beforehand how deep the fall of Israel would be: it displayed not only social injustice, not only idolatry, but the rejection of the Messiah. Therefore, it could hardly be foreseen how magnificent the restoration would be, and by what way—or rather, by what detour—it would be brought about. If the main reason for their being set aside was *their* rejection of their Messiah, the main basis for their re-acceptance will be the re-appearance of the Messiah, *and their acceptance of him.*

Just as in verse 7, Paul spoke here of the "hardening" that has come over Israel. The term "hardening" means that hearts become insensible to God's word; the result is blindness, stubbornness, obstinacy. Viewed from the perspective of human responsibility, hardness means that people themselves choose to be stubborn. Viewed

---

9. Heb. *hoshi'ah na*, which is the "Hosanna" of Matt. 21:9, 15 etc. (see next note).
10. See Matt. 21:9; 23:39; Mark 11:9; Luke 13:35; John 12:13.

from God's standpoint, hardness refers to his judgment upon people. Exodus told us that Pharaoh "hardened" his own heart (8:15, 32; 9:34), but also that *God* "hardened" Pharaoh's heart.[11] Notice these three events:

(1) Here in Romans 11:25, it is God's "hardening" of (the unbelieving majority of) Israel (but the remnant of Israel is ultimately saved).

(2) In Romans 1:26-28, it is God's "hardening" of the pagan world (but again, a remnant from the Gentiles is saved and enters the Ecclesia).

(3) In 2 Thessalonians 2:9-12, it is God's "hardening" of nominal Christianity (but again, the remnant of true believers is saved).

This "hardening" of Israel is both partial—for there is a "remnant, chosen by grace" (vv. 5, 7)—and temporary: it will last until the time of the restoration described in verses 25-27. Before the "fullness" of Israel arrives (v. 12), first a "fullness" from the Gentiles (i.e., a full number, as determined by God) must "come in." The latter presumably means: "come into the olive tree," that is, into the order of the patriarchal promises and blessings). Once this occurs, *then* "all Israel will be saved" (v. 26).

In verse 26, this little word "then" (in italics above) is the Greek word *houtōs*. The usual meaning of this word is "so, thus, in this way," and this is how many translations render it. In our verse as well, this rendering makes perfect sense: "in this way" all Israel will be saved. However, *houtōs* can definitely have a temporal (collateral) meaning as well,[12] as some translations render it: "*then* all Israel will be saved."[13] An example of this can be found in 1 Corinthians 11:28, "Let a person examine himself, and *so* [Gk. *houtōs*] eat of the bread and drink of the cup," for which many translations offer a temporal rendering: ". . . and *then* let him eat . . . ."[14] Other translations supply this temporal connection by using the word

---

11. Exod. 4:21; 7:3; 9:12; 10:1, 20, 27; 11:10; 14:4, 8, 17.

12. *Contra* Bavinck (*RD* 4:670); Van Genderen (2008, 855); O. P. Robertson in Paas (2017, 266); cf. Van der Horst (2000); Van der Kooi and Van den Brink (2017, 356).

13. TLB, NLV, TPT, WE.

14. KJ21, CJB, GNT, ISV, PHILLIPS, NRSV, TPT, TLV, VOICE.

"before": "Everyone ought to examine themselves before they eat . . . ."[15] Another example is 1 Thessalonians 4:17, ". . . and *so* we will always be with the Lord," where the sense is clearly temporal as well: compare CEV: "From that time on"; Phillips: "after that"; NLT: "Then."

In connection with Romans 11:26, the Annotations to the Dutch States Translation explain the "so" in the verse already as "then." There can be no doubt that the sense of verses 25–26 is this: *first*, the fullness of the Gentiles must come in, *then* all Israel will be saved. The Peshitta, the Aramaic translation of the New Testament, says: "*After this* all Israel will be saved."[16]

Supersessionists have opposed the interpretation of *houtōs* here as more or less equivalent to the Greek preposition *tote* ("then").[17] However, in my view the "first . . . then" sequence seems quite apparent: *Israel* will be saved after the "fullness" of the Gentiles has come in. But even if we translate *houtōs* as "so" ("in this way"), the sense is clear: all Israel is saved "in this way," namely, by the "fullness" of the Gentiles coming in first. God first finishes his plan for the Gentile world, but ultimately also "all Israel" will be saved— everything in due time.

14.2.2 When and How?

In Romans 11:26, the "all Israel" (Gk. *pas Israēl*) forms a remarkable contrast with the "remnant" (Gk. *leimma*) of verse 5. One day, when the gathering of the Ecclesia will be finished and the restoration of Israel will arrive, there will no longer be a saved remnant over against a hardened majority of Israel. Thus, it cannot be correct that the salvation of "all Israel" would refer here to the entire period between Pentecost (Acts 2) and the second coming of Christ, as various expositors have asserted.[18] *Today* it is only a "remnant," *then* it will be "all Israel."

---

15. NIV; cf. NCV, NIRV, NLV, NLT.
16. Nierop (2010, 217).
17. Van Leeuwen and Jacobs (1952, 249); Ridderbos (1959, 264); more prudently, Berkouwer (1972, 344, 348).
18. Thus Van Genderen (2008, 856) (pointing to H. Bavinck, H. Ridderbos, and J. P. Versteeg as well); however, he also seemed to leave room for the view being presented here (857).

We find in Isaiah these remarkable promises pertaining to "all Israel":

> In the LORD *all* the offspring of Israel
>   shall be justified and shall glory (45:25).

> Your people shall *all* be righteous;
>   they shall possess the land forever,
> the branch of my planting, the work of my hands,
>   that I might be glorified (60:21)

Or consider the references given by Paul himself in Romans 11:26–27:

> "The Deliverer will come from Zion" (cf. Ps. 14:7; Isa. 59:20a).

> "He will banish ungodliness from Jacob" (cf. Isa. 27:9; 59:20b).

> "[T]his will be my covenant with them
>   when I take away their sins" (cf. Isa. 59:21; Jer. 31:33–34).

The mention here of the Deliverer is of eminent importance: the full restoration, the full redemption for Israel will arrive only when their Redeemer himself arrives.

14.2.3 "Zion"

The reference to Zion is important here, too. Steven Paas argued that nothing in Romans 11 refers to an Israel restored in the Promised Land.[19] However, the apostle Paul was referring here to Isaiah 59:20, where we read: "And a Redeemer will come *to* Zion,[20] to those in Jacob who turn from transgression." The term "Zion" means here what it means everywhere in Isaiah. Especially the next chapters, Isaiah 60–63, explain to us what Zion meant to every Israelite: the earthly Jerusalem (often poetically called "Zion"; cf. the poetic parallelism in 62:1), with the earthly temple mount, as well as the future restoration of Israel in "Zion" during the Messianic kingdom. In other words, Paas again committed the fallacy of begging the question: he began by asserting the very thing that needed first to be proven, namely, that in Isaiah the term "Zion" must be

---

19. Paas (2014, 55), referring also to Robertson (2000).
20. Paul says, "*From* Zion," which for our present argument is irrelevant.

interpreted figuratively. A beautiful example of this literal, earthly Jerusalem that will be fully restored at the beginning of the Messianic kingdom is this:

> Foreigners shall build up your [i.e., Jerusalem's] walls,
>   and their kings shall minister to you . . . .
> The sons of those who afflicted you
>   shall come bending low to you,
> and all who despised you
>   shall bow down at your feet;
> they shall call you the City of the LORD,
>   the Zion of the Holy One of Israel (Isa. 60:11, 14).

In the following verses of Romans 11, Paul underscored again that this complete restoration of Israel cannot be postponed forever because it is rooted in divine election, in "the gifts and the calling of God" that "are irrevocable[21]" (vv. 28–29). That is, God can never revoke the gracious calling of Israel, can never alter his decision once made, and can never transfer it to a fundamentally very different company: the Ecclesia, which in the New Testament is always distinguished from Israel. As surely as the Gentiles, who "were at one time disobedient to God," "now have received mercy," so surely will Israel, too, whose majority does not presently believe in their Messiah, "receive mercy" (v. 31): "For God has [at first] consigned all to disobedience [or, unbelief], that [in the end] he may have mercy on all" (Rom. 11:32). The "all" in this verse is either "all Israel," or all believing Jews and Gentiles together. Paul's point was either that in the end, not only a number of Gentiles but also "all Israel" will be saved (as in v. 26); or his point was that in the end, there will be one large people of God, consisting of Jewish and Gentile Jesus-believers.

14.3 Romans 11 from Various Viewpoints
14.3.1 The Supersessionist View

At this point we have sufficiently demonstrated that according to Romans 11, the repentant and converted portion of *ethnic* Israel will ultimately be saved. However, it is possible that this does not yet adequately explain the expression "all Israel." In what follows, we

---

21. Lit., "are unregrettable," can never be regretted by God; DLNT: "are without-regret"; EHV: "are not regretted."

will consider three main views, followed by a look at Jesus' testimony.²²

(1) the *supersessionist* view ("'all Israel' is the Ecclesia"; see §§14.3.1-2),

(2) the *universalist* view ("'all Israel' encompasses all converted Jews of all time"; see §14.3.2), and

(3) the *particularist* view ("'all Israel' is the converted Israel that will enter the Messianic kingdom"; see §14.3.3).

The supersessionist view understands the phrase "all Israel" to refer to the entire Ecclesia, from Adam to the last day. But as we have seen, in Romans 9–11 the term "Israel" *always* refers to the physical descendants of the patriarchs, and *never* to Gentile believers. Therefore, the supersessionist understanding that Romans 11:26 was speaking about the Ecclesia is quite astonishing. This view was held by John Calvin, mentioned earlier.²³ According to his commentary on Romans, Calvin apparently believed there would be a massive conversion of Israel in the last day, but for the rest his views were thoroughly supersessionist, following in the line of Augustine before him: the "Israel of God" is ostensibly the totality of converted Jews and converted Gentiles. Apparently, Calvin believed that the coming in of the fullness of the Gentiles (v. 25) referred to Gentiles coming into Israel, whereas the apostle Paul was speaking of a coming into the olive tree, which definitely is *not* Israel.

Other Reformers, like Martin Luther, Martin Bucer, Philip Melanchthon, and Johannes Oecolampadius, understood the term "Israel" in Romans 11:26 to refer to the Ecclesia of Jews and Gentiles together, as did Hugo de Groot (or Grotius) and John Lightfoot.²⁴ They were all on the Augustinian wavelength, and none of them imagined that verse 26 could have an interpretation different from all of Romans 9–11. From a psychological viewpoint, it is enor-

---

22. Cf. Maljaars (2015, 16–17); his entire book is an extensive commentary on Romans 11:26, rooted in the biases of supersessionism.

23. Cf. also Kersten (1980, 2:pppp 1947,II, 316); regarding Calvin's view of Israel, see C. Graafland (1978).

24. Van Campen (2007, 436).

mously fascinating that great thinkers can be attached so strongly to a particular paradigm.[25] But perhaps the same is true for all of us; we can be convinced not only by logical arguments, but also by our feelings and emotions.

Other expositors have stated without any basis that the phrase "all Israel" referred to "the called ones from the Gentiles together with the 'remnant' of Israel."[26] Thus, Paul supposedly "does not speak here of a conversion of Israel as a *nation*, as a popular whole, to the Christ, at the end of the days, when the gospel will have been brought to all nations." Thus, whereas everywhere else in Romans 9-11 the term "Israel" referred to ethnic Israel, sharply distinct from the Gentiles, whether believing or not, in verse 26 the term "Israel" suddenly referred to the remnant of Israel plus believing Gentiles?[27] This is another clear example of theological biases governing the exegesis.

However, interestingly enough, Van Leeuwen and Jacobs began to hesitate and to back down: "Many believe that Paul here, until verse 32, teaches a conversion of Israel as a popular whole. The decision is difficult, *perhaps* one may read this into Paul's words."[28] Glorious moment! A glimpse of light broke through! But what happens? In the end, the authors rejected this approach again with the argument that, if Paul had meant this, he should have said so more clearly. One could better argue that if everywhere in Romans 9-11 Paul meant ethnic Israel when he used the word "Israel," but in 11:26 suddenly meant the remnant of Israel plus believing Gentiles, *then he should have said so more clearly.*

---

25. Psychological experiment: if A is longer than B, but nine colleagues say B is longer than A, then the tenth colleague, the subject of the experiment, will usually also say that B is longer; nobody wants to stand alone in their opinion!

26. Van Leeuwen and Jacobs (1952, 227).

27. Maljaars (2015, 36–38) presented the novelty that, in Romans 9–11, we must make a fundamental distinction between "Israel" and "all Israel"! This is absurd not only logically, but also linguistically.

28. Van Leeuwen and Jacobs (1952, 228).

14.3.2 Universalism

The universalist view that is to be rejected asserts that the phrase "all Israel" referred to all Jews who ever lived on earth, all of whom will ultimately be saved.[29] In this case, in contrast with the supersessionist view, the expression does not necessarily refer to the end of time, but it does refer to ethnic Israel. There are, however, at least two problems with this interpretation. The first is that it does not honor the eschatological context of the passage: believing Israelites *will* again be grafted into the olive tree (vv. 23–24), and Israel's restoration will occur when the fullness of the Gentiles has come in (vv. 25–26).

The second problem is that salvation cannot occur without repentance, conversion, and faith, as we have seen. On the universalist view, the Israelites who have passed away would get a chance, after death, to come to repentance and faith. I have explained elsewhere the fundamental biblical objections against such a view.[30]

Various Jesus-believing Jews held and hold the view just described, but other Jesus-believing Jews have sufficiently refuted them.[31] In the Tanakh, the phrase "all Israel" always referred to the nation as a totality, the nation as such, without necessarily including every individual Israelite, however. When it is said that "all Israel" says, hears, does things, this does not mean that every individual Israelite says, hears, or does these things.[32] The phrase "all Israel" does not necessarily mean "all Israelites."

The Mishnah also stated:

> All Israel have a portion in the world to come, for it is written, "Thy people are all righteous; they shall inherit the land forever, the branch

---

29. See Bavinck (*RD*, 4:668–72); Berkhof (1981, 698–700); Hendriksen (1974, 39–52); Ridderbos (1959, ad loc.); 1966, 398–403); Berkouwer (1972, 340–52); Hoekema (1979, 139–47).
30. Ouweneel (2009a, §12.2.1; 2012a, §14.4.1).
31. Stern (1999, 422).
32. See, e.g., Deut. 13:11; 21:21; 27:9; Josh. 3:17; 7:24–25; 8:15, 21, 24, 33; Judg. 8:27; 1 Sam. 2:22; in the New Testament, e.g., Matt. 2:3; 3:5.

of my planting, the work of my hands, that I may be glorified [Isa. 60:21]". But the following have no portion therein: he who maintains that resurrection is not a biblical doctrine, the Torah was not divinely revealed, and an *epikoros*,[33] ....[34]

This is the general pattern: the people as a whole will share in the Messianic kingdom, but as far as individuals are concerned, the wicked will have no part in it. We find the same principle in Revelation 21:5-8: "And he who was seated on the throne said, 'Behold, I am making *all things* new. . . *But* as for the cowardly, the faithless, the detestable, as for murderers, the sexually immoral, sorcerers, idolaters, and all liars, their portion will be in the lake that burns with fire and sulfur, which is the second death." The Mishnah placed more emphasis on unbelievers and heretics, Revelation more on the immoral people in the broadest sense. The excluded wicked Israelites are the exceptions that confirm the rule, and the rule is: "All Israel will be saved."

Herman Ridderbos pointed to the term "fullness" in Romans 11:12, which refers to the spiritual character of the Israel that will ultimately be saved (cf. "fullness" in v. 25).[35] He added:

> Such a universalism [i.e., "all Israel" includes every Jew] would be in total conflict with the entire tenor of Paul's gospel, with the main theme of our letter [Rom.], namely, that the righteous will live by faith, as well as with the wrestling argument of Romans 9-11, wrestling, namely, in order to maintain both the mercy and the severity of God [11:22], both the sovereignty and the faithfulness of God with regard to Israel.[36]

---

33. Comment in the Soncino edition: the *epikoros* is an Epicurean (in the sense of the licentious person), *or* a heretic (Gemarah: one who speaks disparagingly of the Bible and its disciples). Added to these are those who read non-divine books, those who commit sorcery, and those who pronounce "the divine name as it is spelt." Excluded are also three kings (Jeroboam, Ahab and Manasseh [despite 2 Chron. 33:13]) and three "commoners" (Balaam, Doeg, Ahitophel, and Gehazi).
34. Sanhedrin 90a.
35. Ridderbos (1959, 263–64).
36. Ibid., 264.

In other words: no one will ever share in God's salvation without a personal acknowledgement and confession of guilt, personal conversion, and personal faith. If "[i]n the Lord all the offspring of Israel shall be justified" (Isa. 45:25; cf. 53:11), they will be justified (declared righteous) in no different way than every other person throughout all time has been justified: through humbling before God, by faith in the offered salvation of Christ—the coming One, or the One who in the meantime *has* come—and by good works that are the necessary fruits of this faith.[37]

14.3.3 Particularism

Thus, only the third option remains: the phrase "all Israel" referred to all (converted) end-time Israelite believers who are saved, and who together constitute the true Israel of God (the particularist view). They are the believers from Israel in the time of the end, who, after God's judgment upon the wicked Jews, will enter the Messianic kingdom, and will constitute the entire, totally renewed people of Israel.[38] Recall Zechariah 13:8-9, which deals with the end, as we see from its immediate continuation in chapter 14. The prophet told us that the wicked would constitute no less than two-thirds of Israel, whereas the remnant will be only one third of the people, which will be purified through the (spiritual) "fire" of trial and testing. They will call upon the Lord, and he will listen to them. He will call them "My people" (Heb. *'ammi*, cf. Hos. 2:1, 23). This description gives us an excellent picture of what Paul was saying in Romans 11:26: the wicked Jews will be snatched away by the judgments, and what will remain (the "remnant") will be cleansed (cf. Zech. 13:1) and will enter the Messianic kingdom (see 14:9) as the true "Israel of God." The phrase "all Israel" referred to the *true* Israel, the Israel that in Zechariah 13 God can truly call *his* people.

Isaiah 33:14 says about the wicked in Israel at the time of the end (cf. Heb. 12:29):

The sinners in Zion are afraid;

---

37. Cf. Ouweneel (2009b, chapters 7–10).
38. Berkhof (1981, 698–700) called the conversion of the fulness (Gk. *plērōma*) of Israel one of the great events that will precede the second coming of Christ; however, Paul's point was that "all Israel" will be saved *at* Christ's second coming.

trembling has seized the godless:
"Who among us can dwell with the consuming fire?
Who among us can dwell with everlasting burnings?"

Notice here the "fire," which we found in Zechariah 13:9 as well. But there it was a positive image: it was the refining and purifying fire through which the righteous would pass in order that they become the finest gold and silver. But here it is a consuming fire, the devastating fire of God's wrath; compare Isaiah 5:25:

[T]he anger of the LORD was kindled against his people,
and he stretched out his hand against them and struck them,
and the mountains quaked;
and their corpses were as refuse
in the midst of the streets.

Such passages suggest that the number of the wicked might be larger than the two-thirds mentioned in Zechariah 13:8-9. The most pessimistic picture is found in Isaiah 17:4-6:

[I]n that day the glory of Jacob will be brought low,
and the fat of his flesh will grow lean.
And it shall be as when the reaper gathers standing grain
and his arm harvests the ears,
and as when one gleans the ears of grain
in the Valley of Rephaim [cf. 2 Sam. 5:18, 22; 23:13].

Gleanings will be left in it,
as when an olive tree is beaten —
two or three berries
in the top of the highest bough,
four or five
on the branches of a fruit tree.

What a sad picture: some meager gleanings are left over, a few berries at the top of the bush, four or five on the branches — I know of no more pessimistic image of what is literally just a remnant, a small remainder on a once full tree (see also Isa. 56:9–57:13).

14.3.4 Jesus' Testimony

When he was on earth, Jesus himself exposed the wicked condition of the people, a condition that — apart from the *tzaddiqim* — would last until Christ at his second coming puts an end to it. While he was on earth, Jesus earnestly warned the cities rejecting him that they were storing up for themselves great guilt because of their hardened hearts:

> Then he began to denounce the cities where most of his mighty works had been done, because they did not repent. "Woe to you, Chorazin! Woe to you, Bethsaida! For if the mighty works done in you had been done in Tyre and Sidon, they would have repented long ago in sackcloth and ashes. But I tell you, it will be more bearable on the day of judgment for Tyre and Sidon than for you. And you, Capernaum, will you be exalted to heaven? You will be brought down to Hades. For if the mighty works done in you had been done in Sodom, it would have remained until this day. But I tell you that it will be more tolerable on the day of judgment for the land of Sodom than for you." (Matt. 11:20-24; cf. Luke 10:13-16).

When that happens, the wicked in Israel will have remorse and beg for grace, as the rich man did in the "place of torment" (Luke 16:28), but it will be in vain:

> [The Lord] will say, "I tell you, I do not know where you come from. Depart from me, all you workers of evil!" In that place there will be weeping and gnashing of teeth, when you [i.e., the wicked in Israel] see Abraham and Isaac and Jacob and all the prophets in the kingdom of God but you yourselves cast out. And people will come from east and west, and from north and south, and recline at table in the kingdom of God (Luke 13:27-29).

One of the harshest experiences for these wicked, who will consider themselves to be righteous, will be seeing not only how the (Jewish!) tax collectors and the prostitutes enter the kingdom of God *before them* (Matt. 21:31), but how *Gentiles* will "recline at table in the kingdom of God" *instead of them*. This is not because in themselves tax collectors, prostitutes, and Gentiles would be better than these religious Jews—of course not. Here again, the parable of the Pharisee and the tax collector (Luke 18:9-14) is of vital importance: the latter is justified (declared righteous), not because tax collectors are *per se* better than Pharisees—of course they are not—but *because the tax collector repented*, whereas the Pharisee only *boasted*.

Thus, we see how, at Christ's second coming, the faithful in Israel will be redeemed, but the wicked majority of the nation will be condemned. We find this contrast also in the words of Jesus in Matthew 24:37-41:

> [A]s were the days of Noah, so will be the coming of the Son of Man. For as in those days before the flood they were eating and drinking, marrying and giving in marriage, until the day when Noah entered the ark, and they were unaware until the flood came and swept them all away, so will be the coming of the Son of Man. Then two men will be in the field; one will be taken[39] and one left. Two women will be grinding at the mill; one will be taken and one left.

In the days of Noah, too, the great majority of people was unbelieving; they were having a party without bothering about God. Only Noah walked with God (Gen. 6:8-9); we are not told that his sons did. Then came the judgment that destroyed the wicked, but the righteous were saved in the ark, that is, Christ (1 Pet. 3:20-21). It will be similar at the second coming of Christ. The nation—just like Christianity!—will be shown to consist of two groups: those who are snatched away by God's judgment, and those who will stay behind in order to inherit the kingdom. Everywhere, the wicked will be swept away by God's judgment, and what will remain will be the true Israel, the "Israel of God," the "all Israel" of Romans 11:26, the true people of God, who will possess the land in its full expanse.[40]

As to the destiny of the wicked part of the nation, consider Revelation 14:17-20 as well, where we hear of the judgment in the winepress, in which God in his wrath treads the clusters of grapes.[41] These clusters come from the "vine of the earth." In the book of Revelation, the "earth" seems to be a general reference to the place of God's testimony, whether Jewish or Christian. In the Tanakh, the vine, or the vineyard, represents Israel.[42] This vine, or vineyard,

---

39. Gk. *paralambanetai*, i.e., "taken [for judgment]" (AMP, TPT), *not* "shall be received" (GNV, NMB, RGT, YLT).
40. Gen. 13:17; 15:18; Ps. 37:9–11, 20, 22, 28–29, 34; Ezek. 47:13–23; Zech. 9:10.
41. Ouweneel (1990, 121–23).
42. Cf. Ps. 80:8; Isa. 5:1–7; Jer. 2:21; 8:13; 12:10; Hos. 14:7; Joel 1:7, 12; Matt. 21:33–46; sometimes specifically Jerusalem: Ezek. 15.

was planted by God in order that it would produce fruit. However, when the time of the fruit had arrived, he found no grapes or only bad grapes on the vine, or in the vineyard.

It was only that one Man, who is the personification of Israel, and is thus the true vine, who here on earth produced true and perfect fruit for God (John 15:1–8). The Jews were the "branches" on this "vine," as were all confessing Christians later. But again, we find how his people are shown to consist of two groups: on the one hand: "Every branch in me that does not bear fruit he [i.e., the Father, the vinedresser] takes away, and," on the other hand, "every branch that does bear fruit he prunes, that it may bear more fruit" (v. 2). There is an enormous difference between those who do not bear fruit at all—the wicked—and those who bear little fruit, because the latter show that at least the life of the vine is in them. This fruit must become "more fruit," and even "much fruit" (v. 8). But the life of the vine is in them, whereas the former group has no such life. They are branches on the vine, but there is no true living connection between them and the vine. They are the wicked Jews, and later the wicked (nominal) Christians.

14.4 Israel Elsewhere with Paul[43]

14.4.1 Second Corinthians 3:16

In 2 Corinthians 3:13–16 we read about

> ... Moses, who would put a veil over his face so that the Israelites might not gaze at the outcome of what was being brought to an end. But their minds were hardened. For to this day, when they read the old covenant, that same veil remains unlifted, because only through Christ is it taken away. Yes, to this day whenever Moses is read a veil lies over their hearts. But when one [or, it] turns to the Lord, the veil is removed.

Just as in Romans 11:25, we read here about the hardening of Israel, as a consequence of which their heart is veiled whenever they read the Tanakh; they do not understand their own book be-

---

43. Cf. the comparative study by Witherington (1992) regarding the eschatological statement of both Jesus and Paul, also concerning Israel, though he too believed in the notion of a "spiritual Israel."

cause they are lacking the Holy Spirit (see vv. 17–18). Having received the Holy Spirit can be the consequence only of repentance and new birth (Ezek. 36:25-27). Jesus told the Sadducees: "[Y]ou know neither the Scriptures nor the power of God" (Mark 12:24), which might be read as follows: You do not understand the Scriptures *because* you lack the power of God.

After this, we hear this important statement by Paul, which I now quote from the KJV: "[W]hen it shall turn to the Lord, the vail [sic] shall be taken away" (v. 16; cf. ASV, BRG, DARBY, Luther, Segond). The unbiased reader will find in this an announcement of the future conversion of Israel. But many translations render the verse quite differently (partly for supersessionist reasons?): "when(ever) (any) one (or, a person) turns to the Lord, . . ." The Greek says hēnika ean epistrepsēi, "(every time) when it (or he, she) turns to the Lord, . . ."[44] The Greek does not mention a subject, so that the exegete must guess about the identity of the subject. This subject could be "the heart (of a Jew)" (v. 15b), "the Jew," "(the nation of) Israel," or "anyone" (Jew or Gentile).

The aorist tense of the Greek verb points to a single moment of conversion, not a continual turning to the Lord; however, this can be something that repeats itself in the lives of many different persons. Thus, the tense does not help us determine whether we must read "(every time) when anyone (or, a Jew)" *or* "when it (i.e., the nation)." In other words, does the verse refer to the distinct conversion of many Jews throughout the ages, *or* to the conversion of Israel at the end of time? Translators and expositors differ widely on the matter, which phenomenon cannot be separated from their respective dogmatic biases (which, of course, is true about me as well).

The apostle Paul seems to have been alluding here to Exodus 34:34 in the Septuagint: "Whenever Moses went in before the LORD to speak with him, he would remove the veil, until he came out." However, the similarity is limited, and the verbs used are in the imperfect tense, but in 2 Corinthians 3:16 in the aorist. Yet, we can surmise how, because of the similarity, various modern translations

---

44. See the discussion of all the options by Hughes (1962, 113n9); he also pointed to Calvin, who thought that Moses was the subject.

arrived at their rendering.

However, other proposals have been made. Church father Tertullian believed that verse 16 referred "to the Jew on whose face Moses' veil is spread, so that, when he is converted to the faith in Christ, he will understand how Moses has spoken of Christ."[45] In this case, we could just as well read "Israel": when Israel will be converted to Christ, it will finally understand the Tanakh, more specifically, the Torah, more specifically Deuteronomy 18, where Moses speaks of Christ. This also ties in with the translation "their hearts": ". . . when their hearts turn to the Lord."[46] This can be taken to mean the following: ". . . every time the heart of anyone of them turns to the Lord," but also collectively: ". . . when Israel turns to the Lord."

For some Reformed theologians of around 1700, such as Wilhelmus à Brakel, David Flud van Giffen, and Friedrich Adolph Lampe, 2 Corinthians 3:16 was an obvious argument for a future conversion of ethnic Israel.[47] In recent times, Reformed theologian F. W. Grosheide read the verse in a similar way: "We therefore prefer to translate such that we take Israel as the subject of the clause. Conversion is not excluded for Israel."[48] Elsewhere, he wrote:

> Thus, Paul states the possibility (Gk. *hēnika an* with the conjunctive aorist, *as soon as possible*[49]) that the Jews are converted to the Lord, Rom. 11:23, in which *kurios* in this context can refer only to Christ. . . . Paul states the possibility in general that the Jews will convert. When this occurs (and as often as it does), the *kalumma* [veil] *around them is taken away* . . . , then the entire heart becomes free, and the law can find entrance, is written in the heart, v. 3, and understood in the right way.[50]

---

45. Adversus Marcion V.11.
46. Alford (1958, ad loc.); Allo (1956, ad loc.); Hughes (1962, 113n9).
47. See Van Campen (2007, 196, 429, 501).
48. Grosheide (1955, 54).
49. Footnote by Grosheide: "Thus, Paul was not speaking here of a national conversion of Israel, ..."
50. Grosheide (1959, 108).

In summary, 2 Corinthians 3:16 might point to a possible future conversion of Israel, but the wording is not clear enough to view the verse as an unmistakable prediction of a national conversion of Israel.

14.4.2 Second Thessalonians 2:4

In 2 Thessalonians 2:3-4, we read about the "man of lawlessness," the "son of destruction," whom many expositors believe to be identical with the man referred to by the apostle John as the "Antichrist."[51] It is the man "who opposes and exalts himself against every so-called god or object of worship, so that he takes his seat in the temple of God, proclaiming himself to be God" (v. 4).

Elsewhere I have discussed this passage extensively.[52] Here it is necessary only to identify this seemingly Jewish element in the text: the "temple." Many have endeavored to spiritualize this temple, suggesting that the verse was referring to an appearance of the Antichrist within the Christian church.[53] To be sure, the Ecclesia was indeed compared to a temple in the New Testament,[54] but this meaning is hardly fitting in this passage. "Take one's seat in the temple"[55] is too physical an expression to refer to anything other than a literal temple. Every first-century reader would have thought here immediately of the temple in Jerusalem, *not* of some arbitrary pagan temple, for in that case Paul would have used the indefinite article ("*a* temple" instead of "*the* temple"). No, he was referring to what for each Jew and every converted Gentile was "*the* temple of God" (Gk. *ton naon tou theou*): the Second Temple, which at the time this passage was written was still standing in Jerusalem in full splendor.

Of course, we are not claiming that this prediction was not fulfilled because this temple was destroyed in AD 70 without the An-

---

51. This term appears only in 1 John 2:18, 22; 4:3; and 2 John 1:7.
52. Ouweneel (2012a, §8.1.2 and 10.5.2).
53. For Maljaars (2015, 25–26), it is *a priori* certain that the verse has nothing to do with (some temple in) Israel.
54. 1 Cor. 3:16; 2 Cor. 6:16; Eph. 2:20-22.
55. Cf. 1 Sam. 1:9; Matt. 26:55; Luke 2:46; John 2:14; 8:2; Acts 3:10.

tichrist having arrived. "The" temple is always one and the same, even if various distinct forms of the temple appear after each other: the temple of Solomon, the temple of Zerubbabel, the temple of Herod, the temple of the Antichrist (2 Thess. 2:4; Rev. 11:1-2), and the temple of Ezekiel (chapters 40-44).[56]

In the light of Daniel 9:27 and 12:11, we think in 2 Thessalonians 2:4 immediately of "the abomination of desolation" (cf. Matt. 24:15).[57] The reference there is to a future abominable idolatrous image that would be placed in the temple, but in Daniel 11:31 (cf. 8:11-12) the reference was to a similar kind of idolatrous image that Antiochus IV Epiphanes had erected in the Second Temple (167 BC). Antiochus originated from the third (Greco-Macedonian) empire, while the idolatrous image of Daniel 9:27 (and Matt. 24:15) will originate from the empire that had destroyed the temple in Jerusalem again (Dan. 9:26; AD 70), that is the fourth, the Roman Empire. In Revelation 13, we are told that the second "beast," later called the "false prophet" (Rev. 16:13; 19:20; 20:10), commands an idolatrous image to be erected, that is, an image of the Roman ruler (vv. 14-15):

> ... by the signs that it is allowed to work in the presence of the [first] beast it [i.e., the second beast] deceives those who dwell on earth, telling them to make an image for the beast that was wounded by the sword and yet lived. And it was allowed to give breath to the image of the beast, so that the image of the beast might even speak and might cause those who would not worship the image of the beast to be slain.

I cannot doubt that this is the same image intended in Daniel 9:27. A continuous line runs from Antiochus's image of Zeus (supreme deity of the Greek pantheon)[58] to the Roman beast of the end time. In both cases, we are dealing with an image of basically the same supreme deity of the pagan world. In reality, this is a demonic power, which, in the invisible world, stands behind the

---

56. Even the tabernacle in Shiloh is called the "temple of the LORD" (1 Sam. 1:9; 3:3).

57. See more extensively Ouweneel (2012a, §§4.1.1, 6.5.3).

58. 2 Maccabees 6:2: "[The king] was also to defile their [i.e., the Jews'] Temple by dedicating it to the Olympian god Zeus. The temple on Mount Gerizim was to be officially named Temple of Zeus the God of Hospitality, as the people who lived there had requested."

ruler involved, whether King Antiochus or the Roman "beast," or, to put it differently, the power of which this ruler is the physical embodiment.

14.4.3 The Two "Beasts"

Elsewhere, I have discussed whether the Antichrist is the same as the first beast of Revelation 13, that is, the "Roman" supreme leader, or the same as the second "beast," the "false prophet."[59] Or perhaps the two are so strongly connected that together they constitute one single anti-Christian power. Some have compared them to Adolf Hitler and his minister of propaganda, Joseph Goebbels.

At any rate, 2 Thessalonians 2:4 says not only that there will be an idolatrous image in the temple, but that the "man of lawlessness" places *himself* in the temple to have himself worshiped as God, or as a god—and perhaps the image being there, and the man himself being there as well, eventually amounts to the same thing. In order to understand the nature of this divine veneration, we must have knowledge of the angelic prince who stands behind every great, powerful world leader.[60] For instance, Isaiah 14, dealing with the king of Babylon, cannot be understood (especially not vv. 12-15) if we do not perceive "behind" him his angelic prince, an exalted spiritual power in the heavenly spheres, perhaps Satan himself, or an exalted servant of his (cf. 51:9; Jer. 51:34, 44). And in Revelation 12-13, it is the "dragon," that is, Satan himself (12:9; 20:2), who is the angelic prince of the Roman Empire (compare the similarities between 12:3 and 13:1, i.e., between the dragon [Satan] and the "beast," i.e., the Roman Empire as well as the human supreme ruler of this Empire).

The two "beasts," later called "the" beast and the false prophet—are two men, but their real power lies in the higher, invisible world. We see this in three passages:

(a) The "coming of the lawless one is by the activity of Satan with all power and false signs and wonders" (2 Thess. 2:9).

(b) The "dragon" (Rev. 12:9) gives his authority to the beast; apparently, this person has no power in himself, but receives it from the netherworld (Rev. 13:4).

---

59. Ouweneel (2012a, chapter 8).
60. See extensively, Ouweneel (2003a, especially §§4.1, 5.3.3, and 9.1).

(c) The second beast deceivingly looks like the Lamb, but speaks like the dragon, that is, it is Satan speaking through his mouth (Rev. 13:11 GNV).

The two "beasts" are servants or even embodiments, personifications of the "dragon" (Satan). In the book of Revelation, Satan, the angelic prince of the Roman Empire, is essentially the same as the supreme deity of that empire: Jupiter, who is identical with the Greek Zeus, and the Babylonian Bel. Worshiping the image of the Roman beast is not only worshiping a man; it is worshiping Satan, the "dragon," the spiritual power behind the two "beasts" of Revelation 13. Thus, 2 Thessalonians 2 is basically all about Satanism: the beast wants to be worshiped as a god, but in fact this god is his angelic prince, the dragon. In the darkest stage of the end time, in the last three and a half years, the "dragon" (Satan) will be worshiped by apostate humanity, just as the Babylonians once worshiped the "dragon." The temple is the place where the true God must be worshiped. It is this very place that is chosen by the "dragon" to be worshiped "in the beast." I imagine that this will be the absolute nadir in the spiritual history of both ethnic Israel and (nominal) Christianity.

14.5 Israel in Revelation 7–11[61]

14.5.1 Revelation 7:1–8[62]

In Revelation 7:1–8, a very special group of Israelites was separated from the great majority of Israel. In verses 1–2 we hear about angels "who had been given power to harm earth and sea." But another angel says, "Do not harm the earth or the sea or the trees, until

---

61. I have made use of many commentaries, which I will not always mention. Except the ones mentioned in the footnotes below, these are especially Darby (*SYN* 8; *CW* 2, 5, 11, 28, 30); Kelly (1868; 1870; 1970a); Snell (1878); Whybrow (1898); Baines (1879); Grant (1902; n.d.-a; n.d.-b); Chater (1914); Voorhoeve (1918; 1969); Ironside (1930); Burton (1932); Newell (1935); Jennings (1937); Lenski (1943); Lang (1945); Tatford (1947); McDowell (1951); Swete (1951); Lohmeyer (1953); Lilje (1957); Seiss (1957); Cox (1959); Barclay (1960); Van Ryn (1960); Rossier (1961; 1967); Farrer (1964); Glasson (1965); Preston & Hanson (1968); Beasley-Murray (1974); Ford (1975); Kraft (1974); Moffatt (1979); Barnhouse (1985); Tenney (1985); Bellett (n.d.); Coates (n.d.); Dennett (n.d.); Hoste (n.d.); Smith (n.d.); Stanley (n.d.). See also the more extensive bibliography in Ouweneel (1990, 271–77).

62. See Ouweneel (1988, 252–55).

we have sealed the servants of our God on their foreheads." This sealing occurs with a visible seal being put on the foreheads. This "other angel" ascends "from the rising of the sun," that is, from the East, from where the new light is coming: the promise of hope, despite the many judgments that will still come upon the earth. Later, it will be in the East that the sun of righteousness rises, when Christ will appear (Mal. 4:2). This return will be "as the lightning comes from the east and shines as far as the west" (Matt. 24:27).

These "servants of our God" are Israelites, namely, the elect among them; their number is mentioned: "144,000, sealed from every tribe of the sons of Israel" (v. 4), that is, 12,000 from every tribe. We have concluded before that the term "Israel" *nowhere* in the New Testament referred to the Ecclesia of God, or to "the people of God of the new dispensation." On the contrary, it is the ongoing testimony of both the Tanakh and the New Testament that, in the end time, a restoration of ethnic Israel that is both national and spiritual will occur. Therefore, there cannot be the slightest doubt that Revelation 7:1–8 was referring to ethnic Israel.

This thesis is supported by two collateral arguments. First, in this passage we hear not only about Israel, but about the twelve tribes of Israel (cf. §13.6). The notion of a "spiritual Israel" (read, the Ecclesia) is objectionable enough in itself, but exegesis becomes completely confused if we were to spiritualize each of the twelve tribes of Israel.

Second, "Israel" with its "twelve tribes" is clearly distinguished here from the "great multitude that no one could number, from every nation, from all tribes and peoples and languages," viewed here as "standing before the throne and before the Lamb, clothed in white robes, with palm branches in their hands" (v. 9).[63] In my view, it is not possible to identify the 144,000 from Israel with this great *innumerable* "multitude," or to view it as a part of this "multitude," as some have tried.[64] This is impossible

(a) because of the phrase "after this," with which the second company is announced (v.9), as distinct from the former company;

(b) because of the size of these companies: in the first case exact-

---

63. *Contra* Maljaars (2015, 127), who views the two companies as identical, which exegetically is incomprehensible.

64. E.g., Greijdanus (1965, 131–32).

ly 144,000 (irrespective of whether one understands this number to be symbolic; at any rate it is "numbered"), and in the second case "innumerable";

(c) because of the status: the 144,000 are being sealed *before* the "great tribulation," the innumerable multitude comes triumphantly *out of* the "great tribulation."

The prophecies strongly emphasize that, in the end time, all twelve tribes will be represented again in the Holy Land.[65] Actually, it is a mistake to think that after the Babylonian captivity, only Israelites from the tribes of Judah and Benjamin were present in the land of Israel (in spite of Ezra 1:5). Thus, we heard the prophetess Anna confess that she was from the tribe of Asher (Luke 2:36), while there were also Levites in the land.[66] Today, too, many Jews in and outside of Israel trace their origins to tribes other than Judah and Benjamin (and Levi).[67]

In Ezekiel 48, we were told how the division of the land would happen during the Messianic kingdom. The land will be divided up into twelve horizontal strips, that is, very different from the situation in the Tanakh. One reason for this is so that the two tribes and the half tribe beyond Jordan—Reuben, Gad, and half-Manasseh—will finally receive their place—which they despised at the time—within the Holy Land (cf. the earlier situation in Num. 32). Seven tribes will receive an area for living north of the "holy district" (45:1–7)—a special area consecrated to the LORD, where the new temple will be built—and five tribes south of it.

A chapter like Ezekiel 48 is a crystal-clear example of the exegetical problems that supersessionists face repeatedly when trying to spiritualize the prophecies in a plausible way. Just one example: the Annotations to the Dutch States Translation viewed the equality of the portions as a reference to the communion of the saints. This is too egregious for comment.

---

65. Isa. 11:12–13, 16; 27:13 ("those who were lost in the land of Assyria"); Ezek. 20:40; 37:21–22; 48:1–8, 23–29.

66. Luke 10:32; John 1:19; Acts 4:36, and, of course, the many New Testament reference to the priests in Israel, from Matt. 2:4 to Acts 26:12.

67. An Israeli friend and colleague of mine, who claimed to belong to the tribe of Simeon, died in the Yom Kippur war of 1973.

14.5.2 Revelation 10:1–11:13

In Revelation 5, we are told about a scroll (Gk. *biblion*), which relates to the "little scroll" (one word: Gk. *biblaridion*) in Revelation 10:2, 9–10, as the subject of the large book — covering all the earth — relates to that of the little book, which is limited to Israel in the time of the end (see the "temple" and the "holy city" in 11:2).[68] In the light of chapter 11:1–13, and by way of analogy to the scroll in chapter 5,[69] we may assume that the little book of Revelation 10 contains:[70]

(a) Christ's rights of ownership regarding Israel, and especially Jerusalem,

(b) the judgments needed to cleanse Israel and Jerusalem and to restore them to God's blessings,

(c) the revelation of God's counsel with respect to Israel and Jerusalem: the final judgment of his enemies, blessing for the faithful in Israel, renewal of city and land, glorification of God and of the Lamb.

F. F. Bruce believed that Revelation 11:1–13 forms the content of the little book.[71] Expositors who do not link the little book especially with Israel see in this booklet the Word of God, the gospel, or the prophetic Word in its entirety.[72]

After the introduction of the little book in Revelation 10, we find in chapter 11:1–13 this command to the prophet:

> Rise and measure the temple of God and the altar and those who worship there, but do not measure the court outside the temple; leave that out, for it is given over to the nations, and they will trample the holy city for forty-two months. And I will grant authority to my two witnesses, and they will prophesy for 1,260 days, clothed in sackcloth.

The text clearly tells us what period is in view here: it is the last half "week" of Daniel 9:27 (see §13.3): forty-two months (Rev. 11:2;

---

68. See Ouweneel (1990, 27–52).
69. Ouweneel (1988, 219n21).
70. Ouweneel (1990, 30n6).
71. Bruce (1969, 649); cf. Charles (1920, 1:260); Mounce (1977, 216).
72. Greijdanus (1965, 163); Walvoord (1966, 173–74); Morris (1969, 141); Hendriksen (1944, 151).

13:5), or 1,260 days (11:3; 12:6), or "a time [year], and times [two years], and half a time", that is, three and a half years. The text also tells us the location of the events: earthly Jerusalem; see especially Revelation 11:8, which speaks of "the great city that symbolically [or, spiritually] is called Sodom and Egypt, *where their Lord was crucified.*" Because many expositors do not wish to accept that the passage refers to literal Jerusalem, they tell us that Revelation 11:1-13 is exceptionally difficult to explain.[73] The Bible passage deals with Israel and Jerusalem, but supersessionists do not *want* the passage to be about literal Israel, and *therefore* they have a hard time expounding it because of the unnecessary and superfluous exegetical difficulties they have created.

In defense of the literal exegesis of this passage, I point first to the fact that during the Messianic kingdom, Israel will again possess an earthly temple and a literal altar.[74] Shortly before the return of Christ, there will some kind of "holy place," where sacrifices will be brought.[75] The temple and the altar mentioned in Revelation 11:1-2 are the expression of the service of the godly Jews, whereas the court refers to the "outsiders," that is, the wicked Jews together with the wicked Gentiles, who together will "trample" the godly Jews (cf. 13:7; Isa. 10:6; 63:18).

The speculations about the "two witnesses" in Revelation 11:1-13 are numerous.[76] First, we have the supersessionist view, sees the passage as having referred to the Ecclesia, or as having a universal redemptive-historical significance. The "two witnesses" are then viewed as a symbol of, for instance, the Tanakh and the New Testament, or law and prophets, or law and gospel, or Israel and the Word of God. Or these witnesses supposedly symbolized certain historical martyrs (or the totality of all the martyrs[77]), or certain

---

73. E.g., Mounce (1977, 218; Johnson (2006, ad loc.).

74. Isa. 2:2–3; 19:19; 56:7; 60:7; 66:20; Ezek. 40–44; Joel 3:18; Micah 4:1–2; Zech. 6:12–15; 14:20–21.

75. Some orthodox Jews in Israel are preparing the construction of what they call the Third Temple; see, e.g., www.templemountfaithful.org.

76. See the survey in Ouweneel (1990, 44–45n26) with references.

77. Kiddle (1940, ad loc.); Caird (1966, ad loc.); Morris (1969, ad loc.).

groups of martyrs,[78] or they represent the Ecclesia in general,[79] or they refer to two Christian prophets in the end time.[80] In my view, none of these interpretations can do justice to (a) the clearly Jewish context, and (b) the specific, supernatural power of the witnesses (vv. 5-6), and (c) their absolutely exceptional death as well as resurrection (vv. 7-12).

Second, in contrast with the former group, some expositors correctly refer the passage to Israel, although they differ about how many elements in these verses must be taken literally. Some believe that the passage was speaking in very general, symbolic terms about the future restoration of Israel,[81] but in my view this interpretation does not do justice to the many specific details. Therefore, I chose the exegesis according to which these verses speak of the literal temple and city during the Great Tribulation. Some have suggested that the two witnesses are the literally returning[82] Moses and Elijah because one turns water into blood (cf. Exod. 7:19-20), and the other makes all rain to cease (1 Kings 17:1). Others have thought of Enoch and Elijah (Tertullian), or two unnamed prophets,[83] or an indeterminate number of prophets.[84]

The details of the passage do not concern us any further here. My only goal right now is to make it plausible that, Revelation 10:1-11:13 was referring to the time of the end as well as to the literal Jerusalem. In this way, this passage, too, constitutes a piece of teaching concerning the future of ethnic Israel, within the physical land of Israel, in the time of the end.

---

78. See the summary by Ford (1975, 177–78).
79. Greijdanus (1965, ad loc.); Rissi (1968); Bruce (1969, ad loc.); Mounce (1977, ad loc.).
80. Minear (1968, ad loc.); Johnson (2006, ad loc.).
81. Beckwith (1922, ad loc.); Zahn (1924, ad loc.); Ladd (1972, ad loc.).
82. Not necessarily in the sense of some reincarnation; John the Baptist could have been the Elijah who was to come (Matt. 11:14), but then, not literally but as one who came "in the spirit and power of Elijah" (Luke 1:17).
83. Gaebelein (1961, ad loc.).
84. Scott (1920, ad loc.); see Ouweneel (1990, 39–52).

14.6 Revelation 12
14.6.1 The Woman in Revelation 12

In Revelation 12:1-2 and 5 we read:

> And a great sign appeared in heaven: a woman clothed with the sun, with the moon under her feet, and on her head a crown of twelve stars. She was pregnant and was crying out in birth pains and the agony of giving birth. . . . She gave birth to a male child [lit. a male son], one who is to rule all the nations with a rod of iron, but her child was caught up to God and to his throne.

There is wide difference of opinion about this "son";[85] some have suggested that this would be an image of the Ecclesia, which is predestined to rule with Christ, and is "snatched away" (Gk. *hērpastē*) to God (the "rapture"[86] of the Ecclesia[87]). However, the Ecclesia would certainly have been presented as a woman, as in Revelation 19-22. The "son," who moreover is called "male," can be no one other than Christ. He is the only One who was not only "caught up" to God, but also to the latter's throne, whereas the Ecclesia has never had a place at the heavenly throne of God.[88]

On the identity of the "woman" in the quoted passage there is much more difference of opinion.

(1) Alan F. Johnson saw in the woman the covenantal-Messianic community, which began with the Messiah-expecting Jews in whose circle the Messiah was born, and by John the Baptist was separated from the rest of Israel.[89] This circle supposedly culminated in the Ecclesia, the "new Israel." We have already dismissed this supersessionist view. As an additional point, I would point out that this view does not honor the difference between the woman giving birth to the Messiah (Rev. 12) and the woman whom the Messiah marries (Rev. 19-22). Metaphors do must remain plausible: the mother and the wife can hardly be identical.

---

85. See Ouweneel (1990, 64 note 5).
86. Cf. 1 Thess. 4:17, the same verb *harpazō*, "to snatch away, to rapture."
87. See Ouweneel (2012a, chapter 10).
88. Cf. the contrast in Rev. 3:21, and cf. Eph. 1:20 with 2:6: Christ is seated in heaven "at God's right hand," but this is never said of the Ecclesia, though it is said to be seated in heaven as well.
89. Johnson (1981, 514).

In the Tanakh, Israel is often presented as the wife of the LORD, and the LORD as her Husband.[90] When she became apostate and was set aside, Israel was referred to as the rejected one, either a widow or a prostitute.[91] However, in the time of the end she is accepted again as the bride.[92] This extensive imagery supports the understanding that in Revelation 12, only Israel—wife of God and mother of his Son—could have been meant. Only Israel can say, "... *to us* a child is born, *to us* a son is given"[93] (Isa. 9:5; cf. Micah 5:2; Romans 9:5).

(2) In my view, to understand the woman of Revelation 12 as the physical mother of Jesus, as the Roman Catholic tradition does, totally conflicts with the character of Mary in the Gospels. Jesus rejects special privileges for her (Luke 11:28) and never calls her "mother," only "woman."[94] She was never mentioned again after Acts 1:14. Therefore, it would be quite strange if Revelation 12 had suddenly presented her in such magnificent glory. Moreover, the persecution of the woman by the "dragon," and the persecution of the "rest of her offspring" (vv. 13, 17), do not make sense if the woman is understood to be Mary. Actually, Joseph Ratzinger expressed himself in a nuanced way: "When the Book of Revelation speaks of the great sign of a Woman appearing in heaven, she is understood to represent all Israel, indeed, the whole Church. The Church must continually give birth to Christ in pain (cf. Rev 12:1-6)."[95] This is indeed supersessionist, but not Mariocentric.

(3) We pass over here some other interpretations, such as mythological parallelisms (with the Egyptian god Horus, the Babylonian god Marduk, or the Greek god Apollo), or the interpretation related to this that we are dealing here with the birth of the heavenly Mes-

---

90. See especially Isa. 54:5; Jer. 2:2; 3:14; 31:32; Ezek. 16:32; 23:4; Hos. 2:16.
91. Isa. 50:1; 54:4–7; 62:4; Jer. 3:6-10; Hos. 2:1.
92. Isa. 49:18; 54:6–8; 61:10; 62:4–5; Hos. 2:18–19.
93. Normally, a child is always born "to" a man, but there are exceptions: "born to Naomi" (Ruth 4:17).
94. John 2:4; 19:26; cf. Luke 8:19–21; Gal. 4:4; not in any pejorative sense; cf. "dear woman" in many translations, or even "dear lady" (ISV); cf. EXB, "... a respectful form of address in that culture".
95. Ratzinger (2011, 222).

siah from a heavenly mother, possibly before the creation began.[96] It is possible, though, that the book of Revelation was suggesting a contrast with the early deceased son of the Emperor Diocletian, whom the latter declared to be divine, together with his mother. Coins show the young god with a ruler's staff, or with sun, moon, and planets.

(4) The idea that the woman represents Israel has been combated by the supersessionist Hendrik van de Kamp.[97] However, his arguments are not applicable because of a well-known circular argument: his starting point is the very thing that must first be demonstrated, namely, that Revelation 12 wishes to show "to the Christian church the background of its persecution." His second mistaken bias is that no distinct glorious future would be awaiting Israel. As a consequence, Van de Kamp does not see that verse 1 portrays Israel not as it was in the first century, but ideally, that is, in terms of what the people and its future are, and will be, according to God's counsel.

From the latter perspective, the woman is viewed as "clothed with the sun," that is, with the highest authority and power on earth (cf. also Ps. 104:1-2). She has "the moon under her feet," where the moon represents dependent or delegated authority, namely, subordinated to Israel. During the Messianic kingdom, all earthly authorities will be subjected to Israel (cf. Dan. 7:27 ESV with footnotes). Israel will surpass all nations of the world. "[A]nd on her head a crown [or, wreath] of twelve stars." Although the passage speaks of the birth of the Messiah, the woman is portrayed here with the glory with which she will be invested during the Messianic kingdom. Because the Messiah is great, his mother is great. The supersessionist theology of Roman Catholicism has applied this to Mary; a theology that honors the literal interpretation of the Israel prophecies applies this to Israel.

Not as an argument, but as an image, I point here to Song 3:11, where King Solomon, a type of the Messiah, arrives for his wedding, and where his mother, Bathsheba, is mentioned in quite a remarkable role, not with *her* crown but with the one she was holding for her son:

---

96. Rist (1957, 452).

97. Van de Kamp (1990, 210–11).

> Go out, O daughters of Zion,
>> and look upon King Solomon,
> with the crown with which his mother crowned him
>> on the day of his wedding,
>> on the day of the gladness of his heart.

14.6.2 Vicissitudes of the Woman

Revelation 12 continues (v. 2): "She was pregnant and was crying out in birth pains and the agony of giving birth." This is remarkable, for Israel did not experience any birth pains at all when Jesus was born; it hardly noticed his birth (apart from the infanticide at Bethlehem). However, compare here the vernacular of Isaiah 66:7: "Before she was in labor she gave birth; before her pain came upon her she delivered a son." This is quite a conspicuous metaphor; in conflict with the normal order of things, Israel first will "give birth" and only later experience "birth pains"! The latter will be the Great Tribulation, the distress of Jacob (Jer. 30:6–7): "Ask now, and see, can a man bear a child? Why then do I see every man with his hands on his stomach like a woman in labor? Why has every face turned pale? Alas! That day is so great there is none like it; it is a time of distress for Jacob; yet he shall be saved out of it."

Similarly, Micah 5:2 announces the birth of the Messiah, as this took place two thousand years ago, while verses 3–4 speak of the future: "Therefore he shall give them up until the time when she [i.e., Israel] who is in labor has given birth; then the rest of his brothers shall return to the people of Israel."[98]

For this strange sequence, we must remember that the majority of Israel has not yet accepted its Messiah; it is still expecting Messiah's first coming. When Jesus comes again, he will "branch out from his place" (Zech. 6:12). He will "come from Zion" (Rom. 11:26), as if only then he will be "given birth' by the nation. The seeming difficulty in Revelation 12 comes from the fact that the past was being immediately connected with the future, namely, with the birth pains of the "Great Tribulation" (vv. 13–17), which will lead to the second coming (the second "birth") of Christ.

Beginning with Revelation 12:6, we find Israel in the last half "week" (1,260 days; cf. v. 14: "a time, and times, and half a time,"

---

98. See on this, besides Scott (1920, 248–49), e.g., Smith (1961, 181–84).

which is three and a half years), where it will have to fear the terrible tyranny of the "dragon" (Satan; v. 9; 20:2), who will have been cast from heaven (vv. 7–12). His fury will turn especially against Israel, which after all is *the* unique object of God's counsels (vv. 13–18).[99] She receives a hiding place in the "wilderness." Notice here the parallels with the exodus from Egypt:

(a) As the woman fled into the wilderness, Israel fled into the wilderness during the exodus (cf. Exod. 13:18).

(b) As the dragon persecuted the woman, the Pharaoh (whose angelic prince was also a "dragon"! cf. Isa. 51:9) persecuted Israel.[100]

(c) The two wings of the great eagle with which the woman escaped remind us of Exodus 19:4 and Deuteronomy 32:11–12 (about the eagle's wings on which Israel was borne).

(d) The river by which the dragon tried to devour the woman reminds us of the Nile (Exod. 1:22) and the Red Sea (Exod. 14).

(e) The earth that opened its mouth swallowing the river reminds us of Korah and his band, for whom the earth opened its mouth to swallow the band (Num. 16:31–33).

(f) In the wilderness, the woman was miraculously nourished (Rev. 12:14), just as Israel was in the wilderness.[101]

(g) The woman is the mother of the Messiah; thus, Israel in Egypt and the wilderness was in principle already the bearer of the Messiah, "rejoicing over the King" (Num. 23:21 CSB); "a star shall come out of Jacob, and a scepter shall rise out of Israel" (24:17).[102]

Elsewhere, we find similar parallelisms between the exodus from Egypt *and* the exodus from Babylon *and* the restoration of the remnant in the time of the end.[103] In this end time, too, it is as if the faithful in Israel will reach the promised land of the Messianic kingdom through the "wilderness." However, this time it will not take forty years, but "only" three and a half years ("only" between quotation marks: "Indeed, if the length of this time had not been

---

99. Ouweneel (1990, 79–83).

100. Exod. 14:8; Ps. 74:13; 89:10; Isa. 51:9.

101. Exod. 16; Deut. 8:14–16; Ps78:23–29; 105:40.

102. Notice the flexibility of the types: Israel is "firstborn son: (Exod. 4:22), but it is also the "woman" who gives birth to the "firstborn Son" (cf. Heb. 1:6).

103. Isa. 48:20–21; Jer. 31:1–6; Ezek. 20:8–10, 33–38; Hos. 2:14–15.

limited, no one would survive," Matt. 24:22 CJB). For further details concerning Revelation 12, I refer to my comments elsewhere.[104]

14.7 Israel in Revelation 13–16

14.7.1 Revelation 13:14–18

For the two "beasts" mentioned in Revelation 13, I refer to what I have written elsewhere about the Antichrist.[105] Here I will limit myself to verses 14–18, where we hear of an image that can refer to nothing but "the abomination of desolation" mentioned by Daniel (9:27; 12:11) and by Jesus (Matt. 24:15) (see chapter 13 above).[106] In all these cases, we encounter an image of a chief Gentile power that suppresses the faithful in Israel. This image of the Roman beast is not necessarily a literal statue of this dictator, but rather a visible expression of the "beast's" power, in whatever form it may appear. The same occurred in the time of the Babylonian empire of Nebuchadnezzar, who commanded his subjects to bow down before the image that he had erected (Dan. 3). Given the measures of that image (sixty cubits high, six cubits wide) it can hardly have been a statue of the king. However, it did represent his power, and in particular his dark angelic prince.

The measures just given (sixty by six) suggest a link with Revelation 13:18, "This calls for wisdom: let the one who has understanding calculate the number of the beast, for it is the number of a man, and his number is 666." The number six reminds us of the sixth day of creation, the "day of humanity." The 6 x 60 strengthens this, referring to Nebuchadnezzar as the greatest authority on earth in his time, and the number 666 is the climax of this development: the Antichrist is fallen man *par excellence*.

The false prophet receives the power to give "breath" (Gk. *pneuma*) to this image. "Breath" is not the same as life; only the Creator can create life. Apparently, we are dealing here with an imitation of life, which however has the capacity to deceive people (in contrast with this, cf. Rev. 11:11, which speaks of the "breath/spirit [*pneuma*] of life"). Presumably, John was thinking here of the example of his own days: people were forced to worship the statue of the

---

104. Ouweneel (1990, 62–83).

105. Ouweneel (2012a, chapter 8).

106. Ouweneel (1990, 96–101).

emperor, whereby the imperial priests were misleading the people with magic tricks and ventriloquism. In the end times, presumably more will be needed to impress the people: possibly a combination of certain forms of occultism and technology?

I have discussed the details more extensively elsewhere;[107] at present, I wish to emphasize especially that, if we compare here Scripture with Scripture (see in particular Matt. 24:15 and 2 Thess. 2:4), it seems likely that this image of the Roman beast—"the abomination of desolation"—is erected in some restored "holy place" in Jerusalem. Thus, once again: the end times presuppose the people of Israel have returned to the Promised Land, as well as a "holy place" that can pass for a temple, in which the false prophet will erect the image mentioned.

14.7.2 Revelation 14:1–5

In the opening verses of Revelation 14, we see Christ for the first time not on God's throne in heaven, as in chapter 3:21, or before God's throne, as in chapter 5, but on earth, in connection with the 144,000 sealed ones from Israel. The Lamb is standing here on Mount Zion, which in the Bible plays an important role as the place of the temple and of God's presence in the midst of his people. See for instance Psalm 78:67–70:

> [God] rejected the tent of Joseph;
> > he did not choose the tribe of Ephraim,[108]
> but he chose the tribe of Judah,
> > Mount Zion, which he loves.
> He built his sanctuary like the high heavens,
> like the earth, which he has founded forever.
> He chose David his servant. . . . .

Zion—a broad term usually referring to all Jerusalem—was chosen by God in order to establish his sanctuary there, as well as the seat of David's royalty.[109] Consider as well Hebrews 12:22,

---

107. Ibid.

108. Ephraim, though the younger son, received Joseph's birthright (Gen. 48:18–20), just as Joseph, one of Jacob's youngest sons, received Jacob's birthright (1 Chron. 5:1). Great leaders came from Ephraim: Joshua and Jeroboam, but in the end, God's fulfilled his promises to Judah (Gen. 49:8–12).

109. See Ouweneel (2012a, §13.1.2).

where Mount Zion represented in a special way the new spiritual order of God. Mount Sinai is the mountain of the Old Covenant, but Zion is the mountain of the New Covenant, the mountain of God's goodness and mercy.[110]

Apparently, the 144,000 (cf. Rev. 7:1-8) come here out of the Great Tribulation, in which they have continually remained faithful to their Lord (14:4-5). Already before the Messianic kingdom, they were being viewed in the status they will then possess, with the name of the Lamb and the name of his Father on their foreheads. This forms a sharp contrast with those who have the mark of the beast on their right hand or on their forehead, and thus are servants and followers of the beast, the eschatological world power.[111]

The 144,000 are "these who have not defiled themselves with women, for they are virgins" (Rev. 14:4a). This cannot be taken literally, for in that case the 144,000 would consist of men only. In my view, the text implies a contrast with spiritual lewdness.[112] Compare 2 Corinthians 11:2: the Ecclesia has been "betrothed to one husband," to be "a pure virgin to Christ," not intermingling with the evil world around her. The false church is called a prostitute (Rev. 17-18), but the true church is the virgin bride of Christ (19:6-9; 21:2, 9; 22:17). Israel, too, is often compared to a virgin, or called upon to remain a virgin;[113] thus, if it falls into spiritual fornication (linked with idolatry), it is called a prostitute.[114]

The 144,000 are described as followers of the Lamb "wherever he goes," namely, during the Great Tribulation. They follow their beloved Master in the way that he himself went before them, persecuted by the Romans as represented by Pilate, and by their own people as represented by Caiaphas and Herod. In my view, Pilate and Herod may be compared with the first (political) "beast," and Caiaphas with the second (religious) "beast' in Revelation 13. After

---

110. Cf. Gal. 4:24–27, where Zion is implied; cf. v. 27 with Isa. 54:1, and cf. the latter with Isa. 49:14–21 and with 51:1–8; see further Ps. 2:6–8; 48:1–3; 125:1; 126:1; Isa. 24:23; Joel 2:32; Obad. 1:17, 21; Micah 4:2, 7–8; Zeph. 3:14–17; see extensively, Ouweneel (1982, 2:86–87).

111. Rev. 13:16–17; 14:9, 11; 16:2; 19:20; 20:4.

112. Cf. Rev. 2:14, 20–21; 9:21; 14:8; Rev. 17–18 on the "great prostitute"; 19:2.

113. Isa. 37:22; Jer. 18:13; 31:4, 21; Lam. 2:13; Amos 5:2.

114. Jer. 3:6; Ezek. 16:15–17; 23:1–5; Hos. 2:5.

the 144,000 have followed the Lamb in his sufferings, they will also follow him in his glory.[115]

They "have been redeemed from mankind as firstfruits for God and the Lamb" (Rev. 14:4b; cf. v. 3; 5:9): firstfruits of the great harvest in the Messianic kingdom, formed during the Great Tribulation. They are the firstfruits of a very large nation of Israel, the majority of which will be born only *after* the beginning of the Messianic kingdom.[116] These firstlings will always take up a special place among that nation because they are the ones who have passed through the Great Tribulation. "And in their mouth no lie was found, for they are blameless" (v. 5). This is an important fruit of the Spirit, worked in these faithful ones during a period so horrible that one could believe to be able to maintain oneself over against the oppressors only through lies (cf. Zeph. 3:13).

14.7.3 Revelation 16:13–16

> And I saw, coming out of the mouth of the dragon and out of the mouth of the beast and out of the mouth of the false prophet, three unclean spirits like frogs. For they are demonic spirits, performing signs, who go abroad to the kings of the whole world, to assemble them for battle on the great day of God the Almighty. . . . And they assembled them at the place that in Hebrew is called Armageddon.

Here we find the unholy "trinity" of Revelation assembled together: the "dragon," that is, the devil (12:9; 20:2), the "beast," that is, the "beast from the sea" (13:1–10), the Roman ruler, and the "false prophet," that is apparently, the "beast from the earth" (13:11–18), who erects the image for the first beast (see 19:20). Coming forth from these three are "unclean spirits," who in the spiritual world have the form of frogs,[117] and who assemble the earthly hosts of the "beast." The Greek term for "world" here is *oikoumenē*, a term sometimes referring to the Roman Empire (cf. Luke 2:1; Acts 17:6). As by a mysterious hand these armies are directed toward the land of Israel. This is not the hand of the unholy trinity but the hand of

---

115. Cf. Rom. 8:17; 2 Tim. 2:12; 1 Pet. 4:13.
116. Cf. Ps. 22:30; 48:13; 78:4, 6; 102:18; Isa. 65:20–23.
117. Dark spiritual powers are compared to serpents (2 Cor. 11:3; Rev. 12:9), scorpions (Luke 10:19), locusts (Rev. 9:3), frogs (our text), not to mention the "satyrs" (Isa. 13:21 KJV), the "basilisks" (11:8 DRA) and others.

God, if we follow the version that has "he" in verse 16: "*he* gathered them together . . . ." It is not Satan and his companions but God who holds the threads of history in his hand (cf. Prov. 21:1).

The armies gather in Armageddon (v. 16, Gk. *harmagedōn*), a name that presumably is a variation of the Hebrew word *har-m'gid-dōn*, meaning "mountain (ridge) of Megiddo." This mountain (ridge) itself cannot serve as a battlefield; apparently what is intended is the large plain of Jezreel, lying at the foot of the mountain. The size of this plain is 14 by 20 miles or 23 by 32 kilometers, and in the course of history more than two hundred battles have been fought there.[118] Others render Armageddon as "city of Megiddo," or (very differently) as "mountain of destruction" (cf. Jer. 51:25, and read Rome for Babylon), or as "mount of assembly" (cf. Isa. 14:13), as the "mount of his gathering of the troops," or as "his fertile mountain," or the "desired city," that is, Zion or Jerusalem.[119] In the latter case, Armageddon could be associated with the Valley of Jehoshaphat, so that there will not be two final battles, one in the North and one near Jerusalem, but just one.[120]

No matter how these details are decided, Armageddon is the literal place where the great final battle between the Lamb and the beast will take place—just as literal as the second coming of Christ himself. Only after the description of the seventh bowl (Rev. 16:17-21), of the great prostitute, the great Babylon (17:1-19:5), and of the Lamb's marriage (19:6-10), do we hear what will occur in Armageddon: the Lamb will come down from heaven (cf. 17:14), and execute judgment upon the dragon, the beast, and the false prophet (19:19-20:3).

14.8 The Two Jerusalems

14.8.1 The Earthly Jerusalem

The very same book of Revelation spoke of both the earthly and the heavenly Jerusalem, without ever confusing the two. In §14.5.2 we considered the earthly Jerusalem of Revelation 11: it is the city where the believers' Lord was crucified (v. 8). In previous sections we have seen what the book of Revelation told us about the future

---

118. Johnson (1981, 551); see, e.g., Judg. 5:19; 2 Kings 9:27; 23:29.
119. Ibid., 552; Mounce (1977, 301-302).
120. Joel 3:2, 12, 14; cf. Zech. 12:2, 9; 14:1-3; 1 Kings 22.

of ethnic Israel, and thus implicitly about the future of the earthly Jerusalem as well. Only supersessionists could have concluded that the prophecies concerning the earthly Jerusalem are being fulfilled in the heavenly Jerusalem.

The glorious Jerusalem of the Messianic kingdom is indeed very earthly; nothing "heavenly" can be discovered in it, apart from the important fact that it will be in a direct *connection* with heaven, and that all its blessings will descend from there.

(a) Its geographical situation is described precisely in Zechariah 14:10–11:

> The whole land shall be turned into a plain from Geba to Rimmon south of Jerusalem. But Jerusalem shall remain aloft on its site from the Gate of Benjamin to the place of the former gate, to the Corner Gate, and from the Tower of Hananel to the king's winepresses. And it shall be inhabited, for there shall never again be a decree of utter destruction. Jerusalem shall dwell in security.

(b) The nations of the *earth* will go up to *this very* Jerusalem:

> It shall come to pass in the latter days
>   that the mountain of the house of the Lord
> shall be established as the highest of the mountains,
>   and shall be lifted up above the hills;
> and all the nations shall flow to it,
>   and many peoples shall come, and say:
> "Come, let us go up to the mountain of the Lord,
>   to the house of the God of Jacob,
> that he may teach us his ways
>   and that we may walk in his paths."
> For out of Zion shall go forth the law,
>   and the word of the Lord from Jerusalem
> (Isa. 2:2–3; cf. Micah 4:1–2).

(c) *There* the new temple will be built: in the *land of Israel*,[121] in Jerusalem, where the literal descendants of the literal Zadok will perform the priestly ministry (Ezek. 40:46; cf. Zadok during the time of David in 2 Sam. 15:35). *To there* the *Shekhinah* will return (Ezek. 43), that is to say, to exactly the same place from where it had departed (Ezek. 9–11).

---

121. Ezek. 40:2; cf. 37:26–28; Isa. 56:7; Zech. 6:12, 15.

(d) The earthly Jerusalem is just as earthly as the land is earthly: "To your offspring I give this land, from the [literal] river of Egypt[122] to the great river, the [literal] river Euphrates" (Gen. 15:18). Compare Ezekiel 47:13–48:35, and also already the territory over which King Solomon ruled: "Solomon ruled over all the kingdoms from the Euphrates to the land of the Philistines and to the border of Egypt" (1 Kings 4:21).

(e) The nations will help rebuild the walls of the earthly city of Jerusalem (Isa. 60:11), and in other respects contribute to its restoration and splendor. (Consider: in what sense could the nations be thought to help rebuilding the walls of the Ecclesia?)

14.8.2 The Heavenly Jerusalem

The New Testament provides are three referents of the spiritual, heavenly Jerusalem, which overlap, yet are distinct. I mention them briefly here, only for the sake of comparison, and will not discuss the matter any further in order not to draw away the attention from the earthly Israel:

(a) "The Jerusalem [that is] above" (Gal. 4:26) represents the entire spiritual order of Christian freedom, standing over against "the present Jerusalem," which referred not so much to the city as such but rather to the system of Judaist legalism, as represented by the Pharisees and scribes in Jesus' days.

(b) "The heavenly Jerusalem" (Heb. 12:22) referred to what I call the "heavenly capital" of the Messianic kingdom (cf. the world to come, the age to come, the good things to come, the blessings to come, the city to come in Heb. 2:5; 6:5; 10:1; 11:20; 13:14, expressions that all refer to the Messianic kingdom).

(c) "The new Jerusalem" (Rev. 3:12; 21:1–22:5) is explicitly called the bride of the Lamb (21:9), as such forming a contrast with the great prostitute (Rev. 17–18).

If we look at the matter superficially, supersessionism might appear to enjoy some support in the sense that some passages, in the Tanakh referring to earthly Jerusalem, are quoted in Revelation 21 and applied to the new Jerusalem. Examples are the "high moun-

---

122. Not the Nile, but the Wadi el-Arish, which of old has been the boundary river between Israel and Egypt. The Euphrates, however, is much further away from present-day Israel.

tain" (v. 10; cf. Ezek. 40:2), the glory of God (v. 11; cf. Isa. 60:1–2, 19), the offerings of the nations (v. 24; cf. Isa. 60:3, 5). This kind of quotations serve to underline the parallels between the earthly and the heavenly Jerusalem (why else would they carry the same name?). However, they do not mean that the earthly Jerusalem would no longer have any future prospects.[123]

This is a general pattern that we cannot emphasize enough, involving a hermeneutical question of the first order:

(a) The predictions concerning the "new Jerusalem" are *not* the fulfillment of the predictions in the Tanakh concerning the *earthly* Jerusalem; they are only parallels, comparisons, applications.

(b) The statements concerning the Ecclesia as a spiritual temple are *not* the fulfillment of the predictions in the Tanakh concerning the *earthly* temple, which soon will be (re-)built at the beginning of the Messianic kingdom.

(c) The statements concerning the "heavenly country" to which the patriarchs were travelling (Heb. 11:14–16) are *not* the fulfillment of the predictions in the Tanakh concerning the *earthly* Israel.

In short: there will be an earthly Jerusalem just as much as there will be a heavenly Jerusalem during the Messianic kingdom. There is no basis for looking forward to the one any more than to the other — they will form an unbreakable unity.

---

123. *Contra*, e.g., Stewart (2018). There no fewer than eleven "Amsterdams" in the United States, but this does not mean that the original Amsterdam has become irrelevant.

Bibliography

Aalders, G. Ch. 1925. *De profeet Jeremia.* KV. Kampen: Kok.

_____. 1949. *De oud-testamentische profetie en de staat Israël.* Kampen: Kok.

Abma, G. H., L. Den Breejen, M. Van Campen, et al. 2011. *Onopgeefbaar verbonden.* Terschuur: n.p.

Adamek, J. 1938. *Vom römischen Endreich der mittelalterlichen Bibelerklärung.* Würzburg: Triltsch.

Alexander, J. A. 1953 (repr. 1846–1847). *Commentary on the Prophecies of Isaiah.* Grand Rapids, MI: Zondervan.

_____. 1980 (repr. 1846/1847). *Commentary on the Prophecies of Isaiah.* Grand Rapids, MI: Zondervan.

Alexander, R. H. 2010. *Ezekiel.* EBC 7. Grand Rapids, MI: Zondervan.

Alford, H. 1958 (repr. 1849–1861). *The Greek Testament.* 4 vols. Chicago: Moody Press.

Allen, L. C. 1976. *The Books of Joel, Obadiah, Jonah and Micah.* NICOT. Grand Rapids, MI: Eerdmans.

Allen, R. B. 2012. *Numbers.* EBC 2. Grand Rapids, MI: Zondervan.

Allo, E. B. 1956. *Saint Paul: Seconde Épitre aux Corinthiens.* 2nd ed. Paris: Gabalda.

Altaf, S. 2013. *Paul of Tarsus: The Thirteenth Apostle.* CreateSpace.

Anderson, R. 1990. *Daniel in the Critics' Den: A Defense of the Historicity of the Book of Daniel.* Grand Rapids, MI: Kregel.

Ankerberg, J. and J. Weldon. 2011. *The Facts on the New Age Movement.* Plano, TX: ATRI Publishing.

Archbold, N. 1993. *De bergen van Israël: Waarom de Westelijke Jordaanoever bij Israël hoort*. Putten: Shalom Books.

Archer, G. L. 1982. *Encyclopedia of Bible Difficulties*. Grand Rapids, MI: Zondervan.

Armstrong, K. 1993. *A History of God: The 4000-Year Quest of Judaism, Christianity, and Islam*. New York: A. A. Knopf. 2000. *Een geschiedenis van God: Vierduizend jaar jodendom, christendom en islam*. Amsterdam: Flamingo (Ambo | Anthos).

Ashley, T. R. 1993. *The Book of Numbers*. NICOT. Grand Rapids, MI: Eerdmans.

Baarda, T., H. Jansen, S. J. Noorda, and J. S. Vos. 1984. *Paulus en de andere joden: Exegetische bijdragen en discussie*. Delft: Meinema.

Bailey, K. E. 1994. "St. Paul's Understanding of the Territorial Promise of God to Abraham: Romans 4:13 in Its Historical/Theological Context." *Near East School of Theology Review* 15.1:59–69.

Baines, T. B. 1879. *The Revelation of Jesus Christ*. London: G. Morrish.

Baldwin, J. G. 1972. *Haggai, Zechariah, Malachi: An Introduction and Commentary*. Downers Grove, IL: InterVarsity.

Barclay, W. 1960. *The Revelation of John*. 2nd ed. 2 vols. Philadelphia: Westminster.

Barker, K. L. 2008. *Zechariah*. EBC 8. Grand Rapids, MI: Zondervan.

Barnett, P. 1997. *The Second Epistle to the Corinthians*. NICNT. Grand Rapids, MI: Eerdmans.

Barnhouse, D. G. 1985. *Revelation: An Expositional Commentary*. Grand Rapids, MI: Zondervan.

Bartels, W. J. B., G. A. M. Beekelaar, and J. R. T. M. Peters, eds. 1976. *Het beloofde land? Rol van de religies in het Midden-Oostenkonflikt*. Bilthoven: Ambo.

Barth, K. 1956. *Church Dogmatics*. Translated by T. H. L. Parker et al. Vols. 1/1–4/4. Louisville, KY: Westminster John Knox. 1932 etc. *Die kirchliche Dogmatik*, Bd. I,1–IV,4. Zollikon-Zürich: Evangelischer Verlag (afk.: KD).

Bass, C. B. 2005. *Backgrounds to Dispensationalism: Its Historical Genesis and Ecclesiastical Implications*. 5th ed. Grand Rapids, MI: Eerdmans.

Bauer, D. R. 1992. "Son of David." *DJG* 766–69.

Bauman, Z. 1998. *Work, Consumerism and the New Poor.* Philadelphia, PA: Open University Press.

Bavinck, H. 2002–2008. *Reformed Dogmatics.* Edited by J. Bolt. Translated by J. Vriend. 4 vols. Grand Rapids, MI: Baker Academic.

Beasley-Murray, G. R. 1974. *The Book of Revelation.* New Century Bible. London: Oliphants.

Beckwith, I. T. 1922. *The Apocalypse of John.* New York: Macmillan.

Bellett, J. G. n.d. *Musings on the Apocalypse.* Oak Park, IL: Bible Truth Publishers.

Bengel, J. A. 1862 (repr. 1742). *Gnomon Novi Testamenti.* London: Williams & Norgate.

Berkhof, H. 1986. *Christian Faith: An Introduction to the Study of the Faith.* Translated by S. Woudstra. Rev. ed. Grand Rapids, MI: Wm. B. Eerdmans.

Berkhof, L. 1981. *Systematic Theology.* 4th rev. and enlarged ed. Grand Rapids, MI: Eerdmans.

Berkouwer, G. C. 1954. *The Person of Christ.* Translated by J. Vriend. Studies in Dogmatics. Grand Rapids, MI: Eerdmans.

_____. 1965. *The Work of Christ.* Translated by C. Lambregtse. Studies in Dogmatics. Grand Rapids, MI: Eerdmans.

_____. 1972. *The Return of Christ.* Translated by J. Van Oosterom. Studies in Dogmatics. Grand Rapids, MI: Eerdmans.

_____. 1976. *The Church.* Translated by J. E. Davison. Studies in Dogmatics. Grand Rapids, MI: Eerdmans. 1970.

Berkowitz, A. and D. 1999. *Take Hold: Embracing Our Divine Inheritance with Israel.* 2nd ed. Littleton, CO: First Fruits of Zion.

Bernard, J. H. 1979. *The Second Epistle to the Corinthians.* EGT 3. Grand Rapids, MI: Eerdmans.

Bijlsma, R. 1981. *Toch gemeente.* Kampen: Kok.

Bilezikian, G. 2001. *De kerk als gemeenschap.* Hoornaar: Gideon.

Bingham, D. J. and G. R. Kreider, eds. 2016. *Eschatology: Biblical, Historical, and Practical Approaches.* Grand Rapids, MI: Kregel Academic.

Bisschop, R. 1993. *Sions Vorst en volk.* Veenendaal: Kool;

Bloesch, D. G. 1997. *Jesus Christ: Saviour and Lord.* Carlisle: Paternoster.

Boersma, T. J. 1978. *Is the Bible a Jigsaw Puzzle: An Evaluation of Hal Lindsey's Writings.* St. Catharines, ON: Paideia Press.

Bonhoeffer, D. 1997. *Creation and Fall: A Theological Exposition of Genesis 1–3.* Vol. 3. Minneapolis, MN: Fortress.

Boogaard, R., P. den Butter, and E. F. Vergunst. 1992. *Zijn trouw aan Israël nooit gekrenkt.* Houten: Den Hertog.

Boot, B. 1995. *Jeruzalem, de stad van de grote Koning.* Leiden: Groen.

Booth, A. E. 1999. *The Course of Time from Eternity to Eternity.* Neptune, NJ: Loizeaux Brothers.

Bornkamm, H. 1969. *Luther and the Old Testament.* Edited by V. I. Gruhn. Translated by E. W. and R. C. Gritsch. Philadelphia: Fortress Press.

Brakel, W. à. 1949. *De toekomst van Israël.* Oostburg: Pieters.

———. 1995. *The Christian's Reasonable Service.* Translated by J. Beeke and B. Elshout. Vol. 4. Grand Rapids, MI: Reformation Heritage Books.

Bray, J. L. 1996. *Matthew 24 Fulfilled.* Lakeland, FL: John L. Bray Ministries.

Brockhaus, R. n.d. *Meer dan overwinnaars: De brief aan de Romeinen.* Den Haag: J.N. Voorhoeve.

Brown, R. E. 1994. *An Introduction to New Testament Christology.* New York: Paulist Press.

Bruce, F. F. 1969. *The Revelation to John.* New Testament Commentaries. London: Pickering & Inglis.

———. 1988. *The Book of the Acts.* NICNT. Grand Rapids, MI: Eerdmans.

Brueggeman, W. 1977. *The Land: Place as Gift, Promise and Challenge.* Philadelphia, PA: Fortress.

Bruijn, D. J. 1960. *De herleving van Israël en de opstanding.* Doorn: 't Brandpunt.

Buijs, C. J. 1974. *Israëls aanneming: Het leven uit de doden.* Bleiswijk: Tolle Lege.

Bultema, H. 1981. *Commentary on Isaiah.* Grand Rapids, MI: Kregel.

Burton, A. H. 1932. *The Apocalypse Expounded.* London: Advent

Witness Office.

Caird, G. B. 1966. *The Revelation of St. John the Divine.* Harper's New Testament Commentary. New York: Harper & Row.

Calvin, J. n.d. *Commentaries on the Epistles of Paul the Apostle to the Romans.* Translated and edited by J. Owen. Christian Classics Ethereal Library. Grand Rapids, MI. Available at https://ccel.org/ccel/calvin/calcom38/calcom38.i.html.

———. n.d. Commentary upon the Acts of the Apostles. Translated by H. Beveridge. Christian Classics Ethereal Library. Grand Rapids, MI. Available at https://ccel.org/ccel/calvin/calcom36/calcom36.i.html.

Carson, D. A. 2010. *Matthew.* EBC 9. Grand Rapids, MI: Zondervan.

Chafer, L. S. 1983. *Systematic Theology.* 15th ed. 8 vols. Dallas, TX: Dallas Seminary Press.

Chapman, C. 1985. *Whose Promised Land?* Belleville, MI: Lion.

Charles, R. H. 1920. *A Critical and Exegetical Commentary on the Revelation of St. John.* 2 vols. Edinburgh: T. & T. Clark.

Chater, E. H. 1914. *The Revelation of Jesus Christ.* London: G. Morrish.

Chilton, D. 1987. *The Great Tribulation.* Fort Worth, TX: Dominion Press.

———. 2007. *Paradise Restored: A Biblical Theology of Dominion.* Fort Worth, TX: Dominion Press.

Clowney, E. P. 1995. *The Church.* Contours of Christian Theology. Downers Grove, IL: InterVarsity.

Coates, C. A. n.d. *An Outline of the Revelation.* London: Stow Hill Bible & Tract Depot.

Cohen, A., ed. 1980 (repr.). *The Twelve Prophets.* SBB. London: Soncino.

———. 1983. *The Soncino Chumash.* SBB. London: Soncino Press, 1985.

———. 1985. *The Psalms.* SBB. London: Soncino.

Cohen Stuart, G. H. 1989. *Land inzicht: Inzichten in het theologisch denken over het land en de staat Israël.* Kampen: Kok.

Cohn-Sherbok, D. 2006. *The Politics of Apocalypse: The History and Influence of Christian Zionism.* Oxford: Oneworld.

Congar, Y. 1970. *L'Église de S. Augustin à l'époque moderne.* Paris:

Cerf.

Cox, C. C. 1959. *Apocalyptic Commentary*. Cleveland, TN: Pathway Press.

Cranfield, C. E. B. 2004. *The Epistle to the Romans 1-8 (Vol. 1)*. Edinburgh: T & T Clark.

Darby, J. N. n.d.-a *The Collected Writings of J. N. Darby*. Kingston-on-Thames: Stow Hill Bible and Tract Depot.

———. n.d.-b. *Synopsis of the Books of the Bible*. 5 vols. London: G. Morrish.

Davies, W. D. 1969. *The Sermon on the Mount*. Cambridge: Cambridge University Press.

———. 1974. *The Gospel and the Land*. Berkeley, CA: University of California Press.

Davis, J. D. 2004 (repr. 1912). "The Child Whose Name Is Wonderful." In *Biblical and Theological Studies: Commemorating the 100th Anniversary of Princeton Theological Seminary*. By Members of the Faculty of Princeton Theological Seminary. 91-108. New York: Charles Scribners Sons.

De Graaff, F. 1982. *Het geheim van de wereldgeschiedenis*. Kampen: Kok.

De Graaf-van Gelder, R. 1969. *Iets nieuws voor Israël*. Self-published.

———. n.d. *Israël en Kerk*. Self-published.

De Heer, J. 1934. *Het Duizendjarig Vrederijk*. Doorn: Zoeklicht.

———. 1961. *Israëls herstel en terugkeer naar Palestina*. 3rd ed. Driebergen: Zoeklicht.

———. n.d. *Het Joodsche vraagstuk*. Zeist: Zoeklicht.

De Jong, H. 2002. *Van oud naar nieuw: De ontwikkelingsgang van het Oude naar het Nieuwe Testament*. Kampen: Kok.

———. 2011. *De Landbelofte: Een Bijbelstudie over een gevoelig onderwerp*. Baarn: Willem de Zwijgerstichting.

———. 2012. *Twaalf stellingen over Israël*. Hardinxveld: z.u.

Delitzsch, F. 1857. *Commentar zum Briefe an die Hebräer mit archäologischen und dogmatischen Excursen über das Opfer und die Versöhnung*. Leipzig: Dörffling & Franke.

Demarest, B. 1997. *The Cross and Salvation: The Doctrine of Salvation*. Wheaton, IL: Crossway Books.

Den Boer, C., M. Van Campen, and J. Van der Graaf, eds. 1983. *Zicht op Israël: Israël in het licht van de Bijbel en in de traditie van de Reformatie.* Vol. 1. 's-Gravenhage: Boekencentrum.

Den Butter, P. 1978. *Volk tussen eeuwigheid en eenzaamheid.* Lisse: De Orchidee.

Denham Smith, J. n.d. *The Prophet of Glory, or, Zechariah's Visions of the Coming and Kingdom of Christ.* London: James E. Hawkins.

Den Hertog, G. C. 2003. *Hoop die leven doet: Over de samenhang van eschatologie en ethiek.* Apeldoorn: Theologische Universiteit.

Dennett, E. n.d. *The Visions of John in Patmos.* Oak Park, IL: Bible Truth Publishers.

Denney, J. 1979 (repr.). *St. Paul's Epistle to the Romans.* EGT 2. Grand Rapids, MI: Eerdmans.

Dennison, J. T., Jr., ed. 2008–2014. *Reformed Confessions of the 16th and 17th Centuries in English Translation.* 4 vols. Grand Rapids, MI: Reformation Heritage Books.

De Voogd van der Straaten, D. 2007. *Door het oog van een profeet.* Vlissingen: Support Ministries.

De Vries, P. 2013. *De ene olijfboom: De verhouding tussen de christelijke kerk en het Joodse volk.* Putten: Werkgroep Israël.

De Wilde, W. J. 1929. *De messiaansche opvattingen der middeleeuwsche exegeten Rasji, Aben Ezra en Kimchi, vooral volgens hun commentaren op Jesaja.* Wageningen: H. Veenman & Zonen.

Diprose, R. E. 1997. *Israel in the History of Christian Theology.* Leuven: Evangelische Theologische Faculteit.

Douma, J. 1986. "De plaats van Israël in Romeinen 9–11." In *Er staat geschreven . . . Er is geschied.* Ed. by H. J. Boiten. 164–69. Groningen: Bond van Mannenverenigingen op Gereformeerde Grondslag.

———. 1996. *The Ten Commandments: Manual for the Christian Life.* Translated by N. D. Kloosterman. Phillipsburg, NJ: P & R Publishing.

———. 2008. *Christenen voor Israël? Verantwoording van een politieke keus.* Barneveld: De Vuurbaak.

Drost, A. H. 2007. *Is God veranderd?: Een onderzoek naar de relatie God–Israël in de theologie van K.H.Miskotte, A.A. van Ruler en H.*

Berkhof. Zoetermeer: Boekencentrum.

Dulles, A. R. 1987. *Models of the Church*. Garden City, NY: Image Books.

Dunn, J. D. G. 1998. *The Theology of Paul the Apostle*. Edinburgh: T. & T. Clark.

———. 2006. *The Partings of the Ways between Christianity and Judaism and their Significance for the Character of Christianity*. 2nd ed. London: SCM.

Edelkoort, A. H. 1941. *De Christusverwachting in het Oude Testament*. Wageningen: H. Veenman & Zonen.

Edersheim, A. 1971 (repr. 1883). *The Life and Times of Jesus the Messiah*. 2 vols. Grand Rapids, MI: Eerdmans.

Erickson, M. J. 1998 (rev. ed.). *Christian Theology*. Grand Rapids, MI: Baker Book House.

Essid, M. 2009. *Levende verhalen van verzoening*. Soest: Cornerstone Ministries.

Evans, C. A. 1992. "Old Testament in the Gospels." *DJG* 579–90.

Farrer, A. M. 1964. *The Revelation of St. John the Divine*. Oxford: Oxford University Press.

Fijnvandraat, J. G. 1990. *Babylon, beeld en beest: Bijbelstudies over de profetie van Daniël*. Vol. 2: *Hoofdstuk 7–12*. Vaassen: Medema.

Fijnvandraat, J. G., A. Maljaars, and W. J. Ouweneel, W. J. 1979. *De Kerk onder de loep: Een confrontatie tussen de Calvinistische en de chiliastische visie*. Apeldoorn: Medema.

Fisch, S., ed. 1978 (repr.). *Ezekiel*. SBB. London: Soncino.

Flusser, D. 1981. *Die rabbinischen Gleichnisse und der Gleichniserzähler Jesus*. Bern: Lang.

———. 2001. *Jezus*. 2nd ed. Hilversum: B. Folkertsma Stg. voor Talmudica.

Ford, D. 1979. *The Abomination of Desolation in Biblical Eschatology*. Washington, DC: University Press of America.

Ford, J. M. 1975. *Revelation*. AB. Garden City, NY: Doubleday.

France, R. T. 1992. "Servant of Yahweh." *DJG* 744–47.

———. 2007. *The Gospel of Matthew*. NICNT. Grand Rapids, MI: Eerdmans.

Froom, L. E. 1950. *The Prophetic Faith of Our Fathers: The Historical*

Development of Prophetic Interpretation. Vol. 1. Washington, DC: Review & Herald.

Fruchtenbaum, A. G. 1994. *Israelology: The Missing Link in Systematic Theology.* 2nd ed. San Antonio, TX: Ariel Ministries Press.

Fung, R. Y. K. 1988. *The Epistle to the Galatians.* NICNT. Grand Rapids, MI: Eerdmans.

Gäckle, V. 2009. *Das Neue Testament und Israel: Die Bedeutung des jüdischen Volkes für die Christen.* Giessen/Basel: Brunnen.

Gaebelein, A .C. 1910. *The Gospel of Matthew,* Vol. I, II. Wheaton, IL: Van Kampen Press.

_____. 1911. *The Prophet Daniel.* London: Marshall Brothers.

_____. 1961. *The Revelation.* Neptune, NJ: Loizeaux Brothers.

_____. 1965. *The Book of Psalms.* Neptune, NJ: Loizeaux Brothers.

_____. 1970. *Romans.* In: *The Annotated Bible,* Vol. III: *Matthew to Ephesians.* Neptune, NJ: Loizeaux Brothers.

_____. 1972. *The Prophet Ezekiel.* Neptune, NJ: Loizeaux Brothers.

_____. 2017. *Studies in Zechariah.* Collingwood, Vic. (Austr.): Trieste.

Gesenius, W. 2012. *Der Prophet Jesaia.* 3 vols. Charleston, SC: Nabu Press.

Gibbs, J. A. 2001. *Jerusalem and Parousia: Jesus' Eschatological Discourse in Matthew's Gospel.* St. Louis, MO: Concordia Academic Press.

Gispen, W. H. 1974. *Genesis.* Vol. 1. COT. Kampen: Kok.

Glashouwer, W. J. J. 1998. *Israël op weg naar zijn rust.* Heerenveen: Groen.

_____. 2007. *Why Israel?: Understanding Israel, the Church, and the Nations is the Last Days.* Pescara, Italy: Destiny Image Europe.

Glasson, T. F. 1965. *The Revelation of John.* Cambridge: Moody Press.

Godet, F. 1879. *Commentary on the Gospel of Luke.* Edinburgh: T. & T. Clark.

Goldman, S., ed. 1983. *Samuel.* SBB. London: Soncino.

Golverdingen, M. 1971. *Ds. G. H. Kersten: Facetten van zijn leven en werk.* Amersfoort: Bond van Jeugdverenigingen der Gereformeerde Gemeenten.

Goslinga, C. J. 1962. *Het tweede boek Samuël.* COT. Kampen: Kok.

Graafland, C. 1978. *Het vaste verbond: Israël en het Oude Testament bij Calvijn en het gereformeerd protestantisme.* Amsterdam: Bolland.

Grant, F.W. 1897. *The Numerical Bible: The Gospels.* New York: Loizeaux Brothers.

———. 1901. *The Numerical Bible: Acts to II Corinthians.* New York: Loizeaux Brothers.

———. 1902. *The Numerical Bible: Hebrews to Revelation.* New York: Loizeaux Brothers.

———. 1931. *The Numerical Bible: Ezekiel.* New York: Loizeaux Brothers.

———. n.d.-a. *The Revelation of Jesus Christ.* New York: Loizeaux Brothers.

———. n.d.-b. *Present Things As Foreshown in the Book of Revelation.* New York: Loizeaux Brothers.

Green, J. B. and S. McKnight, eds. 1992. *Dictionary of Jesus and the Gospels.* Downers Grove, IL: InterVarsity Press.

Greijdanus, S. 1955. *Het evangelie naar Lucas.* 2 vols. 2nd ed. KV. Kampen: Kok.

———. 1965. *De Openbaring des Heren aan Johannes.* KV. Kampen: Kok.

Groen van Prinsterer, G. 1928. *Handboek der Geschiedenis van het Vaderland.* 8th ed. Baarn: Koning's Uitg.

Groenhuis, G. 1977. *De predikanten: De sociale positie van de gereformeerde predikanten in de Republiek der Verenigde Nederlanden voor ± 1700.* Groningen: Wolters-Noordhoff.

Grogan, G. W. 1986. *Isaiah.* EBC 6. Grand Rapids, MI: Zondervan.

Grosheide, F. W. 1954. *Het heilig evangelie volgens Mattheüs.* 2nd ed. CNT. Kampen: Kok.

———. 1955. *Paulus' tweede brief aan de kerk te Korinthe.* 2nd ed. KV. Kampen: Kok.

———. 1959. *De tweede brief aan de kerk te Korinthe.* CNT. Kampen: Kok.

Grün, A. 2002. *Images of Jesus.* Translated by J. Bowdon. New York: Continuum.

Guthrie, D. 1990. *New Testament Introduction.* Rev. ed. London: InterVarsity Press.

Haacker, K. 1997. "Die Geschichtstheologie von Röm 9–11 im Lichte philosophischer Schriftauslegung." *New Testament Studies* 43:209–222.

Haak, T. 1918 (repr. 1657). *The Dutch Annotations Upon the Whole Bible*. London: Henry Hills.

Habershon, A. R. 1974. *Study of the Types*. Grand Rapids, MI: Kregel Classics.

Haitsma, J. 1991. *Deze, déze is de Messias: De verkondiging van Jezus de Messias door de voormalige rabbi Christiaan Salomon Duijtsch aan Israël*. Leiden: Groen.

Hale, J. K. 1996. "England *as* Israel in Milton's Writings." *Early Modern Literary Studies* 2.2, 3:1–54.

Hamilton, V. P. 1995. *The Book of Genesis Chapters 18–50*. NICOT. Grand Rapids, MI: Eerdmans.

Heidler, R. D. 2006. *The Messiah Church Arising! Restoring the Church to Our Covenant Roots*. Denton, TX: Glory of Zion International Ministries.

Heitink, G. 2007. *Een kerk met karakter: Tijd voor heroriëntatie*. Kampen: Kok.

Hendriksen, W. 1944. *More Than Conquerors: An Interpretation of the Book of Revelation*. 3rd ed. Grand Rapids, MI: Baker.

———. 1959. *The Bible on the Life Hereafter*. Grand Rapids, MI: Baker.

———. 1974. *Israel in Prophecy*. Grand Rapids, MI: Baker.

Hengel, M. 1995. *Studies in Early Christology*. Edinburgh: T. & T. Clark.

Henry, C. F. H., ed. 1962. *Basic Christian Doctrines*. Grand Rapids, MI: Baker.

Hengstenberg, E. W. 1956. *Christology of the Old Testament*. Grand Rapids, MI: Kregel.

Herford, R. T. 2003. *Christianity in Talmud and Midrash*. Eugene, OR: Wipf & Stock.

Herzl, T. 1905. *Zionistische Schriften*. 2 vols. Edited by L. Kellner. Berlin: Jüdischer Verlag.

Heyns, J. A. 1988. *Dogmatiek*. Pretoria: NG Kerkboekhandel.

Hill, C. 1990. *God's Englishman: Oliver Cromwell and the English Revolution*. London: Penguin.

Hill, D. 1972. *The Gospel of Matthew.* Grand Rapids, MI: Eerdmans.

Hirsch, E. 1936. *Das Alte Testament und die Predigt des Evangeliums.* Tübingen: Mohr (Siebeck).

Hoedemaker, Ph. J. 1897. *Heel de kerk en heel het volk! Een protest tegen het optreden der Gereformeerden als partij, en een woord van afscheid aan de Confessioneele Vereeniging.* Sneek: J. Campen.

Hoehner, H. W. 1977. *Chronological Aspects of the Life of Christ.* Grand Rapids, MI: Zondervan.

Hoek, J. 2004. *Hoop op God: Eschatologische verwachting.* 2nd ed. Zoetermeer: Boekencentrum.

———. 2013. *Profetisch licht: Toekomst voor Israël en de kerk.* Heerenveen: Groen.

Hoekema, A. A. 1979. *The Bible and the Future.* Grand Rapids, MI: Eerdmans.

Hoekendijk, B. 2001. *De toekomst van Israël: Interviews met Messiaanse leiders.* Putten: Shalom Books.

Hoste, W. n.d. *The Vision of John the Divine.* Kilmarnock: John Ritchie.

Hughes, P. E. 1962. *Paul's Second Epistle to the Corinthians.* NICNT. Grand Rapids, MI: Eerdmans.

Huisman, C. 1983 *Neerlands Israel: Het natiebesef der traditioneel-gereformeerden in de achttiende eeuw.* Dordrecht: J.P. van den Tol.

Ironside, H. A. 1930. *Lectures on the Book of Revelation.* New York: Loizeaux Brothers.

Jager, H. J. 1978. *Enige opmerkingen over de brief aan de Romeinen: College-dictaat.* Kampen: Van den Berg.

Janse, S. 2000. *Een onderzoek naar de heilshistorische betekenis van Jeruzalem in de brieven van Paulus.* Zoetermeer: Boekencentrum 2000.

Jansen, H. 1981. *Christelijke theologie na Auschwitz.* Vol. 1: *Theologische en kerkelijke wortels van het antisemitisme.* 's-Gravenhage: Boekencentrum.

Jansen, J. G. B. 1999. *Christelijke theologie na Auschwitz: De geschiedenis van 2000 jaar kerkelijk antisemitisme.* 2nd ed. Amsterdam: Blaak.

Jennings, F. C. 1937. *Studies in Revelation.* New York: Loizeaux Brothers.

Johnson, A. F. 2006. *Revelation.* EBC 13. Grand Rapids, MI:

Zondervan.

Jonker, W.D. 1988. *Uit vrye guns alleen: Oor uitverkiesing en verbond.* Pretoria: NG Kerkboekhandel.

Jonkers, J. B. G. and J. Bruinsma-de Beer. 2000. *Gemeente gewogen: Theologen in gesprek over de kerkelijke gemeente.* Kampen: Kok.

Joseph, M. 2005. *Judaism As Creed and Life.* Whitefish, MT: Kessinger.

Jukes, A. 1976. *Types in Genesis.* Grand Rapids, MI: Kregel.

Juster, D. 1995. *Jewish Roots: A Foundation of Biblical Theology.* Shippensburg, PA: Destiny Image Publishers.

Kamsteeg, A. n.d. *Israël, verleden, heden, toekomst.* Groningen: De Vuurbaak.

Kan, R. 2010. *How Warm It Was, and How Far.* CreateSpace (Kindle edition).

Kelly, W., ed. 1856–1920. *Bible Treasury: A Monthly Review of Prophetic and Practical Subjects.* Available at https://bibletruthpublishers.com/bible-treasury/lpvl22465.

_____. 1868. *Lectures on the Book of the Revelation.* London: G. Morrish.

_____. 1870. *Lectures Introductory to the Study of the Acts, the Catholic Epistles, and the Revelation.* London: W.H. Broom.

_____. 1896. *Lectures on the Gospel of Matthew.* London: A.S. Rouse.

_____. 1952. *Notes on the Book of Daniel.* 8th ed. New York: Loizeaux Brothers.

_____. 1970a. *The Revelation.* Winschoten: Uit het Woord der Waarheid.

_____. 1970b. *Lectures Introductory to the Study of the Minor Prophets.* London: Hammond.

Kersten, G. H. 1918. *Een banier tegen de revolutie.* Yerseke: J.J. van der Peijl.

_____. 1980. *Reformed Dogmatics: A Systematic Treatment of Reformed Doctrine.* Translated by J. R. Beeke and J. C. Westrate. 2 vols. Grand Rapids, MI: Eerdmans. 1947. *De gereformeerde dogmatiek voor de gemeenten toegelicht.* 2 vols. Utrecht: De Banier.

Kertelge, K., ed. 1977. *Das kirchliche Amt im Neuen Testament.* Darmstadt: Wissenschaftliche Buchgesellschaft.

Kiddle, M. 1940. *The Revelation of St. John.* Moffet New Testament

Commentary. London: Hodder & Stoughton.

Kimball, W. R. 1984. *What the Bible Says about the Great Tribulation.* Phillipsburg, NJ: Presbyterian & Reformed Publishing Co.

Kitchen, K. A. 2006. *On the Reliability of the Old Testament.* 2nd ed. Grand Rapids, MI: Eerdmans.

Kittel, G. et al., eds. 1964–76. *Theological Dictionary of the New Testament.* Translated by G. W. Bromiley. 10 vols. Grand Rapids, MI: Eerdmans.

Kloosterman, N. D. 2011. "The Old Testament, Ethics, and Preaching: Letting Confessional Light Dispel a Hermeneutical Shadow." *Living Waters from Ancient Springs: Essays in Honor of Cornelis Van Dam.* Edited by Jason Van Vliet. 185–97. Eugene, Oregon: Pickwick Publications.

Knevel, A. G. and M. J. Paul, eds. 1995. *Verkenningen in de oudtestamentische messiasverwachting.* Kampen: Kok Voorhoeve/Hilversum: Evangelische Omroep.

Knight, J. 2004. *Jesus: An Historical and Theological Investigation.* London/New York: T. & T. Clark.

Knowling, R. J. 1979. *The Acts of the Apostles.* EGT 2. Grand Rapids, MI: Eerdmans.

Kocken, E. 1935. *De theorie van de vier wereldrijken en van de overdracht der wereldheerschappij tot op Innocentius III.* Nijmegen: Berkhout.

Kraemer, H. 1941. *Het raadsel der geschiedenis: Gedachten uit Romeinen 9–11.* 's-Gravenhage: Daamen.

Kraft, H. 1974. *Die Offenbarung des Johannes.* Handbuch zum Neuen Testament. Tübingen: Mohr (Siebeck).

Krauss, S. 2009. *Griechische und Lateinische Lehnwörter in Talmud, Midrasch und Targum.* Berlin: Calvary.

Kuhn, T. S. 1996. *The Structure of Scientific Revolutions.* 3rd ed. Chicago: University of Chicago Press.

Kuiper, R. 2009. *Moreel kapitaal: De verbindingskracht van de samenleving.* Amsterdam: Buijten & Schipperheijn Motief.

Küng, H. 1967. *The Church.* Translated by R. and R. Ockenden. London: Burns & Oates.

Küng, H. 1992. *Judaism: Between Yesterday and Tomorrow.* Translated by J. Bowden. New York: Crossroad.

Kuyper, A. 1905. *E Voto Dordraceno: Toelichting op den Heidelbergschen Catechismus.* Vol. 2. Amsterdam: Höveker & Wormser.

_____. 1931. *Van de voleinding.* Vol. 4. Kampen: Kok.

_____. 1934. *Chiliasm or the Doctrine of Premillennialism.* Grand Rapids, MI: Zondervan.

Ladd, G. E. 1959. *The Gospel of the Kingdom: Scriptural Studies in the Kingdom of God.* Grand Rapids, MI: Eerdmans.

_____. 1972. *A Commentary on the Revelation of John.* Grand Rapids, MI: Eerdmans.

Lagrange, M.-J. 1948. *Évangelile selon Saint-Matthieu.* Paris: Lecoffre.

Lambert, L. 1990. *Israël is uniek.* 4th ed. Nijkerk: Chai pers/Stg. Christenen voor Israël.

Lang, G. H. 1942. *The Histories and Prophecies of Daniel.* London: Oliphants.

_____. 1945. *The Revelation of Jesus Christ.* London: Oliphants.

Lapide, P. 1983. *Opstanding: Een joodse geloofservaring.* Kampen: Kok.

_____. 1984. *Is dat niet de zoon van Jozef? Jezus in het hedendaagse jodendom.* Baarn: Ten Have.

_____. 2004. *Er predigte in ihren Synagogen: Jüdische Evangelienauslegung.* 8th ed. Gütersloh: Mohn.

_____. 2011. *Mit einem Juden die Bibel lesen.* Münster: LIT Verlag.

Larsson, G. 1989. *De Joden, majesteit!* 2nd ed. Nijkerk: Centrum voor Bijbelstudie en Onderzoek te Jeruzalem.

Lehman, C. K. 1971. *The Fulfillment of Prophecy.* Rev. ed. Scottdale, PA: Herald Press.

Lenski, R. C. H. 1943. *The Interpretation of St. John's Revelation.* Minneapolis, MN: Augsburg.

Lewis, C. S. 1952. *Mere Christianity.* New York: Macmillan.

Liefeld, W. L. 2009. *Luke.* EBC 10. Grand Rapids, MI: Zondervan.

Lilje, H. 1957. *The Last Book of the Bible: The Meaning of the Revelation of Saint John.* Philadelphia: Muhlenberg Press.

Linnemann, E. 1990. *Historical Criticism of the Bible: Methodology or Ideology?* Translated by R. W. Yarbrough. Grand Rapids, MI: Baker.

Lohmeyer, E. 1953. *Die Offenbarung des Johannes*. 2nd ed. Handbuch zum Neuen Testament. Tübingen: Mohr (Siebeck).

Longenecker, R. N. 2009. *Acts of the Apostles*. EBC 10. Grand Rapids, MI: Zondervan.

Loonstra, B. 1994. *De geloofwaardigheid van de Bijbel*. Zoetermeer: Boekencentrum.

Lueken, M. 1898. *Michael: Eine Darstellung und Vergleichung der jüdischen und der morgenländisch-christlichen Tradition vom Erzengel Michael*. Göttingen: Vandenhoeck & Ruprecht.

Maccoby, H. 1986. *The Mythmaker: Paul and the Invention of Christianity*. New York: Harper & Row.

McComiskey, T. E. 1985. *Micah*. EBC 8. Grand Rapids, MI: Zondervan.

McDowell, E. H. 1951. *The Meaning and Message of the Book of Revelation*. Nashville, TN: Broadman Press.

McDowell, J. 1972. *Evidence That Demands a Verdict*. San Bernardino, CA: Campus Crusade for Christ.

_____. 1979. *Daniel in the Critics' Den: Historical Evidence for the Authenticity of the Book of Daniel*. San Bernardino: Campus Crusade for Christ International.

McGrath, A. E. 2007. *Christian Theology: An Introduction*. Malden, MA: Blackwell Publishers. 1997. *Christelijke theologie: Een introductie*. Kampen: Kok.

Maier, G. 1982. *Der Prophet Daniel*. Wuppertaler Studienbibel. Wuppertal: Brockhaus.

Maljaars, A. 1976. *Niet allen Israël: De verhouding tussen Kerk en Israël in het licht van de Heilige Schrift*. Dordrecht: Van den Tol.

_____. 2015. *Heel Israël zal behouden worden: Een kritisch onderzoek van de gangbare exegese van Romeinen 11, speciaal vs. 26*. Soesterberg: Aspekt.

Marshall, I. H. 1992. "Son of Man." *DJG* 775–81.

Matter, H. M. 1953. *De toekomst van Israël in het licht van het Nieuwe Testament*. Baarn: Bosch & Keuning.

Meeuwse, C. J., G. Roos, and C. Sonneveld, eds 2004. *Trouw aan Israël*. 2nd ed. Houten: Den Hertog.

Mehrtens, G. F., 1987. *De Nieuwe Romeinen: Een cultuurfilosofische verkenning*. Houten: De Haan.

Michel, O. 1992. "*Ho hyios tou anthropou*, the Son of man." In *The New International Dictionary of New Testament Theology*. Edited by C. Brown. 3:613-34. Carlisle: Paternoster.

Michelson, A.U. n.d. *De Joden en Palestina in het licht van de profetie*. Amsterdam: Hebreeuwse Evangelisatie Vereniging.

Minear, P. S. 1960. *Images of the Church in the New Testament*. Philadephia: Westminster Press.

———. 1968. *I Saw a New Earth: An Introduction to the Visions of the Apocalypse*. Washington/Cleveland: Corpus Books.

Miskotte, K. H. 1964. *Het wezen der joodse religie: Bijdrage tot de kennis van het joodse geestesleven*. Haarlem: Holland.

Moerkerken, A. 2004. *Ons troostboek: Verklaring van de Heidelbergse Catechismus*. Houten: Den Hertog.

Moffatt, J. 1979. *The Revelation of St. John the Divine*. EGT 5. Grand Rapids, MI: Eerdmans.

Moltmann, J. 1977. *The Church in the Power of the Spirit: A Contribution to Messianic Ecclesiology*. London: SCM Press. 1975. *Kerk in het krachtveld van de Geest: Bouwstenen voor een messiaanse ekklesiologie*. Baarn: Amboboeken.

———. 1996. *The Coming of God: Christian Eschatology*. Translated by M. Kohl. Minneapolis, MN: Fortress Press.

Montefiore, C. G. 1927. *The Synoptic Gospels*. London: Macmillan.

Moo, D. J. 1996. *The Epistle to the Romans*. NICNT. Grand Rapids, MI: Eerdmans.

Morris, L. 1969. *The Book of Revelation*. TNTC. Grand Rapids, MI: Eerdmans.

Mounce, R. H. 1977. *The Book of Revelation*. NICNT. Grand Rapids, MI: Eerdmans.

Mulder, M. C. and A. Noordegraaf, eds. 2007. *Hoop voor Israël: Perspectieven uit Handelingen*. Zoetermeer: Boekencentrum.

Murray, J. 1968. *The Epistle to the Romans*. NICNT. Grand Rapids, MI: Eerdmans.

Nederbragt, J. A. 1957. *Jeruzalem, indien ik u vergete . . .* 4th ed. Den Haag: Voorhoeve.

Neusner, J., ed. 2008. *The Jerusalem Talmud: A Translation and*

Commentary. Peabody, MA: Hendrickson Publishers.

Newell, W. R. 1935. *The Book of the Revelation*. Chicago: Moody Press.

Nierop, E. 2010. *De heilige boeken van het Nieuwe Testament: Een op de Aramese Peshitta gebaseerde Bijbel*. Eigen uitgave.

Noordmans, O. 1978/1984. *Verzamelde werken*. Vols. 1, 5. Kampen: Kok.

Noordtzij, A. 1932. *De profeet Ezechiël*. 2 vols. KV. Kampen: Kok.

_____. 1934. *Het boek der psalmen*. Vol. 1: *Psalm 1–70*. Kampen: Kok.

North, C. R. 1956. *The Suffering Servant in Deutero-Isaiah: An Historical and Critical Study*. 2nd ed. London: Oxford University Press.

Oegema, G. S. 1991. *De messiaanse verwachtingen ten tijde van Jezus*. Baarn: Ten Have.

Oostland, E. J. and H. J. Siegers. 2016. *Kerk en Israël: Ontwerp voor een gereformeerde visie*. https://yachad.nl/wp-content/uploads/2016/03/GS-Visiedocument-Kerk.pdf.

Op 't Hof, W. J. 1984. *De visie op de Joden in de Nadere Reformatie tijdens het eerste kwart van de zeventiende eeuw*. Amsterdam: Bolland.

Oswalt, J. N. 1986/1998. *The Book of Isaiah*. Vol. 1: *Chapters 1–39*. Vol. 2: *Chapters 40–66*. NICOT. Grand Rapids, MI: Eerdmans.

Ouweneel, W. J. 1973. *Het Hooglied van Salomo*. Winschoten: Uit het Woord der Waarheid.

_____. 1977. *Die Zukunft der Stadt des großen Königs*. Neustadt a/d Weinstraße: Paulus Verlag.

_____. 1981. *Glaube und Werke: Eine Auslegung des Jakobusbriefes*. Schwelm: Heijkoop Verlag.

_____, with V. I. Kerkhof. 1982a. *Het ontstaan van Israël*. Edited by W. J. J. Glashouwer. Hilversum: Evangelische Omroep.

_____. 1982b. *'Wij zien Jezus': Bijbelstudies over de brief aan de Hebreeën*. 2 vols. Vaassen: Medema.

_____. 1988/1990. *De Openbaring van Jezus Christus: Bijbelstudies over het boek Openbaring*. 2 vols. Vaassen: Medema.

_____. 1989. *De profeet Jona*. 2nd ed. Alblasserdam: Stg. Boeken bij de Bijbel.

_____. 1991. *Israël en de Kerk, oftewel: Eén of twee volken van God?: Confrontatie van de verbondsleer en de bedelingenleer*. Vaassen: Medema.

Bibliography

———. 1997. *De vrijheid van de Geest: Bijbelstudies bij de Brief van Paulus aan de Galaten*. Vaassen: Medema.

———. 1998a. *De zevende koningin: Het eeuwig vrouwelijke en de raad van God*. Vol. 2 of *Metahistorische trilogie*. Heerenveen: Barnabas.

———. 1999. *Jeruzalem, de stad van de grote Koning*. Vaassen: Medema.

———. 2000. *Het Jobslijden van Israël: Israëls lijden oplichtend uit het boek Job*. Vaassen: Medema.

———. 2001. *Hoogtijden voor Hem: De bijbelse feesten en hun betekenis voor Joden en christenen*. Vaassen: Medema.

———. 2002. *Israël en de Palestijnen: Waarheid en misleiding*. Heerenveen: Barnabas.

———. 2003a. *De negende Koning: Het laatste der hemelrijken: De triomf van Christus over de machten*. 3rd ed. Vol. 2 of *Metahistorische triologie*. Soesterberg: Aspekt.

———, ed. 2003b. *F.M. Dostojevski: De groot-inquisiteur: Christus door de Kerk verworpen*. Soesterberg: Aspekt.

———. 2007a. *De Geest van God: Ontwerp van een pneumatologie*. EDR 1. Vaassen: Medema.

———. 2007b. *De Christus van God: Ontwerp van een christologie*. EDR 2. Vaassen: Medema.

———. 2008a. *De schepping van God: Ontwerp van een scheppings-, mens- en zondeleer*. EDR 3. Vaassen: Medema.

———. 2008b. *Het plan van God: Ontwerp van een voorbeschikkingsleer*. EDR 4. Vaassen: Medema.

———. 2009a. *Het zoenoffer van God: Ontwerp van een verzoeningsleer*. EDR 5. Vaassen: Medema.

———. 2009b. *Het heil van God: Ontwerp van een soteriologie*. EDR 6. Heerenveen: Medema.

———. 2010a. *De Kerk van God (1): Ontwerp van een elementaire ecclesiologie*. EDR 7. Heerenveen: Medema.

———. 2010b. *De kerk van God (2): Ontwerp van een historische en praktische ecclesiologie*. EDR 8. Heerenveen: Medema.

———. 2011a. *Het verbond en het koninkrijk van God: Ontwerp van een foederologie en basileologie*. EDR9. Heerenveen: Medema.

_____. 2012a. *De toekomst van God: Ontwerp van een eschatologie.* Heerenveen: Medema 2012a.

_____. 2012b. *Vijf nijlpaarden in het kippenhok: Nieuwe brandende onderwerpen waarover christenen verdeeld zijn.* Heerenveen: Medema.

_____. 2012c. *Het Woord van God: Ontwerp van een openbarings- en schriftleer.* EDR 11. Heerenveen: Medema.

_____. 2013. *De glorie van God: Ontwerp van een godsleer en van een theologische vakfilosofie.* EDR 12. Heerenveen: Medema.

_____. 2014. *Een dubbelsnoer van licht: Honderd grootse joodse en christelijke godsmannen door de geschiedenis heen en hun moeizame relaties.* Soesterberg: Aspekt.

_____. 2016. *Dankbaar onderweg: Dagboek bij de Heidelbergse Catechismus.* Utrecht: Kok.

_____. 2017. *The World Is Christ's: A Critique of Two Kingdoms Theology.* Toronto: Ezra Press.

_____. 2018. *Adam, Where Are You?–And Why This Matters: A Theological Evaluation of the Evolutionist Hermeneutic.* Jordan Station, ON: Paideia Press.

_____. 2019a. *Het Israël van God.* Hoornaar: Gideon.

_____. 2019b. *The Eden Story: A History of Paradise, from Its Demise to Its New Rise.* Jordan Station, ON: Paideia Press 2020.

_____. 2020. *The Eternal Torah: Living Under God.* Jordan Station, ONT: Paideia Press.

_____. 2021. *Forever with the Lord.* Jordan Station, ON: Paideia Press.

_____. n.d.-a. *Leviticus: een serie bijbellezingen.* Hengelo: A. Lievers.

_____. n.d.-b. *Het boek Esther.* Alblasserdam: Stg. Boeken bij de Bijbel.

Paas, S. 2012. *Christian Zionism Examined: A Review of Ideas on Israel, the Church and the Kingdom.* Nürnberg: VTR.

_____. 2014. *Israëlvisies in beweging: Gevolgen voor Kerk, geloof en theologie.* Kampen: Brevier.

_____ S. 2015. *Liefde voor Israël nader bekeken: Voor het Evangelie zijn alle volken gelijk.* Kampen: Brevier.

_____, ed. 2017. *Israelism and the Place of Christ: Christocentric*

Interpretation of Biblical Prophecy. Wien: LIT Verlag.

Pannenberg, W. 1998. *Systematic Theology*. Translated by G. Bromiley. Vol. 3. Grand Rapids, MI: Eerdmans.

Paul, M. J. 1987. "The Order of Melchizedek (Ps 110:4 and Heb 7:3)." *Westminster Theological Journal* 49:195-211.

_____. 2013. *Het nieuwe verbond en de uitleg van de profetieën over de toekomst van Israël*. Baarn: Willem de Zwijgerstichting.

Paul, M. J., L. W. G. Blokhuis, and P. A. Siebesma. 1993. *Land voor vrede? Een studie over Israëls landsgrenzen*. Kampen: Kok.

Pawson, D. 1995. *When Jesus Returns*. London: Hodder & Stoughton.

Payne, J. B. 1980. *Encyclopedia of Biblical Prophecy: The Complete Guide to Scriptural Predictions and Their Fulfillment*. Grand Rapids, MI: Baker Books.

Peake, A. S. 1979. *The Epistle to the Colossians*. EGT 3. Grand Rapids, MI: Eerdmans.

Pentecost, J. D. 1964. *Things to Come: A Study in Biblical Eschatology*. Grand Rapids, MI: Academie Books.

Pfisterer, R. 1959. "Antisemitismus und Eschatologie." *Evangelische Theologie* 1959:266-88.

Plaisier, A. and K. Spronk, eds. 2012. *Meervoudig verbonden: Nieuwe perspectieven op vragen rond kerk, Israël en Palestijnen*. Zoetermeer: Boekencentrum.

Plummer, A. 1922. *Gospel According to St. Luke*. 5th ed. International Critical Commentary. Edinburgh: T. & T. Clark.

Pop, F. J. 1999. *Bijbelse woorden en hun geheim*. 10th ed. Zoetermeer: Boekencentrum.

Preston, R. H. and A. T. Hanson. 1968. *The Revelation of Saint John the Divine*. London: SCM-Canterbury Press.

Prince, D. 1994. *De toekomst van Israël en de Kerk*. Gorinchem: Derek Prince Ministries.

Rahner, K. 1966. *De pelgrimerende kerk*. Hilversum/Antwerpen: Paul Brand.

Rahner K. and P. Lapide. 1987. *Encountering Jesus — Encountering Judaism: A Dialogue*. Translated by D. Perkins. New York: Crossroad. Lapide, P. & Rahner, K. 1984. *Heil uit de joden? Een discussie*. Hilversum: Gooi & Sticht.

Ratzinger, J. 2007. *Jesus of Nazareth: From the Baptism in the Jordan to the Transfiguration*. Translated by A. J. Walker. New York, NY: Doubleday.

———. 2011. *Jesus of Nazareth: Holy Week. From the Entrance into Jerusalem to the Resurrection*. San Francisco: Ignatius Press. 2011.

———. 2018. "Grace and Vocation Without Remorse: Comments on the Treatise De Judaeis." Translated by N. J. Healy Jr. *Communio* 45.1 (Spring):163–84.

Raymond, R. L. 2003. *Jesus Divine Messiah: The New and Old Testament Witness*. Fearn: Mentor.

Reitsma, B. 2006. *Wie is onze God? Arabische christenen, Israel en de aard van God*. Amsterdam VBK Media.

Renckens, H. 1962. *De godsdienst van Israël*. Roermond/Maaseik: Romen.

Ridderbos, H. 1959. *Aan de Romeinen*. CNT. Kampen: Kok.

———. 1975. *Paul: An Outline of His Theology*. Translated by J. R. DeWitt. Grand Rapids, MI: Eerdmans.

———. 1987. *Matthew*. Translated by Ray Togtman. Bible Student's Commentary. Grand Rapids, MI: Zondervan.

Ridderbos, J. 1932–1935. *De kleine profeten*.

Ridderbos, J. 1952. *De kleine profeten*. Vol. 3. KV. Kampen: Kok.

3 vols. KV. Kampen: Kok.

———. 1985. *Isaiah*. Translated by J. Vriend. Bible Student's Commentary. Grand Rapids, MI: Zondervan.

1934. *De profeet Jesaja*. Vol. 2: *Hoofdstuk 40–66*. 2nd ed. KV. Kampen: Kok. 1940. *De profeet Jesaja*. Vol. 1: *Hoofdstuk 1–39*. KV. Kampen: Kok.

———. 1955. *De psalmen*. Vol. 1: *Psalm 1–41*. COT. Kampen: Kok.

———. 1958. *De psalmen*. Vol. 2: *Psalm 42–106*. COT. Kampen: Kok.

Rissi, M. 1968. "The Kerygma of the Revelation to John." *Interpretation* 22.1 (January): 3–17.

Rist, M. 1957. "The Revelation of St. John the Divine, Introduction and Exegesis." In *The Interpreter's Bible* 12:345–613. New York: Abingdon.

Robertson, O. P. 2000. *The Israel of God: Yesterday, Today, and Tomorrow*. Phillipsburg, NJ: Presbyterian &Reformed Publishing Co.

Robinson, J. A. T. 2000. *Redating the New Testament*. Eugene, OR: Wipf & Stock.

Roozemeijer, J. H. L. 1911. *De brief van Paulus aan de Romeinen*. Arnhem: G.W. van der Wiel & Co.

Rosenberg, A. 1956. *Michael und der Drache*. Olten: Otto Walter.

Rosenstock-Huessy, E: ed. *Judaism Despite Christianity: The 1916 Wartime Correspondence Between Eugen Rosenstock-Huessy and Franz Rosenzweig*. Chicago: University of Chicago Press.

Rosenzweig, F. 1996. *Stern der Erlösung*. Frankfurt: Suhrkamp.

Rossier, H. 1961. *Le Langage symbolique de l'Apcalypse*. Vevey: Éditions Bibles et Traités Chrétiens.

_____. 1967. *Court exposé et division de l'Apocalypse*. Vevey: Éditions Bibles et Traités Chrétiens.

Rowley, H. H. 1950. "Melchizedek and Zadok." In *Festschrift für Alfred Bertholet zum 80. Geburtstag*. W. Baumgartner et al. Tübingen: Mohr (Siebeck).

_____. 1952. *The Servant of the Lord and Other Essays on the Old Testament*. London: Lutterworth Press.

Ryrie, C. C. 1953. *The Basis of the Premillennial Faith*. Neptune, NJ: Loizeaux Brothers.

_____. 1986. *Basic Theology*. Wheaton, IL: Victor Books.

Sailhamer, J. H. 2008. *Genesis*. EBC 1. Grand Rapids, MI: Zondervan.

Salmond, S. D. F. 1979. *The Epistle to the Ephesians*. EGT 3. Grand Rapids, MI: Eerdmans.

Santala, R. 1997. *Der Messias im Alten Testament im Licht der rabbinischen Schriften*. Neuhausen-Stuttgart: Hänssler-Verlag.

Schaeffer, F. A. 1982. *The Complete Works: A Christian Worldview*. Vol. 2: *A Christian View of the Bible As Truth*. Westchester, IL: Crossway Books.

Schenkle, C., ed. 1987. *Corpus Scriptorum Ecclesiasticorum* Latinorum. Vol. 32/2. Leipzig: Hoelder, Pichler & Tempsky.

Schilder, K. 1949/1950. *Heidelbergsche Catechismus*. Vols. 2–3. Goes: Oosterbaan & Le Cointre.

Schirrmacher, T. 2001. *Christus im Alten Testament*. Hamburg: RVB.

Schlatter, A. 1963. *Der Evangelist Matthäus: Seine Sprache, sein Ziel, seine Selbständigkeit*. 6th ed. Stuttgart: Calwer Verlag.

Schneider, O. 1953. *Das zweite Buch Samuel*. Paderborn: F. Schöningh.

Schniewind, J. 1956. *Das Evangelium nach Matthäus*. Göttingen: Vandenhoeck & Ruprecht.

Schoeps, H. J. 1932. *Jüdischer Glaube in dieser Zeit: Prolegomena zur Grundlegung einer systematischen Theologie des Judentums*. Berlin: Vortrupp.

⸻. 1949. *Theologie und Geschichte des Judenchristentums*. Tübingen: Mohr (Siebeck).

Schoon, S. 1998. *Onopgeefbaar verbonden: Op weg naar vernieuwing in de verhouding tussen de kerk en het volk Israël*. Kampen: Kok.

Schutte, G. J. 1992. "Nederland: een calvinistische natie?" *Bijdragen en Mededelingen betreffende de Geschiedenis der Nederlanden* 107 (1992).4: 790-702703-12.

Schuyler English, E. 1935. *Studies in the Gospel According to Matthew*. New York: Revell.

Scott, W. 1920. *Exposition of the Revelation of Jesus Christ*. London etc.: Pickering & Inglis.

Seiss, J. A. 1957. *The Apocalypse*. Grand Rapids, MI: Kregel.

Sevenster, G. 1986. "Christologie. I. Christologie des Urchristentums." In *Die Religion in Geschichte und Gegenwart: Handwörterbuch für Theologie und Religionswissenschaft*. Edited by K. Galling. 1:1745-1762. Stuttgart: UTB.

Shulam, J. (with Le Cornu, H.) 1998. *A Commentary on the Jewish Roots of Romans*. Baltimore: Messianic Jewish Publishers.

Shulam, J. 2010. *Verborgen schatten: De Joodse manier van uitleg van de Schriften in de eerste eeuw*. Putten: Shalom Books.

Sizer, S. 2004. *Christian Zionism, Road Mapto Armageddon?* Leicester: Inter-Varsity Press.

Sizer, S. 2007. *Zion's Christian Soldiers? The Bible, Israel and the Church*. Leicester: InterVarsity Press.

Skolnik. F. 2007. *Encylopedia Judaica*. 2nd ed. 14 vols. Farmington Hills, MI: Keter Publishing House Ltd.

Slotki, I. W. 1983. *Isaiah*. SBB. London: Soncino.

Slotki, J. J. 1985. *Daniel, Ezra, Nehemiah*. SBB. London: Soncino.

Smith, D. L. 1996. *All God's People: A Theology of the Church*. Wheaton, IL: BridgePoint.

Smith, H. n.d. *The Revelation: An Expository Outline.* Oak Park, IL: Bible Truth Publishers.

Smith, J. B. 1961. *A Revelation of Jesus Christ.* Scottdale, PA: Herald Press.

Smitskamp, H. 1940. *Groen van Prinsterer als historicus.* Amsterdam: H.J. Paris.

_____. 1947. *Calvinistisch nationaal besef in Nederland vóór het midden der 17e eeuw.* 's-Gravenhage: Daamen.

Snell, H. H. 1878. *Notes on the Revelation.* London: W.H. Broom.

CU BS1430 .S6 2008 Spurgeon, C. H. 2008. *The Treasury of David Containing an Original Exposition of the Book of Psalms.* 3 vols. Peabody, MA: Hendrikson.

Stern, D. H. 1997. *Messianic Jewish Manifesto.* 3rd ed. Clarksville, MD: Jewish New Testament Publications.

_____. 1999. *Jewish New Testament Commentary.* 6th ed. Clarksville, MD: Jewish New Testament Publications.

_____. 2009. *Restoring the Jewishness of the Gospel: A Message for Christians.* Clarksville, MD: Messianic Jewish Publishers.

Stewart, A. 2018. "The Future of Israel: Early Christian Hermeneutics, and the Apocalypse of John." *Journal of the Evangelical Theological Society* 61.3:563-75.

Strack, H. L. and P. Billerbeck. 1922-1928 (repr. 1986-97). *Kommentar zum Neuen Testament aus Talmud und Midrasch.* 6 vols. München: Beck.

Strübind, A. 2003. *Eifriger als Zwingli: Die frühe Täuferbewegung in der Schweiz.* Berlin: Duncker und Humblot.

Susman, M. 1996. *Das Buch Hiob und das Schicksal des jüdischen Volkes.* Frankfurt: Jüdischer Verlag.

Swete, H. B. 1951. *The Apocalypse of St. John.* Grand Rapids, MI: Eerdmans.

Tatford, F. A. 1947. *Prophecy's Last Word.* London: Pickering & Inglis.

Te Dorsthorst, W. 1996. *Geestelijk licht op Israël.* Utrecht: Pons Varoli.

Ten Berge, G. 2011. *Land van mensen: Christenen, joden en moslims tussen confrontaties en dialoog.* Nijmegen: Valkhof pers.

Ten Boom, W. et al. 1933. *Het ontwaken van het Joodsche volk.* Den

Haag: Voorhoeve.

Tennenbaum, S. 1982. *Yesterday's Streets*. New York: Ballantine Books.

Tenney, M. C. 1961. *New Testament Survey*. London: InterVarsity Press.

———. 1985. *Interpreting Revelation*. Grand Rapids, MI: Eerdmans.

Thompson, W. M. 1996. *The Struggle for Theology's Soul: Contesting Scripture in Christology*. New York: Crossroad Herder.

Trench, R. C. 1953. *Synonyms of the New Testament*. Grand Rapids, MI: Eerdmans.

———. 2018. *Notes on the Parables of Our Lord*. London: Forgotten Books.

Unger, M. F. 1962. *Zechariah*. Grand Rapids, MI: Zondervan.

Van Barneveld, J. 1998. *Het herstel van Israël*. Puttern: Shalom Books.

———. 2002. *Met Israël op weg naar de eindtijd*. Nijkerk: Chai pers/Stg. Christenen voor Israël.

———. 2009. *Eindtijd, Israël en de Islam*. Doorn: Zoeklicht.

———. 2012. *Met Israël op weg naar de eindtijd*. 3rd ed. Amerongen: Johannnus Multimedia/Nijkerk: Chai pers.

———. 2014. *Het einde van de vervangingsleer*. 3rd ed. Nijkerk: Chai pers/Stg. Christenen voor Israël.

Van Bekkum, K. and M. Mulder, eds. 2010. *Hoe leest u 'Israël'?* Barneveld: Nederlands Dagblad.

Van Bruggen, J. 2013a. *Romeinen: Christenen tussen stad en synagoge*. Commentaar op het Nieuwe Testament, Derde Serie. Utrecht: Kok.

———. 2013b. *Galaten: Het goed recht van gelovige Kelten*. Commentaar op het Nieuwe Testament, Derde Serie. Utrecht: Kok.

Van Campen, M. 2007. *Gans Israël: Voetiaanse en coccejaanse visies op joden gedurende de zeventiende en achttiende eeuw*. 2nd ed. Zoetermeer: Boekencentrum.

Van Campen, M. and G. C. Den Hertog, eds. 2005. *Israël, volk, land en staat: Terugblik en perspectief*. Zoetermeer: Boekencentrum.

Van Campen, M. and P. J. Vergunst. 2015. *Jan Hoek: Theoloog tussen preekstoel en leerstoel*. Zoetermeer: Boekencentrum.

Van de Beek, A. 2002. *De kring om de Messias: Israël als volk van de lijdende Heer*. Zoetermeer: Meinema.

Van de Kamp, H. R. 1990. *Israël in Openbaring*. Kampen: Kok.

Van de Kamp, L. and W. J. Ouweneel. 2013. *Joden en christenen: Overeenkomsten en verschillen*. Heerenveen: Medema.

Van Delden, J. A. 1985. *Israël is Gods volk*. Amsterdam: Buijten & Schipperheijn.

Van der Graaf, J. W. Verboom. 2004. *Vervuld maar (nog) niet voltooid*. Heerenveen: Groen.

Van der Horst, P. W. 2000. "'Pas dan zal heel Israël gered worden'. Hoe moet Romeinen 11:26 vertaald worden?" *Kerk en theologie* 51:183–88.

Van der Kooi, C. and G. Van den Brink. 2017. *Christian Dogmatics: An Introduction*. Translated by R. Bruinsma with J. D. Bratt. Grand Rapid, MI: Eerdmans. 2012. *Christelijke Dogmatiek: Een inleiding*. Zoetermeer: Boekencentrum.

Van der Meer, P. F. 1974. *Het geloof van toen en nu*. Kampen: Van den Berg.

Van der Rhee, F. 1997. *God heeft een zoon! Israël in de Schrift en de betekenis van Israël voor de gemeente*. Delft: Fuma.

Van der Spek-Begemann, G. A. 1991. *Job, het troostboek voor Israël*. 's-Gravenhage: Boekencentrum.

Van der Woude, A. S. 1973. "De oorsprong van Israëls messiaanse verwachtingen in het Oude Testament en in de vroeg-joodse traditie." *Kerk en Theologie* 24:1–11.

Van Dijk, B. 2016. *De vervangingsleer voorbij, maar wat nu? En wat te denken van al die Israëlfans?* Dordrecht: CFI Nederland.

Van Eijnatten, J. 1993. *God, Nederland en Oranje*. Kampen: Kok.

Van Gelder, C. 2000. *The Essence of the Church: A Community Created by the Spirit*. Grand Rapids, MI: Baker Books.

VanGemeren, W. A. 2008. *Psalms*. EBC 5. Grand Rapids, MI: Zondervan.

Van Genderen, J. and W. H. Velema. 2008. *Concise Reformed Dogmatics*. Translated by G. Bilkes and E. M. van der Maas. Phillipsburg, NJ: Presbyterian and Reformed Publishing Company.

Van Hell, E., Mauritz, J.H. and others 1992. *Israël, uitgeheven boven de volkeren*. Woerden: Jeugdbond Gereformeerde Gemeenten.

Van Leeuwen, J. A. C. 1953. *De brief aan de Colossenzen, De brieven aan de Thessalonicensen*. 2nd ed. KV. Kampen: Kok.

_____ and D. Jacobs. 1952. *De brief aan de Romeinen*. 3rd ed. KV. Kampen: Kok.

Van Moolenbroek, A. 2016. *Ezau: Hij is Edom: De verborgen strijd om het koninkrijk*. Driebergen: Aspekt.

Van Ryn, A. 1960. *Notes on the Book of Revelation*. Kansas City: Walterick Publishers.

Van 't Spijker, W, W. Balke, L. Van Driel, K. Exalto, and K. Runia, eds. 1999. *Eschatologie: Handboek over de christelijke toekomstverwachting*. Kampen: De Groot Goudriaan.

Van Veelen, W. 1983. *Israël, verkenning en herkenning langs bijbelse paden*. Heinenoord: Vanderstoep.

Veldhuis, H. 2012. *De muur is afgebroken: Het Israëlisch-Palestijns conflict in het licht van christelijk geloof en internationaal recht*. Kairos Palestina Nederland / Vrienden van Sabeel Nederland.

Verkuyl, J. 1992. *De kern van het christelijk geloof*. Kampen: Kok.

Vermes, G. 1993. *The Religion of Jesus the Jew*. London: SCM.

Vine, W. E. 1971. *Isaiah: Prophecies, Promises, Warnings*. Grand Rapids, MI: Zondervan.

Vischer, W. 1949. *The Witness of the Old Testament to Christ*. Translated by A. B. Crabtree. Vol. 1: *The Pentateuch*. London: Lutterworth Press.

Visser 't Hooft, W. A., ed. 1962. *The New Delhi Report: The Third Assembly of the World Council of Churches*. London: SCM.

Von Rad, G. 1935. "Das Christuszeugnis des Alten Testaments: Eine Auseinandersetzung mit Wilhelm Vischers gleichnamigen Buch." *Theologische Blätter* 14:249–54.

Von Rad, G. 1966. *The Problem of the Hexateuch and Other Essays*. London: Oliver & Boyd.

Voorhoeve, H. C. 1922. *De toekomst onzes Heeren Jezus Christus en de daarmee in verband staande gebeurtenissen*. 8th ed. 's-Gravenhage: J.N. Voorhoeve.

_____. 1969. *Beschouwing over de Openbaring*. Apeldoorn: Medema.

Voorhoeve, J. N. 1918. *Het boek met zeven zegelen*. 's-Gravenhage:

J.N. Voorhoeve.

Vreekamp, H. 1988. *Zonder Israël niet volgroeid: Visie op de verhouding tussen kerk en joodse volk van hervormde zijde*. Kampen: Kok.

Vriezen, Th. C. 1951. *Palestina en Israël*. 2nd ed. Wageningen: Veenman.

Walvoord, J. F. 1966. *The Revelation of Jesus Christ*. Chicago: Moody Press.

_____. 1974. *Matthew: Thy Kingdom Come*. Chicago: Moody Press.

_____. 1991. *Major Bible Prophecies: 37 Crucial prophecies that Affect You Today*. Grand Rapids, MI: Zondervan.

Watson, D. 1978. *I Believe in the Church*. London: Hodder & Stoughton.

Wenger, J. C. 1952. *The Doctrines of the Mennonites*. 2nd ed. Scottdale, PA: Mennonite Publ. House.

_____, ed. 1956. *The Complete Writings of Menno Simons, 1496–1561*. Scottdale, PA: Herald Press.

Wentsel, B. 1981. *Dogmatiek*. Vol. 1: *Het Woord, de Zoon en de dienst*. Kampen: Kok.

_____. 1995. *Dogmatiek*. Vol. 4a: *De Heilige Geest, de kerk en de laatste dingen: De persoon en het werk van de Heilige Geest*. Kampen: Kok.

_____. 1998a. *Dogmatiek*. Vol. 4b: *De Heilige Geest, de kerk en de laatste dingen: De kerk als het saamhorige volk Gods*. Kampen: Kok.

Westerman, E. 2015. *De Messias leren: Israël en de volken – Gods weg nieuw leren lezen*. Zoetermeer: Boekencentrum.

Whybrow, W. T. 1898. *Addresses on the Revelation*. London: James Carter.

Willemse, G. J. 1911. "Overdenking op Dingaansdag." *De Kerkbode*, Dec. 7, 1911.

Wilson, M. R. 1989. *Our Father Abraham: Jewish Roots of the Christian Faith*. Grand Rapids, MI: Eerdmans/Dayton, OH: Center for Judaic-Christian Studies.

Witherington III, B. 1992. *Jesus, Paul, and the End of the World: A Comparative Study in New Testament Eschatology*. Downers Grove, IL: InterVarsity Press.

Wolff, H. W. 1984. *Jesaja 53 im Urchristentum*. 4th ed. Gießen: Brunnen-Verlag.

Wood, L. J. 1985. *Hosea*. EBC 7. Grand Rapids, MI: Zondervan.

Wright, J. S. 2007. *Man in the Process of Time: A Christian Assessment of the Powers and Functions of Human Personality*. Whitefish, MT: Kessinger.

Wright, N. T. 2008. *Surprised by Hope: Rethinking Heaven, the Resurrection, and the Mission of the Church*. New York: HarperOne.

———. 2016. *The Day the Revolution Began: Rethinking the Meaning of Jesus' Crucifixion*. New York: HarperOne.

Young, E. J. 1972. *The Book of Isaiah*, Vol. III: *Chapters 40–66*. Grand Rapids, MI: Eerdmans.

Zahn, Th. 1903. *Das Evangelium des Matthäus*. Leipzig: Deichert.

———. 1924. *Die Offenbarung des Johannes*. Vol. 1. Leipzig: Deichert.

Zwiep, A. 2003. *Jezus en het heil van Israëls God: Verkenningen in het Nieuwe Testament*. Zoetermeer: Boekencentrum.

Scripture Index

OLD TESTAMENT		4:19–22	514	11:10	298
Genesis		4:25–26	302	11:10–27	302
1	121, 328, 329	5	258	11:14–17	27
1–3	124, 510	6–9	302	11:24–43	27
1:2	86, 257, 260, 520, 582	6:5	26	11:27	298, 302
		6:8–9	647	12	48
1:9–10	82, 86	6:9	298	12:1	225, 575
1:30	445	6:11-12	26	12:2	549
2	329	7:11	86	12:2–3	27, 558
2:1	445	8–9	131	12:3	35, 52, 55, 56, 61, 68, 276, 560, 561, 562, 622
2:4	298	8:9	260		
2:15–17	511	8:21	26		
2:23	510	9:13–16	26		
3	124, 328, 401	9:26	26	12:7	33, 225
3:14	124	9:26–27	549	12:17	511
3:15	57, 292, 296, 301, 302	9:27	302	13:14–15	28, 225
		10	63	13:15	33
3:20	57, 301	10:1	298	13:17	647
3:21	124	10:21	27, 302	14	335
4	58	10:24-25	27	14:13	27, 302

14:18	335	19:37–38	562	28:4	33, 303
14:18–20	237, 258	21:3–6	5	28:11	59
15	viii, 34, 131, 559	21:12	303, 304	28:13	33, 303
		22	586, 587	28:14	27, 56, 276, 305, 560, 622
15:6	34, 44, 369, 384, 394, 527, 564	22:2	303		
		22:7–8	537, 587	29:25	472
		22:16	4	31	53
15:10	210	22:18	28, 56, 68, 69, 120, 276, 302, 303, 560, 622	31:55–32:2	8
15:12	59			32	6, 50, 53, 54, 57, 61
15:17	59				
15:18	28, 33, 140, 647, 671			32:2–3	57
		24:7	4, 33	32:20	59
16:3	286	24:16	315	32:22	286
17	viii, 26, 34, 36, 131, 559	24:43	315	32:24	52, 59
		25:1–2	26	32:24–31	51
17:1	35, 69	25:2	303	32:25	5, 53
17:1–2	469	25:12	298	32:25–26	53
17:1–21	34	25:13–15	26	32:26	52, 58
17:4–5	558	25:19	298	32:28	5, 53, 59, 304
17:5	5, 26	25:22	50	32:29	59
17:7	35	25:23	49, 50, 305	32:30	55, 59
17:8	28, 33	25:26	5, 50	32:31	59
17:9	303	25:30	61	32:31–32	53
17:11	36	26:3	4, 33, 303	33	60, 61
17:12	370	26:4	28, 56, 68, 276, 303, 508, 560, 622	33:4	53
17:13	35, 37			33:10	51, 52, 53
17:14	36			33:10–11	60
17:19	35	26:5	69, 469, 564	33:11	61
18:8	56	26:24	303	33:14	61
18:18	28, 68, 276, 560, 622	27	185	33:22	53
		27:29	52, 435, 619	35:10	54, 78, 304
18:19	69, 469, 564	27:36	50, 59	35:11	34
19:23	59	27:39–40	55	35:12	33
19:34–38	422	28:3	34	35:18	331

Scripture Index

35:21–22	304		360, 414	4:20	576
35:22	571	49:2	360	4:21	636
36	26	49:3–7	360	4:22	42, 211, 356, 525, 548, 664
36:1	61, 298	49:8–10	287		
36:9	298	49:8–12	666		
37	362, 453	49:10	75, 291, 292, 306, 339	4:22–23	319
37:3	304			5:1	4, 65, 528, 564, 566
37:7–8	435	49:22–26	306, 361		
37:13	304	49:26	306	5:6–9	578
39	362	49:28	571	6:4	220
40	362	50:24	4	6:7	566
42:5	304			6:12	266
43:6	304	**Exodus**		6:15–19	578
43:8	304	1	57	6:30	266
43:11	304	1:1	572	7	124
44:14	435	1:1–5	578	7:3	578, 636
45	442	1:1–7	538	7:16	566
45–50	361	1:5	57	7:17–21	124
45:21	304	1:11	578	7:19–20	659
45:28	304	1:14	578	8:15	636
46:1–2	304	1:16	579	8:23	578
46:5	304	1:22	579, 664	8:32	636
46:8	304	2:1–13	49	9:12	636
46:26	57	2:2	579	9:34	636
46:29–30	304	2:3–4	579	10:1	636
47:27	304	2:5	579	10:1–2	578
47:29	304	2:24	35	10:20	636
47:31	304	3:1	538	10:27	636
48:4	28, 33, 34	3:5	14, 223	11:10	636
48:15	362	3:6	28	12	537
48:18–20	666	3:7	564	12:3	257
49	26, 307, 311, 360	3:10	564, 566	12:6	257
		3:15-16	28	12:14	585
49:1	201, 306,	3:7	4	12:19	257

705

12:41	98, 111	19:19	582	32:7	4
12:46	348, 442, 587	20	582	32:11–12	4
		20:2	572	32:13	28, 33
12:47	257	20:5	406	32:27	65
13:12–15	370	20:12	29	32:32–33	298
13:18	664	24	38	33:1	33
14	664	24:1	375, 576	33:11	333
14:4	636	24:3	200, 208, 215	33:14	284
14:8	636, 664			33:16	531
14:17	636	24:5	212	33:20–23	333
14:31	384	24:7	200, 208, 215	34:5–6	524
15:5	86			34:6	188, 189, 461
15:13	224	24:9	576		
15:17	224	24:10	65	34:23	65
15:18	505	24:16	223	34:29–30	578
15:24	224	25:8	223	34:34	243, 649
16	664	25:22	20	34:35	578
16:4	576	26:33	20	35:3	157, 282
17:6	576	26:33–34	20	39:30	337
17:16	111	28:3	337	40	97, 221
18:1–12	259	28:36	337	40:34	376
19	286	28:41	337		
19–20	582	29:1	337	**Leviticus**	
19–24	viii, 131	29:7	331	1	385
19:1	572	29:38–46	537, 587	1–7	385
19:4	664	29:38–47	49	2	385
19:5	470, 529, 531, 551	29:21	337	3	385
		29:33	337	4–5	385
19:5–6	461, 566, 627	29:44	337	7	385
		29:45	219	8:12	331, 337
19:6	272, 525	29:45–46	223	8:30	337
19:8	200, 208, 215	30:30	331	12:1–8	370
		31:16	39	12:3	370
19:16	582	31:18	583	16:8	478

16:10	356	2	23, 571	24:14	11, 201, 360, 414
16:14–15	214	3:1–2	442		
16:16	143	3:3	331	24:17	292, 664
16:18	587	3:12–13	213	24:17–19	62, 305
16:20–22	356	3:21	442	24:18–19	62
16:21	143	6	362	24:19	62
16:30	143	6:3	362	25:10–13	336
16:34	143	7:89	20	25:11–13	131
17:11	viii, 367, 387	9:12	348, 442	25:14	359
		9:14	626	26:11	70
18:5	215	10:11	623	27:17	529, 538
20:24	531	11:16	375, 576	30:4	208
23	585	11:24–25	375, 576	30:7	208
23:2	482	11:24–29	535	30:14	208
23:15–21	581	11:25	463	32	575, 656
23:24	586	12:6–8	333	32:11	35
24:2–4	479	12:8	333	33:38	572
24:8	39	14:11–13	359	35:15	626
25:1–7	71	14:21–24	499		
25:23	19, 32, 221, 316, 574, 626	14:22–23	40	**Deuteronomy**	
		15:15	626	1:8	35
		15:17–21	559	1:30–31	209
25:35	626	15:38–40	63	1:31	42
25:47	626	16:31–33	664	1:34	40
25:55	461	16:32	70	4:19	10, 111
26	448	18:20–23	127	4:20	10
26:12	219, 255	21:20	623	4:30	11, 201, 414
26:33	608	22:5	259		
26:38	608	22:23	448	4:40	28
26:41	106, 266	22:31	448	5:5	376
26:42	35, 220	23:19	323	5:6	572
		23:21	664	5:16	29
Numbers		24	305	6:4	410
1:44	375, 576			6:10	35

7:6	40, 531, 551	19:14	395	30:11–14	298
7:6–8	469	21:15–17	287	30:20	35
8:5	42, 209	21:21	642	31:29	414
8:5–6	583	23:3	562	32	77, 415
8:14–16	664	26:2	224	32:4	570
9:5	35	27:9	642	32:6	43
9:10	583	28	77	32:8	19
10:12	106	28–29	448	32:8–9	9, 97
10:15	531	28–32	54	32:10	11, 65, 409
10:16	36, 106, 266	29	415	32:11–12	664
10:17	8	29:1	38	32:15	570
12:5	224	29:1–14	131	32:18	570
12:5–6	224	29:9	38	32:30–31	570
12:11	224	29:12	38	32:35–43	415
12:21	224	29:13	35	32:42	416
13:11	642	29:14	38	32:43	416
14:1	42, 65, 319, 461, 525, 528, 548	29:26	10	33:3	34
		30	77	33:16	14, 223, 362
		30:1–6	142		
14:2	40, 551	30:1–10	228, 415	34:4	35
14:23–24	224	30:2	143, 401	34:10	415, 576
16:2	224	30:2–3	415	34:10–12	333
16:3	585	30:3	143, 229		
16:6	224	30:4–5	417	**Joshua**	
16:9–11	581	30:5	140, 143, 229	2	259
16:11	224			3:17	642
16:12	585	30:5–9	30	4:7	586
17:14–20	332	30:6	36, 106, 266	5:14	8
18	332, 650	30:8	143	6:21	448
18:15	378, 415	30:9	143, 229, 233	7:24–25	642
18:15–16	292			8:15	642
18:15–18	332, 333, 373, 576	30:10	143, 401, 415	8:21	642
				8:24	642
18:18	415	30:11	217	8:33	642

13:3	422	4:17	308, 661	19:20	535
14:9	28	4:18–22	587	19:23	535
22:19	222			28:13	51
23:16	220	**1 Samuel**		31:10	153
24:2	27, 302	1:3	307		
24:2–3	27	1:9	19, 307, 651, 652	**2 Samuel**	
24:16–17	38			2:4	331
24:21	38	1:24	307	2:10	192
		2:7–8	447	3:10	249
Judges		2:22	642	5:2	539
2:1–2	39	3:3	652	5:3	331
2:13	153	3:20	332	5:4	81
3:10	463	4–6	97	5:6–9	71
5:19	669	4:3–4	223	5:7	127, 308
6:34	463	4:4	20, 223, 339, 349	5:9	308
8:27	642			5:14	442
8:30	57	4:21	97	5:17	320
9:13	401	4:21–22	78	5:18	645
10:6	153	6:21	223	5:22	645
11:29	463	7:1–2	223	6:2	20, 223, 339, 349
13:5–6	148	7:3–4	153		
13:25	463	8:5	531	6:10	308
14:6	463	8:20	531	6:10–11	223
14:19	463	10:10	535	6:12	308
15:14	463	12:10	153	6:13–18	335
16:4–21	148	13:14	65, 92, 309	6:14	335
20:2	564	13:19	225	6:16	308
20:27	223	15:12	586	6:17	118
		16:1	308, 309	6:18	335
Ruth		16:11	309	7	313
1–4	259	16:13	331, 535	7:7	539
4	562	16:18	308	7:12	313
4:13–22	562	17:12	308	7:12–16	292, 309, 313, 361
		17:58	308		

7:14	293, 313, 319, 320, 381	7:2	479	6:15–17	9
		8	223	7:6	9
7:16	313	8:1	127	9:27	669
7:23	531	8:6	20, 215	10:33	575
8:2	305	8:14	335	13:23	35
8:13–14	305	8:16	224	14:25	82, 86
8:17	67	8:30–49	85	15:8–11	585
12:24–25	304	8:32	43	18–19	494
14:13	564	8:53	531	19:15	20, 223, 339, 349
15:35	670	8:55	335		
18:18	586	8:62–64	335	19:31	494
23:1–7	335	8:63	118	23:3	38
23:3	305, 493	10	397	23:13	153
23:3–4	296, 348	11:5	153	23:27	224, 468
23:3–5	314	11:15–16	305	23:29	442, 669
23:4	314	11:33	153	24:6	317
23:5	131	11:36	224	24:8–17	370
23:13	645	11:42	81	24:13	19
24:16–17	448	12:21	192	25:27–30	31
24:25	118	13:2	451		
		14:21	514	**1 Chronicles**	
1 Kings		14:31	562	2–4	306
2	168	15:17	86	3:17–18	317
2:11	81	17	259, 513	5:1	306, 666
2:12	232, 249	17:1	341, 451, 659	5:1–2	287, 361
2:25	318	19:16	331	5:26	575
2:27	335	19:18	631	6:3–15	119
2:35	335	22	669	11:3	38
3:4	118, 223	22:19	111	13:6	20, 223, 339, 349
4:21	140, 307, 671				
4:24	307	**2 Kings**		15:1	223
5:3	340	4	259	16:17	35, 39
5:7	259	5	259	16:33	447
6:1	98			16:39	223

21:1	52	**Ezra**		10:3	588
21:28	335	1:1–4	71, 95		
21:29	223	1:3	454	**Job**	
28:5	340	1:4	454	1:6–13	52
29:15	574, 626	1:5	308, 454, 656	2:1–7	52
29:18	564	1:8	308	2:11	259
29:23	75, 93, 111, 234, 340, 418	2:63	455	4:8	477
		2:64	455	9:13	10
29:27	81	3:2	119	14:1–4	215
		3:8	119	15:14–15	215
2 Chronicles		6:12	224	15:15	447
1:3	223	7:12–26	357	22:15	2
1:13	223	9:8–9	578	25:4–6	215
5:7	20	9:9	357	26:12	10
7:1	455			32:2	259
7:20	32	**Nehemiah**		35:7–8	323
9:30	81	1:9	224	42:6	142
15:10–12	581	7:65	455		
15:12–13	38	9:8	220	**Psalms**	
23:3	38	9:17	189	1:2	409
24:20	585	9:36–37	578	2	299, 312, 318, 319, 340
29:10–11	38	9:38	38		
30:9	189	11:1	221	2:1–2	319
33:9	500	11:18	221	2:2	337, 338, 621
33:12–13	500			2:5–7	293
33:13	643	**Esther**		2:6	viii, 23, 320, 505, 621
35:22	442	1:19	422		
36:11–12	82	2:5	331	2:6–8	67, 667
36:20–21	71	3:8	v, 37	2:7	293, 319, 320, 321, 381
36:21	451	3:10	v, 37		
36:22–23	71, 95	8:1	v	2:7–8	289
36:23	227, 549	9:10	v	2:8	120, 307
		9:24	v	2:8–9	319
				2:9	91, 319

5:7	222	22:2	344, 345	40:6–7	385
8	299, 327, 328, 329, 486	22:8–9	345	40:6–8	292, 345, 346
		22:14	345	40:7	348
8:2	327	22:16	281, 302	40:8	208, 217, 409
8:4	88, 324, 379	22:17	345	41:9	348
8:4–6	292, 327, 328	22:19	345	42:7	83
8:5	293, 329	22:23	345	43:3–4	66
8:6	51	22:25	345	45	299, 340, 346, 587
9:10	345	22:28	345		
10:16	505	22:30	668	45:1	346
11:4	222	22:30–31	207	45:1–18	292
14:2	496	22:31	431	45:2	346
14:3	548	24	482	45:3–5	346
14:7	254, 415, 638	24:1	19, 221	45:5	346
16	299, 342, 343, 344	24:7	341	45:6	381
		26:8	223	45:6–7	347
16:1	347	28:8	338	45:7	338, 347
16:1–11	292	28:8–9	338	45:9	6
16:8–11	293, 344	29:10	505	45:11	346
16:9	343	30:13	343	45:14	347
16:10	342, 344	32–42	436	45:14–15	346
17:8	11, 65	32:1–5	401	45:18	587
18:17	330	34:20	348	46:4	19
18:50	337, 338	37:9–11	647	48:1	19, 66, 222
19:4	273	37:20	647	48:1–3	667
19:7–8	409	37:22	647	48:8	19
19:8	583	37:25	345	48:13	668
20:1	596	37:28–29	647	50:2	254
20:2	127	37:31	208	50:15	596
20:6	338	37:34	647	51:5	215
21:5	289	37:39	596	51:10	401
22	296, 299, 344	40	299, 345, 385, 387	51:11	463, 520
22:1	348			51:14	401
22:1–22	292	40:6	293	51:17	388, 401

53:2	496	78:23–29	664	89:27	348
53:3	548	78:25	576	89:38	338
53:6	415	78:27	619	89:51	50, 337, 338
53:7	254	78:54	222	90–100	121
55:6–8	89	78:67–70	666	90:4	245
57:9	343	79:1	222	92	121
68:18	376, 577	80	330, 358	94:8	496
68:33–34	326	80:1	20, 223, 339, 349, 529	94:14	345
69	299, 347			95:3–5	447
69:1–2	83	80:8	88, 331, 358, 528, 647	95:11	4, 40
69:4	292, 347			96:1–3	447
69:5	348	80:8–15	358	96:4	447
69:9	83, 347	80:14	331	96:9–10	447
69:19	348	80:14–17	88	96:11–12	447
69:21	292, 347	80:15	324, 330, 358	97:1	447
69:22–23	347	80:17	324, 330, 331, 358, 379	97:2	326
69:23	631			97:2–5	447
69:25	347	82:6	382	97:7	381
71:17–18	509	83:5–8	488	97:9	447
71:18	509	84:9	338	98:3–4	447
72	299, 307, 321, 339, 340	86:9	544	98:7–8	447
		86:15	189	98:8	448
72:2	339	87	275, 276	99:1	20, 223, 339, 349, 447
72:8	300, 341	87:1	222		
72:8–11	307	87:3	19	99:9	222
72:9	619	87:4	10	100:1	447
74:2	127	88	70	101:6	179
74:12–14	89	89:6	447	101:7–8	179
74:13	664	89:10	664	101:8	19
74:18–19	89	89:11	10	102	299, 382
76:2	127	89:12	447	102:18	668
77:19	50	89:19–29	313	102:24–27	240
78:4	207, 668	89:26	320, 570	102:25–27	382
78:6	431, 668	89:26–27	319	103:8	189, 461

103:8-10	524	118:26	21, 399	132	299, 340
103:13	43, 531	119:11	217	132:4-5	225
104:1-2	662	119:14	588	132:10	337, 338
104:3	326	119:16	588	132:11	76, 419
104:15	401	119:24	588	132:11-12	232
105:8	587	119:34	217	132:15	576
105:9	4	119:35	588	132:17	337, 338
105:10	35, 39	119:36	217	133:3	532
105:15	331	119:44	133, 409	133:3-5	249
105:40	664	119:47	588	136:2	8
106:16	337	119:70	409, 588	137:5	1
109:25	348	119:77	409, 588	137:5-6	15
110	335, 344, 348	119:92	409, 588	138:2	222
110:1	88, 314, 330, 331, 336, 339, 340, 344, 348, 349, 381	119:93	583	144	328
		119:97	409, 589	144:3	324
		119:98	409	144:3-4	328
		119:99-100	374	145:8	189
		119:111-112	588	146:3	323
110:1-7	237, 292	119:112	133, 217, 409	146:10	505
110:4	334				
111:5	587	119:126	198	**Proverbs**	
111:10	496	119:129	217	1:1-7	496
112:6	587	119:143	588	3:3	217
113:1	572	119:144	409	7:2	65, 409
113:7-8	447	119:160	133, 409	7:13	217
114:1	572	119:162	588	8	297, 582
115:3	521	119:163	409	16:33	478
115:16	521	119:165	409	21:1	7, 669
118	350, 482	119:174	409, 588	22:8	477
118:22	350, 425	121:5-6	23	31	510
118:22-23	350	122	14		
118:22-26	292	125:1	667	**Ecclesiastes**	
118:23-27	635	126:1	667	3:12	588
118:25-26	350	130:1-4	401		

Scripture Index

3:12–13	589	4:2	311	8:14	384, 393
3:22	588	5	171	8:14–15	486
4:12	65	5:1–7	358, 400, 528, 647	8:14–18	486
5:2–5	200			8:17	350
5:19	588	5:2	401	8:18	321, 323
7:28	297	5:4	401	9:2	321
8:15	588	5:13	78	9:5	661
9:15	297	5:25	645	9:6	307, 319, 320, 371, 381, 420, 439
11:8–9	588	5:26	203		
11:9	589	6	293, 382		
		6:1	111	9:6–7	46, 68, 76, 203, 227, 232, 250, 292, 311, 313, 316, 317, 320, 340, 379, 418, 419
Song of Solomon		6:1–5	240		
1:8	50	6:9	290, 631		
1:15	89	6:13	311		
2:14	89	7	315, 316		
3:11	347, 662	7:1	316		
4:1	89	7:1–9:7	321		
5:2	89	7:3	253, 495	9:7	107, 203, 300, 316, 322, 335, 367, 418, 419, 420, 445
6:4	347	7:6	321		
6:9	89	7:11–14	316		
		7:13	315, 316		
Isaiah		7:14	292, 309, 313, 315, 316, 321, 322, 417, 420	10	420, 494
1:11	387			10–11	420
1:13	387			10:5	93, 403, 420, 494
1:18–20	43	7:17–18	420		
2:1–4	68, 121, 250, 311, 486	7:20	420	10:6	658
		8:1–4	321	10:12	417, 420, 495
2:2	11, 201, 360, 414, 446	8:3	316	10:20–21	69
		8:4	420	10:20–22	40
2:2–3	583, 658, 670	8:7	420, 491	10:20–25	495
2:2–4	277, 318	8:7–8	425	10:21	498
2:3	23, 65, 235, 587	8:7–10	417	10:21–22	253, 631
2:4	67, 584	8:8	316	10:33–34	311

715

10:33–11:4	420	13:17	72	27:9	137, 638
11	311, 420, 423, 424, 445	13:21	668	27:13	222, 656
		14	653	27:27–29	58
		14:1–2	222	28	425, 487
11:1	232, 310, 318	14:12	305	28–29	425
		14:12–15	97, 653	28–32	417
11:1–5	313	14:13	669	28:2	425
11:1–10	232, 292, 329, 340	14:25	32, 417	28:3	492
		16:4–5	317, 379	28:5	40, 631
11:2	496	16:5	23, 203, 232, 311, 315	28:5–6	340
11:4	311, 424, 445			28:7–19	425
		17:4–6	253, 645	28:15	425
11:4–5	423	17:6	497	28:16	384, 393, 425, 548, 626
11:6	424	17:10	570		
11:6–7	424	17:12	82, 324, 539	28:18	425
11:6–8	444	18	491	29:5–8	340
11:8	446, 668	18:2	491, 492	29:10	631
11:9	222, 420, 446	18:4	492, 493	29:17–18	426
		18:5	493	29:17–24	340
11:9–10	445	18:6	493	29:18	379
11:9–16	424	19:1	326	29:22–24	426
11:10	310	19:19	658	30–32	418
11:11	40, 424, 631	19:23–25	417, 488	30:4–5	155
		21:2	72, 422	30:7	97
11:11–16	421, 488	21:11–12	63	30:18–26	340
11:12	231, 424	22:20–22	350	30:29	570
11:12–13	423, 656	24:5	39, 40, 45, 199	31:4–5	241
11:12–14	203			32:1	155, 340
11:13	231	24:23	667	32:1–2	340
11:14	424	24:23–27:13	340	32:1–3	394, 426
11:14–15	423	25:7	110, 434	32:1–4	241, 379
11:15	424	25:12	619	32:3	340
11:16	631, 656	26:13	10	32:4	340
12:1–6	312	26:19	633	32:5	340

Scripture Index

32:6	340	42:2–4	354	45:4	304, 353, 354, 355
32:7–8	340	42:3	353		
32:9–15	484	42:4	65	45:14	435
32:14–15	484	42:4–7	87	45:22–25	22
32:14–18	203	42:6	45, 194, 204, 353	45:25	253, 462, 469, 631, 638, 644
32:15	438, 463, 535				
33:2	596	42:6–7	353		
33:14	644	42:7	379	46:3	355, 631
34	63	42:19–22	353	46:9–10	6
35:1–2	447	43:6	203	46:10–11	95
35:4–6	624	43:9–12	34	46:11	7
35:5–6	379	43:10	353, 354, 355	48:18	67
36–39	494			48:20	353, 354, 573
37:3	596	43:14–21	453		
37:16	20, 223, 339, 349	43:16–21	22	48:20–21	664
		44:1	304	49:1–5	355
37:22	494, 667	44:1–2	353, 354	49:1–7	292, 350
37:31–32	631	44:1–3	355	49:1–9	350
37:36	417	44:3	260, 438, 463, 484, 535	49:3	87, 304, 353, 354, 399, 529
39	322				
40–53	353				
40:1–11	22	44:6–7	2	49:5–6	304, 307, 353
40:4	446	44:8	34		
40:11	362, 529	44:21	304, 353	49:6	87, 300, 311, 352, 399, 529
41:8	304	44:21–22	353, 355		
41:8–9	353, 354	44:23	171, 355, 447, 448		
41:8–10	355			49:7	353
41:17–20	22	44:24–26	21	49:8	45, 353
41:19	431	44:26	353	49:8–9	353
42–53	88, 296, 456	44:28	7, 22, 71, 95, 227	49:11	446
42:1	354, 355			49:13	447, 448
42:1–4	352	45:1	7, 22, 95, 227	49:14	583
42:1–7	22, 292, 350, 354			49:14–21	667
		45:1–8	71	49:18	528, 661
				49:21	310

717

49:23	435, 619	53:1–6	356	55:12	446, 447, 448
50	141	53:2	311	55:12–13	427, 447
50:1	471, 528, 661	53:2–4	353	55:13	431
50:4	374	53:3	355	56:2	37
50:4–11	292, 350	53:4	352	56:2–6	205
50:6	353	53:4–5	345	56:4	37, 45
50:8–9	348	53:5	281, 302, 352, 355	56:5–7	213, 427
50:10	353			56:6	37, 545
51:1–2	570	53:5–6	386	56:6–7	20, 115, 194, 277
51:1–8	667	53:5–12	353		
51:2	27	53:7	49, 352, 355, 537, 587	56:7	222, 658, 670
51:4	65, 587			56:9–57:13	645
51:7	208, 587	53:7–8	17, 352	57:13	29, 222, 499
51:9	10, 49, 89, 97, 588, 653, 664	53:8	353, 355	57:14–21	253, 401
		53:8–12	355	57:15	143, 388
		53:9	352, 355	57:15–16	92
51:9–11	453	53:10	352, 355, 386	57:17–21	499
51:16	355	53:11	644	57:18–19	499
52–53	80, 352, 354	53:12	352, 354, 355, 427	59:1–8	499
52:1	37, 205			59:9–13	253
52:1–2	221	54	141, 426, 428, 471	59:18–19	499
52:5	524			59:20	137, 499, 638
52:7–10	354	54–56	428	59:20–21	253
52:10	87	54:1	310, 426, 583, 667	59:21	45, 204, 509, 638
52:11	573				
52:11–12	354	54:4–7	661	60	48
52:12	354	54:5	661	60–63	638
52:13	351, 354, 496	54:6	471	60–66	120
52:13–53:12	292, 351, 354, 426	54:6–8	528, 587, 661	60:1	21
		54:10	204	60:1–2	499, 672
52:15	87, 354	54:10–14	427	60:1–3	311, 331
53	18, 294, 295, 300, 351, 352, 355	54:12	427	60:3	672
		54:17	353	60:5	672
		55:3	45, 204, 344	60:7	21, 213, 658

60:11	639, 671	64:1	501	3:17–18	234
60:13	431	64:6	404	3:18	192, 203, 423
60:14	19, 23, 435, 639	64:8	43, 531	3:19	66
		64:9	586	4:1–2	545
60:17–22	203	65	501	4:4	36, 106, 266
60:18–22	501	65:11	222	5:11	192
60:19	672	65:13–14	501	7:1–15	467
60:21	29, 253, 462, 469, 631, 638, 643	65:17–25	501	7:4	19, 467
		65:19–23	207	7:7	29, 140, 225
		65:20	431	7:12	224
61:1	292, 535, 574	65:20–23	668	7:18	153
61:1–2	350, 353	65:21–25	329	7:23	470
61:1–3	334	65:25	124, 222, 301, 431, 445	8:13	647
61:4–11	22			9:4	50
61:6	525	66:7	663	9:25	36
61:7	29, 46, 202	66:8	309, 310	9:25–26	37, 266
61:7–9	45	66:18–21	30	9:26	106
61:8	35, 204	66:19–21	498	10:10	505
61:8–9	193	66:20	203, 213, 222, 227, 230, 658	11:5	4
61:9	76			11:10	192, 199
61:10	528, 587, 661			11:17	192
62:1	638	66:23	37, 205, 312	12:10	647
62:4	661			12:14	192
62:4–5	661	**Jeremiah**		12:14–15	488
62:5	528, 587	2	528	13:11	192
62:6–9	23	2:2	65, 347, 587, 661	13:13	419
62:8	4			15:5	1
62:8–9	4	2:7	32	15:11	596
63	62	2:21	358, 647	16:15	230
63:7–64:12	500	3:6	667	16:16	539
63:11	375, 529	3:6–10	661	16:18	32
63:16	43, 531	3:14	661	16:19	596
63:18	658	3:16	20, 455	17:25	419
63:20–21	582	3:17	75, 111, 277		

18:13	667	30:6–7	663	31:31–3	192, 199
22:2	419	30:6–8	203	31:31–33	204
22:4	419	30:7	202, 210, 439, 596, 597	31:31–34	viii, 38, 137, 207, 214, 255, 428, 549
22:8	77				
22:24	317	30:9	45, 197, 203, 313, 429		
22:30	317, 419				
23	318	30:11	203	31:32	65, 661
23:1–8	452	30:18	429	31:33	133, 195, 208, 423, 587
23:3	230	30:18–20	203		
23:3–8	236	30:18–22	236		
23:5	73, 203, 292, 313, 317, 452	30:21	203	31:33–34	638
		30:21–22	197	31:34	586
23:5–6	318, 430	30:22	219	31:35–37	246
23:8	230	30:24	201, 414	31:38–40	203
23:20	201, 414	31	191, 192, 196, 201	32:37	202, 230, 429
23:29	582			32:37–40	429
24:7	219	31:1	219	32:37–41	45
25:5	29, 140, 225	31:1–6	664	32:38	219
25:11–12	70, 98, 143, 451	31:2–6	470	32:39	216
		31:3	2	32:40	35, 204
25:12	71	31:4	667	32:41	202
25:14	72	31:4–7	203	33	318
25:25	422	31:6	40, 470	33:4	203
25:26	10	31:8	429	33:7	415
27:7	72	31:10	193	33:7–9	193
29:10	70, 98, 143	31:12–14	203	33:11	202, 312, 415
29:10–14	451	31:15	273, 293	33:14	203
29:11–14	72	31:19	429	33:14–16	318, 430
29:14	203, 230	31:21	667	33:14–22	429
29:16	419	31:23	202, 222, 415	33:15	45, 202, 203, 292, 317
30	201	31:24–25	203		
30–31	77, 197, 453	31:27	203	33:17	203, 232, 233, 419
30–33	453, 597	31:30	203		
30:3	202, 423, 429	31:31	201, 203	33:17–18	212, 237

33:21	23	3:39	142	17:22–23	74
33:22	203	3:44	326	17:22–24	452
33:25	131	4:13	142	17:23	313
33:26	415			18:20	203, 406
35	362	**Ezekiel**		18:31	216
35:15	140	1:26	111, 324	19:10	358
36:30	419	2:1	323	20:6	66
37:15–28	203	2:3	323	20:8–10	664
37:24–26	198	2:6	323	20:11	215
38:7–12	259	2:8	323	20:15	66
43:5	203, 230	5:5	19, 23	20:33–38	664
44:17–19	153	6:8	40	20:40	222, 312, 656
44:25	153	9–10	454	20:42	140
46:28	203	9–11	67, 68, 80, 97, 221, 223, 670	21	74
48:47	201, 414, 415			21:18–27	484
49:6	415			21:24–27	75
49:39	201, 414	9:4	497	21:25–27	453
50:4–5	46, 202, 582	10:1	111	21:26–27	484
50:5	35, 204	11:19	216, 401, 461	21:27	308
51	86, 87, 89	11:20	219	21:32	308
51:6	573	12:3–4	78	23	141
51:11	72	14:11	219	23:1–5	667
51:25	669	15	358, 528, 647	23:4	661
51:28	72	16	141, 257, 471, 528	26:20	2
51:34	50, 87, 97, 588, 653	16:1–14	65	29:3	10
				29:14	415
51:44	50, 87, 97, 588, 653	16:8	41, 587	31:3	489
		16:15–17	667	32:7	305
51:45	573	16:32	661	33–39	453
		16:59–61	41	34–37	431
Lamentations		16:60	35, 587	34–48	32
1:3	78	16:60–62	204	34:23	309, 362
1:8	142	17	74, 452	34:23–24	203, 232, 292, 312,
2:13	174, 667	17:3–4	74		

	313, 368, 431, 587	37:14	260, 438, 484, 490	40–44	15, 20, 47, 67, 82, 118, 213, 235, 318, 463, 532, 652, 658
34:24	65	37:15–22	433		
34:25	204	37:15–28	76, 423		
34:27	431	37:16	529		
36	23, 431, 432	37:19	529	40–45	23, 133, 194, 428
36:3–7	431	37:21–22	433, 490, 656		
36:5	32	37:22	446	40–46	387
36:8–12	446	37:24	292, 309, 362, 368	40–48	115
36:8–15	431			40:2	213, 670, 672
36:9	529	37:24–25	66, 203, 312, 313, 431, 587	40:46	67, 119, 336, 670
36:22–32	388			41:4	20
36:23	524	37:24–28	47, 232	42:13	20
36:24	43, 220, 230	37:25	140	42:20	234
36:25–26	526	37:25–26	202	43	78, 81, 454, 588, 670
36:25–27	43, 216, 220, 461, 649	37:26	35, 204		
		37:26–28	193, 670	43:2–5	223
36:26	216, 401	37:27	219, 233, 255	43:4–5	67
36:26–27	208	37:28	234	43:12	20
36:27	260, 438, 463, 484, 535	38–39	32, 489	43:19	67, 119, 336
		38:2–3	489	44:3	97
36:28	43, 140, 226	38:4–5	422	44:7	19, 106, 205
36:29–36	432	38:6	489	44:7–9	266
36:29–39	432	38:12	19, 23	44:9	37, 106, 205
36:31	209	38:15	489	44:13	20
37	197, 232, 432, 433, 441, 489, 490	38:16	32, 201, 360, 414	44:15	67, 119, 336
				44:15–31	212, 213
		38:17	32	44:24	37, 205, 482, 587
37:1–14	137, 633	39:1	489		
37:4–8	137	39:1–5	32	45:1	213
37:8	490	39:2	489	45:1–7	656
37:9–10	490	39:7	32	45:4	213
37:9–14	137	39:25	32	45:7	97
37:11–14	489	39:29	260, 484	45:7–8	213

45:16	213	4	94, 489	7:13	88, 137, 155, 300, 324, 326, 367, 378, 381, 600, 610
45:17	37, 205	4:10	24		
45:22	97, 213	4:11	24		
46:1	37, 205	4:16	96		
46:3-4	37, 205	4:26	131	7:13-14	60, 96, 152, 238, 292, 307, 325, 339, 434
46:12	37, 205	4:34-37	94		
46:16	97	5:4	94		
47:8-10	15	5:11-12	496		
47:13-23	647	5:14	496	7:14	155, 325, 335, 619
47:13-48:35	671	5:18-19	91		
48	65, 571, 656	5:19	71	7:15	434
48:1-8	656	5:20-21	91	7:17	155
48:11	67, 119, 336	5:21	324	7:18	239
48:23-29	656	5:22-28	95	7:22	239, 434
48:29	213	5:28	422	7:23	325
		5:30	72, 95	7:23-24	324
Daniel		6:1	72	7:25	187, 434, 599
1:4	496	6:8	422	7:27	3, 6, 60, 239, 325, 435, 619, 662
1:17	496	6:12	422		
2	62, 90, 96, 151, 152, 157, 489	6:15	422		
		7	62, 90, 152, 238, 239, 323, 324, 325, 326, 379, 489, 608, 609	8	95
				8:3-4	96
2:7	8			8:5	96
2:28	201, 360			8:11-12	652
2:34-35	152			8:13	599
2:37-38	90, 96			8:17	497, 600
2:38	324	7-11	455	8:19	495, 497, 600
2:39	96	7:2	324	8:20	96
2:40-41	96	7:4	96	8:21-22	96
2:41	94	7:4-6	324	9	291, 356, 444
2:44	92, 96	7:5	96	9:2	70, 98, 143, 451
2:45	152	7:6	96		
2:47	8	7:7	96, 324, 325	9:5	143, 406, 444
3	94, 665	7:9	111, 325	9:8	143, 406, 444

9:11	143, 406, 444	11:40	435, 497, 600		471, 472
9:15	143, 406, 444	11:41–43	488	2:1	466, 644, 661
9:24	144, 207, 210, 221, 357, 387, 435, 487, 587	11:44	66	2:5	667
		11:45	222	2:14–15	644
		12	24, 436	2:14–23	65
		12:1	7, 8, 97, 202, 439, 596, 597	2:16	661
9:24–27	187, 291, 356, 435, 487, 599			2:17–20	472
		12:1–2	532, 633	2:18–19	587, 661
		12:1–3	435	2:18–20	528
9:25–26	291	12:3	496	2:22	3, 9, 255, 272
9:26	292, 357, 487, 607, 652	12:4	497, 600	2:23	466, 529, 628, 644
		12:7	187, 599		
9:27	247, 357, 487, 495, 599, 600, 601, 602, 652, 657, 665	12:9	497, 600	3	77, 141, 454
		12:10	436, 496	3:1	473
		12:11	187, 247, 599, 600, 601, 602, 652, 665	3:4	78, 367, 387, 436
				3:4–5	203, 236, 312, 436, 473
10	10				
10:13	7, 8, 97				
10:14	201, 360, 414	12:11–12	599	3:5	66, 201, 360, 414, 587, 629
10:20	7, 8, 97				
10:21	7, 97	Hosea		6:1–3	633
11	19	1–2	11, 255, 569	6:6	367, 387
11–12	9	1:2	472	6:11	415
11:2–4	95	1:3	472	8:13	387
11:4	96	1:6	472	9:3	316
11:16	66	1:6–11	628	9:4	387
11:30	96	1:8	472	10:1	358, 528
11:31	247, 599, 652	1:8–11	466	10:5	78
11:32–33	496	1:9	3, 9, 78, 455	11	358
11:33	436, 496	1:9–10	466	11:1	42, 88, 211, 293, 319, 331, 358, 525, 548
11:35	96, 435, 436, 497, 600	1:10	42, 255, 272, 528, 529, 548		
11:36	8, 495	1:12	3		
11:36–45	435	2	141, 257,	12	61

Scripture Index

12:3–5	53	**Amos**		2:6	86
12:4	54	1–2	531	2:7	222
12:4	50	1:5	78	3	83, 397
12:4–5	52	3:2	468	3:1	87
12:5	53, 54	4:2	4	3:4	83
14:7	647	5:2	667	4:2	189
		5:5	78		
Joel		5:13	496	**Micah**	
1:6	32	5:22	387	1:2	222
1:7	647	6:7	78	1:16	78
1:12	647	7:11	78	2:12	40
2	437	7:17	78	3	485
2:1	222	9:7	468, 531	3:9	485
2:13	189	9:11	203	3:9–4:5	485
2:28	438	9:11–12	314	4:1	201, 202, 360, 414, 485, 486
2:28–29	260	9:11–15	314		
2:28–31	535	9:14	415		
2:28–32	31, 437, 484, 529			4:1–2	21, 658, 670
		Obadiah		4:1–3	277
2:32	548, 667	12	596	4:1–4	250, 485
3	76, 438	14	596	4:2	23, 65, 235, 587, 667
3:1	415	16	222		
3:1–2	31, 237	17	40, 667	4:4	318, 431
3:1–3	438, 609	21	61, 284, 622, 667	4:6–7	624
3:2	15, 32, 669			4:7–8	667
3:8	438, 446			4:9–10	310
3:11–17	31	**Jonah**		4:13	309
3:12	15, 669	1–2	87	4:14	309
3:13–18	237	1:12	83	5	440
3:14	669	1:15	83	5:1	309
3:16–21	439	2	83, 84	5:1–2	309
3:17	222	2:2	86	5:2	292, 309, 310, 313, 320, 335,
3:18	658	2:2–9	85		
		2:4	222		

725

	371, 381, 439, 661, 663	2:9–10	3	6:11	336
		3:12–20	625	6:12	663, 670
5:2–3	309	3:13	40, 668	6:12–13	21, 96, 235, 318, 336, 430
5:2–6	440	3:14–17	667		
5:3	309, 310	3:20	415	6:12–15	213, 658
5:3–4	663			6:13	93, 96, 236, 237, 336, 337
5:3–7	440	**Haggai**			
5:4	309, 310	2:4	454	6:15	670
5:5–6	309, 310	2:6	455	7:5	98
5:5–9	310	2:7–10	318	7:11	563
5:6–7	40			8:3	222
5:7–8	310	**Zechariah**		8:4–5	15
5:8	309	1:7	585	8:8	219
6:6–8	387	1:12	98	8:12	40
7:18–20	70, 450, 481	2:6	99	8:13	203
7:19–20	36	2:7–8	77	8:22–23	235
7:20	4	2:7–12	454	8:23	63
		2:8	11, 65, 409	9:7	40
Nahum		2:10–11	77, 277, 454	9:9	292, 325, 440, 576
1:7	596	2:12	222		
2:3	23	3:1	119	9:9–10	313, 341, 482
2:8	10	3:1–2	52	9:10	341, 441, 647
		3:1–9	336	9:11–10:3	441
Habakkuk		3:8	336	10:6	427
1:6	403	3:8–10	318, 430	10:9	202
2:4	34, 44, 368, 369, 482, 527	3:11	222	10:9–10	230
		4:6–10	336	10:11–12	202
2:20	222	4:14	337	11:1	479
3:16	596	6	318	11:4–7	350
		6:1–8	93	11:9–14	350
Zephaniah		6:5	90	11:12–13	292
1:15	596	6:7	94	12:2	669
2:7	40	6:8	72, 95	12:9	669
2:9	40			12:10	137, 281,

	302, 342, 438, 441, 442, 463, 484, 535	2	196	2:4–6	309
		2:4–5	131	2:5	290
		2:8	131	2:6	537
		2:10	43, 531	2:13–15	579
12:10–14	442	2:14	41, 211	2:15	88, 290, 293, 331, 358
12:12–14	442	2:16	471		
13	644	3:16	20, 80, 547	2:16	579
13–14	442	3:16–17	497	2:17	290
13:1	207, 644	4	549	2:18	273, 293
13:7	230, 350	4:2	59, 296, 314, 655	2:21	225
13:8	497			2:23	290, 311
13:8–9	69, 203, 493, 498, 644, 645	4:4	587	3:3	290, 383
				3:5	642
13:9	645	**NEW TESTAMENT**		3:7–9	560
14	123, 239, 443, 644	**Matthew**		3:9	461, 523
		1:1	80, 300, 303	3:11	261, 521, 535
14:1–3	669	1:1–17	370, 578	3:17	304
14:2–3	233	1:3	306	4:3	52
14:3–11	239, 240	1:6–11	315	4:5	14, 221
14:4	250	1:11–12	370	4:7	383
14:4–5	12	1:12	317	4:10	383
14:5	15, 155	1:16	578	4:14	290
14:8	23	1:18–23	315	4:15–16	321
14:8–11	235	1:20	80, 370, 580	4:17	290
14:9	155, 644	1:20–23	580	4:19	538
14:9–19	250	1:21	370, 392, 580	4:23	290
14:10–11	670	1:22	290	5–7	218, 364, 374, 377, 578, 593, 606
14:16–19	240, 581, 588	1:23	316		
14:16–21	235	2	290, 310		
14:20–21	21, 213, 240, 658	2:1–12	439, 579	5:3	501
		2:1–18	580	5:4	501
		2:2	393, 506, 550	5:10	501
Malachi		2:3	642	5:14–16	529
1:2	305	2:4	656	5:17	37, 39, 101,

	105, 116,	10	604, 610	12:41–42	397
	117, 283,	10:2	571	12:42	313
	409, 518	10:6	550	12:45	246
5:18	115	10:16–23	84	13	398, 400,
5:21–22	295, 378	10:23	379, 600, 603,		538, 539, 610
5:27–28	295, 378		604, 610, 612	13:13–14	291
5:31–32	295, 378	10:25	368	13:14–15	290
5:33	383	10:32	379	13:30	246
5:33–34	295, 378	11:9	373	13:35	290, 552
5:35	66	11:11	517	13:38	398, 402,
5:38–39	295, 378	11:14	659		538, 632
5:43–44	295, 378	11:19	362, 379	13:39–40	594
6:2	366	11:20–24	646	13:40	195, 201
6:5	366	11:21–24	389	13:41	238, 379
6:9–13	372	12	397, 398, 538	13:41–42	603
6:16	366	12:3	195	13:47–48	539
6:21	385	12:7	367	13:49	201, 594
7:5	366	12:15–21	352	13:57	374
7:13–14	390	12:17	290	14:5	373
7:27	261	12:18	304	14:15–21	576
7:29	373, 378	12:18–21	352	15:1	5
8:1–9:34	578	12:23	370	15:7	290, 366
8:10	390	12:24	396	15:20	viii
8:11	34, 195	12:26	396	15:22	370
8:11–12	390, 613	12:26–28	247	15:24	286, 550
8:12	402	12:28	373, 380,	15:28	390
8:16–17	352		397, 583	16	260
8:17	290, 300, 352	12:31–32	397	16:3	595
8:20	238, 379	12:32	116, 195	16:4	246
9:13	367	12:36–37	397	16:14	374
9:15	41	12:39	246	16:16	398
9:20	63	12:40	83, 87, 238,	16:18	260, 401,
9:27	370		298, 379,		460, 509,
9:35	290		397, 588		513, 514,

	567, 570, 612	21:2–7	576	23:8	373
16:21	364	21:4	290	23:13	366
16:27	239	21:4–5	341	23:15	366
16:27–28	238, 379, 600, 603, 610, 611	21:5	441	23:23	366, 394
		21:9	350, 364, 370, 482, 635	23:25	366
				23:27–29	366
16:28	244, 245	21:11	374	23:33	560
17:1–8	238, 611	21:13	428	23:35	58, 301
17:2	296, 578	21:15	350, 370	23:37	403
17:5	304, 576	21:16	327	23:37–39	21, 399, 482
17:9	238, 379	21:23	400	23:39	350, 635
17:12	238	21:26	373	24	181, 244, 246, 247, 250, 592, 593, 594, 596, 601, 603, 604, 606, 607, 608, 610, 630
17:17	246	21:31	390, 646		
17:22	238	21:33–41	400		
17:22–23	385	21:33–46	647		
17:23	364	21:38	400		
18:10–14	529	21:41	400, 402, 632		
18:17	260, 401, 514, 612	21:42	350, 425		
		21:42–43	627	24–25	244, 400, 592, 595
18:20	20, 80, 376, 510, 547	21:43	400, 401, 402, 473		
				24:1–2	594
19	615, 616	22:1–14	402, 476	24:1–44	592
19:8–9	376	22:5	402	24:2	597
19:16	532	22:7	403, 476	24:3	226, 594, 595, 600
19:18	571	22:8–10	404		
19:28	238, 375, 571, 603, 612, 613, 621	22:11	550	24:4	201
		22:14	404	24:4–7	595
		22:18	366	24:4–14	606
20:1–16	403	22:23–32	364	24:4–35	595
20:18	238	22:37	550	24:6	600
20:18–19	385	22:42–45	314	24:8	595, 609
20:28	41, 195, 238, 352, 386	22:43–45	336	24:8–19	606
		22:44	339, 349	24:9–12	595
20:30–31	370	23:2–3	366	24:13	595

Reference	Pages
24:13-14	600
24:14	84, 226, 290, 398, 475, 524, 593, 595, 597, 601, 609, 632
24:14-30	597
24:15	93, 247, 290, 593, 595, 597, 598, 604, 652, 665, 666
24:15-16	238
24:15-20	596, 597, 598, 600, 602, 603, 604, 605
24:15-21	238
24:15-27	591
24:15-28	595, 606
24:15-31	248
24:16-21	602
24:20	602
24:20-22	238
24:20-23	606
24:21	439, 596, 597
24:21-22	203
24:21-30	597
24:22	605, 665
24:23-26	605
24:24	247, 606
24:25-28	607
24:27	238, 248, 379, 603, 610, 655
24:27-30	596, 600, 605
24:29	248, 437, 593, 600, 607
24:29-30	244
24:29-31	606
24:30	238, 249, 364, 379, 601, 610
24:30-31	248, 603
24:31	605
24:34	245, 246, 612
24:36-25:46	595
24:37	379, 600, 601, 603, 610
24:37-39	248
24:37-41	647
24:39	379, 600, 601, 603, 610
24:44	248, 379, 600, 601, 603, 610
24:45-51	180
24:48	244, 610
25	594
25:1-6	245
25:1-13	182
25:5	610
25:19	182, 245, 610
25:21	177
25:23	177
25:31	238, 239, 248, 600, 603, 610
25:31-34	254
25:31-40	84
25:31-46	194, 249, 616
25:32	537
25:34	532, 552
25:40	84
25:46	532
26:2	379
26:24	379
26:25	373
26:28	41, 194, 386, 479
26:31	230, 350, 537
26:49	373
26:54	290
26:55	651
26:56	290
26:64	75, 96, 238, 290, 339, 364, 379, 381, 600, 603, 610
26:64-68	349
27:9	290
27:9-10	350
27:22	377
27:24	160
27:34	83
27:39	299, 345, 348
27:43	299, 345
27:46	299, 345, 348
27:48	83
27:53	14, 221
28	385

Scripture Index

28:16	621	16:14	621	2:4	308, 580
28:18	440, 517	16:15	475	2:7	579
28:18–19	632	16:16	166	2:8–20	537
28:19	398, 475			2:10–11	392
28:20	594	**Luke**		2:11	308
		1:5	585	2:12	579
Mark		1:6	368, 396, 527	2:16	579
1:4	387			2:19	579
1:8	521, 535	1:15	362, 535	2:25	viii
1:11	319	1:17	659	2:28–32	618
1:15	290	1:21	370	2:32	352
1:21–28	379	1:22–24	370	2:36	433, 656
1:24	337	1:31	370	2:41–52	371
9:5	194, 373	1:32	23, 92, 107, 108, 203, 232, 249, 308, 314, 379	2:46	371, 651
9:12	352			2:47	371
9:29	612			2:49	308, 371
10:12–22	396			2:51	579
10:30	116, 195	1:32–33	75, 335, 392, 419	3:16	521, 535
10:51	194, 373			3:21–22	260, 506
11:9	635	1:32–35	371	3:22	319, 373
11:21	194, 373	1:35	320, 376, 547, 578	3:23	372
12:24	649			3:23–38	300, 301, 317, 370
12:36	339, 349	1:36	370		
13	592, 593	1:41	535	3:24	80, 578
13:10	609	1:51–52	447	3:27	317
13:27	90	1:56	579	3:30	80
14:24	41, 194, 352	1:67	535	3:38	548
14:45	194	1:67–79	392, 618	4:1	373
14:51	380	1:68	5	4:5	90
14:61–62	379	1:68–71	viii	4:14	373
15:29	348	1:69	203	4:17–21	334
15:34	345, 348	2:1	90, 383, 579, 668	4:18	574
16	385			4:18–19	350
		2:1–7	439	4:22	346

731

4:34	337	13:24	390	20:36	41
4:43	290	13:27–29	646	20:42	339, 349
5:1–7	538	13:28	34, 195	21	248, 593, 594, 600, 606, 607
5:39	395	13:28–30	390		
6	594	13:33	374		
6:20–49	606	13:34–35	482	21:5–36	592
7:16	374	13:35	635	21:7	594
8:2	370	14:15–24	473	21:20	598
8:19–21	661	15:1–7	350, 537	21:20–24	477, 607
9:29–31	572	16	608	21:22	608
9:33	209	16:8	195	21:24	76, 248, 416, 455, 593, 607, 609
9:34	547, 578	16:16	290		
9:34–35	376	16:28	646		
9:35	377	16:31	376, 577	21:25–26	609
10:1	375, 576, 577	17:21	380, 517, 619	21:25–27	608
				21:27	607
10:13–16	646	17:22	210, 360	21:29–31	488
10:17	375, 576, 577	17:26	210, 360	22	615, 616
		18:4	498	22:18	198
10:19	560, 668	18:9–14	35, 388, 646	22:19	584
10:21	373	18:30	116, 195	22:20	39, 41, 197, 198, 207, 527
10:25	532	18:31	352		
10:27	219	19	594		
10:28	215	19:9	35, 523	22:29–30	612, 613, 616
10:32	433, 656	19:14	403, 477		
10:39	370	19:27	403, 477	22:30	375, 621
11:20	583	19:38–40	364	22:31–32	533
11:28	661	19:41–42	399	22:37	300, 352
11:30	83	19:41–44	477	22:70	379
11:42	395	19:43–44	399	23	124
11:49–51	461	20:16	400, 472, 473	23:45	124
11:51	301			23:50	396
12:8	379	20:34	195	24	385
13:16	35, 523	20:35	116	24:9	621

24:16	350	2:4	661		360, 550, 560
24:25–27	294, 378	2:14	651		
24:26	72, 73	2:16	463, 482, 532	4:31	373
24:27	298			4:34	363
24:33	621	2:17	83, 299, 347	5:1	482
24:44	298	2:19	455, 547, 578	5:1–18	623
24:44–47	294			5:5	623
24:46-49	475	2:19–21	376	5:6	623
27	44	3	500	5:9–16	624
		3–4	500	5:18	381
John		3:1–21	363	5:22	508
1:1–14	310	3:2	373	5:28–29	364
1:4–9	480	3:3	290, 388	5:39	294, 298
1:11	393	3:3–5	461, 462, 526	5:45	294
1:12–13	41, 211, 461, 528, 532			5:45–47	376, 577
		3:3–7	401	5:46	332, 378
		3:5	130, 209, 216, 290, 388	6:4	482
1:17	376, 577			6:14	332, 374, 378
1:18	334, 507				
1:19	433, 656	3:7	388	6:25	373
1:21	332	3:10	388, 500	6:32	375, 576
1:25	332, 334	3:14	375, 577	6:39–40	182
1:29	49, 120, 352, 587	3:14–15	119	6:42	80
		3:16	120	6:44	182
1:33	261, 521, 535	3:19–21	480	6:51	337
		3:22–23	387	6:54	182
1:39	373	3:26	373	6:69	337
1:40–45	537	3:29	517	7:2	482
1:42	292	3:34	373	7:7	403
1:45	80, 294, 332, 370, 378	4	500	7:35	626
		4:5	14, 292	7:37–39	576
		4:19	374	7:39	260, 460, 508
1:47	396	4:22	28, 60, 63, 158, 356,		
1:50	373			7:40	374, 378

7:40–41	334	10:11	350, 362, 397, 537	12:46	480
7:42	309			12:48	182
7:50–51	363	10:12	445	13:18	348
8	388	10:14	350, 537	13:34	462
8:2	651	10:15	397	13:34–35	525
8:12	480, 529	10:16	195, 398, 464, 514, 529, 550	14:1	384
8:29	363			14:1–3	250, 532
8:33	388, 561			14:6	112, 382, 391, 409
8:34–36	389	10:17	397		
8:37	35, 561	10:28	397	14:15	101, 219, 283, 368, 525
8:37–41	523	10:28–30	509		
8:39	35, 265, 389, 461	10:33	381		
		10:33–36	382	14:16	521
8:39–40	276	10:35	295	14:16–17	463, 507, 535
8:39–44	561	11:8	373		
8:44	57, 301, 389, 523	11:24	182	14:21	101, 219, 283, 368, 525
		11:24–25	364		
8:44–45	561	11:50	568		
8:58	310	11:52	259, 331, 398, 513, 514, 532	14:23	368, 525
9	374, 394, 396, 397, 398			14:26	583
				15:1	331, 358
		11:54	433	15:1–2	528
9:2	373	12:13	635	15:1–8	556, 648
9:5	480, 529	12:14–15	341	15:2	648
9:17	374	12:15	441	15:3	290, 388
9:22	396	12:16	259	15:8	648
9:28–29	395	12:32	311	15:9–10	368
9:34	396, 398	12:34	335	15:9–11	589
10	397	12:35–36	480	15:10	101, 219, 525
10:1–18	230	12:37–38	352		
10:2–4	550	12:38	352	15:10–17	283
10:3	398	12:41	240, 293, 382	15:12	525
10:10	397, 509, 532			15:17	525
		12:42	396	15:18	403

15:24	403		522, 617,	2:21	383
15:25	347		618, 620	2:23	80, 301, 443
16:2	396	1:1–3	617	2:24–32	342
16:8	583	1:3	476	2:24	383
16:13	583	1:5	261, 521,	2:25	383
16:27	532		534, 535	2:25–31	293
17:3	532	1:6	464	2:28–29	537
17:4–5	519	1:6–8	617, 620	2:31	299
17:24	310, 552	1:8	475	2:32	383
18:31	308	1:11	12, 239, 250	2:33–34	419
18:36	130	1:14	661	2:34	339, 383
19:12–16	80	1:14–26	621	2:34–35	339, 349
19:15	477	1:20	347	2:36	383, 443
19:18	345	1:21–26	571	2:37	443
19:19	380	1:26	621	2:46	509, 599
19:24	299, 345	2	109, 122,	3	332, 623
19:26	661		132, 257,	3:1	119, 133,
19:28	347		258, 260,		187, 599
19:35–37	441		261, 286,	3:10	651
19:36	348, 587		342, 437,	3:15	80, 301, 383
19:37	137, 281,		438, 449,	3:19–21	350
	342		460, 474,	3:19–26	621
19:38–39	363		504, 511,	3:21	68, 108
20–21	385		514, 520,	3:22	378, 383, 576
20:16	373		522, 535,	3:22–23	332, 373
20:17	345, 532		541, 569,	3:25	27, 560
20:25	345		580, 581,	4:10	383, 443
20:27	345		582, 620, 637	4:11	350, 425
21:1–6	538	2:3	582	4:12	112, 382,
21:2	537	2:4	582		391, 409
21:15–17	537	2:5	522	4:25–26	319
		2:16	437	4:36	433, 656
Acts		2:16–21	535	5:11	514
		2:17	11, 201, 415	5:30	24, 80, 301,
1	239, 261,	2:17–21	437, 529		

	383	9:2	574	13:35	299
5:34	363	9:18	491	13:35–37	342
6:7	363	10	475	13:37	383
7:2	27	10:28	264	13:42	37, 107, 119
7:3	575	10:36	383	13:44	37, 107, 119
7:8	36	10:38	373, 506, 534	13:45	84
7:8–9	65	10:39	24	13:46	465
7:20	579	10:40	383	13:46–47	399
7:20–28	375, 577	10:41	385	13:47	352
7:22	375	10:42	249	14:1	393
7:23–29	375	11:16	261, 521, 535	14:16	26
7:30	476, 538	11:16–17	534	15	115, 283, 314, 536
7:37	373, 378	11:19–20	474		
7:38	110, 257, 449, 504, 509, 513, 514, 567	11:20	383	15:1	271
		11:28	341	15:5	363
		11:50	569	15:7–9	568
7:38–51	583	12:12	370	15:10	208, 215
7:42	476	12:15	51	15:14	465, 528, 531, 564, 567, 568, 569
7:51	106, 266	13	344		
7:51–52	375, 577	13:5	393		
7:51–53	403, 456	13:14	37, 107, 119, 393	15:16–17	314
7:52	80, 301			15:19–21	283
7:55–56	340, 349	13:18	476	15:21	107, 119, 283, 568
7:56	323, 623	13:20	332		
7:57	563	13:22	309	16:3	37
8:1	474, 475, 615	13:22–23	232, 311	16:13	37, 107, 119
8:4	474	13:27	107, 119, 294	17:1–3	393
8:12	290	13:27–29	406	17:2	37, 119
8:30	17	13:28	301	17:5	84
8:30–35	352	13:29	24, 294	17:6	90, 383, 668
8:32–33	17, 300, 352	13:30	383	17:6–7	383
8:32–35	293	13:32–33	320	17:10	393
8:34–35	295	13:33	319, 320	17:31	383
8:35	17	13:34	320, 383	18:4	37, 107, 119,

Scripture Index

	393	25:8	366	2:29	106
19:2	261	26	615, 616	3:1	252
19:8	393	26:5	363	3:1–2	548
19:9	574	26:6–7	613	3:2	370, 549
19:23	574	26:7	613	3:9	113, 251, 391
19:32	110, 257, 449, 504, 509, 514, 567	26:12	656	3:9–12	548
		26:13	296, 578	3:12–29	252
		26:22–23	295	3:19	215, 548
19:39	514	26:23	352	3:19–20	215
19:39-40	110, 257, 449, 504, 509, 567	27	124	3:20	208, 583
		27:27	124	3:22	369
		28:17	107, 133, 187, 366, 599	3:22–24	548
19:41	514			3:22–25	391
20:16	107, 119	28:20	614	3:2–26	113
20:28–29	529	28:25–26	382	3:23	215
21:8	539			3:23–26	518
21:18–26	187	**Romans**		3:24–26	527
21:20	393, 474, 568	1–8	252, 547, 630	3:26	369
		1:4	320	3:30	271
21:21	37	1:16	252, 393, 402, 509	3:31	117, 409, 518
21:21–26	568			4	541
21:26	133, 599	1:17	369, 527	4:1	268
21:39	264	1:22–32	627	4:3	369, 394
22:3	264, 363	1:26–28	636	4:9	369, 394
22:4	574	2:7–10	113	4:11	509, 523, 561
22:11	519	2:9	251	4:11–12	265, 276, 389, 461, 550, 559, 564
23:6	363, 364, 614	2:9–10	393, 402		
		2:12–16	390		
23:6–10	363	2:17–20	34	4:11–13	34
23:8	364	2:19	529	4:13	34
24:12–13	366	2:19–20	84, 87	4:16	509, 523, 561
24:14	574	2:19–24	524	4:16–17	511
24:17	133, 187	2:28–29	36, 265, 267, 407, 464, 553	4:18	369, 394
24:22	574			4:22	369, 394

737

4:24–25	383		630, 640, 641, 643	11	252, 275, 449, 464, 543, 555, 561, 601, 629, 630, 633, 638, 639
4:25	352				
5:6	338	9:1–5	185, 630		
5:8	338	9:1–29	630		
5:20	583	9:3	269, 550		
6:3	375	9:3–4	251		
6:3–4	536	9:4	65, 264, 550	11:1	185, 264, 631
6:4	338	9:4–5	41, 64, 548	11:1–2	550
6:9	338	9:5	35, 559, 661	11:2	467
6:18–22	461	9:6	12, 254, 267, 269, 550, 553, 554	11:2–24	631
6:22	525			11:5	40, 486, 551, 632, 633, 636, 637
6:23	215				
7–8	526	9:8	532, 561		
7:7	208	9:10–13	305	11:5–6	631
7:7–11	583	9:24–25	529	11:7	40, 264, 466, 486, 550, 551, 631, 635, 636
8:3	386, 479	9:24–26	255, 273		
8:3–4	208	9:25–26	464, 628		
8:4	117, 216, 518, 525, 583	9:27	270		
		9:30–10:4	394	11:9–10	347
		9:30–10:21	630	11:11	264, 550, 553, 632
8:5–6	269	9:31	264, 550		
8:14	209, 583	9:32–33	384	11:11–14	632
8:14–16	41, 461, 528	9:33	408, 425	11:11–24	110
8:15–17	532	10:1–13	117	11:12	633, 634, 636, 643
8:17	168, 557, 668	10:4	105, 117, 132, 409		
8:17–18	73			11:14	550, 632
8:19	41	10:6–8	298	11:15	467, 632, 633, 634
8:29	306, 356	10:11	425		
8:29–30	509, 552	10:11–13	548	11:16	276, 559
8:33–34	348	10:12	252, 383	11:16–17	555
8:34	340, 349, 533	10:14–17	509	11:16–19	555
9–11	183, 184, 251, 252, 253, 473, 543, 547, 548, 550, 553, 629,	10:16	352	11:16–24	275, 554
				11:17	556
		10:19	550	11:17–18	558
		10:21	550	11:17–21	276

11:17-24	557	11:29	4, 35, 69, 338, 449, 467	3:8-9	529
11:18	561			3:16	20, 132, 257, 260, 463, 465, 520, 534, 651
11:21	555, 556	11:31	639		
11:21-22	634, 635	11:32	639, 641		
11:22	634, 643	12:1	12		
11:22-23	557	12:3-8	211	3:18	195
11:22-27	557	13:1-7	160	4:14	389
11:23	635, 650	13:2-5	166	5:7	49, 133, 587
11:23-24	634, 642	13:8-10	117, 518, 525	6:2	34, 239
11:24	555, 556	14:9	249, 383	6:11	258
11:24-27	483	14:10	525, 616	6:19	463, 520
11:25	264, 430, 550, 551, 553, 609, 633, 635, 636, 640, 643, 648	14:17	131	7:5	52
		15:3	83, 116, 299, 347	7:14	530
				7:18	272, 283
		15:4	274	7:19	272
		15:8	viii, 286, 338, 550	8:2-6	217
				8:5	10
11:25-26	637, 642	15:8-9	87, 392	9:21	218, 368, 462, 525, 577
11:25-27	137, 416, 457, 636	15:12	232, 310, 311		
		15:16	258	9:24	534
11:26	17, 252, 254, 267, 408, 449, 495, 498, 499, 550, 552, 553, 554, 629, 631, 632, 633, 636, 637, 639, 640, 641, 644, 647, 663	15:21	82, 352	9:25	329
		16	550	9:26	135, 534
		16:6	370	10:1-6	573
		16:20	52, 302	10:1-12	303
		16:25	263, 460, 515	10:2	375, 577
		16:25-26	524	10:6	274
				10:11	116, 201, 274, 415
		1 Corinthians			
		1:8-9	509	10:18	264, 268, 269
		1:20	195	10:32	264, 449, 457, 464, 551
11:26-27	252, 498, 638	1:24	297		
11:28	184, 185, 471, 559	2:6	210, 535	11:24-25	584
		2:6-7	516	11:25	195, 197, 207, 527
11:28-29	483, 639	2:7	460, 515	11:26	198, 509, 584

11:28	636	3:7–8	376, 577	**Galatians**	
12:4–31	211	3:8	214	1:4	116, 195
12:13	261, 463, 521, 535, 540	3:9	214	1:14	366
		3:13–15	434	1:19	314
12:14–31	518	3:13–16	648	2	283
12:28	461	3:14	vii, 299	2:2	534
13:4–7	218	3:14–18	243	2:7–9	475
14:15	536	3:15	649	2:9	271
14:24	535	3:15–16	110	2:12	271
14:26	536	3:16	434, 442, 648, 649, 650, 651	2:14–15	264
15:3	352			2:16	369
15:4–8	385			3	279, 541
15:6	385	3:17	583	3:6	369, 394, 561
15:25	339, 349	3:17–18	649	3:7	35, 195, 276, 278, 461, 523, 560, 561
15:27	328	4:4	195		
15:45	328	5:3	557		
15:46	490	5:10	525, 616	3:7–9	509, 523
15:48–49	325	5:16	269	3:8	560
15:50–57	250	5:17	267	3:9	276
16:8	107	5:19	120	3:11	369, 527
		5:21	214, 352, 479	3:11–12	561
2 Corinthians		6:4	461	3:12	215
1:20	72, 114	6:16	20, 219, 255, 257, 463, 520, 651	3:13	24
1:20–22	370			3:14	276, 509, 523
1:21–22	258, 463, 534			3:15–18	48, 527
1:22	506	6:17–18	573	3:16	298, 302, 303, 623
3:1	39	6:18	41, 461		
3:2–3	195	11:2	41, 470, 528, 667	3:17	98
3:3	133, 208, 210, 214, 218, 583, 650			3:19	376, 583
		11:3	560, 668	3:21	561
		11:14	148	3:24	561
3:6	41, 195, 210, 218, 527, 583	11:22	264	3:26	41, 523, 560, 561
		13:14	532		
3:7	215			3:26–28	268,

Scripture Index

3:27–28	544		110, 266, 269, 407, 449, 464, 501, 523, 530, 627	2:8	461
3:28	263, 267, 474			2:11–13	262
3:29	278, 461, 509, 523, 560, 561			2:11–22	464, 518
				2:12	210
				2:14–15	127
4	117, 139, 277			2:14–16	518
4:1–7	208	**Ephesians**		2:17	87
4:4	370, 371, 661	1:3	16, 115, 119	2:19	269, 534
4:9	117	1:3–4	466	2:19–21	516
4:21	303	1:3–5	551, 552	2:20	425, 460
4:21–31	138, 303, 527	1:4	552	2:20–22	20, 132, 257, 463, 465, 520, 534, 651
4:24–27	583, 667	1:9	264		
4:25	277	1:9–10	68		
4:26	12, 66, 277, 484, 671	1:9–11	460	2:22	260
		1:10	73, 99, 115, 507	3	195
4:27	426, 583, 667			3:1–12	264, 518
4:28	195, 509, 523, 561	1:10–13	509	3:3	263
		1:11	552	3:3–4	460
5	117, 283	1:13	258, 462, 463, 534	3:3–6	262
5:2	271			3:3–11	464
5:6	462	1:13–14	573	3:4–5	516
5:7	534	1:17	311	3:4–6	514
5:13–6:2	583	1:17–18	583	3:5	461, 516
5:16–18	269	1:19–21	533	3:9	460
6	283	1:19–23	519, 533	4:3–6	509
6:2	16, 101, 109, 117, 118, 218, 266, 283, 368, 378, 461, 462, 518, 525, 577	1:20	75, 340, 349, 419, 660	4:8	376, 577
		1:20–23	257, 504, 508	4:8–11	533
		1:21	195	4:9	448
		1:22	328	4:11	461, 516, 537, 539
		1:22–23	132, 460, 463, 507		
				4:11–14	210
6:7	477	2	195	4:15	519
6:15	266	2:5	461	4:15–16	463, 533
6:16	3, 13, 109,	2:6	520, 522, 660	4:22–24	520

741

4:24	325	3:5	264, 433	3:22	268
4:25	217	3:6	363	4:3	264
4:28	217	3:13–14	534	4:11	271
4:30	258, 463, 506, 534, 582	3:20	573		
		3:20–21	250	**1 Thessalonians**	
5:1	41, 532	3:21	519	1:10	83
5:18	521, 534			2:7	389
5:19	536	**Colossians**		2:11	389
5:23	463, 507, 519	1:13	304	3:5	52
5:25	573	1:15	356	3:13	239
5:25–26	217	1:16	329	4:13–17	250
5:25–30	41	1:18	463, 507, 508, 519	4:16	9
5:25–32	528			4:17	186, 637, 660
5:26	290, 388, 509, 582	1:23	557		
		1:24–27	460, 515	**2 Thessalonians**	
5:27	507	1:26	263, 516	2	654
5:32	264, 507	1:26–27	264	2:3–4	651
6:1–3	217	1:28	210	2:3–10	163
6:3	29	2:2	264	2:4	602, 651, 652, 653, 666
6:5	268	2:3	297		
6:12	11	2:8	520	2:8	311
6:12–18	533	2:11–12	38, 106, 205, 536	2:9	653
				2:9–12	636
Philippians		2:15	533		
1:23	108	2:16	536	**1 Timothy**	
2:5–6	368	2:16–17	119	1:2	389
2:6–11	536	2:19	463, 519, 533	1:8–11	117
2:9–11	156	3:1	75, 340, 349	1:15	113
2:10	448	3:1–3	534	1:17	505
2:15	41, 529, 532	3:3	122, 156	1:18	389
2:16	534	3:4	211, 239, 532	2:5	376, 384, 386
3:2–3	271	3:9–11	325, 520	3:16	347
3:3	271, 370	3:11	474	4:1	415
3:4–8	391	3:16	536	6:15	8

Scripture Index

6:17	116, 195			419, 533	4:3	4	
		1:5	293, 309, 313, 319, 381	4:8	337, 370		
2 Timothy				4:9	70, 204, 450		
1:2	389	1:6	356, 381, 664	4:16	533		
2:1	389	1:8	347, 381	5–7	118		
2:12	168, 239, 668	1:10–12	240, 299, 300, 382, 383	5:1–10	119		
2:18	250			5:5	319		
3:1	11, 201, 415	1:13	339, 349, 533	5:6	334		
3:1–5	595	2	327, 329, 486	5:7	345		
3:4–5	402, 462	2:5	204, 245, 278, 415, 486, 671	5:10	334		
3:8	375, 577			5:14	210		
3:16	116			6:5	116, 195, 204, 245, 278, 415, 671		
4:1	249	2:5–9	299, 486				
4:3–4	462	2:6	88, 323, 379				
4:5	539	2:6–8	327	6:13–14	4		
4:7	534	2:6–9	293	6:20	334		
4:8	329	2:7	51	7:1–2	237		
		2:9	327, 486	7:1–10	298		
		2:9–10	73	7:11	334		
Titus		2:11–12	534	7:14	306		
1:4	389	2:11–13	486	7:17	335		
1:10	271	2:12	299, 345	7:22	39, 527		
2:12	116, 195	2:13	323, 347, 350	7:25	212, 533, 534		
2:13–14	564, 566, 567, 573	2:14	302	7:27	133		
		2:17	337, 386, 479	8	viii, 191, 196		
2:14	465, 528, 569	3:1	212	8–9	204		
3:5	290, 401, 461, 613	3:1–6	119, 333, 376, 577	8:1	75, 419		
				8:1–2	213, 534		
		3:6	212, 557	8:3–4	133		
Hebrews		3:11	4, 40	8:6	39, 197, 376, 527		
1	381	3:14	557				
1:1	201	3:18	40	8:7	39		
1:1–2	415	4	450	8:8	39, 198, 201, 210		
1:2	11, 400, 415	4:1	70, 450				
1:3	340, 349,						

8:8–9	192	10:7–9	348	12:18–24	583
8:8–12	207, 464	10:11	346	12:22	278, 408, 484, 666, 671
8:9	209	10:12	419		
8:10	219, 583	10:12–13	339, 349, 533, 534	12:22–24	138
8:11	209			12:23	212, 504
8:12	586	10:12–14	367	12:24	39, 197, 207, 301, 376, 384, 527
8:13	39	10:13	108		
9–10	461	10:18	386		
9:1	39	10:19–20	212	12:28	278, 415
9:1–5	119	10:19–21	214	12:29	644
9:7–26	133	10:19–22	534	13:11	386
9:9	116	10:21	212	13:14	204, 278, 415, 573, 671
9:11–12	214, 480	10:26	386		
9:11–15	206, 479	10:29	207	13:15	534
9:13–14	346, 386, 526	10:38	369, 527	13:20	35, 39, 207, 362, 527, 529, 537
9:14	84	11	108, 369		
9:15	39, 197, 376, 384, 527	11:4	58		
		11:8	575	**James**	
9:18	39	11:10	575	1	615, 616
9:18–23	376, 577	11:13	574, 626	1:1	613, 615, 626
9:20	207	11:13–16	33, 573	1:12	329
9:22	viii, 367, 387	11:14–16	408, 672	1:25	101, 525, 583, 615
9:24	214	11:16	45, 204, 225, 465		
9:25–28	479			2:5	615
9:26	201, 386	11:17–19	120, 304	2:8	101, 525, 615
9:28	352	11:20	204, 415, 671	2:8–12	462
10	346, 385			2:10	208, 215
10:1	204, 671	11:23	579	2:12	101, 525, 583, 615
10:1–14	133, 479	12	139		
10:4	346	12:1–2	534	2:23	369, 394
10:5	293	12:2	75, 419	5:3	11, 201
10:5–7	345, 385	12:12	12	5:7–8	615
10:5–10	299, 386	12:18	204		
10:6	386	12:18–22	376, 577		

1 Peter

1:1	615, 626
1:3	401
1:8	148, 626
1:10–12	348, 626
1:11	72, 294, 352, 451
1:17	574, 626
1:18–19	587
1:19	49, 133, 352
1:19–20	346
1:20	552
1:23	401
2:1–5	535
2:4–5	534
2:5	212, 260, 525, 566
2:6	408
2:6–7	626
2:6–8	384, 425
2:7	350
2:9	212, 461, 525, 529, 535, 566, 569
2:9–10	272, 528, 564, 628
2:9–12	625
2:10	464, 529, 566
2:11	574, 626
2:11–12	573
2:22	300
2:22–25	352
2:24	24, 300
2:25	537
3:6	627
3:18	352
3:20–21	647
3:21–22	533
3:22	340, 349, 419
4:1–3	627
4:5	249
4:6	526
4:12–13	168
4:13	73, 668
4:17	462, 526
5:1	73
5:1–4	537
5:2–3	529
5:4	329, 362, 537
5:8	157, 249, 345
5:10	73

2 Peter

1:15	573
1:16	73
1:16–19	245
1:18	222
1:20	72
3:2	283, 461
3:3	11, 201, 415
3:8	245

1 John

2:1	533
2:1–2	352
2:3–4	219, 283
2:18	163, 201, 318, 415, 651
2:19	509
2:20	463, 534
2:22	163, 318, 651
2:27	463, 534
3:1	532
3:1–2	41
3:5	352
3:8	302
3:8–10	561
3:10	41, 57, 532
3:16	217
3:21	509
3:22	219
3:22–24	283
3:23	525
3:24	219
4:2	318
4:3	163, 651
4:20–21	217
4:21	525
5:2	41, 532
5:2–3	219, 283, 525
5:3	217
5:11–12	532
5:12	532
5:20	532

2 John

1:5–6	525
1:6	283
1:7	163, 318, 651
1:9	375

Jude		4:4	329	11:1	605
1	571	4:10	329	11:1-2	221, 652, 658
9	9, 97	5	657, 666	11:1-13	657, 658
18	415	5-21	587	11:2	14, 187, 599, 657
		5:5	232, 306, 307, 311	11:3	187, 599, 658
Revelation		5:9	307, 668	11:5-6	659
1:5	348	5:10	34, 212, 239, 525, 535	11:7-12	659
1:6	212, 525, 535	6:12	437	11:8	658, 669
1:7	122, 137, 156, 247, 249, 281, 342, 592, 610	7	464, 601, 630	11:11	665
		7-11	654	11:19	214, 587
1:13	323, 324, 529	7:1	90	12	154, 660, 661, 662, 663, 665
1:16	232, 296, 578	7:1-2	506, 654	12-13	24, 97, 653
1:16-17	519	7:1-8	464, 497, 654, 655, 667	12:1-2	660
2	462	7:4	655	12:1-6	661
2-3	109, 526, 567	7:5-8	571	12:2	663
2:1	529	7:9	462, 464, 528, 655	12:3	9, 329, 653
2:5	529			12:3-17	87
2:9	389	7:9-19	84	12:5	660
2:10	329	7:14	439, 596, 597	12:6	187, 599, 658, 663
2:14	667	7:17	537	12:7	97
2:20-21	667	8:4	448	12:7-12	664
2:22	596	8:12	437	12:9	9, 49, 57, 87, 90, 296, 301, 560, 653, 664, 668
2:27	319	9:3	668		
3	462	9:21	667		
3:2	159	10	657		
3:7	350	10:1-11:13	657, 659	12:13	661
3:9	389	10:2	657	12:13-17	663
3:10	186, 203	10:8	448	12:13-18	664
3:12	12, 19, 278, 408, 484, 671	10:9-10	657	12:14	187, 599, 663, 664
3:21	75, 107, 234, 419, 660, 666	10:10	448	12:17	661
		11	601, 669		

Scripture Index

13	91, 425, 489, 652, 653, 654, 665, 667	15:2	602	19:15	311, 493
		15:3	375, 577	19:15–16	92
		15:4	345	19:16	8, 576
13–16	665	15:5–8	587	19:17–18	493
13–19	487	16:2	602, 667	19:19–20	31, 92, 163
13:1	9, 96, 329, 653	16:13	97, 605, 652	19:19–21	319
		16:13–16	31, 668	19:19–20:3	669
13:1–10	668	16:16	15, 669	19:20	602, 605, 652, 667, 668
13:4	653	16:17–21	669		
13:5	187, 599, 658	17	425, 489, 526		
13:7	658	17–18	667, 671	19:21	311
13:8	552	17:1–19:5	669	20	52, 122, 134, 155
13:11	653	17:3	96		
13:11–18	668	17:10–11	576	20:1	302, 448
13:13–15	605	17:14	89, 96, 239, 249, 302, 669	20:1–6	101, 121, 134, 156
13:14–15	602, 652				
13:14–18	665	17:15	82, 324, 539	20:2	9, 49, 57, 87, 90, 97, 296, 301, 560, 653, 664, 668
13:16–17	667	18:4–5	573		
13:18	665	18:20	461		
14	666	19	122, 134, 155		
14:1	408	19–22	660	20:4	239, 250, 602, 616, 667
14:1–5	666	19:2	667		
14:3	668	19:6–9	667		
14:4	667, 668	19:6–10	669	20:4–6	157, 168
14:4–5	667	19:7	257	20:6	212, 239, 250, 525, 535
14:5	668	19:7–9	517		
14:8	667	19:10	72		
14:9	667	19:11	311	20:7–9	319
14:9–11	602	19:11–12	92	20:9	157
14:11	667	19:11–16	30, 96	20:10	63, 302, 605, 652
14:14	323	19:11–21	608		
14:17	587	19:11–20:3	249	20:11–15	616
14:17–20	647	19:12	329	20:15	481
14:18–20	493	19:14	239, 319	21	134, 154,

	155, 157, 671
21:1–8	121
21:1–22:5	671
21:2	12, 41, 221, 278, 347, 408, 484, 528, 667
21:3	285
21:5–8	643
21:7	219
21:9	257, 408, 484, 528, 667, 671
21:9–10	20, 41, 278, 517
21:10	12, 221, 672
21:11	672
21:12	616
21:12–14	572, 621
21:22	121
21:24	672
22:5	239
22:7	245
22:12	245
22:16	305, 311
22:17	41, 667
22:19	221
22:20	245

Subject Index

#

144,000   464, 497, 596, 655, 656, 666, 667, 668

1 Enoch   313, 326

A

'*Ammi*   11, 97, 123, 255, 273, 274, 466, 467, 468, 469, 471, 627, 628, 644

À Brakel, Wilhelmus   12, 13, 17, 436, 437, 503, 542, 551, 650

Aachen   25

Aalders, G. Ch.   38, 429

Aaron   67, 119, 337

Abarbanel, Isaac   322, 351

Abel   57, 58, 138, 197, 258, 301, 513, 537, 565

Abma, G. H.   102

Abomination of desolation   238, 247, 250, 593, 597, 598, 599, 600, 601, 602, 603, 604, 607, 609, 652, 665, 666

Aboth   20, 80, 191, 367, 547, 578

Abraham   2, 5, 26, 27, 28,

Abraham
33, 34, 35, 36,
42, 43, 44, 48,
52, 56, 65, 69,
101, 120, 131,
191, 195, 196,
220, 229, 254,
258, 265, 270,
276, 278, 279,
300, 302, 303,
304, 335, 362,
369, 384, 388,
389, 390, 394,
450, 461, 469,
509, 511, 513,
522, 523, 527,
529, 530, 531,
537, 541, 550,
558, 559, 560,
561, 562, 563,
564, 565, 567,
570, 575, 621,
622, 646

Abraham Ibn Ezra
54, 341

Abrahamic Covenant
34, 35, 40, 114,
131, 195, 536, 559

Abrahamite
254, 270

Abram
26, 27, 34, 48,
225, 558

Absalom
586

Achaz
253

AD
70, 76, 77, 78, 80,
98, 152, 187, 202,
230, 244, 247,
248, 249, 250,
365, 387, 399,
453, 454, 466,
475, 476, 487,
592, 593, 595,
598, 600, 601,
602, 603, 604,
606, 607, 609,
651, 652

Adam
16, 124, 131, 132,
135, 196, 211,
258, 280, 286,
300, 301, 302,
328, 329, 449,
459, 460, 505,
506, 507, 509,
511, 512, 513,
514, 530, 536,
540, 541, 548,
558, 563, 565,
582, 640

Adler, Hermann
335

Adonai
2, 8, 32, 113, 243,
253, 332, 392,
411, 473

Adonijah
167

Adoption
42, 64, 320, 532,
548, 551

Adversus Haereses
317

Adversus Judaeos
  542
Adversus Marcion
  650
Africa
  19, 30, 175
Afrikaners
  175, 176, 220
Afscheiding
  174
Agabus
  341
Against the Jews
  542
Ahab
  451, 643
Ahaz
  315, 316, 420
Ahimaaz
  118
Ahitophel
  643
Al-Aqsa Mosque
  76
Albigenses
  178, 181
Alexander, J. A.
  321, 323, 351, 418
Alexander the Great
  68, 94, 95
Alford, H.
  650
Aliyah
  227, 228, 231, 232
Alkmaar
  173

Almah
  315, 316
All Israel
  17, 137, 172, 252,
  253, 254, 267,
  333, 416, 449,
  483, 495, 498,
  499, 501, 547,
  550, 551, 552,
  553, 554, 610,
  627, 628, 630,
  631, 632, 633,
  636, 637, 639,
  640, 641, 642,
  643, 644, 647, 661
Allen, L. C.
  309, 439
Allo, E. B.
  650
Alphaeus
  571
Altaf, S.
  621
Ambrose
  124, 125, 155, 286
America
  176, 177
American Constitution
  162
Americanism
  177
Americans
  77, 128, 177, 220, 569
Amillennialism
  16, 101, 102, 121,
  133, 169, 170, 178

Amillennialist
122, 156
Amillennialists
101, 121, 122, 126
Amish
168, 169
Amman
422
Ammon
422, 488, 562
Ammonites
421
Amorite
220
Amram
578, 580
Amsterdam
153, 672
Anabaptism
161
Anabaptists
161, 166, 167, 168, 169, 178, 181
Ancient of Days
238, 239, 325
Anderson, R.
357
Andrew
292, 537
Angelic powers
7, 8, 53, 329, 447, 448
Angelic princes
8, 10, 24, 97, 431

Angels
7, 8, 9, 10, 12, 51, 57, 88, 111, 138, 154, 221, 239, 240, 248, 278, 293, 327, 329, 379, 381, 448, 456, 486, 506, 611, 615, 626, 654
Anglicans
153
Anicet-Bourgeois, Auguste
x
Ankerberg, J.
538
Anna
656
Annotations to the Dutch States Translation
183, 267, 276, 426, 446, 492, 542, 598, 637, 656
Anointed One
291, 301, 320, 321, 337, 338, 347, 380
Anti-Messiah
91, 318
Anti-millennialism
150, 155, 158, 159, 160, 161, 162, 164, 182
Anti-Revolutionary Party
164
Anti-Semitism
v, 5, 106, 126, 150, 158, 169,

Subject Index

Antichrist
279, 281, 406, 448, 542
91, 162, 163, 179, 318, 598, 602, 651, 652, 653, 665

Antioch
465, 474

Antiochus IV
247, 455, 585, 586, 598, 599, 652, 653

Apeldoorn
11, 184

Apostasy
70, 77, 436, 450, 452, 454, 471, 482, 555, 556, 557, 605

Apostles
37, 79, 83, 107, 119, 210, 218, 249, 263, 283, 343, 366, 369, 372, 375, 381, 383, 385, 406, 460, 461, 465, 474, 475, 476, 515, 516, 517, 533, 537, 539, 570, 571, 572, 576, 616, 620, 621

Apostles' Creed
249

Apple of God's eye
11, 65, 409

Apollo
661

Aqiva, Rabbi
384

Aquinas, Thomas
279

Arabs
15, 32, 140, 141, 413

Archbold, N.
103

Archer, G. L.
357

Ark of the covenant
20, 78, 119, 214, 223, 339, 349

Armageddon
15, 31, 668, 669

Arminians
166, 181

Armstrong, Karen
134, 367

Artaxerxes I Longimanus
357

Artemis
153

Article
36, 162, 164, 165, 179

Asa
38, 562, 581

Asaph
89

Ascension
73, 75, 108, 239, 339, 349, 419, 463, 507, 508, 519, 521, 585,

Ascension Day
  610, 622
Ashdod
  519, 585
Asher
  422
Asherites
  656
Ashkelon
  433
Ashley, T. R.
  422
Asia
  305
Assyria
  19, 30, 68, 77, 231, 626
Assyrian empire
  19, 93, 202, 230, 310, 311, 417, 418, 420, 421, 422, 424, 425, 440, 488, 489, 494, 495, 611, 656
Assyrians
  90, 422
Astarte
  32, 403, 487, 495
Athanasian Creed
  153
Athanasius
  249
Atonement
  306
  20, 49, 78, 82, 113, 138, 192, 200, 223, 367, 386, 387, 410, 416, 436, 478, 480, 527, 587
Augustus
  25, 383, 579
Auschwitz
  vi, 57, 232, 586
Australia
  76, 168
Australians
  264
Azazel
  478

B

Baal
  631
Baal Shem Tov
  382
Baarda, T.
  553
Babylon
  6, 7, 10, 21, 22, 49, 68, 70, 71, 74, 76, 77, 79, 86, 87, 95, 97, 98, 202, 203, 230, 231, 238, 353, 354, 355, 365, 431, 432, 451, 453, 454, 455, 482, 573, 574, 588, 653, 664, 669
Babylonia
  94, 95

Subject Index

Babylonian captivity
    77, 81, 201, 202,
    203, 229, 230,
    234, 429, 432,
    470, 490, 656
Babylonian empire
    89, 93, 455, 665
Babylonian exile
    21, 22, 45, 46,
    64, 77, 78, 82,
    119, 230, 421,
    427, 429, 453, 454
Babylonian Talmud
    365, 478
Babylonians
    32, 73, 223, 403,
    654
Bagdad
    422
Bailey, K. E.
    34
Baines, T. B.
    654
Balaam
    259, 305, 306, 643
Baldwin, J. G.
    337
Balfour, Arthur J.
    414
Balke, W.
    511
Baptism
    i, 37, 38, 106, 135,
    166, 167, 169,
    192, 205, 206,
    256, 261, 373,
    387, 506, 521,
    522, 530, 535,
    536, 538
Baptist churches
    169
Bar Juda, Jose
    395
Bar Mitzvah
    371
Barclay, W.
    654
Barker, K. L.
    337
Barnabas
    352, 465, 475, 542
Barnett, P.
    218
Barnhouse, D. G.
    654
Bartels, W. J. B.
    38
Bartholomew
    537, 571
Bass, C. B.
    114
Bat Mitzvah
    371
Bathsheba
    662
Battle of Blood River
    175
Bauer, D. R.
    312
Bauman, Z.
    575
Bavinck, Herman
    504, 636, 637, 642

Beasley-Murray, G. R.
654
Beast
31, 63, 90, 91, 92, 96, 213, 324, 325, 425, 445, 446, 487, 602, 603, 605, 608, 652, 653, 654, 665, 666, 667, 668, 669
Beasts
32, 89, 90, 324, 325, 493, 653, 654, 665
Beckwith, I. T.
659
Beelzebub
396
Beelzebul
396, 397
Beersheba
127
Bel
87, 654
Belgic Confession
105, 132, 162, 163, 164, 165, 179, 257, 505, 506, 507, 513, 530
Bellett, J. G.
654
Belshazzar
90, 91, 94, 95
Ben Gershom, Levi
332

Ben Gurion, David
105
Ben Inia, Samuel
455
Ben Meir, Shemuel
305
Ben Yechiel Michel, Meir Leibush
309
Ben Zakkai, Jochanan
367, 479
Ben-Adam
88, 323, 324, 327, 330, 379
Benedict XVI
103
Bengel, J. A.
569
Benjamin
240, 331, 391, 433, 656, 670
Benjaminite
331, 491
Beor
259
Berkhof, H.
102, 184, 185,
Berkhof, L.
510, 566, 567, 642, 644
Berkouwer, G. C.
293, 295, 296, 297, 299, 315, 335, 466, 505, 555, 637, 642

Berkowitz, A.
  103
Berlin
  153
Bernard, J. H.
  218
Beth-aven
  78
Bethel
  54, 55, 78
Bethlehem
  238, 288, 308, 309, 310, 371, 439, 440, 579, 580, 663
Bethsaida
  389, 646
Beveridge, Alfred J.
  177, 178
Bible
  viii, ix, 2, 5, 8, 9, 11, 12, 13, 14, 17, 18, 20, 23, 24, 31, 37, 38, 45, 52, 57, 63, 68, 82, 90, 95, 99, 106, 109, 110, 113, 134, 149, 154, 155, 156, 157, 165, 166, 167, 175, 182, 183, 199, 201, 210, 226, 228, 231, 235, 246, 249, 250, 251, 258, 261, 278, 300, 329, 335, 344, 346, 350, 359, 364, 366, 420, 423, 427, 428, 431, 436, 437, 449, 455, 476, 491, 498, 504, 505, 509, 510, 516, 528, 543, 549, 558, 567, 571, 576, 580, 584, 612, 614, 643, 658, 666

Bible Student's Commentary
  235
Biblia Hebraica Stuttgartensia
  9
Biblical prophecies
  60, 103, 105, 127, 130, 136, 139, 152, 182, 183, 250, 418, 451, 457
Biblical prophecy
  11, 68, 72, 137, 230, 451, 611
Biesma, H.
  38
Bijlsma, R.
  541, 573
Bildad the Shuhite
  259, 513
Bilderdijk, Willem
  173, 182
Bilezikian, G.
  124, 570
Bingham, D. J.
  168

Bisschop, R.
  172
Bithynia
  626
Black, J. Sutherland
  83
Blake, William
  176
Blaising, Craig A.
  459
Blessing
  27, 28, 34, 44, 47,
  48, 51, 55, 56, 58,
  59, 60, 61, 63, 70,
  72, 75, 77, 85,
  115, 142, 194,
  212, 228, 229,
  237, 254, 270,
  292, 302, 335,
  362, 372, 391,
  410, 415, 424,
  454, 462, 463,
  481, 483, 484,
  551, 558, 559,
  560, 561, 575,
  620, 622, 623,
  631, 632, 657
Bloesch, D. G.
  316
Blood of Christ
  84, 192, 206, 207,
  212, 262, 282,
  386, 506, 518, 526
Blood of the covenant
  41, 194, 207
Boaz
  297, 562

Bock, Darrell L.
  459
Body of Christ
  4, 16, 20, 100,
  110, 114, 115,
  123, 146, 174,
  187, 195, 196,
  197, 207, 210,
  211, 262, 263,
  444, 458, 460,
  464, 476, 515,
  516, 521, 522,
  530, 533, 544, 631
Boers
  175
Boersma, T. J.
  38
Bohemian Brethren
  178, 181
Bonhoeffer, Dietrich
  510
Boogaard, R.
  103
Book of Acts
  202, 264, 343,
  363, 365, 383
Book of Ecclesiastes
  588, 589
Book of Job
  88, 142, 297
Book of Jubilees
  581
Book of Revelation
  9, 24, 34, 49, 89,
  93, 96, 139, 148,
  187, 221, 301,
  416, 608, 647,

Subject Index

Book of the Wars of the Lord
332

Boot, B.
102

Booth, A. E.
187

Bornkamm, H.
306

Branch
21, 29, 45, 73, 74,
96, 232, 234, 235,
236, 253, 307,
310, 311, 317,
318, 330, 336,
420, 430, 452,
469, 502, 528,
638, 642, 648, 663

Brandenburg dynasty
176

Bray, J. L.
596,

Bride of Christ
124, 667

Bridegroom
41, 89, 182, 211,
244, 245, 297,
507, 517

British Commonwealth of Nations
176

British-Israel Church of God
168, 176

Britons
32

654, 657, 661,
662, 669

Brockhaus, R.
630

Brown, R. E.
313, 326

Bruce, F. F.
314, 320, 568,
622, 657, 659

Brueggeman, Walter, W.
413

Bruijn, D. J.
103

Bruinsma-de Beer, J.
575

Buber, Martin
391

Bucer, Martin
640

Buchenwald
232

Buenos Aires
227

Buijs, C. J.
102

Buitink-Heijblom
321, 322

Bultema, H.
322, 492

Burton, A. H.
654

C

Caesaropapism
148, 149, 167

Caiaphas
380, 568, 667

Cain
    57, 58, 301
Caird, G. B.
    658
Caleb
    481
Calendar of Saints
    25, 153
Calvary
    24, 133
Calvin, John
    102, 124, 156,
    159, 167, 168,
    252, 279, 319,
    331, 334, 344,
    492, 552, 553,
    617, 640, 649
Calvinism
    41, 102, 161, 176
Calvinists
    161, 167, 176, 536
Canaan
    3, 8, 19, 28, 29,
    47, 51, 66, 220,
    225, 421
Canaanite
    8, 21, 220, 390
Canada
    489
Canadian
    183, 530
Canadian Reformed and American Reformed Churches
    183
Canadians
    220
Canterbury
    20
Cantor, Georg
    512
Cape of Good Hope
    175
Capernaum
    389, 646
Caphtor
    468, 531
Cappadocia
    626
Carson, D. A.
    602, 612, 616
Carthage
    280
Cashdan, Eli
    336, 341, 342
Catechisms
    v, 505
Cathars
    178, 181
Catholic-Apostolic movement
    169
Chafer, L. S.
    205, 459, 513,
    522, 525
Chaldea
    94
Chaldeans
    70, 225, 575
Chaldees
    26, 71

Chapman, C.
    34
Charlemagne
    24, 25, 151, 177
Charles, R. H.
    657
Chasidim
    239, 501, 526
Chater, E. H.
    654
Chelbo, Rabbi
    51
Cherubim
    20, 78, 223
Cheyne, Thomas K.
    83
Children of Abraham
    36, 44, 265, 276,
    278, 279, 389,
    461, 523, 560, 561
Chilton, D.
    244, 596
China
    77, 231
Chorazin
    389, 646
Chosen people
    34, 40, 43, 65,
    120, 259, 387,
    466, 467, 468,
    552, 569, 631, 632
Christenen voor Israël
    169-170,
Christian Ecclesia
    74, 100, 103, 151,
    188, 280, 286

Christian expositors
    64, 74, 78, 83,
    301, 307, 330,
    342, 344, 352, 426
Christian kingdom
    152
Christian nations
    10, 50, 153
Christian Reformed Church
    181
Christian theologians
    v, vi, 300, 322
Christian theology
    vi, 99
Christian world
    50, 58, 147, 400
Christian Zionism
    131, 136
Christianization
    25, 60, 147
Christianity
    ii, vi, 20, 61, 76,
    91, 105, 128, 135,
    145, 146, 148,
    153, 155, 187,
    279, 281, 284,
    343, 350, 351,
    359, 365, 366,
    391, 393, 399,
    405, 434, 507,
    521, 538, 557,
    636, 647, 654
Christians
    ii, v, vi, vii, viii,
    4, 12, 13, 20, 38,
    102, 104, 105,
    109, 110, 118,

127, 128, 135,
140, 141, 145,
146, 147, 148,
149, 150, 152,
156, 157, 160,
165, 168, 169,
172, 175, 178,
182, 183, 185,
186, 195, 204,
205, 220, 225,
231, 265, 267,
279, 280, 281,
283, 284, 288,
292, 299, 300,
327, 351, 352,
363, 365, 366,
367, 368, 369,
371, 372, 373,
387, 389, 392,
393, 395, 396,
402, 405, 406,
407, 408, 409,
410, 411, 417,
424, 434, 437,
441, 462, 468,
479, 480, 491,
519, 521, 524,
525, 536, 538,
539, 540, 555,
556, 557, 562,
563, 574, 575,
598, 599, 600,
615, 620, 648

Christians for Israel
169

Christmas
439, 585

Christology
16, 508

Chrysostom, John
542

Church
ii, 3, 4, 12, 16, 17,
60, 75, 100, 102,
107, 110, 118,
121, 124, 128,
132, 135, 139,
145, 146, 147,
148, 149, 150,
151, 152, 153,
154, 155, 156,
157, 158, 159,
160, 162, 163,
164, 165, 166,
167, 168, 173,
174, 175, 176,
177, 179, 180,
181, 184, 185,
186, 189, 196,
200, 204, 205,
226, 249, 251,
257, 258, 260,
264, 269, 271,
276, 277, 280,
285, 286, 295,
306, 344, 366,
375, 405, 407,
410, 416, 421,
423, 424, 426,
433, 440, 446,
457, 458, 460,
461, 462, 471,
473, 474, 475,
503, 504, 505,
507, 508, 509,

510, 511, 512,
513, 514, 515,
516, 519, 523,
525, 526, 529,
530, 531, 535,
536, 540, 541,
542, 543, 550,
552, 553, 557,
566, 567, 573,
574, 575, 611,
612, 616, 650,
651, 661, 662, 667

Church fathers
121, 146, 147,
150, 151, 154,
306, 344, 375

Church history
154, 155, 162,
180, 204, 249,
366, 473, 557

Church of England
149, 167, 179

Church of the Holy Sepulchre
154

Circumcision
36, 37, 38, 79,
105, 106, 135,
192, 205, 206,
256, 262, 265,
266, 267, 271,
272, 282, 283,
401, 536, 548,
562, 563

City of David
127, 308, 392, 428

Classic dispensationalism
186, 189

Classical dispensationalism
100, 110, 115,
278, 459, 461

Classical dispensationalists
111, 113, 115,
132, 567

Clowney, Edmund P.
526, 528, 541

Coates, C. A.
630, 654

Cocceius, Johannes
172, 416, 436

Codex Bezae
612

Codex Vaticanus
612

Cohen, A.
8, 52, 53, 277,
284, 305, 309,
312, 314, 320,
324, 327, 332,
335, 336, 339,
341, 342, 343,
344, 345, 349,
350, 361, 382, 586

Cohen Stuart, G. H.
102

Cohn-Sherbock, Dan
136

Commandments
30, 65, 67, 69,
101, 105, 107,
109, 110, 133,
139, 143, 156,
208, 215, 216,
217, 218, 219,
226, 229, 272,

283, 368, 369,
373, 378, 390,
396, 405, 469,
524, 526, 527,
562, 564, 589

Commentaar op het Nieuwe Testament, Derde Serie
183

Commentary on the New Testament, Third Series
183

Commonwealth of Israel
210, 262

"Comparison between the Redemption of the Children of Israel and the Liberation of the United Dutch Provinces", poem
171

Confessions
v, 505

Congar, Y.
510

Coniah
317

Constantine
24, 25, 145, 146, 148, 149, 154

Constantinian shift
146, 147, 148, 168

Constantinople
20, 76

Conversion
61, 69, 92, 104, 105, 118, 135, 136, 137, 145, 148, 157, 182, 184, 228, 254, 388, 391, 458, 471, 498, 539, 634, 640, 641, 642, 644, 649, 650, 651

Cornelis
475

Corner Gate
240, 670

Cornu, Francis
x

Council of Nicaea
149

Council of Trent
125

Counter-Reformation
159

Covenant
i, viii, 16, 20, 34, 35, 36, 38, 39, 40, 41, 42, 44, 45, 46, 47, 65, 78, 101, 103, 114, 119, 124, 126, 129, 131, 137, 138, 173, 174, 175, 176, 178, 182, 184, 185, 188, 189, 191, 192, 193, 194, 195, 196, 197, 198, 199, 200, 201, 204, 205, 206, 207, 208, 209, 210, 211, 212, 213, 214, 215, 216, 217,

218, 220, 223, 227, 243, 252, 254, 255, 257, 270, 280, 314, 339, 349, 353, 356, 371, 376, 428, 429, 457, 469, 470, 483, 487, 509, 511, 527, 529, 536, 545, 549, 553, 555, 558, 559, 566, 567, 577, 581, 582, 583, 586, 587, 621, 622, 638, 648, 667

Covenant people
  65, 103, 126, 175, 176, 178, 184, 196, 257, 553, 582

Covenant of grace
  40, 131, 188, 511

Covenant of works
  40, 188, 511

Covenant theology
  i, 131, 178, 188, 189, 428

Covenants
  viii, 16, 34, 35, 38, 40, 41, 42, 64, 131, 188, 191, 205, 210, 211, 218, 219, 225, 262, 527, 541, 549, 581, 586

Cox, C. C.
  654

Craigie, Peter C.
  332, 333

Cranfield, C. E. B.
  117

Creator
  373, 531, 532, 665

Creed of Maimonides
  372

Creeds
  v, 249

Cromwell, Oliver
  176

Crucifixion
  108, 406

Cush
  421, 422, 492

Cushites
  468, 531

Cyprian
  280

Cyrene
  474

Cyrus
  7, 22, 94, 95, 226, 227, 351

D

Da Costa, Isaac
  182, 492

Damascus
  519

Dan
  127, 497, 571

Daniel
  6, 8, 68, 70, 90, 91, 93, 94, 95, 143, 238, 247,

434, 435, 444,
481, 496, 598,
599, 601, 602,
603, 604, 665

Dante Alighieri
24

Darby, J. N.
169, 181, 182,
459, 630, 654

Datheen, Petrus
161, 275

David
23, 25, 38, 45, 46,
47, 52, 65, 66, 71,
73, 74, 75, 76, 77,
80, 81, 82, 89, 92,
107, 108, 118,
119, 120, 127,
130, 145, 151,
168, 170, 176,
179, 197, 198,
202, 203, 212,
214, 223, 227,
228, 232, 234,
235, 236, 237,
249, 284, 289,
292, 297, 300,
303, 304, 307,
308, 309, 311,
312, 313, 314,
315, 316, 317,
318, 319, 320,
321, 322, 328,
330, 335, 336,
339, 340, 342,
343, 344, 345,
347, 348, 349,
360, 361, 364,
365, 367, 368,
370, 379, 380,
381, 387, 392,
418, 419, 420,
428, 429, 430,
431, 434, 436,
442, 445, 451,
452, 453, 454,
463, 473, 482,
524, 529, 537,
562, 580, 587,
619, 629, 666, 670

Davidic king
65, 74, 82, 111,
151, 293, 307,
313, 318, 319,
320, 339, 346,
370, 380, 442, 622

Davidic kingdom
71, 380, 619, 620

Davidic kings
73, 75, 309, 315,
335, 380, 418,
452, 500

Davies, W. D.
375, 413, 577

Davis, J. D.
322

Day of Atonement
82, 478, 480, 587

Day of Pentecost
122, 132, 257,
437, 442, 443,
449, 460, 474,
484, 504, 507,
513, 514, 515,
516, 517, 519,

De Boer
 102
De Brès, Guido
 505
De Cock, Hendrik
 173
De Graaff, F.
 49
De Graaf-van Gelder, R.
 103
De Groot, Hugo
 640
De Heer, Johannes
 102
De Jong, H.
 100, 102, 104, 135, 592
De León, Moses
 351
De Maistre, Joseph
 177
De Voogd van der Straaten, D.
 103
De Vries, P.
 102
De Wilde, W. J.
 342
Dead Sea
 15
Dead Sea scrolls
 307, 313, 320, 336
Death
 vi, 33, 41, 70, 83, 521, 522, 535, 540, 541, 581, 582, 621
 85, 91, 95, 108, 150, 167, 168, 180, 181, 197, 198, 201, 206, 208, 215, 231, 238, 244, 260, 268, 274, 281, 282, 291, 292, 301, 304, 308, 327, 329, 343, 352, 355, 373, 376, 383, 384, 385, 386, 397, 407, 408, 430, 435, 448, 451, 474, 476, 481, 517, 518, 519, 536, 572, 573, 577, 582, 584, 585, 608, 611, 614, 642, 643, 659

Death penalty
 167, 282, 291, 308
Decapolis
 475
Declaration of the Establishment of the State of Israel
 493
Delilah
 148
Delitzsch, F.
 210, 319
Deliverer
 137, 252, 254, 416, 483, 576, 638
Den Boer, C.
 543

Den Butter, P.
  102
Den Hertog, G. C.
  102, 543
Denham Smith, J.
  93, 510
Denney, J.
  630
Dennett, E.
  654
Dennison, J. T., Jr.
  162, 179, 258,
  505, 507, 508
Destruction of Jerusalem
  76, 90, 453, 475,
  476, 478, 481,
  482, 483, 486,
  488, 581, 595,
  598, 606, 607
Devil
  5, 9, 35, 49, 52,
  57, 58, 87, 90,
  249, 296, 301,
  386, 389, 430,
  523, 560, 561, 668
Diaspora
  259, 498, 615, 626
Diocletian
  662
Diprose, R. E.
  103
Disciples
  194, 198, 239,
  240, 245, 246,
  261, 294, 364,
  373, 378, 382,
  387, 395, 398,
  402, 404, 476,
  515, 537, 538,
  570, 571, 594,
  595, 604, 610,
  611, 612, 613,
  617, 618, 619,
  620, 621, 643
Disney World
  262
Dispensation
  99, 100, 187, 510,
  517, 566, 655
Dispensationalism
  18, 100, 110, 114,
  115, 186, 187,
  189, 278, 458,
  459, 461, 592
Dispersion
  103, 210, 230,
  488, 581, 604,
  615, 626
Divorce
  141, 471
Doctrine of the kingdom
  16, 129, 130
Doeg
  643
Dogmatics
  15, 122, 168, 252,
  428, 433
Dome of the Rock
  76, 234
Donatism
  155, 166
Dooyeweerd, Herman
  164

Doppers
176
Dostoevsky, F.
400
Douma, J.
38, 39, 102, 104, 112, 114, 115, 135, 183, 225, 262, 552, 555
Dove
89, 260
Dragon
9, 24, 25, 31, 49, 50, 57, 58, 62, 63, 86, 87, 88, 89, 90, 97, 148, 149, 152, 153, 588, 653, 654, 661, 664, 668, 669
Drost, A. H.
102
Duijtsch, Christiaan Salomon
103
Dulles, A. R.
510
Dunant, Henri
136
Dunn, J. D. G.
363, 553
Dutch Israel
171, 172, 174
Dutch Reformed Church
164, 285
Dutch Second Reformation
128, 159, 416, 436, 489, 542

Dutch States Translation
251, 267, 276, 347, 424, 426, 432, 433, 440, 446, 492, 542, 598, 637, 656

E

Earth
3, 8, 15, 17, 18, 19, 22, 23, 24, 27, 29, 30, 31, 33, 34, 39, 40, 46, 47, 55, 56, 58, 65, 66, 67, 68, 69, 73, 76, 82, 83, 84, 89, 90, 92, 93, 94, 101, 103, 107, 108, 115, 117, 120, 121, 122, 127, 131, 134, 137, 147, 150, 152, 155, 158, 160, 161, 179, 186, 193, 195, 196, 200, 221, 223, 225, 226, 227, 228, 229, 231, 232, 233, 234, 236, 237, 238, 239, 240, 244, 248, 250, 256, 257, 260, 261, 263, 269, 273, 282, 285, 287, 300, 302, 305, 314, 325, 327, 339, 341, 342, 348, 359,

362, 372, 388,
397, 399, 416,
418, 420, 421,
430, 431, 432,
434, 435, 437,
438, 439, 441,
444, 445, 447,
448, 451, 453,
459, 460, 463,
466, 467, 468,
469, 470, 475,
477, 481, 482,
484, 492, 493,
495, 496, 497,
499, 504, 517,
519, 520, 521,
529, 531, 533,
545, 551, 552,
558, 559, 560,
562, 566, 567,
597, 605, 607,
608, 609, 615,
616, 617, 619,
620, 621, 622,
625, 631, 642,
645, 646, 647,
648, 652, 654,
655, 657, 662,
664, 665, 666,
668, 670

Earthly kingdom
67, 108, 434, 618, 620

East Asia
231

Easter
33, 79, 133, 149, 481, 585

Eastern Orthodox churches
102, 146

Eastern Orthodoxy
76, 279

Eastern Roman Empire
76

Ebed-melech
259, 272, 513

Eber
27, 302

Ecclesia
4, 7, 15, 16, 20,
28, 38, 74, 99,
100, 102, 103,
104, 105, 106,
107, 109, 110,
111, 112, 113,
114, 115, 120,
123, 124, 125,
126, 127, 130,
132, 135, 139,
140, 145, 147,
148, 151, 155,
159, 160, 174,
178, 180, 183,
186, 187, 188,
192, 193, 195,
196, 197, 199,
200, 201, 204,
205, 207, 210,
212, 213, 214,
218, 219, 231,
233, 235, 237,
251, 252, 256,
257, 258, 259,
260, 261, 262,
263, 264, 265,
266, 267, 268,

269, 271, 272,
274, 275, 277,
278, 279, 280,
281, 282, 283,
284, 285, 286,
287, 288, 309,
360, 391, 398,
400, 401, 416,
427, 429, 430,
431, 432, 433,
438, 441, 444,
448, 449, 457,
458, 459, 460,
461, 462, 463,
464, 465, 467,
469, 471, 472,
473, 474, 475,
476, 486, 497,
503, 504, 505,
506, 507, 508,
509, 510, 511,
512, 513, 514,
515, 516, 517,
518, 519, 520,
521, 522, 523,
524, 525, 526,
528, 529, 530,
531, 532, 533,
534, 536, 537,
538, 539, 540,
541, 544, 545,
547, 550, 551,
552, 563, 564,
565, 566, 567,
569, 570, 572,
573, 574, 575,
576, 577, 582,
583, 586, 612,
613, 614, 616,
621, 626, 631,
636, 637, 639,
640, 651, 655,
658, 659, 660,
667, 671, 672

Ecclesiology
15, 99, 129, 145,
146, 155, 159,
460, 542

Edelkoort, A. H.
299, 313, 332, 336

Edersheim, Alfred
359

Edict of Milan
146

Edom
32, 50, 51, 52,
55, 57, 58, 59,
61, 62, 63, 64,
284, 305, 314,
421, 422, 424,
438, 488, 611

Edomites
421

Egypt
3, 6, 10, 19, 30,
33, 39, 42, 74, 78,
81, 88, 89, 94, 97,
98, 124, 140, 170,
172, 175, 192,
196, 199, 202,
209, 213, 224,
225, 230, 235,
257, 274, 319,
331, 333, 358,
421, 424, 431,
438, 447, 453,

468, 487, 488,
499, 531, 537,
538, 566, 572,
574, 576, 578,
579, 580, 585,
586, 658, 664, 671

Eighth day
116, 121, 370, 391

Einstein, Albert
512

Ekron
422

El Aqsa Mosque
234

Elam
421, 422, 488

Eldad
375, 576

Eleazar
67

Eleazar, Rabbi
191, 351, 562

Election
i, 16, 26, 129, 305,
387, 466, 467,
469, 471, 483,
543, 550, 551,
552, 559, 631,
632, 639

Electors of Brandenburg
176

Eliakim
350

Elihu
259, 513

Elijah
245, 297, 332,
341, 377, 451,
573, 622, 631, 659

Eliphaz
259, 513

Elisha
9, 297, 622

Elizabeth
216, 370, 527, 579

Elohim
5, 49, 51, 52, 53,
54, 59, 60, 61,
293, 327, 329

Emden, Jakob
392

Encyclopaedia Biblica
83

End time
62, 76, 102, 104,
105, 118, 228,
248, 310, 314,
414, 415, 418,
420, 422, 425,
426, 428, 436,
453, 458, 459,
483, 486, 487,
488, 489, 490,
494, 497, 498,
511, 544, 588,
595, 596, 597,
598, 599, 600,
601, 602, 606,
607, 608, 609,
610, 611, 612,
629, 634, 644,
652, 654, 655,

Subject Index

End Times Sermon
> 656, 659, 664
> 592, 593, 594

England
> 149, 153, 167, 169, 170, 172, 176, 177, 178, 179, 220

English Parliament
> 176

Enoch
> 258, 513, 558, 565, 659

Enosh
> 302

Ephesus
> 110, 153, 257, 261, 449, 504, 509

Ephraim
> 12, 307, 341, 362, 421, 423, 424, 441, 470, 497, 529, 571, 666

Ephraimites
> 433

Ephrathites
> 308

Erickson, Millard J.
> 514

Eschatology
> 11, 16, 101, 129, 145, 146, 147, 151, 155, 156, 158, 159, 160, 166, 364

Esau
> 26, 49, 50, 51, 52, 53, 54, 55, 56, 58, 59, 60, 61, 62, 63, 254, 270, 284, 286, 305, 550

Esther
> 93, 297, 331, 344, 585, 588

Eternal People
> 2, 3, 82

Ethiopian eunuch
> 17, 295, 352

Ethnic Israel
> 3, 4, 13, 15, 17, 28, 39, 40, 44, 100, 101, 102, 103, 104, 106, 107, 109, 110, 112, 118, 126, 127, 130, 136, 139, 150, 151, 175, 199, 204, 205, 250, 251, 252, 253, 254, 255, 256, 258, 264, 270, 273, 279, 280, 281, 401, 416, 427, 443, 444, 448, 449, 452, 458, 459, 462, 465, 466, 467, 468, 472, 481, 513, 541, 551, 553, 554, 613, 614, 616, 639, 641, 642, 650, 654,

Ethnos
655, 659, 670
568, 569,

Euphrates
27, 33, 140, 302,
417, 424, 425,
441, 492, 671

Europe
vii, 19, 24, 30, 68,
76, 158, 176, 274,
487

European Union
489

Europeans
77

Eusebius
154, 155, 249

Evans, C. A.
294

Evangelical free churches
165

Evangelical movement
169

Evangelical Palestinians
vii

Evangelicals
103, 128, 166,
169, 284, 530

Evangelists
131, 210, 533, 539

Eve
16, 57, 124, 211,
258, 301, 449,
459, 460, 505,
506, 510, 513, 514

Everlasting covenant
35, 38, 39, 40, 44,
45, 46, 47, 193,
198, 199, 314, 581

Everlasting Father
46, 227, 321, 322,
381

Exegesis
44, 45, 46, 52, 53,
111, 117, 122,
123, 130, 134,
138, 184, 188,
204, 235, 237,
252, 255, 256,
261, 273, 278,
293, 296, 297,
301, 303, 315,
321, 322, 327,
335, 343, 419,
424, 426, 427,
428, 431, 432,
433, 440, 441,
443, 445, 550,
552, 558, 584,
601, 611, 630,
641, 655, 658, 659

Exodus
3, 10, 40, 78, 81,
140, 192, 196,
210, 274, 459,
537, 572, 573,
574, 585, 664

Ezekiel
70, 73, 121, 351,
451, 452, 481

Subject Index

F

Faith
ii, iii, 34, 35, 37, 40, 44, 100, 103, 109, 111, 113, 147, 149, 156, 159, 197, 205, 210, 211, 226, 255, 256, 264, 267, 268, 276, 278, 299, 304, 363, 368, 369, 389, 390, 391, 393, 405, 409, 413, 443, 458, 462, 467, 482, 498, 500, 504, 509, 523, 524, 525, 526, 527, 530, 534, 541, 544, 552, 556, 557, 558, 561, 565, 567, 568, 615, 622, 626, 631, 634, 642, 643, 644, 650

Fall
40, 188, 258, 260, 328, 445, 510, 511

False prophet
31, 91, 92, 305, 416, 605, 652, 653, 665, 666, 668, 669

Family of God
530, 531, 532

Farrer, A. M.
654

Feast of Booths
240, 581, 585, 588

Feast of the New Covenant
581

Feast of the Old Covenant
581

Feast of the Unleavened Loaves
585

Feast of Weeks
581

Federalism
178, 188, 189

Ferragut
25

Festivals
37, 191, 256, 282, 283, 407, 562, 563, 585, 587

Fijnvandraat, J. G.
135, 263, 357

First beast
91, 652, 653, 668

First exile
76, 77, 78, 98, 453

First World War
488

Fishers of people
537, 538, 539, 540

Flusser, David
372

Foederology
16, 101

Food laws
37, 105, 256, 282, 283, 407, 562, 563

Ford, D.
  601
Ford, J. M.
  654, 659
Fourth Commandment
  105
France
  25, 153, 177
France, R. T.
  351, 600, 603, 612
Frederic the Great
  5
Freedom
  25, 139, 146, 149, 243, 574, 671
Froom, L. E.
  146, 154
Fruchtenbaum, Arnold
  vi, 459, 555, 559
Full preterism
  244, 592, 603
Fung, R. Y. K.
  267, 270

G

Gabriel
  75, 107, 249, 308, 313, 392, 419, 435
Gäckle, V.
  553
Gad
  656
Gaebelein, A. C.
  93, 137, 180, 346, 357, 488, 492, 593, 601, 616, 630, 659
Gaius
  603
Galatia
  266, 626
Galilee
  13, 239, 374, 378
Gamaliel
  363
Garden of Eden
  66, 408, 432, 504, 509
Gate of Benjamin
  240, 670
Gath
  422
Gaza
  422
Geba
  240, 670
Gehazi
  643
Geneva
  20, 160, 167, 181
Gentile Christians
  20, 283, 288
Gentile Jesus-believers
  13, 28, 33, 41, 139, 192, 210, 255, 269, 276, 283, 449, 458, 515, 523, 527, 536, 550, 551, 557, 561, 562, 563, 639
Gentile nations
  48, 193, 194, 235,

255, 273, 392,
433, 548, 562, 630

Gentile world

4, 24, 34, 37, 83,
193, 255, 256,
262, 392, 398,
399, 429, 457,
474, 543, 544,
556, 569, 619, 637

Gentiles

v, 33, 34, 44, 76,
77, 79, 80, 81,
82, 83, 84, 87,
88, 89, 90, 92,
101, 113, 115,
123, 137, 158,
192, 193, 195,
196, 199, 200,
207, 212, 215,
248, 251, 252,
255, 259, 262,
263, 264, 265,
266, 269, 271,
272, 273, 274,
282, 283, 284,
285, 288, 295,
334, 387, 389,
390, 392, 393,
394, 397, 398,
399, 404, 407,
416, 419, 423,
424, 430, 432,
433, 443, 457,
464, 465, 466,
473, 474, 475,
477, 481, 483,
498, 511, 513,
515, 518, 519,
524, 525, 531,
532, 540, 544,
545, 548, 549,
550, 551, 552,
553, 554, 555,
556, 560, 564,
565, 567, 568,
569, 572, 593,
606, 607, 608,
609, 618, 620,
623, 625, 626,
627, 630, 632,
633, 634, 636,
637, 639, 640,
641, 642, 646, 658

German Peasants' War

167

Germany

6, 25, 56, 232

Gersonides

332

Gesenius, W.

351

Ghent

160

Gibbs, J. A.

595, 596

Gibeah

223

Gibeon

223

Gill, John

395

Girgashite

220

Gispen, W. H.

445

Glashouwer, W. J. J.
102, 483, 543

Glasson, T. F.
654

Glorification
292, 339, 349,
419, 460, 508,
517, 519, 520, 657

God of gods
8, 11, 27, 71, 93

God of Israel
viii, 4, 5, 8, 56,
62, 63, 65, 79,
105, 109, 136,
147, 148, 172,
194, 223, 234,
253, 348, 366,
392, 409, 410,
426, 451, 454,
468, 471, 491,
494, 500, 501,
523, 566, 631, 634

God's judgment
71, 74, 83, 84, 91,
94, 404, 416, 491,
525, 557, 609,
644, 647

God's kingdom
62, 116, 197, 404,
543, 634

God's people
i, 3, 52, 63, 84,
231, 255, 267,
272, 273, 338,
353, 404, 421,
450, 455, 467,
468, 470, 472,
479, 484, 486,
540, 541, 562,
563, 564, 569,
583, 588, 596,
618, 625, 627, 634

God's promises
4, 59, 66, 69, 78,
104, 138, 139,
140, 200, 225,
276, 416, 543,
552, 558, 559, 614

God's right hand
89, 107, 124, 263,
331, 339, 340,
349, 463, 508,
517, 519, 521,
563, 660

Godet, F.
317

Gods
8, 9, 10, 11, 27,
51, 71, 79, 93, 94,
147, 152, 153,
157, 199, 220,
236, 312, 327,
329, 410, 416,
432, 436, 447,
448, 473

Goebbels, Joseph
653

Gog
31, 32, 422, 489

Goldman, S.
309, 313

Golgotha
206, 355, 481

Golverdingen, M.
170, 174, 176
Gomer
472, 473
Good Friday
585
Goslinga, C. J.
313, 320
Gospels
106, 202, 238,
294, 323, 332,
365, 516, 591,
592, 593, 606,
610, 616, 661
Goy
vii, 9, 28, 568, 569
Goyyim
26, 28, 59, 558,
559, 568, 569
Graafland, C.
102, 437, 640
Grace
6, 40, 41, 54, 58,
60, 61, 69, 70,
72, 73, 84, 92,
111, 113, 117,
131, 185, 188,
189, 199, 234,
246, 247, 277,
327, 342, 346,
376, 388, 391,
401, 403, 404,
405, 421, 426,
442, 443, 449,
450, 461, 469,
470, 475, 477,
511, 524, 527,
535, 548, 551,
569, 577, 626,
630, 631, 632,
633, 636, 646
Grammatical-historical exegesis
130, 255, 261,
293, 296, 297,
315, 327, 424
Grant, F. W.
137, 207, 323,
346, 475, 488,
559, 593, 601,
616, 630, 654
Gratian
146
Great Britain
492
Great prostitute
526, 667, 669, 671
Great Shift
149, 154, 155,
156, 279
Great Trek
175
Great Tribulation
186, 187, 188,
202, 238, 595,
596, 597, 598,
600, 601, 605,
606, 607, 609,
610, 656, 659,
663, 667, 668
Great white throne
481, 616
Greco-Macedonian empire
94, 652

Greece
  7, 8, 68, 95, 97
Greek empire
  24
Greek Orthodoxy
  76
Greeks
  3, 32, 113, 261,
  264, 308, 391,
  457, 521, 548, 626
Greenland
  231
Greijdanus, S.
  616, 655, 657, 659
Groen van Prinsterer, Guillaume
  173, 178
Groenewegen, Henricus
  416
Groenhuis, Gerrit
  171
Grogan, G. W.
  311, 315, 492
Grosheide, F. W.
  598, 600, 650
Grotius
  640
Grün, A.
  334
Guardian angel
  51, 52, 53, 55, 57,
  60, 61, 63
Gutbrod, W.
  267
Guthrie, D.
  626

H

Ha'Aretz
  7, 14, 47, 79, 80,
  82, 219, 220, 222,
  408
Haacker, K.
  592
Haak, T.
  267, 424, 426,
  433, 440, 446, 598
Habershon, A. R.
  274
Hadad-rimmon
  442
Hades
  260, 389, 448,
  460, 570, 646
Hagar
  138, 286, 303,
  426, 583
Hahn, F.
  513
Haitsma, J.
  103
Hale, J. K.
  176
Halevi, Jehuda
  392
Haman
  v, 37, 93, 586
Hamath
  421
Hamburg
  25
Hamilton, V.
  53, 307

Hannah
446

Hanson, A. T.
654

Hanukkah
585

HaQalir, Eleazar
351

Harun al-Rashid
25

Hasidim
501

Hasmonean dynasty
81

Hays
592

Heaven
6, 12, 33, 34, 55, 60, 68, 73, 74, 75, 88, 90, 91, 92, 94, 95, 96, 107, 108, 111, 112, 115, 117, 122, 123, 127, 131, 138, 147, 152, 153, 154, 155, 156, 163, 186, 187, 195, 196, 200, 201, 204, 211, 212, 213, 214, 226, 229, 230, 234, 238, 239, 240, 244, 245, 247, 248, 249, 250, 257, 260, 261, 278, 281, 282, 285, 298, 300, 324, 325, 339, 349, 361, 364, 367, 372, 375, 377, 379, 381, 382, 389, 390, 391, 396, 417, 419, 430, 431, 432, 434, 445, 447, 448, 463, 476, 478, 496, 501, 504, 507, 508, 516, 517, 519, 520, 521, 522, 529, 533, 536, 538, 539, 544, 545, 573, 574, 576, 585, 592, 597, 600, 602, 605, 606, 607, 608, 610, 616, 619, 621, 622, 623, 626, 646, 660, 661, 664, 666, 669, 670

Heavenly beings
327, 329

Heavenly country
33, 45, 100, 103, 107, 108, 139, 140, 202, 204, 225, 408, 672

Hebrew Bible
226, 549

Hebron
14

Heidelberg Catechism
161, 508

Heidler, R. D.
103
Heitink, G.
573, 574
Hellenbroek, Abraham
172
Hellenism
66, 100
Hellenists
474
Hendriksen, W.
485, 642, 657
Hengel, M.
326, 327, 332, 335
Hengstenberg, E. W.
351, 623
Henry, C. F. H.
511
Henry, Matthew
492, 598
Herford, R. T.
145
Hermon
127
Herod
67, 455, 578, 579,
580, 598, 652, 667
Herzl, Theodor
136, 233, 491
Heyns, J. A.
295, 541, 555, 573
Hezekiah
38, 316, 321, 322,
340, 351, 418,
500, 562

Hildesheim
25
Hill, C.
176
Hill, D.
598
Hillel, Rabbi
344, 364, 374, 382
Hippolytus
155
Hiram
259, 513
Hirsch, E.
293,
Hirsch, Samson Raphael
392
Historia Ecclesiastica
154
Hitler, Adolf
653
Hoedemaker, P. J.
531
Hoek, J.
102, 458, 460, 543
Hoekema, Anthony
598, 642
Hoekendijk, B.
103
Hoehner, H. W.
357
Holocaust
vi, 56, 62, 150
Holy city
14, 66, 144, 214,
220, 221, 222,
278, 356, 435,

Holy Land
487, 605, 657
14, 19, 66, 71,
119, 120, 127,
140, 141, 143,
182, 220, 222,
408, 549, 574,
586, 602, 604,
615, 656

Holy of Holies
20, 435

Holy One of Israel
23, 32, 69, 495,
639

Holy Roman Empire
221

Holy Spirit
4, 16, 41, 69, 83,
110, 111, 113,
131, 132, 137,
200, 208, 211,
214, 215, 216,
217, 218, 219,
220, 224, 257,
258, 260, 261,
262, 263, 282,
373, 382, 397,
401, 410, 437,
442, 450, 455,
456, 460, 461,
462, 463, 475,
476, 484, 491,
494, 505, 506,
507, 508, 515,
516, 517, 520,
521, 522, 526,
530, 532, 534,
535, 536, 541,
544, 568, 580,
582, 583, 585,
593, 606, 617,
618, 620, 626, 649

Horsley, S.
492

Horus
661

Hoste, W.
654

House of David
74, 76, 92, 176,
292, 308, 309,
311, 313, 315,
316, 317, 336,
339, 342, 360,
419, 442, 451,
452, 453

House of the LORD
14, 21, 30, 202,
227, 237, 240,
277, 350, 446,
454, 498, 584,
635, 670

Hughes, P. E.
649, 650

Huisman, C.
172

Human responsibility
40, 69, 270, 450,
469, 471, 525, 635

Hussites
181

Hutzav
10

Huzzab
10

I

Ibn Ezra, Abraham
54, 335, 341, 342, 351

Ichabod
78, 97

Idolatry
79, 93, 162, 164, 179, 482, 549, 605, 627, 635, 667

Imber, Naftali Herz
408

Immanuel
315, 316, 417, 418, 425

India
77

Infant baptism
i, 37, 106, 135, 166, 169, 205, 206, 256, 536

Infidelity
71, 77, 91, 330

Inquisition
157, 160, 282, 407

International law
140, 186

Iran
68, 422, 488

Iranians
3, 32

Iraq
68, 203, 418, 422, 488, 489

Irenaeus
155, 317

Ironside, H. A.
187, 654

Irving, E.
169

Isaac
2, 5, 28, 33, 35, 42, 50, 52, 55, 56, 58, 65, 138, 195, 220, 229, 270, 297, 298, 302, 303, 304, 305, 362, 369, 390, 513, 529, 537, 550, 559, 564, 583, 586, 622, 646

Ishmael
26, 138, 254, 270, 550, 583

Ishtar
153

Islam
77

Israelis
79, 143, 169, 433, 490

Israelism
117, 138

Israelists
112, 116, 117, 118, 138, 468, 469

Israelites
x, 22, 30, 45, 46, 47, 64, 103, 109, 110, 130, 140, 197, 198, 200, 208, 209, 215,

217, 222, 225,
227, 229, 231,
239, 251, 254,
264, 267, 272,
280, 388, 390,
400, 404, 430,
440, 449, 463,
466, 467, 497,
498, 513, 528,
548, 559, 574,
586, 615, 621,
622, 623, 632,
633, 642, 643,
648, 654, 655, 656

Israelology
vi, vii, 4, 11, 15,
18, 45, 46, 99,
118, 126, 129,
131, 132, 134,
135, 138, 139,
146, 147, 155,
156, 159, 160,
188, 189, 279

Istanbul
76

Italy
68

J

Jabbok
51, 53

Jacob
2, 5, 8, 9, 21, 23,
26, 28, 33, 35, 36,
36, 42, 47, 49, 50,
51, 52, 53, 54, 55,
56, 57, 58, 59, 60,
61, 62, 63, 65, 66,
69, 75, 78, 92,
124, 125, 127,
137, 171, 172,
183, 195, 197,
202, 220, 222,
225, 229, 236,
252, 253, 254,
275, 277, 284,
286, 292, 304,
305, 306, 310,
312, 335, 360,
361, 362, 390,
392, 399, 419,
426, 440, 450,
472, 483, 495,
499, 513, 529,
537, 538, 550,
559, 560, 570,
571, 578, 584,
596, 622, 638,
645, 646, 663,
664, 670

Jacobs, D.
630, 637, 641

Jager, H.
183

Jambres
375, 577

Jannaeus, Alexander
359

Jannes
375, 577

Janse, S.
102

Jansen, H.
vi

Jansen, J. G. B.
vi
Japheth
302
Japhethites
302
Javan
30, 498
Jebus
71
Jebusite
220
Jechoniah
317, 370
Jedidiah
304
Jehoiachin
74, 317, 351, 370
Jehovah's Witnesses
182
Jehozadak
118
Jennings, F. C.
654
Jenson, R. W.
106
Jericho
259
Jeroboam
643, 666
Jerome
2, 60, 155
Jerusalem
vii, x, 1, 4, 5, 9, 12, 14, 15, 18, 19, 21, 22, 23, 24, 25, 26, 30, 31, 36, 65, 66, 68, 69, 71, 73, 74, 76, 77, 79, 80, 81, 82, 85, 86, 90, 93, 98, 100, 104, 111, 119, 120, 121, 123, 127, 133, 138, 139, 140, 142, 151, 153, 154, 157, 161, 171, 172, 176, 177, 193, 204, 220, 221, 222, 224, 226, 227, 228, 233, 234, 235, 236, 237, 239, 240, 241, 244, 247, 249, 250, 251, 255, 266, 277, 278, 291, 294, 307, 308, 309, 341, 342, 347, 349, 356, 364, 365, 371, 374, 385, 399, 403, 406, 407, 408, 416, 418, 419, 420, 423, 428, 430, 434, 438, 439, 440, 441, 442, 444, 451, 453, 454, 455, 456, 468, 474, 475, 476, 477, 478, 481, 482, 483, 484, 485, 486, 488, 494, 495,

Subject Index

497, 498, 500,
511, 514, 518,
534, 572, 573,
581, 583, 584,
592, 593, 595,
598, 599, 601,
602, 603, 604,
605, 606, 607,
608, 609, 615,
617, 620, 621,
625, 629, 638,
639, 647, 651,
652, 657, 658,
659, 666, 669,
670, 671, 672

Jerusalem Talmud
308, 478

Jeshua
119, 337, 454

Jesse
232, 308, 310,
311, 335, 420

Jesus-believers
ii, 4, 7, 13, 28, 33,
41, 104, 108, 133,
139, 192, 197,
198, 210, 211,
212, 214, 218,
226, 253, 255,
258, 264, 266,
268, 269, 271,
274, 276, 279,
283, 375, 406,
428, 449, 458,
464, 475, 515,
516, 523, 525,
527, 536, 545,
550, 551, 552,
557, 561, 562,
563, 564, 639

Jesus-believing Gentiles
199, 212, 265,
282, 284, 423,
525, 544, 554,
555, 568, 572

Jesus-believing Jews
viii, 41, 100, 101,
104, 109, 133,
172, 187, 192,
195, 196, 197,
212, 226, 262,
264, 265, 267,
282, 283, 284,
304, 366, 423,
434, 459, 474,
544, 557, 565,
568, 615, 626,
632, 642

Jesus-believing non-Jews
101, 104, 195,
262, 266

Jesus Christ
i, ii, iii, viii, 60,
64, 73, 103, 112,
114, 132, 137,
138, 179, 182,
210, 245, 257,
258, 260, 278,
281, 297, 312,
338, 366, 367,
369, 384, 387,
433, 434, 449,
458, 460, 461,
463, 464, 474,
478, 505, 506,
517, 522, 532,

533, 534, 538,
550, 551, 564,
567, 573, 576,
577, 613, 614,
615, 628

Jesus of Nazareth
281, 285, 294,
299, 300, 332

Jethro
259, 513

Jewish Christians
109, 118, 267

Jewish Council
349, 363

Jewish expositors
60, 300, 301, 305,
309, 319, 321,
325, 342, 347,
381, 419

Jewish people
v, vi, 103, 136,
143, 159, 169,
332, 398, 407,
480, 487, 493,
552, 632

Jewish proselytes
192, 283, 562, 563

Jewish scholars
vii, 52, 291, 300,
309, 392

Jewish state
136, 455, 488, 489

Jewish tradition
8, 50, 53, 62, 228,
291, 311, 350,
570, 578, 580

Jewish War
592, 597, 599,
603, 606, 608

Jewry
vi, 79, 137, 433,
455, 491

Jews
v, vi, vii, viii, 2,
4, 5, 10, 13, 15,
20, 25, 28, 30, 33,
35, 37, 38, 41, 44,
60, 62, 63, 66, 71,
79, 80, 82, 84,
86, 91, 92, 95,
100, 101, 104,
105, 109, 110,
113, 115, 118,
128, 133, 136,
137, 141, 142,
143, 149, 150,
152, 153, 154,
156, 157, 158,
159, 162, 164,
168, 169, 172,
173, 182, 185,
187, 189, 192,
194, 195, 196,
197, 203, 205,
212, 215, 220,
226, 227, 231,
232, 233, 243,
246, 251, 252,
255, 256, 259,
261, 262, 263,
264, 265, 266,
267, 269, 270,
271, 272, 273,
279, 280, 281,

Subject Index

282, 283, 284, 285, 290, 291, 292, 299, 300, 304, 308, 310, 327, 330, 332, 335, 349, 351, 352, 356, 359, 360, 363, 364, 365, 366, 367, 368, 369, 370, 372, 373, 377, 380, 383, 384, 387, 389, 390, 391, 393, 396, 397, 398, 399, 402, 404, 405, 406, 407, 408, 409, 410, 411, 417, 420, 423, 426, 430, 433, 434, 443, 444, 453, 455, 457, 458, 459, 464, 465, 469, 474, 475, 478, 481, 482, 491, 493, 494, 496, 498, 499, 506, 511, 513, 515, 518, 521, 523, 525, 529, 531, 539, 542, 543, 544, 545, 548, 549, 551, 552, 553, 554, 556, 557, 558, 560, 562, 563, 565, 567, 568, 588, 602, 604, 608, 613, 615, 626, 627, 630, 632, 633, 634, 639, 640, 642, 644, 646, 648, 649, 650, 652, 656, 658, 660

Joahaz
315

Joash
38

Jochebed
579

John of Leyden
161, 166, 167

John the Baptist
216, 260, 261, 332, 334, 352, 362, 373, 387, 517, 560, 659, 660

Johnson, Alan F.
658, 659, 660, 669

Jonah
22, 82, 83, 84, 85, 86, 87, 88, 89, 189, 222, 298, 397, 587, 622

Jonker, W.D.
41

Jonkers, J. B. G.
575

Jordan River
475

Joseph, son of Jacob
80, 258, 286, 287, 289, 297, 306, 359, 360, 361, 362, 427, 453,

497, 513, 578, 666

Joseph, husband of Mary
80, 294, 317, 332, 370, 371, 392, 580

Joseph, Morris
191

Josephus, Flavius
580, 603

Joshua, Rabbi
367

Josiah
38, 322, 351, 442, 451, 500, 562

Judah
7, 12, 21, 22, 31, 36, 46, 73, 74, 75, 76, 78, 81, 86, 87, 98, 101, 139, 172, 176, 192, 193, 198, 199, 202, 207, 222, 226, 229, 231, 234, 235, 237, 251, 287, 291, 292, 300, 306, 307, 308, 317, 318, 359, 360, 361, 417, 420, 421, 423, 424, 425, 427, 429, 430, 433, 438, 439, 444, 451, 452, 468, 482, 494, 500, 529, 531, 571, 580, 581, 602, 606, 609, 656, 666

Judaism
vi, 15, 18, 128, 149, 157, 163, 168, 187, 189, 192, 239, 281, 285, 351, 365, 366, 375, 381, 387, 392, 393, 394, 396, 397, 398, 399, 400, 405, 406, 448, 479, 518, 583

Judas the Maccabee
341

Judea
81, 140, 238, 271, 308, 456, 474, 477, 598, 607, 608, 615, 617, 620

Judeans
46, 79, 81, 118, 474, 602

Judgment
26, 31, 52, 60, 70, 71, 73, 74, 75, 83, 84, 91, 92, 93, 94, 119, 177, 185, 230, 237, 239, 307, 330, 340, 376, 389, 397, 404, 416, 432, 438, 450, 453, 471, 476, 477, 481, 484, 485, 486, 493, 525, 557, 577, 583, 589, 609, 611, 616, 629, 636,

Subject Index

Jukes, A.
   125, 274
Juster, D.
   103, 266
Justification
   i, 383, 435, 527, 561
Justin Martyr
   155, 306

K

Kamsteeg, A.
   38
Kan, R.
   vii
Kashrut
   37, 79, 105, 256
Kay, W. A.
   492
Kedar
   21
Keil, C. F.
   309
Kelly, W.
   93, 180, 357, 488, 492, 559, 593, 601, 616, 630, 654
Kersten, G. H.
   174, 175, 617, 618, 640
Kertelge, K.
   513
Keturah
   26
644, 646, 647, 657, 669
Kiddle, M.
   658
Kimball, W. R.
   596
Kimchi, David
   54, 64, 322, 340, 342, 344
King Dingane
   175
King of Babylon
   70, 71, 74, 86, 87, 653
King of Israel
   338, 380, 550, 624
King of kings
   8, 11, 90, 92, 96, 178, 179, 576
King of the Jews
   310, 380, 393, 506
King of the world
   338, 383
Kingdom of God
   16, 116, 122, 130, 131, 163, 167, 198, 216, 226, 247, 284, 285, 290, 380, 387, 388, 389, 390, 394, 397, 400, 401, 402, 403, 404, 444, 473, 488, 500, 506, 517, 540, 545, 574, 575, 615, 617, 646
Kingdom of Heaven
   108, 131, 195,

244, 390, 501,
517, 538, 539
Kingdom of Judea
81
Kingdom of Satan
247
Kir
468, 531
Kiriath-Jearim
223
Kirkpatrick, Alexander F.
335
Kitchen, K. A.
3
Kittim
96
Kloosterman, N. D.
105
Knevel, A. G.
309, 312, 313,
314, 315, 319,
321, 322, 332,
341, 344, 351
Knight, J.
326
Knowling, R. J.
320, 618
Korah
70, 664
Kraemer, H.
466
Kraft, H.
654
Krauss, S.
405

Kreider, G. R.
168
Kuhn, Thomas
134
Kuiper, R.
172
Kümmel, W. G.
129
Küng, Hans
185, 266, 573
Kurds
3, 422
Kuyper, Abraham
122, 164, 165,
174, 175
Kyrios
383

L

Laban
8
Lactantius
155
Ladd, G. E.
540, 659
Lagrange, M.J.
601
LaHaye, Tim
459
Lamb
17, 49, 89, 96,
111, 120, 152,
177, 257, 263,
278, 282, 346,
352, 355, 375,
424, 444, 445,
481, 517, 537,

544, 552, 572,
577, 654, 655,
657, 666, 667,
668, 669, 671

Lambert, L.
103

Lamech
258, 513, 514

Lampe, Friedrich Adolph
650

Lang, G. H.
357, 654

Laodicea
75

Laos
568, 569

Lapide, Pinchas
188, 189, 299,
372, 385

Larsson, G.
5

Lavoisier, Antoine
512

Leah
124, 125, 286,
287, 360, 472, 571

Lebanon
230, 420, 425, 479

Lebbaeus
571

Ledeboer, L. G. C.
174

Legalism
117, 118, 138,
256, 277, 394,
426, 671

Lehman, C. K.
168

Lehrman
312, 314

Lenski, R. C. H.
654

Leo, Heinrich
176

Levey, Samson H.
321

Levi
67, 127, 131, 332,
442, 571, 578,
580, 656

Levites
30, 81, 118, 212,
213, 433, 498, 656

Levitical Covenant
131

Levitical priests
212, 213, 237

Lewis, C. S.
381

Licinius
146

Liefeld, W. L.
616

Lightfoot, John
640

Lightfoot, J. B.
267

Lilje, H.
654

Lindsey, Hal
459

Linnemann, Eta
  134
Literal land promise
  102, 105, 112,
  118, 120, 126,
  204, 226, 256,
  281, 401, 592, 601
Literalism
  99, 100, 123, 130,
  444
Little book
  657
Lo-'Ammi
  3, 9, 11, 78, 79,
  93, 97, 122, 255,
  273, 287, 455,
  466, 467, 468,
  469, 471, 627, 633
Lohmeyer, E.
  654
London
  176
Longenecker, R. N.
  320, 622
Loonstra, B.
  303, 316
Lord of lords
  8, 11, 92, 97, 576
Lord's Prayer
  372
Lord's Supper
  194, 198, 386,
  509, 584, 586
Louis XIV
  5

Lud
  30, 498
Luther, Martin
  102, 156, 159,
  167, 168, 279,
  306, 316, 350,
  510, 553, 640, 649
Lutheran church
  146, 150
Lutherans
  153, 161, 181

M

Maccabees
  80, 81, 436, 497,
  652
Maccoby, H.
  363
Machpelah
  14
Mahanayim
  8
Maier, G.
  357
Maimonides, Moses
  372, 384, 392, 405
Malbim
  309
Maljaars, A.
  17, 102, 104, 129,
  135, 183, 201,
  252, 254, 263,
  265, 267, 271,
  272, 277, 423,
  552, 592, 596,
  597, 614, 615,
  632, 640, 641,

Malta
  124
Mamluks
  32
Manasseh
  362, 497, 500, 571, 643, 656
Mantz, Felix
  167
Marduk
  661
Marshall, I. H.
  323
Martyr, Justin
  155, 306
Martyrs
  456, 497, 658, 659
Mary
  75, 153, 249, 313, 370, 371, 392, 419, 439, 447, 510, 579, 661, 662
Mary Magdalene
  510
Mashiach
  290, 291, 292, 356, 360, 392
Maskilim
  436, 496
Masoretic text
  98, 314, 317, 343
Matter, H. M.
  104
Matthias
  571, 651, 655
Matzot
  585
Maurice of Orange
  161
McComiskey, T. E.
  309, 439
McDowell, E. H.
  654
McDowell, Josh
  301, 357
McGrath, A. E.
  543
Medad
  375, 576
Medema
  630
Medes
  3, 93, 95, 422
Media
  422
Mediator
  138, 197, 206, 298, 376
Mediterranean Sea
  24, 30
Medo-Persian empire
  94, 95
Meeuwse, C. J.
  102
Megiddo
  15, 31, 442, 669
Mehrtens, Gerhard
  177
Melanchthon, Philip
  640

Melchizedek
  118, 237, 258,
  297, 298, 334,
  337, 513
Mennonites
  166, 167, 168, 169
Menorah
  479
Mercy-seat
  20
Meshech
  31
Mesopotamia
  153
Messiah
  viii, 6, 7, 16, 17,
  24, 29, 33, 34, 42,
  45, 46, 47, 48, 49,
  50, 55, 56, 58, 59,
  61, 62, 64, 65, 67,
  70, 72, 73, 74,
  77, 80, 83, 84, 87,
  88, 89, 91, 92,
  93, 95, 96, 97,
  100, 101, 109,
  110, 115, 120,
  124, 128, 132,
  144, 155, 156,
  158, 163, 179,
  185, 197, 201,
  203, 204, 205,
  206, 207, 217,
  219, 226, 227,
  228, 229, 230,
  232, 234, 236,
  237, 238, 239,
  240, 243, 244,
  247, 248, 250,
  254, 258, 267,
  270, 281, 284,
  285, 286, 287,
  288, 289, 290,
  291, 292, 294,
  295, 296, 297,
  298, 299, 300,
  301, 302, 303,
  304, 305, 306,
  307, 308, 309,
  310, 311, 312,
  313, 314, 315,
  316, 317, 318,
  319, 320, 321,
  322, 323, 324,
  325, 326, 328,
  330, 331, 332,
  334, 335, 336,
  337, 338, 339,
  340, 341, 342,
  343, 346, 347,
  348, 349, 350,
  351, 352, 353,
  354, 355, 356,
  357, 358, 359,
  360, 361, 362,
  363, 364, 365,
  367, 368, 373,
  375, 376, 377,
  378, 379, 380,
  381, 384, 390,
  392, 393, 396,
  398, 399, 400,
  405, 407, 409,
  410, 414, 415,
  417, 418, 420,
  423, 426, 429,
  430, 431, 433,
  434, 435, 436,

439, 440, 442,
443, 445, 451,
452, 453, 455,
456, 458, 464,
465, 467, 468,
469, 480, 482,
485, 486, 488,
491, 494, 499,
506, 528, 529,
537, 543, 550,
551, 556, 558,
563, 565, 574,
576, 578, 586,
587, 588, 591,
604, 607, 608,
609, 610, 619,
620, 621, 622,
623, 626, 627,
628, 630, 633,
634, 635, 639,
660, 662, 663, 664

Messianic dispensationalism
459

Messianic expectation
292, 313

Messianic hope
284, 289, 292,
296, 313, 360,
361, 364

Messianic Jews
vii, 13, 20, 109,
133, 226, 256

Messianic kingdom
6, 16, 20, 22, 28,
32, 33, 34, 35,
37, 40, 41, 46,
47, 48, 55, 59, 60,
61, 62, 64, 65,
67, 72, 76, 77, 81,
82, 84, 88, 90,
92, 96, 97, 98,
100, 101, 108,
111, 115, 117,
118, 119, 120,
121, 122, 131,
132, 133, 137,
147, 148, 150,
151, 154, 156,
161, 162, 163,
165, 178, 180,
194, 195, 196,
197, 198, 201,
203, 204, 206,
207, 209, 210,
212, 213, 216,
218, 220, 221,
225, 226, 227,
228, 230, 231,
232, 233, 235,
240, 241, 245,
246, 253, 254,
255, 274, 276,
278, 282, 284,
286, 287, 306,
312, 318, 329,
330, 340, 341,
342, 354, 357,
367, 369, 388,
392, 398, 404,
415, 418, 420,
421, 425, 427,
428, 429, 431,
433, 436, 437,
439, 441, 442,
444, 445, 446,
450, 451, 453,
454, 462, 463,

465, 469, 481,
486, 487, 493,
495, 496, 498,
501, 532, 544,
545, 552, 554,
565, 574, 581,
587, 588, 592,
594, 596, 597,
602, 613, 615,
616, 617, 618,
620, 622, 623,
624, 625, 638,
639, 640, 643,
644, 656, 658,
662, 664, 667,
668, 670, 671, 672

Messianic prophecy
289, 301, 302,
317, 348, 349

Messianic Torah
109, 110, 111,
129, 215, 218,
278, 378, 588

Michael, the archangel
7, 8, 9, 24, 25, 51,
97, 151, 160, 435,
596

Michel, O.
323, 326

Michelangelo
582

Michelson, A.U.
103

Middle Ages
146, 157, 178

Middle East
231, 247, 422,
488, 492

Midrash
51, 52, 53, 293,
343, 344, 351, 578

Midrashim
62

Mighty God
4, 46, 69, 227,
253, 321, 322,
381, 495

Mighty One of Jacob
225, 361

Millennialism
121, 155, 169, 423

Milton, John
176

Minear, P. S.
541, 659

Minor Prophets
82, 436

Minsk
227

Miriam
370, 579

Mishnah
578, 642, 643

Miskotte, K. H.
100, 102

Mo'adim
37, 79, 105

Moab
38, 305, 421, 422,
424, 488, 562, 623

Moabites
421

Mobachius, Joachim
  172
Moerkerken, A.
  509, 619
Moffatt, J.
  654
Moltmann, J.
  185, 574
Mont Saint Michel
  25
Montanism
  166
Montefiore, C. G.
  291
Moo, D. J.
  265, 467, 555,
  559, 630,
Mordecai
  297, 331, 588
Mormons
  182
Morris, L.
  657, 658
Mosaic Covenant
  38
Mosaic Law
  65
Mosaic Torah
  16, 101, 109, 110,
  111, 115, 117,
  129, 132, 133,
  188, 192, 215,
  218, 226, 256,
  266, 278, 283,
  378, 390, 395,
  409, 536, 563,
  568, 577, 588
Moses
  vii, 4, 29, 36, 42,
  77, 101, 115, 119,
  142, 154, 170,
  174, 176, 200,
  216, 223, 224,
  229, 245, 257,
  259, 271, 283,
  294, 295, 297,
  298, 331, 332,
  333, 351, 366,
  368, 370, 372,
  374, 375, 376,
  377, 378, 384,
  392, 395, 413,
  414, 415, 416,
  454, 461, 476,
  481, 529, 537,
  538, 541, 544,
  549, 566, 568,
  573, 576, 577,
  578, 579, 580,
  648, 649, 650, 659
Most Holy Place
  19, 20, 223, 224,
  356, 435, 487
Mother of God
  153
Mounce, R. H.
  657, 658, 659, 669
Mount Esau
  61, 284
Mount Gerizim
  14, 652
Mount Horeb
  223

Mount of Beatitudes
378
Mount of Olives
11, 12, 15, 123, 127, 239, 240, 250
Mount of Transfiguration
222, 377
Mount Sinai
65, 98, 139, 200, 208, 209, 223, 257, 376, 378, 476, 524, 549, 563, 577, 581, 582, 585, 623, 667
Mount Zion
61, 138, 139, 209, 222, 241, 250, 284, 376, 420, 465, 470, 486, 494, 495, 577, 582, 624, 666, 667
Mountain of Megiddo
15, 31
Mudde, J. M.
314, 344
Mulder, M. C.
102, 104, 312, 363
Münster
161, 166, 167
Murray, J.
559
Muslims
140, 234, 408
My-People
255, 471, 627

N
Naamah
514, 562
Naaman
259, 272, 513
Nabonidus
94
Nachmanides
8, 305, 362
Nahor
27
Naomi
661
Nathan
313, 442
Nathanael
332, 378, 537, 571
National angels
7, 10, 88, 221
National church
174, 531
NATO
489
Nazareth
281, 285, 291, 294, 299, 300, 308, 332, 334, 380
Nazi Germany
6, 56
Nazism
542
Nebaioth
21
Nebuchadnezzar
24, 68, 71, 86, 87, 90, 94, 151, 484,

489, 665
Nederbragt, Johan Alexander
     1
Negev desert
     422
Nehemiah
     38, 68, 341, 454
Nehemiah, Rabbi
     145
Neri
     317
Netherlands
     vii, viii, ix, 10, 11,
     12, 25, 103, 117,
     128, 149, 161,
     162, 163, 164,
     165, 166, 169,
     170, 171, 172,
     173, 174, 175,
     177, 179, 181,
     183, 184, 185,
     275, 285, 460
Netherlands Reformed
Congregations
     184
Neusner, J.
     478
New birth
     211, 216, 388,
     401, 649
New Covenant
     38, 39, 40, 41, 44,
     101, 124, 131,
     138, 191, 192,
     194, 195, 196,
     197, 198, 199,
     200, 201, 204,
     205, 206, 207,
     209, 210, 211,
     212, 214, 216,
     217, 218, 255,
     280, 376, 428,
     429, 527, 536,
     549, 577, 581,
     582, 583, 586, 667
New Delhi Report on Witness
     575
New Jerusalem
     12, 19, 100, 111,
     121, 138, 154,
     157, 161, 171,
     177, 221, 278,
     408, 483, 484,
     572, 615, 621,
     671, 672
New Testament
     vi, viii, 2, 12, 13,
     15, 16, 17, 34, 38,
     41, 52, 80, 99,
     100, 102, 103,
     104, 105, 106,
     107, 109, 110,
     111, 113, 114,
     115, 117, 119,
     120, 126, 127,
     130, 132, 136,
     139, 140, 151,
     155, 178, 183,
     187, 188, 191,
     192, 194, 196,
     197, 199, 205,
     211, 219, 225,
     233, 240, 247,
     256, 257, 258,
     266, 268, 272,

273, 274, 275, 277, 278, 279, 281, 282, 284, 285, 286, 290, 292, 293, 295, 296, 297, 299, 300, 310, 311, 319, 321, 322, 323, 325, 326, 328, 332, 334, 336, 338, 339, 342, 344, 347, 348, 349, 350, 351, 352, 354, 355, 358, 366, 370, 371, 375, 383, 396, 398, 400, 401, 410, 414, 424, 425, 427, 428, 433, 443, 449, 455, 458, 459, 460, 463, 464, 476, 481, 487, 498, 503, 504, 505, 506, 507, 508, 509, 510, 511, 512, 514, 516, 517, 518, 522, 524, 526, 527, 529, 530, 532, 533, 535, 536, 540, 541, 543, 549, 551, 565, 566, 567, 571, 574, 576, 577, 580, 583, 591, 592, 601, 612, 613, 614, 617, 629, 630, 635, 637, 639, 642, 651, 655, 656, 658, 671

New Year's Prayer
372

New York
79, 227, 483

New Zealand
76, 231

Newell, W. R.
654

Nicaea
149, 150

Nicene Creed
149, 249

Nicodemus
290, 363, 388

Nida, E.
39

Nierop, E.
637

Nile
57, 140, 492, 579, 664, 671

Nimrod
440

Nineveh
10, 83, 397

Ninevites
83, 85

Noah
26, 248, 258, 302, 513, 558, 563, 565, 647

Noah's Flood
2
Noahic Covenant
16, 42, 131, 549, 581
Noordegraaf, A.
102, 363, 511
Noordmans, O.
175
Noordtzij, A.
323, 345, 432
North, C. R.
352
North America
56, 168, 181, 183, 184
Northern kingdom
81, 423, 497
Not-My-People
9, 78, 255, 273, 455, 471, 627
Nubia
492

O
Obed-Edom
223
Oecolampadius, Johannes
640
Oegema, G. S.
292
Offerings
20, 194, 212, 224, 237, 385, 427, 428, 451, 537, 559, 672

Old Covenant
39, 124, 138, 198, 199, 200, 201, 215, 216, 217, 218, 243, 280, 376, 577, 581, 582, 648, 667
Old Testament
vi, vii, viii, 12, 16, 20, 100, 103, 110, 114, 115, 184, 286, 289, 294, 295, 297, 366, 611
Olive tree
252, 253, 275, 276, 449, 464, 497, 543, 554, 555, 556, 557, 558, 559, 561, 629, 634, 636, 640, 642, 645
On the Consummation
122
Operation Overlord
vii
Op 't Hof, W. J.
172
Oostland, E. J.
104
Orange Free State
175
Origen
405, 510
Orlando
262

Orthodox Jews
    13, 109, 133, 168,
    185, 256, 291,
    300, 365, 366,
    367, 372, 380,
    384, 417, 420,
    434, 481, 494,
    563, 658
Oswalt, John, J. N.
    311, 315, 317,
    321, 351, 445,
    446, 492
Ottoman empire
    488
Ouweneel, W. J.
    i, ii, vi, vii, 7, 16,
    18, 26, 31, 33,
    34, 37, 39, 41,
    49, 62, 66, 69, 73,
    82, 86, 88, 89,
    91, 95, 96, 97,
    105, 108, 116,
    117, 124, 126,
    127, 129, 130,
    131, 132, 133,
    134, 138, 146,
    148, 153, 154,
    158, 164, 174,
    186, 188, 198,
    199, 205, 206,
    209, 211, 216,
    217, 218, 219,
    226, 232, 237,
    240, 259, 261,
    266, 267, 283,
    287, 289, 291,
    293, 295, 297,
    298, 303, 309,
    310, 327, 329,
    330, 335, 340,
    345, 351, 357,
    364, 372, 375,
    380, 381, 392,
    398, 399, 400,
    401, 404, 410,
    417, 426, 429,
    430, 431, 445,
    447, 448, 450,
    458, 460, 461,
    462, 464, 465,
    466, 471, 476,
    483, 487, 503,
    508, 509, 515,
    518, 520, 521,
    526, 530, 532,
    535, 545, 547,
    570, 574, 576,
    578, 581, 582,
    583, 595, 599,
    606, 608, 609,
    611, 615, 616,
    617, 622, 642,
    644, 647, 651,
    652, 653, 654,
    657, 658, 659,
    660, 664, 665,
    666, 667

P

Paas, Steven
    viii, 16, 29, 100,
    102, 104, 112,
    114, 116, 117,
    118, 121, 123,
    128, 135, 138,
    183, 252, 265,
    267, 284, 444,

Subject Index

Packer, J. I.
    468, 510, 552,
    555, 606, 614,
    617, 636, 638
    510, 511
Paddan-aram
    78
Paganism
    153, 157, 163, 609
Palestine
    14, 19, 47, 66,
    127, 136, 421, 422
Palestinian Christians
    viii, 13, 169
Palestinians
    vii, viii, 14, 285,
    488
Pannenberg, W.
    530
Paris
    68, 153
Parry, Hubert
    176
Pascal, Blaise
    5, 160, 310
Passover
    371, 585, 587
Pathros
    421
Patmos
    519,
Patriarchs
    viii, 2, 12, 14, 28,
    33, 35, 36, 42, 56,
    58, 65, 69, 87,
    111, 127, 158,
    220, 225, 254,
    258, 270, 276,
    297, 302, 338,
    362, 392, 413,
    449, 462, 481,
    500, 529, 537,
    549, 550, 554,
    559, 560, 570,
    571, 572, 614,
    618, 621, 622,
    640, 672
Patterson, P.
    168
Paul, the apostle
    3, 33, 34, 36, 37,
    41, 48, 68, 102,
    103, 117, 118,
    124, 129, 130,
    133, 138, 160,
    184, 208, 215,
    216, 218, 251,
    252, 253, 254,
    255, 260, 262,
    263, 264, 265,
    266, 267, 268,
    269, 270, 271,
    272, 273, 274,
    275, 277, 283,
    294, 299, 303,
    305, 309, 310,
    319, 328, 342,
    343, 344, 352,
    363, 366, 369,
    371, 382, 389,
    391, 392, 393,
    398, 406, 409,
    423, 426, 460,
    465, 474, 475,

476, 483, 491,
515, 519, 521,
522, 523, 524,
525, 526, 530,
532, 536, 541,
543, 544, 547,
548, 549, 551,
552, 555, 557,
559, 564, 568,
571, 573, 574,
584, 613, 614,
616, 621, 626,
629, 630, 631,
632, 633, 634,
635, 638, 639,
640, 641, 644,
648, 649, 650, 651

Paul, M. J.
312, 313, 314,
315, 319, 321,
322, 332, 335,
341, 344, 351,
408, 543

Pawson, D.
103

Payne, J. B.
459, 460

Peace of Augsburg
161

Peake, A. S.
536

Peels
313

Pella, Iowa
181

Pennsylvania Dutch
168

Pentateuch
298, 499

Pentecost, J. D.
207

People of God
43, 70, 99, 100,
103, 104, 109,
115, 123, 132,
175, 254, 255,
256, 266, 270,
274, 278, 282,
285, 354, 400,
403, 407, 441,
450, 459, 461,
467, 511, 512,
513, 520, 528,
529, 530, 539,
540, 541, 543,
547, 552, 553,
558, 559, 561,
562, 563, 564,
566, 567, 570,
582, 613, 631,
639, 647, 655

Perizzite
220

Persia
7, 8, 71, 95, 97,
422, 488

Persian empire
94, 95

Persians
3, 32, 71, 93, 94,
95, 308, 422

Pesach
149, 308, 371,
478, 537, 574,

Peshitta
   637
Peter, Simon
   72, 133, 209, 245, 260, 264, 272, 273, 293, 294, 332, 337, 342, 343, 344, 377, 382, 383, 385, 391, 437, 475, 476, 514, 537, 549, 564, 568, 570, 571, 621, 622, 623, 625, 626, 627
Petra
   422
Pfisterer, R.
   466
Pharisees
   349, 359, 362, 363, 364, 365, 366, 388, 394, 396, 397, 646, 671
Pharaoh
   42, 74, 170, 333, 470, 576, 578, 579, 580, 636, 664
Philip
   17, 293, 294, 295, 332, 352, 378, 537
Philip II
   170
Philippines
   177
   585, 587
Philistia
   488
Philistines
   78, 97, 140, 320, 421, 422, 424, 468, 531, 671
Philosophers
   18, 134
Philosophy of science
   17, 18, 129, 135
Philpot, J. C.
   530
Phinehas
   78, 336, 359
Phoenicia
   474
Pirie, Alexander
   331
Plaisier, A.
   102, 106
Plummer, A.
   317
Plymouth Brethren
   13, 169, 181
Poland
   232
Political Reformed Party
   165
Pontius Pilate
   377, 380, 477, 667
Pontus
   626
Pool of Bethesda
   623
Pool of Siloam
   374

Pop, F. J.
  570, 583
Pope
  24, 147, 158, 160,
  163, 179, 405, 570
Pope Francis
  103
Pope John Paul II
  103
Post-millennialism
  101, 416
Post-millennialist
  156
Potgieter, R.
  123
Potiphar
  362
Prayer
  20, 66, 85, 86,
  194, 339, 351,
  372, 393, 427,
  500, 501, 564, 629
Pre-millennialism
  101, 134, 182
Pre-millennialists
  121, 156, 178, 181
Predestination
  466
Present age
  116, 122, 195,
  196, 197, 226,
  594, 595
Preston, R. H.
  654
Preterism
  243, 244, 250,
  592, 603
Preterists
  152, 244, 245,
  247, 248, 249,
  250, 610
Priesthood
  67, 111, 118, 236,
  260, 272, 318,
  335, 336, 337,
  461, 525, 534,
  564, 625, 627
Prince of Peace
  46, 68, 227, 307,
  321, 322
Progressive dispensationalism
  459
Promised Land
  29, 33, 34, 38, 40,
  43, 44, 46, 65,
  77, 78, 79, 88,
  143, 175, 182,
  187, 213, 214,
  220, 221, 223,
  224, 225, 227,
  228, 229, 232,
  236, 274, 303,
  354, 408, 409,
  415, 416, 429,
  431, 469, 470,
  499, 539, 544,
  574, 575, 586,
  611, 612, 638,
  664, 666
Prophecy
  11, 68, 70, 72, 73,
  74, 82, 83, 93,
  114, 115, 119,
  123, 137, 139,

Subject Index

148, 154, 201, 216, 229, 230, 289, 290, 301, 302, 305, 306, 310, 311, 313, 316, 317, 321, 334, 340, 341, 342, 348, 349, 352, 354, 360, 361, 372, 386, 388, 392, 403, 413, 415, 417, 423, 424, 426, 435, 440, 441, 442, 443, 451, 452, 453, 454, 482, 484, 490, 532, 549, 556, 591, 611, 629, 634

Prophetic books
vii, 93, 127, 235, 251, 299, 350, 422

Prophetic promises
44, 67, 592

Prophets
22, 32, 37, 42, 67, 68, 70, 72, 73, 74, 82, 90, 92, 93, 111, 115, 116, 142, 150, 155, 185, 200, 210, 216, 220, 234, 247, 248, 251, 259, 263, 294, 295, 323, 326, 332, 334, 338, 366, 372, 378, 387, 390, 399, 400, 403, 418, 423, 428, 436, 438, 450, 451, 456, 460, 461, 463, 482, 506, 515, 516, 517, 520, 533, 535, 549, 591, 595, 605, 619, 621, 622, 626, 634, 646, 658, 659

Protestant Church in the Netherlands
184, 185, 285

Protestant churches
118, 128

Protestant theologians
542, 551

Protestant theology
542

Protestantism
118, 157, 158, 163, 279, 542

Protestants
102, 108, 125, 128, 148, 149, 151, 155, 168, 178, 181, 279, 284, 504, 510

Prudentius
155

Pseudo-Clement
375, 577

Pul
30, 498

Pulpit Commentary
623

Purification
  84, 107, 206, 346,
  386, 435, 526
Purim
  585, 588
Puritans
  176, 177
Put
  422

Q
Qedushah
  372
Queen of heaven
  153
Queen of the South
  397
Qumran
  9, 306, 581
Quran
  140, 141

R
Rabbinic Judaism
  18, 365, 366, 405
Rabbinic tradition
  50, 322, 327, 339,
  343, 364, 375,
  455, 576
Rabbis
  8, 13, 17, 51, 52,
  53, 93, 121, 188,
  258, 289, 290,
  293, 299, 300,
  308, 310, 324,
  325, 340, 343,
  350, 351, 352,
  363, 366, 372,
  373, 374, 376,
  382, 384, 392,
  478, 479, 480,
  492, 529, 539,
  578, 581, 582, 586
Rachel
  14, 30, 124, 125,
  273, 286, 287,
  360, 472
Rahab
  10, 89, 97, 259,
  447, 510, 513
Rahav
  10
Rahner, K.
  299, 372, 573
Ramah
  273
Ramat Rachel
  14, 30
Rapture
  183, 186, 187, 660
Rashbam
  305, 361
Rashi
  52, 53, 54, 58, 59,
  61, 63, 64, 74, 93,
  284, 305, 309,
  311, 319, 322,
  335, 339, 341,
  342, 351, 361,
  362, 586, 587
Ratzinger, Joseph
  102, 230, 231,
  319, 323, 325,
  331, 333, 337,

338, 339, 482, 598, 599, 609, 661

Raymond, R. L.
290, 360

Rebekah
50, 305, 315

Rebirth
216, 462, 500, 526, 528, 532, 539, 613

Rechabites
362

Recognitiones
375, 577

Red Sea
274, 573, 664

Redeemer
2, 43, 252, 282, 321, 346, 354, 355, 457, 458, 498, 499, 638

Redemption
viii, 113, 171, 206, 209, 214, 333, 334, 353, 354, 355, 391, 415, 448, 480, 498, 500, 526, 548, 614, 618, 630, 638

Redemptive history
19, 80, 117, 186, 210, 363, 455, 458, 463, 565, 588, 631

Reeling Brouwer, R. H.
575

Reformation
12, 118, 128, 146, 147, 155, 156, 159, 160, 166, 170, 171, 177, 416, 436, 489, 503, 542

Reformed Alliance
184

Reformed Baptists
530

Reformed Christians
38, 175, 536

Reformed Church in America
162

Reformed Churches Liberated
183

Reformed covenantal theology
171

Reformed Liberated Churches
275

Reformed magistrates
163

Reformed theologians
102, 103, 188, 189, 416, 460, 489, 542, 650

Reformed theology
40, 205

Reformers
102, 118, 158, 167, 168, 640

Regeneration
40, 106, 157, 177, 206, 216, 388, 401, 462, 528, 529, 571, 613

Rehoboam
514, 562
Reitsma, B.
102, 116
Religious nationalism
178
Remnant
3, 23, 35, 40, 44,
64, 69, 72, 79, 80,
84, 86, 89, 92,
143, 174, 176,
187, 200, 205,
235, 253, 255,
258, 270, 310,
314, 347, 353,
354, 355, 421,
425, 440, 443,
444, 450, 455,
462, 464, 471,
472, 473, 481,
483, 486, 493,
494, 495, 496,
497, 498, 499,
512, 544, 551,
554, 585, 608,
609, 611, 624,
627, 628, 631,
632, 633, 636,
637, 641, 644,
645, 664
Remonstrants
164, 166, 167, 181
Renckens, H.
38
Repentance
ii, 64, 69, 83, 92,
141, 294, 387,
388, 389, 390,
391, 467, 471,
475, 498, 500,
560, 618, 622,
642, 649
Replacement theology
16, 38, 102, 104,
106, 126, 136,
150, 165, 177,
184, 256, 257,
281, 443, 458,
540, 543
Reprobation
i, 466
Restoration
21, 23, 29, 35,
36, 64, 70, 71,
77, 79, 85, 98,
102, 108, 118,
137, 159, 187,
202, 203, 204,
205, 229, 236,
255, 273, 274,
275, 357, 399,
416, 426, 427,
429, 431, 432,
435, 436, 437,
438, 441, 443,
450, 451, 454,
455, 459, 468,
470, 471, 472,
483, 485, 488,
489, 490, 491,
492, 540, 542,
558, 572, 592,
597, 614, 620,
623, 624, 632,
634, 635, 636,
637, 638, 639,

Subject Index

Restoration of Israel
642, 655, 659, 664, 671
23, 35, 36, 64, 79, 102, 187, 202, 203, 204, 229, 274, 275, 399, 416, 429, 431, 436, 441, 488, 489, 540, 542, 558, 597, 624, 634, 635, 637, 638, 639, 659

Resurrection
33, 107, 108, 155, 157, 201, 238, 250, 292, 304, 320, 329, 342, 344, 364, 373, 378, 383, 397, 451, 476, 481, 517, 520, 572, 582, 585, 592, 614, 617, 622, 633, 643, 659

Return of Christ
108, 134, 180, 186, 249, 658

Reuben
286, 287, 361, 656

Réveil
173, 175, 182

Revised dispensationalism
459

Revius, Jacob
275

Rhineland
408

Ridderbos, H.
266, 514, 518, 567, 598, 599, 611, 613, 630, 637, 642, 643

Ridderbos, J.
319, 329, 330, 337, 343, 344, 345, 351, 352, 418, 421, 423, 424, 440, 441, 442, 443

Rimmon
240, 442, 670

Rissi, M.
659

Rist, M.
662

Robertson, O. Palmer
14, 17, 34, 102, 104, 118, 119, 120, 122, 135, 183, 265, 267, 552, 617, 636, 638

Robinson, J. A. T.
476

Rock of Israel
314, 348, 362, 493

Roman beast
90, 605, 652, 654, 665, 666

Roman Catholic catechism
103

Roman Catholic Church
102, 118, 146,

149, 153, 155,
157, 158, 160,
165, 407, 543

Roman Catholicism
163, 185, 279, 662

Roman Catholics
108, 125, 148,
149, 151, 161,
166, 177, 178,
181, 221, 279,
284, 504, 510, 535

Roman Empire
24, 25, 49, 50,
51, 52, 55, 56, 60,
61, 62, 64, 76,
89, 90, 91, 94,
145, 146, 147,
148, 150, 151,
154, 156, 163,
221, 383, 418,
425, 487, 488,
489, 608, 609,
652, 653, 654, 668

Romans
25, 32, 81, 91, 94,
96, 177, 291, 308,
377, 399, 422,
443, 487, 578,
580, 598, 606, 667

Romanticism
178

Rome
20, 23, 24, 25, 57,
59, 62, 63, 68, 97,
145, 147, 151,
156, 157, 158,
177, 221, 288,
366, 538, 576, 669

Roozemeijer, J. H. L.
630

Rosen, Moishe
459

Rosenberg, A.
24

Rosenstock-Huessy, E.
391

Rosenzweig, F.
391, 458

Rosh haShanah
585, 587

Rossier, H.
654

Rowley, H. H.
335, 352

Royal Albert Hall
176

Russia
168, 233, 489

Russian Orthodoxy
76

Ruth
259, 513, 562

Rutishauser, Christian
103

Ryrie, Charles C.
205, 459, 540

S

Sabbath
20, 71, 79, 105,
107, 119, 121,
133, 135, 157,
194, 204, 205,
238, 256, 282,
283, 294, 394,

Subject Index

Sabeans
: 438

Sadducees
: 363, 364, 366, 649

Sailhamer, J. H.
: 307

Saint Denys
: 153

Saint Peter's Basilica
: 151

Salmond, S. D. F.
: 536

Salvation
: viii, 33, 56, 60, 63, 64, 70, 85, 86, 89, 91, 100, 108, 112, 113, 117, 118, 121, 126, 128, 158, 185, 188, 189, 251, 257, 258, 272, 280, 284, 341, 356, 360, 382, 383, 391, 398, 399, 401, 406, 407, 409, 410, 421, 436, 440, 458, 466, 467, 469, 471, 473, 476, 477, 481, 483, 499, 501, 505, 506, 527, 529, 542, 548, 551, 552, 614, 407, 450, 535, 536, 545, 562, 563, 598, 602, 624

Samael
: 52, 63

Samaria
: 140, 470, 474, 615, 617, 620

Samson
: 148

Samuel
: 6, 332, 446, 621

Santala, R.
: 351

Santiago de Compostela
: 575

Sarah
: 27, 138, 303, 426, 510, 570, 583, 627

Satan
: 9, 49, 52, 57, 62, 87, 88, 156, 157, 247, 296, 301, 302, 331, 389, 396, 653, 654, 664, 669

Satanism
: 654

Saturday
: 107, 205, 256

Saudi Arabia
: 488

Saul
: 344, 345, 419, 586

Saul of Tarsus
: 363, 621

621, 622, 626, 629, 630, 633, 637, 642, 644

Savior
92, 150, 226, 281, 322, 392, 400, 538, 564

Scapegoat
356, 478

Scepter
62, 75, 202, 291, 292, 305, 306, 307, 308, 347, 361, 664

Schaeffer, Francis A.
301

Schenkle, C.
125

Schilder, Klaas
298

Schirrmacher, T.
290, 360

Schlatter, A.
601

Schneerson, Menachem Mendel
227

Schneider, O.
320

Schniewind, J.
601

Schoeps, Hans-Joachim
299, 375, 576, 577

Scholte, H. P.
181

Schutte, G. J.
173, 174

Schuyler English, E.
601

Scofield, C. I.
459

Scofield Reference Bible
113

Scott, W.
659, 663

Scripture
i, 4, 12, 32, 33, 72, 114, 116, 126, 159, 165, 188, 295, 303, 342, 363, 366, 376, 442, 516, 548, 666

Scriptures
11, 20, 114, 116, 274, 294, 295, 366, 378, 427, 489, 600, 649

Sea monster
87, 89

Sea of Galilee
378

Seceders
181

Secession
173, 174, 181

Second chariot
93

Second coming of Christ
122, 147, 150, 152, 155, 163, 167, 180, 196, 202, 244, 247, 248, 249, 250, 445, 497, 593, 599, 601, 604, 607, 608, 610,

Subject Index

Second exile
612, 615, 632, 637, 644, 647, 669
64, 76, 77, 97, 98, 453, 455

Second Reformation
12, 128, 159, 170, 171, 177, 416, 436, 489, 503, 542

Second Temple
67, 71, 341, 351, 454, 480, 585, 588, 598, 651, 652

Second Vatican Council
543

Seed of Abraham
48, 303, 522

Seir
61, 62, 63, 64, 284, 286, 305

Seiss, J. A.
654

Sennacherib
417

Septuagint
2, 75, 98, 257, 293, 307, 314, 316, 317, 325, 326, 329, 337, 341, 343, 345, 385, 386, 416, 514, 572, 649

Sermon on the Mount
364, 374, 578, 593

Serpent
57, 87, 119, 124, 296, 301, 577

Servant of the LORD
45, 80, 88, 194, 296, 304, 350, 351, 352, 353, 354, 355, 360, 386, 426, 456

Servetus, Michael
160

Sevenster, G.
323

Seventh day
121, 122, 562, 563

Sforno, Jacob
8, 361, 362

Shabbat
37, 38, 79, 142, 402, 450, 591

Shammai
374, 382

Shavu'ot
581, 582, 585, 587

Shealtiel
317

Sheba
397

Shechem
14

Shekhinah
14, 20, 42, 67, 68, 77, 78, 79, 80, 81, 82, 97, 220, 221, 222, 223, 234, 376, 454, 455, 547, 549, 578, 588, 670

Shem
  16, 26, 302, 549, 558
Shemoneh Esrei
  372
Sheol
  85, 86, 342, 343, 448
Shepherd
  7, 47, 65, 95, 193, 195, 197, 227, 230, 232, 259, 310, 312, 338, 361, 362, 368, 397, 398, 433, 439, 440, 445, 514, 529, 537, 538
Sheshakh
  10
Sheth
  305
Shiloh
  223, 291, 292, 306, 307, 361, 652
Shimei
  442
Shimeites
  442
Shinar
  421
Yitzchaqi, Shlomo
  52, 309
Shoah
  vi, vii, 56, 62, 136, 150, 160, 169, 231

Shulam, J.
  103, 561, 630
Shunammite
  259, 513
Sidon
  389, 646
Siebesma, P.
  341
Siegers, H. J.
  104
Simeon
  571, 618, 656
Simon the Maccabee
  335
Simon the Zealot
  571
Simons, Menno
  166, 167
Sinaitic covenant
  35, 38, 39, 101, 103, 131, 188, 280
Singer, Tovia
  479, 480
Sistine Chapel
  582
Sixteenth century
  125, 159, 170, 542
Sizer, Stephen
  102, 104, 114, 123, 124, 131, 135, 136, 183, 459
Slavery
  5, 139, 170, 175, 274, 277, 453, 532, 572, 574, 580, 586

Slotki, Israel W.
    311, 322, 340,
    420, 492, 570
Slotki, J. J.
    325
Smith, David L.
    540, 559
Smith, H.
    654
Smith, J. B.
    663
Smitskamp, H.
    173, 176
Snell, H. H.
    654
Sodom
    389, 646, 658
Solomon
    25, 66, 81, 118,
    140, 168, 200,
    215, 221, 223,
    234, 298, 303,
    304, 307, 313,
    319, 320, 322,
    335, 339, 340,
    347, 397, 418,
    463, 500, 549,
    562, 587, 652,
    662, 663, 671
Son of Abraham
    35, 254, 270, 300,
    303, 304
Son of David
    47, 80, 145, 203,
    289, 300, 303,
    304, 312, 313,
    314, 319, 320,
    330, 336, 343,
    364, 370, 379,
    380, 381, 419,
    442, 445, 619
Son of Man
    41, 60, 83, 88, 90,
    93, 96, 108, 152,
    163, 195, 210,
    238, 239, 244,
    248, 250, 323,
    324, 325, 326,
    327, 328, 329,
    330, 331, 338,
    358, 360, 364,
    367, 375, 378,
    379, 386, 396,
    434, 486, 489,
    572, 577, 591,
    592, 597, 600,
    602, 603, 604,
    605, 606, 607,
    608, 610, 611,
    612, 613, 619,
    623, 632, 647
Soncino Books of the Bible
    300
Sons of Israel
    9, 306, 572, 616,
    655
Sophia
    582
Souterius, Daniel
    171
South Africa
    175
South America
    3, 76, 231, 233

Southern kingdom
  81, 423
Sovereign grace
  69, 199, 426, 450,
  461, 469
Spain
  172, 575
Spaniards
  173
Spanish Inquisition
  157, 160, 282
Sphere sovereignty
  164, 174
Spirit baptism
  261, 521, 522
Spirit of God
  92, 247, 271, 380,
  397, 490, 491, 583
"Spiritual Battle Cry", poem
  173
Spiritual Israel
  4, 12, 28, 43, 44,
  100, 105, 109,
  110, 130, 132,
  136, 151, 157,
  165, 170, 172,
  177, 178, 179,
  192, 193, 194,
  196, 199, 200,
  204, 205, 231,
  233, 243, 252,
  254, 256, 261,
  264, 266, 268,
  270, 274, 277,
  278, 279, 280,
  281, 286, 401,
  407, 418, 443,
  448, 449, 458,
  459, 463, 464,
  472, 474, 476,
  512, 543, 551,
  555, 563, 565,
  566, 615, 626,
  648, 655
Spiritual Jews
  458, 474, 633
Spiritualism
  99, 100, 130, 136,
  204
Spronk, K.
  102, 106
Spurgeon, C. H.
  330, 331, 346, 530
St. Dionysius
  153
St. George
  153
St. Joseph
  153
St. Nicholas
  153
Stanley
  654
State of Israel
  vi, 13, 32, 57, 77,
  79, 81, 98, 103,
  105, 109, 127,
  128, 136, 137,
  140, 160, 182,
  187, 248, 250,
  280, 408, 422,
  491, 492, 493,
  498, 609

Subject Index

Statenvertaling
149
States-General
149, 164, 165
States Translation of the Bible
167
Stephen
36, 323, 349, 403, 456, 474, 623
Stern, David
103, 187, 246, 266, 283, 450, 630, 642
Stewart, A.
672
Strack, H. L.
327
Substitution theology
102
Substitutionism
102, 150, 256
Sukkot
240, 585
Sukkoth
581, 588
Sunday
13, 37, 38, 105, 107, 135, 205, 256, 407, 535
Supersessionism
viii, 11, 16, 18, 24, 25, 29, 31, 32, 33, 37, 38, 44, 46, 75, 102, 103, 104, 105, 106, 107, 108, 110, 111, 112, 113, 114, 115, 116, 117, 119, 120, 121, 122, 123, 124, 125, 126, 127, 128, 129, 130, 135, 136, 137, 138, 139, 150, 151, 155, 158, 159, 160, 161, 162, 163, 164, 165, 169, 170, 172, 174, 176, 177, 178, 179, 181, 182, 183, 184, 185, 189, 192, 196, 204, 206, 243, 244, 250, 256, 261, 267, 275, 276, 278, 279, 280, 281, 282, 287, 365, 406, 408, 414, 422, 434, 443, 458, 489, 503, 505, 508, 536, 540, 542, 553, 558, 592, 601, 612, 640, 671
Supersessionists
4, 38, 102, 105, 118, 121, 122, 126, 178, 193, 194, 196, 229, 231, 234, 237, 244, 250, 252, 254, 256, 261,

264, 265, 266, 270, 272, 273, 275, 276, 280, 282, 283, 286, 310, 316, 341, 400, 409, 414, 417, 420, 423, 426, 427, 428, 429, 431, 434, 438, 449, 452, 460, 468, 469, 472, 484, 486, 504, 522, 542, 553, 554, 555, 562, 563, 566, 567, 568, 592, 593, 598, 602, 614, 616, 625, 626, 633, 637, 656, 658, 670

Susa
68
Swete, H. B.
654
Sychar
14
Symmachus
9
Synagogues
79, 142, 150, 164, 187, 231, 283, 351, 406, 448, 568
Synod of Dordt
149, 165, 167, 173
Synod of Mainz
24

Syria
9, 418, 422, 474, 488, 489
Syrians
9, 81, 468, 531
Syro-Ephraimite war
321
Syrohexaplaris
9
Systematic theology
v, vi, 11, 15, 18, 99, 101, 135, 145, 184

T
Tabernacle
23, 68, 154, 222, 223, 298, 463, 534, 537, 549, 652
Taborites
178, 181
Talmidim
194, 198, 239
Talmud
20, 54, 62, 63, 70, 79, 80, 99, 142, 145, 189, 191, 259, 289, 300, 308, 311, 317, 321, 325, 327, 339, 359, 363, 364, 365, 373, 376, 402, 405, 455, 478, 479, 480, 529, 547, 562, 578, 581, 629

Subject Index

Tamar
510

Tanakh
vii, viii, 2, 4, 34,
43, 44, 46, 49, 52,
67, 80, 93, 99,
100, 102, 104,
106, 107, 109,
110, 111, 113,
115, 119, 120,
132, 133, 136,
151, 155, 156,
189, 191, 192,
196, 205, 216,
219, 225, 227,
233, 235, 238,
240, 252, 253,
256, 257, 258,
259, 260, 263,
264, 272, 273,
274, 275, 277,
278, 279, 280,
282, 287, 289,
290, 291, 292,
293, 294, 295,
296, 297, 298,
299, 300, 301,
302, 304, 307,
312, 315, 317,
318, 319, 322,
323, 327, 328,
330, 335, 338,
339, 346, 348,
349, 350, 353,
356, 358, 360,
363, 364, 365,
366, 368, 369,
371, 377, 381,
383, 387, 391,
394, 400, 409,
410, 413, 414,
422, 423, 428,
443, 448, 449,
455, 457, 458,
459, 460, 461,
462, 463, 464,
483, 484, 485,
487, 498, 503,
504, 505, 506,
507, 508, 509,
511, 513, 514,
515, 517, 518,
519, 520, 522,
526, 527, 529,
530, 532, 535,
536, 537, 538,
540, 541, 548,
549, 551, 561,
565, 566, 567,
569, 574, 576,
577, 580, 592,
596, 601, 617,
622, 626, 629,
630, 635, 642,
647, 648, 650,
655, 656, 658,
661, 671, 672

Targum
53, 64, 74, 75,
311, 312, 318,
321, 324, 325,
330, 339, 346,
351, 375, 376, 577

Targumim
62

Tarshish
    30, 498
Tatford, F. A.
    654
Te Dorsthorst, W.
    103
Teellinck, Willem
    171
Temple in Jerusalem
    85, 86, 151, 349,
    371, 428, 534,
    592, 651, 652
Temple Mount
    30, 82, 127, 234,
    428, 486, 638
Temple of God
    214, 221, 257 263,
    463, 534, 605,
    651, 657
Temple of Solomon
    221, 223, 549, 652
Temple of the Holy Spirit
    4, 16, 110, 132,
    200, 211, 262,
    263, 282, 460,
    520, 530, 534, 544
Temple of the Lord
    19, 21, 96, 262,
    318, 336, 467, 652
Temple Square
    15, 76, 291, 609
Ten Berge, G.
    102
Ten Boom, W.
    102
Ten Commandments
    105, 133, 215,
    217, 226
Tennenbaum, Silvia
    v
Tenney, M. C.
    475, 627, 654
Terah
    27, 302
Tertullian
    24, 155, 650, 659
Thaddeus
    571
The Christian's Reasonable Service
    12
The Future of Our Lord Jesus Christ
    182
"The Hope", song
    408
The Hope of the Church of Christ
    181
The Lord's Quarrel with his Vineyard
    171
The Miracles of the Most High
    171
Theodosius I
    146
Theodotion
    325
Theologians
    v, vi, 11, 18, 32,
    102, 103, 104,
    112, 118, 130,

Subject Index

Theology of Israel
vi, 126
Third chariot
94
Third exile
97, 98, 453
Third Temple
67, 82, 658
Thompson, W. M.
296
Thousand years
121, 122, 133, 134, 155, 156, 245
Throne of David
23, 46, 75, 82, 107, 108, 130, 151, 168, 176, 214, 227, 228, 232, 234, 284, 300, 316, 317, 321, 364, 365, 379, 418, 419, 434, 445, 451, 452, 453, 619
Throne of the LORD
75, 111, 234, 340, 134, 136, 172, 185, 186, 187, 188, 189, 196, 247, 256, 279, 285, 286, 293, 300, 322, 350, 416, 460, 476, 489, 509, 510, 512, 542, 543, 550, 551, 552, 553, 650
419
Tiberius
25
Tichonius
155
Times of the Gentiles
76, 77, 79, 80, 81, 82, 88, 89, 90, 248, 416, 477, 593, 606, 607, 608, 609
Times of the nations
455, 456, 609
Tish'ah b'Av
142, 143
Titus, Roman commander
476, 484
Toledoth
298
Torah
vii, viii, 16, 21, 23, 34, 37, 42, 65, 79, 80, 84, 101, 105, 109, 110, 111, 115, 117, 118, 129, 132, 133, 137, 186, 188, 191, 192, 200, 208, 209, 215, 217, 218, 219, 226, 243, 250, 252, 256, 258, 264, 266, 278, 281, 282, 283, 294, 295, 297, 298, 299, 302, 303,

335, 363, 364, 366, 367, 368, 370, 371, 372, 373, 376, 377, 378, 382, 383, 384, 390, 393, 394, 395, 401, 409, 449, 450, 456, 461, 462, 474, 480, 491, 497, 500, 518, 523, 524, 525, 526, 536, 544, 547, 548, 549, 563, 568, 577, 580, 581, 582, 583, 584, 585, 586, 587, 588, 589, 615, 630, 643, 650

Torah of Christ
    16, 101, 109, 129, 133, 368, 461, 525, 526, 544, 577, 583

Tower of Hananel
    240, 670

Transfiguration
    222, 238, 245, 377, 572, 611

Transvaal
    175

Trench, Richard
    398, 569

Trinity
    372, 410, 411, 507, 668

Tubal
    30, 31, 498

Tugela River
    175

Turkey
    422, 474

Turks
    32, 76, 182, 232

Twelve tribes of Israel
    65, 168, 191, 192, 195, 200, 213, 527, 571, 572, 613, 614, 615, 616, 621, 655

Twentieth century
    v, 79, 134, 149, 169, 174, 187, 247, 293, 406, 408, 492, 539

Typological exegesis
    296, 297

Tyre
    154, 259, 389, 646

Tzaddiqim
    36, 37, 43, 44, 69, 109, 111, 200, 216, 217, 239, 253, 254, 258, 259, 260, 369, 390, 404, 408, 449, 464, 482, 493, 496, 501, 504, 523, 527, 565, 566, 567, 605, 631, 645

U

Udemans, Godefridus
  171
Unger, M. F.
  337
United Nations
  32
United States
  vii, 128, 168, 177, 489, 672
Ur
  26, 225, 575
Uzziah
  351

V

Valentinian II
  146
Valley of dry bones
  137, 489
Valley of Jehoshaphat
  15, 31, 237, 438, 609, 669
Valley of Jezreel
  15, 31
Valley of Rephaim
  253, 645
Valley of Shittim
  237
Van 't Spijker, W.
  511
Van Barneveld, J.
  103
Van Bekkum, K.
  104

Van Bruggen, Jacob
  183
Van Campen, M.
  102, 128, 172, 184, 416, 437, 503, 542, 543, 640, 650
Van de Beek, A.
  127, 360
Van de Kamp, H. R.
  139, 662
Van de Kamp, Lody
  vi
Van de Velde, Abraham
  171
Van Delden, J. A.
  38, 448
Van den Brink, G.
  102, 184, 185, 186, 189, 285, 286, 555, 636
Van den Vondel, Joost
  171
Van der Graaf, J. W.
  102
Van der Groe, Theodorus
  172, 542
Van der Horst, P. W.
  636
Van der Kooi, C.
  102, 184, 185, 186, 189, 285, 286, 555, 636
Van der Meer, P. F.
  103

Van der Rhee, F.
103
Van der Spek-Begemann, G. A.
102
Van der Woude, A. S.
313
Van Dijk, B.
103
Van Eijnatten, J.
172
Van Estrik
319
Van Gelder, C.
521
Van Genderen, J.
324, 543, 636, 637
Van Giffen, David Flud
416, 650
Van Hell, E.
103
Van Leeuwen, J. A. C.
206, 630, 637, 641
Van Lodensteyn, Jodocus
171
Van Meggelen, J.
617
Van Moolenbroek, A.
103
Van Oldenbarnevelt, Johan
161
Van Oordt family
170
Van Ruler, A. A.
102
Van Ryn, A.
654

Van Veelen, W.
103
VanGemeren, W. A.
319, 330, 335,
339, 343, 344, 345
Vatican
543, 582
Veldhuis, H.
102
Velema, W. H.
324, 543
Velikovsky, Immanuel
395
Verboom, W.
102
Vergunst, E. F.
102
Vergunst, P. J.
184
Verkade, Cor
165
Verkuyl, J.
543, 559, 573
Vermes, G.
295
Versteeg, J. P.
637
Vetus Latina
9
Vilna Gaon
382
Vine
74, 88, 145, 198,
318, 331, 358,
361, 528, 556,
647, 648

Vine, W. E.
    494
Virgin Mary
    153, 313, 510
Vischer, W. E.
    293
Visser 't Hoofd, W. A.
    575
Vita Constantini
    154
Voetius, Gisbertus
    172
Volkskerk
    174, 531
Voltaire
    5
Von Rad, G.
    296, 413
Voorhoeve, H. C.
    182, 183, 186, 187
Voorhoeve, J. N.
    654
Voortrekkers
    175
Vreekamp, H.
    102
Vriezen, T. C.
    103
Vulgate
    2, 24, 99, 155,
    341, 416, 505

W

Wadi El-Arish
    140, 671

Waldenses
    178, 181
Walvoord, John F.
    137, 459, 593,
    601, 616, 657
Washington, D.C.
    69, 177
Water baptism
    261, 387, 521
Watson, D.
    541
Weldon, J.
    538
Wenger, J. C.
    167, 168
Wentsel, B.
    319, 323, 511,
    512, 523, 541,
    542, 555, 570
Wertheim, Eduard
    v
Wesley, John
    598
West Bank
    14, 140
Westcott, B. F.
    623
Westerman, E.
    102
Western church
    405
Western culture
    56, 61, 62, 63
Western Roman Empire
    76

Western Wall
266, 518
Western world
56, 58, 59, 92
Westminster Confession
507
White Anglo-Saxon Protestants
168
Whybrow, W. T.
654
Wilhelmus, Netherlands national anthem
170
Willemse, G. J.
175
William I
181
William III
170
William of Orange
161, 170, 173, 174
William the Silent
161, 170, 174
Willink, G.
169
Wilson, M. R.
188
Wisdom
210, 249, 297, 326, 397, 496, 516, 582, 588, 665
Witherington III, B.
648
Witsius, Herman
171, 172

Wolff, H. W.
351, 352
Wood, L. J.
312
Word of God
96, 163, 399, 465, 515, 657, 658
Wordsworth, C.
623
World dominion
60, 90, 91, 93, 239, 292, 325
World empires
6, 8, 24, 49, 50, 56, 68, 82, 89, 90, 92, 93, 239, 434, 576, 608, 609, 619
Worship
42, 64, 162, 164, 179, 217, 221, 236, 271, 381, 384, 401, 463, 532, 534, 536, 544, 549, 605, 613, 651, 652, 657, 665
Wright, J. S.
572, 574
Wright, N. T.
108, 572, 573, 574

Y

Yalkut Shimeoni
351
Yamim Nora'im
143

Subject Index

Yerushalayim
1, 18, 291, 485

Yeshivas
79

Yeshuah
70, 86, 137, 194, 226, 341, 370, 380, 406, 410

Yesterday's Streets
v

YHWH
2, 111, 171, 318, 382, 383, 410, 454

Yiddish
168

Yitzchaqi, Shlomo
52, 309

Yom Kippur
82, 84, 143, 144, 351, 478, 479, 480, 587, 656

Young, E. J.
334

Z

Zacchaeus
35

Zadok
67, 118, 119, 212, 336, 670

Zahn, Th.
601, 659

Zarephath
259, 513

Zealots
474, 599, 603

Zebedee
571, 575

Zedekiah
74, 75, 315, 318, 452, 453, 454

Zerubbabel
21, 67, 74, 78, 309, 317, 336, 337, 351, 454, 652

Zerwick, M.
267

Zeus
652, 654

Zimri
359

Zion
viii, 21, 23, 46, 61, 65, 66, 67, 77, 121, 123, 127, 137, 138, 139, 172, 174, 209, 221, 222, 237, 241, 250, 251, 252, 254, 255, 276, 277, 284, 309, 310, 341, 347, 354, 376, 393, 408, 409, 416, 420, 425, 426, 438, 439, 440, 441, 444, 454, 465, 470, 483, 485, 486, 494, 495, 498, 499, 505, 544, 577, 580, 581, 582, 583, 584, 619, 622, 624,

        625, 638, 639,
        644, 663, 666,
        667, 669, 670

Zionism
        131, 136

Zohar
        351

Zophar the Naamathite
        259, 513

Zulus
        175

Zwiep, A.
        326

Zwingli, Ulrich
        166, 167

Zwinglianism
        161

Zwinglians
        161

Zwolle
        25

www.ingramcontent.com/pod-product-compliance
Lightning Source LLC
Chambersburg PA
CBHW060332170426
42811CB00131BA/2437/J